Lethbridge—Alberta

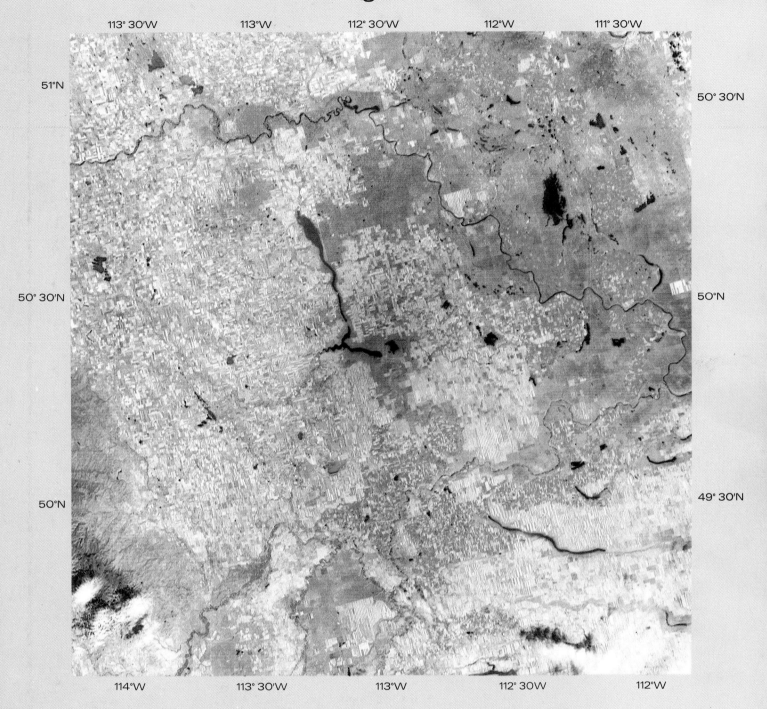

This area of southwestern Alberta is dominated by agriculture with several patterns of land-use. In the northeast, pasture and rangeland with the relative absence of field divisions is brown. The dry high plains of Alberta makes irrigation advisable where possible, and irrigation areas stand out as bright red, growing corn, sugar beet, potatoes and other green crops. Several reservoirs can be seen where rivers have been dammed for irrigation purposes. Wheat and other cereals are grown on the fields with a light tan colour, while mixed farming occupies the remainder of the agricultural area in the smaller, darker, more rectangular fields (especially in the west of the area). In the southwest are the Porcupine Hills – foothills of the Rocky Mountains – covered with forest which gives them a red colour. Lethbridge itself, not clearly visible, lies in the lower centre.

(23 August 1973)

The images shown on the endpapers were produced by the Landsat spacecraft which orbits the earth at an altitude of 900 km. (Images from NASA).

The Atlas of CANADA and the World

Prepared under the direction of

HAROLD FULLARD
Director of Cartography

B. M. WILLETT
Cartographic Editor

GEORGE PHILIP RAINTREE

George Philip Raintree Inc.
205 West Highland Avenue
MILWAUKEE, WISCONSIN 53203, USA

© **1979 George Philip and Son Ltd.**

ISBN 0 89810 001 1 (Standard Edition)
ISBN 0 89810 002 X (Deluxe Edition)
ISBN 0 89810 004 6 (Library Edition)

Printed in Great Britain by George Philip Printers Ltd., London

Preface

The easier and more rapid means of communication, the increase in global trade and exchanges, the growth of world organizations of all kinds and the pace of international events all demand of anyone who is careful to co-ordinate his information a convenient reference source and there is nothing better for this than an atlas. To be of the greatest use, it is essential that the maps should be detailed, accurate, legible and up-to-date; in addition, the index must enable the reader to find any place quickly. Also it is considered helpful that the detailed maps should be complemented by thematic maps, tables and illustrations to analyse and portray on the one hand the physical environment (such as geology, climate and vegetation) and on the other man and his activities, production and trade.

The ATLAS OF CANADA AND THE WORLD, it is hoped, meets these needs. The Atlas is of an easily portable size, convenient for frequent use, and able to stand on a bookshelf. At the same time, the content has been arranged to give regional maps on a large scale because it is only at such scales that a precision and wealth of detail can be satisfactorily presented.

The Atlas gives firstly an overall view of the earth in space, the composition of the earth and its surrounding atmosphere, then physical, demographic, economic and political maps followed by studies in depth of the continents by means of specialized maps and the more detailed regional maps. As befits the requirements of Canadian readers, a considerable section of the Atlas is given to special maps dealing with the country as a whole, as well as with each of the provinces. Thematic maps of Canada portray in the first place the physical conditions – geology, soils, vegetation – followed by specific maps on population and economic activities in agriculture, forestry, fishing, mining, energy production and industry. Regional maps on scales of 1:7M and 1:10M are amplified by larger scale maps, 1:2.5M, of the important more densely settled parts of the provinces, with yet more detailed maps of the Metropolitan regions, whilst the larger cities and capitals are shown on maps of 1:250,000 complemented by photographs. Neighbouring countries in the North and Latin America are given special treatment e.g. Northeastern United States, the Chicago-St. Louis region, California and Washington, Mexico and the Caribbean.

The design of the maps takes advantage of new developments in map reproduction. Lighter yet clearer layer colours have made possible the inclusion of a hill-shading to bring out clearly the character of the land and relief features without impairing the legibility of names, settlements and communications.

The opportunity of new reproduction has been taken to incorporate latest changes up to the date of printing and is shown in the most recent state of boundaries, political and administrative divisions and communications. International boundaries are drawn to show the *de facto* situation where there are rival claims to territory.

Spellings of Canadian names are the forms given in the Gazetteer of Canada by the Canadian Permanent Committee on Geographic Names and in the Répertoire Géographique du Québec by the Commission de Géographie. Spellings of names in other parts of the world are in the forms given in the latest official list and generally agree with the rules of the Permanent Committee on Geographical Names and the United States Board on Geographic Names. The comprehensive index locates over 35,000 places and geographical features by coordinates of latitude and longitude.

H. FULLARD

Contents

Maps 1–136

Contents-II

Canada

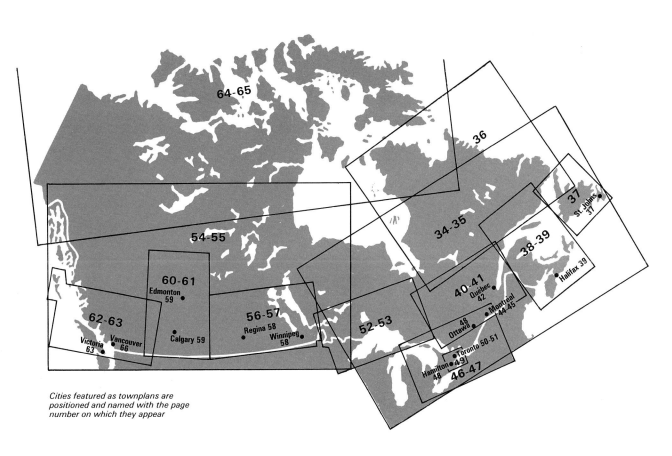

Cities featured as townplans are positioned and named with the page number on which they appear

Contents-III

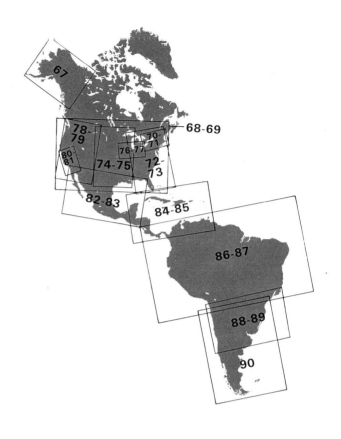

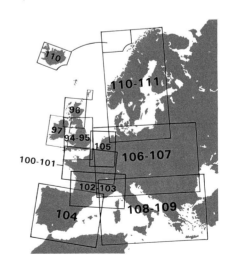

Contents–IV

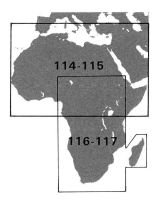

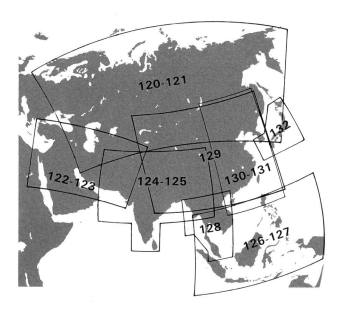

Index

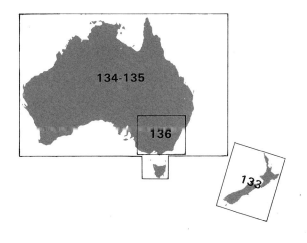

Chart of the Stars

Northern Stars

Stars of the Middle Heavens

Southern Stars

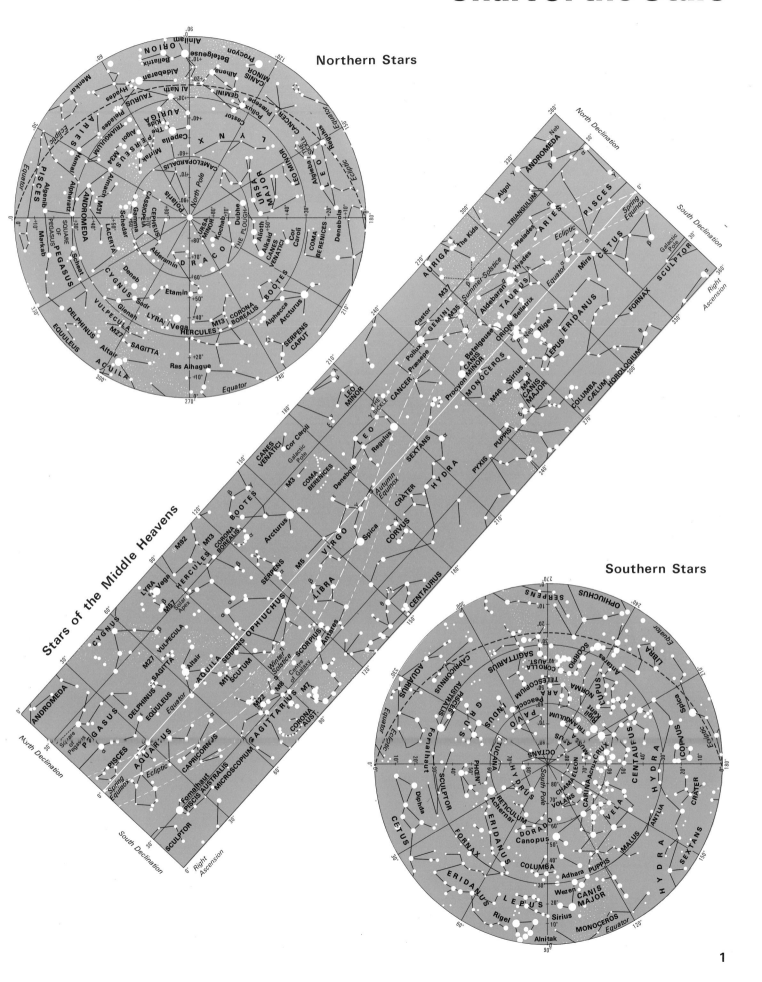

The Solar System

The Solar System is a minute part of one of the innumerable galaxies that make up the universe. Our Galaxy is represented in the drawing to the right and The Solar System (S) lies near the plane of spiral-shaped galaxy, but 27,000 light-years from the centre. The System consists of the Sun at the centre with planets, moons, asteroids, comets, meteors, meteorites, dust and gases revolving around it. It is calculated to be at least 4,700 million years old.

The Solar System can be considered in two parts: the Inner Region planets- Mercury, Venus, Earth and Mars - all small and solid; the Outer Region planets - Jupiter, Saturn, Uranus and Neptune - all gigantic in size, and on the edge of the system the smaller Pluto.

Our galaxy

Inner region planets

Mercury
Venus
Earth
Mars

Outer region planets

Mars
Jupiter
Saturn
Uranus
Neptune
Pluto

The planets

All planets revolve round the Sun in the same direction, and mostly in the same plane. Their orbits are shown (left) - they are not perfectly circular paths.

The table below summarizes the dimensions and movements of the Sun and planets.

The Sun

The Sun has an interior with temperatures believed to be of several million °C brought about by continuous thermo-nuclear fusions of hydrogen into helium. This immense energy is transferred by radiation into surrounding layers of gas the outer surface of which is called the chromosphere. From this "surface" with a temperature of many thousands °C "flames" (solar prominences) leap out into the diffuse corona which can best be seen at times of total eclipse (see photo right). The bright surface of the Sun, the photosphere, is calculated to have a temperature of about 6,000 °C, and when viewed through a telescope has a mottled appearance, the darker patches being called sunspots - the sites of large disturbances of the surface.

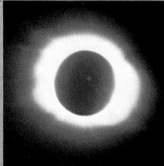
Total eclipse of the sun

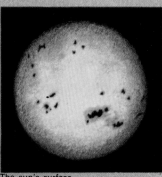
The sun's surface

	Equatorial diameter in km	Mass (earth=1)	Mean distance from sun in millions km	Radii of orbit (earth=1)	Orbital inclination	Sidereal period	Period of rotation on axis	Number of satellites
Sun	1 392 000	333 434	–	–	–	–	25 days 9hrs	–
Mercury	4 840	0·04	58	0·39	7°	88d	59 days	0
Venus	12 300	0·83	108	0·72	3°24'	225d	244 days	0
Earth	12 756	1·00	150	1·00	–	1 year	23hrs56m	1
Mars	6 790	0·11	228	1·52	1°51'	1y 322d	24hrs37m	2
Jupiter	143 200	318	778	5·20	1°18'	11y 315d	9hrs50m	12
Saturn	119 300	95	1 427	9·54	2°29'	29y 167d	10hrs14m	10
Uranus	47 100	15	2 870	19·19	0°46'	84y 6d	10hrs49m	5
Neptune	51 000	17	4 497	30·07	1°46'	164y 288d	15hrs48m	2
Pluto	5 900	0·06	5 950	39·46	17°06'	247y 255d	6d 9hrs 17m	–

The Sun's diameter is 109 times greater than that of the Earth.

Distances from sun in millions km

58 — Mercury
108 — Venus
150 — Earth
228 — Mars

778 — Jupiter

1427 — Saturn

2870 — Uranus

4497 — Neptune

5900 — Pluto

Mercury is the smallest planet and nearest to the Sun. It is composed mostly of metals and probably has an atmosphere of heavy inert gases.

Venus is similar in size to the Earth, and probably in composition. It is, however, much hotter and has a dense atmosphere of carbon dioxide which obscures our view of its surface.

Earth is the largest of the inner planets. It has a dense iron-nickel core surrounded by layers of silicate rock. The surface is approximately $\frac{3}{8}$ land and $\frac{5}{8}$ water, and the lower atmosphere consists of a mixture of nitrogen, oxygen and other gases supplemented by water vapour. With this atmosphere and surface temperatures usually between $-50°C$ and $+40°C$, life is possible.

Mars, smaller than the Earth, has a noticeably red appearance. Recent photographs sent back by satellite show clearly the cratered surface and the ice areas at the poles made from condensed carbon dioxide.

The Asteroids orbit the Sun mainly between Mars and Jupiter. They consist of thousands of bodies of varying sizes with diameters ranging from yards to hundreds of miles.

Jupiter is the largest planet of the Solar System. It shines brightly in the sky (magnitude -2.5), and is notable for its cloud belts and the Great Red Spot.

Saturn, the second largest planet consists of hydrogen, helium and other gases. Its density is less than that of water. It is unique in appearance because of its equatorial rings believed to be made of ice-covered particles.

Uranus was discovered in 1781 by Herschel. It is extremely remote yet faintly visible to the naked eye. Methane in its atmosphere gives it a slightly green appearance.

Neptune, yet more remote than Uranus and larger. It is composed of gases and has a bluish green appearance when seen in a telescope. As with Uranus, little detail can be observed on its surface.

Pluto No details are known of its composition or surface. The existence of this planet was firstly surmised in a computed hypothesis, which was tested by repeated searches by large telescopes until in 1930 the planet was found.

3

The Earth

Seasons, Equinoxes and Solstices

The Earth revolves around the Sun once a year and rotates daily on its axis, which is inclined at $66\frac{1}{2}°$ to the orbital plane and always points into space in the same direction. At midsummer (N.) the North Pole tilts towards the Sun, six months later it points away and half way between the axis is at right angles to the direction of the Sun (right).

Earth data

Maximum distance from the Sun (Aphelion) 152 007 016 km
Minimum distance from the Sun (Perihelion) 147 000 830 km
Obliquity of the ecliptic 23° 27′ 08″
Length of year - tropical (equinox to equinox) 365.24 days
Length of year - sidereal (fixed star to fixed star) 365.26 days
Length of day - mean solar day 24h 03m 56s
Length of day - mean sidereal day 23h 56m 04s

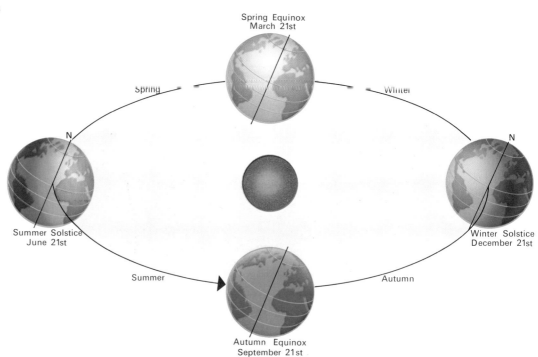

Spring Equinox
March 21st

Spring

Winter

Summer Solstice
June 21st

Winter Solstice
December 21st

Summer

Autumn

Autumn Equinox
September 21st

Length of day and night

At the summer solstice in the northern hemisphere, the Arctic has total daylight and the Antarctic total darkness. The opposite occurs at the winter solstice. At the equator, the length of day and night are almost equal all the year, at 30° the length of day varies from about 14 hours to 10 hours and at 50° from about 16 hours to 8 hours.

Arctic Circle

Sun's rays

Equator

Antarctic Circle

Apparent path of the Sun

The diagrams (right) illustrate the apparent path of the Sun at A the equator, B in mid latitudes say 45°N, C at the Arctic Circle $66\frac{1}{2}°$ and D at the North Pole where there is six months continuous daylight and six months continuous night

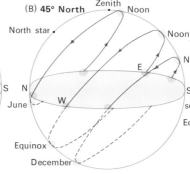

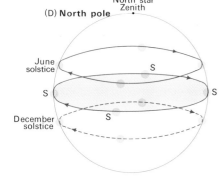

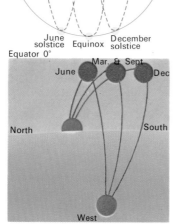

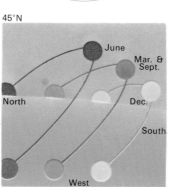

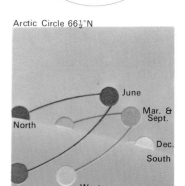

The Moon

The Moon rotates slowly making one complete turn on its axis in just over 27 days. This is the same as its period of revolution around the Earth and thus it always presents the same hemisphere ('face') to us. Surveys and photographs from space-craft have now added greatly to our knowledge of the Moon, and, for the first time, views of the hidden hemisphere.

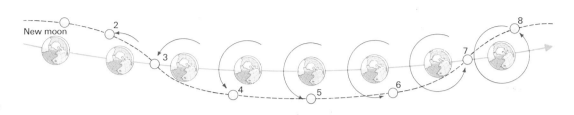

Phases of the Moon

The interval between one full Moon and the next is approximately $29\frac{1}{2}$ days - thus there is one new Moon and one full Moon every month. The diagrams and photographs (right) show how the apparent changes in shape of the Moon from new to full arise from its changing position in relation to the Earth and both to the fixed direction of the Sun's rays.

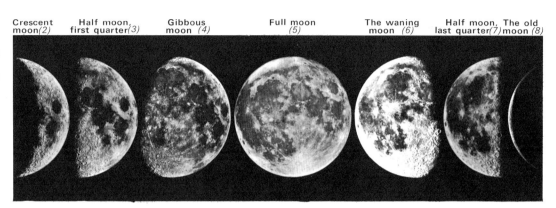

Crescent moon(2)   Half moon, first quarter(3)   Gibbous moon (4)   Full moon (5)   The waning moon (6)   Half moon, last quarter(7) The old moon (8)

Moon data

Distance from Earth 356 410 km to 406 685 km
Mean diameter 3 473 km
Mass approx. $\frac{1}{81}$ of that of Earth
Surface gravity $\frac{1}{6}$ of that of Earth
Atmosphere - none, hence no clouds, no weather, no sound.
Diurnal range of temperature at the Equator +200°C

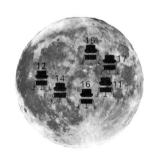

Landings on the Moon

Left are shown the landing sites of the U.S. Apollo programme.
Apollo 11 Sea of Tranquility (1°N 23°E) 1969
Apollo 12 Ocean of Storms (3°S 24°W) 1969
Apollo 14 Fra Mauro (4°S 17°W) 1971
Apollo 15 Hadley Rill (25°N 4°E) 1971
Apollo 16 Descartes (9°S 15°E) 1972
Apollo 17 Sea of Serenity (20°N 31°E) 1972

Eclipses of Sun and Moon

When the Moon passes between Sun and Earth it causes a partial eclipse of the Sun *(right 1)* if the Earth passes through the Moon's outer shadow *(P)*, or a total eclipse *(right 2)*, if the inner cone shadow crosses the Earth's surface.

In a lunar eclipse, the Earth's shadow crosses the Moon and gives either total or partial eclipses.

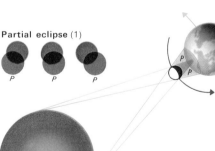

Partial eclipse (1)

Total eclipse (2)

Lunar eclipse

Tides

Ocean water moves around the Earth under the gravitational pull of the Moon, and, less strongly, that of the Sun. When solar and lunar forces pull together - near new and full Moon - high spring tides result. When solar and lunar forces are not combined - near Moon's first and third quarters - low neap tides occur.

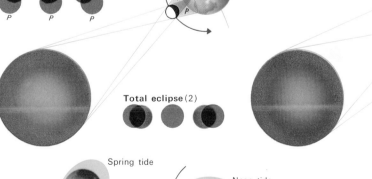

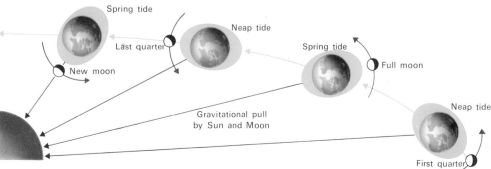

Spring tide   Neap tide   Last quarter   New moon   Spring tide   Full moon   Neap tide   Gravitational pull by Sun and Moon   First quarter

Time

Time measurement

The basic unit of time measurement is the day, one rotation of the earth on its axis. The subdivision of the day into hours and minutes is arbitrary and simply for our convenience. Our present calendar is based on the solar year of $365\frac{1}{4}$ days, the time taken for the earth to orbit the sun. A month was anciently based on the interval from new moon to new moon, approximately $29\frac{1}{2}$ days - and early calendars were entirely lunar.

Rotation of the Earth

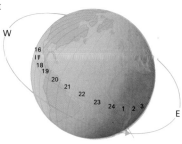

Greenwich Observatory

Prime Meridian

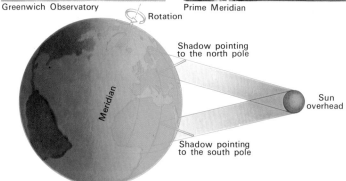

The International Date Line

When it is 12 noon at the Greenwich meridian, 180° east it is midnight of the same day while 180° west the day is only just beginning. To overcome this the International Date Line was established, approximately following the 180° meridian. Thus, for example, if one travelled eastwards from Japan (140° East) to Samoa (170° West) one would pass from Sunday night into Sunday morning.

Time zones

The world is divided into 24 time zones, each centred on meridians at 15° intervals which is the longitudinal distance the sun appears to travel every hour. The meridian running through Greenwich passes through the middle of the first zone. Successive zones to the east of Greenwich zone are ahead of Greenwich time by one hour for every 15° of longitude, while zones to the west are behind by one hour.

Night and day

As the earth rotates from west to east the sun appears to rise in the east and set in the west: when the sun is setting in Shanghai on the directly opposite side of the earth New York is just emerging into sunlight. Noon, when the sun is directly overhead, is coincident at all places on the same meridian with shadows pointing directly towards the poles.

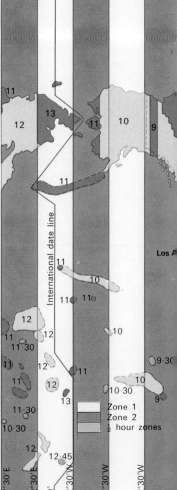

Solar time

The time taken for the earth to complete one rotation about its own axis is constant and defines a day but the speed of the earth along its orbit around the sun is inconstant. The length of day, or 'apparent solar day', as defined by the apparent successive transits of the sun is irregular because the earth must complete more than one rotation before the sun returns to the same meridian.

Sidereal time

The constant sidereal day is defined as the interval between two successive apparent transits of a star, or the first point of Aries, across the same meridian. If the sun is at the equinox and overhead at a meridian on one day, then the next day the sun will be to the east by approximately 1°; thus the sun will not cross the meridian until about 4 minutes after the sidereal noon.

Astronomical clock, Delhi

Sundials

The earliest record of sundials dates back to 741 BC but they undoubtedly existed as early as 2000 BC although probably only as an upright stick or obelisk. A sundial marks the progress of the sun across the sky by casting the shadow of a central style or gnomon on the base. The base, generally made of stone, is delineated to represent the hours between sunrise and sunset.

Kendall's chronometer

Chronometers

With the increase of sea traffic in the 18th century and the need for accurate navigation clockmakers were faced with an intriguing problem. Harrison, an English carpenter, won a British award for designing a clock which was accurate at sea to one tenth of a second per day. He compensated for the effect of temperature changes by incorporating bi-metallic strips connected to thin wires and circular balance wheels

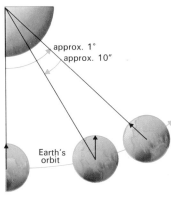

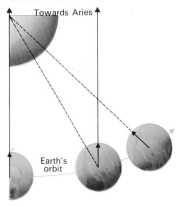

Chronographs

The invention of the chronograph by Charles Wheatstone in 1842 made it possible to record intervals of time to an accuracy of one sixtieth of a second. The simplest form of chronograph is the stopwatch. This was developed to a revolving drum and stylus and later electrical signals. A recent development is the cathode ray tube capable of recording to less than one ten-thousandth of a second.

Quartz crystal clocks

The quartz crystal clock, designed originally in America in 1929, can measure small units of time and radio frequencies. The connection between quartz clocks and the natural vibrations of atoms and molecules mean that the unchanging frequencies emitted by atoms can be used to control the oscillator which controls the quartz clock. A more recent version of the atomic clock is accurate to one second in 300 years.

Progress of the accuracy of timekeepers

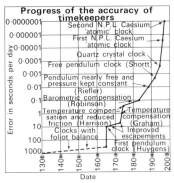

Vibration of quartz ring

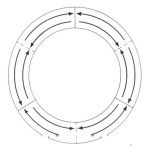

Time difference when travelling by air

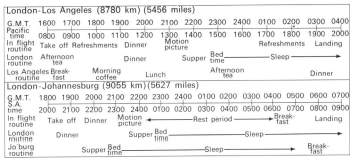

International date line

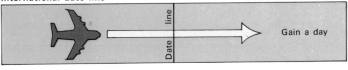

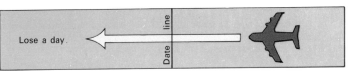

The Atmosphere and Clouds

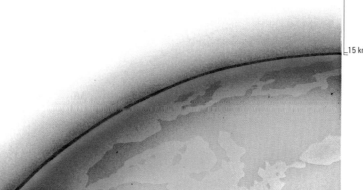

Earth's thin coating *(right)*
The atmosphere is a blanket of protective gases around the earth providing insulation against otherwise extreme alternations in temperature. The gravitational pull increases the density nearer the earth's surface so that 5/6ths of the atmospheric mass is in the first 15 kms. It is a very thin layer in comparison with the earth's diameter of 12 680 kms., like the cellulose coating on a globe.

Exosphere(1)
The exosphere merges with the interplanetary medium and although there is no definite boundary with the ionosphere it starts at a height of about 600 kms. The rarified air mainly consists of a small amount of atomic oxygen up to 600 kms. and equal proportions of hydrogen and helium with hydrogen predominating above 2 400 kms.

Ionosphere(2)
Air particles of the ionosphere are electrically charged by the sun's radiation and congregate in four main layers, D, E, F1 and F2, which can reflect radio waves. Aurorae, caused by charged particles deflected by the earth's magnetic field towards the poles, occur between 65 and 965 kms. above the earth. It is mainly in the lower ionosphere that meteors from outer space burn up as they meet increased air resistance.

Stratosphere(3)
A thin layer of ozone contained within the stratosphere absorbs ultra-violet light and in the process gives off heat. The temperature ranges from about -55°C at the tropopause to about -60°C in the upper part, known as the mesosphere, with a rise to about 2°C just above the ozone layer. This portion of the atmosphere is separated from the lower layer by the tropopause.

Troposphere(4)
The earth's weather conditions are limited to this layer which is relatively thin, extending upwards to about 8 kms. at the poles and 15 kms. at the equator. It contains about 85% of the total atmospheric mass and almost all the water vapour. Air temperature falls steadily with increased height at about 1°C for every 100 metres above sea level.

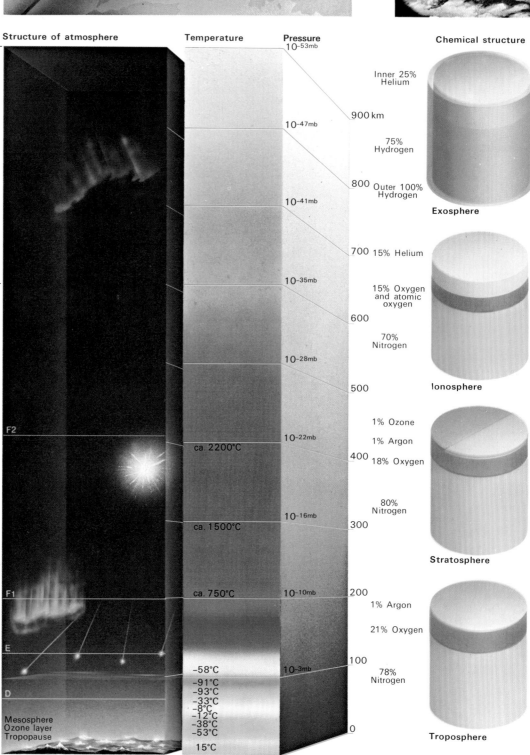

Structure of atmosphere

1

2

F2

F1

E

D

3 Mesosphere
Ozone layer
Tropopause

4

Temperature

ca. 2200°C

ca. 1500°C

ca. 750°C

-58°C
-91°C
-93°C
-33°C
-8°C
-12°C
-38°C
-53°C

15°C

Pressure

$10^{-53}mb$

$10^{-47}mb$

$10^{-41}mb$

$10^{-35}mb$

$10^{-28}mb$

$10^{-22}mb$

$10^{-16}mb$

$10^{-10}mb$

$10^{-3}mb$

$10^{3}mb$

600 km

15 km

900 km

800

700

600

500

400

300

200

100

0

Chemical structure

Inner 25% Helium

75% Hydrogen

Outer 100% Hydrogen

Exosphere

15% Helium

15% Oxygen and atomic oxygen

70% Nitrogen

Ionosphere

1% Ozone

1% Argon

18% Oxygen

80% Nitrogen

Stratosphere

1% Argon

21% Oxygen

78% Nitrogen

Troposphere

Pacific Ocean
Cloud patterns over the Pacific show the paths of prevailing winds.

Circulation of the air

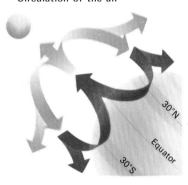

Circulation of the air
Owing to high temperatures in equatorial regions the air near the ground is heated, expands and rises producing a low pressure belt. It cools, causing rain, spreads out then sinks again about latitudes 30° north and south forming high pressure belts.

High and low pressure belts are areas of comparative calm but between them, blowing from high to low pressure, are the prevailing winds. These are deflected to the right in the northern hemisphere and to the left in the southern hemisphere (Corolis effect). The circulations appear in three distinct belts with a seasonal movement north and south following the overhead sun.

Cloud types

Clouds form when damp air is cooled, usually by rising. This may happen in three ways: when a wind rises to cross hills or mountains; when a mass of air rises over, or is pushed up by another mass of denser air; when local heating of the ground causes convection currents.

Cirrus *(1)* are detached clouds composed of microscopic ice crystals which gleam white in the sun resembling hair or feathers. They are found at heights of 6 000 to 12 000 metres.

Cirrostratus *(2)* are a whitish veil of cloud made up of ice crystals through which the sun can be seen often producing a halo of bright light.

Cirrocumulus *(3)* is another high altitude cloud formed by turbulence between layers moving in different directions.

Altostratus *(4)* is a grey or bluish striated, fibrous or uniform sheet of cloud producing light drizzle.

Altocumulus *(5)* is a thicker and fluffier version of cirro cumulus, it is a white and grey patchy sheet of cloud.

Nimbostratus *(6)* is a dark grey layer of cloud obscuring the sun and causing almost continuous rain or snow.

Cumulus *(7)* are detached heaped up, dense low clouds. The sunlit parts are brilliant white while the base is relatively dark and flat.

Stratus *(8)* forms dull overcast skies associated with depressions and occurs at low altitudes up to 1500 metres.

Cumulonimbus *(9)* are heavy and dense clouds associated with storms and rain. They have flat bases and a fluffy outline extending up to great altitudes.

High clouds

Middle clouds

Low clouds

Thousands of metres

1 Cirrus   2 Cirrostratus

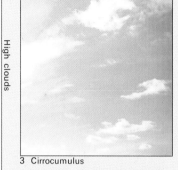

3 Cirrocumulus

4 Altostratus

5 Altocumulus   6 Nimbostratus

7 Cumulus

8 Stratus   9 Cumulonimbus

Climate and Weather

All weather occurs over the earth's surface in the lowest level of the atmosphere, the troposphere. Weather has been defined as the condition of the atmosphere at any place at a specific time with respect to the various elements: temperature, sunshine, pressure, winds, clouds, fog, precipitation. Climate, on the other hand, is the average of weather elements over previous months and years.

Climate graphs *right*
Each graph typifies the kind of climatic conditions one would experience in the region to which it is related by colour to the map. The scale refers to degrees Celsius for temperature and millimetres for rainfall, shown by bars. The graphs show average observations based over long periods of time, the study of which also compares the prime factors for vegetation differences.

Development of a depression *below*
In an equilibrium front between cold and warm air masses (i) a wave disturbance develops as cold air undercuts the warm air (ii). This deflects the air flow and as the disturbance progresses a definite cyclonic circulation with warm and cold fronts is created (iii). The cold front moves more rapidly than the warm front eventually overtaking it, and occlusion occurs as the warm air is pinched out (iv).

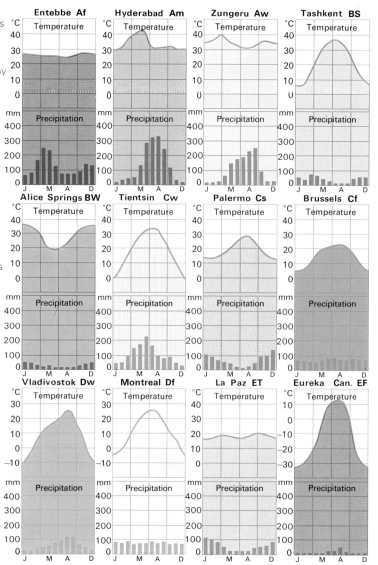

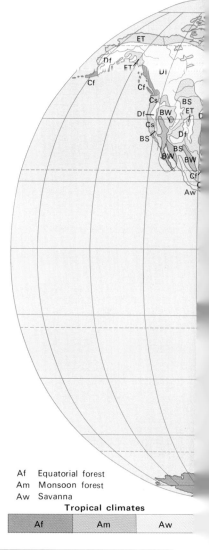

Af Equatorial forest
Am Monsoon forest
Aw Savanna
Tropical climates

| Af | Am | Aw |

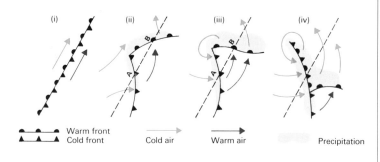

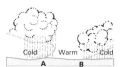 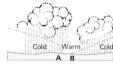 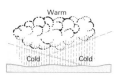

Warm front
Cold front

Cold air   Warm air

Precipitation

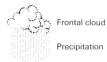

Frontal cloud

Precipitation

The upper diagrams show in plan view stages in the development of a depression.
The cross sections below correspond to stages (ii) to (iv).

Kinds of precipitation
Rain The condensation of water vapour on microscopic particles of dust, sulphur, soot or ice in the atmosphere forms water particles. These combine until they are heavy enough to fall as rain.

Hail Water particles, carried to a great height, freeze into ice particles which fall and become coated with fresh moisture. They are swept up again and refrozen. This may happen several times before falling as hail-stones.

Frost Hoar, the most common type of frost, is precipitated instead of dew when water vapour changes directly into ice crystals on the surface of ground objects which have cooled below freezing point.

Snow is the precipitation of ice in the form of flakes, or clusters, of basically hexagonal ice crystals. They are formed by the condensation of water vapour directly into ice.

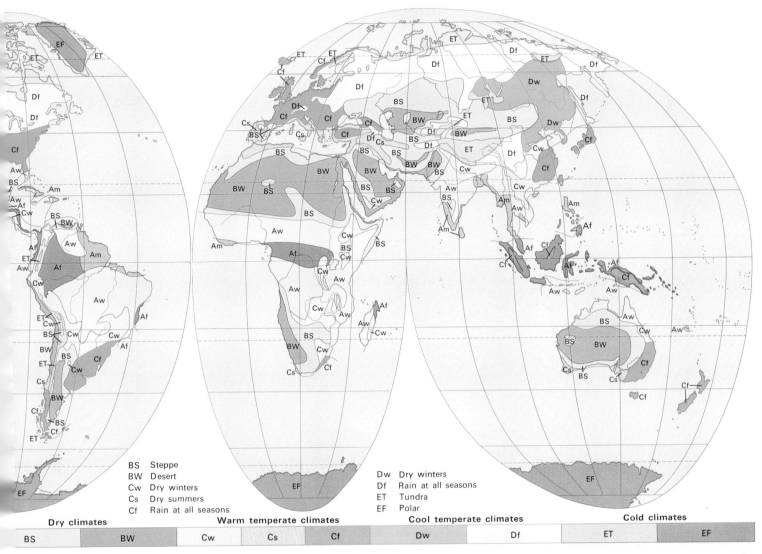

BS Steppe
BW Desert
Cw Dry winters
Cs Dry summers
Cf Rain at all seasons

Dw Dry winters
Df Rain at all seasons
ET Tundra
EF Polar

Dry climates		Warm temperate climates			Cool temperate climates		Cold climates	
BS	BW	Cw	Cs	Cf	Dw	Df	ET	EF

Tropical storm tracks *below*

A tropical cyclone, or storm, is designated as having winds of gale force (60 kph) but less than hurricane force (120 kph). It is a homogenous air mass with upward spiralling air currents around a windless centre, or eye. An average of 65 tropical storms occur each year, over 50% of which reach hurricane force. They originate mainly during the summer over tropical oceans.

Extremes of climate & weather *right*

Tropical high temperatures and polar low temperatures combined with wind systems, altitude and unequal rainfall distribution result in the extremes of tropical rain forests, inland deserts and frozen polar wastes. Fluctuations in the limits of these extreme zones and extremes of weather result in occasional catastrophic heat-waves and drought, floods and storms, frost and snow.

Hurricane devastation

Hot desert

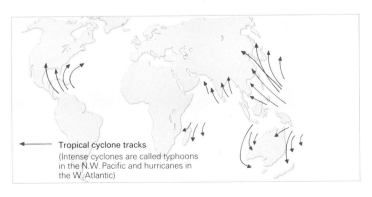
Tropical cyclone tracks
(Intense cyclones are called typhoons in the N.W. Pacific and hurricanes in the W. Atlantic)

Tornado

Arctic dwellings

The Earth from Space

Mount Etna, Sicily *left*
Etna is at the top of the photograph, the Plain of Catania in the centre and the Mediterranean to the right. This is an infra-red photograph; vegetation shows as red, water as blue/black and urban areas as grey. The recent lava flows, as yet with no vegetation, show up as blue/black unlike the cultivated slopes which are red and red/pink.

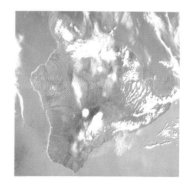

Hawaii, Pacific Ocean *above*
This is a photograph of Hawaii, the largest of the Hawaiian Islands in the Central Pacific. North is at the top of the photograph. The snowcapped craters of the volcanoes Mauna Kea (dormant) in the north centre and Mauna Loa (active) in the south centre of the photograph can be seen. The chief town, Hilo, is on the north east coast.

River Brahmaputra, India *left*
A view looking westwards down the Brahmaputra with the Himalayas on the right and the Khasi Hills of Assam to the left.

Szechwan, China *right*
The River Tachin in the mountainous region of Szechwan, Central China. The lightish blue area in the river valley in the north east of the photograph is a village and its related cultivation.

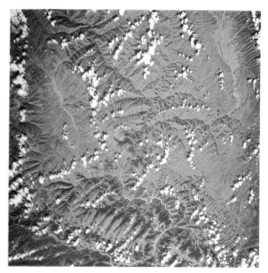

New York, U.S.A. *left*
This infra-red photograph shows the western end of Long Island and the entrance to the Hudson River. Vegetation appears as red, water as blue/black and the metropolitan areas of New York, through the cloud cover, as grey.

The Great Barrier Reef, Australia *right*
The Great Barrier Reef and the Queensland coast from Cape Melville to Cape Flattery. The smoke from a number of forest fires can be seen in the centre of the photograph.

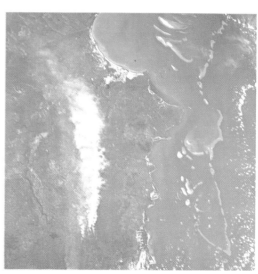

Eastern Himalayas, Asia
above left
A view from Apollo IX looking north-westwards over the snowcapped, sunlit mountain peaks and the head waters of the Mekong, Salween, Irrawaddy and, in the distance, with its distinctive loop, the Brahmaputra.

Atacama Desert, Chile
above right
This view looking eastwards from the Pacific over the Mejillones peninsula with the city of Antofagasta in the southern bay of that peninsula. Inland the desert and salt-pans of Atacama, and beyond, the Andes.

The Alps, Europe *right*
This vertical photograph shows the snow-covered mountains and glaciers of the Alps along the Swiss-Italian-French border. Mont Blanc and the Matterhorn are shown and, in the north, the Valley of the Rhône is seen making its sharp right-hand bend near Martigny. In the south the head waters of the Dora Baltea flow towards the Po and, in the north-west, the Lac d'Annecy can be seen.

The Evolution of the Continents

The origin of the earth is still open to much conjecture although the most widely accepted theory is that it was formed from a solar cloud consisting mainly of hydrogen. Under gravitation the cloud condensed and shrank to form our planets orbiting around the sun. Gravitation forced the lighter elements to the surface of the earth where they cooled to form a crust while the inner material remained hot and molten. Earth's first rocks formed over 3500 million years ago but since then the surface has been constantly altered.

Until comparatively recently the view that the primary units of the earth had remained essentially fixed throughout geological time was regarded as common sense, although the concept of moving continents has been traced back to references in the Bible of a break up of the land after Noah's floods. The continental drift theory was first developed by Antonio Snider in 1858 but probably the most important single advocate was Alfred Wegener who, in 1915, published evidence from geology, climatology and biology. His conclusions are very similar to those reached by current research although he was wrong about the speed of break-up.

The measurement of fossil magnetism found in rocks has probably proved the most influential evidence. While originally these drift theories were openly mocked, now they are considered standard doctrine.

The jigsaw
As knowledge of the shape and structure of the earth's surface grew, several of the early geographers noticed the great similarity in shape of the coasts bordering the Atlantic. It was this remarkable similarity which led to the first detailed geological and structural comparisons. Even more accurate fits can be made by placing the edges of the continental shelves in juxtaposition.

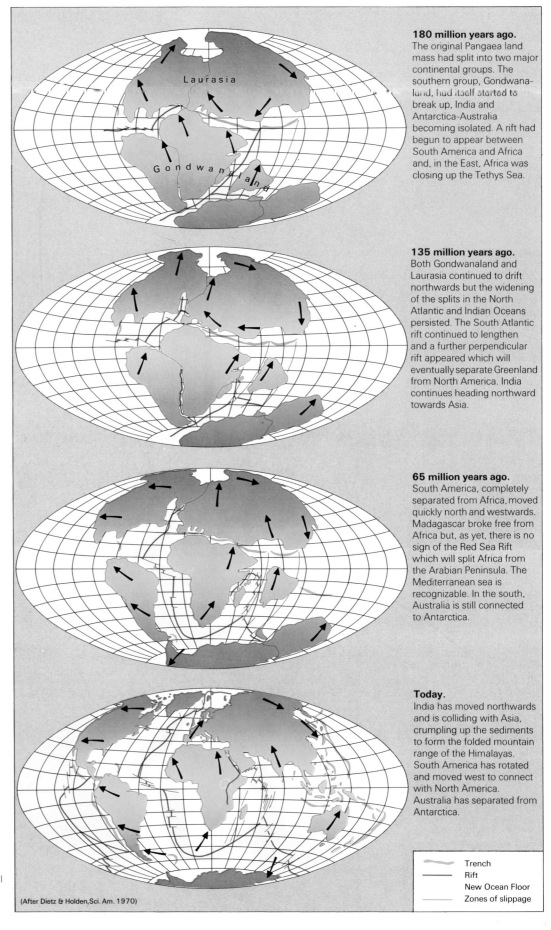

180 million years ago.
The original Pangaea land mass had split into two major continental groups. The southern group, Gondwanaland, had itself started to break up, India and Antarctica-Australia becoming isolated. A rift had begun to appear between South America and Africa and, in the East, Africa was closing up the Tethys Sea.

135 million years ago.
Both Gondwanaland and Laurasia continued to drift northwards but the widening of the splits in the North Atlantic and Indian Oceans persisted. The South Atlantic rift continued to lengthen and a further perpendicular rift appeared which will eventually separate Greenland from North America. India continues heading northward towards Asia.

65 million years ago.
South America, completely separated from Africa, moved quickly north and westwards. Madagascar broke free from Africa but, as yet, there is no sign of the Red Sea Rift which will split Africa from the Arabian Peninsula. The Mediterranean sea is recognizable. In the south, Australia is still connected to Antarctica.

Today.
India has moved northwards and is colliding with Asia, crumpling up the sediments to form the folded mountain range of the Himalayas. South America has rotated and moved west to connect with North America. Australia has separated from Antarctica.

(After Dietz & Holden, Sci. Am. 1970)

Trench
Rift
New Ocean Floor
Zones of slippage

Plate tectonics

The original debate about continental drift was only a prelude to a more radical idea; plate tectonics. The basic theory is that the earth's crust is made up of a series of rigid plates which float on a soft layer of the mantle and are moved about by convection currents in the earth's interior. These plates converge and diverge along margins marked by earthquakes, volcanoes and other seismic activity. Plates diverge from mid-ocean ridges where molten lava pushes upwards and forces the plates apart at a rate of up to 30mm. a year. Converging plates form either a trench, where the oceanic plate sinks below the lighter continental rock, or mountain ranges where two continents collide. This explains the paradox that while there have always been oceans none of the present oceans contain sediments more than 150 million years old.

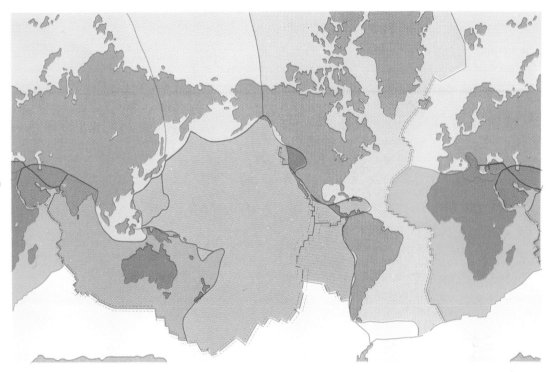

Trench boundary

The present explanation for the comparative youth of the ocean floors is that where an ocean and a continent meet the ocean plate dips under the less dense continental plate at an angle of approximately 45°. All previous crust is then ingested by downward convection currents. In the Japanese trench this occurs at a rate of about 120mm. a year.

Transform fault

The recent identification of the transform, or transverse, fault proved to be one of the crucial preliminaries to the investigation of plate tectonics. They occur when two plates slip alongside each other without parting or approaching to any great extent. They complete the outline of the plates delineated by the ridges and trenches and demonstrate large scale movements of parts of the earth's surface

Ridge boundary

Ocean rises or crests are basically made up from basaltic lavas for although no gap can exist between plates, one plate can ease itself away from another. In that case hot, molten rock instantly rises from below to fill in the incipient rift and forms a ridge. These ridges trace a line almost exactly through the centre of the major oceans.

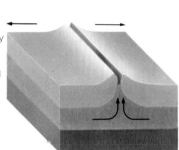

Destruction of ocean plates.

As the ocean plate sinks below the continental plate some of the sediment on its surface is scraped off and piled up on the landward side. This sediment is later incorporated in a folded mountain range which usually appears on the edge of the continent, such as the Andes. Similarly if two continents collide the sediments are squeezed up into new mountains.

Sea floor spreading

Reversals in the earth's magnetic field have occured throughout history. As new rock emerges at the ocean ridges it cools and is magnetised in the direction of the prevailing magnetic field. By mapping the magnetic patterns either side of the ridge a symmetrical stripey pattern of alternating fields can be observed (see inset area in diagram). As the dates of the last few reversals are known the rate of spreading can be calculated.

The Unstable Earth

The earth's surface is slowly but continually being rearranged. Some changes such as erosion and deposition are extremely slow but they upset the balance which causes other more abrupt changes often originating deep within the earth's interior. The constant movements vary in intensity, often with stresses building up to a climax such as a particularly violent volcanic eruption or earthquake.

The crust *(below and right)*
The outer layer or crust of the earth consists of a comparatively low density, brittle material varying from 5 to 50 kilometres deep beneath the continents. Under this is a layer of rock consisting predominately of silica and aluminium; hence it is called 'sial'. Extending under the ocean floors and below the sial is a basaltic layer known as 'sima', consisting mainly of silica and magnesium.

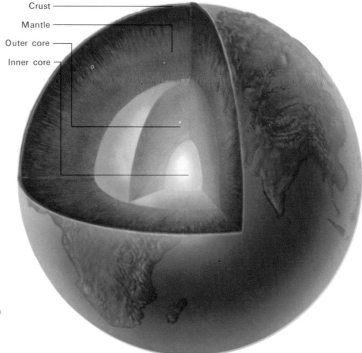

Crust
Mantle
Outer core
Inner core

Continental crust   Ocean crust

Sediment
Granite rock (sial)
Basaltic layer (sima)
Mantle

Volcanoes *(right, below and far right)*
Volcanoes occur when hot liquefied rock beneath the crust reaches the surface as lava. An accumulation of ash and cinders around a vent forms a cone. Successive layers of thin lava flows form an acid lava volcano while thick lava flows form a basic lava volcano. A caldera forms when a particularly violent eruption blows off the top of an already existing cone.

The mantle *(above)*
Immediately below the crust, at the mohorovicic discontinuity line, there is a distinct change in density and chemical properties. This is the mantle - made up of iron and magnesium silicates - with temperatures reaching 1 600°C. The rigid upper mantle extends down to a depth of about 1 000 km., below which is the more viscous lower mantle which is about 1 900 km. thick.

The core *(above)*
The outer core, approximately 2 100 km. thick, consists of molten iron and nickel at 2 000°C to 5 000°C possibly separated from the less dense mantle by an oxidised shell. About 5 000km. below the surface is the liquid transition zone, below which is the solid inner core, a sphere of 2 740km. diameter where rock is three times as dense as in the crust.

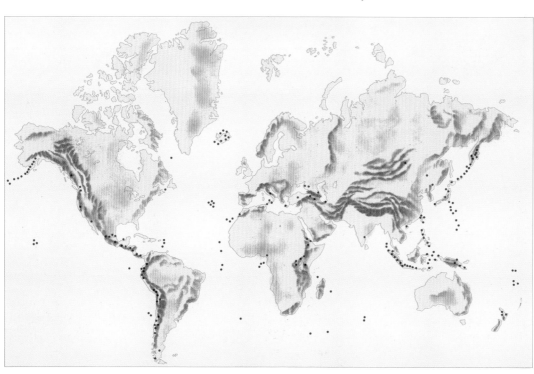

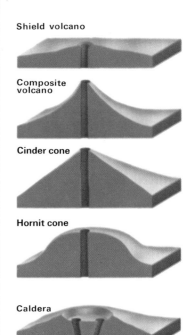

Shield volcano

Composite volcano

Cinder cone

Hornit cone

Caldera

Major earthquakes in the last 100 years	numbers killed
1896 Japan (tsunami)	22 000
1906 San Francisco	destroyed
1906 Chile, Valparaiso	22 000
1908 Italy, Messina	77 000
1920 China, Kansu	180 000
1923 Japan, Tokyo	143 000
1930 Italy, Naples	2 100
1931 Napier	destroyed
1931 Nicaragua, Managua	destroyed
1932 China, Kansu	70 000
1935 India, Quetta	60 000
1939 Chile, Chillan	20 000
1939/40 Turkey, Erzincan	30 000
1948 Japan, Fukui	5 100
1956 N. Afghanistan	2 000
1957 W. Iran	2 500
1960 Morocco, Agadir	12 000
1962 N.W. Iran	10 000
1963 Yugoslavia, Skopje	1 000
1966 U.S.S.R., Tashkent	destroyed
1970 N. Peru	66 800
1972 Nicaragua, Managua	7 000
1974 N. Pakistan	10 000
1975 Turkey, Lice	2 300
1976 China, Tangshan	650 000
1976 Turkey, Van	3 800

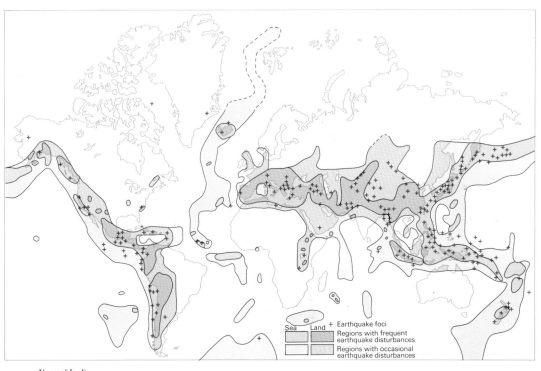

Sea   Land   + Earthquake foci
Regions with frequent earthquake disturbances
Regions with occasional earthquake disturbances

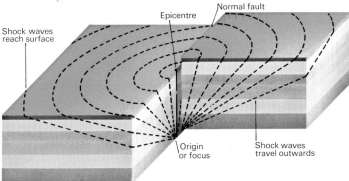

Shock waves reach surface · Epicentre · Normal fault · Origin or focus · Shock waves travel outwards

Earthquakes   *(right and above)*

Earthquakes are a series of rapid vibrations originating from the slipping or faulting of parts of the earth's crust when stresses within build up to breaking point. They usually happen at depths varying from 8-30 km. Severe earthquakes cause extensive damage when they take place in populated areas destroying structures and severing communications. Most loss of life occurs due to secondary causes i.e. falling masonry, fires or tsunami waves.

Alaskan earthquake, 1964

Seismic Waves   *(right)*

The shock waves sent out from the epicentre of an earthquake are of three main kinds each with distinct properties. Primary (P) waves are compressional waves which can be transmitted through both solids and liquids and therefore pass through the earth's liquid core. Secondary (S) waves are shear waves and can only pass through solids. They cannot pass through the core and are reflected at the core-mantle boundary taking a concave course back to the surface. The core also refracts the P waves causing them to alter course, and the net effect of this reflection and refraction is the production of a shadow zone at a certain distance from the epicentre, free from P and S waves. Due to their different properties P waves travel about 1·7 times faster than S waves. The third main kind of wave is a long (L) wave, a slow wave which travels along the earth's surface, its motion being either horizontal or vertical.

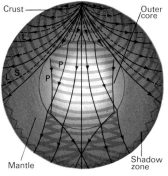

Crust · Outer core · Mantle · Shadow zone

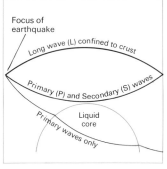

Focus of earthquake · Long wave (L) confined to crust · Primary (P) and Secondary (S) waves · Primary waves only · Liquid core

Wave travel times in hours

Tsunami waves   *(left)*

A sudden slump in the ocean bed during an earthquake forms a trough in the water surface subsequently followed by a crest and smaller waves. A more marked change of level in the sea bed can form a crest, the start of a Tsunami which travels up to 60 kph with waves up to 60 metres high. Seismographic detectors continuously record earthquake shocks and warn of the Tsunami which may follow it.

Horizontal · D · M · P

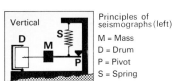

Vertical · D · M · S · P

Principles of seismographs (left)
M = Mass
D = Drum
P = Pivot
S = Spring

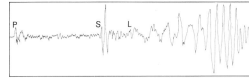

P · S · L

Seismographs are delicate instruments capable of detecting and recording vibrations due to earthquakes thousands of miles away. P waves cause the first tremors. S the second, and L the main shock.

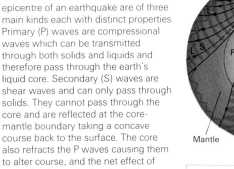

17

The Making of Landscape

The making of landscape

The major forces which shape our land would seem to act very slowly in comparison with man's average life span but in geological terms the erosion of rock is in fact very fast. Land goes through a cycle of transformation. It is broken up by earthquakes and other earth movements, temperature changes, water, wind and ice. Rock debris is then transported by water, wind and glaciers and deposited on lowlands and on the sea floor. Here it builds up and by the pressure of its own weight is converted into new rock strata. These in turn can be uplifted either gently as plains or plateaux or more irregularly to form mountains. In either case the new higher land is eroded and the cycle recommences.

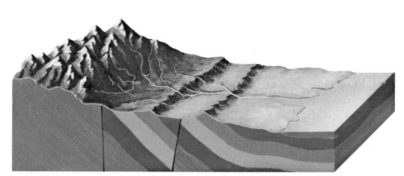
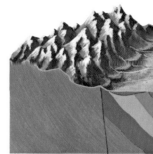

A Peneplain

Uplifted peneplain

Rivers

Rivers shape the land by three basic processes: erosion, transportation and deposition. A youthful river flows fast eroding downwards quickly to form a narrow valley (1) As it matures it deposits some debris and erodes laterally to widen the valley (2). In its last stage it meanders across a wide flat flood plain depositing fine particles of alluvium (3).

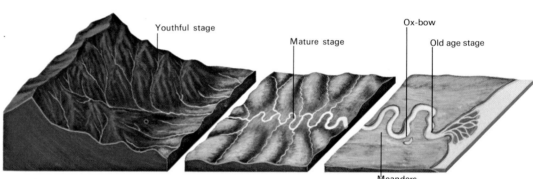

Youthful stage · Mature stage · Ox-bow · Old age stage · Meanders

Underground water

Water enters porous and permeable rocks from the surface moving downward until it reaches a layer of impermeable rock. Joints in underground rock, such as limestone, are eroded to form underground caves and caverns. When the roof of a cave collapses a gorge is formed. Surface entrances to joints are often widened to form vertical openings called swallow holes.

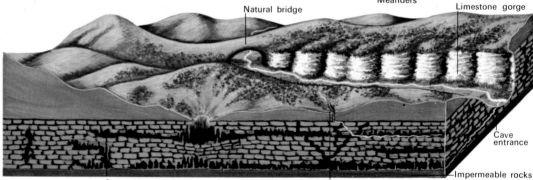

Natural bridge · Limestone gorge · Cave entrance · Impermeable rocks
Cave with stalactites and stalagmites · River disappears down swallow hole

Wind

Wind action is particularly powerful in arid and semi-arid regions where rock waste produced by weathering is used as an abrasive tool by the wind. The rate of erosion varies with the characteristics of the rock which can cause weird shapes and effects (right). Desert sand can also be accumulated by the wind to form barchan dunes (far right) which slowly travel forward, horns first.

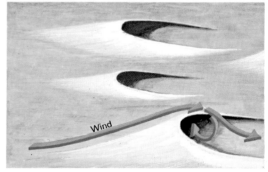

Wind

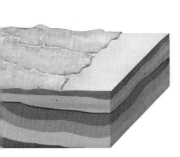

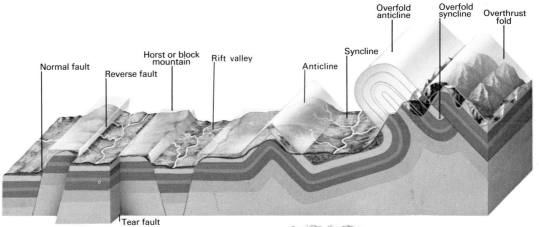

Folding and faulting
A vertical displacement in the earth's crust is called a fault or reverse fault; lateral displacement is a tear fault. An uplifted block is called a horst, the reverse of which is a rift valley. Compressed horizontal layers of sedimentary rock fold to form mountains. Those layers which bend up form an anticline, those bending down form a syncline : continued pressure forms an overfold.

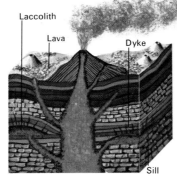

Volcanic activity
When pressure on rocks below the earth's crust is released the normally semi-solid hot rock becomes liquid magma. The magma forces its way into cracks of the crust and may either reach the surface where it forms volcanoes or it may collect in the crust as sills dykes or lacoliths. When magma reaches the surface it cools to form lava.

Waves
Coasts are continually changing, some retreat under wave erosion while others advance with wave deposition. These actions combined form steep cliffs and wave cut platforms. Eroded debris is in turn deposited as a terrace. As the water becomes shallower the erosive power of the waves decreases and gradually the cliff disappears. Wave action can also create other features (far right).

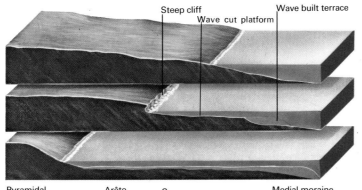

Ice
These diagrams (right) show how a glaciated valley may have formed. The glacier deepens, straightens and widens the river valley whose interlocking spurs become truncated or cut off. Intervalley divides are frost shattered to form sharp aretes and pyramidal peaks. Hanging valleys mark the entry of tributary rivers and eroded rocks form medial moraine. Terminal moraine is deposited as the glacier retreats.

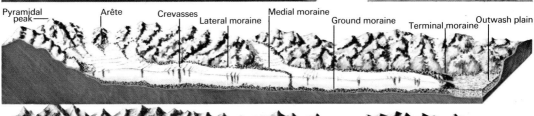

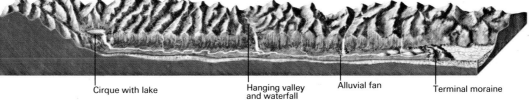

Subsidence and uplift
As the land surface is eroded it may eventually become a level plain - a peneplain, broken only by low hills, remnants of previous mountains. In turn this peneplain may be uplifted to form a plateau with steep edges. At the coast the uplifted wave platform becomes a coastal plain and in the rejuvenated rivers downward erosion once more predominates.

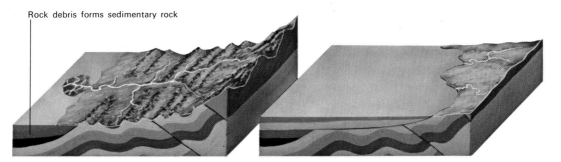

The Earth: Physical Dimensions

Its surface
Highest point on the earth's surface: Mt. Everest, Tibet - Nepal boundary   8 848 m
Lowest point on the earth's surface: The Dead Sea, Jordan   below sea level 395 m
Greatest ocean depth,: Challenger Deep, Mariana Trench   11 022 m
Average height of land   840 m
Average depth of seas and oceans   3 808 m

Dimensions
Superficial area	510 000 000 km²
Land surface	149 000 000 km²
Land surface as % of total area	29·2 %
Water surface	361 000 000 km²
Water surface as % of total area	70·8 %
Equatorial circumference	40 077 km
Meridional circumference	40 009 km
Equatorial diameter	12 756·8 km
Polar diameter	12 713·8 km
Equatorial radius	6 378·4 km
Polar radius	6 356·9 km
Volume of the Earth	1 083 230 x 10⁶ km³
Mass of the Earth	5·9 x 10²¹ tonnes

The Figure of Earth
An imaginary sea-level surface is considered and called a geoid. By measuring at different places the angles from plumb lines to a fixed star there have been many determinations of the shape of parts of the geoid which is found to be an oblate spheriod with its axis along the axis of rotation of the earth. Observations from satellites have now given a new method of more accurate determinations of the figure of the earth and its local irregularities.

Land and Sea Hemispheres.
About 85% of the total land area is contained in the hemisphere centred on a point between Paris and Brussels.

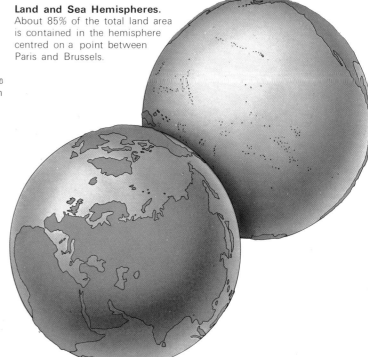

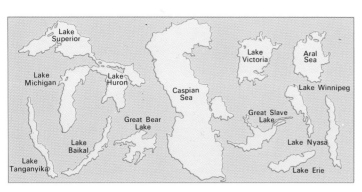

Oceans and Seas
Area in 1000 km²

Pacific Ocean	165 721	North Sea	575
Atlantic Ocean	81 660	Black Sea	448
Indian Ocean	73 442	Red Sea	440
Arctic Ocean	14 351	Baltic Sea	422
Mediterranean Sea	2 966	Persian Gulf	238
Bering Sea	2 274	St. Lawrence, Gulf of	236
Caribbean Sea	1 942	English Channel & Irish Sea	179
Mexico, Gulf of	1 813	California, Gulf of	161
Okhotsk, Sea of	1 528		
East China Sea	1 248		
Hudson Bay	1 230		
Japan, Sea of	1 049		

Lakes and Inland Seas
Areas in 1000 km²

Caspian Sea, Asia	424·2	Lake Ontario, N.America	19·5
Lake Superior, N.America	82·4	Lake Ladoga, Europe	18·4
Lake Victoria, Africa	69·5	Lake Balkhash, Asia	17·3
Aral Sea (Salt), Asia	63·8	Lake Maracaibo, S.America	16·3
Lake Huron, N.America	59·6	Lake Onega, Europe	9·8
Lake Michigan, N.America	58·0	Lake Eyre (Salt), Australia	9·6
Lake Tanganyika, Africa	32·9	Lake Turkana (Salt), Africa	9·1
Lake Baikal, Asia	31·5	Lake Titicaca, S.America	8·3
Great Bear Lake, N.America	31·1	Lake Nicaragua, C.America	8·0
Great Slave Lake, N.America	28·9	Lake Athabasca, N.America	7·9
Lake Nyasa, Africa	28·5	Reindeer Lake, N.America	6·3
Lake Erie, N.America	25·7	Issyk-Kul, Asia	6·2
Lake Winnipeg, N.America	24·3	Lake Torrens (Salt), Australia	6·1
Lake Chad, Africa	20·7	Koko Nor (Salt), Asia	6·0
		Lake Urmia, Asia	6·0
		Vänern, Europe	5·6

Longest rivers
	km.
Nile, Africa	6 690
Amazon, S.America	6 280
Mississipi - Missouri, N.America	6 270
Yangtze, Asia	4 990
Zaïre, Africa	4 670
Amur, Asia	4 410
Hwang Ho (Yellow), Asia	4 350
Lena, Asia	4 260
Mekong, Asia	4 180
Niger, Africa	4 180
Mackenzie, N.America	4 040
Ob, Asia	4 000
Yenisei, Asia	3 800

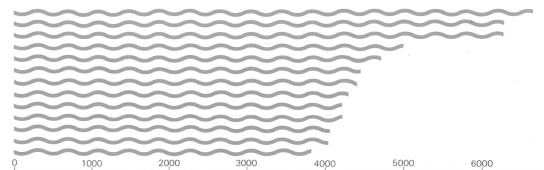

0   1000   2000   3000   4000   5000   6000   70

The Highest Mountains and the Greatest Depths.

Mount Everest defied the world's greatest mountaineers for 32 years and claimed the lives of many men. Not until 1920 was permission granted by the Dalai Lama to attempt the mountain, and the first successful ascent came in 1953. Since then the summit has been reached several times. The world's highest peaks have now been climbed but there are many as yet unexplored peaks in the Himalayas some of which may be over 7 600 m.

The greatest trenches are the Puerto Rico deep (9 200m.). The Tonga (10 822 m) and Mindanao (10 497 m) trenches and the Mariana Trench (11 022 m) in the Pacific. The trenches represent less than 2% of the total area of the sea-bed but are of great interest as lines of structural weakness in the Earth's crust and as areas of frequent earthquakes.

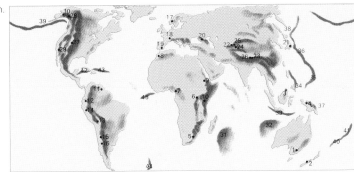

High mountains

Bathyscaphe

Mountain heights in metres

E. India & Oceania — Africa — South America — Europe and Asia — North America

1 Kosciusko 2 230
2 Mt. Cook (N.Z.) 3 764
3 Kinabalu 4 101
4 Jaya (Irian) 5 029
5 Mt. aux Sources 3 299
6 Ruwenzori 5 109
7 Cameroon peak 4 070
8 Dj. Toubkal 4 165
9 Ras Dashen 4 620
10 Kilimanjaro 5 895
11 Roraima 2 810
12 Chimborazo 6 267
13 Illimani 6 462
14 Huascaran 6 768
15 Ojos del Salado 6 863
16 Aconcagua 6 960
17 Galdhøpiggen 2 469
18 Mont Blanc 4 807
19 Mulhacen 3 478
20 Elbrus 5 633
21 Fujiyama 3 776
22 Communism peak 7 495
23 Kanchenjunga 8 598
24 K2 8 611
25 Muztagh 7 723
26 Everest 8 848
27 Mt. Elbert 4 399
28 Mt. Logan 6 050
29 Mt. Whitney 4 418
30 Mt. McKinley 6 194

Ocean depths in metres

Indian Ocean — Pacific Ocean — Atlantic Ocean

31 Mauritius basin 6 400
32 W. Australian basin 6 459
33 Java trench 7 450
34 Mindanao trench 10 497
35 Mariana trench 11 022
36 Japan trench 10 554
37 Bougainville deep 9 140
38 Kuril trench 10 542
39 Aleutian trench 7 822
40 Kermadec trench 10 047
41 Tonga trench 10 822
42 Cayman trough 7 680
43 Puerto Rico trough 9 200
44 S. Sandwich trench 8 428
45 Romanche deep 7 758

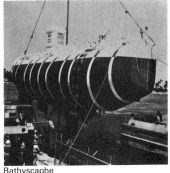

Waterfall

Dam

Notable Waterfalls heights in metres

Angel, Venezuela	980
Tugela, S. Africa	853
Mongefossen, Norway	774
Yosemite, California	738
Mardalsfossen, Norway	655
Cuquenan, Venezuela	610
Sutherland, N.Z.	579
Reichenbach, Switzerland	548
Wollomombi, Australia	518
Ribbon, California	491
Gavarnie, France	422
Tyssefallene, Norway	414
Krimml, Austria	370
King George VI, Guyana	366
Silver Strand, California	356
Geissbach, Switzerland	350
Staubbach, Switzerland	299
Trümmelbach, Switzerland	290
Chirombo, Zambia	268
Livingstone, Zaïre	259
King Edward VIII, Guyana	256
Gersoppa, India	253
Vettifossen Norway	250
Kalambo, Zambia	240
Kaieteur, Guyana	226
Maletsunyane, Lesotho	192
Terui, Italy	180
Murchison, Uganda	122
Victoria, Rhodesia - Zambia	107
Cauvery, India	97
Stanley, Zaïre	61
Niagara, N.America	51
Schaffhausen, Switzerland	30

Notable Dams heights in metres

Africa

Cabora Bassa, Zambezi R.	168
Akosombo Main Dam, Volta R.	141
Kariba, Zambezi R.	128
Aswan High Dam, Nile R.	110

Asia

Nurek, Vakhsh R., U.S.S.R.	317
Bhakra, Sutlej R., India	226
Kurobegawa, Kurobe R., Jap.	186
Charvak, Chirchik R., U.S.S.R.	168
Okutadami, Tadami R., Jap.	157
Bhumiphol, Ping R., Thai.	154

Australasia

Warragamba, N.S.W., Australia	137
Eucumbene, N.S.W., Australia	116

Europe

Grande Dixence, Switz.	284
Vajont, Vajont, R., Italy	261
Mauvoisin, Drance R., Switz.	237
Contra, Verzasca R., Switz.	230
Luzzone, Brenno R., Switz.	208
Tignes, Isère R., France	180
Amir Kabir, Karadj R., U.S.S.R.	180
Vidraru, Arges R., Rum.	165
Kremasta, Acheloos R., Greece	165

North America

Oroville, Feather R.,	235
Hoover, Colorado R.,	221
Glen Canyon, Colorado R.,	216
Daniel Johnson, Can.	214
New Bullards Bar, N. Yuba R.	194
Mossyrock, Cowlitz R.,	184
Shasta, Sacramento R.,	183
W.A.C. Bennett, Canada.	183
Don Pedro, Tuolumne R.,	178
Hungry Horse, Flathead R.,	172
Grand Coulee, Columbia R.,	168

Central and South America

Guri, Caroni R., Venezuela.	106

Distances

Kms (lower-left of each pair shown in kilometres; the upper-right half of the original chart repeats each distance in miles)

	Berlin	Bombay	Buenos Aires	Cairo	Calcutta	Caracas	Chicago	Copenhagen	Darwin	Hong Kong	Honolulu	Johannesburg	Lagos	Lisbon
Berlin														
Bombay	6288													
Buenos Aires	11909	14925												
Cairo	2890	4355	11814											
Calcutta	7033	1664	16524	5699										
Caracas	8435	14522	5096	10203	15464									
Chicago	7084	12953	9011	3206	12839	4027								
Copenhagen	357	6422	12067	9860	7072	8392	6840							
Darwin	12946	7257	14693	11612	6047	18059	15065	12903						
Hong Kong	8754	4317	18478	8150	2659	16360	12526	8671	4271					
Honolulu	11764	12914	12164	14223	11343	9670	6836	11407	8640	8921				
Johannesburg	8870	6974	8088	6267	8459	11019	13984	9225	10639	10732	19206			
Lagos	5198	7612	7916	3915	9216	7741	9612	5530	14222	11845	16308	4505		
Lisbon	2311	8018	9600	3794	9075	6501	6424	2478	15114	11028	12587	8191	3799	
London	928	7190	11131	3508	7961	7507	6356	952	13848	9623	11632	9071	5017	1588
Los Angeles	9311	14000	9852	12200	13120	5812	2804	9003	12695	11639	4117	16676	12414	9122
Mexico City	9732	15656	7389	12372	15280	3586	2726	9514	14631	14122	6085	14585	11071	8676
Moscow	1610	5031	13477	2902	5534	9938	8000	1561	11350	7144	11323	9161	6254	3906
Nairobi	6370	4532	10402	3536	6179	11544	12883	6706	10415	8776	17282	2927	3807	6461
New York	6385	12541	8526	9020	12747	3430	1145	6188	16047	12950	7980	12841	8477	5422
Paris	876	7010	11051	3210	7858	7625	6650	1026	13812	9630	11968	8732	4714	1454
Peking	7822	4757	19268	7544	3269	14399	10603	7202	6011	1963	8160	11710	11457	9668
Reykjavik	2385	8335	11437	5266	8687	6915	4757	2103	13892	9681	9787	10938	6718	2948
Rio de Janeiro	10025	13409	1953	9896	15073	4546	8547	10211	16011	17704	13342	7113	6035	7734
Rome	1180	6175	11151	2133	7219	8363	7739	1531	13265	9284	12916	7743	4039	1861
Singapore	9944	3914	15879	8267	2897	18359	15078	9969	3349	2599	10816	8660	11145	11886
Sydney	16096	10160	11800	14418	9138	15343	14875	16042	3150	7374	8168	11040	15519	18178
Tokyo	8924	6742	18362	9571	5141	14164	10137	8696	5431	2874	6202	13547	13480	11149
Toronto	6497	12488	9093	9233	12561	3873	700	6265	15498	12569	7465	13374	8948	5737
Wellington	18140	12370	9981	16524	11354	13122	13451	17961	5325	9427	7513	11761	16050	19575

Distance chart (miles). City names label each row at right; the diagonal carries the intersecting city names.

City	Values (miles)
Berlin	6047 1000 3958 3967 545 4860 1482 6230 734 6179 10002 5545 4037 11272
Bombay	9728 3126 2816 7793 4356 2956 5179 8332 3837 2432 6313 4189 7760 7686
Buenos Aires	4591 8374 6463 5298 6867 11972 7106 1214 6929 9867 7332 11410 5650 6202
Cairo	7687 1803 2197 5605 1994 4688 3272 6149 1325 5137 8959 5947 5737 10268
Calcutta	9494 3438 3839 7921 4883 2031 5398 9366 4486 1800 5678 3195 7805 7055
Caracas	2228 6175 7173 2131 4738 8947 4297 2825 5196 11407 9534 8801 2406 8154
Chicago	1694 4971 8005 711 4132 6588 2956 5311 4809 9369 9243 6299 435 8358
Copenhagen	5912 970 4167 3845 638 4475 1306 6345 951 6195 9968 5403 3892 11160
Darwin	9091 7053 6472 9971 8582 3735 8632 9948 8243 2081 1957 3375 9630 3309
Hong Kong	8775 4439 5453 8047 5984 1220 6015 11001 5769 1615 4582 1786 7810 5857
Honolulu	3781 7036 10739 4958 7437 5070 6081 8290 8026 6721 5075 3854 4638 4669
Johannesburg	9063 5692 1818 7979 5426 7276 6797 4420 4811 5381 6860 8418 8310 7308
Lagos	6879 3886 2366 5268 2929 7119 4175 3750 2510 6925 9643 8376 5560 9973
Lisbon	5391 2427 4015 3369 903 6007 1832 4805 1157 7385 11295 6928 3565 12163
London	5552 1552 4237 3463 212 5057 1172 5778 889 6743 10558 5942 3545 11691
Los Angeles	1549 6070 9659 2446 5645 6251 4310 6310 6331 8776 7502 5475 2170 6719
Mexico City	6664 9207 2090 5717 7742 4635 4780 6365 10321 8058 7024 2018 6897
Moscow	3942 4666 1545 3600 2053 7184 1477 5237 9008 4651 4637 10283
Nairobi	7358 4029 5727 5395 5548 3350 4635 7552 6996 7570 8490
New York	3626 6828 2613 4832 4280 9531 9935 6741 356 8951
Paris	5106 1384 5708 687 6671 10539 6038 3738 11798
Peking	4897 10773 5049 2783 5561 1304 6557 6700
Reykjavik	6135 2048 7155 10325 5469 2600 10725
Rio de Janeiro	5725 9763 8389 11551 5180 7367
Rome	6229 10143 6127 4399 11523
Singapore	3915 3306 9350 5298
Sydney	4861 9800 1383
Tokyo	6410 5762
Toronto	8820
Wellington	

Lower-left triangle (column labels on diagonal: Mexico City, Moscow, Nairobi, New York, Paris, Peking, Reykjavik, Rio de Janeiro, Rome, Singapore, Sydney, Tokyo, Toronto, Wellington):

	Values (miles)
Peking	10724
Reykjavik	14818 6344
Rio de Janeiro	3364 7510 11842
Rome	9200 2486 6485 5836
Singapore	12460 5794 9216 10988 8217
Sydney	7460 3304 8683 4206 2228 7882
Tokyo	7693 11562 8928 7777 9187 17338 9874
Toronto	10243 2376 5391 6888 1105 8126 3297 9214
Wellington	16610 8428 7460 15339 10737 4478 11514 15712 10025
	12969 14497 12153 15989 16962 8949 16617 13501 16324 6300
	11304 7485 11260 10849 9718 2099 8802 18589 9861 5321 7823
	3247 7462 12183 574 6015 10552 4184 8336 7080 15047 15772 10316
	11100 16549 13664 14405 18987 10782 17260 11855 18545 8526 2226 9273 14194

Miles

23

Water Resources and Vegetation

Water resources and vegetation

Fresh water is essential for life on earth and in some parts of the world it is a most precious commodity. On the other hand it is very easy for industrialised temperate states to take its existence for granted, and man's increasing demand may only be met finally by the desalination of earth's 1250 million cubic kilometres of salt water. 70% of the earth's fresh water exists as ice.

The hydrological cycle

Water is continually being absorbed into the atmosphere as vapour from oceans, lakes, rivers and vegetation transpiration. On cooling the vapour either condenses or freezes and falls as rain, hail or snow. Most precipitation falls over the sea but one quarter falls over the land of which half evaporates again soon after falling while the rest flows back into the oceans.

Distribution of water

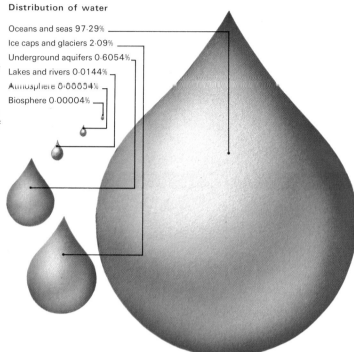

Oceans and seas 97·29%
Ice caps and glaciers 2·09%
Underground aquifers 0·6054%
Lakes and rivers 0·0144%
Atmosphere 0·00034%
Biosphere 0·00004%

Tundra

Mediterranean scrub

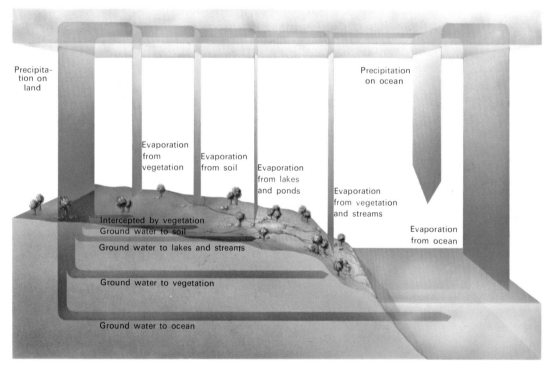

Precipitation on land

Precipitation on ocean

Evaporation from vegetation

Evaporation from soil

Evaporation from lakes and ponds

Evaporation from vegetation and streams

Evaporation from ocean

Intercepted by vegetation
Ground water to soil

Ground water to lakes and streams

Ground water to vegetation

Ground water to ocean

Domestic consumption of water

An area's level of industrialisation, climate and standard of living are all major influences in the consumption of water. On average Europe consumes 636 litres per head each day of which 180 litres is used domestically. In the U.S.A. domestic consumption is slightly higher at 270 litres per day. The graph (right) represents domestic consumption in the U.K. in 1970.

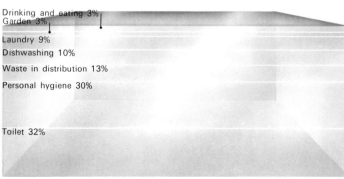

Drinking and eating 3%
Garden 3%
Laundry 9%
Dishwashing 10%
Waste in distribution 13%
Personal hygiene 30%
Toilet 32%

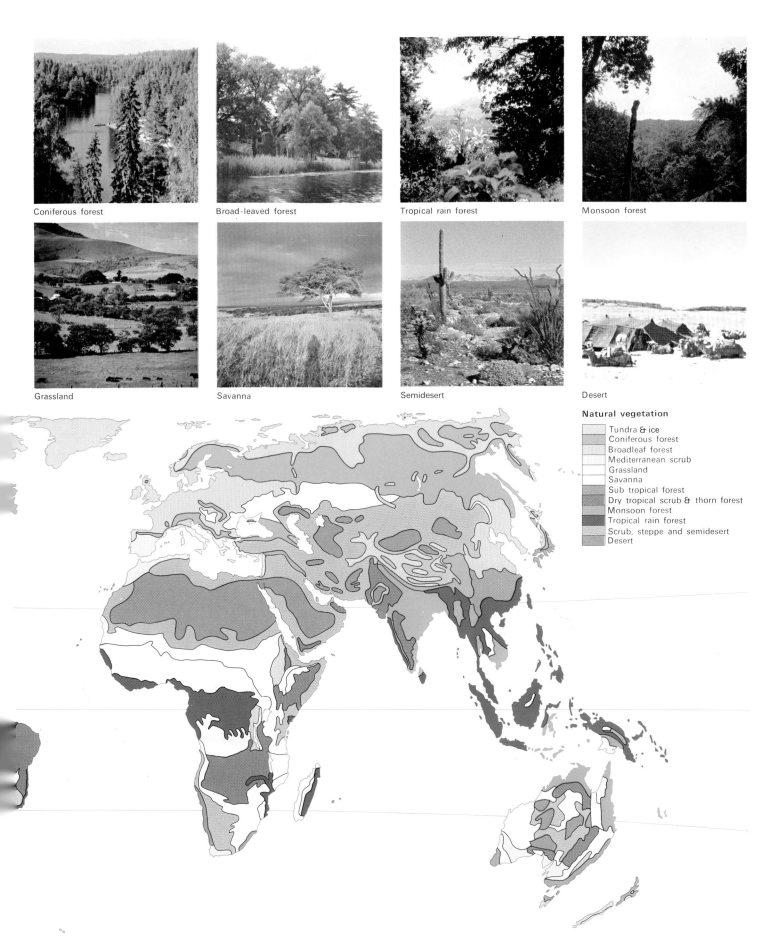

Coniferous forest

Broad-leaved forest

Tropical rain forest

Monsoon forest

Grassland

Savanna

Semidesert

Desert

Natural vegetation

Tundra & ice
Coniferous forest
Broadleaf forest
Mediterranean scrub
Grassland
Savanna
Sub tropical forest
Dry tropical scrub & thorn forest
Monsoon forest
Tropical rain forest
Scrub, steppe and semidesert
Desert

Population

Population distribution
(right and lower right)
People have always been unevenly distributed in the world. Europe has for centuries contained nearly 20% of the world's population but after the 16-19th century explorations and consequent migrations this proportion has rapidly reduced. In 1750 the Americas had 2% of the world's total: in 2000 AD they are expected to contain 16%.

The most densely populated regions are in India, China and Europe where the average density is between 100 and 200 per square km. although there are pockets of extremely high density elsewhere. In contrast Australia has only 1·6 people per square km. The countries in the lower map have been redrawn to make their areas proportional to their populations.

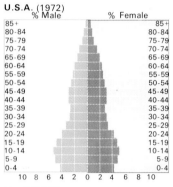

U.S.A. (1972)

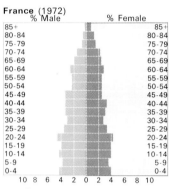

France (1972)

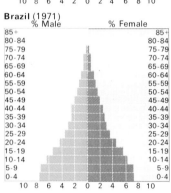

Brazil (1971)

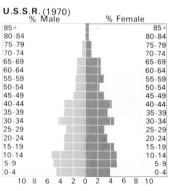

U.S.S.R. (1970)

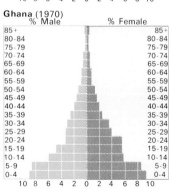

Ghana (1970)

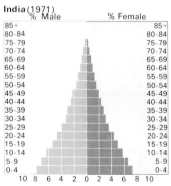

India (1971)

Age distribution
France shows many demographic features characteristic of European countries. Birth and death rates have declined with a moderate population growth - there are nearly as many old as young. In contrast, India and several other countries have few old and many young because of the high death rates and even higher birth rates. It is this excess that is responsible for the world's population explosion.

World population increase
Until comparatively recently there was little increase in the population of the world. About 6000 BC it is thought that there were about 200 million people and in the following 7000 years an increase of just over 100 million. In the 1800's there were about 1000 million; at present there are over 3500 million and by the year 2000 if present trends continue there would be at least 7000 million.

1650   1700   1750   1800

World population distribution

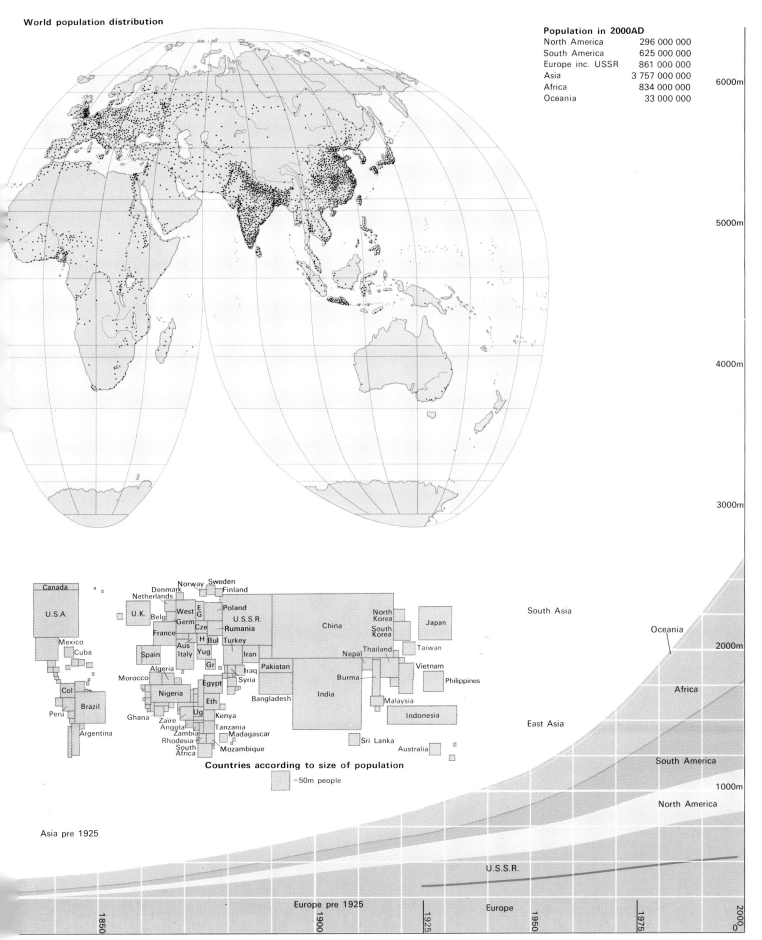

6000m

5000m

4000m

3000m

Canada
U.S.A.
Mexico
Cuba
Col
Peru
Brazil
Argentina

Norway Sweden
Denmark Finland
Netherlands
U.K. Belg West E Poland
Germ G
Cze U.S.S.R.
France H Bul Rumania
Aus Turkey
Spain Italy Yug
Gr Iran
Algeria Iraq
Morocco Pakistan Syria
Egypt
Nigeria Eth
Ghana Zaire Ug Kenya
Angola Tanzania
Zambia Madagascar
Rhodesia
South Mozambique
Africa

China
North Korea
South Korea
Japan
Taiwan
Nepal Thailand
Burma Vietnam
Bangladesh Philippines
India Malaysia
Indonesia
Sri Lanka Australia

South Asia

Oceania

Africa

2000m

South America

1000m

North America

Countries according to size of population

=50m people

East Asia

Asia pre 1925

U.S.S.R.

Europe pre 1925   Europe

1850   1900   1925   1950   1975   2000

Language

Languages may be blamed partly for the division and lack of understanding between nations. While a common language binds countries together it in turn isolates them from other countries and groups. Thus beliefs, ideas and inventions remain exclusive to these groups and different cultures develop.

There are thousands of different languages and dialects spoken today. This can cause strife even within the one country, such as India, where different dialects are enough to break down the country into distinct groups.

As a result of colonization and the spread of internationally accepted languages, many countries have superimposed a completely unrelated language in order to combine isolated national groups and to facilitate international understanding, for example Spanish in South America, English in India.

Assyrian (carved)

Ancient Hebrew (painted)

Egyptian hieroglyphic (painted)

Some modern non-latin type faces

Greek
ΑΒΓΔΕΖΗΘΙΚΛΜΝΞΟΠΡΣΤΥΦΧΨΩΣ

Cyrillic
АБВГДЕЖЗИЙІКΛМΝΟΠΡСΤΥΦΧЏЧШ

Arabic
فى عام ١٨٩٧ وصل إلى إنجلترا أ نموذج

Bengali
১৮৯৭ খ্রীস্টাব্দে আধুনিক মডেলের একটি

Telugu
విన్న సూయింటకె వచ్చిన యథిథ యేమియు

Japanese
国土 の 位 置 と 地形

Chinese
司 父 獨 子 出 有 之 限 地 位 司，
在 提 印 芬 刷 奧 業 司 上 有 能

Related languages

Certain languages showing marked similarities are thought to have developed from common parent languages for example Latin. After the retreat of the Roman Empire wherever Latin had been firmly established it remained as the new nation's language. With no unifying centre divergent development took place and Latin evolved into new languages.

Calligraphy

Writing was originally by a series of pictures, and these gradually developed in styles which were influenced by the tools generally used. Carved alphabets, such as that used by the Sumerians, tended to be angular, while those painted or written tended to be curved, as in Egyptian hieroglyphics development of which can be followed through the West Semitic, Greek and Latin alphabets to our own.

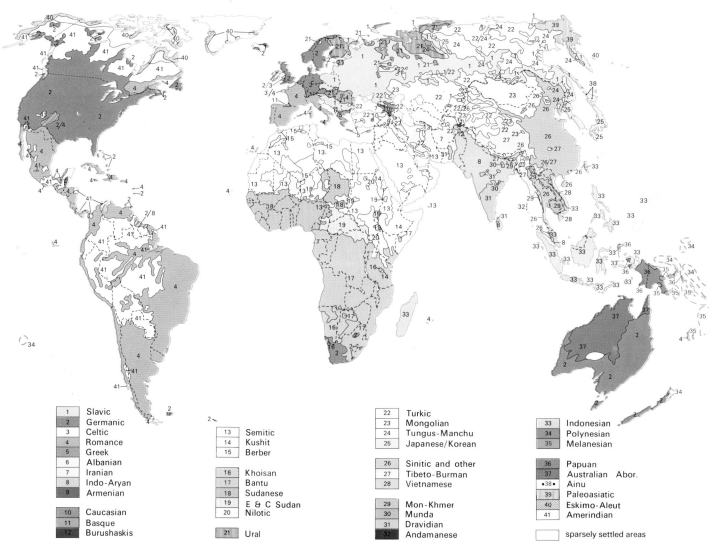

1	Slavic	
2	Germanic	
3	Celtic	
4	Romance	
5	Greek	
6	Albanian	
7	Iranian	
8	Indo-Aryan	
9	Armenian	
10	Caucasian	
11	Basque	
12	Burushaskis	

13	Semitic
14	Kushit
15	Berber
16	Khoisan
17	Bantu
18	Sudanese
19	E & C Sudan
20	Nilotic
21	Ural

22	Turkic
23	Mongolian
24	Tungus-Manchu
25	Japanese/Korean
26	Sinitic and other
27	Tibeto-Burman
28	Vietnamese
29	Mon-Khmer
30	Munda
31	Dravidian
32	Andamanese

33	Indonesian
34	Polynesian
35	Melanesian
36	Papuan
37	Australian Abor.
38	Ainu
39	Paleoasiatic
40	Eskimo-Aleut
41	Amerindian
	sparsely settled areas

Religion

Throughout history man has had beliefs in supernatural powers based on the forces of nature which have developed into worship of a god and some cases gods.

Hinduism honours many gods and goddesses which are all manifestations of the one divine spirit, Brahma, and incorporates beliefs such as reincarnation, worship of cattle and the caste system.

Buddhism, an offshoot of Hinduism, was founded in north east India by Gautama Buddha (563-483 BC) who taught that spiritual and moral discipline were essential to achieve supreme peace.

Confucianism is a mixture of Buddhism and Confucius' teachings which were elaborated to provide a moral basis for the political structure of Imperial China and to cover the already existing forms of ancestor worship.

Judaism dates back to c. 13th century B.C. The Jews were expelled from the Holy Land in AD70 and only reinstated in Palestine in 1948.

Islam, founded in Mecca by Muhammad (570-632 AD) spread across Asia and Africa and in its retreat left isolated pockets of adherent communities.

Christianity was founded by Jesus of Nazareth in the 1st century AD The Papal authority, established in the 4th century, was rejected by Eastern churches in the 11th century. Later several other divisions developed eg. Roman Catholicism, Protestantism.

Christian monastery

Jewish holy place

Hindu temple

Mohammedan mosque

Buddhist temple

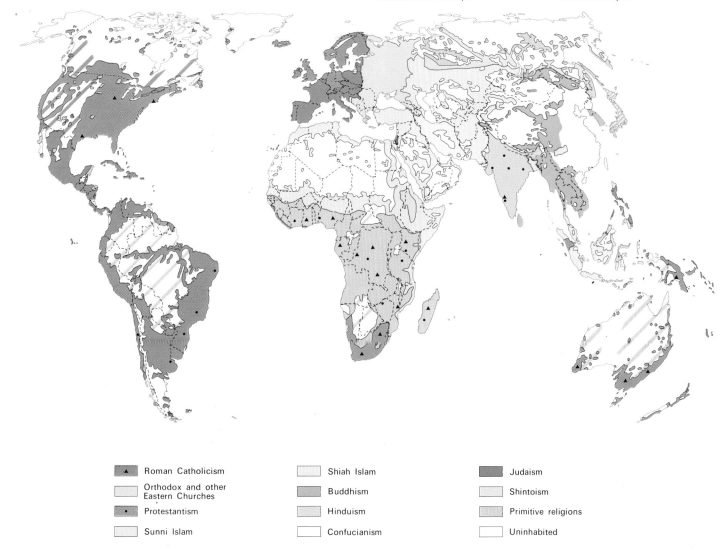

Roman Catholicism	Shiah Islam	Judaism
Orthodox and other Eastern Churches	Buddhism	Shintoism
Protestantism	Hinduism	Primitive religions
Sunni Islam	Confucianism	Uninhabited

The Growth of Cities

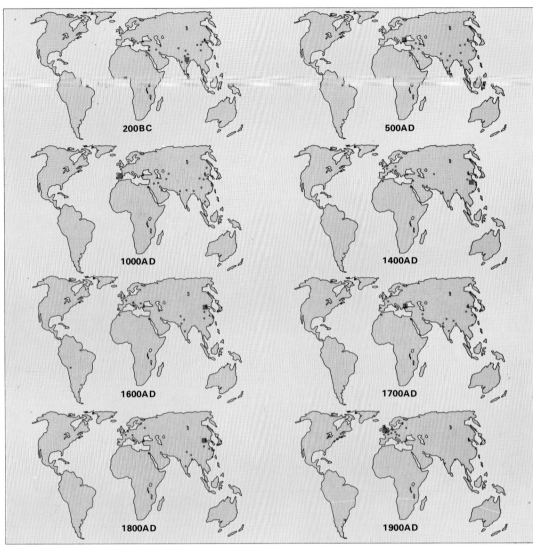

200BC

500AD

1000AD

1400AD

1600AD

1700AD

1800AD

1900AD

Cities through history
The evolution of the semi-perm
anent Neolithic settlements into a
city took from 5000 until 3500 BC.
Efficient communications and
exchange systems were developed
ao population donoitioo inoroaood
as high as 30 000 to 50 000 per
square kilometre in 2000BC
in Egypt and Babylonia,
compared with New York
City today at 10 000.

■ The largest city in
  the world
· The twenty five
  largest cities in
  the world

Sao Paulo

Increase in urbanisation
The increase in urbanisation is
a result primarily of better
sanitation and health resulting in
the growth of population and
secondarily to the movement of
man off the land into industry and
service occupations in the cities.
Generally the most highly
developed industrial nations are the
most intensely urbanised although
exceptions such as Norway and
Switzerland show that rural
industrialisation can exist.

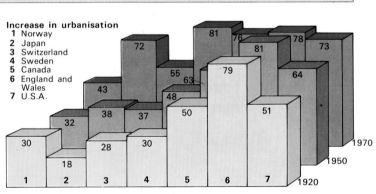

Increase in urbanisation
1 Norway
2 Japan
3 Switzerland
4 Sweden
5 Canada
6 England and
  Wales
7 U.S.A.

1970
1950
1920

Metropolitan areas
A metropolitan area can be
defined as a central city linked
with surrounding communities
by continuous built-up areas
controlled by one municipal
government. With improved
communications the neighbouring
communities generally continue
to provide the city's work-force.
The graph (right) compares the
total populations of the world's
ten largest cities.

City populations

1	Tokyo	11 623 000
2	New York	11 571 000
3	Mexico	11 340 000
4	Shanghai	10 820 000
5	Paris	9 863 000
6	Moscow	7 632 000
7	Peking	7 570 000
8	London	7 168 000
9	Los Angeles	7 032 000
10	Calcutta	7 005 000

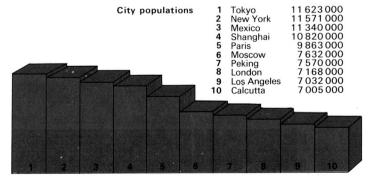

Major cities
Normally these are not only
major centres of population and
wealth but also of political power
and trade. They are the sites of
international airports and
characteristically are great ports
from which imported goods are
distributed using the roads and
railways which focus on the city.
Their staple trades and industries
are varied and flexible and depend
on design and fashion rather
than raw material production.

York

Sydney

Moscow

Tokyo

Hong Kong

Bombay

London

Cairo

Rio de Janeiro

Rome

Cities over 5 000 000 inhabitants

2 000 000 - 5 000 000 inhabitants

1 000 000 - 2 000 000 inhabitants

250 000 - 1 000 000 inhabitants

Food Resources: Vegetable

Cocoa, tea , coffee

These tropical or sub-tropical crops are grown mainly for export to the economically advanced countries. Tea and coffee are the world's principal beverages. Cocoa is used more in the manufacture of chocolate.

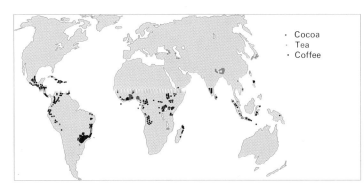

- Cocoa
- Tea
- Coffee

Sugar beet, sugar cane

Cane Sugar - a tropical crop - accounts for the bulk of the sugar entering into international trade. Beet Sugar, on the other hand, demands a temperate climate and is produced primarily for domestic consumption.

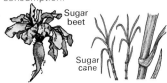

- Sugar beet
- Sugar cane

Cereals

Cereals include those members of the grain family with starchy edible seeds - wheat, maize, barley, oats, rye, rice, millets and sorghums.

Cereals and potatoes (not a cereal but starch producing) are the principal source of food for our modern civilisations because of their high yield in bulk and food value per unit of land and labour required. They are also easy to store and transport, and provide food also for animals producing meat, fat, milk and eggs. Wheat is the principal bread grain of the temperate regions in which potatoe are the next most important food source. Rice is the principal cereal in the hotter. humid regions. especially in Asia. Oats, barley and maize are grown mainly for animal feed; millets and sorghums as main subsistence crops in Africa and India.

Fruit million tonnes

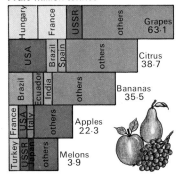

Grapes 63·1
Citrus 38·7
Bananas 35·5
Apples 22·3
Melons 3·9

Wine

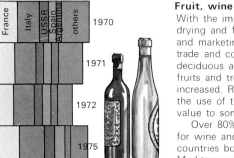

1970
1971
1972
1975

0   120   240   360 million hectolitres

Fruit, wine

With the improvements in canning, drying and freezing, and in transport and marketing, the international trade and consumption of deciduous and soft fruits, citrus fruits and tropical fruits has greatly increased. Recent developments in the use of the peel will give added value to some of the fruit crops.

Over 80% of grapes are grown for wine and over a half in countries bordering the Mediterranean.

Vegetable oilseeds and oils

Despite the increasing use of synthetic chemical products and animal and marine fats, vegetable oils extracted from these crops grow in quantity, value and importance. Food is the major use- in margarine and cooking fats.

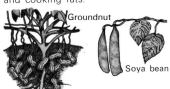

- Groundnuts
- Soya beans

Groundnuts are also a valuable subsistence crop and the meal is used as animal feed. Soya-bean meal is a growing source of protein for humans and animals. The Mediterranean lands are the prime source of olive oil.

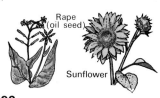

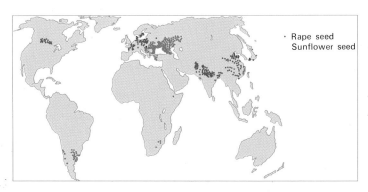

- Rape seed
- Sunflower seed

Maize (or Corn)

Needs plenty of sunshine, summer rain or irrigation and frost free for 6 months. Important as animal feed and for human food in Africa, Latin America and as a vegetable and breakfast cereal.

U.S.A. China Brazil

World production 320·6 million tonnes

Barley

Has the widest range of cultivation requiring only 8 weeks between seed time and harvest. Used mainly as animal-feed and by the malting industry.

U.S.S.R. China France Canada

World production 157·1 million tonnes

Oats

Widely grown in temperate regions with the limit fixed by early autumn frosts. Mainly fed to cattle. The best quality oats are used for oatmeal, porridge and breakfast foods.

U.S.S.R. U.S.A. Canada W.Germany Poland

World production 50·5 million tonnes

Rice

Needs plains or terraces which can be flooded and abundant water in the growing season. The staple food of half the human race. In the husk, it is known as paddy.

China India Indonesia

World production 342·9 million tonnes

Wheat

The most important grain crop in the temperate regions though it is also grown in a variety of climates e.g. in Monsoon lands as a winter crop.

U.S.S.R. U.S.A. China India

World production 362·6 million tonnes

Rye

The hardiest of cereals and more resistant to cold, pests and disease than wheat. An important foodstuff in Central and E. Europe and the U.S.S.R.

U.S.S.R. Poland W. Germany

World production 26·0 million tonnes

Millets

The name given to a number of related members of the grass family, of which sorghum is one of the most important. They provide nutritious grain.

India China U.S.A.

World production 52·3 million tonnes

Potato

An important food crop though less nutritious weight for weight than grain crops. World production is over 300 million tonnes.

U.S.S.R. Poland China

World production 301·6 million tonnes

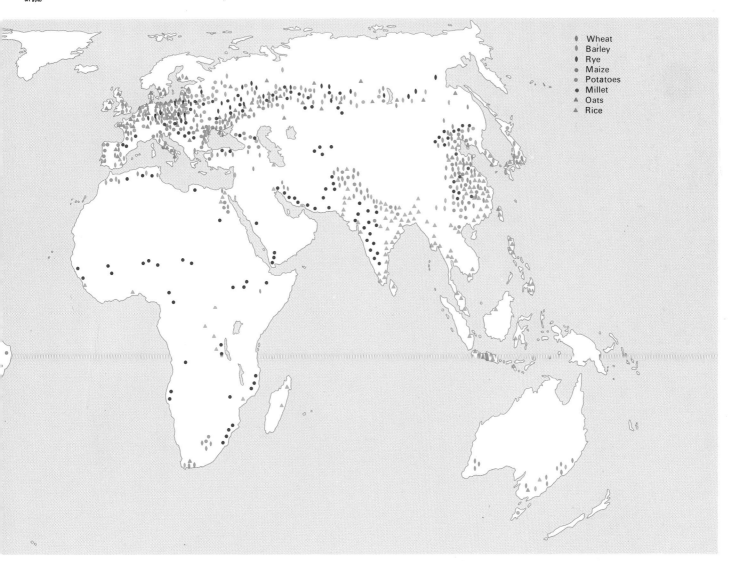

Wheat
Barley
Rye
Maize
Potatoes
Millet
Oats
Rice

Food Resources: Animal

Food resources: Animal
Meat, milk and allied foods are prime protein-providers and are also sources of essential vitamins. Meat is mainly a product of continental and savannah grasslands and the real meat areas, particularly in Europe. Milk and cheese, eggs and fish - though found in some quantity throughout the world - are primarily a product of the temperate zones.

Beef cattle Australia, New Zealand and Argentina provide the major part of international beef exports. Western U.S.A. and Europe have considerable production of beef for their local high demand.

World production 978·8 million head

Dairy Cattle The need of herds for a rich diet and for nearby markets result in dairying being characteristic of densely-populated areas of the temperate zones. U.S.A., N.W. Europe, N.Zealand and S.E. Australia.

World production 200·0 million head

Cheese The principal producers are the U.S.A., India, W. Europe, U.S.S.R., and New Zealand and principal exporters Netherlands, New Zealand, Denmark and France.

World production 10·7 million ton

Sheep Raised mostly for wool and meat, the skins and cheese from their milk are important products in some countries. The merino yields a fine wool and crossbreds are best for meat.

World production 1 046·2 million head

Pigs Can be reared in most climates from monsoon to cool temperate. They are abundant in China, the corn belt of the U.S.A. N.W. and C. Europe, Brazil and U.S.S.R.

World production 674·3 million head

Fish Commercial fishing requires large shoals of fish of one species within reach of markets. Freshwater fishing is also important. A rich source of protein, fish will become an increasingly valuable food source.

World catch 65·7 million tonnes

Butter The biggest producers are U.S.S.R., W. Europe, U.S.A., New Zealand and Australia.

World production 6·3 million tonnes

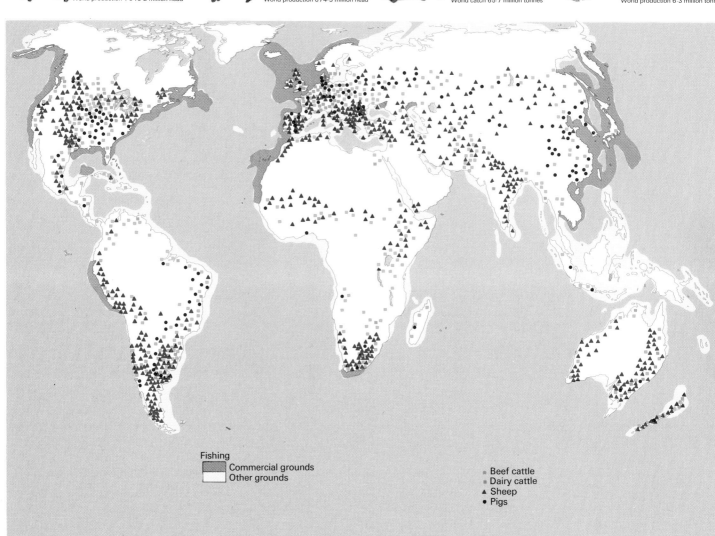

Fishing
☐ Commercial grounds
☐ Other grounds

■ Beef cattle
■ Dairy cattle
▲ Sheep
● Pigs

Foodstuffs fall, nutritionally, into three groups - providers of energy, protein and vitamins. Cereals and oil-seeds provide energy and second-class protein'; milk, meat and allied foods provide protein and vitamins, fruit and vegetables provide vitamins, especially Vitamin C, and some energy. To avoid malnutrition, a minimum level of these three groups of foodstuffs is required: the maps and diagrams show how unfortunately widespread are low standards of nutrition and even malnutrition.

Comparison of daily diets

Far East, Near East, Africa & Latin America

Europe, Oceania & North America

Malnutrition

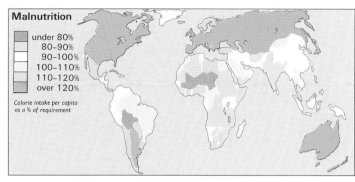

under 80%
80–90%
90–100%
100–110%
110–120%
over 120%

Calorie intake per capita as a % of requirement

Proportions of calories

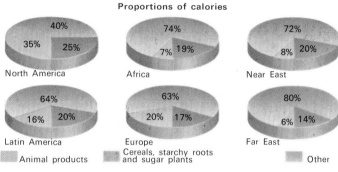

North America — 40% / 35% / 25%

Africa — 74% / 7% / 19%

Near East — 72% / 8% / 20%

Latin America — 64% / 16% / 20%

Europe — 63% / 20% / 17%

Far East — 80% / 6% / 14%

Animal products

Cereals, starchy roots and sugar plants

Other

People and tractors engaged in agriculture

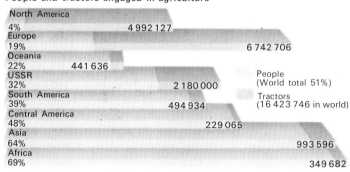

North America 4% — 4 992 127
Europe 19% — 6 742 706
Oceania 22% — 441 636
USSR 32% — 2 180 000
South America 39% — 494 934
Central America 48% — 229 065
Asia 64% — 993 596
Africa 69% — 349 682

People (World total 51%)

Tractors (16 423 746 in world)

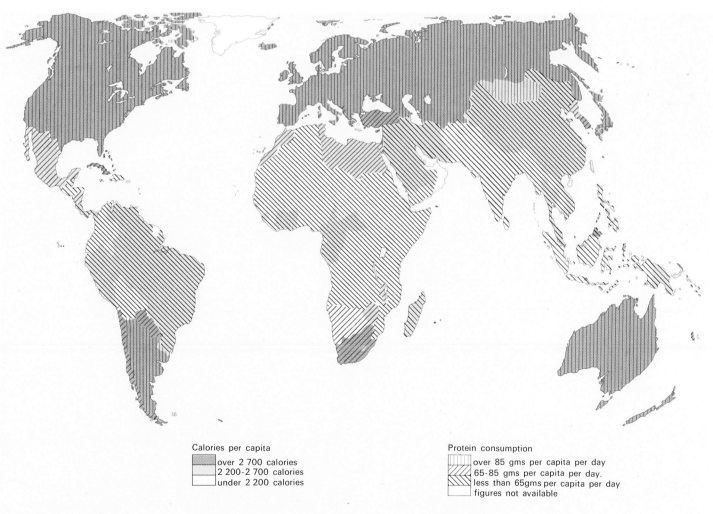

Calories per capita

over 2 700 calories
2 200-2 700 calories
under 2 200 calories

Protein consumption

over 85 gms per capita per day
65-85 gms per capita per day.
less than 65gms per capita per day
figures not available

Mineral Resources I

Primitive man used iron for tools and vessels and its use extended gradually until iron, and later steel, became the backbone of the Modern World with the Industrial Revolution in the late 18th Century. At first, local ores were used, whereas today richer iron ores in huge deposits have been discovered and are mined on a large scale, often far away from the areas where they are used; for example, in Western Australia, Northern Sweden, Venezuela and Liberia. Iron smelting plants are today increasingly located at coastal sites, where the large ore carriers can easily discharge their cargo.

Steel is refined iron with the addition of other minerals, ferro-alloys, giving to the steel their own special properties; for example, resistance to corrosion (chromium, nickel, cobalt), hardness (tungsten, vanadium), elasticity (molybdenum), magnetic properties (cobalt), high tensile strength (manganese) and high ductility (molybdenum).

Production of Ferro-alloy metals

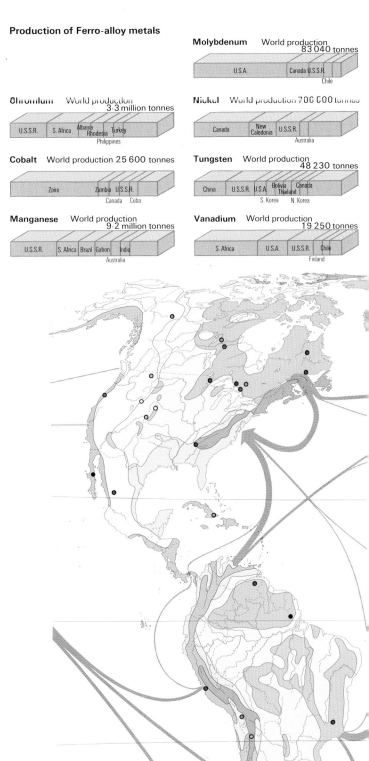

Molybdenum World production 83 040 tonnes — U.S.A., Canada, U.S.S.R., Chile

Chromium World production 3·3 million tonnes — U.S.S.R., S. Africa, Albania, Rhodesia, Turkey, Philippines

Nickel World production 700 000 tonnes — Canada, New Caledonia, U.S.S.R., Australia

Cobalt World production 25 600 tonnes — Zaire, Zambia, U.S.S.R., Canada, Cuba

Tungsten World production 48 230 tonnes — China, U.S.S.R., U.S.A., Bolivia, Thailand, S. Korea, N. Korea, Canada

Manganese World production 9·2 million tonnes — U.S.S.R., S. Africa, Brazil, Gabon, India, Australia

Vanadium World production 19 250 tonnes — S. Africa, U.S.A., U.S.S.R., Chile, Finland

Structural Regions

- Pre-Cambrian shields
- Sedimentary cover on Pre-Cambrian shields
- Palæozoic (Caledonian and Hercynian) folding
- Sedimentary cover on Palæozoic folding
- Mesozoic folding
- Sedimentary cover on Mesozoic folding
- Cainozoic (Alpine) folding
- Sedimentary cover on Cainozoic folding

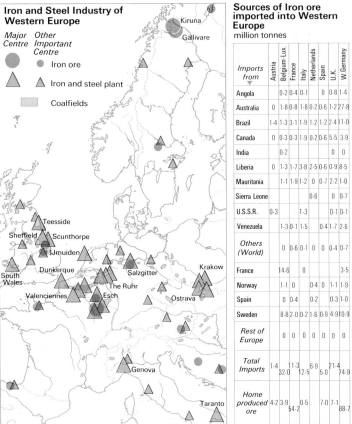

Iron and Steel Industry of Western Europe

Major Centre / Other Important Centre
- Iron ore
- Iron and steel plant
- Coalfields

Kiruna, Gällivare, Teesside, Sheffield, Scunthorpe, IJmuiden, Dunkerque, South Wales, Valenciennes, Esch, The Ruhr, Salzgitter, Krakow, Ostrava, Genova, Taranto

Sources of Iron ore imported into Western Europe
million tonnes

Imports from	Austria	Belgium-Lux.	France	Italy	Netherlands	Spain	U.K.	W. Germany
Angola		0·2	0·4	0·1		0	0·8	1·4
Australia	0	1·8	0·8	1·8	0·2	0·6	1·2	27·8
Brazil	1·4	1·3	3·1	1·9	1·2	1·2	2·4	11·0
Canada	0	0·3	0·3	1·9	0·2	0·6	5·5	3·9
India	0·2						0	0
Liberia	0	1·3	1·7	3·8	2·5	0·6	0·9	8·5
Mauritania		1·1	1·9	1·2		0·7	2·2	1·0
Sierra Leone					0·6		0	0·7
U.S.S.R.	0·3			1·3			0·1	0·1
Venezuela		1·3	0·1	1·5		0·4	1·7	2·6
Others (World)		0·6	0·1	0		0	0·4	0·7
France	14·6		0					3·5
Norway	1·1	0			0·4	0	1·1	1·9
Spain	0	0·4		0·2		0·3	1·0	
Sweden	8·8	2·0		0·2	1·6	0·9	4·9	10·9
Rest of Europe	0	0	0	0	0	0	0	0
Total Imports	1·4	32·0	11·3 12·5	6·9	5·0		21·4	74·9
Home produced ore	4·2	3·9	54·2	0·5		7·0	7·1	88·7

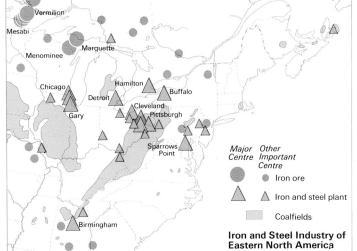

Iron and Steel Industry of Eastern North America

Steep Rock, Vermilion, Mesabi, Menominee, Marquette, Gagnon, Chicago, Hamilton, Detroit, Buffalo, Gary, Cleveland, Pittsburgh, Sparrows Point, Birmingham

Major Centre / Other Important Centre
- Iron ore
- Iron and steel plant
- Coalfields

World production of Pig iron and Ferro-alloys
Total World production 530 million tonnes

Lux.	1%
Rumania	1%
S. Africa	1%
Brazil	1%
Spain	1%
Australia	1%
India	1·5%
Poland	1·5%
Czech.	2%
Canada	2%
Italy	2%
Belg.	2·5%
U.K.	3%
France	4%
China	6%
W. Germany	7%

Others 8·5%
U.S.S.R. 20%
Japan 18%
U.S.A. 16%

Growth of World production of Pig iron and Ferro-alloys

million tonnes
600 — 1976 500
1966 400
1961 300
1956 200
1951 1938 1946 100
0

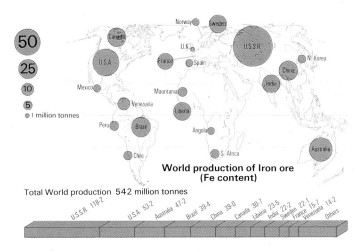

World production of Iron ore (Fe content)

Total World production 542 million tonnes

U.S.S.R. 118·2　U.S.A. 53·2　Australia 47·2　Brazil 39·4　China 39·0　Canada 30·7　Liberia 23·5　India 22·2　Sweden 22·1　France 15·7　Venezuela 14·2　Others

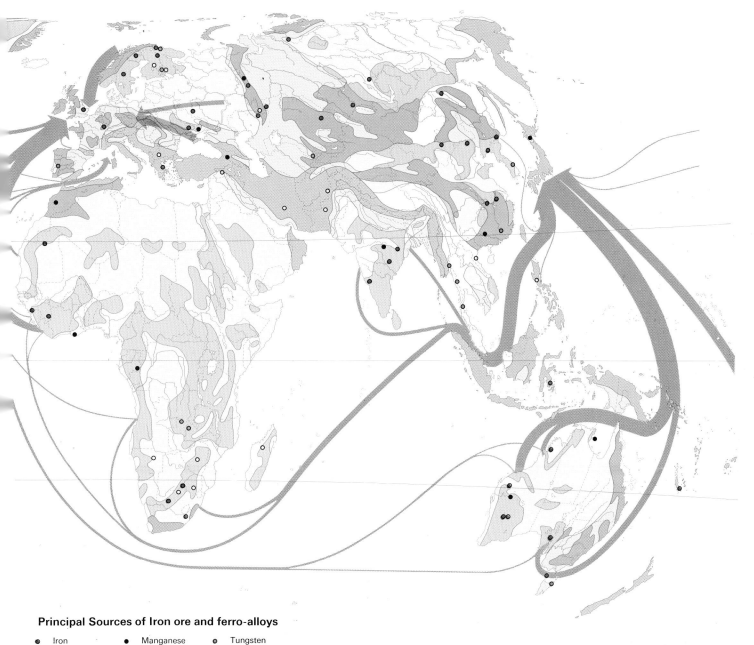

Principal Sources of Iron ore and ferro-alloys

- ◉ Iron
- ○ Chrome
- ◎ Cobalt
- ● Manganese
- ◑ Molybdenum
- ◐ Nickel
- ◒ Tungsten
- ○ Vanadium
- ▨ Iron ore trade flow

Mineral Resources II

Antimony – imparts hardness when alloyed to other metals, especially lead.
Uses: type metal, pigments to paints, glass and enamels, fireproofing of textiles.

World production 78 478 tonnes

S. Africa   China   Bolivia   U.S.S.R. Turkey Thailand

Lead – heavy, soft, malleable, acid resistant.
Uses: storage batteries, sheeting and piping, cable covering, ammunition, type metal, weights, additive to petrol.

World production 3·57 million tonnes

U.S.A.   U.S.S.R. Australia Canada

Tin – resistant to attacks by organic acids, malleable.
Uses: canning, foils, as an alloy to other metals (brass and bronze).

World production 217 200 tonnes

Malaysia   Bolivia   Indonesia   China Thailand

Aluminium – light, resists corrosion, good conductor.
Uses: aircraft, road and rail vehicles, domestic utensils, cables, makes highly tensile and light alloys.

World production 81·22 million tonnes (of Bauxite)

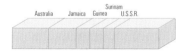

Australia   Jamaica   Surinam Guinea   U.S.S.R.

Gold – untarnishable and resistant to corrosion, highly ductile and malleable, good conductor. The pure metal is soft and it is alloyed to give it hardness.
Uses: bullion, coins, jewellery, gold-leaf, electronics.

World production 1135 tonnes

S. Africa   U.S.S.R.

Copper – excellent conductor of electricity and heat, durable, resistant to corrosion, strong and ductile.
Uses: wire, tubing, brass (with zinc and tin), bronze (with tin), (compounds)   dyeing.

World production 7·89 million tonnes

U.S.A.   U.S.S.R.   Chile Canada Zambia Zaire

Mercury – the only liquid metal, excellent conductor of electricity.
Uses: thermometers, electrical industry, gold and silver ore extraction, (compounds) – drugs, pigments, chemicals, dentistry.

World production 8932 tonnes

U.S.S.R.   Spain   China Italy Mexico

Zinc – hard metal, low corrosion factor.
Uses: brass (with copper and tin), galvanising, diecasting, medicines, paints and dyes.

World production 5·89 million tonnes

Canada   U.S.S.R.   Australia U.S.A. Peru

Diamonds – very hard and resistant to chemical attack, high lustre, very rare.
Uses: jewellery, cutting and abrading other materials.

World production 44·63 million carats

Zaire   U.S.S.R.   S. Africa Ghana Botswana

Silver – ductile and malleable, a soft metal and must be alloyed for use in coinage.
Uses: coins, jewellery, photography, electronics, medicines.

World production 9306 tonnes

U.S.S.R. Canada Peru Mexico U.S.A. Australia

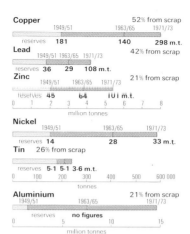

World consumption of non-ferrous metals

These diagrams show the average yearly world consumption of certain refined metals for 1949/51, 1963/65 and 1971/73 and also the percentage of the latter produced from scrap. The figures beneath each diagram show estimates made in 1950, 1964 and 1973 of reserves in the Western World.

While indicating that the reserves are by no means infinite the figures show how widely these estimates have differed over 10 years and take no account of unknown reserves, particularly in the sea-bed, or advances in mining technology which will make it economic to mine low-content ores.

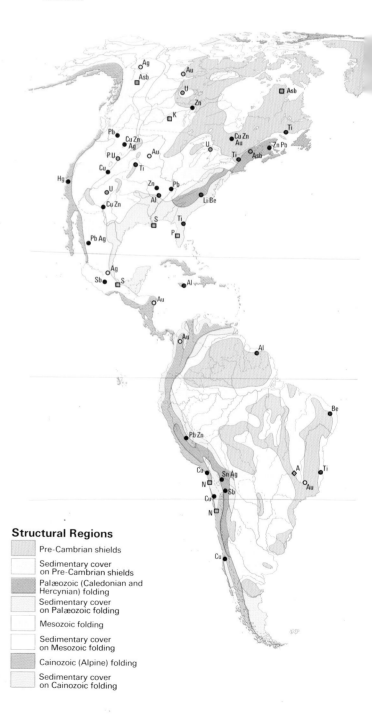

Structural Regions

- Pre-Cambrian shields
- Sedimentary cover on Pre-Cambrian shields
- Palæozoic (Caledonian and Hercynian) folding
- Sedimentary cover on Palæozoic folding
- Mesozoic folding
- Sedimentary cover on Mesozoic folding
- Cainozoic (Alpine) folding
- Sedimentary cover on Cainozoic folding

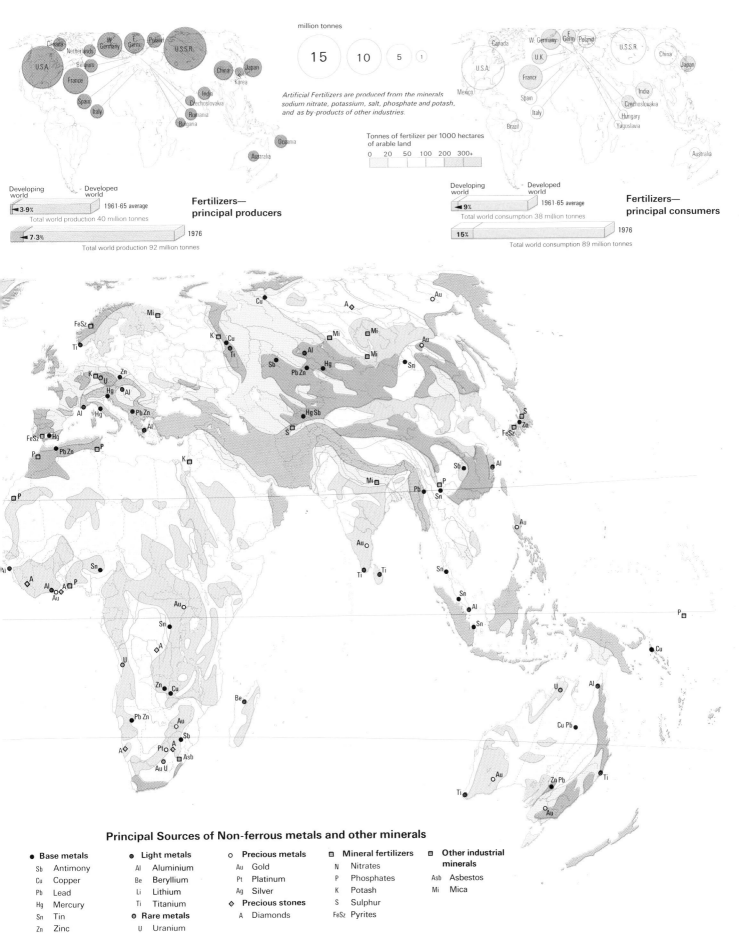

million tonnes

15 10 5 1

Artificial Fertilizers are produced from the minerals
sodium nitrate, potassium, salt, phosphate and potash,
and as by-products of other industries.

Tonnes of fertilizer per 1000 hectares
of arable land

0   20   50   100   200   300+

**Fertilizers—
principal producers**

Developing world | Developed world
◄3.9% | 1961-65 average

Total world production 40 million tonnes

◄7.3% | 1976

Total world production 92 million tonnes

**Fertilizers—
principal consumers**

Developing world | Developed world
◄9% | 1961-65 average

Total world consumption 38 million tonnes

15% | 1976

Total world consumption 89 million tonnes

Principal Sources of Non-ferrous metals and other minerals

● **Base metals**	● **Light metals**	○ **Precious metals**	▣ **Mineral fertilizers**	▣ **Other industrial minerals**
Sb Antimony	Al Aluminium	Au Gold	N Nitrates	
Cu Copper	Be Beryllium	Pt Platinum	P Phosphates	Asb Asbestos
Pb Lead	Li Lithium	Ag Silver	K Potash	Mi Mica
Hg Mercury	Ti Titanium	◇ **Precious stones**	S Sulphur	
Sn Tin	◉ **Rare metals**	A Diamonds	FeSz Pyrites	
Zn Zinc	U Uranium			

Fuel and Energy

Coal

Coal is the result of the accumulation of vegetation over millions of years. Later under pressure from overlying sediments, it is hardened through four stages: peat, lignite, bituminous coal, and finally anthracite. Once the most important source of power, coal's importance now lies in the production of electricity and as a raw material in the production of plastics, heavy chemicals and disinfectants.

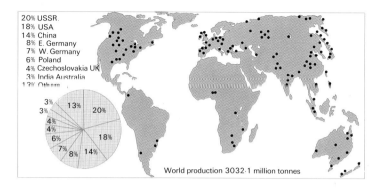

20% USSR.
18% USA
14% China
8% E. Germany
7% W. Germany
6% Poland
4% Czechoslovakia UK
3% India Australia
13% Others

World production 3032·1 million tonnes

Coal mine

Oil

Oil is derived from the remains of marine animals and plants, probably as a result of pressure, heat and chemical action. It is a complex mixture of hydrocarbons which are refined to extract the various constituents. These include products such as gasolene, kerosene and heavy fuel oils. Oil is rapidly replacing coal because of easier handling and reduced pollution.

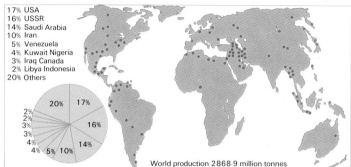

17% USA
16% USSR
14% Saudi Arabia
10% Iran
5% Venezuela
4% Kuwait Nigeria
3% Iraq Canada
2% Libya Indonesia
20% Others

World production 2868·9 million tonnes

Oil derrick

Natural gas

Since the early 1960's natural gas (methane) has become one of the largest single sources of energy. By liquefaction its volume can be reduced to 1/600 of that of gas and hence is easily transported. It is often found directly above oil reserves and because it is both cheaper than coal gas and less polluting it has great potential.

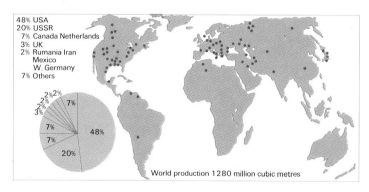

48% USA
20% USSR
7% Canada Netherlands
3% UK
2% Rumania Iran
Mexico
W. Germany
7% Others

World production 1280 million cubic metres

North sea gas rig

Water

Hydro-electric power stations use water to drive turbines which in turn generate electricity. The ideal site is one in which a consistently large volume of water falls a considerable height, hence sources of H.E.P. are found mainly in mountainous areas. Potential sources of hydro-electricity using waves or tides are yet to be exploited widely.

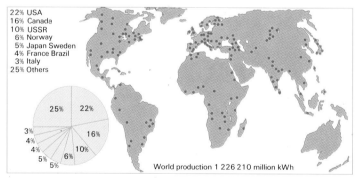

22% USA
16% Canada
10% USSR
6% Norway
5% Japan Sweden
4% France Brazil
3% Italy
25% Others

World production 1 226 210 million kWh

Water power

Nuclear energy

The first source of nuclear power was developed in Britain in 1956. Energy is obtained from heat generated by the reaction from splitting atoms of certain elements, of which uranium and plutonium are the most important. Although the initial installation costs are very high the actual running costs are low because of the slow consumption of fuel. .

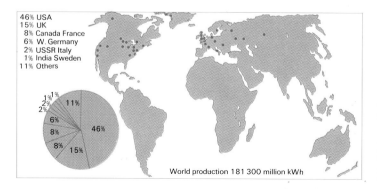

46% USA
15% UK
8% Canada France
6% W. Germany
2% USSR Italy
1% India Sweden
11% Others

World production 181 300 million kWh

Nuclear power station

40

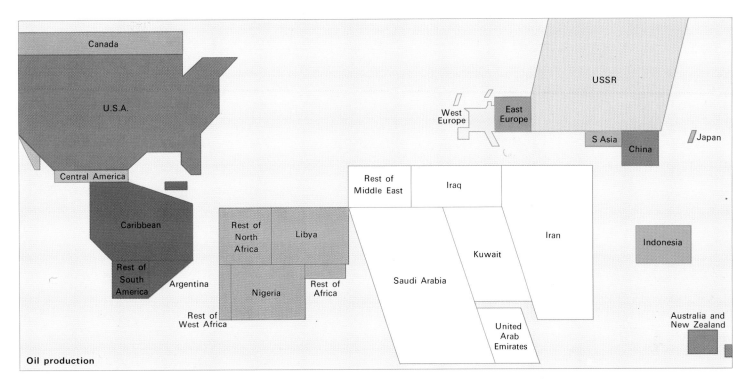

Oil production

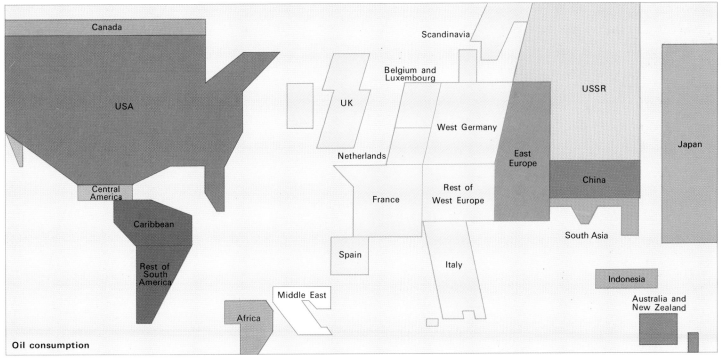

Oil consumption

Oil's new super-powers *above*
When countries are scaled according to their production and consumption of oil they take on new dimensions. At present, large supplies of oil are concentrated in a few countries of the Caribbean, the Middle East and North Africa, except for the vast indigenous supplies of the U.S.A. and U.S.S.R. The Middle East, with 55% of the world's reserves, produces 37% of the world's supply and yet consumes less than 3%. The U.S.A.,

despite its great production, has a deficiency of nearly 300 million tons a year, consuming 30% of the world's total. Estimates show that Western Europe, at present consuming 747 million tons or 27% of the total each year, may by 1980 surpass the U.S. consumption. Japan is the largest importer of crude oil with an increase in consumption of 440% during the period 1963-73.

Energy balance

millions of tons
of coal equivalent

■	−500 to −200
▨	−200 to −50
▨	−50 to 0
☐	0 to +50
▨	+50 to +200
▨	+200 to +500

The figures indicate whether a surplus or deficit exists between home production and home consumption.

Occupations

Proportion employed in

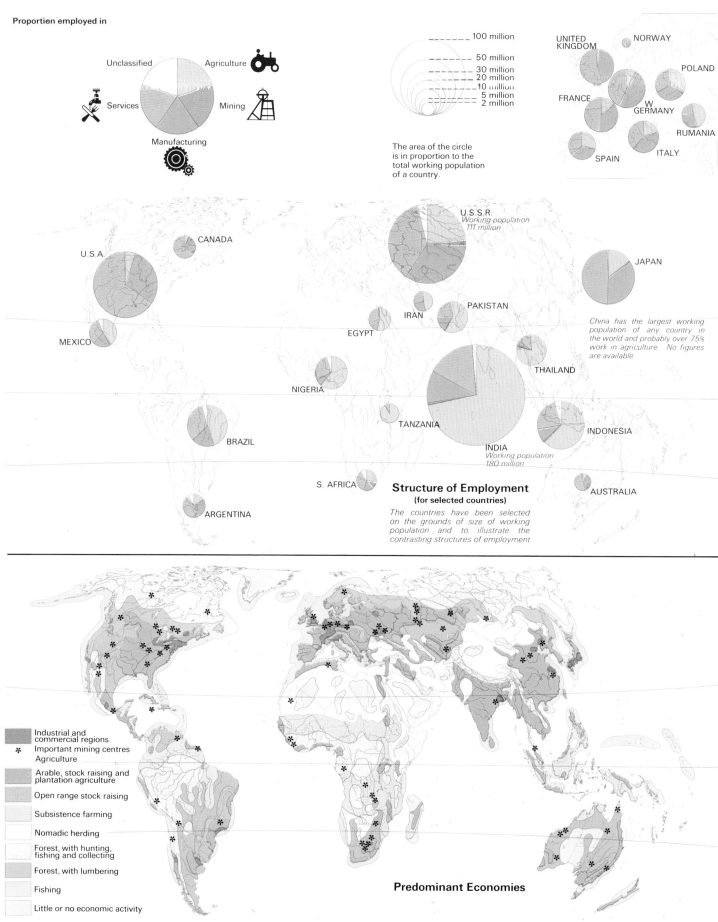

Unclassified Agriculture

Services Mining

Manufacturing

— — — — — 100 million
— — — — — 50 million
— — — — 30 million
— — — 20 million
— — 10 million
— — 5 million
— 2 million

The area of the circle
is in proportion to the
total working population
of a country.

UNITED KINGDOM NORWAY
POLAND
FRANCE W. GERMANY RUMANIA
SPAIN ITALY

CANADA

U.S.S.R.
Working population
111 million

U.S.A.

JAPAN

IRAN PAKISTAN

EGYPT

MEXICO

China has the largest working
population of any country in
the world and probably over 75%
work in agriculture. No figures
are available.

THAILAND

NIGERIA

TANZANIA

INDONESIA

BRAZIL

INDIA
Working population
180 million

S. AFRICA **Structure of Employment**
(for selected countries)

AUSTRALIA

ARGENTINA

The countries have been selected
on the grounds of size of working
population, and to illustrate the
contrasting structures of employment

Industrial and
commercial regions

* Important mining centres
Agriculture

Arable, stock raising and
plantation agriculture

Open range stock raising

Subsistence farming

Nomadic herding

Forest, with hunting,
fishing and collecting

Forest, with lumbering

Fishing

Little or no economic activity

Predominant Economies

42

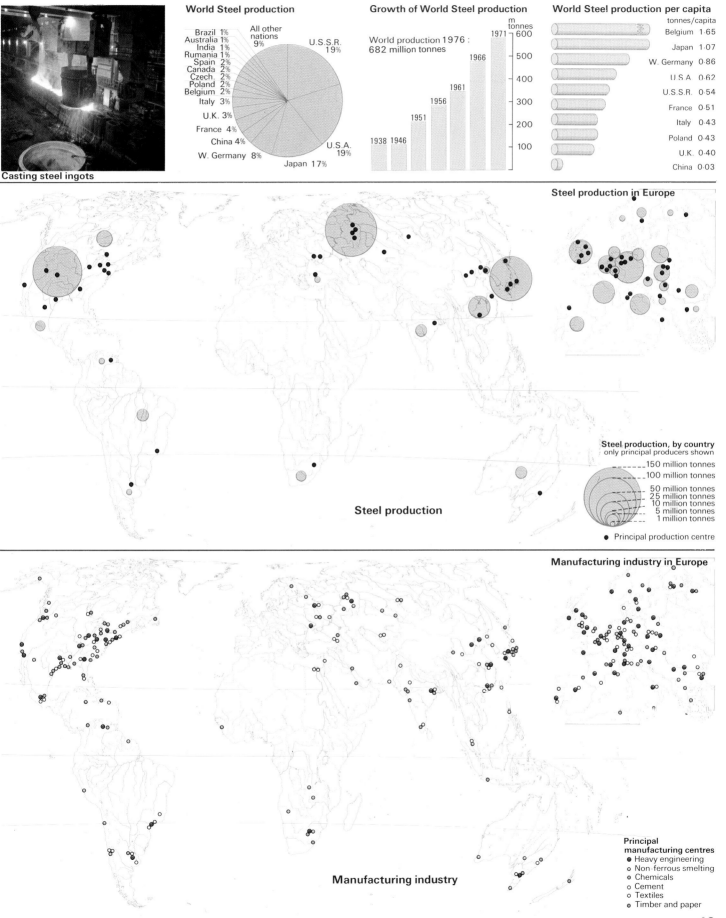

Casting steel ingots

World Steel production

Brazil 1%
Australia 1%
India 1%
Rumania 1%
Spain 2%
Canada 2%
Czech. 2%
Poland 2%
Belgium 2%
Italy 3%
U.K. 3%
France 4%
China 4%
W. Germany 8%
Japan 17%

All other nations 9%
U.S.S.R. 19%
U.S.A. 19%

Growth of World Steel production

World production 1976 : 682 million tonnes

m tonnes

1938 1946 1951 1956 1961 1966 1971

600
500
400
300
200
100

World Steel production per capita

tonnes/capita

Belgium 1·65
Japan 1·07
W. Germany 0·86
U.S.A 0·62
U.S.S.R. 0·54
France 0·51
Italy 0·43
Poland 0·43
U.K. 0·40
China 0·03

Steel production in Europe

Steel production

Steel production, by country
only principal producers shown

150 million tonnes
100 million tonnes
50 million tonnes
25 million tonnes
10 million tonnes
5 million tonnes
1 million tonnes

● Principal production centre

Manufacturing industry in Europe

Manufacturing industry

Principal manufacturing centres
● Heavy engineering
○ Non-ferrous smelting
◑ Chemicals
○ Cement
○ Textiles
◐ Timber and paper

43

Transport

Shipyards

Japan 17 609	
Sweden 2206	
West Germany 2151	
Spain 1428	
France 1349	
U.K. 1281	
Denmark 1125	
Italy 1028	
Norway 1012	
U.S.A. 801	
Yug. 774	
Neth. 723	

Shipbuilding
tonnage launched
in thousand gross
registered tons

● Principal shipbuilding centres

Europe

Japan

Aircraft Industry

In 1975 there were approximately
10 000 civil passenger airliners in
service. This diagram shows where they
were built.

U.S.A. 53%	U.S.S.R. 33%	U.K. 6% Netherlands 3% France 2%

Trade in Aircraft and Aircraft Engines

million U.S. $

	Exports			Imports	
	Aircraft	Engines		Aircraft	Engines
U.S.A.	4143	714	U.S.A.	563	218
U.K.	605	591	Canada	438	108
France	360	150	France	400	250
Canada	325	132	U.K.	389	393
W. Germ.	200		Australia	342	20
Neth.	192	89	W. Germ.	279	
Italy	137		Japan	236	107

Concorde and Boeing 747

● Principal aircraft manufacturing centres

Motor vehicles

Production *thousand units*	Exports *million U.S. $*	Imports *million U.S. $*
U.S.A. 12 638	6076	1005
Japan 7088	4899	193
W. Germany 3949	9107	996
France 3596	3779	1903
U.K. 2164	2701	1599
Italy 1960	1963	1263
Canada 1604	4814	5349
U.S.S.R. 1604	611	240
Belgium 938	2215	1457

Europe

Locomotive works

Railway vehicles

Exports *million U.S. $*		Imports *million U.S. $.*	
U.S.A.	219·2	Yugoslavia	109·2
France	210·2	Brazil	65·8
Japan	186·3	S. Africa	48·4
W. Germany	157·7	W. Germany	47·4
Canada	76·1	U.S.A.	39·0
Yugoslavia	59·6	Belg.-Lux.	34·9
Italy	42·2	Netherlands	34·4
Spain	42·2	France	31·3
U.K.	38·6	Canada	30·0
Sweden	24·2	Argentina	25·7
Belg.-Lux.	22·0	Italy	22·9
Portugal	14·4	Sweden	19·4
Austria	11·8	S. Korea	18·8

● Principal locomotive building centres

Car assembly line

● Principal motor vehicle plants

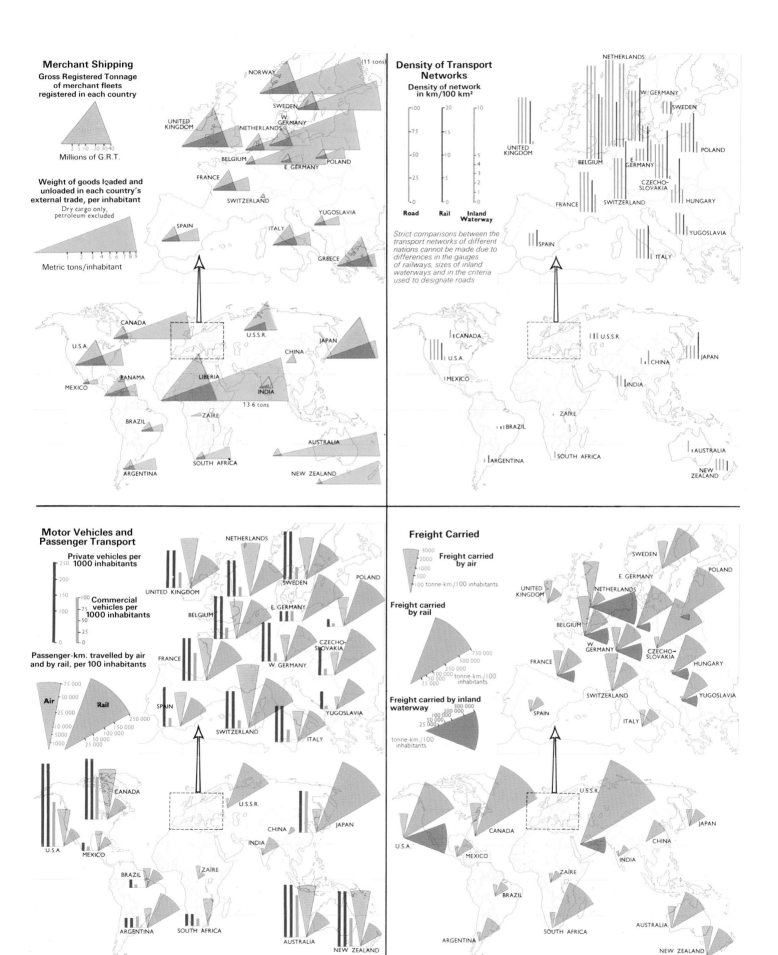

Merchant Shipping

Gross Registered Tonnage of merchant fleets registered in each country

Millions of G.R.T.

2 5 10 20 30 40

Weight of goods loaded and unloaded in each country's external trade, per inhabitant

Dry cargo only, petroleum excluded

1 2 3 4 5 6 7 8 9

Metric tons/inhabitant

NORWAY
SWEDEN
W. GERMANY
UNITED KINGDOM
NETHERLANDS
BELGIUM
E. GERMANY
POLAND
FRANCE
SWITZERLAND
YUGOSLAVIA
SPAIN
ITALY
GREECE
CANADA
U.S.S.R.
JAPAN
U.S.A.
CHINA
PANAMA
MEXICO
LIBERIA
INDIA
BRAZIL
ZAÏRE
AUSTRALIA
SOUTH AFRICA
ARGENTINA
NEW ZEALAND

(11 tons)
13·6 tons

Density of Transport Networks

Density of network in km/100 km²

Road | Rail | Inland Waterway

Strict comparisons between the transport networks of different nations cannot be made due to differences in the gauges of railways, sizes of inland waterways and in the criteria used to designate roads

NETHERLANDS
W. GERMANY
SWEDEN
UNITED KINGDOM
BELGIUM
E. GERMANY
POLAND
FRANCE
SWITZERLAND
CZECHO-SLOVAKIA
HUNGARY
SPAIN
YUGOSLAVIA
ITALY
CANADA
U.S.S.R.
JAPAN
U.S.A.
CHINA
MEXICO
INDIA
ZAÏRE
BRAZIL
ARGENTINA
SOUTH AFRICA
AUSTRALIA
NEW ZEALAND

Motor Vehicles and Passenger Transport

Private vehicles per 1000 inhabitants

250 200 150 100

Commercial vehicles per 1000 inhabitants

100 75 50 25 0

Passenger-km. travelled by air and by rail, per 100 inhabitants

Air | Rail

75 000 50 000 25 000 10 000 5000 1000

250 000 150 000 100 000 50 000

NETHERLANDS
SWEDEN
POLAND
UNITED KINGDOM
E. GERMANY
BELGIUM
CZECHO-SLOVAKIA
FRANCE
W. GERMANY
SPAIN
YUGOSLAVIA
SWITZERLAND
ITALY
CANADA
U.S.S.R.
CHINA
JAPAN
U.S.A.
MEXICO
INDIA
BRAZIL
ZAÏRE
ARGENTINA
SOUTH AFRICA
AUSTRALIA
NEW ZEALAND

Freight Carried

Freight carried by air

3000 2000 1000 500 100 tonne-km./100 inhabitants

Freight carried by rail

750 000 500 000 250 000 100 000 50 000 25 000 tonne-km./100 inhabitants

Freight carried by inland waterway

300 000 200 000 100 000 50 000 25 000 tonne-km./100 inhabitants

SWEDEN
E. GERMANY
POLAND
UNITED KINGDOM
NETHERLANDS
BELGIUM
W. GERMANY
CZECHO-SLOVAKIA
FRANCE
HUNGARY
SWITZERLAND
YUGOSLAVIA
SPAIN
ITALY
U.S.S.R.
CANADA
JAPAN
U.S.A.
CHINA
MEXICO
INDIA
ZAÏRE
BRAZIL
SOUTH AFRICA
ARGENTINA
AUSTRALIA
NEW ZEALAND

Trade

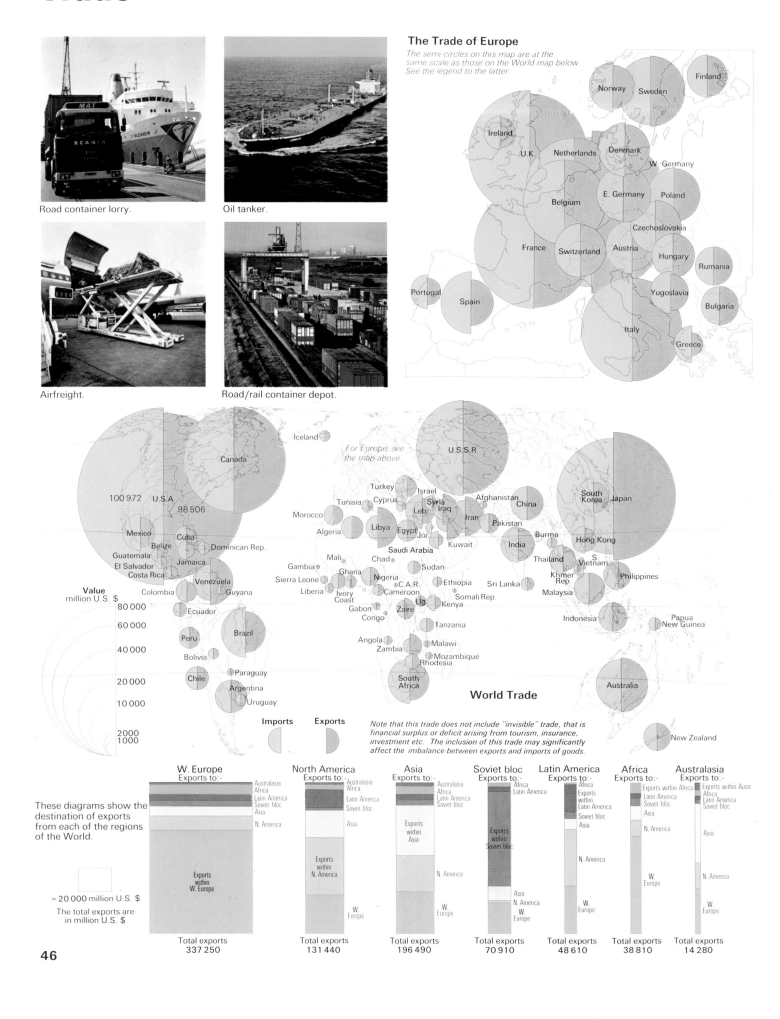

Road container lorry.

Oil tanker.

Airfreight.

Road/rail container depot.

The Trade of Europe

The semi circles on this map are at the same scale as those on the World map below. See the legend to the latter.

Norway · Sweden · Finland · Ireland · U.K. · Netherlands · Denmark · W. Germany · Belgium · E. Germany · Poland · France · Switzerland · Austria · Czechoslovakia · Hungary · Rumania · Portugal · Spain · Yugoslavia · Bulgaria · Italy · Greece

World Trade

For Europe, see the map above.

Iceland · Canada · U.S.A. 100 972 · 98 506 · U.S.S.R. · Mexico · Cuba · Dominican Rep. · Belize · Guatemala · Jamaica · El Salvador · Costa Rica · Venezuela · Guyana · Colombia · Ecuador · Peru · Brazil · Bolivia · Paraguay · Chile · Argentina · Uruguay

Turkey · Israel · Tunisia · Cyprus · Syria · Afghanistan · China · Leb. · Iraq · Morocco · Libya · Egypt · Jor. · Iran · Pakistan · Algeria · Saudi Arabia · Kuwait · India · Burma · South Korea · Japan · Hong Kong · Mali · Chad · Sudan · Thailand · S. Vietnam · Gambia · Ghana · Nigeria · Sri Lanka · Khmer Rep. · Philippines · Sierra Leone · C.A.R. · Ethiopia · Malaysia · Liberia · Ivory Coast · Cameroon · Somali Rep. · Gabon · Zaire · Kenya · Indonesia · Papua New Guinea · Congo · Ug. · Tanzania · Angola · Malawi · Zambia · Mozambique · Rhodesia · South Africa · Australia · New Zealand

Value
million U.S. $

80 000
60 000
40 000
20 000
10 000
2000
1000

Imports · Exports

Note that this trade does not include "invisible" trade, that is financial surplus or deficit arising from tourism, insurance, investment etc. The inclusion of this trade may significantly affect the imbalance between exports and imports of goods.

These diagrams show the destination of exports from each of the regions of the World.

= 20 000 million U.S. $

The total exports are in million U.S. $

W. Europe
Exports to:-
Australasia · Africa · Latin America · Soviet bloc · Asia · N. America
Exports within W. Europe
Total exports
337 250

North America
Exports to:-
Australasia · Africa · Latin America · Soviet bloc · Asia
Exports within N. America
W. Europe
Total exports
131 440

Asia
Exports to:-
Australasia · Africa · Latin America · Soviet bloc
Exports within Asia
N. America
W. Europe
Total exports
196 490

Soviet bloc
Exports to:-
Africa · Latin America
Exports within Soviet bloc
Asia · N. America · W. Europe
Total exports
70 910

Latin America
Exports to:-
Africa · Exports within Latin America · Soviet bloc · Asia · N. America · W. Europe
Total exports
48 610

Africa
Exports to:-
Exports within Africa · Latin America · Soviet bloc · Asia · N. America · W. Europe
Total exports
38 810

Australasia
Exports to:-
Exports within Austr. · Africa · Latin America · Soviet bloc · Asia · N. America · W. Europe
Total exports
14 280

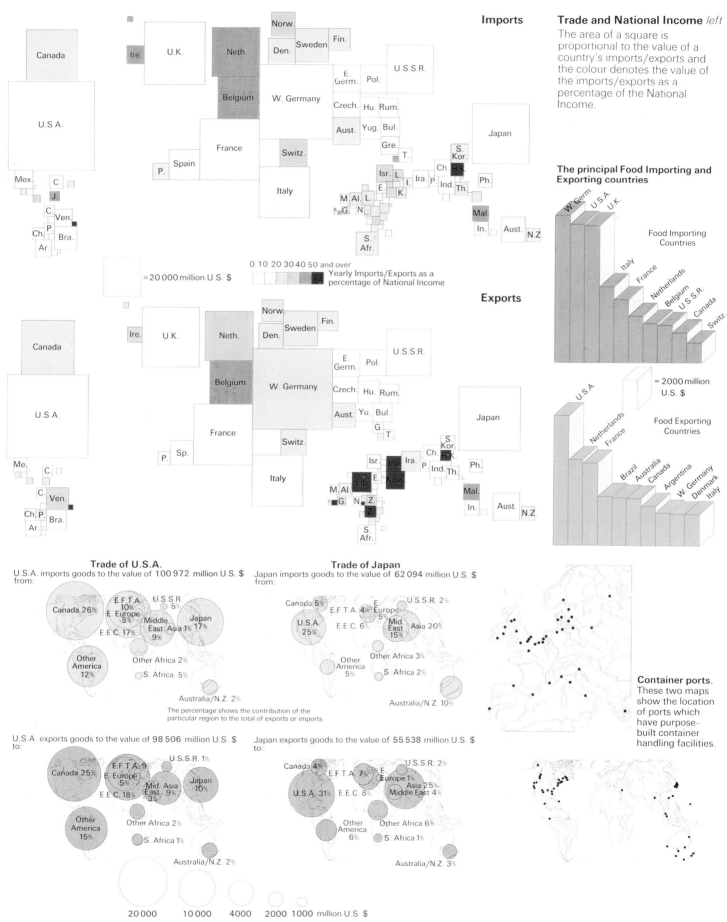

Imports

Trade and National Income *left*
The area of a square is proportional to the value of a country's imports/exports and the colour denotes the value of the imports/exports as a percentage of the National Income.

The principal Food Importing and Exporting countries

Food Importing Countries

W. Germ., U.S.A., U.K., Italy, France, Netherlands, Belgium, U.S.S.R., Canada, Switz.

= 2000 million U.S. $

Food Exporting Countries

U.S.A., Netherlands, France, Brazil, Australia, Canada, Argentina, W. Germany, Denmark, Italy

= 20 000 million U.S. $

0 10 20 30 40 50 and over
Yearly Imports/Exports as a percentage of National Income

Exports

Trade of U.S.A.
U.S.A. imports goods to the value of 100 972 million U.S. $ from:

Canada 26%, E.F.T.A. 10%, E. Europe 5%, U.S.S.R. 5%, Middle East 9%, Asia 1%, Japan 17%, E.E.C. 17%, Other America 12%, Other Africa 2%, S. Africa 5%, Australia/N.Z. 2%

The percentage shows the contribution of the particular region to the total of exports or imports

U.S.A. exports goods to the value of 98 506 million U.S. $ to:

Canada 25%, E.F.T.A. 9%, E. Europe 5%, U.S.S.R. 1%, Mid. East 3%, Asia 9%, Japan 10%, E.E.C. 18%, Other America 15%, Other Africa 2%, S. Africa 1%, Australia/N.Z. 2%

Trade of Japan
Japan imports goods to the value of 62 094 million U.S. $ from:

Canada 5%, E.F.T.A. 4%, E. Europe 5%, U.S.S.R. 2%, U.S.A. 25%, E.E.C. 6%, Mid. East 15%, Asia 20%, Other America 5%, Other Africa 3%, S. Africa 2%, Australia/N.Z. 10%

Japan exports goods to the value of 55 538 million U.S. $ to:

Canada 4%, E.F.T.A. 7%, E. Europe 1%, U.S.S.R. 2%, U.S.A. 31%, E.E.C. 8%, Asia 25%, Middle East 4%, Other America 6%, Other Africa 6%, S. Africa 1%, Australia/N.Z. 3%

20 000 10 000 4000 2000 1000 million U.S. $

Container ports.
These two maps show the location of ports which have purpose-built container handling facilities.

47

Wealth

The living standard of a few highly developed, urbanised, industrialised countries is a complete contrast to the conditions of the vast majority of economically undeveloped, agrarian states. It is this contrast which divides mankind into rich and poor, well fed and hungry. The developing world is still an overwhelmingly agricultural world: over 70% of all its people live off the land and yet the output from that land remains pitifully low. Many Africans, South Americans and Asians struggle with the soil but the bad years occur only too frequently and they seldom have anything left over to save. The need for foreign capital then arises.

National Income *see right*

The gap between developing and developed worlds is in fact widening eg. in 1938 the incomes for the United States and India were in the proportions of 1:15; now they are 1:35.

Islands *see map right*

a Antilles
b Martinique
c Barbados
d Cape Verde
e Bahrein
f Comoro
g Reunion
h Mauritius
j Solomon
k New Hebrides
l Fiji
m New Caledonia
n Tonga

Incomes per capita in U.S. dollars

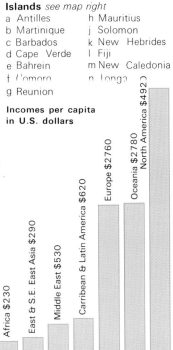

Africa $230
East & S.E. East Asia $290
Middle East $530
Carribean & Latin America $620
Europe $2760
Oceania $2780
North America $4920

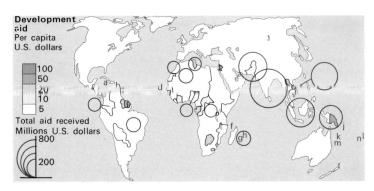

Development aid
Per capita
U.S. dollars

100
50
20
10
5

Total aid received
Millions U.S. dollars
800
200

Development aid

The provision of foreign aid, defined as assistance on concessional terms for promoting development, is today an accepted, though controversial aspect of the economic policies of most advanced countries towards less developed countries. Aid for development is based not merely on economic considerations but also on social, political and historical factors. The most important international committee set up after the war was that of the U.N.; practically all aid however has been given bi-laterally direct from an industrialised country to an under-developed country. Although aid increased during the 1950's the donated proportion of industrialised countries GNP has diminished from 0.5 to 0.4%. Less developed countries share of world trade also decreased and increased population invalidated any progress made:

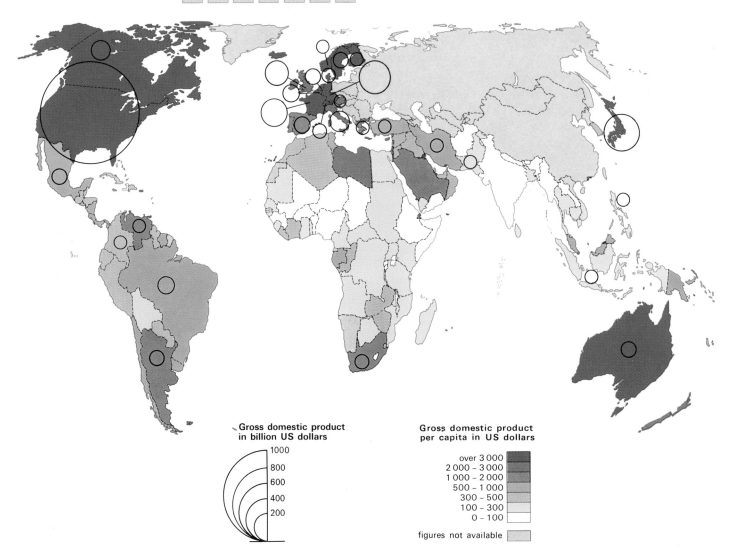

Gross domestic product in billion US dollars

1000
800
600
400
200

Gross domestic product per capita in US dollars

over 3 000
2 000 – 3 000
1 000 – 2 000
500 – 1 000
300 – 500
100 – 300
0 – 100

figures not available

SETTLEMENTS

Settlement symbols in order of size

◻ LONDON
🢭 MONTRÉAL

■ Stuttgart
▫ Hamilton

◉ Sevilla
◎ Moose Jaw

◎ Bergen
◎ Prince Rupert

○ Bath
○ Gaspé

○ Biarritz
  Banff

○ Srikolayatji
  Miquelon

Settlement symbols and type styles vary according to the scale of each map and indicate the importance of towns on the map rather than specific population figures

∴ Sites of Archæological or Historical importance

BOUNDARIES

———— International Boundaries

— ▪▪ — International Boundaries (Undemarcated or Undefined)

▪▪▪▪▪····· Internal Boundaries

International boundaries show the *de facto* situation where there are rival claims to territory

National and Provincial Parks

COMMUNICATIONS

═══ Freeways

▬▬ Principal Railways

············ Principal Canals

═════ Freeways under construction

▬▬ Other Railways

┝━┿━┥ Principal Oil Pipelines

━O━ Trans-Canada Highway

~----~ Railways under construction

_ *3386* _ Principal Shipping Routes (Distances in Nautical Miles)

——— Principal Roads

∃---∈ Railway Tunnels

——— Principal Air Routes

⌒ Other Roads

∃---∈ Road Tunnels

✈ ✛ ✿ Airports

~-----~ Tracks and Seasonal Roads

⌣ Passes

PHYSICAL FEATURES

⌇ Perennial Streams

⬭ Seasonal Lakes, Salt Flats

▭ Permanent Ice

····· Seasonal Streams

Swamps, Marshes

⌣ Wells in Desert

▲ 8848 Spot Height in metres

▼ 8050 Sea Depths. in metres

1134 Height of Lake Surface Above Sea Level, in metres

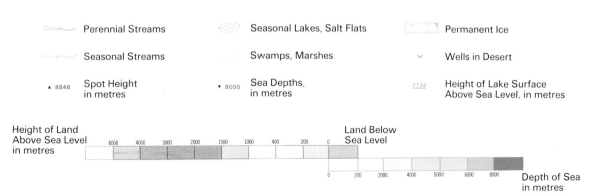

Height of Land Above Sea Level in metres

6000 4000 3000 2000 1500 1000 400 200 0

Land Below Sea Level

0 200 2000. 4000 5000 6000 8000

Depth of Sea in metres

Some of the maps have different contours to highlight and clarify the principal relief features

Abbreviations of measures used   mm Millimetres   m Metres   km Kilometres   °C Degrees Celsius   mb Millibars

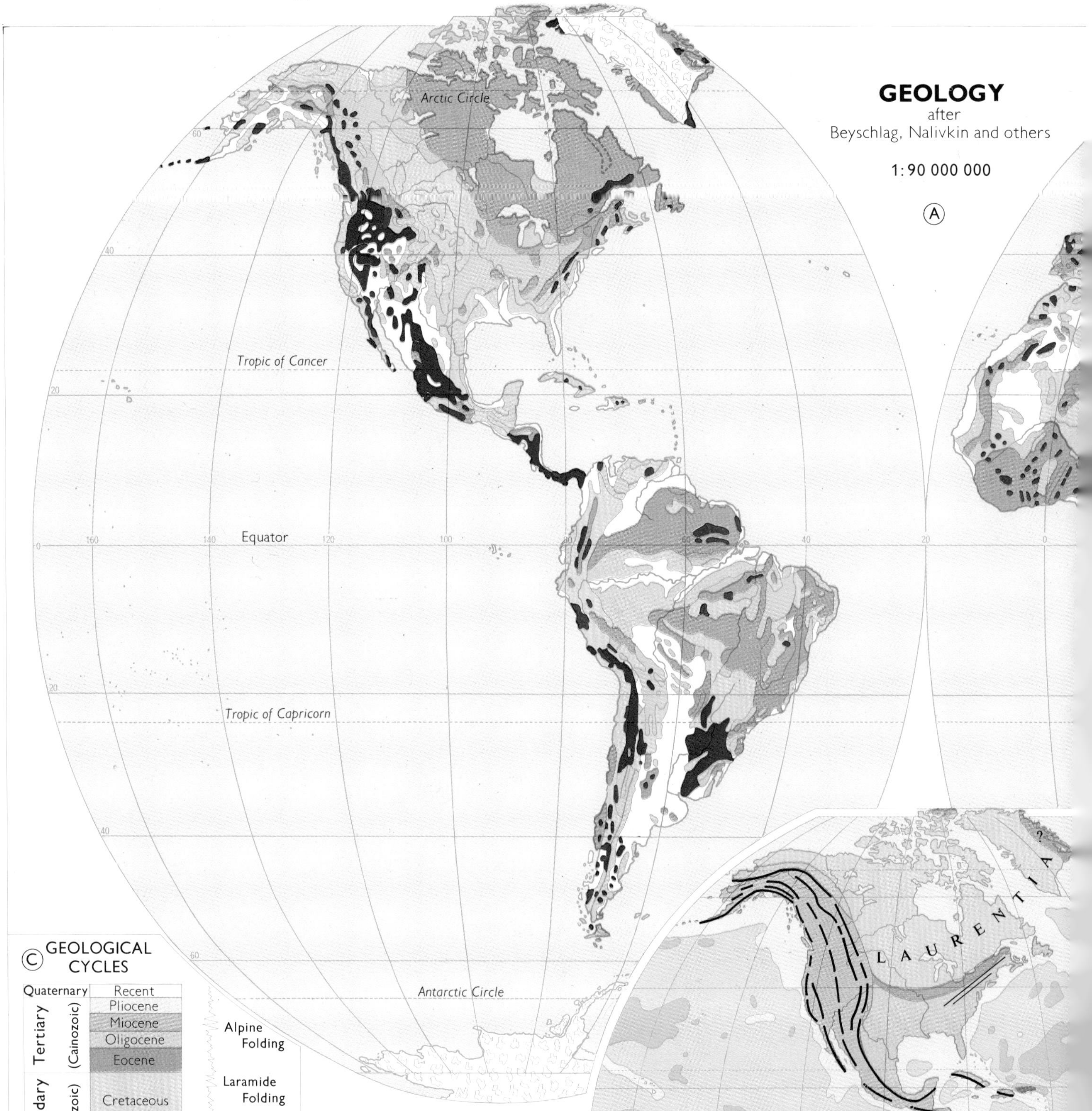

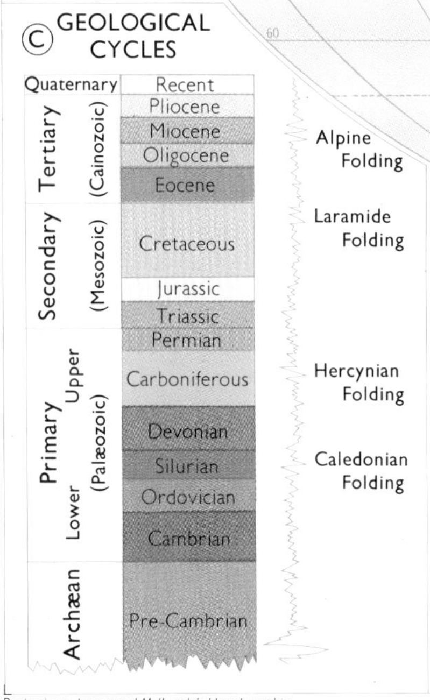

GEOLOGY
after
Beyschlag, Nalivkin and others

1:90 000 000

Ⓐ

Arctic Circle

Tropic of Cancer

Equator

Tropic of Capricorn

Antarctic Circle

LAURENTIA

Ⓒ GEOLOGICAL CYCLES

Quaternary	Recent	
Tertiary (Cainozoic)	Pliocene	
	Miocene	Alpine Folding
	Oligocene	
	Eocene	
Secondary (Mesozoic)	Cretaceous	Laramide Folding
	Jurassic	
	Triassic	
Upper Primary (Palæozoic)	Permian	
	Carboniferous	Hercynian Folding
	Devonian	
Lower	Silurian	Caledonian Folding
	Ordovician	
	Cambrian	
Archæan	Pre-Cambrian	

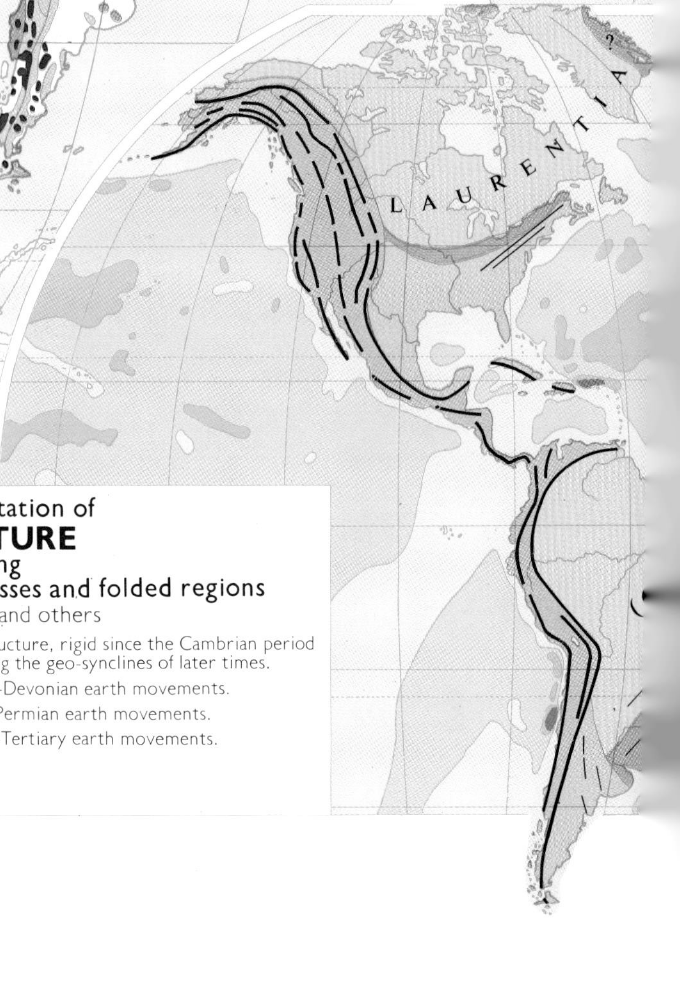

Ⓑ   An Interpretation of
STRUCTURE
showing
the distribution of rigid masses and folded regions
after L. Kober and others

Pre-Cambrian tables composite in structure, rigid since the Cambrian period and forming stable elements separating the geo-synclines of later times.

Regions of Caledonian folding; Siluro-Devonian earth movements.

Regions of Hercynian folding; Carbo-Permian earth movements.

Regions of Tertiary folding; Cretaceo-Tertiary earth movements.

The Great Rift Valley

⟋⟍ Main Trend lines

3

Sedimentary Rocks

Quaternary
Cainozoic
Mesozoic
Upper Palæozoic
Lower Palæozoic
Pre-Cambrian and Metamorphic

Igneous Rocks

Volcanic
Intrusive

Ice caps
Unexplored regions

Arctic Circle

Tropic of Cancer

Equator

Tropic of Capricorn

Sea Depths

m
4000
6000
8000

1:126 000 000

BALTICA

SIBERIAN TABLE
(ANGARALAND)

CHINESE TABLE

N   D   W   A   N   A
L
A
N
D

?

?

COPYRIGHT.GEORGE PHILIP & SON LTD.

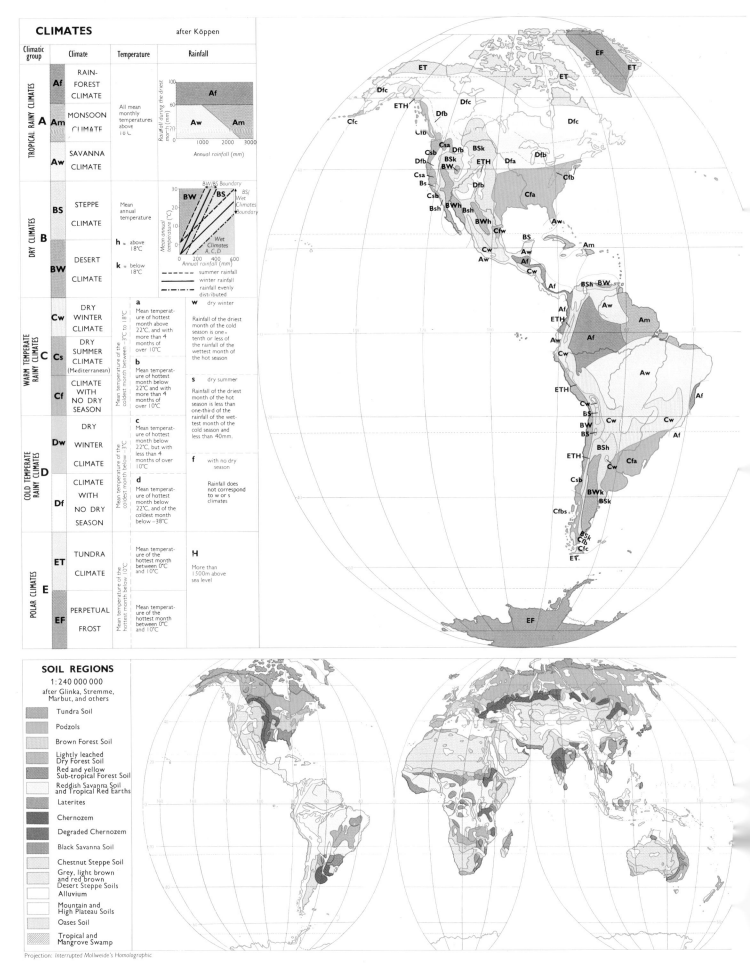

CLIMATES
after Köppen

Climatic group	Climate	Temperature	Rainfall
A TROPICAL RAINY CLIMATES	**Af** RAIN-FOREST CLIMATE	All mean monthly temperatures above 18°C	(rainfall graph) Af / Aw / Am — Rainfall during the driest month (mm) — Annual rainfall (mm)
	Am MONSOON CLIMATE		
	Aw SAVANNA CLIMATE		
B DRY CLIMATES	**BS** STEPPE CLIMATE	Mean annual temperature	(graph) BW/BS Boundary — BW / BS / BS/Wet Climates Boundary — Wet Climates A, C, D — Mean annual temperature (°C) — Annual rainfall (mm)
	BW DESERT CLIMATE	**h** = above 18°C; **k** = below 18°C	summer rainfall / winter rainfall / rainfall evenly distributed
C WARM TEMPERATE RAINY CLIMATES	**Cw** DRY WINTER CLIMATE	Mean temperature of the coldest month between −3°C to 18°C	**a** Mean temperature of hottest month above 22°C, and with more than 4 months of over 10°C
	Cs DRY SUMMER CLIMATE (Mediterranean)		**b** Mean temperature of hottest month below 22°C and with more than 4 months of over 10°C
	Cf CLIMATE WITH NO DRY SEASON		**w** dry winter — Rainfall of the driest month of the cold season is one-tenth or less of the rainfall of the wettest month of the hot season
D COLD TEMPERATE RAINY CLIMATES	**Dw** DRY WINTER CLIMATE	Mean temperature of the coldest month below −3°C	**c** Mean temperature of hottest month below 22°C, but with less than 4 months of over 10°C
	Df CLIMATE WITH NO DRY SEASON		**d** Mean temperature of hottest month below 22°C, and of the coldest month below −38°C
			s dry summer — Rainfall of the driest month of the hot season is less than one-third of the rainfall of the wettest month of the cold season and less than 40mm.
			f with no dry season — Rainfall does not correspond to w or s climates
E POLAR CLIMATES	**ET** TUNDRA CLIMATE	Mean temperature of the hottest month between 0°C and 10°C	**H** More than 1500m above sea level
	EF PERPETUAL FROST	Mean temperature of the hottest month between 0°C and 10°C	

SOIL REGIONS
1:240 000 000
after Glinka, Stremme, Marbut, and others

- Tundra Soil
- Podzols
- Brown Forest Soil
- Lightly leached Dry Forest Soil
- Red and yellow Sub-tropical Forest Soil
- Reddish Savanna Soil and Tropical Red Earths
- Laterites
- Chernozem
- Degraded Chernozem
- Black Savanna Soil
- Chestnut Steppe Soil
- Grey, light brown and red brown Desert Steppe Soils
- Alluvium
- Mountain and High Plateau Soils
- Oases Soil
- Tropical and Mangrove Swamp

Projection: Interrupted Mollweide's Homolographic

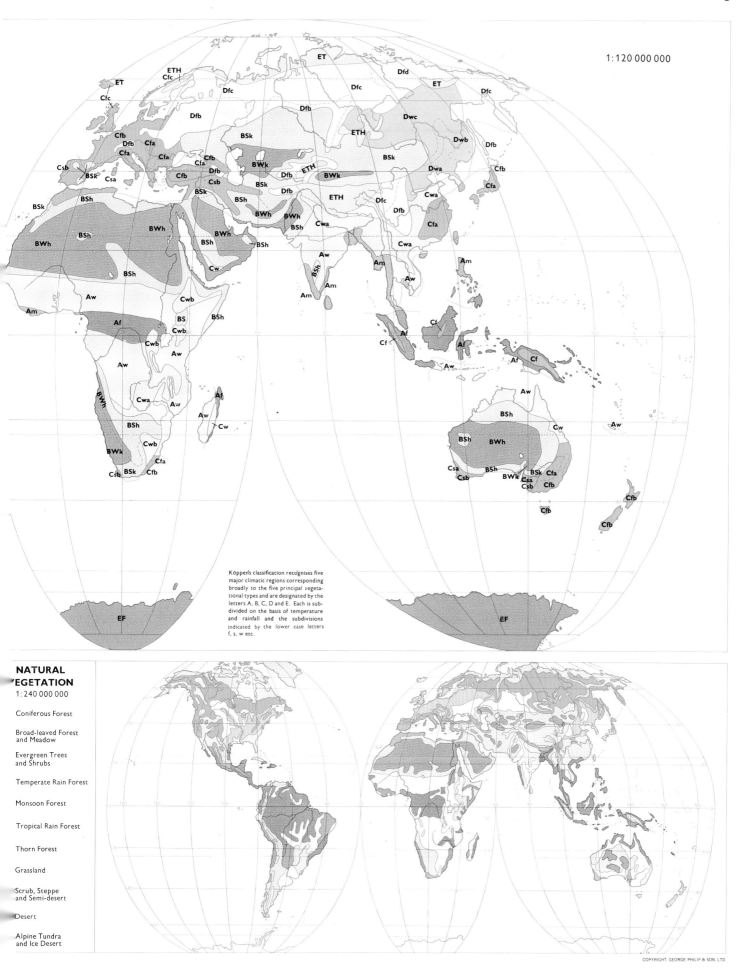

1:120 000 000

ET
ETH
Cfc
ET
Dfd
ET
Cfc
Dfc
Dfc
Dfb
Dfc
Dwc
Dfb
Dwb
Cfb
Dfb
Cfb
ETH
Dfb
Cfb
Dfb
Cfa
Cfa
BSk
Dwa
Cfa
Cfa
Cfa
Cfb
BWk
Cwa
Csb
BSk
Csa
Cfb
Dfb
ETH
Cfa
BWk
Csa
Csb
BSh
BSk
Dfb
ETH
Dfc
Cwa
BSh
BSk
BSh
ETH
Dfb
BSh
Af
BWh
BWh
BSh
BSh
BWh
BSh
BSh
Cw
BSh
BWh
Aw
BSh
Aw
Cwb
Am
Af
Am
Af
Am
Af
BS
Cwb
BSh
Am
Cf
Cwb
Aw
Af
Cf
Af
Aw
Af
Cf
Aw
Af
Cwa
Aw
Aw
Aw
BSh
Cw
Cwb
Aw
Cw
Csa
BSh
BSk
Cfa
Csb
BWk
Csa
Cfa
Csb
BWk
Csb
Cfb
Csb BSk Cfb
Cfb
Cfb
Cfb

EF
EF

Köppen's classification recognises five major climatic regions corresponding broadly to the five principal vegetational types and are designated by the letters A, B, C, D and E. Each is subdivided on the basis of temperature and rainfall and the subdivisions indicated by the lower case letters f, s, w etc.

NATURAL VEGETATION

1:240 000 000

Coniferous Forest

Broad-leaved Forest and Meadow

Evergreen Trees and Shrubs

Temperate Rain Forest

Monsoon Forest

Tropical Rain Forest

Thorn Forest

Grassland

Scrub, Steppe and Semi-desert

Desert

Alpine Tundra and Ice Desert

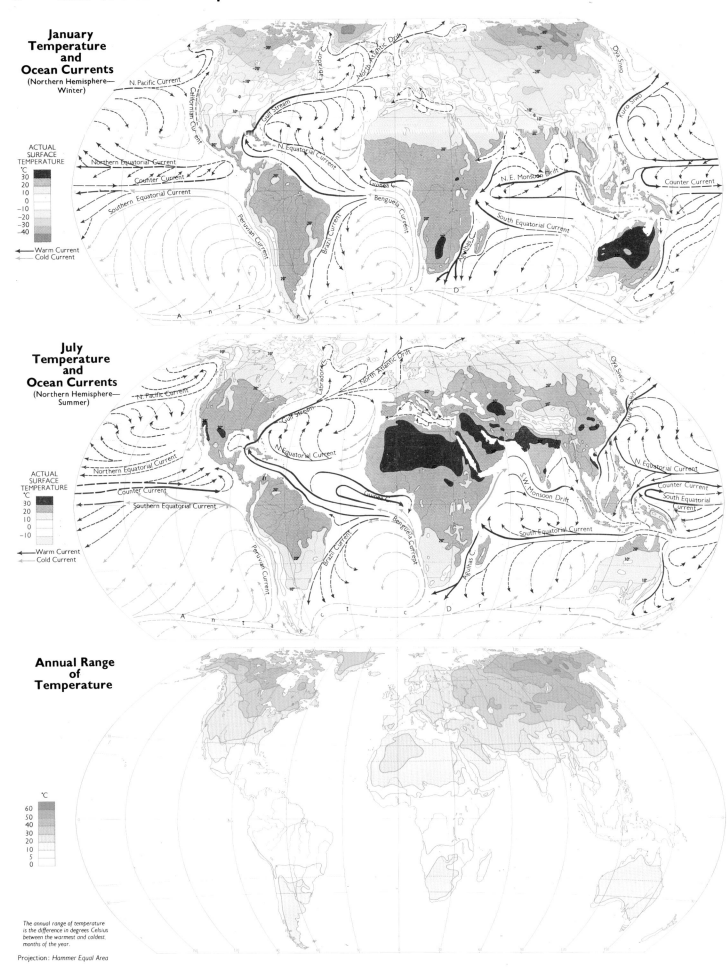

January Temperature and Ocean Currents
(Northern Hemisphere—Winter)

ACTUAL SURFACE TEMPERATURE
°C
30
20
10
0
−10
−20
−30
−40

← Warm Current
← Cold Current

July Temperature and Ocean Currents
(Northern Hemisphere—Summer)

ACTUAL SURFACE TEMPERATURE
°C
30
20
10
0
−10

← Warm Current
← Cold Current

Annual Range of Temperature

°C
60
50
40
30
20
10
5
0

The annual range of temperature is the difference in degrees Celsius between the warmest and coldest months of the year.

Projection: *Hammer Equal Area*

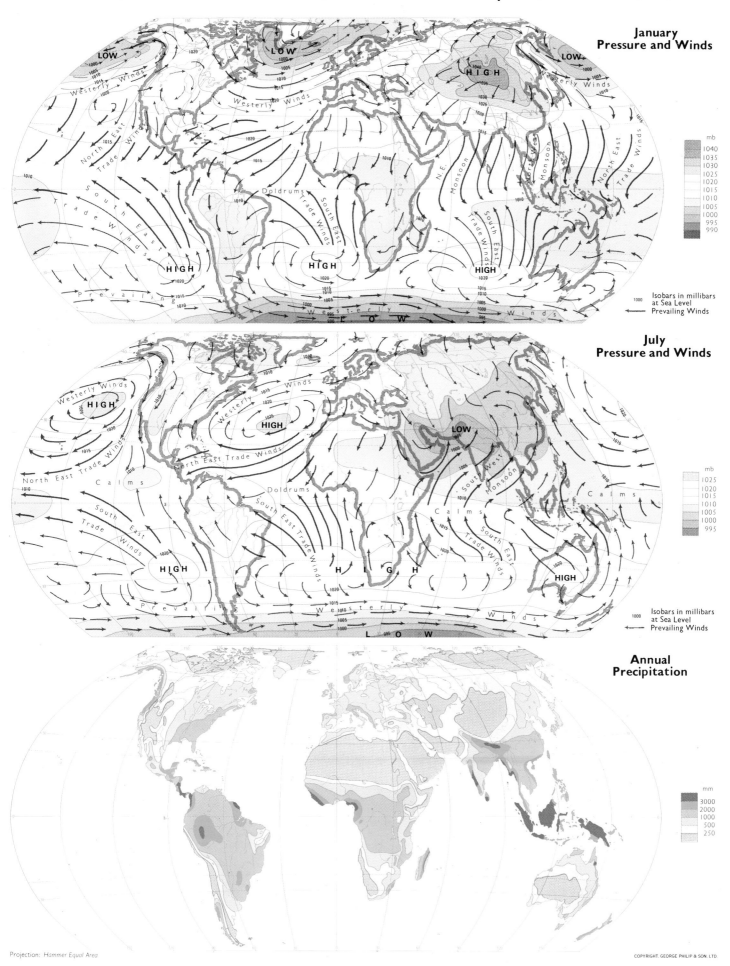

January Pressure and Winds

LOW

LOW

HIGH

LOW

Westerly Winds

Westerly Winds

Westerly Winds

North East Trade Winds

South East Trade Winds

Doldrums

South East Trade Winds

N.E. Monsoon

North West Monsoon

South East Trade Winds

North East Trade Winds

HIGH

HIGH

HIGH

Prevailing

Westerly

Winds

L O W

mb	
	1040
	1035
	1030
	1025
	1020
	1015
	1010
	1005
	1000
	995
	990

1000 Isobars in millibars
at Sea Level
Prevailing Winds

July Pressure and Winds

Westerly Winds

HIGH

HIGH

LOW

Westerly Winds

North East Trade Winds

North East Trade Winds

Calms

Doldrums

South East Trade Winds

South West Monsoon

Calms

South East Trade Winds

Calms

South East Trade Winds

South West Monsoon

Calms

South East Trade Winds

HIGH

H I G H

HIGH

Prevailing

Westerly

Winds

L O W

mb	
	1025
	1020
	1015
	1010
	1005
	1000
	995

1000 Isobars in millibars
at Sea Level
Prevailing Winds

Annual Precipitation

mm	
	3000
	2000
	1000
	500
	250

Projection: Hammer Equal Area

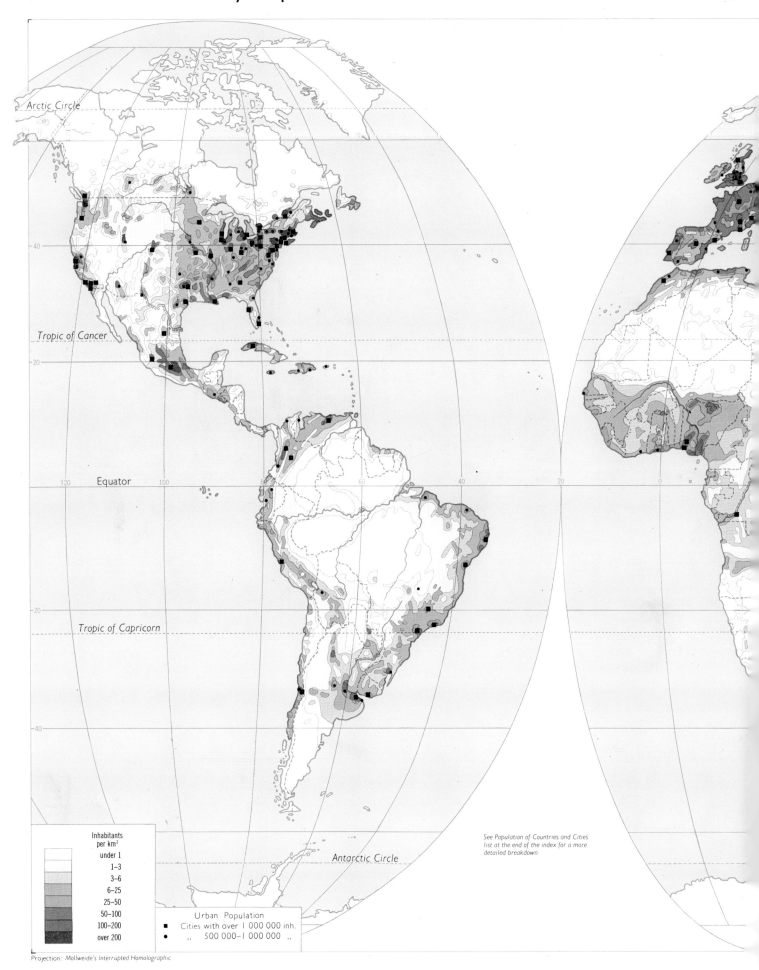

Arctic Circle

Tropic of Cancer

Equator

Tropic of Capricorn

Antarctic Circle

Inhabitants per km²	
under 1	
1–3	
3–6	
6–25	
25–50	
50–100	
100–200	
over 200	

Urban Population
■ Cities with over 1 000 000 inh.
● ,, 500 000–1 000 000 ,,

See Population of Countries and Cities list at the end of the index for a more detailed breakdown

Projection: Mollweide's Interrupted Homolographic

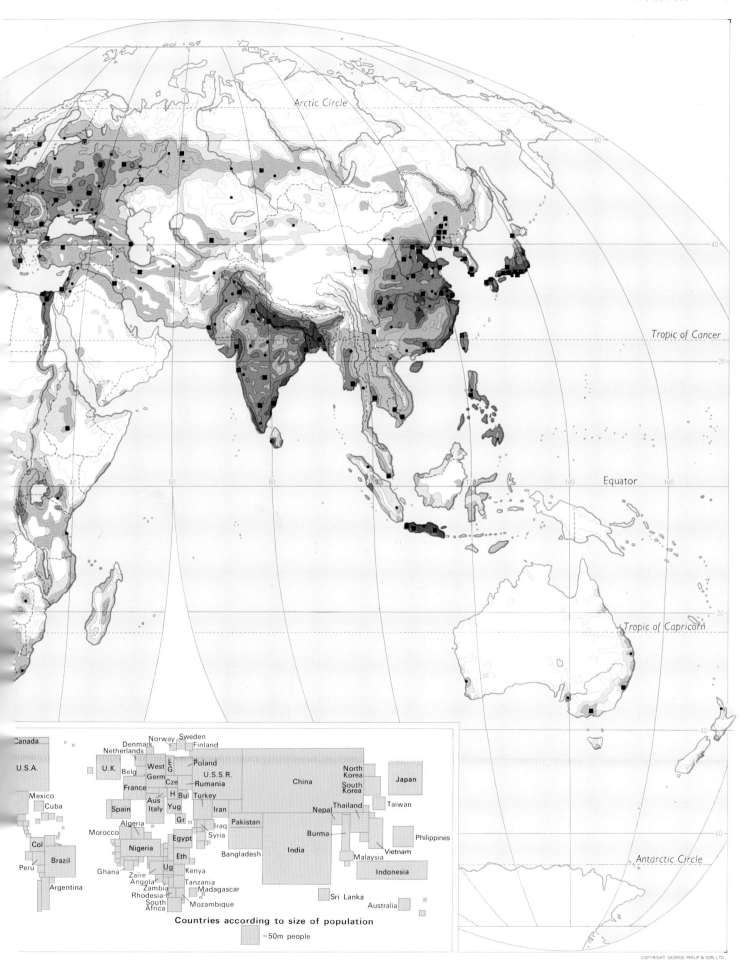

Arctic Circle

Tropic of Cancer

Equator

Tropic of Capricorn

Antarctic Circle

Canada
Norway Sweden
Denmark Finland
Netherlands
U.S.A. U.K. Belg West E Poland U.S.S.R. China North Korea Japan
France Germ G Rumania South Korea
Cze Turkey Taiwan
Mexico Spain Aus H Bul Iran Nepal Thailand
Cuba Italy Yug Gr Pakistan Burma Philippines
Algeria Iraq Bangladesh India Vietnam
Morocco Egypt Syria Malaysia
Col Nigeria Eth Indonesia
Brazil Ghana Ug Kenya
Peru Zaire Tanzania Sri Lanka
Angola Zambia Madagascar Australia
Argentina Rhodesia Mozambique
South
Africa

Countries according to size of population

=50m people

Projection: Hammer Equal Area

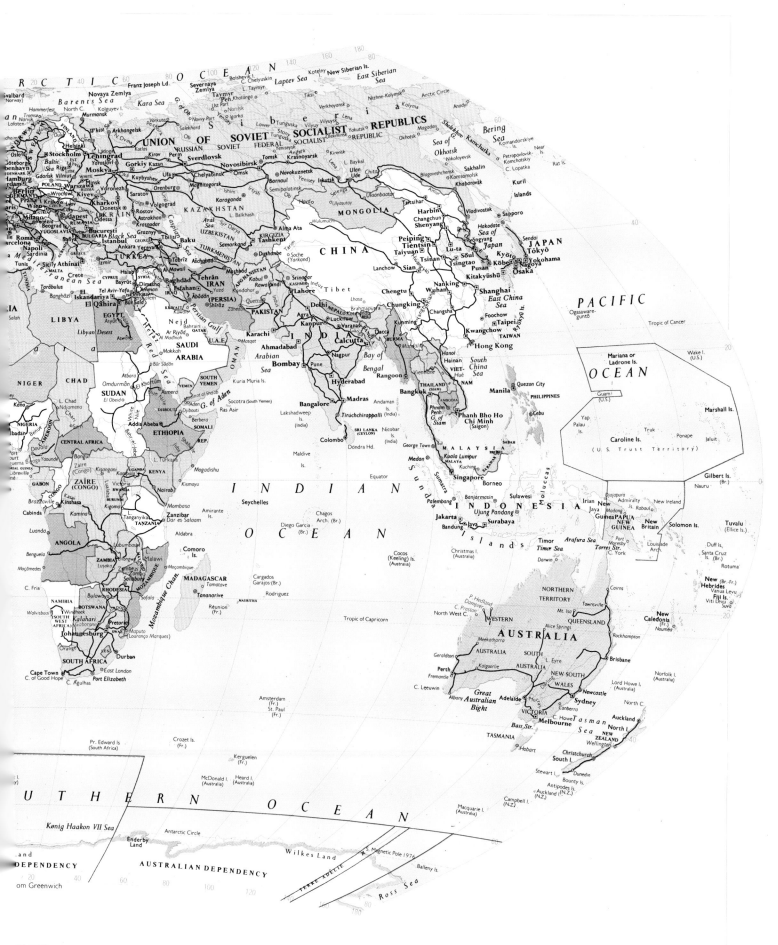

ARCTIC OCEAN

Svalbard
(Norway)
Franz Joseph Ld.
Kotelny New Siberian Is.
Bolshevik I. Chelyuskin
Novaya Zemlya
Severnaya
Zemlya
Taymyr
Pen.
Khatanga
Laptev Sea
East Siberian
Sea

Hammerfest
North C.
Kolguyev I.
Kara Sea
Ust Port
Tiksi
Arctic Circle

Tromsö
Narvik
Murmansk
Arkhangelsk
Vorkuta
Norilsk
Igarka
Verkhoyansk
Nizhne-Kolymsk
Kolyma
Anadyr'

Lofoten
White
N.Dvina
S i b e r i a
Yakutsk
60
Bering
Sea

Helsinki
Ladoga
Kirov
Ob
Lower Tunguska
L.Taymyr
Yakutsk
Skovorodino
Kamchatka
Komandorskiye
Is.

Oslo
Leningrad
RUSSIAN
SOVIET
FEDERAL
Stony Tunguska
Yeniseysk
Angara
SOCIALIST
REPUBLIC
Aldan
Sea of
Okhotsk
Petropavlovsk-
Kamchatskiy
Rat Is.

Stockholm
Gorkiy Kazan
Perm
Sverdlovsk
Tomsk
Krasnoyarsk
Lena
Kirensk
Nikolayevsk
C. Lopatka

Baltic
Sea
Moskva
Kuybyshev Ufa
Chelyabinsk
Omsk
Novokuznetsk
Irkutsk
Ulan
Ude
Chita
Blagoveshchensk
Komsomolsk
Sakhalin
Kuril

Berlin
POLAND
Warszawa
Minsk
Voronezh
Saratov
Orenburg
Magnitogorsk
Ishim
Irtysh
Semipalatinsk
Ulaanbaatar
Amur
Khabarovsk
Islands

Kiyev
UKRAINE
Volga Volgograd
KAZAKHSTAN
Barnaul
Yenisey
Selenga
Tatsihar
Vladivostok
Sapporo

Kharkov
Donetsk
Rostov
Astrakhan
Aral
Sea
L.Balkhash
Hovd
MONGOLIA
Harbin
Changchun
Shenyang
Hakodate
Sea of
Japan
Sendai

Krasnodar
Groznyy
Caspian
Sea
UZBEKISTAN
Syr Darya
Alma Ata
Wulumuchi
Ulaanbaatar
Pyöngyang
Yöngyang
Kyōto
JAPAN

Tbilisi
Baku
Samarkand
Tashkent
KIRGIZIA
Tarim
Peiping
Tientsin
Lu-ta
Seoul
Pusan
Kōbe
Tōkyō
Yokohama

Istanbul
Ankara Yerevan
TURKMENISTAN
Dushanbe
Soche
(Yarkand)
CHINA
Taiyuan
Tsinan
Tsingtao
Kitakyūshū
Osaka

Izmir
TURKEY
Tabriz
Aschabad
AFGHANISTAN
Kabul
Lanchow
Sian
Nanking
Shanghai

Athínai
Halab
SYRIA
Meshed
Srinagar
KASHMIR Indus
Tibet
Chengtu
Wuhan
East China
Sea

Baghdad
Tehrān
Esfahan
Rawalpindi
Lahore
Lhasa
Chungking
Changsha
Foochow

El
Iskandariya
Amman
IRAN
(PERSIA)
Yazd
Quetta
Delhi
NEPAL
Lucknow
Brahmaputra
Kunming
Taipei

El Qâhira
Bûr Said
Shīrāz
Zāhedān
Agra
Kanpur
Varanasi
Dacca
Kwangchow
TAIWAN

LIBYA
EGYPT
Nejd
Ar Riyâd
Persian
Gulf
Karachi
INDIA
Calcutta
BURMA
Mandalay
Hong Kong
PACIFIC

Salah
Libyan Desert
Aswân
Bahrain
QATAR
U.A.E.
Ahmadabad
Nagpur
Bay of
Hanoi
Hainan
South
China
Sea
Ogasawara-
guntō
Wake I.
(U.S.)
Tropic of Cancer

NIGER
CHAD
El Khartûm
Omdurmân
SAUDI
ARABIA
Makkah
Arabian
Sea
Bombay
Pune
Hyderabad
Bengal
Rangoon
Vientiane
VIET-
NAM
Huê
Mariana or
Ladrone Is.
OCEAN

Kano
SUDAN
El Obeid
YEMEN
SOUTH
YEMEN
Madras
Andaman
Is.(India)
Bangalore
THAILAND
(SIAM)
Bangkok
CAMBODIA
Manila
Quezon City
Guam
(U.S.)
Marshall Is.

NIGERIA
Benue
CENTRAL AFRICA
Addis Abeba
DJIBOUTI
Djibouti
Berbera
SOMALI
REP.
Tiruchirappalli
SRI LANKA
(CEYLON)
Nicobar
Is.(India)
Phnom
Penh
G. of
Siam
Phanh Bho Ho
Chi Minh
(Saigon)
Cebu
PHILIPPINES
Yap
Palau
Is.
Caroline Is.
(U. S. Trust Territory)
Truk
Ponape
Jaluit

ETHIOPIA
Colombo
Dóndra Hd.
MALAYSIA
George Town
SABAH
Gilbert Is.
(Br.)

GABON
CONGO
ZAIRE
(CONGO)
Kisangani
UGANDA
KENYA
Nairobi
L. Turkana
Mogadishu
Maldive
Is.
Medan
Kuala Lumpur
MALAYA
Kuching
BRUNEI
SARAWAK
Nauru

EQUATORIAL GUINEA
Brazzaville
Kinshasa
BURUNDI
RWANDA
Victoria
Mombasa
Kismayu
Equator
Singapore
Borneo
INDONESIA
Banjarmasin
Sulawesi
Moluccas
Irian
Jaya
New
Admiralty
Is.
New Ireland
Tuvalu
(Ellice Is.)

Luanda
ANGOLA
Kamina
TANZANIA
Zanzibar
Dar es Salaam
Seychelles
Chagos
Arch.(Br.)
INDIAN
Palembang
Jakarta
Java
Surabaya
Ujung Pandang
PAPUA
NEW
GUINEA
Djajapura
Madong
Rabaul
New
Britain
Solomon Is.
Duff Is.

Benguela
ZAMBIA
Lusaka
Amirante
Is.
Diego Garcia
(Br.)
OCEAN
Bandung
Sunda
Islands
Timor
Timor Sea
Arafura Sea
Port
Moresby
C. York
Louisade
Arch.
Santa Cruz
Is.
Rotuma

Moçâmedes
MALAWI
Moçambique
Christmas I.
(Australia)
Darwin
Torres Str.
New
Hebrides
(Br.-Fr.)
Vanua Levu
Fiji Is.
Viti Levu

C. Fria
RHODESIA
Bulawayo
Salisbury
MOZAMBIQUE
MADAGASCAR
Tamatave
Cargados
Garajos(Br.)
Rodriguez
Cocos
(Keeling) Is.
(Australia)
NORTHERN
TERRITORY
P. Hedland
Dampier
Townsville
Cairns
New
Caledonia
(Fr.)
Nouméa

NAMIBIA
BOTSWANA
Kalahari
Tananarive
MAURITIUS
Réunion
(Fr.)
Tropic of Capricorn
North West C.
C. Preston
WESTERN
Mt. Isa
QUEENSLAND
Rockhampton
Norfolk I.
(Australia)

Walvisbaai
SOUTH
WEST
AFRICA (S.A.)
Windhoek
Gaborone
Pretoria
SWAZILAND
Maputo
(Lourenço Marques)
Meekatharra
WESTERN
AUSTRALIA
Alice Springs
SOUTH
AUSTRALIA
L. Eyre
Brisbane
Lord Howe I.
(Australia)

Johannesburg
Orange
LESOTHO
Durban
Geraldton
Perth
Kalgoorlie
NEW SOUTH
WALES
New

Cape Town
C. of Good Hope
SOUTH AFRICA
East London
Port Elizabeth
Fremantle
Great
Australian
Bight
Albany
C. Leeuwin
Adelaide
Murray
AUSTRALIA
VICTORIA
Canberra
Melbourne
Newcastle
Sydney
Auckland
North I.
NEW
ZEALAND
North C.

C. Agulhas
Amsterdam
(Fr.)
St. Paul
(Fr.)
C. Howe
Bass Str.
Tasman
Sea
Wellington

Pr. Edward Is
(South Africa)
Crozet Is.
(Fr.)
Kerguelen
(Fr.)
TASMANIA
Hobart
Christchurch
South I.
Dunedin

McDonald I.
Heard I.
(Australia)
(Australia)
Stewart I.
Bounty Is.
(N.Z)
Antipodes
Is.(N.Z.)

SOUTHERN OCEAN

Kønig Haakon VII Sea
Enderby
Land
Antarctic Circle
Wilkes Land
S. Magnetic Pole 1976
Macquarie I.
(N.Z.)
Campbell I.
(N.Z.)
Auckland I.(N.Z.)

DEPENDENCY
AUSTRALIAN DEPENDENCY
TERRE ADÉLIE
Ross Sea
Balleny Is.

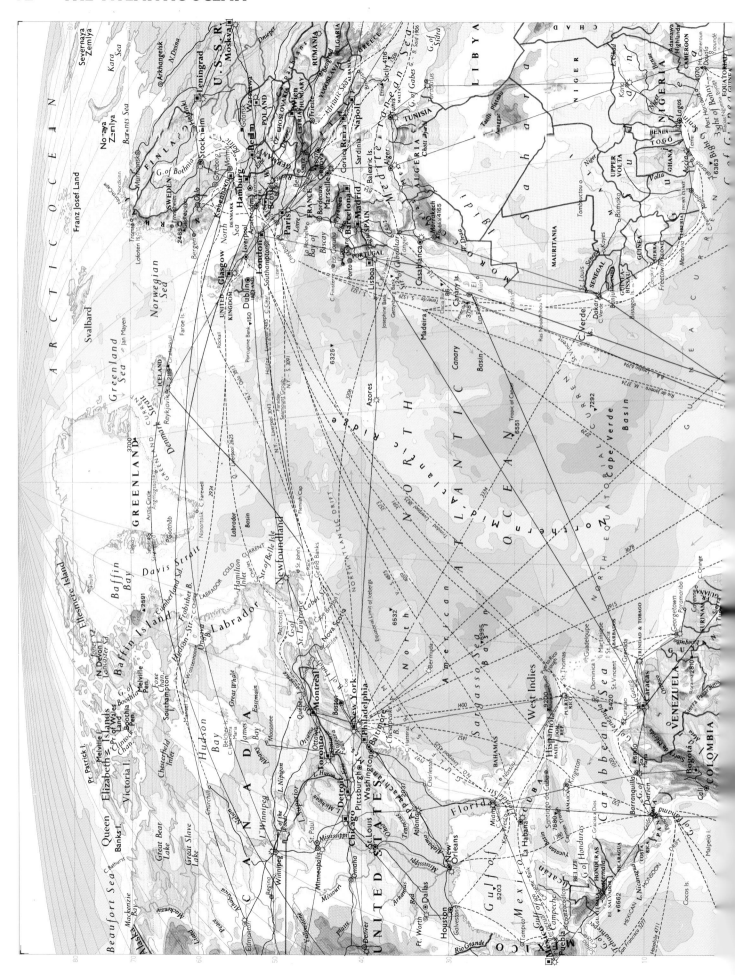

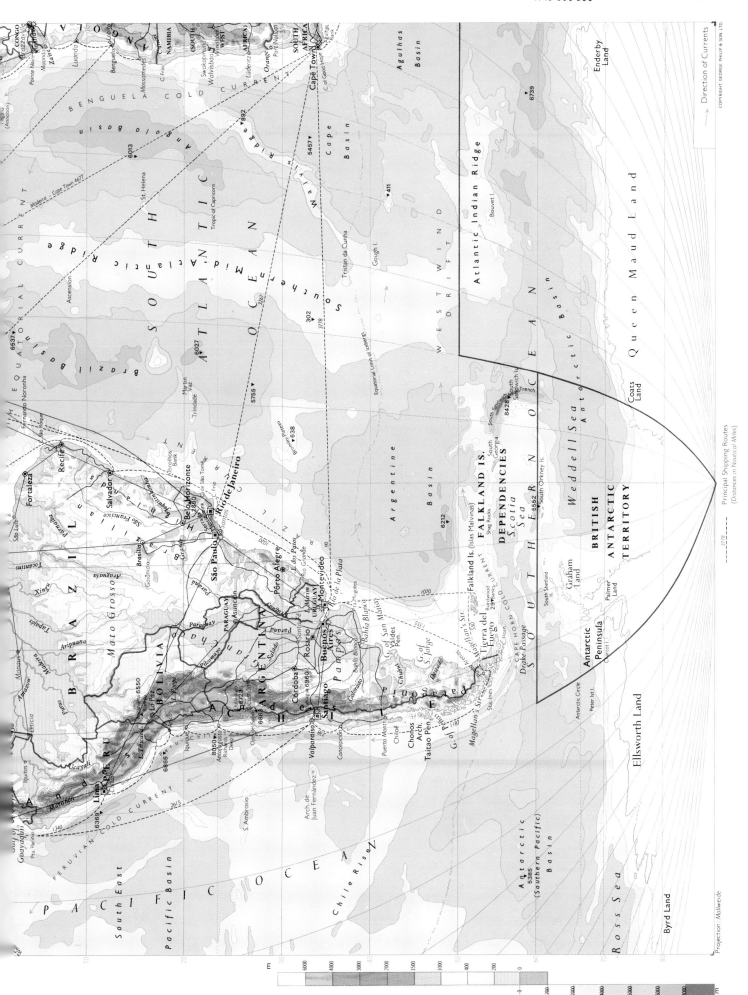

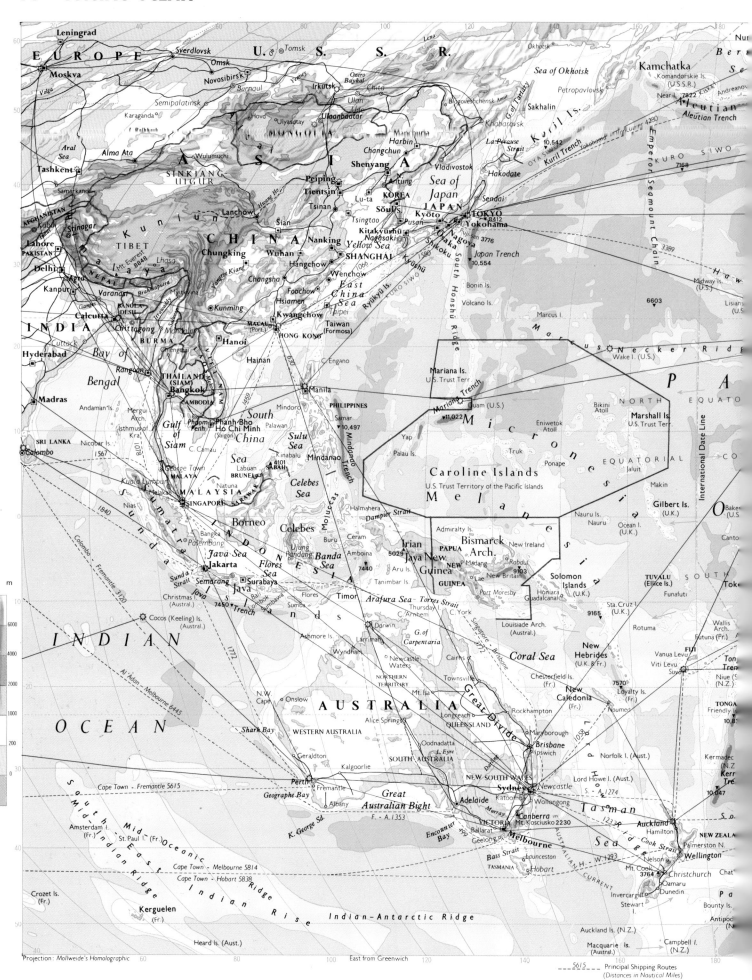

EUROPE

U. S. S. R.

Leningrad
Moskva
Volga
Aral Sea
Tashkent
Samarkand
Sverdlovsk
Omsk
Novosibirsk
Barnaul
Semipalatinsk
Karaganda
Alma Ata
Wulumuchi
Balkhash
Tomsk
Yenisey
Irkutsk
Ozero Baykal
Ulan
Ude
Chita
Hovd
Ulyasutay
Ulaanbaatar
MONGOLIA
Lena
Okhotsk
Sea of Okhotsk
Kamchatka
Komandorskie Is. (U.S.S.R.)
Petropavlovsk
Near I. 7822
KISKA
Andreanof
Aleutian Is.
Aleutian Trench

ASIA

AFGHANISTAN
Kabul
Srinagar
Lahore
PAKISTAN
Delhi
Agra
Kanpur
Varanasi
Calcutta
INDIA
Hyderabad
Madras
SRI LANKA
Colombo

SINKIANG UIGUR
Kun lun
TIBET
Mt. Everest 8848
Lhasa
NEPAL
Himalaya
Kunming

CHINA
Lanchow
Sian
Chungking
Wuhan
Changsha
Hangchow
Foochow
Hsiamen
Kwangchow
MACAU (Port.)
HONG KONG

Peiping
Tientsin
Lu-ta
Tsinan
Tsingtao
Nanking
SHANGHAI
Wenchow

Shenyang
Anting
Harbin
Changchun
Manchuria
KOREA
Söul's
Pusan
Taipei
Taiwan (Formosa)

Vladivostok
Hakodate
Sea of Japan
Sendai
JAPAN
TOKYO
Kyōto
Yokohama
Nagoya
Ōsaka
Shikoku
Kyūshū
Nagasaki
Kitakyūshū
Fuji-san 3776

La Pérouse Strait
Sakhalin
G. of Tartary
Khabarovsk
Amur
Blagoveshchensk
Kuril Is. 10,542
Kuril Trench
OYA SIWO
Yokohama
KURO SIWO 7168
Emperor Seamount Chain
Near 4280

Kunlun 8412
Japan Trench 10,554
Honshu Ridge
Bonin Is.
Volcano Is.
Marcus I.
6603
Lisians (U.S.)
Midway Is. (U.S.)
Haw

INDIA
Bay of Bengal
BANGLA DESH
Chittagong
Mandalay
BURMA
Rangoon
THAILAND (SIAM)
Bangkok
CAMBODIA
Phnom Penh
VIETNAM
Hanoi
Hainan
Phanh Bho
Ho Chi Minh (Saigon)

C. Engano
PHILIPPINES
Manila
Mindoro
Samar
10.497
Palawan
Mindanao Trench
Mindanao

South China Sea
Sulu Sea
Celebes Sea

Mariana Is.
U.S. Trust Terr.
Mariana Trench
11,022
Guam (U.S.)
Yap
Palau Is.
Truk
Ponape
Caroline Islands
U.S. Trust Territory of the Pacific Islands

NORTH
EQUATO
Wake I. (U.S.)
Necker Ridge
Bikini Atoll
Marshall Is.
U.S. Trust Terr.
Eniwetok Atoll
Jaluit
EQUATORIAL
Makin
Gilbert Is. (U.K.)
Ocean I. (U.K.)
Nauru I. Nauru

PA
PA
Micronesia
Melanesia
International Date Line
CO
O
Bake (U.S.
Canto

Andaman Is.
Nicobar Is. 1567
Mergui Arch.
Isthmus of Kra
C. Camau
Kinabalu
SABAH
Labuan
BRUNEI
SARAWAK
MALAYSIA
George Town
Kuala Lumpur
Malacca
SINGAPORE
Sumatra
Nias
Palembang
Bangka
Natuna
Borneo
Celebes
Buru
Ceram
Amboina
Moluccas
Halmahera
Dampier Strait
Admiralty Is.
Bismarck Arch.
New Ireland
New Britain
Rabaul
Madang
Lae
Solomon Islands (U.K.)
Honiara
Guadalcanal
Sta. Cruz I. (U.K.)
9165

Irian Jaya
5029
PAPUA NEW GUINEA
New Guinea
Aru Is.
7440
Port Moresby

Nauru I.
9103

TUVALU (Ellice Is.)
Funafuti
Rotuma
Wallis Arch. (Fr.)
Futuna (Fr.)
FIJI
Vanua Levu
Viti Levu
Suva

SOUTH
Toke
Tren
Niue (N.Z.)
TONGA
Friendly Is.
10.8

INDONESIA
Jakarta
Semarang
Surabaya
Java
Bali
Lombok
Sumbawa
Flores
Sumba
Timor
Java Sea
Flores Sea
Banda Sea
Sunda Strait
Christmas I. (Austral.)
7450
Java Trench
Pandang
Ujung
Tanimbar Is.
Arafura Sea
Torres Strait
Thursday I.
C. Arnhem
C. York
Louisiade Arch. (Austral.)

Coral Sea
New Hebrides (U.K. & Fr.)
Chesterfield Is. (Fr.)
7570
New Caledonia (Fr.)
Noumea
Loyalty Is. (Fr.)
Norfolk I. (Aust.)
Lord Howe I. (Aust.)
S - A 1274

INDIAN OCEAN

Cocos (Keeling) Is. (Austral.)
Al Adon - Melbourne 6445
Colombo - Fremantle 3120
1840
1772

N.W. Cape
Onslow
Ashmore Is.
Darwin
Larrimah
Wyndham
Newcastle Waters
NORTHERN TERRITORY
Alice Springs
Mt. Isa
Cairns
Townsville
G. of Carpentaria

AUSTRALIA
WESTERN AUSTRALIA
Shark Bay
Geraldton
Kalgoorlie
SOUTH AUSTRALIA
Oodnadatta
L. Eyre
Longreach
QUEENSLAND
Rockhampton
Maryborough
Brisbane
Ipswich
Great Divide
Darling

Perth
Fremantle
Geographe Bay
Albany
K. George Sd.
Great Australian Bight
F - A 1353
Encounter Bay
Adelaide
VICTORIA
Ballarat
Geelong
Melbourne
Canberra
Mt. Kosciusko 2230
NEW SOUTH WALES
Sydney
Newcastle
Katoomba
Wollongong
Murray
AUSTRALIAN H.
W. 1293

Cape Town - Fremantle 5615
Cape Town - Melbourne 5814
Cape Town - Hobart 5838
Amsterdam I. (Fr.)
St. Paul I. (Fr.)
Crozet Is. (Fr.)
Kerguelen (Fr.)
South Mid-Indian Ridge
East Indian Ridge
Indian Rise
Indian-Antarctic Ridge
Heard Is. (Aust.)

Bass Strait
Launceston
TASMANIA
Hobart
Tasman Sea
AUSTRALIAN CURRENT
1233
Nelson
Cook Strait
Mt. Cook 3764
Christchurch
Oamaru
Invercargill
Stewart I.
Dunedin
NEW ZEALAND
Auckland
Hamilton
Wellington
Palmerston N.
Kermadec (N.Z.)
Kerr Tre
10.047
Auckland Is. (N.Z.)
Macquarie Is. (Austral.)
Campbell I. (N.Z.)
Chat
Bounty Is.
Antipo

m
6000
4000
2000
1000
200
0
200
2000
4000
6000
8000
m

Projection: Mollweide's Homolographic
East from Greenwich

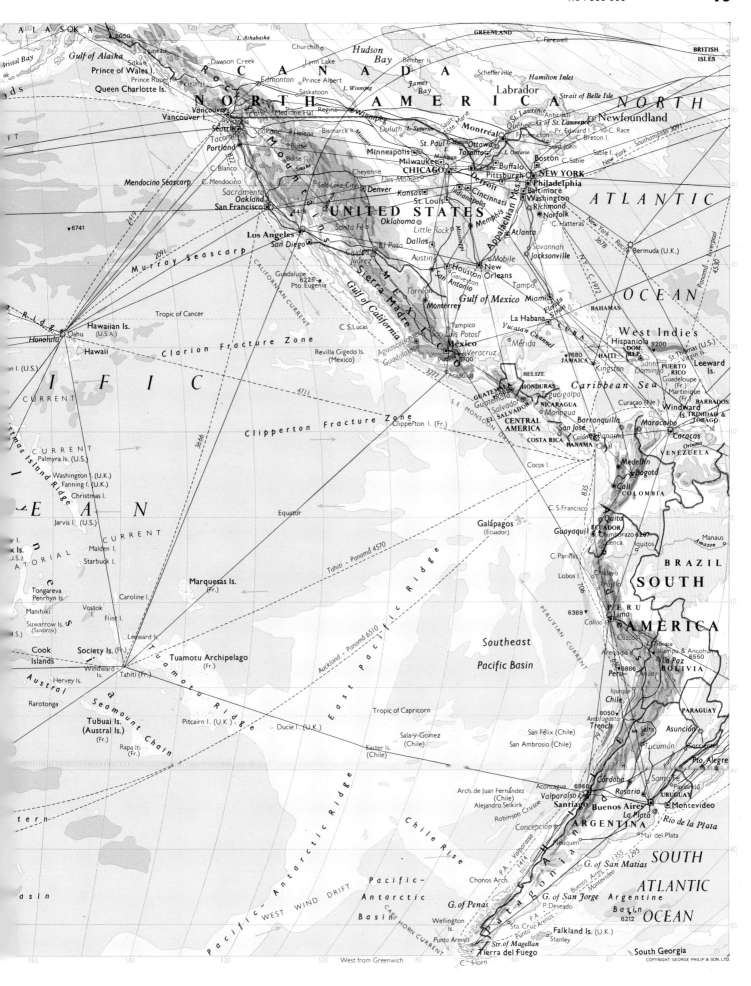

A L A S K A
6050
Bristol Bay
Gulf of Alaska
Juneau
Sitka
Prince of Wales I.
Prince Rupert
Queen Charlotte Is.
Kitimat
L. Athabaska
Churchill
Dawson Creek
Hudson Bay
Belcher Is.
GREENLAND
C. Farewell
BRITISH ISLES

C A N A D A

N O R T H A M E R I C A

NORTH

Edmonton
Prince Albert
Saskatoon
L. Winnipeg
Regina
Medicine Hat
Winnipeg
James Bay
Scheffferville
Labrador
Hamilton Inlet
Strait of Belle Isle

Vancouver
Vancouver I.
Victoria
Seattle
Tacoma
Portland
Spokane
Helena
Butte
Boise
Bismarck
Missouri
Duluth
L. Superior
St. Paul
Minneapolis
Milwaukee
L. Huron
Sault Ste. Marie
St. Lawrence
Ste. Marie
Québec
Montréal
Ottawa
Fredericton
G. of St. Lawrence
Anticosti
Newfoundland
Pr. Edward I.
Saint John
C. Race
Sable I.
Southampton 3091

Mendocino Seascarp
C. Mendocino
Cheyenne
Des Moines
L. Michigan
CHICAGO
Detroit
Toronto
L. Ontario
Buffalo
Boston
C. Sable
New York

6741

Sacramento
Oakland
San Francisco
Salt Lake City
Denver
Kansas
St. Louis
Indianapolis
Cincinnati
Pittsburgh
Baltimore
Washington
Richmond
Norfolk
C. Hatteras
NEW YORK
Philadelphia
ATLANTIC

2419
441B
UNITED STATES
Santa Fé
Oklahoma
Little Rock
Memphis
Atlanta
Savannah
Jacksonville
Bermuda (U.K.)
New York - Recife 3678

Murray Seascarp
2091
Los Angeles
San Diego
El Paso
Ciudad Juárez
Dallas
Austin
San Antonio
Houston
New Orleans
Mobile
Tampa
Miami
BAHAMAS

Tropic of Cancer
Guadalupe
Pto. Eugenia
6225
C. S. Lucas
Torreón
Monterrey
Galveston
Gulf of Mexico
La Habana
Yucatan Channel
CUBA
West Indies

Clarion Fracture Zone
Hawaiian Is. (U.S.A.)
Oahu
Honolulu
Hawaii
Revilla Gigedo Is. (Mexico)
Aguascalientes
Guadalajara
Tampico
San Luis Potosí
Mexico
Veracruz
Puebla 5700
Mérida
Hispaniola
HAITI
JAMAICA
DOM. REP.
Santo Domingo
PUERTO RICO
9200
7680
St. Thomas (U.S.)
Virgin Is.
Leeward Is.

3271
Acapulco
BELIZE
GUATEMALA
HONDURAS
Tegucigalpa
Caribbean Sea
Guadeloupe (Fr.)
Martinique (Fr.)
BARBADOS
TRINIDAD & TOBAGO

P A C I F I C
471L
3666
Clipperton Fracture Zone
Clipperton I. (Fr.)
S. E. MONSOON DRIFT
Guatemala
Salvador
NICARAGUA
Managua
CENTRAL AMERICA
Barranquilla
San José
COSTA RICA
PANAMA
Colón
Panamá
Canal
Windward Is.
Maracaibo
Caracas
Orinoco
VENEZUELA

CURRENT
Christmas Island Ridge
Palmyra Is. (U.S.)
Washington I. (U.K.)
Fanning I. (U.K.)
Christmas I.
Cocos I.
C. S. Francisco
Medellín
Bogotá
Cali
COLOMBIA

O C E A N
Equator
Jarvis I. (U.S.)
CURRENT
Galápagos (Ecuador)
Guayaquil
Quito
ECUADOR
Chimborazo 6267
Cuenca
Iquitos
Manaus
Amazon
BRAZIL

EQUATORIAL CURRENT
Malden I.
Starbuck I.
Tahiti - Panamá 4570
C. Pariñas
Lobos Is.
Chiclayo
Trujillo
SOUTH

Tongareva
Penrhyn Is.
Manihiki
Suwarrow Is. (Suvorov)
Vostok
Flint I.
Marquesas Is. (Fr.)
Caroline I.
East Pacific Ridge
6369
PERU
Lima
Callao
AMERICA

Cook Islands
Society Is. (Fr.)
Windward Is.
Tahiti (Fr.)
Leeward Is.
Tuamotu Ridge
Tuamotu Archipelago (Fr.)
Auckland - Panamá 6510
Southeast
Pacific Basin
Cuzco
Arequipa
La Paz
Titicaca
Ilampu & Ancohuma 6550
BOLIVIA

Austral
Hervey Is.
Rarotonga
Seamount Chain
Pitcairn I. (U.K.)
Ducie I. (U.K.)
Tropic of Capricorn
Iquique
Chile
6866
PERUVIAN CURRENT
Arica
PERU

Tubuai Is. (Austral Is.) (Fr.)
Rapa Iti (Fr.)
Sala-y-Gomez (Chile)
Easter I. (Chile)
San Félix (Chile)
San Ambrosio (Chile)
Antofagasta
Trench
8050
Salta
Tucumán
PARAGUAY
Asunción
Corrientes
Pto. Alegre

Pacific - Antarctic Ridge
Arch. de Juan Fernández (Chile)
Alejandro Selkirk
Robinson Crusoe
Aconcagua 6960
Valparaíso
Santiago
Córdoba
Rosario
Santa Fé
Paraná
Paysandú
URUGUAY
Buenos Aires
La Plata
Montevideo
Río de la Plata
ARGENTINA
Mar del Plata

Chile Rise
Concepción
Neuquén
1355
1295
SOUTH

Pacific - Antarctic Basin
WEST WIND DRIFT
Chonos Arch.
G. of Penas
CAPE HORN CURRENT
Wellington
Sta. Cruz
Punta Arenas
Str. of Magellan
Tierra del Fuego
C. Horn
Patagonian
G. of San Matías
Buenos Aires
Montevideo
G. of San Jorge
P. Deseado
P.A.
Sta. Cruz
1414
Falkland Is. (U.K.)
Stanley
Argentine
Basin
6212
South Georgia
ATLANTIC
OCEAN

160   140   120   West from Greenwich   80   60   40

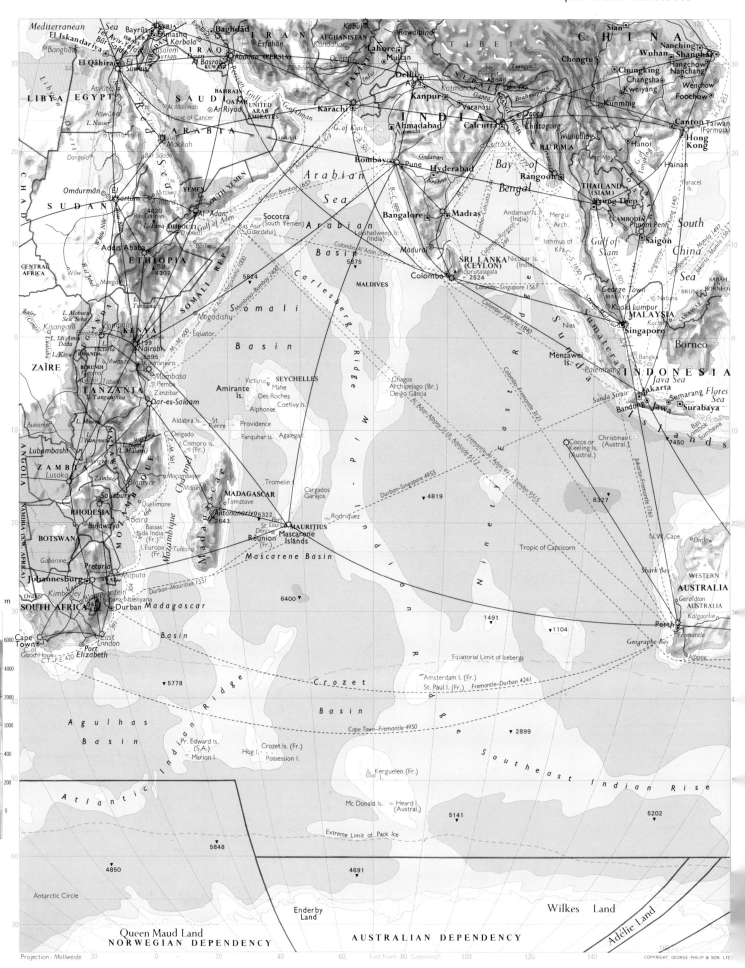

Projection: Mollweide

COPYRIGHT. GEORGE PHILIP & SON LTD.

1:30 000 000

200 0 200 400 600 800 1000 km

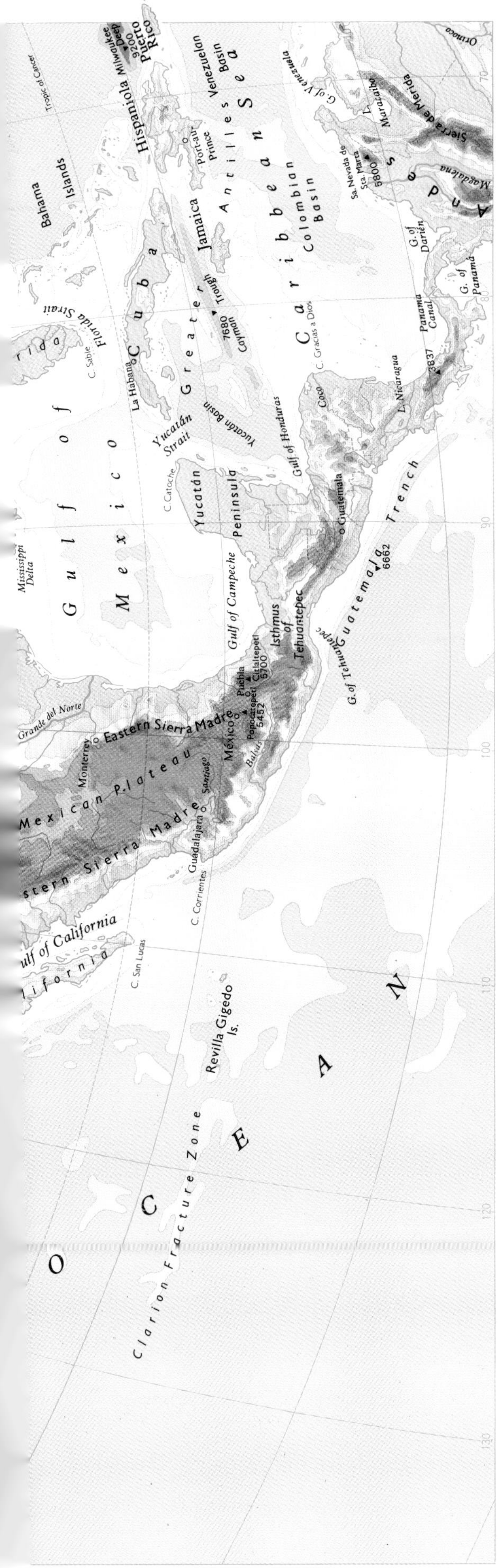

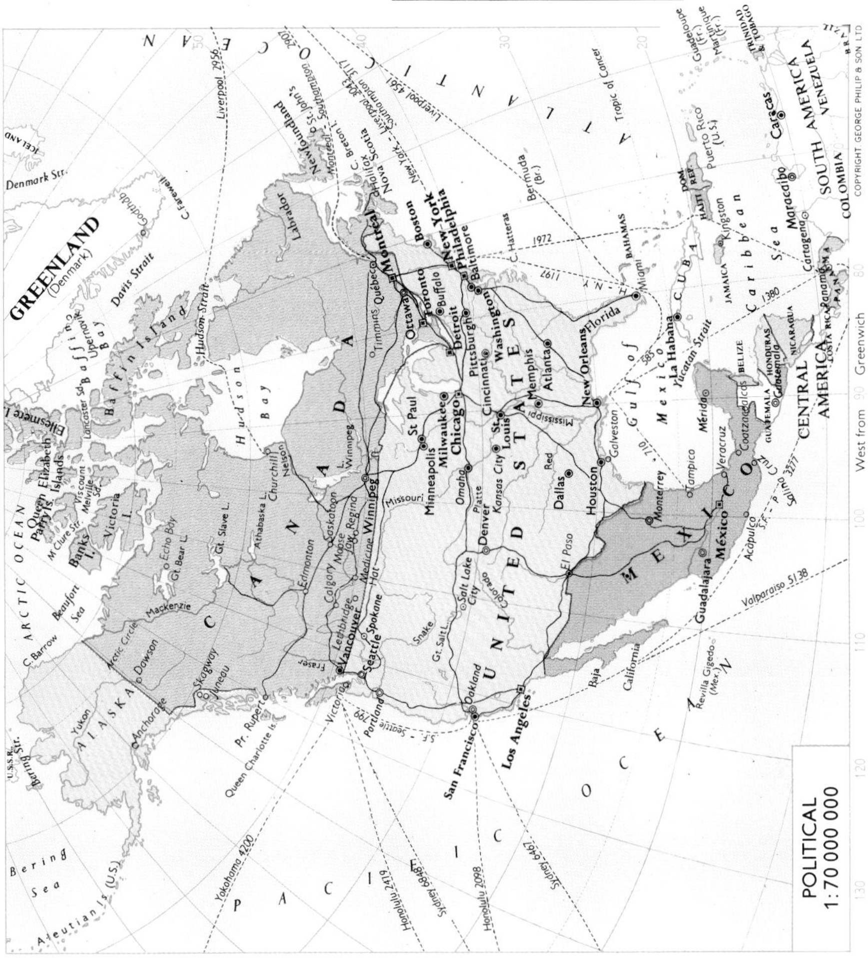

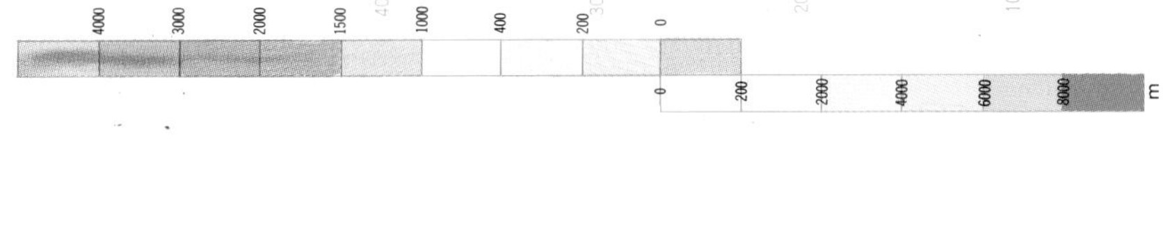

Physical map (left)

Bahama Islands
Tropic of Cancer
Puerto Rico
9200 Milwaukee Deep
Hispaniola
Port-au-Prince
Venezuelan Basin
G. of Venezuela
Sierra de Perija
Orinoco
Maracaibo
Sta. Nevada de Sta. Marta 5800
Antilles Sea
Jamaica
Greater
Cuba
Colombian Basin
Caribbean
La Habana
Florida Strait
C. Sable
Florida
Yucatán Basin
Yucatán Strait
Cayman Trough 7680
C. Catoche
Yucatán Peninsula
Gulf of Honduras
Coco
C. Gracias à Dios
L. Nicaragua
G. of Darién
G. of Panama
Panama Canal
Gulf of Mexico
Gulf of Campeche
Guatemala
7837
Guatemala Trench 6662
Mississippi Delta
Isthmus of Tehuantepec
G. of Tehuantepec
Orizaba 5700
Popocatépetl 5452
Puebla
México
Grande del Norte
Eastern Sierra Madre
Monterrey
Balsas
Sonora
Mexican Plateau
Western Sierra Madre
Gulf of California
Guadalajara
C. Corrientes
C. San Lucas
California
Revilla Gigedo Is.
Clarion Fracture Zone
PACIFIC OCEAN

Political map (top right)

POLITICAL 1:70 000 000

ATLANTIC OCEAN
ARCTIC OCEAN
GREENLAND (Denmark)
Denmark Str.
ICELAND
C. Farewell
Davis Strait
Baffin Bay
Baffin Island
Ellesmere I.
Queen Elizabeth Islands
Parry Is.
Banks I.
Victoria I.
M Clure Str.
Beaufort Sea
C. Barrow
ALASKA (U.S.)
Anchorage
Yukon
Arctic Circle
Pr. Rupert
Queen Charlotte Is.
Bering Sea
Aleutian Is. (U.S.)
Skagway
Juneau
Fraser
Victoria
Vancouver
Seattle
Spokane
Portland
San Francisco
Oakland
Los Angeles
Baja
California
Revilla Gigedo (Mex.)
Hudson Bay
Hudson Str.
Churchill
Gt. Slave L.
Gt. Bear L.
Mackenzie
Arctic Circle
Dawson
Echo Bay
Gt. Slave L.
Athabasca
Lancaster Sd.
Labrador
Newfoundland
St. John's
CANADA
Edmonton
Calgary
Medicine Hat
Lethbridge
Regina
Saskatoon
Winnipeg
Winnipeg
Ottawa
Montreal
Quebec
Toronto
Buffalo
Detroit
Boston
New York
Philadelphia
Baltimore
Washington
Pittsburgh
Cincinnati
St. Paul
Minneapolis
Milwaukee
Chicago
St. Louis
Kansas City
Omaha
Denver
Salt Lake City
Snake
Platte
Missouri
Red
UNITED STATES
Memphis
Atlanta
New Orleans
Dallas
Houston
El Paso
Galveston
Florida
C. Hatteras
Bermuda (Br.)
Liverpool 4964
Liverpool 2956
Tropic of Cancer
BAHAMAS
Miami
La Habana
CUBA
Yucatan Strait
Gulf of Mexico
Tampico
Veracruz
Mérida
Monterrey
MEXICO
Guadalajara
México
Acapulco
Valparaiso 5138
Volcano
CENTRAL AMERICA
GUATEMALA
BELIZE
HONDURAS
NICARAGUA
COSTA RICA
PANAMA
Caribbean
JAMAICA
Kingston
HAITI
Puerto Rico (U.S.)
DOMINICAN REP.
Sierra
TRINIDAD & TOBAGO
Guadeloupe (Fr.)
Martinique (Fr.)
Caracas
Maracaibo
Cartagena
SOUTH AMERICA
VENEZUELA
COLOMBIA
PACIFIC OCEAN
West from 90 Greenwich

Annual rainfall map (bottom right)

ANNUAL RAINFALL 1:70 000 000

Tropic of Cancer
Arctic Circle
West from 90 Greenwich

mm
3000
2000
1000
500
250

Projection: Bonne

m
4000
3000
2000
1500
1000
400
200
0

0
−200
2000
4000
6000
8000
m

1 : 70 000 000

500   0   500   1000   1500   2000   2500 km

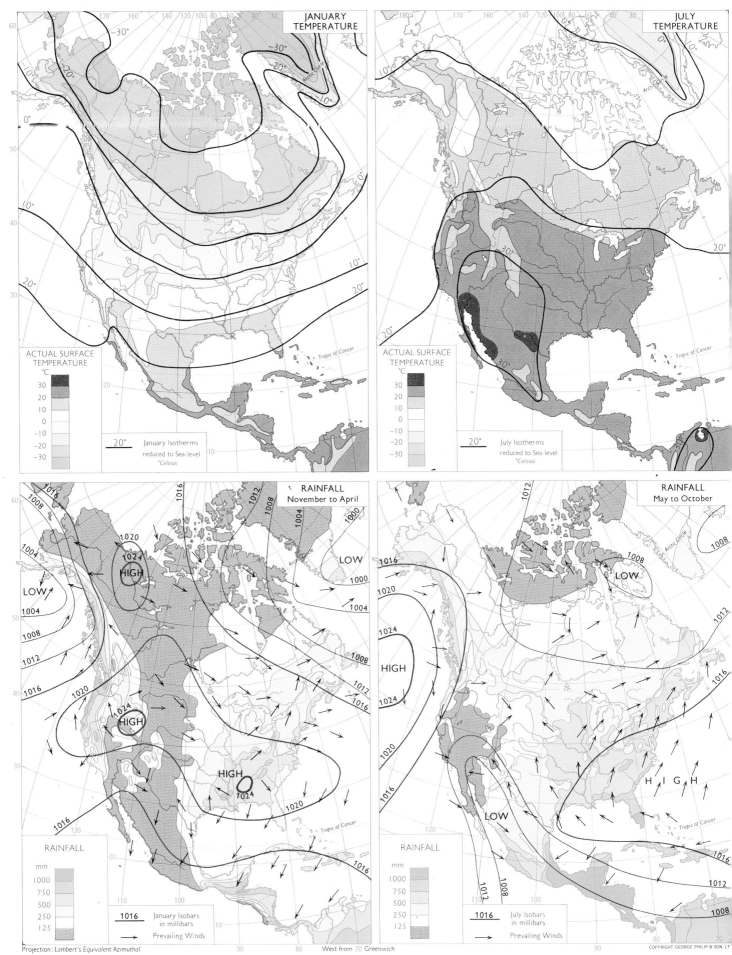

JANUARY
TEMPERATURE

ACTUAL SURFACE
TEMPERATURE
°C

| 30 |
| 20 |
| 10 |
| 0 |
| -10 |
| -20 |
| -30 |

—20°— January Isotherms
reduced to Sea-level
°Celsius

JULY
TEMPERATURE

ACTUAL SURFACE
TEMPERATURE
°C

| 30 |
| 20 |
| 10 |
| 0 |
| -10 |
| -20 |
| -30 |

—20°— July Isotherms
reduced to Sea-level
°Celsius

RAINFALL
November to April

LOW
HIGH
LOW
HIGH
HIGH

RAINFALL
mm

| 1000 |
| 750 |
| 500 |
| 250 |
| 125 |

1016   January Isobars
in millibars
→   Prevailing Winds

RAINFALL
May to October

LOW
HIGH
LOW
H I G H

RAINFALL
mm

| 1000 |
| 750 |
| 500 |
| 250 |
| 125 |

1016   July Isobars
in millibars
→   Prevailing Winds

Projection: Lambert's Equivalent Azimuthal   West from 70 Greenwich   COPYRIGHT GEORGE PHILIP & SON. LT

1:32 000 000

400   0   400   800   1200 km

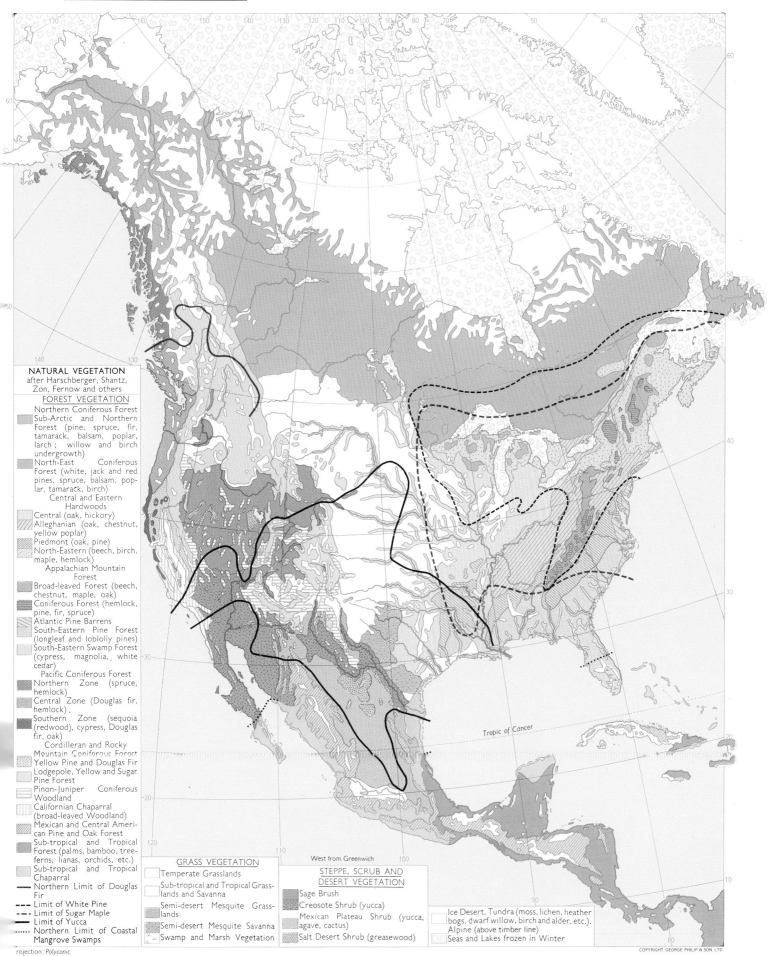

NATURAL VEGETATION
after Harschberger, Shantz,
Zon, Fernow and others

FOREST VEGETATION

Northern Coniferous Forest
Sub-Arctic and Northern Forest (pine, spruce, fir, tamarack, balsam, poplar, larch ; willow and birch undergrowth)
North-East Coniferous Forest (white, jack and red pines, spruce, balsam, poplar, tamarack, birch)

Central and Eastern Hardwoods
Central (oak, hickory)
Alleghanian (oak, chestnut, yellow poplar)
Piedmont (oak, pine)
North-Eastern (beech, birch, maple, hemlock)

Appalachian Mountain Forest
Broad-leaved Forest (beech, chestnut, maple, oak)
Coniferous Forest (hemlock, pine, fir, spruce)
Atlantic Pine Barrens
South-Eastern Pine Forest (longleaf and loblolly pines)
South-Eastern Swamp Forest (cypress, magnolia, white cedar)

Pacific Coniferous Forest
Northern Zone (spruce, hemlock)
Central Zone (Douglas fir, hemlock)
Southern Zone (sequoia (redwood), cypress, Douglas fir, oak)

Cordilleran and Rocky Mountain Coniferous Forest
Yellow Pine and Douglas Fir
Lodgepole, Yellow and Sugar Pine Forest
Pinon-Juniper Coniferous Woodland
Californian Chaparral (broad-leaved Woodland)
Mexican and Central American Pine and Oak Forest
Sub-tropical and Tropical Forest (palms, bamboo, tree-ferns; lianas, orchids, etc.)
Sub-tropical and Tropical Chaparral

——— Northern Limit of Douglas Fir
– – – Limit of White Pine
–·–·– Limit of Sugar Maple
━━━ Limit of Yucca
········· Northern Limit of Coastal Mangrove Swamps

Projection: Polyconic

GRASS VEGETATION
Temperate Grasslands
Sub-tropical and Tropical Grasslands and Savanna
Semi-desert Mesquite Grasslands
Semi-desert Mesquite Savanna
Swamp and Marsh Vegetation

West from Greenwich

STEPPE, SCRUB AND DESERT VEGETATION
Sage Brush
Creosote Shrub (yucca)
Mexican Plateau Shrub (yucca, agave, cactus)
Salt Desert Shrub (greasewood)
Ice Desert, Tundra (moss, lichen, heather bogs, dwarf willow, birch and alder, etc.).
Alpine (above timber line)
Seas and Lakes frozen in Winter

Tropic of Cancer

Projection: Bonne

West from Greenwich

1:17 500 000

200 0 200 400 600 km

GEOLOGY
1:35 000 000

GREENLAND

Baffin Bay

Baffin Island

Victoria I.

Gt. Bear Lake

Gt. Slave Lake

Mackenzie

Rocky Mountains

Coast Range

Athabasca

Nelson

Saskatchewan

L. Winnipeg

Hudson Bay

James Bay

Labrador

Newfoundland

C. Breton I.

Nova Scotia

Laurentian Plateau

St. Lawrence

L. Superior

L. Michigan

L. Huron

L. Ontario

L. Erie

IGNEOUS AND PLUTONIC ROCKS

Volcano	✳
Carbonatite and syenite intrusion	×
Ultrabasic intrusion	⌐
Fault	
Thrust	

Acidic rocks
Basic rocks
Anorthosite
Granitic gneiss
Granulite
Gabbro dyke

SEDIMENTARY AND VOLCANIC ROCKS

Period	Era	Time Scale (million years)
Cenozoic	Tertiary	2·5–65
Mesozoic	Secondary	65–225
Cretaceous		
Paleozoic	Primary	225–570
Late Paleozoic		
Devonian		
Early Paleozoic		
Proterozoic and Paleozoic		
Proterozoic	Precambrian	570–300
Hadrynian		
Helikian		
Neohelikian		
Paleohelikian		
Aphebian		
Archean		

Based on the Atlas of Canada

Hudson Strait

Foxe Basin

Foxe Channel

Cumberland Peninsula

Frobisher Bay

Resolution I.

Ungava Bay

NEW QUEBEC

LABRADOR

NEWFOUNDLAND

St. John's

Gulf of St. Lawrence

Gaspe Pen.

St. Lawrence (St-Laurent)

PR. EDWARD I.

ST. PIERRE & MIQUELON (Fr.)

NEW BRUNSWICK

NOVA SCOTIA

Halifax

Québec

MONTRÉAL

Ottawa

Hull

Toronto

Hamilton

Buffalo

London

DETROIT

Cleveland

Toledo

Boston

Providence

MAINE

VERMONT

NEW HAMPSHIRE

MASS.

NEW YORK

ATLANTIC OCEAN

1:30 000 000

200 0 200 400 600 800 1000 km

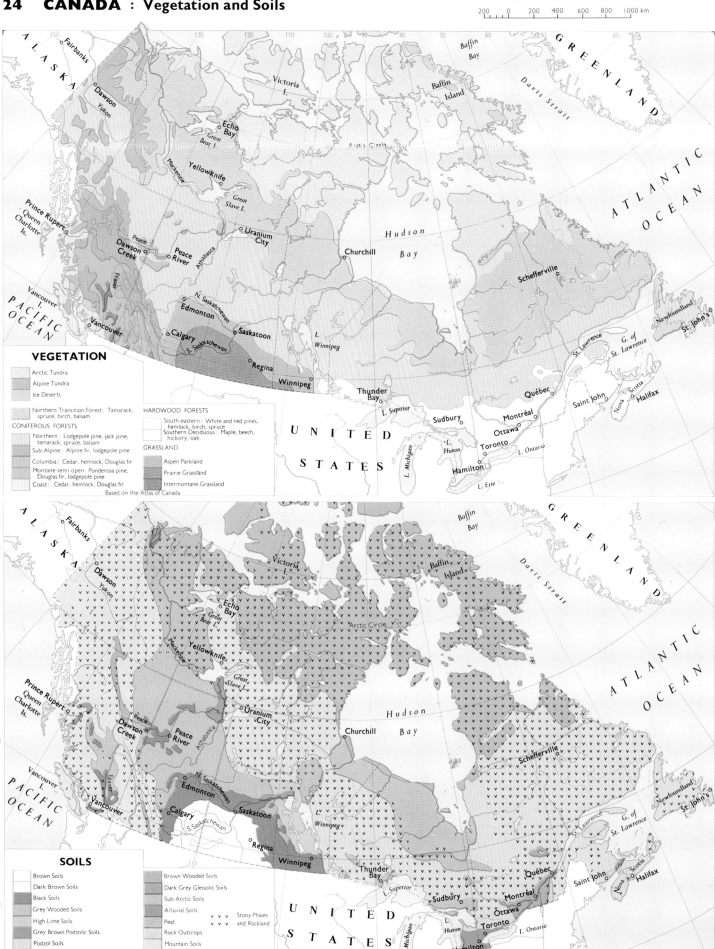

VEGETATION

Arctic Tundra
Alpine Tundra
Ice Deserts

Northern Transition Forest: Tamarack,
spruce, birch, balsam

CONIFEROUS FORESTS

Northern: Lodgepole pine, jack pine,
tamarack, spruce, balsam
Sub-Alpine: Alpine fir, lodgepole pine
Columbia: Cedar, hemlock, Douglas fir
Montane semi-open: Ponderosa pine,
Douglas fir, lodgepole pine
Coast: Cedar, hemlock, Douglas fir

HARDWOOD FORESTS

South-eastern: White and red pines,
hemlock, birch, spruce
Southern Deciduous: Maple, beech,
hickory, oak

GRASSLAND

Aspen Parkland
Prairie Grassland
Intermontane Grassland

Based on the Atlas of Canada

SOILS

Brown Soils
Dark Brown Soils
Black Soils
Grey Wooded Soils
High Lime Soils
Grey Brown Podzolic Soils
Podzol Soils
Brown Podzolic and Brown Forest Soils

Brown Wooded Soils
Dark Grey Gleisolic Soils
Sub-Arctic Soils
Alluvial Soils
Peat
Rock Outcrops
Mountain Soils
Tundra Soils

v v v   Stony Phases
v v v   and Rockland

Based on the Atlas of Canada

West from Greenwich

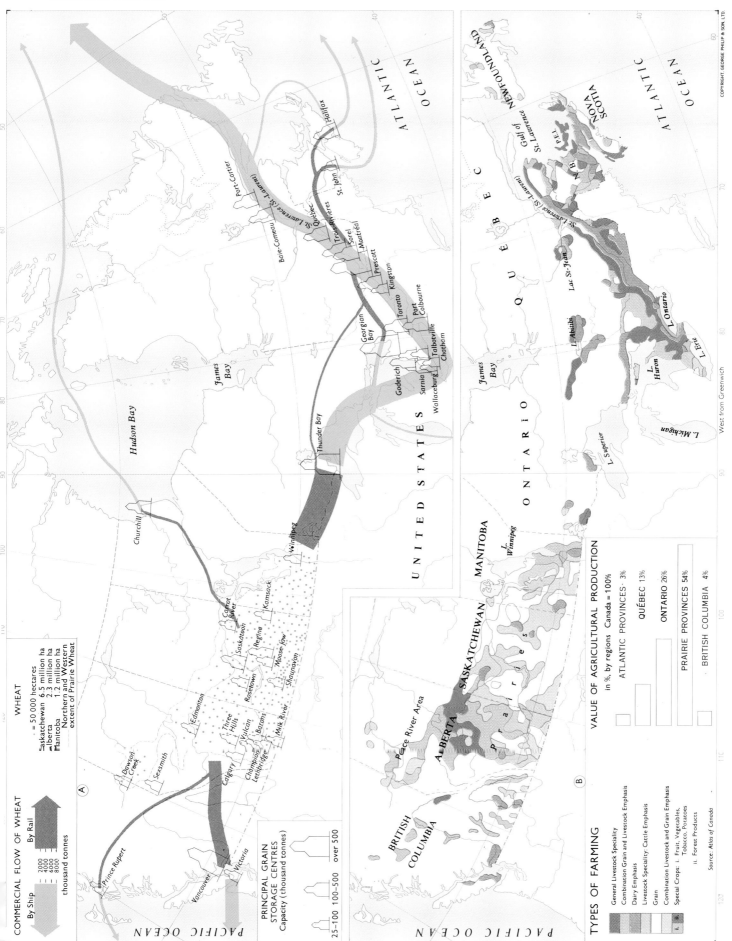

COMMERCIAL FLOW OF WHEAT

By Ship   By Rail

thousand tonnes

- 2000
- 4000
- 8000

WHEAT

= 50 000 hectares

- Saskatchewan 6.5 million ha
- Alberta 2.3 million ha
- Manitoba 1.2 million ha

Northern and Western extent of Prairie Wheat

PRINCIPAL GRAIN STORAGE CENTRES

Capacity (thousand tonnes)

- 25–100
- 100–500
- over 500

A

B

TYPES OF FARMING

- General Livestock Speciality
- Combination Grain and Livestock Emphasis
- Dairy Emphasis
- Livestock Speciality: Cattle Emphasis
- Grain
- Combination Livestock and Grain Emphasis
- Special Crops: i. Fruit, Vegetables, Tobacco, Potatoes
  ii. Forest Products

Source: Atlas of Canada

VALUE OF AGRICULTURAL PRODUCTION

in % by regions   Canada = 100%

- ATLANTIC PROVINCES· 3%
- QUÉBEC 13%
- ONTARIO 26%
- PRAIRIE PROVINCES 54%
- BRITISH COLUMBIA 4%

Scale 1:22 500 000

100 0 200 400 600 km

ATLANTIC OCEAN

PACIFIC OCEAN

Hudson Bay

James Bay

UNITED STATES

QUÉBEC

ONTARIO

MANITOBA

SASKATCHEWAN

ALBERTA

BRITISH COLUMBIA

NEWFOUNDLAND

NOVA SCOTIA

P.E.I.

N.B.

Gulf of St. Lawrence

St. Laurent (St. Lawrence)

L. Ontario

L. Erie

L. Huron

L. Michigan

L. Superior

L. Abitibi

Lac St-Jean

L. Winnipeg

West from Greenwich

Halifax
St. John
Port-Cartier
Baie-Comeau
Québec
Trois-Rivières
Sorel
Montréal
Prescott
Kingston
Toronto
Port Colbourne
Georgian Bay
Talbotville
Chatham
Goderich
Sarnia
Wallaceburg
Thunder Bay
Churchill
Winnipeg
Carrot River
Kamsack
Saskatoon
Regina
Moose Jaw
Rosetown
Shaunavon
Edmonton
Three Hills
Vulcan
Barons
Milk River
Calgary
Champion
Lethbridge
Dawson Creek
Sexsmith
Prince Rupert
Vancouver
Victoria
Peace River Area
Prairies

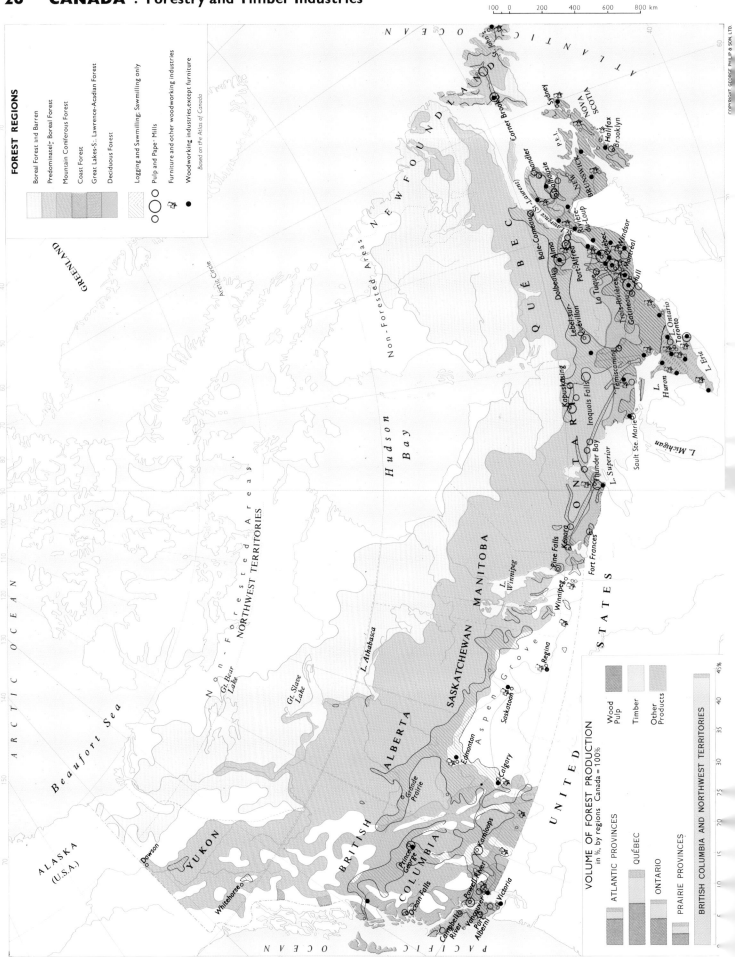

1:22 000 000

100 0   200   400   600   800 km

FOREST REGIONS

Boreal Forest and Barren
Predominately Boreal Forest
Mountain Coniferous Forest
Coast Forest
Great Lakes-S. Lawrence-Acadian Forest
Deciduous Forest

Logging and Sawmilling: Sawmilling only
Pulp and Paper Mills
Furniture and other woodworking industries
Woodworking industries, except furniture

Based on the Atlas of Canada

GREENLAND

ARCTIC OCEAN

Arctic Circle

ATLANTIC OCEAN

Beaufort Sea

ALASKA (U.S.A.)

YUKON

NORTHWEST TERRITORIES

Non - Forested Areas

Gt. Bear Lake

Gt. Slave Lake

L. Athabasca

Dawson

Whitehorse

BRITISH COLUMBIA

Prince George

Kamloops

Ocean Falls

Campbell River

Powell River

Port Alberni

Vancouver

Victoria

ALBERTA

Grande Prairie

Edmonton

Calgary

SASKATCHEWAN

Aspen Grove

Saskatoon

Regina

MANITOBA

Winnipeg

L. Winnipeg

Pine Falls

Kenora

Fort Frances

UNITED STATES

Hudson Bay

Non-Forested Areas

NEWFOUNDLAND

QUÉBEC

ONTARIO

Corner Brook

Sydney

NOVA SCOTIA

Halifax

Brooklyn

P.E.I.

NEW BRUNSWICK

Chandler

Dalhousie

St. Lawrence (S. Laurent)

Baie-Comeau

Rivière-du-Loup

Almo

Port-Alfred

Dolbeau

Québec

Windsor

Montréal

Hull

La Tuque

Trois-Rivières

Gatineau

Lebel-sur-Quévillon

Témiscaming

L. Ontario

Toronto

L. Erie

Kapuskasing

Iroquois Falls

Thunder Bay

Sault Ste. Marie

L. Superior

L. Huron

L. Michigan

PACIFIC OCEAN

VOLUME OF FOREST PRODUCTION
in %, by regions Canada = 100%

Wood Pulp
Timber
Other Products

ATLANTIC PROVINCES

QUÉBEC

ONTARIO

PRAIRIE PROVINCES

BRITISH COLUMBIA AND NORTHWEST TERRITORIES

0   5   10   15   20   25   30   35   40   45%

VALUE OF CATCH in % Canada = 100%

Pacific 32%
SALMON 24%
COD 10%
HERRING 9%
LOBSTER 9%
OTHER 34%
OTHER 8%
6%
Atlantic 62%
Inland 6%

Ⓒ

ATLANTIC COAST FISHERIES
1:9 000 000

Fish Processing Plants

0   200 km
West from Greenwich

Labrador Basin

St. Anthony
Strait of Belle I.
COD

NEWFOUNDLAND
St. John's
COD
Bonavista
MACKEREL
Twillingate COD

Harrington Harbour

Natashquan

Dét. de Jacques-Cartier
I. d'Anticosti
Dét. d'Honguedo
R.-au-Renard
HERRING
COD
MACKEREL

QUÉBEC

Gulf of St. Lawrence

Chaleur Bay
Caraquet
HERRING
MACKEREL
COD

NEW BRUNSWICK

Blacks Harbour
SARDINES
ALEWIVES
Bay of Fundy
HAKE
HADDOCK

St. Lawrence

PRINCE EDWARD I.
PLAICE
HAKE
SHELLFISH
HERRING
MACKEREL
SHAD

NOVA SCOTIA
Halifax
MACKEREL
HAKE
POLLOCK
HERRING
COD
HADDOCK
Yarmouth
Lunenburg

Sydney
Cape Breton I.
CANSO
CANSO BANK
POLLOCK
PLAICE
MISAINE BANK
HADDOCK
BANQUEREAU BANK
ARTIMON BANK
POLLOCK

Channel-Port-aux-Basques
COD
Is. de la Madeleine
REDFISH
BURGEO BANK
COD
90m
HERRING
180m

I. Miquelon (Fr.)
I. St-Pierre (Fr.)
ST. PIERRE BANK
PLAICE
REDFISH
HADDOCK
GREEN BANK

GRAND BANK
HAKE
COD
PLAICE

Sable I.
SABLE I. BANK
HADDOCK
90m
180m

BROWNS BANK
COD

ATLANTIC OCEAN

PLAICE
REDFISH
COD
180m
90m
COD
HADDOCK PLAICE REDFISH

Ⓐ

1:34 000 000

0   400   800   1200 km

Inland Fisheries

Atlantic and Pacific Canadian Fishing Limit

ATLANTIC OCEAN
St. Lawrence

Hudson Bay

Great Slave Lake
TULLIBEE
INCONNU
Peace
Athabasca L.
L. Athabasca
Reindeer L.
Churchill
N. Saskatchewan
S. Saskatchewan
PERCH
PIKE
L. Winnipeg

UNITED STATES

STURGEON
EEL
Ottawa
PIKE
L. Ontario
L. Erie
SMELT
TROUT
L. Huron
L. Michigan
L. Superior

Fraser
PACIFIC OCEAN

PACIFIC COAST FISHERIES
1:7 000 000

0   100   200 km
West from Greenwich

Salmon Fishing Areas
Fish Processing Plants

ALASKA (U.S.A.)

Dixon Entrance
Masset
Queen Charlotte Is.
HALIBUT
COD
HALIBUT
HERRING
SOLE
BRILL
Hecate
Queen Charlotte Sound
COD
SOLE
BRILL
HALIBUT
HERRING

BRITISH COLUMBIA
Prince Rupert
CLAMS
HALIBUT
HERRING
Bella Coola
Namu
Wadhams
HERRING
CLAMS
PRAWNS
CLAMS
Port Hardy
Zeballos
Ucluelet
BRILL
Rock Bay
Vancouver Island
HERRING
HALIBUT
Victoria
Juan de Fuca Strait
Vancouver
PRAWNS
CLAMS
SHRIMPS
HERRING
U.S.A.

PACIFIC OCEAN

Ⓑ

COPYRIGHT GEORGE PHILIP & SON LTD

28 CANADA : Metals and Industrial Minerals

1:22 000 000

100 0 200 400 600 800 km

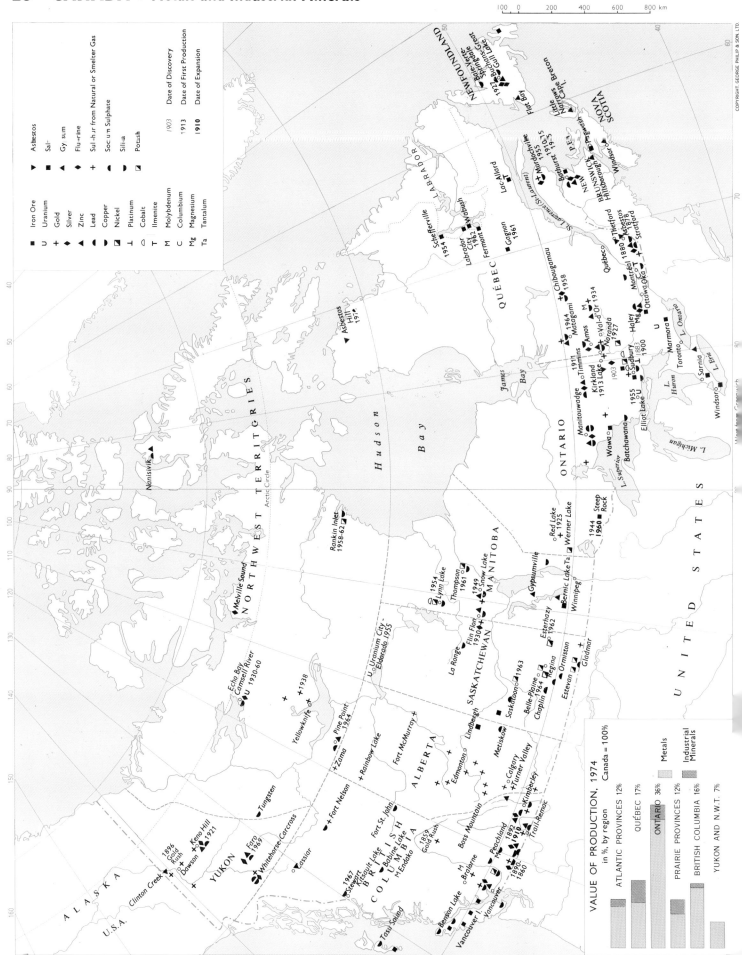

COPYRIGHT. GEORGE PHILIP & SON LTD.

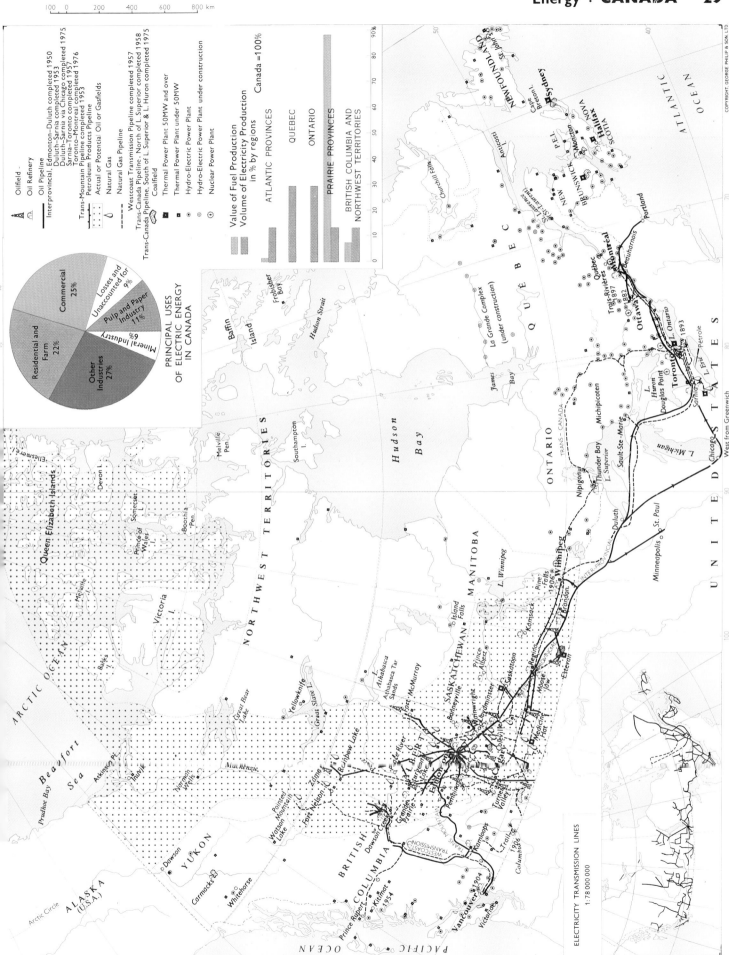

1:22 000 000

100 0 200 400 600 800 km

COPYRIGHT GEORGE PHILIP & SON, LTD

Legend:

▲ Oilfield
⛽ Oil Refinery
— Oil Pipeline
— Interprovincial, Edmonton–Duluth completed 1950
 Duluth–Sarnia completed 1953
 Duluth–Sarnia via Chicago completed 1975
 Sarnia–Toronto completed 1957
 Toronto–Montreal completed 1976
 Petroleum Products Pipeline completed 1953
— Trans-Mountain Pipeline
 Actual or Potential Oil or Gasfields
 Natural Gas
— Natural Gas Pipeline
 Westcoast Transmission Pipeline completed 1957
 Trans-Canada Pipeline, North of L. Superior completed 1958
 Trans-Canada Pipeline, South of L. Superior & L. Huron completed 1975
 Coalfield
■ Thermal Power Plant 50 MW and over
□ Thermal Power Plant under 50 MW
● Hydro-Electric Power Plant
◎ Hydro-Electric Power Plant under construction
⊕ Nuclear Power Plant

Bar chart:
Value of Fuel Production
Volume of Electricity Production
 in % by regions   Canada = 100%

ATLANTIC PROVINCES
QUEBEC
ONTARIO
PRAIRIE PROVINCES
BRITISH COLUMBIA AND
NORTHWEST TERRITORIES

Pie chart: PRINCIPAL USES OF ELECTRIC ENERGY IN CANADA
Commercial 25%
Losses and Unaccounted for 9%
Pulp and Paper Industry 11%
Mineral Industry 6%
Other Industries 27%
Residential and Farm 22%

ELECTRICITY TRANSMISSION LINES
1:78 000 000

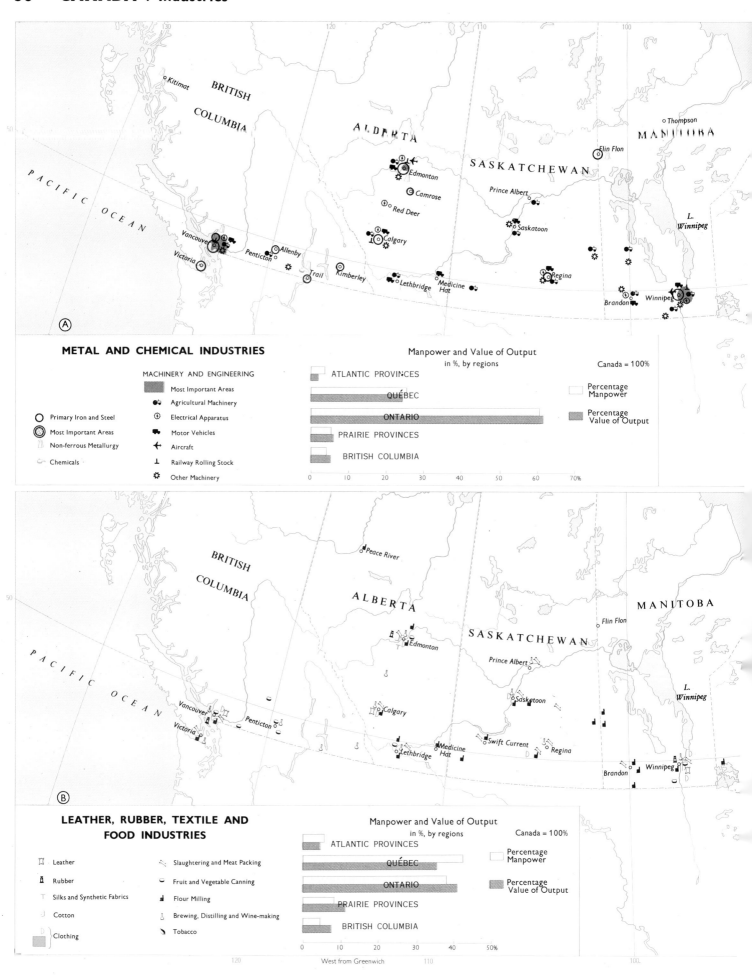

Ⓐ

METAL AND CHEMICAL INDUSTRIES

MACHINERY AND ENGINEERING

▨ Most Important Areas

○ Primary Iron and Steel
◉ Most Important Areas
⚗ Non-ferrous Metallurgy
⚗ Chemicals

🚜 Agricultural Machinery
⊕ Electrical Apparatus
🚚 Motor Vehicles
✈ Aircraft
⊥ Railway Rolling Stock
✿ Other Machinery

Manpower and Value of Output
in %, by regions   Canada = 100%

ATLANTIC PROVINCES
QUÉBEC
ONTARIO
PRAIRIE PROVINCES
BRITISH COLUMBIA

☐ Percentage Manpower
▨ Percentage Value of Output

0   10   20   30   40   50   60   70%

Ⓑ

LEATHER, RUBBER, TEXTILE AND FOOD INDUSTRIES

◫ Leather
🍶 Rubber
⊤ Silks and Synthetic Fabrics
⌇ Cotton
▨ Clothing

⚒ Slaughtering and Meat Packing
⌣ Fruit and Vegetable Canning
⌁ Flour Milling
⚱ Brewing, Distilling and Wine-making
⬂ Tobacco

Manpower and Value of Output
in %, by regions   Canada = 100%

ATLANTIC PROVINCES
QUÉBEC
ONTARIO
PRAIRIE PROVINCES
BRITISH COLUMBIA

☐ Percentage Manpower
▨ Percentage Value of Output

0   10   20   30   40   50%

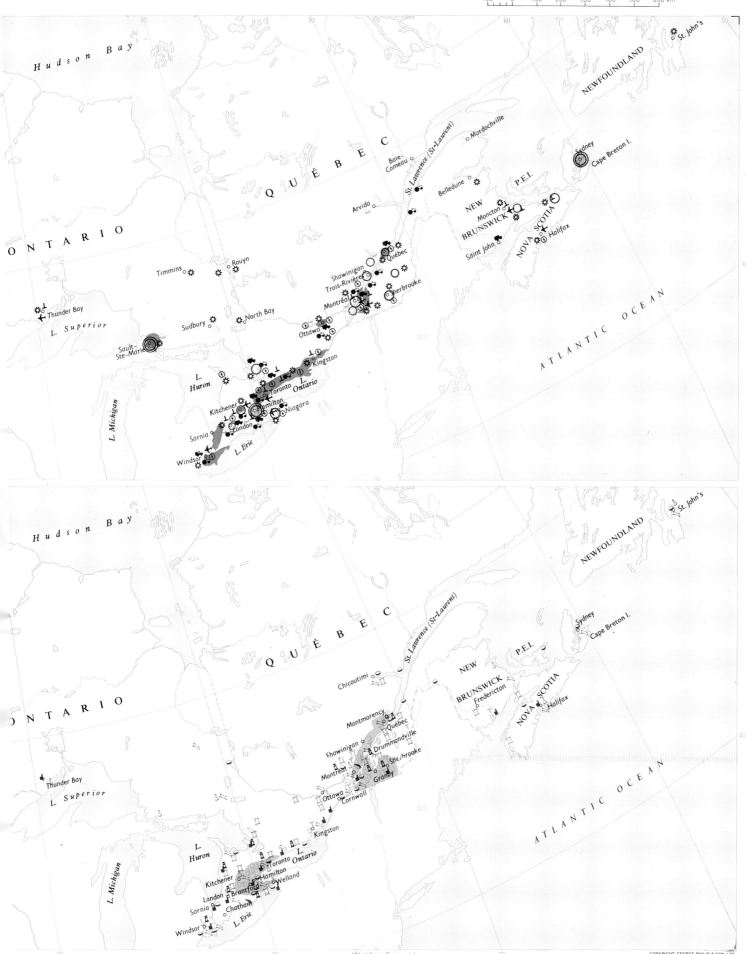

PERCENTAGE DISTRIBUTION OF CANADIAN POPULATION

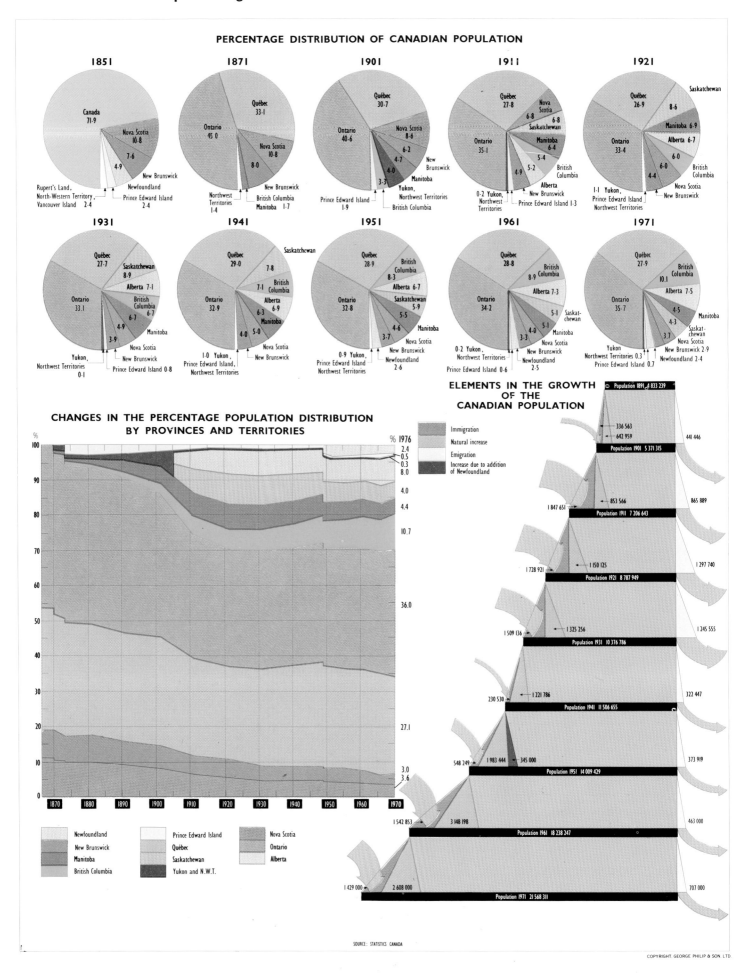

1851
- Canada 71·9
- Nova Scotia 10·8
- 7·6
- 4·9
- New Brunswick
- Rupert's Land, North-Western Territory, Vancouver Island 2·4
- Newfoundland
- Prince Edward Island 2·4

1871
- Québec 33·1
- Ontario 45·0
- Nova Scotia 10·8
- 8·0
- New Brunswick
- Northwest Territories 1·4
- British Columbia
- Manitoba 1·7

1901
- Québec 30·7
- Ontario 40·6
- Nova Scotia 8·6
- 6·2
- 4·7
- 4·0
- 3·3
- New Brunswick
- Manitoba
- Yukon, Northwest Territories
- British Columbia
- Prince Edward Island 1·9

1911
- Québec 27·8
- Nova Scotia 6·8
- 6·8
- Saskatchewan
- Ontario 35·1
- Manitoba 6·4
- 5·4
- British Columbia
- 4·9
- 5·2
- Alberta
- New Brunswick
- 0·2 Yukon, Northwest Territories
- Prince Edward Island 1·3

1921
- Québec 26·9
- Saskatchewan 8·6
- Manitoba 6·9
- Alberta 6·7
- Ontario 33·4
- 6·0
- British Columbia
- 4·4
- Nova Scotia
- New Brunswick
- 1·1 Yukon, Prince Edward Island, Northwest Territories

1931
- Québec 27·7
- Saskatchewan 8·9
- Alberta 7·1
- Ontario 33·1
- British Columbia 6·7
- 6·7
- 4·9
- 3·9
- Manitoba
- Nova Scotia
- New Brunswick
- Prince Edward Island 0·8
- Yukon, Northwest Territories 0·1

1941
- Québec 29·0
- Saskatchewan 7·8
- British Columbia 7·1
- Ontario 32·9
- Alberta 6·9
- 6·3
- Manitoba
- 5·0
- 4·0
- Nova Scotia
- New Brunswick
- 1·0 Yukon, Prince Edward Island, Northwest Territories

1951
- Québec 28·9
- British Columbia 8·3
- Ontario 32·8
- Alberta 6·7
- Saskatchewan 5·9
- 5·5
- Manitoba
- 4·6
- Nova Scotia
- 3·7
- New Brunswick
- Newfoundland 2·6
- 0·9 Yukon, Prince Edward Island, Northwest Territories

1961
- Québec 28·8
- British Columbia 8·9
- Ontario 34·2
- Alberta 7·3
- 5·1 Saskatchewan
- 5·1
- Manitoba
- 4·0
- Nova Scotia
- 3·3
- New Brunswick
- Newfoundland 2·5
- 0·2 Yukon, Northwest Territories
- Prince Edward Island 0·6

1971
- Québec 27·9
- British Columbia 10·1
- Ontario 35·7
- Alberta 7·5
- 4·5
- Manitoba
- 4·3
- Saskatchewan
- 3·7
- Nova Scotia
- New Brunswick 2·9
- Newfoundland 2·4
- Yukon Northwest Territories 0·3
- Prince Edward Island 0·7

CHANGES IN THE PERCENTAGE POPULATION DISTRIBUTION BY PROVINCES AND TERRITORIES

% axis 0–100, years 1870, 1880, 1890, 1900, 1910, 1920, 1930, 1940, 1950, 1960, 1970

% 1976 values: 2.4, 0.5, 0.3, 8.0, 4.0, 4.4, 10.7, 36.0, 27.1, 3.0, 3.6

Legend:
- Newfoundland
- New Brunswick
- Manitoba
- British Columbia
- Prince Edward Island
- Québec
- Saskatchewan
- Yukon and N.W.T.
- Nova Scotia
- Ontario
- Alberta

ELEMENTS IN THE GROWTH OF THE CANADIAN POPULATION

Legend:
- Immigration
- Natural increase
- Emigration
- Increase due to addition of Newfoundland

- Population 1891 4 833 239
- 336 563
- 642 959
- 441 446
- Population 1901 5 371 315
- 853 566
- 1 847 651
- 865 889
- Population 1911 7 206 643
- 1 150 125
- 1 728 921
- 1 297 740
- Population 1921 8 787 949
- 1 325 256
- 1 509 136
- 1 245 555
- Population 1931 10 376 786
- 1 221 786
- 230 530
- 322 447
- Population 1941 11 506 655
- 1 983 444
- 548 249
- 345 000
- 373 919
- Population 1951 14 009 429
- 3 148 198
- 1 542 853
- 463 000
- Population 1961 18 238 247
- 1 429 000
- 2 608 000
- 707 000
- Population 1971 21 568 311

SOURCE: STATISTICS CANADA

1 : 31 500 000

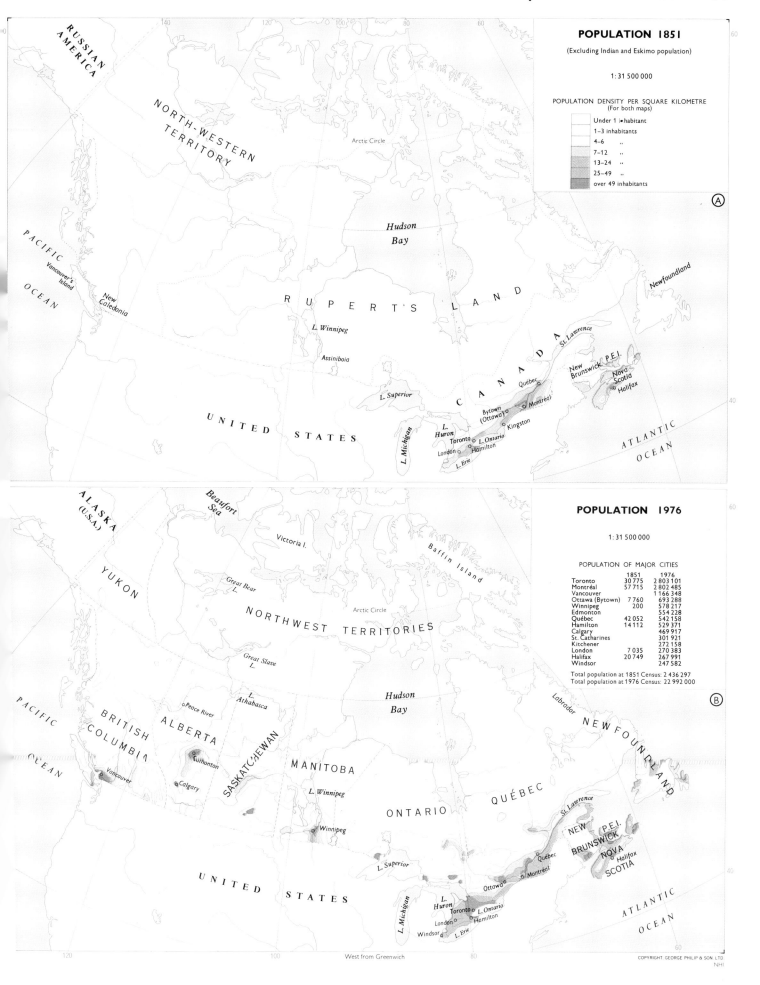

POPULATION 1851

(Excluding Indian and Eskimo population)

1 : 31 500 000

POPULATION DENSITY PER SQUARE KILOMETRE
(For both maps)

	Under 1 inhabitant
	1–3 inhabitants
	4–6 ,,
	7–12 ,,
	13–24 ,,
	25–49 ,,
	over 49 inhabitants

POPULATION 1976

1 : 31 500 000

POPULATION OF MAJOR CITIES

	1851	1976
Toronto	30 775	2 803 101
Montréal	57 715	2 802 485
Vancouver		1 166 348
Ottawa (Bytown)	7 760	693 288
Winnipeg	200	578 217
Edmonton		554 228
Québec	42 052	542 158
Hamilton	14 112	529 371
Calgary		469 917
St. Catharines		301 921
Kitchener		272 158
London	7 035	270 383
Halifax	20 749	267 991
Windsor		247 582

Total population at 1851 Census: 2 436 297
Total population at 1976 Census: 22 992 000

N.W. TERRITORIES

MANITOBA

ONTARIO

HUDSON BAY

JAMES BAY

Belcher Islands

Akimiski I.

LAKE SUPERIOR

LAKE HURON

LAKE ONTARIO

LAKE ERIE

WISCONSIN

MICHIGAN

ILLINOIS

INDIANA

OHIO

PENNSYLVANIA

Thunder Bay

Duluth
Superior

Isle Royale

Sault Ste Marie

Sudbury

North Bay

OTTAWA

TORONTO

Hamilton

BUFFALO

ROCHESTER

SYRACUSE

CLEVELAND

TOLEDO

DETROIT

CHICAGO

MILWAUKEE

Grand Rapids

Madison

Rockford

Timmins

Kirkland Lake

Kapuskasing

Hearst

Cochrane

Moose Factory

Fort Albany

Charlton

Attawapiskat

Winisk

Severn

La Grande

Windsor

London

Kitchener

Niagara Falls

Adirondack Mountains

Georgian Bay

Manitoulin I.

1 : 7 000 000

50   0   50   100   150   200   250   300 km

NEWFOUNDLAND

COAST OF

LABRADOR

South Aulatsivik I.
High I.
Nain
Paul I.
Voisey B.
Kogaluk
Davis Inlet
Nunaksaluk I.
Hopedale
Makkovik
Aillik
Adlavik Is.
C. Harrison
Holton
Indian Harbour
Groswater B.
Rigolet
Cartwright
Sandwich B.
Island of Ponds
Square Islands

Kaniairiktok
Naskaupi
Seal L.
Nipishish L.
Hamilton Inlet
Separation Point
Table B.
L. Melville
Mealy Mts.
North-West River
Goose Bay
Happy Valley
Eagle
Paradise
Alexis
St. Lewis
Mary's Harbour
Battle Harbour
Belle I.
Str. of Belle Isle
Red Bay
L'Anse-au-Loup
Forteau
St. Lunaire-Griguet
St. Anthony
Hare B.

Minipi L.
Little Mecatina
St-Augustin
St-Augustin-Saguenay
Outer I.
Brodore Bay
Lourdes-de-Blanc-Sablon
Flower's Cove
Groais I.
Bell I.
Conche
Englee
Roddickton
White B.
Horse Is.
C. St. John

QUEBEC

Mealy Mts.
I. du Petit-Mécatina
Harrington Harbour
Port Saunders
Daniel's Harbour
Seal Cove
Baie Verte
La Scie
Notre Dame B.
Sop's Arm
Twillingate
Fogo
Fogo I.
Carmanville
C. Freels

L. Musquaro
Etamamu
Trout River
Bay of Islands
Springdale
South Brook
Botwood
Gander
Lewisporte
Wesleyville
Bonavista

Aguanish
Natashquan
Kegaska
Gethsémani
Deer Lake
Howley
Windsor
Grand Falls
Glenwood
Dark Cove
Glovertown
Bonavista
C. Bonavista
Catalina

Long Range Mts.
NEWFOUNDLAND
Corner Brook 814
Buchans
Red Indian L.
Badger
Bishop's Falls
Trinity
Boy de Verde
Trinity B.

Mingan
Havre-St-Pierre
Sheldrake
Aguanus
Natashquan

Long Range Mts.

Port au Port B.
Port au Port
Stephenville
Victoria Res.
Grand L.
Heart's Content
Carbonear
Concepcion B.
Torbay

St. George's
St. George's B.
Long R.
Grey Res.
Salmon Res.
St. John's
Mt. Pearl

GULF OF ST. LAWRENCE

572

Î. d'Anticosti
Jupiter

Dét. de Jacques-Cartier

Heath Pt.

St. David's
South Branch
White Bear Res.
St. Alban's
Terrenceville
Belleoram
Spaniard's Bay
Holyrood
Avalon
Bulls

St. Andrew's
C. Ray
Isle aux Morts
Rose Blanche
Burgeo
Ramea
Hermitage B.
Fortune B.
Harbour Breton
Marystown
Placentia
Argentia
Placentia B.
St. Bride's
C. Race
Trepassey

Channel-Port aux Basques

Miquelon
Grand Bank
Fortune
St. Lawrence
Langlade
St. Pierre

SAINT-PIERRE ET MIQUELON (Fr.)

Cabot Strait

Î. de la Madeleine (Quebec)
Îs. de la Fatima
Cap-aux-Meules
Havre-Aubert
Grande-Entrée
St. Paul
C. North

PRINCE EDWARD ISLAND
Summerside
Kensington
Charlottetown
Souris
East Pt.

Mt. Louis
Grande-Vallée
Mont-St-Pierre
Rivière-au-Renard
C. de Gaspé
Gaspé
Douglastown
Percé
Grande-Rivière
Chandler

Matane
Cap-Chat
Ste-Anne-des-Monts
Mts. Chic-Chocs
Pén. de Gaspé
Mt. Jacques-Cartier 1310
Bonaventure
Paspébiac
Miscou I.
Î. Brion

Rimouski
Bic
Trois-Pistoles
Rivière-du-Loup
Amqui
Causapscal
Matapedia
Dalhousie
Campbellton
Atholville
Belledune
Chaleur Bay
Lamèque
Shippegan
Tracadie

NOVA SCOTIA

Pleasant Bay
Chéticamp
Ingonish
NAT. PARK 532
C. Smokey
Cape Breton Highlands

Cabano
Kedgwick
St. Arthur
Bathurst
Nepisiguit
Miramichi B.
North Pt.
Tignish
Alberton

Edmundston
St-Jacques
Heath Steele
Neguac
Richibucto
Kouchibouguac
Cape Montague
East Pt.
Georgetown
Montague
Murray Hr.
Inverness
N. Sydney
Sydney Mines
New Waterford
Glace Bay

NEW BRUNSWICK
St. Leonard 819
Grand Falls
Plaster Rock
Newcastle
Chatham
Blackville

Van Buren
Caribou
Presque Isle

Ft. Kent
Allagash
Ashland

Notre Dame
Chipman
Minto
Havelock
Petitcodiac
Borden
Cape Tormentine
Pictou
Antigonish
Mulgrave
Canso
Louisbourg
Fourchu

ATLANTIC

Montmagny
Lévis
Pamphile
St-Jean-Port-Joli
Armagh
Beauceville
St-Georges
Thetford Mines
Lac-Mégantic
East Angus
Sherbrooke

MAINE
Eagle L.
Houlton
Island Falls
Patten
Millinocket 1606
Woodstock
Hartland
Stanley
Grand L.
Gagetown
Fredericton
Fredericton Junc.
Oromocto
Chipman
St. John
Shediac
Moncton
Amherst
Springhill
Parrsboro
Truro
New Glasgow
Stellarton
Sherbrooke
Chedabucto B.
Bras d'Or
St. Peters
Î. Madame
Hawkesbury

Moosehead L.
Greenville
Dover-Foxcroft
Danforth
Calais
St. Stephen
St. George
Rothesay
Saint John
Sussex
St. Martins
Chignecto
Joggins
Minas Basin
Windsor
Shubenacadie
Upper Stewiacke
Musquodoboit
Sheet Hr.
Musquodoboit Hr.

Bingham
Skowhegan
Mattawamkeag
Old Town
Brewer
Bangor
Ellsworth
Machias
Jonesport
Eastport
Grand Manan I.
St. Andrews
Blacks Hr.
Bridgetown
Annapolis
Middleton
Kentville
Dartmouth
Halifax

Rumford
Berlin
Bethel
Waterville
Augusta
Belfast
Camden
Rockland
Bar Harbor
Mt. Desert I.
Digby
Weymouth
Yarmouth
Wedgeport
St. Mary's B.
Rossignol Res.
Bridgewater
Mahone Bay
Lunenburg
Liverpool
Port Mouton
Sheet Hr.

Sable I. (Nova Scotia)

Auburn
Lewiston
Bath
Brunswick
Sebago
Portland
Saco
Biddeford
Sanford
Yarmouth
Shelburne
Clark's Harbour
C. Sable
Lockeport

OCEAN

Concord
Dover
Portsmouth
Manchester
Nashua
Haverhill
Lawrence
Gloucester
Lynn
BOSTON
Brockton

West from Greenwich

70   65   60

COPYRIGHT. GEORGE PHILIP & SON. LTD.

1 : 7 000 000

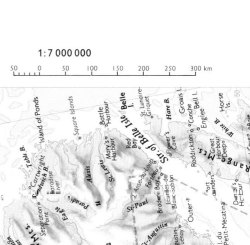

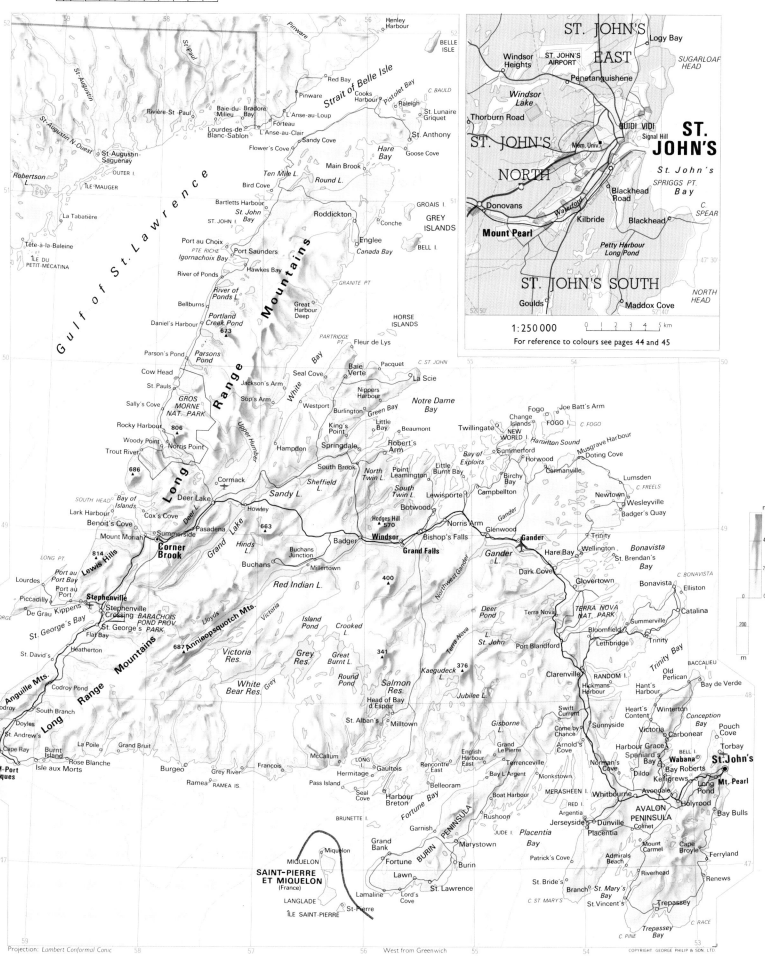

1:2 500 000

10 0 10 20 30 40 50 60 70 80 90 100 km

ST. JOHN'S EAST

Logy Bay

SUGARLOAF
HEAD

Windsor
Heights

ST. JOHN'S
AIRPORT

Penetanguishene

ST. JOHN'S

Windsor
Lake

Thorburn Road

QUIDI VIDI

Signal Hill

**ST.
JOHN'S**

ST. JOHN'S
NORTH

Mem. Univ.

St. John's

SPRIGGS PT.
Bay

Waterford

Blackhead
Road

Donovans

Kilbride

Blackhead

C.
SPEAR

Mount Pearl

47°30'

Petty Harbour
Long Pond

ST. JOHN'S SOUTH

NORTH
HEAD

Goulds

Maddox Cove

52°50'

52°40'

1:250 000

0 1 2 3 4 5 km

For reference to colours see pages 44 and 45

Henley
Harbour

BELLE
ISLE

Red Bay

Strait of Belle Isle

Pinware

Cooks
Harbour

Pistolet Bay

C. BAULD

Raleigh

L'Anse-au-Loup

St. Lunaire
Griquet

Rivière-St-Paul

Baie-du-
Milieu

Bradore
Bay

Forteau

St. Anthony

Lourdes-de-
Blanc-Sablon

L'Anse-au-Clair

Sandy Cove

Goose Cove

Flower's Cove

*Hare
Bay*

St-Augustin-
Saguenay

OUTER I.

*Robertson
L.*

ÎLE MAUGER

Main Brook

Round L.

La Tabatière

Ten Mile L.

Bird Cove

GROAIS I.

Tête-à-la-Baleine

Bartletts Harbour

St. John
Bay

Roddickton

Conche

GREY
ISLANDS

*ÎLE DU
PETIT-MÉCATINA*

ST. JOHN I.

Port au Choix

PTE RICHE

Port Saunders

Englee

BELL I.

Igornachoix Bay

Canada Bay

Hawkes Bay

Gulf of St. Lawrence

River of Ponds

GRANITE PT.

HORSE
ISLANDS

River of
Ponds L.

Bellburns

Great
Harbour
Deep

Portland
Creek Pond

Daniel's Harbour

673

PARTRIDGE
PT.

Fleur de Lys

Parson's Pond

Parsons
Pond

Bay

Pacquet

C. ST. JOHN

Seal Cove

Baie
Verte

Cow Head

White

La Scie

St. Pauls

Jackson's Arm

Nippers
Harbour

Sally's Cove

GROS
MORNE
NAT. PARK

Sop's Arm

Westport

Green Bay

*Notre Dame
Bay*

Fogo

Joe Batt's Arm

Rocky Harbour

806

Burlington

King's
Point

Little
Bay

Change
Islands

FOGO I.

C. FOGO

Woody Point

Norris Point

Upper Humber

Beaumont

NEW
WORLD I.

Hamilton Sound

Trout River

Hampden

Springdale

Robert's
Arm

Twillingate

Musgrave Harbour

686

Cormack

South Brook

North
Twin L.

Point
Leamington

Summerford

Horwood

Doting Cove

Sandy L.

Sheffield
L.

South
Twin L.

Birchy
Bay

Garmanville

Lumsden

SOUTH HEAD

Bay of
Islands

Deer Lake

Howley

Bay of
Exploits

Lewisporte

Campbellton

C. FREELS

Lark Harbour

Cox's Cove

Pasadena

663

Botwood

Newtown

Wesleyville

Benoit's Cove

Deer L.

Hinds
L.

Badger

Hodges Hill
570

Norris Arm

Gander

Badger's Quay

Mount Moriah

Corner
Brook

Grand Lake

Windsor

Bishop's Falls

Glenwood

Trinity

Bonavista
Bay

LONG PT.

Lewis
Hills

814

Buchans
Junction

Grand Falls

Gander
L.

Hare Bay

Wellington

St. Brendan's
Bay

Port au
Port Bay

Buchans

Millertown

Dark Cove

Glovertown

Bonavista

C. BONAVISTA

Lourdes

Port au
Port

Stephenville

Red Indian L.

400

Northwest Gander

TERRA
NOVA
NAT. PARK

Elliston

Piccadilly

Kippens

Victoria

Catalina

De Grau

Stephenville
Crossing

Island
Pond

Deer
Pond

Terra Nova

Summerville

St. George's

BARACHOIS
POND PROV.
PARK

Lloyds

Crooked
L.

Grey
Res.

Terra Nova

TERRA
NOVA

Bloomfield

Lethbridge

Flat Bay

St. George's Bay

687 Annieopsquotch Mts.

Victoria
Res.

Great
Burnt L.

341

St. John

Port Blandford

Trinity

St. David's

Heatherton

White
Bear Res.

Grey

Round
Pond

Salmon
Res.

Kaegudeck
L.

376

Clarenville

RANDOM I.

Trinity Bay

BACCALIEU

Anguille Mts.

Codroy
Pond

Jubilee L.

Hickmans
Harbour

Old
Perlican

Codroy

South Branch

Head of Bay
d'Espoir

Hant's
Harbour

Bay de Verde

Doyles

St. Alban's

Milltown

Swift
Current

Heart's
Content

Winterton

Conception
Bay

St. Andrew's

Cape Ray

Burnt
Island

La Poile

Grand Bruit

McCallum

Gisborne
L.

Come by
Chance

Sunnyside

Victoria

Carbonear

Pouch
Cove

Rose Blanche

François

Grand
Le Pierre

Arnold's
Cove

Harbour
Grace

Torbay

Port-
ques

Isle aux Morts

Burgeo

Grey River

LONG

Gaultois

Hermitage

Rencontre
East

English
Harbour
East

Terrenceville

Norman's
Cove

Spaniard's
Bay

BELL I.

Wabana

Dildo

Kelligrews

St. John's

Ramea

RAMEA IS.

Pass Island

Bay L'Argent

Monkstown

MERASHEEN

Whitbourne

Avondale

Long
Pond

Mt. Pearl

Seal
Cove

Harbour
Breton

Belleoram

Boat Harbour

RED I.

Holyrood

Bay Bulls

BRUNETTE I.

Fortune Bay

BURIN PENINSULA

Rushoon

Argentia

AVALON
PENINSULA

Miquelon

Grand
Bank

Garnish

JUDE I.

Placentia
Bay

Jerseyside

Dunville

Placentia

Colinet

Mount
Carmel

Cape
Broyle

**SAINT-PIERRE
ET MIQUELON**
(France)

MIQUELON

Fortune

Marystown

Patrick's Cove

Admirals
Beach

Ferryland

Lamaline

Lawn

Burin

St. Bride's

Riverhead

Renews

LANGLADE

Lord's
Cove

St. Lawrence

Branch

St. Mary's
Bay

ÎLE SAINT-PIERRE

St-Pierre

C. ST MARY'S

St. Vincent's

Trepassey

C. RACE

Trepassey
Bay

C. PINE

m

400

200

0

200

m

Projection: Lambert Conformal Conic

West from Greenwich

COPYRIGHT GEORGE PHILIP & SON LTD.

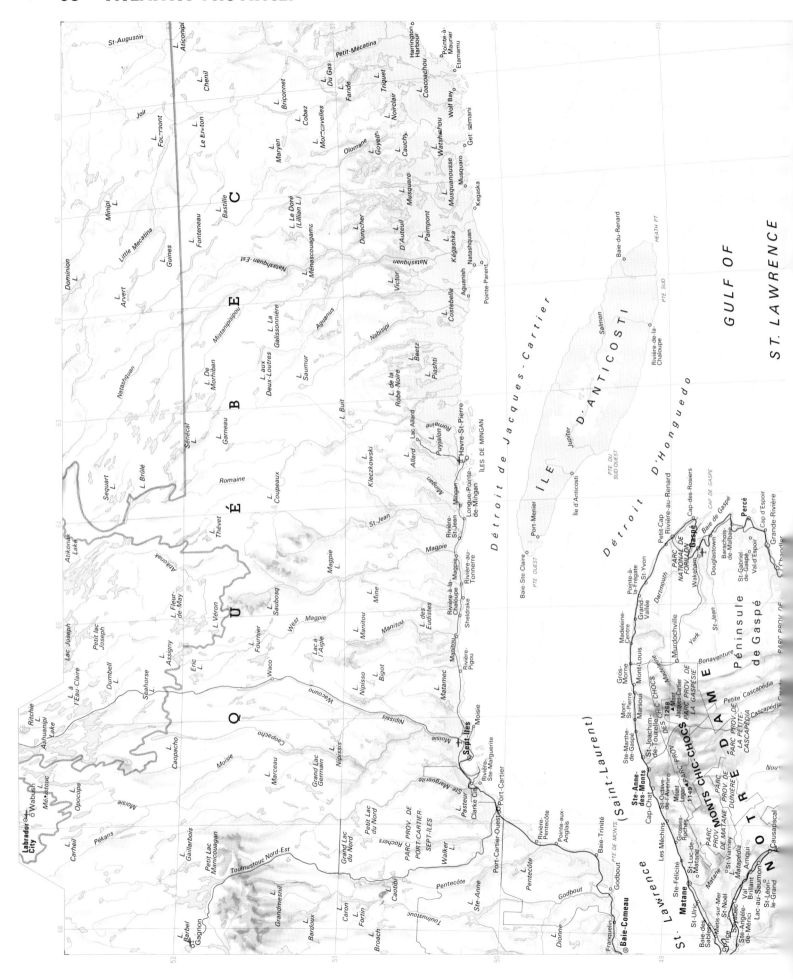

St-Augustin

Aticonipi L.

L. Fox—ront

Chenil

Joir

Le Breton

L. Breton

Petit-Mécatina

Du Gas

Harrington Harbour

Pointe-à-Maurier

Etamamu

Faride

Briconnet

Cobaz

Triquet

Noirclair

Coacoachou

Wolf Bay

Maryen

Mor—velles

Olomane

Goyell

Cauchy

Watshishou

Musquaro

Get semani

Bastille

C

L. Le Doré
(Lillian L.)

Durocher

D'Auteuil

Patmpont

Musquaro

Musquanousse

Musquaro

Kegaska

Minipi L.

Fonteneau

Natashquan-Est

Natashquan

Kegashka

Baie-du-Renard

HEATH PT

Little Mecatina

Guines

É

Victor

Costebelle

Aquanish

Natashquan

Pointe-Parent

GULF OF

Dominion

Arvert

De Morhiban

L. La
Galissonnière

Menascouagams

Nabisipi

Beetz

Piashti

ST. LAWRENCE

Mistanipisipou

L. aux
Deux-Loutres

Aguanus

Saumur

L. de la
Robe-Noire

B

Senécal L.

Garneau

Thévet L.

Romaine

Coupeaux

L. Buit

Allard

Lac Allard

Romaine

Puyjalon

Havre-St-Pierre

ÎLES DE MINGAN

PTE DU
SUD-OUEST

Île d'Anticosti

Jupiter

Salmon

Rivière-de-la-
Chaloupe

PTE SUD

Détroit de Jacques-Cartier

ÎLE D'ANTICOSTI

Détroit D'Honguedo

Atikonak
Lake

L. Fleur-
de-May

L. Véron

St-Jean

Kleczkowski

Mingan

Longue-Pointe-
de-Mingan

Magpie

Rivière-
St-Jean

Baie Ste-Claire

PTE OUEST

Port-Menier

Petit-Cap

Rivière-au-Renard

Cap-des-Rosiers

É

Thévet L.

Magpie L.

Rivière-au-
Tonnerre

Magpie

Pointe-à-
la-Frégate

St-Yvon

CAP DE GASPÉ

Baie de Gaspé

Percé

Cap d'Espoir

Sequart L.

L. Brûlé

Assigny

Eric
L.

Saubosq

West
Magpie

L.
Mine

Manitou

Rivière-à-la-
Chaloupe

Sheldrake

L. des
Eudistes

Dartmuth

Grand-
Vallée

Madeleine-
Centre

Murdochville

St-Jean

Douglastown

PARC
NATIONAL DE
FORILLON

Wakeham

Gaspé

St-Gabriel-
de-Gaspé

Val-d'Espoir

Grande-Rivière

Chandler

Atikonak L.

U

L. à
l'Eau-Claire

Lac Joseph

Petit lac
Joseph

Dumbell
L.

Seahorse
L.

Fournier
L.

Lac à
l'Aigle

L.
Manitou

Matanec

Matamec

Rivière-
Pigou

York

Bonaventure

Gros-
Morne

Mont-
St-Pierre

Marsoui

Mont-Louis

Mont
Jacques-Cartier

DÉS. 1268

CHIC-CHOCS

PARC PROV. DE
LA GASPÉSIE

Petite Cascapédia

Cascapédia

Péninsule
de Gaspé

PARC PROV. DE

Ritchie
L.

Wabush

Ashuanipi
Lake

L. à
l'Eau-Claire

L.
Caopacho

Marceau
L.

Grand Lac
Germain

Nipisso
L.

Bigot
L.

Waco

Nipissis

Moisie

Nipissis

Q

Moisie

Moisie

Nipissis

Waconno

Moisie

Sept-Îles

Rivière-
Ste-Marguerite

Ste-
Marguerite

Mont-
Louis

St-Joachim-
de-Tourelle

CHIC-CHOCS

Mont
Logan
3149

St-Octave-
de-l'Avenir

PARC PROV
DE MATANE

MONTS

CHIC-CHOCS

PARC
PROV. DE
DUNIÈRE

PARC PROV. DE
LA PETITE
CASCAPÉDIA

DAME

Labrador
City

Wabush

L.
Ménistouc

L.
Opocopa

Caopacho

Marceau

Moisie

Petit Lac
du Nord

Grand Lac
du Nord

Rochers

PARC PROV. DE
SEPT-ÎLES

Walker
L.

Ste-Anne-
des-Monts

Cap-Chat

Ste-Marthe-
de-Gaspé

Pasteur

Clarke City

Port-Cartier

Port-Cartier-Ouest

Rivière-
Pentecôte

Pointe-aux-
Anglais

Baie-Trinité

Cap-
Chat

Les Méchins

Grosses-
Roches

St-Luc-de-
Matane

St-Vianney

PROV. DE
MATANE

NOTRE

N

L.
Carheil

Pékans

L.
Gaillarbois

Petit Lac
Manicouagan

Grand Lac
du Nord

PARC PROV. DE
SEPT-ÎLES

Pentecôte

Rivière-
Pentecôte

Pentecôte

Godbout

St-Félicité

Matane

Val-
Brillant

Amqui

Matapédia

Lac-au-Saumon

Causapscal

(Saint-Laurent)

St. Lawrence

St. Lawrence

L.
Barbel

Gagnon

Grandmesnil
L.

Bardoux
L.

Caron
L.

Fortin
L.

Caotibi
L.

Toulnustouc

Godbout

Ste-Anne

Pentecôte
L.

Franquelin

Baie-Comeau

St-Ulric

Baie-des-
Sables

Métis-sur-Mer

St-Noël

Price

Ste-Angèle-
de-Mérici

St-Léon-
le-Grand

Broach
L.

Dionne
L.

Toulnustouc Nord-Est

St-Léon

PTE DE MONTS

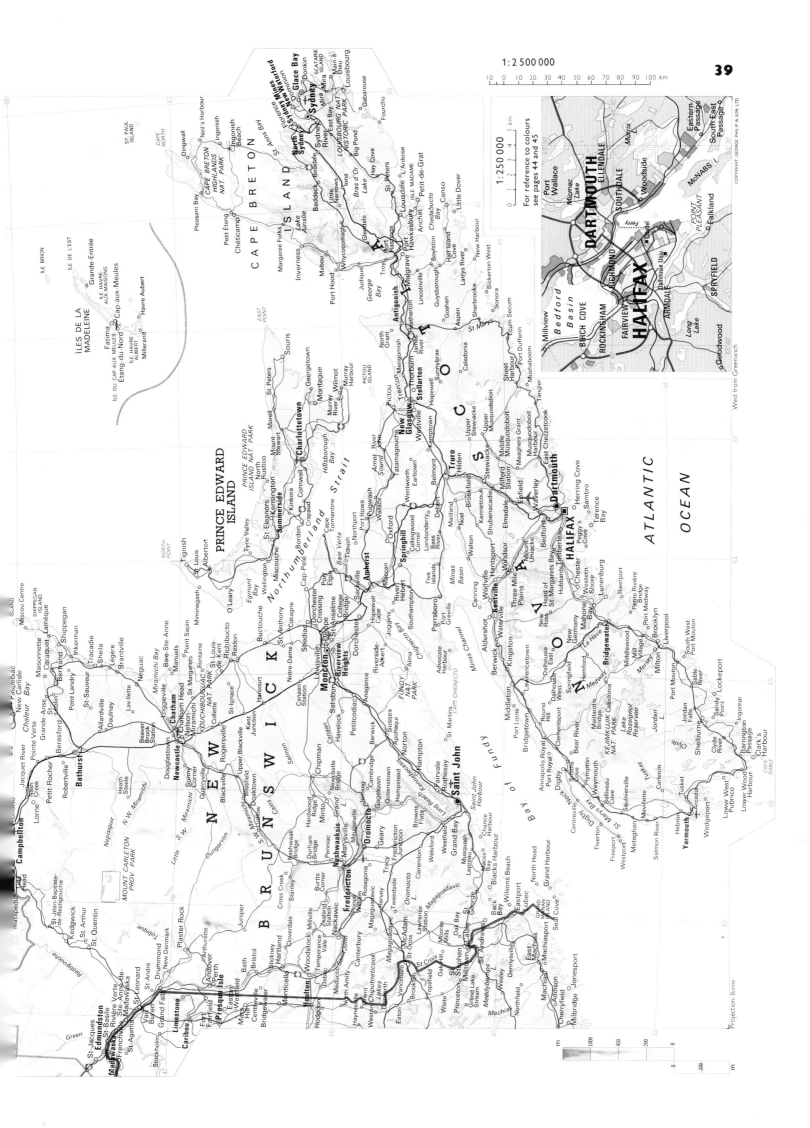

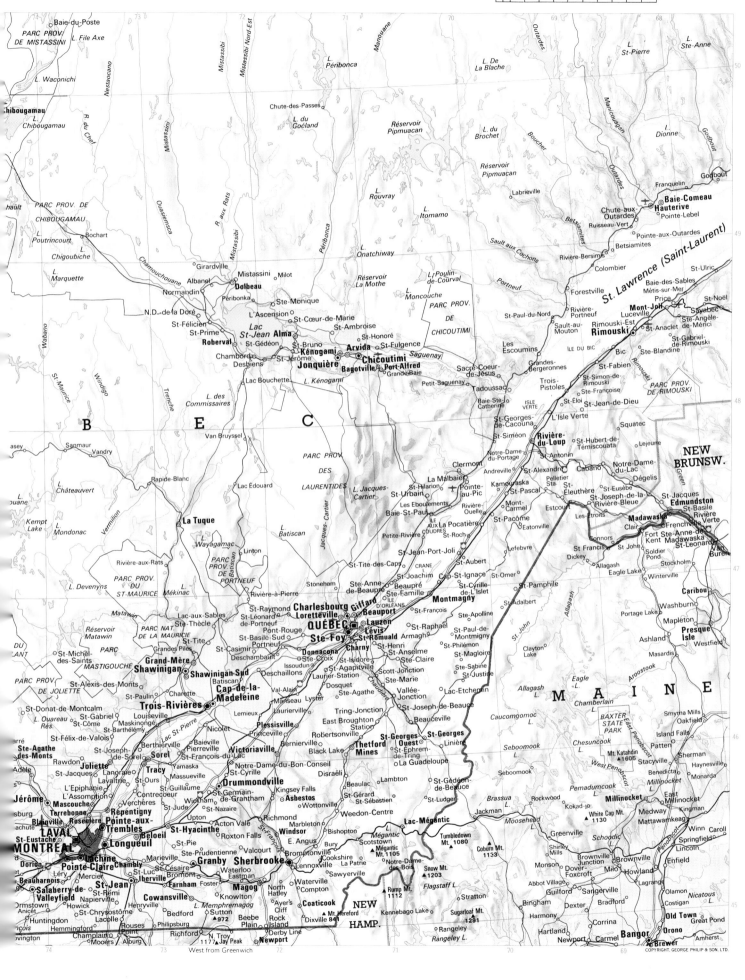

1:250 000

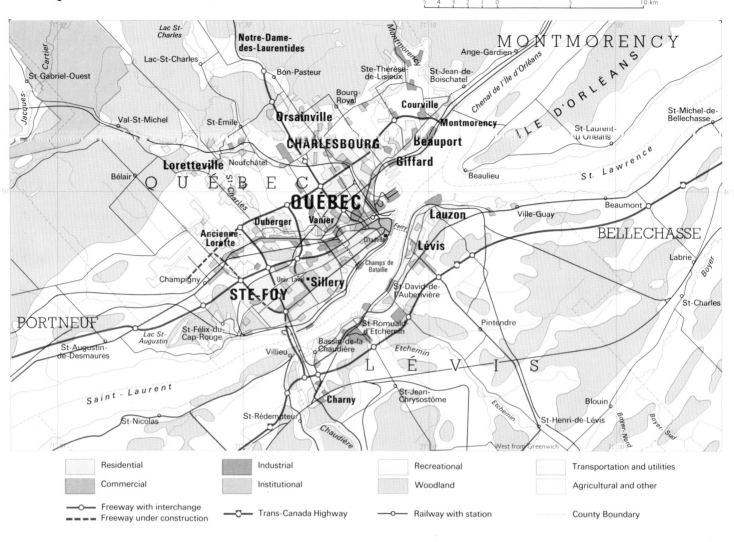

Residential
Commercial
Industrial
Institutional
Recreational
Woodland
Transportation and utilities
Agricultural and other

—○— Freeway with interchange
- - - - Freeway under construction
—◻— Trans-Canada Highway
—○— Railway with station
- - - County Boundary

Projection: *Transverse Mercator*

Québec looking north-east from Parliament Buildings across the St. Lawrence River.

Montréal looking east from Mont-Royal across the St. Lawrence River.

1 : 600 000

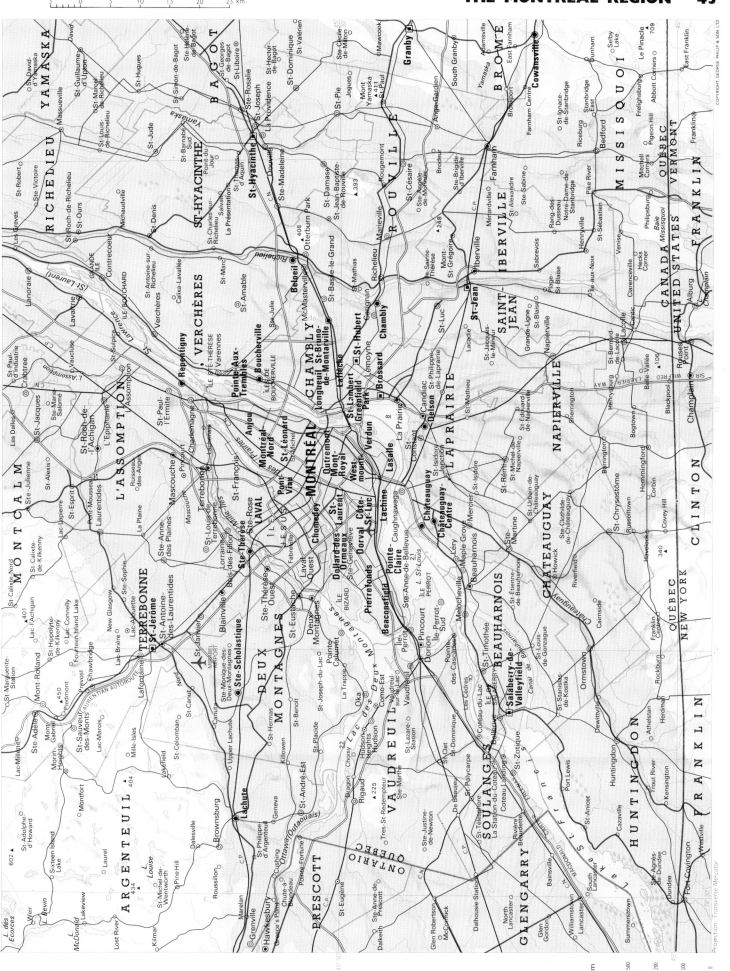

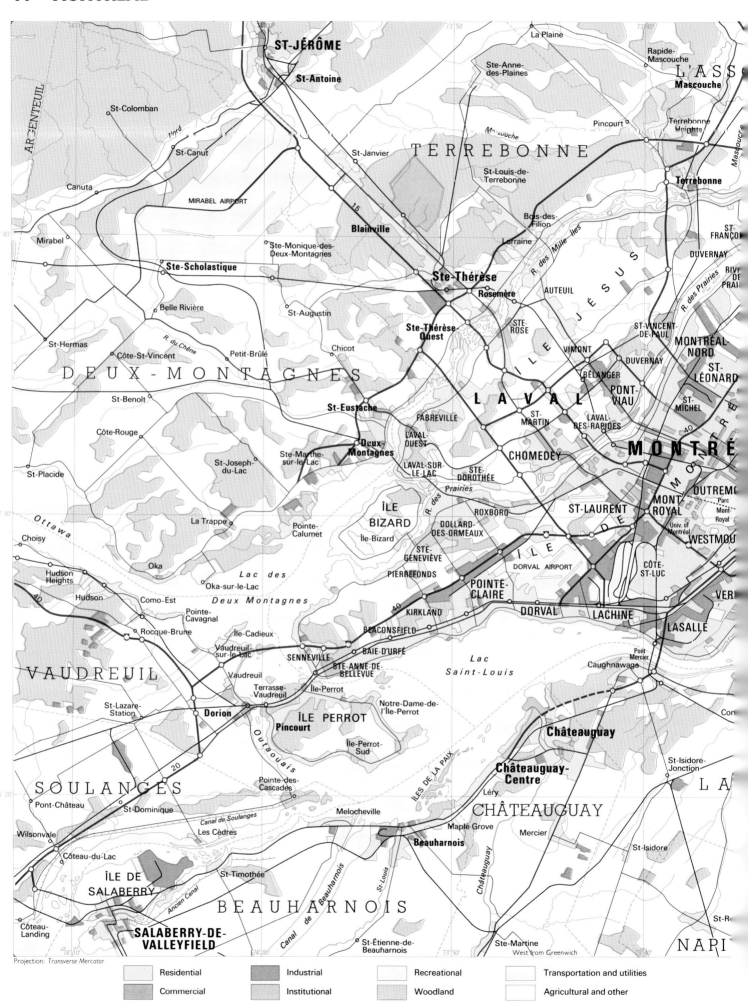

ST-JÉRÔME
St-Antoine
St-Colomban
St-Canut
Canuta
MIRABEL AIRPORT
Mirabel
St-Hermas
Ste-Scholastique
Belle Rivière
Côte-St-Vincent
Petit-Brûlé
St-Benoît
D E U X - M O N T A G N E S
Côte-Rouge
St-Joseph-du-Lac
St-Placide
Ste-Marthe-sur-le-Lac
St-Eustache
Deux-Montagnes
La Trappe
Pointe-Calumet
ÎLE BIZARD
Île-Bizard
Choisy
Hudson Heights
Hudson
Como-Est
Oka
Lac des Oka-sur-le-Lac
Deux Montagnes
Pointe-Cavagnal
Rocque-Brune
Île-Cadieux
Vaudreuil-sur-le-Lac
SENNEVILLE
STE-ANNE-DE-BELLEVUE
BAIE-D'URFÉ
Lac Saint-Louis
V A U D R E U I L
Vaudreuil
St-Lazare-Station
Terrasse-Vaudreuil
Île-Perrot
Dorion
Pincourt
ÎLE PERROT
Notre-Dame-de-l'Île-Perrot
Île-Perrot-Sud
S O U L A N G E S
Pont-Château
St-Dominique
Pointe-des-Cascades
Melocheville
Wilsonvale
Côteau-du-Lac
Canal de Soulanges
Les Cèdres
ÎLE DE SALABERRY
St-Timothée
Ancien Canal
B E A U H A R N O I S
Beauharnois
Maple Grove
Mercier
Côteau-Landing
SALABERRY-DE-VALLEYFIELD
St-Étienne-de-Beauharnois
Ste-Martine
NAPI

La Plaine
Rapide-Mascouche
Ste-Anne-des-Plaines
L'ASS
Mascouche
Pincourt
Terrebonne Heights
T E R R E B O N N E
St-Louis-de-Terrebonne
Terrebonne
Blainville
Ste-Monique-des-Deux-Montagnes
Bois-des-Filion
Lorraine
St-FRANÇO
DUVERNAY
Ste-Thérèse
Rosemère
AUTEUIL
St-Augustin
Ste-Thérèse-Ouest
Chicot
Ste-ROSE
St-VINCENT-DE-PAUL
MONTRÉAL-NORD
St-LÉONARD
VIMONT
DUVERNAY
L A V A L
St-MICHEL
FABREVILLE
St-MARTIN
BÉLANGER
PONT-VIAU
LAVAL-OUEST
LAVAL-DES-RAPIDES
CHOMEDEY
M O N T R É
LAVAL-SUR-LE-LAC
STE-DOROTHÉE
Prairies
ROXBORO
DOLLARD-DES-ORMEAUX
St-LAURENT
MONT-ROYAL
OUTREMO
R. des
STE-GENEVIÈVE
Parc Mont-Royal
Univ. of Montréal
PIERREFONDS
DORVAL AIRPORT
WESTMOU
POINTE-CLAIRE
CÔTE-St-LUC
KIRKLAND
DORVAL
LACHINE
BEACONSFIELD
LASALLE
Pont Mercier
Caughnawaga
VER
Châteauguay
St-Isidore-Jonction
Châteauguay-Centre
L A
Léry
C H Â T E A U G U A Y
St-Isidore
Pont-Château
St-R
West from Greenwich

Ottawa
R. du Chêne
Nord
Outaouais
St-Janvier
ARGENTEUIL

Projection: Transverse Mercator

	Residential		Industrial		Recreational		Transportation and utilities
	Commercial		Institutional		Woodland		Agricultural and other

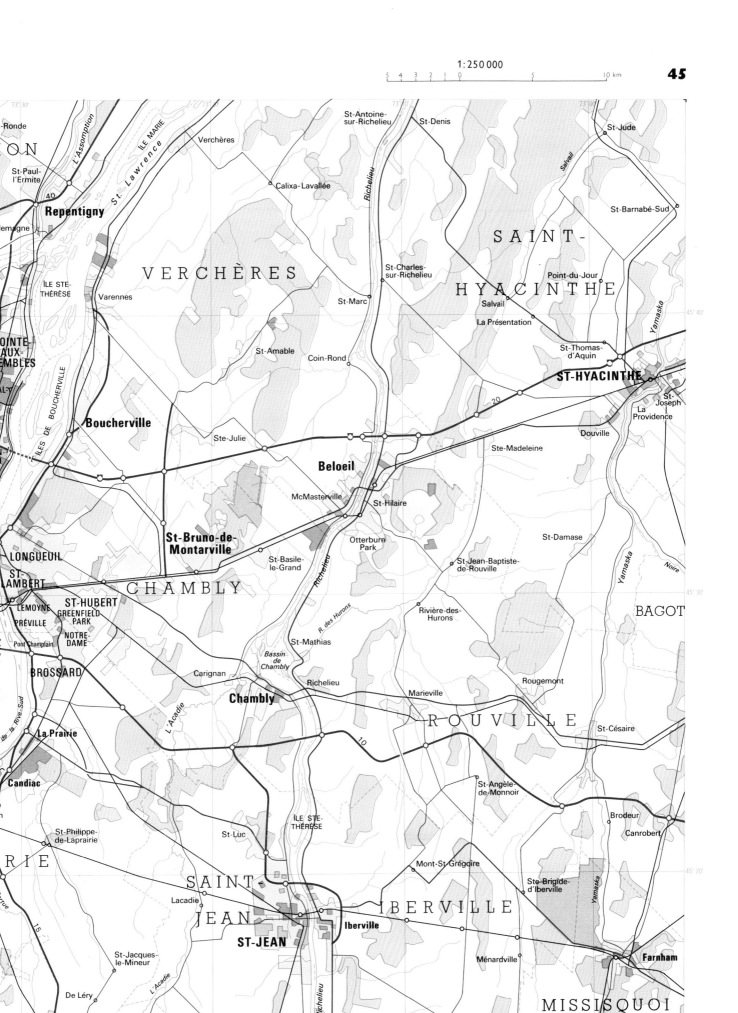

1:250 000

5 4 3 2 1 0   5   10 km

45

Cabane-Ronde

IPTION

St-Paul-l'Ermite

40

Repentigny

Charlemagne

henaie

ÎLE STE-THÉRÈSE

POINTE-AUX-TREMBLES

MONTRÉAL-EST

NJOU

ST-JEAN-DE-DIEU

que

Boucherville

ÎLE STE-HÉLÈNE

Terre des Hommes

LONGUEUIL

ST-LAMBERT

LEMOYNE

Pont Victoria

PRÉVILLE

ST-HUBERT

GREENFIELD PARK

NOTRE-DAME

Pont Champlain

E DES EURS

BROSSARD

La Prairie

Candiac

Delson

St-Philippe-de-Laprairie

St-Jacques-le-Mineur

AIRIE

R. de la Tortue

athieu

De Léry

15

LE

NAPIERVILLE

L'Assomption

ÎLE MARIE

Verchères

St. Lawrence

Calixa-Lavallée

Varennes

V E R C H È R E S

St-Amable

Coin-Rond

Ste-Julie

McMasterville

St-Bruno-de-Montarville

St-Basile-le-Grand

CHAMBLY

Carignan

Bassin de Chambly

St-Mathias

Richelieu

Chambly

L'Acadie

L'Acadie

St-Luc

Lacadie

SAINT JEAN

ST-JEAN

ÎLE STE-THÉRÈSE

St-Antoine-sur-Richelieu

St-Denis

Richelieu

St-Charles-sur-Richelieu

St-Marc

Beloeil

St-Hilaire

Otterburn Park

R. des Hurons

Richelieu

Richelieu

St-Jean-Baptiste-de-Rouville

Rivière-des-Hurons

Marieville

R O U V I L L E

Mont-St-Grégoire

IBERVILLE

Iberville

Ménardville

St-Alexandre

St-Jude

St-Barnabé-Sud

S A I N T -

HYACINTHE

Salvail

La Présentation

Point-du-Jour

St-Thomas-d'Aquin

ST-HYACINTHE

St-Joseph

La Providence

Douville

Ste-Madeleine

Salvail

Yamaska

St-Damase

Yamaska

Noire

BAGOT

Rougemont

St-Césaire

St-Angèle-de-Monnoir

Brodeur

Canrobert

Ste-Brigide-d'Iberville

Yamaska

Farnham

M I S S I S Q U O I

20

10

COPYRIGHT. GEORGE PHILIP & SON. LTD.

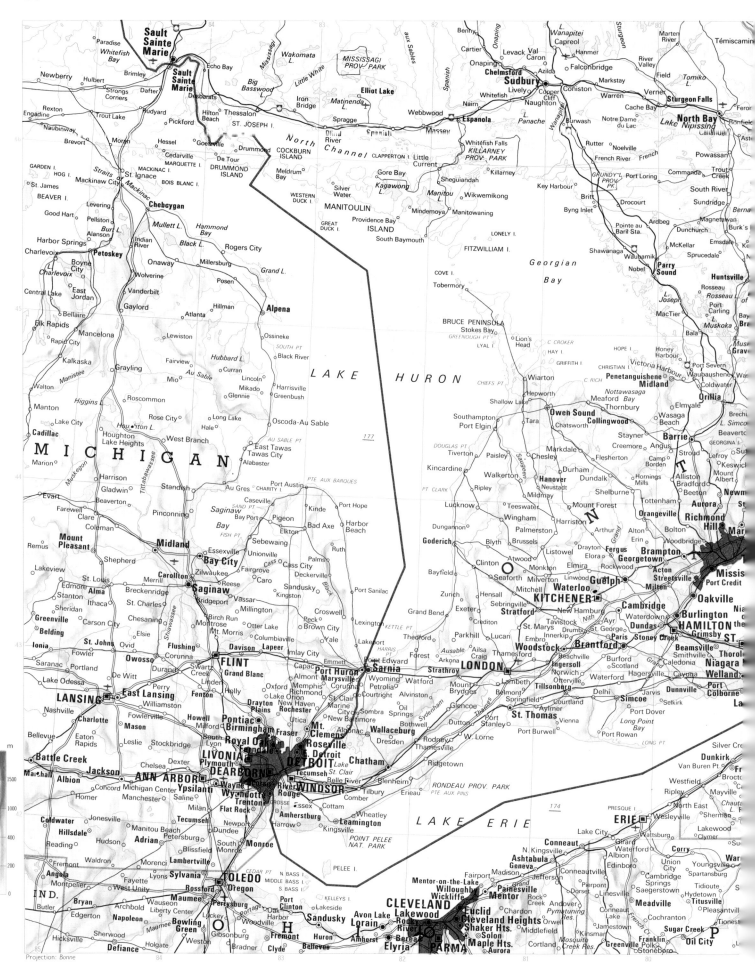

Projection: Bonne

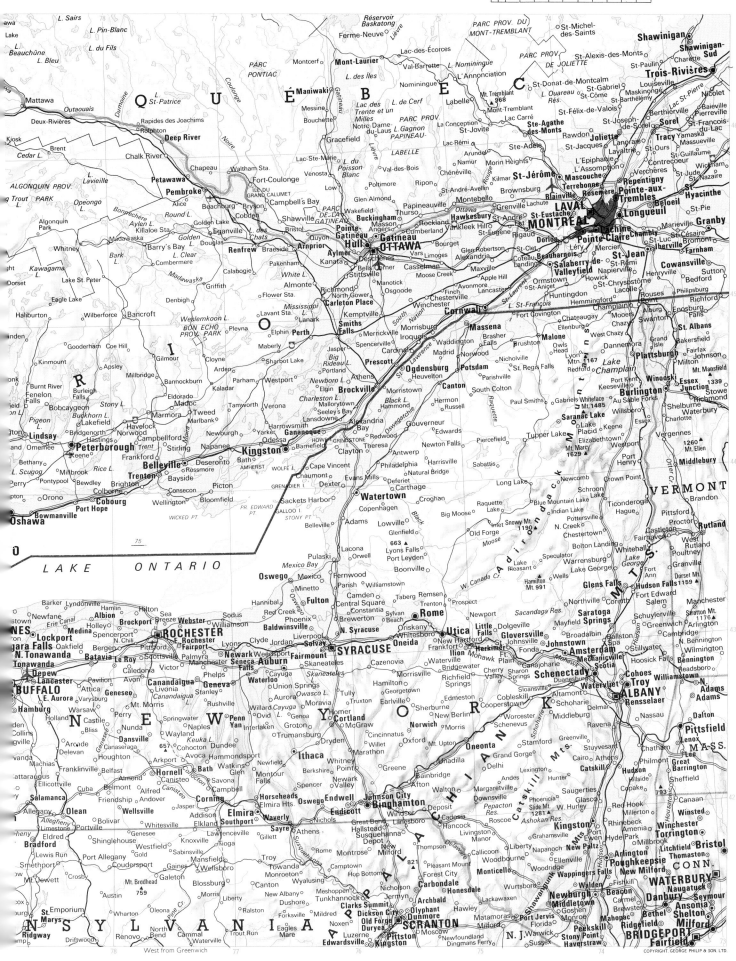

1 : 2 500 000

10 0 10 20 30 40 50 60 70 80 90 100 km

Parliament Hill seen from the air, looking towards Hull.

1:250 000

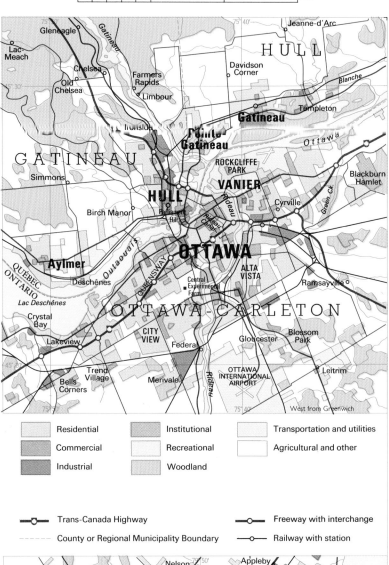

Residential	Institutional	Transportation and utilities
Commercial	Recreational	Agricultural and other
Industrial	Woodland	

—⊙— Trans-Canada Highway   —○— Freeway with interchange

------ County or Regional Municipality Boundary   —○— Railway with station

Hamilton steelworks seen from Hamilton Harbour.

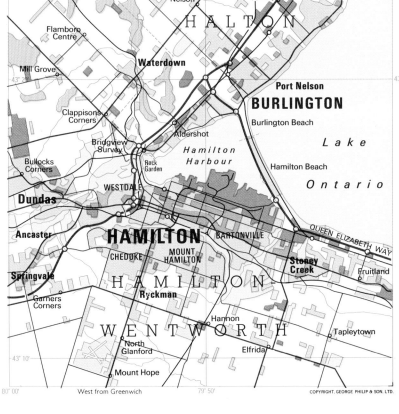

COPYRIGHT. GEORGE PHILIP & SON. LTD.

1:600 000

5 0 5 10 15 20 25 km

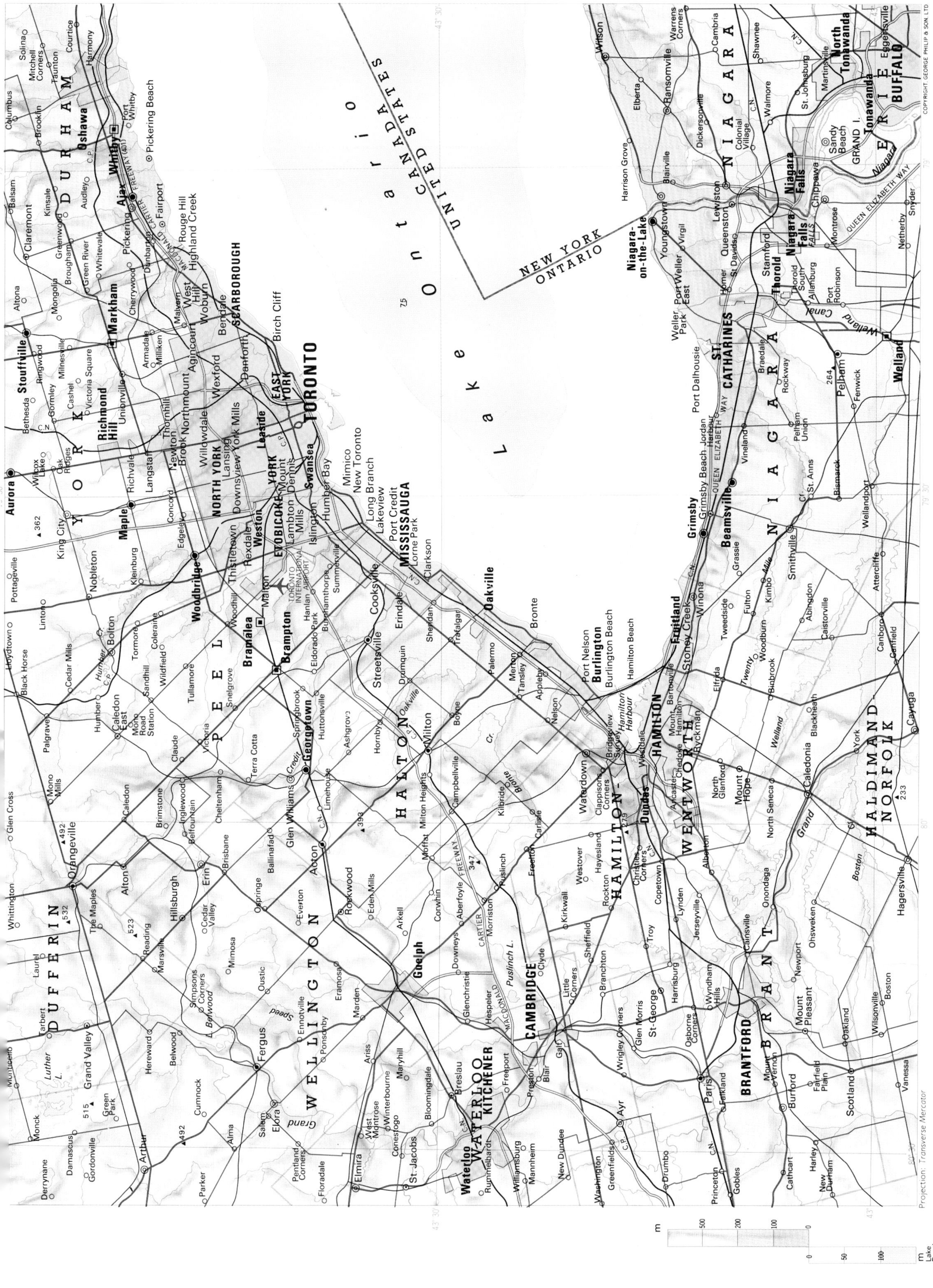

COPYRIGHT GEORGE PHILIP & SON, LTD

Lake Ontario

CANADA
UNITED STATES

NEW YORK
ONTARIO

DURHAM
YORK
PEEL
DUFFERIN
WELLINGTON
WATERLOO
HALTON
HAMILTON-WENTWORTH
BRANT
HALDIMAND-NORFOLK
NIAGARA
ERIE

TORONTO
SCARBOROUGH
NORTH YORK
EAST YORK
YORK
ETOBICOKE
MISSISSAUGA
Oshawa
Whitby
Ajax
Markham
Richmond Hill
Aurora
Stouffville
Maple
Woodbridge
Brampton
Bramalea
Georgetown
Oakville
Burlington
Fruitland
Stoney Creek
Dundas
Waterdown
Grimsby
Beamsville
St CATHARINES
Niagara Falls
Niagara-on-the-Lake
Thorold
Welland
Pelham
BUFFALO
North Tonawanda
Tonawanda
Guelph
CAMBRIDGE
KITCHENER
WATERLOO
BRANTFORD
Paris
Fergus
Elora
Orangeville
Grand Valley

QUEEN ELIZABETH WAY

Welland Canal

Niagara R.

GRAND I.

Lake Depths

Projection Transverse Mercator

m 500 200 100 0

m 50 100 0

NHI

SIMCOE CO.

Lloydtown
Pottageville
Snowball
Aurora
Stouffville
Altona

Linton
Bethesda
Ringwood

Wilcox Lake
Wilcocks Lake
Oak Ridges
Gormley
Cashel
Milnesville

King City
Victoria Square
Green River

Nobleton
Y O R K
RICHMOND HILL
MARKHAM

Bolton
Humber
East Humber
Maple
Richvale
Unionville
Buttonville

Tormore
Kleinburg
Langstaff
Armadale

Wildfield
Coleraine
Humber
West Don
Thornhill
Milliken

Tullamore
West Humber
Edgeley
Pine Grove
Concord
East Don
AGINCOURT
Malvern

Woodbridge
NEWTON BROOK
WILLOWDALE
York Univ.
WOBURN
HIGH C

Woodhill
Mimico Cr.
NORTHMOUNT
BENDALE
WES HILL

THISTLETOWN
NORTH YORK
LANSING
YORK MILLS
WEXFORD
SCARBOROUGH

Malton
REXDALE
DOWNSVIEW
West Don
East Don
SCARBOROUGH

BRAMALEA
T O R O N T O
DON MILLS
DANFORTH

WESTON
LEASIDE

ETOBICOKE
FOREST HILL
Don
BIRCH CLIFF

BRAMPTON
TORONTO INTERNATIONAL AIRPORT
MOUNT DENNIS
Y O R K
EAST YORK
Kew Gardens

P E E L
Etobicoke Cr.
Humber
Mimico Cr.
LAMBTON MILLS
Univ. of Toronto
City Hall

Hanlan
SWANSEA
High Park
C.N. Tower
TORONTO

Eldorado Park
ISLINGTON
Exhibition Park
Credit
O.E.W.
HUMBER BAY
Humber Bay
Toronto Harbour

Burnhamthorpe
Summerville
TORONTO ISLAND
Centre Island Park

MIMICO

NEW TORONTO

LONG BRANCH

Cooksville
Lakeview
Streetsville

Credit
MISSISSAUGA

Erindale
Port Credit

Lorne Park

Sheridan
Clarkson

L a k e

Trafalgar

H A L T O N

OAKVILLE

Projection: *Transverse Mercator*

West from Greenwich

1 : 250 000

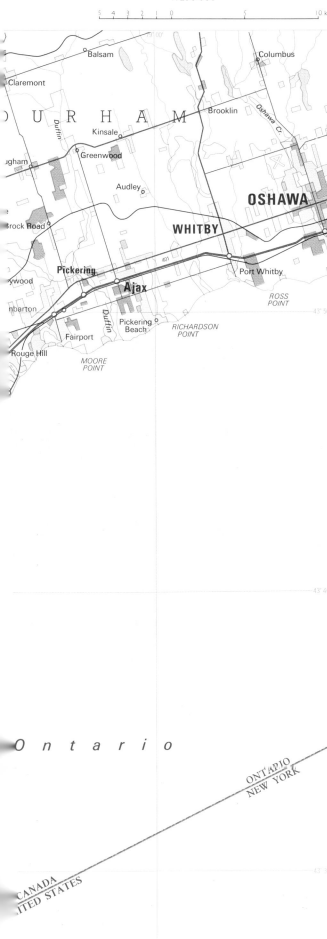

Toronto looking north with CN Tower (553 metres high) in foreground.

	Residential		Institutional		Transportation and utilities
	Commercial		Recreational		Agricultural and other
	Industrial		Woodland		

—○— Freeway with interchange   —— Subway

—○— Trans-Canada Highway   ------ Subway under construction

-·-·- County or Regional Municipality Boundary   —○— Railway with station

Toronto's skyline seen from Toronto Harbour.

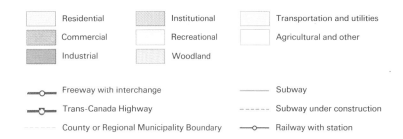

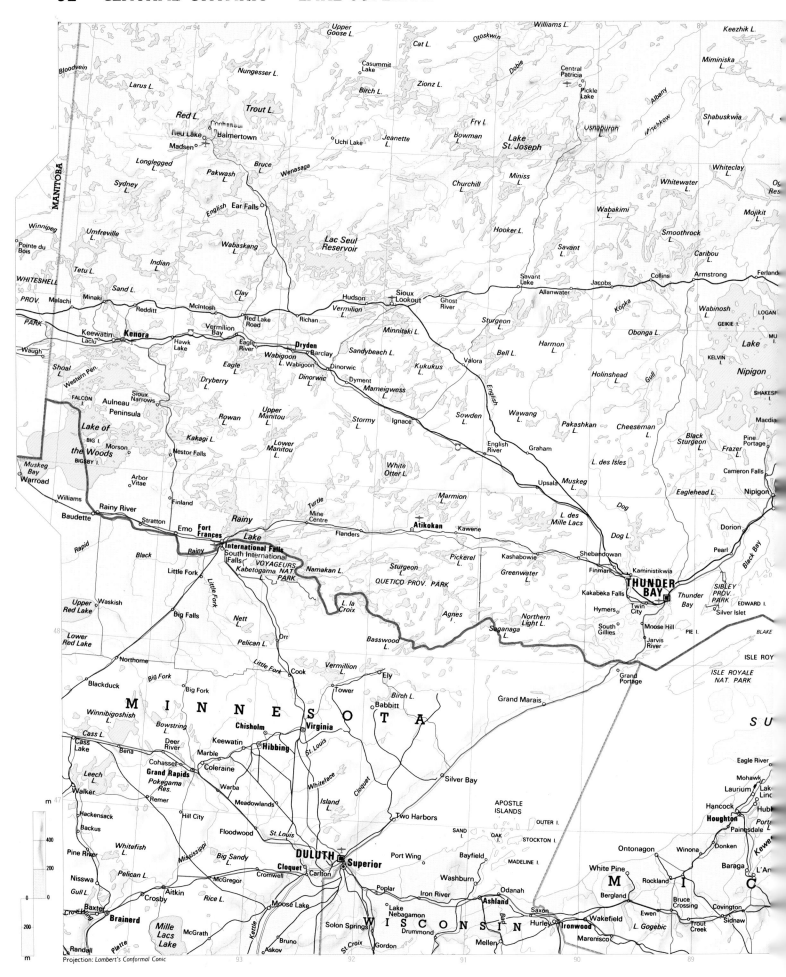

Projection: Lambert's Conformal Conic

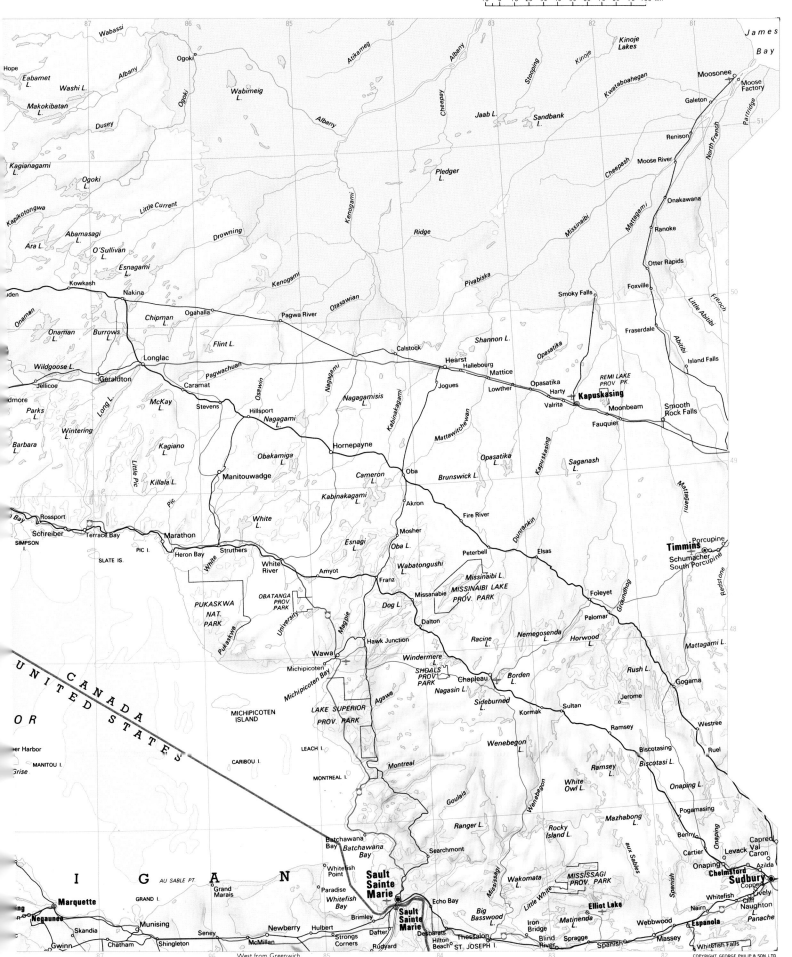

1:2 500 000

10 0 10 20 30 40 50 60 70 80 90 100 km

James Bay

Hope
Eabamet L.
Washi L.
Makokibatan L.
Dusey L.
Albany
Ogoki
Wabassi
Atikameg
Albany
Cheepay
Kinoje
Kinoje Lakes
Moosonee
Moose Factory
Galeton
Renison
Kwetaboahegan
Stooping
Jaab L.
Sandbank
Kagianagami L.
Ogoki L.
Wabimeig L.
Pledger L.
Cheepash
Moose River
Onakawana
Ranoke
North French
Partridge
Kapikotongwa
Little Current
Ogoki
Albany
Ridge
Missinaibi
Mattagami
Otter Rapids
Abamasagi L.
O'Sullivan L.
Drowning
Little Abitibi
Ara L.
Esnagami L.
Kenogami
Pivabiska
Smoky Falls
Foxville
Fraserdale
Abitibi
Island Falls
French
Kowkash
Nakina
Ogahalla
Pagwa River
Otasawian
Calstock
Shannon L.
Opasatika
REMI LAKE PROV PK
Chipman L.
Hearst
Hallebourg
Mattice
Opasatika
Smooth Rock Falls
Wildgoose L.
Longlac
Flint L.
Pagwachuan
Caramat
Jellicoe
Geraldton
Nagagami
Jogues
Lowther
Harty
Kapuskasing
Valrita
Moonbeam
Fauquier
smore
Parks
McKay L.
Stevens
Hillsport
Nagagami L.
Nagagamisis
Mattawitchewan
Opasatika L.
Saganash L.
Long L.
Wintering L.
Kagiano L.
Obakamiga L.
Hornepayne
Oba
Brunswick L.
Kapuskasing
Barbara L.
Killala L.
Little Pic
Manitouwadge
Cameron L.
Oba
Akron
Fire River
Dunrankin
Elsas
Mattagami
Kabinakagami L.
Timmins
Porcupine
Schumacher
South Porcupine
Pic
White L.
Esnagi L.
Mosher
Oba L.
Peterbell
Redstone
Bay
Rossport
Schreiber
Terrace Bay
Marathon
Heron Bay
Struthers
Wabatongushi
Missinaibi L.
Foleyet
Groundhog
SIMPSON
PIC I.
SLATE IS.
White River
Amyot
Franz
Missinabie
MISSINAIBI LAKE PROV. PARK
Palomar
PUKASKWA NAT. PARK
OBATANGA PROV PARK
University
Mespie
Dog L.
Dalton
Racine
Nemegosenda
Horwood
Mattagami L.
er Harbor
Grise
MANITOU I.
Pukaskwa
Hawk Junction
Wawa
Windermere
SHOALS PROV PARK
Chapleau
Borden
Rush L.
Gogama
CARIBOU I.
Michipicoten
Michipicoten Bay
Agawa
Nagasin L.
Jerome
UNITED STATES
CANADA
MICHIPICOTEN ISLAND
LEACH I.
LAKE SUPERIOR PROV. PARK
Sideburned
Kormak
Sultan
Ramsey
Westree
MONTREAL I.
Montreal
Wenebegon L.
Biscotasing
Ruel
Ranger L.
Goulais
White Owl L.
Ramsey L.
Biscotasi L.
Onaping L.
Rocky Island L.
Mazhabong
Pogamasing
Batchawana Bay
Batchawana Bay
Searchmont
Mississagi
aux Sables
Benny
Cartier
Capreol
Val Caron
Whitefish Point
Sault Sainte Marie
MISSISSAGI PROV. PARK
Onaping
Levack
Azilda
Chelmsford
Sudbury
Paradise
Whitefish Bay
Echo Bay
Wakomata
Little White
Elliot Lake
Whitefish
Copper
Lively
Marquette
GRAND I.
AU SABLE PT.
Grand Marais
Brimley
Dafter
Sault Sainte Marie
Desbarats
Big Basswood
Iron Bridge
Matinenda
Webbwood
Nairn
Cliff
Naughton
Panache
Negaunee
Skandia
Munising
Seney
Newberry
Hulbert
Strongs Corners
Rudyard
Hilton Beach
ST. JOSEPH I.
Thessalon
Blind River
Spragge
Spanish
Massey
Espanola
Whitefish Falls
Gwinn
Chatham
Shingleton
McMillan

West from Greenwich

COPYRIGHT. GEORGE PHILIP & SON. LTD.

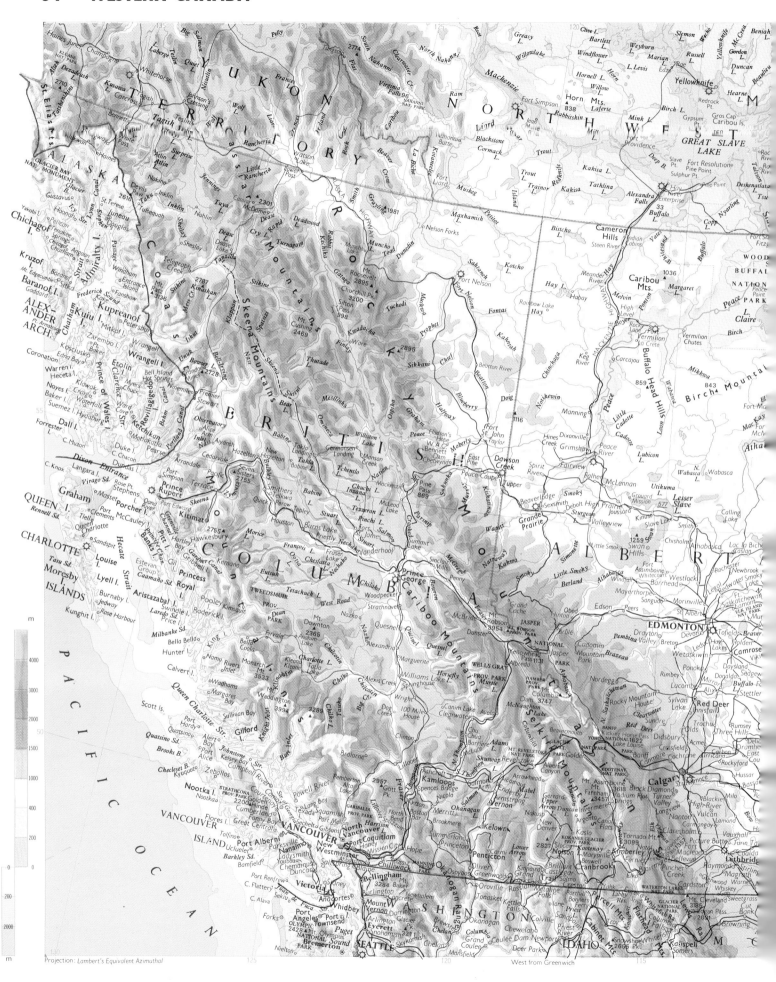

Projection : Lambert's Equivalent Azimuthal   West from Greenwich

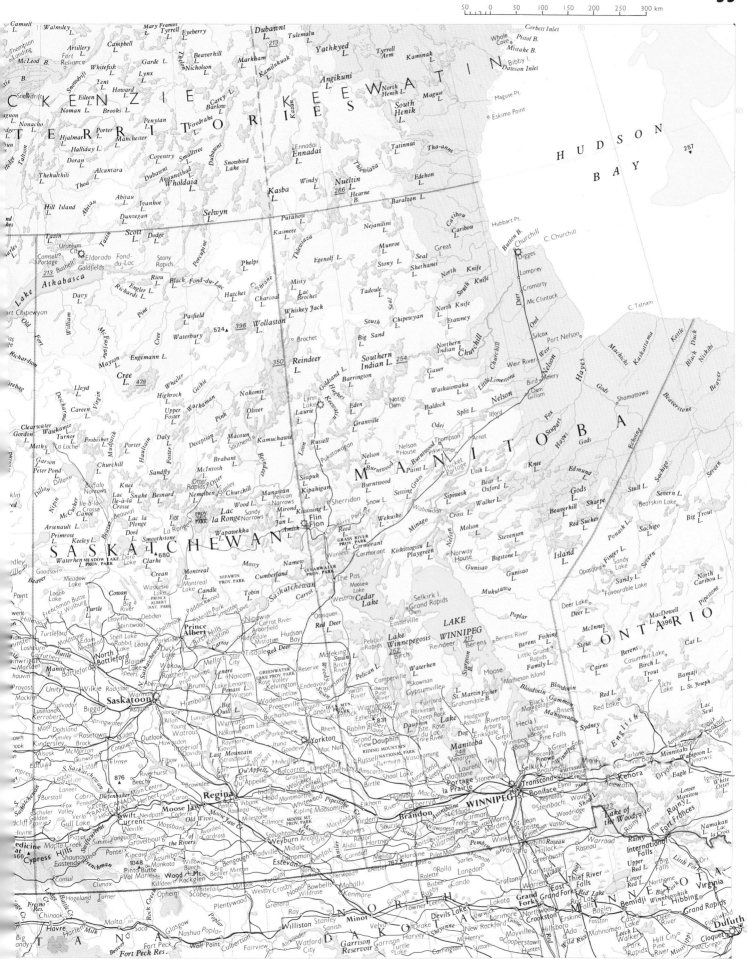

1:7 000 000

50　0　50　100　150　200　250　300 km

HUDSON

BAY

M c K E N Z I E

T E R R I T O R I E S

K E E W A T I N

S A S K A T C H E W A N

M A N I T O B A

O N T A R I O

Lake Athabasca

Lake Winnipegosis

LAKE WINNIPEG

Reindeer L.

Cree L.

Wollaston L.

Churchill

Eskimo Point

C. Churchill

Prince Albert

Saskatoon

Regina

Moose Jaw

Swift Current

Medicine Hat

WINNIPEG

Brandon

Portage la Prairie

Dauphin

Yorkton

Weyburn

Estevan

Kenora

Fort Frances

Duluth

Bemidji

Minot

Williston

Havre

M O N T A N A

N O R T H   D A K O T A

M I N N E S O T A

Fort Peck Res.

Garrison Reservoir

Devils Lake

Grand Forks

International Falls

Lake of the Woods

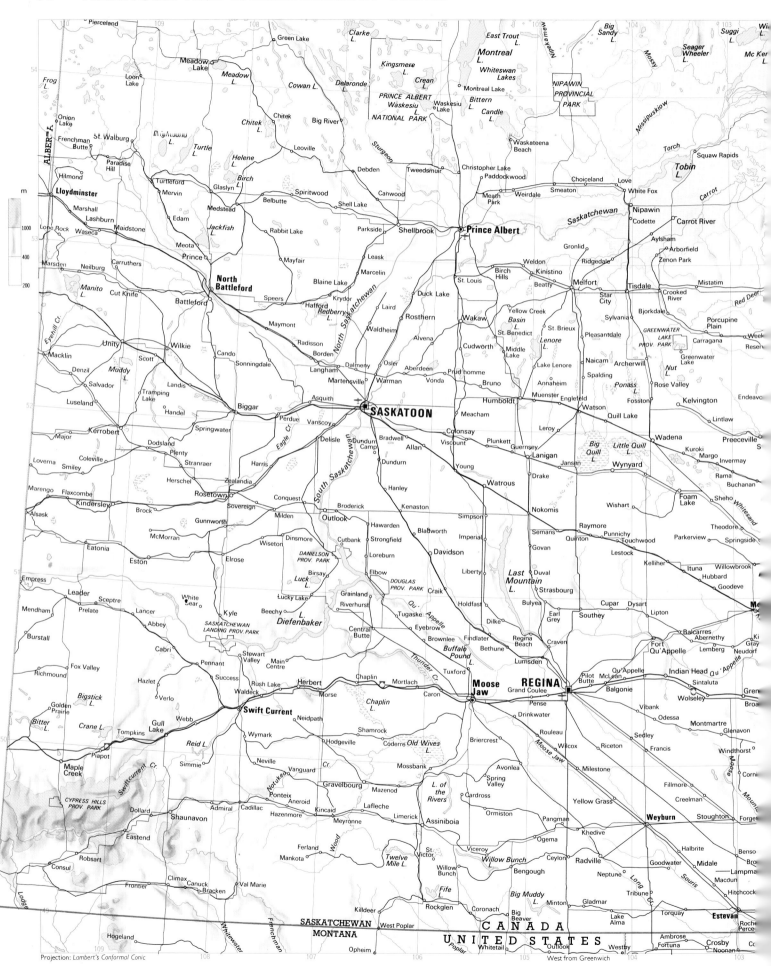

Projection: Lambert's Conformal Conic

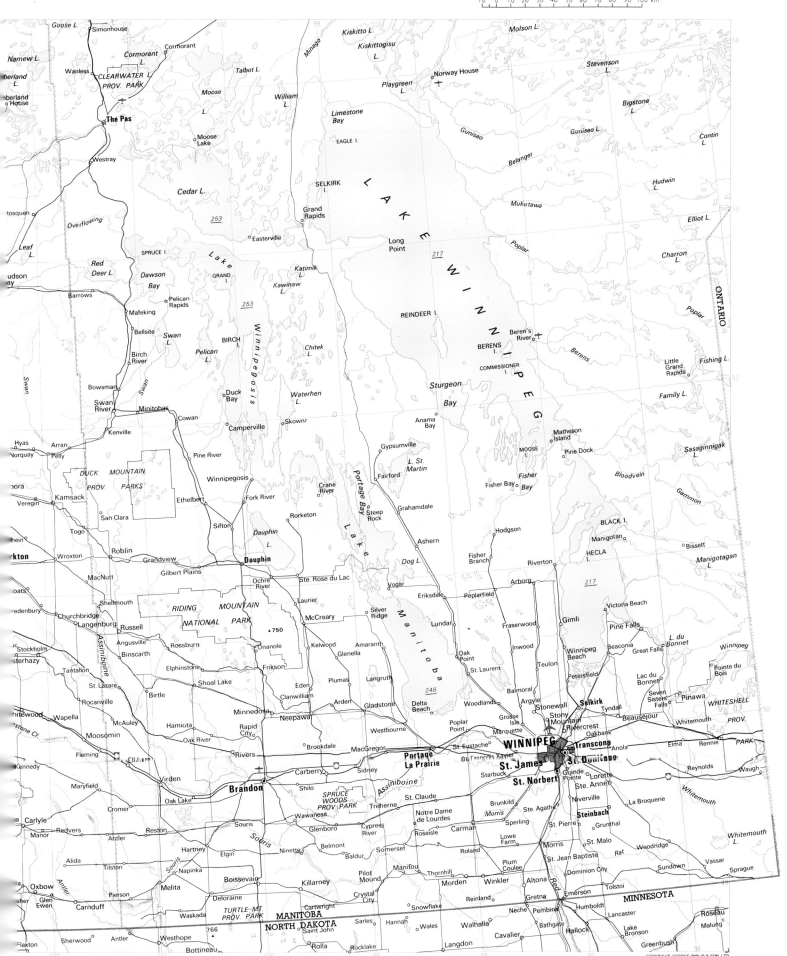

1:2 500 000

10 0 10 20 30 40 50 60 70 80 90 100 km

57

ONTARIO

Namew L.
Goose L.
Simonhouse
101
100
99
Kiskitto L.
Kiskittogisu L.
Molson L.
98
97
96
95
54

Cormorant
Minago
Talbot L.
Stevenson L.

Wanless
CLEARWATER L. PROV. PARK
Moose L.
William L.
Playgreen L.
Norway House
Bigstone L.
Contin

The Pas
Moose Lake
Limestone Bay
Gunisao
Gunisao L.

Westray
EAGLE I.
Belanger
Hudwin

Cedar L.
SELKIRK I.
Mukutawa
Hudwin L.

tosquen
Overflowing
Easterville
Grand Rapids
253
Long Point
217
Poplar
Charron L.
Elliot L.
53

Leaf L.
SPRUCE I.
Lake
REINDEER I.
Poplar
Poplar

udson ay
Red Deer L.
Dawson Bay
GRAND I.
253
Katimik
Kawinaw
Berens River
Berens
Little Grand Rapids
Fishing L.

Barrows
Pelican Rapids
BIRCH
Chitek
Sturgeon Bay
BERENS I.
COMMISSIONER I.
Berens
Family L.
52

Mafeking
Swan L.
Pelican L.
Waterhen L.
Anama Bay
MOOSE I.
Matheson Island
Pine Dock
Sasaginnigak L.

Bellsite
Birch River
Duck Bay
Skownan
Gypsumville
L. St. Martin
Fisher Bay
Fisher Bay
Bloodvein

Bowsman
Camperville
Crane River
Fairford
Grahamdale
Fisher Bay
Gammon

Hyas
Arran
Pelly
Kenville
Cowan
Fork River
Rorketon
Steep Rock
Ashern
Hodgson
BLACK I.
Manigotan
Bissett
51

Norquay
Winnipegosis
Ethelbert
Dauphin L.
Dog L.
Fisher Branch
Riverton
HECLA
Manigotagan L.

rkton
Wroxton
Roblin
Grandview
Gilbert Plains
Dauphin
Ste. Rose du Lac
Vogar
Eriksdale
Arborg
217
Victoria Beach

oats
MacNutt
DUCK MOUNTAIN PROV. PARKS
Ochre River
Laurier
Poplarfield
Lundar
Fraserwood
Gimli
Pine Falls
L. du Bonnet

redenbury
Shellmouth
RIDING MOUNTAIN NATIONAL PARK
McCreary
Silver Ridge
Inwood
Winnipeg Beach
Beaconia
Great Falls
Winnipeg

Churchbridge
Russell
750
Kelwood
Amaranth
Oak Point
St. Laurent
Teulon
Petersfield
Lac du Bonnet
Pointe du Bois

Langenburg
Angusville
Rossburn
Onanole
Glenella
Langruth
248
Balmoral
Argyle
Stonewall
Seven Sisters Falls
Pinawa
WHITESHELL

Stockholm
sterhazy
Binscarth
Elphinstone
Frikson
Eden
Plumas
Langruth
Delta Beach
Woodlands
Grosse Isle
Stony Mountain
Selkirk
Tyndall
Beausejour
Whitemouth
PROV.

Tantallon
St. Lazare
Birtle
Shoal Lake
Clanwilliam
Arden
Gladstone
Poplar Point
Marquette
Rivercrest
Oakbank
Anola
Elma
Rennie
PARK

Rocanville
Minnedosa
Neepawa
Westbourne
WINNIPEG
Transcona
50

whitewood
Wapella
McAuley
Hamiota
Rapid City
Oak River
Brookdale
MacGregor
St. Eustache
Qu francois Xavier
St. James
St. Boniface
Reynolds
Waugh

Fleming
Moosomin
Rivers
Portage La Prairie
Sidney
St. Norbert
Grande Pointe
Lorette
Ste. Anne

Kennedy
Virden
Carberry
Starbuck
Niverville
La Broquerie
Whitemouth

Maryfield
Shilo
Assiniboine
St. Claude
Brunkild
Ste. Agathe
Steinbach
Whitemouth L.

Carlyle
Redvers
Cromer
Oak Lake
SPRUCE WOODS PROV. PARK
Treherne
Notre Dame de Lourdes
Morris
Sperling
St. Pierre
Grunthal

Manor
Antler
Reston
Souris
Wawanesa
Cypress River
Carman
Lowe Farm
Morris
St. Malo
Woodridge

Alida
Hartney
Glenboro
Belmont
Baldur
Somerset
Roseisle
Roland
Plum Coulee
St. Jean Baptiste
Rat
Sundown
Vassar
Sprague

Oxbow
Tilston
Napinka
Elgin
Pilot Mound
Manitou
Thornhill
Dominion City

sher
Glen Ewen
Carnduff
Pierson
Melita
Boissevain
Deloraine
Killarney
Crystal City
Cartwright
Morden
Winkler
Altona
Red
St. Malo
Woodridge

TURTLE MT. PROV. PARK
MANITOBA
Snowflake
Reinland
Gretna
Emerson
MINNESOTA

Flaxton
Sherwood
Antler
Westhope
766
NORTH DAKOTA
Sarles
Hannah
Wales
Walhalla
Neche
Pembina
Humboldt
Lancaster
Roseau
Maling

Bottineau
Rolla
Rocklake
Langdon
Cavalier
Bathgate
Hallock
Lake Bronson
Greenbush
96

COPYRIGHT. GEORGE PHILIP & SON. LTD.

1:250 000

5 4 3 2 1 0 5 10 km

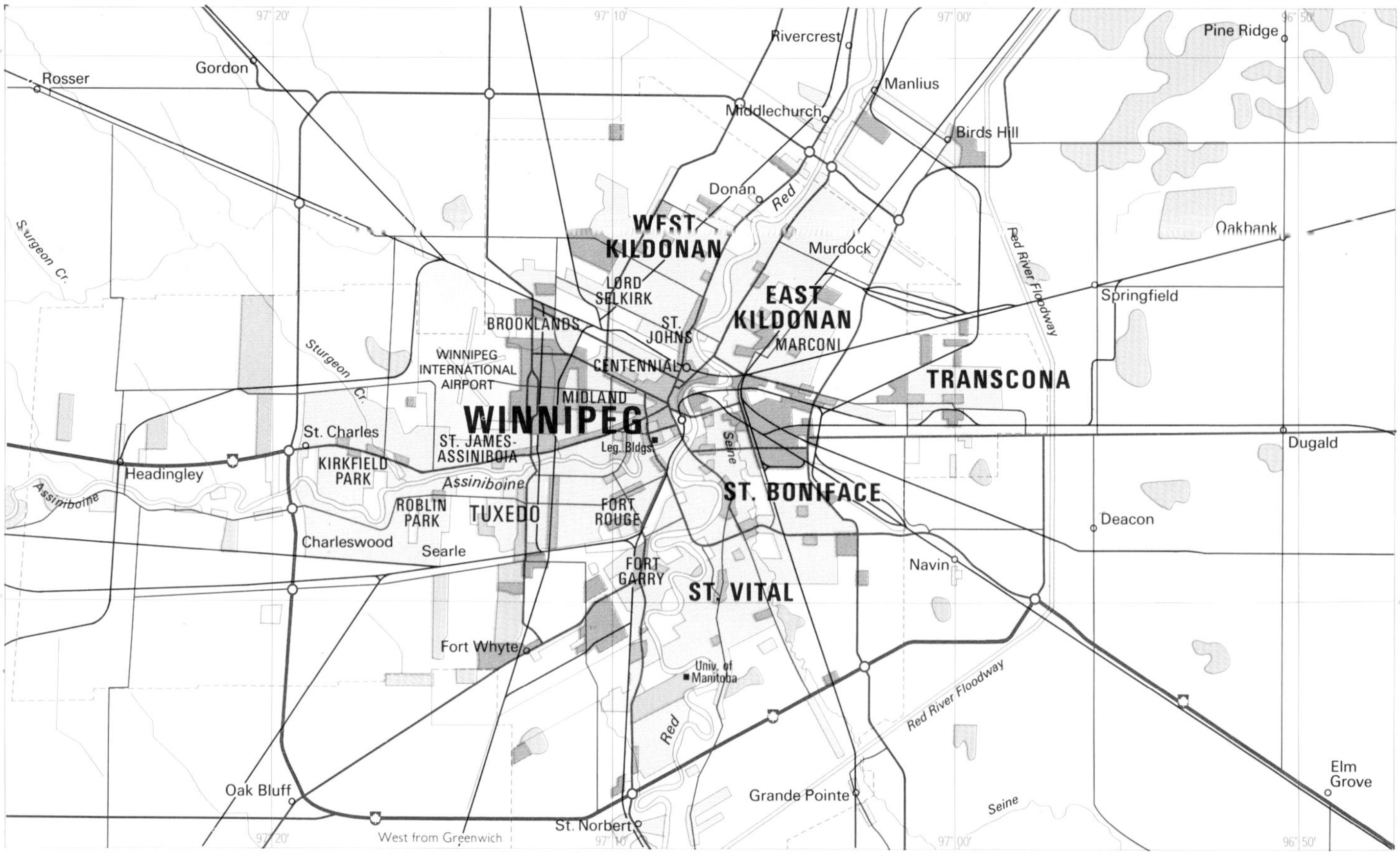

Winnipeg map

Rosser
Gordon
Rivercrest
Pine Ridge
Manlius
Middlechurch
Birds Hill
Donan
Red
Oakbank
WEST KILDONAN
Murdock
LORD SELKIRK
EAST KILDONAN
ST. JOHNS
MARCONI
Springfield
BROOKLANDS
CENTENNIAL
WINNIPEG INTERNATIONAL AIRPORT
TRANSCONA
MIDLAND
Red River Floodway
St. Charles
WINNIPEG
Leg. Bldgs.
Dugald
KIRKFIELD PARK
ST. JAMES-ASSINIBOIA
Headingley
Assiniboine
Seine
Deacon
ROBLIN PARK
TUXEDO
FORT ROUGE
ST. BONIFACE
Charleswood
Searle
FORT GARRY
Navin
ST. VITAL
Fort Whyte
Univ. of Manitoba
Oak Bluff
Red
Red River Floodway
Elm Grove
St. Norbert
Grande Pointe
Seine
West from Greenwich

Sturgeon Cr.
Assiniboine

97°20' 97°10' 97°00' 96°50'
50°00' 49°50' 49°

Legend

Residential — Industrial — Recreational — Transportation and utilities
Commercial — Institutional — Woodland — Agricultural and other

⊶ Freeway with interchange ⊶ Trans-Canada Highway ⊶ Railway with station --- City Boundary

Regina map

Brora
Zehner
Condie Reservoir
Boggy Cr.
Wascana Cr.
UPLANDS
NORMANVIEW
CITY VIEWS
REGINA
REGENT PARK
Boggy Cr.
MOUNT ROYAL
ROSS INDUSTRIAL PARK
ROSEMONT
GLENCAIRN
Wascana Lake
LAKEVIEW
Parl. Bldgs.
Regina Univ.
ALBERT PARK
HILLSDALE
Richardson
Rowatt
Wascana Cr.

104°40' 104°30'
50°30' 50°20'

Projection: Transverse Mercator
West from Greenwich

Winnipeg aerial view looking north.

Regina looking north across Wascana Lake.

1:250 000

5 4 3 2 1 0   5   10 km

*Edmonton looking north with the Legislative Building in the centre and
the city centre beyond.*

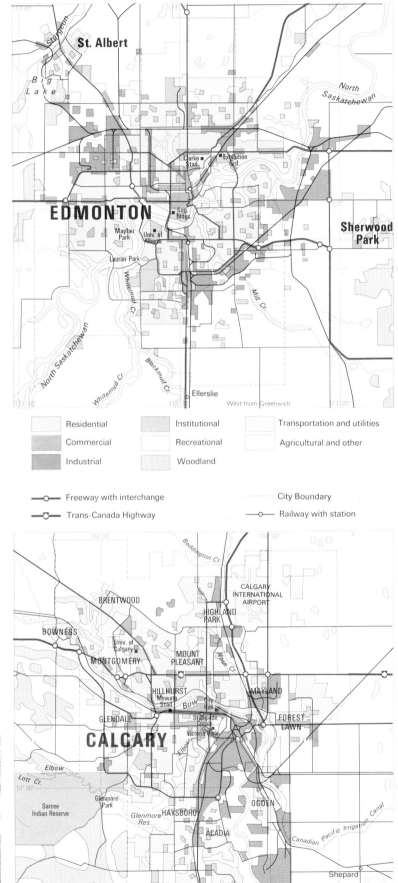

	Residential		Institutional		Transportation and utilities
	Commercial		Recreational		Agricultural and other
	Industrial		Woodland		

Freeway with interchange
Trans-Canada Highway
City Boundary
Railway with station

*Calgary city centre looking south across Bow River, with Calgary Tower
(188 metres high) at left.*

Projection: *Transverse Mercator*

1:2 500 000

10 0 10 20 30 40 50 60 70 80 90 100 km

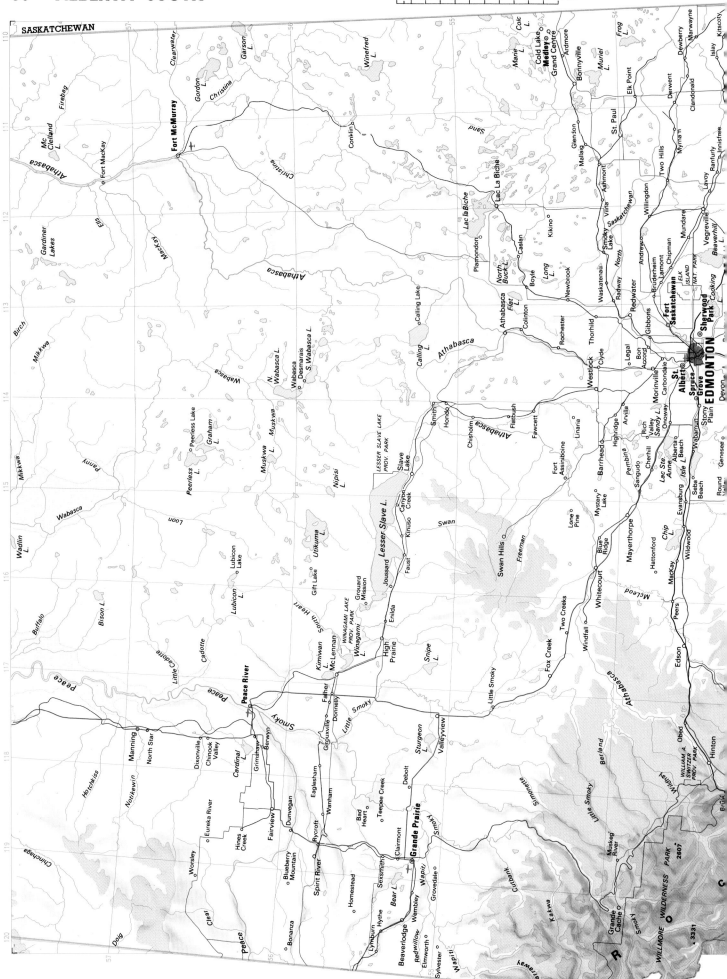

SASKATCHEWAN

Clearwater

Firebag

Gordon L.

Christina

Garson L.

Winefred L.

Mc Clelland L.

Gardiner Lakes

Ells

MacKay

Fort MacKay

Fort McMurray

Athabasca

Birch

Mikkwa

Mikkwa

Panny

Athabasca

Christina

Conklin

Sand

Cold Lake
Medley
Grand Centre

Marie L.

Colc

Ardmore

Bonnyville

Muriel L.

Frog L.

Elk Point

Dewberry

Marwayne

Islay

Kitscoty

Clandonald

Glendon

Mallaig

St. Paul

Myrnam

Derwent

Innisfree

Plamondon

Lac laBiche

Lac La Biche

Smoky Lake

Vilna

Ashmont

Willingdon

Two Hills

Ranfurly

Lavoy

Vegreville

Beauvallon

North Buck L.

Caslan

Kikino

Saskatchewan

North

Andrew

Mundare

Beaverhill

Boyle

Long L.

Newbrook

Waskatenau

Radway

Redwater

Bruderheim

Lamont

Chipman

ELK ISLAND NAT. PARK

Fort Saskatchewan

Cooking

Athabasca

Flat L.

Colinton

Rochester

Thorhild

Clyde

Legal

Bon Accord

Gibbons

Sherwood Park

Calling Lake

Athabasca

Calling L.

Westlock

Morinville

Carbondale

St. Albert

EDMONTON

Spruce Grove

Stony Plain

Devon

Wabasca

N. Wabasca L.

Wabasca L.

Desmarais

S. Wabasca L.

Smith

Hondo

Chisholm

Athabasca

Flatbush

Fawcett

Linaria

Arvilla

Rich Valley

Onoway

Alberta Beach

Seba Beach

Wabamun

Isle L. Beach

Round L.

Genesee

Peerless Lake

Graham L.

Muskwa

Muskwa L.

LESSER SLAVE LAKE PROV. PARK

Slave Lake

Fort Assiniboine

Barrhead

Highridge

Pembina

Cherhill

Sangudo

Lac Ste. Anne

Evansburg

Wildwood

Chip L.

Peerless L.

Nipisi L.

Canyon Creek

Kinuso

Faust

Swan

Swan Hills

Freeman

Lone Pine

Mystery Lake

Blue Ridge

Mayerthorpe

Hattonford

MacKay

Edson

Wadlin L.

Loon

Wabasca

Utikuma L.

Gift Lake

South Heart

Grouard Mission

WINAGAMI LAKE PROV. PARK

Winagami L.

Joussard

Lesser Slave L.

High Prairie

Enilda

Snipe L.

Little Smoky

Two Creeks

Windfall

Whitecourt

Fox Creek

McLeod

Berland

Obed

William A. Switzer Prov. Park

Hinton

Lubicon L.

Lubicon Lake

Kimiwan L.

McLennan

Falher

Donnelly

Girouxville

Little Smoky

Sturgeon L.

Valleyview

Little Smoky

Athabasca

Little Smoky

Simonette

Bison L.

Buffalo

Cadotte

Little Cadotte

Peace

Peace

Peace River

Smoky

Berwyn

Grimshaw

Eaglesham

Wanham

Debolt

Teepee Creek

Clairmont

Grande Prairie

Bad Heart

Smoky

Cutbank

Muskeg River

Kakwa

Grande Cache

WILLMORE WILDERNESS PARK

2607

3331

Hotchkiss

Notikewin

Manning

North Star

Dixonville

Chinook Valley

Cardinal L.

Fairview

Hines Creek

Dunvegan

Rycroft

Spirit River

Homestead

Wembley

Bear L.

Wapiti

Grovedale

Worsley

Eureka River

Blueberry Mountain

Sexsmith

Bonanza

Hythe

Beaverlodge

Redwillow

Elmworth

Sylvester

Wapiti

Peace

Doig

Chinchaga

Wabasca

Smoky

R

Paradise Valley
Battle
Chauvin
Edgerton
Wainwright
Provost
Eyehill Cr.
Sounding
Compeer
Sounding Cr.
Empress
S. Saskatchewan
Many Island
Medicine Hat
Walsh
Irma
Chavin
Altario
Acadia Valley
Hilda
Schuler
Dunmore
CYPRESS HILLS PROV. PARK
Manyberries

Viking
Killam
Sedgewick
Lougheed
Hardisty
Amisk
Czar
Coronation
Veteran
Cereal
Oyen
Youngstown
Chinook
New Brigden
Red
Deer
Cr.
Ralston
Redcliff
Suffield
Bow Island
Burdett
Etzikom
Foremost
Pakowki L.
Sunburst

Wetaskiwin
Camrose
Bawlf
Daysland
Strome
Heisler
Forestburg
Galahad
Castor
Hanna
Wardlow
DINOSAUR PROV. PARK
Duchess
Brooks
Newell
Rolling Hills
Hays
Grassy Lake
Taber
Barnwell
Warner
Milk River
Coutts
MONTANA
Kevin
Cut Bank

New Norway
Ferintosh
Edberg
Bashaw
Donalda
Buffalo L.
Stettler
Erskine
Delia
Morrin
Drumheller
East Coulee
Standard
Hussar
Gem
Rosemary
Bassano
Scandia
Vauxhall
Diamond City
Coaldale
Stirling
Magrath
Raymond
Spring Coulee
WATERTON LAKES

Millet
Battle
Gwynne
Ponoka
Clive
Lacombe
Red Deer
Alix
Mirror
Elnora
Trochu
Three Hills
Carbon
Nacmine
Rockyford
Strathmore
Arrowwood
Milo
McGregor L.
Vulcan
Champion
Travers Reservoir
Barons
Picture Butte
Iron Springs
Oldman
Monarch
Fort Macleod
WATERTON LAKES NAT'L PARK
GLACIER
Logan Pass
St. Mary
NAT'L PARK

Wetaskiwin
Ma-Me-O Beach
Pigeon L.
Winfield
Bluffton
Rimbey
Bentley
Gull L.
Sylvan Lake
Markerville
Torrington
Linden
Acme
Beiseker
Rosebud
Little Bow
Blackie
Cayley
Nanton
Claresholm
Carmangay
Stavely
Granum
Nobleford
Coalhurst
Lethbridge
Coaldale
Glenwood
Hill Spring
Mountain View
Cardston
Waterton Park
St. Mary Reservoir

Buck L.
Buck Lake
College Heights
Blackfalds
Red Deer
Penhold
Innisfail
Bowden
Olds
Didsbury
Carstairs
Crossfield
Airdrie
Cochrane
CALGARY
Black Diamond
Turner Valley
Longview
High River
Hartell
Cayley
Blackie

North Saskatchewan
CRIMSON LAKE PROV. PARK
Crimson Lake
Leslieville
Alhambra
Rocky Mountain House
Caroline
Sundre
Cremona
Madden
Bragg Creek
Eau Claire
Exshaw
Canmore
Banff
Kananaskis
ELK LAKES PROV. PARK
2782
Fording
Elkford
3099
Natal
Crowsnest Pass
Coleman
Blairmore
Bellevue
Lundbreck
Cowley
Pincher Creek
Brocket
Victoria Pk.
2579
Flathead
WATERTON LAKES NATL. PARK
A.
N
S.
Stryker
Eureka

Nordegg
Big Horn Dam
Ram
Clearwater
Red Deer
3162
PARK
NATIONAL
Castle Mountain
Bow Pass
3312
Lake Louise
Vermilion Pass
Sinclair Pass
Mt. Assiniboine
3618
MT. ASSINIBOINE PROV. PARK
KOOTENAY
NATIONAL
PARK
Radium Hot Springs
Edgewater
Invermere
Windermere
Columbia
Canal Flats
3449
Mt. Joffre
TOP OF THE WORLD PROV. PARK
Sparwood
Elko
Fernie
Coal Creek
Elko
Roosville
Newgate
KOOCANUSA
MONTANA

Big Bend Reservoir
Brazeau
North
Ram
BANFF
3612
MOUNTAINS
Donald
Beavermouth
Golden
GLACIER NAT'L PARK
Glacier
Parson
Spillimacheen
Brisco
Toby Creek
Duncan
Marbleheads
Duncan Dam
3468
2865
Meachen
St. Mary
St. Mary's Alpine PROV. PARK
Kimberley
Marysville
Cranbrook
Wardner
KOOCANUSA
Wynndel
Kingsgate
IDAHO

Rocky
Jasper
NATIONAL
PARK
HAMBER PROV. PARK
McNaughton
Mt. Columbia
3747
Mt. Chapman
3075
Mt. Sir Sandford
3522
Mt. Templeman
3070
Gerrard
Trout Lake
Kaslo
Riondel
Boswell
Creston
Porthill
Bonners Ferry
Priest L.

Yellowhead Pass
Valemount
Lucerne
Blue River
Mica Dam
Mica Creek
Mt. Revelstoke NATL. PARK
Revelstoke
Albert Canyon
Arrowhead
2972
MONASHEE PROV. PARK
Sugar
Nakusp
New Denver
Silverton
Slocan
KOKANEE GLACIER PROV. PARK
Kaslo
Balfour
Procter
Kootenay L.
Nelson
Salmo
Creston
Rykerts
Metaline Falls
Ione
Pend Oreille

Albreda
Athabasca
Blue River
Columbia
Seymour Arm
Sicamous
Shuswap L.
Hupel
Mabel L.
Lumby
SILVER STAR PROV. PARK
Cherryville
Burton
Fauquier
Edgewood
Lower Arrow L.
Renata
Castlegar
Brilliant
Kinnaird
Trail
Warfield
Rossland
Montrose
Fruitvale
WASHINGTON

Cariboo Mountains
Adams L.
Sicamous
Swansea
Silver Creek
Enderby
Vernon
Coldstream
Lavington
Upper Arrow Lake
Arrow Park
Cherryville
Granby
Grand Forks
Christina
Eholt
Greenwood
Midway
Kettle
Rock Creek
Republic
Kettle Falls
Colville
Sanpoil

COLUMBIA
BRITISH
S

COPYRIGHT GEORGE PHILIP & SON LTD

West from Greenwich

Projection: Lambert's Conformal Conic

m
3000
2000
1500
1000
400
200

Projection: Lambert's Conformal Conic

West from Greenwich

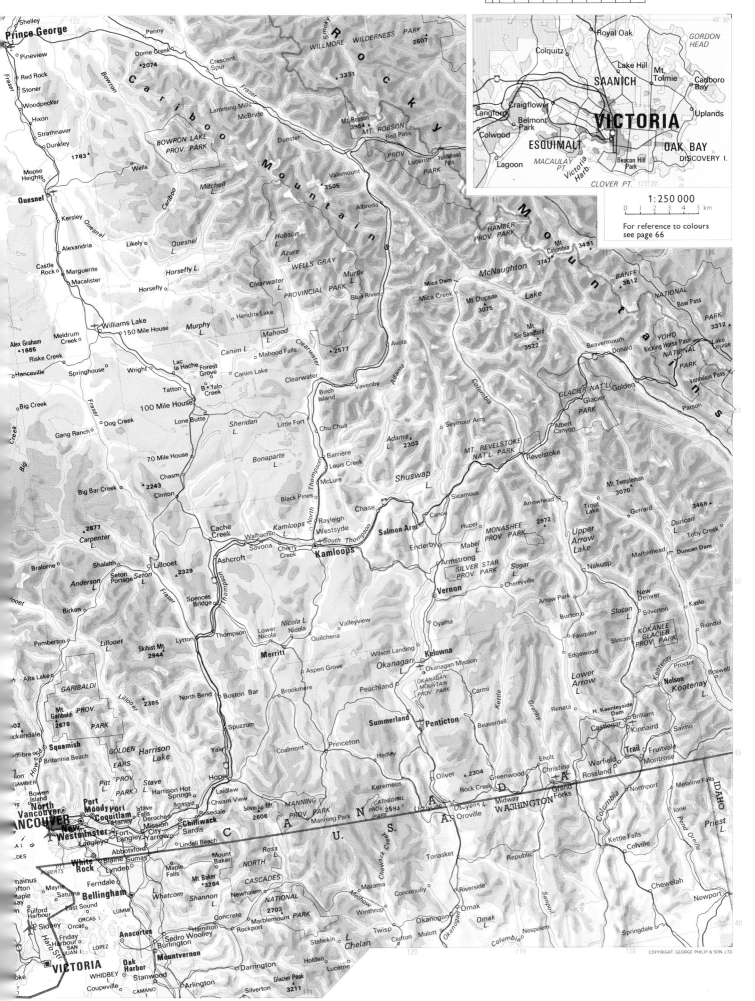

1:2 500 000

10 0 10 20 30 40 50 60 70 80 90 100 km

GORDON
HEAD

Royal Oak

Colquitz

SAANICH   Lake Hill

Mt. Tolmie   Cadboro
Bay

Craigflower   Belmont
Park   Uplands

Langford

Colwood   **VICTORIA**

ESQUIMALT   OAK BAY

MACAULAY   DISCOVERY I.
PT.   Beacon Hill
Park

Lagoon   Victoria
Harb.

CLOVER PT.   123° 20'

1:250 000

0 1 2 3 4 5 km

For reference to colours
see page 66

Shelley

Prince George

Pineview   Penny   WILLMORE WILDERNESS PARK   2607

Red Rock   Dome Creek   2074   Crescent
Spur

Stoner   Fraser   ROCKY

Woodpecker   Lamming Mills   3331

Hixon   McBride   Mt Robson
3954   MT. ROBSON   Red Pass

Strathnaver   Dunkley   BOWRON LAKE
PROV. PARK   Dunster   PROV.   Lucerne   Yellowhead
Pass

Moose   1783   Wells   Valemount   PARK

Heights   3505

Quesnel   Cariboo   Mitchell   Albreda   HAMBER   Mt.   3491
L.   L.   PROV. PARK   Columbia

Kersley   Quesnel   Hobson   McNaughton   3747   BANFF
L.   L.   3612

Alexandria   Likely   Azure   Mica Dam   NATIONAL

Castle   Marguerite   Horsefly L.   Clearwater   Murtle   Mica Creek   Mt Chapman   Bow Pass
Rock   Macalister   L.   L.   3075   Lake

Horsefly   WELLS GRAY   Blue River   Mt   YOHO   3312
Sir Sandford   PARK

Williams Lake   Murphy   PROVINCIAL PARK   2577   3522   Beavermouth   NATIONAL   Lake
Alex Graham   L.   Louise
1665   150 Mile House   Mahood   Clearwater   Donald   Kicking Horse Pass

Riske Creek   Canim L.   L.   GLACIER NAT'L   Golden   PARK

Hanceville   Springhouse   Lac   Forest   Mahood Falls   Avola   PARK   Glacier   Vermilion Pass
la Hache   Grove   Glacier   3468
Big Creek   Wright   Canim Lake   Clearwater   Albert   Parson
Tatton   Canyon
100 Mile House   B'falo   Vavenby   Seymour Arm   Gerrard
Creek   Birch   3070
Dog Creek   Lone Butte   Sheridan   Island   MT. REVELSTOKE   Trout   Duncan
Gang Ranch   L.   Little Fort   Adams   NAT'L PARK   Lake   Toby Creek
70 Mile House   L.   2303   Sicamous   Arrowhead   Marblehead   Duncan Dam
Chasm   Chu Chua   Shuswap   Revelstoke
Big Bar Creek   2243   Barrière   L.   Canoe   Upper
2877   Clinton   Louis Creek   Chase   Hupel   Arrow
Carpenter   McLure   MONASHEE   2972   Lake   Kaslo
Cache   Rayleigh   Salmon Arm   PROV. PARK   Nakusp   KOKANEE
Creek   Black Pines   Westsyde   Enderby   Mabel   Arrow Park   GLACIER
Bralorne   Shalalth   Walhachin   Kamloops   South Thompson   Mabel   Burton   Silverton   PROV. PARK
Lillooet   2329   Savona   L.   Armstrong   L.   New   Riondel
Anderson   Seton   Ashcroft   Cherry   **Kamloops**   SILVER STAR   Sugar   Denver
L.   Seton   Creek   PROV.   L.   Slocan
Portage   PARK   Fauquier
Birken   Thompson   Spences   **Vernon**   Cherryville   Edgewood   Nelson
Pemberton   Skihist Mt.   Bridge   Nicola L.   Oyama   Kootenay
2944   Lytton   Valleyview   Arrow Park   L.
Alta Lake   Thompson   Lower   Nicola   Quilchena   Procter
Nicola   Wilson Landing   Burton   Bpswell
GARIBALDI   **Merritt**   **Kelowna**   Lower   Castlegar
Mt.   Aspen Grove   Okanagan   Okanagan Mission   Arrow   Brilliant
Garibaldi   PROV.   L.   Edgewood   Kinnaird   Salmo
2678   North Bend   2385   OKANAGAN   Carmi   **Trail**   Fruitvale
PARK   Boston Bar   Brookmere   MOUNTAIN   Beaverdell   H. Keenleyside   Montrose
Squamish   GOLDEN   Spuzzum   PROV. PARK   Dam   Warfield   Rossland
fibre   Harrison   Peachland   Renata   Christina   Northport   Metaline Falls
Britannia Beach   EARS   Lake   Yale   **Summerland**   **Penticton**   Eholt   IDAHO
Bowen   PROV.   Coalmont   Princeton   Hedley   Greenwood   Grand   Priest
Island   Pitt   Stave   PARK   Oliver   2304   Rock Creek   Forks   Ione
North   Port   L.   Laidlaw   Keremeos   Midway   WASHINGTON   Pond Orellie
Vancouver   Moody Port   Harrison Hot   Cheam View   Christina   Kettle Falls
Coquitlam   Springs   Agassiz   MANNING   Osoyoos   Oroville   Colville
VANCOUVER   Haney   Deroche   Rosedale   PROV. PARK   CATHEDRAL   Osoyoos L.
**New   Fort   Mission   Silvertip Mt.   PROV.   Republic   Chewelah
Westminster**   Langley   City   Yarrow   2606   Manning Park   2593   Tonasket   Kettle Falls
Abbotsford   Sardis   PARK   Newport
White   Blaine Sumas   Lindell Beach   Mazama   Conconully
Rock   Lynden   Mount   Ross   Columbia
ROBERTS   Ferndale   Maple   Baker   NORTH   Omak   Riverside   Chewelah
Falls   Mt. Baker   L.
Bellingham   Whatcom   3284   CASCADES   Okanogan   Springdale
East Sound   Shannon   Newhalem   NATIONAL   Mazama   Omak   123°
Fulford   Saturna   L.   Concrete   2703   PARK   Methow   L.
Harbour   Marblemount   Winthrop   Nespelem
SAN   Orcas   Hamilton   Marblemount   PARK   Okanogan
JUAN I.   LUMMI   Rockport   Okanogan   Columbia
Friday   Sedro Woolley   Newport
Harbour   LOPEZ   Burlington   Mazama   Malott
Anacortes   Chelan   Winthrop
VICTORIA   Oak   Mountvernon   Stehekin   Twisp   Capton   Nespelem
Harbor   WHIDBEY   Darrington   Holden   Lucerne
Coupeville   Stanwood   Glacier Peak   Chelan   L.
CAMANO   Arlington   Silverton   3211

COPYRIGHT. GEORGE PHILIP & SON. LTD

Projection: Bonne

1:10 000 000

100 0 100 200 300 400 km

C. Thomas Hubbard

United States Range

Alert

Barbeau Pk. 2604

Victoria and Albert Mts.

Nansen Sd.

Greely Fd.

Kane Basin

Humboldt Glacier

Knud Rasmussen Land

GREENLAND

(DENMARK)

Sverdrup Chan.

Princess Margaret Range

Eureka

Fosheim Pen.

Smith Sound

Kennedy Str.

Inglefield Land

Thule (Qanaq)

Inglefield Gulf

2140 Axel Heiberg I.

Raanes Pen.

C. Parry

Dundas (Thule)

C. York

Melville Bay

Kraulshavn

Amund Ringnes I.

Norwegian Bay

Graham I.

Smith B.

Wolstenholme Fjord

Upernavik

Preven

Cornwall I.

Belcher Channel

Simmons Pen.

Grise Fiord

Coburg I.

Svartenhuk Peninsula

Umanak

Nugssuaq Pen.

Penny Str.

Elizabeth Is.

Lady Ann Str.

Jones Sound

Treuter Mts. 1887

Hyde Inlet

C. Cockburn

Baffin

Disko B.

Disko I.

Godhavn

Jakobshavn

magnetic pole +

Bathurst I.

Devon I.

Wellington Chan.

C. Warrender

Bay

Resolute

Cornwallis I.

Lancaster Sound

C. Crauford

2134

Bylot I.

C. Liverpool

Pond Inlet

Nova Zembla I.

C. Hunter

Scott Inlet

Clyde

C. Hewett

Holsteinsborg

Russell I.

Barrow Str.

Prince Regent Inlet

Nunisivik

Arctic Bay

Borden Peninsula

Eclipse Sd.

Pond Inlet

C. Jameson

Bruce Mts.

C. Raper

C. Henry Kater

Somerset I.

Brodeur Peninsula

Home B.

Prince of Wales I.

Ft. Ross

C. Farrand

Admiralty Inlet

Barnes Icecap

Kivitoo

Broughton Island

Padloping Island

Cape Dyer

Bernier B.

Steensby Inlet

Penny Highland 2591

Boothia Peninsula

Gulf of Boothia

673

Fury & Hecla Str.

C. Englefield

Igloolik

Rowley I.

Baird Pen.

Foley I.

Cumberland Peninsula

Pangnirtung

Hoare B.

Gateshead I.

Thom Bay

Hall Lake

Cumberland Sound

C. Mercy

Spence Bay

Simpson Pen.

Melville Peninsula

Prince Charles I.

Air Force I.

Lemieux Islands

King William I.

Pelly Bay

Wales Peninsula

Nettilling L.

Gjoa Haven

Frobisher Bay

Hall Pen.

Adelaide Pen.

Chantrey Inlet

C. Dominion

Amadjuak L.

TERRITORIES

Rae Isthmus

Foxe Basin

Amadjuak

Frobisher Bay

Resolution I.

Macdougall L.

Repulse Bay

Arctic Circle

Vansittart I.

C. Dorchester

Foxe Pen.

Amadjuak

Everett Mts.

Wager L.

Wager B.

Foxe Channel

Cape Dorset

Lake Harbour

C. Chidley

Garry L.

Torsill Mts.

Salisbury I.

Hudson Strait

Southampton I.

Coral Harbour

Bell Pen.

Nottingham I.

Big I.

Port Burwell

Baker Lake

Baker L.

Chesterfield Inlet

Fisher Strait

Melville I.

Nottingham Island

Wolstenholme

Koartac

C. Hopes Advance

Akpatok

Dubawnt L.

Rankin Inlet

Chesterfield Inlet

Coats I.

C. Low

Diggus Is.

C. Wolstenholme

Ivugivik

St. Louis Mts.

Maricourt (Wakeham)

Arnaud (Payne)

Bellin (Payne)

Ungava Bay

Port Nouveau-Quebec (George R.)

Yathkyed L.

Kaminak L.

Whale Cove

Padlei

Tavani

Cape Smith

Povungnituk

Payne L.

Koksoak

Fort-Chimo

KEEWATIN

HUDSON BAY

Portland Promontory

Feuilles (Leaf)

Meleses (Larch)

Caniapiscau

Nueltin L.

Eskimo Point

Thlewiaza

Ottawa Is.

Inoucdjouac (Port Harrison)

L. Minto

L.

1:250 000

5 4 3 2 1 0   5   10 km

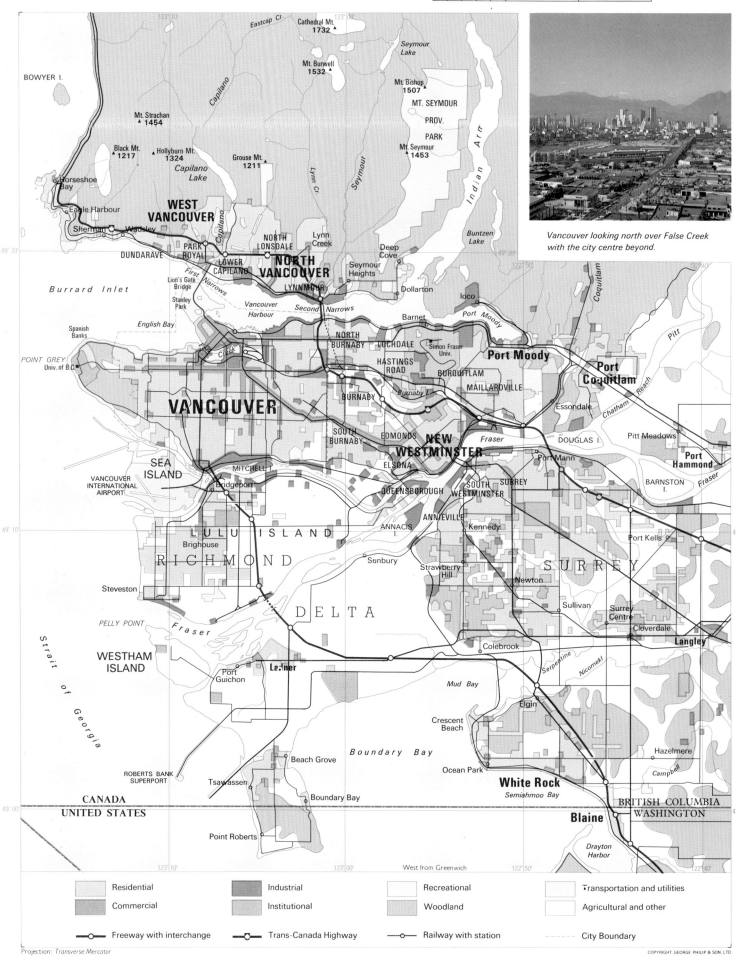

Vancouver looking north over False Creek with the city centre beyond.

BOWYER I.

Eastcap Cr.

Cathedral Mt. 1732 ▲

Seymour Lake

Mt. Burwell 1532 ▲

Capilano

Mt. Bishop 1507 ▲

MT. SEYMOUR

Mt. Strachan 1454 ▲

PROV.

PARK

Black Mt. 1217 ▲   Hollyburn Mt. 1324 ▲   Grouse Mt. 1211 ▲

Mt. Seymour 1453 ▲

Capilano Lake

Horseshoe Bay

Lynn Cr.

Seymour

Indian Arm

Eagle Harbour

WEST VANCOUVER

Sherman   Wadsley

DUNDARAVE

PARK ROYAL

NORTH LONSDALE

Lynn Creek

Buntzen Lake

Deep Cove

LOWER CAPILANO

NORTH VANCOUVER

Lion's Gate Bridge

LYNNMOUR

Seymour Heights

Dollarton

Burrard Inlet

Stanley Park

First Narrows

Vancouver Harbour

Second Narrows

Ioco

Port Moody

Coquitlam

English Bay

Barnet

Spanish Banks

Burrard Creek

NORTH BURNABY

LOCHDALE

Simon Fraser Univ.

Port Moody

POINT GREY Univ. of B.C.

HASTINGS ROAD

BURQUITLAM

Port Coquitlam

VANCOUVER

BURNABY

Burnaby L.

MAILLARDVILLE

Pitt

Essondale

Chatham Reach

SOUTH BURNABY

EDMONDS

NEW WESTMINSTER

Fraser

DOUGLAS I.

Pitt Meadows

SEA ISLAND

MITCHELL

ELSONA

Port Hammond

VANCOUVER INTERNATIONAL AIRPORT

Bridgeport

QUEENSBOROUGH

SOUTH WESTMINSTER

SURREY

Port Mann

BARNSTON I.

ANNACIS I.

ANNIEVILLE

Fraser

Port Kells

L U L U   I S L A N D

Brighouse

Kennedy

49

R I C H M O N D

Sunbury

S U R R E Y

Steveston

Strawberry Hill

Newton

PELLY POINT

Fraser

D E L T A

Sullivan

Surrey Centre

WESTHAM ISLAND

Strait of Georgia

Port Guichon

Ladner

Cloverdale

Langley

Colebrook

Serpentine

Nicomekl

Mud Bay

Elgin

Crescent Beach

Campbell

Hazelmere

ROBERTS BANK SUPERPORT

Beach Grove

Boundary Bay

Ocean Park

White Rock

Semiahmoo Bay

Tsawassen

Boundary Bay

CANADA
UNITED STATES

BRITISH COLUMBIA
WASHINGTON

Blaine

Point Roberts

Drayton Harbor

West from Greenwich

▨ Residential	▨ Industrial	□ Recreational	□ Transportation and utilities
▨ Commercial	▨ Institutional	▨ Woodland	□ Agricultural and other

─○─ Freeway with interchange   ─◎─ Trans-Canada Highway   ─○─ Railway with station   ----- City Boundary

Projection: *Transverse Mercator*

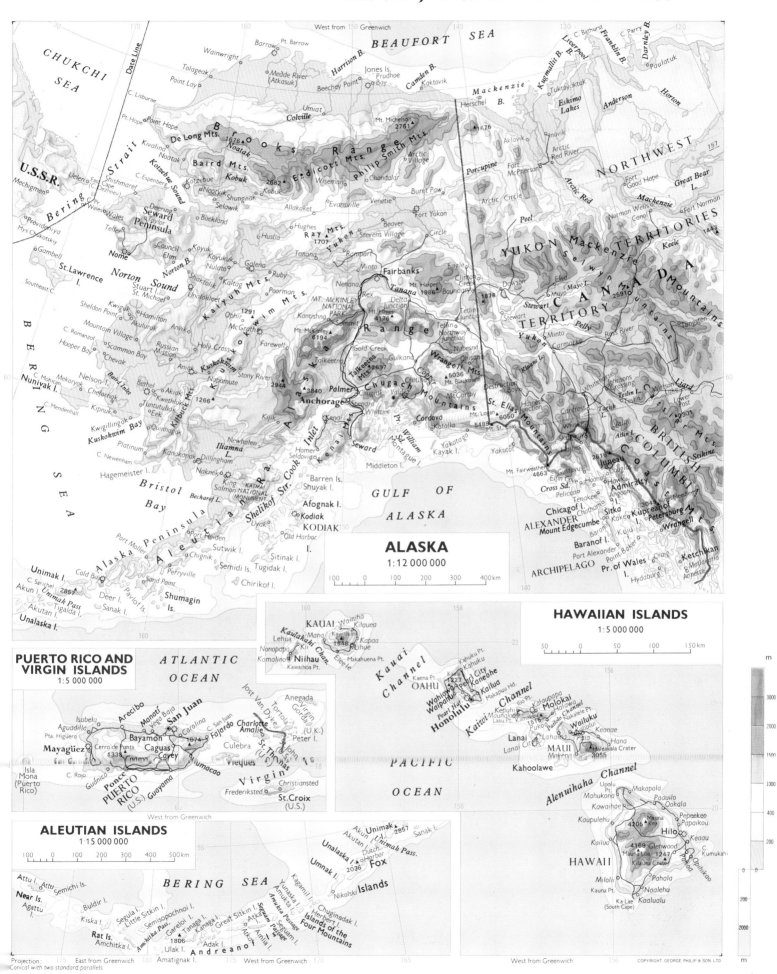

ALASKA
1:12 000 000
100 0 100 200 300 400km

HAWAIIAN ISLANDS
1:5 000 000
50 0 50 100 150 km

PUERTO RICO AND VIRGIN ISLANDS
1:5 000 000

ALEUTIAN ISLANDS
1:15 000 000
100 0 100 200 300 400 500km

Projection:
Conical with two standard parallels

COPYRIGHT GEORGE PHILIP & SON LTD

1:12 000 000

100   0   100   200   300   400   500 km

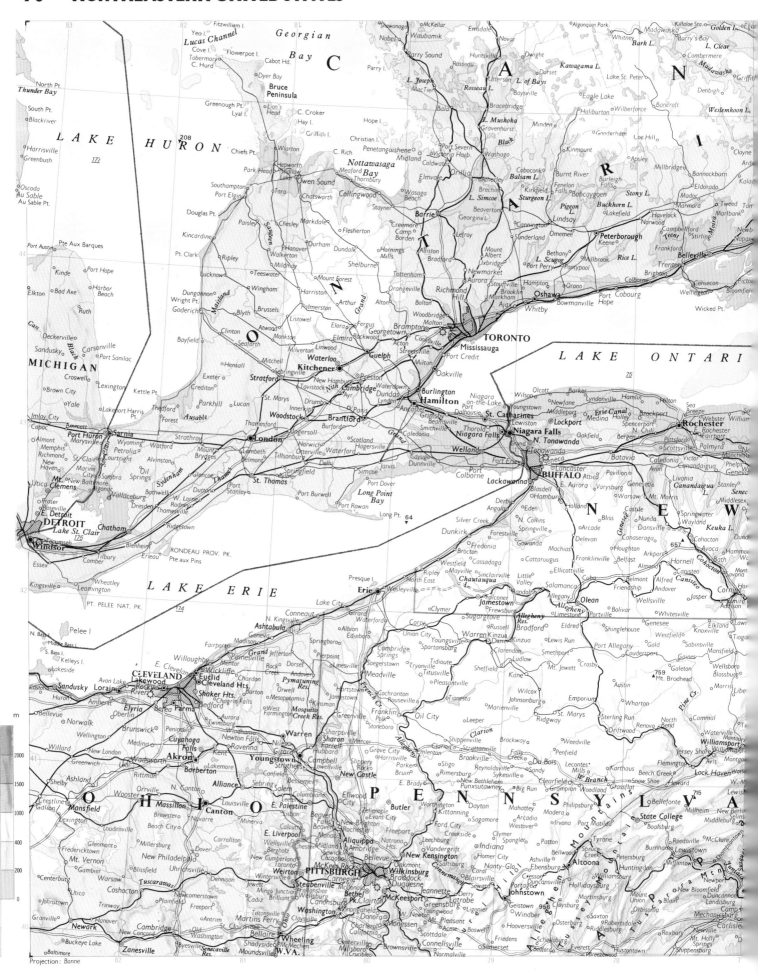

1:2 500 000

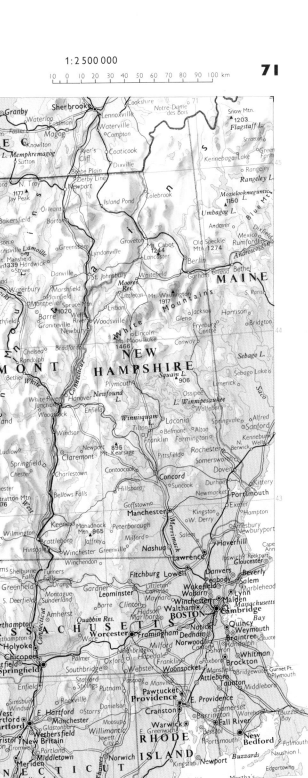
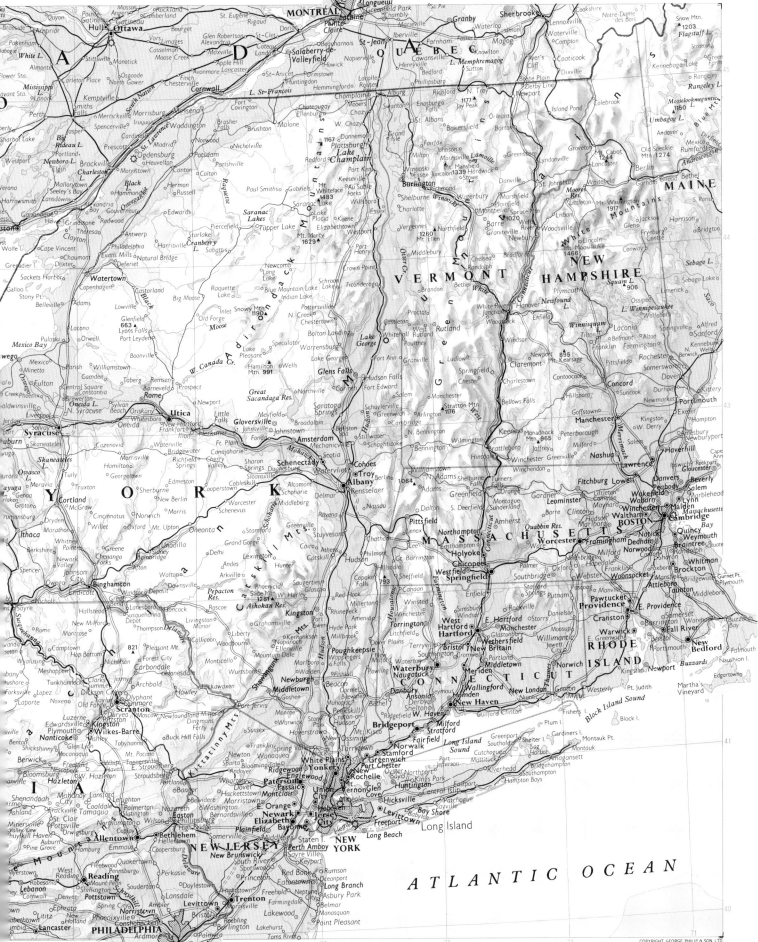

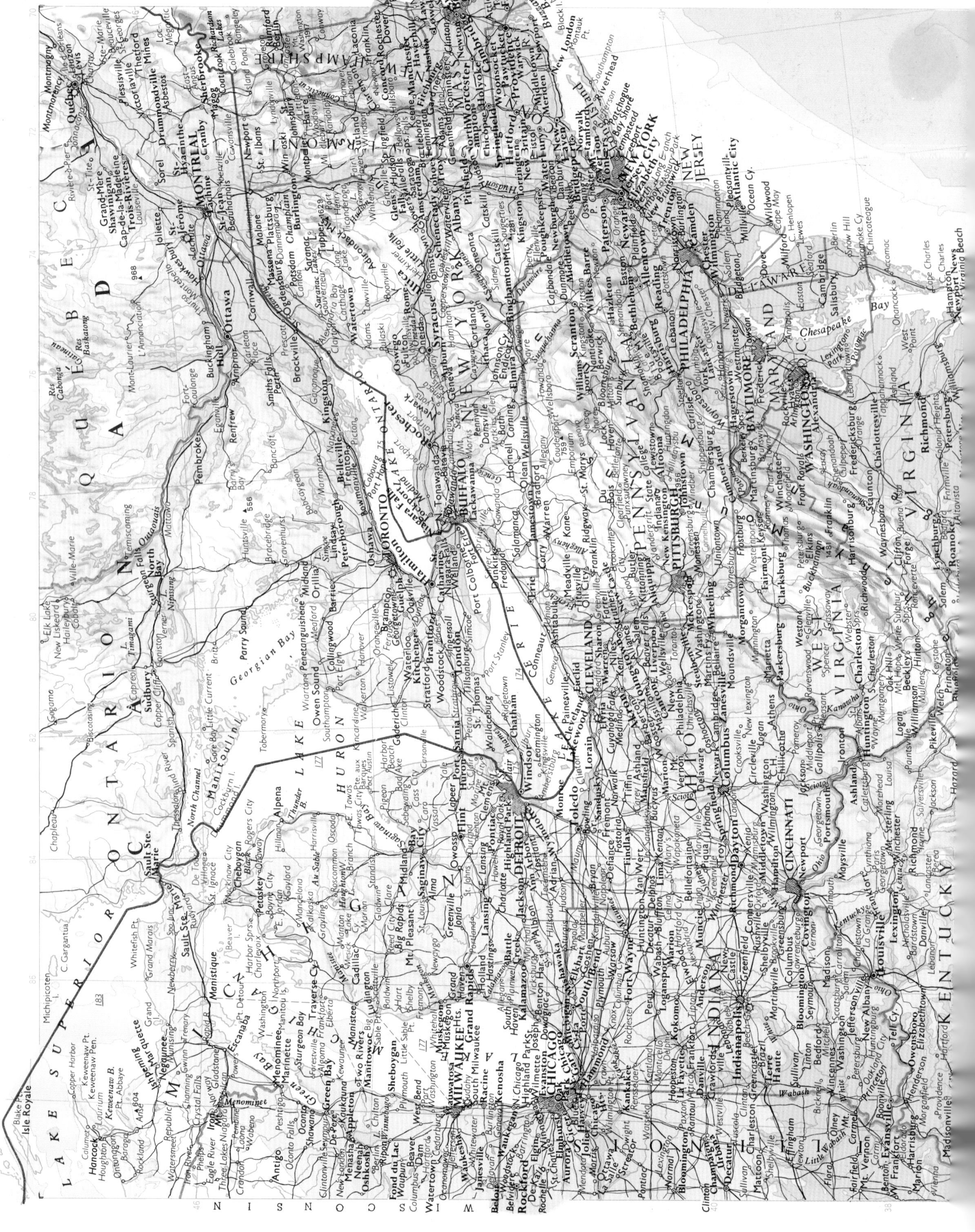
LAKE SUPERIOR
LAKE HURON
LAKE ERIE
LAKE ONTARIO
Georgian Bay
ONTARIO
QUÉBEC
MICHIGAN
WISCONSIN
ILLINOIS
INDIANA
OHIO
KENTUCKY
WEST VIRGINIA
VIRGINIA
PENNSYLVANIA
NEW YORK
NEW JERSEY
MARYLAND
DELAWARE
VERMONT
NEW HAMPSHIRE
MASSACHUSETTS
CONNECTICUT
CHICAGO
MILWAUKEE
DETROIT
CLEVELAND
PITTSBURGH
BUFFALO
TORONTO
MONTREAL
Ottawa
Québec
BOSTON
NEW YORK
PHILADELPHIA
BALTIMORE
WASHINGTON
CINCINNATI
Louisville
Indianapolis
Columbus
Toledo
Hamilton
Rochester
Syracuse
Albany
Richmond
Lexington

1:6 000 000

50   0   50   100   150   200   250 km

Continuation
Eastwards
On same scale

DENSITY OF POPULATION
1:50 000 000

Inhabitants per km²

| under 1 | 1–3 | 3–6 | 6–12 | 12–25 | 25–50 | 50–100 | 100–200 | over 200 |

Towns with over 3 000 000 inh. ▪
1 000 000–3 000 000 ■
500 000–1 000 000 ■

ATLANTIC OCEAN

BAHAMAS

Little Abaco I.
Gt. Abaco I.
Great Abaco I.
Hope Town
Gt. Guana Cay

Grand Cays

Grand
Bahama I.
Settlement
Pt.
Freeport

MAINE

NEW HAMPSHIRE

Pamlico Sound

NORTH CAROLINA

SOUTH CAROLINA

TENNESSEE

GEORGIA

ALABAMA

MISSISSIPPI

FLORIDA

GULF OF MEXICO

West from Greenwich

Projection: Alber's Equal Area with two standard parallels

COPYRIGHT GEORGE PHILIP & SON LTD

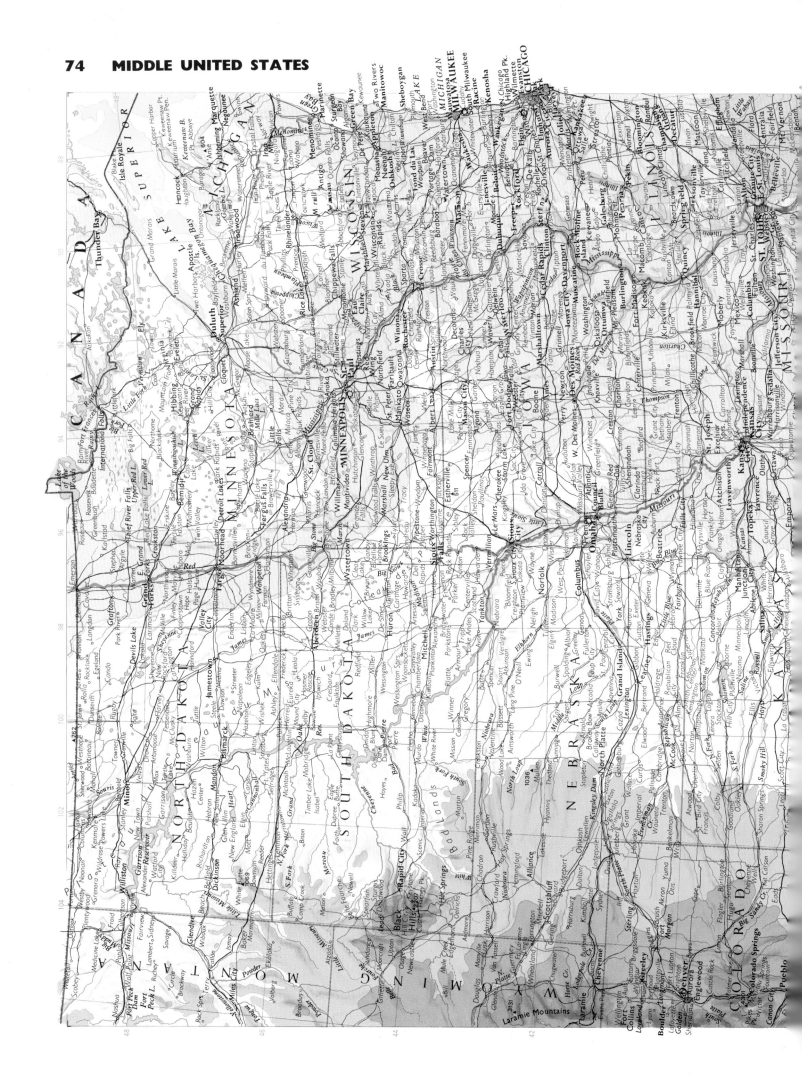

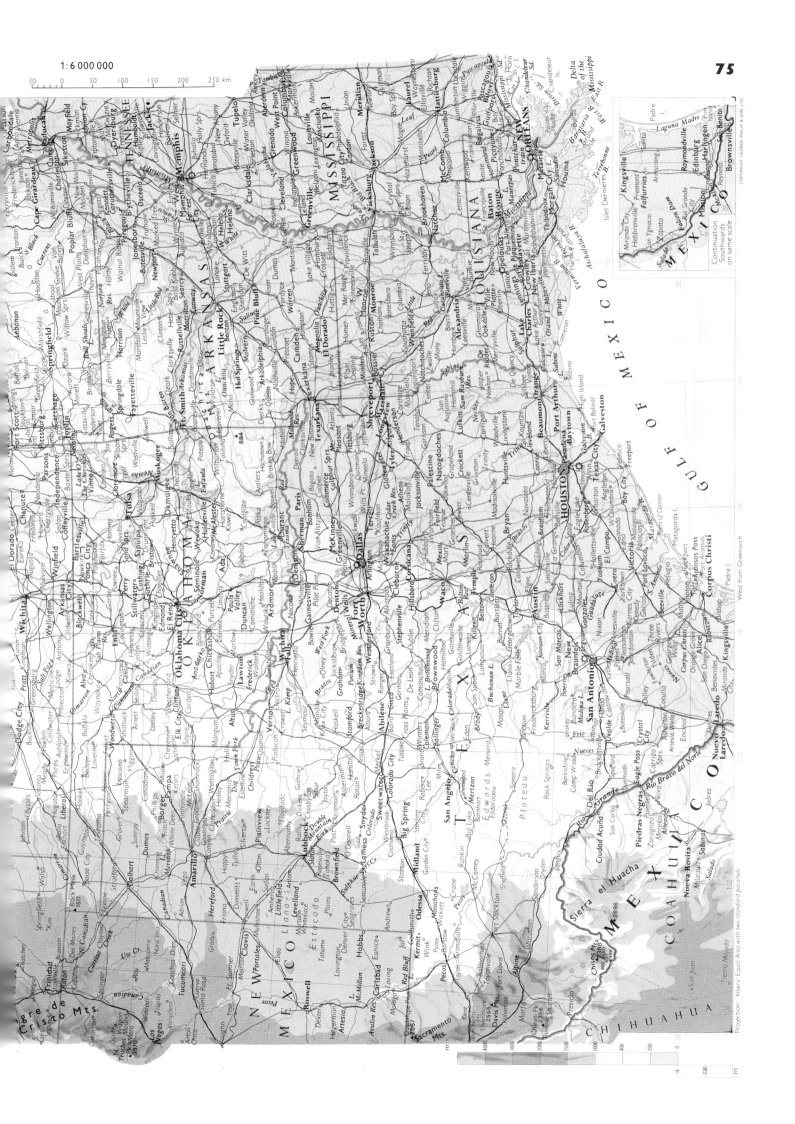

1:6 000 000

50   0   50   100   150   200   250 km

GULF OF MEXICO

TENNESSEE

MISSISSIPPI

ARKANSAS

OKLAHOMA

T E X A S

LOUISIANA

NEW MEXICO

MEXICO

COAHUILA

CHIHUAHUA

Memphis

NEW ORLEANS

Baton Rouge

Little Rock

Shreveport

Dallas

Fort Worth

Houston

San Antonio

Corpus Christi

Austin

Waco

Wichita

Tulsa

Oklahoma City

Amarillo

Lubbock

Odessa

Midland

Laredo

Nuevo Laredo

Galveston

Port Arthur

Beaumont

West from Greenwich

Laguna Madre

MEXICO

Continuation
Southwards
on same scale

Projection : Albers' Equal Area with two standard parallels

COPYRIGHT GEORGE PHILIP & SON, LTD

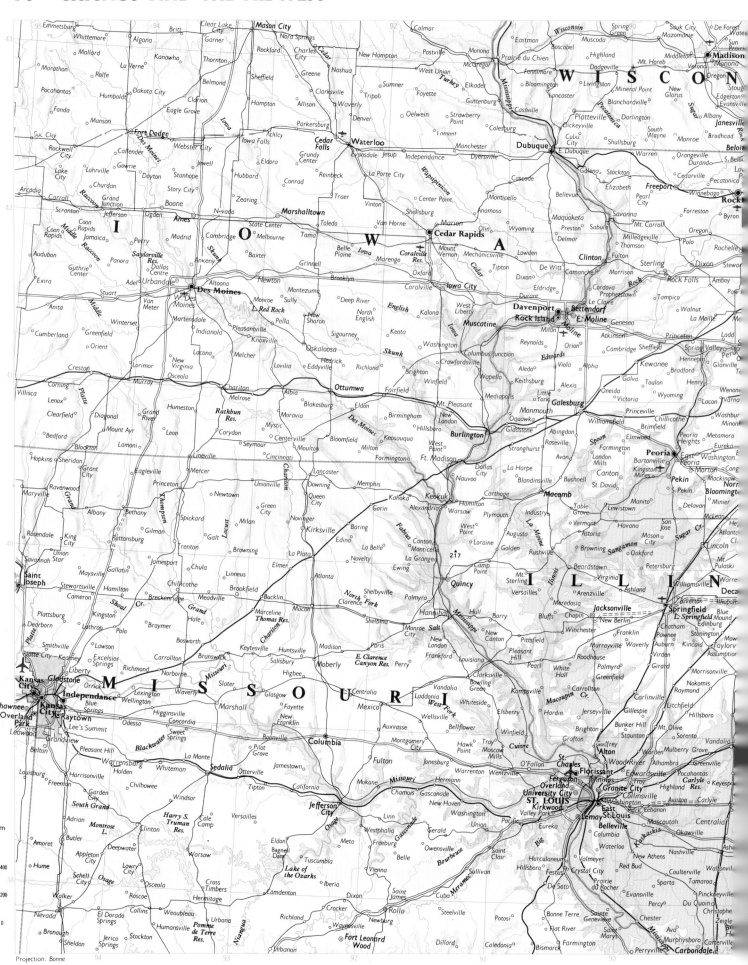

Projection: Bonne

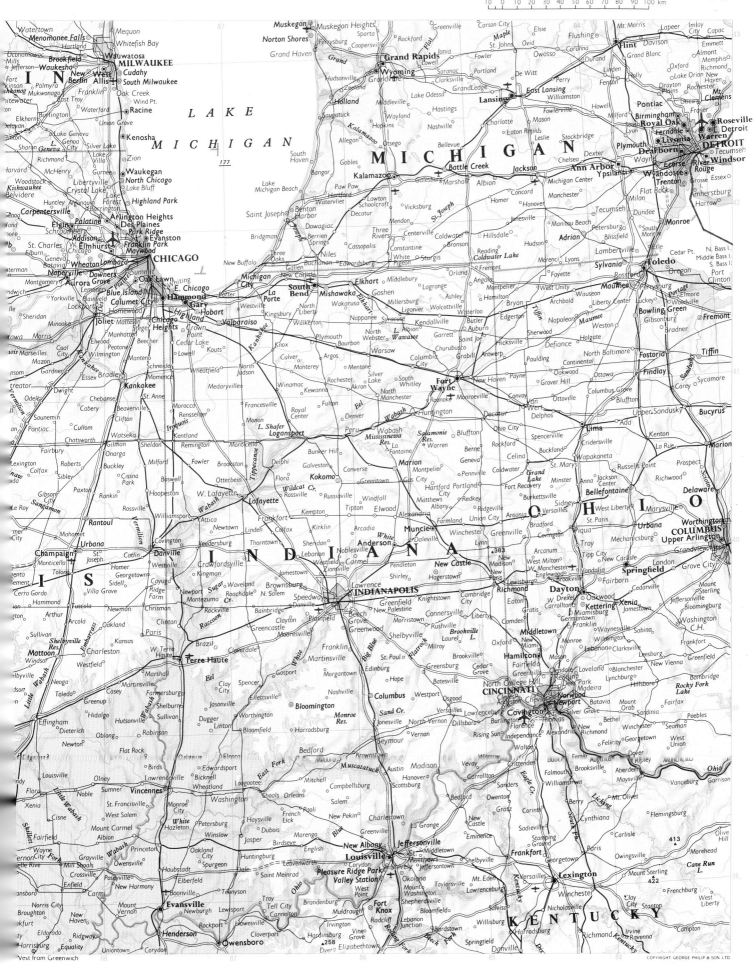

1:2 500 000

10 0 10 20 30 40 50 60 70 80 90 100 km

LAKE
MICHIGAN

MICHIGAN

ILLINOIS

INDIANA

OHIO

KENTUCKY

West from Greenwich

1 : 6 000 000

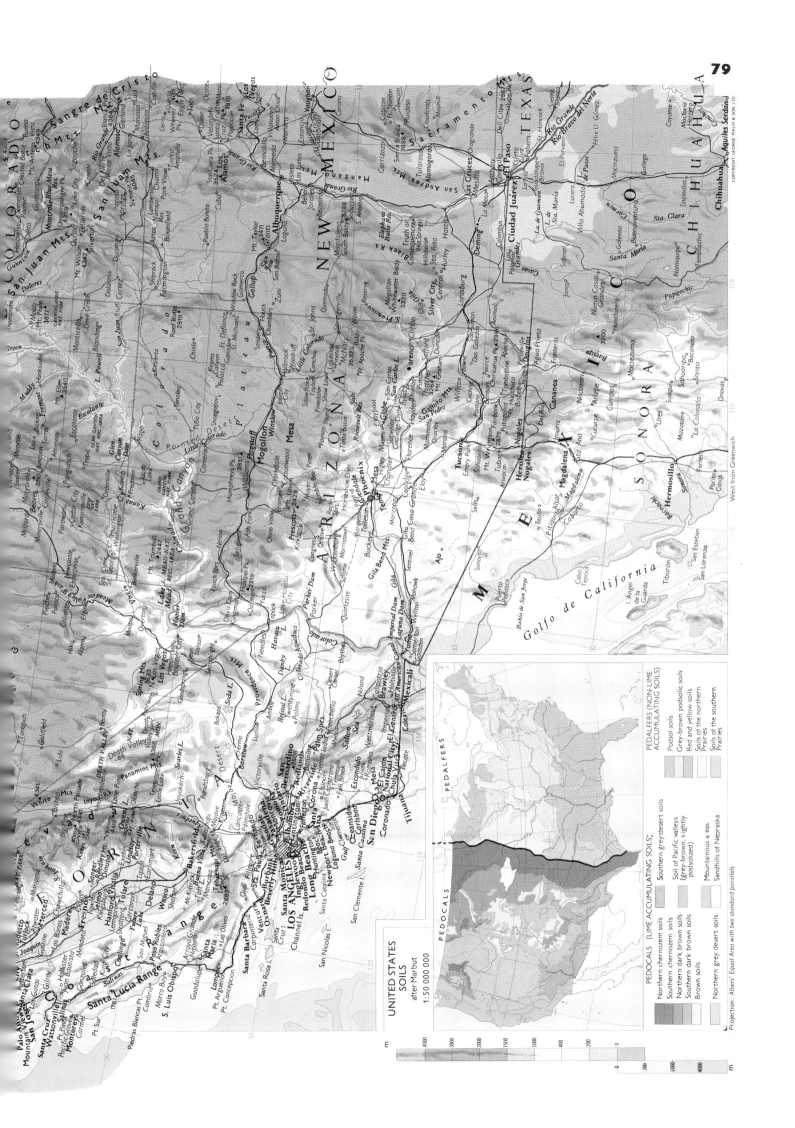

UNITED STATES
SOILS
after Marbut
1:50 000 000

PEDOCALS (LIME ACCUMULATING SOILS)

Northern chernozem soils
Southern chernozem soils
Northern dark brown soils
Southern dark brown soils
Brown soils
Northern grey desert soils
Southern grey-desert soils
Soil of Pacific valleys
(grey-brown, slightly podsolized)
Mountainous areas
Sandhills of Nebraska

PEDALFERS (NON-LIME ACCUMULATING SOILS)

Podsol soils
Grey-brown podsolic soils
Red and yellow soils
Soils of the northern Prairies
Soils of the southern Prairies

PEDALFERS

PEDOCALS

West from Greenwich

Projection: Albers' Equal Area with two standard parallels

COPYRIGHT GEORGE PHILIP & SON, LTD.

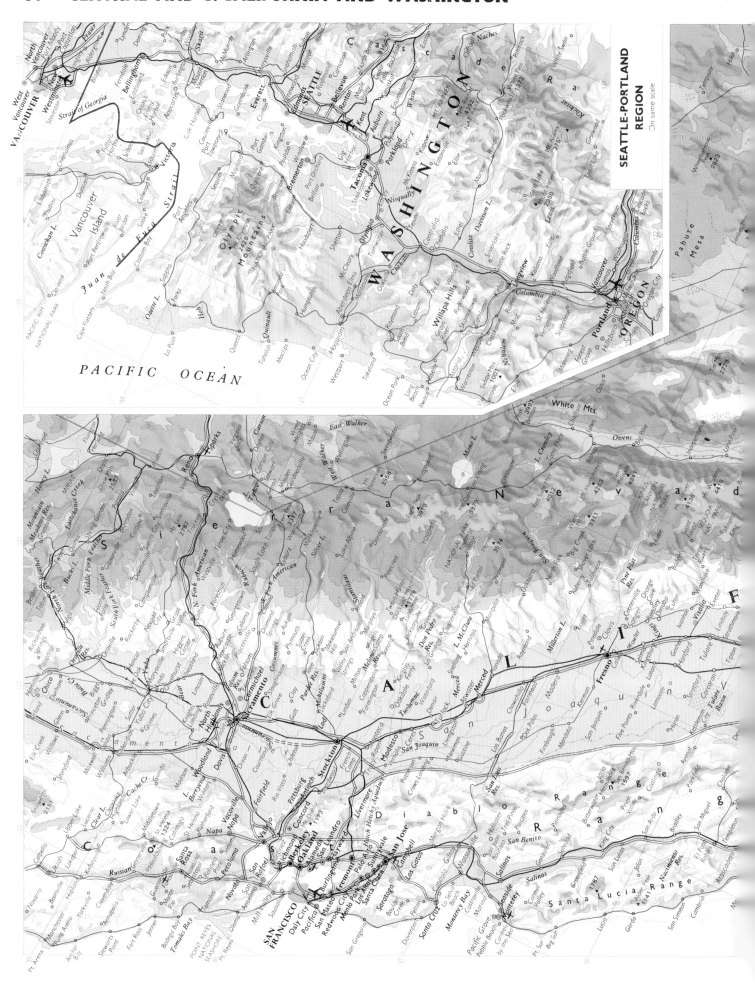

SEATTLE-PORTLAND
REGION
On same scale

PACIFIC OCEAN

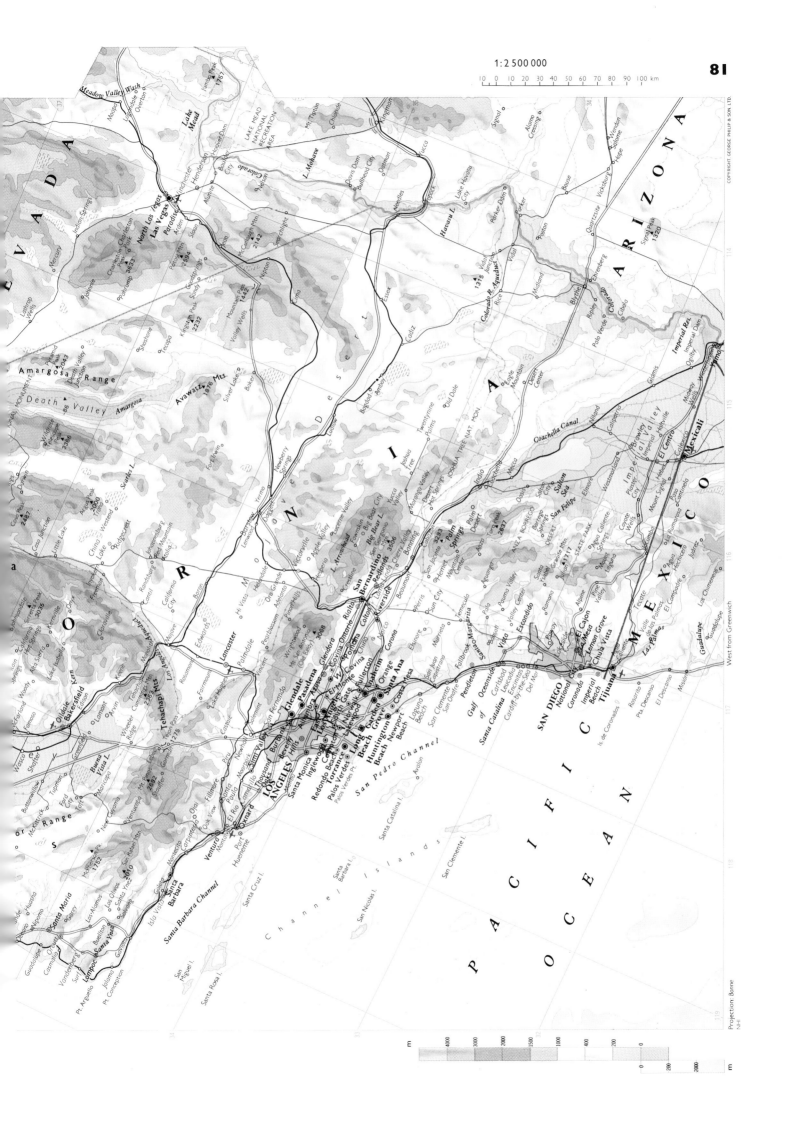

1:2 500 000

10 0 10 20 30 40 50 60 70 80 90 100 km

NEVADA

ARIZONA

CALIFORNIA

MEXICO

PACIFIC OCEAN

LOS ANGELES

San Diego

Las Vegas

Lake Mead

Death Valley

Santa Barbara

Bakersfield

Mexicali

Tijuana

Channel Islands

Projection: Bonne
NHI

West from Greenwich

m 4000 3000 2000 1500 1000 400 200 0

m 2000

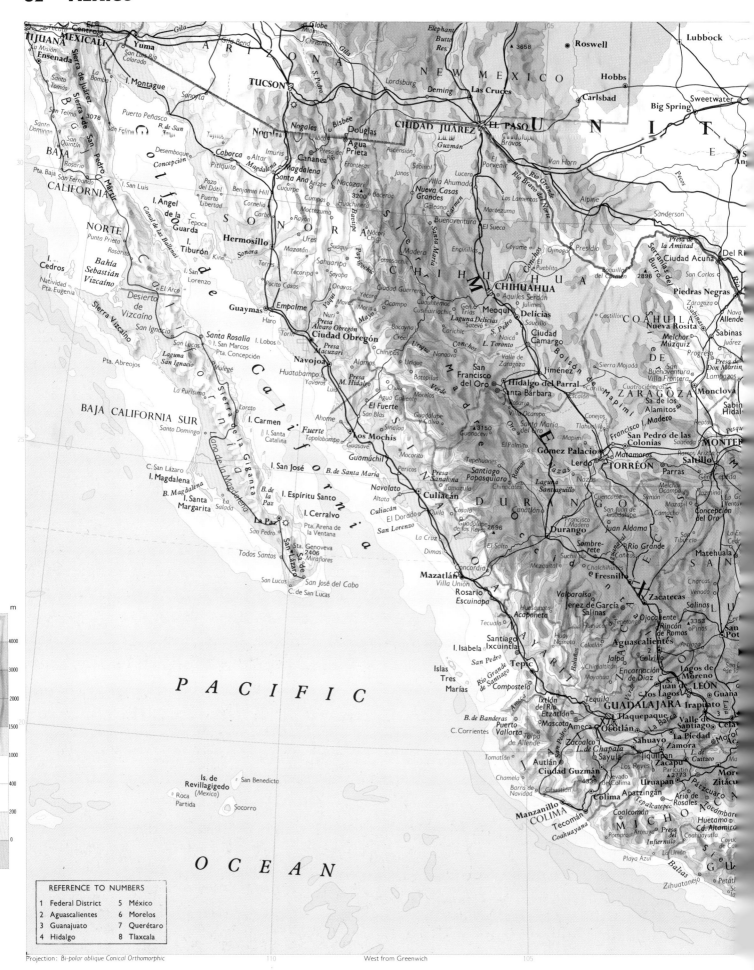

PACIFIC

OCEAN

REFERENCE TO NUMBERS
1	Federal District	5	México
2	Aguascalientes	6	Morelos
3	Guanajuato	7	Querétaro
4	Hidalgo	8	Tlaxcala

m

Projection: Bi-polar oblique Conical Orthomorphic   110   West from Greenwich   105

1:8 000 000

50   0   50   100   150   200 250   300 km

Wichita
Falls
Denison
Sherman   Paris   Red   Hope
Denton   Greenville   ARKANSAS   Greenville   Tuscaloosa   Opelika
Texarkana   El Dorado   Camden   Selma   Columbus   McRae
FORT WORTH   DALLAS   Texarkana   Monroe   MISSISSIPPI   Meridian   Montgomery   Phenix City   Americus   Cordele
Ranger   Longview   Vicksburg   Troy   Albany   Tifton   GEORGIA
lene   Cleburne   Tyler   Shreveport   S   Jackson   A   L   A   B   A   M   A   Dothan   Waycross   Valdosta
Hillsboro   Corsicana   T   Natchez   Laurel   Chattahoochee   Tallahassee
Waco   Palestine   A   Alexandria   Laurel   Hattiesburg   Flomaton   Tallahassee   FLORIDA   Lake
D   Jewett   Lufkin   McComb   Dothan   City
Brownwood   Temple   Trinity   Baton   Bogalusa   MOBILE   Panama City
Austin   Huntsville   Navasota   Rouge   Hammond   Gulfport   Pensacola   Apalachee
Bryan   Beaumont   Lake Charles   NEW   Biloxi   Bay   Suwannee
HOUSTON   Lafayette   ORLEANS   Breton Sound   C. San Blas
SAN   Port   Rosenberg   Mississippi   G   U   L   F   O   F
ANTONIO   Arthur   Galveston   Atchafalaya   Delta
Victoria   Bay   Terrebonne B.   Clearwater
Dilley   Guadalupe
Nueces   Mississippi
Alice   Delta
Laredo   Corpus Christi
Kingsville   G   U   L   F   O   F
vo Laredo   Zapata
Camargo   Laguna Madre   M   E   X   I   C   O
McAllen   Harlingen
Presa   M.R.Reynosa   Brownsville   CUBA
Gomez   Valle Hermoso   Matamoros   La Esperanza   Guane
China   Santa Teresa   La Fé
emorelos   Mendez   Laguna Madre
nares   San Fernando   Isla
Villagran   Desterrada   Canal de Yucatán   C. San Antonio
Santander-Jiménez   Isla Pérez   C.
iudad   La Pesca   Corrientes
toria   Soto la Marina   Pta.   Rio Lagartos   C. Catoche
Ilera   Sierra de   Yalkubul   El Cuyo   Pto. Juárez
Aldama   Tamaulipas   Progreso   Dzilam   Temax   Tizimín   El Díaz
Pta. Jerez   de Bravo   Motul   Puerto Morelos
Ciudad Mante   Altamira   Dzibilchaltún   Izamal   Espita
Ciudad Madero   MÉRIDA   YUCATÁN   Valladolid   Isla
Tampico   Maxcanú   Chichén   Cozumel   Cozumel
Ciudad   Pánuco   Sotuta   Mayapán   Itzá
Valles   Laguna de Tamiahua   Calkiní   Ticul   Peto
SÍ   Uxmal   Tekax
Tempoal   Tenabo   Bolonchenticul   Vigia Chico   B. de la Ascensión
Ozuluama   C. Rojo   Golfo   Campeche   Hopelchén   B. del Espíritu Santo
Tantoyuca   de   Champotón   San José Carpizo   Felipe Carrillo   QUINTANA
Tamazunchale   Campeche   Chenkán   Puerto   Banca
Tuxpan   Juárez   Pedro Antonio Santos   ROO   Chinchorro
Poza Rica   Bacalar   B. de
Papantla   Chetumal   Chetumal
del Río   Nautla   CAMPECHE   Corozal   Ambergris Cay
Pachuca   Huauchinango   Golfo   Ciudad del   Laguna de Términos   Orange Walk   Turneffe Is.
Tulancingo   de   Carmen   Pital   Matamoros   Hondo   Belize   Islas de
Tezlutlán   Campeche   Frontera   Concepción   City   BELIZE   la Bahía
MÉXICO   Jalapa   Zempoala   Coatzacoalcos   Palizada   Belmopan   Stann Creek   Roatán
Tlaxcala   Veracruz   Alvarado   San Andrés   Paraíso   Comalcalco   Uaxactún   Benque   Maya Mts.   Puerto
PUEBLA   Coatepec   Tlacotalpan   Tuxtla   Vela   TABASCO   Villahermosa   Tikal   Viejo   Golfo de Honduras   Castilla
Orizaba   Cosamaloapan   Venta   Cárdenas   Balancán   Monkey River   La Ceiba
Cuernavaca   Córdoba   Acayucan   Minatitlán   Macuspana   Tenosique   San Antonio   Puerto Cortés   Balfate
Tehuacán   Ixtmo   Jesús Carranza   Copainalá   Palenque   L. Petén Itzá   Livingston   Puerto Barrios   Trujillo
Iguala   Acatlán   de   Trinidad   Presa   Chiapa de Corzo   La Libertad   Sava
Chilapa   Nochixtlán   Tehuantepec   Netzahualcoyotl   Ocosingo   Flores   Puerto Cortés   HONDURAS
Chilpancingo   Tlaxiaco   Ixtlán de   San Cristóbal de   Usumacinta   San Pedro Sula   El Joral
del Sur   Oaxaca   Juárez   las Casas   Independencia   San Luis   Santa   Olanchito
capulco   Miahuatlán   Monte Albán   Tuxtla   CHIAPAS   Comitán   Punta   Zacapa   Barbara   Santa Rosa   Il. de
Ometepec   Pinotepa   Gutiérrez   Gorda   La Concordia   Puerto Barrios   de Copán   Comayagua
Nacional   Ixtepec   Chiapa   La Esperanza   Chiquimula   TEGUCIGALPA
Pta.   San Pedro   Juchitán   Arriaga   Madre   Cobán   Chiquimula   Danlí
Maldonado   Tututepec   Salina Cruz   Tonalá   Huehuetenango   Santa   GUATEMALA   La Paz
Puerto   Mixtepec   Golfo de   Mar Muerto   Utatlán   GUATEMALA   La Paz
Escondido   Tehuantepec   Arista   Pijijiapan   San Marcos   Totonicapán   Jalapa   Chiquimula   Cojutepeque   Comayagua
Puerto Ángel   Mapastepec   Huixtla   Quez   Antigua   Esquipulas
Tapachula   V. de Tajumulco   San   Chimaltenango   GUATEMALA
Coatepeque   Mazate   nango   Amatitlán
Retalhuleu   Ocos

COPYRIGHT GEORGE PHILIP & SON LTD.

GULF OF MEXICO

Fort Myers · Fort Lauderdale · Boca Raton · West Palm Beach · West End · Normans Castle · Little Abaco I. · Freeport · Grand Bahama I. · Hope Town · Great Abaco I.
Naples · The Everglades · Hialeah · MIAMI · C. Romano · Bimini Is. · Berry Is. · Nicolls Town · Nassau · New Providence I. · Eleuthera I. · Dunmore
C. Sable · Florida Bay · Key West · Dry Tortugas · Florida City · Florida Keys · Straits of Florida · Cay Sal Bank · Andros Town · Adelaide · Great Exuma

GREAT BAHAMA BANK

Northwest Providence Channel · Northeast Providence Channel · Andros I.

(Havana) LA HABANA · MARIANAO · Guanabacoa · San Antonio de los Baños · Guanajay · La Esperanza · Bahía Honda · Matanzas · Canal Nicolás · Santa Cruz del Norte
Pinar del Río · Guane · Los Palacios · San Luis · La Fé · Güines · Batabanó · Jagüey Grande · Playa Larga · Cárdenas · Colón · Jovellanos · Sagua la Grande · Santa Clara · Caibarién · Placetas · Morón · Cayo Romano
I. de Pinos · Nueva Gerona · Cienfuegos · Trinidad · Sancti-Spíritus · Júcaro · Tunas de Zaza · Ciego de Ávila · Florida · Camagüey · Nuevitas · Puerto Gibara
C. Corrientes · Archipiélago de los Canarreos · GREATER · Arch. de los Jardines de la Reina · Santa Cruz del Sur · Victoria de las Tunas · HOLGUÍN · Bayamo · Palma Soriano
Golfo de Guacanayabo · Manzanillo · Sierra Maestra · SANTIAGO DE CUBA · C. Cruz · 2000

Cayman Islands (Br.) · Cayman Brac · Little Cayman · Georgetown · Grand Cayman

Montego Bay · Falmouth · St. Ann's Bay · Port Maria · Annotto · Lucea · JAMAICA · Savanna la Mar · South Negril Pt. · Black River · May Pen · Spanish Town · KINGSTON · Mandeville · Cambridge
Swan Islands (U.S.A. & Honduras) · Pedro Cays (Jamaica)

Canal de Yucatán

Progreso · Dzilam de Bravo · Yalkubul · Río Lagartos · El Cuyo · C. Catoche · Pta. San Antonio
Mérida · Motul · Dzibilchaltún · Temax · Tizimín · Espita · Pto. Juárez · C. Catoche
Izamal · Sotuta · Mayapán · Chichén Itzá · Valladolid · El Díaz · Isla Cozumel
Campeche · Tekax · Peto · Balanchenticul · Cozumel · Isla Cozumel · Vigía Chico
Champotón · Hopelchén · Chenkán · San José Carpizo · Felipe Carrillo Puerto · B. de la Ascensión
Ciudad del Carmen · Laguna de Términos · Pital · QUINTANA ROO · B. del Espíritu Santo · Banco Chinchorro
Palizada · Balancán · Concepción · Chetumal · B. de Chetumal · Ambergris Cay
Tenosique · Usumacinta · Uaxactún · Orange Walk · Hondo · Turneffe Is.
Palenque · Ocosingo · Tikal · Belize City · BELIZE · Middlesex · Stann Creek
La Independencia · L. Petén Itzá · La Libertad · Flores · Benque Viejo · Maya Mts.
Comitán · San Luis · San Antonio · Monkey River
Lacandón · Punta Gorda · Golfo de Honduras · Islas de la Bahía

GUATEMALA · Cuchumatanes · Cobán · L. de Izabal · Livingston · Puerto Barrios · Puerto Cortés · La Ceiba · Roatán · Puerto Castilla · C. Camarón
Huehuetenango · Utatlán · Sa. de las Minas · Tela · Balfate · Savá · Trujillo · Iriona · Pta. Patuca
San Marcos · Totonicapán · Zacapa · Santa Bárbara · San Pedro Sula · El Progreso · Olanchito · Brus Laguna · Laguna Caratasca
Sololá · Jalapa · Chiquimula · Copán · El Jaral · Yoro · Sulaco · Catacamas · Puerto Lempira
Quezaltenango · Antigua · GUATEMALA · Santa Rosa de Copán · La Esperanza · Comayagua · HONDURAS · Juticalpa · Patuca · C. Falso
Retalhuleu · Mazatenango · Escuintla · Santa Ana · Suchitoto · La Paz · TEGUCIGALPA · Danlí · Coco · (Segovia) · Puerto Cabo Gracias á Dios
Coatepeque · Cojutepeque · Chinameca · Cholbuteca · Pta. Gorda · Cayos Miskitos (Nicaragua)
Ahuachapán · Zacatecoluca · SAN SALVADOR · San Miguel · La Unión · Somoto · Coco · Bonanza · Puerto Cabezas
Acajutla · EL SALVADOR · Golfo de Fonseca · Estelí · Siuna
Usulután · San Miguel · Chinandega · Cord. Isabelia · Jinotega · Matagalpa · I. de Providencia (Colombia)
Corinto · León · Boaco · NICARAGUA · Tuma · San Pedro del Norte · Río Grande · Cayos Roncador (U.S.A. & Colombia)
La Paz Centro · MANAGUA · Masaya · Juigalpa · Santo Domingo · Rama · Prinzapolca · I. de San Andrés (Colombia)
Diriamba · Granada · Lago de Managua · Pta. de Perlas · Cayos de Albuquerque (Colombia)
Rivas · Isla de Ometepe · Lago de Nicaragua · Bluefields · El Bluff · Islas del Maíz (Nicaragua, U.S.A.)
San Juan del Sur · San Carlos · Pta. Mico · Bahía de San Juan del Norte
B. de Salinas · C. Sta. Elena · San Juan · San Juan del Norte
Golfo de Papagayo · C. Velas · Liberia · Cord. de Guanacaste · Cord. Central · COSTA RICA · Guápiles · Siquirres
Santa Cruz · Nicoya · Alajuela · SAN JOSÉ · Cartago · Limón
Puntarenas · Pen. de Nicoya · Esparza · Talamanca · Pta. Mona
C. Blanco · Puerto Quepos · Pen. de Osa · Buenos Aires · Bocas del Toro · Almirante · CANAL ZONE (U.S.A.) · Colón · Nombre de Dios · Portobelo
Bahía de Coronado · Puerto Cortés · Laguna de Chiriquí · Golfo de los Mosquitos · Serranía de Tabasará · La Chorrera · PANAMÁ
Golfo Dulce · David · Remedios · Santiago · Penonomé · Arch. de las Perlas · Golfo del Darién
Puerto Armuelles · Golfo de Chiriquí · Pta. Burica · Chitré · Las Tablas · Golfo de Panamá · El Real

CARIBBEAN

Bajo Nuevo (Colombia) · Mosquitia · Pedro Antonio Santos

1:8 000 000

50   0   50   100   150   200   250   300 km

ATLANTIC

OCEAN

Tropic of Cancer

MAS

r's Town
The Bight
Cat I.
San Salvador
(Watling I., Guanahani)
Conception I.
Rum Cay
Long I.
Clarence Town
Crooked I. Passage
Atwood or Samana Cay
Richmond
Crooked I.
Plana Cays
Albert Town
Snug Corner
Mayaguana I.
ay Verde
Mira por vos Cay
Acklins I.
Santa
go
Hogsty Reef
Little Inagua I.
Caicos Passage
Lake Rose
Matthew Town
Great Inagua I.
Caicos Islands (Br.)
Turks I. Passage
Turks Islands (Br.)
Moa
Baracoa
Pta. de Maisí
I. de la Tortue
Port-de-Paix
C. Frances Viejo
Puerto Plata
La Isabela
ari
Paso de los Vientos
(Windward Passage)
Jean-Rabel
Cap-Haïtien
Fort-Liberté
Monte Cristi
Santiago de los Cabelleros
Vega
San Francisco de Macoris
Sánchez
Sabana de La Mar
uántanamo
Cap-à-Faux
Golfe de la Gonâve
St.-Marc
Gonaïves
Hinche
Cord. Central
3175
Hato Mayor
B. de Samaná
Aguadilla
Arecibo
Bayamón
SAN JUAN
Anegada
Virgin Gorda
Sombrero (Anguilla)
Jérémie
I. de la Gonâve
HAITI
PORT-AU-PRINCE
San Juan
DOMINICAN REP.
San Pedro de Macoris
Higüey
C. Engaño
Fajardo
Virgin Is. (Br.)
Road Town
Virgin Is. Passage
Tortola
Anguilla (Br.)
A.)
Dame
Marie
2280
Enriquillo
La Romana
B. de Yuma
Ponce
Caguas
1338
Virgin Is. (U.S.A.)
St.-Martin (Guad.)
St. Maarten (Neth.)
Saba (Neth.)
St.-Barthélemy (Fr.)
Barbuda (Br.)
C. Carcasse
Les Cayes
Aquin
Jacmel
Godet
Barahona
Pedernales
Compostela
San Cristóbal
I. Saona
I. Mona (U.S.A.)
Mayagüez
Isla Mona
PUERTO RICO (U.S.A.)
Guayama
Charlotte Amalie
St. Croix
Frederiksted
Christiansted
St. Eustatius (Neth.)
Basseterre
Nevis (Br.)
St. Christopher (St. Kitts)
Redonda
St. Johns
Antigua
Pointe-à-Gravois
I.-à-Vache
C. Beata
C. Beata
SANTO DOMINGO
HISPANIOLA
ANTILLES
LESSER
Montserrat (Br.)
Guadeloupe Passage
GUADELOUPE (Fr.)
Ste-Rose
Moule
Désirade
Basse-Terre
Pointe-à-Pitre
Marie-Galante (Fr.)
Grand-Bourge
I. des Saintes (Guad.)
Dominica Passage
Portsmouth
I. de Aves (Bird I.) (Venezuela)
Roseau
Dominica (Br.)
Martinique Passage
Ste-Marie
Mt. Pelée 1397
François
Rivière-Pilot
Fort-de-France
MARTINIQUE
St. Lucia Channel (Fr.)
Castries
Soufrière
St. Lucia (Br.)
BEAN
SEA
St. Vincent Passage
Soufrière 1234
St. Vincent (Br.)
Speightstown
Kingstown
Bridgetown
BARBADOS
WINDWARD ISLANDS
ANTILLES
Hillsborough
The Grenadines
LESSER ANTILLES
St. George's
GRENADA
Aruba (Neth.)
Curaçao (Neth.)
Bonaire (Neth.)
I. Blanquilla (Ven.)
I. Los Hermanos (Ven.)
Tobago
Pta. Gallinas
Willemstad
Is. de Aves (Ven.)
Is. Los Roques (Ven.)
I. Orchila (Ven.)
I. Los Testigos (Ven.)
Port of Spain
Scarborough
Pen. de la Guajira
Pta. Espada
Pen. de Paraguaná
Punta Cardón
Puerto Cumarebo
Coro
La Vela de Coro
Tucacas
Puerto Cabello
Maiquetía
La Guaira
CARACAS
Guaire
I. La Tortuga (Ven.)
I. Margarita
La Asunción
NUEVA ESPARTA
Porlamar
Pen. de Paria
Pta. Peñas
Dragon's Mouth
Galera Pt.
Trinidad
Ríohacha
C. San Román
Uribia
Golfo de Venezuela
Punta Cardón
GUAJIRA
San Rafael
Altogracia
Mene de Mauroa
Tucuyo
MIRANDA
Higuerote
Ocumare del Tuy
Río Chico
Puerto La Cruz
Cumaná
Carúpano
Río Caribe
Güiria
Golfo de Paria
SUCRE
Carúpano
TRINIDAD & TOBAGO
San Fernando
Serpent's Mouth
Santa Marta
C. San Juan de Guía
Cienaga
Sierra Nevada de Santa Marta 5800
MARACAIBO
La Concepción
Santa Rita
Cabimas
Baragua
Carora
Barcelona
Caicara
Maturín
MONAGAS
DELTA-
Tucupita
Soledad
Sabanalarga
Fundación
Calamar
Agustín Codazzi
Valledupar
Villa del Rosario
Machiques
Cuidad Ojeda
Mene Grande
BARQUISIMETO
San Felipe
YARACUY
LARA
Yaritagua de los Morros
Valencia
Villa de Cura
Los Teques
Ocumare del Tuy
San Juan de los Morros de Orituco
Aragua de Barcelona
CARABOBO
Anaco
Cantaura
AMACUR
MAGDALENA
Plato
Zambrano
CÉSAR
Lago de Maracaibo
La Ceiba
TRUJILLO
Acarigua
Trujillo
COJEDES
San Carlos
El Sombrero
GUARICO
Valle de la Pascua
Unare
El Tigre
ANZOATEGUI
Pariaguán
El Pao
Ciudad Guayana
Cotoa
Magangué
Mompos
El Banco
Betijoque
Valera
San Carlos del Zulia
MÉRIDA
Barinas
PORTUGUESA
Guanare
El Baúl
Calabozo
Manapire
Santa María de Ipire
Soledad
Ciudad Bolívar
Sierra Imataca
Upata
AN
Santa
La
Soledad
ZULIA
Catatumbo
NORTE DE SANTANDER
Ocaña
BOLIVAR
Ayapel
Majagual
Caucasia
Simití
Cúcuta
TACHIRA
San Carlos
La Grita
San Cristóbal
Cord. Bolivia
BARINAS
Bruzual
Libertad
San Fernando de Achaguas
Apure
VENEZUELA
Orinoco
Caicara
Mapire
Emb de Guri
Caroní
Guasipati
El Callao
Tumeremo
Ciudad Bolívar

West from Greenwich

COPYRIGHT GEORGE PHILIP & SON, LTD.

m
4000
3000
2000
1500
1000
400
200
0

0
200
2000
4000
6000
8000
m

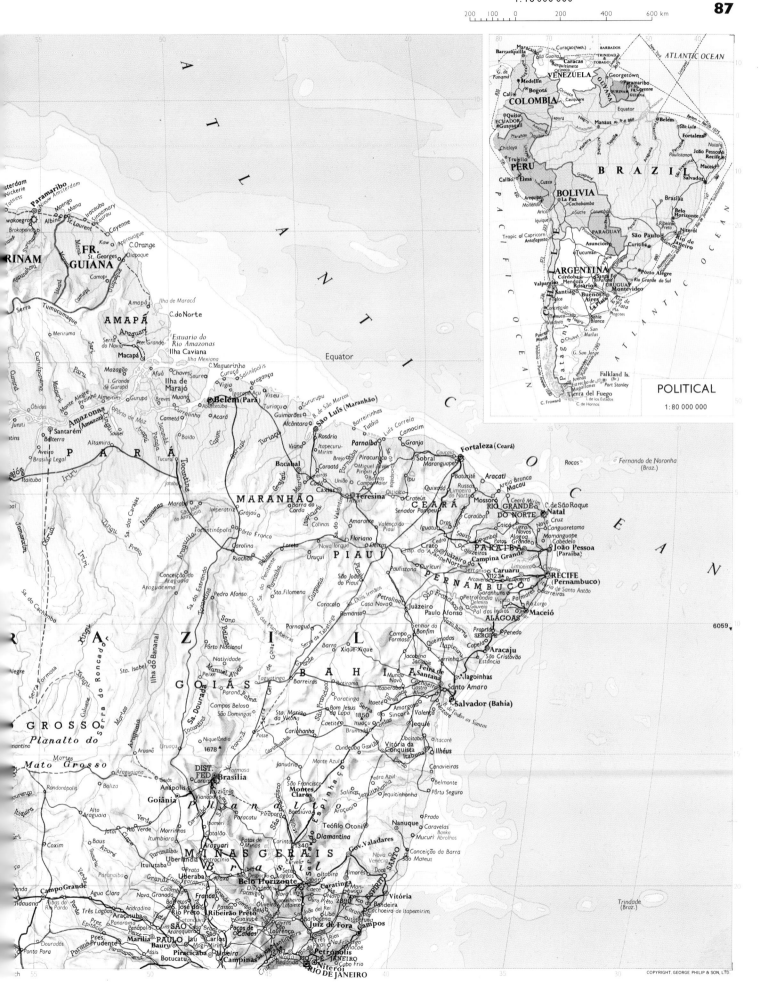

1:16 000 000

200 100 0 200 400 600 km

87

ATLANTIC OCEAN

POLITICAL
1:80 000 000

Amsterdam
Nickerie
Totness
Paramaribo
Nieuw Amsterdam
Albina
Moengo
Mana
Iracoubo
Sinnamary
Kourou
St. Laurent
Cayenne
Brokopondo
SURINAM
FR. GUIANA
St. Georges
Kaw
C.Orange
Camopi
Approuague
Oiapoque
Serra
Tumucumaque

AMAPÁ
Araguari
Amapá
C.do Norte
Macapá
Estuario do
Rio Amazonas
Ilha Caviana
Ilha Mexiana
C.Maguarinho

Amazonas (Amazon)
Santarém
Altamira
Brasília Legal
Itaituba
Tapajós

PARÁ
Belém (Pará)
Ilha de Marajó
Soure
Breves
Muaná
Cametá

Equator

MARANHÃO
São Luís (Maranhão)
Bacabal
Caxias
Teresina

CEARÁ
Fortaleza (Ceará)
Sobral
Maranguape
Aracati
Macau
RIO GRANDE DO NORTE
Natal
C.de São Roque

PIAUÍ
Floriano

PARAÍBA
João Pessoa (Paraíba)
Campina Grande

PERNAMBUCO
Caruaru
RECIFE (Pernambuco)

ALAGOAS
Maceió

Fernando de Noronha
(Braz.)

6059

SERGIPE
Aracaju

GOIÁS
Brasília
DIST. FED.
Anápolis
Goiânia

BAHIA
Barreiras
Feira de Santana
Santo Amaro
Salvador (Bahia)
Jequié
Ilhéus

Planalto do
Mato Grosso
GROSSO

Vitória da Conquista
Itabuna

Montes Claros
Diamantina

Gov. Valadares
Teófilo Otoni
Nanuque
Caravelas

MINAS GERAIS
Araguari
Uberlândia
Uberaba
Belo Horizonte
Juiz de Fora

ESPÍRITO SANTO
Vitória

Campo Grande
Três Lagoas
Araçatuba
Marília
SÃO PAULO
Bauru
Piracicaba
Campinas
Ribeirão Preto
São José do Rio Preto

Petrópolis
RIO DE JANEIRO
Niterói

COPYRIGHT. GEORGE PHILIP & SON, LTD.

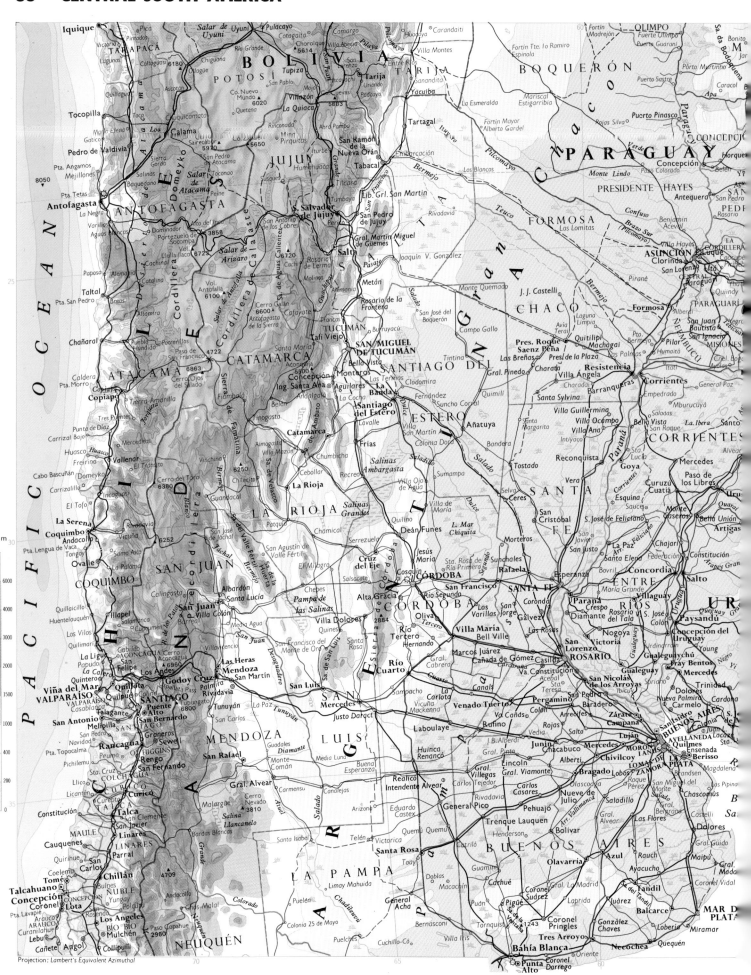

Projection: Lambert's Equivalent Azimuthal

1:8 000 000

50   0   50   100   150   200   250   300 km

ATLANTIC

OCEAN

West from Greenwich

COPYRIGHT. GEORGE. PHILIP & SON. LTD.

1:16 000 000

200 100 0   200   400   600 km

ANTARCTIC REGIONS

1 : 35 000 000

400 0 400 800 1200 km

Sub-Glacial Limits (at Sea Level) of Polar Basins

LITTLE AMERICA

TEMPERATURE Range 41.1°C

PRESSURE M.S.L.

J F M A M J J A S O N D

Little America 78 34'S. 163 56'W.

--- Territory claimed by Argentina

-·-·- Territory claimed by Chile

Antarctic Explorers

Cook 1772–75
Bellingshausen 1819–21
Weddell 1820–24
Biscoe 1831–32
D'Urville 1839–40
Byrd (U.S. Antarctic Service) 1939–41, 1946–47 (bases, Stonington I. & Little America)
····· Trans-Antarctic Route 1958

Wilkes 1839–40
Ross 1840–43
Gerlache 1898–99

Shackleton 1907–9
Scott 1910–13
Amundsen 1911–12
Mawson 1911–14
Byrd 1928–30 (by air)

--- Soviet Expedition 1959

Scott (N.Z.) Permanent Bases

Seas open all year

Extreme limits of drift-ice

Seas covered by pack-ice in Spring

Ice caps and permanent ice shelf

Progress of Exploration

—— Coasts explored between 1800 and 1850
—— Coasts explored since 1900
Byrd 1926 Highest latitudes reached by explorers with date

Projection: Zenithal Equidistant

COPYRIGHT. GEORGE PHILIP & SON LTD.

1 : 20 000 000

200   0   200   400   600   800 km

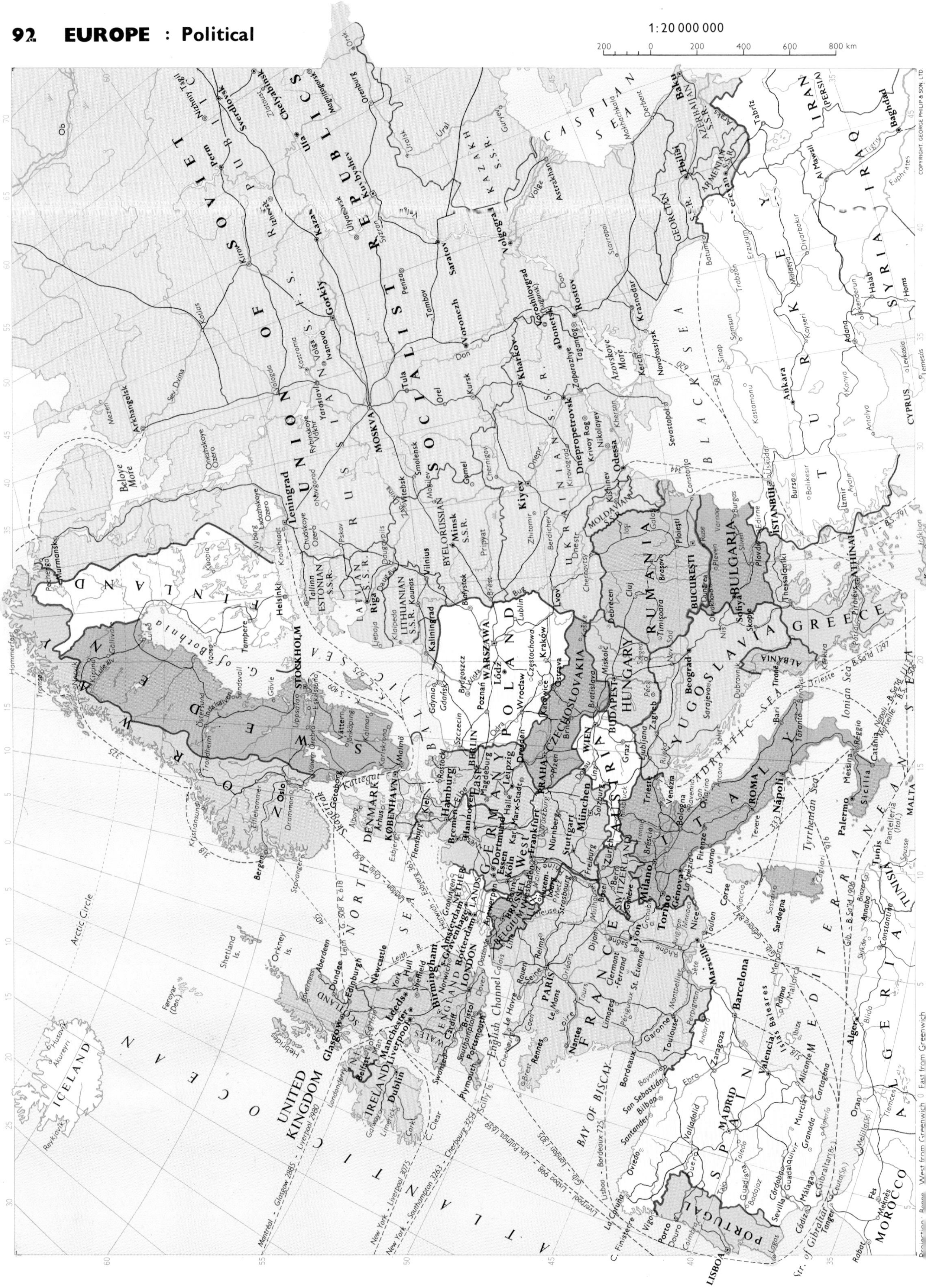

UNION OF SOVIET SOCIALIST REPUBLICS

R U S S I A N   S.F.S.R.

MOSKVA

Leningrad

Gorkiy

Kazan

Kuybyshev

Saratov

Volgograd

Rostov

Kharkov

Kiyev

Donetsk

Dnepropetrovsk

Odessa

U K R A I N I A N   S.S.R.

BYELORUSSIAN S.S.R.

Minsk

ESTONIAN S.S.R.

LATVIAN S.S.R.

Riga

LITHUANIAN S.S.R.

Tallinn

Helsinki

F I N L A N D

N O R W A Y

S W E D E N

STOCKHOLM

Oslo

DENMARK

KØBENHAVN

B A L T I C   S E A

Kaliningrad

P O L A N D

WARSZAWA

Łódź

Wrocław

Kraków

G E R M A N Y

West

BERLIN

Hamburg

Bremen

Hannover

Leipzig

Dresden

Frankfurt

München

Stuttgart

NETHERLANDS

Amsterdam

Rotterdam

BELGIUM

Brussel

LUX.

SWITZERLAND

AUSTRIA

WIEN

CZECHOSLOVAKIA

PRAHA

HUNGARY

BUDAPEST

RUMANIA

BUCUREŞTI

BULGARIA

Sofiya

YUGOSLAVIA

Beograd

Zagreb

ALBANIA

GREECE

ATHINAI

I T A L Y

ROMA

Napoli

Milano

Torino

Genova

Venezia

Firenze

Bologna

SICILIA

SARDEGNA

F R A N C E

PARIS

Lyon

Marseille

Bordeaux

Nantes

BAY OF BISCAY

S P A I N

MADRID

Barcelona

Valencia

PORTUGAL

LISBOA

MOROCCO

ALGERIA

TUNISIA

M E D I T E R R A N E A N   S E A

UNITED KINGDOM

SCOTLAND

Glasgow

Edinburgh

ENGLAND

LONDON

Birmingham

Manchester

Liverpool

Leeds

Newcastle

WALES

Cardiff

IRELAND

Dublin

Belfast

NORTH SEA

ATLANTIC OCEAN

ICELAND

Reykjavik

Arctic Circle

BLACK SEA

CASPIAN SEA

T U R K E Y

Ankara

İSTANBUL

CYPRUS

SYRIA

IRAQ

Baghdad

IRAN (PERSIA)

Tabriz

GEORGIAN S.S.R.

ARMENIAN S.S.R.

AZERBAIJAN

Baku

Tbilisi

Arkhangelsk

Murmansk

Ob

Ural

K A Z A K H

Volga

Don

English Channel

1:20 000 000

200   0   200   400   600   800 km

COPYRIGHT. GEORGE PHILIP & SON LTD

Projection: Bonne   West from Greenwich   East from Greenwich

NORWEGIAN SEA

ATLANTIC OCEAN

NORTH SEA

BALTIC SEA

CASPIAN SEA

BLACK SEA

ADRIATIC SEA

MEDITERRANEAN SEA

Aegean Sea

Ionian Sea

Tyrrhenian Sea

Ligurian Sea

Iberian Peninsula

Scandinavia

Finland

Lapland

Ural Mountains

Obshchi Syrt

Volga Uplands

Central Russian Uplands

Ukraine

Carpathians

Alps

Pyrenees

Apennines

Balkan Peninsula

Anatolia

Caucasus

Kurdistan

Armenia

m 4000 2000 1000 400 200 0 200 2000 4000 m

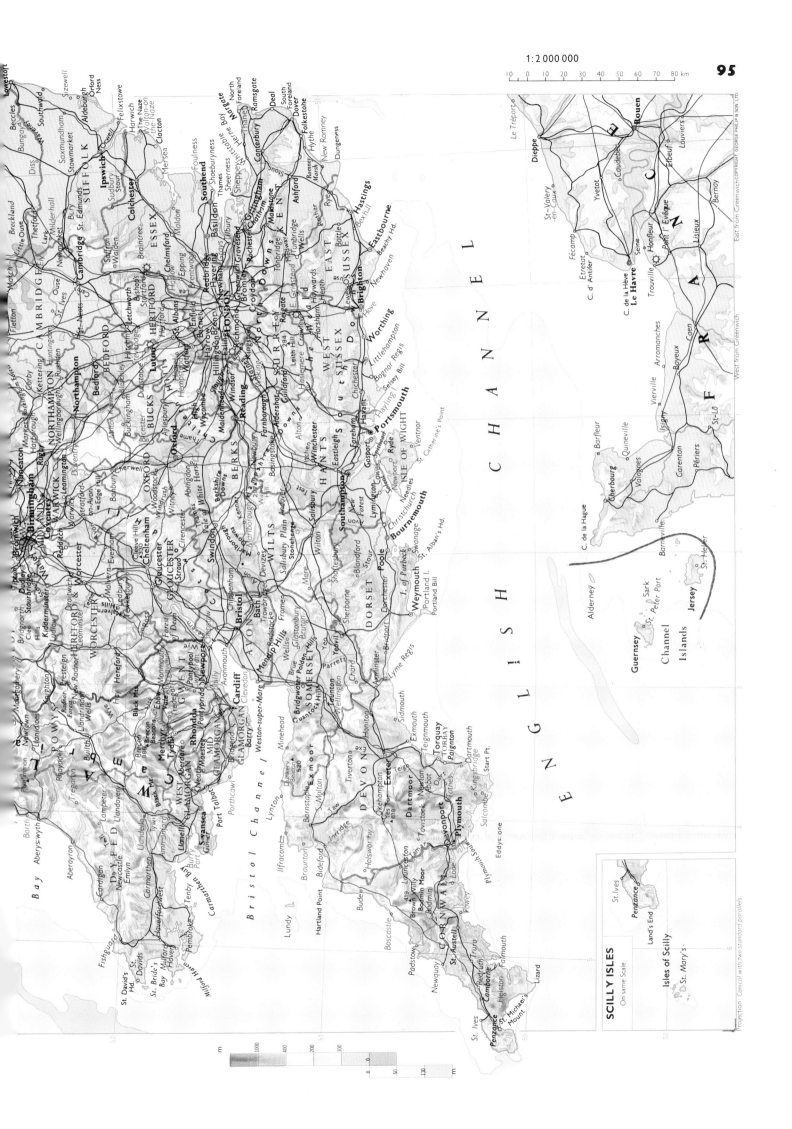

1:2 000 000

SCILLY ISLES
On same Scale

Isles of Scilly

St. Ives
Penzance
Land's End
St. Mary's

Projection: Conical with two standard parallels

East from Greenwich COPYRIGHT GEORGE PHILIP & SON LTD.

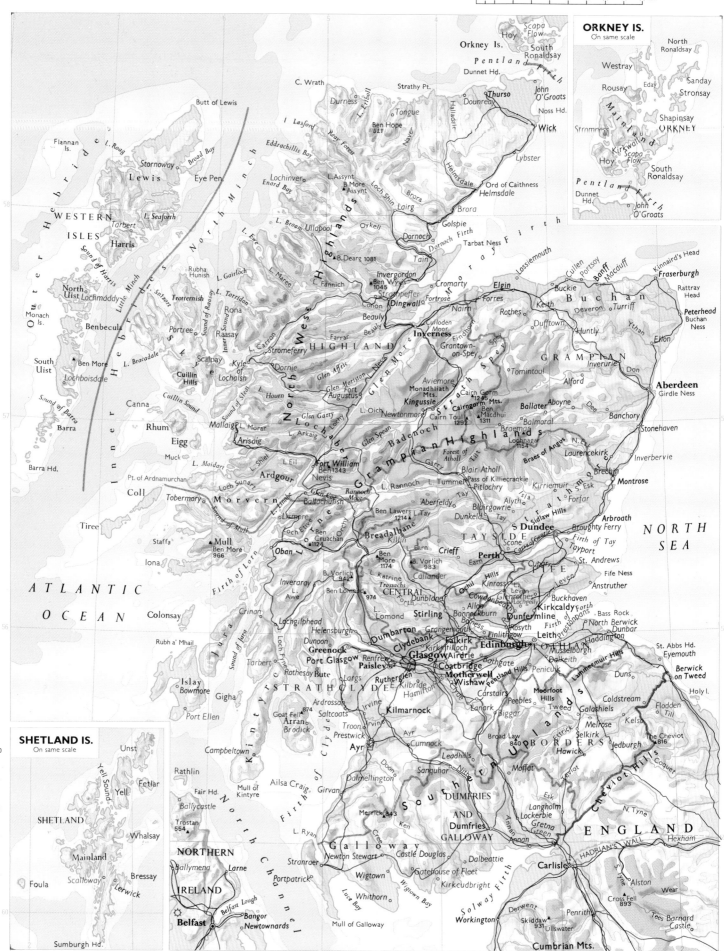

1:2 000 000

10 0 10 20 30 40 50 60 70 80 km

ORKNEY IS.
On same scale

SHETLAND IS.
On same scale

Projection: Conical with two standard parallels.

West from Greenwich

COPYRIGHT. GEORGE PHILIP & SON. LTD.

1:2 000 000

10 0 10 20 30 40 50 60 70 80 km

Towns underlined in Northern Ireland give their
names to the Districts in which they stand

The remaining Districts are:—

1	Fermanagh	5	Castlereagh
2	Moyle	6	Ards
3	Newtownabbey	7	Down
4	North Down	8	Newry & Mourne

Projection: Conical with two standard parallels.   West from Greenwich   COPYRIGHT GEORGE PHILIP & SON, LTD.

1 : 4 000 000

Projection: Conical with two standard parallels

COPYRIGHT. GEORGE PHILIP & SON. LTD.

DÉPARTEMENTS IN THE PARIS AREA

1 Ville de Paris   3 Val-de-Marne

2 Seine-St.-Denis   4 Hauts-de-Seine

Projection: *Conical with two standard parallels*

West from Greenwich   East from Greenwich

1:2 500 000

10 0 10 20 30 40 50 60 70 80 90 100 km

SWITZERLAND

LIGURIAN SEA

Golfo di Génova

CORSICA

DITERRANEAN SEA

COPYRIGHT. GEORGE PHILIP & SON. LTD.

1:5 000 000

50   0   50   100   150   200 km

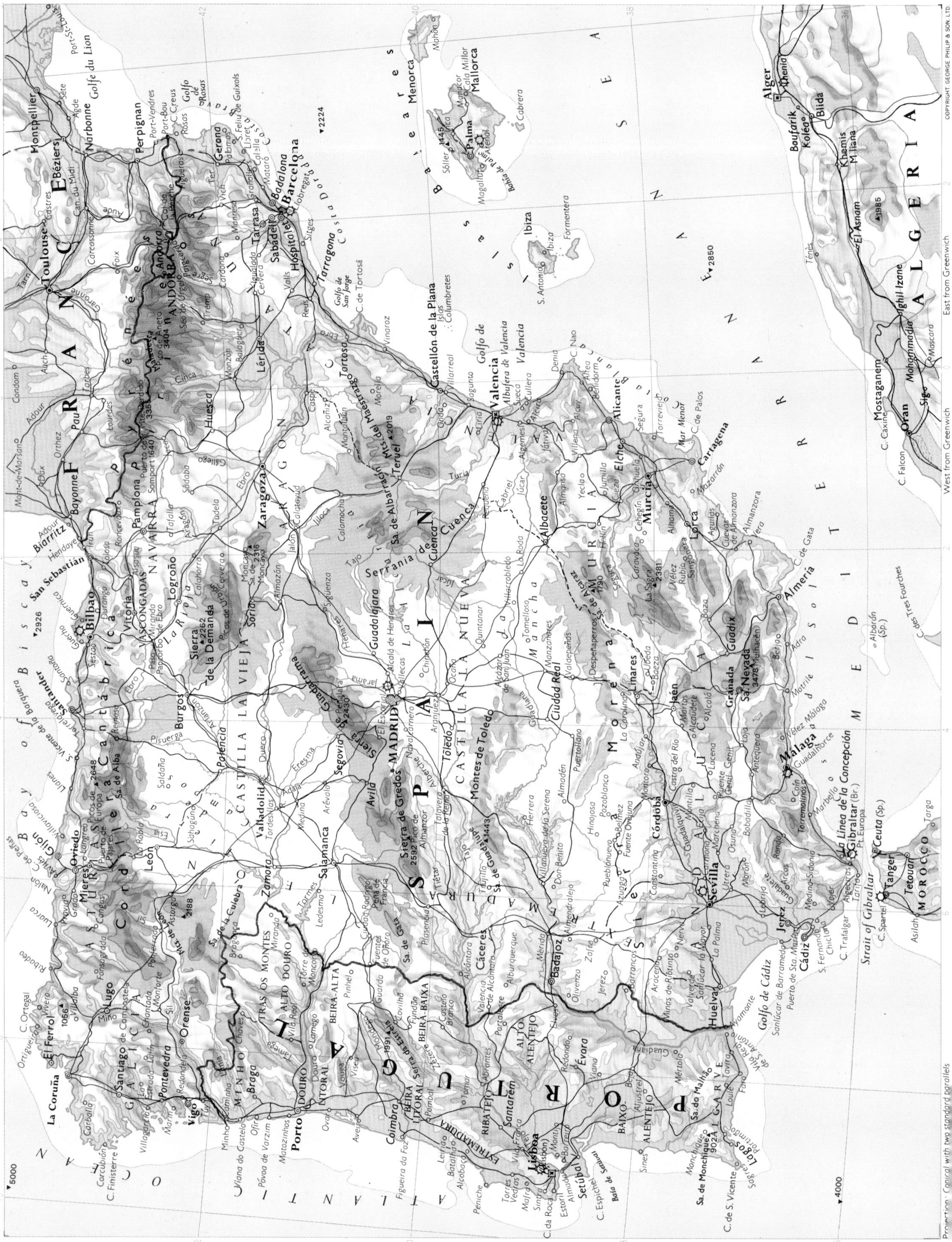

SPAIN

PORTUGAL

FRANCE

ALGERIA

MOROCCO

PYRÉNÉES

Baleares

Mallorca
Menorca
Ibiza
Formentera
Cabrera

MEDITERRANEAN   SEA

ATLANTIC   OCEAN

Bay of Biscay

Golfe du Lion

Golfo de San Jorge

Golfo de Valencia

Golfo de Cádiz

Strait of Gibraltar

Costa Brava
Costa Dorada
Costa del Sol

MADRID
Barcelona
Badalona
Sabadell
Tarrasa
Hospitalet
Sitges
Tarragona
Reus
Valls
Gerona
Perpignan
Figueras
Lérida
Huesca
Zaragoza
Pamplona
Tudela
Logroño
Vitoria
Bilbao
San Sebastián
Bayonne
Biarritz
Toulouse
Béziers
Narbonne
Montpellier
Pau
Andorra

Burgos
Palencia
Valladolid
Zamora
Salamanca
Ávila
Segovia
Soria
León
Oviedo
Gijón
Avilés
Lugo
La Coruña
Santiago de Compostela
Pontevedra
Vigo
Orense

Porto
Braga
Coimbra
Lisboa
Setúbal
Évora
Santarém
Faro
Lagos
Beja

Cáceres
Badajoz
Mérida
Sevilla
Córdoba
Jaén
Linares
Granada
Málaga
Almería
Murcia
Cartagena
Lorca
Alicante
Elche
Valencia
Castellón de la Plana
Albacete
Cuenca
Guadalajara
Toledo
Ciudad Real

Gibraltar
La Línea de la Concepción
Cádiz
Huelva
Jerez
Algeciras
Ceuta
Tánger
Tetouan

Alger
Blida
Boufarik
Koléa
Oran
Mostaganem

Sierra Nevada
Sierra Morena
Sierra de Gredos
Sierra de Guadarrama
Sierra de la Demanda
Cordillera Cantábrica
Montes de Toledo
Serranía de Cuenca
Mts. del Maestrazgo

CASTILLA LA VIEJA
CASTILLA LA NUEVA
ARAGÓN
NAVARRA
CATALUÑA
GALICIA
ASTURIAS
LEÓN
EXTREMADURA
ANDALUCÍA
MURCIA
VALENCIA

Projection : Conical with two standard parallels

m   3000   2000   1500   1000   400   200   0

COPYRIGHT GEORGE PHILIP & SON LTD.

East from Greenwich

West from Greenwich

1:2 000 000

10 0 10 20 30 40 50 60 70 80 km

NORTH SEA

WESTFRIESCHE EILANDEN

Schiermonnikoog · Ostfriesland · Aurich · Jade-busen · Zetel · Varel

Terschelling · Ameland · Dokkum · Zoutkamp · Appingedam · Delfzijl · Emden · Wiesmoor · Aschendorf · Rastede

Vlieland · Leeuwarden · Franeker · Buitenpost · Zuidhorn · Groningen · Weener · Westerstede · Apen · Oldenburg

Texel · Harlingen · Bolsward · Sneek · Drachten · Roden · Veendam · Winschoten · Papenburg · Bad Zwischenahn · Hunte

Den Helder · Den Oever · Workum · Heerenveen · Wolvega · Norg · Stadskanaal · Rhede · Ascendorf · Friesaythe

FRIESLAND · DRENTHE · Assen · Borger · Emmen · Haren · Lathen · Sögel · Cloppenburg · NIEDER

Noordoost Polder · Urk · Emmeloord · Vollenhove · Hoogeveen · Beilen · Coevorden · Meppen · Haselünne · Löningen · SACHSEN · Vechta · Lohne

Alkmaar · Heiloo · Enkhuizen · Hoorn · Kampen · Zwolle · Ommen · Hardenberg · Emlichheim · Lingen · Fürstenau · Bersenbrück · Steinfeld · Damme · Bramsche

Beverwijk · IJmuiden · Velsen · Zaandam · AMSTERDAM · Harderwijk · Elburg · Wezep · OVERIJSSEL · Almelo · Nordhorn · Rheine · Ibbenbüren · Westerkappeln

Haarlem · Heemstede · Hillegom · Bussum · Hilversum · Laren · Baarn · Amersfoort · Apeldoorn · Deventer · Rijssen · Hengelo · Enschede · Gronau · Ochtrup · Emsdetten · Lengerich · Osnabrück

s'GRAVENHAGE (The Hague) · Leiden · Voorburg · Rijswijk · UTRECHT · Zeist · Barneveld · Ede · GELDERLAND · Zutphen · Lochem · Ahaus · Burgsteinfurt · Borghorst · Greven · Münster

Delft · Gouda · Utrecht · IJsselstein · Arnhem · Doesburg · Doetinchem · Winterswijk · Aalten · Stadtlohn · Coesfeld · Warendorf

Hoek van Holland · ROTTERDAM · Wageningen · Tiel · Nijmegen · Kleve · Rees · Bocholt · Borken · Dülmen · Lüdinghausen · Ahlen · Beckum

Vlaardingen · Schiedam · Dordrecht · 's-Hertogenbosch · Oss · Kleve · Rhein · Goch · Kevelaer · Wesel · Dorsten · Marl · Lippe · Datteln · Werne · Hamm

ZUID · Sliedrecht · Gorinchem · Tilburg · Breda · Venray · Geldern · Kamp · Gelsenkirchen · Bottrop · Recklinghausen · Herne · DORTMUND · Bochum · Soest

Goeree · Schouwen · Noord Beveland · Zierikzee · Roosendaal · Oosterhout · Helmond · Venlo · Kempen · Oberhausen · Mülheim · ESSEN · Duisburg · Witten · Iserlohn · Neheim

Walcheren · Middelburg · Goes · Bergen-op-Zoom · Eindhoven · Geldrop · Weert · Roermond · Süchteln · Dülken · Krefeld · Velbert · Gevelsberg · Hagen · Hohenlimburg

Vlissingen (Flushing) · Westerschelde · Terneuzen · Valkenswaard · Mönchen-Gladbach · Viersen · Neuss · DÜSSELDORF · Solingen · Remscheid · Lüdenscheid · Elspe

Oostende (Ostend) · Knokke · Brugge (Bruges) · Eeklo · ANTWERPEN · Turnhout · Maaseik · Erkelenz · Grevenbroich · Rheydt · Opladen · Bergisch Gladbach · Gummersbach · Olpe

Nieuwpoort · Torhout · St-Niklaas · Mechelen · Geel · Leopoldsburg · Genk · Sittard · Geilenkirchen · Jülich · Bedburg · Leverkusen · KÖLN (Cologne) · Overath · Waldbröl · Siegen

Diksmuide · Roeselare · Ghent (Gand) · Boom · Willebroek · Diest · Hasselt · Maastricht · Brunssum · Alsdorf · Düren · Brühl · Siegburg · Morsbach · Eiserfeld

Ieper · Menen · Kortrijk · Aalst · Aarschot · Leuven · Tongeren · Kerkrade · Herzogenrath · Aachen · Eschweiler · Stolberg · Bonn · Bad Godesberg · Königswinter · Hachenburg

Tourcoing · Mouscron · Ronse · BRUSSEL (Bruxelles) · Tienen · St-Troud · Visé · Herstal · Liège · Eupen · Kornelimünster · Euskirchen · Zülpich · Bad Münstereifel · Remagen · Westerwald

Lille · Roubaix · Tournai · Ath · Halle · Wavre · Landen · Jemeppe · Seraing · Verviers · Spa · Malmedy · Schleiden · Gerolstein · Ahrweiler · Neuwied

BELGIUM · Leuze · Nivelles · Gembloux · Namur · Huy · Comblain · Hautes Fagnes · Nürburg · Mayen · Koblenz · Bendorf

Haubourdin · Seclin · HAINAUT · Mons · La Louvière · Charleroi · Fleurus · Theux · Stavelot · St-Vith · Adenau · Andernach

Bully-les-Mines · Lens · Douai · Binche · Jumet · Gilly · Fosse · Dinant · Stoumont · Prüm · Bad Neuenahr · Remagen

Hénin-Beaumont · Valenciennes · Denain · Maubeuge · Thuin · Florennes · Rochefort · Houffalize · Daun · Cochem · Traben-Trarbach · Bingen

Arras · PAS-DE-CALAIS · Cambrai · Solesmes · Avesnes · Philippeville · Cerfontaine · La Roche · Clervaux · Waxweiler · Kyllburg · Wittlich · Bernkastel · Bad Kreuznach

Bapaume · Le Cateau · Fourmies · Mariembourg · Chimay · Givet · St-Hubert · LUXEMBOURG · Bitburg · Traben · Idar-Oberstein

SOMME · Péronne · St-Quentin · Guise · Hirson · Rocroi · Revin · Neufchâteau · Libramont · Diekirch · Ettelbrück · Echternach · Trier · Saarburg · Kirchheim-bolanden

PICARDIE · Ribemont · Vervins · Charleville-Mézières · Sedan · Bouillon · Florenville · LUXEMBOURG · Greven · macher · Konz · Hermeskeil · Lauterecken · Alzey

Noyon · Laon · Craonne · Rethel · Le Chesne · Vouziers · Mouzon · Carignan · Virton · Arlon · Luxembourg · Saarbrücken · Merzig · Idar-Oberstein

Compiègne · Soissons · Aisne · ARDENNES · Attigny · Étain · Longwy · Villerupt · Esch · Differdange · Sierck · Dillingen · Homburg · Zweibrücken · Neustadt

Crépy-en-Valois · Villers-Cotterêts · Reims · Vesle · Plaine de CHAMPAGNE · Ste-Menehould · Verdun · Briey · Thionville · MEURTHE ET · Saarlouis · St-Ingbert · Pirmasens · Landau

Château-Thierry · Épernay · Marne · Suippes · Montigny-lès-Metz · Metz · St-Avold · Sarreguemines · MOSELLE · Forbach · Saarbrücken · Bad Bergzabern

Projection: Conical with two standard parallels · East from Greenwich · COPYRIGHT GEORGE PHILIP & SON LTD.

m · 400 · 200 · 0

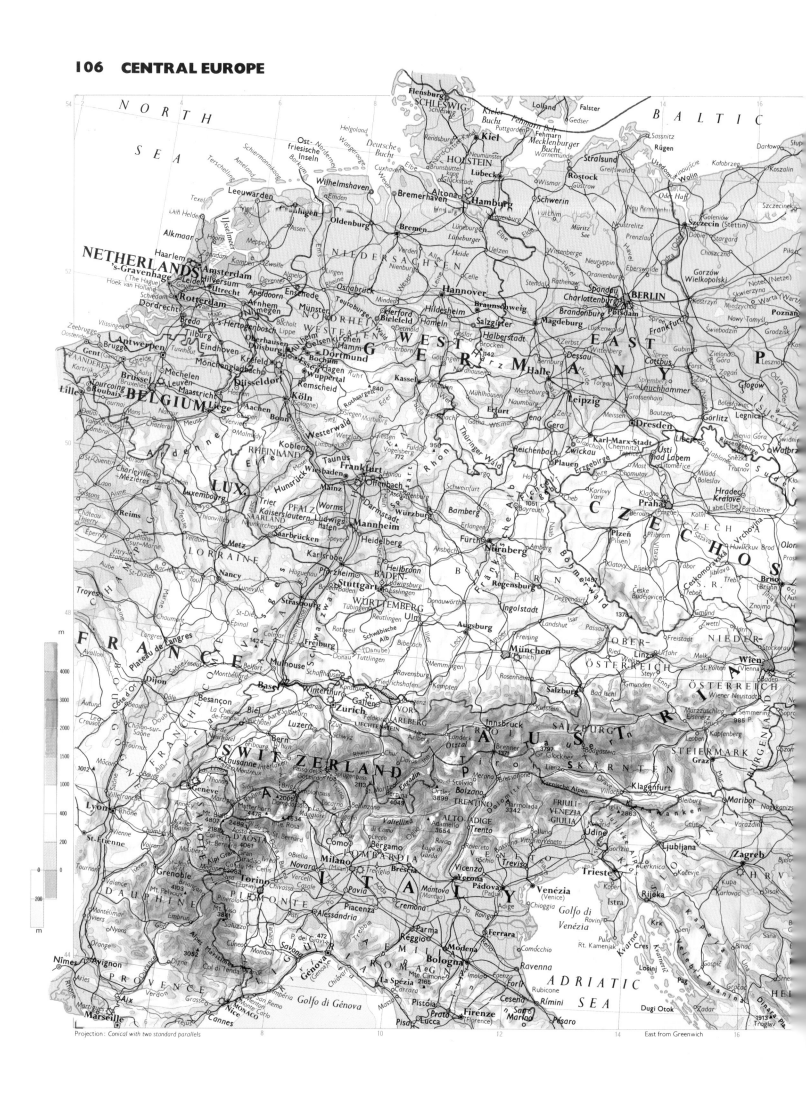

Projection : Conical with two standard parallels

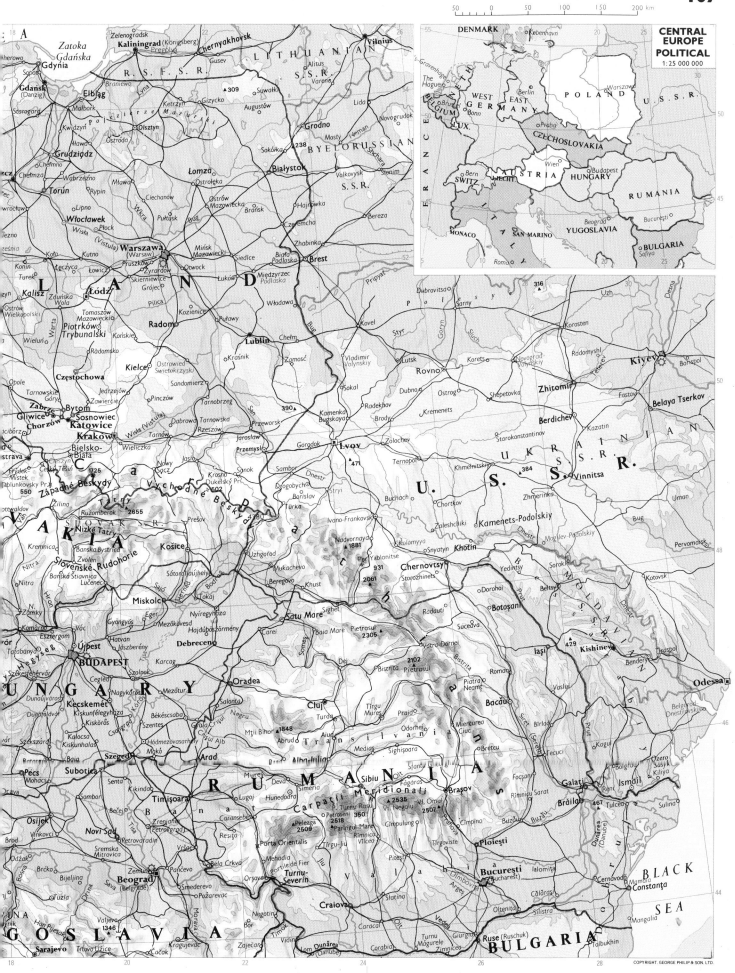

1 : 5 000 000

50   0   50   100   150   200 km

CENTRAL EUROPE POLITICAL
1 : 25 000 000

DENMARK

København

POLAND

Warszawa

U.S.S.R.

The Hague

's-Gravenhage

WEST GERMANY

EAST

Berlin

Bonn

Praha

NETH

BELGIUM

LUX

CZECHOSLOVAKIA

FRANCE

Bern

SWITZ.

LIECHT.

AUSTRIA

Wien

HUNGARY

Budapest

RUMANIA

București

ITALY

SAN MARINO

Beograd

YUGOSLAVIA

MONACO

Roma

BULGARIA

Sofiya

A

Zatoka Gdańska

Zelenograds k

Kaliningrad (Königsberg)

Pregolya

Chernyakhovsk

Gusev

Vilnius

LITHUANIAN

S.S.R.

Alitus

Varena

R.S.F.S.R.

Gdynia

Sopot

Braniewo

Lyna

Suwałki

Lida

Gdańsk (Danzig)

Elbląg

Kętrzyn

Gizycko

Augustów

Malbork

Olsztyn

Grodno

Niemen

Mosty

Szczara

BYELORUSSIAN

Grudziądz

Iława

Ostróda

238

Sokółka

Białystok

Volkovysk

Slonim

Bereza

S.S.R.

Toruń

Chełmno

Wąbrzeźno

Rypin

Mława

Ciechanów

Ostrołęka

Ostrów Mazowiecka

Brańsk

Hajnówka

Lipno

Pułtusk

Bug

Czeremcha

Włocławek

Wisła

Płock

Warszawa (Warsaw)

Mińsk Mazowiecki

Siedlce

Biała Podlaska

Brest

Zhabinka

Pripyat

Konin

Kutno

Łowicz

Pruszków

Żyrardów

Otwock

Łuków

Międzyrzec Podlaski

Kovel

Turek

Skierniewice

Grójec

Pilica

Kozienice

Puławy

Włodawa

L   A   N   D

Łódź

Radom

Chełm

Lublin

Vladimir Volynskiy

Kielce

Krasnik

Zamość

Lutsk

Rovno

316

Sarny

Dubrovitsa

Polesy

Styr

Goryn

Korosten

Uzh

Desna

Kiyev

Borispol

Kalisz

Zduńska Wola

Tomaszów Mazowiecki

Piotrków Trybunalski

Radomsko

Ostrowiec Świętokrzyski

Sandomierz

Sokal

Radekhov

Ostróg

Shepetovka

Zhitomir

Fastov

Belaya Tserkov

Wieluń

Częstochowa

Tarnobrzeg

390

Kamenka Bugskaya

Brody

Kremenets

Berdichev

Kazatin

Opole

Tarnowskie Góry

Pinczów

Przeworsk

Jarosław

Gorodok

Lvov

Zolochev

Ternopol

Starokonstantinov

Zabrze

Bytom

Zawiercie

Dąbrowa Tarnowska

Rzeszów

Przemyśl

471

Khmelnitskiy

384

Vinnitsa

Gliwice

Sosnowiec

Katowice

Wisła (Vistula)

Tarnów

Jasło

Sanok

Sambor

Dnestr

Drogobych

Borislav

Buchach

Chortkov

Zhmerinka

U   K   R   A   I   N   I   A   N

Chorzów

Kraków

Wieliczka

Nowy Sącz

Krosno

Dukelský Pr.

Stryj

Zaleshchiki

Kamenets-Podolskiy

Bug

Uman

Ostrava

Bielsko-Biała

1725

Vychodné Beskyda

502

780

Ivano-Frankovsk

Mogilev-Podolskiy

U.   S.   S.   R.

Pervomalsk

Frýdek-Místek

Jablunkovský Prŭ.

550

Západné Beskydy

Nadvornaya

1881

Kolomyya

Snyatyn

Khotin

Dnestr

Soroki

Kotovsk

Žilina

Ružomberok

2655

Prešov

Uzhgorod

Per. Yablonitse

931

Chernovtsy

Storozhinets

Yedintsy

Beltsy

B

Kremnica

Nízké Tatry

Košice

Mukachevo

2061

E

Dorohoi

Rîbnitsa

Slovenské Rudohorie

Banská Bystrica

Beregovo

Khust

S

Botoșani

M   O   L   D   A   V   I   A   N

Tiraspol

Nitra

Zvolen

Sátoraljaújhely

Bodrog

Sighet

Radauti

Prut

Nitra

Banská Štiavnica

Lučenec

Sajó

Tokaj

Satu Mare

Suceava

Iași

429

Kishinev

Bendery

Miskolc

Hernad

Carei

Baia Mare

Pietrosul

2305

Vatra-Dornei

Roman

Odessa

N. Zámky

Gyöngyös

Eger

Mezőkövesd

Nyíregyháza

Hajdúböszörmény

Someş

Dej

Bistrita

2102

Pietrosul

Bistrița

Vaslui

Belgorod Dnestrovskiy

Komárno

Vác

Hatvan

Jászberény

Debrecen

Bistrița

Roman

Piatra Neamț

Bîrlad

Győr

Esztergom

Újpest

Karcag

Oradea

Cluj

Tîrgu Mureş

Praid

Bacău

Tecuci

Tatabánya

BUDAPEST

Szolnok

Salonta

Turda

Odorhei

Miercurea Ciuc

Kagul

Székesfehérvár

Cegléd

Nagykőrös

Mezőtúr

Crişul Negru

Brețcu

Reni

Dunaújváros

Kecskemét

Kiskunfélegyháza

Crişul Alb

1848

Mții Bihor

Abrud

Aiud

Sighișoara

Focșani

Galați

Ismail

Dunaföldvár

Kiskőrös

Békéscsaba

Szentes

Gyula

T   r   a   n   s   i   l   v   a   n   i   a

Medias

467

Tulcea

Sulina

Szekszárd

Kalocsa

Kiskunhalas

Hódmezővásárhely

Makó

Szeged

Arad

Mureş

Deva

Simeria

Sibiu

Sighișoara

Fágáraş

Brașov

Rîmnicu Sărat

Brăila

Dunărea (Danube)

Pécs

Mohács

Subotica

Senta

Kikinda

R   U   M   A   N   I   A

Vt. Negoiu

Vf. Omul

2507

Cîmpina

Buzău

Sombor

Bačka

Tisza

Timișoara

Lugoj

Hunedoara

Carpaţii Meridionali

2535

P. Turnu Roşu

2543

Cîmpulung

Prahova

Ploiești

Osijek

Novi Sad

Zrenjanin (Petrograd)

Caransebeș

Reșița

Petroșani

350

Paring Mare

Rîmnicu Vîlcea

Tîrgoviște

Bru

BLACK

Brod

Sremska Mitrovica

Petrovaradin

Vršac

2518

Peleaga

2509

Porta Orientalis

Tîrgu-Jiu

V   l   a   h   i   a

Dîmbovita

București (Bucharest)

Cernavodă

Constanța

Brčko

Bijeljina

Bela Crkva

Mehadia

Argeş

Ialomița

Bosna

Drina

Zemun

Pančevo

Orșova

Porțile de Fier

Turnu-Severin

Ozero Sasyk Kiliya

Mangalia

UNA

Tuzla

Beograd (Belgrade)

Smederevo

Požarevac

Iiu

Olt

Pitești

Slatina

Olteniţa

Silistra

Han Pijesak

Sava

Negotin

Craiova

Vedea

Mamaia

SEA

1346

Morava

Timok

Caracal

Turnu Măgurele

Giurgiu

Ruse (Ruschuk)

Talbuhin

G   O   S   L   A   V   I   A

Sarajevo

Titovo Užice

Čačak

Kragujevac

Zaječar

Vidin

Lom

Dunărea (Danube)

Corabia

Zimnicea

BULGARIA

1 : 5 000 000

50   0   50   100   150   200 km

East from Greenwich

COPYRIGHT. GEORGE PHILIP & SON. LTD.

ICELAND
on the same scale
as general map

NORWEGIAN SEA

1:5 000 000

50   100   150   200 km

III

FINLAND

Tampere Lahti Heinola Kotka Lovisa (Lovisa) Kouvola Kymi
Hämeenlinna HÄME Riihimäki Porvoo HELSINKI (Helsingfors)
Rauma Pori SATAKUNTA TURUN JA PORIN Turku (Åbo) Hangö (Hanko)
Uusikaupunki Naantali Ekenäs (Tammisaari)

G. OF FINLAND

ESTONIAN S.S.R.
Tallinn Rakvere Viljandi Valga Pärnu Haapsalu Paldiski
Hiiumaa (Dagö) Saaremaa (Ösel) Kingisepp Kärdla

LATVIA S.S.R.
Riga Valmiera Cēsis Rīgas Jūras Līcis (Gulf of Riga)
Ventspils Kuldīga Tukums Jelgava Bauska Liepāja Tukums

LITHUANIAN S.S.R.
Šiauliai Panevėžys Ukmergė Kaunas Vilnius Telšiai
Klaipėda Taurogė Nemunas Gusev Grodno

R.S.F.S.R.
Sovetsk Kaliningrad Chernyakhovsk

POLAND
Gdynia Gdańsk Zatoka Gdańska Elbląg Malbork Grudziądz
Toruń Bydgoszcz Białystok Łomża Ostrołęka Szczecin
Koszalin Kołobrzeg Darłowo Słupsk

Åland (Ahvenanmaa)
Mariehamn (Maarianhamina)

BALTIC SEA

GULF

Gotska Sandön Fårö **Gotland** Visby Slite Rōnoe Hemse
Burgsvik Hōburgen

SWEDEN

STOCKHOLM Uppsala Gävle Sandviken Söderhamn Hudiksvall
Örebro Västerås Eskilstuna Södertälje Nyköping Oxelösund
Västervik Oskarshamn Kalmar Öland Borgholm
Norrköping Linköping Motala Mjölby Vadstena Tranås
Nässjö Huskvarna Jönköping Vetlanda Växjö Ljungby
Karlskrona Karlshamn **BLEKINGE** Kristianstad
Halmstad Varberg Falkenberg **HALLAND**
GÖTEBORG Borås Alingsås Trollhättan Vänersborg
Uddevalla Lysekil Marstrand Skövde Mariestad Lidköping
Falun Borlänge Hedemora Avesta Fagersta Ludvika Mora
Siljan Orsa **KOPPARBERG** **VÄRMLAND** Karlstad Kristinehamn
Filipstad Arvika Kongsvinger **VÄSTMANLAND** **UPPSALA**

NORWAY
OSLO Drammen Hamar Lillehammer Gjøvik Kongsberg
Drøbak Moss Fredrikstad Sarpsborg Halden Skien Porsgrunn
Larvik Tønsberg Sandefjord Horten Notodden
TELEMARK **BUSKERUD** **AUST-AGDER** **VEST-AGDER** **ROGALAND**
Arendal Grimstad Lillesand Kristiansand Mandal Farsund
Flekkefjord Egersund (Eigersund) Stavanger Sandnes Haugesund
Bergen Hardangerfjorden **HORDALAND** **SOGN OG FJORDANE**

DENMARK
Frederikshavn Hjørring Thisted Aalborg Viborg Randers
Århus Horsens Vejle Fredericia Kolding Esbjerg Ribe
Varde Herning Silkeborg Skive Holstebro Ringkøbing
Odense **Fyn** Svendborg Nyborg Korsør Slagelse Roskilde
København (Copenhagen) Helsingør Hillerød **Sjælland** Køge
Næstved Vordingborg Nykøbing Lolland Falster Møn
Limfjorden Kattegat Store Bælt The Sound

GERMANY (EAST)
Rostock Schwerin Wismar Stralsund Greifswald Rügen Usedom
Warnemünde

GERMANY (WEST)
Hamburg Lübeck Kiel Flensburg Schleswig Neumünster
Bremen Bremerhaven Wilhelmshaven Oldenburg Emden
Bucht Weser Elbe Cuxhaven Helgoland

NETHERLANDS
Groningen Assen

Kattegat Skagerrak Skagen Læsø Anholt

m 2000 1500 1000 400 200 0 200 m

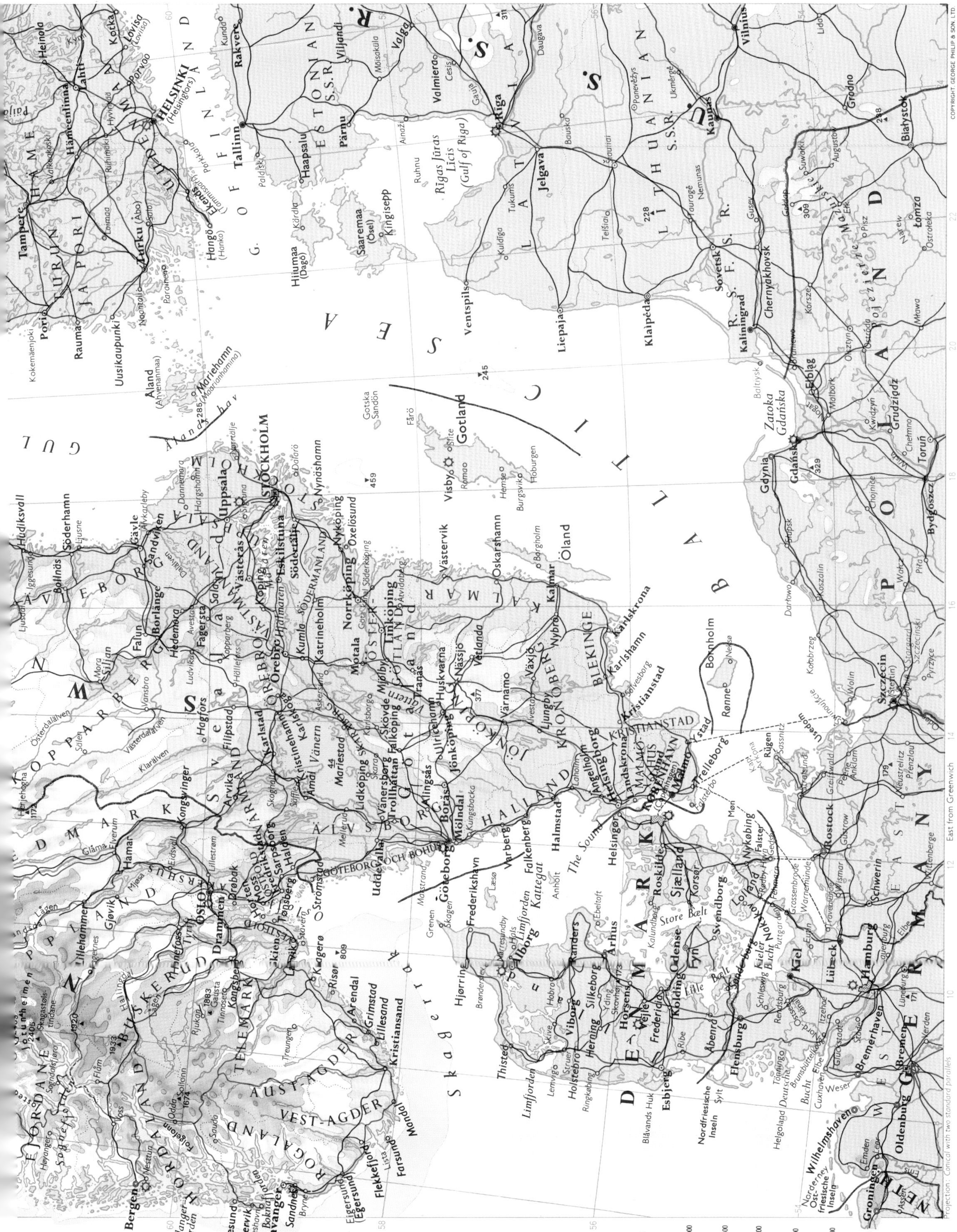

1:40 000 000

400   400   800   1200   1600 km

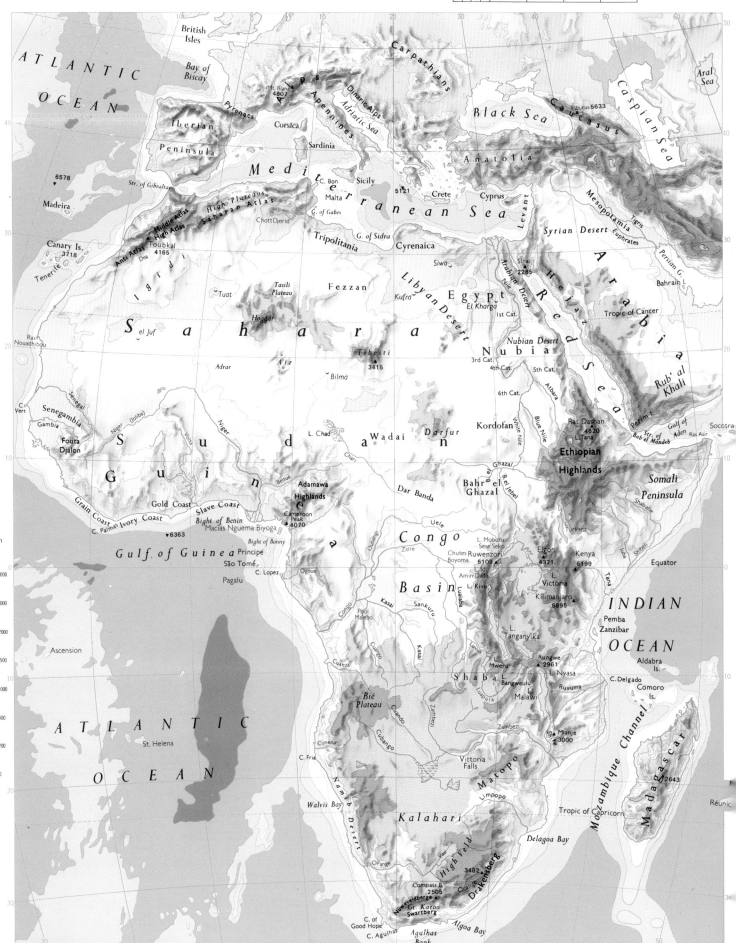

ATLANTIC OCEAN

British Isles

Bay of Biscay

Carpathians

Alps

Mt. Blanc 4807

Pyrenees

Apennines

Dinaric Alps

Adriatic Sea

Black Sea

Caucasus

Elbruz 5633

Aral Sea

Caspian Sea

Iberian Peninsula

Corsica

Sardinia

Anatolia

Mediterranean Sea

6578

Madeira

C. Bon

Sicily

Malta

5121

Crete

Cyprus

Levant

Mesopotamia

Tigris

Euphrates

Persian G.

Canary Is. 3718

Tenerife

Middle Atlas

High Atlas

Anti Atlas

Toubkal

Dra

4165

High Plateaus

Saharan Atlas

Chott Djerid

G. of Gabes

Tripolitania

G. of Sidra

Cyrenaica

Siwa

Libyan Desert

Egypt

Arabian Desert

Sinai 2285

Nile

Syrian Desert

Arabia

Hejaz

Red Sea

Bahrain

Tropic of Cancer

Ras Nouadhibou

Igidi

S. el Juf

Sahara

Tuat

Tasili Plateau

Fezzan

Hoggar

Kufra

El Kharga

1st Cat.

Nubian Desert

3rd Cat.

4th Cat.

5th Cat.

Rub' al Khali

Perim I.

Gulf of Aden

Ras Asir

Socotra

Adrar

Air

Tibesti 3415

Bilma

Wadai

Darfur

Kordofan

White Nile

Blue Nile

Attbara

6th Cat.

Ras Dashan 4620

L. Tana

Str. of Bab el Mandeb

C. Vert

Senegal

Senegambia

Gambia

Fouta Djalon

Niger (Joliba)

Niger

Volta

S u d a n

L. Chad

Chari

Benue

Dar Banda

Bahr el Ghazal

Bahr el Jebel

Ethiopian Highlands

Somali Peninsula

Shabelle

S u i n

G

Grain Coast

C. Palmas Ivory Coast

Gold Coast

Slave Coast

Bight of Benin

Macias Nguema Biyoga

Adamawa Highlands

Cameroon Peak 4070

Oubangi

Uele

Zaïre

Congo

Basin

L. Mobutu Sese Seko

Chutes Boyoma

Ruwenzori 5109

L. Idi Amin Dada

Elgon 4321

Kenya 5199

Equator

6363

Bight of Bonny

Principe

São Tomé

C. Lopez

Ogoue

Gulf of Guinea

Pagalu

Ascension

Congo

Kasai

Sankuru

Kasai

Lualaba

L. Kivu

L. Victoria

Kilimanjaro 5895

Pemba

Zanzibar

INDIAN OCEAN

Aldabra Is.

Comoro Is.

Cuanza

Pool Malebo

L. Tanganyika

Lavua

L. Mweru

Rungwe 2961

L. Bangweulu

Lupula

L. Nyasa

Ruvuma

C. Delgado

ATLANTIC

OCEAN

St. Helena

Bié Plateau

Cuango

Cubango

Cunene

C. Fria

Cuando

Zambezi

Shaba

Malawi

Mlanje 3000

Madagascar

2643

Réunic

Walvis Bay

Namib Desert

Kalahari

Cubango

Victoria Falls

Zambezi

Matopo

Limpopo

Delagoa Bay

Mozambique Channel

Tropic of Capricorn

Orange

Vaal

High Veld

3482

Drakensberg

Orange

Compass B. 2505

Nuweveldberge

Gt. Karroo

Swartberg

Algoa Bay

C. of Good Hope

C. Agulhas

Agulhas Bank

m
4000
3000
2000
1500
1000
400
200
0
0
200
1000
2000
4000
6000
m

1 : 40 000 000

400   0   400   800   1200   1600 km

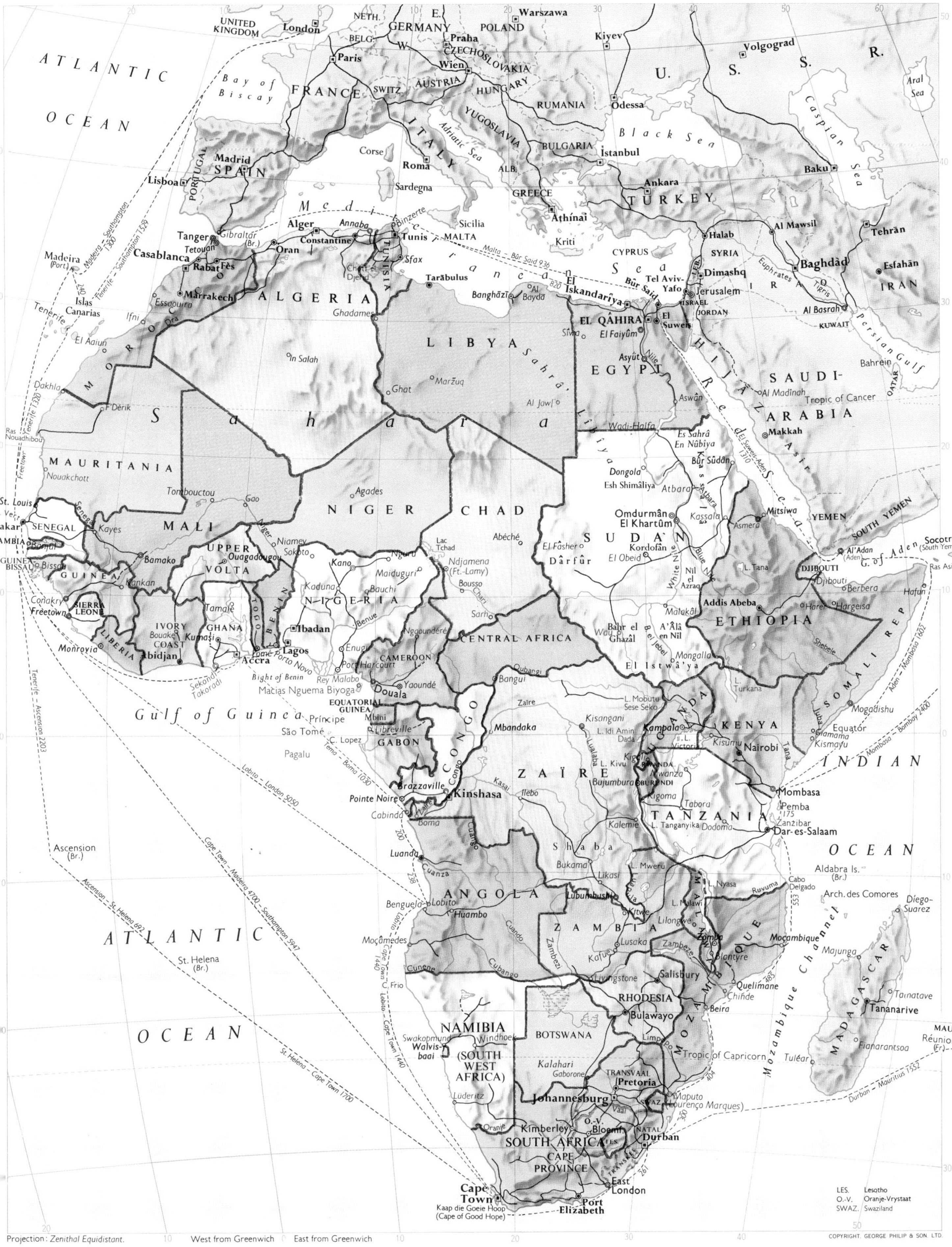

ATLANTIC OCEAN

UNITED KINGDOM
London
NETH.
GERMANY
BELG.
Paris
FRANCE
SWITZ.
AUSTRIA
Wien
HUNGARY
E.
Praha
CZECHOSLOVAKIA
POLAND
Warszawa
Kiyev
Volgograd
U. S. S. R.
RUMANIA
Odessa
BULGARIA
YUGOSLAVIA
ALB.
GREECE
Athínai
Istanbul
Ankara
TURKEY
Aral Sea
Caspian Sea
Baku
Black Sea
Kríti
CYPRUS
SYRIA
Halab
Al Mawsil
Tehrãn
Dimashq
Baghdãd
Esfahãn
IRAN
Tel Aviv-Yafo
Jerusalem
ISRAEL
JORDAN
Al Basrah
KUWAIT
Persian Gulf
Bahrein
QATAR
SAUDI-ARABIA
Al Madînah
Makkah

Bay of Biscay
Madrid
SPAIN
Lisboa
PORTUGAL
Corse
Roma
ITALY
Sardegna
Adriatic Sea
Sicilia
MALTA
Tunis
Bizerte
Annaba
Constantine
Algeri
Oran
TUNISIA
Tarãbulus
Mediterranean Sea
El Iskandarîya
Bûr Saîd
El Suweis
EL QÃHIRA
El Faiyûm
Siwa
Banghãzî
Al Bayda
LIBYA

Tanger
Tetouan
Casablanca
Rabat Fès
MOROCCO
Marrakech
Essaouira
Ifni
El Aiun
Islas Canarias
Madeira (Port.)
Dakhla
F'Dérik
Ras Nouadhibou
Nouakchott
MAURITANIA
Sahara
ALGERIA
In Salah
Ghadames
Ghat
Marzûq
Al Jawf
EGYPT
Asyût
Aswân
Tropic of Cancer
Wadi-Halfa
Es Sahrã En Nûbíya
Bûr Sûdan
Dongola
Esh Shimãlíya
Atbara
Kassala
Omdurmãn
El Khartûm
SUDAN
Kordofãn
El Obeid
Darfûr
El Fãsher
Abéché
Ndjamena (Ft.-Lamy)
Bousso
CHAD
NIGER
Agades
Gao
Tombouctou
MALI
Kayes
SENEGAL
Dakar
St. Louis
C. Vert
GAMBIA
Banjul
GUINEA BISSAU
Bissau
GUINEA
Conakry
Freetown
SIERRA LEONE
LIBERIA
Monrovia
IVORY COAST
Bouaké
Abidjan
Bamako
Kankan
Sokoto
Niamey
UPPER VOLTA
Ouagadougou
Kano
Kaduna
Maiduguri
N I G E R I A
Bauchi
Ibadan
Lagos
Porto Novo
BENIN
TOGO
GHANA
Kumasi
Accra
Tamale
Sekondi Takoradi
Lac Tchad
Benue
Enugu
Port Harcourt
CAMEROON
Yaoundé
Douala
Ngaoundéré
Sarh
CENTRAL AFRICA
Bangui
Bahr el Ghazal
Wau
Malakãl
A'Alã en Nîl
El Istwã'iya
Mongalla
Ethiopia
Addis Abeba
Harer
Hargeisa
Berbera
Hafun
Ras Asir
Al'Adan
Socotra (South Yemen)
SOUTH YEMEN
YEMEN
Asmera
Mitsiwa
DJIBOUTI
Djibouti
L. Tana
Shebele
L. Turkana
Mongalla
SOMALI REP.
Mogadishu
Kismayu
Equator
KENYA
Nairobi
Mombasa
L. Victoria
Kampala
UGANDA
Kisumu
L. Idi Amin Dada
L. Mobutu Sese Seko
Kisangani
ZAÏRE
Mbandaka
Ilebo
Kasai
Zaïre
CONGO
Brazzaville
Kinshasa
Pointe Noire
Cabinda
Boma
Libreville
GABON
São Tomé
Pagalu
Príncipe
EQUATORIAL GUINEA
Rey Malabo
Macías Nguema Biyogo
Bight of Benin
Gulf of Guinea
C. Lopez
Tema
Bôma
ATLANTIC OCEAN
Ascension (Br.)
St. Helena (Br.)

Luanda
Cuanza
ANGOLA
Benguela
Lobito
Huambo
Moçâmedes
Cunene
Cubango
Cuando
BURUNDI
Bujumbura
RWANDA
Kigali
L. Kivu
L. Tanganyika
Kigoma
Tabora
Dodoma
TANZANIA
Dar-es-Salaam
Zanzibar
Pemba
Mwanza
Shaba
Kalemie
Bukama
Lubumbashi
Likasi
Kitwe
L. Mweru
ZAMBIA
Lusaka
Kafue
Kabwe
Livingstone
Zambezi
L. Nyasa
MALAWI
Lilongwe
Blantyre
Zomba
MOZAMBIQUE
Moçambique
Mocuba
Quelimane
Chinde
Beira
Majunga
Tananarive
MADAGASCAR
Tamatave
Fianarantsoa
Tuléar
Diego-Suarez
Cabo Delgado
Ruvuma
Aldabra Is. (Br.)
Arch. des Comores
Réunion (Fr.)
MAURITIUS
INDIAN OCEAN
Durban – Mauritius 1332

RHODESIA
Salisbury
Bulawayo
Limpopo
NAMIBIA (SOUTH WEST AFRICA)
Windhoek
Walvis baai
Swakopmund
Lüderitz
BOTSWANA
Gaborone
Kalahari
Tropic of Capricorn
TRANSVAAL
Pretoria
Johannesburg
Maputo (Lourenço Marques)
SWAZ.
Kimberley
O.V.
Bloemfontein
Orange
Vaal
SOUTH AFRICA
CAPE PROVINCE
NATAL
Durban
East London
Cape Town
Kaap die Goeie Hoop (Cape of Good Hope)
Port Elizabeth

LES. Lesotho
O.-V. Oranje-Vrystaat
SWAZ. Swaziland

Projection: Zenithal Equidistant.
West from Greenwich   East from Greenwich
COPYRIGHT. GEORGE PHILIP & SON LTD.

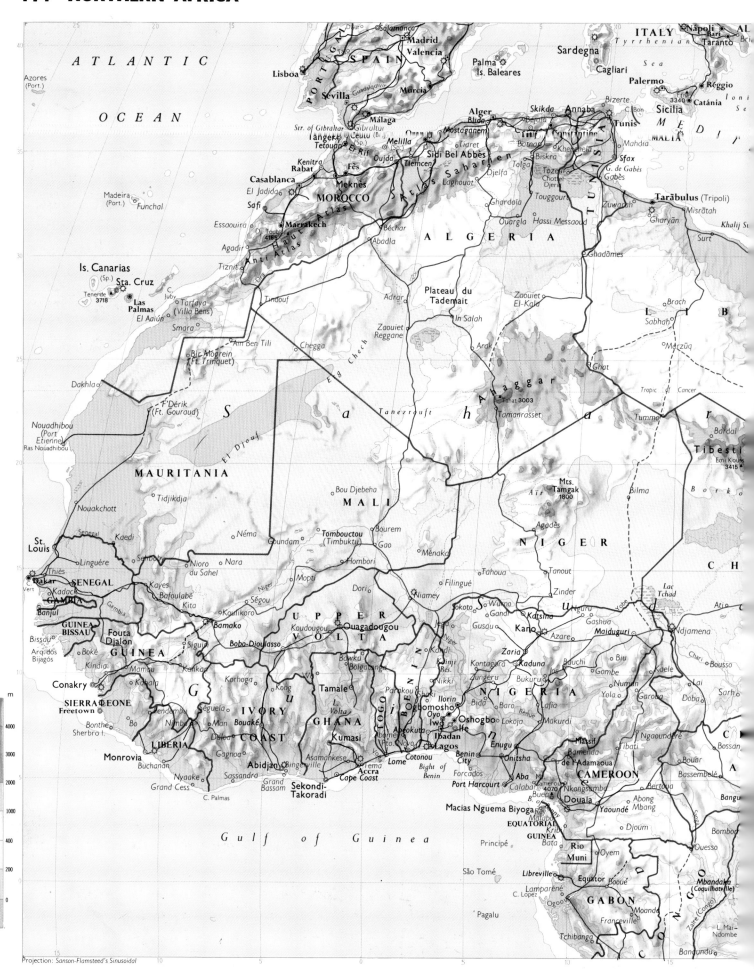

ATLANTIC

OCEAN

ITALY ● Napoli
Tyrrhenian
Sea
Sardegna
Cagliari
Palermo ● Réggio
Bizerte
3340 ● Catánia
Sicilia

Madrid
Valencia
Lisboa
SPAIN
Is. Baleares
Palma
Sevilla
Murcia
Guadalquivir
Málaga
Str. of Gibraltar Gibraltar
Tánger Ceuta (Sp.)
Tetouan El Rif Melilla
Kenitra Oujda
Rabat Fès Tlemcen
Casablanca Meknès
El Jadida Sidi Bel Abbès
Safi
Essaouira Dj. Toubkal Marrakech Béchar
4165 Abadla
Agadir
Tiznit Tindouf

Alger Skikda Annaba
Blida Constantine Tunis
Mostaganem
Oran Batna Sfax
Tiaret Khenchela G. de Gabès
Biskra Gabès
Saharien Djelfa Tolga Tozeur
Laghouat Chottel
Djerid
Ghardaïa Zuwārah
Ouargla TARĀBULUS (Tripoli)
Ghadāmes Gharyān
Misrātah
Khalij S
Surt

MOROCCO
Anti Atlas Haut Atlas

Madeira
(Port.) Funchal

Is. Canarias
(Sp.)
Sta. Cruz
Tenerife Tarfaya
3718 (Villa Bens)
Las El Aaiún
Palmas Smara
C. Juby

ALGERIA
Plateau du
Tademait
Zaouiet
El-Kala
In Salah
Adrar Brach
Zaouiet LIB
Reggane Merzûq
Aïn Ben Tili
Chegga Arak
Egg Chech Ghat
Ahaggar
Tahat 3003 Tropic of Cancer
Tamanrasset
Tummo

Dakhla
F'Dérik
(Ft. Gouraud)
Bîr Mogrein
(Ft. Trinquet)
S a h a r a

Bardaï
Tibesti
Emi Koussi
3415

Nouadhibou
(Port
Etienne)
Ras Nouadhibou

El Djouf

MAURITANIA
Tidjikdja

Bou Djebeha
Mts.
Tamgak
1800
Aïr

MALI

Agadès
NIGER
Bilma

Borko

Nouakchott

St.
Louis
Dakar
C.
Vert
SENEGAL
GAMBIA
Banjul

Kaedi
Linguére
Sélibaby
Kayes
Bafoulabé
Kita
Néma
Nara
Nioro
du Sahel
Tombouctou
(Timbuktu)
Gao
Goundam Bourem
Hombori
Ménaka
Tahoua
Tanout
Zinder
Lac
Tchad

Senegal

Thiès
Kadack

GUINEA
BISSAU
Bissau
Arq. dos
Bijagós
Boké
Kindia
Fouta
Djalon
Siguiri
GUINEA
Kankan
Mamou
Kokala
Conakry
SIERRA LEONE
Freetown
Bonthe
Sherbro I.

Gambia

Bamako
Ségou
Koulikoro
Mopti
Dori
Niamey
Filingué
Sokoto Wurno
Gusau Gandi
Katsina
Kano
Azare
Zaria
Kaduna
Maiduguri
Ndjamena
Ngaru
NIGERIA
Bauchi
Biu
Gombe
Numan
Lai
Garoua
Yola
Doba
CH

UPPER
VOLTA
Ouagadougou
Koudougou
Bobo-Dioulasso
Bawku
Bolgatanga
Korhoga
Kong
Tamale
L.
Volta
GHANA
Kumasi
IVORY
COAST
Bouaké
Séguela
Man
Daloa
Gagnoa
Abidjan
Bingerville
Grand
Bassam
Sekondi-
Takoradi
Cape Coast
Accra
Tema
Lome
Cotonou
Porto-Novo
Lagos

LIBERIA
Monrovia
Buchanan
Nyaake
Grand Cess
C. Palmas
Nimba
Bo
Zwedru

GUINEA
Nikki
Parakou
Kandi
Kainji
Res.
Kontagora
Zungeru
Zaria
Bukuru
Jos
Bida
Lafia
Makurdi
Baro Benue
Ilorin
Oshogbo
Iwo
Ife
Ibadan
Abeokuta
Oyo
Ogbomosho
Enugu
Onitsha
Benin
City
Forcados
Aba
Port Harcourt
Calabar

TOGO
BENIN

Shaki

Lagos

Bight of
Benin

Gulf of Guinea

CAMEROON
Bamenda
Massif
de l'Adamaoua
Tibati
Ngaoundéré
Bertoua
Bafia
Abong
Mbang
Yaoundé
Douala
Kribi
Djoum
Bata
Oyem
Libreville
Equator Booué
Lambaréné
C. Lopez
Pagalu
GABON
Moanda
Franceville
Tchibanga
Bangui

Macias Nguema Biyoga
EQUATORIAL
GUINEA
Rio
Muni
Príncipe
São Tomé

Cameroun
4070
Buea
B.
Nkongsamba

Principé

ZAIRE
Mbandaka
(Coquilhatville)
L. Mar-
Ndombe
Bangundu

m
4000
3000
2000
1000
400
200
0
0
200
m

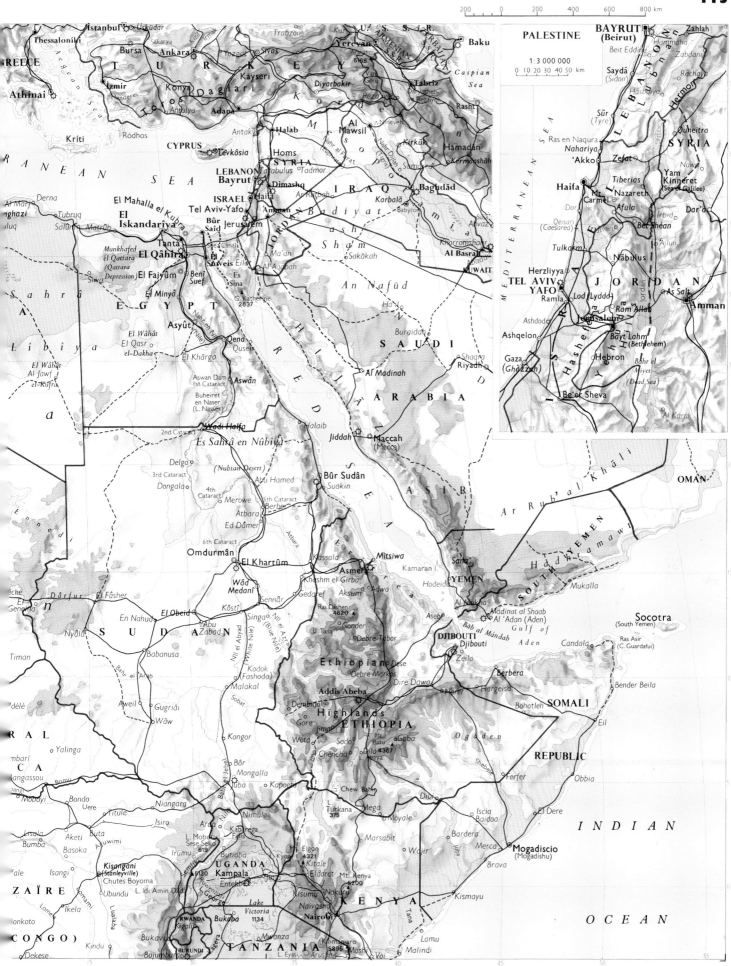

1:20 000 000

200   0   200   400   600   800 km

PALESTINE

1:3 000 000

0 10 20 30 40 50 km

BAYRUT
(Beirut)

Zahlah

Beit Eddine

Hammana

Sayda
(Sidon)

Zabdani

Rachaya

Sûr
(Tyre)

Quneitra

SYRIA

Ras en Naqura
Nahariya
'Akko
Zefat
Naw

Haifa
Mt.
Carmel

Tiberias
Nazareth

Yam
Kinneret
(Sea of Galilee)

Dar'a

Dor

Irbid

Afula

'Ajlun

Qeisari
(Caesarea)

Bet Shéan

Jenin

Tulkarm

Nâbulus

Herzliyya

JORDAN

TEL AVIV-
YAFO

Ramla

Lod Lyddo

Ram Allah

As Salt

Ashdod

Jerusalem

Amman

Ashqelon

Bâyt Lahm
(Bethlehem)

Gaza
(Ghazzah)

Hebron

Bahr el
Miyet
(Dead Sea)

Be'er Sheva

Al Karak

REECE
Istanbul Üsküdar
Thessaloníki
Bursa
Ankara
Sakarya
Trabzon
U. S. S. R.
ARMENIAN
S.S.R.
Yerevan
Baku

Athínai
Izmir
Konya
Kayseri
Sivas
Van
Gölü
5165
Tabriz
Rasht
Caspian
Sea

Kríti
Ródhos
Antalya
Adana
Toros
Dağları
Diyarbakir
Erzurum
Rezaîyeh

CYPRUS
Levkôsia
Al
Mawsil
Ninéveh
Kirkuk
Hamadán
Kermanshäh

RANEAN   SEA
Halab
Homs
Tadmor
IRAQ
Baghdãd
Karbalã
Babylon

Derna
Tubruq
Salûm
Matrûh
SYRIA
LEBANON
Bayrut
Dimashq
Amman
ash
Khorromshahr
Al Basrah

El Mahalla el Kubra
ISRAEL
Tel Aviv-Yafo
Haifa
Badiyat
Sham
KUWAIT

El Iskandariya
Bûr
Saîd
Jerusalem
Ma'an
Sakākah
Shaqra

Tanta
Suez Canal
El Suveis
Es
Sina
Al 'Aqabah
An Nafūd
Buraidah
Riyadh

El Qâhira
El Fajyûm
Beni
Suef
G. Katherine
2637
Ha'il

SAUDI

Munkhafed
el Qattara
(Qattara
Depression)
Siwa
El Minyá
Asyût

El Wâhât
El Qasr
el-Dakhla
El Khârga
Qena
Quseir
Aswân
ARABIA

Sahrâ
Lîbîya
El Wâhât
Al Jawf
el-Kufra
Aswan Dam
1st Cataract
Buheiret
en Naser
(L. Nasser)
Al Madinah

a
Wadi Halfa
2nd Cataract
Halaib
Al Madinah

Es Sahtâ en Nûbiya
Jiddah
Maccah
(Mecca)

Delgo
(Nubian Desert)
3rd Cataract
Abu Hamed
Dongola
4th
Cataract
Merowe
5th Cataract
Berber
Bûr Sudân
Suakin
ASIR
OMAN

Enned
Ed Dâmer
Atbara
Ar Rub' al Khâli

ché
Dârfur
El Fâsher
6th Cataract
Omdurmân
El Khartûm
Kassala
Mîtsiwa
Kamaran I.
YEMEN
Mukalla

Geneina
Wâd
Medanî
Khashm el Girba
Sana'
Hodeida
SOUTH

En Nahud
El Obeid
Sennâr
Gedaref
Aksum
Asmera
Adwa
YEMEN
Al Mukha
Madinat al Shaab
Al 'Adan (Aden)
Socotra
(South Yemen)

Nyâla
SUDAN
Abu
Zabad
Singa
Kôstî
L. Tana
Gander
Bâb al Mándab
Gulf of
Aden
Candala
Ras Asir
(C. Guardafui)

Timan
Babanusa
Nil el Azrag
(Blue Nile)
Debre Tabor
DJIBOUTI
Djibouti
Zeila
Berbera
Bender Beila

Bahr el Arab
Kodok
(Fashoda)
Malakal
Ethiopianese
Debre Markos
Dire Dawa
Harar
Hargeisa
SOMALI

Aweil
Gugriâl
Wâw
Sobat
Addis Abeba
Dembidolo
Highlands
ETHIOPIA
Ogaden
Eil

Yalinga
Bôr
Mongalla
Gore
Jimma
Sodo
Goba
Shebeli
REPUBLIC

ambari
Bomu
Kongor
Wota
Batu
Dila
4307
Ferfer
Obbia

Mobayi
Bondo
Uere
Niangara
Isiro
Kapoeta
Chew Bahir
Dibi
Bardera
Merca

Lisala
Bumba
Aketi
Buta
Titule
Nimule
Mongalla
L. Turkana
375
Mega
Moyale
Marsabit
Wajir
Iscia
Baidoa
El Dere
Mogadiscio
(Mogadishu)

ZAÏRE
Kisangani
(Stanleyville)
Chutes Boyoma
4120
Kampala
Entebbe
Butiaba
Kitale
Mt. Kenya
5200
Brava

Ikela
Ubundu
UGANDA
L. Mobutu
Sese Seko
619
L. Elgon
4321
Eldoret
Kisumu
Nakuru
Naivasha
Kismayu
INDIAN

CONGO)
Dekese
Kindu
RWANDA
Kigali
Bukavu
Bujumbura
BURUNDI
Bukoba
L. Victoria
1134
Mwanza
Nairobi
TANZANIA
5895
Moshi
Arusha
L. Eyasi
Voi
Lamu
Malindi
OCEAN

1:15 000 000

100   0   100   200   300   400   500   600 km

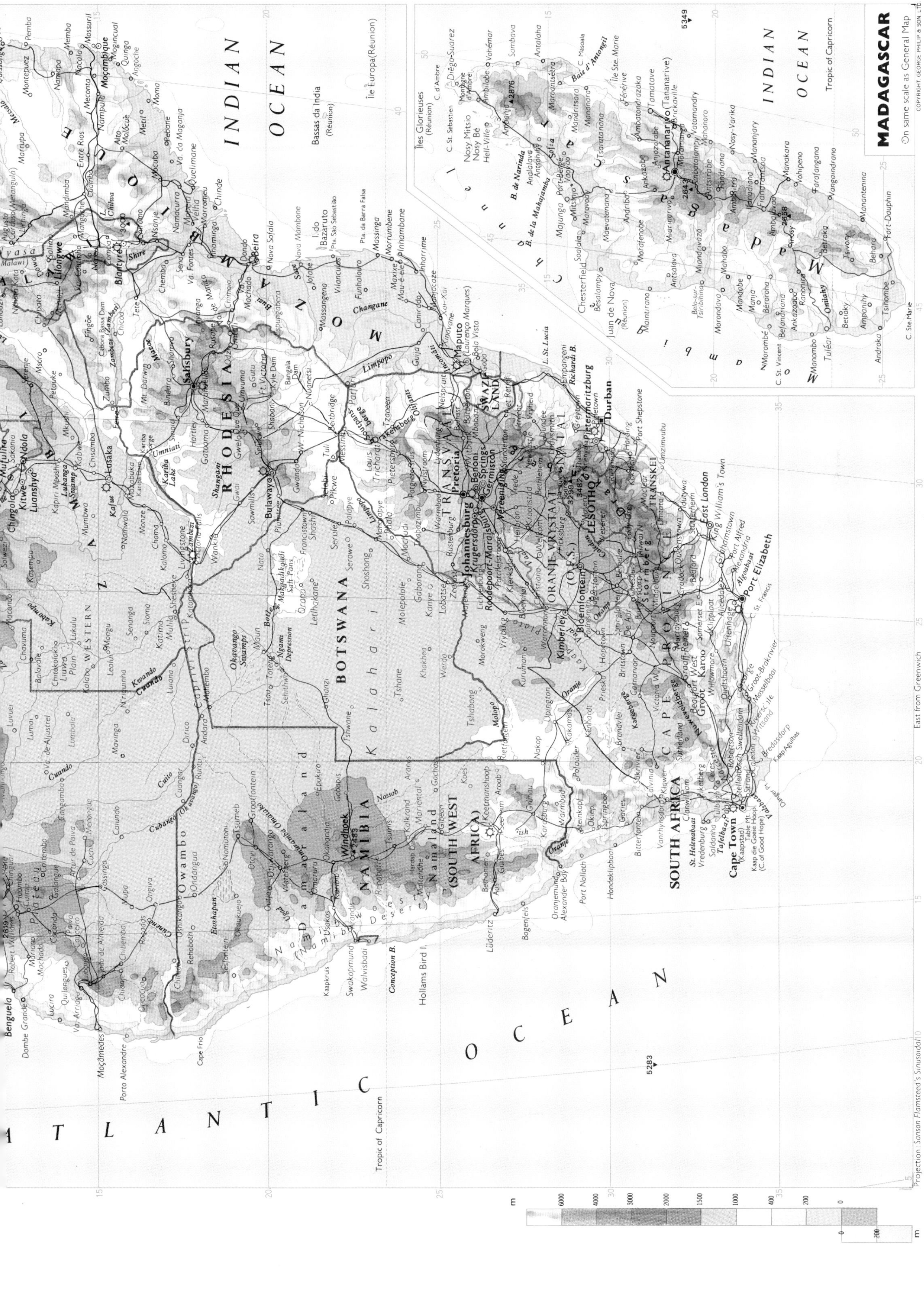

117

MADAGASCAR
On same scale as General Map

COPYRIGHT GEORGE PHILIP & SON LTD

INDIAN   OCEAN

INDIAN   OCEAN

Tropic of Capricorn

RHODESIA

BOTSWANA

Kalahari

NAMIBIA
(SOUTH WEST AFRICA)

SOUTH AFRICA

CAPE   PROVINCE

TRANSVAAL

NATAL

SWAZILAND

LESOTHO

ORANJE VRYSTAAT (O.F.S.)

TRANSKEI

ATLANTIC   OCEAN

Tropic of Capricorn

East from Greenwich

Projection: Sanson Flamsteed's Sinusoidal

m   6000   4000   3000   2000   1500   1000   400   200   0

Johannesburg
Pretoria
Durban
Cape Town
Port Elizabeth
East London
Windhoek
Lusaka
Salisbury
Bulawayo
Maputo
Beira
Blantyre
Lilongwe

1:50 000 000

500   0   500   1000   1500   2000 km

COPYRIGHT GEORGE PHILIP & SON LTD

PACIFIC OCEAN

ARCTIC OCEAN

INDIAN OCEAN

Aleutian Is.
7822
Bering Sea
Kamchatka Peninsula 4760
C. Dezhneva
Bering Str.
Wrangel I. (Kolyma)
New Siberian Is.
Laptev Sea
Kara Sea
Novaya Zemlya
Severnaya Zemlya
Chelyuskin
Taimyr Peninsula
Barents Sea
Kolguyev
Kola Pen.
White Sea
North Cape
Svalbard
Greenland
Iceland
British Isles
North Sea
Baltic Sea
Scandinavia
Finland
North European Plain
Central Russian Uplands
Ural Mountains 1640
West Siberian Plain
Ob
Irtysh
Tobol
Ishim
Yenisei
Angara
Lower Tunguska
Central Siberian Plateau
Lena
Vilyuy
Aldan
Stanovoy Ra.
Yablonovy Ra.
Verkhoyansk Range
Srednny Ra.
Gydan Ra. (Kolyma)
Indigirka
Kolyma
Sea of Okhotsk
Sakhalin
Kuril Is.
Hokkaido
La Perouse Str.
Sea of Japan
Honshu
Shikoku
Kyushu
Korea Str.
Korea
Yellow Sea
Manchurian Plain
Sungari
Amur
Great Khingan Mts.
Hwang
Great Plain of China
Si-kiang
East China Sea
Formosa
Ryukyu Is.
Tropic of Cancer
Bonin Is. 10450
Japan Trench
Guam
Caroline Is.
11022
Pelew Is.
New Guinea
Mindanao 12497
Cape Johnson Deep
Philippine Is.
Luzon
Palawan
Kinabalu 4101
Borneo
Sulu Sea
Celebes Sea
Celebes
Moluccas
Halmahera
Ceram
Banda Sea
Arafura Sea
Australia
Timor
Flores
Bali
Java Sea
Java
East Indies
Makasar Strait
Sunda Str.
Sunda Is.
Sumatra
Str. of Malacca
Malay Peninsula
G. of Siam
Menam
Mekong
Hong (Red)
G. of Tonkin
Hainan
Andaman Is.
Nicobar Is.
Bay of Bengal
Irrawaddy
Salween
Tsangpo
Brahmaputra
Everest 8848
Himalaya
Plateau of Tibet
Kunlun Shan
Koko Nor
Lop Nor
Tarim Basin
Takla Makan
Tsin-ling
Pa Hai
China
Si-kiang
Tien Shan
Turfan Basin
Altai
Bebukha 4506
Sayan Mts.
Selenga
Plateau of Mongolia
Gobi
Ili
L. Balkhash
Chu
Syr Darya
Amu Darya
Aral Sea
Turan Plain
Kara Kum
Pamirs
Communism Pk. 7495
Hindu Kush
Karakoram Ra. 8611
Tarbagatai
Ganga
Indus
Hari-rud
Helmand
Sulaiman Ra.
Thar Desert
Western Ghats
Eastern Ghats
Godavari
Krishna
Narmada
Yamuna
India
Deccan
Polk Strait
Ceylon
C. Comorin
Gulf of Mannar
Maldive Is.
Laccadive Is.
Chagos Arch.
Amirantes
Seychelles
Equator
Socotra
Ras Asir (C. Guardafui)
G. of Aden
Somali Peninsula
Ar Rub' al Khali
Arabia
G. of Oman
Persian Gulf
Arabian Sea
Plateau of Iran
Zagros Mts.
Elburz Mts. 5600
Demavend
Great Salt Desert
Caspian Sea
Caucasus 5633
Ararat 5165
Black Sea
Bosporus
Tigris
Euphrates
Mesopotamia
Syrian Desert
Dead Sea
Nafud
Red Sea
Suez Canal
Sinai Pen.
Nile
Libyan Desert
Mediterranean Sea
Cyprus
Anatolia
Taurus Mts.
Adriatic Sea
Carpathians
Danube
Oder
Elbe
Vistula
Rhine
Dnepr
Don
Volga
Ural
N. Dvina
Narodnaya 1894
Lake Victoria

m
6000 4000 2000 1000 400 200 0
0 200 2000 4000 6000 8000

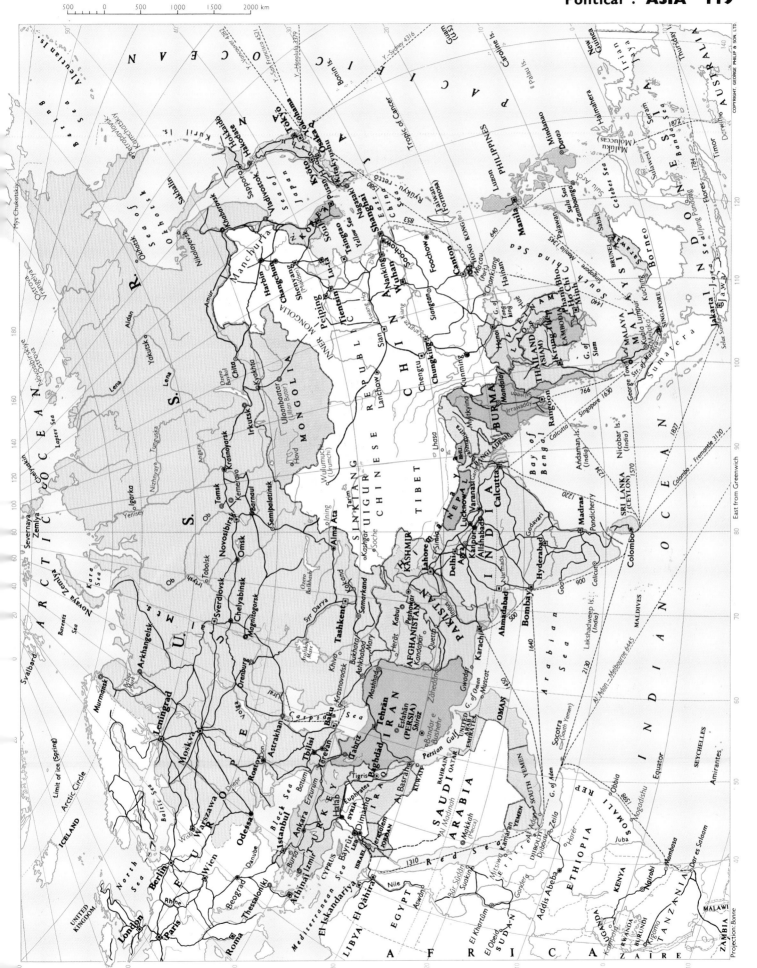

1:50 000 000

500   0   500   1000   1500   2000 km

Projection: Bonne

East from Greenwich

R.S.F.S.R.
1. Daghestan A.S.S.R.
2. Kabardino–Balkar A.S.S.R.
3. Mari A.S.S.R.
4. Mordovian A.S.S.R.
5. North Ossetian A.S.S.R.
6. Tatar A.S.S.R.
7. Udmurt A.S.S.R.
8. Chuvash A.S.S.R.
9. Checheno–Ingush A.S.S.R.
AZERBAIJAN
10. Nakhichevan A.S.S.R.
GEORGIA
11. Abkhaz A.S.S.R.
12. Adzhar A.S.S.R.

Projection: Conical Orthomorphic with two standard parallels

East from Greenwich

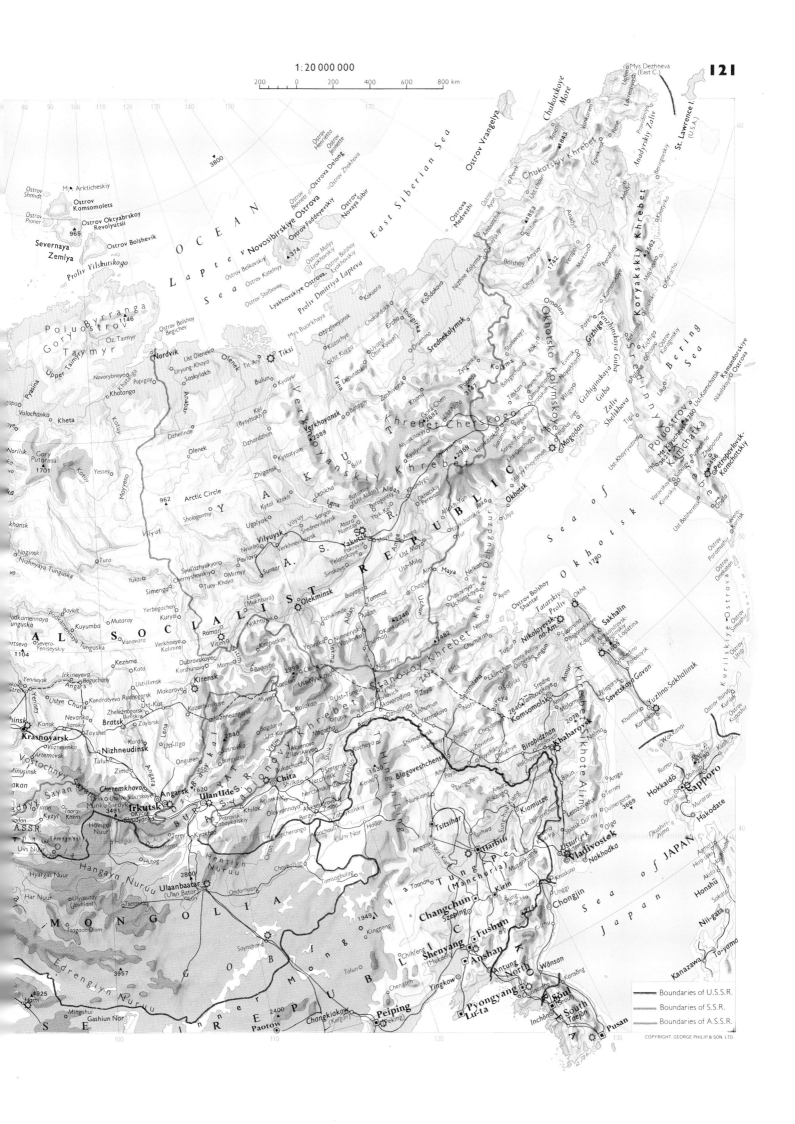

1 : 20 000 000

200   0   200   400   600   800 km

COPYRIGHT. GEORGE PHILIP & SON. LTD.

Boundaries of U.S.S.R.
Boundaries of S.S.R.
Boundaries of A.S.S.R.

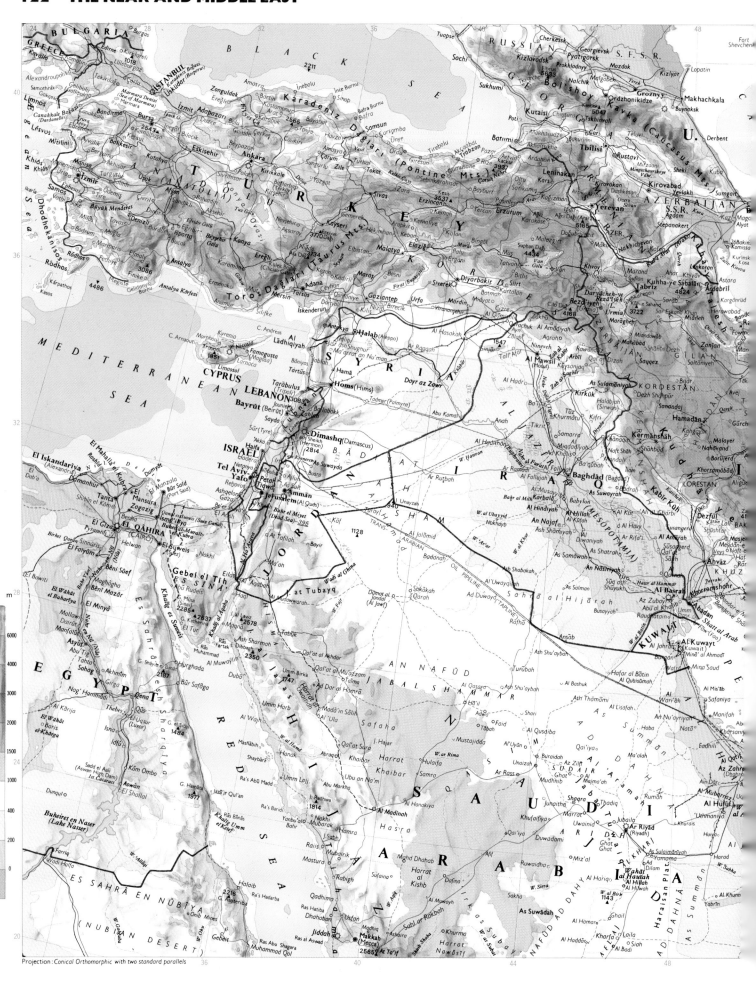

Projection: Conical Orthomorphic with two standard parallels

1:10 000 000

100 0 100 200 300 400 km

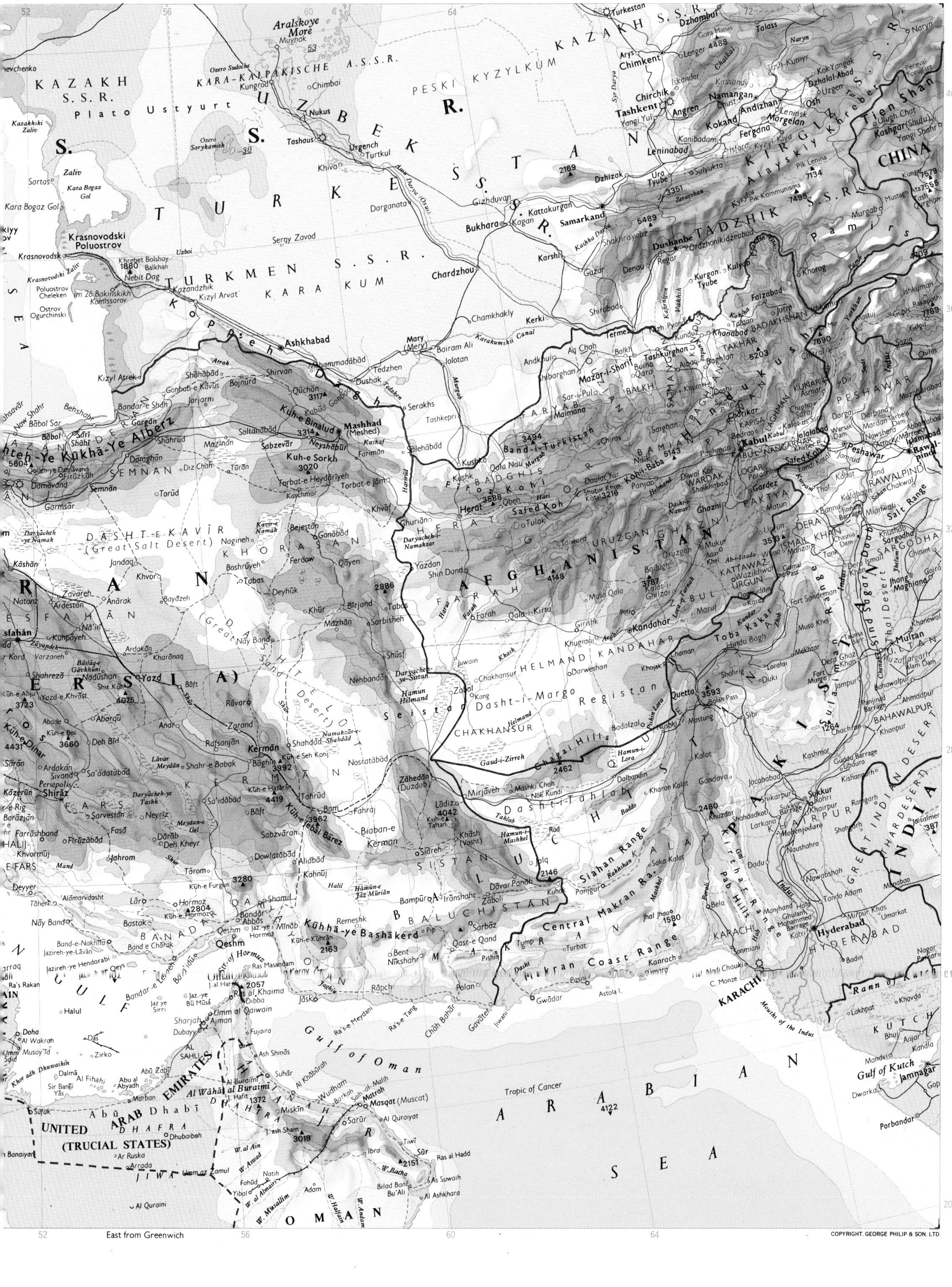

KAZAKH S.S.R.

Plato Ustyurt

KARA-KALPAKISCHE A.S.S.R.

PESKI KYZYLKUM

KAZAKH S.S.R.

U Z B E K S. S. R.

T U R K M E N   S. S. R.

KARA KUM

TADZHIK S.S.R.

KIRGIZ S.S.R.

CHINA

Tien Shan

Pamirs

Ashkhabad

Mashhad (Meshed)

Dushanbe

Kabul

Peshawar

Rawalpindi

DASHT-E KAVIR (Great Salt Desert)

I R A N

KHORASAN

A F G H A N I S T A N

P A K I S T A N

INDIA

Great Indian Desert

Shiraz

Kerman

P E R S I A (FARS)

Dasht-i-Margo

Registan

Kandahar

Quetta

B A L U C H I S T A N

Central Makran Range

Makran Coast Range

Karachi

Gulf of Oman

Tropic of Cancer

A R A B I A N   S E A

Gulf of Kutch

UNITED ARAB EMIRATES (TRUCIAL STATES)

Abu Dhabi

O M A N

Masqat (Muscat)

Ras al Hadd

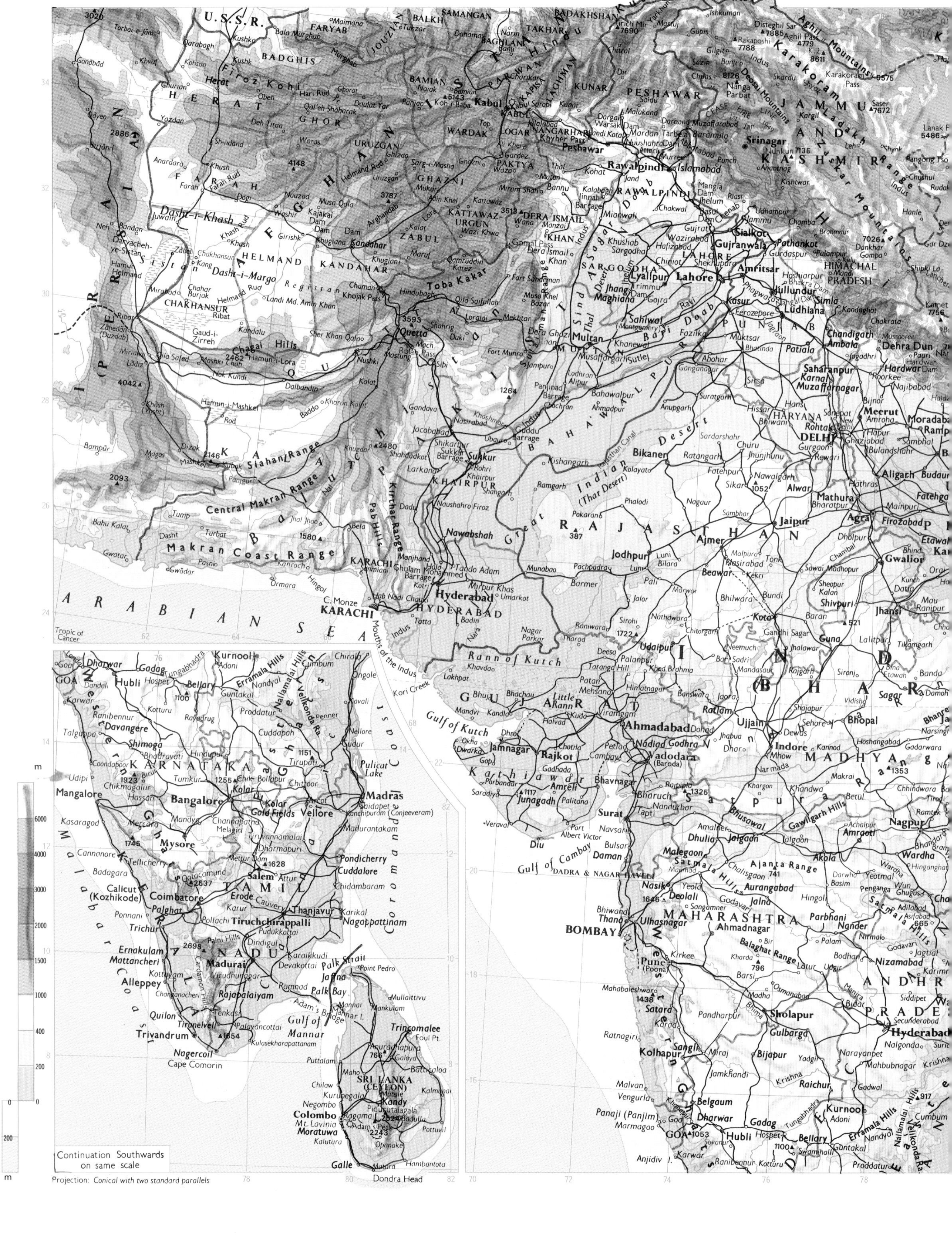

Continuation Southwards on same scale

Projection: Conical with two standard parallels

m
6000
4000
3000
2000
1500
1000
400
200
0
0
200
m

ARABIAN SEA

Tropic of Cancer

U.S.S.R.

AFGHANISTAN

PAKISTAN

INDIA

RAJASTHAN

GUJARAT

MADHYA PRADESH

MAHARASHTRA

ANDHRA PRADESH

KARNATAKA

TAMIL NADU

KERALA

SRI LANKA (CEYLON)

Gulf of Mannar

Palk Strait

Cape Comorin

Dondra Head

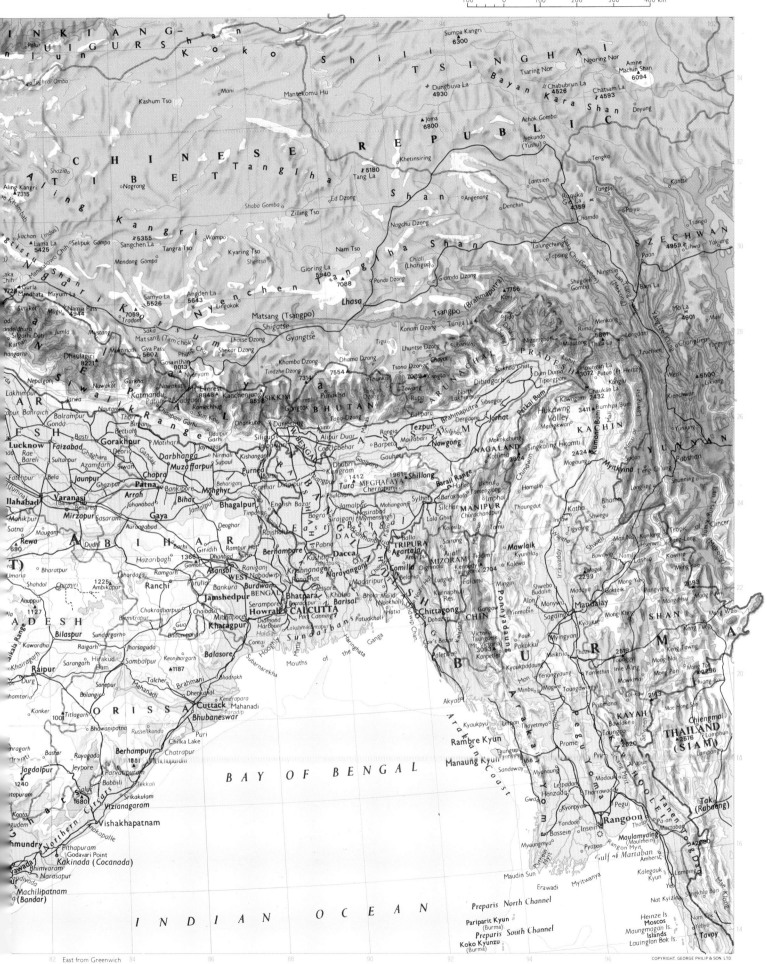

1:10 000 000

100   0   100   200   300   400 km

SINKIANG-UIGUR

Kuen Lun

Koko Shili

Shan

TSINGHAI

Bayan Kara Shan

Amne Machin Shan
6094

SZECHWAN

CHINESE REPUBLIC

TIBET

Tangtha Shan

Nyenchen Tangtha Shan

Lhasa

Tsangpo (Brahmaputra)

ARUNACHAL PRADESH

YUNNAN

NEPAL

Mt. Everest
8848

Kanchenjunga
8598

SIKKIM

BHUTAN

ASSAM

KACHIN

Katmandu

Darjeeling

MEGHALAYA

Shillong

NAGALAND

Lucknow

Gorakhpur

Faizabad

BENGAL

Gauhati

MANIPUR

Imphal

Patna

B I H A R

Bhagalpur

East

DACCA

Sylhet

Mawlaik

Myitkyina

Varanasi

Mirzapur

Gaya

BENGAL

TRIPURA

Agartala

MIZORAM

Mandalay

SHAN

Ranchi

WEST

BENGAL

Dacca

Comilla

CHIN

B U R M A

Jamshedpur

Kharagpur

Howrah

CALCUTTA

Barisal

Chittagong

KAYAH

Raipur

Sundarbans

Mouths of the Ganges

KAYAH

THAILAND
(SIAM)

Chiengmai

ORISSA

Cuttack

Bhubaneswar

Puri

Chilka Lake

Rambre Kyun

Prome

Rangoon

Berhampur

Pegu

Vishakhapatnam

B A Y   O F   B E N G A L

Maulamyaing
(Moulmein)

Gulf of Martaban

Amherst

Machilipatnam
(Bandar)

I N D I A N   O C E A N

Preparis North Channel

Pariparit Kyun
(Burma)
Preparis South Channel

Koko Kyunzu
(Burma)

Tavoy

COPYRIGHT GEORGE PHILIP & SON. LTD

East from Greenwich

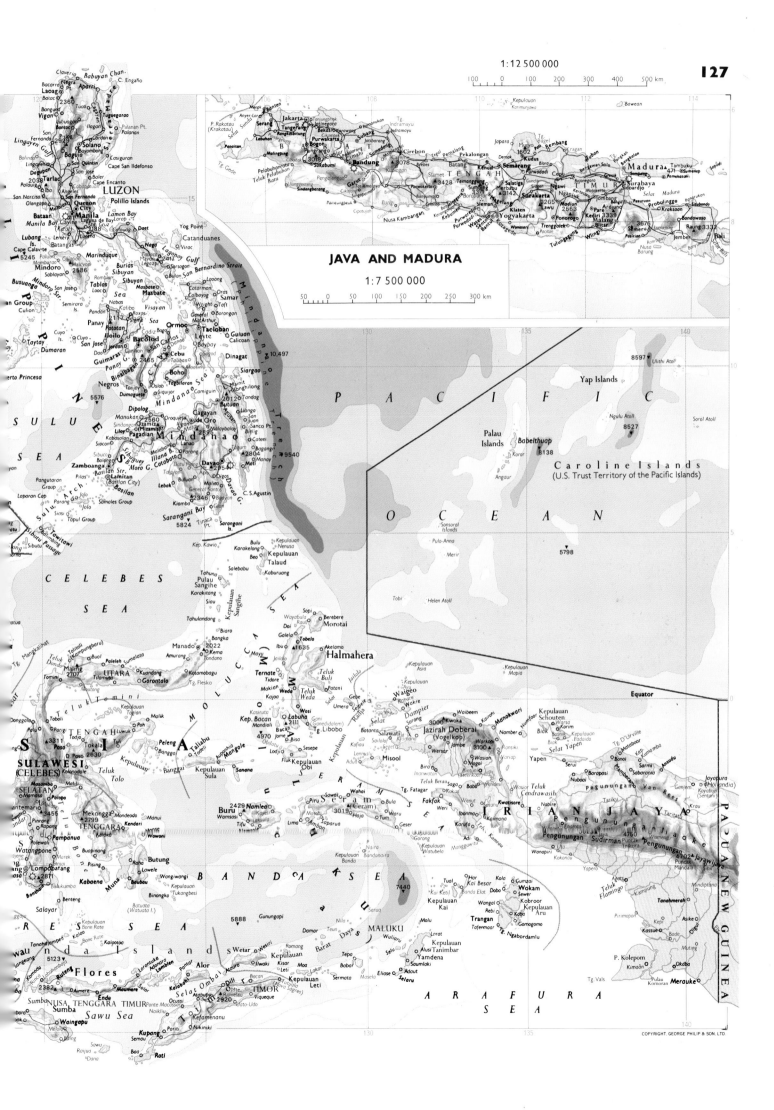

1:10 000 000

100   0   100   200   300   400 km

MALAYA AND SINGAPORE

1:6 000 000

50   0   50   100 km

Projection: Conical with two standard parallels

East from Greenwich

COPYRIGHT GEORGE PHILIP & SON, LTD.

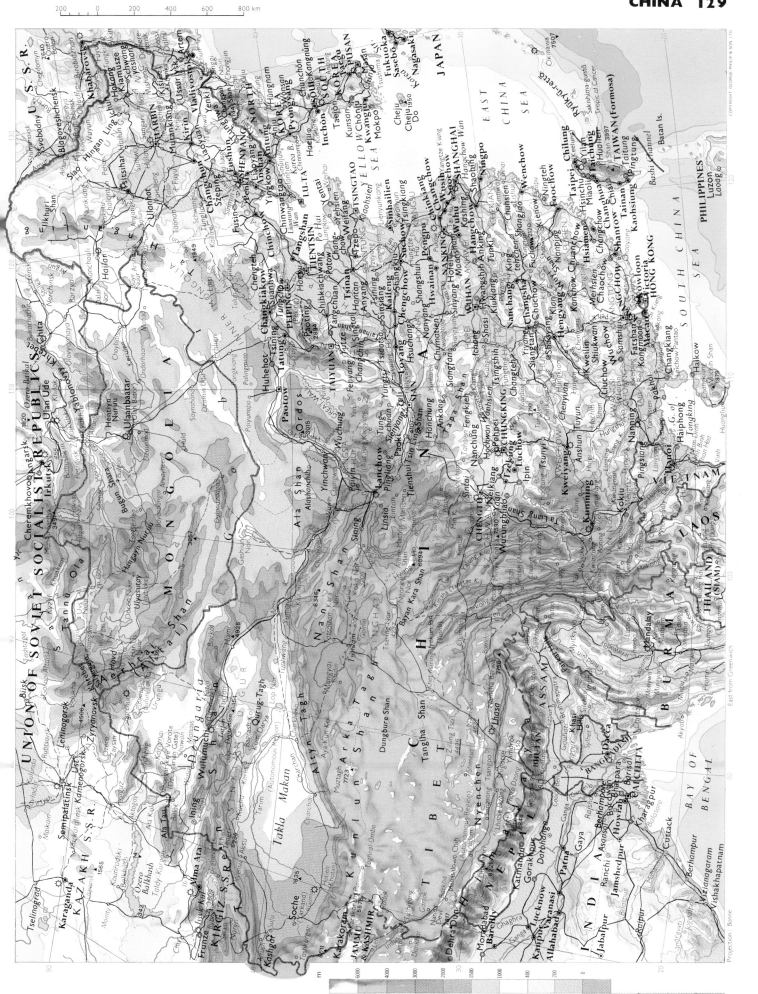

1:20 000 000

1:10 000 000

100   0   100   200   300   400 km

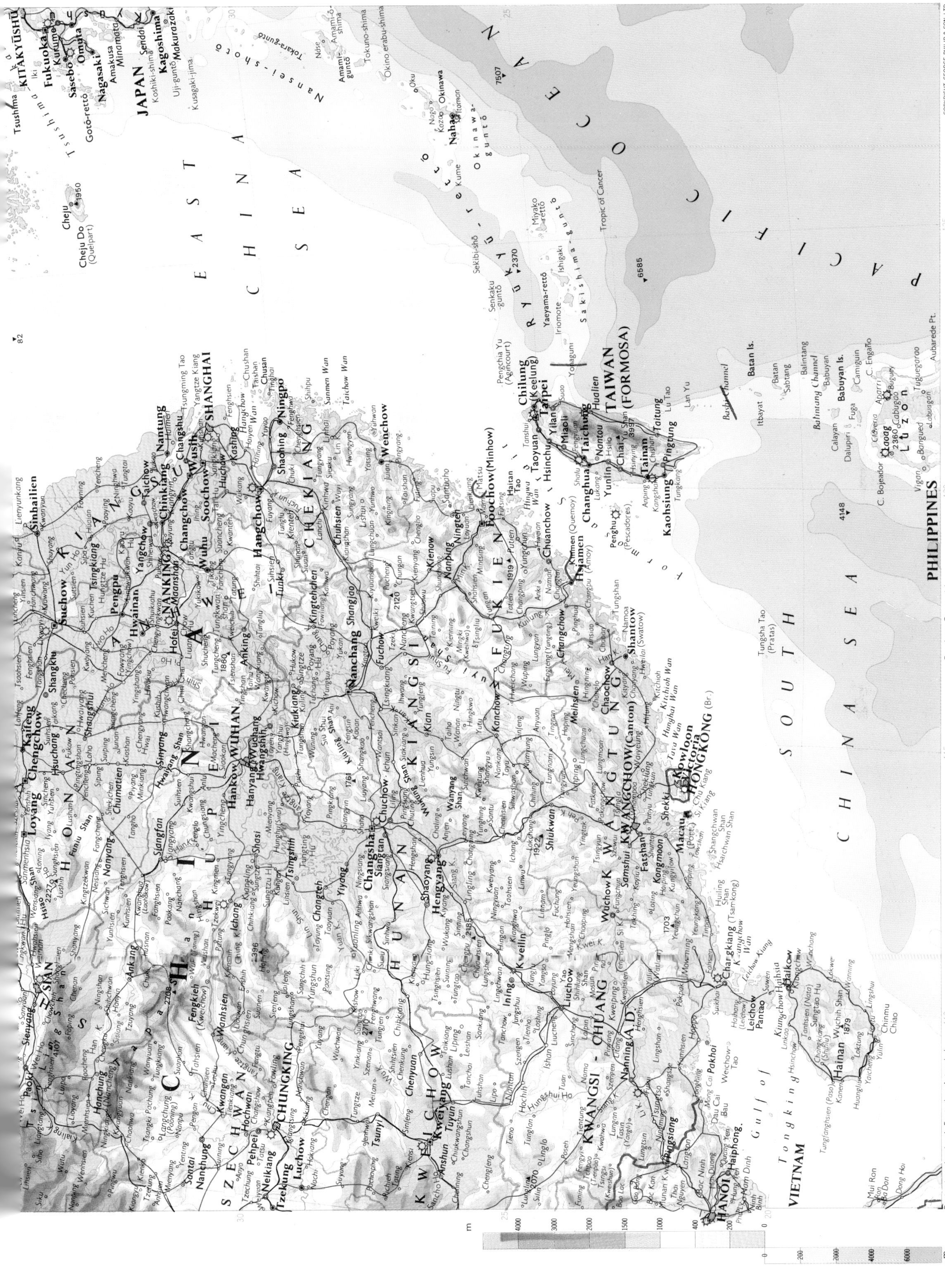

PACIFIC OCEAN

EAST CHINA SEA

JAPAN

KITAKYUSHU
Fukuoka
Kurume
Sasebo
Nagasaki
Omuta
Kagoshima
Amakusa
Minamata
Sendai

Cheju
Cheju Do
(Quelpart)

Nansei-shotō
Tokara-gunto
Amami-guntō
Amami-ō-shima
Okino-erabu-shima
Tokuno-shima
Oku
Okinawa
Naha
Okinawa-guntō
Kume
Miyako
Miyako-rettō
Ishigaki
Iriomote
Yaeyama-guntō
Sakishima-guntō
Sekibi-shō
Senkaku gunto
Yohaguni

Tropic of Cancer

TAIWAN (FORMOSA)
Chilung (Keelung)
Taipei
Taoyuan
Hsinchu
Miaoli
Taichung
Changhua
Nantou
Yunlin
Chiai
Tainan
Kaohsiung
Pingtung
Hualien
Yilan
Taitung
Lan Yu
Lu Tao

PHILIPPINES
Batan Is.
Babuyan Is.
Luzon
C. Bojeador
C. Engaño
Aubarede Pt.
Bashi Channel
Balintang Channel
Babuyan Channel

SOUTH CHINA SEA

KIANGSU
Lienyunkang
Sinhailien
SHANGHAI
NANKING
Suchow
Pengpu
Hwainan
Nantung
Tsungming Tao
Soochow
Wusih
Changchow
Chinkiang
Yangchow
Wuhu
Maanshan

ANHWEI
Hofei
Anking
Wuhan
Hankow
Hanyang
Wuchang

HONAN
Kaifeng
Loyang
Chengchow

CHEKIANG
Hangchow
Ningpo
Shaohing
Wenchow
Chusan
Chushan

KIANGSI
Nanchang
Kiukiang
Kian
Kanchow

HUNAN
Changsha
Hengyang
Shaoyang
Siangtan
Yiyang
Changteh

FUKIEN
Foochow (Minhow)
Amoy
Kinmen (Quemoy)
Nanping
Changchow
Penghu (Pescadores)

KWANGTUNG
KWANGCHOW (Canton)
HONGKONG (Br.)
Kowloon
Victoria
Macau (Port.)
Fatshan
Shekki
Swatow
Shantow
Chaochow
Meihsien

KWANGSI-CHUANG
Nanning
Liuchow
Kweilin
Wuchow
Pakhoi

KWEICHOW
Kweiyang
Tsunyi
Anshun

SZECHWAN
CHUNGKING
Neikiang
Luchow
Tzekung

SHENSI
SIAN
Paoki
Hanchung

VIETNAM
HANOI
Haiphong
Nam Dinh

Gulf of Tonking

Hainan
Hoihow
Haikow
Yaihsien
Wenchang

East from Greenwich

Projection : Lambert's Equivalent Azimuthal

m
4000
3000
2000
1500
1000
400
200

m
200
2000
4000
6000

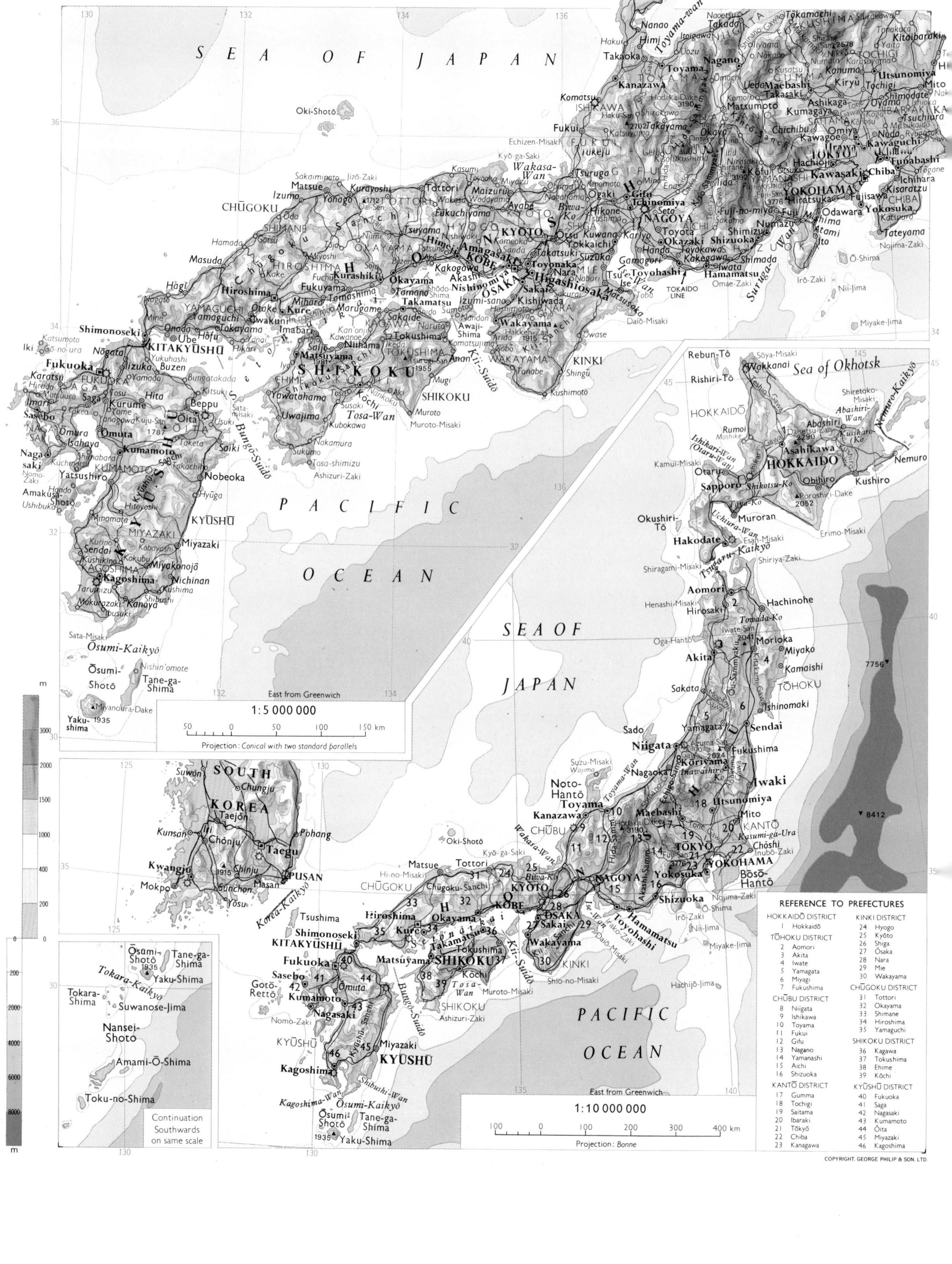

SEA OF JAPAN

CHŪGOKU

PACIFIC OCEAN

SEA OF JAPAN

Sea of Okhotsk

HOKKAIDŌ

KANTŌ

KINKI

SHIKOKU

KYŪSHŪ

TŌHOKU

CHŪBU

SOUTH KOREA

Nansei-Shoto

Continuation Southwards on same scale

1:5 000 000

Projection: Conical with two standard parallels

50   0   50   100   150 km

East from Greenwich

1:10 000 000

100   0   100   200   300   400 km

Projection: Bonne

East from Greenwich

REFERENCE TO PREFECTURES

HOKKAIDŌ DISTRICT		KINKI DISTRICT	
1	Hokkaidō	24	Hyogo
TŌHOKU DISTRICT		25	Kyōto
2	Aomori	26	Shiga
3	Akita	27	Osaka
4	Iwate	28	Nara
5	Yamagata	29	Mie
6	Miyagi	30	Wakayama
7	Fukushima	**CHŪGOKU DISTRICT**	
CHŪBU DISTRICT		31	Tottori
8	Niigata	32	Okayama
9	Ishikawa	33	Shimane
10	Toyama	34	Hiroshima
11	Fukui	35	Yamaguchi
12	Gifu	**SHIKOKU DISTRICT**	
13	Nagano	36	Kagawa
14	Yamanashi	37	Tokushima
15	Aichi	38	Ehime
16	Shizuoka	39	Kōchi
KANTŌ DISTRICT		**KYŪSHŪ DISTRICT**	
17	Gumma	40	Fukuoka
18	Tochigi	41	Saga
19	Saitama	42	Nagasaki
20	Ibaraki	43	Kumamoto
21	Tōkyō	44	Ōita
22	Chiba	45	Miyazaki
23	Kanagawa	46	Kagoshima

1:6 000 000

50 0 50 100 150 200 250 km

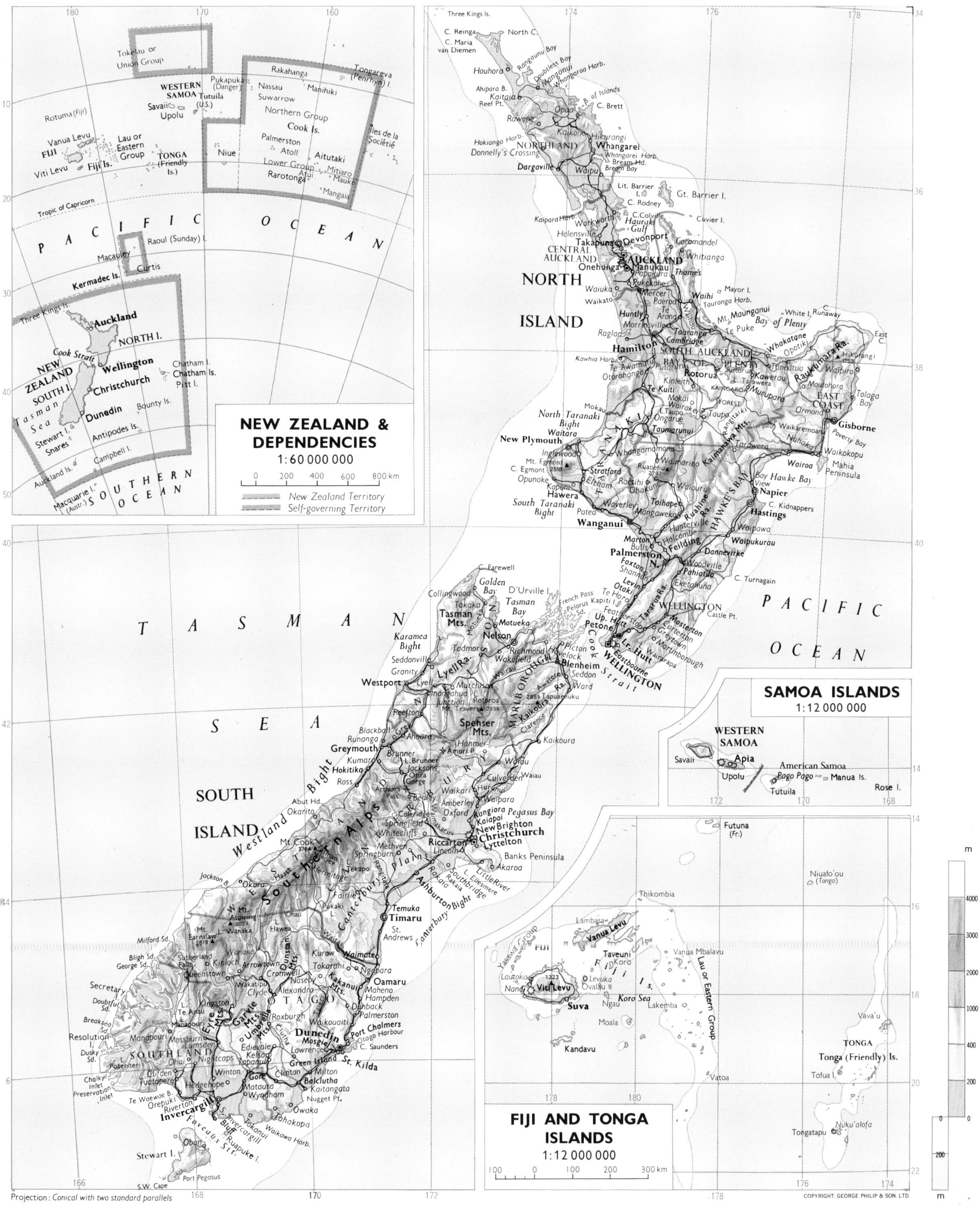

NEW ZEALAND & DEPENDENCIES
1:60 000 000

0 200 400 600 800 km

New Zealand Territory
Self-governing Territory

Tokelau or Union Group

WESTERN SAMOA
Savaii Tutuila (U.S.)
Upolu

Rotuma (Fiji)

Pukapuka (Danger) Nassau Suwarrow
Rakahanga Manihiki
Tongareva (Penrhyn) I.

Northern Group
Cook Is.
Palmerston Atoll
Aitutaki
Iles de la Société
Lower Group
Rarotonga Atiu Mitiaro Mauke

Vanua Levu
Lau or Eastern Group
FIJI
Viti Levu Fiji Is.
TONGA (Friendly Is.)
Niue

Mangaia

Tropic of Capricorn

P A C I F I C   O C E A N

Macauley
Raoul (Sunday) I.
Curtis

Kermadec Is.

Three Kings Is.
Auckland
NORTH I.

NEW ZEALAND
Cook Strait
Wellington
SOUTH I.
Christchurch
Dunedin

Tasman Sea

Stewart I.
Snares
Antipodes Is.
Bounty Is.
Chatham I.
Chatham Is.
Pitt I.

Auckland Is.
Campbell I.
Macquarie I. (Austr.)

S O U T H E R N   O C E A N

Projection: Conical with two standard parallels

NORTH ISLAND

Three Kings Is.
C. Reinga North C.
C. Maria van Diemen
Rangaunu Bay
Houhora
Doubtless Bay
Ahipara B. Mangonui Whangaroa Harb.
Kaitaia
Ahipara Reef Pt.
Rawene
Opua B. of Islands
C. Brett
Hokianga Harb.
Donnelly's Crossing
Hikurangi
NORTHLAND
Whangarei
Dargaville
Whangarei Harb.
Waipu
Bream Hd. Bream Bay

Lit. Barrier I.
Gt. Barrier I.
C. Rodney
Cuvier I.

Kaipara Harb.
Warkworth
Helensville
Takapuna
CENTRAL AUCKLAND
C. Colville
Hauraki Gulf
Coromandel
Whitianga
Devonport
AUCKLAND
Onehunga Manukau
Thames
Waiuku
Pukekohe
Mercer
Mayor I.
Waihi
Tauranga Harb.
Huntly Te Aroha
Waikato
Morrinsville
White I. Runaway
Raglan
Hamilton Cambridge
Mt. Maunganui
Te Puke
Bay of Plenty
Kawhia Harb.
SOUTH AUCKLAND
Whakatane
Otorohanga
BAY OF PLENTY
Opotiki
Rotorua
Hikurangi 1753
Te Kuiti
Kawerau Murupara
EAST COAST
North Taranaki Bight
Mokau Wairakei Taupo
Tolaga Bay
Waitara
Ongarue
Taupo
Waikaremoana
Gisborne
New Plymouth
Whangamomona
Poverty Bay
Mt. Egmont 2518
Stratford
Ruapehu 2797
Wairoa
Opunake
Eltham
Mahia Peninsula
Kapiti
Hawera
Ohakune
Bay Hawke Bay
South Taranaki Bight
Waverley Mangaweka
Napier
Wanganui
Taihape
Hastings
C. Kidnappers
Marton Bulls
Halcombe
Waipukurau
Palmerston N.
Feilding
Dannevirke
Foxton
Shannon
Woodville
Levin
Pahiatua
Otaki
Eketahuna
C. Turnagain
WELLINGTON
Masterton
Carterton
Greytown
Up. Hutt
Lr. Hutt
Eastbourne
WELLINGTON
Petone

SOUTH ISLAND

C. Farewell
Collingwood
Golden Bay
D'Urville I.
Takaka
Tasman Bay
Tasman Mts.
Motueka
French Pass
Pelorus
Nelson
Picton
Karamea Bight
Tadmor
Richmond
Havelock
Seddonville
Wakefield
Blenheim
Granity
Wairau
Seddon
Westport
Lyell Ra.
MARLBOROUGH
Ward
Murchison
Reefton
Rotoroa
Kaikoura
Inangahua Junction
Travers 2338
Tapuaenuku 2885
Blackball Gt.
Spenser Mts.
Clarence
Runanga
Hanmer
Greymouth
Brunner
Amuri P.
Kumara
L. Brunner
Jacksons
Waiau
Hokitika
Otira Gorge
Culverden
Ross
Waikari
Waipara
Amberley
Oxford
Rangiora Pegasus Bay
Abut Hd.
Okarito
Kaiapoi
New Brighton
Coalgate
Christchurch
Springfield
Whitecliffs
Riccarton Lyttelton
Mt. Cook 3764
Methven
Lincoln
Little River
Banks Peninsula
Springburn
L. Ellesmere
Akaroa
Hermitage
Rakaia
Mt. Aspiring 3027
Fairlie
Ashburton
Ashburton Bight
Jackson B.
Okura
Hari Hari
Tekapo
Canterbury Plains
Milford Sd.
Mt. Earnslaw 2819
Wanaka
Temuka
Timaru
Bligh Sd.
George Sd.
Hawea
St. Andrews
Sutherland Falls
Kingston
Cromwell
Waimate
Secretary I.
Doubtful Sd.
Arrowtown
Naseby
Kurow
Queenstown
Alexandra
Maheno
Oamaru
Te Anau
Wakatipu
Clyde
Hampden
Breaksea Sd.
Manapouri
Mossburn
Roxburgh
Waikouaiti
Resolution I.
Lumsden
Lawrence
Palmerston
Dusky Sd.
Clutha
Port Chalmers
Chalky Inlet
SOUTHLAND
Dunedin
Preservation Inlet
Gore
Mosgiel
Green Island
Te Waewae B.
Winton
Clinton
Milton
Orepuki
Balclutha
Riverton
Kaitangata
Invercargill
Mataura
Nugget Pt.
Bluff
Wyndham
Owaka
Foveaux Str.
Oban
Stewart I.
S.W. Cape
Port Pegasus

T A S M A N   S E A

P A C I F I C   O C E A N

SAMOA ISLANDS
1:12 000 000

WESTERN SAMOA
Savaii
Apia
Upolu
American Samoa
Pago Pago
Tutuila
Manua Is.
Rose I.

FIJI AND TONGA ISLANDS
1:12 000 000

100 0 100 200 300 km

Niuafo'ou (Tonga)
Futuna (Fr.)
Thikombia
Lambasa
Vanua Levu
Taveuni
Koro
Vanua Mbalavu
FIJI
Yasawa Group
Lautoka
Lau or Eastern Group
Levuka
Nandi
Viti Levu 1323
Ovalau
Koro Sea
Lakemba
Vatu Vara
Suva
Ngau
Moala
Kandavu
Vatoa
TONGA
Tonga (Friendly) Is.
Tofua I.
Vava'u
Tongatapu
Nuku'alofa

m
4000
3000
2000
1000
400
200
0
200
m

COPYRIGHT. GEORGE PHILIP & SON. LTD.

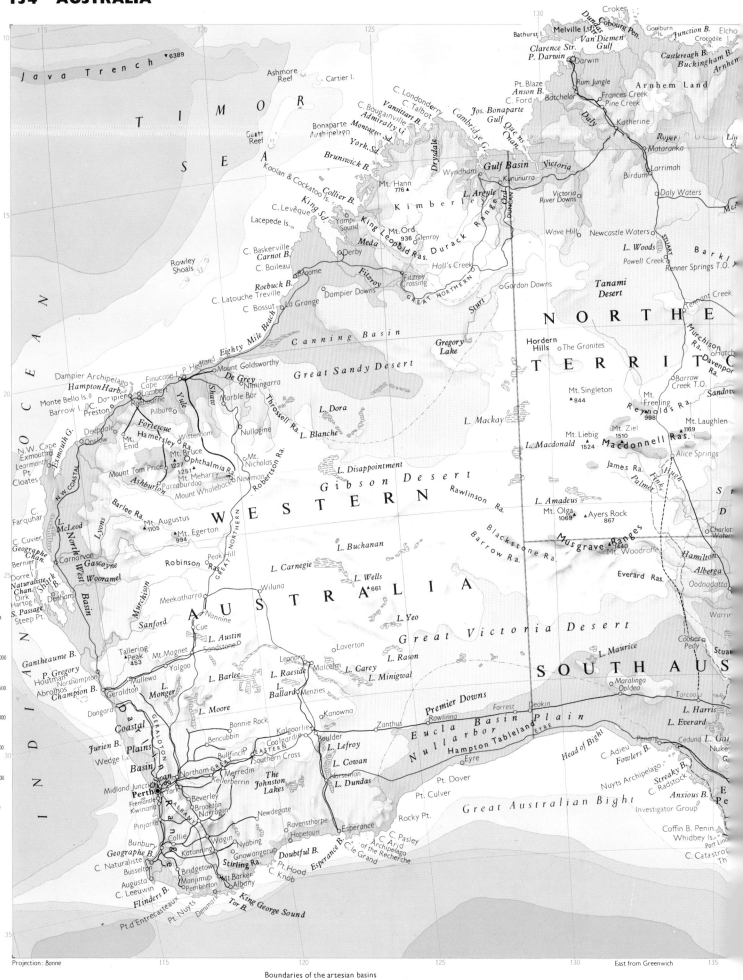

Java Trench ▼6389

TIMOR SEA

OCEAN

INDIAN OCEAN

Projection: Bonne

Boundaries of the artesian basins

East from Greenwich

WESTERN AUSTRALIA

NORTHERN TERRITORY

SOUTH AUS

Croker
Cobourg Pen.
Goulburn
Junction B.
Dundas Str.
Bathurst I. Melville I.
Van Diemen Gulf
Clarence Str.
P. Darwin
Darwin
Castlereagh B.
Buckingham B.
Arnhem

Ashmore Reef
Cartier I.
C. Londonderry
C. Talbot
Vansittart B.
C. Bougainville
Admiralty G.
Bonaparte Archipelago
Montague Sd.
York Sd.
Brunswick B.
Koolan & Cockatoo Is.
Collier B.
King Sd.
C. Lévêque
Lacepede Is.
C. Baskerville
Carnot B.
C. Boileau
Broome
Roebuck B.
C. Latouche Treville
C. Bossut
La Grange

Pt. Blaze
Anson B.
C. Ford
Batchelor
Frances Creek
Pine Creek
Katherine
Roper
Mataranka
Larrimah
Birdum

Cambridge G.
Jos. Bonaparte Gulf
Que ns.
Chan.
Wyndham
Kununurra
Gulf Basin
Victoria
L. Argyle
Drysdale
Mt. Hann 776
Kimberley
Mt. Ord 936
Glenroy
Meda
Derby
Fitzroy
Hall's Creek
Fitzroy Crossing
Gordon Downs
GREAT NORTHERN
Sturt
Dampier Downs
Eighty Mile Beach
Canning Basin
Gregory Lake

Victoria
River Downs
Wave Hill
Newcastle Waters
Powell Creek
Renner Springs T.O.
Daly Waters
L. Woods
Barkly
Tanami Desert
Hordern Hills
The Granites
Tennant Creek
Davenport
Barrow Creek T.O.

Dampier Archipelago
Hampton Harb.
Monte Bello Is.
Barrow I.
Preston
N.W. Cape
Exmouth
Learmonth
Pt. Cloates
C. Farquhar
Geographe Chan.
Bernier I.
Dorre I.
Naturaliste Chan.
Dirk Hartog I.
S. Passage
Steep Pt.
Denham
Shark B.

Finucane I.
P. Hedland
Mount Goldsworthy
Cape Lambert
Dampier
Roebourne
Pilbara
Yule
Shaw
De Grey
Nimingarra
Marble Bar
Deepdale
Onslow
Mt. Enid
Fortescue
Hamersley Ra.
Wittenoom
Mount Tom Price 1251
Mt. Bruce 1227
Ophthalmia Ra.
Ashburton
Parraburdoo
Mt. Meharry
Mount Whaleback
Newman
L. McLeod
Lyons
North West Basin
Gascoyne
Wooramel
Carnarvon
Barlee Ra.
Mt. Augustus 1105
Mt. Egerton 994
Peak Hill
Robinson
Ras.
GREAT NORTHERN

Nullagine
Throssell Ra.
L. Dora
L. Blanche
Mt. Nicholas
Robertson Ra.
L. Disappointment
Great Sandy Desert

Gibson Desert
L. Mackay
L. Macdonald
L. Amadeus
Mt. Olga 1069
Ayers Rock 867
Musgrave Ranges
Blackstone Ra.
Rawlinson Ra.
Barrow Ra.
Everard Ras.

Mt. Singleton 844
Reynolds Ra.
Mt. Freeling 998
Mt. Ziel 1510
Mt. Liebig
Mt. Laughlen 1169
Macdonnell Ras.
Alice Springs
James Ra.
Palmer
Hugh
Finke
Mt. Woodroffe 1440
Oodnadatta
Alberga
Warrir
Coober Pedy
Stua

Meekatharra
Sanford
Nannine
Cue
L. Austin
Sandstone
Wiluna
L. Carnegie
L. Buchanan
L. Wells 661
L. Yeo
Great Victoria Desert
L. Maurice
Maralinga
Ooldea
Tarcoola
L. Harris

Tallering Peak 453
Mt. Magnet
Yalgoo
Mullewa
Northampton
Houtman Abrolhos
Champion B.
Geraldton
Dangara
L. Monger
L. Barlee
Leonora
Malcolm
Menzies
L. Raeside
L. Ballard
L. Carey
L. Minigwal
L. Rason
Laverton
Premier Downs
Forrest
Deakin
Rawlinna
Zanthus
Eucla Basin
Nullarbor Plain
Hampton Tableland
EYRE
Forrest

Jurien B.
Wedge I.
Coastal Plains Basin
L. Moore
Bonnie Rock
Bencubbin
Bullfinch
Southern Cross
Kalgoorlie
Coolgardie
Boulder
Kanowna
L. Lefroy
L. Cowan
Norseman
L. Dundas
Pt. Dover
Pt. Culver
Eyre
Rocky Pt.
Great Australian Bight
Head of Bight
C. Adieu
Fowlers B.
Ceduna
L. Gai
Nuke
Penang
Streaky B.
C. Radstock
Nuyts Archipelago
Anxious B.
Investigator Group
Coffin B. Penin.
Whidbey Is.
Port Lin
C. Catastro
Pe

Perth
Fremantle
Kwinana
Midland Junction
Swan
York
Beverley
Brookton
Narrogin
Northam
Merredin
Kellerberrin
The Johnston Lakes
Newdegate
Ravensthorpe
Hopetoun
Esperance
Esperance B.
C. Arid
Archipelago of the Recherche
C. le Grand
Pt. Hood
C. Pasley
C. Knob

Pinjarra
Bunbury
Collie
Katanning
Geographe B.
C. Naturaliste
Busselton
Augusta
C. Leeuwin
Flinders B.
Bridgetown
Manjimup
Pemberton
Wagin
Nyabing
Gnowangerup
Doubtful B.
Stirling Ra.
Mt. Barker
Albany
Denmark
Tor B.
King George Sound
Pt. Nuyts
Pt. d'Entrecasteaux

m
2000
1500
1000
400
200
0
200
2000
4000
6000
m

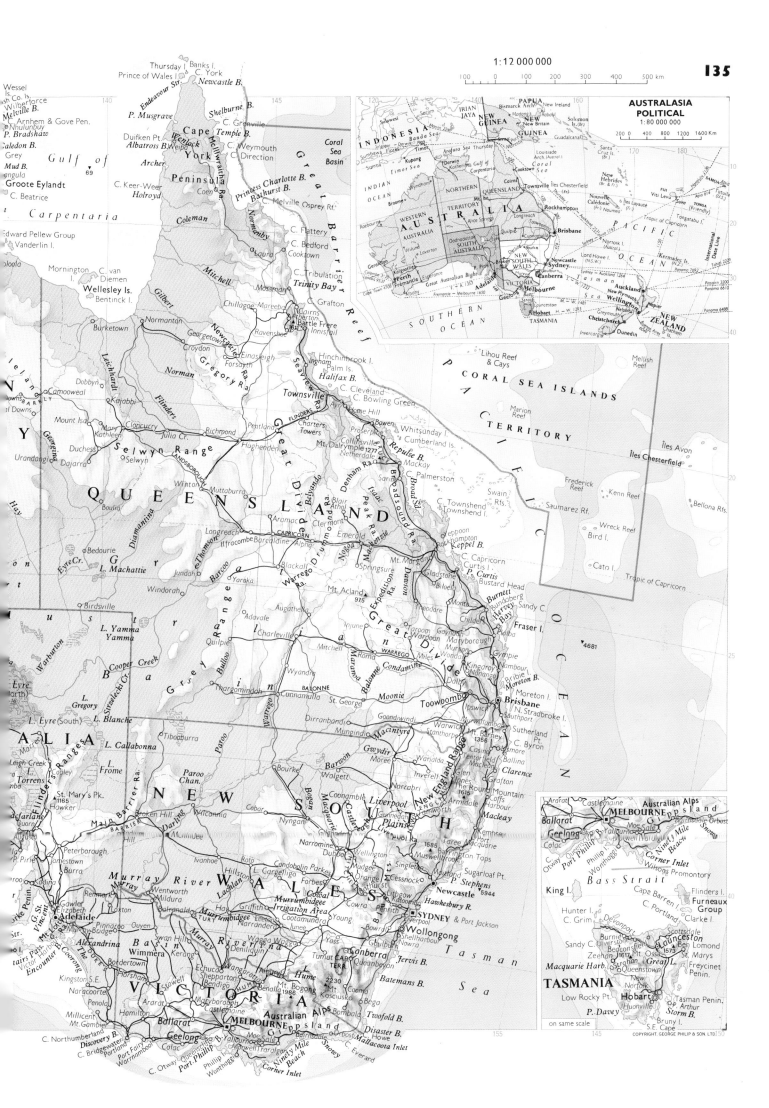

1:12 000 000

100   0   100   200   300   400   500 km

AUSTRALASIA POLITICAL
1:80 000 000

200 0   400   800   1200 1600 Km

INDONESIA

PAPUA NEW GUINEA

IRIAN JAYA

NEW GUINEA

NORTHERN TERRITORY

WESTERN AUSTRALIA

SOUTH AUSTRALIA

QUEENSLAND

NEW SOUTH WALES

VICTORIA

Perth

Adelaide

Sydney

Canberra

Melbourne

Hobart

TASMANIA

NEW ZEALAND

Auckland

Wellington

Christchurch

Dunedin

PACIFIC OCEAN

SOUTHERN OCEAN

CORAL SEA ISLANDS TERRITORY

Gulf of Carpentaria

Cape York Peninsula

Groote Eylandt

QUEENSLAND

Mount Isa

Cloncurry

Townsville

Cairns

Rockhampton

Gladstone

Brisbane

Toowoomba

Tropic of Capricorn

NEW SOUTH WALES

Broken Hill

Dubbo

Newcastle

SYDNEY

Wollongong

Canberra

ALIA

SOUTH AUSTRALIA

Adelaide

L. Eyre

VICTORIA

MELBOURNE

Geelong

Ballarat

Bass Strait

King I.

Flinders I.
Furneaux Group

TASMANIA

Launceston

Hobart

PACIFIC OCEAN

Tasman Sea

COPYRIGHT. GEORGE PHILIP & SON. LTD

1:4 500 000

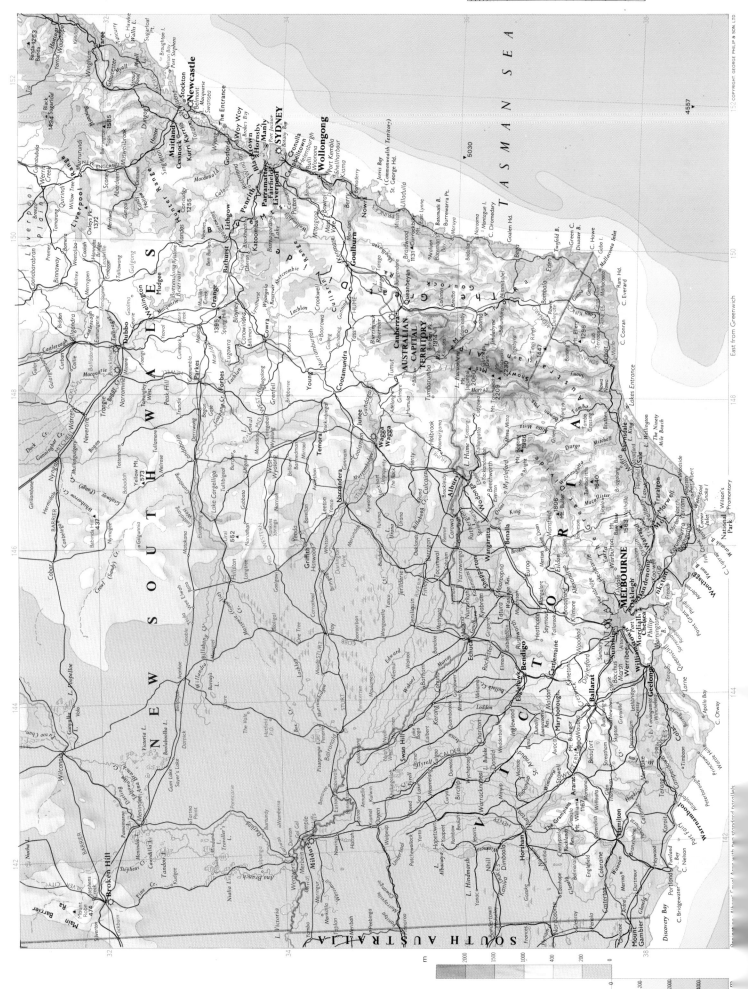

Index

The number printed in bold type against each index entry indicates the map page where the feature will be found. The geographical coordinates which follow the name are sometimes only approximate but are close enough for the place name to be located.

An open square □ signifies that the name refers to an administrative subdivision of a country while a solid square ■ follows the name of a country.

The alphabetical order of names composed of two or more words is governed primarily by the first word and then by the second. This rule applies even if the second word is a description or its abbreviation, R.,L.,I. for example. Names

composed of a proper name (St. Lawrence) and a description (Gulf of) are positioned alphabetically by the proper name. If the same place name occurs twice or more times in the index and all are in the same country, each is followed by the name of the administrative subdivision in which it is located. The names are placed in the alphabetical order of the subdivisions. If the same place name occurs twice or more in the index and the places are in different countries they will be followed by their country names, the latter governing the alphabetical order. In a mixture of these situations the primary order is fixed by the alphabetical sequence of the countries and the secondary order by that of the country subdivisions.

A. C. T. – Australian Capital Territory
A. R. – Autonomous Region
A. S. S. R. – Autonomous Soviet Socialist Republic
Afghan. – Afghanistan
Afr. – Africa
Ala. – Alabama
Alas. – Alaska
Alg. – Algeria
Alta. – Alberta
Amer. – America
And. P. – Andhra Pradesh
Ang. – Angola
Arch. – Archipelago
Argent. – Argentina
Ariz. – Arizona
Ark. – Arkansas
Atl. Oc. – Atlantic Ocean
Austral. – Australia
B. – Baie, Bahía, Bay, Bucht, Bugt
B.A. – Buenos Aires
B.C. – British Columbia
Bangla. – Bangladesh
Barr. – Barrage
Bay. – Bayern
Belg. – Belgium
Bol. – Bolshoi
Bots. – Botswana
Br. – British
Bri. – Bridge
Bt. – Bight
Bulg. – Bulgaria
C. – Cabo, Cap, Cape
C. Prov. – Cape Province
C. Rica – Costa Rica
Calif. – California
Camb. – Cambodia
Cambs. – Cambridgeshire
Can. – Canada
Cat. – Cataract, Cataracta
Cent. – Central
Chan. – Channel
Co. – Country
Colo. – Colorado
Conn. – Connecticut
Cord. – Cordillera
Cr. – Creek
Cumb. – Cumbria
Cy. – City
Czech. – Czechoslovakia
D.C. – District of Columbia
Del. – Delaware
Dep. – Dependency
Des. – Desert
Dist. – District
Dj. – Djebel
Dom. Rep. – Dominican Republic
E. – East
Eng. – England
Eq. Guinea – Equatorial Guinea

Fed. – Federal, Federation
Fla. – Florida
For. – Forest
Fr. – France, French
Fr. Gui. – French Guiana
Fs. – Falls
Ft. – Fort
G. – Golf, Golfo, Gulf, Guba
Ga. – Georgia
Germ. – Germany
Gib. – Gibraltar
Gr. – Grande, Great, Greater, Group
Guat. – Guatemala
H.K. – Hong Kong
H.P. – Himachal Pradesh
Hants. – Hampshire
Harb. – Harbor, Harbour
Hd. – Head
Hung. – Hungary
I. of W. – Isle of Wight
I.(s). – Île, Ilha, Insel, Isla, Island
Id. – Idaho
Ill. – Illinois
Ind. – Indiana
Ind. Oc. – Indian Ocean
Ivory C. – Ivory Coast
J. – Jabal, Jabel, Jazira
Junc. – Junction
K. – Kap, Kapp
K. – Kuala
Kal. – Kalmyk A.S.S.R.
Kans. – Kansas
Kor. – Korea
Kpl. – Kapell
Ky. – Kentucky
L. – Lac, Lacul, Lago, Lagoa, Lake, Limni, Loch, Lough
La. – Louisiana
Lancs. – Lancashire
Leb. – Lebanon
Lincs. – Lincolnshire
Lit. – Little
Lr. – Lower
Lt. Ho. – Light House
Mad. P. – Madhya Pradesh
Madag. – Madagascar
Malay. – Malaysia
Man. – Manitoba
Mass. – Massachusetts
Md. – Maryland
Me. – Maine
Mend. – Mendoza
Mer. – Méridionale
Mich. – Michigan
Mid. – Middle
Minn. – Minnesota
Miss. – Mississippi
Mo. – Missouri
Mong. – Mongolia
Mont. – Montana
Moroc. – Morocco
Mozam. – Mozambique

Mt.(e). – Mont, Monte, Monti, Montaña, Mountain
Mys. – Mysore
N. – North, Northern, Nouveau
N.B. – New Brunswick
N.C. – North Carolina
N.D. – North Dakota
N.H. – New Hampshire
N.I. – North Island
N.J. – New Jersey
N. Mex. – New Mexico
N.S. – Nova Scotia
N.S.W. – New South Wales
N.T. – Northern Territory
N.W.T. – North West Territory
N.Y. – New York
N.Z. – New Zealand
Nat. – National
Nat. Mon. – National Monument
Nat. Park. – National Park
Nebr. – Nebraska
Neth. – Netherlands
Nev. – Nevada
Newf. – Newfoundland
Nic. – Nicaragua
Northants. – Northamptonshire
O. – Oued, ouadi
O.F.S. – Orange Free State
Okla. – Oklahoma
Ont. – Ontario
Or. – Orientale
Oreg. – Oregon
Os. – Ostrov
Oz. – Ozero
P. – Pass, Passo, Pasul, Pulau
P.E.I. – Prince Edward Island
P.N.G. – Papua New Guinea
P.O. – Post Office
P. Rico – Puerto Rico
Pa. – Pennsylvania
Pac. Oc. – Pacific Ocean
Pak. – Pakistan
Para Prov. – Para Provincial
Pass. – Passage
Pen. – Peninsula, Peninsule
Phil. – Philippines
Pk. – Park, Peak
Plat. – Plateau
P-ov. – Poluostrov
Port. – Portugal, Portuguese
Prom. – Promontory
Prov. – Province, Provincial
Pt. – Point
Pta. – Ponta, Punta
Pte. – Pointe
Qué. – Québec
Queens. – Queensland
R. – Rio, River
R.I. – Rhode Island
R.S.F.S.R. – Russian Soviet Federal Socialist Republic
Ra.(s). – Range(s)

Raj. – Rajasthan
Reg. – Region
Rep. – Republic
Res. – Reserve, Reservoir, Reservation
Rhod. – Rhodesia
S. – San, South
S. Afr. – South Africa
S. Arab. – Saudi Arabia
S. Austral. – South Australia
S.C. – South Carolina
S.D. – South Dakota
S.I. – South Island
S. Leone – Sierra Leone
S.S.R. – Soviet Socialist Republic
Sa. – Serra, Sierra
Sard. – Sardinia
Sask. – Saskatchewan
Scot. – Scotland
Sd. – Sound
Sept. – Septentrionale
Sib. – Siberia
Span. – Spanish
Sprs. – Springs
St. – Saint
Sta. – Santa, Station
Ste. – Sainte
Sto. – Santo
Str. – Strait, Stretto
Switz. – Switzerland
T.O. – Telegraph Office
Tanz. – Tanzania
Tas. – Tasmania
Tenn. – Tennessee
Terr. – Territory
Tex. – Texas
Tg. – Tanjung
Thai. – Thailand
Trans. – Transvaal
Trin. – Trinidad
U.K. – United Kingdom
U.S.A. – United States of America
U.S.S.R. – Union of Soviet Socialist Republics
Ukr. – Ukraine
Ut.P. – Uttar Pradesh
Va. – Virginia
Vdkhr. – Vodokhranilishche
Venez. – Venezuela
Vic. – Victoria
Viet. – Vietnam
Vol. – Volcano
Vt. – Vermont
W. – Wadi, West
W.A. – Western Australia
W. Isles – Western Isles
Wash. – Washington
Wis. – Wisconsin
Wlkp. – Wielkopolski
Wyo. – Wyoming
Yorks. – Yorkshire
Yugo. – Yugoslavia

Aachen Al Madīnah

A

Aachen 105 50 47N 6 4 E
Aadorf 13 47 30N 8 55 E
Aalsmeer 105 52 17N 4 43 E
Aalst, Neth. 54 50 57N 4 20 E
Aalst, Neth. 105 51 23N 5 29 E
Aalten 105 51 56N 6 35 E
Aarau 106 47 23N 8 4 E
Aare, R. 106 47 33N 8 14 E
Aarschot 105 50 59N 4 49 E
Aba 114 5 10N 7 19 E
Abadan 122 30 22N 48 20 E
Abade 123 31 8N 52 40 E
Abadla 114 31 2N 2 45W
Abaetetuba 87 1 40S 48 50W
Abai 89 25 58S 55 54W
Abakan 121 53 40N 91 10 E
Aballetuba 87 1 40S 51 15W
Abamasagi L. 53 50 28N 87 15W
Abarqū 123 31 10N 53 20 E
Abashiri 132 44 0N 144 15 E
Abaya L. 115 6 30N 37 50 E
Abbaye, Pt. 72 46 58N 88 4W
Abbeville, France 101 50 6N 1 49 E
Abbeville, La., U.S.A. 75 30 0N 92 7W
Abbeville, S.C., U.S.A. 73 34 12N 82 21W
Abbey 56 50 44N 108 45W
Abbotabad 124 34 10N 73 15 E
Abbotsford, B.C., Can. 63 49 5N 122 20W
Abbotsford, Que., Can. 71 45 25N 72 53W
Abbotsford, U.S.A. 74 44 55N 90 20W
Abbott Corners 43 45 3N 72 48W
Abéché 115 13 50N 20 35 E
Åbenrå 111 55 3N 9 25 E
Abeokuta 114 7 3N 3 19 E
Aberaeron 95 52 15N 4 16W
Aberayron = Aberaeron 95 52 15N 4 16W
Abercorn = Mbala 116 8 46S 31 17 E
Abercrombie, R. 136 33 54S 149 8 E
Aberdare 95 51 43N 3 27W
Aberdaron 95 52 48N 4 41W
Aberdeen, Austral. 136 32 9S 150 56 E
Aberdeen, Can. 56 52 20N 106 8W
Aberdeen, U.K. 96 57 9N 2 6W
Aberdeen, Ohio, U.S.A. 77 38 39N 83 46W
Aberdeen, S.D., U.S.A. 74 45 30N 98 30W
Aberdeen, Wash., U.S.A. 80 47 0N 123 50W
Aberdovey 95 52 33N 4 3W
Aberfeldy 96 56 37N 3 50W
Aberfoyle 49 43 28N 80 9W
Abernathy 75 33 49N 101 49W
Abernethy 56 50 45N 103 25W
Aberystwyth 95 52 25N 4 6W
Abidjan 114 5 26N 3 58W
Abilene, Kans., U.S.A. 74 39 0N 97 16W
Abilene, Texas, U.S.A. 75 32 22N 99 40W
Abingdon, Can. 49 43 5N 79 41W
Abingdon, U.K. 95 51 40N 1 17W
Abingdon, Ill., U.S.A. 76 40 53N 90 23W
Abingdon, Va., U.S.A. 73 36 46N 81 56W
Abitau L. 55 60 27N 107 15W
Abitau, R. 55 59 53N 109 3W
Abitibi L. 34 48 40N 79 40W
Abitibi, R. 53 51 3N 80 55W
Abkhaz A.S.S.R. □ 120 43 0N 41 0 E
Abkit 121 64 10N 157 10 E
Åbo = Turku 111 60 27N 22 14 E
Abohar 124 30 10N 74 10 E
Abomey 114 7 10N 2 5 E
Abondance 103 46 18N 6 42 E
Abong Mbang 116 4 0N 13 8 E
Aboyne 96 57 4N 2 48W
Abqaiq 122 26 0N 49 45 E
Abra Pampa 88 22 43S 65 42W
Abrantes 104 39 24N 8 7W
Abreojos, Pta. 82 26 50N 113 40W
Abreschviller 101 48 39N 7 6 E
Abrets, Les 103 45 32N 5 35 E
Abrolhos, Arquipélago dos 87 18 0S 38 30W
Abrud 107 46 19N 23 5 E
Abruzzi □ 108 42 15N 14 0 E
Absaroka Ra. 78 44 40N 110 0W
Abū al Khasib 122 30 25N 48 0 E
Abū 'Ali 122 27 20N 49 27 E
Abū Dhabī 123 24 28N 54 36 E
Abu Hamed 115 19 32N 33 13 E
Abu Kamal 122 34 30N 41 0 E
Abu Markha 122 25 4N 38 22 E
Abû Zabad 115 12 25N 29 10 E
Abukumagawa 132 37 30N 140 30 E
Abunā 86 9 40S 65 20W
Abuná, R. 86 9 41S 65 20W
Abut Hd. 133 43 7S 170 15 E
Acacias 86 3 59N 73 46W
Acadia 59 50 58N 114 4W
Acadia Valley 61 51 8N 110 13W
Acadie, L', R. 45 45 29N 73 16W
Acajutla 84 13 36N 89 50W
Acámbaro 82 20 0N 100 40W
Acaponeta 82 22 30N 105 20W
Acapulco de Juárez 83 16 51N 99 56W
Acarai, Serra 87 1 50N 57 50W
Acarigua 86 9 33N 69 12W
Acatlan 83 18 10N 98 3W
Acayucán 83 17 59N 94 58W
Accomac 72 37 43N 75 40W
Accra 114 5 35N 0 6W
Accrington 94 53 46N 2 22W
Acebal 88 33 20S 60 50W
Aceh □ 126 4 0N 97 30 E
Achaguas 86 7 46N 68 14W
Achalpur 124 21 22N 77 32 E
Achill 97 53 56N 9 55W
Achill Hd. 97 53 59N 10 15W
Achill I. 97 53 58N 10 5W
Achill Sd. 97 53 53N 9 55W
Achinsk 121 56 20N 90 20 E
Ackerman 75 33 20N 89 8W
Ackley 76 42 33N 93 3W
Acklin's I. 85 22 30N 74 0W
Acland, Mt. 135 24 50S 148 20 E
Acme 61 51 33N 113 30W
Aconcagua 88 32 50S 70 0W
Aconcagua □ 88 32 15S 70 30W
Aconcagua, Cerro 88 32 39S 70 0W
Aconquija, Mt. 88 27 0S 66 0W
Açores, Is. dos 12 38 44N 29 0W
Acre = 'Akko 115 32 35N 35 4 E
Acre □ 86 9 1S 71 0W
Acre, R. 86 10 45S 68 25W
Actinolite 70 44 34N 77 20W
Acton 49 43 38N 80 3W
Acton Vale 41 45 39N 72 34W
Ad Dammam 122 26 20N 50 5 E
Ad Dar al Hamrā 122 27 20N 37 45 E
Ad Dawhah 123 25 15N 51 35 E
Ad Dilam 122 23 55N 47 10 E
Ada, Minn., U.S.A. 74 47 20N 96 30W
Ada, Ohio, U.S.A. 77 40 46N 83 49W
Ada, Okla., U.S.A. 75 34 50N 96 45W
Adair C. 17 71 50N 71 0W
Adaja, R. 104 41 15N 4 50W
Adam 123 22 15N 57 28 E
Adamaoua, Massif de l' 114 7 20N 12 20 E
Adamawa Highlands = Adamaoua 114 7 20N 12 20 E
Adamello, Mt. 108 46 10N 10 34 E
Adaminaby 136 36 0S 148 45 E
Adams, Mass., U.S.A. 71 42 38N 73 8W
Adams, N.Y., U.S.A. 71 43 50N 76 3W
Adams, Wis., U.S.A. 74 43 59N 89 50W
Adam's Bridge 124 9 15N 79 40 E
Adams Center 71 43 51N 76 1W
Adams L. 63 51 10N 119 40W
Adams Mt. 80 46 10N 121 28W
Adam's Peak 124 6 55N 80 45 E
Adams, R. 63 51 25N 119 27W
Adamsville 45 45 17N 72 47W
Adana 122 37 0N 35 16 E
Adapazari 122 40 48N 30 25 E
Adare, C. 91 71 0S 171 0 E
Adavale 135 25 52S 144 32 E
Adda, R. 108 45 25N 9 30 E
Addie 61 48 55N 116 10W
Addis Ababa = Addis Abeba 115 9 2N 38 42 E
Addis Abeba 115 9 2N 38 42 E
Addison, Ill., U.S.A. 77 41 56N 87 59W
Addison, N.Y., U.S.A. 70 42 9N 77 15W
Addison, Vt., U.S.A. 71 44 6N 73 18W
Addu Atoll 119 0 30S 73 0 E
Addyston 77 39 8N 84 43W
Adel, Ga., U.S.A. 73 31 10N 83 28W
Adel, Iowa, U.S.A. 76 41 37N 94 1W
Adelaide, Austral. 135 34 52S 138 30 E
Adelaide, Bahamas 84 25 0N 77 31W
Adelaide I. 91 67 15S 68 30W
Adelaide Pen. 65 68 15N 97 30W
Adelanto 81 34 35N 117 22W
Adélie, Terre 91 67 0S 140 0 E
Aden 115 12 50N 45 0 E
Aden, G. of 115 13 0N 50 0 E
Adi 127 4 15S 133 30 E
Adieu, C. 134 32 0S 132 10 E
Adige, R. 108 45 9N 11 25 E
Adilabad 124 19 33N 78 35 E
Adin 78 41 10N 121 0W
Adin Khel 124 32 45N 68 5 E
Adirondack Mts. 71 44 0N 74 15W
Adlavik Is. 36 55 2N 58 45W
Admiral 56 49 43N 108 1W
Admiral's Beach 37 47 1N 53 39W
Admiralty B. 91 62 0S 59 0W
Admiralty G. 134 14 20S 125 55 E
Admiralty I., Can. 65 69 25N 101 10W
Admiralty I., U.S.A. 67 57 40N 134 35W
Admiralty In. 65 72 30N 86 0W
Admiralty Inlet 78 48 0N 122 40W
Admiralty Ra. 91 72 0S 164 0 E
Adonara 127 8 15S 123 5 E
Adoni 124 15 33N 77 18W
Adour, R. 102 43 32N 1 32W
Adra 104 36 43N 3 3W
Adrano 108 37 40N 14 49 E
Adrar 114 27 51N 0 11W
Adrian, Mich., U.S.A. 77 41 55N 84 0W
Adrian, Mo., U.S.A. 76 38 24N 94 21W
Adrian, Tex., U.S.A. 75 35 19N 102 37W
Adriatic Sea 108 43 0N 16 0 E
Adua 127 1 45S 129 50 E
Advocate Harbour 39 45 20N 64 47W
Adwa, Ethiopia 115 14 15N 38 52 E
Adwa, Si Arab. 122 27 15N 42 35 E
Adzhar A.S.S.R. □ 120 42 0N 42 0 E
Ægean Sea 109 37 0N 25 0 E
Aerht'ai Shan 129 46 40N 92 45 E
Afars Issas, Terr. of ■ 115 11 30N 42 15 E
Affric, R. 96 57 15N 4 50W
Afghanistan ■ 124 33 0N 65 0 E
Afif 122 23 53N 42 56 E
Afognak I. 67 58 10N 152 50W
Africa 112 10 0N 20 0 E
Afton 71 42 14N 75 31W
Afuá 87 0 15S 50 10W
Afula 115 32 37N 35 17 E
Afyon Karahisar 122 38 45N 30 33 E
Agades 114 16 58N 7 59 E
Agadir 114 30 28N 9 35W
Agano, R. 132 37 50N 139 30 E
Agapa 121 71 27N 89 15 E
Agartala 125 23 50N 91 23 E
Agassiz 63 49 14N 121 46W
Agattu I. 67 52 25N 172 30 E
Agawa, R. 53 47 23N 84 40W
Agde 102 43 19N 3 28 E
Agde, C. d' 102 43 16N 3 28 E
Agen 102 44 12N 0 38 E
Aghil Mts. 124 36 0N 77 0 E
Aghil Pass 124 36 15N 76 35 E
Agincourt 50 43 47N 79 17W
Aginskoye 121 51 6N 114 32 E
Agly, R. 102 42 46N 3 3 E
Agnes L. 52 48 15N 91 20W
Agon 100 49 2N 1 34W
Agout, R. 102 43 47N 1 41 E
Agra 124 27 17N 77 58 E
Agrado 86 2 15N 75 46W
Ağri Daği 122 39 50N 44 15 E
Agri, R. 108 40 17N 16 15 E
Agrigento 108 37 19N 13 33 E
Agrinion 109 38 37N 21 27 E
Agua Caliente, Mexico 82 26 30N 108 20W
Agua Caliente, U.S.A. 81 32 29N 116 59W
Agua Caliente Springs 81 32 56N 116 19W
Agua Clara 87 20 25S 52 45W
Agua Hechicero 81 32 26N 116 14W
Agua Prieta 82 31 20N 109 32W
Aguadas 86 5 40N 75 38W
Aguadilla 85 18 27N 67 10W
Aguadulce 84 8 15N 80 32W
Aguanaval, R. 82 23 45N 103 10W
Aguanga 81 33 27N 116 51W
Aguanus, R. 38 50 13N 62 5W
Aguapey, R. 88 29 7S 56 36W
Aguaray Guazú, R. 88 24 47S 57 19W
Aguarico, R. 86 0 0 77 30W
Aguas Blancas 88 24 15S 69 55W
Aguas Calientes, Sierra de 88 25 26S 67 27W
Aguascalientes 82 22 0N 102 12W
Aguascalientes □ 82 22 0N 102 20W
Aguilares 88 27 26S 65 35W
Aguilas 104 37 23N 1 35W
Aguja, C. de la 86 11 18N 74 12W
Aguja, Pta. 86 6 0S 81 0W
Agulhas Basin 16 45 0S 25 0 E
Agulhas, Kaap 117 34 52S 20 0 E
Agung 126 8 20S 115 28 E
Agusan, R. 127 9 20N 125 50 E
Ahaggar 114 23 0N 6 30 E
Ahar 122 38 35N 47 0 E
Ahaura 133 42 20S 171 32 E
Ahimanawa Ra. 14 39 5S 176 30 E
Ahipara B. 133 35 5S 173 5 E
Ahiri 124 19 30N 80 0 E
Ahlen 105 51 45N 7 52 E
Ahmadabad (Ahmedabad) 124 23 0N 72 40 E
Ahmadnagar (Ahmednagar) 124 19 7N 74 46 E
Ahmadpur 124 29 12N 71 10 E
Ahome 82 25 55N 109 11W
Ahsā, Wahatā al 122 25 50N 49 0 E
Ahuachapán 84 13 54N 89 52W
Ahvāz 122 31 20N 48 40 E
Ahvenanmaa 111 60 15N 20 0 E
Aibaq 123 36 15N 68 5 E
Aichi-ken □ 132 35 0N 137 15 E
Aignay-le-Duc 101 47 40N 4 43 E
Aigre 102 45 54N 0 1 E
Aigua 89 34 13S 54 46W
Aiguebelle, Parc 40 48 30N 78 45W
Aigueperse 102 46 3N 3 13 E
Aigues-Mortes 103 43 35N 4 12 E
Aiguilles 103 44 47N 6 51 E
Aiguillon 102 44 18N 0 21 E
Aiguillon, L' 102 46 20N 1 16W
Aigurande 102 46 27N 1 49 E
Aihun 130 49 55N 127 30 E
Aija 86 9 50S 77 45W
Aijal 125 23 40N 92 44 E
Aiken 73 33 34N 81 50W
Aillant-sur-Tholon 101 47 52N 3 20 E
Aillik 36 55 11N 59 18W
Ailly-sur-Noye 101 49 45N 2 20 E
Ailsa Craig 46 43 8N 81 33W
Ailsa Craig, I. 96 55 15N 5 7W
Aim 121 59 0N 133 55 E
Aimere 127 8 45S 121 3 E
Aimogasta 88 28 33S 66 50W
Aimorés 87 19 30S 41 4W
Aimorés, Serra dos 87 17 50S 40 30W
Ain □ 103 46 5N 5 20 E
Ain Banaiyan 123 23 0N 51 0 E
Ain Dār 122 25 55N 49 10 E
Ain, R. 103 45 52N 5 11 E
Ainslie, L. 39 46 8N 61 11W
Ainsworth 74 42 33N 99 52W
Aion 121 69 50N 169 0 E
Aipe 86 3 13N 75 15W
Aïr 114 18 30N 8 0 E
Air Force I. 65 67 58N 74 5W
Airaines 101 49 58N 1 55 E
Aird, The, C. 96 57 26N 4 30W
Airdrie, Can. 61 51 18N 114 2W
Airdrie, U.K. 96 55 53N 3 57W
Aire 101 50 37N 2 22 E
Aire, R., France 101 49 18N 5 0 E
Aire, R., U.K. 94 53 42N 1 30W
Aire-sur-l'Adour 102 43 42N 0 15W
Airvault 100 46 50N 0 8W
Aishihik 67 61 40N 137 46W
Aisne □ 101 49 42N 3 40 E
Aisne, R. 101 49 26N 2 50 E
Aitkin 52 46 32N 93 43W
Aitush 129 39 54N 75 40 E
Aiud 107 46 19N 23 44 E
Aix-en-Provence 103 43 32N 5 27 E
Aix-la-Chapelle = Aachen 105 50 47N 6 4 E
Aix-les-Bains 103 45 41N 5 53 E
Aix-sur-Vienne 102 45 48N 1 8 E
Aiyansh 54 55 17N 129 2W
Aiyina 109 37 45N 23 26 E
Aiyion 109 38 15N 22 5 E
Aizenay 100 46 44N 1 38W
Ajaccio 103 41 55N 8 40 E
Ajaccio, G. d' 103 41 52N 8 40 E
Ajalpán 83 18 22N 97 15W
Ajanta Ra. 124 20 28N 75 50 E
Ajax 51 43 50N 79 1W
'Ajlun 115 32 18N 35 47 E
Ajman 123 25 25N 55 30 E
Ajmer 124 26 28N 74 37 E
Ajo 79 32 18N 112 54W
Ak Dağ 122 36 30N 30 0 E
Akaroa 133 43 49S 172 59 E
Akaroa Harb. 15 43 54S 172 59 E
Akashi 132 34 45N 135 0 E
Akelamo 127 1 35N 129 40 E
Akershus Fylke □ 111 60 10N 11 15 E
Aketi 116 2 38N 23 47 E
Akhelóös, R. 109 39 5N 21 25 E
Akhisar 122 38 56N 27 48 E
Akiak 67 60 50N 161 12W
Akimiski I. 34 52 50N 81 30W
Akita 132 39 45N 140 0 E
Akita-ken □ 132 39 40N 140 30 E
'Akko 115 32 35N 35 4 E
Akkol 120 43 36N 70 45 E
Aklavik 64 68 12N 135 0W
Akola 124 20 42N 77 2 E
Akpatok I. 36 60 25N 68 8W
Akranes 110 64 19N 22 6W
Akron, Can. 53 48 55N 84 7W
Akron, Colo., U.S.A. 74 40 13N 103 15W
Akron, Ind., U.S.A. 77 41 2N 86 1W
Akron, Ohio, U.S.A. 70 41 7N 81 31W
Akrotíri, Ákra 109 40 26N 25 27W
Aksaray 122 38 25N 34 2 E
Aksarka 120 66 31N 67 50 E
Aksehir 122 38 18N 31 30 E
Aksenovo Zilovskoye 121 53 20N 117 40 E
Aksu 129 41 4N 80 5 E
Aksum 115 14 5N 38 40 E
Aktogay 120 44 25N 76 44 E
Aktyubinsk 120 50 17N 57 10 E
Akulurak 67 62 40N 164 35W
Akun I. 67 54 15N 165 30W
Akureyri 110 65 40N 18 6W
Akutan I. 67 53 30N 166 0W
Al Ahmadiyah 122 37 5N 43 30 E
Al Amārah 122 31 55N 47 15 E
Al 'Aqabah 122 29 37N 35 0 E
Al Ashkhara 123 21 50N 59 30 E
Al Badi 122 22 0N 46 35 E
Al Basrah 122 30 30N 47 50 E
Al Dīwaniyah 122 32 0N 45 0 E
Al Fallujah 122 33 20N 43 55 E
Al Fāw 122 30 0N 48 30 E
Al Hadithan 122 34 0N 41 13 E
Al Hāmad 122 31 30N 39 30 E
Al Hamar 122 22 23N 46 6 E
Al Hariq 122 23 29N 46 27 E
Al Hasakah 122 36 35N 40 45 E
Al Havy 122 32 5N 46 5 E
Al Hillah, Iraq 122 32 30N 44 25 E
Al Hillah, Si Arab. 122 23 35N 46 50 E
Al Hilwah 122 23 24N 46 48 E
Al Hindiyah 122 32 30N 44 10 E
Al Hūfuf 122 25 25N 49 45 E
Al Ittihad = Madinat al Shaab 115 12 50N 45 0 E
Al Jahrah 122 29 25N 47 40 E
Al Jalāmid 122 31 20N 39 45 E
Al Jawf 115 24 10N 23 24 E
Al Jubail 122 27 0N 49 50 E
Al Khābūrah 123 23 57N 57 5 E
Al Kūt 122 32 30N 46 0 E
Al Kuwayt 122 29 20N 48 0 E
Al Lādhiqiyah 122 35 30N 35 45 E
Al Madīnah 122 24 35N 39 52 E

Al Majma'ah **Ambato**

Al Majma'ah **122** 25 57N 45 22 E
Al Manamāh **123** 26 10N 50 30 E
Al Marj **115** 32 25N 20 30 E
Al Mawsil **122** 36 15N 43 5 E
Al Miqdadīyah **122** 34 0N 45 0 E
Al Mubarraz **122** 25 30N 49 40 E
Al Muharraq **123** 26 15N 50 40 E
Al Musayyib **122** 32 40N 44 25 E
Al Muwaylih **122** 27 40N 35 30 E
Al Qāmishli **122** 37 10N 41 10 E
Al Qatif **122** 26 35N 50 0 E
Al Quaisūmah **122** 28 10N 46 20 E
Al Quraiyat **123** 23 17N 58 53 E
Al Qurnah **122** 31 1N 47 25 E
Al 'Ula **122** 26 35N 38 0 E
Al Uqayr **122** 25 40N 50 15 E
Al' Uwayqilah **122** 30 30N 42 10 E
Al 'Uyūn **122** 26 30N 43 50 E
Al Wakrah **123** 25 10N 51 40 E
Al Warī 'ah **122** 27 50N 47 30 E
Ala Shan **129** 40 0N 104 0 E
Alabama □ **73** 33 0N 87 0W
Alabama, R. **73** 31 30N 87 35W
Alabaster **46** 44 10N 83 33W
Alagôa Grande **87** 7 3 S 35 35W
Alagôas □ **87** 9 0 S 36 0W
Alagoinhas **87** 12 0 S 38 20W
Alajuela **84** 10 2N 84 8W
Alameda, Can. **57** 49 16N 102 17W
Alameda, Calif., U.S.A. **80** 37 46N 122 15W
Alameda, Idaho, U.S.A. **78** 43 2N 112 30W
Alameda, N. Mex., U.S.A. **79** 35 10N 106 43W
Alamitos, Sierra de los **82** 26 30N 102 20W
Alamo **81** 37 21N 115 10W
Alamo Crossing **81** 34 16N 113 33W
Alamogordo **79** 32 59N 106 0W
Alamos **82** 27 0N 109 0W
Alamosa **79** 37 30N 106 0W
Åland **111** 60 15N 20 0 E
Ålands hav **111** 60 10N 19 30 E
Alanson **46** 45 27N 84 47W
Alanya **122** 36 38N 32 0 E
Alapayevsk **120** 57 52N 61 42 E
Alashanchih **130** 38 58N 105 14 E
Alaska □ **67** 65 0N 150 0W
Alaska, G. of **67** 58 0N 145 0W
Alaska Highway **54** 60 0N 130 0W
Alaska Pen. **67** 56 0N 160 0W
Alaska Range **67** 62 50N 151 0W
Alatyr **120** 54 45N 46 35 E
Alausí **86** 2 0 S 78 50W
Alava, C. **78** 48 10N 124 40W
Alba **108** 44 41N 8 1 E
Alba-Iulia **107** 46 8N 23 39 E
Albacete **104** 39 0N 1 50W
Albanel **41** 48 53N 72 27W
Albanel, L. **36** 50 55N 73 12W
Albania ■ **109** 41 0N 20 0 E
Albany, Austral. **134** 35 1 S 117 58 E
Albany, Ga., U.S.A. **73** 31 40N 84 10W
Albany, Ind., U.S.A. **77** 40 18N 85 13W
Albany, Minn., U.S.A. **74** 45 37N 94 38W
Albany, Mo., U.S.A. **76** 40 15N 94 20W
Albany, N.Y., U.S.A. **71** 42 35N 73 47W
Albany, Oreg., U.S.A. **78** 44 41N 123 0W
Albany, Tex., U.S.A. **75** 32 45N 99 20W
Albany, Wis., U.S.A. **76** 42 43N 89 26W
Albany, R. **34** 52 17N 81 31W
Albardón **88** 31 20 S 68 30W
Albarracín, Sierra de **104** 40 30N 1 30W
Albatross B. **135** 12 45 S 141 30 E
Albemarle **73** 35 27N 80 15W
Albemarle Sd. **73** 36 0N 76 30W
Alberche, R. **104** 40 10N 4 30W
Alberdi **88** 26 14 S 58 20W
Alberga, R. **134** 26 50 S 133 40 E
Alberni **54** 49 20N 124 50W
Albert, Can. **35** 45 51N 64 38W
Albert, France **101** 50 0N 2 38 E
Albert Canyon **63** 51 8N 117 41W
Albert L. **78** 42 40N 120 8W
Albert Lea **74** 43 32N 93 20W
Albert, L. = Mobutu Sese Seko, L. **116** 1 30N 31 0 E
Albert Nile, R. **116** 3 16N 31 38 E
Albert Park **58** 50 24N 104 38W
Albert Town **85** 22 37N 74 33 E
Alberta □ **54** 54 40N 115 0W
Alberta Beach **60** 53 40N 114 21W
Alberti **88** 35 1 S 60 16W
Alberton, Ont., Can. **49** 43 11N 80 5W
Alberton, P.E.I., Can. **39** 46 50N 64 0W
Albertville **103** 45 40N 6 22 E
Albertville = Kalemie **116** 5 55 S 29 9 E
Alberz, Reshteh-Ye Kūkhā-Ye **123** 36 0N 52 0 E
Albi **102** 43 56N 2 9 E
Albia **76** 41 0N 92 50W
Albina **87** 5 37N 54 15W
Albion, Idaho, U.S.A. **78** 42 21N 113 37W
Albion, Ill., U.S.A. **77** 38 23N 88 4W
Albion, Ind., U.S.A. **77** 41 24N 85 25W
Albion, Mich., U.S.A. **77** 42 15N 84 45W
Albion, Nebr., U.S.A. **74** 41 47N 98 0W
Albion, Pa., U.S.A. **70** 41 53N 80 21W
Ålborg **111** 57 2N 9 54 E
Albreda **63** 52 35N 119 10W
Albuquerque **79** 35 5N 106 47W
Albuquerque, Cayos de **84** 12 10N 81 50W
Alburg **43** 44 58N 73 19W
Alburquerque **104** 39 15N 6 59W
Alcalá de Henares **104** 40 28N 3 22W
Alcalá la Real **104** 37 27N 3 57W
Alcamo **108** 37 59N 12 55 E
Alcaníz **104** 41 2N 0 8W
Alcântara **87** 2 20 S 44 30W
Alcántara **104** 39 41N 6 57W
Alcantara L. **55** 60 57N 108 9W
Alcaraz, Sierra de **104** 38 40N 2 20W
Alcaudete **104** 37 35N 4 5W
Alcázar de San Juan **104** 39 24N 3 12W
Alcira **104** 39 9N 0 30W
Alcoa **73** 35 50N 84 0W
Alcobaça **104** 39 32N 9 0W
Alcova **78** 42 37N 106 52W
Alcoy **104** 38 43N 0 30W
Aldabra Is. **16** 9 22 S 46 28 E
Aldama **83** 22 25N 98 4W
Aldan **121** 58 40N 125 30 E
Aldan, R. **121** 62 30N 135 10 E
Aldeburgh **95** 52 9N 1 35 E
Alder **78** 45 27N 112 3W
Alder Pk. **80** 35 53N 12 22W
Alderney, I. **100** 49 42N 2 12W
Aldershot, N.S., Can. **39** 45 6N 64 31W
Aldershot, Ont., Can. **48** 43 18N 79 51W
Aldershot, U.K. **95** 51 15N 0 43W
Aldersyde **54** 50 40N 113 53W
Aledo **76** 41 10N 90 50W
Alegre **89** 20 50 S 41 30W
Alegrete **89** 29 40 S 56 0W
Aleisk **120** 52 40N 83 0 E
Alejandro Selkirk, I. **15** 33 50 S 80 15W
Aleksandrov Gay. **120** 50 15N 48 35 E
Aleksandrovsk-Sakhaliniskiy **121** 50 50N 142 20 E
Aleksandrovskiy Zavod **121** 50 40N 117 50 E
Aleksandrovskoye **120** 60 35N 77 50 E
Além Paraíba **89** 21 52 S 42 41W
Alemania, Argent. **88** 25 40 S 65 30W
Alemania, Chile **88** 25 10 S 69 55W
Alençon **100** 48 27N 0 4 E
Alentejo, Alto- **104** 39 0N 7 40W
Alentejo, Baixo- **104** 38 0N 8 30W
Alenuihaha Chan. **67** 20 25N 156 0W
Aleppo **122** 36 10N 37 15 E
Aléria **103** 42 5N 9 26 E
Alert **65** 83 2N 60 0W
Alert B. **62** 50 30N 127 35W
Alès **103** 44 9N 4 5 E
Alessándria **108** 44 54N 8 37 E
Ålesund **111** 62 28N 6 12 E
Alet-les-Bains **102** 43 0N 2 14 E
Aleutian Is. **67** 52 0N 175 0W
Aleutian Ra. **67** 55 0N 155 0W
Alex Graham, Mt. **63** 52 4N 122 52W
Alexander **74** 47 51N 103 40W
Alexander Arch. **67** 57 0N 135 0W
Alexander B. **117** 28 36 S 16 33 E
Alexander City **73** 32 58N 85 57W
Alexander I. **91** 69 0 S 70 0W
Alexandra, Austral. **136** 37 8 S 145 40 E
Alexandra, N.Z. **133** 45 14 S 169 25 E
Alexandra Falls **54** 60 29N 116 18W
Alexandretta = Iskenderun **129** 36 32N 36 10 E
Alexandria, B.C., Can. **63** 52 35N 122 27W
Alexandria, Ont., Can. **47** 45 19N 74 38W
Alexandria, S. Afr. **117** 33 38 S 26 28 E
Alexandria, Ind., U.S.A. **77** 40 18N 85 40W
Alexandria, Ky., U.S.A. **77** 38 58N 84 23W
Alexandria, La., U.S.A. **75** 31 20N 92 30W
Alexandria, Minn., U.S.A. **74** 45 50N 95 20W
Alexandria, Mo., U.S.A. **76** 40 27N 91 28W
Alexandria, S.D., U.S.A. **74** 43 40N 97 45W
Alexandria, Va., U.S.A. **72** 38 47N 77 1W
Alexandria = El Iskandarîya **115** 31 0N 30 0 E
Alexandria Bay **71** 44 20N 75 52W
Alexandrina, L. **135** 35 25 S 139 10 E
Alexandroúpolis **109** 40 50N 25 54 E
Alexis **76** 41 4N 90 33W
Alexis Creek **62** 52 10N 123 20W
Alexis, R. **36** 52 33N 56 8W
Alfenas **89** 21 40 S 44 0W
Alford **96** 57 13N 2 42W
Alfred, Me., U.S.A. **71** 43 28N 70 40W
Alfred, N.Y., U.S.A. **70** 42 15N 77 45W
Alfreton **94** 53 6N 1 22W
Alftanes **110** 64 29N 22 10W
Alga **120** 49 53N 57 20 E
Alganac **70** 42 36N 82 34W
Algarve **104** 37 15N 8 10W
Algeciras **104** 36 9N 5 28W
Algemesí **104** 39 11N 0 27W
Alger **114** 36 42N 3 8 E
Algeria ■ **114** 35 10N 3 11 E
Alghero **108** 40 34N 8 20 E
Algiers = Alger **114** 36 42N 3 8 E
Algoabaai **117** 33 50 S 25 45 E
Algoma, Oreg., U.S.A. **78** 42 25N 121 54W
Algoma, Wis., U.S.A. **72** 44 35N 87 27W
Algona **76** 43 1N 94 10W
Algonac **46** 42 37N 82 32W
Algonquin **77** 42 10N 88 18W
Algonquin Prov. Pk. **47** 45 50N 78 30W
Alhama de Murcia **104** 37 51N 1 25W
Alhambra, Can. **61** 52 20N 114 40W
Alhambra, Calif., U.S.A. **81** 34 8N 118 10W
Alhambra, Ill., U.S.A. **76** 38 52N 89 45W
Ali al Gharbi **122** 32 30N 46 45 E
Ali Khel **124** 33 56N 69 35 E
Aliābād **123** 28 10N 57 35 E
Aliakmon, R. **109** 40 10N 22 0 E
Alicante **104** 38 23N 0 30W
Alice, Can. **47** 45 47N 77 14W
Alice, U.S.A. **75** 27 47N 98 1W
Alice Arm **54** 55 29N 129 31W
Alice Springs **134** 23 40 S 135 50 E
Alicedale **124** 33 15 S 26 4 E
Aliceville **73** 33 9N 88 10W
Alida **57** 49 25N 101 55W
Aligarh **124** 27 55N 78 10 E
Aligudarz **122** 33 25N 49 45 E
Aling Kangri, Range **125** 31 45N 84 45 E
Alingsås **111** 57 56N 12 31 E
Alipur **124** 29 25N 70 55 E
Alipur Duar **125** 26 30N 89 35 E
Aliquippa **70** 40 38N 80 18W
Aliwal North **117** 30 45 S 26 45 E
Alix **61** 52 24N 113 11W
Aljustrel **104** 37 55N 8 10W
Alkmaar **105** 52 37N 4 45 E
All American Canal **79** 32 45N 115 0W
Allahabad **125** 25 25N 81 58 E
Allakaket **67** 66 30N 152 45W
Allakh Yun **121** 60 50N 137 5 E
Allan **56** 51 53N 106 4W
Allanburg **49** 43 5N 79 12W
Allanche **102** 45 14N 2 57 E
Allanwater **52** 50 14N 90 10W
Allard, L. **38** 50 32N 63 31W
Allardville **39** 47 28N 65 29W
Allassac **102** 45 15N 1 29 E
Allegan **77** 42 32N 85 52W
Allegany **70** 41 30N 78 30W
Allegheny Mts. **72** 38 0N 80 0W
Allegheny, R. **70** 41 14N 79 50W
Allegheny Res. **70** 42 0N 78 55W
Allègre **102** 45 12N 3 41 E
Allen, Bog of **97** 53 15N 7 0W
Allen, L. **97** 54 30N 8 5W
Allende **82** 28 20N 100 50W
Allentown **71** 40 36N 75 30W
Alleppey **124** 9 30N 76 28 E
Allevard **103** 45 24N 6 5 E
Alliance, Can. **61** 52 26N 111 47W
Alliance, Nebr., U.S.A. **74** 42 10N 102 50W
Alliance, Ohio, U.S.A. **70** 40 53N 81 7W
Allier □ **102** 46 25N 3 0 E
Allier, R. **101** 46 57N 3 4 E
Alliford Bay **62** 53 12N 131 58W
Allison **76** 42 45N 92 48W
Allison Harbour **62** 51 2N 127 29W
Alliston **46** 44 9N 79 52W
Alloa **96** 56 7N 3 49W
Allos **103** 44 15N 6 38 E
Alluviaq, Fj. **36** 59 27N 65 10W
Alma, N.B., Can. **39** 45 36N 64 57W
Alma, Ont., Can. **49** 43 44N 80 30W
Alma, Qué., Can. **41** 48 35N 71 40W
Alma, Kans., U.S.A. **74** 39 1N 96 22W
Alma, Mich., U.S.A. **46** 43 25N 84 40W
Alma, Nebr., U.S.A. **74** 40 10N 99 25W
Alma, Wis., U.S.A. **74** 44 19N 91 54W
Alma Ata **120** 43 15N 76 57 E
Almada **104** 38 40N 9 9W
Almadén **104** 38 49N 4 52W
Almanor, L. **78** 40 15N 121 11W
Almansa **104** 38 51N 1 5W
Almanzor, Pico de **104** 40 15N 5 18W
Almanzora, R. **104** 37 22N 2 21W
Almazán **104** 41 30N 2 30W
Almeirim **87** 1 30 S 52 0W
Almelo **105** 52 22N 6 42 E
Almendralejo **104** 38 41N 6 26W
Almería **104** 36 52N 2 32W
Almirante **84** 9 10N 82 30W
Almont **46** 42 53N 83 2W
Almonte **47** 45 14N 76 12W
Almora **124** 29 38N 79 4 E
Alnwick **94** 55 25N 1 42W
Alo Tau, mts. **129** 45 30N 80 40 E
Alon **125** 22 12N 95 5 E
Alonsa **55** 50 50N 99 0W
Alor, I. **127** 8 15 S 124 30 E
Alor Setar **128** 6 7N 100 22 E
Alpaugh **80** 35 53N 119 29W
Alpena **46** 45 6N 83 24W
Alpes-de-Haute-Provence □ **103** 44 8N 6 10 E
Alpes-Maritimes □ **103** 43 55N 7 10 E
Alpha, Austral. **135** 23 39 S 146 37 E
Alpha, U.S.A. **76** 41 11N 90 23W
Alphen **105** 51 29N 4 58 E
Alphonse, I. **16** 7 0 S 52 45 E
Alpi Craie **101** 45 40N 7 0 E
Alpine, Ariz., U.S.A. **79** 33 57N 109 4W
Alpine, Calif., U.S.A. **81** 32 50N 116 46W
Alpine, Tex., U.S.A. **75** 30 25N 103 35W
Alps **106** 47 0N 8 0 E
Alsace **101** 48 15N 7 25 E
Alsask **56** 51 21N 109 59W
Alsásua **104** 42 54N 2 10W
Alsdorf **105** 50 53N 6 10 E
Alsten **110** 65 58N 12 40 E
Alta **110** 69 57N 23 10 E
Alta Gracia **88** 31 40 S 64 30W
Alta Lake **63** 50 10N 123 0W
Alta Sierra **81** 35 42N 118 33W
Alta Vista **48** 45 23N 75 40W
Altaelva **110** 69 46N 23 45 E
Altafjorden **110** 70 5N 23 5 E
Altagracia **86** 10 45N 71 30W
Altai **129** 48 6N 87 2 E
Altai = Aerhatai Shan **129** 46 40N 92 45 E
Altamaha, R. **73** 31 50N 82 0W
Altamira, Brazil **87** 3 0 S 52 10W
Altamira, Chile **88** 25 47 S 69 51W
Altamira, Colomb. **86** 2 3N 75 47W
Altamira, Mexico **83** 22 24N 97 55W
Altamont, Ill., U.S.A. **77** 39 4N 88 45W
Altamont, N.Y., U.S.A. **71** 42 43N 74 3W
Altanbulag **130** 50 16N 106 30 E
Altar **82** 30 40N 111 50W
Altario **61** 51 55N 110 9W
Altata **82** 24 30N 108 0W
Altavista **72** 37 9N 79 22W
Altkirch **101** 47 37N 7 15 E
Alto Araguaia **87** 17 15 S 53 20W
Alto Cuchumatanes **82** 15 30N 91 10W
Alto del Inca **88** 24 10 S 68 10W
Alto Molocue **117** 15 50 S 37 35 E
Alto Paraná □ **89** 25 0 S 54 50W
Alto Uruguay, R. **89** 27 0 S 53 30W
Alton, Can. **49** 43 54N 80 5W
Alton, U.S.A. **76** 38 55N 90 5W
Altona, Austral. **136** 37 51 S 144 50 E
Altona, Man., Can. **57** 49 6N 97 33W
Altona, Ont., Can. **50** 43 58N 79 12W
Altona, Ger. **106** 53 32N 9 56 E
Altoona, Iowa, U.S.A. **76** 41 39N 93 28W
Altoona, Pa., U.S.A. **70** 40 32N 78 24W
Alturas **78** 41 36N 120 37W
Altus **75** 34 30N 99 25W
Altyn Tagh **129** 39 0N 90 0 E
Alunite **81** 35 59N 114 55W
Alusi **127** 7 35 S 131 40 E
Alva **75** 36 50N 98 50W
Alvarado, Mexico **83** 18 40N 95 50W
Alvarado, U.S.A. **75** 32 25N 97 15W
Alvaro Obregón, Presa **82** 27 55N 109 52W
Alvear **88** 29 5 S 56 30W
Alvena **56** 52 31N 106 1W
Alvesta **111** 56 54N 14 35 E
Alvin **75** 29 23N 95 12W
Alvinston **46** 42 49N 81 52W
Älvkarleby **111** 60 32N 17 40 E
Älvsborgs län □ **111** 58 30N 12 30 E
Älvsbyn **110** 65 40N 20 0 E
Alwar **124** 27 38N 76 34 E
Alyangula **135** 13 55 S 136 30 E
Alyaskitovyy **121** 64 45N 141 30 E
Alzada **74** 45 3N 104 22W
Am Timan **115** 11 0N 20 10 E
Amadeus, L. **134** 24 54 S 131 0 E
Amadi **116** 3 40N 26 40 E
Amadia **122** 37 6N 43 30 E
Amadjuak **65** 64 0N 72 39W
Amadjuak L. **65** 65 0N 71 8W
Amadore **70** 43 12N 82 36W
Amaga **86** 6 3N 75 42W
Amagasaki **132** 34 42N 135 20 E
Amakusa-Shotō **132** 32 15N 130 10 E
Amål **111** 59 2N 12 40 E
Amalfi **86** 6 55N 75 4W
Amalner **124** 21 5N 75 5 E
Amambaí **89** 23 5 S 55 13W
Amambai, R. **89** 23 22 S 53 56W
Amambay □ **89** 23 0 S 56 0W
Amambay, Cordillera de **89** 20 30 S 56 0W
Amami-guntō **131** 28 0N 129 0 E
Amanda Park **80** 47 28N 123 55W
Amangeldy **120** 50 10N 65 10 E
Amapá **87** 2 5N 50 50W
Amapá □ **87** 1 40N 52 0W
Amara **122** 31 57N 47 12 E
Amarante **87** 6 14 S 42 50W
Amaranth **57** 50 36N 98 43W
Amaravati = Amraoti **124** 20 45N 77 45 E
Amargosa **87** 13 2 S 39 36W
Amargosa, R. **81** 36 14N 116 51W
Amargosa Ra., mts **81** 36 25N 116 40W
Amarillo **75** 35 14N 101 46W
Amaro, Mt. **108** 42 5N 14 6 E
Amarpur **125** 23 30N 91 45 E
Amasra **122** 41 45N 32 30 E
Amasya **122** 40 40N 35 50 E
Amatignak I. **67** 51 19N 179 10W
Amatitlán **84** 14 29N 90 38W
Amazon, R. **87** 2 0 S 53 30W
Amazonas □, Brazil **86** 4 20 S 64 0W
Amazonas □, Colomb. **86** 1 0 S 72 0W
Amazonas □, Venez. **86** 3 30N 66 0W
Amazonas, R. **87** 2 0 S 53 30W
Ambala **124** 30 23N 76 56 E
Ambalavao **117** 21 50 S 46 56 E
Ambam **116** 2 20N 11 15 E
Ambanja **117** 13 40 S 48 27 E
Ambarchik **121** 69 40N 162 20 E
Ambato **86** 1 5 S 78 42W

Ambato, Sierra de **Aquiles Serdán**

Ambato, Sierra de	**88**	28 25N	66 10W
Ambatolampy	**117**	19 20S	47 35E
Ambatondrazaka	**117**	17 55S	48 28E
Ambeno	**127**	9 20S	124 30E
Amberg	**106**	49 25N	11 52E
Ambergris Cay	**83**	18 0N	88 0W
Ambérieu-en-Bugey	**103**	45 57N	5 20E
Amberley	**133**	43 9S	172 44E
Ambert	**102**	45 33N	3 44E
Ambikapur	**125**	23 15N	83 15E
Ambilobé	**117**	13 10S	49 3E
Ambleside	**94**	54 26N	2 58W
Ambo	**86**	10 5S	76 10W
Ambon	**127**	3 35S	128 20E
Ambositra	**117**	20 31S	47 25E
Amboy, Calif., U.S.A.	**81**	34 33N	115 51W
Amboy, Ill., U.S.A.	**76**	41 44N	89 20W
Amboy, N.J., U.S.A.	**71**	40 31N	74 18W
Ambre, C. d'	**117**	12 40S	49 10E
Ambre, Mt. d'	**117**	12 30S	49 10E
Ambridge	**70**	40 36N	80 15W
Ambriz	**116**	7 48S	13 8E
Ambrizete	**116**	7 10S	12 52E
Ambrose	**56**	48 57N	103 29W
Amchitka I.	**67**	51 30N	179 0W
Amchitka P.	**67**	51 30N	179 0W
Amderma	**120**	69 45N	61 30E
Ameca	**82**	20 30N	104 0W
Ameca, R.	**82**	20 40N	105 15W
Amecameca	**83**	19 10N	98 57W
Ameland	**105**	53 27N	5 45E
Amélie-les-Bains-Palalda	**102**	42 29N	2 41E
Amen	**121**	68 45N	180 0E
American Falls	**78**	42 46N	112 56W
American Falls Res.	**78**	43 0N	112 50W
American Highland	**91**	73 0S	75 0E
American Samoa	**133**	14 20S	170 40W
Americana	**89**	22 45S	47 20W
Americus	**73**	32 0N	84 10W
Amersfoort	**105**	52 9N	5 23E
Amery	**55**	56 34N	94 3W
Ames	**76**	42 0N	93 40W
Amesbury	**71**	42 50N	70 52W
Amesdale	**55**	50 2N	92 55W
Ameson	**34**	49 50N	84 35W
Amet Sound	**39**	45 47N	63 10W
Amga, R.	**121**	61 0N	132 0E
Amgu	**121**	45 45N	137 15E
Amgun, R.	**121**	52 50N	138 0E
Amherst, Burma	**125**	16 2N	97 20E
Amherst, Can.	**39**	45 48N	64 8W
Amherst, Mass., U.S.A.	**71**	42 21N	72 30W
Amherst, Ohio, U.S.A.	**70**	41 23N	82 15W
Amherst, Tex., U.S.A.	**75**	34 0N	102 24W
Amherst I.	**47**	44 8N	76 43W
Amherstburg	**46**	42 6N	83 6W
Amiata Mte.	**108**	42 54N	11 40E
Amiens	**101**	49 54N	2 16E
Amirante Is.	**16**	6 0S	53 0E
Amisk	**61**	52 33N	111 4W
Amisk L.	**55**	54 35N	102 15W
Amistati, Presa	**82**	29 24N	101 0W
Amite	**75**	30 47N	90 31W
Amlia I.	**67**	52 5N	173 30W
Amlwch	**94**	53 24N	4 21W
'Ammān	**115**	32 0N	35 52E
Amne Machin Shan	**129**	34 25N	99 40E
Amnéville	**101**	49 16N	6 9E
Amoret	**76**	38 15N	94 35W
Amorgós	**109**	36 50N	25 57E
Amos	**40**	48 35N	78 5W
Amoy = Hsiamen	**131**	24 25N	118 4E
Amoy Hsiamen	**131**	24 25N	118 4E
Amozoc	**83**	19 2N	98 3W
Ampanihy	**117**	24 40S	44 45E
Amqui	**38**	48 28N	67 27W
Amraoti	**124**	20 55N	77 45E
Amreli	**124**	21 35N	71 17E
Amritsar	**124**	31 35N	74 57E
Amroha	**124**	28 53N	78 30E
Amsterdam, Neth.	**105**	52 23N	4 54E
Amsterdam, U.S.A.	**71**	42 58N	74 10W
Amsterdam, Î.	**16**	37 30S	77 30E
Amu Darya, R.	**120**	37 50N	65 0E
Amuay	**86**	11 50N	70 10W
Amukta I.	**67**	52 29N	171 20W
Amund Ringnes I.	**65**	78 20N	96 25W
Amundsen Gulf	**64**	71 0N	124 0W
Amundsen Sea	**91**	72 0S	115 0W
Amuntai	**126**	2 28S	115 25E
Amur, R.	**121**	53 30N	122 30E
Amurang	**127**	1 5N	124 40E
Amuri Pass	**133**	42 31S	172 11E
Amurzet	**121**	47 50N	131 5E
Amyot	**53**	48 29N	84 57W
An Nafūd	**122**	28 15N	41 0E
An Najaf	**122**	32 3N	44 15E
An Nasiriyah	**122**	31 0N	46 15E
An Nhon (Binh Dinh)	**128**	13 55N	109 7E
An Nu'ayriyah	**122**	27 30N	48 30E
An Uaimh, Ireland	**97**	53 39N	6 40W
An Uaimh, Ireland	**97**	53 39N	6 40W
Ana Branch, R.	**136**	32 20S	143 0E
Anaco	**86**	9 27N	64 28W
Anaconda	**78**	46 7N	113 0W
Anacortes	**80**	48 30N	122 40W
Anadarko	**75**	35 4N	98 15W
Anadolu	**122**	38 0N	29 0E
Anadyr	**121**	64 35N	177 20E
Anadyr, R.	**121**	66 50N	171 0E
Anadyrskiy Zaliv	**121**	64 0N	180 0E
Anah	**122**	34 25N	42 0E
Anaheim	**81**	33 50N	118 0W
Anahim Lake	**62**	52 28N	125 18W
Anáhuac	**82**	27 14N	100 9W
Anakapalle	**125**	17 42N	83 06E
Analalava	**117**	14 35S	48 0E
Anama Bay	**57**	51 58N	98 4W
Anambas, Kepulauan	**126**	3 20N	106 30E
Anamoose	**74**	47 55N	100 20W
Anamosa	**76**	42 7N	91 30W
Anamur	**122**	36 8N	32 58E
Anan	**132**	33 54N	134 40E
Anantnag	**124**	33 45N	75 10E
Anápolis	**87**	16 15S	48 50W
Anar	**123**	30 55N	55 13E
Anārak	**123**	33 25N	53 40E
Anatolia = Anadolu	**122**	38 0N	29 0E
Anatone	**78**	46 9N	117 4W
Añatuya	**88**	28 20S	62 50W
Anaunethad L.	**55**	60 55N	104 25W
Ancaster	**48**	43 13N	79 59W
Ancenis	**100**	47 21N	1 10W
Anchor Bay	**80**	38 48N	123 34W
Anchorage	**67**	61 10N	149 50W
Ancien Canal	**44**	45 19N	74 2W
Ancienne-Lorette	**42**	46 48N	71 21W
Ancohuma, Nevada	**86**	16 0S	68 50W
Ancon	**82**	8 57N	79 33W
Ancón	**86**	11 50S	77 10W
Ancona	**108**	43 37N	13 30E
Ancud	**90**	42 0S	73 50W
Ancud, G. de	**90**	42 0S	73 0W
Andacollo, Argent.	**88**	37 10S	70 42W
Andacollo, Chile	**88**	30 15S	71 10W
Andalgalá	**88**	27 40S	66 30W
Åndalsnes	**110**	62 35N	7 43E
Andalucia	**104**	37 35N	5 0W
Andalusia	**73**	31 25N	86 30W
Andalusia = Andalucía	**104**	37 35N	5 0W
Andaman Is.	**128**	12 30N	92 30E
Andaman Sea	**128**	13 0N	96 0E
Andaman Str.	**128**	12 15N	92 20E
Andara	**117**	18 2S	21 9E
Andelot	**101**	46 51N	5 56E
Andelys, Les	**100**	49 15N	1 25E
Anderlues	**105**	50 25N	4 16E
Andernach	**105**	50 24N	7 25E
Andernos-les-Bains	**102**	44 44N	1 6W
Anderson, Calif., U.S.A.	**78**	40 30N	122 19W
Anderson, Ind., U.S.A.	**77**	40 5N	85 40W
Anderson, Mo., U.S.A.	**75**	36 43N	94 29W
Anderson, S.C., U.S.A.	**73**	34 32N	82 40W
Anderson L.	**63**	50 37N	122 25W
Anderson, R.	**64**	69 42N	129 0W
Andes, mts.	**86**	20 0S	68 0W
Andfjorden	**110**	69 10N	16 20E
Andhra Pradesh □	**124**	15 0N	80 0E
Andikíthira	**109**	35 52N	23 15E
Andizhan	**120**	41 10N	72 0E
Andkhui	**123**	36 52N	65 8E
Ando	**136**	36 43S	149 16E
Andorra ■	**104**	42 30N	1 30E
Andorra La Vella	**104**	42 31N	1 32E
Andover, Can.	**39**	46 45N	67 42W
Andover, U.K.	**95**	51 13N	1 29W
Andover, N.Y., U.S.A.	**70**	42 11N	77 48W
Andover, Ohio, U.S.A.	**70**	41 35N	80 35W
Andreanof Is.	**67**	51 0N	178 0W
Andreville	**41**	47 41N	69 44W
Andrew	**60**	53 53N	112 21W
Andrews, S.C., U.S.A.	**73**	33 29N	79 30W
Andrews, Tex., U.S.A.	**75**	32 18N	102 33W
Ándria	**108**	41 13N	16 17E
Andriba	**117**	17 30S	46 58E
Androka	**117**	24 58S	44 2E
Andros	**109**	37 50N	24 50E
Andros I.	**84**	24 30N	78 0W
Andros Town	**84**	24 43N	77 47W
Andújar	**104**	38 3N	4 5W
Anegada I.	**85**	18 45N	64 20W
Aneroid	**56**	49 43N	107 18W
Aneto, Pico de	**104**	42 37N	0 40E
Ang Thong	**128**	14 35N	100 31E
Anga	**121**	60 35N	132 0E
Angamos, Punta	**88**	23 1S	70 32W
Angangki	**130**	47 9N	123 48E
Angara, R.	**121**	58 30N	97 0E
Angarsk	**121**	52 30N	104 0E
Ånge	**110**	62 31N	15 35E
Ange-Gardien	**42**	45 22N	72 57W
Ángel de la Guarda, I.	**82**	29 30N	113 30W
Ängelholm	**111**	56 15N	12 58E
Angels Camp	**80**	38 8N	120 30W
Ångermanälven	**110**	62 40N	18 0E
Angers, Can.	**40**	45 31N	75 29W
Angers, France	**100**	47 30N	0 35W
Ångerville	**101**	48 19N	2 0E
Ångesån	**110**	66 50N	22 15E
Angikuni L.	**55**	62 0N	100 0W
Angkor	**128**	13 22N	103 50E
Anglesey, I.	**94**	53 17N	4 20W
Anglet	**102**	43 29N	1 31W
Angleton	**75**	29 12N	95 23W
Angliers	**40**	47 33N	79 14W
Anglure	**101**	48 35N	3 50E
Angmagssalik	**17**	65 40N	37 20W
Ango	**116**	4 10N	26 5E
Angoche, I.	**117**	16 20S	39 50E
Angol	**88**	37 56S	72 45W
Angola, Ind., U.S.A.	**77**	41 40N	85 0W
Angola, N.Y., U.S.A.	**70**	42 38N	79 2W
Angola ■	**117**	12 0S	18 0E
Angoon	**67**	57 40N	134 40W
Angoulême	**102**	45 39N	0 10E
Angoumois	**102**	45 50N	0 25E
Angra dos Reis	**89**	23 0S	44 10W
Angran	**120**	80 59N	69 3E
Anguilla, I.	**85**	18 14N	63 5W
Anguille Mts.	**37**	48 0N	59 11W
Angus	**46**	44 19N	79 53W
Angus, Braes of	**96**	56 51N	3 0W
Angusville	**57**	50 44N	101 1W
Anhanduí, R.	**89**	21 46S	52 9W
Anholt	**111**	56 42N	11 33E
Anhwa	**131**	28 18N	111 25E
Ani	**131**	28 50N	115 29E
Aniak	**67**	61 58N	159 50W
Animas	**79**	31 58N	108 58W
Anin	**128**	15 36N	97 50E
Anita	**76**	41 27N	94 46W
Anjen	**131**	26 42N	113 19E
Anjidiv I.	**124**	14 40N	74 10E
Anjou, Can.	**43**	45 36N	73 33W
Anjou, France	**100**	47 20N	0 15W
Anjozorobe	**117**	18 22S	47 52E
Anju	**130**	39 40N	125 45E
Ankang	**131**	32 38N	109 5E
Ankara	**122**	40 0N	32 54E
Ankazoabo	**117**	22 18S	44 31E
Ankazobé	**117**	18 20S	47 10E
Ankeny	**76**	41 44N	93 36W
Anki	**131**	25 1N	118 4E
Anking	**131**	30 34N	117 1E
Ankoro	**116**	6 45S	26 55E
Anlu	**131**	31 12N	113 38E
Ann Arbor	**46**	42 17N	83 45W
Ann C., Antarct.	**91**	66 30S	50 30E
Ann C., U.S.A.	**71**	42 39N	70 37W
Anna, Ill., U.S.A.	**75**	37 28N	89 10W
Anna, Ohio, U.S.A.	**77**	40 24N	84 11W
Annaba	**114**	36 50N	7 46E
Annacis I.	**66**	49 10N	122 57W
Annaheim	**56**	52 19N	104 49W
Annalee, R.	**97**	54 3N	7 15W
Annalera Telegraph Office	**136**	41 16S	143 59E
Annam = Trung-Phan	**128**	16 30N	107 30E
Annamitique, Chaîne	**128**	17 0N	106 0E
Annan	**96**	55 0N	3 17W
Annan, R.	**96**	54 58N	3 18W
Annapolis Royal	**39**	44 44N	65 32W
Annecy	**103**	45 55N	6 8E
Annecy, L. d'	**103**	45 52N	6 10E
Annemasse	**103**	46 12N	6 16E
Annette	**67**	55 2N	131 35W
Annieopsquotch Mts.	**37**	48 20N	57 30W
Annieville	**66**	49 11N	122 55W
Anning	**129**	24 58N	102 30E
Anniston	**73**	33 45N	85 50W
Annobón = Pagalu	**112**	1 35S	3 35E
Annonay	**103**	45 15N	4 40E
Annonciation, L', Can.	**34**	46 25N	74 55W
Annonciation, L', Qué., Can.	**40**	46 25N	74 55W
Annot	**103**	43 58N	6 38E
Annotto Bay	**84**	18 17N	77 3W
Annville	**71**	40 18N	76 32W
Anoka	**74**	45 10N	93 26W
Anola	**57**	49 53N	96 38W
Anping	**131**	23 0N	120 6E
Ansbach	**106**	49 17N	10 34E
Anse-au-Clair, L'	**37**	51 25N	57 5W
Anse au Loup, L'	**37**	51 32N	56 50W
Anse, L'	**52**	46 47N	88 28W
Anserma	**86**	5 13N	75 48W
Anshun	**131**	26 2N	105 57E
Ansi	**130**	40 21N	96 10E
Ansley	**74**	41 19N	99 24W
Anson	**75**	32 46N	99 54W
Anson B.	**134**	13 20S	130 6E
Ansonia, Conn., U.S.A.	**71**	41 21N	73 6W
Ansonia, Ohio, U.S.A.	**77**	40 13N	84 38W
Ansonville	**34**	48 46N	80 43W
Anstruther	**96**	56 14N	2 40W
Anstruther, E. and W.	**96**	56 14N	2 40W
Ansudu	**127**	2 11S	139 22E
Anta	**130**	46 18N	125 34E
Antabamba	**86**	14 40S	73 0W
Antakya	**122**	36 14N	36 10E
Antalaha	**117**	14 57S	50 20E
Antalya	**122**	36 52N	30 45E
Antalya Körfezi	**122**	36 15N	31 30E
Antananarivo	**117**	18 55S	47 35E
Antarctic Pen.	**91**	67 0S	60 0W
Antarctica	**91**	90 0S	0 0
Antequera, Parag.	**88**	24 8S	57 7W
Antequera, Spain	**104**	37 5N	4 33W
Antero Mt.	**79**	38 45N	106 15W
Anthony, Kans., U.S.A.	**75**	37 8N	98 2W
Anthony, N. Mex., U.S.A.	**79**	32 1N	106 37W
Anti Atlas, Mts.	**114**	30 30N	6 30W
Antibes	**103**	43 34N	7 6E
Antibes, C. d'	**103**	43 31N	7 7E
Anticosti, Î. d'	**38**	49 30N	63 0W
Antifer, C. d'	**100**	49 41N	0 10E
Antigo	**74**	45 8N	89 5W
Antigonish	**39**	45 38N	61 58W
Antigua	**84**	14 34N	90 41W
Antigua Bahama, Canal de la	**84**	22 10N	77 30W
Antigua, I.	**85**	17 0N	61 50W
Antilla	**84**	20 40N	75 50W
Antimony	**79**	38 7N	112 0W
Antioch	**80**	38 7N	121 45W
Antioche, Pertuis d'	**102**	46 6N	1 20W
Antioquia	**86**	6 40N	75 55W
Antioquia □	**86**	7 0N	75 30W
Antipodes Is.	**14**	49 45S	178 40E
Antler, Can.	**57**	49 34N	101 27W
Antler, U.S.A.	**57**	48 58N	101 18W
Antler, R.	**57**	49 8N	101 0W
Antlers	**75**	34 15N	95 35W
Antofagasta	**88**	23 50S	70 30W
Antofagasta □	**88**	24 0S	69 0W
Antofagasta de la Sierra	**88**	26 5S	67 20W
Antofallá	**88**	25 30S	68 5W
Antofalla, Salar de	**88**	25 40S	67 45W
Anton	**75**	33 49N	102 5W
Anton Chico	**79**	35 12N	105 5W
Antongil, B. d'	**117**	15 30S	49 50E
Antonina	**89**	25 26S	48 42W
Antonito	**79**	37 4N	106 1W
Antrain	**100**	48 28N	1 30W
Antrim	**97**	54 43N	6 13W
Antrim □	**97**	54 42N	6 20W
Antrim Co.	**97**	54 58N	6 20W
Antrim, Mts. of	**97**	54 57N	6 8W
Antsalova	**117**	18 40S	44 37E
Antsirabé	**117**	19 55S	47 2E
Antsohihy	**117**	14 50S	47 50E
Antung	**130**	40 10N	124 18E
Antwerp, N.Y., U.S.A.	**71**	44 12N	75 36W
Antwerp, Ohio, U.S.A.	**77**	41 11N	84 45W
Antwerp = Antwerpen	**105**	51 13N	4 25E
Antwerpen	**105**	51 13N	4 25E
Antwerpen □	**105**	51 15N	4 40E
Anupgarh	**124**	29 10N	73 10E
Anuradhapura	**124**	8 22N	80 28E
Anvers I.	**91**	64 30S	63 40W
Anvik	**67**	62 37N	160 20W
Anxious B.	**134**	33 24S	134 45E
Anyang	**130**	36 7N	114 26E
Anyer-Lor	**127**	6 6S	105 56E
Anyi	**131**	35 0N	110 44E
Anyuan	**131**	24 59N	115 31E
Anza	**81**	33 35N	116 39W
Anzhero-Sudzhensk	**120**	56 10N	83 40E
Ánzio	**108**	41 28N	12 37E
Aomori	**132**	40 45N	140 45E
Aomori-ken □	**132**	40 45N	140 45E
Aosta	**108**	45 43N	7 20E
Apa, R.	**88**	22 6S	58 2W
Apache, Ariz., U.S.A.	**79**	31 46N	109 6W
Apache, Okla., U.S.A.	**75**	34 53N	98 22W
Apalachee B.	**73**	30 0N	84 0W
Apalachicola	**73**	29 40N	85 0W
Apaporis, R.	**86**	0 30S	70 30W
Aparri	**127**	18 22N	121 38E
Aparurén	**86**	5 6N	62 8W
Apatzingán	**82**	19 0N	102 20W
Apeldoorn	**105**	52 13N	5 57E
Apenam	**126**	8 35S	116 13E
Apennines	**93**	44 20N	10 20E
Apia	**86**	5 5N	75 58W
Apia	**133**	13 50S	171 50W
Apiacás, Serra dos	**86**	9 50S	57 0W
Apiaí	**86**	24 31S	48 50W
Apizaco	**83**	19 26N	98 9W
Aplao	**86**	16 0S	72 40W
Apo, Mt.	**127**	6 53N	125 14E
Apohaqui	**39**	45 42N	65 36W
Apollo Bay	**136**	38 45S	143 40E
Apolo	**86**	14 30S	68 30W
Apostle Is.	**52**	47 0N	90 30W
Apóstoles	**89**	28 0S	56 0W
Apoteri	**86**	4 2N	58 32W
Appalachian Mts.	**72**	38 0N	80 0W
Appalachicola, R.	**73**	30 0N	85 0W
Appennini	**108**	41 0N	15 0E
Appingedam	**105**	53 19N	6 51E
Apple Hill	**47**	45 13N	74 46W
Apple Valley	**81**	34 30N	117 11W
Appleby, Can.	**48**	43 23N	79 46W
Appleby, U.K.	**94**	54 35N	2 29W
Appleton	**72**	44 17N	88 25W
Appleton City	**76**	38 11N	94 2W
Approuague	**87**	4 20N	52 0W
Apsley	**47**	44 45N	78 6W
Apt	**103**	43 53N	5 24E
Apucarana	**89**	23 55S	51 33W
Apulia = Puglia	**108**	41 0N	16 30E
Apure □	**86**	7 10N	68 50W
Apure, R.	**86**	8 0N	69 20W
Apurimac, R.	**86**	12 10S	73 30W
Apurito, R.	**86**	7 50N	67 0W
Aq Chah	**123**	37 0N	66 5E
'Aqaba, Khalīj al	**122**	28 15N	33 20E
'Aqrah	**122**	36 46N	43 45E
Aqsu	**129**	41 10N	80 15E
Aquanish	**38**	50 14N	62 2W
Aquidauana	**87**	20 30S	55 50W
Aquila, L'	**108**	42 21N	13 24E
Aquiles Serdán	**82**	28 37N	105 54W

Aquin Assis

Aquin 85 18 16N 73 24W
Ar Ramadi 122 33 25N 43 20 E
Ar Raqqah 122 36 0N 38 55 E
Ar Rass 122 25 50N 43 40 E
Ar Rifai 122 31 50N 46 10 E
Ar Riyâd 122 24 41N 46 42 E
Ar Rub 'al Khālī 115 21 0N 51 0 E
Ar Ruṭbah 122 33 0N 40 15 E
Ara L. 53 50 33N 87 28W
Arab, Shatt al 122 30 0N 48 31 E
Arabelo 86 4 55N 64 13W
Arabia 118 25 0N 45 0 E
Arabian Sea 118 16 0N 65 0 E
Aracajú 87 10 55 S 37 4W
Aracataca 86 10 38N 74 9W
Aracati 87 4 30 S 37 44W
Araçatuba 89 21 10 S 50 30W
Aracena 104 37 53N 6 38W
Aracruz 87 19 49 S 40 16W
Araçuaí 87 16 52 S 42 4W
Arad 107 46 10N 21 20 E
Arafura Sea 127 10 0 S 135 0 E
Aragón 104 41 25N 1 0W
Aragón, R. 104 42 35N 0 50W
Aragua □ 86 10 0N 67 10W
Aragua de Barcelona 86 9 28N 64 49W
Araguacema 87 8 50 S 49 20W
Araguaia, R. 87 7 0 S 49 15W
Araguari 87 18 38 S 48 11W
Araguari, R. 87 1 0N 51 40W
Arak 114 25 20N 3 45 E
Arāk 122 34 0N 49 40 E
Arakan Coast 125 19 0N 94 0 E
Arakan Yoma 125 20 0N 94 30 E
Araks, R. = Aras, Rud-e 122 39 10N 47 10 E
Aral Sea = Aralskoye More 120 44 30N 60 0 E
Aralsk 120 46 50N 61 20 E
Aralskoye More 120 44 30N 60 0 E
Aramac 135 22 58 S 145 14 E
Aran, I. 97 55 0N 8 30W
Aran Is. 97 53 5N 9 42W
Aranjuez 104 40 1N 3 40W
Aranos 117 24 9 S 19 7 E
Aransas Pass 75 27 55N 97 9W
Aranyaprathet 128 13 41N 102 30 E
Aranzazu 86 5 16N 75 30W
Arapahoe 74 40 22N 99 53W
Arapawa I. 15 41 13 S 174 20 E
Arapey Grande, R. 88 30 55 S 57 49W
Arapkir 122 39 5N 38 30 E
Arapongas 89 23 29 S 51 28W
Arapuni 14 38 3 S 175 37 E
Araranguá 89 29 0 S 49 30W
Araraquara 87 21 50 S 48 0W
Araras 89 5 15 S 60 35W
Ararás, Serra dos 89 25 0 S 53 10W
Ararat 136 37 16 S 143 0 E
Ararat, Mt. = Ağri Daği 122 39 50N 44 15 E
Araruama, Lagoa de 89 22 53 S 42 12W
Aras, Rud-e 122 39 10N 47 10 E
Arauca 86 7 0N 70 40W
Arauca □ 86 6 40N 71 0W
Arauca, R. 86 7 30N 69 0W
Arauco 88 37 16 S 73 25W
Arauco □ 88 37 40 S 73 25W
Arauquita 86 7 2N 71 25W
Araure 86 9 34N 69 13W
Araxá 87 19 35 S 46 55W
Araya, Pen. de 86 10 40N 64 0W
Arbatax 108 39 57N 9 42 E
Arbeláez 86 4 17N 74 26W
Arbīl 122 36 15N 44 5 E
Arbois 101 46 55N 5 46 E
Arbor Vitae 52 48 54N 94 18W
Arborfield 56 53 6N 103 39W
Arborg 57 50 54N 97 13W
Arbresle, L' 103 45 50N 4 26 E
Arbroath 96 56 34N 2 35W
Arbuckle 80 39 3N 122 2W
Arc 101 47 28N 5 34 E
Arcachon 102 44 40N 1 10W
Arcachon, Bassin d' 102 44 42N 1 10W
Arcade 70 42 34N 78 25W
Arcadia, Can. 39 43 50N 66 4W
Arcadia, Fla., U.S.A. 73 27 20N 81 50W
Arcadia, Ind., U.S.A. 77 40 10N 86 1W
Arcadia, Iowa, U.S.A. 76 42 5N 95 3W
Arcadia, La., U.S.A. 75 32 34N 92 53W
Arcadia, Nebr., U.S.A. 74 41 29N 99 4W
Arcadia, Pa., U.S.A. 70 40 46N 78 54W
Arcadia, Wis., U.S.A. 74 44 13N 91 29W
Arcanum 77 39 59N 84 33W
Arcata 78 40 55N 124 4W
Arcen 131 51 29N 6 11 E
Archangel = Arkhangelsk 120 64 40N 41 0 E
Archbald 71 41 30N 75 31W
Archbold 77 41 31N 84 18W
Archer, R. 135 13 25 S 142 50 E
Archerwill 56 52 26N 103 51W
Arcis-sur-Aube 101 48 32N 4 10 E
Arco 78 43 45N 113 16W
Arcola, Can. 57 49 40N 102 30W
Arcola, U.S.A. 77 39 41N 88 19W
Arcos 104 41 12N 2 16W
Arcot 124 12 53N 79 20 E
Arcoverde 87 8 25 S 37 4W
Arctic B. 65 73 1N 85 7W
Arctic Ocean 17 78 0N 160 0W
Arctic Red, R. 67 66 0N 132 0W
Arctic Red River 64 67 15N 134 0W
Arctic Village 67 68 5N 145 45W
Arda, R. 109 41 40N 25 40 E
Ardabrīl 122 38 15N 48 18 E
Ardakan 123 30 20N 52 5 E
Ardbeg 46 45 38N 80 5W
Ardèche □ 103 44 42N 4 16 E
Ardee 97 53 51N 6 32W
Arden, Man., Can. 57 50 17N 99 16W
Arden, Ont., Can. 47 44 43N 76 56W
Arden, U.S.A. 81 36 1N 115 14W
Ardennes 106 49 30N 5 10 E
Ardennes □ 101 49 35N 4 40 E
Ardentes 101 46 45N 1 50 E
Ardestān 123 33 20N 52 25 E
Ardgour 96 56 45N 5 25W
Ardlethan 136 34 22 S 146 53 E
Ardmore, Can. 60 54 20N 110 29W
Ardmore, Okla., U.S.A. 75 34 10N 97 5W
Ardmore, Pa., U.S.A. 71 39 58N 75 18W
Ardmore, S.D., U.S.A. 74 43 0N 103 40W
Ardnacrusha 97 52 43N 8 38W
Ardnamurchan Pt. 96 56 44N 6 14W
Ardoise, L' 39 45 37N 60 45W
Ardres 101 50 50N 2 0 E
Ardrossan 96 55 39N 4 50W
Ards □ 97 54 35N 5 30W
Ards Pen. 97 54 30N 5 25W
Arecibo 85 18 29N 66 42W
Areia Branca 87 5 0 S 37 0W
Arena de la Ventana, Punta 82 24 4N 109 52W
Arena, Pt. 80 38 57N 123 44W
Arenales, Cerro 90 47 5 S 73 40W
Arenas, Pta. 86 10 20N 62 39W
Arendal 111 58 28N 8 46 E
Arendonk 105 51 19N 5 5 E
Arenzville 76 39 53N 90 22W
Arequipa 86 16 20 S 71 30W
Arès 102 44 47N 1 8W
Arévalo 104 41 3N 4 43W
Arezzo 108 43 28N 11 50 E
Argelès-Gazost 102 43 0N 0 6W
Argelès-sur-Mer 102 42 34N 3 1 E
Argent-sur-Sauldre 101 47 33N 2 25 E
Argenta, Can. 54 50 20N 116 55W
Argenta, U.S.A. 77 39 59N 88 49W
Argentan 100 48 45N 0 1W
Argentário, Mte. 108 42 23N 11 11 E
Argentat 102 45 6N 1 56 E
Argenteuil 101 48 57N 2 14 E
Argenteuil □ 43 45 50N 74 30W
Argentia 37 47 18N 53 58W
Argentina 86 0 34N 74 17W
Argentina ■ 90 35 0 S 66 0W
Argentino, L. 90 50 10 S 73 0W
Argenton-sur-Creuse 102 46 36N 1 30 E
Argentré 100 48 5N 0 40W
Argeş, R. 107 44 30N 25 50 E
Arghandab, R. 124 32 15N 66 23 E
Argolikós Kólpos 109 37 20N 22 52 E
Argonne 101 49 0N 5 20 E
Argos 109 37 40N 22 43 E
Argos 77 41 14N 86 15W
Argostólion 109 38 12N 20 33 E
Arguello, Pt. 81 34 34N 120 40W
Argun, R. 121 53 20N 121 28 E
Argus Pk. 81 35 52N 117 26W
Argyle, Can. 57 50 11N 97 27W
Argyle, U.S.A. 74 48 23N 96 49W
Århus 111 56 8N 10 11 E
Ariake-wan 132 31 30N 131 10 E
Arica, Chile 86 18 32 S 70 20W
Arica, Colomb. 86 2 0 S 71 50W
Arica, Peru 86 1 30 S 75 30W
Arichat 39 45 31N 61 1W
Arid, C. 134 34 1 S 123 10 E
Ariège □ 102 42 56N 1 30 E
Ariège, R. 102 43 30N 1 25 E
Arima 85 10 38N 61 17W
Arinos, R. 86 11 15 S 57 0W
Ario de Rosales 82 19 12N 101 42W
Aripuanã 86 9 25 S 60 30W
Aripuanã, R. 86 7 30 S 60 25W
Ariquemes 86 9 55 S 63 6W
Arisaig 96 56 55N 5 50W
Arismendi 86 8 29N 68 22W
Ariss 49 43 35N 80 22W
Aristazabal, I. 62 52 40N 129 10W
Arivaca 79 31 37N 111 25W
Arizaro, Salar de 88 24 40 S 67 50W
Arizona 88 35 45 S 65 25W
Arizona □ 79 34 20N 111 30W
Arizpe 82 30 20N 110 11W
Arjeplog 110 66 3N 18 2 E
Arjona 86 10 14N 75 22W
Arjuno 127 7 49 S 112 19 E
Arka 121 60 15N 142 0 E
Arka Tagh 129 36 30N 90 0 E
Arkadelphia 75 34 5N 93 0W
Arkaig, L. 96 56 58N 5 10W
Arkansas □ 75 35 0N 92 30W
Arkansas City 75 37 4N 97 3W
Arkansas, R. 75 35 20N 93 30W
Arkell 49 43 32N 80 10W
Arkhangelsk 120 64 40N 41 0 E
Arklow 97 52 48N 6 10W
Arkona 46 43 4N 81 50W
Arkticheskiy, Mys 121 81 10N 95 0 E
Arlanc 102 45 25N 3 42 E
Arlanzón, R. 104 42 12N 4 0W
Arlberg Pass 106 49 9N 10 12 E
Arlee 78 47 10N 114 4W
Arles 103 43 41N 4 40 E
Arlington, Oreg., U.S.A. 78 45 48N 120 6W
Arlington, S.D., U.S.A. 74 44 25N 97 4W
Arlington, Wash., U.S.A. 80 48 11N 122 4W
Arlington Heights 77 42 5N 87 59W
Arlon 105 49 42N 5 49 E
Armadale 50 43 50N 79 15W
Armagh, Can. 41 46 41N 70 32W
Armagh, U.K. 97 54 22N 6 40W
Armagh □ 97 54 18N 6 37W
Armagh Co. 97 54 16N 6 35W
Armagnac 102 43 44N 0 10 E
Armançon, R. 101 47 59N 3 30 E
Armavir 120 45 2N 41 7 E
Armenia 86 4 35N 75 45W
Armentières 101 50 40N 2 50 E
Armero 86 4 58N 74 54W
Armidale, Austral. 135 30 30 S 151 40 E
Armidale, Can. 39 44 37N 63 38W
Armour 74 43 20N 98 25W
Arms 34 49 34N 86 3W
Armstead 78 45 0N 112 56W
Armstrong, B.C., Can. 63 50 25N 119 10W
Armstrong, Ont., Can. 52 50 18N 89 4W
Armstrong, U.S.A. 75 26 59N 97 48W
Arnarfjörður 110 65 48N 23 40W
Arnaud, R. 36 59 59N 69 46W
Arnay-le-Duc 101 47 10N 4 27 E
Arnes 110 66 1N 21 31W
Arnett 75 36 9N 99 44W
Arnhem 105 51 58N 5 55 E
Arnhem B. 134 12 20 S 136 10 E
Arnhem, C. 135 12 20 S 137 0 E
Arnhem Ld. 134 13 10 S 135 0 E
Arno, R. 108 43 44N 10 20 E
Arnold, Calif., U.S.A. 80 38 15N 120 20W
Arnold, Nebr., U.S.A. 74 41 29N 100 10W
Arnold, Pa., U.S.A. 70 40 36N 79 44W
Arnot 55 55 56N 96 41W
Arnøy 110 70 9N 20 40 E
Arnprior 47 45 26N 76 21W
Arntfield 40 48 12N 79 15W
Aroa 86 10 26N 68 54W
Aroab 117 26 41 S 19 39 E
Arpajon, Cantal, France 102 44 54N 2 28 E
Arpajon, Seine et Oise, France 101 48 37N 2 12 E
Arrah 125 25 35N 84 32 E
Arraiján 84 8 56N 79 36W
Arran 57 51 53N 101 43W
Arran, I. 96 55 34N 5 12W
Arrandale 54 54 57N 130 0W
Arras 101 50 17N 2 46 E
Arreau 102 42 54N 0 22 E
Arrecifes 88 34 06 S 60 9W
Arrée, Mts. d' 100 48 26N 3 55W
Arriaga, Chiapas, Mexico 83 16 15N 93 52W
Arriaga, San Luís de Potosi, Mexico 82 21 55N 101 23W
Arromanches-les-Bains 100 49 20N 0 38W
Arrou 100 48 6N 1 8 E
Arrow L. 97 54 3N 8 20W
Arrow Park 63 50 6N 117 57W
Arrow Rock Res. 78 43 45N 115 50W
Arrowhead 63 50 40N 117 55W
Arrowhead, L. 81 34 16N 117 10W
Arrowtown 133 44 57 S 168 50 E
Arrowwood 61 50 44N 113 9W
Arroyo Grande 81 35 9N 120 32W
Ars 102 46 13N 1 30W
Ars-sur-Moselle 101 49 5N 6 4 E
Arsenault L. 55 55 6N 108 32W
Arshan 130 46 59N 120 0 E
Árta 109 39 8N 21 2 E
Arteaga 82 18 50N 102 20W
Artenay 101 48 5N 1 50 E
Artesia 75 32 55N 104 25W
Artesia Wells 75 28 17N 99 18W
Artesian 74 44 2N 97 54W
Arthez-de-Béarn 102 43 29N 0 38W
Arthur, Can. 49 43 50N 80 32W
Arthur, U.S.A. 77 39 43N 88 28W
Arthurette 39 46 47N 67 29W
Arthur's Pass 133 42 54 S 171 35 E
Arthur's Town 85 24 38N 75 42W
Artigas 88 30 20 S 56 30W
Artillery L. 55 63 9N 107 52W
Artois 101 50 20N 2 30 E
Arts Bogd Uul, mts. 130 44 40N 102 20 E
Artvin 122 41 14N 41 44 E
Aru, Kepulauan 127 6 0 S 134 30 E
Arua 116 3 1N 30 58 E
Aruanã 87 15 0 S 51 10W
Aruba I. 85 12 30N 70 0W
Arudy 102 43 7N 0 28W
Arunachal Pradesh □ 125 28 0N 95 0 E
Arundel 40 45 58N 74 37W
Arusha 116 3 20 S 36 40 E
Aruwimi, R. 116 1 30N 25 0 E
Arvada 78 44 43N 106 6W
Arvayheer 130 46 15N 102 45 E
Arve, R. 103 46 11N 6 8 E
Arvert, L. 38 52 18N 61 45W
Arvida 41 48 25N 71 14W
Arvidsjaur 110 65 35N 19 10 E
Arvika 111 59 40N 12 36 E
Arvilla 60 53 59N 114 0W
Arvin 81 35 12N 118 50W
Arys 120 42 26N 68 48 E
Arzamas 120 55 27N 43 55 E
As Salt 115 32 2N 35 43 E
As Samāwah 122 31 15N 45 15 E
As Shatrah 122 31 30N 46 10 E
As Sulaimānīyah 122 35 35N 45 29 E
As Suwaih 123 22 10N 59 33 E
As Suwayda 122 32 40N 36 30 E
As Suwayrah 122 32 55N 45 0 E
Asadabad 122 34 50N 48 10 E
Asahi-dake, mt. 132 43 42N 142 54 E
Asahigawa 132 43 45N 142 30 E
Asahikawa 132 43 45N 142 30 E
Asamankese 114 5 50N 0 40W
Asansol 125 23 40N 87 1 E
Asbestos 35 45 47N 71 58W
Asbury Park 71 40 15N 74 1W
Ascensión 82 31 6N 107 59W
Ascensión, B. de la 83 19 50N 87 20W
Ascension, I. 13 8 0 S 14 15W
Aschaffenburg 106 49 58N 9 8 E
Áscoli Piceno 108 42 51N 13 34 E
Ascope 86 7 46 S 79 8W
Ascotán 88 21 45 S 68 17W
Aseb 115 13 0N 42 40 E
Asfeld 101 49 27N 4 5 E
Ash Fork 79 35 14N 112 32W
Ash Grove 75 37 21N 93 36W
Ash Shām, Bādiyat 122 31 30N 40 0 E
Ash Shāmīyah 122 31 55N 44 35 E
Ashan 130 41 3N 122 58 E
Ashburn 73 31 42N 83 40W
Ashburton 133 43 53 S 171 48 E
Ashburton, R., Austral. 134 21 40 S 114 56 E
Ashburton, R., N.Z. 15 44 2 S 171 50 E
Ashby-de-la-Zouch 94 52 45N 1 29W
Ashcroft 63 50 40N 121 20W
Ashdod 115 31 49N 34 35 E
Asheboro 73 35 43N 79 46W
Ashern 57 51 11N 98 21W
Asherton 75 28 25N 99 43W
Asheville 73 35 39N 82 30W
Asheweig, R. 34 54 17N 87 12W
Ashford, U.K. 95 51 8N 0 53 E
Ashford, U.S.A. 78 46 45N 122 2W
Ashgrove 49 43 36N 79 53W
Ashikaga 132 36 28N 139 29 E
Ashizuri-Zaki 132 32 35N 132 50 E
Ashkhabad 120 38 0N 57 50 E
Ashland, U.S.A. 76 39 53N 90 0W
Ashland, Kans., U.S.A. 75 37 13N 99 43W
Ashland, Ky., U.S.A. 72 38 25N 82 40W
Ashland, Me., U.S.A. 35 46 34N 68 26W
Ashland, Mont., U.S.A. 78 45 41N 106 12W
Ashland, Nebr., U.S.A. 74 41 5N 96 27W
Ashland, Ohio, U.S.A. 70 40 52N 82 20W
Ashland, Oreg., U.S.A. 78 42 10N 122 38W
Ashland, Pa., U.S.A. 71 40 45N 76 22W
Ashland, Va., U.S.A. 72 37 46N 77 30W
Ashland, Wis., U.S.A. 52 46 40N 90 52W
Ashley, Ill., U.S.A. 76 38 20N 89 11W
Ashley, Ind., U.S.A. 77 41 32N 85 4W
Ashley, Mich., U.S.A. 77 43 11N 84 29W
Ashley, N.D., U.S.A. 74 46 3N 99 23W
Ashley, Pa., U.S.A. 71 41 12N 75 55W
Ashmont 60 54 7N 111 35W
Ashmore Reef 134 12 14 S 123 5 E
Ashquelon 115 31 42N 34 55 E
Ashtabula 70 41 52N 80 50W
Ashton 78 44 6N 111 30W
Ashton-u.-Lyne 94 53 30N 2 8 E
Ashuanipi, L. 38 52 45N 66 15W
Ashun 131 25 10N 106 0 E
Asia 118 45 0N 75 0 E
Asia, Kepulauan 127 1 0N 131 13 E
Asifabad 124 19 30N 79 24 E
Asinara, G. dell' 108 41 0N 8 30 E
Asinara I. 108 41 5N 8 15 E
Asino 120 57 0N 86 0 E
Asir 115 18 40N 42 30 E
Asir, Ras 115 11 55N 51 10 E
Askersund 111 58 53N 14 55 E
Askja 110 65 3N 16 48W
Askov 52 46 12N 92 51W
Asmar 123 35 10N 71 27 E
Asmara = Asmera 115 15 19N 38 55 E
Asmera 115 15 19N 38 55 E
Aso 132 33 0N 130 42 E
Aspen, Can. 39 45 18N 62 3W
Aspen, U.S.A. 79 39 12N 106 56W
Aspen Grove 63 49 57N 120 37W
Aspermont 75 33 11N 100 15W
Aspiring, Mt. 133 44 23 S 168 46 E
Aspres 103 44 32N 5 44 E
Asquith 56 52 8N 107 13W
Assam □ 125 25 45N 92 30 E
Assen 105 53 0N 6 35 E
Assigny, L. 38 52 0N 65 20W
Assiniboia 56 49 40N 105 59W
Assiniboine, R. 58 49 53N 97 8W
Assinica L. 34 50 30N 75 20W
Assis 89 22 40 S 50 20W

Assisi Bagan Siapiapi

Assisi	**108**	43 4N	12 36 E
Assomption, L'	**43**	45 50N	73 25W
Assomption, L' □	**43**	45 49N	73 30W
Assomption, L', R.	**43**	45 43N	73 29W
Assumption	**76**	39 31N	89 3W
Assynt	**96**	58 25N	5 10W
Assynt, L.	**96**	58 25N	5 15W
Astaffort	**102**	44 4N	0 40 E
Asti	**108**	44 54N	8 11 E
Astipálaia	**109**	36 32N	26 22 E
Astorga	**104**	42 29N	6 8W
Astoria, Ill., U.S.A.	**76**	40 14N	90 21W
Astoria, Oreg., U.S.A.	**80**	46 10N	123 50W
Astorville	**46**	46 11N	79 17W
Astrakhan	**120**	46 25N	48 5 E
Asturias	**104**	43 15N	6 0W
Asunción	**88**	25 21 S	57 30W
Asunción, La	**86**	11 2N	63 53W
Aswân	**115**	24 4N	32 57 E
Aswân Dam	**115**	24 5N	32 57 E
Asyût	**115**	27 11N	31 4 E
At Tafilah	**122**	30 45N	35 30 E
Atacama	**88**	25 40 S	67 40W
Atacama □	**88**	27 30 S	70 0W
Atacama, Desierto de	**90**	24 0 S	69 20W
Atacama, Salar de	**88**	24 0 S	68 20W
Ataco	**86**	3 35N	75 23W
Atalaia	**112**	9 25 S	36 0W
Atalaya	**86**	10 45 S	73 50W
Atami	**132**	35 0N	139 55 E
Atara	**121**	63 10N	129 10 E
Atascadero	**81**	35 32N	120 44W
Atasu	**120**	48 30N	71 0 E
Atauro	**127**	8 10 S	125 30 E
Atbara, R.	**115**	17 40N	33 56 E
Atchafalaya B.	**75**	29 30N	91 20W
Atchison	**74**	39 40N	95 10W
Ath	**105**	50 38N	3 47 E
Ath Thamami	**122**	27 45N	35 30 E
Athabasca	**60**	54 45N	113 20W
Athabasca, L.	**55**	59 15N	109 15W
Athabasca, R.	**55**	58 40N	110 50W
Athboy	**97**	53 37N	6 55W
Athelstan	**43**	45 2N	74 10W
Athenry	**97**	53 18N	8 45W
Athens, Can.	**47**	44 38N	75 57W
Athens, Ala., U.S.A.	**73**	34 49N	86 58W
Athens, Ga., U.S.A.	**73**	33 56N	83 24W
Athens, N.Y., U.S.A.	**71**	42 15N	73 48W
Athens, Ohio, U.S.A.	**72**	39 25N	82 6W
Athens, Pa., U.S.A.	**71**	41 57N	76 36W
Athens, Tex., U.S.A.	**75**	32 11N	95 48W
Athens = Athínai	**109**	37 58N	23 46 E
Atherly	**70**	44 37N	79 20W
Atherton	**135**	17 17 S	145 30 E
Athínai	**109**	37 58N	23 46 E
Athlone	**97**	53 26N	7 57W
Atholl, Forest of	**96**	56 51N	3 50W
Atholville	**39**	47 59N	66 43W
Áthos, Mt.	**109**	40 9N	24 22 E
Athy	**97**	53 0N	7 0W
Ati	**114**	13 5N	29 2 E
Atico	**86**	16 14 S	73 40W
Aticonipi, L.	**38**	51 52N	59 22W
Atikokan	**52**	48 45N	91 37W
Atikonak L.	**38**	52 40N	64 32W
Atikonak, R.	**38**	52 51N	65 16W
Atka, U.S.A.	**67**	52 5N	174 40W
Atka, U.S.S.R.	**121**	60 50N	151 48 E
Atkasuk (Meade River)	**67**	70 30N	157 20W
Atkinson, Ill., U.S.A.	**76**	41 25N	90 1W
Atkinson, Nebr., U.S.A.	**74**	42 35N	98 59W
Atlanta, Ga., U.S.A.	**73**	33 50N	84 24W
Atlanta, Ill., U.S.A.	**76**	40 16N	89 14W
Atlanta, Mich., U.S.A.	**46**	45 0N	84 9W
Atlanta, Mo., U.S.A.	**76**	39 54N	92 29W
Atlanta, Tex., U.S.A.	**75**	33 7N	94 8W
Atlantic	**74**	41 25N	95 0W
Atlantic City	**72**	39 25N	74 25W
Atlantic Ocean	**12**	0 0	20 0W
Atlántico □	**86**	10 45N	75 0W
Atlas, Great, Mts.	**112**	33 0N	5 0W
Atlas Saharien	**114**	33 30N	1 0 E
Atlin	**67**	59 31N	133 41W
Atlin, L.	**67**	59 26N	133 45W
Atmore	**73**	31 2N	87 30W
Atnarko	**54**	52 25N	126 0W
Atoka	**75**	34 22N	96 10W
Atolia	**81**	35 19N	117 37W
Atotonilco el Alto	**82**	20 20N	98 40W
Atoyac, R.	**83**	16 30N	97 31W
Atrak, R.	**123**	37 50N	57 0 E
Atrato, R.	**86**	6 40N	77 0W
Attalla	**73**	34 2N	86 5W
Attawapiskat	**34**	52 56N	82 24W
Attawapiskat, L.	**34**	52 18N	87 54W
Attawapiskat, R.	**34**	52 57N	82 18W
Attercliffe	**49**	42 59N	79 36W
Attica	**77**	40 20N	87 15W
Attichy	**101**	49 25N	3 3 E
Attigny	**101**	49 28N	4 35 E
Attikamagen L.	**36**	55 0N	66 30W
Attleboro	**71**	41 56N	71 18W
Attock	**124**	33 52N	72 20 E
Attopeu	**128**	14 48N	106 50 E
Attu	**67**	52 55N	173 10W
Attur	**124**	11 35N	78 30 E
Attwood, R	**52**	51 15N	88 30W
Atuel, R.	**88**	36 17 S	66 50W
Atunze = Tehtsin	**129**	28 45N	98 58 E
Atvidaberg	**111**	58 12N	16 0 E
Atwater	**80**	37 21N	120 37W
Atwood, Can.	**46**	43 40N	81 1W
Atwood, U.S.A.	**74**	39 52N	101 3W
Au Gres	**46**	44 3N	83 42W
Au Sable Pt., U.S.A.	**46**	44 20N	83 20W
Au Sable Pt., U.S.A.	**53**	46 40N	86 10W
Au Sable, R.	**46**	44 25N	83 20W
Aubagne	**103**	43 17N	5 37 E
Aubarede Pt.	**127**	17 15N	122 20 E
Aube □	**101**	48 15N	4 0 E
Aubel	**105**	50 42N	5 51 E
Aubenas	**103**	44 37N	4 24 E
Aubenton	**101**	49 50N	4 12 E
Auberry	**81**	37 7N	119 29W
Aubigny-sur-Nère	**101**	47 30N	2 24 E
Aubin	**102**	44 33N	2 15 E
Aubrac, Mts. d'	**102**	44 38N	2 58 E
Aubry L.	**64**	67 23N	126 30W
Auburn, Ala., U.S.A.	**73**	32 37N	85 30W
Auburn, Calif., U.S.A.	**80**	38 50N	121 4W
Auburn, Ill., U.S.A.	**76**	39 36N	89 45W
Auburn, Ind., U.S.A.	**77**	41 20N	85 0W
Auburn, Nebr., U.S.A.	**74**	40 25N	95 50W
Auburn, N.Y., U.S.A.	**71**	42 57N	76 39W
Auburn, Wash., U.S.A.	**80**	47 18N	122 13W
Auburndale	**73**	28 5N	81 45W
Aubusson	**102**	45 57N	2 11 E
Auch	**102**	43 39N	0 36 E
Auchel	**101**	50 30N	2 29 E
Auckland	**133**	36 52 S	174 46 E
Auckland □	**133**	38 35 S	177 0 E
Auckland Is.	**133**	51 0 S	166 0 E
Aude □	**102**	43 8N	2 28 E
Aude, R.	**102**	44 13N	3 15 E
Auden	**53**	50 14N	87 53W
Auderville	**100**	49 43N	1 57W
Audierne	**100**	48 1N	4 34W
Audincourt	**101**	47 30N	6 50 E
Audley	**51**	43 54N	79 1W
Audubon	**76**	41 43N	94 56W
Auffay	**100**	49 43N	1 07 E
Augathella	**135**	25 48 S	146 35 E
Augsburg	**106**	48 22N	10 54 E
Augusta, Italy	**108**	37 14N	15 12 E
Augusta, U.S.A.	**76**	40 14N	90 57W
Augusta, U.S.A.	**77**	38 47N	84 0W
Augusta, Ark., U.S.A.	**75**	35 17N	91 25W
Augusta, Ga., U.S.A.	**73**	33 29N	81 59W
Augusta, Kans., U.S.A.	**75**	37 40N	97 0W
Augusta, Me., U.S.A.	**35**	44 20N	69 46 E
Augusta, Mont., U.S.A.	**78**	47 30N	112 29W
Augusta, Wis., U.S.A.	**74**	44 41N	91 8W
Augustines, L. des	**40**	47 37N	75 56W
Augusto Cardosa	**117**	12 40 S	34 50 E
Augustów	**107**	53 51N	23 00 E
Augustus, Mt.	**134**	24 20 S	116 50 E
Aukum	**80**	38 34N	120 43W
Aulnay	**102**	46 2N	0 22W
Aulne, R.	**100**	48 17N	4 16W
Aulneau Pen.	**52**	49 23N	94 29W
Ault	**74**	40 40N	104 42W
Ault-Onival	**100**	50 5N	1 29 E
Aulus-les-Bains	**102**	42 49N	1 19 E
Aumale	**101**	49 46N	1 46 E
Aumont-Aubrac	**102**	44 43N	3 17 E
Aunis	**102**	46 0N	0 50W
Auponhia	**127**	1 58 S	125 27 E
Aups	**103**	43 37N	6 15 E
Aurangabad, Bihar, India	**125**	24 45N	84 18 E
Aurangabad, Maharashtra, India	**124**	19 50N	75 23 E
Auray	**100**	47 40N	3 0W
Aurillac	**102**	44 55N	2 26 E
Aurora, Can.	**49**	44 0N	72 30 E
Aurora, Colo., U.S.A.	**74**	39 44N	104 55W
Aurora, Ill., U.S.A.	**77**	41 42N	88 12W
Aurora, Mo., U.S.A.	**75**	36 58N	93 42W
Aurora, Nebr., U.S.A.	**74**	40 55N	98 0W
Aurora, Ohio, U.S.A.	**70**	41 21N	81 20W
Aus	**117**	26 35 S	16 12 E
Ausable, R.	**46**	43 19N	81 46W
Aust-Agder fylke □	**111**	58 55N	7 40 E
Austerlitz = Slavikov	**106**	49 10N	16 52 E
Austin, Ind., U.S.A.	**77**	38 45N	85 49W
Austin, Minn., U.S.A.	**74**	43 37N	92 59W
Austin, Nev., U.S.A.	**78**	39 30N	117 1W
Austin, Pa., U.S.A.	**70**	41 40N	78 7W
Austin, Tex., U.S.A.	**75**	30 20N	97 45W
Austin Chan.	**65**	75 35N	103 25W
Austin, L.	**134**	27 40 S	118 0 E
Austral Downs	**135**	20 30 S	137 45 E
Austral Is. = Toubouai, Îles	**15**	25 0 S	150 0W
Australia ■	**135**	23 0 S	135 0 E
Australian Alps	**136**	36 30 S	148 8 E
Australian Cap. Terr. □	**136**	35 15 S	149 8 E
Australian Dependency	**91**	73 0 S	90 0 E
Austria ■	**106**	47 0N	14 0 E
Austvågøy	**110**	68 20N	14 40 E
Auterive	**102**	43 21N	1 29 E
Auteuil	**44**	45 38N	73 46W
Auteuil, L.d'	**38**	50 38N	61 17W
Authie, R.	**101**	50 22N	1 38 E
Autlan	**82**	19 40N	104 30W
Autun	**101**	46 58N	4 17 E
Auvergne	**102**	45 20N	3 0 E
Auxerre	**101**	47 48N	3 32 E
Auxi-le-Château	**101**	50 15N	2 8 E
Auxonne	**101**	47 10N	5 20 E
Auxvasse	**76**	39 1N	91 54W
Auzances	**102**	46 2N	2 30 E
Ava	**76**	37 53N	89 30W
Avallon	**101**	47 30N	3 53 E
Avalon	**81**	33 21N	118 20W
Avalon Pen.	**37**	47 30N	53 20W
Avalon Res.	**75**	32 30N	104 30W
Avaré	**89**	23 4 S	48 58W
Avawata Mts	**81**	35 30N	116 20W
Aveiro, Brazil	**87**	3 10 S	55 5W
Aveiro, Port.	**104**	40 37N	8 38W
Avej	**122**	35 40N	49 15 E
Avellaneda	**88**	34 50 S	58 10W
Avellino	**108**	40 54N	14 46 E
Avenal	**80**	36 0N	120 8W
Aversa	**108**	40 58N	14 11 E
Avery	**78**	47 22N	115 56W
Aves, Islas de	**86**	12 0N	67 40W
Avesnes-sur-Helpe	**101**	50 8N	3 55 E
Avesta	**111**	60 9N	16 10 E
Aveyron □	**102**	44 22N	2 45 E
Aviá Terai	**88**	26 45 S	60 50W
Avignon	**103**	43 57N	4 50 E
Ávila	**104**	40 39N	4 43W
Avila Beach	**81**	35 11N	120 44W
Avilés	**104**	43 35N	5 57W
Aviston	**76**	38 36N	89 36W
Avize	**101**	48 59N	4 0 E
Avoca, Austral.	**136**	37 5 S	143 26 E
Avoca, U.S.A.	**70**	42 24N	77 25W
Avoca, R., Austral.	**136**	35 40 S	143 43 E
Avoca, R., Ireland	**97**	52 48N	6 10W
Avola	**63**	51 45N	119 19W
Avon, Ill., U.S.A.	**76**	40 40N	90 26W
Avon, N.Y., U.S.A.	**70**	43 0N	77 42W
Avon, S.D., U.S.A.	**74**	43 0N	98 3W
Avon □	**95**	51 30N	2 40W
Avon Downs	**135**	19 58 S	137 25 E
Avon Is.	**135**	19 37 S	158 17 E
Avon Lake	**70**	41 28N	82 3W
Avon, R., Avon, U.K.	**95**	51 30N	2 43W
Avon, R., Hants., U.K.	**95**	50 44N	1 45W
Avon, R., Warwick, U.K.	**95**	52 0N	2 9W
Avondale	**37**	47 25N	53 12W
Avonlea	**56**	50 0N	105 0W
Avonmore	**47**	45 10N	74 58W
Avonmouth	**95**	51 30N	2 42W
Avranches	**100**	48 40N	1 20W
Avrillé	**102**	46 28N	1 28W
Awali	**123**	26 0N	50 30 E
Awatere, R.	**133**	41 37 S	174 10 E
Awe, L.	**96**	56 15N	5 15W
Aweil	**115**	8 42N	27 20 E
Ax-les-Thermes	**102**	42 44N	1 50 E
Axarfjörður	**110**	66 15N	16 45W
Axel Heiberg I.	**65**	80 0N	90 0W
Axminster	**95**	50 47N	3 1W
Ay	**101**	49 3N	4 0 E
Ayabaca	**86**	4 40 S	79 53W
Ayabe	**132**	35 20N	135 20 E
Ayacucho, Argent.	**88**	37 5 S	58 20W
Ayacucho, Peru	**86**	13 0 S	74 0W
Ayaguz	**120**	48 10N	80 0 E
Ayamonte	**104**	37 12N	7 24W
Ayan	**121**	56 30N	138 16 E
Ayapel	**86**	8 19N	75 9W
Ayapel, Sa. de	**86**	7 45N	75 30W
Ayaviri	**86**	14 50 S	70 35W
Aydın □	**122**	37 40N	27 40 E
Ayeritam	**128**	5 24N	100 15 E
Ayer's Cliff	**41**	45 10N	72 3W
Ayers Rock	**134**	25 23 S	131 5 E
Áyios Evstrátios	**109**	39 34N	24 58 E
Aylen L.	**47**	45 37N	77 51W
Aylesbury	**95**	51 48N	0 49W
Aylmer, Ont., Can.	**46**	42 46N	80 59W
Aylmer, Ont., Can.	**48**	45 23N	75 50W
Aylmer, Qué., Can.	**40**	45 24N	75 51W
Aylmer L.	**64**	64 0N	110 8W
Aylsham	**56**	53 12N	103 49W
Ayn Zālah	**122**	36 45N	42 35 E
Ayolas	**88**	27 10 S	56 59W
Ayon, Ostrov	**121**	69 50N	169 0 E
Ayr, Austral.	**135**	19 35 S	147 25 E
Ayr, Can.	**49**	43 17N	80 27W
Ayr, U.K.	**96**	55 28N	4 37W
Ayr, R.	**96**	55 29N	4 40W
Ayre, Pt. of I.o.M.	**94**	54 27N	4 21W
Aytos	**109**	42 47N	27 16 E
Ayu, Kepulauan	**127**	0 35N	131 5 E
Ayutla, Guat.	**84**	14 40N	92 10W
Ayutla, Mexico	**83**	16 58N	99 17W
Ayutthaya = Phra Nakhon Si A.	**128**	14 25N	100 30 E
Ayvalık	**122**	39 20N	26 46 E
Az Zahrān	**122**	26 10N	50 7 E
Az-Zilfī	**122**	26 12N	44 52 E
Az Zubayr	**122**	30 20N	47 50 E
Azamgarh	**125**	26 35N	83 13 E
Azārbāijān □	**122**	37 0N	44 30 E
Azare	**114**	11 55N	10 10 E
Azay-le-Rideau	**100**	47 16N	0 30 E
Azbine = Aïr	**114**	18 0N	8 0 E
Azerbaijan S.S.R. □	**120**	40 20N	48 0 E
Azilda	**46**	46 33N	81 6W
Azogues	**86**	2 35 S	78 0W
Azores, Is.	**12**	38 44N	29 0W
Azov Sea = Azovskoye More	**120**	46 0N	36 30 E
Azovskoye More	**120**	46 0N	36 30 E
Azovy	**120**	64 55N	64 35 E
Aztec	**79**	36 54N	108 0W
Azúa de Compostela	**85**	18 25N	70 44W
Azuaga	**104**	38 16N	5 39W
Azúcar, Presa del	**83**	26 0N	99 5W
Azuero, Pen. de	**84**	7 30N	80 30W
Azul	**88**	36 42 S	59 43W
Azure L.	**63**	52 22N	120 3W
Azusa	**81**	34 8N	117 52W

B

Ba Don	**128**	17 45N	106 26 E
Ba Ngoi = Cam Lam	**128**	11 50N	109 10 E
Baa	**127**	10 50 S	123 0 E
Baarle Nassau	**105**	51 27N	4 56 E
Baarn	**105**	52 12N	5 17 E
Bāb el Māndeb	**115**	12 35N	43 25 E
Babahoyo	**86**	1 40 S	79 30W
Babar, I.	**127**	8 0 S	129 30 E
Babb	**78**	48 56N	113 27W
Babbitt	**52**	47 43N	91 57W
Babinda Hill	**136**	31 55 S	146 28 E
Babine L.	**54**	54 48N	126 0W
Babine, R.	**54**	55 45N	127 44W
Babo	**127**	2 30 S	133 30 E
Bābol	**123**	36 40N	52 50 E
Bābol Sar	**123**	36 45N	52 45 E
Babuyan Is.	**131**	19 10N	121 40 E
Babylon, Iraq	**122**	32 40N	44 30 E
Babylon, U.S.A.	**71**	40 42N	73 20W
Bac Kan	**128**	22 5N	105 50 E
Bac Lieu = Vinh Loi	**128**	9 17N	105 43 E
Bac Ninh	**128**	21 13N	106 4 E
Bac Phan	**128**	22 0N	105 0 E
Bac Quang	**128**	22 30N	104 48 E
Bacabal	**87**	4 15N	44 45W
Bacalar	**83**	18 12N	87 53W
Bacan, Pulau	**127**	0 50 S	127 30 E
Bacarès, Le	**102**	42 47N	3 3 E
Bacarra	**127**	18 15N	120 37 E
Bacău	**107**	46 35N	26 55 E
Baccalieu I.	**37**	48 8N	52 48W
Baccarat	**101**	48 28N	6 42 E
Bacchus Marsh	**136**	37 40 S	144 27 E
Bacerac	**82**	30 18N	108 50W
Bachaquero	**86**	9 56N	71 8W
Bacharach	**105**	50 3N	7 46 E
Bachclina	**120**	57 45N	67 20 E
Back Bay	**39**	45 3N	66 52W
Back, R.	**64**	67 15N	95 15W
Backstairs Passage	**135**	35 40 S	138 5 E
Backus	**52**	46 51N	94 31W
Bacolod	**127**	10 40N	122 57 E
Bacqueville	**100**	49 47N	1 0 E
Bacuit	**127**	11 20N	119 20 E
Bad Axe	**46**	43 48N	82 59W
Bad Godesberg	**105**	50 41N	7 4 E
Bad Heart	**60**	55 30N	118 18W
Bad Ischl	**106**	47 44N	13 38 E
Bad Kreuznach	**105**	49 47N	7 47 E
Bad Lands	**74**	43 40N	102 10W
Bad, R., U.S.A.	**52**	46 38N	90 40W
Bad, R., U.S.A.	**74**	44 10N	100 50W
Badagara	**124**	11 35N	75 40 E
Badajoz	**104**	38 50N	6 59W
Badakhshan □	**123**	36 30N	71 0 E
Badalona	**104**	41 26N	2 15 E
Badampahar	**125**	22 10N	86 10 E
Badanah	**122**	30 58N	41 30 E
Badas	**126**	4 33N	114 25 E
Badas, Kepulauan	**126**	0 45N	107 5 E
Baddeck	**39**	46 6N	60 45W
Baddo, R.	**124**	28 15N	65 0 E
Bade	**127**	7 10 S	139 35 E
Baden, Austria	**106**	48 1N	16 13 E
Baden, Can.	**70**	43 14N	80 40W
Baden-Baden	**106**	48 45N	8 15 E
Baden-Württemberg □	**106**	48 40N	9 0 E
Badenoch	**96**	58 16N	4 5W
Badgastein	**106**	47 7N	13 9 E
Badger, Can.	**37**	49 0N	56 4W
Badger, U.S.A.	**80**	36 38N	119 1W
Badger's Quay	**37**	49 7N	53 35W
Badghis □	**124**	35 0N	63 0 E
Badin	**124**	24 38N	68 54 E
Badrinath	**124**	30 45N	79 30 E
Badulla	**124**	7 1N	81 7 E
Baetas	**86**	6 5 S	62 15W
Baeza, Ecuador	**86**	0 25 S	77 45W
Baeza, Spain	**104**	37 57N	3 25W
Baffin Bay	**65**	72 0N	64 0W
Baffin I.	**65**	68 0N	75 0W
Bafia	**116**	4 40N	11 10 E
Bafoulabé	**114**	13 50N	10 55W
Bafq	**123**	31 40N	55 20 E
Bafra	**122**	41 34N	35 54 E
Bāft, Iran	**123**	29 15N	56 38 E
Bāft, Iran	**123**	31 40N	55 25 E
Bafwasende	**116**	1 3N	27 5 E
Bagamoyo	**116**	6 28 S	38 55 E
Bagan Siapiapi	**126**	2 12N	100 50 E

Baganga Barkah

Baganga 127 7 34N 126 33 E
Bagdad 81 34 35N 115 53W
Bagdarin 121 54 26N 113 36 E
Bagé 89 31 20 S 54 15W
Baggs 78 41 8N 107 46W
Baghdād 122 33 20N 44 30 E
Bāghīn 123 30 12N 56 45 E
Baghlan 124 36 12N 69 0 E
Baghlan □ 123 36 0N 68 30 E
Bagley 74 47 30N 95 22W
Bagnell Dam 76 38 14N 92 36W
Bagnères-de-Bigorre 102 43 5N 0 9 E
Bagnères-de-Luchon 102 42 47N 0 38 E
Bagnoles-de-l'Orne 100 48 32N 0 25W
Bagnols-les-Bains 102 44 30N 3 40 E
Bagnols-sur-Cèze 103 44 10N 4 36 E
Bagot □ 45 45 35N 72 45W
Bagotville 41 48 22N 70 54W
Bagrash Kol 129 42 0N 87 0 E
Baguio 127 16 26N 120 34 E
Bahama, Canal Viejo de 84 22 10N 77 30W
Bahama Is. 85 24 40N 74 0W
Bahamas■ 85 24 0N 74 0W
Bahau 128 2 48N 102 26 E
Bahawalpur 124 29 37N 71 40 E
Bahawalpur □ 124 29 5N 71 3 E
Bahía = Salvador 87 13 0 S 38 30W
Bahía Blanca 88 38 35 S 62 13W
Bahía de Caráquez 86 0 40 S 80 27W
Bahía Honda 84 22 54N 83 10W
Bahía, Islas de la 84 16 45N 86 15W
Bahía Laura 90 48 10 S 66 30W
Bahía Negra 86 20 5 S 58 5W
Bahr el 'Arab, R. 115 10 0N 26 0 E
Bahr el Ghazâl □ 116 7 0N 28 0 E
Bahr el Jebel 115 7 30N 30 30 E
Bahra 122 21 25N 39 32 E
Bahraich 125 27 38N 81 50 E
Bahrain ■ 123 26 0N 50 35 E
Bahramabad 123 30 28N 56 2 E
Bahu Kalat 123 25 50N 61 20 E
Baia-Mare 107 47 40N 23 17 E
Baie Comeau 38 49 12N 68 10W
Baie de l'Abri 35 50 3N 67 0W
Baie-des-Sables 38 48 43N 67 54W
Baie-du-Poste 41 50 24N 73 56W
Baie-du-Renard 38 49 17N 61 50W
Baie Johan Beetz 35 50 18N 62 50W
Baie-St-Paul 41 47 28N 70 32W
Baie-Ste-Anne 39 47 3N 64 58W
Baie-Ste-Catherine 41 48 6N 69 44W
Baie-Ste-Claire 38 49 54N 64 30W
Baie Trinité 38 49 25N 67 20W
Baie Verte, N.B., Can. 39 46 1N 64 6W
Baie Verte, Newf., Can. 37 49 55N 56 12W
Baieville 41 46 8N 72 43W
Baignes 102 45 28N 0 25W
Baigneux-les-Juifs 101 47 31N 4 39 E
Ba'ijī 122 35 0N 43 30 E
Baikal, L. 121 53 0N 108 0 E
Baile Atha Cliath = Dublin 97 53 20N 6 18W
Bailleul 101 50 44N 2 41 E
Bain-de-Bretagne 100 47 50N 1 40W
Bainbridge, Ga., U.S.A. 73 30 53N 84 34W
Bainbridge, Ind., U.S.A. 77 39 46N 86 49W
Bainbridge, N.Y., U.S.A. 71 42 17N 75 29W
Bainbridge, Ohio, U.S.A. 77 39 14N 83 16W
Baing 127 10 14 S 120 34 E
Bainsville 43 45 10N 74 25W
Bainville 74 48 8N 104 10W
Baird 75 32 25N 99 25W
Baird Inlet 67 64 49N 164 18W
Baird Mts. 67 67 10N 160 15W
Baird Pen. 65 68 55N 76 4W
Bairnsdale 136 37 48 S 147 36 E
Baissoklyn 130 47 55N 102 20 E
Baitadi 125 29 35N 80 25 E
Baja 107 46 12N 18 59 E
Baja California 82 32 10N 115 12W
Baja, Pta. 82 29 50N 116 0W
Bajo Boquete 85 8 49N 82 27W
Bakala 116 6 15N 20 20 E
Baker, Calif., U.S.A. 81 35 16N 116 8W
Baker, Mont., U.S.A. 74 46 22N 104 12W
Baker, Nev., U.S.A. 78 38 59N 114 7W
Baker, Oreg., U.S.A. 78 44 50N 117 55W
Baker Is. 14 0 10N 176 35 E
Baker, L. 65 64 0N 96 0W
Baker Lake 65 64 20N 96 3W
Baker Mt. 63 48 50N 121 49W
Baker's Dozen Is. 36 56 45N 78 45W
Bakersfield, Calif., U.S.A. 81 35 25N 119 0W
Bakersfield, Vt., U.S.A. 71 44 46N 72 48W
Bakhtiari □ 122 32 0N 49 0 E
Bakinskikh Komissarov 122 39 20N 49 15 E
Bakkafjörδr 110 66 2N 14 48W
Bakkagerδi 110 65 31N 13 49W
Bakony Forest = Bakony Hegység 107 47 10N 17 30 E
Bakony Hegység 107 47 10N 17 30 E
Bakouma 116 5 40N 22 56 E
Baku 120 40 25N 49 45 E
Bala, Can. 46 45 1N 79 37W
Bala, U.K. 94 52 54N 3 36W
Bala, L. = Tegid, L. 94 52 53N 3 38W
Balabac I. 126 8 0N 117 0 E
Balabac, Selat 126 7 53N 117 5 E
Balabakk 122 34 0N 36 10 E
Balabalangan, Kepulauan 126 2 20 S 117 30 E
Balaghat 124 21 49N 80 12 E
Balaghat Ra. 124 18 50N 76 30 E
Balaguer 104 41 50N 0 50 E
Balakovo 120 52 4N 47 55 E
Balancán 83 17 48N 91 32W
Balasore 125 21 35N 87 3 E
Balaton 107 46 50N 17 40 E
Balboa 84 9 0N 79 30W
Balboa Hill 84 9 6N 79 44W
Balbriggan 97 53 35N 6 10W
Balcarce 88 38 0 S 58 10W
Balcarres 56 50 50N 103 35W
Balchik 109 43 28N 28 11 E
Balclutha 133 46 15 S 169 45 E
Bald Knob 75 35 20N 91 35W
Baldock L. 55 56 33N 97 57W
Baldur 57 49 23N 99 15W
Baldwin, Fla., U.S.A. 72 30 15N 82 10W
Baldwin, Mich., U.S.A. 72 43 54N 85 53W
Baldwinsville 71 43 10N 76 19W
Baleares, Islas 104 39 30N 3 0 E
Balearic Is. = Baleares, Islas 104 39 30N 3 0 E
Baler 127 15 46N 121 34 E
Balfate 84 15 48N 86 25W
Balgonie 56 50 29N 104 16W
Bali □ 126 8 20 S 115 0 E
Bali, I. 126 8 20 S 115 0 E
Bali, Selat 127 8 30 S 114 35 E
Balikesir 122 39 35N 27 58 E
Balikpapan 126 1 10 S 116 55 E
Balimbing 127 5 10N 120 3 E
Baling 128 5 41N 100 55 E
Balintang Chan. 131 19 50N 122 0 E
Balintang Is. 131 19 55N 122 0 E
Balipara 125 26 50N 92 45 E
Baliston Spa 71 43 0N 73 52W
Baliza 87 16 0 S 52 20W
Balkan Mts. = Stara Planina 109 43 15N 23 0 E
Balkan Pen. 93 42 0N 22 0 E
Balkh = Wazirabad 123 36 44N 66 47 E
Balkh □ 123 36 30N 67 0 E
Balkhash 120 46 50N 74 50 E
Balkhash, Ozero 120 40 0N 74 50 E
Balla 125 24 10N 91 35 E
Ballachulish 96 56 40N 5 10W
Balladoran 136 31 52 S 148 39 E
Ballarat 136 37 33 S 143 50 E
Ballard, L. 134 29 20 S 120 10 E
Ballater 96 57 2N 3 2W
Ballenas, Canal de las 82 29 10N 113 45W
Balleny Is. 91 66 30 S 163 0 E
Ballina, Austral. 135 28 50 S 153 31 E
Ballina, Mayo, Ireland 97 54 7N 9 10W
Ballina, Tipp., Ireland 97 52 49N 8 27W
Ballinafad 49 43 42N 80 1W
Ballinasloe 97 53 20N 8 12W
Ballinger 75 31 45N 99 58W
Ballinrobe 97 53 36N 9 13W
Ballinskelligs 97 51 50N 10 17W
Ballinskelligs B. 97 51 46N 10 11W
Ballivian 88 22 41 S 62 10W
Ballycastle 97 55 12N 6 15W
Ballymena 97 54 53N 6 18W
Ballymena □ 97 54 53N 6 18W
Ballymoney 97 55 5N 6 30W
Ballymoney □ 97 55 5N 6 23W
Ballyshannon 97 54 30N 8 10W
Balmaceda 90 46 0 S 71 50W
Balmertown 52 51 4N 93 41W
Balmoral, Austral. 136 37 15 S 141 48 E
Balmoral, Can. 57 50 15N 97 19W
Balmoral, U.K. 96 57 3N 3 13W
Balmorhea 75 31 2N 103 41W
Balonne, R. 135 28 47 S 147 56 E
Balovale 117 13 30 S 23 15 E
Balpunga 136 33 46 S 141 45 E
Balrampur 125 27 30N 82 20 E
Balranald 136 34 38 S 143 33 E
Balsam 51 43 59N 79 4W
Balsam L. 70 44 35N 78 50W
Balsas 83 18 0N 99 40W
Balsas, R. 82 18 30N 101 20W
Balta 74 48 12N 100 7W
Baltic Sea 111 56 0N 20 0 E
Baltimore, Can. 70 44 2N 78 10W
Baltimore, Ireland 97 51 29N 9 22W
Baltimore, U.S.A. 72 39 18N 76 37W
Baluchistan □ 124 27 30N 65 0 E
Balygychan 121 63 56N 154 12 E
Bam 123 29 7N 58 14 E
Bamako 114 12 34N 7 55W
Bambari 116 5 40N 20 35 E
Bamberg, Ger. 106 49 54N 10 53 E
Bamberg, U.S.A. 73 33 19N 81 1W
Bambili 116 3 40N 26 0 E
Bamfield 62 48 45N 125 10W
Bamian □ 124 35 0N 67 0 E
Bampūr 123 27 15N 60 21 E
Bampur, R. 123 27 20N 59 30 E
Ban Ban 128 19 31N 103 15 E
Ban Bua Chum 128 15 11N 101 12 E
Ban Bua Yai 128 15 33N 102 26 E
Ban Houei Sai 128 20 22N 100 32 E
Ban Kantang 128 7 25N 99 31 E
Ban Khe Bo 128 19 10N 104 39 E
Ban Khun Yuam 128 18 49N 97 57 E
Ban Me Thuot 128 12 40N 108 3 E
Ban Phai 128 16 4N 102 44 E
Ban Takua Pa 128 8 55N 98 25 E
Ban Thateng 128 15 25N 106 27 E
Banadar Daryay Oman □ 123 25 30N 56 0 E
Banadia 86 6 54N 71 49W
Banalia 116 1 32N 25 5 E
Banam 128 11 20N 105 17 E
Bananal, I. do 87 11 30 S 50 30W
Banaras = Varanasi 125 25 22N 83 8 E
Banat □ 107 45 45N 21 15 E
Banbridge 97 54 21N 6 17W
Banbridge □ 97 54 21N 6 16W
Banbury 95 52 4N 1 21W
Banchory 96 57 3N 2 30W
Bancroft 47 45 3N 77 51W
Bancroft = Chililabombwe 117 12 18 S 27 43 E
Band-i-Turkistan, Ra. 123 35 2N 64 0 E
Banda 124 25 30N 80 26 E
Banda Aceh 126 5 35N 95 20 E
Banda Banda, Mt. 136 31 10 S 152 28 E
Banda Elat 127 5 40 S 133 5 E
Banda, Kepulauan 127 4 37 S 129 50 E
Banda, La 88 27 45 S 64 10W
Banda, Punta 82 31 47N 116 50W
Banda Sea 127 6 0 S 130 0 E
Bandar = Masulipatnam 125 16 12N 81 12 E
Bandār 'Abbās 123 27 15N 56 15 E
Bandar-e Būshehr 123 28 55N 50 55 E
Bandar-e Chārak 123 26 45N 54 20 E
Bandar-e Deylam 122 30 5N 50 10 E
Bandar-e Lengeh 123 26 35N 54 58 E
Bandar-e Ma'shur 122 30 35N 49 10 E
Bandar-e-Nakhīlū 123 26 58N 53 30 E
Bandar-e Rīg 123 29 30N 50 45 E
Bandar-e Shāh 123 37 0N 54 10 E
Bandar-e-Shāhpūr 122 30 30N 49 5 E
Bandar-i-Pahlavi 122 37 30N 49 30 E
Bandar Maharani = Muar 128 2 3N 102 34 E
Bandar Penggaram = Batu Pahat 128 1 50N 102 56 E
Bandar Seri Begawan 126 4 52N 115 0 E
Bandawe 117 11 58 S 34 5 E
Bandeira, Pico da 89 20 26 S 41 47W
Bandera, Argent. 88 28 55 S 62 20W
Bandera, U.S.A. 75 29 45N 99 3W
Banderas, Bahía de 82 20 40N 105 30W
Bandi-San 132 37 36N 140 4 E
Bandirma 122 40 20N 28 0 E
Bandon 97 51 44N 8 45W
Bandon, R. 97 51 40N 8 11W
Bandundu 116 3 15 S 17 22 E
Bandung 127 6 36 S 107 48 E
Banes 85 21 0N 75 42W
Banff, Can. 61 51 10N 115 34W
Banff, U.K. 96 57 40N 2 32W
Banff Nat. Park 61 51 30N 116 15W
Bang Hieng, R. 128 16 24N 105 40 E
Bang Lamung 128 13 3N 100 56 E
Bang Saphan 128 11 14N 99 28 E
Bangala Dam 117 21 7 S 31 25 E
Bangalore 124 12 59N 77 40 E
Bangassou 116 4 55N 23 55 E
Banggai 127 1 40 S 123 30 E
Banggi, P. 126 7 50N 117 0 E
Banghāzī 115 32 11N 20 3 E
Bangil 127 7 36 S 112 50 E
Bangka, Pulau, Celebes, Indon. 127 1 50N 125 5 E
Bangka, Pulau, Sumatera, Indon. 126 2 0 S 105 50 E
Bangka, Selat, Indon. 126 2 30 S 105 30 E
Bangka, Selat, Indon. 126 3 30 S 105 30 E
Bangkalan 127 7 2 S 112 46 E
Bangkinang 126 0 18N 100 5 E
Bangko 126 2 5 S 102 9 E
Bangkok = Krung Thep 128 13 45N 100 31 E
Bangladesh ■ 125 24 0N 90 0 E
Bangor, Me., U.S.A. 35 44 48N 68 42W
Bangor, Mich., U.S.A. 77 42 18N 86 7W
Bangor, Pa., U.S.A. 71 40 51N 75 13W
Bangor, N.I., U.K. 97 54 40N 5 40W
Bangor, Wales, U.K. 94 53 13N 4 9W
Bangued 127 17 40N 120 37 E
Bangui 116 4 23N 18 35 E
Bangweulu, L. 116 11 0 S 30 0 E
Bangweulu Swamp 116 11 20 S 30 15 E
Bani 85 18 16N 70 22W
Bāniyas 122 35 10N 36 0 E
Banja Luka 108 44 49N 17 26 E
Banjak, Kepulauan 126 2 10N 97 10 E
Banjar 127 7 24 S 108 30 E
Banjarmasin 126 3 20 S 114 35 E
Banjarnegara 127 7 24 S 109 42 E
Banjul 114 13 28N 16 40W
Bankipore 125 25 35N 85 10 E
Banks I., B.C., Can. 62 53 20N 130 0W
Banks I., N. W. Terr., Can. 64 73 15N 121 30W
Banks I., P.N.G. 135 10 10 S 142 15 E
Banks Peninsula 133 43 45 S 173 15 E
Bankura 125 23 11N 87 18 E
Bann, R. 97 55 2N 6 35W
Bann R. 97 54 30N 6 31W
Bannalec 100 47 57N 3 42W
Banning, Can. 34 48 44N 91 56W
Banning, U.S.A. 81 33 58N 116 58W
Banningville = Bandundu 116 3 15 S 17 22 E
Bannockburn, Can. 47 44 39N 77 33W
Bannockburn, U.K. 96 56 5N 3 55W
Bannu 124 33 0N 70 18 E
Banon 103 44 2N 5 38 E
Banská Bystrica 107 48 46N 19 14 E
Banská Stiavnica 107 48 25N 18 55 E
Banswara 124 23 32N 74 24 E
Banten 127 6 5 S 106 8 E
Bantry 97 51 40N 9 28W
Bantry, B. 97 51 35N 9 50W
Bantul 127 7 55 S 110 19 E
Banu 124 35 35N 69 5 E
Banyuls 102 42 29N 3 8 E
Banyumas 127 7 32 S 109 18 E
Banyuwangi 127 8 13 S 114 21 E
Banzare Coast 91 66 30 S 125 0 E
Bapatla 125 15 55N 80 30 E
Bapaume 101 50 7N 2 50 E
Baqūbah 122 33 45N 44 50 E
Baquedano 88 23 20 S 69 52W
Bar 109 42 8N 19 8 E
Bar Harbor 35 44 15N 68 20W
Bar-le-Duc 101 48 47N 5 10 E
Bar-sur-Aube 101 48 14N 4 40 E
Bar-sur-Seine 101 48 7N 4 20 E
Barabai 126 2 32 S 115 34 E
Barabinsk 120 55 20N 78 20 E
Baraboo 74 43 28N 89 46W
Barachois-de-Malbaie 38 48 37N 64 17W
Barachois Pond Prov. Park 37 48 28N 58 15W
Baracoa 85 20 20N 74 30W
Baradero 88 33 52 S 59 29W
Baraga 52 46 49N 88 29W
Barahona 85 18 13N 71 7W
Barail Range 125 25 15N 93 20 E
Barakhola 125 25 0N 92 45 E
Baralzon L. 55 60 0N 98 3W
Baramula 124 34 15N 74 20 E
Baran 124 25 9N 76 40 E
Baranoa 86 10 48N 74 55W
Baranof I. 67 57 0N 135 10W
Baranovichi 120 53 10N 26 0 E
Barão de Melgaço 86 11 50 S 60 45W
Barapasi 127 2 15 S 137 5 E
Barat Daya,Kepuluan 127 7 30 S 128 0 E
Barataria B. 75 29 15N 89 45W
Baraya 86 3 10N 75 4W
Barbacena 89 21 15 S 43 56W
Barbacoas, Colomb. 86 1 45N 78 0W
Barbacoas, Venez. 86 9 29N 66 58W
Barbados ■ 85 13 0N 59 30W
Barbara L. 53 49 20N 87 47W
Barbeau Pk. 65 81 54N 75 1W
Barbel, L. 38 51 55N 68 13W
Barberton, S. Afr. 117 25 42 S 31 2 E
Barberton, U.S.A. 70 41 0N 81 40W
Barbourville 73 36 57N 83 52W
Barbuda I. 85 17 30N 61 40W
Barca, La 82 20 20N 102 40W
Barcaldine 135 23 33 S 145 13 E
Barce = Al Marj 115 32 25N 20 40 E
Barcelona, Spain 104 41 21N 2 10 E
Barcelona, Venez. 86 10 10N 64 40W
Barcelonette 103 44 23N 6 40 E
Barcelos 86 1 0 S 63 0W
Barclay 52 49 47N 92 43W
Barcoo, R. 135 28 29 S 137 46 E
Bardai 114 21 25N 17 0 E
Bardas Blancas 88 35 49 S 69 45W
Bardera 115 2 20N 42 27 E
Bardoux, L. 38 51 9N 67 50W
Bardsey, I. 94 52 46N 4 47W
Bardstown 77 37 50N 85 29W
Bareilly 124 28 22N 79 27 E
Barentin 100 49 33N 0 58 E
Barenton 100 48 38N 0 50W
Barents Sea 17 73 0N 39 0 E
Barfleur 100 49 40N 1 17W
Barge, La 78 42 12N 110 4W
Barguzin 121 53 37N 109 37 E
Barham 136 35 36 S 144 8 E
Barhi 125 24 15N 85 25 E
Bari 108 41 6N 16 52 E
Bari Doab 124 30 20N 73 0 E
Baria = Phuoc Le 128 10 39N 107 19 E
Barinas 86 8 36N 70 15W
Barinas □ 86 8 10N 69 50W
Baring 76 40 15N 92 12W
Baring C. 64 70 0N 117 30W
Baringo 116 0 47N 36 16 E
Baringo, L. 116 0 47N 36 16 E
Barinitas 86 8 45N 70 25W
Barisal 125 22 30N 90 20 E
Barisan, Bukit 126 3 30 S 102 15 E
Barito, R. 126 2 50 S 114 50 E
Barjac 103 44 20N 4 22 E
Barjols 103 43 34N 6 2 E
Bark L 47 45 27N 77 51W
Bark L. 34 46 58N 82 25W
Barkah 123 23 40N 58 0 E

Bédarrides Beuil

Bédarrides 103 44 2N 4 54 E
Beddington Cr. 59 51 9N 114 3W
Bedford, N.S., Can. 39 44 44N 63 40W
Bedford, Qué., Can. 43 45 7N 72 59W
Bedford, S. Afr. 117 32 40 S 26 10 E
Bedford, U.K. 95 52 8N 0 29W
Bedford, Ind., U.S.A. 77 38 50N 86 30W
Bedford, Iowa, U.S.A. 76 40 40N 94 41W
Bedford, Ky., U.S.A. 77 38 36N 85 19W
Bedford, Ohio, U.S.A. 70 41 23N 81 32W
Bedford, Pa., U.S.A. 70 40 1N 78 30W
Bedford, Va., U.S.A. 72 37 25N 79 30W
Bedford □ 95 52 4N 0 28W
Bedford Basin 39 44 42N 63 38W
Bedford, C. 135 15 14 S 145 21 E
Bednesti 54 53 50N 123 10W
Bedourie 135 24 30 S 139 30 E
Beebe Plain 41 45 1N 72 9W
Beech Forest 136 38 37 S 143 37 E
Beech Fork, R. 77 37 55N 85 50W
Beech Grove 77 39 40N 86 2W
Beecher 77 41 21N 87 38W
Beechey Hd. 63 48 10N 123 30W
Beechey Point 67 70 27N 149 18W
Beechworth 136 36 22 S 146 43 E
Beechy 56 50 53N 107 24W
Beemunnel 136 31 40 S 147 51 E
Be'er Sheva' 115 31 15N 34 48 E
Beeston 94 52 55N 1 11W
Beeton 46 44 5N 79 47W
Beetz, L. 38 50 34N 62 42W
Beeville 75 28 27N 97 44W
Befale 116 0 25N 20 45 E
Befandriana 117 21 55 S 44 0 E
Bega 136 36 41 S 149 51 E
Béhagle = Lai 114 9 25N 16 30 E
Behara 117 24 55 S 46 20 E
Behbehan 122 30 30N 50 15 E
Behshahr 123 36 45N 53 35 E
Beilen 105 52 52N 6 27 E
Beira 117 19 50 S 34 52 E
Beira-Alta 104 40 35N 7 35W
Beira-Baixa 104 40 2N 7 30W
Beira-Litoral 104 40 5N 8 30W
Beirut = Bayrūt 115 33 53N 35 31 E
Beiseker 61 51 23N 113 32W
Beitbridge 117 22 12 S 30 0 E
Beja 104 38 2N 7 53W
Béjaïa 114 36 42N 5 2 E
Bejestān 123 34 30N 58 5 E
Bekasi 127 6 20 S 107 0 E
Békéscsaba 107 46 40N 21 10 E
Bekok 128 2 20N 103 7 E
Bela, India 125 25 50N 82 0 E
Bela, Pak. 124 26 12N 66 20 E
Bela Crkva 109 44 55N 21 27 E
Bela Vista, Brazil 89 22 12 S 56 20W
Bela Vista, Mozam. 117 26 10 S 32 44 E
Bélâbre 102 46 34N 1 8 E
Bélair 42 46 51N 71 26W
Bélanger 44 45 36N 73 43W
Belanger, R. 57 53 27N 97 41W
Belawan 126 3 33N 98 32 E
Belaya Tserkov 120 49 45N 30 10 E
Belbutte 56 53 22N 107 49W
Belcher, C. 17 75 0N 160 0W
Belcher Chan. 65 77 15N 95 0W
Belcher Is. 36 56 15N 78 45W
Belcourt 40 48 24N 77 21W
Belden 80 40 2N 121 17W
Belém (Pará) 87 1 20 S 48 30W
Belén, Argent. 88 27 40 S 67 5W
Belén, Colomb. 86 1 26N 75 56W
Belén, Parag. 88 23 30 S 57 6W
Belen 79 34 40N 106 50W
Bélesta 102 42 55N 1 56 E
Belfair 80 47 27N 122 50W
Belfast, S. Afr. 117 25 42 S 30 2 E
Belfast, U.K. 97 54 35N 5 56W
Belfast, Maine, U.S.A. 35 44 30N 69 0W
Belfast, N.Y., U.S.A. 70 42 21N 78 9W
Belfast □ 97 54 35N 5 56W
Belfast, L. 97 54 40N 5 50W
Belfield 74 46 54N 103 11W
Belfort 101 47 38N 6 50 E
Belfort □ 101 47 38N 6 52 E
Belfountain 49 43 48N 80 1W
Belfry 78 45 10N 109 2W
Belgaum 124 15 55N 74 35 E
Belgium ■ 105 51 30N 5 0 E
Belgorod 120 50 35N 36 35 E
Belgrade 78 45 50N 111 10W
Belgrade = Beograd 109 44 50N 20 37 E
Belhaven 73 35 34N 76 35W
Beli Drim, R. 109 42 25N 20 34 E
Belinga 116 1 10N 13 2 E
Belinyu 126 1 35 S 105 50 E
Belitung, P. 126 3 10 S 107 50 E
Belize ■ 83 17 0N 88 30W
Belize City 83 17 25N 88 0W
Belize Inlet 62 51 8N 127 20W
Bell I., Newf., Can. 37 47 38N 52 58W
Bell I., Newf., Can. 37 50 46N 55 35W
Bell Irving, R. 54 56 12N 129 5W
Bell L. 52 49 48N 90 58W
Bell Peninsula 65 63 50N 82 0W
Bell, R. 40 49 48N 77 38W
Bell Ville 88 32 40 S 62 40W
Bella Bella 62 52 10N 128 10W
Bella Coola 62 52 25N 126 40W
Bella Unión 88 30 15 S 57 40W
Bella Vista, Corrientes, Argent. 88 28 33 S 59 0W
Bella Vista, Tucuman, Argent. 88 27 10 S 65 25W
Bellaire, Mich., U.S.A. 46 44 59N 85 13W
Bellaire, Ohio, U.S.A. 70 40 1N 80 46W
Bellary 124 15 10N 76 56 E
Bellburns 37 50 20N 57 32W
Belle 76 38 17N 91 43W
Belle Fourche 74 44 43N 103 52W
Belle Fourche, R. 74 44 25N 105 0W
Belle Glade 73 26 43N 80 38W
Belle-Ile 100 47 20N 3 10W
Belle Isle 37 51 57N 55 25W
Belle-Isle-en-Terre 100 48 33N 3 23W
Belle Isle, Str. of 37 51 30N 56 30W
Belle, La, Fla., U.S.A. 73 26 45N 81 22W
Belle, La, Mo., U.S.A. 76 40 7N 91 55W
Belle Plaine, Iowa, U.S.A. 76 41 51N 92 18W
Belle Plaine, Minn., U.S.A. 74 44 35N 93 48W
Belle Rive 77 38 14N 88 45W
Belle River 46 42 18N 82 43W
Belle Rivière 44 45 37N 74 6W
Belle-Vallée 43 45 4N 73 26W
Bellechasse □ 42 46 47N 71 14W
Belledonne 103 45 11N 6 0 E
Belledune 35 47 55N 65 50W
Bellefontaine 77 40 20N 83 45W
Bellefonte 70 40 56N 77 45W
Bellegarde, Ain, France 103 46 4N 5 49 E
Bellegarde, Creuse, France 101 45 59N 2 19 E
Bellegarde, Loiret, France 101 48 0N 2 26 E
Belleoram 37 47 31N 55 25W
Bellerive 43 45 15N 74 10W
Belleterre 40 47 25N 78 41W
Belleville, Can. 47 44 10N 77 23W
Belleville, Rhône, France 103 46 7N 4 45 E
Belleville, Vendée, France 100 46 48N 1 28W
Belleville, Ill., U.S.A. 77 38 30N 90 0W
Belleville, Kans., U.S.A. 74 39 51N 97 38W
Belleville, N.Y., U.S.A. 71 43 46N 76 10W
Bellevue, Can. 61 49 35N 114 22W
Bellevue, Idaho, U.S.A. 78 43 25N 144 23W
Bellevue, Iowa, U.S.A. 76 42 16N 90 26W
Bellevue, Mich., U.S.A. 77 42 27N 85 1W
Bellevue, Ohio, U.S.A. 70 41 20N 82 48W
Bellevue, Pa., U.S.A. 70 40 29N 80 3W
Bellevue, Wash., U.S.A. 80 47 37N 122 12W
Belley 103 45 46N 5 41 E
Bellflower 76 39 0N 91 21W
Bellin (Payne Bay) 36 60 0N 70 0W
Bellingham 80 48 45N 122 27W
Bellingshausen Sea 91 66 0 S 80 0W
Bellinzona 106 46 11N 9 1 E
Belliveau Cove 39 44 23N 66 4W
Bello 86 6 20N 75 33W
Bellona Reefs 135 21 26 S 159 0 E
Bellows Falls 71 43 10N 72 30W
Bells Corners 48 45 19N 75 50W
Bellsite 57 52 35N 101 4W
Belluno 108 46 8N 12 6 E
Bellville, Ohio, U.S.A. 70 40 38N 82 32W
Bellville, Tex., U.S.A. 75 29 58N 96 18W
Bellwood 70 40 36N 78 21W
Belly, R. 61 49 46N 113 2W
Belmar 71 40 10N 74 2W
Bélmez 104 38 17N 5 17W
Belmond 76 42 51N 93 37W
Belmont, Austral. 136 33 4 S 151 42 E
Belmont, Man., Can. 57 49 25N 99 27W
Belmont, N.S., Can. 39 45 25N 63 23W
Belmont, Ont., Can. 46 42 53N 81 5W
Belmont, U.S.A. 70 42 14N 78 3W
Belmont Park 63 48 27N 123 27W
Belmonte 87 16 0 S 39 0W
Belmopan 83 17 18N 88 30W
Belmullet 97 54 13N 9 58W
Belo Horizonte 87 19 53 S 43 56W
Belo-sur-Tsiribihana 117 19 40 S 43 30 E
Beloeil 45 45 34N 73 12W
Belogorsk 121 51 0N 128 20 E
Beloit, Kans., U.S.A. 74 39 32N 98 9W
Beloit, Wis., U.S.A. 76 42 35N 89 0W
Belomorsk 120 64 35N 34 30 E
Belonia 125 23 15N 91 30 E
Belot, L. 64 66 53N 126 16W
Belovo 120 54 30N 86 0 E
Beloye Ozero 120 45 15N 46 50 E
Belozersk 120 60 0N 37 30 E
Belterra 87 2 45 S 55 0W
Belton, S.C., U.S.A. 73 34 31N 82 39W
Belton, Tex., U.S.A. 75 31 4N 97 30W
Belturbet 97 54 6N 7 28W
Belukha 120 49 50N 86 50 E
Beluran 126 5 48N 117 35 E
Belvès 102 44 46N 1 0 E
Belvidere, Ill., U.S.A. 77 42 15N 88 55W
Belvidere, N.J., U.S.A. 71 40 48N 75 5W
Belwood 49 43 47N 80 19W
Belwood, L. 49 43 46N 80 20W
Belyando, R. 135 21 38 S 146 50 E
Belyj Jar 120 58 26N 84 39 E
Belyy, Ostrov 120 73 30N 71 0 E
Belzoni 75 33 12N 90 30W
Bement 77 39 55N 88 34W
Bemidji 74 47 30N 94 50W
Ben Cruachan, Mt. 96 56 26N 5 8W
Ben Dearg, mt. 96 56 54N 3 49W
Ben Hope, mt. 96 58 24N 4 36W
Ben Lawers, mt. 96 56 33N 4 13W
Ben Lomond 135 41 38 S 147 42 E
Ben Lomond, mt. 96 56 12N 4 39W
Ben Macdhui 96 57 4N 3 40W
Ben Mhor 96 57 16N 7 21W
Ben More, Mull, U.K. 96 56 26N 6 2W
Ben More, Perth, U.K. 96 56 23N 4 31W
Ben More Assynt 96 58 7N 4 51W
Ben Nevis, mt. 96 56 48N 5 0W
Ben Vorlich, Strathclyde, U.K. 96 56 17N 4 47W
Ben Vorlich, Tayside, U.K. 96 56 22N 4 15W
Ben Wyvis, mt. 96 57 40N 4 35W
Bena 52 47 19N 94 8W
Bena Dibele 116 4 4 S 22 50 E
Benalla 136 36 30 S 146 0 E
Benambra, Mt. 136 36 31 S 147 34 E
Benares = Varanasi 125 25 22N 83 8 E
Benavides 75 27 35N 98 28W
Benbecula, I. 96 57 26N 7 21W
Bencubbin 134 30 48 S 117 52 E
Bend 78 44 2N 121 15W
Bendale 50 43 46N 79 14W
Bender Beila 115 9 30N 50 48 E
Bendigo 136 36 40 S 144 15 E
Bénestroff 101 48 54N 6 45 E
Benet 102 46 22N 0 35W
Benevento 108 41 7N 14 45 E
Benfeld 101 48 22N 7 34 E
Bengal, Bay of 125 15 0N 00 90 E
Bengawan Solo 127 7 5 S 112 25 E
Benghazi = Banghāzī 115 32 11N 20 3 E
Bengkalis 126 1 30N 102 10 E
Bengkulu 126 3 50 S 102 12 E
Bengkulu □ 126 3 48 S 102 16 E
Bengough 56 49 25N 105 10W
Benguela 117 12 37 S 13 25 E
Beni 116 0 30N 29 27 E
Beni, R. 86 10 30 S 66 0W
Benī Suêf 115 29 5N 31 6 E
Beniah L. 54 63 23N 112 17W
Benicia 80 38 3N 122 9W
Benidorm 104 38 33N 0 9W
Benin ■ 114 10 0N 2 0 E
Benin, Bight of 114 5 0N 3 0 E
Benin City 114 6 20N 5 31 E
Benjamin Aceval 88 24 58 S 57 34W
Benjamin Constant 86 4 40 S 70 15W
Benjamin Hill 82 30 10N 111 10W
Benkelman 74 40 7N 101 32W
Bennett 67 59 56N 134 53W
Bennettsville 73 34 38N 79 39W
Bennington 71 42 52N 73 12W
Benny 46 46 47N 81 38W
Benoa 126 8 50 S 115 20 E
Bénodet 100 47 53N 4 7W
Benoit's Cove 37 49 1N 58 7W
Benoni 117 26 11 S 28 18 E
Benque Viejo 83 17 5N 89 8W
Benson, Can. 56 49 27N 103 1W
Benson, U.S.A. 79 31 59N 110 19W
Bent 123 26 20N 59 25 E
Benteng 127 6 10 S 120 30 E
Bentinck I. 135 17 3 S 139 35 E
Bentley 61 52 28N 114 4W
Bento Gonçalves 89 29 10 S 51 31W
Benton, Ark., U.S.A. 75 34 30N 92 35W
Benton, Calif., U.S.A. 80 37 48N 118 32W
Benton, Ill., U.S.A. 76 38 0N 88 55W
Benton Harbor 77 42 10N 86 28W
Bentong 128 3 31N 101 55 E
Benue, R. 114 7 50N 6 30 E
Beo 127 4 25N 126 50 E
Beograd 109 44 50N 20 37 E
Beowawe 78 40 45N 116 30W
Beppu 132 33 15N 131 30 E
Berber 115 18 0N 34 0 E
Berbera 115 10 30N 45 2 E
Berbérati 116 4 15N 15 40 E
Berbice, R. 86 5 20N 58 10W
Berck-sur-Mer 101 50 25N 1 36 E
Berdsk 120 54 47N 83 2 E
Berea, Kentucky, U.S.A. 72 37 35N 84 18W
Berea, Ohio, U.S.A. 70 41 21N 81 50W
Berebere 127 2 25N 128 45 E
Berens I. 57 52 18N 97 18W
Berens, R. 57 52 25N 96 55W
Berens River 57 52 25N 97 0W
Beresford 39 47 42N 65 42W
Bereziuk, L. 36 54 0N 76 18W
Berezniki 120 59 24N 56 46 E
Berezovo 120 64 0N 65 0 E
Bergama 122 39 8N 27 15 E
Bérgamo 108 45 42N 9 40 E
Bergen, Norway 111 60 23N 5 20 E
Bergen, U.S.A. 70 43 5N 77 56W
Bergen-Binnen 105 52 40N 4 43 E
Bergen-op-Zoom 105 51 30N 4 18 E
Bergerac 102 44 51N 0 30 E
Bergisch-Gladbach 105 50 59N 7 9 E
Bergland 52 46 35N 89 34W
Bergues 101 50 58N 2 24 E
Bergum 105 53 13N 5 59 E
Berhala, Selat 126 1 0 S 104 15 E
Berhampore 125 24 2N 88 27 E
Berhampur 125 19 15N 84 54 E
Bering Sea 14 58 0N 167 0 E
Bering Str. 67 66 0N 170 0W
Beringovskiy 121 63 3N 179 19 E
Berisso 88 34 40 S 58 0W
Berja 104 36 50N 2 56W
Berkeley 80 37 52N 122 20W
Berkeley Springs 72 39 38N 78 12W
Berkner I. 91 79 30 S 50 0W
Berkshire □ 95 51 30N 1 20W
Berkshire Downs 95 51 30N 1 30W
Berlaar 105 51 7N 4 39 E
Berland, R. 60 54 0N 116 50W
Berlin, Ger. 106 52 32N 13 24 E
Berlin, Md., U.S.A. 72 38 19N 75 12W
Berlin, N.H., U.S.A. 71 44 29N 71 10W
Bermejo, R., Formosa, Argent. 88 26 30 S 58 50W
Bermejo, R., San Juan, Argent. 88 30 0 S 68 0W
Bermen, L. 36 53 35N 68 55W
Bermuda, I. 10 32 45N 65 0W
Bern (Berne) 106 46 57N 7 28 E
Bernalillo 79 35 17N 106 37W
Bernam, R. 128 3 45N 101 5 E
Bernard L. 46 45 45N 79 23W
Bernardo de Irigoyen 89 26 15 S 53 40W
Bernasconi 88 37 55 S 63 44W
Bernay 100 49 5N 0 35 E
Bernburg 106 51 40N 11 42 E
Berne 77 40 39N 84 57W
Berne = Bern 106 46 57N 7 28 E
Bernier B. 65 71 5N 88 15W
Bernier I. 134 24 50 S 113 12 E
Bernierville 41 46 6N 71 34W
Beroroha 117 21 40 S 45 10 E
Beroun 106 49 57N 14 5 E
Berowra 136 33 35 S 151 12 E
Berre 103 43 28N 5 11 E
Berre, Étang de 103 43 27N 5 5 E
Berrien Springs 77 41 57N 86 20W
Berrigan 136 35 38 S 145 49 E
Berry, France 101 47 0N 2 0 E
Berry, U.S.A. 77 38 31N 84 23W
Berry Cr. 61 50 50N 111 37W
Berry Is. 84 25 40N 77 50W
Berryessa, L. 80 38 31N 122 6W
Berryville 75 36 23N 93 35W
Berthaund 74 40 21N 105 5W
Berthierville 41 46 5N 73 10W
Berthold 74 48 19N 101 45W
Bertincourt 101 50 5N 2 58 E
Bertoua 116 4 30N 13 45 E
Bertrand, Can. 39 47 45N 65 4W
Bertrand, U.S.A. 74 40 35N 99 38W
Berufjörður 110 64 48N 14 29W
Berwick, N.B., Can. 39 45 47N 65 36W
Berwick, N.S., Can. 39 45 3N 64 44W
Berwick, U.S.A. 71 41 4N 76 17W
Berwick-upon-Tweed 94 55 47N 2 0W
Berwyn 60 56 9N 117 44W
Berwyn Mts. 94 52 54N 3 26W
Besalampy 117 16 43 S 44 29 E
Besançon 101 47 9N 6 0 E
Besar 126 2 40 S 116 0 E
Beserah 128 3 50N 103 21 E
Besnard L. 55 55 25N 106 0W
Bessèges 103 44 18N 4 8 E
Bessemer 74 46 27N 90 0W
Bessin 100 49 21N 1 0W
Bessines-sur-Gartempe 100 46 6N 1 22 E
Bet She'an 115 32 30N 35 30 E
Bete Grise B. 53 47 26N 87 53W
Bethanien 117 26 31 S 17 8 E
Bethany, Can. 47 44 11N 78 34W
Bethany, Ill., U.S.A. 77 39 39N 88 45W
Bethany, Mo., U.S.A. 76 40 18N 94 0W
Bethel, Alaska, U.S.A. 67 60 50N 161 50W
Bethel, Ohio, U.S.A. 77 38 58N 84 5W
Bethel, Pa., U.S.A. 70 40 20N 80 2W
Bethel, Vt., U.S.A. 71 43 50N 72 37W
Bethesda 50 43 58N 79 21W
Bethlehem, S. Afr. 117 28 14 S 28 18 E
Bethlehem, U.S.A. 71 40 39N 75 24W
Bethlehem = Bayt Lahm 115 31 43N 35 12 E
Bethulie 117 30 30 S 25 59 E
Bethune 56 50 43N 105 13W
Béthune 101 50 30N 2 38 E
Béthune, R. 100 49 56N 1 5 E
Betijoque 86 9 23N 70 44W
Betioky 117 23 48 S 44 20 E
Beton Bazoches 101 48 42N 3 15 E
Betong 128 5 45N 101 5 E
Betroka 117 23 16 S 46 0 E
Betsiamites 41 48 56N 68 40W
Betsiamites, R. 41 48 56N 68 38W
Bettendorf 76 41 32N 90 30W
Bettiah 125 26 48N 84 33 E
Bettles 67 66 54N 150 50W
Betul 124 21 48N 77 59 E
Betung 126 2 0 S 103 10 E
Beuil 103 44 6N 7 0 E

Beulah **Blåvands Huk**

Beulah, Can. 55 50 16N 101 02W
Beulah, U.S.A. 74 47 18N 101 47W
Beverley, Austral. 134 32 9S 116 56E
Beverley, U.K. 94 53 52N 0 26W
Beverly, Can. 54 53 36N 113 21W
Beverly, Mass., U.S.A. 71 42 32N 70 50W
Beverly, Wash., U.S.A. 78 46 55N 119 59W
Beverly Hills 81 34 4N 118 29W
Beverwijk 105 52 28N 4 38E
Bevin, L. 43 45 57N 74 35W
Bewdley 47 44 5N 78 19W
Beynat 107 45 8N 1 44E
Beyneu 120 45 10N 55 3E
Beypazarı 122 40 10N 31 48E
Beyşehir Gölü 122 37 40N 31 45E
Bezhitsa 120 53 19N 34 17E
Béziers 102 43 20N 3 12E
Bezwada = Vijayawada 125 16 31N 80 39E
Bhachau 124 23 20N 70 16E
Bhadrakh 125 21 10N 86 30E
Bhadravati 124 13 49N 76 15E
Bhagalpur 125 25 10N 87 0E
Bhakra Dam 124 31 30N 76 45E
Bhamo 125 24 15N 97 15E
Bhandara 124 21 5N 79 42E
Bhanrer Ra. 124 23 40N 79 45E
Bharat = India 124 24 0N 78 0E
Bharatpur 124 27 15N 77 30E
Bhatpara 125 22 50N 88 25E
Bhaunagar = Bhavnagar 124 21 45N 72 10E
Bhavnagar 124 21 45N 72 10E
Bhawanipatna 125 19 55N 83 30E
Bhilsa = Vidisha 124 23 28N 77 53E
Bhilwara 124 25 25N 74 38E
Bhima, R. 124 17 20N 76 30E
Bhimvaram 125 16 30N 81 30E
Bhind 124 26 30N 78 46E
Bhiwandi 124 19 15N 73 0E
Bhiwani 124 28 50N 76 9E
Bhola 125 22 45N 90 35E
Bhopal 124 23 20N 77 53E
Bhubaneswar 125 20 15N 85 50E
Bhuj 124 23 15N 69 49E
Bhusaval 124 21 15N 69 49E
Bhutan ■ 125 27 25N 89 50E
Biafra, B. of = Bonny, Bight of 116 3 30N 9 20E
Biak 127 1 0S 136 0E
Biała Podlaska 107 52 4N 23 6E
Białystok 107 53 10N 23 10E
Biaro 127 2 5N 125 26E
Biarritz 102 43 29N 1 33W
Bibby I. 55 61 55N 93 0W
Biberach 106 48 5N 9 49E
Bic 41 48 20N 68 41W
Bic, Île du 41 48 24N 68 52W
Bicester 95 51 53N 1 9W
Biche, L. la 60 54 50N 112 3W
Biche, La, R. 54 59 57N 123 50W
Bickerton West 39 45 6N 61 44W
Bicknell, Ind., U.S.A. 77 38 50N 87 20W
Bicknell, Utah, U.S.A. 79 38 16N 111 35W
Bida 114 9 3N 5 58E
Bidar 124 17 55N 77 35E
Biddeford 35 43 30N 70 28W
Bideford 95 51 1N 4 13W
Bidor 128 4 6N 101 15E
Bié Plateau 117 12 0S 16 0E
Bieber 78 41 4N 121 6W
Biel (Bienne) 106 47 8N 7 14E
Bielé Karpaty 107 49 5N 18 0E
Bielefeld 106 52 2N 8 31E
Biella 108 45 33N 8 3E
Bielsko-Biała 107 49 50N 19 8E
Bien Hoa 128 10 57N 106 49E
Bienfait 56 49 10N 102 50W
Bienne = Biel 106 47 8N 7 14E
Bienville, L. 36 55 5N 72 40W
Big B. 36 55 43N 60 35W
Big Bar Creek 63 51 12N 122 7W
Big Basswood L. 46 46 25N 83 23W
Big Bay 53 46 49N 87 44W
Big Bear City 81 34 16N 116 51W
Big Bear L. 81 34 15N 116 56W
Big Beaver 56 49 10N 105 10W
Big Beaver House 34 52 59N 89 50W
Big Belt Mts. 78 46 50N 111 30W
Big Bend Nat. Park 75 29 15N 103 15W
Big Bend Res. 61 52 59N 115 30W
Big Black, R. 75 32 35N 90 30W
Big Blue, R., Ind., U.S.A. 77 39 12N 85 56W
Big Blue, R., Kans., U.S.A. 74 40 20N 96 40W
Big Cr. 63 51 42N 122 41W
Big Creek, Can. 63 51 43N 123 2W
Big Creek, U.S.A. 80 37 11N 119 14W
Big Cypress Swamp 73 26 12N 81 10W
Big Delta 67 64 15N 145 0W
Big Falls 52 48 11N 93 48W
Big Fork 52 47 45N 93 39W
Big Fork, R. 52 48 31N 93 43W
Big Horn 78 46 11N 107 25W
Big Horn Dam 61 52 20N 116 20W
Big Horn Mts. = Bighorn Mts. 78 44 30N 107 30W
Big Horn R. 78 45 30N 108 10W
Big I., N.W.T., Can. 65 62 43N 70 43W
Big I., Ont., Can. 52 49 9N 94 40W
Big L. 59 53 37N 113 42W
Big Lake 75 31 12N 101 25W
Big Moose 71 43 49N 74 58W
Big Muddy L. 56 49 9N 104 51W
Big Muddy, R 76 38 0N 89 0W
Big Muddy, R. 74 48 25N 104 45W
Big Pine 80 37 12N 118 17W
Big Piney 78 42 32N 110 3W
Big Pond 39 45 57N 60 32W
Big Quill L. 56 51 55N 104 22W
Big, R., Can. 36 54 50N 58 55W
Big, R., U.S.A. 76 38 27N 90 37W
Big Rapids 72 43 42N 85 27W
Big Rideau L. 47 44 40N 76 15W
Big River 56 53 50N 107 0W
Big Run 70 40 57N 78 55W
Big Sable Pt. 72 44 5N 86 30W
Big Salmon 67 61 50N 136 0W
Big Sand L. 55 57 45N 99 45W
Big Sandy 78 48 12N 110 9W
Big Sandy Cr. 74 38 52N 103 11W
Big Sandy L., Can. 56 54 27N 104 6W
Big Sandy L., U.S.A. 52 46 45N 93 20W
Big Sioux, R. 74 44 20N 96 53W
Big Snowy Mt. 78 46 50N 109 15W
Big Spring 75 32 10N 101 25W
Big Springs 74 41 4N 102 3W
Big Stone City 74 45 20N 96 30W
Big Stone Gap 73 36 52N 82 45W
Big Stone L. 74 45 30N 96 35W
Big Sur 80 36 15N 121 48W
Big Trout L., Ont., Can. 34 53 40N 90 0W
Big Trout L., Ont., Can. 47 45 46N 78 37W
Big Valley 61 52 2N 112 46W
Biganos 102 44 39N 0 59W
Bigfork 78 48 3N 114 2W
Biggar 56 52 4N 108 0W
Biggs 80 39 24N 121 43W
Bighorn Mts. 78 44 30N 107 30W
Bigniba, R. 40 49 18N 77 20W
Bigot, L. 38 50 50N 65 39W
Bigsby I 52 49 4N 94 34W
Bigstick L. 56 50 16N 109 20W
Bigstone L. 57 53 42N 95 44W
Bigtimber 78 45 53N 110 0W
Bihać 108 44 49N 15 57E
Bihar 125 25 5N 85 40E
Bihar □ 125 25 0N 86 0E
Bihé Plateau 117 12 0S 16 0E
Bihor, Munţii 107 46 29N 22 47E
Bijagós, Arquipélago dos 114 11 15N 16 10W
Bijapur, Mad. P., India 125 18 50N 80 50E
Bijapur, Mysore, India 124 16 50N 75 55E
Bijär 122 35 52N 47 35E
Bijeljina 109 44 46N 19 17E
Bijnor 124 29 27N 78 11E
Bikaner 124 28 2N 73 18E
Bikin 121 46 50N 134 20E
Bikini, atoll 14 12 0N 167 30E
Bikoro 116 0 48S 18 15E
Biläd Banī Bū 'Alt 123 22 0N 59 20E
Bilara 124 26 14N 73 53E
Bilaspur 125 22 2N 82 15E
Bilauk Taungdan 128 13 0N 99 0E
Bilbao 104 43 16N 2 56W
Bildudalur 110 65 41N 23 36W
Bilecik 122 40 5N 30 5E
Bilibino 121 68 3N 166 20E
Bilir 121 65 40N 131 20E
Bill 74 43 18N 105 18W
Billabong Creek 136 35 5S 144 2E
Billingham 94 54 36N 1 18W
Billings 78 45 43N 108 29W
Billiton Is = Belitung 126 3 10S 107 50E
Billom 102 45 43N 3 20E
Bilma 114 18 50N 13 30E
Biloxi 75 30 30N 89 0W
Bima 127 8 22S 118 49E
Bimberi Peak, mt. 136 35 44S 148 51E
Bimbo 116 4 15N 18 33E
Bina-Etawah 124 24 13N 78 14E
Binalbagan 127 10 12N 122 50E
Binalong 136 34 40S 148 39E
Binatang 126 2 10N 111 40E
Binbrook 49 43 7N 79 48W
Binche 105 50 26N 4 10E
Bindura 117 17 18S 31 18E
Bingen 105 49 57N 7 53E
Bingerville 114 5 18N 3 49W
Bingham 35 45 5N 69 50W
Bingham Canyon 78 40 31N 112 10W
Binghamton 71 42 9N 75 54W
Bingöl 122 39 20N 41 0E
Binh Dinh = An Nhon 128 13 55N 109 7E
Binh Son 128 15 20N 108 40E
Binjai 126 3 50N 98 30E
Binnaway 136 31 28S 149 24E
Binongko 127 5 55S 123 55E
Binscarth 57 50 37N 101 17W
Bint 123 26 22N 59 25E
Bintan 126 1 0N 104 0E
Bintulu 126 3 10N 113 0E
Binzert = Bizerte 114 37 15N 9 50E
Bío-Bío □ 88 37 35S 72 0W
Bir 124 19 0N 75 54E
Bir Mogreïn, (Fort Trinquet) 114 25 10N 11 25W
Bira 127 2 3S 132 2E
Birch Cliff, Ont., Can. 49 43 41N 79 18W
Birch Cliff, Ont., Can. 50 43 41N 79 17W
Birch Cove 39 44 42N 63 41W
Birch Hills 56 52 59N 105 25W
Birch I. 57 52 26N 99 54W
Birch Island 63 51 37N 119 54W
Birch L., Alta., Can. 60 53 19N 111 35W
Birch L., N.W.T., Can. 54 62 4N 116 33W
Birch L., Ont., Can. 52 51 23N 92 18W
Birch L., Sask., Can. 56 53 27N 108 10W
Birch L., U.S.A. 52 47 48N 91 43W
Birch Manor 48 45 26N 75 46W
Birch Mts. 54 57 30N 113 10W
Birch River 57 52 24N 101 6W
Birch Run 46 43 15N 83 48W
Birchip 136 35 56S 142 55E
Birchy Bay 37 49 21N 54 44W
Bird 55 56 30N 94 13W
Bird City 74 39 48N 101 33W
Bird Cove 37 51 3N 56 56W
Bird I. 135 22 10S 155 28E
Birds 77 38 50N 87 40W
Birds Hill 58 49 59N 97 0W
Birdseye 77 38 19N 86 42W
Birdsville 135 25 51S 139 20E
Birdum 134 15 39S 133 13E
Birecik 122 37 0N 38 0E
Bireuen 126 5 14N 96 39E
Birigui 89 21 18S 50 16W
Birjand 123 32 57N 59 10E
Birken 63 50 28N 122 37W
Birkenhead 94 53 24N 3 1W
Bîrlad 107 46 15N 27 38E
Birmingham, U.K. 95 52 30N 1 55W
Birmingham, U.S.A. 46 42 33N 83 15W
Birmingham, Ala., U.S.A. 73 33 31N 86 50W
Birmingham, Iowa, U.S.A. 76 40 53N 91 57W
Birmitrapur 125 22 30N 84 10E
Birobidzhan 121 48 50N 132 50E
Biron 38 48 12N 66 16W
Birr 97 53 7N 7 55W
Birsay 56 51 6N 106 59W
Birsk 120 55 25N 55 30E
Birtle 57 50 30N 101 5W
Birur 124 13 30N 75 55E
Bisa 127 1 10S 127 40E
Bisbee 79 31 30N 110 0W
Biscay, B. of 12 45 0N 2 0W
Biscayne B. 73 25 40N 80 12W
Bischwiller 101 48 41N 7 50E
Biscoe I. 91 66 0S 67 0W
Biscostasing 53 47 18N 82 9W
Biscotasi L. 53 47 22N 82 1W
Biscucuy 86 9 22N 69 59W
Bishop, Calif., U.S.A. 80 37 20N 118 26W
Bishop, Tex., U.S.A. 75 27 35N 97 49W
Bishop Auckland 94 54 40N 1 40W
Bishop, Mt. 66 49 26N 122 56W
Bishop's Falls 37 49 2N 55 30W
Bishop's Stortford 95 51 52N 0 11E
Bishopton 41 45 35N 71 35W
Biskra 114 34 50N 5 44E
Bislig 127 8 15N 126 27E
Bismarck, Can. 49 43 3N 79 30W
Bismarck, Mo., U.S.A. 76 37 46N 90 38W
Bismarck, N.Dak., U.S.A. 74 46 49N 100 49W
Bismarck Arch. 14 2 30S 150 0E
Bison 74 45 34N 102 28W
Bison L. 60 57 12N 116 8W
Bispfors 110 63 1N 16 39E
Bissagos = Bijagós 114 11 15N 16 10W
Bissau 114 11 45N 15 45W
Bissett 57 51 2N 95 41W
Bistcho L. 54 59 45N 118 50W
Bistriţa 107 47 9N 24 35E
Bistriţa, R. 107 47 10N 24 30E
Bitam 116 2 5N 11 25E
Bitche 101 48 58N 7 25E
Bitlis 122 38 20N 42 3E
Bitola (Bitolj) 109 41 5N 21 10E
Bitter Creek 78 41 39N 108 36W
Bitter L. 56 50 7N 109 48W
Bitterfontein 117 31 0S 18 32E
Bittern L., Alta., Can. 61 53 3N 113 5W
Bittern L., Sask., Can. 56 53 56N 105 45W
Bitteroot, R. 78 46 30N 114 20W
Bitterroot Range 78 46 0N 114 20W
Bitterwater 80 36 23N 121 0W
Bitumount 54 57 26N 111 40W
Biu 114 10 40N 12 3E
Biwa-Ko 132 35 15N 135 45E
Biwabik 74 47 33N 92 19W
Biysk 120 52 40N 85 0E
Bizard, Île 44 45 29N 73 54W
Bizerte (Binzert) 114 37 15N 9 50E
Bjargtangar 110 65 30N 24 30W
Bjelovar 108 45 56N 16 49E
Bjorkdale 56 52 43N 103 39W
Blache, L. de la 41 50 5N 69 29W
Black B. 52 48 40N 88 25W
Black Creek 62 49 49N 125 7W
Black Diamond 61 50 45N 114 14W
Black Hills 74 44 0N 103 50W
Black Horse 49 43 59N 79 49W
Black I. 57 51 12N 96 30W
Black L., Can. 55 59 12N 105 15W
Black L., U.S.A. 46 45 28N 84 15W
Black Lake 41 46 1N 71 22W
Black Mesa, Mt. 75 36 57N 102 55W
Black Mt. 66 49 23N 123 13W
Black Mt. = Mynydd Du 95 51 45N 3 45W
Black Mts. 95 51 52N 3 5W
Black Pines 63 50 57N 120 15W
Black, R., Can. 46 44 42N 79 19W
Black, R., Ark., U.S.A. 75 36 15N 90 45W
Black, R., Mich., U.S.A. 46 43 3N 82 37W
Black, R., Minn., U.S.A. 52 48 32N 93 51W
Black, R., N.Y., U.S.A. 71 43 59N 76 40W
Black, R., Wis., U.S.A. 74 44 18N 90 52W
Black Range, Mts. 79 33 30N 107 55W
Black River, Jamaica 84 18 0N 77 50W
Black River, U.S.A. 46 44 53N 83 18W
Black Rock Pt. 36 60 2N 64 10W
Black Sea 92 43 30N 35 0E
Black Sturgeon L. 52 49 20N 88 53W
Black Sugarloaf, Mt. 136 31 18S 151 35E
Black Warrior, R. 73 33 0N 87 45W
Blackall 135 24 25S 145 45E
Blackball 133 42 22S 171 26E
Blackburn 94 53 44N 2 30W
Blackburn Hamlet 48 45 26N 75 33W
Blackburn, Mt. 67 61 5N 142 3W
Blackduck 52 47 43N 94 32W
Blackfalds 61 52 23N 113 47W
Blackfoot, Can. 60 53 17N 110 10W
Blackfoot, U.S.A. 78 43 13N 112 12W
Blackfoot, R. 78 47 0N 113 35W
Blackhead 37 47 32N 52 39W
Blackhead Road 37 47 33N 52 43W
Blackheath 49 43 4N 79 49W
Blackie 61 50 36N 113 37W
Blackmud Cr. 59 53 27N 113 33W
Blackpool, Can. 43 45 1N 73 28W
Blackpool, U.K. 94 53 48N 3 3W
Blackriver 70 44 46N 83 17W
Blacks Harbour 42 45 3N 66 49W
Blacksburg 72 37 17N 80 23W
Blacksod B. 97 54 6N 10 0W
Blackstone 72 37 6N 78 0W
Blackstone, R. 54 61 5N 122 55W
Blackstone Ra. 134 26 00S 129 00E
Blackville 39 46 44N 65 50W
Blackwater 54 53 20N 123 0W
Blackwater, R., Cork, Ireland 97 52 5N 9 3W
Blackwater, R., Limerick, Ireland 97 51 55N 7 50W
Blackwater, R., Meath, Ireland 97 53 46N 7 0W
Blackwater, R., U.K. 97 54 31N 6 35W
Blackwater, R., U.S.A. 76 38 59N 92 59W
Blackwell 75 36 55N 97 20W
Blackwells Corner 81 35 37N 119 47W
Bladworth 56 51 22N 106 8W
Blaenau Ffestiniog 94 53 0N 3 57W
Blagnac 102 43 38N 1 24E
Blagoveshchensk 121 50 20N 127 30E
Blaine 66 48 59N 122 43W
Blaine Lake 56 52 51N 106 52W
Blainville, Can. 44 45 40N 73 52W
Blainville, France 101 48 33N 6 23E
Blair, Can. 49 43 23N 80 23W
Blair, U.S.A. 74 41 38N 96 10W
Blair Athol 135 22 42S 147 31E
Blair Atholl 96 56 46N 3 50W
Blairgowrie 96 56 36N 3 20W
Blairmore 61 49 40N 114 25W
Blairs Mills 70 40 17N 77 45W
Blairsden 80 39 47N 120 37W
Blairsville 70 40 27N 79 15W
Blairville 49 43 14N 79 2W
Blake Pt. 52 48 12N 88 27W
Blakely 73 31 22N 85 0W
Blakesburg 76 40 58N 92 38W
Blâmont 101 48 35N 6 50E
Blanc, Le 102 46 37N 1 3E
Blanc, Mont 103 45 48N 6 50E
Blanca, Bahía 90 39 10S 61 30W
Blanca Peak 79 37 35N 105 29W
Blanchard 75 35 8N 97 40W
Blanchardville 76 42 48N 89 52W
Blanche L., S. Austral., Austral. 134 29 15S 139 40E
Blanche L., W. Austral., Austral. 135 22 25S 123 17E
Blanche, R. 48 45 30N 75 33W
Blanchester 77 39 17N 83 59W
Blanco 75 30 7N 98 30W
Blanco, C., C. Rica 84 9 34N 85 8W
Blanco, C., Peru 86 4 10S 81 10W
Blanco, C., U.S.A. 78 42 50N 124 40W
Blanco, R. 88 31 54S 69 42W
Blanda 110 65 20N 19 40W
Blandford Forum 95 50 52N 2 10W
Blanding 79 37 35N 109 30W
Blandinsville 76 40 33N 90 52W
Blankenberge 105 51 20N 3 9E
Blanquefort 102 44 55N 0 38W
Blanquilla, La 86 11 51N 64 37W
Blanquillo 89 32 53S 55 37W
Blantyre 117 15 45S 35 0E
Blarney 97 51 57N 8 35W
Blåvands Huk 111 55 33N 8 4E

Blaydon **Bowbells**

Place	Page	Lat.	Long.
Blaydon	**94**	54 56N	1 47W
Blaye	**102**	45 8N	0 40W
Blaye-les-Mines	**102**	44 1N	2 8E
Blayney	**136**	33 32S	149 14E
Blaze, Pt.	**134**	12 56S	130 11E
Blednaya, Gora	**120**	65 50N	65 30E
Bleiburg	**106**	46 35N	14 49E
Blekinge län □	**111**	56 20N	15 20E
Blenheim, Can.	**46**	42 20N	82 0W
Blenheim, N.Z.	**133**	41 38S	174 5E
Bléone, R.	**103**	44 5N	6 0E
Bletchley	**95**	51 59N	0 44W
Bleu, L.	**40**	46 35N	78 24W
Bleymard, Le	**102**	44 30N	3 42E
Blida	**114**	36 30N	2 49E
Bligh Sound	**133**	44 47S	167 32E
Blind River	**46**	46 10N	82 58W
Blissfield, Can.	**39**	46 36N	66 5W
Blissfield, U.S.A.	**77**	41 50N	83 52W
Blitar	**127**	8 5S	112 11E
Block I., U.S.A.	**71**	41 11N	71 35W
Block I., U.S.A.	**71**	41 13N	71 35W
Block Island Sound	**71**	41 17N	71 35W
Blockton	**76**	40 37N	94 29W
Bloemfontein	**117**	29 6S	26 14E
Bloemhof	**117**	27 38S	25 32E
Blois	**100**	47 35N	1 20E
Blonduōs	**110**	65 40N	20 12W
Bloodvein, R.	**57**	51 47N	96 43W
Bloody Foreland	**97**	55 10N	8 18W
Bloomer	**74**	45 8N	91 30W
Bloomfield, Newf., Can.	**37**	48 23N	53 54W
Bloomfield, Ont., Can.	**47**	43 59N	77 14W
Bloomfield, Ind., U.S.A.	**77**	39 1N	86 57W
Bloomfield, Iowa, U.S.A.	**76**	40 44N	92 26W
Bloomfield, Ky., U.S.A.	**77**	37 55N	85 19W
Bloomfield, N. Mexico, U.S.A.	**79**	36 46N	107 59W
Bloomfield, Nebr., U.S.A.	**74**	42 38N	97 40W
Bloomingburg	**77**	39 36N	83 24W
Bloomingdale	**49**	43 31N	80 27W
Bloomington, Ill., U.S.A.	**76**	40 49N	89 0W
Bloomington, Ind., U.S.A.	**77**	39 10N	86 30W
Bloomington, Wis., U.S.A.	**76**	42 53N	90 55W
Bloomsburg	**71**	41 0N	76 30W
Blora	**127**	6 57S	111 25E
Blossburg	**70**	41 40N	77 4W
Blossom Park	**48**	45 21N	75 37W
Blouin	**42**	46 2N	71 0W
Blountstown	**73**	30 28N	85 5W
Blubber Bay	**62**	49 47N	124 37W
Blue Hills	**64**	75 34N	114 30W
Blue I.	**77**	41 40N	87 40W
Blue Lake	**78**	40 53N	124 0W
Blue Mesa Res.	**79**	38 30N	107 15W
Blue Mound	**76**	39 42N	89 7W
Blue Mountain Peak	**85**	18 0N	76 40W
Blue Mts., Austral.	**136**	33 40S	150 0E
Blue Mts., Jamaica	**85**	18 0N	76 40W
Blue Mts., Ore., U.S.A.	**78**	45 15N	119 0W
Blue Mts., Pa., U.S.A.	**71**	40 30N	76 0W
Blue Mud B.	**135**	13 30S	136 0E
Blue Nile, R. = Nîl el Azraq	**114**	10 30N	35 0E
Blue, R.	**77**	38 11N	86 18W
Blue Ridge	**60**	54 8N	115 22W
Blue Ridge, Mts.	**73**	36 30N	80 15W
Blue River	**63**	52 6N	119 18W
Blue Springs	**76**	39 1N	94 17W
Blue Stack Mts.	**97**	54 46N	8 5W
Blueberry Mountain	**60**	55 56N	119 9W
Blueberry, R.	**54**	56 45N	120 49W
Bluefield	**72**	37 18N	81 14W
Bluefields	**84**	12 0N	83 50W
Bluenose L.	**64**	68 30N	119 35W
Bluestack, mt.	**97**	54 46N	8 5W
Bluff, N.Z.	**133**	46 37S	168 20E
Bluff, U.S.A.	**67**	64 50N	147 15W
Bluffs	**76**	39 45N	90 32W
Bluffton, Can.	**61**	52 45N	114 17W
Bluffton, Ind., U.S.A.	**77**	40 43N	85 9W
Bluffton, Ohio, U.S.A.	**77**	40 54N	83 54W
Bluford	**77**	38 20N	88 45W
Blumenau	**89**	27 0S	49 0W
Blunt	**74**	44 32N	100 0W
Bly	**78**	42 23N	121 0W
Blyth, Can.	**46**	43 44N	81 26W
Blyth, U.K.	**94**	55 8N	1 32W
Blythe	**81**	33 40N	114 33W
Blytheswood	**70**	42 8N	82 37W
Bo	**114**	7 55N	11 50W
Bo Duc	**128**	11 58N	106 50E
Boa Vista	**86**	2 48N	60 30W
Boaco	**84**	12 29N	85 35W
Boat Harbour	**37**	47 24N	54 50W
Bobbili	**125**	18 35N	83 30E
Bobcaygeon	**47**	44 33N	78 33W
Bobo-Dioulasso	**114**	11 8N	4 13W
Bóbr, R.	**106**	51 50N	15 15E
Bobruysk	**120**	53 10N	29 15E
Bobundara	**136**	36 32S	148 59E
Bobures	**86**	9 15N	71 11W
Boca de Uracoa	**86**	9 8N	62 20W
Bôca do Acre	**86**	8 50S	67 27W
Boca, La	**84**	9 0N	79 30W
Bocage	**99**	49 0N	1 0W
Bocaiúva	**87**	17 7S	43 49W
Bocaranga	**116**	7 0N	15 35E
Bocas del Dragon	**86**	11 0N	61 50W
Bocas del Toro	**84**	9 15N	82 20W
Bochart	**41**	49 10N	73 30W
Bocholt	**106**	51 50N	6 35E
Bochum	**105**	51 28N	7 12E
Bocoyna	**82**	27 52N	107 35W
Boda	**116**	4 19N	17 26E
Bodaybo	**121**	57 50N	114 0E
Bodega Bay	**80**	38 20N	123 3W
Boden	**110**	65 50N	21 42E
Bodensee	**106**	47 35N	9 25E
Bodhan	**124**	18 40N	77 55E
Bodmin	**95**	50 28N	4 44W
Bodmin Moor	**95**	50 33N	4 36W
Bodrog, R.	**107**	48 15N	21 35E
Bodrum	**122**	37 5N	27 30E
Boën	**103**	45 44N	4 0E
Boende	**116**	0 24S	21 12E
Boerne	**75**	29 48N	98 41W
Bogalusa	**75**	30 50N	89 55W
Bogan Gate	**136**	33 7S	147 49E
Bogan, R.	**136**	32 45S	148 8E
Bogandyera, Mt.	**136**	35 50S	147 5E
Bogata	**75**	33 26N	95 10W
Bogenfels	**117**	27 25S	15 25E
Boggeragh Mts.	**97**	52 2N	8 55W
Boggy Cr.	**58**	50 40N	104 50W
Bognor Regis	**95**	50 47N	0 40W
Bogo	**127**	11 3N	124 0E
Bogor	**127**	6 36S	106 48E
Bogoro	**116**	9 37N	9 29E
Bogorodskoye	**121**	52 22N	140 30E
Bogotá	**86**	4 34N	74 0W
Bogotol	**120**	56 15N	89 50E
Bogra	**125**	24 51N	89 22E
Bogtown	**43**	45 5N	73 31W
Boguchany	**121**	58 40N	97 30E
Bohain	**101**	49 59N	3 28E
Bohemian Forest = Böhmerwald	**106**	49 30N	12 40E
Böhmerwald	**106**	49 30N	12 40E
Boholl, I.	**127**	9 50N	124 10E
Bohotleh	**115**	8 20N	46 25E
Boi, Pta. de	**89**	23 55S	45 15W
Boiestown	**35**	46 27N	66 26W
Boileau, C.	**134**	17 40S	122 7E
Bois Blanc I.	**46**	45 50N	84 30W
Bois-des-Filion	**44**	45 40N	73 45W
Bois, L. des	**64**	66 50N	125 9W
Boisdale	**39**	46 6N	60 30W
Boise	**78**	43 43N	116 9W
Boise City	**75**	36 45N	102 30W
Boissevain	**57**	49 15N	100 5W
Bojana, R.	**109**	41 52N	19 22E
Bojnürd	**123**	37 30N	57 20E
Bojonegoro	**127**	7 11S	111 54E
Boké	**114**	10 56N	14 17W
Boknafjorden	**111**	59 14N	5 40E
Bokote	**116**	0 12S	21 8E
Bokpyin	**128**	11 18N	98 42E
Bokungu	**116**	0 35S	22 50E
Bolan Pass	**124**	29 50N	67 20E
Bolaños, R.	**82**	22 0N	104 10W
Bolbec	**100**	49 30N	0 30E
Bolchereche	**120**	56 4N	74 45E
Bolesławiec	**106**	51 17N	15 37E
Bolgatanga	**114**	10 44N	0 53W
Bolinao C.	**127**	16 30N	119 55E
Bolívar, Argent.	**88**	36 15S	60 53W
Bolívar, Antioquía, Colomb.	**86**	5 50N	76 1W
Bolívar, Cauca, Colomb.	**86**	2 0N	77 0W
Bolivar, Mo., U.S.A.	**75**	37 38N	93 22W
Bolivar, Tenn., U.S.A.	**75**	35 14N	89 0W
Bolívar □	**86**	9 0N	74 40W
Bolivia ■	**86**	17 6S	64 0W
Bollène	**103**	44 18N	4 45E
Bollnäs	**111**	61 21N	16 24E
Bolobo	**116**	2 6S	16 20E
Bologna	**108**	44 30N	11 20E
Bologne	**101**	48 10N	5 8E
Bologoye	**120**	57 55N	34 0E
Bolomba	**116**	0 35N	19 0E
Bolonchenticul	**83**	20 0N	89 49W
Bolong	**127**	6 6N	122 16E
Boloven, Cao Nguyen	**128**	15 10N	106 30E
Bolsena, L. di	**108**	42 35N	11 55E
Bolshereche	**120**	56 5N	74 40E
Bolshevik, Ostrov	**121**	78 30N	102 0E
Bolshoi Kavkas	**120**	42 50N	44 0E
Bolshoy Atlym	**120**	62 25N	66 50E
Bolsward	**105**	53 3N	5 32E
Bolton, Can.	**50**	43 54N	79 45W
Bolton, U.K.	**94**	53 35N	2 26W
Bolu	**122**	40 45N	31 35E
Bolvadin	**122**	38 45N	31 57E
Bolzano (Bozen)	**108**	46 30N	11 20E
Bom Despacho	**87**	19 43S	45 15W
Bom Jesus da Lapa	**87**	13 15S	43 25W
Boma	**116**	5 50S	13 4E
Bomaderry	**136**	34 52S	150 37E
Bomba, La	**82**	31 53N	115 2W
Bombay	**124**	18 55N	72 50E
Bomboma	**116**	2 25N	18 55E
Bomda	**129**	29 59N	96 25E
Bomili	**116**	1 45N	27 5E
Bomongo	**116**	1 27N	18 21E
Bomu, R.	**116**	4 40N	23 30E
Bon Accord	**60**	53 50N	113 25W
Bon C.	**114**	37 1N	11 2E
Bon Echo Prov. Pk.	**47**	45 0N	77 20W
Bon-Pasteur	**42**	46 54N	71 18W
Bonaduz	**13**	46 49N	9 25E
Bonaire, I.	**85**	12 10N	68 15W
Bonanza, Can.	**60**	55 55N	119 49W
Bonanza, Nic.	**84**	13 54N	84 35W
Bonaparte Archipelago	**134**	14 0S	124 30E
Bonaparte L.	**63**	51 15N	120 34W
Bonaventure	**39**	48 5N	65 32W
Bonavista	**37**	48 40N	53 5W
Bonavista B.	**37**	48 45N	53 25W
Bonavista, C.	**37**	48 42N	53 5W
Bondo	**116**	3 55N	23 53E
Bone Rate, I.	**127**	7 25S	121 5E
Bone Rate, Kepulauan	**127**	6 30S	121 10E
Bone, Teluk	**127**	4 10S	120 50E
Bo'ness	**96**	56 0N	3 38W
Bonfield	**46**	46 14N	79 9W
Bong Son = Hoai Nhon	**128**	14 26N	109 1E
Bongandanga	**116**	1 24N	21 3E
Bonham	**75**	33 30N	96 10W
Bonifacio	**103**	41 24N	9 10E
Bonifacio, Bouches de	**108**	41 12N	9 15E
Bonilla I.	**62**	53 28N	130 37W
Bonin Is.	**14**	27 0N	142 0E
Bonn	**105**	50 43N	7 6E
Bonnat	**102**	46 20N	1 53E
Bonne B.	**35**	40 31N	58 0W
Bonne Espérance, I.	**35**	51 24N	57 40W
Bonne Terre	**76**	37 57N	90 33W
Bonnechere, R.	**47**	45 35N	77 50W
Bonners Ferry	**61**	48 38N	116 21W
Bonnet, Lac du	**57**	50 22N	95 55W
Bonnétable	**100**	48 11N	0 25E
Bonneuil Matours	**100**	46 41N	0 34E
Bonneville	**103**	46 5N	6 24E
Bonnie Rock	**134**	30 29S	118 22E
Bonny	**101**	47 34N	2 50E
Bonny, Bight of	**116**	3 30N	9 20E
Bonnyville	**60**	54 20N	110 45W
Bonoi	**127**	1 45S	137 41E
Bonsall	**81**	33 16N	117 14W
Bontang	**126**	0 10N	117 30E
Bonthain	**127**	5 34S	119 56E
Bonthe	**114**	7 30N	12 33W
Booker	**75**	36 29N	100 30W
Boolaboolka, L.	**136**	32 38S	143 10E
Boom	**105**	51 6N	4 20E
Boone, Iowa, U.S.A.	**76**	42 5N	93 53W
Boone, N.C., U.S.A.	**73**	36 14N	81 43W
Booneville, Ark., U.S.A.	**75**	35 10N	93 54W
Booneville, Miss., U.S.A.	**73**	34 39N	88 34W
Boonville, Calif., U.S.A.	**80**	39 1N	123 22W
Boonville, Ind., U.S.A.	**77**	38 3N	87 13W
Boonville, Mo., U.S.A.	**76**	38 57N	92 45W
Boonville, N.Y., U.S.A.	**71**	43 31N	75 20W
Boorowa	**136**	34 28S	148 44E
Boothia, Gulf of	**65**	71 0N	91 0W
Boothia Pen.	**65**	71 0N	94 0W
Bootle, Cumb., U.K.	**94**	54 17N	3 24W
Bootle, Merseysude, U.K.	**94**	53 28N	3 1W
Booué	**116**	0 5S	11 55E
Boquete	**84**	8 46N	82 27W
Boquillas	**82**	29 17N	102 53W
Bôr	**115**	6 10N	31 40E
Bor	**109**	44 8N	22 7E
Borah, Mt.	**78**	44 19N	113 46W
Borås	**111**	57 43N	12 56E
Borāzjan	**123**	29 22N	51 10E
Borba	**86**	4 12S	59 34W
Bordeaux	**102**	44 50N	0 36W
Borden, P.E.I., Can.	**39**	46 18N	63 47W
Borden, Sask., Can.	**56**	52 27N	107 14W
Borden I.	**64**	78 30N	111 30W
Borden L.	**53**	47 50N	83 17W
Borden Pen.	**65**	73 0N	83 0W
Borders □	**96**	55 45N	2 50W
Bordertown	**136**	36 19S	140 45E
Borðeyri	**110**	65 12N	21 6W
Borgarnes	**110**	64 32N	21 55W
Borgefjellet	**110**	65 20N	13 45E
Borger, Neth.	**105**	52 54N	6 33E
Borger, U.S.A.	**75**	35 40N	101 20W
Borgholm	**111**	56 52N	16 39E
Borisoglebsk	**120**	51 27N	42 5E
Borja	**86**	4 20S	77 40W
Borkou	**114**	18 15N	18 50E
Borkum I.	**106**	53 38N	6 41E
Borlänge	**111**	60 29N	15 26E
Borley, C.	**91**	66 15S	52 30E
Borneo, I.	**126**	1 0N	115 0E
Bornholm, I.	**111**	55 10N	15 0E
Borogontsy	**121**	62 42N	131 8E
Boron	**81**	35 0N	117 39W
Borongan	**127**	11 37N	125 26E
Borrego Springs	**81**	33 15N	116 23W
Borroloola	**135**	16 4S	136 17E
Bort-les-Orgues	**102**	45 24N	2 29E
Borujerd	**122**	33 55N	48 50E
Borzya	**121**	50 24N	116 31E
Bos. Gradiška	**108**	45 10N	17 15E
Bosa	**108**	40 17N	8 32E
Boscobel	**76**	43 8N	90 42W
Boshrūyeh	**123**	33 50N	57 30E
Bosna i Hercegovina □	**108**	44 0N	18 0E
Bosna, R.	**109**	44 50N	18 10E
Bosnik	**127**	1 5S	136 10E
Bōsō-Hantō	**132**	35 20N	140 20E
Bosobolo	**116**	4 15N	19 50E
Bosporus = Karadeniz Boğazı	**122**	41 10N	29 10E
Bossangoa	**116**	6 35N	17 30E
Bossekop	**110**	69 57N	23 15E
Bossembélé	**114**	5 25N	17 40E
Bossier City	**75**	32 28N	93 48W
Bossut C.	**134**	18 42S	121 35E
Boston, Can.	**49**	42 59N	80 16W
Boston, U.K.	**94**	52 59N	0 2W
Boston, U.S.A.	**71**	42 20N	71 0W
Boston Bar	**63**	49 52N	121 30W
Boston Cr.	**49**	43 2N	79 56W
Boswell, Can.	**63**	49 28N	116 45W
Boswell, Ind., U.S.A.	**77**	40 30N	87 23W
Boswell, Okla., U.S.A.	**75**	34 1N	95 50W
Boswell, Pa., U.S.A.	**70**	40 9N	79 2W
Bosworth	**76**	39 28N	93 20W
Bothnia, G. of	**110**	63 0N	21 0E
Bothwell, Ont., Can.	**46**	42 38N	81 52W
Bothwell, Ont., Can.	**46**	42 38N	81 52W
Botletle R.	**117**	20 10S	24 10E
Botoşani	**107**	47 42N	26 41E
Botswana ■	**117**	22 0S	24 0E
Bottineau	**57**	48 49N	100 25W
Bottrop	**105**	51 34N	6 59E
Botucatu	**89**	22 55S	48 30W
Botwood	**37**	49 6N	55 23W
Bou Djébéha	**114**	18 25N	2 45W
Bouaké	**114**	7 40N	5 2W
Bouar	**116**	6 0N	15 40E
Bouca	**116**	6 45N	18 25E
Boucau	**102**	43 32N	1 29W
Bouchard, Ile	**43**	45 49N	73 21W
Boucher, R.	**41**	49 10N	69 6W
Boucherville	**45**	45 36N	73 27W
Boucherville, Îes de	**45**	45 37N	73 28W
Bouches-du-Rhône □	**103**	43 37N	5 2E
Bouchette	**40**	46 12N	75 57W
Bouchier, L.	**40**	50 6N	77 48W
Bougainville C.	**134**	13 57S	126 4E
Bougie = Béjaïa	**114**	36 42N	5 2E
Boulder, Austral.	**134**	30 46S	121 30E
Boulder, Colo., U.S.A.	**74**	40 3N	105 10W
Boulder, Mont., U.S.A.	**78**	46 14N	112 4W
Boulder City	**81**	36 0N	114 50W
Boulder Creek	**80**	37 7N	122 7W
Boulder Dam = Hoover Dam	**79**	36 0N	114 45W
Bouleau, Lac au	**34**	47 40N	77 35W
Boulia	**135**	22 52S	139 51E
Bouligny	**101**	49 17N	5 45E
Boulogne, R.	**100**	46 50N	1 25W
Boulogne-sur-Gesse	**102**	43 18N	0 38E
Boulogne-sur-Mer	**101**	50 42N	1 36E
Boundary	**67**	64 11N	141 2W
Boundary B.	**66**	49 2N	122 57W
Boundary Bay	**66**	49 0N	123 2W
Boundary Pk.	**80**	37 51N	118 21W
Bountiful	**78**	40 57N	111 58W
Bounty I.	**14**	46 0S	180 0E
Bour Khaya	**121**	71 50N	133 10E
Bourbeuse, R.	**76**	38 24N	90 54W
Bourbon	**77**	41 18N	86 7W
Bourbon-l'Archambault	**102**	46 36N	3 4E
Bourbon-Lancy	**102**	46 37N	3 45E
Bourbonnais	**102**	46 28N	3 0E
Bourbonne	**101**	47 59N	5 45E
Bourem	**114**	17 0N	0 24W
Bourg	**102**	45 3N	0 34W
Bourg-Argental	**103**	45 18N	4 32E
Bourg-de-Péage	**103**	45 2N	5 3E
Bourg-en-Bresse	**103**	46 13N	5 12E
Bourg-Royal	**42**	46 53N	71 15W
Bourg-St.-Andéol	**103**	44 23N	4 39E
Bourg-St.-Maurice	**103**	45 35N	6 45E
Bourganeuf	**102**	45 57N	1 45E
Bourges	**101**	47 9N	2 25E
Bourget	**45**	45 26N	75 9W
Bourget, L. du	**103**	45 44N	5 52E
Bourgneuf	**100**	47 2N	1 58W
Bourgneuf, B. de	**100**	47 3N	2 10W
Bourgneuf, Le	**100**	48 10N	0 59W
Bourgogne	**101**	47 0N	4 30E
Bourgoin-Jallieu	**103**	45 36N	5 17E
Bourlamaque	**34**	48 5N	77 56W
Bournemouth	**95**	50 43N	1 53W
Bourriot-Bergonce	**102**	44 7N	0 14W
Bouscat, Le	**102**	44 53N	0 32W
Bouse	**81**	33 55N	114 0W
Boussac	**102**	46 22N	2 13E
Boussens	**102**	43 12N	0 58E
Bousso	**114**	10 34N	16 52E
Bouthillier, Le	**35**	47 47N	64 55W
Bouvet I.	**13**	55 0S	3 30E
Bouzonville	**101**	49 17N	6 32E
Bovigny	**105**	50 12N	5 55E
Bovill	**78**	46 58N	116 27W
Bow Island	**61**	49 50N	111 23W
Bow Pass	**61**	51 43N	116 30W
Bow, R.	**61**	49 57N	111 41W
Bowbells	**74**	48 47N	102 19W

Bowden **Bruce Crossing**

Bowden 61 51 55N 114 2W
Bowdle 74 45 30N 99 40W
Bowen 135 20 0S 148 16E
Bowen Island 63 49 23N 123 20W
Bowie, Ariz., U.S.A. 79 32 15N 109 30W
Bowie, Tex., U.S.A. 75 33 33N 97 50W
Bowland, Forest of 94 54 0N 2 30W
Bowling Green, Ky., U.S.A. 72 37 0N 86 25W
Bowling Green, Mo., U.S.A. 76 39 21N 91 12W
Bowling Green, Ohio, U.S.A. 77 41 22N 83 40W
Bowling Green, C. 135 19 19S 147 25E
Bowman 74 46 12N 103 21W
Bowman, I. 91 65 0S 104 0E
Bowman L. 52 51 10N 91 25W
Bowmanville 47 43 55N 78 41W
Bowmore 96 55 45N 6 18W
Bowness 59 51 5N 114 10W
Bowral 136 34 26S 150 27E
Bowron Lake Prov. Park 63 53 10N 121 5W
Bowron, R. 63 54 3N 121 50W
Bowser 62 49 27N 124 40W
Bowser L. 54 56 30N 129 30W
Bowsman 57 52 14N 101 12W
Bowstring L. 52 47 34N 93 52W
Bowyer I. 66 49 26N 123 16W
Boxelder Creek 78 47 20N 108 30W
Boxtel 105 51 36N 5 9E
Boyacá □ 86 5 30N 72 30W
Boyce 75 31 25N 92 39W
Boyd L. 36 52 46N 76 42W
Boyer-Nord, R. 42 46 44N 70 58W
Boyer, R., Alta., Can. 54 58 27N 115 57W
Boyer, R., Qué., Can. 42 46 53N 70 52W
Boyer-Sud, R. 42 46 44N 70 58W
Boyle, Can. 60 54 35N 112 49W
Boyle, Ireland 97 53 58N 8 19W
Boylston 39 45 26N 61 30W
Boyne 49 43 29N 79 50W
Boyne City 46 45 13N 85 1W
Boyne, R. 97 53 40N 6 34W
Boynton Beach 73 26 31N 80 3W
Bozeman 78 45 40N 111 0W
Bozouls 102 44 28N 2 43E
Bozoum 116 6 25N 16 35E
Brabant □ 105 50 46N 4 30E
Brabant L. 55 55 58N 104 5W
Brač 108 43 20N 16 40E
Bracadale, L. 96 57 20N 6 30W
Bracciano, L. di 108 42 8N 12 11E
Bracebridge 46 45 2N 79 19W
Brach 114 27 31N 14 20E
Bracieux 101 47 30N 1 30E
Bräcke 110 62 45N 15 26E
Bracken 56 49 11N 108 6W
Brackendale 63 49 48N 123 8W
Brackenridge 70 40 38N 79 44W
Brackettville 75 29 21N 100 20W
Brad 107 46 10N 22 50E
Braddock 70 40 24N 79 51W
Bradenton 73 27 25N 82 35W
Bradford, Can. 46 44 7N 79 34W
Bradford, U.K. 94 53 47N 1 45W
Bradford, Ill., U.S.A. 76 41 11N 89 39W
Bradford, Ohio, U.S.A. 77 40 8N 84 27W
Bradford, Pa., U.S.A. 70 41 58N 78 41W
Bradford, Vt., U.S.A. 71 43 59N 72 9W
Bradley, Ark., U.S.A. 75 33 7N 93 39W
Bradley, Calif., U.S.A. 80 35 52N 120 48W
Bradley, Ill., U.S.A. 77 41 9N 87 52W
Bradley, S.D., U.S.A. 74 45 10N 97 40W
Bradore Bay 37 51 27N 57 18W
Bradshaw 135 15 21S 130 16E
Bradwell 56 51 57N 106 14W
Brady 75 31 8N 99 25W
Braedale 49 43 8N 79 14W
Braeside 47 45 28N 76 24W
Braga 104 41 35N 8 25W
Bragado 88 35 2S 60 27W
Bragança, Brazil 87 1 0S 47 2W
Bragança, Port. 104 41 48N 6 50W
Bragança Paulista 89 22 55S 46 32W
Bragg Creek 61 50 57N 114 35W
Brahmanbaria 125 23 50N 91 15E
Brahmani, R. 125 21 0N 85 15E
Brahmaputra, R. 125 26 30N 93 30E
Brahmaur 124 32 28N 76 32E
Braich-y-Pwll 94 52 47N 4 46W
Braidwood 136 35 27S 149 49E
Brăila 107 45 19N 27 59E
Brainerd 52 46 20N 94 10W
Braintree, U.K. 95 51 53N 0 34E
Braintree, U.S.A. 71 42 11N 71 0W
Bralorne 63 50 50N 123 45W
Bramalea 50 43 44N 79 43W
Brampton 50 43 45N 79 45W
Branch 37 46 53N 53 57W
Branchton 49 43 18N 80 15W
Branco, R. 86 0 0 61 15W
Brandenburg, Ger. 106 52 24N 12 33E
Brandenburg, U.S.A. 77 38 0N 86 10W
Brandon, Can. 57 49 50N 99 57W
Brandon, U.S.A. 71 43 48N 73 4W
Brandon B. 97 52 17N 10 8W
Brandon, Mt. 97 52 15N 10 15W
Brandsen 88 35 10S 58 15W
Brandvlei 117 30 25S 20 30E
Branford 71 41 15N 72 48W
Braniewo 107 54 25N 19 50E
Bransfield Str. 91 63 0S 59 0W
Brańsk 107 52 45N 22 50E
Branson, Colo., U.S.A. 75 37 4N 103 53W
Branson, Mo., U.S.A. 75 36 40N 93 18W
Brant □ 49 43 10N 80 20W
Brantford 49 43 10N 80 15W
Brantôme 102 45 22N 0 39E
Brantville 39 47 22N 64 58W
Bras d'or, L. 39 45 50N 60 50W
Brasiléia 86 11 0S 68 45W
Brasília 87 15 47S 47 55E
Braşov 107 45 38N 25 35E
Brasschaat 105 51 19N 4 27E
Brassey, Barisan 126 5 0N 117 15E
Brasstown Bald, Mt. 73 34 54N 83 45W
Bratislava 106 48 10N 17 7E
Bratsk 121 56 10N 101 30E
Brattleboro 71 42 53N 72 37W
Braunschweig 106 52 17N 10 28E
Brava 115 1 20N 44 8E
Bravo del Norte, R. 82 30 30N 105 0W
Brawley 81 32 58N 115 30W
Bray 97 53 12N 6 6W
Bray, Pays de 101 49 15N 1 40E
Bray-sur-Seine 101 48 25N 3 14E
Braymer 76 39 35N 93 48W
Brazeau, R. 61 52 55N 115 14W
Brazil 77 39 32N 87 8W
Brazil ■ 86 5 0N 20 0W
Brazilian Highlands 87 18 0S 46 30W
Brazo Sur, R. 88 25 30S 58 0W
Brazos, R. 75 30 30N 96 20W
Brazzaville 116 4 9S 15 12E
Brčko 109 44 54N 18 46E
Breadalbane 96 56 30N 4 15W
Breaksea Sd. 133 45 35S 166 35E
Bream Bay 133 35 56S 174 28E
Bream Head 133 35 51S 174 36E
Breas 88 25 29S 70 24W
Brebes 127 6 52S 109 3E
Brechin, Can. 46 44 32N 79 10W
Brechin, U.K. 96 56 44N 2 40W
Breckenridge, Colo., U.S.A. 78 39 30N 106 2W
Breckenridge, Mich., U.S.A. 46 43 24N 84 29W
Breckenridge, Minn., U.S.A. 74 46 20N 96 36W
Breckenridge, Mo., U.S.A. 76 39 46N 93 48W
Breckenridge, Tex., U.S.A. 75 32 48N 98 55W
Breckland 98 52 30N 0 40E
Brecon 95 51 57N 3 23W
Brecon Beacons 95 51 53N 3 27W
Breda 105 51 35N 4 45E
Bredasdorp 117 34 33S 20 2E
Bredenbury 57 50 57N 102 3W
Bregenz 106 47 30N 9 45E
Bréhal 100 48 53N 1 30W
Bréhat, I. de 100 48 51N 3 0W
Breiðafjörður 110 65 15N 23 15W
Breil 103 43 56N 7 31E
Bremen 106 53 4N 8 47E
Bremerhaven 106 53 34N 8 35E
Bremerton 80 47 30N 122 38W
Brenham 75 30 5N 96 27W
Brenner Pass 106 47 0N 11 30E
Brent, Can. 47 46 2N 78 29W
Brent, U.K. 95 51 33N 0 18W
Brentwood 59 51 7N 114 9W
Bréscia 108 45 33N 10 13E
Breslau 49 43 28N 80 25W
Breslau = Wrocław. 106 51 5N 17 5E
Bresle, R. 100 50 4N 1 21E
Bresles 101 49 25N 2 13E
Bressanone 108 46 43N 11 40E
Bressay I. 96 60 10N 1 5W
Bresse, La 101 48 0N 6 53E
Bresse, Plaine de 101 46 50N 5 10E
Bressuire 100 46 51N 0 30W
Brest, France 100 48 24N 4 31W
Brest, U.S.S.R. 120 52 10N 23 40E
Bretagne 100 48 0N 3 0W
Bretçu 107 46 7N 26 18E
Breteuil, Eur, France 100 48 50N 0 53E
Breteuil, Oise, France 101 49 38N 2 18E
Breton 61 53 7N 114 28W
Breton, Le, L. 38 51 53N 60 9W
Breton, Pertuis 102 46 17N 1 25W
Breton Sd. 75 29 40N 89 12W
Brett, C. 133 35 10S 174 20E
Brevard 73 35 19N 82 42W
Brevort 46 46 2N 85 2W
Brewer 35 44 43N 68 50W
Brewer, Mt. 80 36 44N 118 28W
Brewster, N.Y., U.S.A. 71 41 23N 73 37W
Brewster, Wash., U.S.A. 78 48 10N 119 51W
Brewster, Kap 17 70 7N 22 0W
Brewton 73 31 9N 87 2W
Bria 116 6 30N 21 58E
Briançon 103 44 54N 6 39E
Briare 101 47 38N 2 45E
Bribie I. 135 27 0S 152 58E
Brickaville 117 18 49S 49 4E
Bricon 101 48 5N 5 0E
Briçonnet, L. 38 51 27N 60 10W
Bricquebec 100 49 29N 1 39W
Bridge River 54 50 50N 122 40W
Bridgehampton 71 40 56N 72 19W
Bridgeman 77 41 57N 86 33W
Bridgend 95 51 30N 3 35W
Bridgenorth 47 44 23N 78 23W
Bridgeport, B.C., Can. 66 49 12N 123 8W
Bridgeport, Ont., Can. 46 43 29N 80 29W
Bridgeport, Calif., U.S.A. 80 38 14N 119 15W
Bridgeport, Conn., U.S.A. 71 41 12N 73 12W
Bridgeport, Mich., U.S.A. 46 43 22N 83 53W
Bridgeport, Nebr., U.S.A. 74 41 42N 103 10W
Bridgeport, Tex., U.S.A. 75 33 15N 97 45W
Bridger 78 45 20N 108 58W
Bridgeton 72 39 29N 75 10W
Bridgetown, Austral. 134 33 58S 116 7E
Bridgetown, Barbados 85 13 0N 59 30W
Bridgetown, Can. 39 44 55N 65 18W
Bridgeview Survey 48 43 18N 79 54W
Bridgewater, Can. 39 44 25N 64 31W
Bridgewater, Mass., U.S.A. 71 41 59N 70 56W
Bridgewater, S.D., U.S.A. 74 43 34N 97 29W
Bridgewater, C. 136 38 23S 141 23E
Bridgnorth 95 52 33N 2 25W
Bridgton 71 44 5N 70 41W
Bridgwater 95 51 7N 3 0W
Bridlington 94 54 6N 0 11W
Bridport 95 50 43N 2 45W
Brie-Comte-Robert 101 48 40N 2 35E
Brie, Plaine de 101 48 35N 3 10E
Briec 100 48 6N 4 0W
Brienne-le-Château 101 48 24N 4 30E
Brienon 101 48 0N 3 35E
Briercrest 56 50 10N 105 16W
Briey 101 49 14N 5 57E
Brig 106 46 18N 7 59E
Brigg 94 53 33N 0 30W
Briggsdale 74 40 40N 104 20W
Brigham City 78 41 30N 112 1W
Brighouse 66 49 10N 123 8W
Bright 136 36 42S 146 56E
Brighton, Can. 47 44 2N 77 44W
Brighton, U.K. 95 50 50N 0 9W
Brighton, Colo., U.S.A. 74 39 59N 104 50W
Brighton, Ill., U.S.A. 76 39 2N 90 8W
Brighton, Iowa, U.S.A. 76 41 10N 91 49W
Brighton, Pa., U.S.A. 70 40 42N 80 19W
Brightsand L. 56 53 36N 108 53W
Brignogan-Plage 100 48 40N 4 20W
Brignoles 103 43 25N 6 5E
Brilliant, Can. 63 49 19N 117 38W
Brilliant, U.S.A. 70 40 15N 80 39W
Brimfield 76 40 50N 89 53W
Brimley 46 46 25N 84 41W
Brimstone 49 43 48N 80 0W
Brindisi 109 40 39N 17 55E
Brinkley 75 34 55N 91 15W
Brinnon 80 47 41N 122 54W
Brion I. 39 47 46N 61 26W
Brionne 100 49 11N 0 43E
Brioude 102 45 18N 3 23E
Briouze 100 48 42N 0 23W
Brisbane, Austral. 135 27 25S 153 2E
Brisbane, Can. 49 43 44N 80 4W
Bristol, N.B., Can. 39 46 28N 67 35W
Bristol, Qué., Can. 40 45 32N 76 28W
Bristol, U.K. 95 51 26N 2 35W
Bristol, Conn., U.S.A. 71 41 44N 72 57W
Bristol, R.I., U.S.A. 71 41 40N 71 15W
Bristol, S.D., U.S.A. 74 45 25N 97 43W
Bristol B. 67 58 0N 160 0W
Bristol Channel 95 51 18N 4 30W
Bristol I. 91 58 45S 28 0W
Bristol L. 79 34 23N 116 50W
Bristow 75 35 55N 96 28W
Britannia Beach 63 49 38N 123 12W
British Antarctic Territory 91 66 0S 45 0W
British Columbia □ 54 55 0N 125 15W
British Guiana = Guyana 86 5 0N 59 0W
British Honduras = Belize 83 17 0N 88 30W
British Isles 93 55 0N 4 0W
British Mts. 64 68 50N 140 0W
Britstown 117 30 37S 23 30E
Britt, Can. 46 45 46N 80 34W
Britt, U.S.A. 76 43 6N 93 48W
Brittany = Bretagne 100 48 0N 3 0W
Britton 74 45 50N 97 47W
Brive-la-Gaillarde 102 45 10N 1 32E
Brlik 120 44 0N 74 5E
Brno 106 49 10N 16 35E
Broach, L. 38 50 45N 67 59W
Broad B. 96 58 14N 6 16W
Broad Haven 97 54 20N 9 55W
Broad Law, Mt. 96 55 30N 3 22W
Broad, R. 73 34 30N 81 26W
Broad Sd. 135 22 0S 149 45E
Broadback, R. 36 51 21N 78 52W
Broadford 136 37 14S 145 4E
Broads, The 94 52 45N 1 30E
Broadsound Ra. 135 22 50S 149 30E
Broadus 74 45 28N 105 27W
Broadview 56 50 22N 102 35W
Brochet, Man., Can. 55 57 53N 101 40W
Brochet, Québec, Can. 34 47 12N 72 42W
Brochet, L. 55 58 36N 101 35W
Brochet, L. du 41 49 40N 69 37W
Brock 56 51 26N 108 43W
Brock I. 64 77 52N 114 19W
Brock, R. 40 50 0N 75 5W
Brock Road 51 43 53N 79 5W
Brocken 106 51 48N 10 40E
Brockport 70 43 12N 77 56W
Brockton 71 42 8N 71 2W
Brockville 47 44 35N 75 41W
Brockway 74 47 18N 105 46W
Brockwayville 70 41 14N 78 48W
Brocton 70 42 25N 79 26W
Brod 109 41 35N 21 17E
Broderick 56 51 30N 106 55W
Brodeur 45 45 22N 72 59W
Brodeur Pen. 65 72 30N 88 10W
Brodhead 76 42 37N 89 22W
Brodick 96 55 34N 5 9W
Brogan 78 44 14N 117 32W
Broglie 100 49 0N 0 30E
Broken Bay 136 33 30S 151 15E
Broken Bow, Nebr., U.S.A. 74 41 25N 99 35W
Broken Bow, Okla., U.S.A. 75 34 2N 94 43W
Broken Hill 136 31 58S 141 29E
Broken, R. 136 36 24S 145 24E
Bromhead 55 49 18N 103 40W
Bromley 95 51 20N 0 5E
Bromont 41 45 17N 72 39W
Bromptonville 41 45 28N 71 57W
Bronaugh 76 37 41N 94 28W
Brønderslev 111 57 16N 9 57E
Bronson 77 41 52N 85 12W
Bronte, Can. 49 43 24N 79 43W
Bronte, U.S.A. 75 31 54N 100 18W
Bronte Cr. 49 43 24N 79 43W
Brookdale 57 50 3N 99 34W
Brookfield, Can. 39 45 15N 63 17W
Brookfield, Ill., U.S.A. 77 41 50N 87 51W
Brookfield, Mo., U.S.A. 76 39 50N 92 55W
Brookhaven 75 31 40N 90 25W
Brookings, Oreg., U.S.A. 78 42 4N 124 10W
Brookings, S.D., U.S.A. 74 44 20N 96 45W
Brooklands 58 49 55N 97 12W
Brooklin 51 43 55N 78 55W
Brooklyn, Can. 39 44 3N 64 42W
Brooklyn, Iowa, U.S.A. 76 41 44N 92 27W
Brooklyn, N.Y., U.S.A. 71 40 45N 73 58W
Brookmere 63 49 52N 120 53W
Brookport 43 45 15N 72 50W
Brooks 61 50 35N 111 55W
Brooks B. 62 50 15N 127 55W
Brooks L. 55 61 55N 106 35W
Brooks Ra. 67 68 40N 147 0W
Brookston 77 40 36N 86 52W
Brooksville, Fla., U.S.A. 73 28 32N 82 21W
Brooksville, Ky., U.S.A. 77 38 41N 84 4W
Brookton 134 32 22S 116 57E
Brookville, Ind., U.S.A. 77 39 25N 85 0W
Brookville, Pa., U.S.A. 70 41 10N 79 6W
Broom, L. 96 57 55N 5 15W
Broome 134 18 0S 122 15E
Broons 100 48 20N 2 16W
Brora 58 50 35N 104 41W
Brora, R. 96 58 4N 3 52W
Brosna, R. 97 53 8N 8 0W
Brossard 45 45 26N 73 29W
Brothers 78 43 56N 120 39W
Brougham 51 43 55N 79 6W
Broughton 77 37 56N 88 27W
Broughton I. 62 50 48N 126 42W
Broughton Island 65 67 33N 63 0W
Broughty Ferry 96 56 29N 2 50W
Browerville 74 46 3N 94 50W
Brown City 46 43 13N 82 59W
Brown Willy, Mt. 95 50 35N 4 34W
Brownfield 75 33 10N 102 15W
Browning, Can. 56 49 27N 102 38W
Browning, Ill., U.S.A. 76 40 7N 90 22W
Browning, Mo., U.S.A. 76 40 3N 93 12W
Browning, Mont., U.S.A. 78 48 35N 113 0W
Brownlee 56 50 43N 106 1W
Browns Flats 39 45 28N 66 8W
Browns Line 50 43 36N 79 32W
Brownsburg, Can. 43 45 41N 74 25W
Brownsburg, U.S.A. 77 39 50N 86 26W
Brownstown 77 38 53N 86 3W
Brownsville, Oreg., U.S.A. 78 44 29N 123 0W
Brownsville, Tenn., U.S.A. 75 35 35N 89 15W
Brownsville, Tex., U.S.A. 75 25 56N 97 25W
Brownwood 75 31 45N 99 0W
Brownwood, L. 75 31 51N 98 35W
Bruas 128 4 31N 100 46E
Bruay-en-Artois 101 50 29N 2 33E
Bruce 61 53 10N 112 2W
Bruce Crossing 52 46 38N 89 9W

Bruce L Cáceres

Bruce L.	**52**	50 49N	93 20W
Bruce Mines	**34**	46 20N	83 45W
Bruce, Mt.	**134**	22 37S	118 8E
Bruce Mts.	**65**	71 12N	72 15W
Bruce Pen.	**46**	45 0N	81 30W
Bruck a.d. Leitha	**106**	48 1N	16 47E
Bruderheim	**60**	53 47N	112 56W
Brue, R.	**95**	51 10N	2 59W
Bruges = Brugge	**105**	51 13N	3 13E
Brugge	**105**	51 13N	3 13E
Brühl	**105**	50 49N	6 51E
Brûlé	**60**	53 15N	117 58W
Brûlé, L.	**38**	52 30N	63 40W
Brûlon	**100**	47 58N	0 15W
Brumado	**87**	14 14S	41 40W
Brumath	**101**	48 43N	7 40E
Brundidge	**73**	31 43N	85 45W
Bruneau	**78**	42 57N	115 55W
Bruneau, R.	**78**	42 45N	115 50W
Brunei = Bandar Seri Begawan	**126**	4 52N	115 0E
Brunei ■	**126**	4 50N	115 0E
Brunette I.	**37**	47 16N	55 55W
Brunkild	**57**	49 36N	97 35W
Brunner	**133**	42 27S	171 20E
Brunner, L.	**133**	42 27S	171 20E
Bruno, Can.	**56**	52 20N	105 30W
Bruno, U.S.A.	**52**	46 17N	92 44W
Brunsbüttelkoog	**106**	53 52N	9 13E
Brunswick, Ga., U.S.A.	**73**	31 10N	81 30W
Brunswick, Md., U.S.A.	**72**	39 20N	77 38W
Brunswick, Me., U.S.A.	**35**	43 53N	69 50W
Brunswick, Mo., U.S.A.	**76**	39 26N	93 10W
Brunswick, Ohio, U.S.A.	**70**	41 15N	81 50W
Brunswick = Braunschweig	**106**	52 17N	10 28E
Brunswick B.	**134**	15 15S	124 50E
Brunswick L.	**53**	48 58N	83 23W
Brunswick, Pen. de	**90**	53 30S	71 30W
Bruny I.	**135**	43 20S	147 15E
Brus Laguna	**84**	15 47N	84 35W
Brush	**74**	40 17N	103 33W
Brushton	**71**	44 50N	74 62W
Brusque	**89**	27 5S	49 0W
Brussel	**105**	50 51N	4 21E
Brussels, Can.	**70**	43 45N	81 25W
Brussels, Ont., Can.	**46**	43 44N	81 15W
Brussels = Bruxelles	**105**	50 51N	4 21E
Bruxelles	**105**	50 51N	4 21E
Bruyères	**101**	48 10N	6 40E
Bryan, Ohio, U.S.A.	**77**	41 30N	84 30W
Bryan, Texas, U.S.A.	**75**	30 40N	96 27W
Bryansk	**120**	53 13N	34 25E
Bryne	**111**	58 44N	5 38E
Bryson	**40**	45 41N	76 37W
Bryson City	**73**	35 28N	83 25W
Bryte	**80**	38 35N	121 33W
Buapinang	**127**	4 40S	121 30E
Buayan	**127**	5 3N	125 28E
Bucaramanga	**86**	7 0N	73 0W
Buchan	**96**	57 32N	2 8W
Buchan Ness	**96**	57 29N	1 48W
Buchanan, Can.	**56**	51 40N	102 45W
Buchanan, Liberia	**114**	5 57N	10 2W
Buchanan, U.S.A.	**77**	41 50N	86 22W
Buchanan, L., Austral.	**134**	25 33S	123 2E
Buchanan, L., U.S.A.	**75**	30 50N	98 25W
Buchans	**37**	48 50N	56 52W
Buchans Junction	**37**	48 51N	56 28W
Bucharest = Bucureşti	**107**	44 27N	26 10E
Buchon, Pt.	**80**	35 15N	120 54W
Buck L.	**61**	52 59N	114 46W
Buck Lake	**61**	52 57N	114 47W
Buckeye	**79**	33 28N	112 40W
Buckhannon	**72**	39 2N	80 10W
Buckhaven	**96**	56 10N	3 2W
Buckhorn L.	**47**	44 29N	78 23W
Buckie	**96**	57 40N	2 58W
Buckingham, Can.	**40**	45 37N	75 24W
Buckingham, U.K.	**95**	52 0N	0 59W
Buckingham □	**95**	51 50N	0 55W
Buckingham B.	**134**	12 10S	135 40E
Buckland, Alaska, U.S.A.	**67**	66 0N	161 5W
Buckland, Ohio, U.S.A.	**77**	40 37N	84 16W
Buckland Newton	**70**	50 50N	2 57W
Buckley, Ill., U.S.A.	**77**	40 35N	88 2W
Buckley, Wash., U.S.A.	**78**	47 10N	122 2W
Bucklin, Kans., U.S.A.	**75**	37 37N	99 40W
Bucklin, Mo., U.S.A.	**76**	39 47N	92 53W
Bucks L.	**80**	39 54N	121 12W
Bucquoy	**101**	50 9N	2 43E
Buctouche	**39**	46 30N	64 45W
Bucureşti	**107**	44 27N	26 10E
Bucyrus	**77**	40 48N	83 0W
Budacul, Munte	**99**	47 5N	25 40E
Budalin	**125**	22 20N	95 10E
Budapest	**107**	47 29N	19 5E
Budaun	**124**	28 5N	79 10E
Budd Coast	**91**	67 0S	112 0E
Bude	**95**	50 49N	4 33W
Búdir	**110**	64 49N	23 23W
Budjala	**116**	2 50N	19 40E
Buea	**114**	4 10N	9 9E
Buellton	**81**	34 37N	120 12W
Buena Vista, Colo., U.S.A.	**79**	38 56N	106 6W
Buena Vista, Va., U.S.A.	**72**	37 47N	79 23W
Buena Vista L.	**81**	35 15N	119 21W
Buenaventura	**82**	29 50N	107 30W
Buenaventura, B. de	**86**	3 48N	77 17W
Buenos Aires, Argent.	**88**	34 30S	58 20W
Buenos Aires, Colomb.	**86**	1 36N	73 18W
Buenos Aires, C. Rica	**84**	9 10N	83 20W
Buenos Aires □	**88**	36 30S	60 0W
Buenos Aires, Lago	**90**	46 35S	72 30W
Buesaco	**86**	1 23N	77 9W
Buffalo, Can.	**55**	50 49N	110 42W
Buffalo, Mo., U.S.A.	**76**	37 40N	93 5W
Buffalo, N.Y., U.S.A.	**49**	42 55N	78 50W
Buffalo, Okla., U.S.A.	**75**	36 55N	99 42W
Buffalo, S.D., U.S.A.	**75**	45 39N	103 31W
Buffalo, Wyo., U.S.A.	**78**	44 25N	106 50W
Buffalo Center	**67**	64 2N	145 50W
Buffalo Creek	**63**	51 44N	121 9W
Buffalo Head Hills	**54**	57 25N	115 55W
Buffalo L.	**61**	52 27N	112 54W
Buffalo Narrows	**55**	55 51N	108 29W
Buffalo Pound L.	**56**	50 39N	105 30W
Buffalo, R.	**54**	60 5N	115 5W
Buford	**73**	34 5N	84 0W
Bug, R.	**107**	51 20N	23 40E
Buga	**86**	4 0N	77 0W
Bugeat	**102**	45 36N	1 55E
Buggs I. L.	**73**	36 20N	78 30W
Bugsuk, I.	**126**	8 15N	117 15E
Bugue, Le	**102**	44 55N	0 56E
Bugun Shara	**130**	49 0N	104 0E
Buguruslan	**120**	53 39N	52 26E
Buhl, Idaho, U.S.A.	**78**	42 35N	114 54W
Buhl, Minn., U.S.A.	**74**	47 30N	92 46W
Buick	**75**	37 38N	91 2W
Builth Wells	**95**	52 10N	3 26W
Buina Qara	**123**	36 20N	67 0E
Buis-les-Baronnies	**103**	44 17N	5 16E
Buit, L.	**38**	50 59N	63 13W
Buitenpost	**105**	53 15N	6 9E
Bujnurd	**123**	37 35N	57 15E
Bujumbura (Usumbura)	**116**	3 16S	29 18E
Bukachacha	**121**	52 55N	116 50E
Bukama	**116**	9 10S	25 50E
Bukavu	**116**	2 20S	28 52E
Bukene	**116**	4 15S	32 48E
Bukhara	**120**	39 48N	64 25E
Bukittinggi	**126**	0 20S	100 20E
Bukoba	**116**	1 20S	31 49E
Bukuru	**114**	9 42N	8 48E
Bulak	**129**	45 2N	82 5E
Bulan	**127**	12 40N	123 52E
Bulandshahr	**124**	28 28N	77 58E
Bulawayo	**117**	20 7S	28 32E
Buldir I.	**67**	52 20N	175 55E
Bulgan	**130**	48 35N	103 34E
Bulgaria ■	**109**	42 35N	25 30E
Buli, Teluk	**127**	1 5N	128 25E
Buliluyan, C.	**126**	8 20N	117 15E
Bulkley, R.	**54**	55 15N	127 40W
Bulkur	**121**	71 50N	126 30E
Bull, R.	**62**	49 18N	115 18W
Bull Shoals L.	**75**	36 40N	93 5W
Buller, Mt.	**136**	37 10S	146 28E
Bullfinch	**134**	30 58S	119 3E
Bullhead City	**81**	35 11N	114 33W
Bullocks Corners	**48**	43 17N	79 59W
Bulls	**133**	40 10S	175 24E
Bully-les-Mines	**101**	50 27N	2 44E
Bulnes	**88**	36 42S	72 19W
Bulsar	**124**	20 40N	72 58E
Bulu Karakelong	**127**	4 35N	126 50E
Buluan	**127**	9 0N	125 30E
Bulukumba	**127**	5 33S	120 11E
Bulun	**121**	70 37N	127 30E
Bulun Tokhai = Puluntohai	**129**	47 2N	87 29E
Bulyea	**56**	50 59N	104 52W
Bumba	**116**	2 13N	22 30E
Bumble Bee	**79**	34 8N	112 18W
Bumhpa Bum	**125**	26 51N	97 14E
Buna	**116**	2 58N	39 30E
Bunaiyin	**122**	23 10N	51 8E
Bunaloo	**136**	35 47S	144 35E
Bunbury	**134**	33 20S	115 35E
Buncrana	**97**	55 8N	7 28W
Bundaberg	**135**	24 54S	152 22E
Bundi	**124**	25 30N	75 35E
Bundoran	**97**	54 24N	8 17W
Bundure	**136**	35 10S	146 1E
Bungendore	**136**	35 14S	149 30E
Bungō-Suidō	**132**	33 0N	132 15E
Bunguran N. Is.	**126**	4 45N	108 0E
Bungwahl	**136**	32 25S	153 0E
Bunia	**116**	1 35N	30 20E
Bunji	**124**	35 45N	74 40E
Bunju	**126**	3 35N	117 50E
Bunker Hill, Ill., U.S.A.	**76**	39 3N	89 57W
Bunker Hill, Ind., U.S.A.	**77**	40 40N	86 6W
Bunkerville	**79**	36 47N	114 6W
Bunkie	**75**	31 1N	92 12W
Bunnell	**73**	29 28N	81 12W
Buntok	**126**	1 40S	114 58E
Buntzen L.	**66**	49 21N	122 52W
Búoareyri	**110**	65 2N	14 13W
Buol	**127**	1 15N	121 32E
Buorkhaya, Mys	**121**	71 50N	133 10E
Bûr Sa'îd	**115**	31 16N	32 18E
Bûr Sûdân	**115**	19 32N	37 9E
Bura	**116**	1 4S	39 58E
Buraidah	**122**	26 20N	44 8E
Buraimī, Al Wāhāt al	**123**	24 15N	55 43E
Buras	**75**	29 20N	89 33W
Burbank	**81**	34 9N	118 23W
Burcher	**136**	33 30S	147 16E
Burchun	**129**	48 0N	86 7E
Burdett	**61**	49 50N	111 32W
Burdur	**122**	37 45N	30 22E
Burdwan	**125**	23 16N	87 54E
Bure, R.	**94**	52 38N	1 45E
Burford	**49**	43 7N	80 27W
Burgan	**122**	29 0N	47 57E
Burgas	**109**	42 33N	27 29E
Burgenland □	**106**	47 20N	16 20E
Burgeo	**37**	47 37N	57 38W
Burgersdorp	**117**	31 0S	26 20E
Burgos	**104**	42 21N	3 41W
Burgsvik	**111**	57 3N	18 19E
Burgundy = Bourgogne	**101**	47 0N	4 30E
Burhou Rocks	**100**	49 45N	2 15W
Burias, I.	**127**	12 55N	123 5E
Burica, Punta	**84**	8 3N	82 51W
Burin	**37**	47 1N	55 14W
Burin Peninsula	**37**	47 0N	55 40W
Buriram	**128**	15 0N	103 0E
Burkburnett	**75**	34 7N	98 35W
Burke	**78**	47 31N	115 56W
Burke Chan.	**62**	52 10N	127 30W
Burketown	**135**	17 45S	139 33E
Burkettsville	**77**	40 21N	84 39W
Burk's Falls	**46**	45 37N	79 24W
Burleigh Falls	**47**	44 33N	78 12W
Burley	**78**	42 37N	113 55W
Burlingame	**80**	37 35N	122 21W
Burlington, Newf., Can.	**37**	49 45N	56 1W
Burlington, Ont., Can.	**48**	43 18N	79 45W
Burlington, Colo., U.S.A.	**74**	39 21N	102 18W
Burlington, Ill., U.S.A.	**77**	42 43N	88 33W
Burlington, Iowa, U.S.A.	**76**	40 50N	91 5W
Burlington, Kans., U.S.A.	**74**	38 15N	95 47W
Burlington, Ky., U.S.A.	**77**	39 2N	84 43W
Burlington, N.C., U.S.A.	**73**	36 7N	79 27W
Burlington, N.J., U.S.A.	**71**	40 5N	74 50W
Burlington, Vt., U.S.A.	**71**	44 27N	73 14W
Burlington, Wash., U.S.A.	**80**	48 29N	122 19W
Burlington, Wis., U.S.A.	**72**	42 41N	88 18W
Burlington Beach	**48**	43 18N	79 48W
Burlyu-Tyube	**120**	46 30N	79 10E
Burma ■	**125**	21 0N	96 30E
Burnaby	**66**	49 15N	123 0W
Burnaby I.	**62**	52 25N	131 19W
Burnaby L.	**66**	49 14N	122 56W
Burnet	**75**	30 45N	98 11W
Burnett, R.	**135**	24 45S	152 23E
Burney	**78**	40 56N	121 41W
Burnham	**70**	40 37N	77 34W
Burnhamthorpe	**50**	43 37N	79 36W
Burnie	**135**	41 4S	145 56E
Burnley	**94**	53 47N	2 15W
Burns, Oreg., U.S.A.	**78**	43 40N	119 4W
Burns, Wyo., U.S.A.	**74**	41 13N	104 18W
Burns Lake	**54**	54 20N	125 45W
Burnside, R.	**64**	66 51N	108 4W
Burnt Island	**37**	47 36N	58 53W
Burnt L.	**36**	53 35N	64 4W
Burnt Paw	**67**	67 2N	142 43W
Burnt, R.	**70**	44 40N	78 42W
Burnt River	**47**	44 41N	78 42W
Burntwood L.	**55**	55 22N	100 26W
Burntwood, R.	**55**	56 8N	96 34W
Burquitlam	**66**	49 16N	122 54W
Burra	**135**	33 40S	138 55E
Burragorang, L.	**136**	33 52S	150 37E
Burrard Inlet	**66**	49 18N	123 15W
Burrendong Res.	**136**	32 45S	149 10E
Burrewarra Pt.	**136**	35 50S	150 15E
Burrinjuck Dam	**136**	35 0S	148 34E
Burrinjuck Res.	**136**	35 0S	148 36E
Burro, Serranias del	**82**	29 0N	102 0W
Burrows L.	**53**	49 57N	86 44W
Burruyacú	**88**	26 30S	64 40W
Bursa	**122**	40 15N	29 5E
Burstall	**56**	50 39N	109 54W
Burt L.	**46**	45 27N	84 40W
Burton	**63**	50 0N	117 53W
Burton L.	**36**	54 45N	78 20W
Burton-upon-Trent	**94**	52 48N	1 39W
Burtts Corner	**39**	46 3N	66 52W
Buru, I.	**127**	3 30S	126 30E
Burujird	**122**	33 58N	48 41E
Burundi ■	**116**	3 15S	30 0E
Burung	**126**	0 21N	108 25E
Burwash	**46**	46 14N	80 51W
Burwash Landing	**67**	61 21N	139 0W
Burwell	**74**	41 49N	99 8W
Burwell, Mt.	**66**	49 27N	123 1W
Bury, Can.	**41**	45 28N	71 30W
Bury, U.K.	**94**	53 36N	2 19W
Bury St. Edmunds	**95**	52 15N	0 42E
Buryat A.S.S.R. □	**121**	53 0N	110 0E
Busayyah	**122**	30 0N	46 10E
Busby	**54**	53 55N	114 0W
Bushell	**55**	59 31N	108 45W
Bushnell, Ill., U.S.A.	**74**	40 32N	90 30W
Bushnell, Nebr., U.S.A.	**74**	41 18N	103 50W
Businga	**116**	3 16N	20 59E
Buskerud fylke □	**111**	60 13N	9 0E
Busra	**122**	32 30N	36 25E
Bussang	**101**	47 50N	6 50E
Busselton	**134**	33 42S	115 15E
Bussum	**105**	52 16N	5 10E
Bustard Hd.	**135**	24 0S	151 48E
Busto Arsizio	**108**	45 40N	8 50E
Busu-Djanoa	**116**	1 50N	21 5E
Busuangal, I.	**127**	12 10N	120 0E
Buta	**116**	2 50N	24 53E
Butare	**116**	2 31S	29 52E
Bute Inlet	**62**	50 40N	124 53W
Butedale	**62**	53 8N	128 42W
Butembo	**116**	0 9N	29 18E
Butiaba	**116**	1 50N	31 20E
Butler, Ind., U.S.A.	**77**	41 26N	84 52W
Butler, Ky., U.S.A.	**77**	38 47N	84 22W
Butler, Mo., U.S.A.	**76**	38 17N	94 18W
Butler, Pa., U.S.A.	**70**	40 52N	79 52W
Butte, Mont., U.S.A.	**78**	46 0N	112 31W
Butte, Nebr., U.S.A.	**74**	42 56N	98 54W
Butte Creek, R.	**80**	39 12N	121 56W
Butterworth	**128**	5 24N	100 23E
Buttle L.	**62**	49 42N	125 33W
Button B.	**55**	58 45N	94 23W
Button Is.	**36**	60 38N	64 40W
Buttonville	**50**	43 51N	79 21W
Buttonwillow	**81**	35 24N	119 28W
Butuan	**127**	8 57N	125 33E
Butung, I.	**127**	5 0S	122 45E
Buxton	**94**	53 16N	1 54W
Buxy	**101**	46 44N	4 40E
Buyaga	**121**	59 50N	127 0E
Buyr Nuur	**130**	47 50N	117 35E
Büyük Menderes, R.	**122**	37 45N	27 40E
Buzançais	**100**	46 54N	1 25E
Buzău	**107**	45 10N	26 50E
Buzău, R.	**107**	45 10N	27 20E
Buzen	**132**	33 35N	131 5E
Buzi, R.	**117**	19 52S	34 30E
Buzuluk	**120**	52 48N	52 12E
Buzzards Bay	**71**	41 45N	70 38W
Byam Martin I.	**64**	75 15N	104 15W
Bydgoszcz	**107**	53 10N	18 0E
Byelorussian S.S.R. □	**120**	53 30N	27 0E
Byers	**74**	39 46N	104 13W
Byesville	**70**	39 56N	81 32W
Byhalia	**75**	34 53N	89 41W
Bylas	**79**	33 11N	110 9W
Bylot I.	**65**	73 13N	78 34W
Byng Inlet	**46**	45 46N	80 33W
Byrd Land = Marie Byrd Land	**91**	79 30S	125 0W
Byrd Sub-Glacial Basin	**91**	82 0S	120 0W
Byron	**76**	42 8N	89 15W
Byron B.	**35**	54 42N	57 40W
Byron, C.	**135**	28 38S	153 40E
Byrranga, Gory	**121**	75 0N	100 0E
Byske	**110**	64 57N	21 11E
Byske, R.	**110**	65 20N	20 0E
Bytom	**107**	50 25N	19 0E

C

Ca Mau = Quan Long	**128**	9 7N	105 8E
Ca Mau, Mui = Bai Bung	**128**	8 35N	104 42E
Caacupé	**88**	25 23S	57 5W
Caamano Sd.	**62**	52 55N	129 25W
Caatingas	**87**	7 0S	52 30W
Caazapá	**88**	26 8S	56 19W
Caazapá □	**89**	26 10S	56 0W
Cabanatuan	**127**	15 30N	121 5E
Cabane-Ronde	**45**	45 47N	73 33W
Cabano	**41**	47 40N	68 56E
Cabazon	**81**	33 55N	116 47W
Cabedelo	**87**	7 0S	34 50W
Cabery	**77**	41 0N	88 12W
Cabildo	**88**	32 30S	71 5W
Cabimas	**86**	10 30N	71 25W
Cabinda	**116**	5 40S	12 11E
Cabinda □	**116**	5 0S	12 30E
Cabinet Mts.	**78**	48 0N	115 30W
Cabo Blanco	**90**	47 56S	65 47W
Cabo Frio	**89**	22 51S	42 3W
Cabo Pantoja	**86**	1 0S	75 10W
Cabonga Réservoir	**40**	47 20N	76 40W
Cabool	**75**	37 10N	92 8W
Cabora Bassa Dam	**117**	15 20S	32 50E
Caborca (Heroica)	**82**	30 40N	112 10W
Cabot Hd.	**70**	45 14N	81 18W
Cabot, Mt.	**71**	44 30N	71 25W
Cabot Strait	**35**	47 15N	59 40W
Cabrera, I.	**104**	39 6N	2 59E
Cabri	**56**	50 35N	108 25W
Cabriel, R.	**104**	39 20N	1 20W
Cabruta	**86**	7 50N	66 10W
Caburan	**127**	6 3N	125 45E
Çabuyaro	**86**	4 18N	72 49W
Čačak	**109**	43 54N	20 20E
Cáceres, Brazil	**86**	16 5S	57 40W

Cáceres **Canyon Creek**

Cáceres, Colomb. **86** 7 35N 75 20W
Cáceres, Spain **104** 39 26N 6 23W
Cache B. **34** 46 26N 80 1W
Cache Bay **46** 46 22N 80 0W
Cache Cr. **80** 38 45N 121 43W
Cache Creek **63** 50 48N 121 19W
Cachi **88** 25 5 S 66 10W
Cachimbo, Serra do **87** 9 30 S 55 0W
Cáchira **86** 7 21N 73 17W
Cachoeira **87** 12 30 S 39 0W
Cachoeira de
Itapemirim **89** 20 51 S 41 7W
Cachoeira do Sul **89** 30 3 S 52 53W
Cacolo **116** 10 9 S 19 21 E
Caconda **117** 13 48 S 15 8 E
Cadboro Bay **63** 48 28N 123 17W
Caddo **75** 34 8N 96 18W
Cader Idris **94** 52 43N 3 56W
Cadereyta Jiménez **83** 25 40N 100 0W
Cadillac, Qué., Can. **40** 48 14N 78 23W
Cadillac, Sask., Can. **56** 49 44N 107 44W
Cadillac, France **102** 44 38N 0 20W
Cadillac, U.S.A. **46** 44 16N 85 25W
Cadiz **127** 11 30N 123 15 E
Cádiz **104** 36 30N 6 20W
Cadiz **70** 40 13N 81 0W
Cádiz, G. de **104** 36 40N 7 0W
Cadomin **61** 53 2N 117 20W
Cadotte, R. **60** 56 43N 117 10W
Cadours **102** 43 44N 1 2 E
Caen **100** 49 10N 0 22W
Caergwrle **95** 53 6N 3 3W
Caernarfon **94** 53 8N 4 17W
Caernarfon B. **94** 53 4N 4 40W
Caernarvon =
Caernarfon **94** 53 8N 4 17W
Cæsarea = Qesari **115** 32 30N 34 53 E
Caeté **87** 20 0 S 43 40W
Caetité **87** 13 50 S 42 50W
Cafayate **88** 26 2 S 66 0W
Cagayan de Oro **127** 8 30N 124 40 E
Cagayan, R. **127** 18 25N 121 42 E
Cágliari **108** 39 15N 9 6 E
Cágliari, G. di **108** 39 8N 9 10 E
Cagnes-sur-Mer **103** 43 40N 7 9 E
Caguas **85** 18 14N 66 4W
Caha Mts. **97** 51 45N 9 40W
Cahir **97** 52 23N 7 56W
Cahirciveen **97** 51 57N 10 13W
Cahore Pt. **97** 52 34N 6 11W
Cahors **102** 44 27N 1 27 E
Cahuapanas **86** 5 15 S 77 0W
Caibarién **84** 22 30N 79 30W
Caicara **86** 7 38N 66 10W
Caicó **87** 6 20 S 37 0W
Caicos Is. **85** 21 40N 71 40W
Caicos Passage **85** 22 45N 72 45W
Caihaique **90** 45 30 S 71 45W
Cains, R. **39** 46 40N 65 47W
Cainsville **49** 43 9N 80 15W
Caird Coast **91** 75 0 S 25 0W
Cairn Gorm **96** 57 7N 3 40W
Cairn Toul **96** 57 3N 3 44W
Cairngorm Mts. **96** 57 6N 3 42W
Cairns **135** 16 57 S 145 45 E
Cairnside **43** 45 7N 73 54W
Cairo, Ga., U.S.A. **73** 30 52N 84 12W
Cairo, Illinois, U.S.A. **75** 37 0N 89 10W
Cairo = El Qâhira **115** 30 1N 31 14 E
Caistorville **49** 43 3N 79 44W
Caithness, Ord of, C. **96** 58 35N 3 37W
Caiundo **117** 15 50 S 17 52 E
Caiza **86** 20 2 S 65 40W
Cajamarca **86** 7 5 S 78 28W
Cajarc **102** 44 29N 1 50 E
Cajàzeiros **87** 7 0 S 38 30W
Calabar **114** 4 57N 8 20 E
Calabogie **47** 45 18N 76 43W
Calabozo **86** 9 0N 67 20W
Calábria □ **108** 39 24N 16 30 E
Calafate **90** 50 25 S 72 25W
Calahorra **104** 42 18N 1 59W
Calais, France **101** 50 57N 1 56 E
Calais, U.S.A. **35** 45 5N 67 20W
Calais, Pas de **78** 50 57N 1 20 E
Calalaste, Sierra de **88** 25 0 S 67 0W
Calama, Brazil **86** 8 0 S 62 50W
Calama, Chile **88** 22 30 S 68 55W
Calamar, Bolívar,
Colomb. **86** 10 15N 74 55W
Calamar, Vaupés,
Colomb. **86** 1 58N 72 32W
Calamian Group **127** 11 50N 119 55 E
Calamocha **104** 40 50N 1 17W
Calanaque **86** 0 5 S 64 0W
Calang **126** 4 30N 95 43 E
Calapan **127** 13 25N 121 7 E
Calatayud **104** 41 20N 1 40W
Calauag **127** 13 55N 122 15 E
Calavite, Cape **127** 13 26N 120 10 E
Calayan, I. **131** 19 20N 121 30 E
Calca **86** 13 10 S 72 0W
Calcutta **125** 22 36N 88 24 E
Caldas □ **86** 5 15N 75 30W
Calder, R. **94** 53 44N 1 21W
Caldera **88** 27 5 S 70 55W
Caldiran **122** 39 7N 44 0 E
Caldwell, Idaho, U.S.A. **78** 43 45N 116 42W
Caldwell, Kans., U.S.A. **75** 37 5N 97 37W
Caldwell, Texas, U.S.A. **75** 30 30N 96 42W
Caledon, Can. **49** 43 52N 80 0W
Caledon, S. Afr. **117** 34 14 S 19 26 E
Caledon B. **135** 12 45 S 137 0 E
Caledon East **49** 43 52N 79 52W
Caledon, R. **117** 30 0 S 26 46 E
Caledonia, N.S., Can. **39** 44 22N 65 2W
Caledonia, N.S., Can. **39** 45 17N 62 33W
Caledonia, Ont., Can. **49** 43 7N 79 58W
Caledonia, Mo., U.S.A. **76** 37 45N 90 46W
Caledonia, N.Y., U.S.A. **70** 42 57N 77 54W
Calella **104** 41 37N 2 40 E
Calera, La **88** 32 50 S 71 10W
Calexico **81** 32 40N 115 33W
Calf of Man **94** 54 4N 4 48W
Calgary **59** 51 0N 114 10W
Calgary International
Airport **59** 51 4N 114 1W
Calhoun **73** 34 30N 84 55W
Cali **86** 3 25N 76 35W
Calicoan, I. **127** 10 59N 125 50 E
Calicut, (Kozhikode) **124** 11 15N 75 43 E
Caliente **79** 37 43N 114 34W
California, Mo., U.S.A. **76** 38 37N 92 30W
California, Pa., U.S.A. **70** 40 4N 79 55W
California □ **78** 37 25N 120 0W
California, Baja **82** 32 10N 115 12W
California, Baja, T.N. □ **82** 30 0N 115 0W
California, Baja, T.S. □ **82** 25 50N 111 50W
California City **81** 35 7N 117 57W
California, Golfo de **82** 27 0N 111 0W
California Hot Springs **81** 35 51N 118 41W
California, Lr. =
California, Baja **82** 25 50N 111 50W
Calilegua **88** 23 45 S 64 42W
Calingasta **88** 31 15 S 69 30W
Calipatria **81** 33 8N 115 30W
Calistoga **80** 38 36N 122 32W
Calixa-Lavallée **45** 45 45N 73 17W
Calkiní **83** 20 21N 90 3W
Callabonna, L. **135** 29 40 S 140 5 E
Callac **100** 48 25N 3 27W
Callan **97** 52 33N 7 25W
Callander **46** 46 13N 79 22W
Callao **86** 12 0 S 77 0W
Callaway **74** 41 20N 99 56W
Callender **76** 42 22N 94 17W
Calles **83** 23 2N 98 42W
Calling L. **60** 55 15N 113 20W
Calling Lake **60** 55 15N 113 12W
Calmar, Can. **60** 53 16N 113 49W
Calmar, U.S.A. **76** 43 11N 91 52W
Calpella **80** 39 14N 123 12W
Calpine **80** 39 40N 120 27W
Calstock **53** 49 47N 84 9W
Caltagirone **108** 37 13N 14 30 E
Caltanissetta **108** 37 30N 14 3 E
Caluire-et-Cuire **103** 45 49N 4 51 E
Calulo **116** 10 1 S 14 56 E
Calumbo **116** 9 0 S 13 20 E
Calumet City **77** 41 37N 87 32W
Calvados □ **100** 49 5N 0 15W
Calvert **75** 30 59N 96 50W
Calvert C. **62** 51 25N 127 53W
Calvert I. **62** 51 30N 128 0W
Calvi **108** 42 34N 8 45 E
Calvillo **82** 21 51N 102 43W
Calvinia **117** 31 28 S 19 45 E
Calwa **80** 36 42N 119 46W
Cam Lam **128** 11 54N 109 10 E
Cam, R. **95** 52 21N 0 16 E
Cam Ranh **128** 11 54N 109 12 E
Camabatela **116** 8 20 S 15 26 E
Camachigama, L. **40** 47 50N 76 19W
Camacho **82** 24 25N 102 18W
Camaguán **86** 8 6N 67 36W
Camagüey **84** 21 20N 78 0W
Camaná **86** 16 30 S 72 50W
Camanche **76** 41 47N 90 15W
Camano I. **63** 48 10N 122 30W
Camaquã, R. **89** 30 50 S 52 50W
Camaret **100** 48 16N 4 37W
Camargo **86** 20 38 S 65 15 E
Camargue **103** 43 34N 4 34 E
Camarillo **81** 34 13N 119 2W
Camarón, C. **84** 16 0N 85 0W
Camarones, Argent. **90** 44 50 S 65 40W
Camarones, Chile **86** 19 0 S 69 58W
Camas **80** 45 35N 122 24W
Camas Valley **78** 43 0N 123 46W
Cambará **89** 23 2 S 50 5W
Cambay **124** 22 23N 72 33 E
Cambay, G. of **124** 20 45N 72 30 E
Cambo-les-Bains **102** 43 22N 1 23W
Cambodia ■ **128** 12 15N 105 0 E
Camborne **95** 50 13N 5 18W
Cambrai **101** 50 11N 3 14 E
Cambria, Calif., U.S.A. **80** 35 44N 121 6W
Cambria, N.Y., U.S.A. **49** 43 11N 78 49W
Cambrian Mts. **95** 52 25N 3 52W
Cambridge, N.B., Can. **39** 45 50N 65 58W
Cambridge, Ont., Can. **49** 43 23N 80 15W
Cambridge, Jamaica **84** 18 18N 77 54W
Cambridge, N.Z. **133** 37 54 S 175 29 E
Cambridge, U.K. **95** 52 13N 0 8 E
Cambridge, Idaho,
U.S.A. **78** 44 36N 116 52W
Cambridge, Ill., U.S.A. **76** 41 18N 90 12W
Cambridge, Iowa,
U.S.A. **76** 41 54N 93 32W
Cambridge, Mass.,
U.S.A. **72** 42 20N 71 8W
Cambridge, Md., U.S.A. **72** 38 33N 76 2W
Cambridge, Minn.,
U.S.A. **74** 45 34N 93 15W
Cambridge, Nebr.,
U.S.A. **74** 40 20N 100 12W
Cambridge, N.Y.,
U.S.A. **71** 43 2N 73 22W
Cambridge, Ohio,
U.S.A. **70** 40 1N 81 35W
Cambridge Bay **64** 69 10N 105 0W
Cambridge City **77** 39 49N 85 10W
Cambridge Gulf **134** 14 45 S 128 0 E
Cambridge Springs **70** 41 47N 80 4W
Cambridgeshire □ **95** 52 12N 0 7 E
Cambuci **89** 21 35 S 41 55W
Camden, Ala., U.S.A. **73** 31 59N 87 15W
Camden, Ark., U.S.A. **75** 33 40N 92 50W
Camden, Me., U.S.A. **35** 44 14N 69 6W
Camden, N.J., U.S.A. **72** 39 57N 75 1W
Camden, Ohio, U.S.A. **77** 39 38N 84 39W
Camden, S.C., U.S.A. **73** 34 17N 80 34W
Camden, B. **67** 71 0N 145 0W
Camdenton **76** 38 1N 92 45W
Camembert **100** 48 53N 0 10 E
Cameron, Ariz., U.S.A. **79** 35 55N 111 31W
Cameron, La., U.S.A. **75** 29 50N 93 18W
Cameron, Mo., U.S.A. **76** 39 42N 94 14W
Cameron, Tex., U.S.A. **75** 30 53N 97 0W
Cameron Falls **52** 49 8N 88 19W
Cameron Highlands **128** 4 27N 101 22 E
Cameron Hills **54** 59 48N 118 0W
Cameron L. **53** 49 1N 84 17W
Cameroon ■ **114** 3 30N 12 30 E
Cameroun, Mt. **116** 4 45N 8 55 E
Cametá **87** 2 0 S 49 30W
Camiguin, I. **131** 19 55N 122 0 E
Caminha **104** 41 50N 8 50W
Camino **80** 38 47N 120 40W
Camlachie **70** 43 3N 82 9W
Cammal **70** 41 24N 77 28W
Camocim **87** 2 55 S 40 50W
Camooweal **135** 19 56 S 138 7 E
Camopi, R. **87** 3 12N 52 17W
Camp Borden **46** 44 18N 79 56W
Camp Crook **74** 45 36N 103 59W
Camp Nelson **81** 36 8N 118 39W
Camp Point **76** 40 3N 91 4W
Camp Wood **75** 29 47N 100 0W
Campagna **108** 40 40N 15 5 E
Campana **88** 34 10 S 58 55W
Campana, I. **90** 48 20 S 75 10W
Campania □ **108** 40 50N 14 45 E
Campania I. **62** 53 5N 129 25W
Campbell **80** 37 17N 121 57W
Campbell Island **62** 52 8N 128 12W
Campbell L. **55** 63 14N 106 55W
Campbell, R. **66** 49 1N 122 47W
Campbell River **62** 50 5N 125 20W
Campbellford **47** 44 18N 77 48W
Campbell's Bay **40** 45 44N 76 36W
Campbellsburg, Ind.,
U.S.A. **77** 38 39N 86 16W
Campbellsburg, Ky.,
U.S.A. **77** 38 31N 85 12W
Campbellsville **72** 37 23N 85 12W
Campbellton, Alta.,
Can. **54** 53 32N 113 15W
Campbellton, N.B.,
Can. **39** 47 57N 66 43W
Campbellton, Newf.,
Can. **37** 49 17N 54 56W
Campbelltown **136** 34 4 S 150 49 E
Campbellville **49** 43 29N 79 59W
Campbeltown **96** 55 25N 5 36W
Campeche **83** 19 50N 90 32W
Campeche □ **83** 19 50N 90 32W
Campeche, Golfo de **83** 19 30N 93 0W
Camperdown **136** 38 14 S 143 9 E
Camperville **57** 51 59N 100 9W
Campina Grande **87** 7 20 S 35 47W
Campinas **89** 22 50 S 47 0W
Campinho **87** 14 30 S 39 10W
Campo **116** 2 15N 9 58 E
Campo Beló **87** 21 0 S 45 30W
Campo Formoso **87** 10 30 S 40 20W
Campo Grande **87** 20 25 S 54 40W
Campo Maior **87** 4 50 S 42 12W
Campoalegre **86** 2 41N 75 20W
Campobasso **108** 41 34N 14 40 E
Campos **89** 21 50 S 41 20W
Campos Belos **87** 13 10 S 46 45W
Campos Novos **89** 27 21 S 51 20W
Campsie Fells **98** 56 2N 4 20W
Campton **77** 37 44N 83 33W
Camptonville **80** 39 27N 121 3W
Campuya, R. **86** 1 10 S 74 0W
Camrose **61** 53 0N 112 50W
Camsall L. **55** 72 32N 106 47W
Camsell Portage **55** 59 37N 109 15W
Can Tho **128** 10 2N 105 46 E
Canaan **71** 42 1N 73 20W
Canaan, R. **39** 45 55N 65 47W
Canaan Station **39** 46 15N 65 4W
Canada ■ **22** 60 0N 100 0W
Canada B. **37** 50 43N 56 8W
Canadian **75** 35 56N 100 25W
Canadian Pacific
Irrigation Canal **59** 51 0N 114 0W
Canadian, R. **75** 36 0N 98 45W
Canakkale **122** 40 8N 26 30 E
Canakkale Boğazi **109** 40 0N 26 0 E
Canal de l'Est **101** 48 45N 5 35 E
Canal Flats **61** 50 10N 115 48W
Canal latéral à la
Garonne **102** 44 25N 0 15 E
Canalejas **88** 35 15 S 66 34W
Canals **88** 33 35 S 62 40W
Canandaigua **70** 42 55N 77 10W
Cananea **82** 31 0N 110 20W
Canarias, Islas **114** 29 30N 17 0W
Canarreos, Arch. de los **84** 21 35N 81 40W
Canary Is. = Canarias,
Islas **114** 29 30N 17 0W
Canatlán **82** 24 31N 104 47W
Canaveral, C. **73** 28 28N 80 31W
Canavieiras **87** 15 39 S 39 0W
Canberra **136** 35 15 S 149 8 E
Canboro **49** 42 59N 79 41W
Canby, Calif., U.S.A. **78** 41 26N 120 58W
Canby, Minn., U.S.A. **74** 44 44N 96 15W
Canby, Ore., U.S.A. **80** 45 16N 122 42W
Cancale **100** 48 40N 1 50W
Candala **115** 11 30N 49 58 E
Candé **100** 47 34N 1 0W
Candelaria **89** 27 29 S 55 44W
Candiac **45** 45 23N 73 31W
Candle L. **56** 53 50N 105 18W
Cando, Can. **56** 52 23N 108 14W
Cando, U.S.A. **74** 48 30N 99 14W
Canelones **88** 34 32 S 56 10W
Canet-Plage **102** 42 41N 3 2 E
Cañete, Chile **88** 37 50 S 73 30W
Cañete, Cuba **85** 20 36N 74 43W
Cañete, Peru **86** 13 0 S 76 30W
Canfield **49** 42 58N 79 45W
Cangamba **117** 13 40 S 19 54 E
Cangas **104** 42 16N 8 47W
Canguaretama **87** 6 20 S 35 5W
Canguçu **89** 31 22 S 52 43W
Canicado **117** 24 2 S 33 2 E
Canim, L. **63** 51 45N 120 50W
Canim Lake **63** 51 47N 120 54W
Canipaan **126** 8 33N 117 15 E
Canisteo **70** 42 17N 77 37W
Canisteo, R. **70** 42 15N 77 30W
Cañitas **82** 23 36N 102 43W
Cankırı **122** 40 40N 33 30 E
Canlaon, Mt. **127** 9 27N 118 25 E
Canmore **61** 51 7N 115 18W
Canna I. **96** 57 3N 6 33W
Cannanore **124** 11 53N 75 27 E
Cannelton **77** 37 55N 86 45W
Cannes **103** 43 32N 7 0 E
Canning **39** 45 9N 64 25W
Canning Basin **134** 19 50 S 124 0 E
Cannington **70** 44 20N 79 2W
Cannock **94** 52 42N 2 2W
Cannock Chase, hills **98** 52 43N 2 0W
Cannon Ball, R. **74** 46 20N 101 20W
Caño Colorado **86** 2 18N 68 22W
Canoe **63** 50 45N 119 13W
Canoe L. **55** 55 10N 108 15W
Canol **67** 65 15N 126 50W
Canon City **74** 39 30N 105 20W
Canonba **136** 31 21 S 147 22 E
Canora **57** 51 40N 102 30W
Canourgue, Le **102** 44 26N 3 13 E
Canowindra **136** 33 35 S 148 38 E
Canrobert **45** 45 21N 72 56W
Canso **39** 45 20N 61 0W
Cantabrian Mts. =
Cantábrica **104** 43 0N 5 10W
Cantábrica, Cordillera **104** 43 0N 5 10W
Cantal □ **102** 45 4N 2 45 E
Cantaura **86** 9 19N 64 21W
Canterbury, Can. **39** 45 53N 67 29W
Canterbury, U.K. **95** 51 17N 1 5 E
Canterbury □ **133** 43 45 S 171 19 E
Canterbury Bight **133** 44 16 S 171 55 E
Canterbury Plains **133** 43 55 S 171 22 E
Cantic **43** 45 4N 73 21W
Cantil **81** 35 18N 117 58W
Canton, Ga., U.S.A. **73** 34 13N 84 29W
Canton, Ill., U.S.A. **76** 40 32N 90 0W
Canton, Mass., U.S.A. **71** 42 8N 71 8W
Canton, Miss., U.S.A. **75** 32 40N 90 1W
Canton, Mo., U.S.A. **76** 40 10N 91 33W
Canton, N.Y., U.S.A. **71** 44 32N 75 3W
Canton, Ohio, U.S.A. **70** 40 47N 81 22W
Canton, Okla., U.S.A. **75** 36 5N 98 36W
Canton, S.D., U.S.A. **74** 43 20N 96 35W
Canton = Kwangchow **131** 23 10N 113 10 E
Canton I. **14** 2 30 S 172 0W
Canton L. **75** 36 12N 98 40W
Canuck **56** 49 12N 108 13W
Canudos **86** 7 13 S 58 5W
Canulloit **79** 31 58N 106 36W
Canuta **44** 45 42N 74 9W
Canutama **86** 6 30 S 64 20W
Canwood **56** 53 22N 106 36W
Canyon, Can. **67** 47 25N 84 36W
Canyon, Texas, U.S.A. **75** 35 0N 101 57W
Canyon, Wyo., U.S.A. **78** 44 43N 110 36W
Canyon Creek **60** 55 22N 115 5W

Catlin **Charleswood**

Catlin **77** 40 4N 87 42W
Cato I. **135** 23 15S 155 32E
Catoche, C. **83** 21 40N 87 0W
Catrimani **86** 0 27N 61 41W
Catskill **71** 42 14N 73 52W
Catskill Mts. **71** 42 15N 74 15W
Cattaraugus **70** 42 22N 78 52W
Cauca □ **86** 2 30N 76 50W
Cauca, R. **86** 7 25N 75 30W
Caucasia **86** 8 0N 75 12W
Caucasus Mts. = Bolshoi Kavkas **120** 42 50N 44 0E
Cauchy, L. **38** 50 36N 60 46W
Caudebec-en-Caux **100** 49 30N 0 42E
Caudry **101** 50 7N 3 22E
Caughnawaga **44** 45 25N 73 41W
Caulfield **66** 49 21N 123 15W
Caulnes **100** 48 18N 2 10W
Caungula **116** 8 15S 18 50E
Cáuquenes **88** 36 0S 72 30W
Caura, R. **86** 6 20N 64 30W
Causapscal **38** 48 19N 67 12W
Causapscal, Parc Prov. de **38** 48 15N 67 0W
Caussade **102** 44 10N 1 33E
Cauterets **102** 42 52N 0 8W
Caution C. **62** 51 10N 127 47W
Cauvery, R. **124** 12 0N 77 45E
Caux, Pays de **100** 49 38N 0 35E
Cavaillon **103** 43 50N 5 2E
Cavalaire-sur-Mer **103** 43 10N 6 33E
Cavalerie, La **102** 44 0N 3 10E
Cavalier **57** 48 50N 97 39W
Cavallo, I. de **103** 41 22N 9 16E
Cavan **97** 54 0N 7 22W
Cavan □ **97** 53 58N 7 10W
Cave City **72** 37 13N 85 57W
Cavers **34** 48 55N 87 41W
Caviana, Ilha **87** 0 15N 50 0W
Cavite **127** 14 20N 120 55E
Cawasachouane, L. **40** 47 27N 77 45W
Caxias **86** 5 0S 43 27W
Caxias do Sul **89** 29 10S 51 10W
Cay Sal Bank **84** 23 45N 80 0W
Cayambe **86** 0 3N 78 22W
Cayce **73** 33 59N 81 2W
Caycuse **62** 48 53N 124 22W
Cayenne **87** 5 0N 52 18W
Cayes, Les **85** 18 15N 73 46W
Cayeux-sur-Mer. **101** 50 10N 1 30E
Cayey **67** 18 7N 66 10W
Cayley **61** 50 27N 113 51W
Caylus **102** 44 15N 1 47E
Cayman Brac, I. **84** 19 43N 79 49W
Cayman Is. **84** 19 40N 79 50W
Cayo **83** 17 10N 89 0W
Cayo Romano, I. **85** 22 0N 73 30W
Cayuga, Can. **49** 42 59N 79 50W
Cayuga, Ind., U.S.A. **77** 39 57N 87 38W
Cayuga, N.Y., U.S.A. **71** 42 54N 76 44W
Cayuga L. **71** 42 45N 76 45W
Cazaux et de Sanguinet, Étang de **102** 44 29N 1 10W
Cazaville **43** 45 5N 74 22W
Cazères **102** 43 13N 1 5E
Cazombo **117** 12 0S 22 48E
Cazorla **86** 8 1N 67 0W
Ceanannas Mor **97** 53 42N 6 53W
Ceará □ **87** 5 0S 40 0W
Ceará Mirim **87** 5 38S 35 25W
Cebaco, I. **84** 7 33N 81 9W
Cebollar **88** 29 10S 66 35W
Cebú **127** 10 18N 123 54E
Cebú, I. **127** 10 15N 123 40E
Cedar City **79** 37 41N 113 3W
Cedar Creek Res. **75** 32 15N 96 0W
Cedar Falls, Iowa, U.S.A. **76** 42 39N 92 29W
Cedar Falls, Wash., U.S.A. **80** 47 25N 121 45W
Cedar Grove **77** 39 22N 84 56W
Cedar Key **73** 29 9N 83 5W
Cedar L., Man., Can. **57** 53 20N 100 10W
Cedar L., Ont., Can. **47** 46 2N 78 30W
Cedar Lake **77** 41 20N 87 25W
Cedar Mills **49** 43 55N 79 48W
Cedar Point **77** 41 44N 83 21W
Cedar, R. **76** 41 17N 91 21W
Cedar Rapids **76** 42 0N 91 38W
Cedar Springs **77** 43 13N 85 33W
Cedar Valley **49** 43 46N 80 10W
Cedarburg **72** 43 18N 87 55W
Cedartown **73** 34 1N 85 15W
Cedarvale **54** 55 1N 128 22W
Cedarville, Calif., U.S.A. **78** 41 37N 120 13W
Cedarville, Ill., U.S.A. **76** 42 23N 89 38W
Cedarville, Mich., U.S.A. **46** 46 0N 84 22W
Cedarville, Ohio, U.S.A. **77** 39 44N 83 49W
Cedral **82** 23 50N 100 42W
Cèdres, Les **44** 45 18N 74 3W
Cedro **87** 6 34S 39 3W
Cedros, I. de **82** 28 10N 115 20W
Ceduna **134** 32 7S 133 46E
Ceepeecee **54** 49 52N 126 42W
Cefalù **108** 38 3N 14 1E
Cegléd **107** 47 11N 19 47E
Cehegín **104** 38 6N 1 48W
Ceiba, La **84** 15 40N 86 50W
Celaya **82** 20 31N 100 37W
Celbridge **97** 53 20N 6 33W
Celebes I. = Sulawesi **127** 2 0S 120 0E
Celebes Sea **127** 3 0N 123 0E
Celina **77** 40 32N 84 31W
Celje **108** 46 16N 15 18E
Celle **106** 52 37N 10 4E
Cement **75** 34 56N 98 8W
Cenis, Col du Mt. **103** 45 15N 6 55E
Cenon **102** 44 50N 0 33W
Centennial **58** 49 54N 97 9W
Center, N.D., U.S.A. **74** 47 9N 101 17W
Center, Texas, U.S.A. **75** 31 50N 94 10W
Center Point **76** 42 12N 91 46W
Centerfield **78** 39 9N 111 56W
Centerville, Ala., U.S.A. **73** 32 55N 87 7W
Centerville, Calif., U.S.A. **80** 36 44N 119 30W
Centerville, Iowa, U.S.A. **76** 40 45N 92 57W
Centerville, Mich., U.S.A. **77** 41 55N 85 32W
Centerville, Miss., U.S.A. **75** 31 10N 91 3W
Centerville, Pa., U.S.A. **70** 40 3N 79 59W
Centerville, S.D., U.S.A. **74** 43 10N 96 58W
Centerville, Tenn., U.S.A. **73** 35 46N 87 29W
Centerville, Tex., U.S.A. **75** 31 15N 95 56W
Central □ **96** 56 0N 4 30W
Central African Empire ■ **116** 7 0N 20 0E
Central Butte **56** 50 48N 106 31W
Central City, Ky., U.S.A. **72** 37 20N 87 7W
Central City, Nebr., U.S.A. **74** 41 8N 98 0W
Central, Cordillera, C. Rica **84** 10 10N 84 5W
Central, Cordillera, Dom. Rep. **85** 19 15N 71 0W
Central Islip **71** 40 49N 73 13W
Central Lake **46** 45 4N 85 16W
Central Makran Range **124** 26 30N 64 15E
Central Patricia **52** 51 30N 90 9W
Central Russian Uplands **93** 54 0N 36 0E
Central Siberian Plateau **121** 65 0N 105 0E
Centralia, Ill., U.S.A. **76** 38 32N 89 5W
Centralia, Mo., U.S.A. **76** 39 12N 92 6W
Centralia, Wash., U.S.A. **80** 46 46N 122 59W
Centreville, N.B., Can. **39** 46 26N 67 43W
Centreville, N.S., Can. **39** 44 33N 66 1W
Ceram I. = Seram I. **127** 3 10S 129 0E
Ceram Sea = Seram Sea **127** 2 30S 128 30E
Cerbère **102** 42 26N 3 10E
Cerbicales, Îles **103** 41 33N 9 22E
Cereal **61** 51 25N 110 48W
Ceres, Argent. **88** 29 55S 61 55W
Ceres, S. Afr. **117** 33 21S 19 18E
Ceres, U.S.A. **80** 37 35N 120 57W
Céret **102** 42 30N 2 42E
Cereté **86** 8 53N 75 48W
Cerf, L. de **40** 46 16N 75 30W
Cerfontaine **105** 50 11N 4 26E
Cerignola **108** 41 17N 15 53E
Cérilly **102** 46 37N 2 50E
Cerisiers **101** 48 8N 3 30E
Cerizay **100** 46 50N 0 40W
Çerkeş **122** 40 40N 32 58E
Cerknica **108** 45 48N 14 21E
Cernavodă **107** 44 22N 28 3E
Cernay **101** 47 44N 7 10E
Cerralvo, I. **82** 24 20N 109 45E
Cerritos **82** 22 20N 100 20W
Cerro **79** 36 47N 105 36W
Cerro de Punta, Mt. **67** 18 10N 67 0W
Cerro Gordo **77** 39 53N 88 44W
Cervera **104** 41 40N 1 16E
Cervera del Río Alhama **104** 42 2N 1 58W
Cervione **103** 42 20N 9 29E
César □ **86** 9 0N 73 30W
Çesena **108** 44 9N 12 14E
Česke Budějovice **106** 48 55N 14 25E
Český TěV5n **107** 49 45N 18 39E
Cessnock **136** 32 50S 151 21E
Cetinje **109** 42 23N 18 59E
Ceuta **114** 35 52N 5 18W
Cévennes, mts. **102** 44 10N 3 50E
Ceylon **56** 49 27N 104 36W
Ceylon = Sri Lanka ■ **124** 7 30N 80 50E
Cha Pa. **128** 22 20N 103 47E
Chaati I. **62** 53 7N 132 30W
Chabeuil **103** 44 54N 5 1E
Chablais **103** 46 20N 6 36E
Chablis **101** 47 47N 3 48E
Chacabuco **88** 34 40S 60 27W
Chachapoyas **86** 6 15S 77 50W
Chachran **124** 28 55N 70 30E
Chaco □ **88** 25 0S 61 0W
Chaco Austral **90** 27 30S 61 40W
Chaco Boreal **88** 22 30S 60 10W
Chaco Central **90** 24 0S 61 0W
Chad ■ **114** 12 30N 17 15E
Chad, L. = Tchad, L. **114** 13 30N 14 30E
Chadan **121** 51 17N 91 35E
Chadileuvú, R. **88** 37 0S 65 55W
Chadron **74** 42 50N 103 0W
Chafurray **86** 3 10N 73 14W
Chagai **123** 29 30N 63 0E
Chagai Hills **124** 29 30N 63 0E
Chagda **121** 58 45N 130 30E
Chagny **101** 46 57N 4 45E
Chagos Arch. **16** 6 0S 72 0E
Chágres, R. **84** 9 5N 79 40W
Chãh Bahãr **123** 25 20N 60 40E
Chahar Buriak **124** 30 15N 62 0E
Chãhr-e Babak **123** 30 10N 55 20E
Chaibasa **125** 22 42N 85 49E
Chaillé-les-Marais **102** 46 25N 1 2W
Chaise-Dieu, La **102** 45 20N 3 40E
Chaize-le-Vicomté, La **100** 46 40N 1 18W
Chajari **88** 30 42N 58 0W
Chakhansur **124** 31 10N 62 0E
Chakonipau, L. **36** 56 18N 68 30W
Chakradharpur **125** 22 45N 85 40E
Chakwal **124** 32 50N 72 45E
Chala **86** 15 48S 74 20W
Chalainor **130** 49 31N 117 30E
Chalais **102** 45 16N 0 3E
Chalantun = Putehachi **130** 48 4N 122 45E
Chalcatongo **83** 17 4N 97 34W
Chalchihuites **82** 23 29N 103 53W
Chaleur B. **39** 47 55N 65 30W
Chalfant **80** 37 32N 118 21W
Chalhuanca **86** 14 15S 73 5W
Chaling **131** 26 47N 113 35E
Chalisgaon **124** 20 30N 75 10E
Chalk River **47** 46 1N 77 27W
Chalky Inlet **133** 46 3S 166 31E
Challans **100** 46 50N 1 52W
Challapata **86** 19 0S 66 50W
Challerange **101** 49 18N 4 46E
Challis **78** 44 32N 114 25W
Chalon-sur-Saône **101** 46 48N 4 50E
Chalonnes **100** 47 20N 0 45W
Châlons-sur-Marne **101** 48 58N 4 20E
Châlus **102** 45 39N 0 58E
Chaman **124** 30 58N 66 25E
Chamba, India **124** 32 35N 76 10E
Chamba, Tanz. **117** 11 37S 37 0E
Chambal, R. **124** 26 0N 76 55E
Chamberlain **74** 43 50N 99 21W
Chambers **79** 35 13N 109 30W
Chambersburg **72** 39 53N 77 41W
Chambéry **103** 45 34N 5 55E
Chambeshi, R. **116** 10 20S 31 58E
Chambly **45** 45 27N 73 17W
Chambly □ **45** 45 30N 73 30W
Chambly, Bassin de **45** 45 27N 73 17W
Chambois **100** 48 48N 0 6E
Chambon-Feugerolles, Le **103** 45 24N 4 18E
Châmbon, Le **103** 45 35N 4 26E
Chambord **41** 48 25N 72 6W
Chamboulive **102** 45 26N 1 42E
Chamdo **129** 31 21N 97 2E
Chamela **82** 19 32N 105 5W
Chamical **88** 30 22S 66 27W
Chamois **76** 38 41N 91 46W
Chamonix **103** 45 55N 6 51E
Chamouchouane, R. **41** 48 37N 72 20W
Champagne, Can. **54** 60 49N 136 30W
Champagne, France **101** 49 0N 4 40E
Champagnole **101** 46 45N 5 55E
Champaign **77** 40 8N 88 14W
Champain, L. **43** 44 45N 73 15W
Champaubert **101** 48 50N 3 45E
Champdeniers **102** 46 29N 0 25W
Champdoré, L. **36** 55 55N 65 49W
Champeix **102** 45 37N 3 8E
Champerico **84** 14 18N 91 55W
Champigny **42** 46 47N 71 21W
Champion, Can. **61** 50 14N 113 9W
Champion, U.S.A. **53** 46 31N 87 58W
Champion B. **134** 28 44S 114 36E
Champlain, Can. **35** 46 27N 72 24W
Champlain, U.S.A. **43** 44 59N 73 27W
Champlain, L. **71** 44 30N 73 20W
Champneuf **40** 48 35N 77 30W
Champotón **83** 19 20N 90 50W
Chan-chŏsujigjin **130** 40 21N 127 20E
Chañaral **88** 26 15S 70 50W
Chance Harbour **39** 45 7N 66 21W
Chanda **124** 19 57N 79 25E
Chandalar **67** 67 30N 148 35W
Chandeleur Sd. **75** 29 58N 88 40W
Chandigarh **124** 30 30N 76 58E
Chandler, Can. **38** 48 18N 64 46W
Chandler, Ariz., U.S.A. **79** 33 20N 111 56W
Chandler, Okla., U.S.A. **75** 35 43N 97 20W
Chandmani **129** 45 22N 98 2E
Chandpur **125** 22 8N 90 55E
Changanacheri **124** 9 25N 76 31E
Changane, R. **117** 23 30S 33 50E
Changchow, Fukien, China **131** 24 32N 117 44E
Changchow, Shantung, China **130** 36 55N 118 3E
Changchun **130** 43 58N 125 19E
Change Islands **37** 49 40N 54 25W
Changhua **131** 24 2N 120 30E
Changkiakow **130** 40 52N 114 45E
Changkiang **131** 21 7N 110 21E
Changkiang (Shihlu) **131** 19 25N 108 57E
Changkwansai Ling **130** 44 40N 129 0E
Changlo **131** 24 0N 115 33E
Changning **131** 26 25N 112 15E
Changpai Shan, mts. **130** 42 25N 129 0E
Changping **130** 40 15N 116 15E
Changpu **131** 24 2N 117 31E
Changsha **131** 28 5N 113 1E
Changshow **131** 29 49N 107 10E
Changshu **131** 31 33N 120 45E
Changtai **131** 24 34N 117 50E
Changteh **131** 29 12N 111 43E
Changting **131** 25 52N 116 20E
Changwu **130** 42 21N 122 45E
Changyeh **129** 38 56N 100 37E
Chankiang (Tsamkong) **131** 21 7N 110 21E
Channapatna **124** 12 40N 77 15E
Channel Is. **100** 49 30N 2 40W
Channel Islands **81** 33 30N 119 0W
Channel-Port aux Basques **37** 47 30N 59 9W
Channing, Mich., U.S.A. **72** 46 9N 88 1W
Channing, Tex., U.S.A. **75** 35 45N 102 20W
Chantada **104** 42 36N 7 46W
Chanthaburi **128** 12 38N 102 12E
Chantilly **101** 49 12N 2 29E
Chantonnay **100** 46 40N 1 3W
Chantrey Inlet **65** 67 48N 96 20W
Chanute **75** 37 45N 85 25W
Chanyi **129** 25 56N 104 1E
Chao Phraya, R. **128** 13 32N 100 36E
Chaoan **131** 23 41N 116 38E
Chaochow **131** 23 45N 116 32E
Chaohwa **131** 32 16N 105 41E
Chaoping **131** 24 1N 110 59E
Chaotung **129** 27 19N 103 42E
Chaoyan **130** 37 23N 120 29E
Chaoyang, Kwangtung, China **131** 23 10N 116 30E
Chaoyang, Liaoning, China **130** 41 46N 120 16E
Chap Kuduk **120** 48 45N 55 5E
Chapais **40** 49 47N 74 51W
Chapala, Lago de **82** 20 10N 103 20W
Chapayevo **120** 50 25N 51 10E
Chapayevsk **120** 53 0N 49 40E
Chapeau **40** 45 54N 77 4W
Chapecó **89** 27 14S 52 41W
Chapel Hill **73** 35 53N 79 3W
Chapelle-d'Angillon, La **101** 47 21N 2 25E
Chapelle Glain, La **100** 47 38N 1 11W
Chapleau **53** 47 50N 83 24W
Chaplin, Can. **56** 50 28N 106 40W
Chaplin, U.S.A. **76** 39 46N 90 24W
Chaplin L. **56** 50 22N 106 36W
Chapman, Mt. **63** 51 56N 118 20W
Chapra **125** 25 48N 84 50E
Chara **121** 56 54N 118 12E
Charadai **88** 27 35S 60 0W
Charagua **86** 19 45S 63 10W
Charak **123** 26 46N 54 18E
Charalá **86** 6 17N 73 10W
Charaña **86** 17 30S 69 35W
Charapita **86** 0 37S 74 21W
Charata **88** 27 13S 61 14W
Charcas **82** 23 10N 101 20W
Charchan **129** 38 4N 85 16E
Charcoal L. **55** 58 49N 102 22W
Charcot I. **91** 70 0S 75 0W
Chard, Can. **55** 55 55N 111 10W
Chard, U.K. **95** 50 52N 2 59W
Chardara **120** 41 16N 67 59E
Chardon **70** 41 34N 81 17W
Chardzhou **120** 39 6N 63 34E
Charente-Maritime □ **102** 45 30N 0 35W
Charente □ **102** 45 50N 0 16E
Charente, R. **102** 45 41N 0 30W
Charette **41** 46 27N 72 56W
Chari, R. **114** 13 0N 15 20E
Charikar **124** 35 0N 69 10E
Charité, La **101** 47 10N 3 0E
Chariton **76** 41 1N 93 19W
Chariton R. **76** 39 19N 92 58W
Charity I. **46** 44 3N 83 27W
Charkhlikh **129** 39 16N 88 17E
Charlemagne **45** 45 43N 73 29W
Charleroi **105** 50 24N 4 27E
Charlerol **70** 40 8N 79 54W
Charles, C. **72** 37 10N 75 52W
Charles City **76** 43 2N 92 41W
Charles L. **55** 59 50N 110 33W
Charles Town **72** 39 20N 77 50W
Charlesbourg **42** 46 51N 71 16W
Charleston, Ill., U.S.A. **77** 39 30N 88 10W
Charleston, Miss., U.S.A. **75** 34 2N 90 3W
Charleston, Mo., U.S.A. **75** 36 52N 89 20W
Charleston, S.C., U.S.A. **73** 32 47N 79 56W
Charleston, W. Va., U.S.A. **73** 38 24N 81 36W
Charleston L. **47** 44 32N 76 0W
Charleston Park **81** 36 17N 115 37W
Charleston Pk., mt. **81** 36 16N 115 42W
Charlestown **77** 38 29N 85 40W
Charlesville **116** 5 27S 20 59E
Charleswood **58** 49 51N 97 17W

Charleville Chinmu Chiao

Charleville 135 26 24 S 146 15 E
Charleville-Mézières 101 49 44N 4 40 E
Charleville = Rath Luirc 97 52 21N 8 40W
Charlevoix 46 45 19N 85 14W
Charlevoix, L. 46 45 15N 85 8W
Charlieu 103 46 10N 4 10 E
Charlo 39 47 59N 66 17W
Charlotte, Mich., U.S.A. 77 42 36N 84 48W
Charlotte, N.C., U.S.A. 73 35 16N 80 46W
Charlotte Amalie 85 18 22N 64 56W
Charlotte Harb. 73 26 45N 82 10W
Charlotte L. 62 52 12N 125 19W
Charlotte Waters 134 25 56 S 134 54 E
Charlottesville 72 38 1N 78 30W
Charlottetown 39 46 14N 63 8W
Charlton, Austral. 136 36 16 S 143 24 E
Charlton, U.S.A. 74 40 59N 93 20W
Charlton I. 36 52 0N 79 20W
Charmes 101 48 22N 6 17 E
Charnwood Forest 98 52 43N 1 18W
Charny 42 46 43N 71 15W
Charolles 103 46 27N 4 16 E
Charost 101 47 0N 2 7 E
Charron L. 57 52 44N 95 15W
Charroux 102 46 9N 0 25 E
Charters Towers 135 20 5 S 146 13 E
Chartre, La 100 47 42N 0 34 E
Chartres 100 48 29N 1 30 E
Chascomús 88 35 30 S 58 0W
Chase 63 50 50N 119 41W
Chasm 63 51 13N 121 30W
Chasseneuil-sur-Bonnieure 102 45 52N 0 29 E
Châtaigneraie, La 100 46 38N 0 45W
Château-Chinon 101 47 4N 3 56 E
Château-du-Loir 100 47 40N 0 25 E
Château Gontien 100 47 50N 0 42W
Château-la-Vallière 100 47 30N 0 20 E
Château-Landon 101 48 8N 2 40 E
Château, Le 102 45 52N 1 12W
Château Porcien 101 49 31N 4 13 E
Château Renault 100 47 36N 0 56 E
Château-Salins 101 48 50N 6 30 E
Château-Thierry 101 49 3N 3 20 E
Châteaubourg 100 48 7N 1 25W
Châteaubriant 100 47 43N 1 23W
Châteaudun 100 48 3N 1 20 E
Châteaugiron 100 48 3N 1 30W
Châteauguay 44 45 23N 73 45W
Châteauguay □ 44 45 11N 73 45W
Châteauguay-Centre 44 45 21N 73 45W
Châteauguay, L. 36 56 26N 70 3W
Châteauguay, R. 44 45 23N 73 45W
Châteaulin 100 48 11N 4 8W
Châteaumeillant 102 46 35N 2 12 E
Châteauneuf 100 48 35N 1 15 E
Châteauneuf-du-Faou 100 48 11N 3 50W
Châteauneuf-sur-Charente 102 45 36N 0 3W
Châteauneuf-sur-Cher 101 46 52N 2 18 E
Châteauneuf-sur-Loire 101 47 52N 2 13 E
Châteaurenard 103 43 53N 4 51 E
Châteauroux 101 46 50N 1 40 E
Châteauvert, L. 41 47 39N 73 56W
Châtelaillon-Plage 102 46 5N 1 5W
Châtelaudren 100 48 33N 2 59W
Chatelet 105 50 24N 4 32 E
Châtelet, Le, Cher, France 102 46 40N 2 20 E
Châtelet, Le, Seine-et-Marne, France 101 48 30N 2 47 E
Châtelguyon 102 45 55N 3 4 E
Châtellerault 100 46 50N 0 30 E
Châtelus-Malvaleix 102 46 18N 2 1 E
Chatham, N.B., Can. 39 47 2N 65 28W
Chatham, Ont., Can. 46 42 24N 82 11W
Chatham, U.K. 95 51 22N 0 32 E
Chatham, Alaska, U.S.A. 67 57 30N 135 0W
Chatham, Ill., U.S.A. 76 39 40N 89 42W
Chatham, La., U.S.A. 75 32 22N 92 26W
Chatham, Mich., U.S.A. 53 46 20N 86 56W
Chatham, N.Y., U.S.A. 71 42 21N 73 32W
Chatham Head 39 47 0N 65 33W
Chatham Is. 14 44 0 S 176 40W
Chatham Reach 66 49 15N 122 44W
Chatham Str. 54 57 0N 134 40W
Châtillon, Loiret, France 101 47 36N 2 44 E
Châtillon, Marne, France 101 49 5N 3 43 E
Châtillon-Coligny 101 47 50N 2 51 E
Châtillon-en-Bazois 101 47 3N 3 39 E
Châtillon-en-Diois 103 44 41N 5 29 E
Châtillon-sur-Seine 101 47 50N 4 33 E
Châtillon-sur-Sèvre 100 46 56N 0 45W
Chatrapur 125 19 22N 85 2 E
Châtre, La 102 46 35N 1 59 E
Chats, L. des 47 45 30N 76 20W
Chatsworth, Can. 46 44 27N 80 54W
Chatsworth, U.S.A. 77 40 45N 88 18W
Chattahoochee 73 30 43N 84 51W
Chattanooga 73 35 2N 85 17W
Chaudes-Aigues 102 44 51N 3 1 E
Chaudière, R. 41 46 45N 71 17W
Chauffailles 103 46 13N 4 20 E
Chaukan La 125 27 0N 97 15 E
Chaulnes 101 49 48N 2 47 E
Chaumont, France 101 48 7N 5 8 E
Chaumont, U.S.A. 71 44 4N 76 9W
Chaumont-en-Vexin 101 49 16N 1 53 E
Chaumont-sur-Loire 100 47 29N 1 11 E
Chaunay 102 46 13N 0 9 E
Chauny 101 49 37N 3 12 E
Chausey, Îs. 100 48 52N 1 49W
Chaussin 101 46 59N 5 22 E
Chautauqua 70 42 17N 79 30W
Chauvin 61 52 45N 110 10W
Chaux de Fonds, La 106 47 7N 6 50 E
Chaves, Brazil 87 0 15 S 49 55W
Chaves, Port. 104 41 45N 7 32W
Chavigny, L. 36 58 12N 75 8W
Chavuma 117 13 10 S 22 55 E
Chazelles-sur-Lyon 103 45 39N 4 22 E
Chazy 71 44 52N 73 28W
Cheam View 63 49 15N 121 40W
Cheb (Eger) 106 50 9N 12 20 E
Chebanse 77 41 0N 87 54W
Cheboksary 120 56 8N 47 30 E
Cheboygan 46 45 38N 84 29W
Checheng 131 34 4N 115 33 E
Checheno-Ingush, A.S.S.R. □ 120 43 30N 45 29 E
Checleset B. 62 50 5N 127 35W
Checotah 75 35 31N 95 30W
Chedabucto B. 39 45 25N 61 8W
Chedoke 48 43 14N 79 53W
Cheepash, R. 53 51 3N 80 59W
Cheepay, R. 53 51 25N 83 26W
Cheeseman L. 52 49 27N 89 20W
Chef-Boutonne 102 46 7N 0 4W
Chef, R. du 41 49 21N 73 25W
Chefornak 67 60 10N 164 15W
Chegdomyn 121 51 7N 132 52 E
Chegga 114 25 15N 5 40W
Chehalis 80 46 44N 122 59W
Cheju 131 33 28N 126 30 E
Cheju Do 131 33 29N 126 34 E
Chekiang □ 131 29 30N 120 0 E
Chelan, Can. 55 52 38N 103 22 E
Chelan, U.S.A. 78 47 49N 120 0W
Chelan, L. 63 48 5N 120 30W
Cheleken 120 39 26N 53 7 E
Chelforó 90 39 0 S 66 40W
Chelkar 120 47 40N 59 32 E
Chelkar Tengiz, Solonchak 120 48 0N 62 30 E
Chelles 101 48 52N 2 33 E
Chełm 107 51 8N 23 30 E
Chełmno 107 53 20N 18 30 E
Chelmsford 95 51 44N 0 29 E
Chełmża 107 53 10N 18 39 E
Chelsea, Austral. 136 38 5 S 145 8 E
Chelsea, Can. 48 45 30N 75 47W
Chelsea, Mich., U.S.A. 77 42 19N 84 1W
Chelsea, Okla., U.S.A. 75 36 35N 95 35W
Chelsea, Vermont, U.S.A. 71 43 59N 72 27W
Cheltenham, Can. 49 43 45N 79 55W
Cheltenham, U.K. 95 51 55N 2 5W
Chelyabinsk 120 55 10N 61 24 E
Chelyuskin, C. 118 77 30N 103 0 E
Chemainus 63 48 55N 123 48W
Chemillé 100 47 14N 0 45W
Chemnitz = Karl-Marx-Stadt 106 50 50N 12 55 E
Chemor 128 4 44N 101 6 E
Chemult 78 43 14N 121 54W
Chemung 71 42 2N 76 37W
Chen, Gora 121 65 10N 141 20 E
Chenab, R. 124 30 40N 73 30 E
Chenango Forks 71 42 15N 75 51W
Chencha 115 6 15N 37 32 E
Chêne, R. du 44 45 33N 73 54W
Chénéville 40 45 53N 75 3W
Cheney 78 47 38N 117 34W
Chenfeng 131 25 25N 105 51 E
Chengan 131 28 30N 107 30 E
Chengchow 131 34 47N 113 46 E
Chengho 131 27 25N 118 46 E
Chenghsien 131 29 30N 120 40 E
Chengkiang 129 24 58N 102 59 E
Chengkung 131 27 8N 108 57 E
Chengpu 131 26 12N 110 5 E
Chengteh 130 41 0N 117 55 E
Chengtu 129 30 45N 104 0 E
Chenhsien 131 25 46N 112 59 E
Chenil, L. 38 51 51N 59 41W
Chenkán 83 19 8N 90 58W
Chenki 131 28 1N 110 2 E
Chenning 131 25 57N 105 51 E
Chenoa 77 40 45N 88 42W
Chentung 130 46 2N 123 1 E
Chenyuan, Kansu, China 130 35 59N 107 2 E
Chenyuan, Kweichow, China 131 27 0N 108 20 E
Cheo Reo = Hau Bon 128 13 25N 108 28 E
Cheom Ksan 128 14 13N 104 56 E
Chepén 86 7 10 S 79 15W
Chepes 88 31 20 S 66 35W
Chepo 84 9 10N 79 6W
Chequamegon B. 74 46 40N 90 30W
Cher □ 101 47 10N 2 30 E
Chér, R. 101 47 10N 2 10 E
Cheraw 73 34 42N 79 54W
Cherbourg 100 49 39N 1 40W
Cherdyn 120 60 24N 56 29 E
Cheremkhovo 121 53 32N 102 40 E
Cherepanovo 120 54 15N 83 30 E
Cherepovets 120 59 5N 37 55 E
Cherhill 60 53 49N 114 41W
Cherkassy 120 49 30N 32 0 E
Cherlak 120 54 15N 74 55 E
Chernigov 120 51 28N 31 20 E
Chernogorsk 121 54 5N 91 10 E
Chernovtsy 120 48 0N 26 0 E
Chernoye 121 70 30N 89 10 E
Chernyakhovsk 120 54 29N 21 48 E
Chernyshevskiy 121 62 40N 112 30 E
Cherokee, Iowa, U.S.A. 74 42 40N 95 30W
Cherokee, Okla., U.S.A. 75 36 45N 98 25W
Cherokees, L. O'The 75 36 50N 95 12W
Cherquenco 90 38 35 S 72 0W
Cherrapunji 125 25 17N 91 47 E
Cherry Creek, Can. 63 50 43N 120 40W
Cherry Creek, Nev., U.S.A. 78 39 50N 114 58W
Cherry Creek, N.Y., U.S.A. 70 42 18N 79 6W
Cherry Valley 81 33 59N 116 57W
Cherryvale 75 37 20N 95 33W
Cherryville 63 50 15N 118 37W
Cherrywood 51 43 52N 79 8W
Cherskiy 121 68 45N 161 18 E
Cherskogo Khrebet 121 65 0N 143 0 E
Cherwell, R. 95 51 46N 1 18W
Chesaning 46 43 11N 84 7W
Chesapeake Bay 72 38 0N 76 12W
Chesha B. = Cheshskaya G. 120 67 20N 47 0 E
Cheshire □ 94 53 14N 2 30W
Chesil Beach 98 50 37N 2 33W
Cheslatta 62 53 48N 125 48W
Cheslatta L. 62 53 49N 125 20W
Chesley 46 44 17N 81 5W
Chesne, Le 101 49 30N 4 45 E
Chester, Can. 39 44 33N 64 15W
Chester, U.K. 94 53 12N 2 53W
Chester, Calif., U.S.A. 78 40 22N 121 22W
Chester, Ill., U.S.A. 76 37 58N 89 50W
Chester, Mont., U.S.A. 78 48 31N 111 0W
Chester, N.Y., U.S.A. 71 41 22N 74 16W
Chester, Pa., U.S.A. 72 39 54N 75 20W
Chester, S.C., U.S.A. 73 34 44N 81 13W
Chesterfield 94 53 14N 1 26W
Chesterfield I. 117 16 20 S 43 58 E
Chesterfield, Îles 135 19 52 S 158 15 E
Chesterfield In. 65 63 25N 90 45W
Chesterfield Inlet 65 63 30N 90 45W
Chesterville 47 45 6N 75 14W
Chesuncook L. 35 46 0N 69 10W
Chéticamp 39 46 37N 60 59W
Chetumal 83 18 30N 88 20W
Chetumal, Bahía de 83 18 40N 88 10W
Chetwynd 54 55 45N 121 45W
Chevanceaux 102 45 18N 0 14W
Cheviot 77 39 10N 84 37W
Cheviot Hills 94 55 20N 2 30W
Cheviot, The 94 55 29N 2 8W
Chew Bahir 115 4 40N 30 50 E
Chewelah 63 48 17N 117 43W
Cheyenne, Okla., U.S.A. 75 35 35N 99 40W
Cheyenne, Wyo., U.S.A. 74 41 9N 104 49W
Cheyenne, R. 74 44 50N 101 0W
Cheyenne Wells 74 38 51N 102 23W
Cheylard, Le 103 44 55N 4 25 E
Chezacut 62 52 24N 124 1W
Chhang 126 12 15N 104 14 E
Chhatarpur 124 24 55N 79 43 E
Chhindwara 124 22 2N 78 59 E
Chhlong 128 12 15N 105 58 E
Chi, R. 128 15 11N 104 43 E
Chiai 131 23 29N 120 25 E
Chiang Mai 128 18 47N 98 59 E
Chianie 117 15 35 S 13 40 E
Chiapa de Corzo 83 16 42N 93 0W
Chiapa, R. 83 16 42N 93 0W
Chiapas □ 83 17 0N 92 45W
Chiautla 83 18 18N 98 34W
Chiba 132 35 30N 140 7 E
Chiba-ken □ 132 35 30N 140 20 E
Chibemba 117 15 48 S 14 8 E
Chibougamau 41 49 56N 74 24W
Chibougamau L. 41 49 50N 74 20W
Chibougamau, Parc Prov. de 41 49 15N 73 45W
Chibougamau, R. 40 49 42N 75 57W
Chic-Chocs, Mts. 38 48 55N 66 0W
Chic-Chocs, Parc Prov. des 38 48 55N 66 20W
Chicago 77 41 53N 87 40W
Chicago Heights 77 41 29N 87 37W
Chichagof I. 54 58 0N 136 0W
Chichén Itzá 83 20 40N 88 32W
Chichester 95 50 50N 0 47W
Chichibu 132 36 5N 139 10 E
Chichirin 130 50 35N 123 45 E
Chichiriviche 86 10 56N 68 16W
Chichow 130 38 30N 115 25 E
Chickasha 75 35 0N 98 0W
Chicken Hd. 94 58 10N 6 15W
Chiclana de la Frontera 104 36 26N 6 9W
Chiclayo 86 6 42 S 79 50W
Chico 80 39 45N 121 54W
Chico, R., Chubut, Argent. 78 44 0 S 67 0W
Chico, R., Santa Cruz, Argent. 90 49 30 S 69 30W
Chicoa 117 15 35 S 32 20 E
Chicobi, L. 40 48 53N 78 30W
Chicontepec 83 20 58N 98 10W
Chicopee 71 42 6N 72 37W
Chicot 44 45 36N 73 56W
Chicoutimi 35 48 28N 71 5W
Chicoutimi, Parc Prov. de 41 48 30N 70 20W
Chidambaram 124 11 20N 79 45 E
Chidley C. 36 60 23N 64 26W
Chiefs Pt. 46 44 41N 81 18W
Chiengi 116 8 45 S 29 10 E
Chiese, R. 108 45 45N 10 35 E
Chieti 108 42 22N 14 10 E
Chignecto B. 39 45 30N 64 40W
Chignecto, Cape 39 45 20N 64 57W
Chignik 67 56 15N 158 27W
Chigorodó 86 7 41N 76 42W
Chigoubiche, L. 41 49 7N 73 30W
Chiguana 88 21 0 S 67 50W
Chihfeng 130 42 18N 118 57 E
Chihing 131 25 2N 113 45 E
Chihkiang, Hunan, China 131 27 21N 109 45 E
Chihkiang, Hupei, China 131 30 25N 111 30 E
Chihkin 131 26 30N 105 45 E
Chihli, G. of (Po Hai) 130 38 30N 119 0 E
Chihsien (Weihwei) 131 35 29N 114 1 E
Chihuahua 82 28 40N 106 3W
Chihuahua □ 82 28 40N 106 3W
Chihuatlán 82 19 14N 104 35W
Chik Ballapur 124 13 25N 77 45 E
Chikmagalur 124 13 15N 75 45 E
Chilac 83 18 20N 97 24W
Chilako, R. 62 53 53N 122 57W
Chilanko Forks 62 52 7N 124 5W
Chilanko, R. 62 52 7N 123 41W
Chilapa 83 17 40N 99 20W
Chilas 124 35 25N 74 5 E
Chilaw 124 7 30N 79 50 E
Chilco 62 54 3N 123 49W
Chilcotin, R. 63 51 44N 122 23W
Childers 135 25 15 S 152 17 E
Childress 75 34 30N 100 15W
Chile ■ 90 35 0 S 71 15W
Chilecito 88 29 0 S 67 40W
Chilete 86 7 10 S 78 50W
Chilhowee 76 38 36N 93 51W
Chililabombwe (Bancroft) 117 12 18 S 27 43 E
Chilka L. 125 19 40N 85 25 E
Chilko, L. 62 51 20N 124 10W
Chilko, R. 62 52 6N 123 40W
Chillagoe 135 17 14 S 144 33 E
Chillán 88 36 40 S 72 10W
Chillicothe, Ill., U.S.A. 76 40 55N 89 32W
Chillicothe, Mo., U.S.A. 76 39 45N 93 30W
Chillicothe, Ohio, U.S.A. 72 39 20N 82 58W
Chilliwack 63 49 10N 122 0W
Chiloé, I. de 90 42 50 S 73 45W
Chilpancingo 83 17 30N 99 40W
Chiltern Hills 95 51 44N 0 42W
Chilton 72 44 1N 88 12W
Chiluage 116 9 15 S 21 42 E
Chilung 131 25 3N 121 45 E
Chilwa, L. (Shirwa) 117 15 15 S 35 40 E
Chimacum 78 48 1N 122 53W
Chimai 129 33 35N 102 10 E
Chimaltitán 82 21 46N 103 50W
Chimán 84 8 45N 78 40W
Chimay 105 50 3N 4 20 E
Chimbay 120 42 57N 59 47 E
Chimborazo 86 1 20 S 78 55W
Chimbote 86 9 0 S 78 35W
Chimkent 120 42 18N 69 36 E
Chin □ 125 22 0N 93 0 E
Chin Chai 131 31 58N 115 59 E
China 82 25 40N 99 20W
China ■ 129 30 0N 110 0 E
China Lake 81 35 44N 117 37W
Chinacates 82 25 0N 105 14W
Chinacota 86 7 37N 72 36W
Chinandega 84 12 30N 87 0W
Chinati Pk. 75 30 0N 104 25W
Chincha Alta 86 13 20 S 76 0W
Chinchaga, R. 60 58 53N 118 20W
Chinchón 104 40 9N 3 26W
Chinchorro, Banco 83 18 35N 87 20W
Chinchow 130 41 10N 121 2 E
Chincoteague 72 37 58N 75 21W
Chinde 117 18 45 S 36 30 E
Chindwin, R. 125 21 26N 95 15 E
Ching Ho, R. 131 34 20N 109 0 E
Chinghai □ 129 36 0N 97 0 E
Chingola 117 12 31 S 27 53 E
Chinguar 117 12 18 S 16 45 E
Chiniot 124 31 45N 73 0 E
Chinipas 82 27 22N 108 32W
Chinkiang 131 32 2N 119 29 E
Chinle 79 36 14N 109 38W
Chinmu Chiao 131 18 10N 109 35 E

Chinnampo Clinton

Chinnampo 130 38 52N 125 28E
Chino 81 34 1N 117 41W
Chino Valley 79 34 54N 112 28W
Chinon 100 47 10N 0 15E
Chinook, Can. 61 51 28N 110 59W
Chinook, U.S.A. 78 48 35N 109 19W
Chinook Valley 60 56 29N 117 39W
Chinsali 116 10 30S 32 2E
Chinwangtao 130 40 0N 119 31E
Chióggia 108 45 13N 12 15E
Chip L. 60 53 40N 115 23W
Chip Lake 54 53 35N 115 35W
Chipai L. 54 52 56N 87 53W
Chipata (Ft. Jameson) 117 13 38S 32 28E
Chipewyan L. 55 58 0N 98 27W
Chipley 73 30 45N 85 32W
Chipman, Alta., Can. 60 53 42N 112 38W
Chipman, N.B., Can. 39 46 6N 65 53W
Chipman L. 53 49 58N 86 15W
Chippawa 49 43 5N 79 2W
Chippenham 95 51 27N 2 7W
Chippewa Falls 74 44 55N 91 22W
Chippewa, R. 74 44 45N 91 55W
Chiputneticook Lakes 39 45 37N 67 40W
Chiquian 86 10 10S 77 0W
Chiquimula 84 14 51N 89 37W
Chiquinquirá 86 5 37N 73 50W
Chirala 124 15 50N 80 20E
Chiras 123 35 14N 65 40E
Chirchik 120 41 29N 69 35E
Chiricahua Pk. 79 31 53N 109 14W
Chirikof I. 67 55 50N 155 40W
Chiriquí, Golfo de 84 8 0N 82 10W
Chiriquí, Lago de 84 9 10N 82 0W
Chiriquí, Vol. 84 8 55N 82 35W
Chirmiri 125 23 15N 82 20E
Chiromo 117 16 30S 35 7E
Chirripó Grande, cerro 84 9 29N 83 29W
Chisamba 117 14 55S 28 20E
Chisapani Garhi 125 27 30N 84 2E
Chishan 131 22 44N 120 31E
Chisholm, Can. 60 54 55N 114 10W
Chisholm, U.S.A. 52 47 29N 92 53W
Chisos Mts. 75 29 20N 103 15W
Chistopol 120 55 25N 50 38E
Chita, Colomb. 86 6 11N 72 28W
Chita, U.S.S.R. 121 52 0N 113 25E
Chitado 117 17 10S 14 8E
Chitek 56 53 48N 107 45W
Chitek L., Man., Can. 57 52 25N 99 25W
Chitek L., Sask., Can. 56 53 45N 107 47W
Chitembo 117 13 30S 16 50E
Chitina 67 61 30N 144 30W
Chitokoloki 117 13 43S 23 4E
Chitorgarh 124 24 52N 74 43E
Chitral 124 35 50N 71 56E
Chitré 85 7 59N 80 27W
Chittagong 125 22 19N 91 55E
Chittagong □ 125 24 5N 91 25E
Chittoor 124 13 15N 79 5E
Chiusi 108 43 1N 11 58E
Chivasso 108 45 10N 7 52E
Chivilcoy 88 35 0S 60 0W
Chkalov = Orenburg 120 52 0N 55 5E
Chloride 81 35 25N 114 12W
Choahsien 130 37 48N 114 46E
Chocó □ 86 6 0N 77 0W
Chocontá 86 5 9N 73 41W
Choele Choel 90 39 11S 65 40W
Choelquoit L. 62 51 42N 124 12W
Choiceland 56 53 29N 104 29W
Choiseul I. 14 7 0S 156 40E
Choisy 44 45 29N 74 13W
Choisy-le-Roi 101 48 45N 2 24E
Choix 82 26 40N 108 10W
Chojnice 107 53 42N 17 40E
Chokurdakh 121 70 38N 147 55E
Cholame 80 35 44N 120 18W
Cholet 100 47 4N 0 52W
Choluteca 84 13 20N 87 14W
Choluteca, R. 84 13 5N 87 20W
Choma 117 16 48S 26 59E
Chomedey 44 45 32N 73 45W
Chomutov 106 50 28N 13 23E
Chŏnan 130 36 48N 127 9E
Chonburi 128 13 21N 101 1E
Chone 86 0 40S 80 0W
Chongjin 130 41 47N 129 50E
Chŏngju 130 36 39N 127 27E
Chŏnju 130 35 50N 127 4E
Chonos, Arch. de los 90 45 0S 75 0W
Chopim, R. 89 25 35S 53 5W
Chorley 94 53 39N 2 39W
Chorolque, Cerro 88 20 59S 66 5W
Chorrera, La 84 8 50N 79 50W
Chŏrwŏn 130 38 15N 127 10E
Chorzów 107 50 18N 19 0E
Chos-Malal 88 37 15S 70 5W
Choshi 132 35 45N 140 45E
Choszczno 106 53 7N 15 25E
Choteau 78 47 50N 112 10W
Chotila 124 22 30N 71 15E
Chow Hu 131 31 35N 117 30E
Chowchilla 80 37 11N 120 12W
Choybalsan 130 48 3N 114 28E
Choyr 130 46 24N 108 30E
Chrisman 77 39 48N 87 41W
Christchurch, N.Z. 133 43 33S 172 47E
Christchurch, U.K. 95 50 44N 1 47W
Christian I. 46 44 50N 80 12W
Christiana 117 27 52S 25 8E
Christiansted 85 17 45N 64 42W
Christie B. 55 62 32N 111 10W
Christies Corners 49 43 16N 80 2W
Christina, L. 63 49 3N 118 12W
Christina, R. 60 56 40N 111 3W
Christmas I., Ind. Oc. 16 10 0S 105 40E
Christmas I., Pac. Oc. 15 1 58N 157 27W
Christopher Lake 56 53 32N 105 48W
Chu 120 43 36N 73 42E
Chu Chua 63 51 22N 120 10W
Chu Kiang 131 22 15N 113 45E
Chu, R. 128 19 53N 105 45E
Chuanchow 131 24 57N 118 31E
Chuanhsien 131 25 50N 111 12E
Chūbu □ 132 36 45N 137 30E
Chubut, R. 90 43 0S 70 0W
Chuchi L. 54 55 12N 124 30W
Chuchow 131 27 56N 113 3E
Chuchow (Lishui) 131 28 30N 119 50E
Chugach Mts. 67 62 0N 146 0W
Chugiak 67 61 7N 149 10W
Chuginadak I. 67 52 50N 169 45W
Chūgoku □ 132 35 0N 133 0E
Chūgoku-Sanchi 132 35 0N 133 0E
Chugwater 74 41 48N 104 47W
Chuho = Shangchih 130 45 10N 127 59E
Chuhsien, Chekiang, China 130 28 57N 118 58E
Chuhsien, Shantung, China 131 35 31N 118 45E
Chuhsien, Szechwan, China 131 30 51N 107 1E
Chukai 128 4 13N 103 25E
Chuki, Chekiang, China 131 29 30N 120 4E
Chuki, Hupei, China 131 32 26N 110 0E
Chukotskiy Khrebet 121 68 0N 175 0E
Chukotskiy, Mys 121 66 10N 169 3E
Chukotskoye More 121 68 0N 175 0W
Chula 76 39 55N 93 29W
Chula Vista 81 32 39N 117 8W
Chulucanas 86 5 0S 80 0W
Chumatien 131 33 0N 114 4E
Chumbicha 88 29 0S 66 10W
Chumikan 121 54 40N 135 10E
Chumphon 128 10 35N 99 14E
Chunchŏn 130 37 58N 127 44E
Chungan 131 27 45N 118 0E
Chunghsien 131 30 17N 108 4E
Chungking 131 29 30N 106 30E
Chungsiang 131 31 14N 112 42E
Chunya 116 8 30S 33 27E
Chuquibamba 86 15 47N 72 44W
Chuquicamata 88 22 15S 69 0W
Chuquisaca □ 88 23 30S 63 30W
Chur 106 46 52N 9 32E
Churachandpur 125 24 20N 93 40E
Church House 54 50 20N 125 10W
Churchbridge 57 50 54N 101 54W
Churchill 55 58 47N 94 11W
Churchill, C. 55 58 46N 93 12W
Churchill Falls 36 53 36N 64 19W
Churchill L., Ont., Can. 52 50 50N 91 10W
Churchill L., Sask., Can. 55 55 55N 108 20W
Churchill Pk. 54 58 10N 125 10W
Churchill, R., Man., Can. 55 58 47N 94 12W
Churchill, R., Newf., Can. 36 53 19N 60 10W
Churchill, R., Sask., Can. 55 58 47N 94 12W
Churdan 76 42 9N 94 29W
Churu 124 28 20N 75 0E
Churubusco 77 41 14N 85 19W
Churuguaro 86 10 49N 69 32W
Chusan 131 30 0N 122 20E
Chushul 124 33 40N 78 40E
Chusnan 131 32 14N 110 30E
Chusovoy 120 58 15N 57 40E
Chute-à-Blondeau 43 45 35N 74 28W
Chute-aux-Outardes 41 49 7N 68 24W
Chute-des-Passes 41 49 52N 71 16W
Chuting 131 27 28N 113 1E
Chuvash A.S.S.R. □ 120 55 30N 48 0E
Chwangho 130 39 41N 123 2E
Cibola 81 33 17N 114 9W
Cicero 72 41 48N 87 48W
Ciechanów 107 52 52N 20 38E
Ciego de Avila 84 21 50N 78 50W
Ciénaga 86 11 1N 74 15W
Ciénaga de Oro 86 8 53N 75 37W
Cienfuegos 84 22 10N 80 30W
Cierp 102 42 55N 0 40E
Cieszyn 107 49 45N 18 35E
Cieza 104 38 17N 1 23W
Cijulang 127 7 42S 108 27E
Cikampek 127 6 23S 107 28E
Cilacap 127 7 43S 109 0E
Cilician Gates P. 122 37 20N 34 52E
Cilician Taurus 122 36 40N 34 0E
Cima 81 35 14N 115 30W
Cimarron, Kans., U.S.A. 75 37 50N 100 20W
Cimarron, N. Mex., U.S.A. 75 36 30N 104 52W
Cimarron, R. 75 37 10N 102 10W
Cimone, Mte. 108 44 10N 10 40E
Cîmpina 107 45 10N 25 45E
Cîmpulung 107 45 17N 25 3E
Cinca, R. 104 42 20N 0 9E
Cinch, R. 73 36 0N 84 15W
Cincinnati, Iowa, U.S.A. 76 40 38N 92 56W
Cincinnati, Ohio, U.S.A. 77 39 10N 84 26W
Cinto, Mt. 103 42 24N 8 54E
Ciotat, La 103 43 12N 5 36E
Circle, Alaska, U.S.A. 67 65 50N 144 10W
Circle, Montana, U.S.A. 74 47 26N 105 35W
Circleville, Ohio, U.S.A. 72 39 35N 82 57W
Circleville, Utah, U.S.A. 79 38 12N 112 24W
Cirebon 127 6 45S 108 32E
Cirencester 95 51 43N 1 59W
Cirey-sur-Vezouze 101 48 35N 6 57E
Cisco 75 32 25N 99 0W
Cisne 77 38 31N 88 26W
Cisneros 86 6 33N 75 4W
Cissna Park 77 40 34N 87 54W
Citlaltépetl, mt. 83 19 0N 97 20W
City View, Ont., Can. 48 45 21N 75 45W
City View, Sask., Can. 58 50 28N 104 37W
Ciudad Acuña 82 29 20N 101 10W
Ciudad Altamirano 82 18 20N 100 40W
Ciudad Bolívar 86 8 5N 63 30W
Ciudad Camargo 82 27 41N 105 10W
Ciudad de Valles 83 22 0N 98 30W
Ciudad del Carmen 83 18 20N 97 50W
Ciudad Delicias = Delicias 82 28 10N 105 30W
Ciudad Guerrero 82 28 33N 107 28W
Ciudad Guzmán 82 19 40N 103 30W
Ciudad Juárez 82 31 40N 106 28W
Ciudad Madero 83 22 19N 97 50W
Ciudad Mante 83 22 50N 99 0W
Ciudad Obregón 82 27 28N 109 59W
Ciudad Piar 86 7 27N 63 19W
Ciudad Real 104 38 59N 3 55W
Ciudad Rodrigo 104 40 35N 6 32W
Ciudad Trujillo = Sto. Domingo 85 18 30N 70 0W
Ciudad Victoria 83 23 41N 99 9W
Civitanova Marche 108 43 18N 13 41E
Civitavécchia 108 42 6N 11 46E
Civray 102 46 10N 0 17E
Çivril 122 38 20N 29 55E
Cizre 122 37 19N 42 10E
Clacton-on-Sea 95 51 47N 1 10E
Clairambault, L. 36 54 29N 69 0W
Claire 41 47 15N 68 40W
Claire, L. 54 58 35N 112 5W
Claire, Le 76 41 36N 90 21W
Clairemont 75 33 9N 100 44W
Clairmont 60 55 16N 118 47W
Clairton 70 40 18N 79 54W
Clairvaux-les-Lacs 103 46 35N 5 45E
Clallam Bay 80 48 15N 124 16W
Clamecy 101 47 28N 3 30E
Clandonald 60 53 34N 110 44W
Clanton 73 32 48N 86 36W
Clanwilliam, Can. 57 50 22N 99 49W
Clanwilliam, S. Afr. 117 32 11S 18 52E
Clapperton I. 46 46 0N 82 14W
Clappisons Corners 48 43 18N 79 55W
Clara 97 53 20N 7 38W
Claraville 81 35 24N 118 20W
Clare, Austral. 136 33 50S 138 37E
Clare, U.S.A. 46 43 47N 84 45W
Clare □ 97 52 20N 7 38W
Clare I. 97 53 48N 10 0W
Clare, I. 97 53 48N 10 0W
Clare, R. 97 53 20N 9 0W
Claremont, Can. 51 43 58N 79 7W
Claremont, U.S.A. 71 43 23N 72 20W
Claremore 75 36 40N 95 20W
Claremorris 97 53 45N 9 0W
Clarence 76 39 45N 92 16W
Clarence I. 91 61 30S 53 50W
Clarence, I. 90 54 0S 72 0W
Clarence, R., Austral. 135 29 25S 153 22E
Clarence, R., N.Z. 133 42 10S 173 56E
Clarence Str., Austral. 134 12 0S 131 0E
Clarence Str., U.S.A. 54 55 40N 132 10W
Clarence Town 85 23 6N 74 59W
Clarenceville 43 45 4N 73 15W
Clarendon, Can. 39 45 29N 66 26W
Clarendon, Ark., U.S.A. 75 34 41N 91 20W
Clarendon, Tex., U.S.A. 75 34 58N 100 54W
Clarenville 37 48 10N 54 1W
Claresholm 61 50 0N 113 45W
Clarie Coast 91 67 0S 135 0E
Clarinda 74 40 45N 95 0W
Clarion, Iowa, U.S.A. 76 42 41N 93 46W
Clarion, Pa., U.S.A. 70 41 12N 79 22W
Clarion, R. 70 41 19N 79 10W
Clark 74 44 55N 97 45W
Clark Fork 78 48 9N 116 9W
Clark Fork, R. 78 48 0N 115 40W
Clark Hill Res. 73 33 45N 82 20W
Clark, Pt. 46 44 4N 81 45W
Clarkdale 79 34 53N 112 3W
Clarke City 38 50 12N 66 38W
Clarke, I. 135 40 32S 148 10E
Clarke L. 56 54 24N 106 54W
Clarkefield 136 37 30S 44 40E
Clark's Fork, R. 78 45 0N 109 30W
Clark's Harbour 39 43 25N 65 38W
Clarks Summit 71 41 31N 75 44W
Clarksburg 72 39 18N 80 21W
Clarksdale 75 34 12N 90 33W
Clarkson 50 43 31N 79 37W
Clarkston 78 46 28N 117 2W
Clarksville, Ark., U.S.A. 75 35 29N 93 27W
Clarksville, Iowa, U.S.A. 76 42 47N 92 40W
Clarksville, Mich., U.S.A. 77 42 50N 85 15W
Clarksville, Ohio, U.S.A. 77 39 24N 83 59W
Clarksville, Tenn., U.S.A. 73 36 32N 87 20W
Clarksville, Tex., U.S.A. 75 33 37N 94 59W
Clatskanie 80 46 9N 123 12W
Claude, Can. 49 43 47N 79 54W
Claude, U.S.A. 75 35 8N 101 22W
Claveria 127 18 37N 121 15E
Clay 80 38 17N 121 10W
Clay Center 74 39 27N 97 9W
Clay City, Ind., U.S.A. 77 39 17N 87 7W
Clay City, Ky., U.S.A. 77 37 52N 83 55W
Clay L. 52 50 3N 93 30W
Clayette, La 103 46 17N 4 19E
Claypool 79 33 27N 110 55W
Claysville 70 40 5N 80 25W
Clayton, Idaho, U.S.A. 78 44 12N 114 31W
Clayton, Ind., U.S.A. 77 39 41N 86 31W
Clayton, N. Mex., U.S.A. 75 36 30N 103 10W
Cle Elum 78 47 15N 120 57W
Clear L. 80 39 5N 122 47W
Clear C. 97 51 26N 9 30W
Clear I. 97 51 26N 9 30W
Clear, L. 47 45 26N 77 12W
Clear Lake, S.D., U.S.A. 74 44 48N 96 41W
Clear Lake, Wash., U.S.A. 78 48 27N 122 15W
Clear Lake City 76 43 8N 93 23W
Clear Lake Res. 78 41 55N 121 10W
Clear, R. 60 56 11N 119 42W
Clearfield, Iowa, U.S.A. 76 40 48N 94 29W
Clearfield, Pa., U.S.A. 72 41 0N 78 27W
Clearfield, Utah, U.S.A. 78 41 10N 112 0W
Clearlake Highlands 80 38 57N 122 38W
Clearmont 78 44 43N 106 29W
Clearwater, Can. 63 51 38N 120 2W
Clearwater, U.S.A. 73 27 58N 82 45W
Clearwater Cr. 54 61 36N 125 30W
Clearwater L. 63 52 15N 120 13W
Clearwater, Mts. 78 46 20N 115 30W
Clearwater Prov. Park 57 54 0N 101 0W
Clearwater, R., Alta., Can. 60 56 44N 111 23W
Clearwater, R., Alta., Can. 61 52 22N 114 57W
Clearwater, R., B.C., Can. 63 51 38N 120 3W
Cleburne 75 32 18N 97 25W
Clee Hills 98 52 26N 2 35W
Cleethorpes 94 53 33N 0 2W
Cleeve Cloud 95 51 56N 2 0W
Cleeve Hill 95 51 54N 2 0W
Clelles 103 44 50N 5 38E
Clementsport 39 44 40N 65 37W
Clendale 77 39 16N 84 28W
Clerks Rocks 91 56 0S 36 30W
Clermont, Austral. 135 22 49S 147 39E
Clermont, Can. 41 47 41N 70 14W
Clermont-en-Argonne 101 49 5N 5 4E
Clermont-Ferrand 102 45 46N 3 4E
Clermont-l'Hérault 102 43 38N 3 26E
Clerval 101 47 25N 6 30E
Cléry-Saint-André 101 47 50N 1 46E
Cleveland, U.K. 94 54 29N 1 0W
Cleveland, Miss., U.S.A. 75 33 43N 90 43W
Cleveland, Ohio, U.S.A. 70 41 28N 81 43W
Cleveland, Okla., U.S.A. 75 36 21N 96 33W
Cleveland, Tenn., U.S.A. 73 35 9N 84 52W
Cleveland, Tex., U.S.A. 75 30 18N 95 0W
Cleveland □ 94 54 35N 1 8E
Cleveland, C. 135 19 11S 147 1E
Cleveland Heights 70 41 32N 81 30W
Clevelândia 89 26 24S 52 23W
Cleves 77 39 10N 84 45W
Clevvaux 105 50 4N 6 2E
Clew Bay 97 53 54N 9 50W
Clewiston 73 26 44N 80 50W
Clifden, Ireland 97 53 30N 10 2W
Clifden, N.Z. 133 46 1S 167 42E
Cliff 79 33 0N 108 44W
Cliffdell 80 46 44N 120 42W
Clifton, Ariz., U.S.A. 79 33 8N 109 23W
Clifton, Ill., U.S.A. 77 40 56N 87 56W
Clifton, Tex., U.S.A. 75 31 46N 97 35W
Clifton Forge 72 37 49N 79 51W
Climax 56 49 10N 108 20W
Clingmans Dome 73 35 35N 83 30W
Clint 79 31 37N 106 11W
Clinton, B.C., Can. 63 51 6N 121 35W
Clinton, Ont., Can. 46 43 37N 81 32W
Clinton, N.Z. 133 46 12S 169 23E

Clinton **Concots**

Clinton, Ark., U.S.A. 75 35 37N 92 30W
Clinton, Ill., U.S.A. 74 40 8N 89 0W
Clinton, Ind., U.S.A. 77 39 40N 87 22W
Clinton, Iowa, U.S.A. 76 41 50N 90 12W
Clinton, Mass., U.S.A. 71 42 26N 71 40W
Clinton, Mo., U.S.A. 76 38 20N 93 46W
Clinton, N.C., U.S.A. 73 35 5N 78 15W
Clinton, Okla., U.S.A. 75 35 30N 99 0W
Clinton, S.C., U.S.A. 73 34 30N 81 54W
Clinton, Tenn., U.S.A. 73 36 6N 84 10W
Clinton, Wash., U.S.A. 80 47 59N 122 22W
Clinton, Wis., U.S.A. 77 42 34N 88 52W
Clinton Colden L. 64 64 58N 107 27W
Clinton Creek 64 64 25N 140 37W
Clintonville 74 44 35N 88 46W
Clisson 100 47 5N 1 16W
Clive 61 52 28N 113 27W
Clive L. 54 63 13N 118 54W
Clodomira 88 27 35S 64 14W
Clonakilty 97 51 37N 8 53W
Clonakilty B. 97 51 33N 8 50W
Cloncurry 135 20 40S 140 28E
Clones 97 54 10N 7 13W
Clonmel 97 52 22N 7 42W
Cloquet 52 46 40N 92 30W
Cloquet, R. 52 46 52N 92 35W
Clorinda 88 25 16S 57 45W
Cloud Peak 78 44 30N 107 10W
Cloudcroft 79 33 0N 105 48W
Clova 40 48 7N 75 22W
Clover Pt. 63 48 24N 123 21W
Cloverdale, B.C., Can. 66 49 7N 122 44W
Cloverdale, N.B., Can. 39 46 17N 67 22W
Cloverdale, Calif., U.S.A. 80 38 49N 123 0W
Cloverdale, Ind., U.S.A. 77 39 31N 86 47W
Cloverport 77 37 50N 86 38W
Clovis, Calif., U.S.A. 80 36 54N 119 45W
Clovis, N. Mex., U.S.A. 75 34 20N 103 10W
Cloyne 47 44 49N 77 11W
Cluculz L. 62 53 53N 123 33W
Cluj 107 46 47N 23 38E
Cluny 103 46 26N 4 38E
Cluses 103 46 5N 6 35E
Clutha, R. 133 46 20S 169 49E
Clwyd □ 94 53 5N 3 20W
Clwyd, R. 94 53 12N 3 30W
Clyde, Alta., Can. 60 54 9N 113 39W
Clyde, N.W.T., Can. 65 70 30N 68 30W
Clyde, Ont., Can. 49 43 22N 80 14W
Clyde, N.Z. 133 45 12S 169 20E
Clyde, N.Y., U.S.A. 70 43 8N 76 52W
Clyde, Ohio, U.S.A. 76 41 18N 82 59W
Clyde, Firth of 96 55 20N 5 0W
Clyde, R., Can. 39 43 35N 65 27W
Clyde, R., U.K. 96 55 46N 4 58W
Clyde River 39 43 38N 65 29W
Clydebank 96 55 54N 4 25W
Clymer 70 42 3N 79 39W
Coachella 81 33 44N 116 13W
Coachella Canal 81 32 43N 114 57W
Coachman's Cove 35 50 6N 56 20W
Coacoachou, L. 38 50 25N 60 14W
Coahoma 75 32 17N 101 20W
Coahuayana, R. 82 18 41N 103 45W
Coahuayutla 82 18 19N 101 42W
Coahuila □ 82 27 0N 112 30W
Coal City 77 41 17N 88 17W
Coal Creek 61 49 30N 114 59W
Coal Harbour 62 50 36N 127 35W
Coal, R. 54 59 39N 126 57W
Coalcomán 82 18 40N 103 10W
Coaldale 61 49 45N 112 35W
Coalgate 75 34 35N 96 13W
Coalhurst 61 49 45N 112 56W
Coalinga 80 36 10N 120 21W
Coalmont 63 49 32N 120 42W
Coalspur 54 53 15N 117 0W
Coalville, U.K. 94 52 43N 1 21W
Coalville, U.S.A. 78 40 58N 111 24W
Coamo 67 18 5N 66 22W
Coari 86 4 8S 63 7W
Coast Mts. 62 52 0N 126 0W
Coast Range 80 40 0N 124 0W
Coastal Plains Basin 134 30 10S 115 30E
Coatbridge 96 55 52N 4 2W
Coatepec 83 19 27N 96 58W
Coatepeque 84 14 46N 91 55W
Coatesville 72 39 59N 75 55W
Coaticook 41 45 10N 71 46W
Coats I. 65 62 30N 83 0W
Coats Land 91 77 0S 25 0W
Coatzacoalcos 83 18 7N 94 35W
Cobalt 34 47 25N 79 42W
Cobán 84 15 30N 90 21W
Cobar 136 31 27S 145 48E
Cobaz, L. 38 51 15N 60 21W
Cobden 47 45 38N 76 53W
Cóbh 97 51 50N 8 18W
Cobija 86 11 0S 68 50W
Cobleskill 71 42 40N 74 30W
Coboconk 47 44 39N 78 48W
Cobourg 47 43 58N 78 10W
Cobourg Pen. 134 11 20S 132 15E
Cobram 136 35 54S 145 40E
Cobre 78 41 6N 114 25W
Cóbué 117 12 0S 34 58E
Coburg 106 50 15N 10 58E
Coburg I. 65 75 57N 79 26W
Coca, R. 86 0 25S 77 5W
Cocagne 39 46 20N 64 37W
Cocha, La 88 27 50S 65 40W
Cochabamba 86 17 15S 66 20W
Coche, I. 86 10 47N 63 56W
Cochenour 52 51 5N 93 48W
Cochilha Grande de Albardão 89 28 30S 51 30W
Cochin China = Nam-Phan 128 10 30N 106 0E
Cochise 79 32 6N 109 58W
Cochran 73 32 25N 83 23W
Cochrane, Alta., Can. 61 51 11N 114 30W
Cochrane, Ont., Can. 34 49 0N 81 0W
Cochrane, L. 90 47 10S 72 0W
Cochrane, R. 55 57 53N 101 34W
Cockatoo I. 134 16 6S 123 37E
Cockburn 136 32 5S 141 0E
Cockburn, Canal 90 54 30S 72 0W
Cockburn, C. 65 74 52N 79 24W
Cockburn I. 46 45 55N 83 22W
Coco Chan. 128 13 50N 93 25E
Coco, Pta. 86 2 58N 77 43W
Coco, R. (Wanks) 84 14 10N 85 0W
Coco Solo 84 9 22N 79 53W
Cocoa 73 28 22N 80 40W
Cocobeach 116 0 59N 9 34E
Cocos, Is. 16 12 10S 96 50E
Cocos (Keeling) Is. 11 12 12S 96 54E
Cod, C. 72 42 8N 70 10W
Cod I. 36 57 47N 61 47W
Codajás 86 3 40S 62 0W
Codera, C. 86 10 35N 66 4W
Coderre 56 50 11N 106 31W
Codette 56 53 16N 104 0W
Codó 87 4 30S 43 55W
Codroy 37 47 53N 59 24W
Codroy Pond 37 48 4N 58 52W
Cody 78 44 35N 109 0W
Coe Hill 47 44 52N 77 50W
Coelemu 88 36 30S 72 48W
Coen 135 13 52S 143 12E
Coesfeld 105 51 56N 7 10E
Coetivy Is. 16 7 8S 56 16E
Coeur d'Alene 78 47 45N 116 51W
Coffeyville 75 37 0N 95 40W
Coffs Harbour 135 30 16S 153 5E
Cofre de Perote, Cerro 83 19 30N 97 10W
Coghinas, R. 108 40 55N 8 48E
Cognac 102 45 41N 0 20W
Cohagen 78 47 2N 106 45W
Cohasset 52 47 18N 93 39W
Cohoes 71 42 47N 73 42W
Cohuna 136 35 45S 144 15E
Coiba I. 84 7 30N 81 40W
Coig, R. 90 51 0S 70 20W
Coimbatore 124 11 2N 76 59E
Coimbra 104 40 15N 8 27W
Coin 104 36 40N 4 48W
Coin-Rond 45 45 38N 73 13W
Cojedes □ 86 9 20N 68 20W
Cojimies 86 0 20N 80 0W
Cojutepequé 84 13 41N 88 54W
Cokeville 78 42 4N 111 0W
Colac 136 38 21S 143 35E
Colbinabbin 136 36 38S 144 48E
Colborne 47 44 0N 77 53W
Colby 74 39 27N 101 2W
Colchagua □ 88 34 30S 71 0W
Colchester 95 51 54N 0 55E
Cold L. 60 54 33N 110 5W
Cold Lake 60 54 27N 110 10W
Coldstream 96 55 39N 2 14W
Coldwater, Can. 46 44 42N 79 40W
Coldwater, Kans., U.S.A. 75 37 18N 99 24W
Coldwater, Mich., U.S.A. 77 41 57N 85 0W
Coldwater, Ohio, U.S.A. 77 40 29N 84 38W
Coldwater, L. 77 41 48N 84 59W
Coldwell 34 48 45N 86 30W
Cole Camp 76 38 28N 93 12W
Colebrook, Can. 66 49 6N 122 52W
Colebrook, U.S.A. 71 44 54N 71 29W
Coleman, Can. 61 49 40N 114 30W
Coleman, Mich., U.S.A. 46 43 46N 84 35W
Coleman, Tex., U.S.A. 75 31 52N 99 30W
Coleman, R. 135 15 6S 141 38E
Coleraine, Austral. 136 37 36S 141 40E
Coleraine, Can. 50 43 49N 79 41W
Coleraine, U.K. 97 55 8N 6 40E
Coleraine, U.S.A. 52 47 17N 93 27W
Coleraine □ 97 55 8N 6 40E
Coleridge, L. 133 43 17S 171 30E
Colesberg 117 30 45S 25 5E
Colesburg 76 42 38N 91 12W
Coleville, Can. 56 51 43N 109 15W
Coleville, U.S.A. 80 38 44N 119 30W
Colfax, Calif., U.S.A. 80 39 6N 120 57W
Colfax, Ill., U.S.A. 77 40 34N 88 37W
Colfax, Ind., U.S.A. 77 40 12N 86 40W
Colfax, La., U.S.A. 75 31 35N 92 39W
Colfax, Wash., U.S.A. 78 46 57N 117 28W
Colhué Huapi, L. 90 45 30S 69 0W
Colima 82 19 10N 103 40W
Colima □ 82 19 10N 103 40W
Colima, Nevado de 82 19 30N 103 40W
Colina 88 33 13S 70 45W
Colinas 87 6 0S 44 10W
Colinet 37 47 13N 53 33W
Colinton, Austral. 136 35 50S 149 10E
Colinton, Can. 60 54 37N 113 15W
Coll, I. 96 56 40N 6 35W
Collaguasi 88 21 5S 68 45W
Collbran 79 39 16N 107 58W
College Bridge 39 45 59N 64 33W
College Heights 61 52 28N 113 45W
College Park 73 33 42N 84 27W
Collette 35 46 40N 65 30W
Colleymount 62 54 2N 126 19W
Collie 134 33 22S 116 8E
Collier B. 134 16 10S 124 15E
Collingwood, Can. 46 44 29N 80 13W
Collingwood, N.Z. 133 40 25S 172 40E
Collingwood Corner 39 45 37N 63 56W
Collins, Can. 52 50 17N 89 27W
Collins, U.S.A. 76 37 54N 93 37W
Collinson Pen 65 69 58N 101 24W
Collinsville, Austral. 135 20 30S 147 56E
Collinsville, U.S.A. 76 38 40N 89 59W
Collipulli 88 37 55S 72 30W
Collonges 103 46 9N 5 52E
Collooney 97 54 11N 8 28W
Colmar 101 48 5N 7 20E
Colmars 103 44 11N 6 39E
Colmor 75 36 18N 104 36W
Colne 94 53 51N 2 11W
Colnett, Cabo 82 31 0N 116 20W
Colo, R. 136 33 25S 150 52E
Cologne = Koln 105 50 56N 9 58E
Colombey-les-Belles 101 48 32N 5 54E
Colombey-les-Deux Églises 101 48 20N 4 50E
Colombia 86 3 24N 79 49W
Colombia ■ 86 3 45N 73 0W
Colombier 41 48 52N 68 51W
Colombo 124 6 56N 79 58E
Colombus, Kans., U.S.A. 75 37 15N 94 30W
Colombus, Nebr., U.S.A. 74 41 30N 97 25W
Colombus, N.Mex., U.S.A. 79 31 54N 107 43W
Colome 74 43 20N 99 44W
Colón, Argent. 88 32 12S 58 30W
Colón, Cuba 84 22 42N 80 54W
Colón, Panama 84 9 20N 80 0W
Colonel Hill 85 22 50N 74 21W
Colonia del Sacramento 89 34 25S 57 50W
Colonia Dora 88 28 34S 62 59W
Colonia Las Heras 90 46 30S 69 0W
Colonia Sarmiento 90 45 30S 68 15W
Colonial Hts. 72 37 19N 77 25W
Colonial Village 49 43 12N 78 59W
Colonsay 56 51 59N 105 52W
Colonsay, I. 96 56 4N 6 12W
Colorado □ 68 37 40N 106 0W
Colorado Aqueduct 81 34 17N 114 10W
Colorado City 75 32 25N 100 50W
Colorado Desert 68 34 20N 116 0W
Colorado, I. 84 9 12N 79 50W
Colorado Plateau 79 36 40N 110 30W
Colorado, R., Argent. 88 37 30S 69 0W
Colorado, R., Ariz., U.S.A. 79 33 30N 114 30W
Colorado, R., Calif., U.S.A. 79 34 0N 114 33W
Colorado, R., Tex., U.S.A. 75 29 40N 96 30W
Colorado Springs 74 38 55N 104 50W
Colotepec 83 15 47N 97 3W
Colotlán 82 22 6N 103 16W
Colquitz 63 48 29N 123 24W
Colton, Calif., U.S.A. 81 34 4N 117 20W
Colton, N.Y., U.S.A. 71 44 34N 74 58W
Colton, Wash., U.S.A. 78 46 41N 117 6W
Columa 80 38 48N 120 53W
Columbia, Ill., U.S.A. 76 38 26N 90 12W
Columbia, La., U.S.A. 75 32 7N 92 5W
Columbia, Miss., U.S.A. 75 31 16N 89 50W
Columbia, Mo., U.S.A. 76 38 58N 92 20W
Columbia, Pa., U.S.A. 71 40 2N 76 30W
Columbia, S.C., U.S.A. 73 34 0N 81 0W
Columbia, Tenn., U.S.A. 73 35 40N 87 0W
Columbia, C. 17 83 0N 70 0W
Columbia City 77 41 8N 85 30W
Columbia, District of □ 72 38 55N 77 0W
Columbia Falls 78 48 25N 114 16W
Columbia Heights 74 45 5N 93 10W
Columbia L. 61 50 15N 115 52W
Columbia, Mt. 63 52 8N 117 20W
Columbia Plateau 78 47 30N 118 30W
Columbia, R. 78 45 49N 120 0W
Columbiana 70 40 53N 80 40W
Columbiaville 46 43 9N 83 25W
Columbretes, Is. 104 39 50N 0 50E
Columbus, Can. 51 43 59N 78 55W
Columbus, Ga., U.S.A. 73 32 30N 84 58W
Columbus, Ind., U.S.A. 72 39 14N 85 55W
Columbus, Miss., U.S.A. 73 33 30N 88 26W
Columbus, Mont., U.S.A. 78 45 45N 109 14W
Columbus, N.D., U.S.A. 56 48 52N 102 48W
Columbus, Ohio, U.S.A. 77 39 57N 83 1W
Columbus, Tex., U.S.A. 75 29 42N 96 33W
Columbus, Wis., U.S.A. 74 43 20N 89 2W
Columbus Grove 77 40 55N 84 4W
Columbus Junction 76 41 17N 91 22W
Colusa 80 39 15N 122 1W
Colville 63 48 33N 117 54W
Colville, C. 133 36 29S 175 21E
Colville Lake 64 67 2N 126 7W
Colville, R. 67 69 15N 152 0W
Colwood 63 48 26N 123 29W
Colwyn Bay 94 53 17N 3 44W
Com-Est 44 45 27N 74 7W
Comácchio 108 44 41N 12 10E
Comalcalco 83 18 16N 93 13W
Comallo 90 41 0S 70 5W
Comanche, Okla., U.S.A. 75 34 27N 97 58W
Comanche, Tex., U.S.A. 75 31 55N 98 35W
Comayagua 84 14 25N 87 37W
Combahee, R. 73 32 45N 80 50W
Combeaufontaine 101 47 38N 5 54E
Comber 46 42 14N 82 33W
Combermere 47 45 22N 77 37W
Comblain 105 50 29N 5 35E
Combles 101 50 0N 2 50E
Combourg 100 48 25N 1 46W
Combronde 102 45 58N 3 5E
Come by Chance 37 47 51N 54 0W
Comeragh Mts. 97 52 17N 7 35W
Comilla 125 23 28N 91 10E
Comino I. 108 36 0N 14 22E
Comitán 83 16 18N 92 9W
Commanda 46 45 57N 79 36W
Commentry 102 46 20N 2 46E
Commerce, Ga., U.S.A. 73 34 10N 83 25W
Commerce, Tex., U.S.A. 75 33 15N 95 50W
Commercy 101 48 40N 5 34E
Commissaires, L. des 41 48 10N 72 16W
Commissioner I. 57 52 10N 97 16W
Committee B. 65 68 30N 86 30W
Commonwealth B. 91 67 0S 144 0E
Communism Pk. = Kommunisma, Pk. 123 38 40N 72 20E
Como 108 45 48N 9 5E
Como, L. di 108 46 5N 9 17E
Comodoro Rivadavia 90 45 50S 67 40W
Comores, Arch. des 11 10 0S 50 0E
Comores, Is. 11 12 10S 44 15E
Comorin, C. 124 8 3N 77 40E
Comoro Is. 11 12 10S 44 15E
Comox 62 49 42N 124 55W
Compeer 61 51 52N 110 0W
Compiègne 101 49 24N 2 50E
Compostela 82 21 15N 104 53W
Comprida, I. 89 24 50S 47 42W
Compton, Can. 41 45 14N 71 49W
Compton, U.S.A. 81 33 54N 118 13W
Côn Dao 128 8 45N 106 45E
Conakry 114 9 29N 13 49W
Conatlán 82 24 30N 104 42W
Concarneau 100 47 52N 3 56W
Conceiç o da Barra 87 18 35S 39 45W
Conceiç o do Araguaia 87 8 0S 49 2W
Concepción, Argent. 88 27 20S 65 35W
Concepción, Boliv. 86 15 50S 61 40W
Concepción, Chile 88 36 50S 73 0W
Concepción, Colomb. 86 0 5N 75 37W
Concepción, Mexico 83 18 15N 90 5W
Concepción, Parag. 88 23 30S 57 20W
Concepción, Venez. 86 10 48N 71 46W
Concepción □ 88 37 0S 72 30W
Concepcion, C. 68 34 30N 120 34W
Concepción del Oro 82 24 40N 101 30W
Concepción del Uruguay 88 32 35S 58 20W
Concepción, L. 86 17 20S 61 10W
Concepción, Punta 82 26 55N 111 50W
Concepción, R. 82 30 32N 113 2W
Conception B., Can. 37 47 45N 53 0W
Conception B., Namibia 117 23 55S 14 22E
Conception I. 85 23 52N 75 9W
Concepcion, La 40 46 9N 74 42W
Conchas Dam 75 35 25N 104 10W
Conche 37 50 48N 55 58W
Concho 79 34 32N 109 43W
Concho, R. 75 31 30N 100 8W
Conchos, R., Chihnahua, Mexico 82 29 20N 105 0W
Conchos, R., Tamaulipas, Mexico 83 25 0N 97 32W
Concon 88 32 56S 71 33W
Conconully 63 48 31N 119 45W
Concord, Can. 50 43 48N 79 29W
Concord, Calif., U.S.A. 80 37 59N 122 2W
Concord, Mich., U.S.A. 77 42 11N 84 38W
Concord, N.C., U.S.A. 73 35 28N 80 35W
Concord, N.H., U.S.A. 71 43 12N 71 30W
Concórdia, Argent. 88 31 20S 58 2W
Concórdia, Brazil 86 4 36S 66 36W
Concordia, Colomb. 86 2 39N 72 47W
Concordia, Mexico 82 23 18N 106 2W
Concordia, U.S.A. 76 38 59N 93 34W
Concordia, Kans., U.S.A. 74 39 35N 97 40W
Concordia, La 83 16 8N 92 38W
Concots 102 44 26N 1 40E

Concrete **Craon**

Concrete **63** 48 35N 121 49W
Condamine, R. **135** 27 7 S 149 48 E
Condat **102** 45 21N 2 46 E
Condé **101** 50 26N 3 34 E
Conde **74** 45 13N 98 5W
Condé-sur-Noireau **100** 48 51N 0 33W
Condeúba **87** 15 0 S 42 0W
Condie Res. **58** 50 34N 104 43W
Condobolin **136** 33 4 S 147 6 E
Condom **102** 43 57N 0 22 E
Condon **78** 45 15N 120 8W
Conejos **82** 26 14N 103 53W
Conemaugh, R. **70** 40 24N 79 0W
Conestogo **49** 43 32N 80 30W
Conflans-en-Jarnisy **101** 49 10N 5 52 E
Confolens **102** 46 2N 0 40 E
Confuso, R. **88** 24 10 S 59 0W
Congleton **94** 53 10N 2 12W
Congnarauya **36** 58 35N 68 1W
Congo ■ **116** 1 0 S 16 0 E
Congo Basin **112** 0 10 S 24 30 E
Congo (Kinshasa) ■ =
 Zaïre ■ **116** 1 0 S 16 0 E
Congo, R. = Zaïre, R. **116** 1 30N 28 0 E
Congonhas **89** 20 30 S 43 52W
Congress **79** 34 11N 112 56W
Congucu **113** 31 25 S 52 30W
Coniston **46** 46 29N 80 51W
Conjeevaram =
 Kanchipuram **124** 12 52N 79 45 E
Conklin **60** 55 38N 111 5W
Conn, L. **97** 54 3N 9 15W
Connacht **97** 53 23N 8 40W
Conneaut **70** 41 55N 80 32W
Connecticut □ **71** 41 40N 72 40W
Connecticut, R. **71** 41 17N 72 21W
Connell **78** 46 45N 118 58W
Connemara **97** 53 29N 9 45W
Conner, La **78** 48 22N 122 27W
Connersville **77** 39 40N 85 10W
Connolsville **70** 40 5N 79 32W
Connors **41** 47 10N 68 52W
Conoble **136** 32 55 S 144 42 E
Conon, R. **96** 57 33N 4 45W
Cononaco, R. **86** 1 20 S 76 30W
Conquest **56** 51 32N 107 14W
Conquet, Le **100** 48 21N 4 46W
Conrad, Iowa, U.S.A. **76** 42 14N 92 52W
Conrad, Mont., U.S.A. **78** 48 11N 112 0W
Conroe **75** 30 15N 95 28W
Consecon **47** 44 0N 77 31W
Conselheiro Lafaiete **89** 20 40 S 43 48W
Conshohocken **71** 40 5N 75 18W
Consort **61** 52 1N 110 46W
Constanţa **107** 44 14N 28 38 E
Constantina **104** 37 51N 5 40W
Constantine, Alg. **114** 36 25N 6 42 E
Constantine, U.S.A. **77** 41 50N 85 40W
Constitución, Chile **88** 35 20 S 72 30W
Constitución, Uruguay **88** 31 0 S 58 10W
Consul **56** 49 20N 109 30W
Contact **78** 41 50N 114 56W
Contai **125** 21 54N 87 55 E
Contamana **86** 7 10 S 74 55W
Contas, R. **87** 13 5 S 41 53W
Contes **103** 43 49N 7 19 E
Contin L. **57** 53 25N 95 10W
Continental **77** 41 6N 84 16W
Contoocook **71** 43 13N 71 45W
Contrecoeur **43** 45 51N 73 14W
Contres **100** 47 24N 1 26 E
Contrexéville **101** 48 6N 5 53 E
Contwoyto L. **64** 65 42N 110 50W
Convención **86** 8 28N 73 21W
Converse **77** 40 34N 85 52W
Convoy **77** 40 55N 84 43W
Conway, Ark., U.S.A. **75** 35 5N 92 30W
Conway, N.H., U.S.A. **71** 43 58N 71 8W
Conway, S.C., U.S.A. **73** 33 49N 79 2W
Conway = Conwy **94** 53 17N 3 50W
Conway, R. = Conwy **94** 53 10N 3 50W
Conwy **94** 53 17N 3 50W
Conwy, R. **94** 53 18N 3 50W
Coober Pedy **134** 29 1 S 134 43 E
Cooch Behar **125** 26 22N 89 29 E
Cook **52** 47 49N 92 39W
Cook, Bahía **90** 55 10 S 70 0W
Cook Inlet **67** 59 0N 151 0W
Cook Is. **15** 20 0 S 160 0W
Cook, Mt. **133** 43 36 S 170 9 E
Cook Strait **133** 41 15 S 174 29 E
Cookeville **73** 36 12N 85 30W
Cooking L. **60** 53 26N 113 2W
Cook's Harbour **37** 51 36N 55 52W
Cookshire **41** 45 25N 71 38W
Cookstown **97** 54 40N 6 43W
Cookstown □ **97** 54 40N 6 43W
Cooksville **50** 43 36N 79 35W
Cooktown **135** 15 30 S 145 16 E
Coolah **136** 31 48 S 149 41 E
Coolamon **136** 34 46 S 147 8 E
Coolgardie **134** 30 55 S 121 8 E
Coolidge **79** 33 1N 111 35W
Coolidge Dam **79** 33 10N 110 30W
Cooma **136** 36 12 S 149 8 E
Coombs **62** 49 18N 124 25W
Coon Rapids **76** 41 53N 94 41W
Coonabarabran **136** 31 14 S 149 18 E
Coonamble **135** 30 56 S 148 27 E
Coondapoor **124** 13 42N 74 40 E
Cooper **75** 33 20N 95 40W
Cooper, R. **73** 33 0N 79 55W
Cooperstown, N.D.,
 U.S.A. **74** 47 30N 98 14W
Cooperstown, N.Y.,
 U.S.A. **71** 42 42N 74 57W
Coopersville **77** 43 4N 85 57W
Coorong, The **135** 35 50 S 139 20 E
Coos Bay **78** 43 26N 124 7W
Cootamundra **136** 34 36 S 148 1 E
Cootehill **97** 54 5N 7 5W
Copahué, Paso **88** 37 49 S 71 8W
Copainalá **83** 17 8N 93 11W
Copán **84** 14 50N 89 9W
Cope **74** 39 44N 102 50W
Copenhagen =
 København **111** 55 41N 12 34 E
Copetown **49** 43 14N 80 4W
Copiapó **88** 27 15 S 70 20 E
Copiapó, R. **88** 27 19 S 70 56W
Copp L. **54** 60 14N 114 40W
Copper Center **67** 62 10N 145 25W
Copper Cliff **46** 46 28N 81 4W
Copper Harbor **53** 47 31N 87 55W
Copper Mountain **54** 49 20N 120 30W
Copper, R. **67** 61 30N 144 30W
Coppermine **64** 67 50N 115 5W
Coppermine, R. **64** 67 49N 115 4W
Copperopolis **80** 37 58N 120 38W
Coquet, R. **94** 55 18N 1 45W
Coquille **78** 43 15N 124 6W
Coquimbo **88** 30 0 S 71 20W
Coquimbo □ **88** 31 0 S 71 0W
Coquitlam, R. **66** 49 13N 122 48W
Corabia **107** 43 48N 24 30 E
Coracora **86** 15 5 S 73 45W
Coral Harbour **65** 64 8N 83 10W
Coral Rapids **34** 50 20N 81 40W
Coral Sea **135** 15 0 S 150 0 E
Coral Sea Islands Terr. **135** 20 0 S 155 0 E
Corangamite, L. **136** 38 0 S 143 30 E
Coraopolis **70** 40 30N 80 10W
Corato **108** 41 12N 16 22 E
Corbeil-Essonnes **101** 48 36N 2 26 E
Corbie **101** 49 54N 2 30 E
Corbières, mts. **102** 42 55N 2 35 E
Corbigny **101** 47 16N 3 40 E
Corbin, Can. **43** 45 3N 73 41W
Corbin, U.S.A. **72** 37 0N 84 3W
Corby, Lincs., U.K. **95** 52 49N 0 31W
Corby, Northants.,
 U.K. **95** 52 29N 0 41W
Corcoran **80** 36 6N 119 35W
Corcubión **104** 42 56N 9 12W
Cord. de Caravaya **86** 14 0 S 70 30W
Cordele **73** 31 55N 83 49W
Cordell **75** 35 18N 99 0W
Cordes **102** 44 5N 1 57 E
Cordillera Oriental **86** 5 0N 74 0W
Córdoba, Argent. **88** 31 20 S 64 10W
Córdoba, Mexico **83** 18 50N 97 0W
Córdoba, Spain **104** 37 50N 4 50W
Córdoba □, Argent. **88** 31 22 S 64 15W
Córdoba □, Colomb. **86** 8 20N 75 40W
Córdoba, Sierra de **88** 31 10 S 64 25W
Cordon **127** 16 42N 121 32 E
Cordova, Ala., U.S.A. **73** 33 45N 87 12W
Cordova, Alaska,
 U.S.A. **67** 60 36N 145 45W
Cordova, Ill., U.S.A. **76** 41 41N 90 19W
Corfu = Kerkira **109** 39 38N 19 50 E
Coricudgy, Mt. **136** 32 51 S 150 24 E
Corigliano Cálabro **108** 39 36N 16 31 E
Corinth, Ky., U.S.A. **77** 38 30N 84 34W
Corinth, Miss., U.S.A. **73** 34 54N 88 30W
Corinth, N.Y., U.S.A. **71** 43 15N 73 50W
Corinto, Brazil **87** 18 20 S 44 30W
Corinto, Nic. **84** 12 30N 87 10W
Cork **97** 51 54N 8 30W
Cork □ **97** 51 50N 8 50W
Cork Harbour **97** 51 46N 8 16W
Corlay **100** 48 20N 3 5W
Çorlu **122** 41 11N 27 49 E
Cormack **37** 49 18N 57 23W
Cormack L. **54** 60 56N 121 37W
Cormorant **57** 54 14N 100 35W
Cormorant L. **57** 54 15N 100 50W
Corn Is. **85** 12 0N 83 0W
Cornelio **82** 29 55N 111 8W
Cornélio Procópio **89** 23 7 S 50 40W
Cornell, U.S.A. **74** 45 10N 91 8W
Cornell, U.S.A. **77** 40 58N 88 43W
Corner Brook **37** 48 57N 57 58W
Corner Inlet **136** 38 45 S 146 20 E
Corning, Can. **56** 49 58N 102 58W
Corning, Ark., U.S.A. **75** 36 27N 90 34W
Corning, Calif., U.S.A. **78** 39 56N 122 9W
Corning, Iowa, U.S.A. **76** 40 57N 94 40W
Corning, N.Y., U.S.A. **70** 42 10N 77 3W
Cornwall, Can. **39** 46 14N 63 13W
Cornwall, Ont., Can. **47** 45 2N 74 44W
Cornwall □ **95** 50 26N 4 40W
Cornwall I. **65** 77 37N 94 38W
Cornwallis I. **65** 75 8N 95 0W
Coro **86** 11 25N 69 41W
Coroatá **87** 4 20 S 44 0W
Corocoro **86** 17 15 S 69 19W
Coroico **86** 16 0 S 67 50W
Coromandel **133** 36 45 S 175 31 E
Coromandel Coast **124** 12 30N 81 0 E
Corona, Calif., U.S.A. **81** 33 49N 117 36W
Corona, N. Mex.,
 U.S.A. **79** 34 15N 105 32W
Coronach **56** 49 7N 105 31W
Coronada B. **84** 9 0N 83 40W
Coronadas, Is. de **81** 32 25N 117 15W
Coronado **81** 32 45N 117 9W
Coronado, Bahía de **84** 9 0N 83 40W
Coronation **61** 52 5N 111 27W
Coronation Gulf **64** 68 25N 112 0W
Coronation I., Antarct. **91** 60 45 S 46 0W
Coronation I., U.S.A. **54** 55 52N 134 20W
Coronda **88** 31 58 S 60 56W
Coronel **88** 37 0 S 73 10W
Coronel Bogado **88** 27 11 S 56 18W
Coronel Dorrego **88** 38 40 S 61 10W
Coronel Oviedo **88** 25 24 S 56 30W
Coronel Pringles **88** 38 0 S 61 30W
Coronel Suárez **88** 37 30 S 62 0W
Coronel Vidal **88** 37 28 S 57 45W
Coronie **87** 5 55N 56 25W
Corowa **136** 35 58 S 146 21 E
Corozal, Belize **83** 18 30N 88 30W
Corozal, Colomb. **86** 9 19N 75 18W
Corozal, Pan. C. Z. **84** 8 59N 79 34W
Corps **103** 44 50N 5 56 E
Corpus **89** 27 10 S 55 30W
Corpus Christi **75** 27 50N 97 28W
Corpus Christi L. **75** 28 5N 97 54W
Corque **86** 18 10 S 67 50W
Corrèze □ **102** 45 20N 1 45 E
Corrib, L. **97** 53 25N 9 10W
Corrientes **88** 27 30 S 58 45W
Corrientes □ **88** 28 0 S 57 0W
Corrientes, C., Colomb. **86** 5 30N 77 34W
Corrientes, C., Cuba **84** 21 43N 84 30W
Corrientes, C., Mexico **82** 20 25N 105 42W
Corrientes, R., Argent. **88** 30 21 S 59 33W
Corrientes, R., Colomb. **86** 3 15 S 75 58W
Corrigan **75** 31 0N 94 48W
Corry **70** 41 55N 79 39W
Corse, C. **103** 43 1N 9 25 E
Corse-du-Sud □ **103** 41 45N 9 0 E
Corse, Î **103** 42 0N 9 0 E
Corsica = Corse **103** 42 0N 9 0 E
Corsicana **75** 32 5N 96 30W
Corté **103** 42 19N 9 11 E
Cortez **79** 37 24N 108 35W
Cortland **71** 42 35N 76 11W
Cortona **108** 43 16N 12 0 E
Çorum **122** 40 30N 35 5 E
Corumbá, Goias, Brazil **87** 16 0 S 48 50W
Corumbá, Mato Grosso,
 Brazil **86** 19 0 S 57 30W
Coruña, La **104** 43 20N 8 25W
Corunna, Can. **46** 42 53N 82 26W
Corunna, U.S.A. **46** 42 59N 84 7W
Corunna = La Coruña **104** 43 20N 8 25W
Coruripe **87** 10 5 S 36 10W
Corvallis **78** 44 36N 123 15W
Corvette, L. de la **36** 53 25N 74 3W
Corwhin **49** 43 31N 80 6W
Corydon, Ind., U.S.A. **77** 38 13N 86 7W
Corydon, Iowa, U.S.A. **76** 40 42N 93 22W
Corydon, Ky., U.S.A. **77** 37 44N 87 43W
Cosalá **82** 24 28N 106 40W
Cosamaloapán **83** 18 23N 95 50W
Cosenza **108** 39 17N 16 14 E
Coshocton **70** 40 17N 81 51W
Cosne-s.-Loire **101** 47 24N 2 54 E
Coso Junction **81** 36 3N 117 57W
Coso Pk. **81** 36 13N 117 44W
Cosquín **88** 31 15 S 64 30W
Cossé-le-Vivien **100** 47 57N 0 54W
Costa Blanca **104** 38 25N 0 10W
Costa Brava **104** 41 30N 3 0 E
Costa del Sol **104** 36 30N 4 30W
Costa Dorada **104** 40 45N 1 15 E
Costa Mesa **81** 33 39N 117 55W
Costa Rica **82** 31 20N 112 40W
Costa Rica ■ **84** 10 0N 84 0W
Costebelle, L. **38** 50 19N 62 23W
Costilla **79** 37 0N 105 30W
Cosumnes, R. **80** 38 14N 121 25W
Cotabato **127** 7 14N 124 15 E
Cotagaita **88** 20 45 S 65 30W
Côte d'Azur **103** 43 25N 6 50 E
Côte d'Or **101** 47 10N 4 50 E
Côte d'Or □ **101** 47 30N 4 50 E
Côte-Rouge **44** 45 33N 74 6W
Côte-St. André, La **103** 45 24N 5 15 E
Côte-St-Luce **44** 45 28N 73 40W
Côte-St-Vincent **44** 45 36N 74 8W
Coteau des Prairies **74** 44 30N 97 0W
Coteau-du-Lac **44** 45 18N 74 11W
Coteau du Missouri,
 Plat. du **68** 47 0N 101 0W
Coteau Landing **43** 45 15N 74 13W
Coteau Sta. **71** 45 17N 74 14W
Cotentin **100** 49 30N 1 30W
Côtes de Meuse **101** 49 15N 5 22 E
Côtes-du-Nord □ **100** 48 25N 2 40W
Cotonou **114** 6 20N 2 25 E
Cotopaxi, Vol. **86** 0 30 S 78 30W
Cotswold Hills **95** 51 42N 2 10W
Cottage Grove **78** 43 48N 123 2W
Cottam **46** 42 8N 82 45W
Cottbus **106** 51 44N 14 20 E
Cottonwood, Can. **54** 53 5N 121 50W
Cottonwood, U.S.A. **79** 34 48N 112 1W
Coubre, Pte. de la **102** 45 42N 1 15W
Couches **101** 46 53N 4 30 E
Coudersport **70** 41 45N 77 40W
Coudres, Île aux **41** 47 24N 70 23W
Couëron **100** 47 13N 1 44W
Couesnon, R. **100** 48 20N 1 15W
Couhé-Vérac **102** 46 18N 0 12 E
Coulanges **101** 47 30N 3 30 E
Coulee City **78** 47 44N 119 12W
Coulman I. **91** 73 35 S 170 0 E
Coulommiers **101** 48 50N 3 3 E
Coulonge, R. **40** 45 52N 76 46W
Coulonges **102** 46 58N 0 35W
Coulterville, Calif.,
 U.S.A. **80** 37 42N 120 12W
Coulterville, Ill., U.S.A. **76** 38 11N 89 36W
Council **67** 64 55N 163 45W
Council Bluffs **74** 41 20N 95 50W
Council Grove **74** 38 41N 96 30W
Coupeaux, L. **38** 51 27N 63 58W
Coupeville **80** 48 13N 122 41W
Courantyne, R. **86** 5 0N 57 45W
Courçon **102** 46 15N 0 50W
Cours **103** 46 7N 4 19 E
Courseulles **100** 49 20N 0 29W
Courtenay **62** 49 45N 125 0W
Courtice **49** 43 55N 78 46W
Courtine, La **102** 45 43N 2 16 E
Courtland, Can. **46** 42 51N 80 38W
Courtland, U.S.A. **80** 38 20N 121 34W
Courtright **46** 42 49N 82 28W
Courville, Can. **42** 46 53N 71 10W
Courville, France **100** 48 28N 1 15 E
Coutances **100** 49 3N 1 28W
Couterne **100** 48 30N 0 25W
Coutras **102** 45 3N 0 8W
Coutts **61** 49 0N 111 57W
Couture, L. **36** 60 7N 75 20W
Couvin **105** 50 3N 4 29 E
Cove I. **46** 45 17N 81 44W
Coventry **95** 52 25N 1 31W
Coventry L. **55** 61 15N 106 15W
Covey Hill **43** 45 1N 73 46W
Covilhã **104** 40 17N 7 31W
Covina **81** 34 5N 117 52W
Covington, Ga., U.S.A. **73** 33 36N 83 50W
Covington, Ind., U.S.A. **77** 40 9N 87 24W
Covington, Ky., U.S.A. **77** 39 5N 84 30W
Covington, Mich.,
 U.S.A. **52** 46 30N 88 35W
Covington, Ohio,
 U.S.A. **77** 40 8N 84 20W
Covington, Okla.,
 U.S.A. **75** 36 21N 97 36W
Covington, Tenn.,
 U.S.A. **75** 35 34N 89 39W
Cow Head **37** 49 55N 57 48W
Cowal, L. **136** 33 40 S 147 25 E
Cowan **57** 52 5N 100 45W
Cowan, L. **134** 31 45 S 121 45 E
Cowan L., Can. **56** 54 0N 107 0W
Cowan L., Sask., Can. **55** 54 0N 107 15W
Cowansville **43** 45 14N 72 46W
Cowden **77** 39 15N 88 52W
Cowdenbeath **96** 56 7N 3 20W
Cowes **95** 50 45N 1 18W
Cowichan L. **62** 48 53N 124 17W
Cowley **61** 49 34N 114 5W
Cowlitz, R **80** 46 5N 122 53W
Cowra **136** 33 49 S 148 42 E
Cox I. **62** 50 48N 128 36W
Coxim **87** 18 30 S 54 55W
Cox's Bazar **125** 21 26N 91 59 E
Cox's Cove **37** 49 7N 58 5W
Coyame **82** 29 28N 105 6W
Coyote Wells **81** 32 44N 115 58W
Coyuca de Benítez **83** 17 1N 100 8W
Coyuca de Catalán **82** 18 58N 100 41W
Cozad **74** 40 55N 99 57W
Cozumel **83** 20 31N 86 55W
Cozumel, Isla de **83** 20 30N 86 40W
Craboon **136** 32 3 S 149 30 E
Crabtree **43** 45 58N 73 28W
Cracroft Is. **62** 50 32N 126 25W
Cradock **117** 32 8 S 25 36 E
Crafton **70** 40 25N 80 4W
Craig, Alaska, U.S.A. **67** 55 30N 133 5W
Craig, Colo., U.S.A. **78** 40 32N 107 44W
Craigavon = Portadown **97** 54 27N 6 26W
Craigavon □ **97** 54 30N 6 25W
Craigavon = Lurgan **97** 54 28N 6 20W
Craigflower **63** 48 27N 123 26W
Craigmyle **61** 51 40N 112 15W
Craik **56** 51 3N 105 49W
Craiova **107** 44 21N 23 48 E
Crampel **116** 7 8N 19 81 E
Cranberry Portage **55** 54 35N 101 23W
Cranbrook **61** 49 30N 115 46W
Crandon **74** 45 32N 88 52W
Crane, Oregon, U.S.A. **78** 43 21N 118 39W
Crane, Texas, U.S.A. **75** 31 26N 102 27W
Crane I. **41** 47 4N 70 33W
Crane L. **56** 50 5N 109 5W
Crane River **57** 51 50N 99 14W
Cranston **71** 41 47N 71 27W
Craon **100** 47 50N 0 58W

Craonne Dâmboviţa, R

Craonne	101	49 27N	3 46E
Crapaud	39	46 14N	63 30W
Crater, L.	78	42 55N	122 3W
Crateús	87	5 10S	40 50W
Crato	87	7 10S	39 25W
Crau	103	43 32N	4 40E
Crauford, C.	65	73 44N	84 51W
Craven	56	50 42N	104 49W
Craven, L.	36	54 20N	76 56W
Crawford	74	42 40N	103 25W
Crawfordsville	77	40 2N	86 51W
Crawley	95	51 7N	0 10W
Crazy Mts.	78	46 14N	110 30W
Crean L.	56	54 5N	106 9W
Crèche, La	102	46 23N	0 19W
Crécy-en-Brie	101	48 50N	2 53E
Crécy-en-Ponthieu	101	50 15N	1 53E
Crécy-sur-Serre	101	49 40N	3 32E
Credit, R.	50	43 33N	79 35W
Crediton	46	43 17N	81 33W
Cree L.	55	57 30N	106 30W
Cree, R., Can.	55	58 57N	105 47W
Cree, R., U.K.	96	54 51N	4 24W
Creede	79	37 56N	106 59W
Creel	82	27 45N	107 38W
Creelman	56	49 49N	103 18W
Creemore	46	44 19N	80 6W
Creighton	74	42 30N	97 52W
Creil	101	49 15N	2 34E
Cremona, Can.	61	51 33N	114 29W
Cremona, Italy	108	45 8N	10 2E
Crépy	101	49 37N	3 32E
Crépy-en-Valois	101	49 14N	2 54E
Cres	108	44 58N	14 25E
Cresbard	74	45 13N	98 57W
Crescent, Okla., U.S.A.	75	35 58N	97 36W
Crescent, Oreg., U.S.A.	78	43 30N	121 37W
Crescent Beach	66	49 3N	122 53W
Crescent City	78	41 45N	124 12W
Crescent Spur	63	53 34N	120 42W
Crespo	88	32 2S	60 19W
Cressman	34	47 40N	72 55W
Cressy	136	38 2S	143 40E
Crest	103	44 44N	5 2E
Crested Butte	79	38 57N	107 0W
Crestline, Calif., U.S.A.	81	34 14N	117 18W
Crestline, Ohio, U.S.A.	70	40 46N	82 45W
Creston, Can.	61	49 10N	116 31W
Creston, Calif., U.S.A.	80	35 32N	120 33W
Creston, Iowa, U.S.A.	76	41 0N	94 20W
Creston, Wash., U.S.A.	78	47 47N	118 36W
Creston, Wyo., U.S.A.	78	41 46N	107 50W
Crestone	79	35 2N	106 0W
Crestview, Calif., U.S.A.	80	37 46N	118 58W
Crestview, Fla., U.S.A.	73	30 45N	86 35W
Creswick	136	37 25S	143 51E
Crete	74	40 38N	96 58W
Crete, La	54	58 11N	116 24W
Creus, C.	104	42 20N	3 19E
Creuse □	102	46 0N	2 0E
Creuse, R.	102	47 0N	0 34E
Creusot, Le	101	46 50N	4 24E
Crèvecœur-le-Grand	101	49 37N	2 5E
Crewe	94	53 6N	2 28W
Criciúma	89	28 40S	49 23W
Cridersville	77	40 39N	84 9W
Crieff	96	56 22N	3 50W
Crillon, Mt.	54	58 39N	137 14W
Crimea = Krymskaya	120	45 0N	34 0E
Crimson Lake	61	52 27N	115 2W
Crimson Lake Prov. Park	61	52 28N	114 54W
Crinan	96	56 6N	5 34W
Cristóbal	84	9 10N	80 0W
Crişul Alb, R.	107	46 25N	21 40E
Crişul Negru, R.	107	46 38N	22 26E
Crittenden	77	38 47N	84 36W
Crna Gora □	109	42 40N	19 20E
Crna Gora, Mts.	109	42 10N	21 30E
Crna, R.	109	41 20N	21 59E
Croagh Patrick, mt.	97	53 46N	9 40W
Crocker	76	37 57N	92 16W
Crocker, Barisan	126	5 0N	116 30E
Crockett	75	31 20N	95 30W
Crocodile Is.	134	11 43S	135 8E
Crocq	102	45 52N	2 21E
Crofton	63	48 52N	123 38W
Croisic, Le	100	47 18N	2 30W
Croisic, Pte. du.	100	47 19N	2 31W
Croix, La, L.	52	48 20N	92 15W
Croker, C.	46	44 58N	80 59W
Croker, I.	134	11 12S	132 32E
Cromarty, Can.	55	58 3N	94 9W
Cromarty, U.K.	96	57 40N	4 2W
Cromer, Can.	57	49 44N	101 14W
Cromer, U.K.	94	52 56N	1 18E
Cromwell, N.Z.	133	45 3S	169 14E
Cromwell, U.S.A.	52	46 42N	92 51W
Cronat	101	46 43N	3 40E
Cronulla	136	34 3S	151 8E
Crooked I.	85	22 50N	74 10W
Crooked Island Passage	85	23 0N	74 30W
Crooked L.	37	48 24N	56 17W
Crooked, R., Can.	54	54 10N	122 35W
Crooked, R., U.S.A.	78	44 30N	121 0W
Crooked River	56	52 51N	103 44W
Crookston, Minn., U.S.A.	74	47 50N	96 40W
Crookston, Nebr., U.S.A.	74	42 56N	100 45W
Crooksville	72	39 45N	82 8W
Crookwell	136	34 28S	149 24E
Crosby, Minn., U.S.A.	52	46 28N	93 57W
Crosby, N.D., U.S.A.	56	48 55N	103 18W
Crosby, Pa., U.S.A.	70	41 45N	78 23W
Crosbyton	75	33 37N	101 12W
Cross City	73	29 35N	83 5W
Cross Creek	39	46 19N	66 43W
Cross Fell	94	54 44N	2 29W
Cross L.	55	54 45N	97 30W
Cross Plains	75	32 8N	99 7W
Cross, R.	95	4 46N	8 20E
Cross Sound	67	58 20N	136 30W
Cross Timbers	76	38 1N	93 14W
Crosse, La, Kans., U.S.A.	74	38 33N	99 20W
Crosse, La, Wis., U.S.A.	74	43 48N	91 13W
Crossett	75	33 10N	91 57W
Crossfield	61	51 25N	114 0W
Crosshaven	97	51 48N	8 19W
Crossville	77	38 10N	88 4W
Croswell	46	43 16N	82 37W
Croton-on-Hudson	71	41 12N	73 55W
Crotone	108	39 5N	17 6E
Crow Agency	78	45 40N	107 30W
Crow Hd.	97	51 34N	10 9W
Crow, R.	54	59 41N	124 20W
Crow Wing R.	52	46 19N	94 20W
Crowell	75	33 59N	99 45W
Crowes	136	38 43S	143 24E
Crowley	75	30 15N	92 20W
Crowley, L.	80	37 53N	118 42W
Crown Point	77	41 24N	87 23W
Crows Landing	80	37 23N	121 6W
Crowsnest Pass	61	49 40N	114 40W
Croydon, Austral.	135	18 13S	142 14E
Croydon, U.K.	95	51 18N	0 5W
Crozet Basin	16	46 0S	52 0E
Crozet, Île	16	46 27S	52 0E
Crozon	100	48 15N	4 30W
Cruz, C.	84	19 50N	77 50W
Cruz del Eje	88	30 45S	64 50W
Cruz, La, Colomb.	86	1 35N	76 58W
Cruz, La, C. Rica	84	11 4N	85 39W
Cruz, La, Mexico	82	23 55N	106 54W
Cruzeiro	89	22 50S	45 0W
Cruzeiro do Oeste	89	23 46S	53 4W
Cruzeiro do Sul	86	7 35S	72 35W
Cry L.	54	58 45N	128 5W
Crystal Bay, Can.	48	45 22N	75 51W
Crystal Bay, U.S.A.	80	39 15N	120 0W
Crystal City, Can.	57	49 9N	98 57W
Crystal City, Mo., U.S.A.	76	38 15N	90 23W
Crystal City, Tex., U.S.A.	75	28 40N	99 50W
Crystal Falls	72	46 9N	88 11W
Crystal Lake	77	42 14N	88 19W
Crystal River	73	28 54N	82 35W
Crystal Springs	75	31 59N	90 25W
Csongrád	107	46 43N	20 12E
Ctesiphon	122	33 9N	44 35E
Cu Lao Hon	128	10 54N	108 18E
Cuamba = Nova Freixo	117	14 45S	36 22E
Cuando, R.	117	14 0S	19 30E
Cuango	116	6 15S	16 35E
Cuarto, R.	88	33 25S	63 2W
Cuatrociénegas de Carranza	82	26 59N	102 5W
Cuauhtémoc	82	28 25N	106 52W
Cuba, Mo., U.S.A.	76	38 4N	91 24W
Cuba, N. Mex., U.S.A.	79	36 0N	107 0W
Cuba, N.Y., U.S.A.	70	42 12N	78 18W
Cuba ■	84	22 0N	79 0W
Cuba City	76	42 36N	90 26W
Cubango, R.	117	16 15S	17 45E
Cuchi	117	14 37S	17 10E
Cuchumatanes, Sierra de los	84	15 35N	91 25W
Cucurpe	82	30 20N	110 43W
Cucurrupí	86	4 23N	76 56W
Cúcuta	86	7 54N	72 31W
Cudahy	77	42 54N	87 50W
Cuddalore	124	11 46N	79 45E
Cuddapah	124	14 30N	78 47E
Cudworth	56	52 30N	105 44W
Cue	134	27 25S	117 54E
Cuenca, Ecuador	86	2 50S	79 9W
Cuenca, Spain	104	40 5N	2 10W
Cuenca, Serranía de	104	39 55N	1 50W
Cuencamé	82	24 53N	103 41W
Cuernavaca	83	18 50N	99 20W
Cuero	75	29 5N	97 17W
Cuers	103	43 14N	6 5E
Cuervo	75	35 5N	104 25W
Cuevas del Almanzora	104	37 18N	1 58W
Cuevo	86	20 25N	63 30W
Cuhimbre	86	0 10S	75 23W
Cuiabá	87	15 30S	56 0W
Cuiabá, R.	87	16 50S	56 30W
Cuidad Bolivar	86	8 21N	70 34W
Cuilco	84	15 24N	91 58W
Cuillin Hills	96	57 14N	6 15W
Cuillin Sd.	96	57 4N	6 20W
Cuima	117	13 0S	15 45E
Cuiseaux	103	46 30N	5 22E
Cuito, R.	117	16 50S	19 30E
Cuitzeo, L.	82	19 55N	101 5W
Cuivre, R.	76	38 55N	90 44W
Culan	102	46 34N	2 20E
Cŭlaraşi	101	44 14N	27 23E
Culbertson	74	48 9N	104 30W
Culcairn	136	35 41S	147 3E
Culebra, I.	67	18 19N	65 17W
Culebra, Sierra de la	104	41 55N	6 20W
Culiacán	82	24 50N	107 40W
Culiacán, R.	82	24 30N	107 42W
Culion, I.	127	11 54N	120 1E
Cullarin Range	136	34 30S	149 30E
Cullen	96	57 45N	2 50W
Cullera	104	39 9N	0 17W
Cullman	73	34 13N	86 50W
Culloden Moor	96	57 29N	4 7W
Cullom	77	40 53N	88 16W
Culoz	103	45 47N	5 46E
Culpeper	72	38 29N	77 59W
Culuene, R.	87	12 15S	53 10W
Culver	77	41 13N	86 25W
Culver, Pt.	134	32 54S	124 43E
Culverden	133	42 47S	172 49E
Cumaná	86	10 30N	64 5W
Cumberland, B.C., Can.	62	49 40N	125 0W
Cumberland, Ont., Can.	47	45 29N	75 24W
Cumberland, Qué., Can.	71	45 30N	75 24W
Cumberland, Iowa, U.S.A.	76	41 16N	94 52W
Cumberland, Md., U.S.A.	72	39 40N	78 43W
Cumberland, Wis., U.S.A.	74	45 32N	92 3W
Cumberland House	57	53 58N	102 16W
Cumberland I.	73	30 52N	81 30W
Cumberland Is.	135	20 35S	149 10E
Cumberland L.	57	54 3N	102 18W
Cumberland Pen.	65	67 0N	64 0W
Cumberland Plat.	73	36 0N	84 30W
Cumberland, R.	73	36 15N	87 0W
Cumberland Sound	65	65 30N	67 0W
Cumbria □	94	54 35N	2 55W
Cumbrian Mts.	94	54 30N	3 0W
Cumbum	124	15 40N	79 10E
Cummings Mt.	81	35 2N	118 34W
Cumnock	49	43 46N	80 27W
Cumpas	82	30 0N	109 48W
Cumshewa Inlet	62	53 3N	131 50W
Cumuruxatiba	87	17 6S	39 13W
Cuñaré	86	0 49N	72 32W
Cuncumén	88	31 53S	70 38W
Cundinamarca □	86	5 0N	74 0W
Cunene, R.	117	17 0S	15 0E
Cúneo	108	44 23N	7 31E
Cunlhat	102	45 38N	3 32E
Cunnamulla	135	28 2S	145 38E
Cupar, Can.	56	50 57N	104 10W
Cupar, U.K.	96	56 20N	3 0W
Cupica	86	6 50N	77 30W
Cupica, Golfo de	86	6 25N	77 30W
Curaçao, I.	85	12 10N	69 0W
Curanilahue	88	37 29S	73 28W
Curaray, R.	86	1 30S	75 30W
Curatabaca	86	6 19N	62 51W
Curbarado	86	7 3N	76 54W
Curepto	88	35 8S	72 1W
Curiapo	86	8 33N	61 5W
Curicó	88	34 55S	71 20W
Curicó □	88	34 50S	71 15W
Curiplaya	86	0 16N	74 52W
Curitiba	89	25 20S	49 10W
Curlwaa	136	34 2S	141 59E
Currais Novos	87	6 13S	36 30W
Curralinho	87	1 35S	49 30W
Curran	46	44 41N	83 47W
Currant	78	38 51N	115 32W
Current, R.	75	37 15N	91 10W
Currie	78	40 16N	114 45W
Currituck Sd.	73	36 20N	75 50W
Currockbilly Mt.	136	35 25S	150 0E
Curtis	74	40 41N	100 32W
Curtis, I.	135	23 35S	151 10E
Curtis, Pt.	135	23 53S	151 21E
Curuapanema, R.	87	7 0S	54 30W
Curuçá	87	0 35S	47 50W
Curuguaty	89	24 19S	55 49W
Curundu	84	8 59N	79 38W
Curupira, Serra	86	1 25N	64 30W
Cururupu	87	1 50S	44 50W
Curuzú Cuatiá	88	29 50S	58 5W
Curvelo	87	18 45S	44 27W
Cushing	43	45 36N	74 28W
Cushing, Mt.	54	57 35N	126 57W
Cusihuiriáchic	82	28 10N	106 50W
Cusset	102	46 8N	3 28E
Cusson, Pte.	36	60 23N	77 46W
Custer	74	43 45N	103 38W
Cut Bank	61	48 40N	112 15W
Cut Knife	56	52 45N	109 1W
Cutbank	56	51 18N	106 51W
Cutbank, R.	60	54 43N	118 32W
Cuthbert	73	31 47N	84 47W
Cutler	80	36 31N	119 17W
Cuttack	125	20 25N	85 57E
Cuvier, C.	134	23 14S	113 22E
Cuvier I.	133	36 27S	175 50E
Cuxhaven	106	53 51N	8 41E
Cuyabeno	86	0 16S	75 53W
Cuyahoga Falls	70	41 8N	81 30W
Cuyahoga, R.	70	41 20N	81 35W
Cuyo	127	10 50N	121 5E
Cuyuni, R.	87	7 0N	59 30W
Cuzco	86	13 32S	72 0W
Cuzco, Mt.	86	20 0S	66 50W
Cynthia	60	53 17N	115 25W
Cynthiana	77	38 23N	84 10W
Cypress Hills	55	49 40N	109 30W
Cypress Hills Prov. Park	56	49 40N	109 30W
Cypress River	57	49 34N	99 5W
Cyprus ■	122	35 0N	33 0E
Cyrville	48	45 25N	75 38W
Czar	61	52 27N	110 50W
Czech S.R. □	106	49 30N	15 0E
Czechoslovakia ■	106	49 0N	17 0E
Czeremcha	107	52 32N	23 20E
Częstochowa	107	50 49N	19 7E

D

Da Lat	128	11 56N	108 25E
Da Nang	128	16 4N	108 13E
Da, R.	128	21 15N	105 20E
Dabajuro	86	11 2N	70 40W
Dabie	106	53 27N	14 45E
Dabrowa Tarnówska	107	50 10N	20 59E
Dacca	125	23 43N	90 26E
Dacca □	125	24 0N	90 25E
Dadanawa	86	3 0N	59 30W
Dade City	73	28 20N	82 12W
Dadra and Nagar Haveli □	124	20 5N	73 0E
Dadu	124	26 45N	67 45E
Daet	127	14 2N	122 55E
Dafter	46	46 21N	84 27W
Dagestan, A.S.S.R. □	120	42 30N	47 0E
Daggett	81	34 43N	116 52W
Dagupan	127	16 3N	120 20E
Dagus Mines	70	41 20N	78 36W
Dahlgren	77	38 12N	88 41W
Dahlonega	73	34 35N	83 59W
Dahomey ■ = Benin ■	114	8 0N	2 0E
Daingean	97	53 18N	7 15W
Daintree	97	16 20S	145 20E
Daiō-Misaki	132	34 15N	136 45E
Dairen = Lu-ta	130	39 0N	121 31E
Dakar	114	14 34N	17 29W
Dakhla	114	23 50N	15 53W
Dakhla, El Wâhât el-	115	25 30N	28 50E
Dakota City, Iowa, U.S.A.	76	42 43N	94 12W
Dakota City, Nebr., U.S.A.	74	42 27N	96 28W
Đakovica	109	42 22N	20 26E
Dalälven, L.	111	61 27N	17 15E
Dalandzadgad	130	43 37N	104 30E
Dalarö	111	59 8N	18 24E
Dalat	128	12 3N	108 32E
Dalbandin	124	29 0N	64 23E
Dalbeattie	96	54 55N	3 50W
Dalby	135	27 10S	151 17E
Dale	77	38 10N	86 59W
Dalesville	43	45 42N	74 24W
Daleville	77	40 7N	85 33W
Dalhart	75	36 10N	102 30W
Dalhousie	39	48 5N	66 26W
Dalhousie East	39	44 43N	64 48W
Dalhousie Station	43	45 18N	74 27W
Dalhousie West	39	44 43N	65 13W
Dalj	86	45 28N	18 58E
Dalkeith, Can.	43	45 27N	74 32W
Dalkeith, U.K.	96	55 54N	3 5W
Dall I.	54	54 59N	133 25W
Dallas, Oregon, U.S.A.	78	45 0N	123 15W
Dallas, Texas, U.S.A.	75	32 50N	96 50W
Dallas Center	76	41 41N	93 58W
Dallas City	76	40 38N	91 10W
Dalles, Les	43	45 59N	73 31W
Dalmacija	108	43 20N	17 0E
Dalmatia = Dalmacija	108	43 20N	17 0E
Dalmeny	56	52 20N	106 46W
Dalneretchensk	121	45 50N	133 40E
Daloa	114	7 0N	6 30W
Dalrymple, Mt.	135	21 1S	148 39E
Dalton, Can.	53	48 11N	84 1W
Dalton, Ga., U.S.A.	127	34 45N	85 0W
Dalton, Mass., U.S.A.	71	42 28N	73 11W
Dalton, Nebr., U.S.A.	74	41 27N	103 0W
Dalton Post	54	66 42N	137 0W
Dalupuri, I.	131	19 2N	121 8E
Dalvík	110	65 58N	18 32W
Daly City	80	37 42N	122 28W
Daly L.	55	56 32N	105 39W
Daly, R.	134	13 21S	130 18E
Daly Waters	134	16 15S	133 24E
Dam	87	4 45N	55 0W
Daman	124	20 25N	72 57E
Daman □	124	20 25N	72 58E
Damar, I.	127	7 15S	128 30E
Damaraland	117	21 0S	17 0E
Damascus	49	43 55N	80 29W
Damascus = Dimashq	122	33 30N	36 18E
Damāvand	123	36 0N	52 0E
Damāvand, Qolleh-ye	123	35 45N	52 10E
Damba	116	6 44S	15 29E
Dâmboviţa, R.	107	44 40N	26 0E

Dame Marie **Deva**

Dame Marie	**85**	18 36N	74 26W
Dāmghān	**123**	36 10N	54 17E
Damin	**123**	27 30N	60 40E
Damman	**122**	26 25N	50 2E
Dammarie	**101**	48 20N	1 30E
Dammartin	**101**	49 3N	2 41E
Damme	**105**	52 32N	8 12E
Damoh	**124**	23 50N	79 28E
Dampier	**134**	20 41S	116 42E
Dampier Arch.	**134**	20 38S	116 32E
Dampier Downs	**134**	18 24S	123 5E
Dampier, Selat	**127**	0 40S	131 0E
Damville	**100**	48 51N	1 5E
Damvillers	**101**	49 20N	5 21E
Dana	**127**	11 0S	122 52E
Dana, Lac	**36**	50 53N	77 20W
Dana, Mt	**80**	37 54N	119 12W
Danao	**127**	10 31N	124 1E
Danbury	**71**	41 23N	73 29W
Danby L.	**79**	34 17N	115 0W
Dandeldhura	**125**	29 20N	80 35E
Dandeli	**124**	15 5N	74 30E
Dandenong	**136**	38 0S	145 15E
Danforth, Can.	**50**	43 43N	79 15W
Danforth, U.S.A.	**35**	45 39N	67 57W
Dang Raek	**128**	14 40N	104 0E
Danger Is.	**15**	10 53S	165 49W
Danger Pt.	**117**	34 40S	19 17E
Daniel	**78**	42 56N	110 2W
Daniel's Harbour	**37**	50 13N	57 35W
Danielson	**71**	41 50N	71 52W
Danielson Prov. Park	**56**	51 16N	106 50W
Dankhar Gompa	**124**	32 10N	78 10E
Danlí	**84**	14 4N	86 35W
Dannemora, Sweden	**111**	60 12N	17 51E
Dannemora, U.S.A.	**71**	44 41N	73 44W
Dannevirke	**133**	40 12S	176 8E
Dansalan	**127**	8 2N	124 30E
Danskin	**62**	53 59N	125 47W
Dansville	**70**	42 32N	77 41W
Danube, R.	**106**	45 0N	28 20W
Danvers	**71**	42 34N	70 55E
Danville, Ill., U.S.A.	**77**	40 10N	87 40W
Danville, Ind., U.S.A.	**77**	39 46N	86 32W
Danville, Ky., U.S.A.	**77**	37 40N	84 45W
Danville, Va., U.S.A.	**73**	36 40N	79 20W
Danzig = Gdansk	**107**	54 22N	18 40E
Dão	**127**	10 30N	122 6E
Daoulas	**100**	48 22N	4 17W
Dar al Hamrā, Ad	**122**	27 22N	37 43E
Dar es Salaam	**116**	6 50S	39 12E
Dar'á	**115**	32 36N	36 7E
Dārāb	**123**	28 50N	54 30E
Darband	**124**	34 30N	72 50E
Darbhanga	**125**	26 15N	86 8E
Darby	**78**	46 2N	114 7W
D'Arcy	**54**	50 35N	122 30W
Dardanelle	**80**	38 2N	119 50W
Dardanelles = Canakkale Bğazi	**122**	40 0N	26 20E
Dardenelle	**75**	35 12N	93 9W
Dargai	**124**	34 25N	71 45E
Dargan Ata	**120**	40 40N	62 20E
Dargaville	**133**	35 57S	173 52E
Darhan	**130**	49 27N	105 57E
Darién	**84**	9 7N	79 46W
Darién, G. del	**86**	9 0N	77 0W
Darién, Serranía del	**86**	8 30N	77 30W
Darjeeling	**125**	27 3N	88 18E
Dark Cove	**37**	48 47N	54 13W
Darling, R.	**136**	34 4S	141 54E
Darling Ra.	**134**	32 30S	116 0E
Darlington, U.K.	**94**	54 33N	1 33W
Darlington, S.C., U.S.A.	**73**	34 18N	79 50W
Darlington, Wis., U.S.A.	**76**	42 43N	90 7W
Darlington Point	**136**	34 37S	146 1E
Darłowo	**106**	54 25N	16 25E
Darmstadt	**106**	49 51N	8 40E
Darnétal	**100**	49 25N	1 10E
Darney	**101**	48 5N	6 0E
Darnick	**136**	32 48S	143 38E
Darnley B.	**67**	69 30N	123 30W
Darnley, C.	**91**	68 0S	69 0E
Darrington	**63**	48 14N	121 37W
Dart, R.	**95**	50 24N	3 36W
Dartmoor	**95**	50 36N	4 0W
Dartmouth, Can.	**39**	44 40N	63 30W
Dartmouth, U.K.	**95**	50 21N	3 35W
Dartmouth, R.	**38**	48 53N	64 34W
Darvel Bay	**127**	4 50N	118 20E
Darwha	**124**	20 15N	77 45E
Darwin, Austral.	**134**	12 25S	130 51E
Darwin, U.S.A.	**81**	36 15N	117 35W
Daryacheh-ye-Sistan	**123**	31 0N	61 0E
Dashinchilen	**130**	48 0N	105 59E
Dasht-e Kavīr	**123**	34 30N	55 0E
Dasht-e Lūt	**123**	31 30N	58 0E
Dasht-i-Khash	**124**	32 0N	62 0E
Dasht-i-Margo	**124**	30 40N	62 30E
Dasht, R.	**124**	25 40N	62 20E
Dasserat, L.	**40**	48 16N	79 25W
Datia	**124**	25 39N	78 27E
Datteln	**105**	51 39N	7 23E
Daugavpils	**120**	55 53N	26 32E
Daulat Yar	**123**	34 30N	65 45E
Daulnay	**39**	47 25N	65 28W
Dauphin	**57**	51 9N	100 5W
Dauphin I.	**73**	30 16N	88 10W
Dauphin L.	**57**	51 20N	99 45W
Dauphiné	**103**	45 15N	5 25E
Davangere	**124**	14 25N	75 50E
Davao	**127**	7 0N	125 40E
Davao, G. of	**127**	6 30N	125 48E
Dāvar Panāh	**123**	27 25N	62 15E
Davenport, Calif., U.S.A.	**80**	37 1N	122 12W
Davenport, Iowa, U.S.A.	**76**	41 30N	90 40W
Davenport, Wash., U.S.A.	**78**	47 40N	118 5W
Davenport Ra.	**134**	20 28S	134 0E
Daventry	**95**	52 16N	1 10W
David	**84**	8 30N	82 30W
David City	**74**	41 18N	97 10W
David, R.	**43**	45 58N	72 54W
Davidson	**56**	51 16N	105 59W
Davis	**80**	38 33N	121 45W
Davis Dam	**81**	35 11N	114 35W
Davis Inlet	**36**	55 50N	60 59W
Davis Mts.	**75**	30 42N	104 15W
Davis Str.	**65**	65 0N	58 0W
Davison	**46**	43 2N	83 31W
Davisson, L.	**80**	46 30N	122 20W
Davos	**106**	46 48N	9 49E
Davy L.	**55**	58 53N	108 18W
Dawson, Can.	**64**	64 10N	139 30W
Dawson, Ga., U.S.A.	**73**	31 45N	84 28W
Dawson, N.D., U.S.A.	**74**	46 56N	99 45W
Dawson B.	**57**	52 53N	100 49W
Dawson Creek	**54**	55 45N	120 15W
Dawson, I.	**90**	53 50S	70 50W
Dawson Inlet	**55**	61 50N	93 25W
Dawson, R.	**135**	23 25S	150 10E
Daylesford	**136**	37 21S	144 9E
Dayr az Zawr	**122**	35 20N	40 5E
Daysland	**61**	52 50N	112 20W
Dayton, Iowa, U.S.A.	**76**	42 14N	94 6W
Dayton, Ky., U.S.A.	**77**	39 7N	84 28W
Dayton, Nev., U.S.A.	**80**	39 15N	119 34W
Dayton, Ohio, U.S.A.	**72**	39 45N	84 10W
Dayton, Pa., U.S.A.	**70**	40 54N	79 18W
Dayton, Tenn., U.S.A.	**73**	35 30N	85 1W
Dayton, Wash., U.S.A.	**78**	46 20N	118 10W
Daytona Beach	**73**	29 14N	81 0W
Dayville	**78**	44 33N	119 37W
De Aar	**117**	30 39S	24 0E
De Beaujeu	**43**	45 19N	74 20W
De Forest	**76**	43 15N	89 20W
De Funiak Springs	**73**	30 42N	86 10W
De Grau	**37**	48 29N	59 9W
De Grey	**134**	20 12S	119 12E
De Land	**73**	29 1N	81 19W
De Leon	**75**	32 9N	98 35W
De Léry	**45**	45 15N	73 26W
De Long Mts.	**67**	68 10N	163 0W
De Long, Ostrova	**121**	76 40N	149 20E
De Morhiban, L.	**38**	51 50N	62 54W
De Pere	**72**	44 28N	88 1W
De Queen	**75**	34 3N	94 24W
De Quincy	**75**	30 30N	93 27W
De Ridder	**75**	30 48N	93 15W
De Smet	**74**	44 25N	97 35W
De Soto	**76**	38 7N	90 33W
De Tour	**46**	45 59N	83 56W
De Witt, Ark., U.S.A.	**75**	34 19N	91 20W
De Witt, Iowa, U.S.A.	**76**	41 49N	90 33W
De Witt, Mich., U.S.A.	**77**	42 50N	84 33W
Deacon	**58**	49 51N	96 56W
Dead Sea = Miyet, Bahr el	**115**	31 30N	35 30E
Deadwood L.	**54**	59 10N	128 30W
Deakin	**134**	30 46S	129 58E
Deal	**95**	51 13N	1 25E
Dean Chan.	**62**	52 30N	127 15W
Dean, Forest of	**95**	51 50N	2 35W
Deán Funes	**88**	30 20S	64 20W
Dean, R.	**62**	52 49N	126 58W
Dearborn, U.S.A.	**46**	42 18N	83 15W
Dearborn, U.S.A.	**76**	39 32N	94 46W
Dease Arm	**106**	66 52N	119 37W
Dease L.	**54**	58 40N	130 5W
Dease Lake	**54**	58 25N	130 6W
Dease, R.	**54**	59 56N	128 32W
Death Valley	**81**	36 27N	116 52W
Death Valley Junc.	**81**	36 21N	116 30W
Death Valley Nat. Monument	**81**	36 30N	117 0W
Deauville	**100**	49 23N	0 2E
Debar	**109**	41 21N	20 37E
Debden	**56**	53 30N	106 50W
Debec	**39**	46 4N	67 41W
Debert	**39**	45 26N	63 28W
Debolt	**60**	55 12N	118 1W
Debre Markos	**115**	10 20N	37 40E
Debre Tabor	**115**	11 50N	38 26E
Debrecen	**107**	47 33N	21 42E
Decatur, Ala., U.S.A.	**73**	34 35N	87 0W
Decatur, Ga., U.S.A.	**73**	33 47N	84 17W
Decatur, Ill., U.S.A.	**76**	39 50N	89 0W
Decatur, Ind., U.S.A.	**72**	40 52N	85 28W
Dĕcatur, Ind., U.S.A.	**77**	40 50N	84 56W
Decatur, Mich., U.S.A.	**77**	42 7N	85 58W
Decatur, Texas, U.S.A.	**75**	33 15N	97 35W
Decazeville	**102**	44 34N	2 15E
Deccan	**124**	14 0N	77 0E
Decelles, Rés	**40**	47 42N	78 8W
Déception, B.	**36**	62 8N	74 41W
Deception I.	**91**	63 0S	60 15W
Deception L.	**55**	56 33N	104 13W
Decize	**101**	46 50N	3 28E
Deckerville	**46**	43 33N	82 46W
Decorah	**74**	43 20N	91 50W
Dedham	**71**	42 14N	71 10W
Dee, R., Scot., U.K.	**96**	57 4N	2 7W
Dee, R., Wales, U.K.	**94**	53 15N	3 7W
Deep B.	**54**	61 15N	116 35W
Deep Cove	**66**	49 20N	122 56W
Deep River	**76**	41 35N	92 22W
Deepdale	**134**	26 22S	114 20E
Deepwater	**76**	38 18N	93 46W
Deer I.	**67**	54 55N	162 20W
Deer, L.	**37**	49 6N	57 35W
Deer Lake, Newf., Can.	**37**	49 11N	57 27W
Deer Lake, Ontario, Can.	**55**	52 36N	94 20W
Deer Lodge	**78**	46 25N	112 40W
Deer Park, Ohio, U.S.A.	**77**	39 13N	84 23W
Deer Park, Wash., U.S.A.	**78**	47 55N	117 21W
Deer Pond	**37**	48 30N	54 45W
Deer, R.	**55**	58 23N	94 13W
Deer River	**52**	47 21N	93 44W
Deering	**67**	66 5N	162 50W
Deesa	**124**	24 18N	72 10E
Defiance	**77**	41 20N	84 20W
Dégelis	**41**	47 30N	68 35W
Deggendorf	**106**	48 49N	12 59E
Deh Bīd	**123**	30 39N	53 11E
Deh Kheyr	**123**	28 45N	54 40E
Deh Titan	**124**	33 45N	63 50E
Dehkareqan	**122**	37 50N	45 55E
Dehra Dun	**124**	30 20N	78 4E
Deinze	**105**	50 59N	3 32E
Dej	**107**	47 10N	23 52E
Dekalb	**77**	41 55N	88 45W
Dekese	**116**	3 24S	21 24E
Del Mar	**81**	32 58N	117 16W
Del Norte	**79**	37 47N	106 27W
Del Rio, Mexico	**82**	29 22N	100 54W
Del Rio, U.S.A.	**75**	29 15N	100 50W
Delagua	**75**	32 35N	104 40W
Delano	**81**	35 48N	119 13W
Delaronde L.	**56**	54 3N	107 3W
Delavan, Ill., U.S.A.	**76**	40 22N	89 33W
Delavan, Wis., U.S.A.	**77**	42 40N	88 39W
Delaware	**77**	40 20N	83 0W
Delaware □	**72**	39 0N	75 40W
Delaware, R.	**71**	39 20N	75 25W
Delburne	**61**	52 12N	113 14W
Delft	**105**	52 1N	4 22E
Delgado, C.	**116**	10 45S	40 40E
Delgo	**115**	20 6N	30 40E
Delhi, Can.	**46**	42 51N	80 30W
Delhi, India	**124**	28 38N	77 17E
Delhi, U.S.A.	**71**	42 17N	74 56W
Delia	**61**	51 38N	112 23W
Delice, R.	**122**	39 45N	34 15E
Delicias	**82**	28 10N	105 30W
Delicias, Laguna	**82**	28 7N	105 40W
Delisle	**56**	51 55N	107 8W
Dell City	**79**	31 58N	105 19W
Dell Rapids	**74**	43 53N	96 44W
Delle	**101**	47 30N	7 2E
Delmar, Iowa, U.S.A.	**76**	42 0N	90 37W
Delmar, N.Y., U.S.A.	**71**	42 37N	73 47W
Delmiro	**87**	9 24S	38 6W
Deloraine	**57**	49 15N	100 29W
Delorme, L.	**56**	54 31N	69 52W
Delphi	**77**	40 37N	86 40W
Delphos	**77**	40 51N	84 17W
Delray Beach	**73**	26 27N	80 4W
Delson	**45**	45 22N	73 33W
Delta, Colo., U.S.A.	**79**	38 44N	108 5W
Delta, Utah, U.S.A.	**78**	39 21N	112 29W
Delta □	**66**	49 7N	123 0W
Delta Amacuro □	**86**	8 30N	61 30W
Delta Beach	**57**	50 11N	98 19W
Demak	**127**	6 50S	110 40E
Demanda, Sierra de la	**104**	42 15N	3 0W
Demba	**116**	5 28S	22 15E
Dembidolo	**115**	8 34N	34 50E
Demer, R.	**105**	51 0N	5 8E
Demerais, L.	**34**	47 35N	77 0W
Demerara, R.	**86**	7 0N	58 0W
Deming, N.Mex., U.S.A.	**79**	32 10N	107 50W
Deming, Wash., U.S.A.	**80**	48 49N	122 13W
Demini, R.	**86**	0 46N	62 56W
Demmit	**54**	55 20N	119 50W
Demopolis	**73**	32 30N	87 48W
Dempo, Mt.	**126**	4 10S	103 15E
Den Burg	**105**	53 3N	4 47E
Den Haag = 's Gravenhage	**105**	52 7N	4 17E
Den Helder	**105**	52 57N	4 45E
Den Oever	**105**	52 56N	5 2E
Denain	**101**	50 20N	3 22E
Denair	**80**	37 32N	120 48W
Denau	**120**	38 16N	67 54E
Denbigh, Can.	**47**	45 8N	77 15W
Denbigh, U.K.	**94**	53 12N	3 26W
Dendang	**126**	3 7S	107 56E
Denham	**134**	25 56S	113 31E
Denham Ra.	**135**	21 55S	147 46E
Denholm	**55**	52 40N	108 0W
Denia	**104**	38 49N	0 8E
Deniliquin	**136**	35 30S	144 58E
Denison, Iowa, U.S.A.	**74**	42 0N	95 18W
Denison, Texas, U.S.A.	**75**	33 50N	96 40W
Denison Range	**135**	28 30S	136 5E
Denizli	**122**	37 42N	29 2E
Denman Island	**62**	49 33N	124 48W
Denmark	**134**	34 59S	117 18E
Denmark ■	**111**	55 30N	9 0E
Denmark Str.	**12**	66 0N	30 0W
Dennison	**70**	40 21N	81 21W
Denpasar	**126**	8 45S	115 5E
Denton, Mont., U.S.A.	**78**	47 25N	109 56W
Denton, Texas, U.S.A.	**75**	33 12N	97 10W
Denver, Colo., U.S.A.	**74**	39 45N	105 0W
Denver, Ind., U.S.A.	**77**	40 52N	86 5W
Denver, Iowa, U.S.A.	**76**	42 40N	92 20W
Denver City	**75**	32 58N	102 48W
Denzil	**56**	52 14N	109 39W
Deoghar	**125**	24 30N	86 59E
Deolali	**124**	19 50N	73 50E
Deoria	**125**	26 31N	83 48E
Deosai, Mts.	**124**	35 40N	75 0E
Departure Bay	**62**	49 13N	123 57W
Depew	**70**	42 55N	78 43W
Deposit	**71**	42 5N	75 23W
Depot Harbour	**70**	45 18N	80 5W
Deputatskiy	**121**	69 18N	139 54E
Dera Ghazi Khan	**124**	30 5N	70 43E
Dera Ismail Khan	**124**	31 50N	70 50E
Dera Ismail Khan □	**124**	32 30N	70 0E
Derbent	**120**	42 5N	48 15E
Derby, Austral.	**134**	17 18S	123 38E
Derby, U.K.	**94**	52 55N	1 28W
Derby, Conn., U.S.A.	**71**	41 20N	73 5W
Derby, N.Y., U.S.A.	**70**	42 40N	78 59W
Derby, Ohio, U.S.A.	**77**	39 46N	83 13W
Derby □	**94**	52 55N	1 28W
Derg, L.	**97**	53 0N	8 20W
Derg, R.	**97**	54 42N	7 26W
Dergaon	**125**	26 45N	94 0E
Derna	**115**	32 40N	22 35E
Dernieres Isles	**75**	29 0N	90 45W
Deroche	**63**	49 12N	122 4W
Derrynane	**49**	43 56N	80 35W
Derryveagh Mts.	**97**	55 0N	8 40W
Derval	**100**	47 40N	1 41W
Derwent	**60**	53 41N	110 58W
Derwent, R., Cumb., U.K.	**94**	54 42N	3 22W
Derwent, R., Derby, U.K.	**94**	52 53N	1 17W
Derwent, R., N. Yorks., U.K.	**94**	53 45N	0 57W
Derwentwater, L.	**94**	53 34N	3 9W
Des Moines, Iowa, U.S.A.	**76**	41 35N	93 37W
Des Moines, N. Mex., U.S.A.	**75**	36 50N	103 51W
Des Moines, R.	**74**	40 23N	91 25W
Des Plaines	**77**	42 3N	87 52W
Des Plaines, R.	**77**	41 23N	88 15W
Desaguadero, R., Argent.	**88**	33 28S	67 15W
Desaguadero, R., Boliv.	**86**	17 30S	68 0W
Desbarats	**46**	46 20N	83 56W
Desbiens	**41**	48 25N	71 57W
Descanso	**81**	32 12N	116 58W
Descanso, Pta.	**81**	32 21N	117 3W
Deschaillons	**41**	46 32N	72 7W
Deschambault	**41**	46 39N	71 56W
Descharme, R.	**55**	56 51N	109 13W
Deschênes, Ont., Can.	**48**	45 25N	75 49W
Deschênes, Qué., Can.	**40**	45 23N	75 48W
Deschênes, L.	**48**	45 22N	75 51W
Deschutes, R.	**78**	45 30N	121 0W
Dese	**115**	11 5N	39 40E
Deseado, R.	**90**	40 0S	69 0W
Desemboque	**82**	30 30N	112 27W
Deseronto	**47**	44 12N	77 3W
Desert Center	**81**	33 45N	115 27W
Desert Hot Springs	**81**	33 58N	116 30W
Désirade, I.	**85**	16 18N	61 3W
Deskenatlata L.	**54**	60 55N	112 3W
Desmarais	**60**	55 56N	113 49W
Desmaraisville	**40**	49 32N	76 9W
Desméloizes	**40**	48 57N	79 29W
Desolación, I.	**90**	53 0S	74 0W
Desolation Sound Prov. Marine Park	**62**	50 5N	124 25W
Despeñaperros, Paso	**104**	38 24N	3 30W
Dessau	**106**	51 49N	12 15E
Destruction Bay	**64**	61 15N	138 48W
Desvrès	**101**	50 40N	1 48E
Detmold	**106**	51 55N	8 50E
Detour Pt.	**72**	45 37N	86 35W
Detroit, Mich., U.S.A.	**46**	42 13N	83 22W
Detroit, Tex., U.S.A.	**75**	33 40N	95 10W
Detroit Lakes	**74**	46 50N	95 50W
Dettifoss	**110**	65 49N	16 24W
Deurne, Belg.	**105**	51 12N	4 24E
Deurne, Neth.	**105**	51 27N	5 49E
Deutsche Bucht	**106**	54 10N	7 51E
Deux-Loutres, L. aux	**38**	51 31N	62 28W
Deux Montagnes	**44**	45 32N	73 53W
Deux Montagnes □	**44**	45 40N	74 0W
Deux Montagnes, Lac des	**44**	45 28N	73 59W
Deux-Sèvres □	**100**	46 35N	0 20W
Deva	**107**	45 53N	22 55E

Devakottai	**124**	9 55N	78 45 E
Devastation Chan.	**62**	53 40N	128 50W
Deventer	**105**	52 15N	6 10 E
Devenyns, L.	**41**	47 5N	73 50W
Deveron, R.	**96**	57 40N	2 31W
Devils Den	**80**	35 46N	119 58W
Devils Lake	**74**	48 5N	98 50W
Devils Paw, mt.	**54**	58 47N	134 0W
Devizes	**95**	51 21N	2 0W
Devon	**60**	53 24N	113 44W
Devon I.	**65**	75 47N	88 0W
Devonport, Austral.	**135**	41 10 S	146 22 E
Devonport, N.Z.	**133**	36 49 S	174 49 E
Devonport, U.K.	**95**	50 23N	4 11W
Devonshire □	**95**	50 50N	3 40W
Dewas	**124**	22 59N	76 3 E
Dewberry	**60**	53 35N	110 32W
Dewittville	**43**	45 7N	74 5W
Dewsbury	**94**	53 42N	1 38W
Dexter, U.S.A.	**77**	42 20N	83 53W
Dexter, Mo., U.S.A.	**75**	36 50N	90 0W
Dexter, N. Mex., U.S.A.	**75**	33 15N	104 25W
Deyhūk	**123**	33 15N	57 30 E
Deyyer	**123**	27 55N	51 55 E
Dezadeash L.	**54**	60 28N	136 58W
Dezfūl	**122**	32 20N	48 30 E
Dezh Shāhpūr	**122**	35 30N	46 25 E
Dezhneva, Mys	**121**	66 10N	169 3 E
Dhaba	**122**	27 25N	35 40 E
Dhahran	**122**	26 9N	50 10 E
Dhamtari	**125**	20 42N	81 35 E
Dhanbad	**125**	23 50N	86 30 E
Dhangarhi	**125**	28 55N	80 40 E
Dhankuta	**125**	26 55N	87 20 E
Dhar	**124**	22 35N	75 26 E
Dharmapuri	**124**	12 10N	78 10 E
Dhaulagiri Mt.	**125**	28 45N	83 45 E
Dhenkanal	**125**	20 45N	85 35 E
Dhidhimótikhon	**109**	41 22N	26 29 E
Dhikti, Mt.	**109**	35 8N	25 29 E
Dhirfis, Mt.	**109**	38 40N	23 54 E
Dhodhekánisos	**109**	36 35N	27 0 E
Dholpur	**124**	26 45N	77 59 E
Dhrol	**124**	22 40N	70 25 E
Dhubaibah	**123**	23 25N	54 35 E
Dhubri	**125**	26 2N	90 2 E
Dhulia	**124**	20 58N	74 50 E
Di Linh, Cao Nguyen	**128**	11 30N	108 0 E
Diable, Mt.	**80**	37 53N	121 56W
Diablo Heights	**84**	8 58N	79 34W
Diablo Range	**80**	37 0N	121 5W
Diagonal	**76**	40 49N	94 20W
Diamante	**88**	32 5 S	60 40W
Diamante, R.	**88**	34 31 S	66 56W
Diamantina	**87**	18 5 S	43 40W
Diamantina, R.	**135**	22 25 S	142 20 E
Diamantino	**87**	14 30 S	56 30W
Diamond City	**61**	49 48N	112 51W
Diamond Harbour	**125**	22 11N	88 14 E
Diamond Mts.	**78**	40 0N	115 58W
Diamond Springs	**80**	38 42N	120 49W
Diamondville	**78**	41 51N	110 30W
Diana B.	**36**	61 20N	70 0W
Diaole, Î. du.	**87**	5 15N	52 45W
Dibai (Dubai)	**123**	25 15N	55 20 E
Dibaya	**116**	6 20 S	22 0 E
Dibaya Lubue	**116**	4 12 S	19 54 E
Dibba	**123**	25 45N	56 16 E
Dibega	**122**	35 50N	43 46 E
Dibi	**115**	4 10N	41 52 E
Dibrugarh	**125**	27 29N	94 55 E
Dibulla	**86**	11 17N	73 19W
Dickersonville	**49**	43 14N	78 53W
Dickeyville	**76**	42 38N	90 36W
Dickinson	**74**	46 50N	102 40W
Dickson	**73**	36 5N	87 22W
Dickson City	**71**	41 29N	75 40W
Didsbury	**61**	51 35N	114 10W
Die	**103**	44 47N	5 22 E
Diefenbaker L.	**55**	51 0N	106 55W
Diego Garcia, I.	**16**	9 50 S	75 0 E
Diégo Suarez	**117**	12 25 S	49 20 E
Diekirch	**105**	49 52N	6 10 E
Diélette	**100**	49 33N	1 52W
Diên Biên Phu	**128**	21 20N	103 0 E
Diepenbeek	**105**	50 54N	5 25 E
Dieppe, Can.	**39**	46 6N	64 45W
Dieppe, France	**100**	49 54N	1 4 E
Dieren	**105**	52 3N	6 6 E
Dierks	**75**	34 9N	94 0W
Diest	**105**	50 58N	5 4 E
Dieterich	**77**	39 4N	88 23W
Dieulefit	**103**	44 32N	5 4 E
Dieuze	**101**	48 30N	6 40 E
Differdange	**105**	49 81N	5 54 E
Digby	**39**	44 38N	65 50W
Digby Neck	**39**	44 30N	66 5W
Digges	**55**	58 40N	94 0W
Digges Is.	**36**	62 40N	77 50W
Dighinala	**125**	23 15N	92 5 E
Dighton	**74**	38 30N	100 26W
Digne	**103**	44 5N	6 12 E
Digoin	**102**	46 29N	3 58 E
Digos	**127**	6 45N	125 20 E
Digranes	**110**	66 4N	14 44 E
Dihang, R.	**125**	27 30N	96 30 E
Dijlah	**122**	37 0N	42 30 E
Dijon	**101**	47 20N	5 0 E
Diksmuide	**105**	51 2N	2 52 E
Dikson	**120**	73 40N	80 5 E
Dila	**115**	6 14N	38 22 E
Dilam	**122**	23 55N	47 10 E
Dildo	**37**	47 34N	53 33W
Dili	**127**	8 39 S	125 34 E
Dilke	**56**	50 52N	105 15W
Dillard	**76**	37 44N	91 13W
Dilley	**75**	28 40N	99 12W
Dillingham	**67**	59 5N	158 30W
Dillon, Can.	**55**	55 56N	108 56W
Dillon, Mont., U.S.A.	**78**	45 9N	112 36W
Dillon, S.C., U.S.A.	**73**	34 26N	79 20W
Dillon, R.	**55**	55 56N	108 56W
Dillsboro	**77**	39 1N	85 4W
Dilolo	**12**	10 28 S	22 18 E
Dimas	**82**	23 43N	106 47W
Dimashq	**122**	33 30N	36 18 E
Dimbelenge	**116**	4 30N	23 0 E
Dimboola	**136**	36 28 S	142 0 E
Dimitriya Lapteva, Proliv	**121**	73 0N	140 0 E
Dimitrovgrad	**109**	42 5N	25 35 E
Dimmitt	**75**	34 36N	102 16W
Dinagat I.	**127**	10 10N	125 40 E
Dinajpur	**125**	25 33N	88 43 E
Dinan	**100**	48 28N	2 2W
Dinant	**105**	50 16N	4 55 E
Dinar	**122**	38 5N	30 15 E
Dinara Planina, mts.	**108**	44 0N	16 30 E
Dinard	**100**	48 38N	2 6W
Dinaric Alps	**93**	44 0N	17 30 E
Dindigul	**124**	10 25N	78 0 E
Dingle	**97**	52 9N	10 17W
Dingle B.	**97**	52 3N	10 20W
Dingmans Ferry	**71**	41 13N	74 55W
Dingwall, Can.	**39**	46 54N	60 28W
Dingwall, U.K.	**96**	57 36N	4 26W
Dinorwic	**52**	49 41N	92 30W
Dinorwic L.	**52**	49 37N	92 33W
Dinosaur National Monument	**78**	40 30N	108 45W
Dinosaur Prov. Park	**61**	50 47N	111 30W
Dinsmore	**56**	51 20N	107 26W
Dinuba	**80**	36 37N	119 22W
Dionne, L.	**38**	49 26N	67 55W
Dipolog	**127**	8 36N	123 20 E
Dir	**124**	35 08N	71 59 E
Dire Dawa	**115**	9 35N	41 45 E
Direction, C.	**135**	12 51 S	143 32 E
Diriamba	**84**	11 51N	86 19W
Dirico	**117**	17 50 S	20 42 E
Dirk Hartog I.	**134**	25 50 S	113 5 E
Dirranbandi	**135**	28 33 S	148 17 E
Disappointment, C.	**78**	46 20N	124 0W
Disappointment L.	**134**	23 20 S	122 40 E
Disaster B.	**135**	37 15 S	150 0 E
Discovery B.	**136**	38 10 S	140 40 E
Disko	**17**	69 45N	53 30W
Disko Bugt	**65**	69 10N	52 0W
Disko I.	**65**	69 30N	54 30W
Disraëli	**41**	45 54N	71 21W
Disteghil Sar	**124**	36 20N	75 5 E
Distrito Federal □	**86**	10 30N	66 55W
Diu, I.	**124**	20 45N	70 58 E
Diver	**34**	46 44N	79 30W
Dives, R.	**100**	49 18N	0 7W
Dives-sur-Mer	**100**	49 18N	0 8W
Divide	**78**	45 48N	112 47W
Dix, R.	**77**	37 49N	84 44W
Dixie	**78**	45 37N	115 27W
Dixie Mt.	**80**	39 55N	120 16W
Dixon, Calif., U.S.A.	**80**	38 27N	121 49W
Dixon, Ill., U.S.A.	**76**	41 50N	89 30W
Dixon, Iowa, U.S.A.	**76**	41 45N	90 47W
Dixon, Mo., U.S.A.	**76**	37 59N	92 6W
Dixon, Mont., U.S.A.	**78**	47 19N	114 25W
Dixon, N. Mex., U.S.A.	**79**	36 15N	105 57W
Dixon Entrance	**54**	54 30N	132 0W
Dixonville	**60**	56 32N	117 40W
Dixville	**41**	45 4N	71 46W
Diyarbakir	**122**	37 55N	40 18 E
Djakarta = Jakarta	**127**	6 9 S	106 49 E
Djambala	**116**	2 20 S	14 30 E
Djawa = Jawa	**127**	7 0 S	110 0 E
Djelfa	**114**	34 40N	3 15 E
Djema	**116**	6 9N	25 15 E
Djibouti	**115**	11 30N	43 5 E
Djibouti ■	**115**	11 30N	42 15 E
Djirlange	**128**	11 44N	108 15 E
Djolu	**116**	0 45N	22 5 E
Djoum	**116**	2 41N	12 35 E
Djugu	**116**	1 55N	30 35 E
Djúpivogur	**110**	64 39N	14 17W
Dmitriya Lapteva, Proliv	**121**	73 0N	140 0 E
Dneiper, R. = Dnepr	**120**	52 29N	35 10 E
Dnepr, R.	**120**	50 0N	31 0 E
Dneprodzerzhinskoye Vdkhr.	**121**	49 0N	34 0 E
Dnepropetrovsk	**120**	48 30N	35 0 E
Dnestr, R.	**120**	48 30N	26 30 E
Dniester = Dnestr	**120**	48 30N	26 30 E
Doaktown	**39**	46 33N	66 8W
Doba	**114**	8 40N	16 50 E
Dobbyn	**135**	19 44 S	139 59 E
Doberai, Jazirah	**127**	1 25 S	133 0 E
Dobie, R.	**52**	51 41N	90 29W
Doblas	**88**	37 5 S	64 0W
Dobo	**127**	5 45 S	134 15 E
Dobruja, reg.	**107**	44 30N	28 30 E
Dodecanese = Dhodhekánisos	**109**	36 35N	27 0 E
Dodge Center	**74**	44 1N	92 57W
Dodge City	**75**	37 42N	100 0W
Dodge L.	**55**	59 50N	105 36W
Dodgeville	**76**	42 55N	90 8W
Dodoma	**116**	6 8 S	35 45 E
Dodsland	**56**	51 50N	108 45W
Dodson	**78**	48 23N	108 4W
Doesburg	**105**	52 1N	6 9 E
Doetinchem	**105**	51 59N	6 18 E
Dog Creek	**63**	51 35N	122 14W
Dog L., Man., Can.	**54**	51 2N	98 31W
Dog L., Ont., Can.	**52**	48 40N	89 30W
Dog L., Ont., Can.	**53**	48 17N	84 8W
Dog, R.	**52**	48 32N	89 39W
Dogi	**124**	32 20N	62 50 E
Dohad	**124**	22 50N	74 15 E
Dohazari	**125**	22 10N	92 5 E
Doheny	**34**	47 4N	72 35W
Doherty	**34**	46 58N	79 44W
Doi, I.	**127**	2 21N	127 49 E
Doi Luang	**128**	18 20N	101 30 E
Doig, R., Alta., Can.	**54**	56 57N	120 0W
Doig, R., B.C., Can.	**54**	56 25N	120 40W
Dojran	**109**	41 10N	22 45 E
Dokkum	**105**	53 20N	5 59 E
Dol	**100**	48 34N	1 47W
Dolak, Pulau = Kolepom, P.	**127**	8 0 S	138 30 E
Doland	**74**	44 55N	98 5W
Dolbeau	**41**	48 53N	72 18W
Dole	**101**	47 7N	5 31 E
Dolgellau	**94**	52 44N	3 53W
Dolgelly = Dolgellau	**94**	52 44N	3 53W
Dolisie	**116**	4 0 S	13 10 E
Dollard	**56**	49 37N	108 35W
Dollard-des-Ormeaux	**44**	45 29N	73 49W
Dollarton	**66**	49 18N	122 57W
Dolomites = Dolomiti	**108**	46 30N	11 40 E
Dolomiti	**108**	46 30N	11 40 E
Dolores, Argent.	**88**	36 20 S	57 40W
Dolores, Mexico	**82**	28 53N	108 27W
Dolores, Uruguay	**88**	33 34 S	58 15W
Dolores, Colo., U.S.A.	**79**	37 30N	108 30W
Dolores, Tex., U.S.A.	**75**	27 40N	99 38W
Dolores, R.	**75**	38 30N	108 55W
Dolphin and Union Str.	**64**	69 5N	114 45W
Dolphin C.	**90**	51 10 S	50 0W
Dom Pedrito	**89**	31 0 S	54 40W
Dombarovskiy	**120**	50 46N	59 32 E
Dombås	**111**	62 6N	9 4 E
Dombasle	**101**	49 8N	5 10 E
Dombe Grande	**117**	12 56 S	13 8 E
Dombes	**103**	46 3N	5 0 E
Dome Creek	**63**	53 44N	121 1W
Domel, I = Letsok-aw-kyun	**128**	11 30N	98 25 E
Domérat	**102**	46 21N	2 32 E
Domeyko	**88**	29 0 S	71 30W
Domeyko, Cordillera	**88**	24 30 S	69 0W
Domfront	**100**	48 37N	0 40W
Dominador	**88**	24 21 S	69 20W
Dominica I.	**85**	15 20N	61 20W
Dominica Passage	**85**	15 10N	61 20W
Dominican Rep. ■	**85**	19 0N	70 30W
Dominion	**39**	46 13N	60 1W
Dominion, C.	**65**	65 30N	74 28W
Dominion City	**57**	49 9N	97 9W
Dominion L.	**38**	52 40N	61 45W
Domme	**102**	44 48N	1 12 E
Domodossóla	**106**	46 6N	8 19 E
Dompaire	**101**	48 14N	6 14 E
Dompierre-sur-Besbre	**102**	46 31N	3 41 E
Domrémy	**101**	48 26N	5 40 E
Don Benito	**104**	38 53N	5 51W
Don Martín, Presa de	**82**	27 30N	100 50W
Don Mills	**50**	43 42N	79 21W
Don Pedro Res.	**80**	37 43N	120 24W
Don Pen.	**62**	52 25N	128 12W
Don, R., Can.	**50**	43 39N	79 21W
Don, R., Eng., U.K.	**94**	53 41N	0 51W
Don, R., Scot., U.K.	**96**	57 14N	2 5W
Don, R., U.S.S.R.	**120**	49 35N	41 40 E
Donaghadee	**97**	54 38N	5 32W
Donald, Austral.	**136**	36 23 S	143 0 E
Donald, Can.	**63**	51 29N	117 10W
Donalda	**61**	52 35N	112 34W
Donaldsonville	**75**	30 2N	91 0W
Donalsonville	**73**	31 3N	84 52W
Donan	**58**	49 57N	97 6W
Donau, R.	**107**	47 55N	17 20 E
Donauwörth	**106**	48 42N	10 47 E
Doncaster	**94**	53 31N	1 9W
Dondo, Angola	**110**	9 45 S	14 25 E
Dondo, Mozam.	**116**	19 33 S	34 46 E
Dondo, Teluk	**127**	0 29N	120 45 E
Dondra Head	**124**	5 55N	80 40 E
Donegal	**97**	54 39N	8 8W
Donegal □	**97**	54 53N	8 0W
Donegal B.	**97**	54 30N	8 35W
Donetsk	**120**	48 0N	37 45 E
Dongara	**134**	29 14 S	114 57 E
Dongen	**105**	51 38N	4 56 E
Donges	**100**	47 18N	2 4W
Donggala	**127**	0 30 S	119 40 E
Dongou	**116**	2 0N	18 5 E
Doniphan	**75**	36 40N	90 50W
Donjon, Le	**102**	46 22N	3 48 E
Donken	**52**	46 58N	88 51W
Donkin	**39**	46 11N	59 52W
Donna	**110**	66 6N	12 30 E
Donna	**75**	26 12N	98 2W
Donnaconna	**41**	46 41N	71 41W
Donnelly	**60**	55 44N	117 6W
Donnelly's Crossing	**133**	35 42 S	173 38 E
Donora	**70**	40 11N	79 50W
Donovans	**37**	47 32N	52 50W
Donzère-Mondragon	**103**	44 28N	4 43 E
Donzy	**101**	47 20N	3 6 E
Doon, R.	**96**	55 26N	4 41W
Dor (Tantura)	**115**	32 37N	34 55 E
Dora Báltea, R.	**108**	45 42N	7 25 E
Dora, L.	**134**	22 0 S	123 0 E
Dorada, La	**86**	5 30N	74 40W
Doran L.	**55**	61 13N	108 6W
Dorat, Le	**102**	46 14N	1 5 E
Dorchester, Can.	**39**	45 54N	64 31W
Dorchester, U.K.	**95**	50 42N	2 28W
Dorchester, C.	**65**	65 27N	77 27W
Dorchester Crossing	**39**	46 10N	64 34W
Dordogne □	**102**	45 5N	0 40 E
Dordogne, R.	**102**	45 2N	0 36W
Dordrecht	**105**	51 48N	4 39 E
Doré L.	**55**	54 46N	107 17W
Doré Lake	**55**	54 38N	107 54W
Doré, Le, L.	**38**	51 17N	61 23W
Dore, Mt.	**102**	45 32N	2 50 E
Dore, R.	**102**	45 59N	3 28 E
Dori	**114**	14 3N	0 2W
Dorion, Ont., Can.	**52**	48 47N	88 39W
Dorion, Qué., Can.	**44**	45 23N	74 3W
Dorion-Vaudreuil	**71**	45 25N	75 4W
Dornes	**101**	46 48N	3 18 E
Dornoch	**96**	57 52N	4 0W
Dornoch Firth	**96**	57 52N	4 0W
Dorohoi	**107**	47 56N	26 30 E
Döröö Nuur	**129**	48 0N	93 0 E
Dorre I.	**134**	25 13 S	113 12 E
Dorris	**78**	41 59N	121 58W
Dorset, Can.	**47**	45 14N	78 54W
Dorset, U.S.A.	**70**	41 41N	8 42W
Dorset □	**95**	50 48N	2 25W
Dorsten	**105**	51 40N	6 55 E
Dortmund	**105**	51 32N	7 28 E
Dörtyol	**122**	36 52N	36 12 E
Doruma	**116**	4 42N	27 33 E
Dorval	**44**	45 27N	73 44W
Dorval Airport	**44**	45 28N	73 44W
Dos Bahías, C.	**90**	44 58 S	65 32W
Dos Cabezas	**79**	32 10N	109 37W
Dos Palos	**80**	36 59N	120 37W
Doshi	**123**	35 35N	68 50 E
Dosquet	**41**	46 28N	71 32W
Dot	**54**	50 12N	121 25W
Dothan	**73**	31 10N	85 25W
Doting Cove	**37**	49 27N	53 57W
Doty	**80**	46 38N	123 17W
Douai	**101**	50 21N	3 4 E
Douala	**116**	4 0N	9 45 E
Douarnenez	**100**	48 6N	4 21W
Doubs □	**101**	47 10N	6 20 E
Doubs, R.	**101**	46 53N	5 1 E
Doubtful B.	**134**	34 15 S	119 28 E
Doubtful Sd.	**133**	45 20 S	166 49 E
Doubtless B.	**133**	34 55 S	173 26 E
Doucet	**34**	48 15N	76 35W
Doudeville	**100**	49 43N	0 47 E
Doué	**100**	47 11N	0 20W
Douglas, Can.	**47**	45 31N	76 56W
Douglas, U.K.	**94**	54 9N	4 29W
Douglas, Alaska, U.S.A.	**67**	58 23N	134 32W
Douglas, Ariz., U.S.A.	**79**	31 21N	109 30W
Douglas, Ga., U.S.A.	**73**	31 32N	82 52W
Douglas, Wyo., U.S.A.	**74**	42 45N	105 20W
Douglas Chan.	**62**	53 40N	129 20W
Douglas I.	**66**	49 13N	122 47W
Douglas Pt.	**46**	44 19N	81 37W
Douglas Prov. Park	**56**	51 3N	106 28W
Douglastown, N.B., Can.	**38**	48 46N	64 24W
Douglastown, N.B., Can.	**39**	47 1N	65 30W
Douglasville	**73**	33 40N	84 43W
Doulevant	**101**	48 22N	4 53 E
Doullens	**101**	50 10N	2 20 E
Doumé	**116**	4 15N	13 25 E
Dounreay	**96**	58 40N	3 28W
Dourados	**89**	22 9 S	54 50W
Dourados, R.	**89**	21 58 S	54 18W
Dourdan	**101**	48 30N	2 0 E
Douro Litoral □	**104**	41 10N	8 20W
Douro, R.	**104**	41 1N	8 16W
Douvaine	**103**	46 19N	6 16 E
Douville	**45**	45 36N	72 59W
Dove Creek	**79**	37 53N	108 59W
Dove, R., N. Yorks, U.K.	**94**	54 20N	0 55W
Dove, R., Staffs., U.K.	**94**	52 51N	1 36W
Dover, U.K.	**95**	51 7N	1 19 E
Dover, Del., U.S.A.	**72**	39 10N	75 31W
Dover, Ky., U.S.A.	**77**	38 43N	83 52W
Dover, N.H., U.S.A.	**71**	43 5N	70 51W
Dover, N.J., U.S.A.	**71**	40 53N	74 34W
Dover, Ohio, U.S.A.	**70**	40 32N	81 30W
Dover-Foxcroft	**35**	45 14N	69 14W
Dover Plains	**71**	41 43N	73 35W

E

Eatonton **Emmeloord**

Eatonton **73** 33 22N 83 24W
Eatonville, Can. **41** 47 20N 69 41W
Eatonville, U.S.A. **80** 46 52N 122 16W
Eau Claire, S.C., U.S.A. **73** 34 5N 81 2W
Eau Claire, Wis., U.S.A. **74** 44 46N 91 30W
Eau-Claire, L. à l' **38** 52 36N 65 50W
Eau Claire, L. à l' **36** 56 10N 74 25W
Eauze **102** 43 53N 0 7 E
Ebbw Vale **95** 51 47N 3 12W
Ebeltoft **111** 56 12N 10 41 E
Ebensburg **70** 40 29N 78 43W
Eberswalde **106** 52 49N 13 50 E
Eboli **108** 40 39N 15 2 E
Ebolowa **116** 2 55N 11 10 E
Eboulements, Les **41** 47 28N 70 21W
Ebro, R. **104** 41 49N 1 5W
Éceuillé **100** 47 10N 1 19 E
Echaneni **121** 27 33 S 32 6 E
Echelles, Les **103** 45 27N 5 45 E
Echo Bay **46** 46 29N 84 4W
Echo Bay (Port Radium) **64** 66 05N 117 55W
Echoing, R. **55** 55 51N 92 5W
Échouani, L. **40** 47 46N 75 42W
Echternach **105** 49 49N 6 3 E
Echuca **136** 36 3 S 144 46 E
Ecija **104** 37 30N 5 10W
Eckville **61** 52 21N 114 22W
Eclipse Sd. **65** 72 38N 79 0W
Écommoy **100** 47 50N 0 17 E
Écorce, L. de l' **40** 47 5N 76 24W
Ecorces, L. des **43** 46 0N 74 32W
Ecorse **77** 42 14N 83 10W
Écos **101** 49 9N 1 35 E
Écouché **100** 48 42N 0 10W
Ecuador ■ **86** 2 0 S 78 0W
Ecueils, Pte. aux **36** 59 47N 77 50W
Ecum Secum **39** 44 58N 62 8W
Ed Damer **115** 17 27N 34 0 E
Edam, Can. **56** 53 11N 108 46W
Edam, Neth. **105** 52 31N 5 3 E
Eday, I. **96** 59 11N 2 47W
Edberg **61** 52 47N 112 47W
Eddrachillis B. **96** 58 16N 5 10W
Eddystone **95** 50 11N 4 16W
Eddyville **76** 41 9N 92 38W
Ede **105** 52 4N 5 40 E
Édea **116** 3 51N 10 9 E
Edehon L. **55** 60 25N 97 15W
Eden, Austral. **136** 37 3 S 149 55 E
Eden, Can. **57** 50 23N 99 28W
Eden, N.Y., U.S.A. **70** 42 39N 78 55W
Eden, Tex., U.S.A. **75** 31 16N 99 50W
Eden, Wyo., U.S.A. **78** 42 2N 109 27W
Eden L. **55** 56 38N 100 15W
Eden Mills **49** 43 35N 80 9W
Eden, R. **94** 54 57N 3 2W
Edenderry **97** 53 21N 7 3W
Edenton **73** 36 5N 76 36W
Edgar **74** 40 25N 98 0W
Edgartown **71** 41 22N 70 28W
Edge Hill **95** 52 7N 1 28W
Edge I. **17** 77 45N 22 30 E
Edgefield **73** 33 43N 81 59W
Edgeley, Can. **50** 43 48N 79 31W
Edgeley, U.S.A. **74** 46 27N 98 41W
Edgemont **74** 43 15N 103 53W
Edgeøya **17** 77 45N 22 30 E
Edgerton, Can. **61** 52 45N 110 27W
Edgerton, Ohio, U.S.A. **77** 41 27N 84 45W
Edgerton, Wis., U.S.A. **76** 42 50N 89 4W
Edgewater **61** 50 42N 116 5W
Edgewood, Can. **63** 49 47N 118 8W
Edgewood, U.S.A. **77** 38 55N 88 40W
Edgington **70** 45 24N 79 46W
Edhessa **109** 40 48N 22 5 E
Edievale **133** 45 49 S 169 22 E
Edina **76** 40 6N 92 10W
Edinburg, Ill., U.S.A. **76** 39 39N 89 23W
Edinburg, Ind., U.S.A. **77** 39 21N 85 58W
Edinburg, Tex., U.S.A. **75** 26 22N 98 10W
Edinburgh **96** 55 57N 3 12W
Edirne **109** 41 40N 26 45 E
Edison, Calif., U.S.A. **81** 35 21N 118 52W
Edison, Wash., U.S.A. **80** 48 33N 122 27W
Edmeston **71** 42 42N 75 15W
Edmond **75** 35 37N 97 30W
Edmonds, Can. **66** 49 13N 122 57W
Edmonds, U.S.A. **80** 47 47N 122 22W
Edmonton **59** 53 30N 113 30W
Edmore **46** 43 25N 85 3W
Edmund L. **55** 54 45N 93 17W
Edmundston **39** 47 23N 68 20W
Edna **75** 29 0N 96 40W
Edna Bay **54** 55 55N 133 40W
Edremit **122** 39 40N 27 0 E
Edsel Ford Ra. **91** 77 0 S 143 0W
Edson **60** 53 35N 116 28W
Eduardo Castex **88** 35 50 S 64 25W
Edward I. **52** 48 22N 88 37W
Edward, L. = Idi Amin Dada, L. **116** 0 25 S 29 40 E
Edward, R. **136** 35 0 S 143 30 E
Edward VII Pen. **91** 80 0 S 160 0W
Edwards **81** 34 55N 117 51W
Edwards Plat. **75** 30 30N 101 5W
Edwards, R. **76** 41 10N 90 59W
Edwardsburg **77** 41 48N 86 6W
Edwardsport **77** 38 49N 87 15W
Edwardsville, Ill., U.S.A. **76** 38 49N 89 57W
Edwardsville, Pa., U.S.A. **71** 41 15N 75 56W
Edzo **54** 62 49N 116 4W
Eek **67** 60 10N 162 0W
Eekloo **105** 51 11N 3 33 E
Eel, R., Ind., U.S.A. **77** 39 7N 86 58W
Eel, R., Ind., U.S.A. **77** 40 45N 86 22W
Eel River Crossing **39** 48 1N 66 25W
Eernegem **105** 51 8N 3 2 E
Effingham **77** 39 8N 88 30W
Égadi, Ísole **108** 37 55N 12 10 E
Eganville **47** 45 32N 77 5W
Egeland **74** 48 42N 99 6W
Egenolf L. **55** 59 3N 100 0W
Eger **107** 47 53N 20 27 E
Egersund = Eigersund **111** 58 26N 6 1 E
Egerton, Mt. **134** 24 42 S 117 44 E
Egg L. **55** 55 5N 105 30W
Eggertsville **49** 42 58N 78 46W
Égletons **102** 45 24N 2 3 E
Eglington I. **64** 75 48N 118 30W
Egmont **62** 49 45N 123 56W
Egmont B. **39** 46 29N 64 6W
Egmont, C. **133** 39 16 S 173 45 E
Egmont, Mt. **133** 39 17 S 174 5 E
Eğridir Gölü **122** 37 53N 30 50 E
Egua **86** 5 5N 68 0W
Éguzon **102** 46 27N 1 33 E
Egvekinot **121** 66 19N 179 50W
Egypt■ **115** 28 0N 31 0 E
Ehime-ken □ **132** 33 30N 132 40 E
Eholt **63** 49 10N 118 34W
Ehrenburg **81** 33 36N 114 31W
Eidsvoll **111** 60 19N 11 14 E
Eifel **105** 50 10N 6 45 E
Eigersund **111** 58 26N 6 1 E
Eigg, I. **96** 56 54N 6 10W
Eighty Mile Beach **134** 19 30 S 120 40 E
Eil **115** 8 0N 49 50 E
Eil, L. **96** 56 50N 5 15W
Eilat **122** 29 30N 34 56 E
Eildon, L. **136** 37 10 S 146 0 E
Eileen L. **55** 62 16N 107 37W
Einasleigh **135** 18 32 S 144 5 E
Eindhoven **105** 51 26N 5 30 E
Eiriksjökull **110** 64 46N 20 24W
Eirunepé **86** 6 35 S 70 0W
Eisenach **106** 50 58N 10 18 E
Eisenerz **106** 47 32N 14 54 E
Ejido **86** 8 33N 71 14W
Ejutla **83** 16 34N 96 44W
Ekalaka **74** 45 55N 104 30W
Eketahuna **133** 40 38 S 175 43 E
Ekibastuz **120** 51 40N 75 22 E
Ekimchan **121** 53 0N 133 0W
Ekwan Pt. **34** 53 16N 82 7W
Ekwan, R. **34** 53 12N 82 15W
El Baúl **86** 8 57N 68 17W
El Bluff **84** 11 59N 83 40W
El Cajon **81** 32 49N 117 0W
El Callao **86** 7 25N 61 50W
El Campo **75** 29 10N 96 20W
El Carmen **86** 1 16N 66 52W
El Centro **81** 32 50N 115 40W
El Cerro **86** 17 30 S 61 40W
El Cocuy **86** 6 25N 72 27W
El Compadre **81** 32 20N 116 14W
El Cuy **90** 39 55 S 68 25W
El Cuyo **83** 21 30N 87 40W
El Dátil **82** 30 7N 112 15W
El Dere **115** 3 50N 47 8 E
El Díaz **83** 21 1N 87 17W
El Dificul **86** 9 51N 74 14W
El Díos **82** 20 40N 87 20W
El Diviso **86** 1 22N 78 14W
El Djouf **114** 20 0N 11 30 E
El Dorado, Colomb. **86** 1 11N 71 52W
El Dorado, Ark., U.S.A. **75** 33 10N 92 40W
El Dorado, Kans., U.S.A. **75** 37 55N 96 56W
El Dorado, Venez. **86** 6 55N 61 30W
El Dorado Springs **76** 37 54N 93 59W
El Escorial **104** 40 35N 4 7W
El Faiyûm **115** 29 19N 30 50 E
El Fâsher **115** 13 33N 25 26 E
El Ferrol **104** 43 29N 3 14W
El Fuerte **82** 26 30N 108 40W
El Iskandarîya **115** 31 0N 30 0 E
El Khârga **115** 25 30N 30 33 E
El Khartûm **115** 15 31N 32 35 E
El Ladhiqiya **122** 35 20N 35 30 E
El Mahalla el Kubra **115** 31 0N 31 0 E
El Mansûra **122** 31 0N 31 19 E
El Mantico **86** 7 27N 62 32W
El Miamo **86** 7 39N 61 46W
El Milagro **88** 30 59 S 65 59W
El Minyâ **115** 28 7N 30 33 E
El Monte **81** 34 4N 118 2W
El Obeid **115** 13 8N 30 10 E
El Oro = Sta. María del Oro **82** 25 50N 105 20W
El Oro de Hidalgo **83** 19 48N 100 8W
El Palmar **86** 7 58N 61 53W
El Palmito, Presa **82** 25 40N 105 3W
El Pao **86** 9 38N 68 8W
El Paso, Ill., U.S.A. **76** 40 44N 89 1W
El Paso, Tex., U.S.A. **79** 31 50N 106 30W
El Paso Robles **80** 35 38N 120 41W
El Pilar **86** 10 32N 63 9W
El Portal **80** 37 44N 119 49W
El Porvenir, Mexico **82** 31 15N 105 51W
El Porvenir, Venez. **86** 4 42N 71 19W
El Progreso **84** 15 26N 87 51W
El Pueblito **82** 29 3N 105 4W
El Qahira **115** 30 1N 31 14 E
El Qasr **115** 25 44N 28 42 E
El Reno **75** 35 30N 98 0W
El Rio **81** 34 14N 119 10W
El Salado **86** 8 56N 73 55W
El Salto **82** 23 47N 105 22W
El Salvador ■ **84** 13 50N 89 0W
El Sauce **84** 13 0N 86 40W
El Suweis **115** 29 58N 32 31 E
El Temblador **86** 8 59N 62 44W
El Tigre **86** 8 55N 64 15W
El Tocuyo **86** 9 47N 69 48W
El Tofo **88** 29 22 S 71 18W
El Tránsito **88** 28 52 S 70 17W
El Turbio **90** 51 30 S 72 40W
El Vigía **86** 8 38N 71 39W
El Wak **116** 2 49N 40 56 E
Elaho, R. **62** 50 7N 123 23W
Elat **127** 5 40 S 133 5 E
Elâziğ **122** 38 37N 39 22 E
Elba **73** 31 27N 86 4W
Elba, I. **108** 42 48N 10 15 E
Elbasani **109** 41 9N 20 9 E
Elbe **80** 46 45N 121 49W
Elbe, R. **106** 53 15N 10 7 E
Elberfeld **77** 38 10N 87 27W
Elbert, Mt. **79** 39 12N 106 36W
Elberta, Mich., U.S.A. **72** 44 35N 86 14W
Elberta, N.Y., U.S.A. **49** 43 16N 78 52W
Elberton **73** 34 7N 82 51W
Elbeuf **100** 49 17N 1 2 E
Elblag **107** 54 10N 19 25 E
Elbow **56** 51 7N 106 35W
Elbow, R. **59** 51 3N 114 2W
Elbrus, Mt. **120** 43 30N 42 30 E
Elburg **105** 52 26N 5 50 E
Elburn **77** 41 54N 88 28W
Elburz Mts. = Alborz **123** 36 0N 52 0 E
Elche **104** 38 15N 0 42W
Elcho I. **134** 11 55 S 135 45 E
Eldon, Iowa, U.S.A. **76** 40 50N 92 12W
Eldon, Mo., U.S.A. **76** 38 20N 92 38W
Eldora **76** 42 20N 93 5W
Eldorado, Argent. **89** 26 28 S 54 43W
Eldorado, Ont., Can. **47** 44 35N 77 31W
Eldorado, Sask., Can. **55** 59 35N 108 30W
Eldorado, Mexico **82** 24 0N 107 30W
Eldorado, Ill., U.S.A. **77** 37 50N 88 25W
Eldorado, Tex., U.S.A. **75** 30 52N 100 35W
Eldorado Park **50** 43 39N 79 46W
Eldoret **116** 0 30N 35 25 E
Eldred **70** 41 57N 78 24W
Eldridge **76** 41 39N 90 35W
Electra **75** 34 0N 99 0W
Eleele **67** 21 54N 159 35W
Elephant Butte Res. **79** 33 45N 107 30W
Elephant I. **91** 61 0 S 55 0W
Eleuthera I. **84** 25 0N 76 20W
Elfin Cove **67** 58 11N 136 20W
Elfrida **48** 43 10N 79 47W
Elgin, B.C., Can. **66** 49 4N 122 49W
Elgin, Man., Can. **57** 49 27N 100 16W
Elgin, N.B., Can. **35** 45 48N 65 10W
Elgin, Ont., Can. **47** 44 36N 76 13W
Elgin, Ont., Can. **71** 44 37N 76 15W
Elgin, U.K. **96** 57 39N 3 20W
Elgin, Ill., U.S.A. **77** 42 0N 88 20W
Elgin, N.D., U.S.A. **74** 46 24N 101 46W
Elgin, Nebr., U.S.A. **74** 41 58N 98 3W
Elgin, Nev., U.S.A. **79** 37 27N 114 36W
Elgin, Oreg., U.S.A. **78** 45 37N 118 0W
Elgin, Texas, U.S.A. **75** 30 21N 97 22W
Elgon, Mt. **116** 1 10N 34 30 E
Eliase **127** 8 10 S 130 55 E
Elida **75** 33 56N 103 41W
Elie **55** 49 48N 97 52W
Elim **67** 64 35N 162 20W
Elisabethville = Lubumbashi **117** 11 32 S 27 38 E
Elista **120** 46 16N 44 14 E
Elizabeth, Austral. **135** 34 42 S 138 41 E
Elizabeth, Ill., U.S.A. **76** 42 19N 90 13W
Elizabeth, N.J., U.S.A. **71** 40 37N 74 12W
Elizabeth City **73** 36 18N 76 16W
Elizabethton **73** 36 20N 82 13W
Elizabethtown, Ill., U.S.A. **77** 37 27N 88 18W
Elizabethtown, Ky., U.S.A. **72** 37 40N 85 54W
Elizabethtown, N.Y., U.S.A. **71** 44 13N 73 36W
Elizabethtown, Pa., U.S.A. **71** 40 8N 76 36W
Elk City **75** 35 25N 99 25W
Elk Creek **80** 39 36N 122 32W
Elk Grove **80** 38 25N 121 22W
Elk Island Nat. Park **60** 53 35N 112 59W
Elk Lake **34** 47 40N 80 25W
Elk Lakes Prov. Pzrk **61** 50 30N 115 10W
Elk Point **60** 53 54N 110 55W
Elk, R. **61** 49 11N 115 14W
Elk Rapids **46** 44 54N 85 25W
Elk River, Idaho, U.S.A. **78** 46 50N 116 8W
Elk River, Minn., U.S.A. **74** 45 17N 93 34W
Elkader **76** 42 51N 91 24W
Elkford **61** 49 52N 114 53W
Elkhart, Ind., U.S.A. **77** 41 42N 85 55W
Elkhart, Kans., U.S.A. **75** 37 3N 101 54W
Elkhart, R. **77** 41 41N 85 58W
Elkhorn, Can. **57** 49 59N 101 14W
Elkhorn, U.S.A. **77** 42 40N 88 33W
Elkhorn, R. **74** 42 0N 98 15W
Elkhovo **109** 42 10N 26 40 E
Elkin **73** 36 17N 80 50W
Elkins **72** 38 53N 79 53W
Elko, Can. **61** 49 20N 115 10W
Elko, U.S.A. **78** 40 50N 115 50W
Elkton **46** 43 49N 83 11W
Ellef Ringnes I. **65** 78 30N 102 2W
Ellen, Mt. **79** 38 4N 110 56W
Ellendale, Can. **39** 44 41N 63 33W
Ellendale, U.S.A. **74** 46 3N 98 30W
Ellensburg **78** 47 0N 120 30W
Ellenville **71** 41 42N 74 23W
Ellerslie **59** 53 26N 113 30W
Ellery, Mt. **136** 37 28 S 148 40 E
Ellesmere I. **65** 79 30N 80 0W
Ellesmere, L. **15** 43 46 S 172 27 E
Ellesworth Land **91** 74 0 S 85 0W
Ellettsville **77** 39 14N 86 38W
Ellice Is. **14** 8 0 S 176 0 E
Ellinwood **74** 38 27N 98 37W
Elliot L. **57** 52 54N 95 18W
Elliot Lake **46** 46 25N 82 35W
Ellis **74** 39 0N 99 39W
Elliston **37** 48 38N 53 3W
Ellisville **73** 31 38N 89 12W
Ellon **96** 57 21N 2 5W
Ellore = Eluru **125** 16 48N 81 8 E
Ells, R. **60** 57 18N 111 40W
Ellsworth **74** 38 47N 98 15W
Ellsworth Land **91** 76 0 S 89 0W
Ellwood City **70** 40 52N 80 19W
Elm Grove **58** 49 47N 96 49W
Elma, Can. **57** 49 52N 95 55W
Elma, U.S.A. **80** 47 0N 123 30 E
Elmer **76** 39 57N 92 39W
Elmhurst **77** 41 52N 87 58W
Elmira, Ont., Can. **49** 43 36N 80 33W
Elmira, P.E.I., Can. **35** 46 30N 61 59W
Elmira, U.S.A. **70** 42 8N 76 49W
Elmore, Austral. **136** 36 30 S 144 37 E
Elmore, Calif., U.S.A. **81** 33 7N 115 49W
Elmore, Minn., U.S.A. **77** 41 29N 83 18W
Elmsdale **39** 44 58N 63 30W
Elmvale **46** 44 35N 79 52W
Elmwood, Can. **70** 44 14N 81 3W
Elmwood, U.S.A. **76** 40 47N 89 58W
Elmworth **60** 55 3N 119 37W
Elnora, Can. **61** 51 59N 113 12W
Elnora, U.S.A. **77** 38 53N 87 5W
Elora **49** 43 41N 80 26W
Elorza **86** 7 3N 69 31W
Eloy **79** 32 46N 111 46W
Éloyes **101** 48 6N 6 36 E
Elphin **47** 44 55N 76 37W
Elphinstone **57** 50 32N 100 30W
Elrose **56** 51 12N 108 0W
Elsa **64** 63 55N 135 29W
Elsas **53** 48 32N 82 55W
Elsie, Mich., U.S.A. **46** 43 5N 84 23W
Elsie, Oreg., U.S.A. **80** 45 52N 123 35W
Elsinore, Cal., U.S.A. **81** 33 40N 117 15W
Elsinore, Utah, U.S.A. **79** 38 40N 112 2W
Elson **80** 47 32N 123 4W
Elsona **66** 49 12N 122 57W
Elst **105** 51 55N 5 51 E
Eltham **133** 39 26 S 174 19 E
Eluru **125** 16 48N 81 8 E
Elvas **104** 38 50N 7 17W
Elven **100** 47 44N 2 36W
Elverum **111** 60 53N 11 34 E
Elvire, Mt. **136** 29 14 S 119 33 E
Elwood, Ill., U.S.A. **77** 41 24N 88 7W
Elwood, Ind., U.S.A. **77** 40 20N 85 50W
Elwood, Nebr., U.S.A. **74** 40 38N 99 51W
Ely, U.K. **95** 52 24N 0 16 E
Ely, Minn., U.S.A. **52** 47 54N 91 52W
Ely, Nev., U.S.A. **78** 39 10N 114 50W
Elyria **70** 41 22N 82 8W
Emba **120** 48 50N 58 8 E
Emba, R. **120** 48 0N 56 0 E
Embarcación **88** 23 10 S 64 0W
Embarras Portage **55** 58 27N 111 28W
Embarrass, R. **77** 38 39N 87 37W
Embro **46** 43 9N 80 54W
Embrun **103** 44 34N 6 30 E
Embu **116** 0 32 S 37 38 E
Emden **105** 53 22N 7 12 E
Emerald **135** 23 32 S 148 10 E
Emeril **36** 47 26N 75 47W
Emerson **57** 49 0N 97 10W
Emery **79** 38 59N 111 17W
Emery Park **79** 32 10N 110 59W
Emi Koussi, Mt. **114** 20 0N 18 55 E
Emilia-Romagna □ **108** 44 33N 10 40 E
Eminence **77** 38 22N 85 11W
Emlenton **70** 41 11N 79 41W
Emmeloord **105** 52 44N 5 46 E

Emmen Eyre Pen

Emmen 105 52 48N 6 57 E
Emmerich 105 51 50N 6 12 E
Emmetsburg 76 43 3N 94 40W
Emmett, Idaho, U.S.A. 78 43 51N 116 33W
Emmett, Mich., U.S.A. 46 42 59N 82 46W
Emo 52 48 38N 93 50W
Empalme 82 28 1N 110 49W
Empangeni 117 28 50S 31 52 E
Empedrado 88 28 0S 58 46W
Emporia, Kans., U.S.A. 74 38 25N 96 16W
Emporia, Va., U.S.A. 73 36 41N 77 32W
Emporium 70 41 30N 78 17W
Empress 61 50 57N 110 0W
Ems, R. 105 52 37N 7 16 E
Emsdale 46 45 32N 79 19W
Emsdetten 105 52 11N 7 31 E
En Nahud 115 12 45N 28 25 E
Enambú 86 1 1N 70 17W
Enard B. 96 58 5N 5 20W
Encantadas, Serra 89 30 40S 53 0W
Encanto, Cape 127 15 44N 121 40 E
Encarnación 89 27 15S 56 0W
Encarnación de Diaz 82 21 30N 102 20W
Encinal 75 28 3N 99 25W
Encinillas 82 33 3N 117 17W
Encinitas 81 33 3N 117 17W
Encino 79 34 38N 105 40W
Encounter B. 135 35 45S 138 45 E
Endako 62 54 6N 125 2W
Endau 128 2 40N 103 38 E
Endau, R. 128 2 30N 103 30 E
Ende 127 8 45S 121 30 E
Endeavour 56 52 10N 102 39W
Endeavour Str. 135 10 45S 142 0 E
Enderbury I. 15 3 8S 171 5W
Enderby 63 50 35N 119 10W
Enderby Land 91 66 0S 53 0 E
Enderlin 74 46 45N 97 41W
Endicott, N.Y., U.S.A. 71 42 6N 76 2W
Endicott, Wash., U.S.A. 78 47 0N 117 45W
Endicott Mts. 67 68 0N 152 30W
Enez 109 40 45N 26 5 E
Enfield, Can. 39 44 56N 63 32W
Enfield, U.K. 95 51 39N 0 4W
Enfield, U.S.A. 77 38 6N 88 20W
Engadin 106 46 45N 10 10 E
Engadine 46 46 4N 85 38W
Engano, C. 85 18 30N 68 20W
Engaño, C. 127 18 35N 122 23 E
Engels 120 51 28N 46 6 E
Engemann L. 55 58 0N 106 55W
Enggano, I. 126 5 20S 102 40 E
Enghien 105 50 37N 4 2 E
Engkilili 126 1 3N 111 42 E
England 75 34 30N 91 58W
England □ 94 53 0N 2 0W
Englee 37 50 45N 56 5W
Englefeld 56 52 10N 104 39W
Englefield, C. 65 69 49N 85 34W
Englehart 34 47 49N 79 52W
Engler L. 55 59 8N 106 52W
Englewood, U.S.A. 77 39 53N 84 18W
Englewood, Colo., U.S.A. 74 39 40N 105 0W
Englewood, Kans., U.S.A. 75 37 7N 99 59W
English 77 38 20N 86 28W
English B. 66 49 17N 123 11W
English Bazar 125 24 58N 88 21 E
English Channel 95 50 0N 2 0W
English Company Is. 135 12 0S 137 0 E
English Harbour East 37 47 38N 54 54W
English, R., Ont., Can. 52 50 35N 93 30W
English, R., Ont., Can. 52 49 12N 91 5W
English, R., U.S.A. 76 41 29N 91 32W
English River 52 49 20N 91 0W
Engteng (Yungting) 131 24 46N 116 45 E
Enid 75 36 26N 97 52W
Enilda 60 55 25N 116 18W
Eniwetok 15 11 30N 152 16 E
Enkhuizen 105 52 42N 5 17 E
Enna 108 37 34N 14 15 E
Ennadai 55 61 8N 100 53W
Ennadai L. 55 61 0N 101 0W
Ennedi, reg. 115 19 20N 28 0 E
Ennis, Ireland 97 52 51N 8 59W
Ennis, Mont., U.S.A. 78 45 27N 111 48W
Ennis, Texas, U.S.A. 75 32 15N 96 40W
Enniscorthy 97 52 30N 6 35W
Enniskillen 97 54 20N 7 40W
Ennistimon 97 52 56N 9 18W
Ennotville 49 43 39N 80 20W
Enns, R. 106 48 8N 14 27 E
Enontekiö 110 68 23N 23 37 E
Enriquillo, L. 85 18 20N 72 5W
Enschede 105 52 13N 6 53 E
Ensenada, Argent. 88 34 55S 57 55W
Ensenada, Mexico 82 31 50N 116 50W
Enshih 131 30 18N 109 27 E
Ensisheim 101 47 50N 7 20 E
Entebbe 116 0 4N 32 28 E
Enterprise, Can. 54 60 47N 115 45W
Enterprise, Oreg., U.S.A. 78 45 30N 117 11W
Enterprise, Utah, U.S.A. 79 37 37N 113 36W
Entiako L. 62 53 13N 125 31W
Entrance 54 53 25N 117 50W
Entre Rios, Boliv. 88 21 30S 64 25W
Entre Ríos, Mozam. 117 14 57S 37 20 E
Entre Ríos □ 88 30 30S 58 30W
Entrecasteaux, Pt. d' 134 34 50S 115 56 E
Entwistle 54 53 30N 115 0W
Enugu 114 6 30N 7 30 E
Enumclaw 80 47 12N 122 0W
Envermeu 100 49 53N 1 15 E
Envigado 86 6 10N 75 35W
Eólie o Lípari, Is. 108 38 30N 14 50 E
Epe 105 52 21N 5 59 E
Épernay 101 49 3N 3 56 E
Épernon 101 48 35N 1 40 E
Ephesus 122 38 0N 27 30 E
Ephraim 78 39 30N 111 37W
Ephrata 78 47 28N 119 32W
Épinac-les-Mines 101 46 59N 4 31 E
Épinal 101 48 19N 6 27 E
Epiphanie, L' 43 45 51N 73 29W
Epping 95 51 42N 0 8 E
Epukiro 117 21 30S 19 0 E
Equality 77 37 44N 88 20W
Equatorial Guinea ■ 116 2 0S 78 0W
Équeurdreville-Hainneville 100 49 40N 1 40W
Er Rif 114 35 1N 4 1W
Eramosa 49 43 37N 80 13W
Ercha 121 69 45N 147 20 E
Erciyas Daği 122 38 30N 35 30 E
Erdene 130 44 30N 111 10 E
Erdenedalay 130 46 3N 105 1 E
Erebus, Mt. 91 77 35S 167 0 E
Erechim 89 27 35S 52 15W
Ereğli 122 41 15N 31 30 E
Eresma, R. 104 41 13N 4 30W
Erewadi Myitwanya 125 15 30N 95 0 E
Erfurt 106 50 58N 11 2 E
Erg Chech, dist. 114 50 59N 11 0 E
Ergani 122 38 26N 39 49 E
Ergene, R. 109 41 20N 27 0 E
Erhlien 130 43 42N 112 2 E
Erhtao Kiang 130 42 40N 127 10 E
Eriboll, L. 96 58 28N 4 41W
Eric 36 51 56N 65 45W
Eric L. 38 51 55N 65 36W
Érice 108 38 4N 12 34 E
Erie, Mich., U.S.A. 77 41 47N 83 31W
Erie, Pa., U.S.A. 70 42 10N 80 7W
Erie □ 49 42 58N 78 56W
Erie Canal 70 43 15N 78 0W
Erie, L. 46 42 15N 81 0W
Erieau 46 42 16N 81 57W
Eriksdale 57 50 52N 98 7W
Erimanthos 109 37 57N 21 50 E
Erimo-misaki 132 41 50N 143 15 E
Erin 49 43 45N 80 7W
Erindale 50 43 32N 79 39W
Erith 54 53 25N 116 46W
Eritrea □ 115 14 0N 41 0 E
Erlandson, L. 36 57 3N 68 28W
Erlangen 106 49 35N 11 0 E
Ermenak 122 36 44N 33 0 E
Ermoúpolis = Siros 109 37 28N 24 57 E
Ernakulam 124 9 59N 76 19 E
Erne, Lough 97 54 26N 7 46W
Erne, R. 97 54 30N 8 16W
Ernée 100 48 18N 0 56W
Erode 124 11 24N 77 45 E
Erquy 100 48 38N 2 29W
Erquy, Cap d' 100 48 39N 2 29W
Erramala Hills 124 15 30N 78 15 E
Errigal, Mt. 97 55 2N 8 8W
Erris Hd. 97 54 19N 10 0W
Erskine, Can. 61 52 20N 112 53W
Erskine, U.S.A. 74 47 37N 96 0W
Erstein 101 48 25N 7 38 E
Ervy-le-Châtel 101 48 2N 3 55 E
Erwin 73 36 10N 82 28W
Erzgebirge 106 50 25N 13 0 E
Erzin 121 50 15N 95 10 E
Erzincan 122 39 46N 39 30 E
Erzurum 122 39 57N 41 15 E
Es Sînâ' 115 29 0N 34 0 E
Esan-misaki 132 41 40N 141 10 E
Esbjerg 111 55 29N 8 29 E
Escalante 79 37 47N 111 37W
Escalante, R. 79 37 45N 111 0W
Escalón 82 26 40N 104 20W
Escambia, R. 73 30 45N 87 15W
Escanaba 72 45 44N 87 5W
Esch 105 51 37N 5 17 E
Eschweiler 105 50 49N 6 14 E
Escobal 84 9 6N 80 1W
Escondida, La 82 24 6N 99 55W
Escondido 81 33 9N 117 4W
Escoumins, Les 41 48 21N 69 24W
Escuinapa 82 22 50N 105 50W
Escuintla 84 14 20N 90 48W
Escuminac 35 48 0N 67 0W
Escutillas = Ceba 86 6 33N 70 24W
Esfahān □ 123 33 0N 53 0 E
Esh Sham = Dimashq 122 33 30N 36 18 E
Esk, R., Dumfries, U.K. 96 54 58N 3 4W
Esk, R., N. Yorks., U.K. 94 54 27N 0 36W
Esker 36 53 53N 66 25W
Eskifjördur 110 65 3N 13 55W
Eskilstuna 111 59 22N 16 32 E
Eskimo Ls. 67 69 15N 132 17W
Eskimo Pt. 55 61 10N 94 3W
Eskişehir 122 39 50N 30 35 E
Esla, R. 104 41 45N 5 50W
Esmeralda, La 88 22 16S 62 33W
Esmeraldas 86 1 0N 79 40W
Esnagami L. 53 50 19N 86 51W
Esnagi L. 53 48 36N 84 33W
Espada, Pta. 86 12 5N 71 7W
Espalion 102 44 32N 2 47 E
Espanola 46 46 15N 81 46W
Esparta 84 9 59N 84 40W
Espenberg, C. 67 66 35N 163 40W
Esperance 134 33 45S 121 55 E
Esperance B. 134 33 48S 121 55 E
Esperanza, Argent. 88 31 29S 61 3W
Esperanza, Can. 62 49 52N 126 43W
Esperanza Inlet 62 49 51N 126 55W
Esperanza, La, Argent. 88 24 9S 64 52W
Esperanza, La, Boliv. 86 14 20S 62 0W
Esperanza, La, Cuba 84 22 46N 83 44W
Esperanza, La, Hond. 84 14 15N 88 10W
Espéraza 102 42 56N 2 14 E
Espichel, C. 104 38 22N 9 16W
Espigão, Serra do 89 26 35S 50 30W
Espinal 86 4 9N 74 53W
Espinilho, Serra do 89 28 30S 55 0W
Espino 86 8 34N 66 1W
Espíritu Santo, B. del 83 19 15N 79 40W
Espíritu Santo, I. 82 24 30N 110 23W
Espita 83 21 1N 88 19W
Espungabera 117 20 29S 32 45 E
Esquel 90 42 40S 71 20W
Esquimalt 63 48 26N 123 25W
Esquina 88 30 0S 59 30W
Essaouira 114 31 32N 9 42W
Essarts, Les 100 46 47N 1 12W
Essen, Belg. 105 51 28N 4 28 E
Essen, Ger. 105 51 28N 6 59 E
Essequibo, R. 86 5 45N 58 50W
Essex, Can. 46 42 10N 82 49W
Essex, Calif., U.S.A. 81 34 44N 115 15W
Essex, Ill., U.S.A. 77 41 11N 88 11W
Essex, N.Y., U.S.A. 71 44 17N 73 21W
Essex □ 95 51 48N 0 30 E
Essexville 46 43 37N 83 50W
Esslingen 106 48 43N 9 19 E
Essondale 66 49 14N 122 48W
Essonne □ 101 48 30N 2 20 E
Est, L.de l' 39 47 37N 61 23W
Estados, I. de los 90 54 40S 64 30W
Estagel 102 42 47N 2 40 E
Estância 87 11 16S 37 26W
Estancia 79 34 50N 106 1W
Estats, Pic d' 102 42 40N 1 40 E
Estcourt 41 47 28N 69 14W
Estelí 84 13 9N 86 22W
Estelline, S.D., U.S.A. 74 44 39N 96 52W
Estelline, Texas, U.S.A. 75 34 35N 100 27W
Esterhazy 57 50 37N 102 5W
Esternay 101 48 44N 3 33 E
Estevan 56 49 10N 102 59W
Estevan Group 62 53 3N 129 38W
Estevan Sd. 62 53 5N 129 34W
Estherville 74 43 25N 94 50W
Estissac 101 48 16N 3 48 E
Eston 56 51 8N 108 40W
Estonian S.S.R. □ 120 48 30N 25 30 E
Estoril 104 38 42N 9 23W
Estrada, La 104 42 43N 8 27W
Estrêla, Serra da 104 40 10N 7 45W
Estremadura 104 39 0N 9 0W
Estrondo, Serra do 87 7 20S 48 0W
Esztergom 107 47 47N 18 44 E
Étables-sur-Mer 100 48 38N 2 51W
Étain 101 49 13N 5 38 E
Étamamu 38 50 18N 59 59W
Étampes 101 48 26N 2 10 E
Étang 101 46 52N 4 10 E
Étang-du-Nord 39 47 22N 61 57W
Étaples 101 50 30N 1 39 E
Etawah 124 26 48N 79 6 E
Etawah, R. 73 34 20N 84 15W
Etawney L. 55 57 50N 96 50W
Etchemin, R. 42 46 46N 71 14W
Ethel 80 46 32N 122 46W
Ethelbert 57 51 32N 100 25W
Ethiopia ■ 115 8 0N 40 0 E
Ethiopian Highlands 112 10 0N 37 0 E
Etive, L. 96 56 30N 5 12W
Etna, Mt. 108 37 45N 15 0 E
Etobicoke 50 43 42N 79 34W
Etobicoke Cr. 50 43 35N 79 32W
Etolin I. 54 56 5N 132 20W
Etoshapan 117 18 40S 16 30 E
Etowah 73 35 20N 84 30W
Étrépagny 100 49 18N 1 36 E
Étretat 100 49 42N 0 12 E
Étroits, Les 41 47 24N 68 54W
Ettelbrück 105 49 50N 6 5 E
Ettrick Water 96 55 31N 2 55W
Etzatlán 82 20 48N 104 5W
Etzikom 61 49 29N 111 6W
Etzna 83 19 35N 90 15W
Eu 100 50 3N 1 26 E
Euabalong West 136 33 3S 146 23 E
Euboea = Évvoia 109 38 40N 23 40 E
Eucla Basin 134 31 19S 126 9 E
Euclid 70 41 32N 81 31W
Eucumbene, L. 136 36 2S 148 40 E
Eudistes, L. des 38 50 30N 65 15W
Eudora 75 33 5N 91 17W
Eufaula, Ala., U.S.A. 73 31 55N 85 11W
Eufaula, Okla., U.S.A. 75 35 20N 95 33W
Eufaula, L. 75 35 15N 95 28W
Eugene 78 44 0N 123 8W
Eugenia, Punta 82 27 50N 115 5W
Eugowra 136 33 22S 148 24 E
Eunice, La., U.S.A. 75 30 35N 92 28W
Eunice, N. Mex., U.S.A. 75 32 30N 103 10W
Eupen 105 50 37N 6 3 E
Euphrates = Furat, Nahr al 122 33 30N 43 0 E
Eure □ 100 49 6N 1 0 E
Eure-et-Loir □ 100 48 22N 1 30 E
Eureka, Can. 65 80 0N 85 56W
Eureka, Calif., U.S.A. 78 40 50N 124 0W
Eureka, Ill., U.S.A. 76 40 43N 89 16W
Eureka, Kans., U.S.A. 75 37 50N 96 20W
Eureka, Mo., U.S.A. 76 38 30N 90 38W
Eureka, Mont., U.S.A. 61 48 53N 115 6W
Eureka, Nev., U.S.A. 78 39 32N 116 2W
Eureka, S.D., U.S.A. 74 45 49N 99 38W
Eureka, Utah, U.S.A. 78 40 0N 112 0W
Eureka River 60 56 27N 118 44W
Euroa 136 36 44S 145 35 E
Europa, Île 117 22 20S 40 22 E
Europa, Picos de 104 43 10N 5 0W
Europa Pt. 104 36 2N 6 32W
Europe 93 20 0N 20 0 E
Europoort 105 51 57N 4 10 E
Eustis 73 28 54N 81 36W
Eutsuk L. 62 53 20N 126 45W
Évain 40 48 14N 79 8W
Evans 74 40 25N 104 43W
Evans L. 36 50 50N 77 0W
Evans Mills 71 44 6N 75 48W
Evans P. 74 41 0N 105 35W
Evansburg 60 53 36N 114 59W
Evansdale 76 42 30N 92 17W
Evanston, Ill., U.S.A. 77 42 0N 87 40W
Evanston, Wy., U.S.A. 78 41 10N 111 0W
Evansville, Ill., U.S.A. 76 38 5N 89 56W
Evansville, Ind., U.S.A. 77 38 0N 87 35W
Evansville, Wis., U.S.A. 76 42 47N 89 18W
Évart 46 43 54N 85 8W
Évaux-les-Bains 102 46 12N 2 29 E
Eveleth 74 47 29N 92 30W
Evensk 121 61 57N 159 14 E
Everard, C. 136 37 49S 149 17 E
Everard, L. 134 31 30S 135 0 E
Everard Ras. 134 27 5S 132 28 E
Everest, Mt. 125 28 5N 86 58 E
Everett, Pa., U.S.A. 70 40 2N 78 24W
Everett, Wash., U.S.A. 80 48 0N 122 10W
Everglades 73 26 0N 80 30W
Evergreen 73 31 28N 86 55W
Everrett Mts. 65 62 45N 67 12W
Everson 78 48 57N 122 22W
Everton 49 43 40N 80 9W
Evesham 95 52 6N 1 57W
Evian-les-Bains 103 46 24N 6 35 E
Evinayong 116 1 50N 10 35 E
Évisa 103 42 15N 8 48 E
Évora 104 38 33N 7 57W
Évreux 100 49 0N 1 8 E
Évron 100 48 23N 1 58W
Évvoia 109 38 30N 24 0 E
Ewe, L. 96 57 49N 5 38W
Ewen 52 46 32N 89 17W
Ewing, Mo., U.S.A. 76 40 6N 91 43W
Ewing, Nebr., U.S.A. 74 42 18N 98 22W
Ewo 116 0 48S 14 45 E
Exaltación 86 13 10S 65 20W
Excelsior Springs 76 39 20N 94 10W
Excideuil 102 45 20N 1 4 E
Exe, R. 95 50 38N 3 27W
Exeter, Can. 46 43 21N 81 29W
Exeter, U.K. 95 50 43N 3 31W
Exeter, Calif., U.S.A. 80 36 17N 119 9W
Exeter, Nebr., U.S.A. 74 40 43N 97 30W
Exeter, N.H., U.S.A. 71 43 0N 70 58W
Exira 76 41 35N 94 52W
Exmes 100 48 45N 0 10 E
Exmoor 95 51 10N 3 59W
Exmouth, Austral. 134 22 6S 114 0 E
Exmouth, U.K. 95 50 37N 3 26W
Exmouth G. 134 22 15S 114 15 E
Expedition Range 135 24 30S 149 12 E
Exploits, B. of 37 49 20N 55 0W
Exshaw 61 51 3N 115 9W
Extremadura 104 39 30N 6 5W
Exuma Sound 84 24 30N 76 20W
Eyasi, L. 116 3 30S 35 0 E
Eyeberry L. 55 63 8N 104 43W
Eyebrow 56 50 48N 106 9W
Eyehill Cr., Alta., Can. 61 52 14N 110 0W
Eyehill Cr., Sask., Can. 56 52 40N 109 39W
Eyemouth 96 55 53N 2 5W
Eygurande 102 45 40N 2 26 E
Eyjafjorður 110 66 15N 18 30W
Eymet 102 44 40N 0 25 E
Eymoutiers 102 45 40N 1 45 E
Eyrarbakki 110 63 52N 21 9W
Eyre 134 32 15S 126 18 E
Eyre Cr. 135 26 40S 139 0 E
Eyre, L. 135 29 30S 137 26 E
Eyre Mts. 133 45 25S 168 25 E
Eyre Pen. 134 33 30S 137 17 E

Fabens **Flat Bay**

F

Fabens 79 31 30N 106 8W
Fabre 40 47 12N 79 22W
Fabreville 44 45 34N 73 51W
Fabriano 108 43 20N 12 52 E
Fabrizia 101 38 29N 16 19 E
Facatativá 86 4 49N 74 22W
Facture 102 44 39N 0 58W
Faddeyevski, Ostrov 121 76 0N 150 0 E
Fadhili 122 26 55N 49 10 E
Faenza 108 44 17N 11 53 E
Făgăraş 107 45 48N 24 58 E
Fagatogo 133 14 17 S 170 41W
Fagernes 111 60 59N 9 14 E
Fagersta 111 60 1N 15 46 E
Fagnano, L. 90 54 30 S 68 0W
Fagnières 101 48 58N 4 20 E
Fahraj 123 29 0N 59 0 E
Fahsien 131 21 19N 110 33 E
Fahūd 123 22 18N 56 28 E
Faid 122 27 1N 42 52 E
Faillon, L. 40 48 21N 76 39W
Fair Harbour 62 50 4N 127 10W
Fair Hd. 97 55 14N 6 10W
Fair Isle 98 59 30N 1 40W
Fair Oaks 80 38 39N 121 16W
Fair Play 76 37 38N 93 35W
Fairbank 79 31 44N 110 12W
Fairbanks 67 64 59N 147 40W
Fairborn 77 39 42N 84 2W
Fairbury, U.S.A. 77 40 45N 88 31W
Fairbury, Nebr., U.S.A. 74 40 5N 97 5W
Fairfax, Ohio, U.S.A. 77 39 5N 83 37W
Fairfax, Okla., U.S.A. 75 36 37N 96 45W
Fairfield, Austral. 136 33 53 S 150 57 E
Fairfield, Ala., U.S.A. 73 33 30N 87 0W
Fairfield, Calif., U.S.A. 80 38 14N 122 1W
Fairfield, Conn., U.S.A. 71 41 8N 73 16W
Fairfield, Idaho, U.S.A. 78 43 27N 114 52W
Fairfield, Ill., U.S.A. 77 38 20N 88 20W
Fairfield, Iowa, U.S.A. 76 41 0N 91 58W
Fairfield, Mont., U.S.A. 78 47 40N 112 0W
Fairfield, Ohio, U.S.A. 77 39 21N 84 34W
Fairfield, Texas, U.S.A. 75 31 40N 96 0W
Fairfield Plain 49 43 3N 80 24W
Fairford 57 51 37N 98 38W
Fairgrove 46 43 31N 83 33W
Fairhope 73 30 35N 87 50W
Fairlie 133 44 5 S 170 49 E
Fairmead 80 37 5N 120 10W
Fairmont, Minn., U.S.A. 74 43 37N 94 30W
Fairmont, W. Va., U.S.A. 72 39 29N 80 10W
Fairmont Hot Springs 54 50 20N 115 56W
Fairmount 81 34 45N 118 26W
Fairplay 79 39 9N 105 40W
Fairport, Can. 51 43 49N 79 5W
Fairport, N.Y., U.S.A. 70 43 8N 77 29W
Fairport, Ohio, U.S.A. 70 41 45N 81 17W
Fairvale 39 45 25N 66 0W
Fairview, Can. 39 44 40N 63 38W
Fairview, Alta., Can. 60 56 5N 118 25W
Fairview, Mich., U.S.A. 46 44 44N 84 3W
Fairview, N. Dak., U.S.A. 74 47 49N 104 7W
Fairview, Okla., U.S.A. 75 36 19N 98 30W
Fairview, Utah, U.S.A. 78 39 50N 111 0W
Fairweather, Mt. 67 58 55N 137 45W
Faith 74 45 2N 102 4W
Faizabad, Afghan. 123 37 7N 70 33 E
Faizabad, India 125 26 45N 82 10 E
Fajardo 85 18 20N 65 39W
Fakfak 127 3 0 S 132 15 E
Fakiya 87 42 10N 27 4 E
Falaise 100 48 54N 0 12W
Falcón □ 86 11 0N 69 50W
Falcon Dam 75 26 50N 99 20W
Falcon I. 52 49 23N 94 45W
Falconbridge 46 46 35N 80 45W
Falconer 70 42 7N 79 13W
Falfurrias 75 27 8N 98 8W
Falher 60 55 44N 117 15W
Falkenberg, Can. 70 45 9N 79 21W
Falkenberg, Sweden 111 56 54N 12 30 E
Falkirk 96 56 0N 3 47W
Falkland, N.S., Can. 39 44 37N 63 34W
Falkland, Ont., Can. 49 43 10N 80 26W
Falkland Is. 90 51 30 S 59 0W
Falkland Is. Dep. 91 57 0 S 40 0W
Falkland Sd. 90 52 0 S 60 0W
Falköping 111 58 12N 13 33 E
Fall Brook 79 33 25N 117 12W
Fall River 71 41 45N 71 5W
Fall River Mills 78 41 1N 121 30W
Fallbrook 81 33 23N 117 15W
Fallon, Mont., U.S.A. 74 46 52N 105 8W
Fallon, Nev., U.S.A. 78 39 31N 118 51W
Falls City, Nebr., U.S.A. 74 40 0N 95 40W
Falls City, Oreg., U.S.A. 78 44 54N 123 29W
Falls Creek 70 41 8N 78 49W
Falmouth, Jamaica 84 18 30N 77 40W
Falmouth, U.K. 95 50 9N 5 5W
Falmouth, U.S.A. 77 38 40N 84 20W
Falmouth B. 95 50 7N 5 3 E
False Cr. 66 49 15N 123 8W
Falso, C. 84 15 12N 83 21W
Falsterbo 111 55 23N 12 50 E
Falun 111 60 37N 15 37 E
Famagusta 122 35 8N 33 55 E
Famatina, Sierra, de 88 29 5 S 68 0W
Family L. 57 51 54N 95 27W
Famoso 81 35 37N 119 12W
Fancheng 131 31 2N 118 13 E
Fandriana 117 20 14 S 47 21 E
Fangcheng 131 33 16N 112 59 E
Fankiatun 130 43 50N 125 6 E
Fannich, L. 96 57 40N 5 0W
Fanning I. 15 3 51N 159 22W
Fanny Bay 62 49 27N 124 48W
Fano 108 43 50N 13 0 E
Fanshaw 54 57 11N 133 30W
Fao (Al Fāw) 122 30 0N 48 30 E
Far Mt. 62 52 47N 125 20W
Faraday Seamount Group 12 50 0N 27 0W
Faradje 116 3 50N 29 45 E
Farafangana 117 22 49 S 47 50 E
Farah 124 32 20N 62 7 E
Farah □ 124 32 25N 62 10 E
Fareham 95 50 52N 1 11W
Farewell, Alaska, U.S.A. 67 62 30N 154 0W
Farewell, Mich., U.S.A. 46 43 52N 84 55W
Farewell, C. 133 40 29 S 172 43 E
Farewell C. = Farvel, K. 17 59 48N 43 55W
Farfán 86 0 16N 76 41W
Fargeville, La 71 44 12N 75 58W
Fargo 74 47 0N 97 0W
Faribault 74 44 15N 93 19W
Faride, L. 38 50 58N 59 55W
Faridpur 125 18 14N 79 34 E
Farimān 123 35 40N 60 0 E
Farmer City 77 40 15N 88 39W
Farmers Rapids 48 45 30N 75 45W
Farmersburg 77 39 15N 87 23W
Farmerville 75 32 48N 92 23W
Farmington, Calif., U.S.A. 80 37 56N 121 0W
Farmington, Ill., U.S.A. 76 40 42N 90 0W
Farmington, Iowa, U.S.A. 76 40 38N 91 44W
Farmington, Mo., U.S.A. 76 37 47N 90 25W
Farmington, N. Mex., U.S.A. 79 36 45N 108 28W
Farmington, N.H., U.S.A. 71 43 25N 71 7W
Farmington, Utah, U.S.A. 78 41 0N 111 58W
Farmington, R. 71 41 51N 72 38W
Farmland 77 40 15N 85 5W
Farmville 72 37 19N 78 22W
Farnborough 95 51 17N 0 46W
Farne Is. 94 55 38N 1 37W
Farnham 45 45 17N 72 59W
Farnham Centre 43 45 15N 72 50W
Farnham, Mt. 54 45 20N 72 55W
Faro, Brazil 87 2 0 S 56 45W
Faro, Can. 64 62 11N 133 22W
Faro, Port. 104 37 2N 7 55W
Fårö 111 58 0N 19 10 E
Faroe Is. 93 62 0N 7 0W
Farquhar, C. 134 23 38 S 113 36 E
Farquhar Is. 16 11 0 S 52 0 E
Farrand, C. 65 71 45N 90 0W
Farrāshband 123 28 57N 52 5 E
Farrell 70 41 13N 80 29W
Fars □ 123 29 30N 55 0 E
Fársala 109 39 17N 22 23 E
Farsund 111 58 5N 6 55 E
Fartura, Serra da 89 26 21 S 52 52W
Farvel, Kap 17 59 48N 43 55W
Farwell 75 34 25N 103 0W
Faryab 124 28 7N 57 14 E
Fasā 123 29 0N 53 32 E
Fastnet Rock 97 51 22N 9 37W
Fatehgarh 124 27 25N 79 35 E
Fatehpur, Raj., India 124 28 0N 75 4 E
Fatehpur, Ut. P., India 125 27 8N 81 7 E
Fati 131 23 10N 113 10 E
Fatima 39 47 24N 61 53W
Fatkeng 131 23 58N 113 29 E
Fatshan 131 23 0N 113 4 E
Faucilles, Monts 101 48 5N 5 50 E
Faulkton 74 45 4N 99 8W
Faulquemont 101 49 3N 6 36 E
Fauquembergues 101 50 36N 2 5 E
Fauquier, B.C., Can. 63 49 52N 118 5W
Fauquier, Ont., Can. 53 49 18N 82 3W
Fauresmith 117 29 44 S 25 17 E
Fauske 110 67 17N 15 25 E
Faust 60 55 19N 115 38W
Favara 108 37 19N 13 39 E
Favignana 108 37 56N 12 18 E
Favone 103 41 47N 9 26 E
Favourable Lake 34 52 50N 93 39W
Fawcett 60 54 32N 114 5W
Fawn, R. 34 52 22N 88 20W
Fawnskin 81 34 16N 116 56W
Faxaflói 110 64 29N 23 0W
Fayence 103 43 38N 6 42 E
Fayette, Ala., U.S.A. 73 33 40N 87 50W
Fayette, Iowa, U.S.A. 76 42 51N 91 48W
Fayette, Mo., U.S.A. 76 39 10N 92 40W
Fayette, Ohio, U.S.A. 77 41 40N 84 20W
Fayette, La. 72 40 22N 86 52W
Fayetteville, Ark., U.S.A. 75 36 0N 94 5W
Fayetteville, N.C., U.S.A. 73 35 0N 78 58W
Fayetteville, Tenn., U.S.A. 73 35 20N 86 50W
Fazilka 124 30 27N 74 2 E
F'Derik 114 22 40N 12 45W
Fé, La 84 22 2N 84 15W
Feale, R. 97 52 26N 9 28W
Fear, C. 73 33 45N 78 0W
Feather Falls 80 39 36N 121 16W
Feather, R. 78 39 30N 121 20W
Featherston 133 41 6 S 175 20 E
Fécamp 100 49 45N 0 22 E
Federación 88 31 0 S 57 55W
Federal 48 45 20N 75 42W
Fehmarn 106 54 26N 11 10 E
Fehmarn Bælt 106 54 35N 11 20 E
Feilding 133 40 13 S 175 35 E
Feira 117 15 35 S 30 16 E
Feldkirch 106 47 15N 9 37 E
Felicity 77 38 51N 84 6W
Felipe Carrillo Puerto 83 19 38N 88 3W
Felixstowe 95 51 58N 1 22W
Felletin 102 45 53N 2 11 E
Felton 80 37 3N 122 4W
Femunden 110 62 10N 11 53 E
Fen Ho, R. 130 35 25N 110 30 E
Fenelon Falls 47 44 32N 78 45W
Fénérive 117 17 22 S 49 25 E
Fengcheng, Heilungkiang, China 130 45 41N 128 54 E
Fengcheng, Kiangsi, China 131 28 2N 115 46 E
Fengcheng, Liaoning, China 130 40 28N 124 4 E
Fengfeng 130 36 40N 114 24 E
Fenghsien 131 33 56N 106 41 E
Fenghwa 131 29 37N 121 29 E
Fengkieh (Kweichow) 131 31 0N 109 33 E
Fenglo 131 31 30N 112 29 E
Fengsiang 131 34 27N 107 30 E
Fengsin 131 28 41N 115 11 E
Fengtai 130 39 57N 116 21 E
Fengtu 131 29 58N 107 59 E
Fengy 131 23 48N 106 50 E
Fengyi 131 25 31N 100 13 E
Fengyuan 131 24 10N 120 45 E
Fenit 97 52 17N 9 51W
Fennimore 76 42 58N 90 41W
Feno, C. de 103 41 58N 8 33 E
Fens, The 94 52 45N 0 2 E
Fenton, Can. 55 53 0N 105 35W
Fenton, U.S.A. 46 42 47N 83 44W
Fenwick 49 43 1N 79 22W
Fenyang 130 37 19N 111 46 E
Feodosiya 120 45 2N 35 28 E
Ferdows 123 33 58N 58 2 E
Fère-Champenoise 101 48 45N 4 0 E
Fère-en-Tardenois 101 49 10N 3 30 E
Fère, La 101 49 40N 3 20 E
Ferfer 115 5 18N 45 20 E
Fergana 120 40 23N 71 46 E
Fergus 49 43 43N 80 24W
Fergus Falls 74 46 25N 96 0W
Ferguson, Can. 34 47 50N 73 30W
Ferguson, U.S.A. 76 38 45N 90 18W
Ferintosh 61 52 46N 112 58W
Ferland, Ont., Can. 52 50 19N 88 27W
Ferland, Sask., Can. 56 49 27N 106 57W
Fermanagh (□) 97 54 21N 7 40W
Ferme-Neuve 40 46 42N 75 27W
Fermoy 97 52 4N 8 18W
Fernández 88 27 55 S 63 50W
Fernandina Beach 73 30 40N 81 30W
Fernando de Noronha, I. 87 4 0 S 33 10W
Fernando do Noronho □ 87 4 0 S 33 10W
Fernando Póo = Macias Nguema Biyoga 113 3 30N 8 40 E
Ferndale, U.S.A. 46 42 26N 83 6W
Ferndale, Calif., U.S.A. 78 40 37N 124 12W
Ferndale, Wash., U.S.A. 80 48 51N 122 41W
Fernie 61 49 30N 115 5W
Fernley 78 39 42N 119 20W
Feronia 46 46 22N 79 19W
Ferozepore 124 30 55N 74 40 E
Ferrara 108 44 50N 11 36 E
Ferreñafe 86 6 35 S 79 50W
Ferret, C. 102 44 38N 1 15W
Ferrette 101 47 30N 7 20 E
Ferriday 75 31 35N 91 33W
Ferrières 101 48 5N 2 48 E
Ferron 78 39 3N 111 3W
Ferryland 37 47 2N 52 53W
Ferrysburg 77 43 5N 86 13W
Ferté Bernard, La 100 48 10N 0 40 E
Ferté, La 101 48 57N 3 6 E
Ferté-Mace, La 100 48 35N 0 21W
Ferté-St. Aubin, La 101 47 42N 1 57 E
Ferté-Vidame, La 100 48 37N 0 53 E
Fertile 74 47 37N 96 18W
Fès 114 34 0N 5 0W
Feshi 116 6 0 S 18 10 E
Fessenden 74 47 42N 99 44W
Festus 76 38 13N 90 24W
Fethiye 122 36 36N 29 10 E
Fetlar, I. 96 60 36N 0 52W
Feuilles, B. aux 36 58 55N 69 20W
Feuilles, R. 36 58 47N 70 4W
Feurs 103 45 45N 4 13 E
Ffestiniog 94 52 58N 3 56W
Fiambalá 88 27 45 S 67 37W
Fianarantsoa 117 21 20 S 46 45 E
Fichtelgebirge 106 50 10N 12 0 E
Field 46 46 31N 80 1W
Fife □ 96 56 13N 3 2W
Fife L. 56 49 14N 105 53W
Fife Ness 96 56 17N 2 35W
Figeac 102 44 37N 2 2 E
Figueira da Foz 104 40 7N 8 54W
Figueras 104 42 18N 2 58 E
Fiji ■ 133 17 20 S 179 0 E
Fiji Is. 133 17 20 S 179 0 E
Filadelfia 88 22 25 S 60 0W
Filchner Ice Shelf 91 78 0 S 60 0W
File Axe, L. 41 50 18N 73 34W
Filer 78 42 30N 114 35W
Filey 94 54 13N 0 18W
Filiatrá 109 37 9N 21 35 E
Filipstad 111 59 43N 14 9 E
Fillmore, Can. 56 49 50N 103 25W
Fillmore, U.S.A. 81 34 23N 118 58W
Fils, L. du 40 46 37N 78 7W
Filyos çayi 122 41 35N 32 10 E
Finch 47 45 11N 75 7W
Findhorn, R. 96 57 38N 3 38W
Findlater 56 50 47N 105 24W
Findlay 77 41 0N 83 41W
Finger L. 62 53 33N 124 18W
Fingõe 117 15 12 S 31 50 E
Finike 122 36 21N 30 10 E
Finistère □ 100 48 20N 4 0W
Finisterre, C. 104 42 50N 9 19W
Finke, R. 134 24 54 S 134 16 E
Finland 52 48 51N 93 55W
Finland ■ 111 64 0N 27 0 E
Finland, G. of 111 60 0N 26 0 E
Finlay, R. 54 56 50N 125 10W
Finley, Austral. 136 35 38 S 145 35 E
Finley, U.S.A. 74 47 35N 97 50W
Finmark 52 48 35N 89 45W
Finn, R. 97 54 50N 7 55W
Finnmark fylke □ 110 69 30N 25 0 E
Finucanel I. 134 20 19 S 118 30 E
Fiora, R. 108 42 25N 11 35 E
Fire River 53 48 47N 83 36W
Firebag, R. 60 57 45N 111 21W
Firebaugh 80 36 52N 120 27W
Firedrake L. 55 61 25N 104 30W
Firenze 108 43 47N 11 15 E
Firmi 102 44 32N 2 19 E
Firminy 103 45 23N 4 18 E
Fīroz Kohi 124 34 45N 63 0 E
Firozabad 124 27 10N 78 25 E
First Narrows 66 49 19N 123 8W
Fīrūzābād 123 28 52N 52 35 E
Fīrūzkūh 123 35 50N 52 40 E
Firvale 62 52 27N 126 13W
Fish Cr. 59 50 54N 114 1W
Fish Pt. 46 43 43N 83 38W
Fish, R. 117 27 40 S 17 30 E
Fisher B. 57 51 35N 97 13W
Fisher Bay 57 51 29N 97 18W
Fisher Branch 57 51 5N 97 13W
Fisher Str. 65 63 15N 83 30W
Fishguard 95 51 59N 4 59W
Fishing L. 57 52 10N 95 24W
Fiskivõtn 110 64 50N 20 45W
Fismes 101 49 20N 3 40 E
Fitchburg 71 42 35N 71 47W
Fitz Hugh Sd. 62 51 40N 127 55W
Fitz Roy 90 47 10 S 67 0W
Fitzgerald, Can. 54 59 51N 111 36W
Fitzgerald, U.S.A. 73 31 45N 83 10W
Fitzpatrick 34 47 29N 72 46W
Fitzroy Crossing 134 18 9 S 125 38 E
Fitzroy, R. 134 17 25 S 124 0 E
Fitzwilliam I. 46 45 30N 81 45W
Fiume = Rijeka 108 45 20N 14 21 E
Five Islands 39 45 23N 64 6W
Five Points 80 36 26N 120 6W
Fizi 116 4 17 S 28 55 E
Flagler 74 39 20N 103 4W
Flagstaff 79 35 10N 111 40W
Flagstone 54 49 4N 115 10W
Flaherty, I. 36 56 15N 79 15W
Flåm 111 60 52N 7 14 E
Flambeau, R. 74 45 40N 90 50W
Flamboro Centre 48 43 22N 79 56W
Flamborough Hd. 94 54 8N 0 4W
Flaming Gorge Dam 78 40 50N 109 25W
Flaming Gorge L. 78 41 15N 109 30W
Flamingo, Teluk 127 5 30 S 138 0 E
Flanagan 77 40 53N 88 52W
Flanders 52 48 44N 92 5W
Flandre 106 51 10N 3 15 E
Flandre Occidental □ 105 51 0N 3 0 E
Flandreau 74 44 5N 96 38W
Flanigan 80 40 10N 119 53W
Flannan Is. 96 58 9N 7 52W
Flåsjön 110 64 5N 15 50 E
Flat Bay 37 48 24N 58 36W

Flat L **Frederick Sd**

Flat L.	**60**	54 38N	112 54W
Flat, R., Can.	**54**	61 51N	128 0W
Flat, R., U.S.A.	**77**	42 56N	85 15W
Flat River	**75**	37 50N	90 30W
Flat Rock, Ill., U.S.A.	**77**	38 54N	87 40W
Flat Rock, Mich., U.S.A.	**46**	42 6N	83 18W
Flatbush	**60**	54 42N	114 9W
Flatey, Barðastrandarsýsla, Iceland	**110**	66 10N	17 52W
Flatey, Suður-þingeyjarsýsla, Iceland	**110**	65 22N	22 56W
Flathead L.	**78**	47 50N	114 0W
Flatrock, R.	**77**	38 46N	85 10W
Flattery, C.	**80**	48 21N	124 43W
Flavy-le-Martel	**101**	49 43N	3 12 E
Flaxcombe	**56**	51 29N	109 36W
Flaxton	**57**	48 52N	102 24W
Flèche, La	**100**	47 42N	0 5W
Fleetwood	**94**	53 55N	3 1W
Fleming	**57**	50 4N	101 31W
Flemingsburg	**77**	38 25N	83 45W
Flemington	**70**	41 7N	77 28W
Flensburg	**106**	54 46N	9 28 E
Flers	**100**	48 47N	0 33W
Flesherton	**46**	44 16N	80 33W
Fletton	**95**	52 34N	0 13W
Fleur de Lys	**37**	50 7N	56 8W
Fleur-de-May, L.	**38**	52 0N	65 5W
Fleurance	**102**	43 52N	0 40 E
Flin Flon	**55**	54 46N	101 53W
Flinders I.	**135**	40 0 S	148 0 E
Flint, U.K.	**94**	53 15N	3 7W
Flint, U.S.A.	**46**	43 5N	83 40W
Flint, I.	**15**	11 26 S	151 48W
Flint L.	**53**	49 52N	85 53W
Flint, R.	**73**	31 20N	84 10W
Flixecourt	**101**	50 0N	2 5 E
Flodden	**94**	55 37N	2 8W
Floodwood	**52**	46 55N	92 55W
Flora, Ill., U.S.A.	**72**	38 40N	88 30W
Flora, Ind., U.S.A.	**77**	40 33N	86 31W
Florac	**102**	44 20N	3 37 E
Floradale	**49**	43 37N	80 35W
Florala	**73**	31 0N	86 20W
Florence, Can.	**39**	46 16N	60 16W
Florence, Ala., U.S.A.	**73**	34 50N	87 50W
Florence, Ariz., U.S.A.	**79**	33 0N	111 25W
Florence, Colo., U.S.A.	**74**	38 26N	105 0W
Florence, Ky., U.S.A.	**77**	39 0N	84 38W
Florence, Oreg., U.S.A.	**78**	44 0N	124 3W
Florence, S.C., U.S.A.	**73**	34 5N	79 50W
Florence = Firenze	**108**	43 47N	11 15 E
Florensac	**102**	43 23N	3 28 E
Flores, Azores	**93**	39 13N	31 13W
Flores, Guat.	**84**	16 50N	89 40W
Flores I.	**62**	49 20N	126 10W
Flores, I.	**127**	8 35 S	121 0 E
Flores Sea	**126**	6 30 S	124 0 E
Floresville	**75**	29 10N	98 10W
Floriano	**87**	6 50 S	43 0W
Florianópolis	**89**	27 30 S	48 30W
Florida, Cuba	**84**	21 32N	78 14W
Florida, Uruguay	**89**	34 7 S	56 10W
Florida □	**73**	28 30N	82 0W
Florida B.	**85**	25 0N	81 20W
Florida Keys	**85**	25 0N	80 40W
Florida, Strait of	**85**	25 0N	80 0W
Florissant	**76**	38 48N	90 20W
Florø	**111**	61 35N	5 1 E
Flower Sta.	**47**	45 10N	76 41W
Flower's Cove	**37**	51 14N	56 46W
Floydada	**75**	33 58N	101 18W
Fluk	**127**	1 42 S	127 38 E
Flushing	**46**	43 4N	83 51W
Flushing = Vlissingen	**105**	51 26N	3 34 E
Foam Lake	**56**	51 40N	103 32W
Fogo	**37**	49 43N	54 17W
Fogo, C.	**37**	49 40N	54 0W
Fogo I.	**37**	49 40N	54 5W
Foins, L. aux	**40**	47 5N	78 11W
Foix	**102**	42 58N	1 38 E
Folda, Nord-Trøndelag, Norway	**110**	64 41N	10 50 E
Folda, Nordland, Norway	**110**	67 38N	14 50 E
Folette, La	**73**	36 23N	84 9W
Foley I.	**65**	68 32N	75 5W
Foleyet	**53**	48 15N	82 25W
Folkestone	**95**	51 5N	1 11 E
Folkston	**73**	30 55N	82 0W
Follett	**75**	36 30N	100 12W
Folsom	**80**	38 41N	121 7W
Folsom Res.	**80**	38 42N	121 9W
Fond-du-Lac	**55**	59 19N	107 12W
Fond du lac	**74**	43 46N	88 26W
Fond-du-Lac, R.	**55**	59 17N	106 0W
Fonda, Iowa, U.S.A.	**76**	42 35N	94 51W
Fonda, N.Y., U.S.A.	**71**	42 57N	74 23W
Fonseca, G. de	**84**	13 10N	87 40W
Fontaine	**39**	46 51N	64 58W
Fontaine-Française	**101**	47 32N	5 21 E
Fontaine, La	**77**	40 40N	85 43W
Fontainebleau	**101**	48 24N	2 40 E
Fontas, R.	**54**	58 14N	121 48W
Fonte Boa	**86**	2 25 S	66 0W
Fontenay-le-Comte	**102**	46 28N	0 48W
Fonteneau, L.	**38**	51 55N	61 30W
Fontenelle	**35**	48 54N	64 33W
Fontur	**110**	66 23N	14 32W
Foochow (Minhow)	**131**	26 2N	119 25 E
Foothills	**61**	53 4N	116 47W
Forbach	**101**	49 10N	6 52 E
Forcalquier	**103**	43 58N	5 47 E
Ford City, Calif., U.S.A.	**81**	35 9N	119 27W
Ford City, Pa., U.S.A.	**70**	40 47N	79 31W
Fording	**61**	50 12N	114 52W
Fordongianus	**102**	40 0N	8 50 E
Fordyce	**75**	33 50N	92 20W
Forel	**17**	66 52N	36 55W
Foremost	**61**	49 26N	111 25W
Forest, Can.	**46**	43 6N	82 0W
Forest, U.S.A.	**75**	32 21N	89 27W
Forest City, Iowa, U.S.A.	**74**	43 12N	93 39W
Forest City, N.C., U.S.A.	**73**	35 23N	81 50W
Forest City, Pa., U.S.A.	**71**	41 39N	75 29W
Forest Grove, Can.	**63**	51 46N	121 5W
Forest Grove, U.S.A.	**80**	45 31N	123 4W
Forest Hill	**50**	43 42N	79 25W
Forest Lawn	**59**	51 2N	113 58W
Forestburg	**61**	52 35N	112 1W
Foresthill	**80**	39 1N	120 49W
Forestville, Can.	**41**	48 48N	69 2W
Forestville, Calif., U.S.A.	**80**	38 28N	122 54W
Forestville, Wis., U.S.A.	**72**	44 41N	87 29W
Forez, Mts. du	**102**	45 40N	3 50 E
Forfar	**96**	56 40N	2 53W
Forges-les-Eaux	**101**	49 37N	1 30 E
Forget	**56**	49 39N	102 52W
Forillon, Parc National	**38**	48 46N	64 12W
Fork River	**57**	51 31N	100 1W
Forks	**80**	47 56N	124 23W
Forli	**108**	44 14N	12 2 E
Forman	**74**	46 9N	97 43W
Formby Pt.	**94**	53 33N	3 7W
Formentera, I.	**104**	38 40N	1 30 E
Formiguères	**102**	42 37N	2 5 E
Formosa	**88**	26 15 S	58 10W
Formosa = Taiwan	**131**	23 30N	121 0 E
Formosa = Taiwan ■	**131**	24 0N	121 0 E
Formosa □	**88**	26 5 S	58 10W
Formosa Bay	**116**	2 40 S	40 20 E
Formosa Str.	**131**	24 40N	120 0 E
Forres	**96**	57 37N	3 38W
Forrest City	**75**	35 0N	90 50W
Forreston	**76**	42 8N	89 35W
Forsyth, Ga., U.S.A.	**73**	33 4N	83 55W
Forsyth, Mont., U.S.A.	**78**	46 14N	106 37W
Forsythe	**40**	48 14N	76 26W
Fort Albany	**34**	52 15N	81 35W
Fort Amador	**84**	8 56N	79 32W
Fort Apache	**79**	33 50N	110 0W
Fort Assiniboine	**60**	54 20N	114 45W
Fort Atkinson	**77**	42 56N	88 50W
Fort Augustus	**96**	57 9N	4 40W
Fort Babine	**54**	55 22N	126 37W
Fort Benton	**78**	47 50N	110 40W
Fort Bragg	**78**	39 28N	123 50W
Fort Bridger	**78**	41 22N	110 20W
Fort Chimo	**36**	58 6N	68 25W
Fort Chipewyan	**55**	58 42N	111 8W
Fort Clayton	**84**	9 0N	79 35W
Fort Collins	**74**	40 30N	105 4W
Fort-Coulonge	**40**	45 50N	76 45W
Fort Covington	**43**	44 59N	74 30W
Fort-Dauphin	**117**	25 2 S	47 0 E
Fort Davis, Pan. C. Z.	**84**	9 17N	79 56W
Fort Davis, U.S.A.	**75**	30 38N	103 53W
Fort-de-France	**85**	14 36N	61 2W
Fort Defiance	**79**	35 47N	109 4W
Fort Dodge	**74**	42 29N	94 10W
Fort Edward	**71**	43 16N	73 35W
Fort Frances	**52**	48 36N	93 24W
Fort Fraser	**62**	54 4N	124 33W
Fort Garland	**79**	37 28N	105 30W
Fort Garry	**58**	49 50N	97 9W
Fort George	**36**	53 50N	79 0W
Fort George, R.	**34**	53 50N	77 0W
Fort Good-Hope	**67**	66 14N	128 40W
Fort Grahame	**54**	56 30N	124 35W
Fort Hancock	**79**	31 19N	105 56W
Fort Hauchuca	**79**	31 32N	110 30W
Fort Hertz (Putao)	**125**	27 28N	97 30 E
Fort Hope	**53**	51 30N	88 0W
Fort Irwin	**81**	35 16N	116 34W
Fort Jameson = Chipata	**117**	13 38 S	32 38 E
Fort Kent	**35**	47 12N	68 30W
Fort Klamath	**78**	42 45N	122 0W
Fort Knox	**77**	38 50N	85 0W
Fort Langley	**63**	49 10N	122 35W
Fort Laramie	**74**	42 15N	104 30W
Fort Lauderdale	**73**	26 10N	80 5W
Fort Leonard Wood	**76**	37 46N	92 11W
Fort Liard	**54**	60 20N	123 30W
Fort Liberté	**85**	19 42N	71 51W
Fort Lupton	**74**	40 8N	104 48W
Fort Mackay	**60**	57 12N	111 41W
Fort McKenzie	**36**	57 20N	69 0W
Fort Macleod	**61**	49 45N	113 30W
Fort McMurray	**60**	56 44N	111 23W
Fort McPherson	**67**	67 30N	134 55W
Fort Madison	**74**	40 39N	91 20W
Fort Meade	**73**	27 45N	81 45W
Fort Morgan	**74**	40 10N	103 50W
Fort Myers	**73**	26 30N	81 50W
Fort Nelson	**54**	58 50N	122 38W
Fort Nelson, R.	**54**	59 32N	124 0W
Fort Norman	**67**	64 57N	125 30W
Fort Payne	**73**	34 25N	85 44W
Fort Peck	**78**	48 1N	106 30W
Fort Peck Dam	**78**	48 0N	106 20W
Fort Peck L.	**78**	47 40N	107 0W
Fort Pierce	**74**	27 29N	80 19W
Fort Pierre	**74**	44 25N	100 25W
Fort Plain	**71**	42 56N	74 39W
Fort Portal	**116**	0 40N	30 20 E
Fort Providence	**54**	61 21N	117 40W
Fort Qu'Appelle	**56**	50 45N	103 50W
Fort Randall	**67**	55 10N	162 48W
Fort Randolph	**84**	9 23N	79 53W
Fort Recovery	**77**	40 25N	84 47W
Fort Resolution	**54**	61 10N	113 40W
Fort Ross, Can.	**65**	72 0N	94 14W
Fort Ross, U.S.A.	**80**	38 32N	123 13W
Fort Rouge	**58**	49 52N	97 9W
Fort Rupert	**62**	50 42N	127 23W
Fort Rupert (Rupert House)	**36**	51 30N	78 40W
Fort St. James	**54**	54 30N	124 10W
Fort St. John	**54**	56 15N	120 50W
Fort Sandeman	**124**	31 20N	69 25 E
Fort Saskatchewan	**60**	53 40N	113 15W
Fort Scott	**75**	37 50N	94 40W
Fort Selkirk	**67**	62 43N	137 22W
Fort Severn	**34**	56 0N	87 40W
Fort Sherman	**84**	9 22N	79 56W
Fort Shevchenko	**120**	44 30N	50 10W
Fort Simpson	**54**	61 45N	121 23W
Fort Smith, Can.	**54**	60 0N	111 51W
Fort Smith, U.S.A.	**75**	35 25N	94 25W
Fort Stanton	**79**	33 33N	105 36W
Fort Stockton	**75**	30 48N	103 2W
Fort Sumner	**75**	34 24N	104 8W
Fort Thomas, Ariz., U.S.A.	**79**	33 2N	109 59W
Fort Thomas, Ky., U.S.A.	**77**	39 5N	84 27W
Fort Valley	**73**	32 33N	83 52W
Fort Vermilion	**54**	58 24N	116 0W
Fort Victoria	**117**	20 8 S	30 55 E
Ft. Walton Beach	**73**	30 25N	86 40W
Fort Wayne	**72**	41 5N	85 10W
Fort Whyte	**58**	49 49N	97 13W
Fort William	**96**	56 48N	5 8W
Fort William = Thunder Bay	**34**	48 20N	89 10W
Fort Worth	**75**	32 45N	97 25W
Fort Yates	**74**	46 8N	100 38W
Fort Yukon	**67**	66 35N	145 12W
Fortaleza	**87**	3 35 S	38 35W
Forte Coimbra	**86**	19 55 S	57 48W
Forteau	**36**	51 28N	56 58W
Forth, Firth of	**96**	56 5N	2 55W
Forth, R.	**96**	56 9N	4 18W
Fortín Corrales	**86**	22 21 S	60 35W
Fortín Guachalla	**86**	22 22 S	62 23W
Fortin, L.	**38**	50 50N	67 46W
Fortín Rojas Silva	**88**	22 40 S	59 3W
Fortín Siracuas	**86**	21 3 S	61 46W
Fortín Teniente Montania	**88**	22 1 S	59 45W
Fortrose	**96**	57 35N	4 10W
Fortuna, Cal., U.S.A.	**78**	48 38N	124 8W
Fortuna, N.D., U.S.A.	**56**	48 55N	103 48W
Fortune	**37**	47 4N	55 50W
Fortune B.	**37**	47 30N	55 22W
Forty Mile	**67**	64 20N	140 30W
Forūr	**123**	26 20N	54 30 E
Fos do Jordão	**86**	9 30 S	72 14W
Fos-sur-Mer	**103**	43 26N	4 56 E
Fosheim Pen.	**65**	80 0N	85 0W
Fossil	**78**	45 0N	120 9W
Fosston, Can.	**56**	52 12N	103 49W
Fosston, U.S.A.	**74**	47 33N	95 39W
Foster, Can.	**41**	45 17N	72 30W
Foster, U.S.A.	**77**	38 48N	84 13W
Foster, R.	**55**	55 47N	105 49W
Fostoria	**72**	41 8N	83 25W
Fougamou	**116**	1 38 S	11 39 E
Fougères	**100**	48 21N	1 14W
Foul Pt.	**124**	8 35N	81 25 E
Foula, I.	**96**	60 10N	2 5W
Fountain, Colo., U.S.A.	**74**	38 42N	104 40W
Fountain, Utah, U.S.A.	**78**	39 41N	111 50W
Fountain Springs	**81**	35 54N	118 51W
Four Mts., Is. of the	**67**	52 0N	170 30W
Fourchambault	**101**	47 0N	3 3 E
Fourchu	**39**	45 43N	60 17W
Fourmies	**101**	50 1N	4 2 E
Fourmont, L.	**38**	52 5N	60 27W
Fournier, L.	**38**	51 33N	65 25W
Fours	**101**	46 50N	3 42 E
Fourteen Island Lake	**43**	45 54N	74 2W
Fouta Djalon	**114**	11 20N	12 10W
Foux, Cap-à-	**85**	19 43N	73 27W
Foveaux Str.	**133**	46 42 S	168 10 E
Fowler, Calif., U.S.A.	**80**	36 41N	119 41W
Fowler, Colo., U.S.A.	**74**	38 10N	104 0W
Fowler, Ind., U.S.A.	**77**	40 37N	87 19W
Fowler, Kans., U.S.A.	**75**	37 28N	100 7W
Fowler, Mich., U.S.A.	**77**	43 0N	84 45W
Fowlerton	**75**	28 26N	98 50W
Fowlerville	**77**	42 40N	84 4W
Fowliang	**131**	27 8N	117 12 E
Fowling	**131**	29 39N	107 29 E
Fox Creek	**60**	54 24N	116 48W
Fox Is.	**67**	52 30N	166 0W
Fox, R., Can.	**55**	56 3N	93 18W
Fox, R., U.S.A.	**76**	40 21N	91 28W
Fox Valley	**56**	50 30N	109 25W
Foxe Basin	**65**	66 0N	77 0W
Foxe Chan.	**65**	65 0N	80 0W
Foxe Pen.	**65**	65 0N	76 0W
Foxpark	**78**	41 4N	106 6W
Foxton	**133**	40 29 S	175 18 E
Foxville	**53**	50 4N	81 38W
Foyle, Lough	**97**	55 6N	7 8W
Foynes	**97**	52 30N	9 5W
Foz do Gregório	**86**	6 47 S	71 0W
Foz do Iguaçu	**89**	25 30 S	54 30W
Frackville	**71**	40 46N	76 15W
Framlingham	**71**	42 18N	71 26W
Franca	**87**	20 25 S	47 30W
Francavilla Fontana	**109**	40 32N	17 35 E
France ■	**99**	47 0N	3 0 E
Frances Creek	**134**	13 25 S	132 3 E
Frances L.	**54**	61 23N	129 30W
Frances, R.	**54**	60 16N	129 10W
Francés Viejo, C.	**85**	19 40N	70 0W
Francesville	**77**	40 59N	86 53W
Franceville	**116**	1 40 S	13 32 E
Franche Comté	**101**	46 30N	5 50 E
Francis	**56**	50 6N	103 52W
Francis Harbour	**35**	52 34N	55 44W
Francisco I. Madero, Coahuila, Mexico	**82**	25 48N	103 18W
Francisco I. Madero, Durango, Mexico	**82**	24 32N	104 22W
Francistown	**117**	21 7 S	27 33 E
François	**37**	47 35N	56 45W
François L.	**62**	54 0N	125 30W
François, Le	**85**	14 38N	60 57W
Franeker	**105**	53 12N	5 33 E
Frankford, Can.	**47**	44 12N	77 36W
Frankford, U.S.A.	**76**	39 29N	91 19W
Frankfort, Ind., U.S.A.	**77**	40 20N	86 33W
Frankfort, Kans., U.S.A.	**74**	39 42N	96 26W
Frankfort, Ky., U.S.A.	**77**	38 12N	84 52W
Frankfort, Mich., U.S.A.	**72**	44 38N	86 14W
Frankfort, Ohio, U.S.A.	**77**	39 24N	83 11W
Frankfurt am Main	**106**	50 7N	8 40 E
Frankfurt an der Oder	**106**	52 50N	14 31 E
Fränkische Alb	**106**	49 20N	11 30 E
Franklin, Ill., U.S.A.	**76**	39 37N	90 3W
Franklin, Ind., U.S.A.	**77**	39 29N	86 3W
Franklin, Ky., U.S.A.	**73**	36 40N	86 30W
Franklin, La., U.S.A.	**75**	29 45N	91 30W
Franklin, Mass., U.S.A.	**71**	42 4N	71 23W
Franklin, Nebr., U.S.A.	**74**	40 9N	98 55W
Franklin, N.H., U.S.A.	**71**	43 28N	71 39W
Franklin, N.J., U.S.A.	**71**	41 9N	74 38W
Franklin, Ohio, U.S.A.	**77**	39 34N	84 18W
Franklin, Pa., U.S.A.	**70**	41 22N	79 45W
Franklin, Tenn., U.S.A.	**73**	35 54N	86 53W
Franklin, Va., U.S.A.	**73**	36 40N	76 58W
Franklin, Vt., U.S.A.	**43**	44 59N	72 55W
Franklin, W. Va., U.S.A.	**72**	38 38N	79 21W
Franklin, Wis., U.S.A.	**77**	42 53N	88 1W
Franklin □	**64**	71 0N	99 0W
Franklin B.	**67**	69 45N	126 0W
Franklin Centre	**43**	45 2N	73 55W
Franklin D. Roosevelt L.	**78**	48 30N	118 16W
Franklin I.	**91**	76 10 S	168 30 E
Franklin, L.	**78**	40 20N	115 26W
Franklin Mts.	**64**	65 0N	125 0W
Franklin Park	**77**	41 56N	87 51W
Franklin River	**62**	49 7N	124 48W
Franklin Str.	**65**	72 0N	96 0W
Franklinton	**75**	30 53N	90 10W
Franklinville	**70**	42 21N	78 28W
Franks Peak	**78**	43 50N	109 5W
Frankston	**136**	38 8 S	145 8 E
Franquelin	**38**	49 18N	67 54W
Frantsa Josifa, Zemlya	**120**	79 0N	62 0 E
Franz	**53**	48 25N	84 30W
Franz Josef Fd.	**17**	73 20N	22 0 E
Franz Josef Land = Frantsa Josifa	**120**	76 0N	62 0 E
Fraser	**46**	42 32N	82 57W
Fraser I.	**135**	25 15 S	153 10 E
Fraser Lake	**62**	54 0N	124 50W
Fraser, R., B.C., Can.	**66**	49 7N	123 11W
Fraser, R., Newf., Can.	**36**	56 39N	62 10W
Fraserburgh	**96**	57 41N	2 0W
Fraserdale	**53**	49 55N	81 37W
Fraserwood	**57**	50 38N	97 13W
Frasne	**101**	46 50N	6 10 E
Frater	**34**	47 20N	84 25W
Fray Bentos	**88**	33 10 S	58 15W
Frazer L.	**52**	49 15N	88 40W
Fredericia	**111**	55 34N	9 45 E
Frederick, Md., U.S.A.	**72**	39 25N	77 23W
Frederick, Okla., U.S.A.	**75**	34 22N	99 0W
Frederick, S.D., U.S.A.	**74**	45 55N	98 29W
Frederick Reef	**135**	20 58 S	154 23 E
Frederick Sd.	**54**	57 10N	134 0W

Fredericksburg Gatun

Fredericksburg, Tex., U.S.A. 75 30 17N 98 55W
Fredericksburg, Va., U.S.A. 72 38 16N 77 29W
Frederickstown 75 37 35N 90 15W
Fredericton 39 45 57N 66 40W
Fredericton Junc. 39 45 41N 66 40W
Frederikshåb 17 62 0N 49 30W
Frederikshavn 111 57 28N 10 31E
Frederiksted 85 17 43N 64 53W
Fredonia, Ariz., U.S.A. 79 36 59N 112 36W
Fredonia, Kans., U.S.A. 75 37 34N 95 50W
Fredonia, N.Y., U.S.A. 70 42 26N 79 20W
Fredrikstad 111 59 13N 10 57E
Freeburg 76 38 19N 91 56W
Freehold 71 40 15N 74 18W
Freel Pk. 80 38 52N 119 53W
Freeland 71 41 3N 75 48W
Freeling, Mt. 134 22 35S 133 06E
Freels, C. 37 49 15N 53 30W
Freelton 49 43 24N 80 2W
Freeman, Calif., U.S.A. 81 35 35N 117 53W
Freeman, Mo., U.S.A. 76 38 37N 94 30W
Freeman, S.D., U.S.A. 74 43 25N 97 20W
Freeman, R. 60 54 19N 114 47W
Freeport, Bahamas 85 25 45N 88 30E
Freeport, N.S., Can. 39 44 15N 66 20W
Freeport, Ont., Can. 49 43 25N 80 25W
Freeport, Ill., U.S.A. 76 42 18N 89 40W
Freeport, Tex., U.S.A. 75 28 55N 95 22W
Freetown 114 8 30N 13 10W
Frégate, L. 36 53 15N 74 45W
Fréhel, C. 100 48 40N 2 20W
Freiberg 106 50 55N 13 20E
Freire 90 39 0S 72 50W
Freirina 88 28 30S 70 27W
Freising 106 48 24N 11 47E
Freistadt 106 48 30N 14 30E
Fréjus 103 43 25N 6 44E
Frelighsburg 43 45 3N 72 50W
Fremantle 134 32 1S 115 47E
Fremont, Calif., U.S.A. 80 37 32N 122 57W
Fremont, Ind., U.S.A. 77 41 44N 84 56W
Fremont, Mich., U.S.A. 72 43 29N 85 59W
Fremont, Nebr., U.S.A. 74 41 30N 96 30W
Fremont, Ohio, U.S.A. 77 41 20N 83 5W
Fremont, L. 78 43 0N 109 50W
Fremont, R. 79 38 15N 110 20W
French Camp 80 37 53N 121 16W
French Cr. 70 41 30N 80 2W
French Guiana ■ 87 4 0N 53 0W
French I. 136 38 20S 145 22E
French Lick 77 38 33N 86 37W
French, R., Ont., Can. 46 46 2N 80 34W
French, R., Ont., Can. 53 50 40N 80 59W
French River 46 46 2N 80 34W
French Terr. of Afars & Issas □ = Djibouti 115 11 30N 42 15E
Frenchburg 77 37 57N 83 38W
Frenchglen 78 42 56N 119 0W
Frenchman Butte 56 53 35N 109 38W
Frenchman Creek, R. 74 40 34N 101 35W
Frenchman, R. 78 49 25N 108 20W
Fresco, R. 87 7 15S 51 30W
Freshfield, C. 91 68 25S 151 10E
Fresnillo 82 23 10N 103 0W
Fresno 80 36 47N 119 50W
Fresno Res. 78 48 47N 110 0W
Frévent 101 50 15N 2 17E
Freycinet Pen. 135 42 10S 148 25E
Fria, La 86 8 13N 72 15W
Friant 80 36 59N 119 43W
Frias 88 28 40S 65 5W
Fribourg 106 48 0N 7 52E
Friday Harbor 80 48 32N 123 1W
Friedberg 10 50 19N 8 45E
Friedrichshafen 106 47 39N 9 29E
Friendly (Tonga) Is. 133 19 50S 174 30W
Friesland □ 105 53 5N 5 50E
Frigate, L. 34 53 15N 74 45W
Frijoles 84 9 11N 79 48W
Frikson 57 50 30N 99 55W
Frio, C. 117 18 0S 12 0E
Frio, R. 75 29 40N 99 40W
Friona 75 34 40N 102 42W
Fritch 75 35 40N 101 35W
Friuli-Venezia Giulia □ 108 46 0N 13 0E
Frobisher 57 49 12N 102 26W
Frobisher B. 65 63 0N 67 0W
Frobisher Bay 65 63 44N 68 31W
Frobisher L. 55 56 20N 108 15W
Frog L. 60 53 55N 110 20W
Frohavet 110 64 5N 9 35E
Froid 74 48 20N 104 29W
Fromberg 78 45 19N 108 58W
Frome 95 51 16N 2 17W
Frome, L. 135 30 45S 139 45E
Fromentine 100 46 53N 2 9W
Front Range 78 40 0N 105 10W
Front Royal 72 38 55N 78 10W
Frontera 83 18 30N 92 40W
Frontier 56 49 12N 108 34W
Frontignan 102 43 27N 3 45E
Frosinone 108 41 38N 13 20E
Frostburg 72 39 43N 78 57W
Frostisen 110 68 14N 17 10E
Frouard 101 48 47N 6 8E
Fröya I. 110 63 45N 8 45E
Fruges 101 50 30N 2 8E
Fruitland 48 43 13N 79 43W
Fruitvale 63 49 7N 117 33W
Frunze 120 42 54N 74 36E
Frutal 87 20 0S 49 0W
Fry L. 52 51 14N 91 19W
Frýdek-Místek 107 49 40N 18 20E
Fuchin 130 47 10N 132 0E
Fuchow, Kiangsi, China 131 27 50N 116 14E
Fuchow, Liaoning, China 130 39 45N 121 45E
Fuchun K. 131 30 1N 120 1E
Fuchung 131 24 25N 110 16E
Fucino, L. 102 42 0N 13 30E
Fuente Ovejuna 104 38 15N 5 25W
Fuentes de Oñoro 104 40 33N 6 52W
Fuerte Olimpo 88 21 0S 58 0W
Fuerte, R. 82 26 0N 109 0W
Fuga, I. 131 19 55N 121 10E
Fugløysund 110 70 15N 20 20E
Fujaira 123 25 7N 56 18E
Fuji-no-miya 132 35 20N 138 40E
Fuji-San 132 35 22N 138 44E
Fujisawa 132 35 22N 139 29E
Fukien □ 131 26 0N 117 30E
Fukow 131 34 11N 114 36E
Fukuchiyama 132 35 25N 135 9E
Fukui 132 36 0N 136 10E
Fukui-ken □ 132 36 0N 136 12E
Fukuoka 132 33 30N 130 30E
Fukuoka-ken □ 132 33 30N 131 0E
Fukushima-ken □ 132 37 30N 140 15E
Fukuyama 132 34 35N 133 20E
Fulda 106 50 32N 9 41E
Fulda, R. 106 50 37N 9 40E
Fulford Harbour 63 48 47N 123 27W
Fullerton, Calif., U.S.A. 81 33 52N 117 58W
Fullerton, Nebr., U.S.A. 74 41 25N 98 0W
Fulton, Can. 49 43 8N 79 40W
Fulton, Ill., U.S.A. 76 41 52N 90 11W
Fulton, Ind., U.S.A. 77 40 57N 86 16W
Fulton, Mo., U.S.A. 76 38 50N 91 55W
Fulton, N.Y., U.S.A. 71 43 20N 76 22W
Fumay 101 50 0N 4 40E
Fumel 102 44 30N 0 58E
Funabashi 132 35 45N 140 0E
Funafuti, I. 14 8 30S 179 0E
Funchal 114 32 45N 16 55W
Fundación 86 10 31N 74 11W
Fundão 104 40 8N 7 30W
Fundy, B. of 39 45 0N 66 0W
Fundy Nat. Park 39 45 35N 65 10W
Funes 86 1 0N 77 28W
Fungchun 131 23 27N 111 30E
Funing 131 23 45N 105 30E
Furat, Nahr al 122 33 30N 43 0E
Furbero 83 20 22N 97 31W
Furnas, Reprêsa de 89 20 50S 45 0W
Furneaux Group 135 40 10S 147 50E
Furness 94 54 14N 3 8W
Furness, Pen. 94 54 12N 3 10W
Fürth 106 49 29N 11 0E
Fury and Hecla Str. 65 69 56N 84 0W
Fusagasugá 86 4 21N 74 22W
Fuse 132 34 40N 135 37E
Fushun 130 41 50N 123 55E
Fusin 130 42 12N 121 33E
Fusui 131 22 35N 107 58E
Futing 131 27 15N 120 10E
Futsing 131 25 46N 119 29E
Futuna I. 14 14 25S 178 20E
Fuyang Ho 131 38 14N 116 5E
Fuyuan 130 48 9N 134 3E
Fwaka 117 12 5S 29 25E
Fyekundo = Yushu 129 33 6N 96 48E
Fylde 94 53 50N 2 58W
Fyn 111 55 20N 10 30E
Fyne, L. 96 56 0N 5 20W

G

Gabarouse 39 45 50N 60 9W
Gabela 116 11 0S 14 37E
Gaberones = Gaborone 117 24 37S 25 57E
Gabès 114 33 53N 10 2E
Gabès, Golfe de 114 34 0N 10 30E
Gabon ■ 116 0 10S 10 0E
Gaborone 117 24 37S 25 57E
Gabriels 71 44 26N 74 12W
Gabriola I. 63 49 9N 123 47W
Gabrovo 109 42 52N 25 27E
Gacé 100 48 49N 0 20E
Gach Sārān 123 30 15N 50 45E
Gadag 124 15 30N 75 45E
Gadarwara 124 22 50N 78 50E
Gadhada 124 22 0N 71 35E
Gadsden, Ala., U.S.A. 73 34 1N 86 0W
Gadsden, Ariz., U.S.A. 79 32 35N 114 47W
Gadwal 124 16 10N 77 50E
Gaffney 73 35 10N 81 31W
Gagetown 39 45 46N 66 10W
Gagnoa 114 6 4N 5 55W
Gagnon 38 51 50N 68 5W
Gagnon, L., N.W.T., Can. 55 62 3N 110 27W
Gagnon, L., Qué., Can. 40 46 7N 75 7W
Gail 75 32 48N 101 25W
Gaillac 102 43 54N 1 54E
Gaillarbois, L. 38 52 0N 67 27W
Gaillon 100 49 10N 1 20E
Gaines 70 41 45N 77 35W
Gainesville, Fla., U.S.A. 73 29 38N 82 20W
Gainesville, Ga., U.S.A. 73 34 17N 83 47W
Gainesville, Mo., U.S.A. 75 36 35N 92 26W
Gainesville, Tex., U.S.A. 75 33 40N 97 10W
Gainsborough 94 53 23N 0 46W
Gairdner L. 134 31 30S 136 0E
Gairloch L. 96 57 43N 5 45W
Galahad 61 52 31N 111 56W
Galán, Cerro 88 25 55S 66 52W
Galangue 117 13 48S 16 3E
Galápagos, Is. 15 0 0 89 0W
Galas, R. 128 4 55N 101 57E
Galashiels 96 55 37N 2 50W
Galaţi 107 45 27N 28 2E
Galatina 109 40 10N 18 10E
Galax 73 36 42N 80 57W
Galdhøpiggen 111 61 38N 8 18E
Galeana 82 24 50N 100 4W
Galela 127 1 50N 127 55E
Galena, Alaska, U.S.A. 67 64 42N 157 0W
Galena, Ill., U.S.A. 76 42 25N 90 26W
Galeota Point 85 10 8N 61 0W
Galera, Pta. de la 86 10 48N 75 16W
Galesburg, Ill., U.S.A. 76 40 57N 90 23W
Galesburg, Mich., U.S.A. 77 42 17N 85 26W
Galeton, Can. 53 51 8N 80 55W
Galeton, U.S.A. 70 41 43N 77 40W
Galicia 104 42 43N 8 0W
Galien 77 41 48N 86 30W
Galilee, S. of = Kinneret, L. 115 32 49N 35 36E
Galion 70 40 43N 82 48W
Galissonnière, La, L. 38 51 25N 62 0W
Galiuro Mts. 79 32 40N 110 30W
Gallatin, Mo., U.S.A. 76 39 55N 93 58W
Gallatin, Tenn., U.S.A. 73 36 24N 86 27W
Galle 124 6 5N 80 10E
Gallego 82 29 49N 106 22W
Gállego, R. 104 42 23N 0 30W
Gallegos, R. 90 51 50S 71 0W
Galley Hd. 97 51 32N 8 56W
Gallinas, Pta. 86 12 28N 71 40W
Gallípoli 109 40 8N 18 0E
Gallipoli = Gelibolu 109 40 28N 26 43E
Gallipolis 72 38 50N 82 10W
Gallitzin 70 40 28N 78 32W
Gällivare 110 67 9N 20 40E
Galloway 96 55 0N 4 25W
Galloway, Mull of 96 54 38N 4 50W
Gallup 79 35 30N 108 54W
Galoya 124 8 10N 80 55E
Galt, Can. 49 43 22N 80 19W
Galt, Calif., U.S.A. 80 38 15N 121 18W
Galt, Mo., U.S.A. 76 40 8N 93 23W
Galty Mts. 97 52 22N 8 10W
Galtymore, Mt. 97 52 22N 8 12W
Galva 76 41 10N 90 0W
Galveston, Ind., U.S.A. 77 40 35N 86 11W
Galveston, Tex., U.S.A. 75 29 15N 94 48W
Galveston B. 75 29 30N 94 50W
Gálvez 88 32 0S 61 20W
Galway 97 53 16N 9 4W
Galway □ 97 53 16N 9 3W
Galway B. 97 53 10N 9 20W
Gamarra 86 8 20N 73 45W
Gambell 67 63 55N 171 50W
Gambia ■ 114 13 25N 16 0W
Gambia, R. 114 13 20N 15 45W
Gambier I. 63 49 30N 123 23W
Gamboa 84 9 8N 79 42W
Gamboma 116 1 55S 15 52E
Gameleira 87 7 50S 50 0W
Gamerco 79 35 33N 108 56W
Gammelgarn 87 57 24N 18 49E
Gammon, R. 57 51 24N 95 44W
Gan 102 43 12N 0 27W
Gan (Addu Atoll) 119 0 10S 71 10E
Ganado, Ariz., U.S.A. 79 35 46N 109 41W
Ganado, Tex., U.S.A. 75 29 4N 96 31W
Gananoque 47 44 20N 76 10W
Ganaveh 123 29 35N 50 35E
Gand 105 51 2N 3 37E
Gandak, R. 125 27 0N 84 8E
Gandava 124 28 32N 67 32E
Gander 37 48 58N 54 35W
Gander L. 37 48 58N 54 35W
Gander, R. 37 49 16N 54 30W
Gand = Gent 105 51 2N 3 37E
Gandhi Sagar 124 24 40N 75 40E
Gandi 114 12 55N 5 49E
Ganedidalem = Gani 127 0 48S 128 14E
Gang Ranch 63 51 33N 122 20W
Ganga, R. 125 25 0N 88 0E
Ganganagar 124 29 56N 73 56E
Gangaw 125 22 5N 94 15E
Ganges 102 43 56N 3 42E
Ganges = Ganga, R. 125 25 0N 88 0E
Ganges, Mouth of the 125 21 30N 90 0E
Gangtok 125 27 20N 88 37E
Gannat 102 46 7N 3 11E
Gannett Pk. 78 43 15N 109 47W
Gannvalley 74 44 3N 98 57W
Gantheaume B. 134 27 40S 114 10E
Gao 114 16 15N 0 5W
Gao Bang 128 22 37N 106 18E
Gap 103 44 33N 6 5E
Gar Dzong 124 32 20N 79 55E
Garachiné 84 8 0N 78 12W
Garanhuns 87 8 50S 36 30W
Garber 75 36 30N 97 36W
Garberville 78 40 11N 123 50W
Gard □ 103 44 2N 4 10E
Garda, L. di 108 45 40N 10 40E
Gardanne 103 43 27N 5 27E
Garde L. 55 62 50N 106 13W
Garden City, Kans., U.S.A. 75 38 0N 100 45W
Garden City, Mo., U.S.A. 76 38 34N 94 12W
Garden City, Tex., U.S.A. 75 31 52N 101 28W
Garden Grove 81 33 47N 117 55W
Garden I. 46 45 49N 85 30W
Gardez 124 33 31N 68 59E
Gardiner, Can. 34 49 19N 81 2W
Gardiner, Mont., U.S.A. 78 45 3N 110 53W
Gardiner, N. Mex., U.S.A. 75 36 55N 104 29W
Gardiner Ls. 60 57 32N 112 30W
Gardiners I. 71 41 4N 72 5W
Gardner, Ill., U.S.A. 77 41 12N 88 17W
Gardner, Mass., U.S.A. 71 42 35N 72 0W
Gardner Canal 62 53 27N 128 8W
Gardnerville 80 38 59N 119 47W
Gareloi I. 67 51 49N 178 50W
Garey 81 34 53N 120 19W
Garfield, Utah, U.S.A. 78 40 45N 112 15W
Garfield, Wash., U.S.A. 78 47 3N 117 8W
Gargano, Mte. 108 41 43N 15 43E
Gargans, Mt. 102 45 37N 1 39E
Gargantua, C. 34 47 35N 85 0W
Garibaldi 54 49 56N 123 15W
Garibaldi, Mt. 63 49 51N 123 0W
Garibaldi Prov. Park 63 49 50N 122 40W
Garies 117 30 32S 17 59E
Garigliano, R. 108 41 13N 13 44E
Garland 78 41 47N 112 10W
Garm 120 39 0N 70 20E
Garmsār 123 35 20N 52 25E
Garneau, L. 38 51 43N 63 22W
Garner 76 43 4N 93 37W
Garners Corners 48 43 12N 79 57W
Garnett 74 38 18N 95 12W
Garnish 37 47 14N 55 22W
Garonne, R. 102 45 2N 0 36W
Garoua 114 9 19N 13 21E
Garrett 77 41 21N 85 8W
Garrigues 102 43 40N 3 30E
Garrison, Ky., U.S.A. 77 38 36N 83 10W
Garrison, Mont., U.S.A. 78 46 37N 112 56W
Garrison, N.D., U.S.A. 74 31 50N 94 28W
Garrison, Tex., U.S.A. 75 47 39N 101 27W
Garrison Res. 74 47 30N 102 0W
Garry, Glen 96 57 3N 5 7W
Garry L., Can. 65 65 58N 100 18W
Garry L., U.K. 96 57 5N 4 52W
Garry, R. 96 56 47N 3 47W
Garsen 116 2 20S 40 5E
Garson L. 60 56 19N 110 2W
Garson, R.. 55 56 20N 110 1W
Gartempe, R. 102 46 47N 0 49E
Gartok 129 31 59N 80 30E
Garupá 87 1 25S 51 35W
Garut 127 7 14S 107 53E
Garvie Mts. 133 45 30S 168 50E
Gary 77 41 35N 87 20W
Garzón 86 2 10N 75 40W
Gas City 77 40 29N 85 36W
Gasan Kuli 120 37 40N 54 20E
Gascogne 102 43 45N 0 20E
Gasconade 76 38 40N 91 33W
Gasconade R. 76 38 41N 91 33W
Gascons 38 48 11N 64 51W
Gascony = Gascogne 102 43 45N 0 20E
Gascoyne, R. 134 24 52S 113 37E
Gashiun Nor 129 42 20N 100 40E
Gashua 114 12 54N 11 0E
Gaspé 38 48 52N 64 30W
Gaspé, Baie de 38 48 46N 64 17W
Gaspé, C. 38 48 48N 64 7W
Gaspé Pen. 38 48 45N 65 40W
Gaspé, Péninsule de 38 48 30N 65 30W
Gaspésie, Parc Prov. de la 38 48 55N 65 50W
Gassaway 72 38 42N 80 43W
Gastonia 73 35 17N 81 10W
Gastre 90 42 10S 69 15W
Gata, C. de 104 36 41N 2 13W
Gata, Sierra de 104 40 20N 6 20W
Gataga, R. 54 58 35N 126 59W
Gateshead 94 54 57N 1 37W
Gateshead I. 65 70 36N 100 26W
Gatesville 75 31 29N 97 45W
Gatico 88 22 40S 70 20W
Gâtinais 101 48 5N 2 40E
Gâtine, Hauteurs de 102 46 35N 0 45W
Gatineau, Ont., Can. 48 45 29N 75 39W
Gatineau, Qué., Can. 40 45 29N 75 38W
Gatineau, Parc de la 40 45 40N 76 0W
Gatineau, R. 48 45 27N 75 42W
Gatooma 117 18 20S 29 52E
Gatun 84 9 16N 79 55W

Gatun Dam Gobles

Gatun Dam 84 9 16N 79 55W
Gatun, L. 84 9 7N 79 56W
Gatun Locks 84 9 16N 79 55W
Gaud-i-Zirreh 124 29 45N 62 0E
Gauer L. 55 57 0N 97 50W
Gauhati 125 26 10N 91 45E
Gaula, R. 110 62 57N 11 0E
Gaultois 37 47 36N 55 54W
Gaussberg, Mt. 91 66 45S 89 0E
Gausta, Mt. 111 59 48N 8 40E
Gavarnie 102 42 44N 0 3W
Gavăter 123 25 10N 61 23E
Gaviota 81 34 29N 120 13W
Gavle 111 60 41N 17 13E
Gävleborgs Lan □ 111 61 20N 16 15E
Gavray 100 48 55N 1 20W
Gawilgarh Hills 124 21 15N 76 45E
Gawler 135 34 30S 138 42E
Gawler Ranges 134 32 30S 135 45E
Gaya 125 24 47N 85 4E
Gaylord 46 45 1N 84 35W
Gayndah 135 25 35S 151 39E
Gayot, L. 36 55 43N 70 50W
Gaza 115 31 30N 34 28E
Gaziantep 122 37 6N 37 23E
Gdansk 107 54 22N 18 40E
Gdanska, Zatoka 107 54 30N 19 20E
Gdynia 107 54 35N 18 33E
Geary 39 45 46N 66 29W
Gebe, I. 127 0 5N 129 25E
Gedaref 115 14 2N 35 28E
Gèdre 102 42 47N 0 2E
Gedser 111 54 35N 11 55E
Geel 105 51 10N 4 59E
Geelong 136 38 10S 144 22E
Geikie I. 52 50 0N 88 35W
Geikie, R. 55 57 45N 103 52W
Geita 116 2 48S 32 12E
Gela 108 37 6N 14 18E
Gelderland □ 105 52 5N 6 10E
Geldermalsen 105 51 53N 5 17E
Geldrop 105 51 25N 5 32E
Geleen 105 50 57N 5 49E
Gelibolu 109 40 28N 26 43E
Gelsenkirchen 105 51 30N 7 5E
Gem 61 50 57N 112 11W
Gemas 128 2 37N 102 36E
Gembloux 105 50 34N 4 43E
Gemena 116 3 20N 19 40E
Gemerek 122 39 15N 36 10E
Gemert 105 51 33N 5 41E
Gemlik 122 40 28N 29 13E
Gençay 102 46 23N 0 23E
General Acha 88 37 20S 64 38W
General Alvear, B. A., Argent. 88 36 0S 60 0W
General Alvear, Mend., Argent. 88 35 0S 67 40W
General Artigas 88 26 52S 56 16W
General Belgrano 88 36 0S 58 30W
General Cabrera 88 32 53S 63 58W
General Cepeda 82 25 23N 101 27W
General Guido 88 36 40S 57 50W
General Juan Madariaga 88 37 0S 57 0W
General La Madrid 88 37 30S 61 10W
General MacArthur 127 11 18N 125 28E
General Martin Miguel de Güemes 88 24 50S 65 0W
General Paz 88 27 45S 57 36W
General Paz, L. 90 44 0S 72 0W
General Pico 88 35 45S 63 50W
General Pinedo 88 27 15S 61 30W
General Pinto 88 34 45S 61 50W
General Roca 90 30 0S 67 40W
General Santos 127 6 12N 125 14E
General Treviño 83 26 14N 99 29W
General Trías 82 28 21N 106 22W
General Viamonte 88 35 1S 61 3W
General Villegas 88 35 0S 63 0W
Genesee, Can. 60 53 21N 114 20W
Genesee, Idaho, U.S.A. 78 46 31N 116 59W
Genesee, Mich., U.S.A. 70 43 7N 83 38W
Genesee, Pa., U.S.A. 70 42 0N 77 54W
Genesee, R. 70 41 35N 78 0W
Geneseo, Ill., U.S.A. 76 41 25N 90 10W
Geneseo, Kans., U.S.A. 74 38 32N 98 8W
Geneseo, N.Y., U.S.A. 70 42 49N 77 49W
Geneva, Can. 43 45 36N 74 20W
Geneva, Ala., U.S.A. 73 31 2N 85 52W
Geneva, Ill., U.S.A. 77 41 53N 88 18W
Geneva, Nebr., U.S.A. 74 40 35N 97 35W
Geneva, N.Y., U.S.A. 70 42 53N 77 0W
Geneva, Ohio, U.S.A. 70 41 49N 80 58W
Geneva = Genève 106 46 12N 6 9E
Geneva, L. 77 42 38N 88 30W
Geneva, L. = Léman, Lac 106 46 26N 6 30E
Genève 106 46 12N 6 9E
Geneve 77 40 36N 84 57W
Genil, R. 104 37 12N 3 50W
Génissiat, Barrage de 103 46 1N 5 48E
Genk 105 50 58N 5 32E
Genlis 101 47 15N 5 12E
Gennargentu, Mt. del 108 40 0N 9 10E
Gennes 100 47 20N 0 17W
Genoa, Ill., U.S.A. 77 42 6N 88 42W
Genoa, Nebr., U.S.A. 74 41 31N 97 44W
Genoa, Nev., U.S.A. 80 39 2N 119 50W
Genoa, N.Y., U.S.A. 71 42 40N 76 32W
Genoa = Génova 108 44 24N 8 57E
Genoa City 77 42 30N 88 20W
Génova 108 44 24N 8 56E
Génova, Golfo di 108 44 0N 9 0E
Gent 105 51 2N 3 37E
Genteng 127 7 25S 106 23E
Geographe B. 134 33 30S 113 20E
Geographe Chan. 134 24 30S 113 0E
George, Can. 35 46 12N 62 32W
George, S. Afr. 117 33 58S 22 29E
George B. 39 45 45N 61 45W
George, L., N.S.W., Austral. 136 35 10S 149 25E
George, L., S. Austral., Austral. 136 37 25S 140 0E
George, L., Uganda 116 0 5N 30 10E
George, L., Fla., U.S.A. 73 29 15N 81 35W
George, L., N.Y., U.S.A. 71 43 30N 73 30W
George, R., Qué., Can. 35 58 49N 66 10W
George, R., Qué., Can. 36 49 21N 67 59W
George River = Port Nouveau-Québec 36 58 32N 65 54W
George Sound 133 44 52S 167 25E
George Town, Bahamas 84 23 33N 75 47W
George Town, Malay. 128 5 25N 100 19E
George V Coast 91 67 0S 148 0E
George West 75 28 18N 98 5W
Georgetown, Austral. 135 18 17S 143 33E
Georgetown, Ont., Can. 49 43 40N 79 56W
Georgetown, P.E.I., Can. 39 46 13N 62 24W
Georgetown, Cay. Is. 84 19 20N 81 24W
Georgetown, Guyana 86 6 50N 58 12W
Georgetown, Calif., U.S.A. 80 38 54N 120 50W
Georgetown, Colo., U.S.A. 78 39 46N 105 49W
Georgetown, Ill., U.S.A. 77 39 59N 87 38W
Georgetown, Ky., U.S.A. 77 38 13N 84 33W
Georgetown, Ohio, U.S.A. 72 38 50N 83 50W
Georgetown, S.C., U.S.A. 73 33 22N 79 15W
Georgetown, Tex., U.S.A. 75 30 40N 97 45W
Georgia □ 72 32 0N 82 0W
Georgia, Str. of 62 49 25N 124 0W
Georgian B. 46 45 15N 81 0W
Georgian S.S.R. □ 120 41 0N 45 0E
Georgievsk 120 44 12N 43 28E
Georgina I. 46 44 22N 79 17W
Georgina, R. 135 23 30S 139 47E
Georgiu-Dezh 120 51 3N 39 20E
Gera 106 50 53N 12 5E
Geraardsbergen 105 50 45N 3 53E
Geral de Goias, Serra 87 12 0S 46 0W
Geral, Serra 89 26 25S 50 0W
Gerald 76 38 24N 91 21W
Geraldine 78 47 45N 110 18W
Geraldton, Austral. 134 28 48S 114 32E
Geraldton, Can. 53 49 44N 86 59W
Gérardmer 101 48 3N 6 50E
Gerdine, Mt. 67 61 32N 152 30W
Gerede 122 40 45N 32 10E
Gerik 128 5 25N 100 8E
Gering 74 41 51N 103 40W
Gerlach 78 40 43N 119 27W
Germain, Grand L. 38 51 12N 66 41W
Germansen Landing 54 55 43N 124 40W
Germantown 77 39 38N 84 22W
Germany, East ■ 106 52 0N 12 0E
Germany, West ■ 106 52 0N 9 0E
Germiston 117 26 11S 28 10E
Gerona 104 41 58N 2 46E
Gerrard 63 50 30N 117 17W
Gers □ 102 43 35N 0 38E
Gerze 122 41 45N 35 10E
Geser 127 3 50N 130 35E
Gethsémani 36 50 13N 60 40W
Gettysburg, Pa., U.S.A. 72 39 47N 77 18W
Gettysburg, S.D., U.S.A. 74 45 3N 99 56W
Getz Ice Shelf 91 75 0S 130 0W
Gévaudan 102 44 40N 3 40E
Gevelsberg 105 51 21N 7 7E
Gex 103 46 21N 6 3E
Geyser 78 47 17N 110 30W
Geyserville 80 38 42N 122 54W
Geysir 110 64 19N 20 18W
Ghaghara, R. 125 26 0N 84 20E
Ghail 122 21 40N 46 20E
Ghana ■ 114 6 0N 1 0W
Ghanzi 117 21 50S 21 45E
Ghardaïa 114 32 31N 3 37E
Gharyān 114 32 10N 13 0E
Ghāt 114 24 59N 10 19E
Ghat Ghat 122 24 40N 46 15E
Ghawdex = Gozo, I. 108 36 0N 14 13E
Ghaziabad 124 28 42N 77 35E
Ghazipur 125 25 38N 83 35E
Ghazni 124 33 30N 68 17E
Ghazni □ 124 33 0N 68 0E
Ghent = Gand 105 51 4N 3 43E
Ghisonaccia 103 42 1N 9 26E
Ghizao 124 33 30N 65 59E
Ghorat □ 124 34 0N 64 20E
Ghost River 52 50 12N 91 30W
Ghugus 124 20 0N 79 0E
Ghurian 124 34 17N 61 25E
Gia Lai = Pleiku 128 14 3N 108 0E
Gia Nghia 128 12 0N 107 42E
Giant Forest 80 36 36N 118 43W
Giant's Causeway 97 55 15N 6 30W
Giarre 108 37 44N 15 10E
Gibara 84 21 0N 76 20W
Gibbon 74 40 49N 98 45W
Gibbons 60 53 50N 113 20W
Gibeon 117 25 7S 17 45E
Gibraltar 104 36 7N 5 22W
Gibraltar, Str. of 104 35 55N 5 40W
Gibson City 77 40 28N 88 22W
Gibson Des. 134 24 0S 126 0E
Gibsonburg 77 41 23N 83 19W
Gibsons 63 49 24N 123 32W
Gibsonville 80 39 46N 120 54W
Gida. G. 17 72 30N 77 0E
Giddings 75 30 11N 96 58W
Gien 101 47 40N 2 36E
Giessen 106 50 34N 8 40E
Giffard 42 46 51N 71 12W
Gift Lake 60 55 53N 115 49W
Gifu 132 35 30N 136 45E
Gifu-ken □ 132 36 0N 137 0E
Gig Harbor 80 47 20N 122 35W
Giganta, Sa. de la 82 25 30N 111 30W
Gigha, I. 96 55 42N 5 45W
Gignac 102 43 39N 3 32E
Gijón 104 43 32N 5 42W
Gil I. 62 53 12N 129 15W
Gila Bend 79 33 0N 112 46W
Gila Bend Mts. 79 33 15N 113 0W
Gila, R. 79 33 5N 108 40W
Gilbert Is. 14 1 0S 176 0E
Gilbert, Mt. 62 50 52N 124 16W
Gilbert Plains 57 51 9N 100 28W
Gilbert, R. 135 16 35S 141 15E
Gilford I. 62 50 40N 126 30W
Gilgandra 136 31 43S 148 39E
Gilgit 124 35 50N 74 15E
Gillam 55 56 20N 94 40W
Gillespie 76 39 7N 89 49W
Gillette 74 44 20N 105 38W
Gillies Bay 62 49 42N 124 29W
Gillingham 95 51 23N 0 34E
Gilman, Ill., U.S.A. 77 40 46N 88 0W
Gilman, Mo., U.S.A. 76 40 8N 93 53W
Gilmer 75 32 44N 94 55W
Gilmour 47 44 48N 77 37W
Gilroy 80 37 1N 121 37W
Gimli 55 50 40N 97 10W
Gimont 102 43 38N 0 52E
Gióna, Óros 109 38 38N 22 14E
Giong, Teluk 127 4 50N 118 20E
Giovi, P. dei 103 44 30N 8 55E
Gippsland 135 37 45S 147 15E
Girard, Ill., U.S.A. 76 39 27N 89 48W
Girard, Kans., U.S.A. 75 37 30N 94 50W
Girard, Ohio, U.S.A. 70 41 10N 80 42W
Girard, Pa., U.S.A. 70 42 1N 80 21W
Girardot 86 4 18N 74 48W
Girardville 41 49 0N 72 32W
Girdle Ness 96 57 9N 2 2W
Giresun 122 40 45N 38 30E
Giridih 125 24 10N 86 21E
Girishk 124 31 47N 64 24E
Giromagny 101 47 44N 6 50E
Gironde □ 102 44 45N 0 30W
Gironde, R. 102 45 27N 0 53W
Girouxville 60 55 45N 117 20W
Girvan 96 55 15N 4 50W
Gisborne 133 38 39S 178 5E
Gisborne L. 37 47 48N 54 49W
Gisenyi 116 1 41S 29 30E
Gisors 101 49 15N 1 40E
Giurgiu 107 43 52N 25 57E
Givet 101 50 8N 4 49E
Givors 103 45 35N 4 45E
Givry 101 46 41N 4 46E
Gizhiga 121 62 0N 150 27E
Gizhiginskaya, Guba 121 61 0N 158 0E
Gizycko 107 54 2N 21 48E
Gjirokastër 109 40 7N 20 16E
Gjoa Haven 65 68 38N 95 53W
Gjøvik 111 60 47N 10 43E
Glace Bay 39 46 11N 59 58W
Glacier B. 54 58 30N 136 10W
Glacier Nat. Park 63 51 15N 117 30W
Glacier National Park 61 48 35N 113 40W
Glacier Peak Mt. 63 48 7N 121 7W
Glacier Str. 65 76 12N 79 15W
Gladewater 75 32 30N 94 58W
Gladmar 56 49 10N 104 27W
Gladstone, Austral. 136 23 52S 151 16E
Gladstone, Can. 57 50 13N 98 57W
Gladstone, Mich., U.S.A. 72 45 52N 87 1W
Gladstone, Mo., U.S.A. 76 39 13N 94 35W
Gladwin 46 43 59N 84 29W
Gladys L. 54 59 50N 133 0W
Gláma 110 65 48N 23 0W
Glåma, R. 111 60 30N 12 8E
Glamis 81 33 0N 115 4W
Glamorgan (□) 95 51 37N 3 35W
Glamorgan, Vale of 98 50 45N 3 15W
Glan 127 5 45N 125 20E
Glanville 76 41 17N 89 15W
Glasco, Kans., U.S.A. 74 39 25N 97 50W
Glasco, N.Y., U.S.A. 71 42 3N 73 57W
Glasgow, U.K. 96 55 52N 4 14W
Glasgow, Ky., U.S.A. 72 37 2N 85 55W
Glasgow, Mo., U.S.A. 76 39 14N 92 51W
Glasgow, Mont., U.S.A. 78 48 12N 106 35W
Glaslyn 56 53 22N 108 21W
Glastonbury, U.K. 95 51 9N 2 42W
Glastonbury, U.S.A. 71 41 42N 72 27W
Glauchau 106 50 50N 12 33E
Glazov 120 58 9N 52 40E
Gleichen 54 50 50N 113 0W
Glen 71 44 7N 71 10W
Glen Affric 96 57 15N 5 0W
Glen Almond 40 45 42N 75 29W
Glen Canyon Dam 79 37 0N 111 25W
Glen Canyon Nat. Recreation Area 79 37 30N 111 0W
Glen Coe 98 56 40N 5 0W
Glen Cove 71 40 51N 73 37W
Glen Cross 49 43 59N 80 3W
Glen Ewen 57 49 12N 102 1W
Glen Garry 96 57 3N 5 7W
Glen Gordon 43 45 10N 74 32W
Glen Innes 135 29 40S 151 39E
Glen Lyon 71 41 10N 76 7W
Glen Mor 96 57 12N 4 37E
Glen Moriston 96 57 10N 4 58W
Glen Morris 49 43 16N 80 21W
Glen Robertson 43 45 22N 74 30W
Glen Thompson 136 37 38S 142 35E
Glen Ullin 74 46 48N 101 46W
Glen Williams 49 43 40N 79 55W
Glénans, Îs. de 100 47 42N 4 0W
Glenavon 56 50 12N 103 8W
Glenboro 57 49 33N 99 17W
Glenbrook 133 33 46S 150 37E
Glenburnie 136 37 51S 140 50E
Glencairn 58 50 26N 104 33W
Glenchristie 49 43 28N 80 17W
Glencoe, Can. 46 42 45N 81 43W
Glencoe, U.S.A. 74 44 45N 94 10W
Glendale, Alta., Can. 59 51 2N 114 9W
Glendale, N.S., Can. 39 45 49N 61 18W
Glendale, Ariz., U.S.A. 79 33 40N 112 8W
Glendale, Calif., U.S.A. 81 34 7N 118 18W
Glendale, Oreg., U.S.A. 78 42 44N 123 29W
Glendive 74 47 7N 104 40W
Glendo 74 42 30N 105 0W
Glendon 60 54 15N 111 10W
Glendora 81 34 8N 117 52W
Gleneagle 48 45 32N 75 48W
Glenelg, R. 136 38 4S 140 59E
Glenella 57 50 33N 99 11W
Glengariff 97 51 45N 9 33W
Glengarry □ 43 45 15N 74 30W
Glenmoor Res. 59 50 59N 114 8W
Glenmora 75 31 1N 92 34W
Glenn 80 39 31N 122 1W
Glennie 46 44 32N 83 39W
Glennie's Creek 136 32 30S 151 8E
Glenns Ferry 78 43 0N 115 15W
Glenrock 78 42 53N 105 55W
Glenroy 134 26 23S 28 17E
Glens Falls 71 43 20N 73 40W
Glenties 97 54 48N 8 18W
Glenville 72 38 56N 80 50W
Glenwood, Alta., Can. 61 49 21N 113 31W
Glenwood, Newf., Can. 37 49 0N 54 47W
Glenwood, Ark., U.S.A. 75 34 20N 93 30W
Glenwood, Hawaii, U.S.A. 67 19 29N 155 10W
Glenwood, Iowa, U.S.A. 74 41 7N 95 41W
Glenwood, Minn., U.S.A. 74 45 38N 95 21W
Glenwood, Wash., U.S.A. 80 46 1N 121 17W
Glenwood Sprs. 78 39 39N 107 15W
Glettinganes 110 65 30N 13 37W
Gliwice 107 50 22N 18 41E
Globe 79 33 25N 110 53W
Głogów 106 51 37N 16 5E
Gloria, La 86 8 37N 73 48W
Glorieuses, Îs. 117 11 30S 47 20E
Glossop 94 53 27N 1 56W
Gloucester, Can. 48 45 21N 75 39W
Gloucester, U.K. 95 51 52N 2 15W
Gloucester, U.S.A. 71 42 38N 70 39W
Gloucestershire □ 95 51 44N 2 10W
Gloversville 71 43 5N 74 18W
Glovertown 35 48 40N 54 03W
Glückstadt 106 53 46N 9 28E
Gmünd 106 48 45N 15 0E
Gmunden 106 47 55N 13 48E
Gniezno 107 52 30N 17 35E
Gnowangerup 134 33 58S 117 59E
Go Cong 128 10 22N 106 40E
Goa 124 15 33N 73 59E
Goa □ 124 15 33N 73 59E
Goalen Hd. 136 36 33S 150 4E
Goalpara 125 26 10N 90 40E
Goat Fell 96 55 37N 5 11W
Goba, Ethiopia 115 7 1N 39 59E
Goba, Mozam. 117 26 15S 32 13E
Gobabis 117 22 16S 19 0E
Gobi, desert 129 44 0N 111 0E
Gobles, Can. 49 43 9N 80 34W

Gobles Great Central

Gobles, U.S.A. 77 42 22N 85 53W
Gochas 117 24 59S 19 25E
Godavari Point 125 17 0N 82 20E
Godavari, R. 125 19 5N 79 0E
Godbout 38 49 20N 67 38W
Godbout, R. 38 49 19N 67 36W
Goderich 46 43 45N 81 41W
Goderville 100 49 38N 0 22E
Godfrey 76 38 57N 90 11W
Godham 65 60 55N 60 40W
Godhavn 17 69 15N 53 38W
Godhra 124 22 49N 73 40E
Godoy Cruz 88 32 56S 68 52W
Gods L. 55 54 40N 94 15W
Gods, R. 55 56 22N 92 51W
Godthåb 17 64 10N 51 46W
Goeie Hoop, Kaap die 117 34 24S 18 30E
Goéland, L. du 41 49 47N 71 43W
Goéland, L.au 40 49 50N 76 48W
Goeree 105 51 50N 4 0E
Goes 105 51 30N 3 55E
Goetzville 46 46 3N 84 5W
Gogama 53 47 35N 81 43W
Gogebic, L. 52 46 30N 89 34W
Gogriâl 115 8 30N 28 0E
Goiânia 87 16 35S 49 20W
Goiás 87 15 55S 50 10W
Goiás □ 87 12 10S 48 0W
Goirle 105 51 31N 5 4E
Gojra 124 31 10N 72 40E
Gokteik 125 22 26N 97 0E
Golchikha 17 71 45N 84 0E
Golconda 78 40 58N 117 32W
Gold Beach 78 42 25N 124 25W
Gold Creek 67 62 45N 149 45W
Gold Hill 78 42 28N 123 2W
Gold River 62 49 40N 126 10E
Golden, Can. 63 51 20N 117 59W
Golden, Colo., U.S.A. 74 39 42N 105 30W
Golden, Ill., U.S.A. 76 40 7N 91 1W
Golden Bay 133 40 40S 172 50E
Golden Ears Prov. Park 63 49 30N 122 25W
Golden Gate 78 37 54N 122 30W
Golden Hinde, mt. 62 49 40N 125 44W
Golden Lake 47 45 34N 77 21W
Golden Prairie 56 50 13N 109 37W
Golden Vale 97 52 33N 8 17W
Goldendale 78 45 53N 120 48W
Goldfield 79 37 45N 117 13W
Goldfields 55 59 28N 108 29W
Goldpines 55 50 45N 93 05W
Goldsand L. 55 57 2N 101 8W
Goldsboro 73 35 24N 77 59W
Goldsmith 75 32 0N 102 40W
Goldthwaite 75 31 25N 98 32W
Goleniów 106 53 35N 14 50E
Goleta 81 34 27N 119 50W
Golfito 84 8 41N 83 5W
Goliad 75 28 40N 97 22W
Golmo 129 36 30N 95 10E
Golo, R. 103 42 31N 9 32E
Golspie 96 57 58N 3 58W
Goma 116 2 11S 29 18E
Gombe 114 10 19N 11 2E
Gomel 120 52 28N 31 0E
Gómez Palacio 82 25 40N 104 40W
Gomogomo 127 6 25S 134 53E
Gomoh 125 23 52N 86 10E
Gonābād 123 34 15N 58 45E
Gonaïves 85 19 20N 72 50W
Gonâve, G. de la 85 19 29N 72 42W
Gonâve, I. de la 85 18 45N 73 0W
Gonda 125 27 9N 81 58E
Gondab-e Kāvūs 123 37 20N 55 25E
Gonder 115 12 23N 37 30E
Gondia 124 21 30N 80 10E
Gondrecourt-le-Château 101 48 26N 5 30E
Gonno-Altaysk 120 51 50N 86 5E
Gonzales, Calif., U.S.A. 80 36 35N 121 30W
Gonzales, Tex., U.S.A. 75 29 30N 97 30W
González Chaves 88 38 02S 60 05W
Goobang Cr. 136 33 20S 147 50E
Good Hart 46 45 34N 85 7W
Good Hope, C. of = Goeie Hoop 117 34 24S 18 30E
Good Hope Mt. 62 51 9N 124 10W
Good Spirit L. 56 51 34N 102 40W
Gooderham 47 44 54N 78 21W
Goodeve 56 51 4N 103 10W
Gooding 78 43 0N 114 50W
Goodland 74 39 22N 101 44W
Goodnight 75 35 4N 101 13W
Goodsoil 55 54 24N 109 13W
Goodsprings 79 35 51N 115 30W
Goodwater 56 49 24N 103 42W
Goodwood 39 44 37N 63 40W
Goole 94 53 42N 0 52W
Goolgowi 136 33 58S 145 41E
Goolma 136 32 18S 149 10E
Goondiwindi 135 28 30S 150 21E
Goose Bay 36 53 15N 60 20W
Goose Cove 37 51 18N 55 38W
Goose I. 62 51 57N 128 26W
Goose L., Can. 57 54 28N 101 30W
Goose L., U.S.A. 78 42 0N 120 30W
Goose R. 36 53 20N 60 35W
Gop 124 22 5N 69 50E
Gorakhpur 125 26 47N 83 32E
Gorda 80 35 53N 121 26W
Gorda, Punta 84 14 10N 83 10W
Gordon, Can. 58 50 0N 97 21W
Gordon, Nebr., U.S.A. 74 42 49N 102 6W
Gordon, Wis., U.S.A. 52 46 15N 91 48W
Gordon Downs 134 18 48S 128 40E
Gordon Hd. 63 48 29N 123 18W
Gordon L., Alta., Can. 60 56 30N 110 25W
Gordon L., N.W.T., Can. 54 63 5N 113 11W
Gordonville 49 43 54N 80 33W
Gore, Ethiopia 115 8 12N 35 32E
Gore, N.Z. 133 46 5S 168 58E
Gore Bay 46 45 57N 82 28W
Gorey 97 52 41N 6 18W
Gorgān 123 36 55N 54 30E
Gorgona, I. 86 3 0N 78 10W
Gorham 71 44 23N 71 10W
Gorham Mt. 71 43 42N 70 37W
Gorin 76 40 22N 92 1W
Gorinchem 105 51 50N 4 59E
Gorizia 108 45 56N 13 37E
Gorki = Gorkiy 120 56 20N 44 0E
Gorkiy 120 57 20N 44 0E
Görlitz 106 51 10N 14 59E
Gorman, Calif., U.S.A. 81 34 47N 118 51W
Gorman, Tex., U.S.A. 75 32 15N 98 43W
Gormley 50 43 56N 79 23W
Gorna Oryakhovitsa 109 43 7N 25 40E
Gorno Filinskoye 120 60 5N 70 0E
Gorong, Kepulauan 127 4 5S 131 15E
Gorontalo 127 0 35N 123 13E
Gorron 100 48 25N 0 50W
Gort 97 53 4N 8 50W
Gorzów Wielkopolski 106 52 43N 15 15E
Gosainthan, Mt. 125 28 20N 85 45E
Goschen I. 62 53 48N 130 33W
Gosford 136 33 23N 151 18E
Goshen, Can. 39 45 23N 61 59W
Goshen, Calif., U.S.A. 80 36 21N 119 25W
Goshen, Ind., U.S.A. 77 41 36N 85 46W
Goshen, N.Y., U.S.A. 71 41 23N 74 21W
Goslar 106 51 55N 10 23E
Gospič 108 44 35N 15 23E
Gosport, U.K. 95 50 48N 1 8W
Gosport, U.S.A. 77 39 21N 86 40W
Göta Kanal 111 58 35N 14 15E
Götaland, reg. 111 58 0N 14 0E
Göteborg 111 57 43N 11 59E
Göteborg & Bohus □ 111 58 20N 11 50E
Gotha 106 50 56N 10 42E
Gothenburg 74 40 58N 100 8W
Gothenburg & Goteborg 111 57 43N 11 59E
Gotōr-rettō 132 32 55N 129 5E
Gotska Sandön 111 58 24N 19 15E
Göttingen 106 51 31N 9 55E
Gottwaldov (Zlin) 107 49 14N 17 40E
Gouda 105 52 1N 4 42E
Gough I. 13 40 10S 9 45W
Gough L. 61 52 2N 112 28W
Gouin Rés. 40 48 35N 74 40W
Goulais, R. 53 46 43N 84 27W
Goulburn, Austral. 136 34 44S 149 44E
Goulburn, N.S.W., Austral. 136 32 22S 149 31E
Goulburn Is. 134 11 40S 133 20E
Goulburn, R. 136 36 6S 144 55E
Goulds 37 47 29N 52 46W
Goundam 114 16 25N 3 45W
Gourdon 102 44 44N 1 23E
Gournay-en-Bray 101 49 29N 1 44E
Gourock Ra. 136 36 0S 149 25E
Gouverneur 71 44 18N 75 30W
Gouzon 102 46 12N 2 14E
Govan 56 51 20N 105 0W
Gove 135 12 25S 136 55E
Governador Valadares 87 18 15S 41 57W
Governor's Harbour 84 25 10N 76 14W
Gowanda 70 42 29N 78 58W
Gower, The 95 51 35N 4 10W
Gowna, L. 97 53 52N 7 35W
Gowrie 76 42 17N 94 17W
Goya 88 29 10S 59 10W
Goyelle, L. 38 50 47N 60 45W
Goyllarisquizga 86 10 19S 76 31W
Gozo, I. 108 36 0N 14 13E
Graaff-Reinet 117 32 13S 24 32E
Grabill 77 41 13N 84 57W
Gračac 108 44 18N 15 57E
Graçay 101 47 10N 1 50E
Grace 78 42 38N 111 46W
Gracefield 40 46 6N 76 3W
Graceville 74 45 36N 96 23W
Gracias a Dios, C. 84 15 0N 83 20W
Grado 104 43 23N 6 4W
Grady 75 34 52N 103 15W
Graénalon, L. 110 64 10N 17 20W
Grafton, Austral. 135 29 38S 152 58E
Grafton, Ill., U.S.A. 76 38 58N 90 26W
Grafton, N.Dak., U.S.A. 74 48 30N 97 25W
Grafton, C. 135 16 51S 146 0E
Graham, Can. 52 49 20N 90 30W
Graham, N.C., U.S.A. 73 36 5N 79 22W
Graham, Tex., U.S.A. 75 33 7N 98 38W
Graham Bell, Os. 120 80 5N 70 0E
Graham I., B.C., Can. 62 53 40N 132 30W
Graham I., N.W.T., Can. 65 77 25N 90 30W
Graham L. 60 56 35N 114 33W
Graham Land 91 65 0S 64 0W
Graham Mt. 79 32 46N 109 58W
Graham, R. 54 56 31N 122 17W
Grahamdale 57 51 23N 98 30W
Grahamstown 117 33 19S 26 31E
Grainland 56 50 59N 106 33W
Grajaú 87 5 50S 46 30W
Gramat 102 44 48N 1 43E
Grampian □ 96 57 0N 3 0W
Gramsh 96 40 52N 20 12E
Gran Chaco 130 25 0S 61 0W
Gran Paradiso 108 49 33N 7 17E
Gran Sabana, La 86 5 30N 61 30W
Gran Sasso d'Italia, Mt. 102 42 25N 13 30E
Granada, Nic. 84 11 58N 86 0W
Granada, Spain 104 37 10N 3 35W
Granada, U.S.A. 74 38 5N 102 13W
Granard 97 53 47N 7 30W
Granbury 75 32 28N 97 48W
Granby 41 45 25N 72 45W
Granby, R. 63 49 2N 118 27W
Grand Bahama I. 84 26 40N 78 30W
Grand Bank 37 47 6N 55 48W
Grand Bassam 114 5 10N 3 49W
Grand Bay 39 45 18N 66 12W
Grand Bend 46 43 19N 81 45W
Grand Blanc 46 42 56N 83 38W
Grand-Bourg 85 15 53N 61 19W
Grand Bruit 37 47 40N 58 14W
Grand Calumet, Île du 40 45 44N 76 41W
Grand Canal = Yun Ho 129 35 0N 117 0E
Grand Canyon National Park 79 36 15N 112 20W
Grand Cayman 84 19 20N 81 20W
Grand Centre 60 54 25N 110 13W
Grand Cess 114 4 40N 8 12W
Grand-Combe, La 103 44 13N 4 2E
Grand Coulee, Can. 56 50 26N 104 49W
Grand Coulee, U.S.A. 78 47 48N 119 1W
Grand Coulee Dam 78 48 0N 118 50W
Grand Falls 39 48 56N 55 40W
Grand Forks, Can. 63 49 0N 118 30W
Grand Forks, U.S.A. 74 48 0N 97 3W
Grand Fougeray, Le 100 47 44N 1 43W
Grand Harbour 39 44 41N 66 46W
Grand Haven 77 43 3N 86 13W
Grand I., Can. 57 52 51N 100 0W
Grand I., Mich., U.S.A. 53 46 30N 86 40W
Grand I., N.Y., U.S.A. 49 43 2N 78 59W
Grand Island 74 40 59N 98 25W
Grand Isle 75 29 15N 89 58W
Grand Junction, Colo., U.S.A. 79 39 0N 108 30W
Grand Junction, Iowa, U.S.A. 76 42 2N 94 14W
Grand L., N.B., Can. 39 45 57N 66 7W
Grand L., Newf., Can. 35 48 45N 57 45W
Grand L., Newf., Can. 36 53 40N 60 30W
Grand L., Newf., Can. 37 49 0N 57 30W
Grand L., Louis., U.S.A. 75 29 55N 92 45W
Grand L., Mich., U.S.A. 46 45 18N 83 30W
Grand L., Ohio, U.S.A. 77 40 32N 84 25W
Grand Lac 34 47 35N 77 35W
Grand Lake 78 40 20N 105 54W
Grand le Pierre 37 47 41N 54 47W
Grand Ledge 77 42 45N 84 45W
Grand-Lieu, Lac de 100 47 6N 1 40W
Grand Manan I. 39 44 45N 66 52W
Grand Marais, Can. 52 47 45N 90 25W
Grand Marais, U.S.A. 53 46 39N 85 59W
Grand Mère 41 46 36N 72 40W
Grand Motte, La 103 48 35N 1 4E
Grand Piles 41 46 40N 72 40W
Grand Portage 52 47 58N 89 41W
Grand Pressigny, Le 100 46 55N 0 48E
Grand, R., Can. 49 42 51N 79 34W
Grand, R., Mich., U.S.A. 77 43 4N 86 15W
Grand, R., Mo., U.S.A. 78 39 23N 93 27W
Grand, R., S.D., U.S.A. 78 45 45N 101 30W
Grand Rapids, Can. 57 53 12N 99 19W
Grand Rapids, Mich., U.S.A. 77 42 57N 85 40W
Grand Rapids, Minn., U.S.A. 52 47 15N 93 29W
Grand River 76 40 49N 93 58W
Grand Teton 78 43 54N 111 57W
Grand Valley, Can. 49 43 54N 80 19W
Grand Valley, U.S.A. 78 39 30N 108 2W
Grand View 57 51 10N 100 42W
Grande 87 11 30S 44 30W
Grande-Anse 39 47 48N 65 11W
Grande, B. 90 50 30S 68 20W
Grande Baie 41 48 19N 70 52W
Grande Baleine, R. de la 36 55 16N 77 47W
Grande Cache 60 53 53N 119 8W
Grande-Cascapédia 38 48 15N 65 54W
Grande, Coxilha 89 28 18S 51 30W
Grande de Santiago, R. 82 21 20N 105 50W
Grande-Entrée 39 47 30N 61 40W
Grande, Île 43 45 52N 73 14W
Grande, La 78 45 15N 118 0W
Grande, La, R. 36 53 50N 79 0W
Grande-Ligne 43 45 14N 73 22W
Grande Pointe 58 49 46N 97 3W
Grande Prairie 60 55 10N 118 50W
Grande, R., Jujuy, Argent. 88 23 9S 65 52W
Grande, R., Mendoza, Argent. 88 36 52S 69 45W
Grande R. 86 18 35S 63 0W
Grande, R., Brazil 87 20 0S 50 0W
Grande, R., U.S.A. 75 29 20N 100 40W
Grande-Rivière 38 48 26N 64 30W
Grande, Serra 87 4 30S 41 20W
Grande-Vallée 38 49 14N 65 8W
Grandes-Bergeronnes 41 48 16N 69 35W
Grandfalls 75 31 21N 102 51W
Grandmesnil, L. 38 51 19N 67 33W
Grandoe Mines 54 56 29N 129 54W
Grandpré 101 49 20N 4 50E
Grandview, Mo., U.S.A. 76 38 53N 94 32W
Grandview, Wash., U.S.A. 78 46 13N 119 58W
Grandview Heights 77 39 58N 83 2W
Grandville 77 42 54N 85 46W
Grandvilliers 101 49 40N 1 57E
Graneros 88 34 5S 70 45W
Granet, L. 40 47 47N 77 31W
Grange, La, Austral. 134 18 45S 121 43E
Grange, La, U.S.A. 80 37 42N 120 27W
Grange, La, Ga., U.S.A. 73 33 4N 85 0W
Grange, La, Ky., U.S.A. 72 38 20N 85 20W
Grange, La, Mo., U.S.A. 76 40 3N 91 35W
Grange, La, Tex., U.S.A. 75 29 54N 96 52W
Grangemouth 96 56 1N 3 43W
Granger 78 46 25N 120 5W
Grangeville 78 45 57N 116 4W
Granite, Pk. 78 45 8N 109 52W
Granite City 76 38 45N 90 3W
Granite Falls 74 44 45N 95 35W
Granite Mtn. 81 33 5N 116 28W
Granite Pt. 37 50 31N 56 17W
Granity 133 41 39S 171 51E
Granja 87 3 17S 40 50W
Granollers 104 41 39N 2 18E
Grant, Can. 34 50 6N 86 18W
Grant, U.S.A. 74 40 53N 101 42W
Grant City 76 40 30N 94 25W
Grant, Mt. 80 38 34N 118 48W
Grant, Pt. 136 38 32S 145 6E
Grant Range Mts. 79 38 30N 115 30W
Grantham 94 52 55N 0 39W
Grantown-on-Spey 96 57 19N 3 36W
Grants 79 35 14N 107 57W
Grants Pass 78 42 30N 123 22W
Grantsburg 74 45 46N 92 44W
Grantsville 78 40 35N 112 32W
Granville, France 100 48 50N 1 35W
Granville, N.D., U.S.A. 74 48 18N 100 48W
Granville, N.Y., U.S.A. 72 43 24N 73 16W
Granville L. 55 56 18N 100 30W
Grapeland 75 31 30N 95 25W
Gras, L. de 64 64 30N 110 30W
Grass, R. 55 56 3N 96 33W
Grass Range 78 47 0N 109 0W
Grass River Prov. Park 55 54 40N 100 50W
Grass Valley, Calif., U.S.A. 80 39 18N 121 0W
Grass Valley, Oreg., U.S.A. 78 45 28N 120 48W
Grasse 103 43 38N 6 56E
Grasset, L. 40 49 55N 78 10W
Grassie 49 43 9N 79 37W
Grassy Lake 61 49 49N 111 43W
Grate's Cove 35 48 8N 53 0W
Gratis 77 39 38N 84 32W
Gratz 77 38 28N 84 57W
Graulhet 102 43 45N 1 58E
Grave, Pte. de 102 45 34N 1 4W
Gravelbourg 56 49 50N 106 35W
Gravelines 101 51 0N 2 10E
's-Gravenhage 105 52 7N 4 17E
Gravenhurst 46 44 52N 79 20W
Gravesend 95 51 25N 0 22E
Gravois, Pointe-à 85 16 15N 73 45W
Gravone, R. 103 41 58N 8 45E
Gray 101 47 27N 5 35E
Grayling 46 44 40N 84 42W
Grayling, R. 54 59 21N 125 0W
Grays Harbor 78 46 55N 124 8W
Grays L. 78 43 8N 111 30W
Grays River 80 46 21N 123 37W
Grayson 56 50 45N 102 40W
Grayville 77 38 16N 88 0W
Graz 106 47 4N 15 27E
Greasy L. 54 62 55N 122 12W
Great Abaco I. 84 26 15N 77 10W
Great Australia Basin 135 26 0S 140 0E
Great Australian Bight 134 33 30S 130 0E
Great Barrier I. 133 36 11S 175 25E
Great Barrier Reef 135 19 0S 149 0E
Great Barrington 71 42 11N 73 22W
Great Basin 68 40 0N 116 30W
Great Bear L. 64 65 30N 120 0W
Great Bear, R. 64 65 0N 124 0W
Great Bena 71 41 57N 75 45W
Great Bend 74 38 25N 98 55W
Great Blasket, I. 97 52 5N 10 30W
Great Britain 93 54 0N 2 15W
Great Burnt L. 37 48 20N 56 20W
Great Central 62 49 20N 125 10W

Great Central L — Gunisao, R

Great Central L.	**62**	49 22N	125 10W
Great Coco I.	**128**	14 10N	93 25E
Great Divide	**135**	23 0S	146 0E
Great Duck I.	**46**	45 40N	82 57W
Great Exuma I.	**84**	23 30N	75 50W
Great Falls, Can.	**57**	50 27N	96 1W
Great Falls, U.S.A.	**78**	47 27N	111 12W
Great Guana Cay	**84**	24 0N	76 20W
Great Harbour Deep	**37**	50 25N	56 25W
Great I.	**55**	58 53N	96 35W
Great Inagua I.	**85**	21 0N	73 20W
Gt. Indian Desert = Thar Desert	**124**	28 0N	72 0E
Great Jarvis	**35**	47 39N	57 12W
Great Karoo = Groot Karoo	**117**	32 30S	23 0E
Great Lake	**135**	41 50S	146 30E
Great Lakes	**55**	44 0N	82 0W
Great Orme's Head	**94**	53 20N	3 52W
Great Ouse, R.	**94**	52 20N	0 8E
Great Ruaha, R.	**116**	7 30S	35 0E
Gt. St. Bernard P.	**106**	45 50N	7 10E
Great Salt Lake	**78**	41 0N	112 30W
Great Salt Lake Desert	**78**	40 20N	113 50W
Great Salt Plains Res.	**75**	36 40N	98 15W
Great Sandy Desert	**134**	21 0S	124 0E
Great Sandy I. = Fraser I.	**135**	25 15S	153 0E
Great Sitkin I.	**67**	52 0N	176 10W
Great Slave L.	**54**	61 23N	115 38W
Great Stour, R.	**95**	51 21N	1 15E
Gt. Victoria Des.	**134**	29 30S	126 30E
Great Wall	**130**	38 30N	109 30E
Great Whale, R.	**34**	55 20N	75 30W
Great Whernside, mt.	**85**	54 9N	1 59W
Great Yarmouth	**94**	52 40N	1 45E
Greater Antilles	**85**	17 40N	74 0W
Greater Manchester □	**94**	53 30N	2 15W
Gredos, Sierra de	**104**	40 20N	5 0W
Greece ■	**109**	40 0N	23 0E
Greece's Point	**43**	45 36N	74 30W
Greeley, Colo., U.S.A.	**74**	40 30N	104 40W
Greeley, Nebr., U.S.A.	**74**	41 36N	98 32W
Greely Fd.	**65**	80 30N	85 0W
Green B., Can.	**37**	49 45N	55 55W
Green B., U.S.A.	**72**	45 0N	87 30W
Green Bay	**72**	44 30N	88 0W
Green C.	**136**	37 13S	150 1E
Green City	**76**	40 16N	92 57W
Green Cove Springs	**73**	29 59N	81 40W
Green Cr.	**48**	45 28N	75 34W
Green Island	**133**	45 55S	170 26E
Green Lake	**56**	54 17N	107 47W
Green Park	**49**	43 52N	80 27W
Green, R.	**39**	47 18N	68 9W
Green R., Ky., U.S.A.	**77**	37 54N	87 30W
Green R., Utah, U.S.A.	**79**	39 0N	110 6W
Green R., Wyo., U.S.A.	**78**	43 2N	110 2W
Green R., Wyo., U.S.A.	**78**	41 44N	109 28W
Green River	**50**	43 53N	79 11W
Greenbank	**80**	48 6N	122 34W
Greenbush, Mich., U.S.A.	**46**	44 35N	83 19W
Greenbush, Minn., U.S.A.	**57**	48 46N	96 10W
Greencastle	**77**	39 40N	86 48W
Greene, U.S.A.	**76**	42 54N	92 48W
Greene, N.Y., U.S.A.	**71**	42 20N	75 45W
Greenfield, Calif., U.S.A.	**80**	36 19N	121 15W
Greenfield, Calif., U.S.A.	**81**	35 15N	119 0W
Greenfield, Ill., U.S.A.	**76**	39 21N	90 12W
Greenfield, Ind., U.S.A.	**77**	39 47N	85 51W
Greenfield, Iowa, U.S.A.	**76**	41 18N	94 28W
Greenfield, Mass., U.S.A.	**71**	42 38N	72 38W
Greenfield, Miss., U.S.A.	**75**	37 28N	93 50W
Greenfield, Ohio, U.S.A.	**77**	39 21N	83 23W
Greenfield Park	**45**	45 29N	73 29W
Greenfields	**49**	43 18N	80 29W
Greenhills	**77**	39 16N	84 32W
Greening	**34**	48 10N	74 55W
Greenland	**17**	66 0N	45 0W
Greenland Sea	**17**	73 0N	10 0W
Greenock	**96**	55 57N	4 46W
Greenore	**97**	54 2N	6 8W
Greenore Pt.	**97**	52 15N	6 20W
Greenough Pt.	**46**	44 58N	81 26W
Greenport	**71**	41 5N	72 23W
Greensboro, Ga., U.S.A.	**73**	33 34N	83 12W
Greensboro, N.C., U.S.A.	**73**	36 7N	79 46W
Greensburg, Ind., U.S.A.	**77**	39 20N	85 30W
Greensburg, Kans., U.S.A.	**75**	37 38N	99 20W
Greensburg, Pa., U.S.A.	**70**	40 18N	79 31W
Greentown	**77**	40 29N	85 58W
Greenup	**77**	39 15N	88 10W
Greenville, Ala., U.S.A.	**73**	31 50N	86 37W
Greenville, Calif., U.S.A.	**80**	40 8N	121 0W
Greenville, Ill., U.S.A.	**76**	38 53N	89 22W
Greenville, Ind., U.S.A.	**77**	38 22N	85 59W
Greenville, Me., U.S.A.	**35**	45 30N	69 32W
Greenville, Mich., U.S.A.	**77**	43 12N	85 14W
Greenville, Miss., U.S.A.	**75**	33 25N	91 0W
Greenville, N.C., U.S.A.	**73**	35 37N	77 26W
Greenville, Ohio, U.S.A.	**77**	40 5N	84 38W
Greenville, Pa., U.S.A.	**70**	41 23N	80 22W
Greenville, S.C., U.S.A.	**73**	34 54N	82 24W
Greenville, Tenn., U.S.A.	**73**	36 13N	82 51W
Greenville, Tex., U.S.A.	**75**	33 5N	96 5W
Greenwater L.	**52**	48 34N	90 26W
Greenwater Lake	**56**	52 30N	103 31W
Greenwater Lake Prov. Park	**56**	52 32N	103 30W
Greenwich, U.K.	**95**	51 28N	0 0
Greenwich, N.Y., U.S.A.	**71**	43 2N	73 36W
Greenwich, Ohio, U.S.A.	**70**	41 1N	82 32W
Greenwood, B.C., Can.	**63**	49 10N	118 40W
Greenwood, Ont., Can.	**51**	43 56N	79 3W
Greenwood, Ind., U.S.A.	**77**	39 37N	86 7W
Greenwood, Miss., U.S.A.	**75**	33 30N	90 4W
Greenwood, S.C., U.S.A.	**73**	34 13N	82 13W
Gregory	**74**	43 14N	99 20W
Gregory, L.	**135**	28 55S	139 0E
Gregory Lake	**134**	20 10S	127 30E
Gregory Ra.	**135**	19 30S	143 40E
Greifswald	**106**	54 6N	13 23E
Gremikha	**120**	67 50N	39 40E
Grenada	**75**	33 45N	89 50W
Grenada I. ■	**85**	12 10N	61 40W
Grenade	**102**	43 47N	1 17E
Grenadines	**85**	12 40N	61 20W
Grenen	**111**	57 44N	10 40E
Grenfell, Austral.	**136**	33 52S	148 8E
Grenfell, Can.	**56**	50 30N	102 56W
Grenoble	**103**	45 12N	5 42E
Grenora	**74**	48 38N	103 54W
Grenville	**43**	45 37N	74 36W
Grenville, C.	**135**	12 0S	143 13E
Grenville Chan.	**62**	53 40N	129 46W
Gréoux-les-Bains	**103**	43 45N	5 52E
Gresham	**80**	45 30N	122 31W
Gresik	**127**	9 13S	112 38E
Gretna, Can.	**57**	49 1N	97 34W
Gretna, U.S.A.	**75**	30 0N	90 2W
Gretna Green	**96**	55 0N	3 3W
Grevenmacher	**105**	49 41N	6 26E
Greves, Les	**43**	45 59N	73 11W
Grey, C.	**135**	13 0S	136 35E
Grey Is.	**37**	50 50N	55 35W
Grey, Pt.	**66**	49 16N	123 16W
Grey, R., Can.	**37**	47 34N	57 6W
Grey, R., N.Z.	**133**	42 27S	171 12E
Grey Range	**135**	27 0S	143 30E
Grey Res.	**37**	48 20N	56 30W
Grey River	**37**	47 35N	57 6W
Greybull	**78**	44 30N	108 3W
Greytown, N.Z.	**133**	41 5S	175 29E
Greytown, S. Afr.	**117**	29 1S	30 36E
Gribbell I.	**62**	53 23N	129 0W
Gridley	**80**	39 27N	121 47W
Griffin	**73**	33 17N	84 14W
Griffith, Austral.	**136**	34 18S	146 2E
Griffith, Can.	**47**	45 15N	77 10W
Griffith I.	**46**	44 50N	80 55W
Griffith Mine	**55**	50 47N	93 25W
Grijalva, R.	**82**	16 20N	92 20W
Grim, C.	**135**	40 45S	144 45E
Grimari	**116**	5 43N	20 0E
Grimes	**80**	39 4N	121 54W
Grimsby, Can.	**49**	43 12N	79 34W
Grimsby, U.K.	**94**	53 35N	0 5W
Grimsby Beach	**49**	43 12N	79 32W
Grimsey	**110**	66 33N	18 0W
Grimshaw	**60**	56 10N	117 40W
Grimstad	**111**	58 22N	8 35E
Grindstone I.	**47**	44 43N	76 14W
Grindstone Island	**35**	47 25N	62 0W
Grinnell	**76**	41 45N	92 43W
Grise Fiord	**65**	76 25N	82 57W
Grisolles	**102**	43 49N	1 19E
Grita, La	**86**	8 8N	71 59W
Griz Nez, C.	**101**	50 50N	1 35E
Groais I.	**37**	50 55N	55 35W
Grodno	**120**	53 42N	23 52E
Grodzisk Wlkp.	**106**	52 15N	16 22E
Groesbeck	**75**	31 32N	96 34W
Groix	**100**	47 38N	3 29W
Groix, I. de	**100**	47 38N	3 28W
Grójec	**107**	51 50N	20 58E
Gronau	**105**	52 13N	7 2E
Grong	**110**	64 25N	12 8E
Groningen	**105**	53 15N	6 35E
Groningen □	**105**	53 16N	6 40E
Gronlid	**56**	53 6N	104 28W
Groom	**75**	35 12N	100 59W
Groot-Brakrivier	**117**	34 2S	22 18E
Groot Karoo	**117**	32 35S	23 0E
Groot Namakwaland = Namaland	**117**	26 0S	18 0E
Groote Eylandt	**135**	14 0S	136 50E
Grootfontein	**117**	19 31S	18 6E
Gros C.	**54**	61 59N	113 32W
Gros-Morne	**38**	49 15N	65 34W
Gros Morne Nat. Park	**37**	49 40N	57 50W
Grosne, R.	**103**	46 30N	4 40E
Gross Glockner	**106**	47 5N	12 40E
Grossa, Pta.	**87**	1 20N	50 0W
Grosse I.	**46**	42 8N	83 9W
Grosse Isle	**57**	50 4N	97 27W
Grossenhain	**106**	51 17N	13 32E
Grosses-Roches	**38**	48 57N	67 5W
Grosseto	**108**	42 45N	11 7E
Groswater B.	**36**	54 20N	57 40W
Groton	**71**	41 22N	72 12W
Grouard Mission	**60**	55 33N	116 9W
Grouin, Pointe du	**100**	48 43N	1 51W
Groundhog, R.	**53**	48 45N	82 20W
Grouse Creek	**78**	41 51N	113 57W
Grove City, Ohio, U.S.A.	**77**	39 53N	83 6W
Grove City, Pa., U.S.A.	**70**	41 10N	80 5W
Grovedale	**60**	55 3N	118 52W
Groveland	**80**	37 50N	120 14W
Grover City	**81**	35 7N	120 37W
Grover Hill	**77**	41 1N	84 29W
Groveton, N.H., U.S.A.	**71**	44 34N	71 30W
Groveton, Tex., U.S.A.	**75**	31 5N	95 4W
Groznyy	**120**	43 20N	45 45E
Grudziadz	**107**	53 30N	18 47E
Gruissan	**102**	43 8N	3 7E
Grünau	**117**	27 45S	18 26E
Grundy Center	**76**	42 22N	92 45W
Grundy Prov. Pk.	**46**	45 58N	80 30W
Grunthal	**57**	49 24N	96 51W
Gruver	**75**	36 19N	101 20W
Gryazi	**120**	52 30N	39 58E
Gryazovets	**120**	58 50N	40 20E
Grytviken	**91**	53 50S	37 10W
Gua	**125**	22 18N	85 20E
Guacanayabo, G. de	**84**	20 40N	77 20W
Guacara	**86**	10 14N	67 53W
Guachípas	**88**	25 40S	65 30W
Guachiría, R.	**86**	5 30N	71 30W
Guadalajara, Mexico	**82**	20 40N	103 20W
Guadalajara, Spain	**104**	40 37N	3 12W
Guadalcanal, I.	**14**	9 32S	160 12E
Guadales	**88**	34 30S	67 55W
Guadalete, R.	**104**	36 45N	5 47W
Guadalhorce, R.	**104**	36 50N	4 42W
Guadalquivir, R.	**104**	38 0N	4 0W
Guadalupe, Mexico	**81**	32 4N	116 32W
Guadalupe, U.S.A.	**81**	34 59N	120 33W
Guadalupe Bravos	**82**	31 20N	106 10W
Guadalupe de los Reyes	**82**	25 23N	104 15W
Guadalupe Pk.	**79**	31 50N	105 30W
Guadalupe, R., Mexico	**81**	32 6N	116 51W
Guadalupe, R., U.S.A.	**75**	29 25N	97 30W
Guadalupe, Sierra de	**104**	39 28N	5 30W
Guadalupe y Calvo	**82**	26 6N	106 58W
Guadarrama, Sierra de	**104**	41 0N	4 0W
Guadeloupe, I.	**85**	16 20N	61 40W
Guadeloupe, La	**41**	45 57N	70 56W
Guadeloupe Passage	**85**	16 50N	68 15W
Guadiana, R.	**104**	37 45N	7 35W
Guadix	**104**	37 18N	3 11W
Guafo, Boca del	**90**	43 35S	74 0W
Guaina	**86**	5 9N	63 36W
Guainía □	**86**	2 30N	69 00W
Guaíra	**89**	24 5S	54 10W
Guaira, La	**86**	10 36N	66 56W
Guaitecas, Islas	**90**	44 0S	74 30W
Guajará-Mirim	**86**	10 50S	65 20W
Guajira, La □	**86**	11 30N	72 30W
Guajira, Pen. de la	**85**	12 0N	72 0W
Gualan	**84**	15 8N	89 22W
Gualeguay	**88**	33 10S	59 20W
Gualeguaychú	**88**	33 3S	58 31W
Guam I.	**14**	13 27N	144 45E
Guama	**86**	10 16N	68 49W
Guamareyes	**86**	0 30S	73 0W
Guaminí	**88**	37 1S	62 28W
Guampí, Sierra de	**86**	6 0N	65 35W
Guamuchil	**82**	25 25N	108 3W
Guanabacoa	**84**	23 8N	82 18W
Guanabara □	**89**	23 0S	43 25W
Guanacaste	**84**	10 40N	85 30W
Guanacaste, Cordillera del	**84**	10 40N	85 4W
Guanacevío	**82**	25 40N	106 0W
Guanajay	**84**	22 56N	82 42W
Guanajuato	**82**	21 0N	101 20W
Guanajuato □	**82**	20 40N	101 20W
Guanare	**86**	8 42N	69 12W
Guanare, R.	**86**	8 50N	68 50W
Guandacol	**88**	29 30S	68 40W
Guane	**84**	22 10N	84 0W
Guanica	**67**	17 58N	66 55W
Guanipa, R.	**86**	9 20N	63 30W
Guanta	**86**	10 14N	64 36W
Guantánamo	**85**	20 10N	75 20W
Guapí	**86**	2 36N	77 54W
Guápiles	**84**	10 10N	83 46W
Guaporé	**89**	12 0S	64 0W
Guaporé, R.	**86**	13 0S	63 0W
Guaqui	**86**	16 41S	68 54W
Guarapari	**89**	20 40S	40 30W
Guarapuava	**87**	25 20S	51 30W
Guaratinguetá	**89**	22 49S	45 9W
Guaratuba	**89**	25 53S	48 38W
Guarda	**104**	40 32N	7 20W
Guardafui, C. = Asir, Ras	**115**	11 55N	51 10E
Guaria □	**88**	25 45N	56 30W
Guárico □	**86**	8 40N	66 35W
Guarujá	**89**	24 2S	46 25W
Guarus	**89**	21 30S	41 20W
Guasave	**82**	25 34N	108 27W
Guasdualito	**86**	7 15N	70 44W
Guasipati	**86**	7 28N	61 54W
Guatemala	**84**	14 40N	90 30W
Guatemala ■	**84**	15 40N	90 30W
Guatire	**86**	10 28N	66 32W
Guaviare, R.	**86**	3 30N	71 0W
Guaxupé	**89**	21 10S	47 5W
Guayabal	**86**	4 43N	71 37W
Guayama	**85**	17 59N	66 7W
Guayaquil	**86**	2 15S	79 52W
Guayaquil, G. de	**86**	3 10S	81 0W
Guaymallen	**88**	32 50S	68 45W
Guaymas	**82**	27 50N	111 0W
Guchil	**128**	5 35N	102 10E
Guchin-Us	**130**	45 28N	102 10E
Gudbransdal	**111**	61 33N	10 0E
Guddu Barrage	**71**	28 30N	69 50E
Gudivada	**125**	16 30N	81 15E
Gudur	**124**	14 12N	79 55E
Guebwiller	**101**	47 55N	7 12E
Guecho	**104**	43 21N	2 59W
Guéguen, L.	**40**	48 6N	77 13W
Guelph	**49**	43 35N	80 20W
Guéméné-Penfao	**100**	47 38N	1 50W
Guéméné-sur-Scorff	**100**	48 4N	3 13W
Güemes	**88**	24 50S	65 0W
Guer	**100**	47 54N	2 8W
Guérande	**100**	47 20N	2 26W
Guerche, La	**100**	47 57N	1 16W
Guerche-sur-l'Aubois, La	**101**	46 58N	2 56E
Guéret	**102**	46 11N	1 51E
Guérigny	**101**	47 6N	3 10E
Guerneville	**80**	38 30N	123 0W
Guernica	**104**	43 19N	2 40W
Guernsey, Can.	**56**	51 53N	105 11W
Guernsey, U.S.A.	**74**	42 19N	104 45W
Guernsey I.	**100**	49 30N	2 35W
Guerrero □	**83**	17 30N	100 0W
Gueugnon	**103**	45 36N	4 3E
Gueydan	**75**	30 3N	92 30W
Guhra	**123**	27 36N	56 8E
Guia Lopes da Laguna	**89**	21 26S	56 7W
Guiana Highlands	**86**	5 0N	60 0W
Guibes	**117**	26 41S	16 49E
Guigues	**40**	47 28N	79 26W
Guija	**117**	34 35S	33 15E
Guildford	**95**	51 14N	0 34W
Guilford	**35**	45 12N	69 25W
Guillaume-Delisle, L.	**36**	56 15N	76 17W
Guillaumes	**103**	44 5N	6 52E
Guillestre	**103**	44 39N	6 40E
Guilvinec	**100**	47 48N	4 17W
Guimarães	**87**	2 9S	44 35W
Guimaras I.	**127**	10 35N	122 37E
Guinda	**80**	38 50N	122 12W
Guinea ■	**114**	10 20N	10 0W
Guinea Bissau ■	**114**	12 0N	15 0W
Guinea, Gulf of	**114**	3 0N	2 30E
Guinea, Port. = Guinea Bissau	**114**	12 0N	15 0W
Güines	**84**	22 50N	82 0W
Guines, L.	**38**	52 8N	61 25W
Guingamp	**100**	48 34N	3 10W
Guipavas	**100**	48 26N	4 29W
Güiria	**86**	10 32N	62 18W
Guiscard	**101**	49 40N	3 0E
Guise	**101**	49 52N	3 35E
Guivan	**127**	11 5N	125 55E
Gujan-Mestras	**102**	44 38N	1 4W
Gujarat □	**124**	23 20N	71 0E
Gujranwala	**124**	32 10N	74 12E
Gujrat	**124**	32 40N	74 2E
Gukhothae	**128**	17 2N	99 50E
Gulargambone	**136**	31 20S	148 30E
Gulbahar	**123**	35 5N	69 10E
Gulbargâ	**124**	17 20N	76 50E
Gulf Basin	**134**	15 20S	129 0E
Gulfport	**75**	30 28N	89 3W
Gulgong	**136**	32 20S	149 30E
Gulkana	**67**	62 15N	145 48W
Gull L., Can.	**61**	52 34N	114 0W
Gull L., U.S.A.	**52**	46 30N	94 21W
Gull Lake	**56**	50 10N	108 29W
Gull, R.	**52**	49 45N	89 0W
Gulpaigan	**122**	33 26N	50 20E
Gulshad	**120**	46 45N	74 25E
Gulu	**116**	2 48N	32 17E
Gum Lake	**136**	32 42S	143 9E
Guma	**129**	37 37N	78 18E
Gumma-ken □	**132**	36 30N	138 20E
Gummersbach	**105**	51 2N	7 32E
Gümüsane	**122**	40 30N	39 30E
Gumzai	**127**	5 28S	134 42E
Guna	**124**	24 40N	77 19E
Gundagai	**136**	35 3S	148 6E
Gundih	**127**	7 10S	110 56E
Gungu	**116**	5 43S	19 20E
Gunisao L.	**57**	53 33N	96 15W
Gunisao, R.	**57**	53 56N	97 53W

Gunnedah

Harry S. Truman Res

Gunnedah	135	30 59S	150 15E
Gunning	136	34 47S	149 14E
Gunnison, Colo., U.S.A.	79	38 32N	106 56W
Gunnison, Utah, U.S.A.	78	39 11N	111 48W
Gunnison, R.	79	38 50N	108 30W
Guntakal	124	15 11N	77 27E
Guntersville	73	34 18N	86 16W
Guntur	125	16 23N	80 30E
Gunung-Sitoli	126	1 15N	97 30E
Gunungap	127	6 45S	126 30E
Gunungsugih	126	4 58S	105 7E
Gunworth	55	51 20N	108 10W
Gupis	124	36 15N	73 20E
Gūrchañ	122	34 55N	49 25E
Gurdaspur	124	32 5N	75 25E
Gurdon	75	33 55N	93 10W
Gurgaon	124	28 33N	77 10E
Gurkha	125	28 5N	84 40E
Gurnee	77	42 22N	87 55W
Gurun	128	5 49N	100 27E
Gürün	122	38 41N	37 22E
Gurupá	87	1 20S	51 45W
Gurupá, I. Grande de	87	1 0S	51 45W
Gurupi, R.	87	3 20S	47 20W
Gurvandzagal	130	49 35N	115 2E
Guryev	120	47 5N	52 0E
Gusau	114	12 18N	6 31E
Gusinoczersk	130	51 16N	106 27E
Gustavus	67	58 25N	135 58W
Gustine	80	37 21N	121 0W
Güstrow	106	53 47N	12 12E
Guthega Dam	136	36 20S	148 27E
Guthrie	75	35 55N	97 30W
Guthrie Center	76	41 41N	94 30W
Guttenberg	76	42 46N	91 10W
Guyana ■	86	5 0N	59 0W
Guyenne	102	44 30N	0 40E
Guymon	75	36 45N	101 30W
Guysborough	39	45 23N	61 30W
Guzmán, Laguna de	82	31 25N	107 25W
Gwa	125	17 30N	94 40E
Gwādar	124	25 10N	62 18E
Gwalior	124	26 12N	78 10E
Gwanda	117	20 55S	29 0E
Gweebarra B.	97	54 52N	8 21W
Gweedore	97	55 4N	8 15W
Gwelo	117	19 28S	29 45E
Gwent □	95	51 45N	2 55W
Gwinn	53	46 15N	87 29W
Gwydir, R.	135	29 27S	149 48E
Gwynedd □	94	53 0N	4 0W
Gya La	125	28 45N	84 45E
Gyangtse	125	28 50N	89 33E
Gydanskiy P-ov.	120	70 0N	78 0E
Gympie	135	26 11S	152 38E
Gyoda	132	36 10N	139 30E
Gyöngyös	107	47 48N	20 15E
Györ	107	47 41N	17 40E
Gypsum Pt.	54	61 53N	114 35W
Gypsumville	57	51 45N	98 40W
H			
Ha Nam = Phu-Ly	128	20 35N	105 50E
Haapamäki	110	62 18N	24 28E
Haarlem	105	52 23N	4 39E
Haast, R.	133	43 50S	169 2E
Hab Nadi Chauki	124	25 0N	66 50E
Haba	122	27 10N	47 0E
Habana, La	84	23 8N	82 22W
Habaswein	116	1 2N	39 30E
Habay	54	58 50N	118 44W
Hachijō-Jima	132	33 5N	139 45E
Hachinohe	132	40 30N	141 29E
Hachiōji	132	35 30N	139 30E
Hackensack	52	46 56N	94 29W
Hackett	54	52 9N	112 28W
Hadd, Ras al	123	22 35N	59 50E
Haddington	96	55 57N	2 48W
Hadhramaut = Hadramawt	115	15 30N	49 30E
Hadramawt	115	15 30N	49 30E
Hadrians Wall	94	55 0N	2 30W
Haeju	130	38 3N	125 45E
Hafar al Bātin	122	28 25N	46 50E
Hafford	56	52 43N	107 21W
Hafizabad	124	32 5N	73 40E
Haflong	125	25 10N	93 5E
Hafnarfjörður	110	64 4N	21 57W
Haft-Gel	122	31 30N	49 32E
Hagemeister I.	67	58 42N	161 0W
Hagen	105	51 21N	7 29E
Hagensborg	62	52 23N	126 32W
Hagerman	75	33 5N	104 22W
Hagerstown, Ind., U.S.A.	77	39 55N	85 10W
Hagerstown, Md., U.S.A.	72	39 39N	77 46W
Hagersville	49	42 58N	80 3W
Hagetmau	102	43 39N	0 37W
Hagfors	111	60 3N	13 45E
Hagi, Iceland	110	65 28N	23 25W
Hagi, Japan	132	34 30N	131 30E
Hags Hd.	97	52 57N	9 30W
Hague, C. de la	100	49 44N	1 56W
Hague, The = 's-Gravenhage	105	52 7N	4 17E
Haguenau	101	48 49N	7 47E
Haicheng	130	40 56N	122 51E
Haifa	115	32 46N	35 0E
Haihang	131	20 55N	110 3E
Haik'ou	131	20 5N	110 20E
Haikow	131	20 0N	110 20E
Hā'il	122	27 28N	42 2E
Hailar	130	49 12N	119 37E
Hailar Ho	130	49 30N	118 30E
Hailey	78	43 30N	114 15W
Haileybury	34	47 30N	79 38W
Hailun	130	47 24N	127 0E
Hailuoto	110	65 3N	24 45E
Haimen	131	31 48N	121 8E
Hainan, I.	131	19 0N	110 0E
Hainan Str. = Ch'iungcho Haihsia	131	20 10N	110 15E
Hainaut □	105	50 30N	4 0E
Haines, Alaska, U.S.A.	67	59 20N	135 36W
Haines, Oreg., U.S.A.	78	44 51N	117 59W
Haines City	73	28 6N	81 35W
Haines Junction	67	60 45N	137 30W
Haining	131	30 23N	120 30E
Haiphong	128	20 47N	106 35E
Haitan Tao	131	25 30N	119 45E
Haiti ■	85	19 0N	72 30W
Haiyen	131	30 28N	120 57E
Haiyuan	130	36 32N	105 31E
Haja	127	3 19S	129 37E
Hajdúböszörmény	107	47 40N	21 30E
Haji Langar	124	35 50N	79 20E
Hajnówka	107	52 45N	23 32E
Hajr	123	24 0N	56 34E
Hakken-Zan	132	34 10N	135 54E
Hakodate	132	41 45N	140 44E
Hala	124	25 43N	68 20E
Halab = Aleppo	122	36 10N	37 15E
Halabjah	122	35 10N	45 58E
Halaib	115	22 5N	36 30E
Halawa	67	21 9N	156 47W
Halberstadt	106	51 53N	11 2E
Halbrite	56	49 30N	103 33W
Halcombe	133	40 8S	175 30E
Halcyon, Mt.	127	13 0N	121 30E
Haldia	125	22 5N	88 3E
Haldimand-Norfolk □	49	42 57N	79 50W
Haldwani	124	29 25N	79 30E
Hale, Mich., U.S.A.	46	44 18N	83 48W
Hale, Mo., U.S.A.	76	39 36N	93 20W
Haleakala Crater	67	20 43N	156 12W
Haleyville	73	34 15N	87 40W
Half Island Cove	39	45 21N	61 12W
Halfway	78	44 56N	117 8W
Halfway, R.	54	56 12N	121 32W
Haliburton	47	45 3N	78 30W
Halifax, Can.	39	44 38N	63 35W
Halifax, U.K.	94	53 43N	1 51W
Halifax B.	135	18 50S	147 0E
Halil, R.	123	27 40N	58 30E
Halkirk	61	52 17N	112 9W
Hall Beach	65	68 46N	81 12W
Hall Land	17	81 20N	60 0W
Hall Pen.	65	63 30N	66 0W
Halland	111	56 55N	12 50E
Halle	105	51 29N	12 0E
Hallebourg	53	49 40N	83 31W
Hallettsville	75	29 28N	96 57W
Halley Bay	91	75 31S	26 36W
Halliday	74	47 20N	102 25W
Halliday L.	55	61 21N	108 56W
Hallingdal, R.	111	60 34N	9 12E
Hällnäs	110	64 19N	19 36E
Hallock	57	48 47N	97 0W
Hall's Creek	134	18 16S	127 46E
Hallstead	71	41 56N	75 45W
Halmahera, I.	127	0 40N	128 0E
Halmstad	111	56 41N	12 52E
Hals	111	56 59N	10 18E
Halstad	74	47 21N	96 41W
Halton □	48	43 30N	79 53W
Hamā	122	35 5N	36 40E
Hamada	132	34 50N	132 10E
Hamadān	122	34 52N	48 32E
Hamadān □	122	35 0N	49 0E
Hamamatsu	132	34 45N	137 45E
Hamar	111	60 48N	11 7E
Hamarøy	110	68 5N	15 38E
Hambantota	124	6 10N	81 10E
Hamber Prov. Park	63	52 20N	118 0W
Hamburg, Ger.	106	53 32N	9 59E
Hamburg, Ark., U.S.A.	75	33 15N	91 47W
Hamburg, Iowa, U.S.A.	74	40 37N	95 38W
Hamburg, N.Y., U.S.A.	70	42 44N	78 50W
Hamburg, Pa., U.S.A.	71	40 33N	76 0W
Hame	111	61 30N	24 0E
Hämeenlinna	111	61 0N	24 28E
Hameln	106	52 7N	9 24E
Hamer	71	42 38N	76 11W
Hamersley Ra.	134	22 0S	117 45E
Hamhung	130	40 0N	127 30E
Hamilton, Austral.	136	37 45S	142 2E
Hamilton, Can.	48	43 15N	79 50W
Hamilton, N.Z.	133	37 47S	175 19E
Hamilton, U.K.	96	55 47N	4 2W
Hamilton, Alas., U.S.A.	67	62 55N	164 0W
Hamilton, Ill., U.S.A.	76	40 24N	91 21W
Hamilton, Ind., U.S.A.	77	41 33N	84 56W
Hamilton, Mo., U.S.A.	96	39 45N	93 59W
Hamilton, Mont., U.S.A.	78	46 20N	114 6W
Hamilton, N.Y., U.S.A.	71	42 49N	75 31W
Hamilton, Ohio, U.S.A.	77	39 20N	84 35W
Hamilton, Tex., U.S.A.	75	31 40N	98 5W
Hamilton, Wash., U.S.A.	63	48 31N	121 59W
Hamilton Beach	48	43 17N	79 47W
Hamilton City	80	39 45N	122 1W
Hamilton Harbour	48	43 18N	79 50W
Hamilton Inlet	35	54 0N	57 30W
Hamilton, R.	134	26 40S	134 20E
Hamilton Sound	37	49 35N	54 15W
Hamilton-Wentworth □	48	43 15N	79 49W
Hamiota	57	50 11N	100 38W
Hamlet	73	34 56N	79 40W
Hamlin, N.Y., U.S.A.	70	43 17N	77 55W
Hamlin, Tex., U.S.A.	75	32 58N	100 8W
Hamm	105	51 40N	7 58E
Hammenton	72	39 40N	74 47W
Hammerfest	110	70 39N	23 41E
Hammond, Can.	71	45 26N	75 15W
Hammond, Ill., U.S.A.	77	39 48N	88 36W
Hammond, Ind., U.S.A.	77	41 40N	87 30W
Hammond, La., U.S.A.	75	30 32N	90 30W
Hammond B.	46	45 31N	84 0W
Hampden, Can.	37	49 33N	56 51W
Hampden, N.Z.	133	45 18S	170 50E
Hampshire □	95	51 3N	1 20W
Hampshire Downs	95	51 10N	1 10W
Hampstead	39	45 37N	66 5W
Hampton, N.B., Can.	39	45 32N	65 51W
Hampton, Ont., Can.	47	43 58N	78 45W
Hampton, Ark., U.S.A.	75	33 35N	92 29W
Hampton, Iowa, U.S.A.	76	42 42N	93 12W
Hampton, N.H., U.S.A.	71	42 56N	70 48W
Hampton, S.C., U.S.A.	73	32 52N	81 2W
Hampton, Va., U.S.A.	72	37 4N	76 18W
Hampton Harbour	134	20 30S	116 30E
Hampton Tableland	134	32 0S	127 0E
Hamra	122	24 2N	38 55E
Hamun Helmand	123	31 15N	61 15E
Hamun-i-Lora	124	29 38N	64 58E
Hamun-i-Mashkel	124	28 30N	63 0E
Han K., Hupei, China	131	31 40N	112 20E
Han K., Kwangtung, China	131	23 45N	116 35E
Han Kiang R.	131	31 40N	112 20E
Han Pijesak	109	44 0N	19 0E
Hana	67	20 45N	155 59W
Hanau	106	50 8N	8 56E
Hanbagd	130	43 12N	107 10E
Hanceville	63	51 55N	123 2W
Hancheng	130	35 14N	110 22E
Hanchow Wan	131	35 0N	119 0E
Hancock, Mich., U.S.A.	52	47 10N	88 40W
Hancock, Minn., U.S.A.	74	45 26N	95 46W
Hancock, Pa., U.S.A.	71	41 57N	75 19W
Handa	132	34 53N	137 0E
Handel	56	52 4N	108 42W
Handeni	116	5 25S	38 2E
Handlová	69	48 45N	18 35E
Handshur	130	48 29N	118 2E
Haney	63	49 12N	122 40W
Hanford	80	36 25N	119 39W
Hangchow	131	30 12N	120 1E
Hangchow Wan	131	30 30N	121 30E
Hangchwang	131	34 34N	117 27E
Hangö (Hanko)	111	59 59N	22 57E
Hanh	130	51 32N	100 35E
Hankinson	74	46 9N	96 58W
Hanko = Hangö	111	59 59N	22 57E
Hankow	131	30 32N	114 20E
Hanksville	79	38 19N	110 45W
Hanku	130	39 16N	117 50E
Hanlan	50	43 39N	79 39W
Hanle	124	32 42N	79 4E
Hanley	56	51 38N	106 26W
Hanmer, Can.	46	46 39N	80 56W
Hanmer, N.Z.	133	42 32S	172 50E
Hann, Mt.	134	16 0S	126 0E
Hanna	61	51 40N	111 54W
Hannaford	74	47 23N	98 18W
Hannah	57	48 58N	98 47W
Hannah B.	34	51 40N	80 0W
Hannibal	76	39 42N	91 22W
Hannon	48	43 11N	79 50W
Hannover	106	52 23N	9 43E
Hanoi	128	21 5N	105 55E
Hanover, Can.	46	44 9N	81 2W
Hanover, U.S.A.	77	38 43N	85 28W
Hanover, N.H., U.S.A.	71	43 43N	72 17W
Hanover, Ohio, U.S.A.	70	40 5N	82 17W
Hanover, Pa., U.S.A.	72	39 46N	76 59W
Hanover = Hannover	106	52 23N	9 43E
Hanover, I.	90	51 0S	74 50W
Hansi	124	29 10N	75 57E
Hanson Range	134	27 0S	136 30E
Hantan	130	36 42N	114 30E
Hant's Harbour	37	48 1N	53 16W
Hantsport	39	45 4N	64 11W
Hanuy Gol	130	48 20N	101 30E
Hanwood	136	34 22S	146 2E
Hanyang	131	30 32N	114 10E
Haparanda	110	65 52N	24 8E
Happy	75	34 47N	101 50W
Happy Camp	78	41 52N	123 30W
Happy Valley	36	53 15N	60 20W
Hapur	124	28 45N	77 45E
Haql	122	29 10N	35 0E
Har	127	5 16S	133 14E
Har-Ayrag	130	45 47N	109 16E
Har Us Nuur	129	48 0N	92 0E
Hara Narinula, (Lang Shan)	130	41 30N	107 0E
Haraa Gol	129	49 0N	106 0E
Harad	122	24 15N	49 0E
Haradh	122	24 15N	49 0E
Haran	122	36 48N	39 0E
Harbin	130	45 46N	126 51E
Harbor Beach	46	43 50N	82 38W
Harbor Springs	46	45 28N	85 0W
Harbour Breton	37	47 29N	55 50W
Harbour Deep	35	50 25N	56 30W
Harbour Grace	37	47 40N	53 22W
Harburg	106	53 27N	9 58E
Harcourt	39	46 27N	65 15W
Hardangerfjorden.	111	60 15N	6 0E
Hardap Dam	117	24 32S	17 50E
Hardenberg	105	52 34N	6 37E
Harderwijk	105	52 21N	5 38E
Hardin, Ill., U.S.A.	76	39 9N	90 37W
Hardin, Mont., U.S.A.	78	45 50N	107 35W
Harding	117	30 22S	29 55E
Hardinsburg	77	37 47N	86 28W
Hardinxveld	105	51 49N	4 53E
Hardisty	61	52 40N	111 18W
Hardman	78	45 12N	119 49W
Hardoi	124	27 26N	80 15E
Hardwar	124	29 58N	78 16E
Hardwick	71	44 30N	72 20W
Hardwicke I.	62	50 27N	125 50W
Hardwicke Island	62	50 26N	125 55W
Hardwood Ridge	39	46 10N	66 1W
Hardy	75	36 20N	91 30W
Hardy, Pen.	90	55 30S	68 20W
Hare B.	37	51 15N	55 45W
Hare Bay	37	48 51N	54 1W
Harelbeke	105	50 52N	3 20E
Harer	115	9 20N	42 8E
Harfleur	100	49 30N	0 10E
Hargeisa	115	9 30N	44 2E
Hargshamn	111	60 12N	18 30E
Hari, R., Afghan.	124	34 20N	64 30E
Hari, R., Indon.	126	1 10S	101 50E
Haringhata, R.	125	22 0N	89 58E
Harirūd	123	35 0N	61 0E
Harlan, Iowa, U.S.A.	74	41 37N	95 20W
Harlan, Tenn., U.S.A.	73	36 58N	83 20W
Harlech	94	52 52N	4 7W
Harlem	78	48 29N	108 39W
Harley	49	43 4N	80 29W
Harlingen, Neth.	105	53 11N	5 25E
Harlingen, U.S.A.	75	26 20N	97 50W
Harlowton	78	46 30N	109 54W
Harmon L.	52	49 56N	90 13W
Harmony	49	43 54N	78 50W
Harney Basin	78	43 30N	119 0W
Harney L.	78	43 0N	119 0W
Harney Pk.	74	43 52N	103 33W
Harnösand	110	62 38N	18 5E
Haro, C.	82	27 50N	110 55W
Haro Str.	63	48 30N	123 15W
Harp L.	36	55 5N	61 50W
Harpe, La	76	40 30N	91 0W
Harper Mt.	67	64 15N	143 57W
Harput	122	38 48N	39 15E
Harrat al Kishb	122	22 30N	40 15E
Harrat al Uwairidh	122	26 50N	38 0E
Harricana, R.	40	50 56N	79 32W
Harriman	73	36 0N	84 35W
Harrington Harbour	38	50 31N	59 30W
Harris, Can.	56	51 44N	107 35W
Harris, U.K.	96	57 50N	6 55W
Harris L.	134	31 10S	135 10E
Harris Pt.	46	43 6N	82 9W
Harris, Sd. of	96	57 44N	7 6W
Harrisburg, Can.	49	43 14N	80 13W
Harrisburg, Ill., U.S.A.	77	37 42N	88 30W
Harrisburg, Nebr., U.S.A.	74	41 36N	103 46W
Harrisburg, Oreg., U.S.A.	78	44 26N	123 10W
Harrisburg, Pa., U.S.A.	70	40 18N	76 52W
Harrison, Ark., U.S.A.	75	36 10N	93 4W
Harrison, Idaho, U.S.A.	78	47 30N	116 51W
Harrison, Mich., U.S.A.	46	44 1N	84 48W
Harrison, Nebr., U.S.A.	74	42 42N	103 52W
Harrison, Ohio, U.S.A.	77	39 16N	84 49W
Harrison B.	67	70 25N	151 0W
Harrison, C.	36	54 55N	57 55W
Harrison Grove	49	43 18N	78 58W
Harrison Hot Springs	63	49 18N	121 47W
Harrison L.	63	49 33N	121 50W
Harrisonburg	72	38 28N	78 52W
Harrisonville	76	38 39N	94 21W
Harriston	46	43 57N	80 53W
Harrisville	46	44 40N	83 19W
Harrodsburg, Ind., U.S.A.	77	39 1N	86 33W
Harrodsburg, Ky., U.S.A.	77	37 46N	84 51W
Harrogate	94	53 59N	1 32W
Harrow, Can.	46	42 2N	82 55W
Harrow, U.K.	95	51 35N	0 15W
Harrowsmith	47	44 24N	76 40W
Harry S. Truman Res	76	38 14N	93 30W

Harstad Highland

Harstad	**110**	68 48N	16 30 E
Hart	**72**	43 42N	86 21W
Hartell	**61**	50 36N	114 14W
Hartford, Conn., U.S.A.	**71**	41 47N	72 41W
Hartford, Ky., U.S.A.	**72**	37 26N	86 50W
Hartford, Mich., U.S.A.	**77**	42 13N	86 10W
Hartford, S.D., U.S.A.	**74**	43 40N	96 58W
Hartford, Wis., U.S.A.	**74**	43 18N	88 25W
Hartford City	**77**	40 22N	85 20W
Hartland, Can.	**39**	46 20N	67 32W
Hartland, U.S.A.	**77**	43 6N	88 21W
Hartland Pt.	**95**	51 2N	4 32W
Hartlepool	**94**	54 42N	1 11W
Hartley	**117**	18 10 S	30 7 E
Hartley Bay	**62**	53 25N	129 15W
Hartney	**57**	49 30N	100 35W
Hartselle	**73**	34 25N	86 55W
Hartshorne	**75**	34 51N	95 30W
Hartsville	**73**	34 23N	80 2W
Hartwell	**73**	34 21N	82 52W
Harty	**53**	49 29N	82 41W
Harvard	**77**	42 25N	88 37W
Harvard, Mt.	**79**	39 0N	106 5W
Harvey, Can.	**39**	45 43N	67 1W
Harvey, Ill., U.S.A.	**77**	41 40N	87 40W
Harvey, N.D., U.S.A.	**74**	47 50N	99 58W
Harwich	**95**	51 56N	1 18 E
Harwood	**70**	44 7N	78 11W
Haryana □	**124**	29 0N	76 10 E
Harz	**106**	51 40N	10 40 E
Hasa	**122**	26 0N	49 0 E
Hasbaiya	**115**	33 25N	35 41 E
Hashefela	**115**	31 30N	34 43 E
Haskell, Okla., U.S.A.	**75**	35 51N	95 40W
Haskell, Tex., U.S.A.	**75**	33 10N	99 45W
Hasparren	**102**	43 24N	1 18W
Hassan	**122**	13 0N	76 5 E
Hasselt, Belg.	**105**	50 56N	5 21 E
Hasselt, Neth.	**105**	52 36N	6 6 E
Hassi Messaoud	**114**	31 43N	6 8 E
Hassi Taguenza	**88**	29 8N	0 23W
Hastings, Can.	**47**	44 18N	77 57W
Hastings, N.Z.	**133**	39 39 S	176 52 E
Hastings, U.K.	**95**	50 51N	0 36 E
Hastings, Mich., U.S.A.	**77**	42 40N	85 20W
Hastings, Minn., U.S.A.	**74**	44 41N	92 51W
Hastings, Nebr., U.S.A.	**74**	40 34N	98 22W
Hastings, Pa., U.S.A.	**70**	40 40N	78 45W
Hastings Road	**66**	49 16N	122 56W
Hat Nhao	**128**	14 46N	106 32 E
Hatch	**79**	32 45N	107 8W
Hatches Creek	**134**	20 56 S	135 12 E
Hatchet L.	**55**	58 36N	103 40W
Hatfield Post Office	**136**	33 54N	143 49 E
Hathras	**124**	27 36N	78 6 E
Hatia	**125**	22 30N	91 5 E
Hato de Corozal	**86**	6 11N	71 45W
Hato Mayor	**85**	18 46N	69 15W
Hattem	**105**	52 28N	6 4 E
Hatteras, C.	**73**	35 10N	75 30W
Hattiesburg	**75**	31 20N	89 20W
Hatton	**55**	50 2N	109 50W
Hattonford	**60**	53 46N	115 42W
Hatvan	**107**	47 40N	19 45 E
Hau Bon (Cheo Reo)	**128**	13 25N	108 28 E
Haubstadt	**77**	38 12N	87 34W
Hauchinango	**82**	20 12N	97 45W
Haugesund	**111**	59 23N	5 13 E
Haultain, R.	**55**	55 51N	106 46W
Hauraki Gulf	**133**	36 35 S	175 5 E
Haut Atlas	**114**	32 30N	7 0W
Haut-Rhin □	**101**	48 0N	7 15 E
Hauta Oasis	**122**	23 40N	47 0 E
Hautah, Wahāt al	**122**	23 40N	47 0 E
Haute-Corse □	**103**	42 30N	9 30 E
Haute-Garonne □	**102**	43 28N	1 30 E
Haute-Loire □	**102**	45 5N	3 50 E
Haute-Marne □	**101**	48 10N	5 20 E
Haute-Saône □	**101**	47 45N	6 10 E
Haute-Savoie □	**103**	46 0N	6 20 E
Haute-Vienne □	**102**	45 50N	1 10 E
Hauterive	**41**	49 10N	68 16W
Hautes-Alpes □	**103**	44 42N	6 20 E
Hautes-Pyrénées □	**102**	43 0N	0 10 E
Hauteville-Lompnes	**103**	45 59N	5 35 E
Hautmont	**101**	50 15N	3 55 E
Hauts-de-Seine □	**101**	48 52N	2 15 E
Havana	**76**	40 19N	90 3W
Havana = La Habana	**84**	23 8N	82 22W
Havasu, L.	**81**	34 18N	114 28W
Havel, R.	**106**	52 40N	12 15 E
Havelange	**105**	50 23N	5 15 E
Havelock, N.B., Can.	**39**	46 2N	65 24W
Havelock, Ont., Can.	**47**	44 26N	77 53W
Havelock, Qué., Can.	**43**	45 3N	73 45W
Havelock, N.Z.	**133**	41 17 S	173 48 E
Havelock I.	**128**	11 55N	93 2 E
Haverfordwest	**95**	51 48N	4 59W
Haverhill	**71**	42 50N	71 2W
Havering	**95**	51 33N	0 20 E
Haverstraw	**71**	41 12N	73 58W
Havlíčkův Brod	**106**	49 36N	15 33 E
Havre	**78**	48 40N	109 34W
Havre-St.-Pierre	**38**	50 18N	63 33W
Havre-Aubert	**39**	47 12N	61 56W
Havre Aubert, Î.	**39**	47 13N	61 57W
Havre-aux-Maisons, Î.	**39**	47 25N	61 47W
Havre, Le	**100**	49 30N	0 5 E
Havza	**122**	41 0N	35 35 E
Haw, R.	**73**	37 43N	80 52W
Hawaii □	**67**	20 30N	157 0W
Hawaii I.	**67**	20 0N	155 0W
Hawaiian Is.	**67**	20 30N	156 0W
Hawarden, Can.	**56**	51 25N	106 36W
Hawarden, U.S.A.	**74**	43 2N	96 28W
Hawea Lake	**133**	44 28 S	169 19 E
Hawera	**133**	39 35 S	174 19 E
Hawesville	**77**	37 54N	86 45W
Hawick	**96**	55 25N	2 48W
Hawk Junction	**53**	48 5N	84 38W
Hawk Lake	**52**	49 48N	93 59W
Hawk Point	**76**	38 58N	91 8W
Hawke B.	**133**	39 25N	177 20 E
Hawke, C.	**136**	32 13 S	152 34 E
Hawker	**94**	31 59 S	138 22 E
Hawkes Bay	**37**	50 36N	57 10W
Hawke's Bay □	**133**	39 45 S	176 35 E
Hawkesbury	**43**	45 37N	74 37W
Hawkesbury I.	**62**	53 37N	129 3W
Hawkesbury River	**136**	33 50 S	151 44W
Hawkestone	**70**	44 31N	79 27W
Hawkinsville	**73**	32 17N	83 30W
Hawley	**74**	46 58N	96 20W
Hawthorne	**78**	38 31N	118 37W
Haxtun	**74**	40 40N	102 39W
Hay, Austral.	**136**	34 30 S	144 51 E
Hay, U.K.	**95**	52 4N	3 9W
Hay, C.	**64**	74 25N	113 0W
Hay Cove	**39**	45 45N	60 44W
Hay I.	**46**	44 53N	80 58W
Hay L.	**54**	58 50N	118 50W
Hay Lakes	**61**	53 12N	113 2W
Hay, R., Austral.	**135**	24 10 S	137 20 E
Hay, R., Can.	**54**	60 0N	116 56W
Hay River	**54**	60 51N	115 44W
Hay Springs	**74**	42 40N	102 38W
Hayange	**101**	49 20N	6 2 E
Haycock	**67**	65 10N	161 20W
Hayden, Ariz., U.S.A.	**79**	33 2N	110 54W
Hayden, Colo., U.S.A.	**78**	40 30N	107 22W
Haye Descartes, La	**100**	46 58N	0 42 E
Haye-du-Puits, La	**100**	49 17N	1 33W
Hayes	**74**	44 22N	101 1W
Hayes Pen.	**17**	75 30N	65 0W
Hayes, R.	**55**	57 3N	92 12W
Haymana	**122**	39 30N	32 35 E
Haynesville	**75**	33 0N	93 7W
Hays, Can.	**61**	50 6N	111 48W
Hays, U.S.A.	**74**	38 55N	99 25W
Haysboro	**59**	50 59N	114 5W
Haysville	**77**	38 28N	86 55W
Hayward, Calif., U.S.A.	**80**	37 40N	122 5W
Hayward, Wis., U.S.A.	**74**	46 2N	91 30W
Hayward's Heath	**95**	51 0N	0 5W
Hazard	**72**	37 18N	83 10W
Hazaribagh	**125**	23 58N	85 26 E
Hazebrouck	**101**	50 42N	2 31 E
Hazelmere	**66**	49 2N	122 43W
Hazelton, Can.	**54**	55 20N	127 42W
Hazelton, U.S.A.	**74**	46 30N	100 15W
Hazen	**78**	39 37N	119 2W
Hazenmore	**56**	49 42N	107 8W
Hazlehurst	**73**	31 50N	82 35W
Hazlet	**56**	50 24N	108 36W
Hazleton, Ind., U.S.A.	**77**	38 29N	87 34W
Hazleton, Pa., U.S.A.	**71**	40 58N	76 0W
Hazrat Imam	**123**	37 15N	68 50 E
Head of Bay d'Espoir	**37**	47 56N	55 45W
Head of Bight	**134**	31 30 S	131 25 E
Head of St. Margarets Bay	**39**	44 41N	63 55W
Headingley	**58**	49 53N	97 24W
Healdsburg	**80**	38 33N	122 51W
Healdton	**75**	34 16N	97 31W
Healesville	**136**	37 35 S	145 30 E
Heanor	**94**	53 1N	1 20W
Heard I.	**16**	53 0 S	74 0 E
Hearne	**75**	30 54N	96 35W
Hearne B.	**55**	60 10N	99 10W
Hearne L.	**54**	62 20N	113 10W
Hearst	**53**	49 40N	83 41W
Heart, R.	**74**	46 40N	101 30W
Heart's Content	**37**	47 54N	53 27W
Heath Pt.	**38**	49 8N	61 40W
Heath Steele	**39**	47 17N	66 5W
Heatherton, Newf., Can.	**37**	48 17N	58 45W
Heatherton, N.S., Can.	**39**	45 35N	61 47W
Heavener	**75**	34 54N	94 36W
Hebbronville	**75**	27 20N	98 40W
Heber	**81**	32 44N	115 32W
Heber Springs	**75**	35 29N	91 59W
Hebert	**56**	50 30N	107 10W
Hebgen, L.	**78**	44 50N	111 15W
Hebrides, U.K.	**96**	57 30N	7 0W
Hebrides, Inner Is., U.K.	**96**	57 20N	6 40W
Hebrides, Outer Is., U.K.	**96**	57 50N	7 25W
Hebron, Newf., Can.	**36**	58 12N	62 38W
Hebron, N.S., Can.	**39**	43 53N	66 5W
Hebrón	**115**	31 32N	35 6 E
Hebron, Ind., U.S.A.	**77**	41 19N	87 17W
Hebron, N.D., U.S.A.	**74**	46 56N	102 2W
Hebron, Nebr., U.S.A.	**74**	40 15N	97 33W
Hebron Fd.	**36**	58 9N	62 45W
Hecate I.	**62**	51 42N	128 0W
Hecate Str.	**62**	53 10N	130 30W
Hecks Corner	**43**	45 4N	73 12W
Hecla	**74**	45 56N	98 8W
Hecla I.	**57**	51 10N	96 43W
Hédé	**100**	48 18N	1 49W
Hede	**110**	62 23N	13 30 E
Hedemora	**111**	60 18N	15 58 E
Hedley, Can.	**63**	49 22N	120 4W
Hedley, U.S.A.	**75**	34 53N	100 39W
Hedley B.	**64**	73 0N	108 0W
Hedmark □	**111**	61 17N	11 40 E
Hedrick	**76**	41 11N	92 19W
Heemstede	**105**	52 22N	4 37 E
Heerenveen	**105**	52 57N	5 55 E
Heerlen	**105**	50 55N	6 0 E
Heidelberg	**106**	49 23N	8 41 E
Heilbron	**117**	27 16 S	27 59 E
Heilbronn	**106**	49 8N	9 13 E
Heilungkiang □	**130**	47 30N	129 0 E
Heinola	**111**	61 13N	26 24 E
Heinsburg	**55**	53 50N	110 30W
Heinze Is.	**128**	14 25N	97 45 E
Heisler	**61**	52 41N	112 13W
Hejaz = Hijāz	**122**	26 0N	37 30 E
Hekimhan	**122**	38 50N	38 0 E
Hekla	**110**	63 56N	19 35W
Helena, Ark., U.S.A.	**75**	34 30N	90 35W
Helena, Mont., U.S.A.	**78**	46 40N	112 0W
Helendale	**81**	34 45N	117 19W
Helene L.	**56**	53 33N	108 12W
Helensburgh, Austral.	**136**	34 11 S	151 1 E
Helensburgh, U.K.	**96**	56 0N	4 44W
Helensville	**133**	36 41 S	174 29 E
Helgeland	**110**	66 20N	13 30 E
Helgoland, I.	**106**	54 10N	7 51 E
Heligoland = Helgoland	**106**	54 10N	7 51 E
Hell-Ville	**117**	13 25 S	48 16 E
Hellick Kenyon Plateau	**91**	82 0 S	110 0W
Hellin	**104**	38 31N	1 40W
Helmand □	**124**	31 20N	64 0 E
Helmand, R.	**124**	34 0N	67 0 E
Helmond	**105**	51 29N	5 41 E
Helmsdale	**96**	58 7N	3 40W
Helmsdale, R.	**96**	58 10N	3 50W
Helper	**78**	39 44N	110 56W
Helsingborg	**111**	56 3N	12 42 E
Helsingfors = Helsinki	**111**	60 15N	25 3 E
Helsingør	**111**	56 2N	12 35 E
Helsinki (Helsingfors)	**111**	60 15N	25 3 E
Helvellyn	**94**	54 31N	3 1W
Hemet	**81**	33 45N	116 59W
Hemford	**39**	44 30N	64 47W
Hemingford	**74**	42 21N	103 4W
Hemmingford	**43**	45 3N	73 35W
Hemphill	**75**	31 21N	93 49W
Hempstead	**75**	30 5N	96 5W
Hemse	**111**	57 15N	18 22 E
Henares, R.	**104**	40 55N	3 0W
Hendaye	**102**	43 23N	1 47W
Henderson, Argent.	**88**	36 18 S	61 43W
Henderson, Ky., U.S.A.	**77**	37 50N	87 38W
Henderson, Nev., U.S.A.	**81**	36 2N	115 0W
Henderson, Pa., U.S.A.	**73**	35 25N	88 40W
Henderson, Tex., U.S.A.	**75**	32 5N	94 49W
Henderson, Mt.	**62**	54 16N	128 4W
Hendersonville	**73**	35 21N	82 28W
Hendrix Lake	**63**	52 5N	120 48W
Hengelo	**105**	52 16N	6 48 E
Henghsien	**131**	22 36N	109 16 E
Hengshan	**130**	27 10N	112 45 E
Hengyang	**131**	26 51N	112 30 E
Hénin-Beaumont	**101**	50 25N	2 58 E
Henley Harbour	**37**	52 2N	55 51W
Henlopen, C.	**72**	38 48N	75 5W
Hennebont	**100**	47 49N	3 19W
Hennepin	**76**	41 15N	89 21W
Hennessy	**75**	36 8N	97 53W
Henribourg	**55**	53 25N	105 38W
Henrichemont	**101**	47 20N	2 21 E
Henrietta	**75**	33 50N	98 15W
Henrietta Maria C.	**34**	55 9N	82 20W
Henry	**76**	41 5N	89 20W
Henry Kater, C.	**65**	69 8N	66 30W
Henryetta	**75**	35 30N	96 0W
Henrysburg	**43**	45 5N	73 27W
Henryville	**43**	45 8N	73 11W
Hensall	**46**	43 26N	81 30W
Hentiyn Nuruu	**130**	48 30N	108 30 E
Henty	**136**	35 30N	147 0 E
Henzada	**125**	17 38N	95 35 E
Heppner	**78**	45 27N	119 34W
Hepworth	**46**	44 37N	81 9W
Héraðsflói	**110**	65 42N	14 12W
Héradsvötn	**110**	65 25N	19 5W
Herät	**124**	34 20N	62 7 E
Herät □	**124**	35 0N	62 0 E
Hérault □	**102**	43 34N	3 15 E
Hérault, R.	**102**	43 20N	3 32 E
Herbert I.	**67**	52 49N	170 10W
Herbert Inlet	**62**	49 20N	125 58W
Herbiers, Les	**100**	46 52N	1 0W
Herbignac	**100**	47 27N	2 18W
Hercegnovi	**109**	42 30N	18 33 E
Herculaneum	**76**	38 16N	90 23W
Herðubreið	**110**	65 11N	16 21W
Herdman	**43**	45 2N	74 6W
Hereford, U.K.	**95**	52 4N	2 42W
Hereford, U.S.A.	**75**	34 50N	102 28W
Hereford and Worcester □	**95**	52 10N	2 30W
Hereford, Mt.	**41**	45 5N	71 36W
Herentals	**105**	51 12N	4 51 E
Hereward	**49**	43 50N	80 19W
Herford	**106**	52 7N	8 40 E
Héricourt	**101**	47 32N	6 55 E
Herington	**74**	38 43N	97 0W
Heriot Bay	**62**	50 7N	125 13W
Hérisson	**102**	46 32N	2 42 E
Herjehogna	**111**	61 43N	12 7 E
Herkimer	**71**	43 0N	74 59W
Herlong	**80**	40 8N	120 8W
Herm I.	**100**	49 30N	2 28W
Herman	**74**	45 51N	96 8W
Hermandez	**80**	36 24N	120 46W
Hermann	**74**	38 40N	91 25W
Herment	**102**	45 45N	2 24 E
Hermidale	**136**	31 30 S	146 42 E
Hermiston	**78**	45 50N	119 16W
Hermitage, Can.	**37**	47 33N	55 56W
Hermitage, N.Z.	**133**	43 44 S	170 5 E
Hermitage, U.S.A.	**76**	37 56N	93 19W
Hermitage B.	**35**	47 33N	56 10W
Hermite, Is.	**90**	55 50 S	68 0W
Hermon, Mt.	**115**	33 20N	36 0 E
Hermon, Mt. = Sheikh, J. ash	**115**	33 20N	36 0 E
Hermosillo	**82**	29 10N	111 0W
Hernad, R.	**107**	48 20N	21 15 E
Hernandarias	**89**	25 20 S	54 40W
Hernando, Argent.	**88**	32 28 S	63 40W
Hernando, U.S.A.	**75**	34 50N	89 59W
Herne	**105**	51 33N	7 12 E
Herne Bay	**95**	51 22N	1 8 E
Herning	**111**	56 8N	8 58 E
Heroica Nogales	**82**	31 14N	110 56W
Heron Bay	**53**	48 40N	86 25W
Hérons, Ile aux	**44**	45 25N	73 35W
Herreid	**74**	45 53N	100 5W
Herrera	**104**	39 12N	4 50W
Herrero, Punta	**83**	19 17N	87 27W
Herrin	**76**	37 50N	89 0W
Herring Cove	**39**	44 34N	63 34W
Herschel	**56**	51 38N	108 21W
Herschel I.	**67**	69 35N	139 5W
Herstal	**105**	50 40N	5 38 E
Hertford	**95**	51 47N	0 4W
Hertford □	**95**	51 51N	0 5W
's-Hertogenbosch	**105**	51 42N	5 17 E
Hervey B.	**135**	25 0 S	152 52 E
Hervey Is.	**15**	19 30 S	159 0W
Hervey Junction	**34**	46 50N	72 29W
Herzliyya	**115**	32 10N	34 50 E
Hesdin	**101**	50 21N	2 0 E
Hespeler	**49**	43 26N	80 19W
Hesperia	**81**	34 25N	117 18W
Hesse = Hessen	**106**	50 40N	9 20 E
Hessel	**46**	46 1N	84 28W
Hessen □	**106**	50 40N	9 20 E
Hetch Hetchy Aqueduct	**80**	37 36N	121 25W
Hettinger	**74**	46 8N	102 38W
Hève, C. de la	**100**	49 30N	0 5 E
Hewett, C.	**65**	70 16N	67 45W
Hexham	**94**	54 58N	2 7W
Heyfield	**136**	37 59 S	146 47 E
Heysham	**94**	54 5N	2 53W
Heywood	**136**	38 8 S	141 37 E
Hi-no-Misaki	**132**	35 26N	132 38 E
Hi Vista	**81**	34 44N	117 46W
Hiawatha, Kans., U.S.A.	**74**	39 55N	95 33W
Hiawatha, Utah, U.S.A.	**78**	39 37N	111 1W
Hibben I.	**62**	53 0N	132 18W
Hibbing	**52**	47 30N	93 0W
Hickman	**75**	36 35N	89 8W
Hickmans Harbour	**37**	48 6N	53 44W
Hickory	**73**	35 46N	81 17W
Hicksville, N.Y., U.S.A.	**71**	40 46N	73 30W
Hicksville, Ohio, U.S.A.	**77**	41 18N	84 46W
Hida-Sammyaku	**132**	36 30N	137 40 E
Hida-sammyaku	**132**	36 30N	137 40 E
Hidalgo	**77**	39 9N	88 9W
Hidalgo □	**82**	20 30N	99 10W
Hidalgo del Parral	**82**	26 58N	105 40W
Hidalgo, Presa M.	**82**	26 30N	108 35W
Hifung	**131**	22 59N	115 17 E
Higashiōsaka	**132**	34 40N	135 37 E
Higbee	**76**	39 19N	92 31W
Higgins	**75**	36 9N	100 1W
Higgins Corner	**80**	39 2N	121 5W
Higgins L.	**46**	44 30N	84 45W
Higginsville	**76**	39 4N	93 43W
Higgs I. L.	**73**	36 20N	78 30W
High Atlas = Haut Atlas	**114**	32 30N	5 0W
High I., Newf., Can.	**35**	56 40N	61 10W
High I., Newf., Can.	**36**	52 28N	55 40W
High Island	**75**	29 32N	94 22W
High Level	**54**	58 31N	117 8W
High Point	**73**	35 57N	79 58W
High Prairie	**60**	55 30N	116 30W
High River	**61**	50 30N	113 50W
High Springs	**73**	29 50N	82 40W
High Wycombe	**95**	51 37N	0 45W
Highland, U.S.A.	**77**	41 33N	87 28W
Highland, Ill., U.S.A.	**76**	38 44N	89 41W

Highland Huanglui

Highland, Wis., U.S.A. 76 43 6N 90 21W
Highland □ 96 57 30N 5 0W
Highland Creek 50 43 47N 79 10W
Highland Park 59 51 6N 114 4W
Highland Pk., Ill., U.S.A. 77 42 10N 87 50W
Highland Pk., Mich., U.S.A. 70 42 25N 83 6W
Highmore 74 44 35N 99 26W
Highridge 60 54 3N 114 8W
Highrock L. 55 57 5N 105 32W
Higley 79 33 27N 111 46W
Higüay 85 18 37N 68 42W
Higüero, Pta. 85 18 22N 67 16W
Hiko 80 37 30N 115 13W
Hikone 132 35 15N 136 10 E
Hikurangi 133 37 55 S 178 4 E
Hilda 61 50 28N 110 3W
Hilden 39 45 18N 63 18W
Hildesheim 106 52 9N 9 55 E
Hill 47 45 40N 74 45W
Hill City, Idaho, U.S.A. 78 43 20N 115 2W
Hill City, Kans., U.S.A. 74 39 25N 99 51W
Hill City, Minn., U.S.A. 52 46 57N 93 35W
Hill City, S.D., U.S.A. 74 43 58N 103 35W
Hill Island L. 55 60 30N 109 50W
Hill Spring 61 49 17N 113 38W
Hilla, Iraq 122 32 30N 44 27 E
Hilla, Si Arab. 122 23 35N 46 50 E
Hillegom 105 52 18N 4 35 E
Hillhurst 59 51 3N 114 7W
Hillingdon 95 51 33N 0 29W
Hillman 46 45 5N 83 52W
Hillmond 56 53 26N 109 41W
Hillsboro, Ill., U.S.A. 76 39 9N 89 29W
Hillsboro, Iowa, U.S.A. 76 40 50N 91 42W
Hillsboro, Kans., U.S.A. 74 38 28N 97 10W
Hillsboro, Mo., U.S.A. 76 38 14N 90 34W
Hillsboro, N. Mex., U.S.A. 79 33 0N 107 35W
Hillsboro, N.D., U.S.A. 74 47 23N 97 9W
Hillsboro, N.H., U.S.A. 71 43 8N 71 56W
Hillsboro, Ohio, U.S.A. 77 39 12N 83 37W
Hillsboro, Oreg., U.S.A. 80 45 31N 123 0W
Hillsboro, Tex., U.S.A. 75 32 0N 97 10W
Hillsborough 85 12 28N 61 28W
Hillsborough B. 39 46 8N 63 5W
Hillsburgh 49 43 47N 80 9W
Hillsdale, Can. 58 50 25N 104 37W
Hillsdale, Mich., U.S.A. 77 41 55N 84 40W
Hillsdale, N.Y., U.S.A. 71 42 11N 73 30W
Hillsport 53 49 27N 85 34W
Hillston 136 33 30 S 145 31 E
Hilo 67 19 44N 155 5W
Hilonghilong, mt. 127 9 10N 125 45 E
Hilton 70 43 16N 77 48W
Hilton Beach 46 46 15N 83 53W
Hilversum 105 52 14N 5 10 E
Himachal Pradesh □ 124 31 30N 77 0 E
Himalaya, mts. 124 29 0N 84 0 E
Himatnagar 124 23 37N 72 57 E
Himeji 132 34 50N 134 40 E
Himi 132 36 50N 137 0 E
Hims = Homs 122 34 40N 36 45 E
Hinako, Kepulauan 126 0 50N 97 20 E
Hinche 85 19 9N 72 1W
Hinckley, U.K. 95 52 33N 1 21W
Hinckley, U.S.A. 78 39 18N 112 41W
Hindmarsh L. 136 36 5 S 141 55 E
Hinds L. 37 48 58N 57 0W
Hindu Kush 124 36 0N 71 0 E
Hindubagh 124 30 56N 67 57 E
Hindupur 124 13 49N 77 32 E
Hines Creek 60 56 20N 118 40W
Hingan 131 25 39N 110 43 E
Hinganghat 124 20 30N 78 59 E
Hingham 78 48 40N 110 29W
Hingi 131 25 4N 105 2 E
Hingkwo 131 26 15N 115 13 E
Hingning 131 24 2N 115 55 E
Hingol, R. 124 25 30N 65 30 E
Hingoli 124 19 41N 77 15 E
Hinlopenstretet 17 79 33N 18 40 E
Hinnøy 110 68 40N 16 28 E
Hinojosa 104 38 30N 5 17W
Hinsdale 78 48 26N 107 2W
Hinton, Can. 60 53 26N 117 34W
Hinton, U.S.A. 72 37 40N 80 51W
Hirakud Dam 125 21 32N 83 45 E
Hiratsuka 132 35 19N 139 21 E
Hirosaki 132 40 34N 140 28 E
Hiroshima 132 34 30N 132 30 E
Hiroshima-ken □ 132 34 50N 133 0 E
Hirson 101 49 55N 4 4 E
Hispaniola, I. 83 19 0N 71 0W
Hissar 124 29 12N 75 45 E
Hita 132 33 20N 130 58 E
Hitachi 132 16 40N 140 35 E
Hitchcock 56 49 14N 103 7W
Hitchin 95 51 57N 0 16W
Hitoyoshi 132 32 13N 130 45 E
Hitra 110 63 30N 8 45 E
Hiungyao 130 40 10N 122 9 E
Hixon 63 53 25N 122 35W
Hjalmar L. 55 61 33N 109 25W
Hjälmaren 111 59 18N 15 40 E
Hjørring 111 57 29N 9 59 E
Ho Chi Minh, Phanh Bho 128 10 58N 106 40 E
Hoa Binh 128 20 50N 105 20 E
Hoa Da (Phan Ri) 128 11 16N 108 40 E
Hoadley 54 52 45N 114 30W
Hoai Nhon (Bon Son) 128 14 28N 109 1 E
Hoare B. 65 65 17N 62 0W
Hobart, Austral. 135 42 50 S 147 21 E
Hobart, Ind., U.S.A. 77 41 32N 87 15W
Hobart, Okla., U.S.A. 75 35 0N 99 5W
Hobbs 75 32 40N 103 3W
Hobo 86 2 35N 75 30W
Hoboken, Belg. 105 51 11N 4 21 E
Hoboken, U.S.A. 71 40 45N 74 4W
Hobro 111 56 39N 9 46 E
Hobson L. 63 52 35N 120 15W
Hoburgen 111 56 55N 18 7 E
Hochatown 75 34 11N 94 39W
Hochih 131 24 43N 107 43 E
Hochwan 131 30 0N 106 15 E
Hodeïda 115 14 50N 43 0 E
Hodges Hill 37 49 4N 55 53W
Hodgeville 56 50 7N 106 58W
Hodgson 57 51 13N 97 36W
Hódmezövásárhely 107 46 28N 20 22 E
Hodonín 106 48 50N 17 0 E
Hoëdic, I. 100 47 21N 2 52W
Hoek van Holland 105 52 0N 4 7 E
Hof, Ger. 106 50 18N 11 55 E
Hof, Iceland 110 64 33N 14 40W
Höfðakaupstaður 110 65 50N 20 19W
Hofei 131 31 52N 117 15 E
Hofeng 131 29 55N 110 5 E
Hofsjökull 110 64 49N 18 48W
Hofsós 110 65 53N 19 26W
Hōfu 132 34 3N 131 34 E
Hofuf 122 25 20N 49 40 E
Hog I. 46 45 48N 85 22W
Hogansville 73 33 14N 84 50W
Hogeland 56 48 51N 108 40W
Hogsty Reef 85 21 41N 73 48W
Hoh, R. 80 47 45N 124 29W
Hohenlimburg 105 51 21N 7 35 E
Hohenwald 73 35 35N 87 30W
Hohpi 130 35 59N 114 13 E
Hôi An 128 15 30N 108 19 E
Hoi Xuan 128 20 25N 105 9 E
Hoiping 131 22 30N 112 12 E
Hoisington 74 38 33N 98 50W
Hokang 130 47 36N 130 28 E
Hokiang 131 28 50N 105 50 E
Hokianga Harbour 133 35 31 S 173 22 E
Hokitika 133 42 42 S 171 0 E
Hokkaidō 132 43 30N 143 0 E
Hokow 128 22 39N 103 57 E
Hokowchen 130 40 16N 111 4 E
Holan Shan 130 38 40N 105 50 E
Holberg 62 50 40N 128 0W
Holbrook, Austral. 136 35 42 S 147 18 E
Holbrook, U.S.A. 79 35 0N 110 0W
Holden, Can. 60 53 13N 112 11W
Holden, Mo., U.S.A. 76 38 43N 94 0W
Holden, Wash., U.S.A. 63 48 12N 120 47W
Holden Fillmore 78 39 0N 112 26W
Holdenville 75 35 5N 96 25W
Holderness 94 53 45N 0 5W
Holdfast 56 50 58N 105 25W
Holdrege 74 40 25N 99 30W
Holgate 77 41 15N 84 8W
Holguín 85 20 50N 76 20W
Holinshead L. 52 49 39N 89 40W
Hollams Bird I. 117 24 40 S 14 30 E
Holland, U.K. 94 52 50N 0 10W
Holland, U.S.A. 77 42 47N 86 7W
Holland Landing 70 44 7N 79 30W
Hollandia = Jayapura 127 2 28 S 140 38 E
Hollidaysburg 70 40 26N 78 25W
Hollis 75 34 45N 99 55W
Hollister, Calif., U.S.A. 80 36 51N 121 24W
Hollister, Idaho, U.S.A. 70 42 21N 114 36W
Holly, U.S.A. 46 42 48N 83 38W
Holly, Colo., U.S.A. 74 38 7N 102 7W
Holly Hill 73 29 15N 81 3W
Holly Springs 75 34 45N 89 25W
Hollywood, Calif., U.S.A. 68 34 7N 118 25W
Hollywood, Fla., U.S.A. 73 26 0N 80 9W
Holman 64 70 44N 117 44W
Hólmavík 110 65 42N 21 40W
Holmsund 110 63 41N 20 20 E
Holroyd, R. 135 14 10 S 141 36 E
Holsteinsborg 65 66 40N 53 30W
Holt 110 63 33N 19 48W
Holton 36 54 31N 57 12W
Holtville 81 32 50N 115 27W
Holy Cross 67 62 10N 159 52W
Holy I., England, U.K. 94 55 42N 1 48W
Holy I., Wales, U.K. 94 53 17N 4 37W
Holyhead 94 53 18N 4 38W
Holyhead B. 94 53 20N 4 35W
Holyoke, Colo., U.S.A. 74 40 39N 102 18W
Holyoke, Mass., U.S.A. 71 42 14N 72 37W
Holyrood 37 47 27N 53 8W
Homalin 125 24 55N 95 0 E
Homathko, R. 62 51 0N 124 56W
Hombori 114 15 20N 1 38W
Homburg 105 49 19N 7 21 E
Home B. 65 68 40N 67 10W
Home Hill 135 19 43 S 147 25 E
Homedale 78 43 42N 116 59W
Homer, Can. 49 43 10N 79 11W
Homer, Alaska, U.S.A. 67 59 40N 151 35W
Homer, Ill, U.S.A. 77 40 4N 87 57W
Homer, La., U.S.A. 75 32 50N 93 4W
Homer, Mich., U.S.A. 77 42 9N 84 49W
Homestead, Can. 60 55 31N 119 22W
Homestead, Fla., U.S.A. 73 25 29N 80 27W
Homestead, Idaho, U.S.A. 70 45 3N 116 58W
Homewood, Calif., U.S.A. 80 39 4N 120 8W
Homewood, Ill., U.S.A. 77 41 34N 87 40W
Hominy 75 36 26N 96 24W
Homs (Hims) 122 34 40N 36 45 E
Hon Chong 128 10 16N 104 38 E
Honan □ 131 33 50N 113 15 E
Honcut 80 39 20N 121 32W
Honda 86 5 12N 74 45W
Hondeklipbaai 117 30 19 S 17 17 E
Hondo, Can. 60 55 4N 114 2W
Hondo, U.S.A. 75 29 22N 99 6W
Hondo, R. 83 18 25N 88 21W
Honduras ■ 84 14 40N 86 30W
Honduras, Golfo de 84 16 50N 87 0W
Hönefoss 111 60 10N 10 12 E
Honesdale 71 41 34N 75 17W
Honey Harbour 46 44 52N 79 49W
Honey L. 80 40 13N 120 14W
Honfleur 100 49 25N 0 13 E
Hong Kong ■ 131 22 11N 114 14 E
Hongha, R. 128 22 0N 104 0 E
Honghai B. 131 22 45N 115 15 E
Hongkong ■ 131 22 11N 114 14 E
Honguedo, Détroit d' 38 49 15N 64 0W
Honiton 95 50 48N 3 11W
Honolulu 67 21 19N 157 52W
Honshū 132 36 0N 138 0 E
Hood Mt. 78 45 30N 121 50W
Hood, Pt. 134 34 23 S 119 34 E
Hood River 78 45 45N 121 37W
Hoodsport 80 47 24N 123 7W
Hoogeveen 105 52 44N 6 30 E
Hoogezand 105 53 11N 6 45 E
Hooghly, R. 125 21 59N 88 10 E
Hooglede 105 50 59N 3 5 E
Hook Hd. 97 52 8N 6 57W
Hooker 75 36 55N 101 10W
Hooker L. 52 50 35N 91 1W
Hoonah 67 58 15N 135 30W
Hooper Bay 67 61 30N 166 10W
Hoopeston 77 40 30N 87 40W
Hoorn 105 52 38N 5 4 E
Hoosick Falls 71 42 54N 73 21W
Hoover Dam 81 36 0N 114 45W
Hooversville 70 40 8N 78 57W
Hop Bottom 71 41 41N 75 47W
Hope, B.C., Can. 63 49 25N 121 25 E
Hope, Ont., Can. 50 43 53N 79 31W
Hope, Ariz., U.S.A. 81 33 43N 113 42W
Hope, Ark., U.S.A. 75 33 40N 93 30W
Hope, Ind., U.S.A. 77 39 18N 85 46W
Hope, N.D., U.S.A. 74 47 21N 97 42W
Hope Bay 91 65 0 S 55 0W
Hope I., B.C., Can. 62 50 55N 127 53W
Hope I., Ont., Can. 46 44 55N 80 11W
Hope Pt. 67 68 20N 166 50W
Hope Town 73 26 30N 76 30W
Hopedale 36 55 28N 60 13W
Hopelchén 83 19 46N 89 50W
Hopes Advance, C. 36 61 4N 69 34W
Hopetoun 136 33 57 S 120 7 E
Hopetown 117 29 34 S 24 3 E
Hopewell 39 45 29N 62 42W
Hopewell Cape 39 45 51N 64 35W
Hoping 131 24 31N 115 2 E
Hopkins, Mich., U.S.A. 77 42 37N 85 46W
Hopkins, Mo., U.S.A. 76 40 31N 94 45W
Hopkins, R. 136 37 55 S 142 40 E
Hopkinsville 73 36 52N 87 26W
Hopland 80 39 0N 123 7W
Hoppo 131 21 32N 109 6 E
Hoquiam 80 46 50N 123 55W
Hordaland fylke □ 111 60 25N 6 15 E
Hordern Hills 134 20 40 S 130 20 E
Horlick Mts. 91 84 0 S 102 0W
Hormoz 123 27 35N 55 0 E
Hormuz, I. 123 27 8N 56 28 E
Hormuz Str. 123 26 30N 56 30 E
Horn, Austria 106 48 39N 15 40 E
Horn, Ísafjarðarsýsla, Iceland 110 66 28N 22 28W
Horn, Suður-Múlasýsla, Iceland 110 65 10N 13 31W
Horn, Cape = Hornos, C. de 90 55 50 S 67 30W
Horn Head 97 55 13N 8 0W
Horn, I. 73 30 17N 88 40W
Horn Mts. 54 62 15N 119 15W
Horn, R. 54 61 30N 118 1W
Hornaday, R. 64 69 19N 123 48W
Hornavan 110 66 15N 17 30 E
Hornbeck 75 31 22N 93 20W
Hornbrook 78 41 58N 122 37W
Hornby 49 43 34N 79 50W
Horncastle 94 53 13N 0 8W
Hornell 70 42 23N 77 41W
Hornell L. 54 62 20N 119 25W
Hornepayne 53 49 14N 84 48W
Hornings Mills 46 44 9N 80 12W
Hornitos 80 37 30N 120 14W
Hornos, Cabo de 90 55 50 S 67 30 E
Hornoy 101 49 50N 1 54 E
Hornsby 136 33 42 S 151 2 E
Hornsea 94 53 55N 0 10W
Hornu 105 50 26N 3 50 E
Horoshiri Dake 132 42 40N 142 40 E
Horqueta 88 23 15 S 56 55W
Horse Cr. 74 41 33N 104 45W
Horse Is. 37 50 15N 55 50W
Horsefly 63 52 20N 121 25W
Horsefly L. 63 52 25N 121 0W
Horsens 111 55 52N 9 51 E
Horseshoe Bay 66 49 22N 123 17W
Horseshoe Dam 79 33 45N 111 35W
Horsham, Austral. 136 36 44 S 142 13 E
Horsham, U.K. 95 51 4N 0 20W
Horten 111 59 25N 10 32 E
Horton 74 39 42N 95 30W
Horton, R. 67 69 56N 126 52W
Horwood 37 49 27N 54 32W
Horwood, L. 53 48 5N 82 20W
Hose, Pegunungan 126 2 5N 114 6 E
Hoshangabad 124 22 45N 77 45 E
Hoshiarpur 124 31 30N 75 58 E
Hosmer 74 45 36N 99 29W
Hospet 124 15 15N 76 20 E
Hospitalet de Llobregat 104 41 21N 2 6 E
Hospitalet, L' 102 42 36N 1 47 E
Hoste, I. 90 55 0 S 69 0W
Hostens 102 44 30N 0 40W
Hot 128 18 8N 98 29 E
Hot Creek Ra. 78 39 0N 116 0W
Hot Springs, Ark, U.S.A. 75 34 30N 93 0W
Hot Springs, S.D., U.S.A. 74 43 25N 103 30W
Hotagen, L. 110 63 50N 14 30 E
Hotchkiss 79 38 55N 107 47W
Hotchkiss, R. 60 57 2N 117 28W
Hotien (Khotan) 129 37 6N 79 59 E
Hoting 110 64 8N 16 15 E
Hottah L. 64 65 4N 118 30W
Hotte, Massif de la 85 18 30N 73 45W
Houat, I. 100 47 24N 2 58W
Houck 79 35 15N 109 15W
Houdan 101 48 48N 1 35 E
Houffalize 105 50 8N 5 48 E
Houghton 52 47 9N 88 39W
Houghton L. 46 44 20N 84 40W
Houghton Lake Heights 46 44 18N 84 51W
Houghton-le-Spring 94 54 51N 1 28W
Houhora 133 34 49 S 173 9 E
Houlton 35 46 5N 68 0W
Houma 75 29 35N 90 50W
Hourtin 102 45 11N 1 4W
Houston, Can. 54 54 25N 126 30W
Houston, Mo., U.S.A. 75 37 20N 92 0W
Houston, Tex., U.S.A. 75 29 50N 95 20W
Hovd (Jargalant) 129 48 2N 91 37 E
Hove 95 50 50N 0 10W
Hövsgöl Nuur 130 51 0N 100 30 E
Howard, Kans., U.S.A. 75 37 30N 96 16W
Howard, Penn., U.S.A. 70 41 0N 77 40W
Howard, S.D., U.S.A. 74 44 2N 97 30W
Howard L. 55 62 15N 105 57W
Howe 78 43 48N 113 0W
Howe, C. 136 37 30 S 150 0 E
Howe I. 47 44 16N 76 17W
Howe Sd. 63 49 35N 123 15W
Howell 46 42 38N 83 56W
Howick 43 45 11N 73 51W
Howley 37 49 12N 57 2W
Howrah 125 22 37N 88 27 E
Howth Hd. 97 53 21N 6 0W
Hoy I. 96 58 50N 3 15W
Høyanger 111 61 25N 6 50 E
Hpungan Pass 125 27 30N 96 55 E
Hrádec Králové 106 50 15N 15 50 E
Hron, R. 107 48 0N 18 4 E
Hrvatska 108 45 20N 16 0 E
Hsaichwan Shan 131 21 34N 112 30 E
Hsiao Shan 131 34 0N 111 30 E
Hsenwi 125 23 22N 97 55 E
Hsiamen 131 24 30N 118 7 E
Hsinchow 131 19 37N 109 17 E
Hsinchu 131 24 48N 120 58 E
Hsinhsing 131 22 45N 112 11 E
Hua Hin 128 12 34N 99 58 E
Huachacalla 82 18 45 S 68 17W
Huachinera 82 30 9N 108 55W
Huachipato 88 36 45 S 73 09W
Huacho 86 11 10 S 77 35W
Huachón 86 10 35 S 76 0W
Huacrachuco 86 8 35 S 76 50W
Huaian 131 33 28N 119 5 E
Huain 131 36 26N 119 12 E
Huajuapan 83 17 50N 98 0W
Hualien 131 24 0N 121 30 E
Huallaga, R. 86 5 30 S 76 10W
Hualpai Pk. 79 35 8N 113 58W
Huancabamba 86 5 10 S 79 15W
Huancané 86 15 10 S 69 50W
Huancapi 86 13 25 S 74 0W
Huancavelica 86 12 50 S 75 5W
Huancayo 86 12 5 S 75 0W
Huanglui 131 18 30N 108 46 E

Huangnipo Incomáti, R

Huangnipo 131 27 40N 105 10 E
Huánuco 86 9 55 S 76 15W
Huaraz 86 9 30 S 77 32W
Huarmey 86 10 5 S 78 5W
Huasamota 82 22 30N 104 30W
Huascarán 86 9 0 S 77 30W
Huasco 88 28 24 S 71 15W
Huasco, R. 88 28 27 S 71 13W
Huasna 81 35 6N 120 24W
Huatabampo 82 26 50N 109 50W
Huauchinango 83 20 11N 98 3W
Huautla 82 10 20N 96 50W
Huautla de Jiménez 83 18 8N 96 51W
Huay Namota 82 21 56N 104 30W
Huayllay 86 11 03 S 76 21W
Hubbard, Can. 56 51 8N 103 22W
Hubbard, Iowa, U.S.A. 76 42 18N 93 18W
Hubbard, Tex., U.S.A. 75 31 50N 96 50W
Hubbard L. 46 44 49N 83 34W
Hubbards 39 44 38N 64 4W
Hubbart Pt. 55 59 21N 94 41W
Hubbell 52 47 11N 88 26W
Hubli-Dharwar 124 15 22N 75 15 E
Huchow 131 30 57N 120 1 E
Huchuetenango 82 15 25N 91 30W
Huddersfield 94 53 38N 1 49W
Hudiksvall 111 61 43N 17 10 E
Hudson, Ont., Can. 52 50 6N 92 09W
Hudson, Qué., Can. 44 45 27N 74 9W
Hudson, Mass., U.S.A. 71 42 23N 71 35W
Hudson, Mich., U.S.A. 77 41 50N 84 20W
Hudson, N.Y., U.S.A. 71 42 15N 73 46W
Hudson, Wis., U.S.A. 74 44 57N 92 45W
Hudson, Wyo., U.S.A. 78 42 54N 108 37W
Hudson B. 55 59 0N 91 0W
Hudson Bay, Can. 65 60 0N 86 0W
Hudson Bay, Sask., Can. 57 52 51N 102 23W
Hudson Falls 71 43 18N 73 34W
Hudson Heights 44 45 28N 74 10W
Hudson Hope 54 56 0N 121 54W
Hudson, R. 71 40 42N 74 2W
Hudson Str. 65 62 0N 70 0W
Hudsonville 77 42 52N 85 52W
Hudwin L. 57 53 12N 95 41W
Hué 128 16 30N 107 35 E
Huehuetenango 84 15 20N 91 28W
Huejúcar 82 22 21N 103 13W
Huelgoat 100 48 22N 3 46W
Huelva 104 37 18N 6 57W
Huentelauquén 88 31 38 S 71 33W
Huerta, Sa. de la 88 31 10 S 67 30W
Huesca 104 42 8N 0 25W
Huétamo 82 18 36N 100 54W
Hugh, R. 134 25 1 S 134 10 E
Hughenden 135 20 52 S 144 10 E
Hughes 67 66 0N 154 20W
Hugo, Colo., U.S.A. 74 39 12N 103 27W
Hugo, Okla., U.S.A. 75 34 0N 95 30W
Hugoton 75 37 18N 101 22W
Huhehot 130 40 52N 111 36 E
Huichapán 83 20 24N 99 40W
Huila □ 86 2 30N 75 45W
Huila, Nevado del 86 3 0N 76 0W
Huiling Shan 131 21 35N 111 57 E
Huinan 130 42 40N 126 5 E
Huinca Renancó 88 34 51 S 64 22W
Huixtla 83 15 9N 92 28W
Huiya 122 24 40N 49 15 E
Huizen 105 52 18N 5 14 E
Hukawng Valley 125 26 30N 96 30 E
Hukow 131 29 38N 116 25 E
Hulaifa 122 25 58N 41 0 E
Hulan 130 46 0N 126 44 E
Hulbert 46 46 21N 85 9W
Huld 130 45 5N 105 30 E
Hulin 130 45 45N 133 0 E
Hull, Can. 48 45 25N 75 44W
Hull, U.K. 94 53 45N 0 20W
Hull, U.S.A. 76 39 43N 91 13W
Hull, R. 94 53 55N 0 23W
Hulst 105 51 17N 4 2 E
Huma 130 51 44N 126 42 E
Humacao 67 18 9N 65 50W
Humahuaca 88 23 10 S 65 25W
Humaitá 86 7 35 S 62 40W
Humaita 88 27 2 S 58 31W
Humansville 76 37 48N 93 35W
Humber 49 43 54N 79 49W
Humber B. 50 43 38N 79 28W
Humber Bay 50 43 38N 79 27W
Humber, R., Can. 50 43 38N 79 28W
Humber, R., U.K. 94 53 40N 0 10W
Humberside □ 94 53 50N 0 30W
Humberstone 70 42 53N 79 16W
Humble 75 29 59N 95 10W
Humboldt, Can. 56 52 15N 105 9W
Humboldt, Iowa, U.S.A. 76 42 42N 94 15W
Humboldt, Minn., U.S.A. 57 48 53N 97 7W
Humboldt, Tenn., U.S.A. 73 35 50N 88 55W
Humboldt Gletscher 65 79 30N 62 0W
Humboldt, R. 78 40 55N 116 0W
Hume, Calif., U.S.A. 80 36 48N 118 54W
Hume, Kans., U.S.A. 76 38 5N 94 35W
Hume, L. 136 36 0 S 147 0 E
Humeston 76 40 51N 93 30W
Humphreys, Mt. 80 37 17N 118 40W
Humphreys Pk. 79 35 24N 111 38W
Humptulips 80 47 14N 123 57W
Huna Floi 110 65 50N 20 50W
Hunan □ 131 27 30N 111 30 E
Hunchun 130 42 49N 130 31 E
Hundred and Fifty Mile House 63 52 7N 121 57W
Hundred Mile House 63 51 38N 121 18W
Hunedoara 107 45 40N 22 50 E
Hung Ho, R. 131 32 25N 115 35 E
Hungary ■ 107 47 20N 19 20 E
Hungary, Plain of 93 47 0N 20 0 E
Hunghai Wan 131 22 45N 115 15 E
Hunghu (Sinti) 131 29 49N 113 30 E
Hungkiang 131 27 0N 109 49 E
Hŭngnam 130 39 55N 127 45 E
Hungshui Ho, R. 131 23 24N 110 12 E
Hungtze Hu 131 33 20N 118 35 E
Hunsrück, mts. 105 49 30N 7 0 E
Hunstanton 94 52 57N 0 30 E
Hunstsville 77 40 26N 83 48W
Hunter, N.D., U.S.A. 74 47 12N 97 17W
Hunter, N.Y., U.S.A. 71 42 13N 74 13W
Hunter, C. 65 71 42N 72 30W
Hunter, I. 135 40 30 S 144 54 E
Hunter I. 62 51 55N 128 0W
Hunter, R. 136 32 52 S 151 46 E
Hunter Ra. 136 32 45 S 150 15 E
Hunterville 133 39 56 S 175 35 E
Huntingburg 77 38 20N 86 58W
Huntingdon, Can. 43 45 6N 74 10W
Huntingdon, U.K. 95 52 20N 0 11W
Huntingdon, N.Y., U.S.A. 71 40 52N 73 25W
Huntingdon, Pa., U.S.A. 70 40 28N 78 1W
Huntingdon □ 43 45 5N 74 15W
Huntington, Ind., U.S.A. 77 40 52N 85 30W
Huntington, Oreg., U.S.A. 78 44 22N 117 21W
Huntington, Ut., U.S.A. 78 39 24N 111 1W
Huntington, W. Va., U.S.A. 72 38 20N 82 30W
Huntington Beach 81 33 40N 118 0W
Huntington Park 79 33 58N 118 15W
Huntington, Resr. 77 40 49N 85 25W
Huntley 77 42 10N 88 26W
Huntly, N.Z. 133 37 34 S 175 11 E
Huntly, U.K. 96 57 27N 2 48W
Huntsville, Can. 46 45 20N 79 14W
Huntsville, Ala., U.S.A. 73 34 45N 86 35W
Huntsville, Mo., U.S.A. 76 39 26N 92 33W
Huntsville, Tex., U.S.A. 75 30 45N 95 35W
Huonville 135 43 0 S 147 5 E
Hupei □ 131 31 5N 113 5 E
Hupel 63 50 37N 118 44W
Hurd C. 70 45 15N 81 40W
Hurley, N. Mex., U.S.A. 79 32 45N 108 7W
Hurley, Wis., U.S.A. 52 46 26N 90 10W
Huron, Calif., U.S.A. 80 36 12N 120 6W
Huron, Ohio, U.S.A. 70 41 22N 82 34W
Huron, S.D., U.S.A. 74 44 30N 98 20W
Huron B. 52 46 57N 88 9W
Huron, L. 46 45 0N 83 0W
Hurons, R. des 45 45 28N 73 16W
Hurricane 79 37 10N 113 12W
Hurstbridge 136 37 40 S 145 10 E
Hurunui, R. 133 42 54 S 173 18 E
Húsavík 110 66 3N 17 21W
Huskvarna 111 57 47N 14 15 E
Huslia 67 65 40N 156 30W
Hussar 61 51 3N 112 41W
Hutag 130 49 25N 102 34 E
Hutchinson, Kans., U.S.A. 75 38 3N 97 59W
Hutchinson, Minn, U.S.A. 74 44 50N 94 22W
Huto Ho 130 38 30N 113 45 E
Hutsonville 77 39 6N 87 40W
Hutte Sauvage, L. de la 36 56 15N 64 45W
Huttig 75 33 5N 92 10W
Huttonsville 49 43 38N 79 48W
Huy 105 50 31N 5 15 E
Hvammsfjörður 110 65 4N 22 5W
Hvammur 110 65 13N 21 49W
Hvar, I. 108 43 11N 16 28 E
Hvítá, Arnessýsla, Iceland 110 64 0N 20 58W
Hvítá, Mýrasýsla, Iceland 110 64 40N 21 5W
Hvítárvatn 110 63 37N 19 50W
Hwachwan 130 47 1N 130 50 E
Hwai Ho 131 32 20N 114 30 E
Hwainan 131 32 44N 117 1 E
Hwaiyang 131 33 50N 115 2 E
Hwan Ho 130 37 10N 117 30 E
Hwang-ho, R. 130 40 50N 107 30 E
Hwangan 131 31 30N 114 40 E
Hwangshih 131 30 27N 115 0 E
Hwangyen 131 28 34N 121 12 E
Hwanjen 130 41 24N 125 26 E
Hwateh 130 41 58N 113 58 E
Hwatien 130 43 0N 126 52 E
Hweian 131 25 2N 118 56 E
Hweichang 131 25 33N 115 41 E
Hweihsien 131 35 30N 113 46 E
Hweilai 131 23 0N 116 15 E
Hweimin 130 37 36N 117 30 E
Hweining 130 35 45N 105 0 E
Hweitseh 129 26 32N 103 6 E
Hwokiu 131 32 23N 116 16 E
Hyannis 74 42 0N 101 45W
Hyas 57 51 54N 102 16W
Hyattsville 72 38 59N 76 55W
Hydaburg 67 55 15N 132 45W
Hyde In. 65 75 2N 80 0W
Hyderabad, India 124 17 10N 78 29 E
Hyderabad, Pak. 124 25 23N 68 36 E
Hyderabad □ 124 25 3N 68 24 E
Hyères 103 43 8N 6 9 E
Hyères, Is. d' 103 43 0N 6 28 E
Hyesan 130 41 20N 128 10 E
Hyland, R. 54 59 52N 128 12W
Hymers 52 48 18N 89 43W
Hyndman Pk. 78 43 50N 114 0W
Hyōgo-ken □ 132 35 15N 135 0 E
Hyrum 78 41 35N 111 56W
Hysham 78 46 21N 107 11W
Hythe, Can. 60 55 20N 119 33W
Hythe, U.K. 95 51 4N 1 5 E
Hyvinkä 111 60 38N 24 50 E

I

Iaco, R. 86 10 25 S 70 30W
Ialomiţa, R. 107 44 45N 27 57 E
Ian L. 62 53 50N 132 45W
Iaşi 107 47 10N 27 40 E
Iauaretê 86 0 30N 69 5W
Iba 127 15 22N 120 0 E
Ibadan 114 7 22N 3 58 E
Ibagué 86 4 27N 73 14W
Ibar, R. 109 43 15N 20 40 E
Ibaraki-ken □ 132 36 10N 140 10 E
Ibarra 86 0 21N 78 7W
Ibera, Laguna 88 28 30 S 57 9W
Iberia 76 38 5N 92 18W
Iberian Peninsula 93 40 0N 5 0W
Iberville 45 45 19N 73 17W
Iberville □ 45 45 15N 73 10W
Iberville, Lac d' 36 55 55N 73 15W
Iberville, Mt. d' 36 58 50N 63 50W
Ibiá 87 19 30 S 46 30W
Ibicuy 88 33 55 S 59 10W
Ibiracu 87 19 50 S 40 30W
Ibiza 104 38 54N 1 26 E
Ibiza, I. 104 39 0N 1 30 E
Ibo 117 12 22 S 40 32 E
Ibonma 127 3 22 S 133 31 E
Ibotirama 87 12 13 S 43 12W
Ibu 127 1 35N 127 25 E
Ica 86 14 0 S 75 30W
Ica, R. 86 2 55 S 69 0W
Icabarú 86 4 20N 61 45W
Içana 86 1 21N 69 0W
Iceland, I. ■ 110 65 0N 19 0W
Icha 121 55 30N 156 0 E
Ichang 131 30 48N 111 29 E
Ichchapuram 125 19 10N 84 40 E
Ichihara 132 35 28N 140 5 E
Ichikawa 132 35 44N 139 55 E
Ichilo, R. 86 16 30 S 64 45W
Ichinomiya 132 35 18N 136 48 E
Ichun, Heilungkiang, China 129 47 42N 129 8 E
Ichun, Kiangsi, China 131 27 51N 114 12 E
Ichun, Shensi, China 130 35 24N 109 9 E
Ichung 131 25 30N 112 29 E
Ichwan 130 36 9N 109 58 E
Icy C. 17 70 25N 162 0W
Icy Str. 54 58 20N 135 30W
Ida 77 41 55N 83 34W
Ida Grove 74 42 20N 95 25W
Idabel 75 33 53N 94 50W
Idaho □ 78 44 10N 114 0W
Idaho City 78 43 50N 115 52W
Idaho Falls 78 43 30N 112 10W
Idaho Springs 78 39 49N 105 30W
Idar-Oberstein 105 49 43N 7 19 E
Idhi Oros 109 35 15N 24 45 E
Idhra 109 37 20N 23 28 E
Idi 126 4 55N 97 45 E
Idi Amin Dada, L. 116 0 25 S 29 40 E
Idiofa 116 4 55 S 19 42 E
Idria 80 36 25N 120 41W
Idutywa 117 32 8 S 28 18 E
Ieper 105 50 51N 2 53 E
Ierápetra 109 35 0N 25 44 E
Ierzu 108 39 48N 9 32 E
Ifanadiana 117 21 29 S 47 39 E
Ife 114 7 30N 4 31 E
Igarapava 87 20 3 S 47 47W
Igarapé Açu 87 1 4 S 47 33W
Igarka 121 67 30N 87 20 E
Igatimi 89 24 5 S 55 30W
Iggesund 111 61 39N 17 10 E
Iglésias 108 39 19N 8 27 E
Igloolik 65 69 20N 81 30W
Ignace 52 49 30N 91 40W
Igornachoix Bay 37 50 40N 57 25W
Iguaçu, Cat. del 89 25 41N 54 26W
Iguaçu, R. 89 25 30 S 53 10W
Iguala 83 18 20N 99 40W
Igualada 104 41 37N 1 37 E
Iguape, R. 89 24 40 S 48 0W
Iguassu = Iguaçu 89 25 41N 54 26W
Iguatu 87 6 20 S 39 18W
Iguéla 116 2 0 S 9 16 E
Ihing 131 31 21N 119 51 E
Ihosy 117 22 24 S 46 8 E
Ihsien 130 41 45N 121 3 E
Ihwang 131 27 30N 116 2 E
Ii 110 65 15N 25 30 E
Iida 132 35 35N 138 0 E
Iijoki 110 65 20N 26 15 E
Iisalmi 110 63 32N 27 10 E
Iizuka 132 33 38N 130 42 E
IJmuiden 105 52 28N 4 35 E
IJsselmeer 105 52 45N 5 20 E
IJsselstein 105 52 1N 5 2 E
Ijuí, R. 89 27 58 S 55 20W
Ikamatua 99 42 15 S 171 41 E
Ikaria, I. 109 37 35N 26 10 E
Ikela 116 1 0 S 23 35 E
Iki 132 33 45N 129 42 E
Ilan 130 46 14N 129 33 E
Ilanskiy 121 56 14N 96 3 E
Ile-à-la Crosse 55 55 27N 107 53W
Ile-à-la-Crosse, Lac 55 55 40N 107 45W
Île-aux-Noix 43 45 8N 73 17W
Île-Bizard 44 45 29N 73 53W
Île-Bouchard, L' 100 47 7N 0 26 E
Île-Cadieux 44 45 25N 74 1W
Île de France □ 101 49 0N 2 20 E
Ile d'Orleans, Chenal de l' 42 46 58N 71 0W
Île-Perrot 44 45 23N 73 57W
Île-Perrot-Sud 44 45 21N 73 54W
Île-Sainte-Thérèse 43 45 22N 73 15W
Ile-sur-le-Doubs, L' 101 47 26N 6 34 E
Ilebo 116 4 17 S 20 47 E
Ilek 120 51 30N 53 21 E
Ilek, R. 120 51 30N 53 22 E
Îles, L. des 40 46 20N 75 18W
Ilford 55 56 4N 95 35W
Ilfracombe, Austral. 135 23 30 S 144 30 E
Ilfracombe, U.K. 95 51 13N 4 8W
Ilheus 87 14 49 S 39 2W
Iliamna L. 67 59 35N 155 30W
Ilich 120 40 50N 68 27 E
Ilico 88 34 50 S 72 20W
Iliff 74 40 50N 103 3W
Ilio Pt. 67 21 13N 157 16W
Iliodhrómia 109 39 12N 23 50 E
Ilion 71 43 0N 75 3W
Iliysk 120 44 10N 77 20 E
Ilkeston 94 52 59N 1 19W
Ilkhuri Shan 130 51 30N 124 0 E
Ilkley 92 53 56N 1 49W
Illana B. 127 7 35N 123 45 E
Illapel 88 32 0 S 71 10W
Ille 102 42 40N 2 37 E
Ille-et-Vilaine □ 100 48 10N 1 30W
Iller, R. 106 47 53N 10 10 E
Illimani, Mte. 86 16 30 S 67 50W
Illinois □ 69 40 15N 89 30W
Illinois R. 76 38 5N 90 28W
Illiopolis 76 39 51N 89 15W
Illukotat, R. 36 60 48N 78 11W
Ilo 86 17 40 S 71 20W
Iloilo 127 10 45N 122 33 E
Ilorin 114 8 30N 4 35 E
Ilwaco 80 46 19N 124 3W
Ilwaki 127 7 55 S 126 30 E
Imabari 132 34 4N 133 0 E
Iman = Dalneretchensk 121 45 50N 133 40 E
Imandra, Oz. 120 67 45N 33 0 E
Imari 132 33 15N 129 52 E
Imbler 78 45 31N 118 0W
Imeni Poliny Osipenko 121 55 25N 136 29 E
Imeri, Serra 86 0 50N 65 25W
Imienpo 130 45 0N 128 16 E
Imlay 78 40 45N 118 9W
Imlay City 46 43 0N 83 2W
Immingham 94 53 37N 0 12W
Immokalee 73 26 25N 81 20W
Imola 108 44 20N 11 42 E
Imperatriz 87 5 30 S 47 29W
Impéria 108 43 52N 8 0 E
Imperial, Can. 56 51 21N 105 28W
Imperial, Calif., U.S.A. 81 32 52N 115 34W
Imperial, Nebr., U.S.A. 74 40 38N 101 39W
Imperial Beach 81 32 35N 117 8W
Imperial Dam 81 32 50N 114 30W
Imperial Res. 81 32 53N 114 28W
Imperial Valley 81 32 55N 115 30W
Impfondo 116 1 40N 18 0 E
Imphal 125 24 48N 93 56 E
Imphy 101 46 56N 3 15 E
Imuruan B. 127 10 40N 119 10 E
In Salah 114 27 10N 2 32 E
Ina 132 35 50N 138 0 E
Inangahua Junc. 133 41 52 S 171 59 E
Inanwatan 127 2 10 S 132 5 E
Iñapari 86 11 0 S 69 40W
Inari 110 68 54N 27 5 E
Inari, L. 110 69 0N 28 0 E
Inawashir-Ko 132 37 28N 140 2 E
Inca 104 39 43N 2 54 E
Incaguasi 88 29 12 S 71 5W
İnce Burnu 122 42 2N 35 0 E
Inchŏn 130 37 32N 126 45 E
Incomáti, R. 117 25 15 S 32 35 E

Incudine, Mte. l' **Jacmel**

Incudine, Mte. l' **103** 41 50N 9 12 E
Indalsälven **110** 62 36N 17 30 E
Indaw **125** 24 15N 96 5 E
Independence, Calif., U.S.A. **80** 36 51N 118 7W
Independence, Iowa, U.S.A. **76** 42 27N 91 52W
Independence, Kans., U.S.A. **75** 37 10N 95 50W
Independence, Ky., U.S.A. **77** 38 57N 84 33W
Independence, Mo., U.S.A. **76** 39 3N 94 25W
Independence, Oreg., U.S.A. **78** 44 53N 123 6W
Independence Fjord **17** 82 10N 29 0W
Independence Mts. **78** 41 30N 116 2W
Independencia, La **83** 16 31N 91 47W
Index **80** 47 50N 121 33W
India ■ **119** 20 0N 80 0 E
Indian Arm **66** 49 23N 122 53W
Indian Cabins **54** 59 52N 117 2W
Indian Harbour **36** 54 27N 57 13W
Indian Head **56** 50 30N 103 35W
Indian L. **52** 50 14N 94 5W
Indian Ocean **11** 5 0 S 75 0 E
Indian Springs **81** 36 35N 115 40W
Indiana **70** 40 38N 79 9W
Indiana □ **72** 40 0N 86 0W
Indianapolis **77** 39 42N 86 10W
Indianola, Iowa, U.S.A. **76** 41 20N 93 38W
Indianola, Miss., U.S.A. **75** 33 27N 90 40W
Indiga **120** 67 50N 48 50 E
Indigirka, R. **121** 69 0N 147 0 E
Indio **81** 33 46N 116 15W
Indonesia ■ **126** 5 0 S 115 0 E
Indore **124** 22 42N 75 53 E
Indramaju **127** 6 21 S 108 20 E
Indramaju, Tg. **127** 6 20 S 108 20 E
Indravati, R. **125** 19 0N 81 15 E
Indre □ **101** 47 12N 1 39 E
Indre-et-Loire □ **100** 47 12N 0 40 E
Indre, R. **100** 47 2N 1 8 E
Indus, R. **124** 28 40N 70 10 E
Industry **76** 40 20N 90 36W
İnebolu **122** 41 55N 33 40 E
Infiernillo, Presa del **82** 18 9N 102 0W
Ingelmunster **105** 50 56N 3 16 E
Ingende **116** 0 12 S 18 57 E
Ingenio Santa Ana **88** 27 25 S 65 40W
Ingersoll **46** 43 4N 80 55W
Ingham **135** 18 43 S 146 10 E
Ingleborough, mt. **94** 54 11N 2 23W
Inglefield G. **65** 77 30N 67 0W
Inglega **136** 31 20 S 147 50 E
Inglewood, Queensland, Austral. **136** 28 25 S 151 8 E
Inglewood, Vic., Austral. **136** 36 29 S 143 53 E
Inglewood, Can. **49** 43 47N 79 56W
Inglewood, N.Z. **133** 39 9 S 174 14 E
Inglewood, U.S.A. **81** 33 58N 118 21W
Ingólfshöfði **110** 63 48N 16 39W
Ingolstadt **106** 48 45N 11 26 E
Ingomar, Can. **39** 43 34N 65 22W
Ingomar, U.S.A. **78** 46 43N 107 37W
Ingonish **39** 46 42N 60 18W
Ingonish Beach **39** 46 38N 60 25W
Inhambane **117** 23 54 S 35 30 E
Inhaminga **117** 18 26 S 35 0 E
Inharrime **117** 24 30 S 35 0 E
Ining **131** 25 8N 109 57 E
Ining (Kuldja) **129** 43 57N 81 20 E
Inírida, R. **86** 3 0N 68 40W
Inishbofin I. **97** 53 35N 10 12W
Inishmore, I. **97** 53 8N 9 45W
Inishowen, Pen. **97** 55 14N 7 15W
Injune **135** 25 46 S 148 32 E
Inkerman **39** 47 40N 64 49W
Inklin **54** 58 56N 133 5W
Inklin, R. **54** 58 50N 133 10W
Inkom **78** 42 51N 112 7W
Inkpen Beacon **95** 51 22N 1 28W
Inle Aing **125** 20 30N 96 58 E
Inn, R. **106** 48 35N 13 28 E
Inner Hebrides, Is. **96** 57 0N 6 30W
Inner Mongolia □ **130** 44 50N 117 40 E
Inner Sound **96** 57 30N 5 55W
Innerkip, Can. **70** 43 12N 80 41W
Innerkip, Ont., Can. **46** 43 13N 80 42W
Innetalling I. **36** 56 0N 79 0W
Innisfail, Austral. **135** 17 33 S 146 5 E
Innisfail, Can. **61** 52 0N 113 57W
Innisfree **60** 53 22N 111 32W
Innsbruck **106** 47 16N 11 23 E
Inongo **116** 1 35 S 18 30 E
Inosu **86** 12 22N 71 38W
Inoucdjouac (Port Harrison) **36** 58 27N 78 6W
Inowrocław **107** 52 50N 18 20 E
Inquisivi **86** 16 50 S 66 45W
Intata Reach **62** 53 38N 125 30W
Intendente Alvear **88** 35 12 S 63 32W
Interior **74** 43 46N 101 59W
Interlaken **101** 46 41N 7 50 E
International Falls **52** 48 36N 93 25W
Interview I. **128** 12 55N 92 42 E
Inthanon, Mt. **128** 18 35N 98 29 E
Intiyaco **88** 28 50 S 60 0W
Inútil, B. **90** 53 30 S 70 15W
Inuvik **67** 68 16N 133 40W
Inveraray **96** 56 13N 5 5W
Inverbervie **96** 56 50N 2 17W
Invercargill **133** 46 24 S 168 24 E
Inverell **135** 29 45 S 151 8 E
Invergordon **96** 57 41N 4 10W
Invermay **56** 51 48N 103 9W
Invermere **61** 50 30N 116 2W
Inverness, Can. **39** 46 15N 61 19W
Inverness, U.K. **96** 57 29N 4 12W
Inverness, U.S.A. **73** 28 50N 82 20W
Inverurie **96** 57 15N 2 21W
Investigator Group **134** 34 45 S 134 20 E
Investigator Str. **135** 35 30 S 137 0 E
Invona **70** 40 46N 78 35W
Inwood **57** 50 30N 97 30W
Inyo Range **79** 37 0N 118 0W
Inyokern **81** 35 37N 117 54W
Inza **120** 53 55N 46 25 E
Ioánnina (Janinà) □ **109** 39 39N 20 57 E
Ioco **66** 49 18N 122 53W
Iola **75** 38 0N 95 20W
Iona **39** 45 58N 60 48W
Iona I. **96** 56 20N 6 25W
Ione, Calif., U.S.A. **80** 38 20N 121 0W
Ione, Wash., U.S.A. **63** 48 44N 117 29W
Ionia **77** 42 59N 85 7W
Ionian Is. = Ionioi Nisoi **109** 38 40N 20 0 E
Ionian Sea **109** 37 30N 17 30 E
Iónioi Nísoi **109** 38 40N 20 8 E
Íos, I. **109** 36 41N 25 20 E
Iowa □ **74** 42 18N 93 30W
Iowa City **76** 41 40N 91 35W
Iowa Falls **76** 42 30N 93 15W
Iowa, R. **76** 41 10N 91 1W
Ipameri **87** 17 44 S 48 9W
Ipiales **86** 0 50N 77 37W
Ipin **129** 28 48N 104 33 E
Ípiros □ **109** 39 30N 20 30 E
Ipixuna **86** 7 0 S 71 40W
Ipoh **128** 4 35N 101 5 E
Ippy **116** 6 5N 21 7 E
Ipswich, Austral. **135** 27 35 S 152 46 E
Ipswich, U.K. **95** 52 4N 1 9 E
Ipswich, N.H., U.S.A. **71** 42 40N 70 50W
Ipswich, S.D., U.S.A. **74** 45 28N 99 20W
Ipu **87** 4 23 S 40 44W
Iquique **86** 20 19 S 70 5W
Iquitos **86** 3 45 S 73 10W
Iracoubo **87** 5 30N 53 10W
Iráklion **109** 35 20N 25 12 E
Irala **89** 25 55 S 54 35W
Iran ■ **123** 33 0N 53 0 E
Iran, Pegunungan **126** 2 20N 114 50 E
Iran, Plateau of **101** 33 00N 55 0 E
Irānshahr **123** 27 75N 60 40 E
Irapa **86** 10 34N 62 35W
Irapuato **82** 20 40N 101 40W
Iraq ■ **122** 33 0N 44 0 E
Irati **89** 25 25 S 50 38W
Irbid **115** 32 35N 35 48 E
Irebu **116** 0 40 S 17 55 E
Ireland ■ **97** 53 0N 8 0W
Ireland's Eye **97** 53 25N 6 4W
Irentala Steppe **130** 43 45N 112 15 E
Iret **121** 60 10N 154 5 E
Irian Jaya □ **127** 4 0 S 137 0 E
Iringa **116** 7 48 S 35 43 E
Iriomote **131** 24 25N 123 58 E
Iriona **84** 15 57N 85 11W
Irish Republic ■ **97** 53 0N 8 0 E
Irish Sea **94** 54 0N 5 0W
Irish Town **124** 40 55 S 145 9 E
Irkutsk **121** 52 10N 104 20 E
Irma **61** 52 55N 111 14W
Irmak **122** 39 58N 33 25 E
Iroise, Mer d' **100** 48 15N 4 45W
Iron Bridge **46** 46 17N 83 14W
Iron Knob **135** 32 46 S 137 8 E
Iron Mountain **72** 45 49N 88 4W
Iron River, Mich., U.S.A. **74** 46 6N 88 40W
Iron River, Wis., U.S.A. **52** 46 34N 91 24W
Iron Springs **61** 49 56N 112 41W
Ironbridge **95** 52 38N 2 29W
Irondale **70** 44 51N 78 30W
Ironside **48** 45 27N 75 45W
Ironton, Mo., U.S.A. **75** 37 40N 90 40W
Ironton, Ohio, U.S.A. **72** 38 35N 82 40W
Ironwood **52** 46 30N 90 10W
Iroquois **47** 44 51N 75 19W
Iroquois Falls **34** 48 46N 80 41W
Iroquois, R. **77** 41 5N 87 49W
Irrawaddy, R. **125** 15 50N 95 6 E
Irshih **130** 47 8N 119 57 E
Irtysh, R. **120** 53 36N 75 30 E
Irumu **116** 1 32N 29 53 E
Irún **104** 43 20N 1 52W
Irvine, Can. **61** 49 57N 110 16W
Irvine, U.K. **96** 55 37N 4 40W
Irvine, U.S.A. **72** 37 42N 83 58W
Irvine, R. **96** 55 35N 4 40W
Irvinestown **97** 54 28N 7 38W
Irvington **77** 37 53N 86 17W
Irymple **136** 34 14 S 142 8 E
Is-sur-Tille **101** 47 30N 5 10 E
Isaac, R. **135** 22 55 S 149 20 E
Isabel **74** 45 27N 101 22W
Isabela, Dom. Rep. **85** 19 58N 71 2W
Isabela, Pto Rico **67** 18 30N 67 01W
Isabela, Cord. **84** 13 30N 85 25W
Isabela, I. **82** 21 51N 105 55W
Isachsen **65** 78 47N 103 30W
Ísafjarðardjúp **110** 66 10N 23 0W
Ísafjörður **110** 66 5N 23 9W
Isangi **116** 0 52N 24 10 E
Isar, R. **106** 48 40N 12 30 E
Isbergues **101** 50 36N 2 24 E
Íschia, I. **108** 40 45N 13 51 E
Iscuandé **86** 2 28N 77 59W
Ise **132** 34 25N 136 45 E
Ise-Wan **132** 34 43N 136 43 E
Isère □ **103** 45 15N 5 40 E
Isère, R. **102** 45 15N 5 30 E
Iserlohn **105** 51 22N 7 40 E
Ishan **130** 24 30N 108 41 E
Ishigaki **131** 24 26N 124 10 E
Ishikari-Wan **132** 43 20N 141 20 E
Ishikawa-ken □ **132** 36 30N 136 30 E
Ishim **120** 56 10N 69 18 E
Ishim, R. **120** 57 45N 71 10 E
Ishinomaki **132** 38 32N 141 20 E
Ishkuman **124** 36 30N 73 50 E
Ishpeming **53** 46 30N 87 40W
Isigny-sur-Mer **100** 49 19N 1 6W
Isil Kul **120** 54 55N 71 16 E
Isili **102** 39 45N 9 6 E
Isiolo **116** 0 24N 37 33 E
Isiro **116** 2 53N 27 58 E
İskenderun **122** 36 32N 36 10 E
Iskut, R. **54** 56 45N 131 49W
Isla, La **86** 6 51N 76 56W
Isla, R. **96** 56 32N 3 20W
Islamabad **124** 33 40N 73 0 E
Island Falls, Can. **53** 49 35N 81 20W
Island Falls, U.S.A. **35** 46 0N 68 25W
Island L., Can. **55** 53 47N 94 25W
Island L., U.S.A. **52** 47 7N 92 10W
Island Pond, Can. **37** 48 25N 56 23W
Island Pond, U.S.A. **71** 44 50N 71 50W
Island, R. **54** 60 25N 121 12W
Islands, B. of, Can. **37** 49 11N 58 15W
Islands, B. of, N.Z. **133** 35 20 S 174 20 E
Islay **60** 53 24N 110 33W
Islay, I. **96** 55 46N 6 10W
Islay Sound **96** 55 45N 6 5W
Isle-Adam, L' **101** 49 6N 2 14 E
Isle aux Morts **37** 47 35N 59 0W
Isle-Jourdain, L', Gers, France **102** 43 36N 1 5 E
Isle-Jourdain, L', Vienne, France **100** 46 13N 0 31 E
Isle L. **60** 53 38N 114 44W
Isle of Wight □ **95** 50 40N 1 20W
Isle Pierre **62** 53 57N 123 16W
Isle Royale **52** 48 0N 88 50W
Isle Royale Nat. Park **52** 48 0N 89 0W
Isle-sur-la-Sorgue, L' **103** 43 55N 5 2 E
Isle Verte, L' **41** 48 1N 69 20W
Isle Vista **81** 34 27N 119 52W
Isles, L. des **52** 49 10N 89 40W
Islet, L' **35** 47 4N 70 23W
Isleta **79** 34 58N 106 46W
Isleton **80** 38 10N 121 37W
Islington **50** 43 38N 79 32W
Ismâ'ilîya **122** 30 37N 32 18 E
Ismay **74** 46 33N 104 44W
Isparta **122** 37 47N 30 30 E
Íspica **108** 36 47N 14 53 E
Israel ■ **115** 32 0N 34 50 E
Issoire **102** 45 32N 3 15 E
Issoudun, Can. **41** 46 35N 71 38W
Issoudun, France **101** 46 57N 2 0 E
Issyk-Kul, Ozero **120** 42 25N 77 15 E
İstanbul **122** 41 0N 29 0 E
Istiaía **86** 38 57N 23 10 E
Istmina **86** 5 10N 76 39W
Istokpoga, L. **73** 27 22N 81 14W
Istra **108** 45 10N 14 0 E
Istres **103** 43 31N 4 59 E
Istria = Istra **108** 45 10N 14 0 E
Itó **88** [illegible] 57 21W
Itabaiana **87** 7 18 S 35 19W
Itaberaba **87** 12 32 S 40 18W
Itabira **87** 19 37 S 43 13W
Itabirito **89** 20 15 S 43 48W
Itabuna **87** 14 48 S 39 16W
Itaete **87** 13 0 S 41 5W
Itaituba **87** 4 10 S 55 50W
Itajaí **89** 27 0 S 48 45W
Itajubá **89** 22 24 S 45 30W
Italy ■ **108** 42 0N 13 0 E
Itambe, mt. **87** 18 30 S 43 15W
Itapecuru, R. **87** 3 20 S 44 15W
Itaperuna **87** 21 10 S 42 0W
Itapetininga **89** 23 36 S 48 7W
Itapeva **89** 23 59 S 48 59W
Itapicuru, R., Bahia, Brazil **87** 10 50 S 38 40W
Itapicuru, R., Maranhão, Brazil **87** 5 40 S 44 30W
Itapuá □ **89** 26 40 S 55 40W
Itaquari **89** 20 12 S 40 25W
Itaquatiana **86** 2 58 S 58 30W
Itaquí **88** 29 0 S 56 30W
Itararé **89** 24 6 S 49 23W
Itatí **88** 27 16 S 58 15W
Itatuba **86** 5 40 S 63 20W
Itbayat I. **131** 20 45N 121 50 E
Itchen, R. **95** 50 57N 1 20W
Ithaca, Mich., U.S.A. **46** 43 18N 84 36W
Ithaca, N.Y., U.S.A. **71** 42 25N 76 30W
Itháki **109** 38 25N 20 43 E
Ito **132** 34 58N 139 5 E
Itomamo, L. **41** 49 11N 70 28W
Itoman **131** 26 7N 127 40 E
Itonamas, R. **86** 13 0 S 64 25W
Itu **89** 23 10 S 47 15W
Ituaçu **87** 13 50 S 41 18W
Ituango **86** 7 4N 75 45W
Ituiutaba **87** 19 0 S 49 25W
Ituliho **129** 50 40N 121 30 E
Itumbiara **87** 18 20 S 49 10W
Ituna **56** 51 10N 103 30W
Itung **130** 43 25N 125 21 E
Iturbe **88** 23 0 S 65 25W
Iturup, Ostrov **121** 45 0N 148 0 E
Ituyuro, R. **88** 22 40 S 63 50W
Iuka **77** 38 37N 88 47W
Ivalo **110** 68 38N 27 35 E
Ivalojoki **110** 68 30N 27 0 E
Ivanhoe, Austral. **136** 32 56 S 144 20 E
Ivanhoe, U.S.A. **80** 36 23N 119 13W
Ivanhoe L. **55** 60 25N 106 30W
Ivano-Frankovsk, (Stanislav) **120** 49 0N 24 40 E
Ivanovo **120** 52 7N 25 29 E
Ivinheima, R. **89** 21 48 S 54 15W
Iviza = Ibiza **104** 39 0N 1 30 E
Ivory Coast ■ **114** 7 30N 5 0W
Ivrea **108** 45 30N 7 52 E
Ivugivik, (N.D. d'Ivugivic) **36** 62 24N 77 55W
Iwahig **126** 8 35N 117 32 E
Iwakuni **132** 34 15N 132 8 E
Iwata **132** 34 49N 137 59 E
Iwate-ken □ **132** 39 30N 141 30 E
Iwo **114** 7 39N 4 9 E
Ixiamas **86** 13 50 S 68 5W
Ixtepec **83** 16 40N 95 10W
Ixtlán de Juárez **83** 17 23N 96 28W
Ixtlán del Rio **82** 21 5N 104 28W
Iyang **131** 28 36N 112 20 E
Izabal, L. **84** 15 30N 89 10W
Izamal **83** 20 56N 89 1W
Izegem **105** 50 55N 3 12 E
Izhevsk **120** 56 51N 53 14 E
Izmail **120** 45 22N 28 46 E
İzmir (Smyrna) **122** 38 25N 27 8 E
İzmit **122** 40 45N 29 50 E
Izumisano **132** 34 40N 135 43 E
Izumo **132** 35 20N 132 55 E

J

Jaab L. **53** 51 10N 82 58W
Jabalpur **124** 23 9N 79 58 E
Jablah **122** 35 20N 36 0 E
Jablanica, Mt. **109** 41 20N 20 30 E
Jablonec **106** 50 43N 15 10 E
Jaboticabal **89** 21 15 S 48 17W
Jaburu **86** 5 30 S 64 0W
Jaca **104** 42 35N 0 33W
Jacala **83** 21 1N 99 11W
Jacareí **89** 23 20 S 46 0W
Jacarèzinho **89** 23 5 S 50 0W
Jáchal **88** 30 5 S 69 0W
Jack Lane B. **35** 55 45N 60 35W
Jackfish **34** 48 45N 87 0W
Jackfish L. **56** 53 9N 108 29W
Jackman **35** 45 35N 70 17W
Jacksboro **75** 33 14N 98 15W
Jackson, Ala., U.S.A. **73** 31 32N 87 53W
Jackson, Calif., U.S.A. **80** 38 25N 120 47W
Jackson, Ky., U.S.A. **72** 37 35N 83 22W
Jackson, Mich., U.S.A. **77** 42 18N 84 25W
Jackson, Minn., U.S.A. **74** 43 35N 95 0W
Jackson, Miss., U.S.A. **75** 32 20N 90 10W
Jackson, Mo., U.S.A. **75** 37 23N 89 42W
Jackson, Ohio, U.S.A. **72** 39 0N 82 40W
Jackson, Tenn., U.S.A. **73** 35 40N 88 50W
Jackson, Wyo., U.S.A. **78** 43 30N 110 49W
Jackson Bay, Can. **54** 50 32N 125 57W
Jackson Bay, N.Z. **133** 43 58 S 168 42 E
Jackson Center **77** 40 27N 84 4W
Jackson, L. **78** 43 55N 110 40W
Jacksons **133** 42 46 S 171 32 E
Jackson's Arm **37** 49 52N 56 47W
Jacksonville, Ala., U.S.A. **73** 33 49N 85 45W
Jacksonville, Calif., U.S.A. **80** 37 52N 120 24W
Jacksonville, Fla., U.S.A. **73** 30 15N 81 38W
Jacksonville, Ill., U.S.A. **76** 39 42N 90 15W
Jacksonville, N.C., U.S.A. **73** 34 50N 77 29W
Jacksonville, Oreg., U.S.A. **78** 42 13N 122 56W
Jacksonville, Tex., U.S.A. **75** 31 58N 95 12W
Jacksonville Beach **73** 30 19N 81 26W
Jacmel **85** 18 20N 72 40W

Jacob Lake Jundiaí

Place	Page	Lat.	Long.
Jacob Lake	79	36 45N	112 12W
Jacobabad	124	28 20N	68 29 E
Jacobina	87	11 11 S	40 30W
Jacobs	52	50 15N	89 50W
Jacques-Cartier	41	45 31N	73 29W
Jacques Cartier, Dét. de	36	50 0N	63 30W
Jacques-Cartier, L.	41	47 35N	71 13W
Jacques-Cartier, Mt.	38	48 57N	66 0W
Jacques Cartier Pass	35	49 50N	62 30W
Jacques-Cartier, R.	41	46 40N	71 45W
Jacquet River	39	47 55N	66 0W
Jacuí, R.	89	30 2 S	51 15W
Jacuipe, R.	87	12 30 S	39 5W
Jacumba	81	32 37N	116 11W
Jacundá, R.	87	1 57 S	50 26W
Jaén, Peru	86	5 25 S	78 40W
Jaén, Spain	104	37 44N	3 43W
Jaffna	124	9 45N	80 2 E
Jagadhri	124	30 10N	77 20 E
Jagdalpur	125	19 3N	82 6 E
Jagersfontein	117	29 44 S	25 27 E
Jagraon	124	30 50N	75 25 E
Jagtial	124	18 50N	79 0 E
Jaguariaíva	89	24 10 S	49 50W
Jaguaribe, R.	87	6 0 S	38 35W
Jagüey	84	22 35N	81 7W
Jagungal, Mt.	136	36 12 S	148 28 E
Jahrom	122	28 30N	53 31 E
Jainti	125	26 45N	89 40 E
Jaipur	124	27 0N	76 10 E
Jakarta	127	6 9 S	106 49 E
Jakobshavn	65	68 0N	51 0W
Jakobstad (Pietarsaari)	110	63 40N	22 43 E
Jal	75	32 8N	103 8W
Jala	123	27 30N	62 40 E
Jalalabad	124	34 30N	70 29 E
Jalama	81	34 29N	120 29W
Jalapa, Guat.	84	14 45N	89 59W
Jalapa, Mexico	83	19 30N	96 50W
Jalas, Jabal al	122	27 30N	36 30 E
Jalgaon, Maharashtra, India	124	21 2N	76 31 E
Jalgaon, Maharashtra, India	124	21 0N	75 42 E
Jalisco □	82	20 0N	104 0W
Jalna	124	19 48N	75 57 E
Jalón, R.	104	41 20N	1 40W
Jalpa	82	21 38N	102 58W
Jalpaiguri	125	26 32N	88 46 E
Jalq	123	27 35N	62 33 E
Jaluit I.	14	6 0N	169 30 E
Jamaica	76	41 51N	94 18W
Jamaica, I. ■	84	18 10N	77 30W
Jamalpur, Bangla.	125	24 52N	90 2 E
Jamalpur, India	125	25 18N	86 28 E
Jamanxim, R.	87	6 30 S	55 50W
Jambe	127	1 15 S	132 10 E
Jambi	126	1 38 S	103 30 E
Jamdena, I. = Yamdena	127	7 45 S	131 20 E
James B.	53	51 30N	80 0W
James, R.	74	44 50N	98 0W
James Ranges	134	24 10 S	132 0 E
James River	39	45 35N	62 7W
James Ross I.	91	63 58 S	50 94W
Jameson, C.	65	72 5N	74 14W
Jamesport	76	39 58N	93 48W
Jamestown, Austral.	135	33 10 S	138 32 E
Jamestown, Ind., U.S.A.	77	39 56N	86 38W
Jamestown, Ky., U.S.A.	72	37 0N	85 5W
Jamestown, Mo., U.S.A.	76	38 48N	92 30W
Jamestown, N.D., U.S.A.	74	47 0N	98 45W
Jamestown, N.Y., U.S.A.	70	42 5N	79 18W
Jamestown, Ohio, U.S.A.	77	39 39N	83 44W
Jamestown, Penn., U.S.A.	70	41 22N	80 27W
Jamestown, Tenn., U.S.A.	73	36 25N	85 0W
Jamiltepec	83	16 17N	97 49W
Jamkhandi	124	16 30N	75 15 E
Jammu	124	32 43N	74 54 E
Jammu & Kashmir □	124	34 25N	77 0 E
Jamnagar	124	22 30N	70 0 E
Jamshedpur	125	22 44N	86 20 E
Jämtlands län □	110	62 40N	13 50 E
Jan L.	55	54 56N	102 55W
Jan Mayen Is.	17	71 0N	11 0W
Jand	124	33 30N	72 0 E
Jandaq	122	34 3N	54 22 E
Janesville	76	42 39N	89 1W
Jani Khel	123	32 45N	68 25 E
Janos	82	30 45N	108 10W
Jansen	56	51 54N	104 45W
Januária	87	15 25 S	44 25W
Janville	101	48 10N	1 50 E
Janzé	100	47 55N	1 28W
Jaoho	130	47 12N	134 15 E
Jaora	124	23 40N	75 10 E
Japan ■	132	36 0N	136 0 E
Japan, Sea of	132	40 0N	135 0 E
Japara	127	6 30 S	110 40 E
Japen, I. = Yapen	127	1 50 S	136 0 E
Japurá	86	1 48 S	66 30W
Japurá, R.	86	3 8 S	64 46W
Jaque	86	7 27N	78 15W
Jaques-Cartier, Détroit de	38	50 0N	63 30W
Jara, La	79	37 16N	106 0W
Jarales	79	34 39N	106 51W
Jarama, R.	104	40 50N	3 20W
Jarbridge	78	41 56N	115 27W
Jardim	88	21 28 S	56 9W
Jardines de la Reina, Is.	84	20 50N	78 50W
Jargalant	130	47 2N	115 1 E
Jargalant (Kobdo)	129	48 0N	91 43 E
Jargeau	101	47 50N	2 7 E
Jarjarni	123	37 5N	56 20 E
Jarnac	102	45 40N	0 11W
Jarny	101	49 9N	5 53 E
Jarosław	107	50 2N	22 42 E
Jarvis	46	42 53N	80 6W
Jarvis I.	15	0 15 S	159 55W
Jarvis River	52	48 7N	89 21W
Jarwa	125	27 45N	82 30 E
Jasin	128	2 20N	102 26 E
Jāsk	123	25 38N	57 45 E
Jasło	107	49 45N	21 30 E
Jasonville	77	39 10N	87 13W
Jasper, Alta., Can.	61	52 55N	118 5W
Jasper, Ont., Can.	47	44 50N	75 56W
Jasper, Ont., Can.	71	44 52N	75 57W
Jasper, Ala., U.S.A.	73	33 48N	87 16W
Jasper, Fla., U.S.A.	73	30 31N	82 58W
Jasper, Ind., U.S.A.	77	38 24N	86 56W
Jasper, La., U.S.A.	75	30 59N	93 58W
Jasper, Minn., U.S.A.	74	43 52N	96 22W
Jasper Nat. Park	61	52 50N	118 8W
Jasper Place	54	53 33N	113 25W
Jászberény	107	47 30N	19 55 E
Jataí	87	17 50 S	51 45W
Jatibarang	127	6 28 S	108 18 E
Jatinegara	127	6 13 S	106 52 E
Játiva	104	39 0N	0 32W
Jatobal	87	4 35 S	49 33W
Jaú	89	22 10 S	48 30W
Jauja	86	11 45 S	75 30W
Jaunpur	125	25 46N	82 44 E
Java = Jawa	127	7 0 S	110 0 E
Java Sea	126	4 35 S	107 15 E
Javhlant = Ulyasutay	129	47 42N	13 10 E
Javron	100	48 25N	0 25W
Jawa	127	7 0 S	110 0 E
Jay	75	36 17N	94 46W
Jayapura	127	2 28 S	140 38 E
Jayawijaya, Pengunungan	127	7 0 S	139 0 E
Jaydot	55	49 15N	110 15W
Jaynagar	125	26 43N	86 9 E
Jayton	75	33 17N	100 35W
Jazminal	82	24 56N	101 25W
Jean	81	35 47N	115 20W
Jean Marie River	54	61 32N	120 38W
Jean Rabel	85	19 50N	73 30W
Jeanerette	75	29 52N	91 38W
Jeanette L.	52	51 5N	92 5W
Jeanne-d'Arc	48	45 32N	75 38W
Jeannette	70	40 20N	79 36W
Jedburgh	96	55 28N	2 33W
Jedrzejów	107	50 35N	20 15 E
Jedway	62	52 17N	131 14W
Jefferson, Iowa, U.S.A.	76	42 3N	94 25W
Jefferson, Ohio, U.S.A.	70	41 40N	80 46W
Jefferson, Tex., U.S.A.	75	32 45N	94 23W
Jefferson, Wis., U.S.A.	77	43 0N	88 49W
Jefferson City, Mo., U.S.A.	76	38 34N	92 10W
Jefferson City, Tenn., U.S.A.	73	36 8N	83 30W
Jefferson, Mt., Nev., U.S.A.	78	38 51N	117 0W
Jefferson, Mt., Oreg., U.S.A.	78	44 45N	121 50W
Jeffersontown	77	38 17N	85 44W
Jeffersonville, Ind., U.S.A.	77	38 20N	85 42W
Jeffersonville, Ohio, U.S.A.	77	39 38N	83 34W
Jega	114	12 15N	4 23 E
Jelenia Góra	106	50 50N	15 45 E
Jelgava	111	56 41N	22 49 E
Jellicoe	53	49 40N	87 30W
Jemaja	126	3 5N	105 45 E
Jemappes	105	50 27N	3 54 E
Jember	127	8 11 S	113 41 E
Jembongan, I.	126	6 45N	117 20 E
Jemeppe	105	50 37N	5 30 E
Jemseg	39	45 50N	66 7W
Jena, Ger.	106	50 56N	11 33 E
Jena, U.S.A.	75	31 41N	92 7W
Jenhwai	131	28 5N	106 10 E
Jenin	115	32 28N	35 18 E
Jenkins	72	37 13N	82 41W
Jenner	80	38 27N	123 7W
Jennings, La., U.S.A.	75	30 10N	92 45W
Jennings, Mo., U.S.A.	76	38 43N	90 16W
Jennings, R.	54	59 38N	132 5W
Jequié	87	13 51 S	40 5W
Jequitinhonha	87	16 30 S	41 0W
Jequitinhonha, R.	87	15 51 S	38 53W
Jerantut	128	3 56N	102 22 E
Jérémie	85	18 40N	74 10W
Jerez de García Salinas	82	22 39N	103 0W
Jerez de la Frontera	104	36 41N	6 7W
Jerez de los Caballeros	104	38 20N	6 45W
Jerez, Punta	83	22 58N	97 40W
Jerico Springs	76	37 37N	94 1W
Jerilderie	136	35 20 S	145 41 E
Jermyn	71	41 31N	75 31W
Jerome, Can.	53	47 37N	82 14W
Jerome, U.S.A.	79	34 50N	112 0W
Jersey City	71	40 41N	74 8W
Jersey, I.	100	49 13N	2 7W
Jersey Shore	70	41 17N	77 18W
Jerseyside	37	47 16N	53 58W
Jerseyville, Can.	49	43 12N	80 7W
Jerseyville, U.S.A.	76	39 5N	90 20W
Jerusalem	115	31 47N	35 10 E
Jervis B.	136	35 8 S	150 46 E
Jervis Inlet	62	50 0N	123 57W
Jesselton = Kota Kinabalu	126	6 0N	116 12 E
Jessore	125	23 10N	89 10 E
Jesup, U.S.A.	73	31 30N	82 0W
Jesup, U.S.A.	76	42 29N	92 4W
Jesús Carranza	83	17 28N	95 1W
Jesus, Île	44	45 35N	73 45W
Jesús María	88	30 59 S	64 5W
Jetmore	75	38 10N	99 57W
Jewell	76	42 20N	93 39W
Jewett, Ohio, U.S.A.	70	40 22N	81 2W
Jewett, Tex., U.S.A.	75	31 20N	96 8W
Jewett City	71	41 36N	72 0W
Jeypore	125	18 50N	82 38 E
Jhal Jhao	124	26 20N	65 35 E
Jhalawar	124	24 35N	76 10 E
Jhang Maghiana	124	31 15N	72 15 E
Jhansi	124	25 30N	78 36 E
Jharsaguda	125	21 50N	84 5 E
Jhelum	124	33 0N	73 45 E
Jhelum, R.	124	31 50N	72 10 E
Jhunjhunu	124	28 10N	75 20 E
Jicarón, I.	84	7 10N	81 50W
Jiddah	122	21 29N	39 16 E
Jido	125	29 2N	94 58 E
Jihchao	131	35 18N	119 28 E
Jihlava	106	49 28N	15 35 E
Jihlava R.	106	49 21N	15 38 E
Jiloca, R.	104	41 0N	1 20W
Jima	115	7 40N	36 55 E
Jiménez	82	27 10N	105 0W
Jindabyne	136	36 25 S	148 35 E
Jindabyne L.	136	36 20N	148 38 E
Jinja	116	0 25N	33 12 E
Jinnah Barrage	124	32 58N	71 33 E
Jinné	130	51 32N	121 25 E
Jinotega	84	13 6N	85 59W
Jinotepe	84	11 50N	86 10W
Jiparaná (Machado), R.	86	8 45 S	62 20W
Jipijapa	86	1 0 S	80 40W
Jiquilpán	82	19 57N	102 42W
Jis rash Shughur	122	35 49N	36 18 E
Jitra	128	6 16N	100 25 E
Jiu, R.	107	44 50N	23 20 E
Joaçaba	89	27 5 S	51 31W
João de Almeida	117	15 10 S	13 50 E
João Pessoa	87	7 10 S	34 52W
Joaquín V. González	88	25 10 S	64 0W
Jobourg, Nez de	100	49 41N	1 57W
Jodhpur	124	26 23N	73 2 E
Joe Batt's Arm	37	49 44N	54 10W
Jœuf	101	49 12N	6 1 E
Jofane	117	21 15 S	34 18 E
Joffre, Mt.	61	50 32N	115 13W
Joggins	39	45 42N	64 27W
Jogjakarta = Yogyakarta	127	7 49 S	110 22 E
Jogues, Ont., Can.	53	49 36N	83 45W
Jogues, Qué., Can.	43	45 29N	72 49W
Johannesburg, S. Afr.	117	26 10 S	28 8 E
Johannesburg, U.S.A.	81	35 22N	117 38W
John Days, R.	78	45 0N	120 0W
John o' Groats	96	58 39N	3 3W
Johnnie	81	36 25N	116 5W
Johnson	75	37 35N	101 48W
Johnson City, Ill., U.S.A.	76	37 49N	88 56W
Johnson City, Tenn., U.S.A.	73	36 18N	82 21W
Johnson City, Tex., U.S.A.	75	30 15N	98 24W
Johnson Cy.	71	42 9N	67 0W
Johnsonburg	70	41 30N	78 40W
Johnsondale	81	35 58N	118 32W
Johnson's Crossing	54	60 29N	133 18W
Johnston I.	15	17 10N	169 8 E
Johnston Lakes	134	32 20 S	120 45 E
Johnstone Str.	62	50 28N	126 0W
Johnstown, N.Y., U.S.A.	71	43 1N	74 20W
Johnstown, Pa., U.S.A.	70	40 19N	78 53W
Johor □	128	2 5N	103 20 E
Johor Baharu	128	1 45N	103 47 E
Joigny	101	48 0N	3 20 E
Joinvile	89	26 15 S	48 55 E
Joinville	101	48 27N	5 10 E
Joinville I.	91	63 15N	55 30W
Joir, R.	38	51 59N	60 12W
Jojutla	83	18 37N	99 11W
Jokkmokk	110	66 35N	19 50 E
Jökulsá á Brú	110	65 40N	14 16W
Jökulsá! Fjöllum	110	65 30N	16 15W
Jökulsa R.	110	65 30N	16 15W
Jolan	80	35 58N	121 9W
Joliet	77	41 30N	88 0W
Joliette	41	46 3N	73 24W
Joliette, Parc. Prov. de	41	46 30N	74 0W
Jolo I.	127	6 0N	121 0 E
Jome, I.	127	1 16 S	127 30 E
Jones C.	34	54 33N	79 35W
Jones Sound	65	76 0N	89 0W
Jonesboro, Ark., U.S.A.	75	35 50N	90 45W
Jonesboro, Ill., U.S.A.	75	37 26N	89 18W
Jonesboro, La., U.S.A.	75	32 15N	92 41W
Jonesburg	76	38 51N	91 18W
Jonesport	35	44 32N	67 38W
Jonesville, Ind., U.S.A.	77	39 5N	85 54W
Jonesville, Mich, U.S.A.	77	41 59N	84 40W
Jönköping	111	57 45N	14 10 E
Jönköpings län □	111	57 30N	14 30 E
Jonquière	41	48 27N	71 14W
Jonzac	102	45 27N	0 28W
Joplin	75	37 0N	94 25W
Jordan, Phil.	127	10 41N	122 38 E
Jordan, U.S.A.	78	47 25N	106 58W
Jordan ■	122	31 0N	36 0 E
Jordan Falls	39	43 49N	65 14W
Jordan Harbour	49	43 11N	79 23W
Jordan, L.	39	44 5N	65 14W
Jordan, R.	115	32 10N	35 32 E
Jordan Valley	78	43 0N	117 2W
Jorhat	125	26 45N	94 20 E
Jörn	110	65 4N	20 1 E
Jorquera, R.	88	28 3 S	69 58W
Jos	114	9 53N	8 51 E
José Batlle y OrdóPez	89	33 20 S	55 10W
Joseph	78	45 27N	117 13W
Joseph City	79	35 0N	110 16W
Joseph, L.	46	45 10N	79 44W
Joseph, Lac	38	52 45N	65 18W
Joseph, Petit lac	38	52 36N	65 5W
Joshua Tree	81	34 8N	116 19W
Joshua Tree Nat. Mon.	81	33 56N	116 5W
Josselin	100	47 57N	2 33W
Jostedal	111	61 35N	7 15 E
Jotunheimen	111	61 35N	8 25 E
Jounieh	122	33 59N	35 30 E
Jourdanton	75	28 54N	98 32W
Joussard	60	55 22N	115 57W
Jouzjan □	123	36 10N	66 0 E
Jovellanos	84	22 40N	81 10W
Joy B.	36	61 30N	72 0W
Joyeuse	103	44 29N	4 16 E
Juan Aldama	82	24 20N	103 23W
Juan Bautista	79	36 55N	121 33W
Juan Bautista Alberdi	88	34 26 S	61 48W
Juan de Fuca Str.	80	48 15N	124 0W
Juan de Nova, I.	117	17 3 S	42 45 E
Juan Fernández, Arch. de	15	33 50 S	80 0W
Juan José Castelli	88	25 27 S	60 37W
Juan L. Lacaze	88	34 26 S	57 25W
Juan Perez Sd.	62	52 32N	131 30W
Juárez, Argent.	88	37 40 S	59 43W
Juárez, Mexico	82	27 37N	100 44W
Juárez, U.S.A.	81	32 20N	115 57W
Juárez, Sierra de	82	32 0N	116 0W
Juàzeiro	87	9 30 S	40 30W
Juàzeiro do Norte	87	7 10 S	39 18W
Jûbâ	115	4 57N	31 35 E
Juba, R.	115	1 30N	42 35 E
Jubaila	122	24 55N	46 25 E
Jubilee L.	37	48 3N	55 11W
Juby, C.	114	28 0N	12 59W
Júcar, R.	104	40 8N	2 13W
Júcaro	84	21 37N	78 51W
Juchitán	83	16 27N	95 5W
Judaea = Yehuda	115	31 35N	34 57 E
Jude I.	37	47 15N	54 49W
Judique	39	45 52N	61 30W
Judith Gap	78	46 48N	109 46W
Judith Pt.	71	41 20N	71 30W
Judith, R.	78	47 30N	109 30W
Juian	131	27 45N	120 38 E
Juigalpa	84	12 6N	85 26W
Juillac	102	45 20N	1 19 E
Juiz de Fora	87	21 43 S	43 19W
Jujuy	88	24 10 S	65 25W
Jujuy □	88	23 20 S	65 40W
Jukao	131	32 24N	120 35 E
Julesberg	74	41 0N	102 20W
Juli	86	16 10 S	69 25W
Julia Creek	135	20 39 S	141 44 E
Juliaca	86	15 25 S	70 10W
Julian	81	33 4N	116 38W
Julian L.	36	54 25N	77 57W
Julianehåb	17	60 43N	46 0W
Julimes	82	28 25N	105 27W
Jullundur	124	31 20N	75 40 E
Jumbo Pk.	81	36 12N	114 11W
Jumento, Cayos	85	23 0N	75 40 E
Jumet	105	50 27N	4 25 E
Jumilla	104	38 28N	1 19W
Jumla	125	29 15N	82 13 E
Jumna, R. = Yamuna	125	27 0N	78 30 E
Junagadh	124	21 30N	70 30 E
Junction, Tex., U.S.A.	75	30 29N	99 48W
Junction, Utah, U.S.A.	79	38 10N	112 15W
Junction B.	134	11 52 S	133 55 E
Junction City, Kans., U.S.A.	74	39 4N	96 55W
Junction City, Oreg., U.S.A.	78	44 20N	123 12W
Jundah	135	24 46 S	143 2 E
Jundiaí	89	23 10 S	47 0W

Kashabowie **Kiangyin**

Kashabowie **52** 48 40N 90 26W
Kāshān **123** 34 5N 51 30 E
Kashgar **129** 39 46N 75 52 E
Kashing **131** 30 45N 120 41 E
Kaskaskia, R. **76** 37 58N 89 57W
Kaskattama, R. **55** 57 3N 90 4W
Kaskinen (Kaskö) **110** 62 22N 21 15 E
Kaskö (Kaskinen) **110** 62 22N 21 15 E
Kaslo **63** 49 55N 116 55W
Kasmere L. **55** 59 34N 101 10W
Kasongo **116** 4 30S 26 33 E
Kasongo Lunda **116** 6 35S 17 0 E
Kásos, I. **109** 35 20N 26 55 E
Kassala **115** 15 23N 36 26 E
Kassala □ **116** 15 20N 36 26 E
Kassel **106** 51 19N 9 32 E
Kassue **127** 6 58S 139 21 E
Kastamonu **122** 41 25N 33 43 E
Kastoria **109** 40 30N 21 19 E
Kasulu **116** 4 37S 30 5 E
Kasur **124** 31 5N 74 25 E
Kata **121** 58 46N 102 40 E
Katako Kombe **116** 3 25S 24 20 E
Katalla **67** 60 10N 144 35W
Katangi **124** 21 56N 79 50 E
Katangli **121** 51 42N 143 14 E
Katanning **134** 33 40S 117 33 E
Katha **125** 24 10N 96 30 E
Katherina, Gebel **115** 28 30N 33 57 E
Katherine **134** 14 27S 132 20 E
Kathiawar, dist. **124** 22 20N 71 0 E
Katiet **126** 2 21S 99 44 E
Katihar **125** 25 34N 87 36 E
Katima Mulilo **117** 17 28S 24 13 E
Katimik L. **57** 52 53N 99 21W
Katmai Nat. Monument **67** 58 30N 155 0W
Katmai, vol. **67** 58 20N 154 59W
Katmandu **125** 27 45N 85 12 E
Katompi **116** 6 2S 26 23 E
Katoomba **136** 33 41S 150 19 E
Katowice **107** 50 17N 19 5 E
Katrine L. **96** 56 15N 4 30W
Katrineholm **111** 59 9N 16 12 E
Katsina **114** 7 10N 9 20 E
Katsuura **132** 35 15N 140 20 E
Kattawaz **124** 32 48N 68 23 E
Kattawaz-Urgun □ **124** 32 10N 68 20 E
Kattegat **111** 57 0N 11 20 E
Katwijk-aan-Zee **105** 52 12N 4 24 E
Kau Tao **128** 10 6N 99 48 E
Kauai Chan. **67** 21 45N 158 50W
Kauai, I. **67** 19 30N 155 30W
Kaufman **75** 32 35N 96 20W
Kaukauna **72** 44 20N 88 13W
Kaukonen **110** 67 31N 24 53 E
Kauliranta **110** 66 27N 23 41 E
Kaunas **120** 54 54N 23 54 E
Kaupulehu **67** 19 43N 155 53W
Kautokeino **110** 69 0N 23 4 E
Kavacha **121** 60 16N 169 51 E
Kavali **124** 14 55N 80 1 E
Kaválla **109** 40 57N 24 28 E
Kavanayén **86** 5 38N 61 48W
Kaw = Caux **87** 4 30N 52 15W
Kawagama L., Can. **70** 45 18N 78 45W
Kawagama L., Ont., Can. **47** 45 18N 78 45W
Kawagoe **132** 35 55N 139 29 E
Kawaguchi **132** 35 52N 138 45 E
Kawaihae **67** 20 3N 155 50W
Kawaihoa Pt. **67** 21 47N 160 12W
Kawaikini, Mt. **67** 22 0N 159 30W
Kawambwa **116** 9 48S 29 3 E
Kawana **132** 35 5N 135 27 E
Kawardha **125** 22 0N 81 17 E
Kawasaki **132** 35 35N 138 42 E
Kawene **52** 48 45N 91 15W
Kawerau **133** 38 7S 176 42 E
Kawhia Harbour **133** 38 5S 174 51 E
Kawinawl **57** 52 50N 99 30W
Kawthaung **128** 10 5N 98 36 E
Kawthoolei □ = Kawthuk **125** 18 0N 97 30 E
Kawthuk □ **125** 18 0N 97 30 E
Kayah □ **125** 19 15N 97 15 E
Kayak I. **67** 60 0N 144 30W
Kaycee **78** 43 45N 106 46W
Kayenta **79** 36 46N 110 15W
Kayes **114** 14 25N 11 30W
Kayseri **122** 38 45N 35 30 E
Kaysville **78** 41 2N 111 58W
Kazachinskoye **121** 56 16N 107 36 E
Kazachye **121** 70 52N 135 58 E
Kazakh S.S.R. □ ♦ **120** 50 0N 58 0 E
Kazan **120** 55 48N 49 3 E
Kazan, R. **55** 64 2N 95 30W
Kazanluk **109** 42 38N 25 35 E
Kāzerūn **123** 29 38N 51 40 E
Kazumba **116** 6 25S 22 5 E
Kazvin **122** 36 15N 50 0 E
Kazym, R. **120** 63 40N 68 30 E
Kéa **109** 37 35N 24 22 E
Keaau **67** 19 37N 155 3W
Keams Canyon **79** 35 53N 110 9W
Keanae **67** 20 52N 156 9W
Kearney, Can. **46** 45 33N 79 13W
Kearney, U.S.A. **76** 39 22N 94 22W
Kearney, Nebr., U.S.A. **74** 40 45N 99 3W
Keban **122** 38 50N 38 50 E
Kebnekaise, mt. **110** 67 54N 18 33 E
Kebumen **127** 7 42S 109 40 E
Kechika, R. **54** 59 41N 127 12W
Kecskemét **107** 46 57N 19 35 E
Kedah □ **128** 5 50N 100 40 E
Kedgwick **39** 47 40N 67 20W
Kediri **127** 7 51S 112 1 E
Keefers **54** 50 0N 121 40W
Keele, R. **67** 64 15N 127 0W
Keeler **80** 36 29N 117 52W
Keeley L. **55** 54 54N 108 8W
Keeling Is. = Cocos Is. **16** 12 12S 96 54 E
Keelung = Chilung **131** 25 3N 121 45 E
Keene, Can. **47** 44 15N 78 10W
Keene, Calif., U.S.A. **81** 35 13N 118 33W
Keene, N.H., U.S.A. **71** 42 57N 72 17W
Keeper, Mt. **97** 52 46N 8 17W
Keer-Weer, C. **135** 14 0S 141 32 E
Keeseville **71** 44 29N 73 30W
Keetmanshoop **117** 26 35S 18 8 E
Keewatin, Can. **52** 49 46N 94 34W
Keewatin, U.S.A. **52** 47 23N 93 0W
Keewatin □ **55** 63 20N 94 40W
Keewatin, R. **55** 56 29N 100 46W
Keezhik L. **52** 51 45N 88 30W
Kefallinía, I. **109** 38 28N 20 30 E
Kefamenanu **127** 9 28S 124 38 E
Keflavík **110** 64 2N 22 35W
Keg River **54** 57 54N 117 7W
Kegashka **38** 50 9N 61 18W
Kégashka, L. **38** 50 20N 61 25W
Keglo, B. **36** 58 40N 66 0W
Keighley **94** 53 52N 1 54W
Keith **96** 57 33N 2 58W
Keith Arm **64** 64 20N 122 15W
Keithsburg **76** 41 6N 90 56W
Kejimkujik Nat. Park **39** 44 25N 65 25W
Kekri **124** 26 0N 75 10 E
Kël **121** 69 30N 124 10 E
Kelang **128** 3 2N 101 26 E
Kelantan □ **128** 5 10N 102 0 E
Kelantan, R. **128** 6 13N 102 14 E
Kellé **116** 0 8S 14 38 E
Keller **78** 48 2N 118 44W
Kellerberrin **134** 31 36S 117 38 E
Kellett C. **64** 72 0N 126 0W
Kellett Str. **64** 75 45N 117 30W
Kelleys I. **70** 41 35N 82 42W
Kelligrews **37** 47 30N 53 1W
Kelliher **56** 51 16N 103 44W
Kellogg **78** 47 30N 116 5W
Kelloselkä **110** 66 56N 28 53 E
Kells = Ceanannas Mor **97** 53 42N 6 53W
Kelowna **63** 49 50N 119 25W
Kelsey Bay **62** 50 25N 126 0W
Kelseyville **80** 38 59N 122 50W
Kelso, N.Z. **133** 45 54S 169 15 E
Kelso, U.K. **96** 55 36N 2 27W
Kelso, U.S.A. **80** 46 10N 122 57W
Keluang **128** 2 3N 103 18 E
Kelvin I. **52** 49 51N 88 40W
Kelvington **56** 52 10N 103 30W
Kelwood **57** 50 37N 99 28W
Kem **120** 65 0N 34 38 E
Kema **127** 1 22N 125 8 E
Kemah **122** 39 32N 39 5 E
Kemano **62** 53 35N 128 0W
Kemerovo **120** 55 20N 85 50 E
Kemi **110** 65 44N 24 34 E
Kemi älv = Kemijoki **110** 65 47N 24 32 E
Kemijärvi **110** 66 43N 27 22 E
Kemijoki **110** 65 47N 24 32 E
Kemmerer **78** 41 52N 110 30W
Kemmuna = Comino, I. **108** 36 0N 14 20 E
Kemp Coast **91** 69 0S 55 0 E
Kemp L. **75** 33 45N 99 15W
Kempsey **135** 31 1S 152 50 E
Kempt, L. **41** 47 25N 74 22W
Kempten **106** 47 42N 10 18 E
Kempton **77** 40 56N 86 14W
Kemptown **39** 45 28N 63 5W
Kemptville **47** 45 0N 75 38W
Ken L. **96** 55 0N 4 8W
Kenai **67** 60 35N 151 20W
Kenai Mts. **67** 60 0N 150 0W
Kenaston **56** 51 30N 106 17W
Kendal, Indon. **127** 6 56S 110 14 E
Kendal, U.K. **94** 54 19N 2 44W
Kendall **136** 31 35S 152 44 E
Kendallville **77** 41 25N 85 15W
Kendari **127** 3 50S 122 30 E
Kendawangan **126** 2 32S 110 17 E
Kendrapara **125** 20 35N 86 30 E
Kendrick **78** 46 43N 116 41W
Keng Tawng **125** 20 45N 98 18 E
Keng Tung **125** 21 0N 99 30 E
Kenge **116** 4 50S 16 55 E
Kenhardt **117** 29 19S 21 12 E
Kenho **130** 50 43N 121 30 E
Kenitra **114** 34 15N 6 40W
Kenmare, Ireland **97** 51 52N 9 35W
Kenmare, U.S.A. **74** 48 40N 102 4W
Kenmare, R. **97** 51 40N 10 0W
Kenmore **136** 34 44S 149 45 E
Kenn Reef **135** 21 12S 155 46 E
Kennaway **70** 45 9N 78 11W
Kennebec **74** 43 56N 99 54W
Kennebecasis, R. **39** 45 19N 66 4W
Kennedy, B.C., Can. **66** 49 10N 122 53W
Kennedy, Sask., Can. **57** 50 1N 102 21W
Kennedy I. **62** 54 3N 130 11W
Kennedy L. **62** 49 3N 125 32W
Kennedy, Mt. **64** 81 2N 78 55W
Kennedy Taungdeik **125** 23 35N 94 4 E
Kennet, R. **95** 51 24N 1 7W
Kennetcook **39** 45 11N 63 44W
Kennett **75** 36 7N 90 0W
Kennewick **78** 46 11N 119 2W
Keno Hill **96** 63 57N 135 18W
Kénogami **41** 48 25N 71 15W
Kénogami, L. **41** 48 20N 71 23W
Kenogami, R. **53** 51 6N 84 28W
Kenora **52** 49 47N 94 29W
Kenosha **77** 42 33N 87 48W
Kensington, P.E.I., Can. **39** 46 28N 63 34W
Kensington, Qué., Can. **43** 45 1N 74 18W
Kensington, U.S.A. **74** 39 48N 99 2W
Kent, Ohio, U.S.A. **70** 41 8N 81 20W
Kent, Oreg., U.S.A. **78** 45 11N 120 45W
Kent, Tex., U.S.A. **75** 31 5N 104 12W
Kent, Wash., U.S.A. **80** 47 23N 122 14W
Kent □ **95** 51 12N 0 40 E
Kent Junction **39** 46 35N 65 20W
Kent Pen. **64** 68 30N 107 0W
Kent, Vale of **98** 51 12N 0 30 E
Kentau **120** 43 32N 68 36 E
Kentland **77** 40 45N 87 25W
Kenton **77** 40 40N 83 35W
Kentucky □ **72** 37 20N 85 0W
Kentucky Dam **72** 37 2N 88 15W
Kentucky L. **73** 36 0N 88 0W
Kentucky, R. **77** 38 41N 85 11W
Kentville **39** 45 6N 64 29W
Kentwood **75** 31 0N 90 30W
Kenville **57** 52 0N 101 20W
Kenya ■ **116** 2 20N 38 0 E
Kenya, Mt. **116** 0 10S 37 18 E
Keokuk **76** 40 25N 91 24W
Keosauqua **76** 40 44N 91 58W
Keota **76** 41 22N 91 57W
Kepi **127** 6 32S 139 19 E
Keppel B. **135** 23 21S 150 55 E
Kepsut **122** 39 40N 28 15 E
Kepuhi **67** 22 13N 159 21W
Kepulauan, R. **127** 5 30S 139 0 E
Kepulauan Sunda, Ketjil Barat □ **126** 8 50S 117 30 E
Kepulauan Sunda, Ketjil Timor □ **127** 9 30S 122 0 E
Kerala □ **124** 11 0N 76 15 E
Kerang **136** 35 40S 143 55 E
Keray **123** 26 15N 57 30 E
Kerch **120** 45 20N 36 20 E
Keremeos **63** 49 13N 119 50W
Kerguelen I. **16** 48 15S 69 10 E
Kericho **116** 0 22S 35 15 E
Kerinci **126** 2 5S 101 0 E
Kerki **120** 37 50N 65 12 E
Kérkira **109** 39 38N 19 50 E
Kermadec Is. **14** 31 8S 175 16W
Kermān **123** 30 15N 57 1 E
Kerman **80** 36 43N 120 4W
Kermān □ **123** 30 0N 57 0 E
Kermānshāh **122** 34 23N 47 0 E
Kermānshāh □ **122** 34 0N 46 30 E
Kermit **75** 31 56N 103 3W
Kern, R. **81** 35 16N 119 18W
Kernville **81** 35 45N 118 26W
Kerrobert **73** 52 0N 109 11W
Kerrville **75** 30 1N 99 8W
Kerry □ **97** 52 7N 9 35W
Kerry Hd. **97** 52 26N 9 56W
Kersley **63** 52 49N 122 25W
Kertosono **127** 7 38S 112 9 E
Kerulen, R. **130** 48 48N 117 0 E
Kesagami L. **34** 50 23N 80 15W
Kesagami, R. **34** 51 4N 79 45W
Keski Suomen □ **110** 62 45N 25 15 E
Kessel-Lo **105** 50 53N 4 43 E
Kestenga **120** 66 0N 31 50 E
Keswick, Can. **46** 44 15N 79 28W
Keswick, U.K. **94** 54 35N 3 9W
Ketapang **126** 1 55S 110 0 E
Ketchikan **67** 55 25N 131 40W
Ketchum **78** 43 50N 114 27W
Kettering, U.K. **95** 52 24N 0 44W
Kettering, U.S.A. **77** 39 41N 84 10W
Kettle Falls **63** 48 41N 118 2W
Kettle Pt. **46** 43 13N 82 1W
Kettle, R., B.C., Can. **63** 48 41N 118 7W
Kettle, R., Man., Can. **55** 56 23N 94 34W
Kettle R. **52** 46 22N 92 53W
Kettleman City **80** 36 1N 119 58W
Kevin **61** 48 45N 111 58W
Kewanee **76** 41 18N 90 0W
Kewanna **77** 41 1N 86 25W
Kewaunee **72** 44 27N 87 30W
Keweenaw B. **52** 46 56N 88 23W
Keweenaw Pen. **72** 47 30N 88 0W
Keweenaw Pt. **72** 47 26N 87 40W
Key Harbour **46** 45 50N 80 45W
Key West **84** 24 40N 82 0W
Keyesport **76** 38 45N 89 17W
Keyport **71** 40 26N 74 12W
Keyser **72** 39 26N 79 0W
Keystone, S.D., U.S.A. **74** 43 54N 103 27W
Keystone, W. Va., U.S.A. **72** 37 30N 81 30W
Keytesville **76** 39 26N 92 56W
Kezhma **121** 59 15N 100 57 E
Khabarovo **120** 69 30N 60 30 E
Khabarovsk **121** 48 20N 135 0 E
Khaibar **122** 25 38N 39 28 E
Khairpur **124** 27 32N 68 49 E
Khairpur □ **124** 23 30N 69 8 E
Khakhea **117** 24 48S 23 22 E
Khalij-e-Fars □ **123** 28 20N 51 45 E
Khalkis **109** 38 27N 23 42 E
Khalmer-Sede = Tazovskiy **120** 67 30N 78 30 E
Khalmer Yu **120** 67 58N 65 1 E
Khalturin **120** 58 40N 48 50 E
Khan Tengri **129** 42 25N 80 10 E
Khanabad **123** 36 45N 69 5 E
Khānaqin **122** 34 23N 45 25 E
Khandwa **124** 21 49N 76 22 E
Khandyga **121** 62 30N 134 50 E
Khanewal **124** 30 20N 71 55 E
Khaniá **109** 35 30N 24 4 E
Khanion Kólpos **109** 35 33N 23 55 E
Khanka, Oz. **120** 45 0N 132 30 E
Khanty-Mansiysk **120** 61 0N 69 0 E
Kharagpur **125** 22 20N 87 25 E
Kharan Kalat **124** 28 34N 65 21 E
Kharānaq **123** 32 20N 54 45 E
Kharda **124** 18 40N 75 40 E
Kharfa **122** 22 0N 46 35 E
Kharg, Jazireh **122** 29 15N 50 28 E
Khargon **124** 21 45N 75 35 E
Kharkov **120** 49 58N 36 20 E
Kharsaniya **122** 27 10N 49 10 E
Khartoum = El Khartûm **115** 15 31N 32 35 E
Khasab **123** 26 14N 56 15 E
Khāsh **124** 28 15N 61 5 E
Khashm el Girba **115** 14 59N 35 58 E
Khaskovo **109** 41 56N 25 30 E
Khatanga **121** 72 0N 102 20 E
Khatanga, Zaliv **17** 66 0N 112 0 E
Khatyrka **121** 62 3N 175 15 E
Khavar □ **122** 37 20N 46 0 E
Khed Brahma **124** 24 7N 73 5 E
Khedive **56** 49 37N 104 31W
Khemmarat **128** 16 10N 105 15 E
Khenmarak Phouminville **126** 11 40N 102 58 E
Kherson **120** 46 35N 32 35 E
Khetinsiring **129** 32 52N 92 21 E
Khilok **121** 51 30N 110 45 E
Khingan, mts. **118** 47 0N 119 30 E
Khios **109** 38 27N 26 9 E
Khíos, I. **109** 38 20N 26 0 E
Khiva **120** 41 30N 60 18 E
Khiyāv **122** 38 30N 47 45 E
Khlong, R. **128** 15 30N 98 50 E
Khmelnitsky **107** 49 23N 27 0 E
Khmer Republic ■ = Cambodia **128** 12 15N 105 0 E
Khoi **122** 38 40N 45 0 E
Khojak P. **124** 30 55N 66 30 E
Kholm **120** 57 10N 31 15 E
Kholmsk **121** 35 5N 139 48 E
Khomayn **122** 33 40N 50 7 E
Khon Kaen **128** 16 30N 102 47 E
Khong **128** 13 55N 105 56 E
Khong, R. **128** 15 0N 106 50 E
Khonh Hung (Soc Trang) **128** 9 37N 105 50 E
Khonu **121** 66 30N 143 25 E
Khoper, R. **120** 52 0N 43 20 E
Khorasan □ **123** 34 0N 58 0 E
Khorat = Nakhon Ratchasima **128** 14 59N 102 12 E
Khorat, Cao Nguyen **128** 15 30N 102 50 E
Khorat Plat. **128** 15 30N 102 50 E
Khorog **120** 37 30N 71 36 E
Khorramābād **122** 33 30N 48 25 E
Khorromshahr **122** 30 29N 48 15 E
Khotan = Hotien **129** 37 6N 79 59 E
Khu Khan **128** 14 42N 104 12 E
Khufaifiya **122** 24 50N 44 35 E
Khugiani **124** 31 28N 66 14 E
Khulna **125** 22 45N 89 34 E
Khulna □ **125** 22 45N 89 35 E
Khūr **123** 32 55N 58 18 E
Khurais **122** 24 55N 48 5 E
Khurma **122** 21 58N 42 3 E
Khush **124** 32 55N 62 10 E
Khushab **124** 32 20N 72 20 E
Khuzdar **124** 27 52N 66 30 E
Khuzestan □ **122** 31 0N 50 0 E
Khvor **123** 33 45N 55 0 E
Khvormūj **123** 28 40N 51 30 E
Khvoy **122** 38 35N 45 0 E
Khwaja Muhammad **123** 36 0N 70 0 E
Khyber Pass **124** 34 10N 71 8 E
Kiahsien **130** 38 10N 110 8 E
Kiama **136** 34 40S 150 50 E
Kiamusze **130** 46 45N 130 30 E
Kian **131** 27 1N 114 58 E
Kianghwa **131** 25 26N 111 29 E
Kiangling **131** 30 28N 113 16 E
Kiangpeh **131** 29 40N 106 30 E
Kiangshan **131** 28 51N 118 38 E
Kiangsi □ **131** 27 20N 115 40 E
Kiangsu □ **131** 33 0N 119 50 E
Kiangyin **131** 31 51N 120 0 E

Kiangyu Kokand

Kiangyu 131 31 41N 104 26 E
Kiaochow Wan 130 36 10N 120 15 E
Kiaohsien 130 36 20N 120 0 E
Kiawang 131 34 23N 117 28 E
Kibangou 116 3 18 S 12 22 E
Kibombo 116 3 57 S 25 53 E
Kibondo 116 3 35 S 30 45 E
Kibwesa 116 6 30 S 29 58 E
Kibwezi 116 2 27 S 37 57 E
Kichiga 121 59 50N 163 5 E
Kichow 131 30 0N 115 30 E
Kicking Horse Pass 63 51 28N 116 16W
Kidderminster 95 52 24N 2 13W
Kidnappers, C. 133 39 38 S 177 5 E
Kiel 106 54 16N 10 8 E
Kielce 107 50 58N 20 42 E
Kieler Bucht 106 54 30N 10 30 E
Kienhinghsien 131 26 50N 116 50 E
Kienhsien 131 34 30N 108 16 E
Kienko 131 31 50N 105 30 E
Kienning 131 27 4N 118 21 E
Kienow 131 27 0N 118 16 E
Kienshui 129 23 57N 102 45 E
Kiensi 131 26 58N 106 0 E
Kienteh 131 29 30N 119 28 E
Kienyang, Fukien, China 131 27 30N 118 0 E
Kienyang, Hunan, China 131 27 10N 109 50 E
Kiev = Kiyev 120 50 30N 30 28 E
Kifri 122 34 45N 45 0 E
Kigali 116 1 5 S 30 4 E
Kiglapait Mts. 36 57 6N 61 22W
Kigoma-Ujiji 116 5 30 S 30 0 E
Kihsien 130 36 20N 110 35 E
Kii-Suido 132 33 40N 135 0 E
Kijik 67 60 20N 154 20W
Kikiang 131 28 58N 106 44 E
Kikinda 109 45 50N 20 30 E
Kikino 60 54 27N 112 8W
Kikkatla 62 53 47N 130 25W
Kikládhes □ 109 37 0N 25 0 E
Kikládhes, Is. 109 37 20N 24 30 E
Kikwit 116 5 5 S 18 45 E
Kilauea 67 22 13N 159 25W
Kilauea Crater 67 19 24N 155 17W
Kilbride, Newf., Can. 37 47 32N 52 45W
Kilbride, Ont., Can. 49 43 25N 79 56W
Kilbuck Mts. 67 60 30N 160 0W
Kildala Arm 62 53 50N 128 29W
Kildare 97 53 10N 6 50W
Kildare □ 97 53 10N 6 50W
Kilembe 116 0 15N 30 3 E
Kilgore 75 32 22N 94 55W
Kilimanjaro, Mt. 116 3 7 S 37 20 E
Kilindini 116 4 4 S 39 40 E
Kilis 122 36 50N 37 10 E
Kilkee 97 52 41N 9 40W
Kilkenny 97 52 40N 7 17W
Kilkenny □ 97 52 35N 7 15W
Kilkieran B. 97 53 18N 9 45W
Killala 97 54 13N 9 12W
Killala B. 97 54 20N 9 12W
Killala L. 53 49 5N 86 32W
Killaloe 97 52 48N 8 28W
Killaloe Sta. 47 45 33N 77 25W
Killaly 56 50 45N 102 50W
Killam 61 52 47N 111 51W
Killarney, Man., Can. 34 49 10N 99 40W
Killarney, Ont., Can. 55 45 55N 81 30W
Killarney, Ireland 97 52 2N 9 30W
Killarney, L's. of 97 52 0N 9 30W
Killarney Prov. Park 46 46 2N 81 35W
Killary Harb. 97 53 38N 9 52W
Killbuck 70 40 29N 81 58W
Killdeer, Can. 56 49 6N 106 22W
Killdeer, U.S.A. 74 47 26N 102 48W
Killeen 75 31 7N 97 45W
Killiecrankie P. 96 56 44N 3 46W
Killinek I. 36 60 24N 64 37W
Killíni, Mts. 109 37 54N 22 25 E
Killowen 43 45 36N 74 15W
Killybegs 97 54 38N 8 26W
Kilmar 43 45 46N 74 37W
Kilmarnock 96 55 36N 4 30W
Kilmore 136 37 25 S 144 53 E
Kilosa 116 6 48 S 37 0 E
Kilrush 97 52 39N 9 30W
Kilwa Kisiwani 116 8 58 S 39 32 E
Kilwa Kivinje 116 8 45 S 39 25 E
Kim 75 37 18N 103 20W
Kimba 134 33 8 S 136 23 E
Kimball, Nebr., U.S.A. 74 41 17N 103 40W
Kimball, S.D., U.S.A. 74 43 47N 98 57W
Kimberley, Austral. 134 16 20 S 127 0 E
Kimberley, Can. 61 49 40N 115 59W
Kimberley, S. Afr. 117 28 43 S 24 46 E
Kimberly 78 42 33N 114 25W
Kimbo 49 43 7N 79 36W
Kimchaek 130 40 40N 129 10 E
Kimiwan L. 60 55 45N 116 55W
Kimsquit 62 52 45N 126 57W
Kinabalu, mt. 126 6 0N 116 0 E
Kinaskan L. 54 57 38N 130 8W
Kincaid 56 49 40N 107 0W
Kincald 76 39 35N 89 25W
Kincardine 46 44 10N 81 40W
Kinchwan 130 42 28N 126 6 E
Kinde 46 43 56N 83 0W
Kindersley 56 51 30N 109 10W
Kindia 114 10 0N 12 52W
Kindu 116 2 55 S 25 50 E
King City, Can. 50 43 56N 79 32W
King City, U.S.A. 76 40 3N 94 31W
King City, Calif., U.S.A. 80 36 11N 121 8W
King Frederick VI Land 17 63 0N 43 0W
King Frederick VIII Land 17 77 30N 25 0W
King George B. 90 51 30 S 60 30W
King George I. 91 60 0 S 60 0W
King George Is. 36 57 20N 78 25W
King George Sd. 134 35 5 S 118 0 E
King I., Austral. 135 39 50 S 144 0 E
King I., Can. 62 52 10N 127 40W
King I. = Kadah Kyun 128 12 30N 98 20 E
King Leopold Ranges 134 17 20 S 124 20 E
King Sd. 134 16 50 S 123 20 E
King William I. 65 69 10N 97 25W
King William's Town 117 32 51 S 27 22 E
Kingaroy 135 26 32 S 151 51 E
Kingcome Inlet 62 50 56N 126 29W
Kingfisher 75 35 50N 97 55W
Kinghorn 50 43 55N 79 34W
Kingku 129 23 49N 100 30 E
Kingman, U.S.A. 77 39 58N 87 18W
Kingman, Ariz., U.S.A. 81 35 12N 114 2W
Kingman, Kans., U.S.A. 75 37 41N 98 9W
Kingmen 131 31 10N 112 15 E
Kingning 131 27 55N 119 30 E
Kingpeng 130 43 10N 117 25 E
Kings B. 17 78 0N 15 0 E
Kings Canyon National Park 80 37 0N 118 35W
King's Lynn 94 52 45N 0 25 E
Kings Mountain 73 35 13N 81 20W
King's Peak 78 40 46N 110 27W
King's Point 37 49 35N 56 11W
Kings, R. 80 36 10N 119 50W
Kingsburg 80 36 35N 119 36W
Kingsbury 77 41 31N 86 42W
Kingscourt 97 53 55N 6 48W
Kingsey Falls 41 45 51N 72 4W
Kingsgate 61 49 1N 116 11W
Kingsley 74 42 37N 95 58W
Kingsley Dam 74 41 20N 101 40W
Kingsmere L. 56 54 6N 106 27W
Kingsport 73 36 33N 82 36W
Kingston, N.S., Can. 39 44 59N 64 57W
Kingston, Ont., Can. 47 44 14N 76 30W
Kingston, Jamaica 84 18 0N 76 50W
Kingston, N.Z. 133 45 20 S 168 43 E
Kingston, Mich., U.S.A. 46 43 29N 83 11W
Kingston, Mo., U.S.A. 76 39 38N 94 2W
Kingston, N.Y., U.S.A. 71 41 55N 74 0W
Kingston, Pa., U.S.A. 71 41 19N 75 58W
Kingston, R.I., U.S.A. 71 41 29N 71 30W
Kingston, Wash., U.S.A. 80 47 48N 122 30W
Kingston Mines 76 40 34N 89 47W
Kingston Pk. 81 35 45N 115 54W
Kingstown 85 13 10N 61 10W
Kingstree 73 33 40N 79 48W
Kingsville, Can. 46 42 2N 82 45W
Kingsville, U.S.A. 75 27 30N 97 53W
Kingtai 130 37 4N 103 59 E
Kingtehchen (Fowliang) 131 29 8N 117 21 E
Kingtzekwan 131 33 25N 111 10 E
Kingussie 96 47 3N 4 2W
Kingyang 130 36 6N 107 49 E
Kinhsien 130 36 6N 107 49 E
Kinhwa 131 29 5N 119 32 E
Kinistino 56 52 57N 105 2W
Kinkala 116 4 18 S 14 49 E
Kinkora 39 46 19N 63 36W
Kinleith 133 38 20 S 175 56 E
Kinloch 133 44 51 S 168 20 E
Kinmen (Quemoy) Is. 131 24 25N 118 24 E
Kinmount 47 44 48N 78 45W
Kinmundy 77 38 46N 88 51W
Kinnaird 63 49 17N 117 39W
Kinnaird's Hd. 96 57 40N 2 0W
Kino 82 28 45N 111 59W
Kinoje Ls. 53 51 35N 81 48W
Kinoje, R. 34 52 8N 81 25W
Kinping 128 22 56N 103 15 E
Kinross 96 56 13N 3 25W
Kinsale, Can. 51 43 56N 79 2W
Kinsale, Ireland 97 51 42N 8 31W
Kinsale Harbour 97 51 40N 8 30W
Kinsale Old Hd. 97 51 37N 8 32W
Kinsha (Yangtze) 129 32 30N 98 30 E
Kinshasa 116 4 20 S 15 15 E
Kinsiang 131 35 4N 116 25 E
Kinsley 75 37 57N 99 30W
Kinston 73 35 18N 77 35W
Kintap 126 3 51 S 115 13 E
Kintyre, Mull of 96 55 17N 5 4W
Kintyre, pen. 96 55 30N 5 35W
Kinushseo, R. 34 55 15N 83 45W
Kinuso 60 55 20N 115 25W
Kinzua 70 41 52N 78 58W
Kinzua Dam 70 41 53N 79 0W
Kioshan 131 32 50N 114 0 E
Kiosk 47 46 6N 78 53W
Kiowa, Kans., U.S.A. 75 37 3N 98 30W
Kiowa, Okla., U.S.A. 75 34 45N 95 50W
Kipahigan L. 55 55 20N 101 55W
Kiparissia 109 37 15N 21 40 E
Kiparissiakós Kólpos 109 37 25N 21 25 E
Kipawa 40 46 47N 78 59W
Kipawa L. 40 46 50N 79 0W
Kipawa, Parc de 40 47 0N 78 50W
Kipawa Res. Prov. Park 34 47 0N 78 30W
Kipembawe 116 7 38 S 33 27 E
Kipili 116 7 28 S 30 32 E
Kipling 56 50 6N 102 38W
Kipnuk 67 59 55N 164 7W
Kippens 37 48 33N 58 38W
Kippure, Mt. 97 53 11N 6 23W
Kipushi 117 11 48 S 27 12 E
Kirensk 121 57 50N 107 55 E
Kirgiz S.S.R. □ 120 42 0N 75 0 E
Kiri 116 1 29 S 19 25 E
Kirikkale 122 39 51N 33 32 E
Kirin 130 43 58N 126 31 E
Kirin □ 130 43 50N 125 45 E
Kirkcaldy 96 56 7N 3 10W
Kirkcudbright 96 54 50N 4 3W
Kirkee 124 18 34N 73 56 E
Kirkenes 110 69 40N 30 5 E
Kirkfield 47 44 34N 78 59W
Kirkfield Park 58 49 53N 97 17W
Kirkintilloch 96 55 57N 4 10W
Kirkjubæjarklaustur 110 63 47N 18 4W
Kirkland, Can. 44 45 27N 73 52W
Kirkland, U.S.A. 77 42 5N 88 51W
Kirkland, Ariz., U.S.A. 79 34 29N 112 46W
Kirkland, Wash., U.S.A. 78 47 40N 122 10W
Kirkland Lake 34 48 9N 80 2W
Kırklareli 109 41 44N 27 15 E
Kirklin 77 40 12N 86 22W
Kirksville 76 40 8N 92 35W
Kirkūk 122 35 30N 44 21 E
Kirkwall, Can. 49 43 21N 80 10W
Kirkwall, U.K. 96 58 59N 2 59W
Kirkwood 76 38 35N 90 24W
Kirov, R.S.F.S.R., U.S.S.R. 120 58 35N 49 40 E
Kirov, R.S.F.S.R., U.S.S.R. 120 58 35N 49 40 E
Kirovabad 120 40 45N 46 10 E
Kirovograd 120 48 35N 32 20 E
Kirovsk 120 67 48N 33 50 E
Kirriemuir 55 51 56N 110 20W
Kirşehir 122 39 14N 34 5 E
Kirthar Range 124 27 0N 67 0 E
Kiruna 110 67 52N 20 15 E
Kirundu 116 0 50 S 25 35 E
Kiryū 132 36 24N 139 20 E
Kisalaya 84 14 40N 84 3W
Kisangani 116 0 35N 25 15 E
Kisar, I. 127 8 5 S 127 10 E
Kisaran 126 2 47N 99 29 E
Kisaratzu 132 35 25N 139 59 E
Kisbey 56 49 39N 102 40W
Kiselevsk 120 54 5N 86 6 E
Kishanganj 125 26 3N 88 14 E
Kishangarh 124 27 50N 70 30 E
Kishinev 120 47 0N 28 50 E
Kishiwada 132 34 28N 135 22 E
Kishow 131 28 16N 109 47 E
Kishtwar 124 33 20N 75 48 E
Kishwaukee, R. 77 42 12N 89 8W
Kisi 130 45 21N 131 0 E
Kisii 116 0 40 S 34 45 E
Kisiju 116 7 23 S 39 19 E
Kiska I. 67 52 0N 177 30 E
Kiskatinaw, R. 54 56 8N 120 10W
Kiskitto L. 57 54 16N 98 30W
Kiskittogisu L. 57 54 13N 98 20W
Kiskörös 107 46 37N 19 20 E
Kiskunfelégyháza 107 46 42N 19 53 E
Kiskunhalas 107 46 28N 19 37 E
Kismayu 113 0 20 S 42 30 E
Kiso-Gawa 132 35 20N 137 0 E
Kiso-Sammyaku 132 35 30N 137 45 E
Kissimmee 73 28 18N 81 22W
Kissimmee, R. 73 27 20N 81 0W
Kississing L. 55 55 10N 101 10W
Kisumu 116 0 3 S 34 45 E
Kit Carson 74 38 48N 102 45W
Kita 114 13 5N 9 25W
Kitab 120 39 7N 66 52 E
Kitai 129 44 0N 89 27 E
Kitaibaraki 132 36 50N 140 45 E
Kitakami-Gawa 132 39 30N 141 15 E
Kitakyūshū 132 33 50N 130 50 E
Kitale 116 1 0N 35 12 E
Kitchener 49 43 27N 80 29W
Kitchigami, R. 34 50 35N 78 5W
Kitchioh 131 22 57N 116 2 E
Kitega = Citega 116 3 30 S 29 58 E
Kitgum Matidi 116 3 17N 32 52 E
Kíthira 109 36 9N 23 0 E
Kíthira, I. 109 36 15N 23 0 E
Kíthnos 109 37 26N 24 27 E
Kíthnos, I. 109 37 25N 24 25 E
Kitimat 62 54 3N 128 38W
Kitimat Arm 62 53 55N 128 42W
Kitimat Ranges 62 54 0N 129 15W
Kitinen, R. 110 67 34N 26 40 E
Kitscoty 60 53 20N 110 20W
Kittanning 70 40 49N 79 30W
Kittatinny Mts. 71 41 0N 75 0W
Kittertoksoak, I. 36 58 50N 65 50W
Kittery 71 43 7N 70 42W
Kitui 116 1 17 S 38 0 E
Kitwe 117 12 54 S 28 7 E
Kityang 131 23 30N 116 29 E
Kiuchuan 129 39 51N 98 30 E
Kiukiang 131 29 37N 116 2 E
Kiuling Shan, mts. 131 28 30N 114 30 E
Kiungchow 131 19 57N 110 17 E
Kiungchow Haihsia 131 20 40N 110 0 E
Kivalina 67 67 45N 164 40W
Kivalo 110 66 18N 26 0 E
Kivitoo 65 67 56N 64 52W
Kivu, L. 116 1 48 S 29 0 E
Kiyang 131 26 36N 111 42 E
Kiyev 120 50 30N 30 28 E
Kiyuanshan 131 28 6N 117 46 E
Kizil Kiya 120 40 20N 72 35 E
Kizlyar 120 43 51N 46 40 E
Kizyl-Arvat 120 38 58N 56 15 E
Klabat, Teluk 126 1 30 S 105 40 E
Kladno 106 50 10N 14 7 E
Klagenfurt 106 46 38N 14 20 E
Klaipeda 120 55 43N 21 10 E
Klamath Falls 78 42 20N 121 50W
Klamath Mts. 78 41 20N 123 0W
Klamath, R. 78 41 40N 123 30W
Klang = Kelang 128 3 1N 101 33 E
Klappan, R. 54 58 0N 129 43W
Klarälven 111 60 32N 13 15 E
Klaten 127 7 43 S 110 36 E
Klatovy 106 49 23N 13 18 E
Klawak 54 55 35N 133 0W
Klawer 117 31 44 S 18 36 E
Kleczkowski, L. 38 50 48N 63 27W
Kleena Kleene 62 52 0N 124 50W
Klein 78 46 26N 108 31W
Kleinburg 50 43 50N 79 38W
Kleindale 62 49 38N 123 58W
Klemtu 54 52 35N 128 55W
Klerksdorp 117 26 51 S 26 38 E
Kletskaïa Kletskiy 120 49 20N 43 0 E
Kletskiy 120 49 20N 43 0 E
Kleve 105 51 46N 6 10 E
Klickitat 78 45 50N 121 10W
Klickitat, R. 80 45 42N 121 17W
Klin 120 56 28N 36 48 E
Klinaklini, R. 62 51 21N 125 40W
Kłodzko 106 50 28N 16 38 E
Klondike 64 64 0N 139 26W
Klotz, L. 36 60 32N 73 40W
Kluane L. 64 61 15N 138 40W
Kluang = Keluang 128 1 59N 103 20 E
Knaresborough 94 54 1N 1 29W
Knee L., Man., Can. 55 55 3N 94 45W
Knee L., Sask., Can. 55 55 51N 107 0W
Knewstubb L. 62 53 33N 124 55W
Knight Inlet 62 50 45N 125 40W
Knighton 95 52 21N 3 2W
Knights Ferry 80 37 50N 120 40W
Knight's Landing 80 38 50N 121 43W
Knightstown 77 39 49N 85 32W
Knob, C. 134 34 32 S 119 16 E
Knockmealdown Mts. 97 52 16N 8 0W
Knokke 105 51 20N 3 17 E
Knossos 109 35 18N 25 10 E
Knowlton 41 45 13N 72 31W
Knox 77 41 18N 86 36W
Knox, C. 62 54 11N 133 5W
Knox City 75 33 26N 99 38W
Knox Coast 91 66 30 S 108 0 E
Knoxville, Iowa, U.S.A. 76 41 20N 93 5W
Knoxville, Pa., U.S.A. 73 41 57N 77 26W
Knoxville, Tenn., U.S.A. 73 35 58N 83 57W
Knud Rasmussen Land 65 79 0N 60 0W
Ko Chang 128 12 0N 102 20 E
Ko Kut 128 11 40N 102 32 E
Ko Phangan 128 9 45N 100 10 E
Ko Phra Thong 128 9 6N 98 15 E
Ko Samui 128 9 30N 100 0 E
Koartac (Notre Dame de Koartac) 36 61 5N 69 36 E
Koba, Aru, Indon. 127 6 37 S 134 37 E
Koba, Bangka, Indon. 126 2 26 S 106 14 E
Kobarid 108 46 15N 13 30 E
Kobayashi 132 31 56N 130 59 E
Kōbe 132 34 45N 135 10 E
København 111 55 41N 12 34 E
Koblenz 105 50 21N 7 36 E
Kobroor, Kepulauan 127 6 10 S 134 30 E
Kobuk 67 66 55N 157 0W
Kobuk, R. 67 66 55N 157 0W
Kočani 109 41 55N 22 25 E
Kočevje 108 45 39N 14 50 E
Kōchi 132 33 30N 133 35 E
Kōchi-ken □ 132 33 40N 133 30 E
Kodiak 67 57 30N 152 45W
Kodiak I. 67 57 30N 152 45W
Kodiang 128 6 21N 100 18 E
Koes 117 26 0 S 19 15 E
Köflach 91 47 4N 15 4 E
Kōfu 132 35 40N 138 30 E
Kogaluk, R. 36 56 12N 61 44W
Koh-i-Baba, mts. 124 34 30N 67 0 E
Kohat 124 33 40N 71 29 E
Kohima 125 25 35N 94 10 E
Kohler Ra. 91 77 0N 110 0W
Kojabuti 127 2 36 S 140 37 E
Kokand 120 40 30N 70 57 E

Place	Page	Lat.	Long.
Kokanee Glacier Prov. Park	**63**	49 47N	117 10W
Kokas	**127**	2 42S	132 26E
Kokchetav	**120**	53 20N	69 10E
Kokemäenjoki	**111**	61 32N	21 44E
Kokiu	**129**	23 30N	103 0E
Kokkola (Gamlakarleby)	**110**	63 50N	23 8E
Koko Kyunzu	**128**	14 10N	93 25E
Koko-Nor	**129**	37 0N	100 0E
Koko Shili	**125**	35 20N	91 0E
Kokomo	**72**	40 30N	86 6W
Kokoura	**121**	71 35N	144 50E
Kokstad	**117**	30 32S	29 29E
Kola	**120**	68 45N	33 8E
Kola, I.	**127**	5 35S	134 30E
Kola Pen. = Kolskiy P-ov.	**120**	67 30N	38 0E
Kolagede	**127**	7 54S	110 26E
Kolaka	**127**	4 3S	121 46E
Kolar	**124**	13 12N	78 15E
Kolar Gold Fields	**124**	12 58N	78 16E
Kolari	**110**	67 20N	23 48E
Kolarovgrad	**109**	43 27N	26 42E
Kolayat	**124**	27 50N	72 50E
Koldewey I.	**17**	77 0N	18 0W
Kolding	**111**	55 30N	9 29E
Kole	**116**	3 16S	22 42E
Kolepom, Pulau	**127**	8 0S	138 30E
Kolguyev, Ostrov	**120**	69 20N	48 30E
Kolhapur	**124**	16 43N	74 15E
Kolín	**106**	50 2N	15 9E
Köln	**105**	50 56N	9 58E
Koło	**107**	52 14N	18 40E
Kołobrzeg	**106**	54 10N	15 35E
Kolomna	**120**	55 8N	38 45E
Kolonodale	**127**	2 3S	121 25E
Kolosib	**125**	24 15N	92 45E
Kolpashevo	**120**	58 20N	83 5E
Kolskiy Poluostrov	**120**	67 30N	38 0E
Kolwezi	**116**	10 40S	25 25E
Kolyma, R.	**121**	64 40N	153 0E
Kolymskoye, Okhotsko	**121**	63 0N	157 0E
Komandorskiye Ostrava	**121**	55 0N	167 0E
Komárno	**107**	47 49N	18 5E
Komi, A.S.S.R. □	**120**	64 0N	55 0E
Kommunizma, Pik	**120**	39 0N	72 2E
Komodo	**127**	8 37S	119 20E
Komono	**116**	3 15S	13 20E
Komoran, Pulau	**127**	8 18S	138 45E
Komotiri	**109**	41 9N	25 26E
Kompong Cham	**128**	11 54N	105 30E
Kompong Chhnang	**128**	12 20N	104 35E
Kompong Speu	**128**	11 26N	104 32E
Kompong Thom	**128**	12 35N	104 51E
Komsomolets, Ostrov	**121**	80 30N	95 0E
Komsomolsk	**121**	50 30N	137 0E
Konawa	**75**	34 59N	96 46W
Kondoa	**116**	4 55S	35 50E
Kondratyevo	**121**	57 30N	98 30E
Kong	**114**	8 54N	4 36W
Kong Christian IX.s Land	**17**	68 0N	36 0W
Kong Christian X.s Land	**17**	74 0N	29 0W
Kong Frederik VIII.s Land	**17**	78 30N	26 0W
Kong Frederik VI.s Kyst	**17**	63 0N	43 0W
Kong, Koh	**128**	11 20N	103 0E
Kong Oscar Fjord	**17**	72 20N	24 0W
Kongmoon	**131**	22 35N	113 1E
Kongolo	**116**	5 22S	27 0E
Kongsberg	**111**	59 39N	9 39E
Kongsvinger	**111**	60 12N	12 2E
Konin	**107**	52 12N	18 15E
Konjic	**109**	43 42N	17 58E
Konosha	**120**	61 0N	40 5E
Konotop	**120**	51 12N	33 7E
Konskie	**107**	51 15N	20 23E
Konstanz	**106**	47 39N	9 10E
Kontagora	**114**	10 23N	5 27E
Kontum	**128**	14 24N	108 0E
Konya	**122**	37 52N	32 35E
Konza	**116**	1 45S	37 0E
Koo-wee-rup	**136**	38 13S	145 28E
Koocanusa, L.	**61**	49 20N	115 15W
Koog	**17**	52 27N	4 49E
Koolan I.	**134**	16 0S	123 45E
Kooloonong	**136**	34 48S	143 10E
Koorakee	**136**	34 27S	142 56E
Koorawatha	**136**	34 2S	148 33E
Kooskia	**78**	46 9N	115 59W
Koostatak	**55**	51 26N	97 26W
Kootenai, R.	**78**	48 30N	115 30W
Kootenay L.	**63**	49 45N	116 50W
Kootenay Nat. Park	**61**	51 0N	116 0W
Kootingal	**89**	31 1S	151 3E
Kopaonik Planina	**109**	43 10N	21 50E
Kópavogur	**110**	64 6N	21 55W
Koper	**108**	45 31N	13 44E
Kopervik	**111**	59 17N	5 17E
Kopeysk	**120**	55 7N	61 37E
Köping	**111**	59 31N	16 3E
Kopka, R.	**52**	50 4N	89 1W
Kopparberg	**111**	59 52N	15 0E
Kopparbergs län □	**67**	61 20N	14 15E
Koppeh Dāgh	**123**	38 0N	58 0E
Korab, mt.	**109**	41 44N	20 40E
Korça	**109**	40 37N	20 50E
Korčula, I.	**108**	42 57N	17 0E
Kordestān □	**122**	36 0N	47 0E
Kordestan, reg.	**122**	37 30N	42 0E
Korea, South ■	**130**	36 0N	128 0E
Korea Strait	**118**	34 0N	129 30E
Korea, North ■	**130**	40 0N	127 0E
Korhogo	**114**	9 29N	5 28W
Korim	**127**	0 58S	136 10E
Korinthiakós Kólpos	**109**	38 16N	22 30E
Kórinthos	**109**	37 56N	22 55E
Koriyama	**132**	37 24N	140 23E
Korla	**129**	41 45N	86 4E
Kormack	**53**	47 38N	82 59W
Koro, I.	**133**	17 19S	179 23E
Koroc, R.	**36**	58 50N	65 50W
Korogwe	**116**	5 5S	38 25E
Koroit	**136**	38 18S	142 24E
Koror	**127**	7 20N	134 28E
Körös, R.	**107**	46 45N	20 20E
Korsakov	**121**	46 30N	142 42E
Korshunovo	**121**	58 37N	110 10E
Korsör	**111**	55 20N	11 9E
Kortrijk	**105**	50 50N	3 17E
Koryakskiy Khrebet	**121**	61 0N	171 0E
Kos	**109**	36 52N	27 19E
Kos, I.	**109**	36 50N	27 15E
Kosciusko	**75**	33 3N	89 34W
Kosciusko, I.	**54**	56 0N	133 40W
Kosciusko, Mt.	**136**	36 27S	148 16E
Koshkonong, L.	**77**	42 53N	88 58W
Košice	**107**	48 42N	21 15E
Kosŏnf	**130**	38 40N	128 22E
Kosovska-Mitrovica	**109**	42 54N	20 52E
Kosścian	**106**	52 5N	16 40E
Kôstî	**115**	13 8N	32 43E
Kostroma	**120**	57 50N	41 58E
Kostrzyn	**106**	52 24N	17 14E
Koszalin	**106**	54 12N	16 8E
Kota	**124**	25 14N	75 49E
Kota Baharu	**128**	6 7N	102 14E
Kota Kinabalu	**126**	6 0N	116 12E
Kota Tinggi	**128**	1 44N	103 53E
Kotaagung	**126**	5 38S	104 29E
Kotabaru	**126**	3 20S	116 20E
Kotabumi	**126**	4 49S	104 46E
Kotamobagu	**127**	0 57N	124 31E
Kotaneelee, R.	**54**	60 11N	123 42W
Kotawaringin	**126**	2 28S	111 27E
Kotcho L.	**54**	59 7N	121 12W
Kotelnich	**120**	58 20N	48 10E
Kotelnikovo	**120**	47 45N	43 15E
Kotelnyy, Ostrov	**121**	75 10N	139 0E
Kotka	**111**	60 28N	26 58E
Kotlas	**120**	61 15N	47 0E
Kotor	**109**	42 25N	18 47E
Kotri	**124**	25 22N	68 22E
Kottayam	**124**	9 35N	76 33E
Kotturu	**124**	14 45N	76 10E
Kotuy, R.	**121**	70 30N	103 0E
Kotzebue	**67**	66 50N	162 40W
Kotzebue Sd.	**67**	66 30N	164 0W
Kouango	**116**	5 0N	20 10E
Kouchibouguac Nat. Park	**39**	46 50N	65 20W
Koudougou	**114**	12 10N	2 20W
Kouilou, R.	**116**	4 10S	12 5E
Kouki	**116**	7 22N	17 3E
Koula Moutou	**116**	1 15S	12 25E
Koulen	**128**	13 50N	104 40E
Koulikoro	**114**	12 40N	7 50W
Koumradskiy	**120**	47 20N	75 0E
Kountze	**75**	30 20N	94 22W
Kouts	**77**	41 18N	87 2W
Kovel	**120**	51 10N	24 20E
Kovic, B.	**36**	61 35N	77 36W
Kowkash	**53**	50 20N	87 12W
Kowloon	**131**	22 20N	114 15E
Kowpangtze	**130**	41 24N	121 56E
Koyan, Pegunungan	**126**	3 15N	114 30E
Koyiu	**131**	23 2N	112 28E
Koyuk	**67**	64 55N	161 20W
Koyukuk, R.	**67**	65 45N	156 30W
Koza	**131**	26 20N	127 47E
Kozan	**122**	37 35N	35 50E
Kozàni	**109**	40 19N	21 47E
Kozhikode = Calicut	**124**	11 15N	75 43E
Kra Buri	**128**	10 22N	98 46E
Kra, Isthmus of = Kra, Kho Khot	**128**	10 15N	99 30E
Kra, Kho Khot	**128**	10 15N	99 30E
Kragan	**127**	6 43S	111 38E
Kragerø	**111**	58 52N	9 25E
Kragujevac	**109**	44 2N	20 56E
Krakatau = Rakata, Pulau	**126**	6 10S	105 20E
Kraków	**107**	50 4N	19 57E
Kraksaan	**127**	7 43S	113 23E
Kraljevo	**109**	43 44N	20 41E
Kramer	**79**	35 0N	117 38W
Kramfors	**110**	62 55N	17 48E
Kraskino	**121**	42 44N	130 48E
Krasnoarmeysk	**120**	50 32N	45 50E
Krasnodar	**120**	45 5N	38 50E
Krasnoïarsk	**121**	56 8N	93 0E
Krasnoperekopsk	**120**	46 0N	33 54E
Krasnoselkupsk	**120**	65 20N	82 10E
Krasnoturinsk	**120**	59 46N	60 12E
Krasnoufimsk	**120**	56 57N	57 46E
Krasnouralsk	**120**	58 21N	60 3E
Krasnovodsk	**120**	40 0N	52 52E
Krasnoyarsk	**121**	56 8N	93 0E
Kraśnik	**107**	50 55N	22 5E
Kratie	**128**	12 32N	106 10E
Kravanh, Chuor Phnum	**128**	12 0N	103 32E
Krawang	**127**	6 19N	107 18E
Krefeld	**105**	51 20N	6 22E
Kremenchug	**120**	49 5N	33 25E
Kremmling	**78**	40 10N	106 30W
Kremnica	**107**	48 45N	18 50E
Kribi	**116**	2 57N	9 56E
Krishna, R.	**124**	16 30N	77 0E
Krishnanagar	**125**	23 24N	88 33E
Kristiansand	**111**	58 9N	8 1E
Kristianstad	**111**	56 2N	14 9E
Kristianstad □	**111**	56 15N	14 0E
Kristiansund	**110**	63 7N	7 45E
Kristiinankaupunki	**110**	62 16N	21 21E
Kristinehamn	**111**	59 18N	14 13E
Kristinestad	**110**	62 16N	21 21E
Kríti, I.	**109**	35 15N	25 0E
Krivoy Rog	**120**	47 51N	33 20E
Krk, I.	**108**	45 8N	14 40E
Kroeng Krai	**128**	14 55N	98 30E
Kronobergs län □	**111**	56 45N	14 30E
Kronprins Harald Kyst	**91**	70 0S	35 1E
Kronprins Olav Kyst	**91**	69 0S	42 0E
Kronprinsesse Märtha Kyst	**91**	73 30S	10 0W
Kronshtadt	**120**	60 5N	29 35E
Kroonstad	**117**	27 43S	27 19E
Kropotkin	**121**	45 25N	40 35E
Krosno	**107**	49 35N	21 56E
Krotoszyn	**107**	51 42N	17 23E
Krugersdorp	**117**	26 5S	27 46E
Krung Thep	**128**	13 45N	100 35E
Kruševac	**109**	43 35N	21 28E
Kruzof I.	**54**	57 10N	135 40W
Krydor	**56**	52 47N	107 4W
Krymskaya	**120**	45 0N	34 0E
Kuala	**126**	2 46N	105 47E
Kuala Kangsar	**128**	4 46N	100 56E
Kuala Kerai	**128**	5 30N	102 12E
Kuala Kubu Baharu	**128**	3 34N	101 39E
Kuala Lipis	**128**	4 10N	102 3E
Kuala Lumpur	**128**	3 9N	101 41E
Kuala Sedili Besar	**128**	1 55N	104 5E
Kuala Trengganu	**128**	5 20N	103 8E
Kualakahi Chan	**67**	22 2N	159 53W
Kualakapuas	**126**	2 55S	114 20E
Kualakurun	**126**	1 10S	113 50E
Kualapembuang, Indon.	**126**	2 52S	111 45E
Kualapembuang, Indon.	**126**	3 14S	112 38E
Kuandang	**127**	0 56N	123 1E
Kuantan	**128**	3 49N	103 20E
Kuba	**120**	41 21N	48 32E
Kucha	**129**	41 50N	82 30E
Kuchen	**131**	33 29N	117 27E
Kuching	**126**	1 33N	110 25E
Kuda	**124**	23 10N	71 15E
Kudat	**126**	6 55N	116 55E
Kudus	**127**	6 48S	110 51E
Kudymkar	**120**	59 1N	54 39E
Kufra, El Wâhât el	**115**	24 17N	23 15E
Kufstein	**106**	47 35N	12 11E
Kugaluk, B.	**36**	59 10N	78 40W
Kugmallit B.	**67**	69 0N	134 0W
Kugong, I.	**36**	56 18N	79 50W
Kūh-e-Aliju	**123**	31 30N	51 41E
Kūh-e-Dinar	**123**	30 10N	51 0E
Kūh-e-Hazārān	**123**	29 35N	57 20E
Kūh-e-Jebāl Bārez	**123**	29 0N	58 0E
Kūh-e-Sorkh	**123**	35 30N	58 45E
Kūh-e-Taftan	**123**	28 40N	61 0E
Kūhak	**123**	27 12N	63 10E
Kūhhā-ye-Bashākerd	**123**	26 45N	59 0E
Kūhhā-ye Sabalān	**123**	38 15N	47 45E
Kūhpāyeh	**123**	32 44N	52 20E
Kuinre	**105**	52 47N	5 51E
Kuiu I.	**67**	56 40N	134 15W
Kukukus L.	**52**	49 47N	91 41W
Kulai	**128**	1 44N	103 35E
Kulasekharapattanam	**124**	8 20N	78 0E
Kuldja = Ining	**129**	43 57N	81 20E
Kulm	**74**	46 22N	98 58W
Kulsary	**120**	46 59N	54 1E
Kulu	**130**	37 12N	115 2E
Kulunda	**120**	52 45N	79 15E
Kulunkai	**130**	42 46N	121 55E
Kulwin	**136**	35 0S	142 42E
Kulyab	**120**	37 55N	69 50E
Kum Darya	**129**	41 0N	89 0E
Kum Tekei	**120**	43 10N	79 30E
Kuma, R.	**120**	44 55N	45 57E
Kumagaya	**132**	36 9N	139 22E
Kumamoto	**132**	32 45N	130 45E
Kumamoto-ken □	**132**	32 30N	130 40E
Kumanovo	**109**	42 9N	21 42E
Kumara	**133**	42 37S	171 12E
Kumasi	**114**	6 41N	1 38W
Kumba	**116**	4 36N	9 24E
Kume-guntō	**131**	26 8N	126 45E
Kumla	**111**	59 8N	15 10E
Kumon Bum	**125**	26 30N	97 15E
Kumukahi, C.	**67**	19 31N	154 49W
Kunar	**124**	34 30N	71 3E
Kunashir, Ostrov	**121**	44 0N	146 0E
Kunch	**124**	26 0N	79 10E
Kunduz	**123**	36 50N	68 50E
Kunduz □	**123**	36 50N	68 50E
Kungan	**131**	30 0N	112 2E
Kungchuling	**130**	43 31N	124 58E
Kunghit I.	**62**	52 6N	131 3W
Kungho	**129**	36 28N	100 45E
Kungrad	**120**	43 6N	58 54E
Kungsbacka	**111**	57 30N	12 5E
Kungur	**120**	57 25N	56 57E
Kungyifow	**131**	22 24N	112 41E
Kunhsien	**131**	33 30N	111 17E
Kuningan	**127**	6 59S	108 29E
Kunlong	**125**	23 20N	98 50E
Kunlun Shan	**129**	36 0N	86 30E
Kunming	**129**	25 11N	102 37E
Kunsan	**130**	35 59N	126 45E
Kunshan	**131**	31 16N	121 0E
Kununurra	**134**	15 40S	128 39E
Kuopio	**110**	62 53N	27 35E
Kuopion Lääni □	**110**	63 25N	27 10E
Kupa, R.	**108**	45 30N	16 10E
Kupang	**127**	10 19S	123 39E
Kupreanof I.	**67**	56 50N	133 30W
Kupyansk	**120**	49 45N	37 35E
Kurashiki	**132**	34 40N	133 50E
Kurayoshi	**132**	35 26N	133 50E
Kure	**132**	34 14N	132 32E
Kurgaldzhino	**120**	50 35N	70 20E
Kurgan, R.S.F.S.R., U.S.S.R.	**120**	55 26N	65 18E
Kurgan, R.S.F.S.R., U.S.S.R.	**121**	64 5N	172 50W
Kurigram	**125**	25 49N	89 39E
Kurilskiye Ostrova	**121**	45 0N	150 0E
Kurnool	**124**	15 45N	78 0E
Kuroki	**56**	51 52N	103 29W
Kurow	**133**	44 4S	170 29E
Kurri Kurri	**136**	32 50S	151 28E
Kursk	**120**	51 42N	36 11E
Kuršumlija	**109**	43 9N	21 19E
Kurtalān	**122**	37 55N	41 40E
Kuruman	**117**	27 28S	23 28E
Kurume	**132**	33 15N	130 30E
Kurunegala	**124**	7 30N	80 18E
Kurya	**121**	61 15N	108 10E
Kusagaki	**131**	30 54N	129 28E
Kusawa L.	**54**	60 20N	136 13W
Kushan	**130**	39 58N	123 30E
Kushih	**131**	32 12N	115 43E
Kushiro	**132**	43 0N	144 25E
Kushirogawa	**132**	43 0N	144 30E
Kushk	**124**	34 55N	62 30E
Kushka	**120**	35 20N	62 18E
Kushtia	**125**	23 55N	89 5E
Kuskokwim Bay	**67**	59 50N	162 56W
Kuskokwim Mts.	**67**	63 0N	156 0W
Kuskokwim, R.	**67**	61 48N	157 0W
Kustanay	**120**	53 10N	63 35E
Kutahya	**122**	39 30N	30 2E
Kutaisi	**120**	42 19N	42 40E
Kutaradja = Banda Aceh	**126**	5 35N	95 20E
Kutatjane	**126**	3 45N	97 50E
Kutch, G. of	**124**	22 50N	69 15E
Kutch, Rann of	**124**	24 0N	70 0E
Kutno	**107**	52 15N	19 23E
Kutu	**116**	2 40S	18 11E
Kuwait = Al Kuwayt	**122**	29 30N	47 30E
Kuwait ■	**122**	29 30N	47 30E
Kuyang	**130**	41 8N	110 1E
Kuybyshev	**120**	55 27N	78 19E
Kuyung	**131**	32 0N	119 8E
Kvænangen	**110**	69 55N	21 15E
Kvarken	**111**	63 30N	21 0E
Kvarner	**108**	44 50N	14 10E
Kvarnerič	**108**	44 43N	14 37E
Kwadacha, R.	**54**	57 28N	125 38W
Kwakoegron	**87**	5 25N	55 25W
Kwando, R.	**117**	16 48S	22 45E
Kwangan	**131**	30 35N	106 40E
Kwangchow	**131**	23 10N	113 10E
Kwangchow Wan.	**131**	21 0N	111 0E
Kwangju	**130**	35 9N	126 55E
Kwangnan	**129**	24 10N	105 0E
Kwangping	**130**	36 40N	114 41E
Kwangshui	**131**	31 45N	114 0E
Kwangsi-Chuang □	**131**	23 30N	108 55E
Kwangtseh	**131**	27 30N	117 25E
Kwangtsi	**131**	30 2N	115 46E
Kwangtung	**131**	23 35N	114 0E
Kwangyuan	**131**	32 30N	105 49E
Kwanhsien	**129**	30 59N	103 40E
Kwantung	**129**	25 12N	101 37E
Kwanyun	**131**	34 28N	119 29E
Kwataboahegan, R.	**53**	51 9N	80 50W
Kwatisore	**127**	3 7S	139 59E
Kweichih	**131**	30 40N	117 30E
Kweichow = Fengkieh	**131**	31 0N	109 33E
Kweichow □	**131**	27 20N	107 0E
Kweihsien	**131**	22 59N	109 44E
Kweihwa = Mingki	**131**	26 10N	117 14E
Kweiki	**131**	28 10N	117 8E
Kweilin	**131**	25 16N	110 15E
Kweiping	**131**	23 12N	110 0E
Kweishun = Tsingsing	**131**	38 1N	114 4E
Kweitung	**131**	26 0N	113 35E
Kweiyang, Hunan, China	**131**	25 50N	112 25E

Kweiyang
Laois □

Kweiyang, Kweichow, China **131** 26 30N 106 35 E
Kwethluk **67** 60 45N 161 34W
Kwidzyn **107** 54 45N 18 58 E
Kwigillingok **67** 59 50N 163 10W
Kwiguk **67** 63 45N 164 35W
Kwinana **134** 32 15 S 115 47 E
Kwinitsa **62** 54 19N 129 22W
Kwo Ho **131** 33 20N 116 50 E
Kwohwa **131** 23 10N 107 0 E
Kwoyang **131** 33 35N 116 15 E
Kyabram **136** 36 19 S 145 4 E
Kyaikto **128** 17 20N 97 3 E
Kyakhta **121** 50 30N 106 25 E
Kyargas Nuur **129** 49 0N 93 0 E
Kyaukpadaung **125** 20 52N 95 8 E
Kyaukpyu **125** 19 28N 93 30 E
Kyaukse **125** 21 36N 96 10 E
Kyburz **80** 38 47N 120 18W
Kyle **56** 50 50N 108 2W
Kyle Dam **117** 20 15 S 31 0 E
Kyle of Lochalsh **96** 57 17N 5 43W
Kyneton **136** 37 10 S 144 29 E
Kynoch Inlet **62** 52 45N 128 0W
Kyō-ga-Saki **132** 35 45N 135 15 E
Kyoga, L. **116** 1 35N 33 0 E
Kyongju **130** 35 50N 129 13 E
Kyongpyaw **125** 17 12N 95 10 E
Kyōto **132** 35 0N 135 45 E
Kyōto-fu □ **132** 35 15N 135 30 E
Kyrenia **122** 35 20N 33 20 E
Kystatyam **121** 67 20N 123 10 E
Kytalktakh **121** 65 30N 123 40 E
Kyulyunken **121** 64 10N 137 5 E
Kyunhla **125** 23 25N 95 15 E
Kyuquot **62** 50 3N 127 25W
Kyūshū **132** 33 0N 131 0 E
Kyushu, I. **132** 32 30N 131 0 E
Kyūshū-Sanchi **132** 32 45N 131 40 E
Kyustendil **109** 42 25N 22 41 E
Kyusyur **121** 70 39N 127 15 E
Kywong **136** 34 58 S 146 44 E
Kyzyl **121** 51 50N 94 30 E
Kyzyl-Kiya **120** 40 16N 72 8 E
Kyzyl Orda **120** 44 56N 65 30 E
Kyzyl Rabat **120** 37 45N 74 55 E
Kyzylkum **120** 42 30N 65 0 E
Kzyl-orda **120** 44 48N 65 28 E

L

La Broquerie **57** 49 25N 96 30W
La Havre, R. **39** 44 14N 64 20W
La Push **80** 47 55N 124 38W
Laau Pt. **67** 21 57N 159 40W
Labastide **102** 43 28N 2 39 E
Labastide-Murat **102** 44 39N 1 33 E
Labe, R. **106** 50 3N 15 20 E
Laberge, L. **54** 61 11N 135 12W
Labis **128** 2 22N 103 2 E
Laboa **127** 8 6 S 122 50 E
Labouheyre **102** 44 13N 0 55W
Laboulaye **88** 34 10 S 63 30W
Labrador City **38** 52 57N 66 55W
Labranzagrande **86** 5 33N 72 34W
Lábrea **86** 7 15 S 64 51W
Labrède **102** 44 41N 0 32W
Labrie **42** 46 48N 70 56W
Labrieville **41** 49 18N 69 34W
Labuan, I. **126** 5 15N 115 38W
Labuha **127** 0 30 S 127 30 E
Labuhan **127** 6 26 S 105 50 E
Labuhanbajo **127** 8 28 S 120 1 E
Labuk, Telok **126** 6 10N 117 50 E
Lac Allard **38** 50 33N 63 24W
Lac-Alouette **43** 45 49N 73 58W
Lac-au-Saumon **38** 48 25N 67 22W
Lac-aux-Sables **41** 46 51N 72 24W
Lac Bouchette **41** 48 16N 72 11W
Lac-Brière **43** 45 50N 73 58W
Lac Carré **41** 46 7N 74 29W
Lac-des-Écorces **40** 46 34N 75 22W
Lac du Bonnet **57** 50 15N 96 4W
Lac du Flambeau **74** 46 1N 89 51W
Lac Édouard **41** 47 40N 72 16W
Lac-Etchemin **41** 46 24N 70 30W
Lac la Biche **60** 54 45N 111 58W
Lac la Hache **63** 51 49N 121 27W
Lac la Martre **64** 63 8N 117 16W
Lac-l'Achigan **43** 45 57N 73 59W
Lac-Lapierre **43** 45 56N 73 47W
Lac-Marois **43** 45 51N 74 8W
Lac-Meach **48** 45 32N 75 51W
Lac-Mégantic **41** 45 35N 70 53W
Lac-Millette **43** 45 58N 74 12W
Lac-Rémi **40** 46 1N 74 46W
Lac-St-Charles **42** 46 54N 71 23W
Lac-Ste-Marie **40** 45 57N 75 57W
Lac Seul **55** 50 28N 92 0W
Lacadie **45** 45 19N 73 21W
Lacanau, Étang de **102** 44 58N 1 7W
Lacanau Médoc **102** 44 59N 1 5W
Lacantum, R. **83** 16 36N 90 40W
Lacaune **102** 43 43N 2 40 E
Lacaune, Mts. de **102** 43 43N 2 50 E
Laccadive Is. = Lakshadweep Is. **118** 10 0N 72 30 E
Lacepede Is. **134** 16 55 S 122 0 E
Lacey **80** 47 7N 122 49W
Lachenaie **45** 45 42N 73 33W
Lachine **44** 45 30N 73 40W
Lachlan, R. **136** 34 22 S 143 55 E
Lachute **43** 45 39N 74 21W
Lackawanna **70** 42 49N 78 50W
Laclu **52** 49 46N 94 41W
Lacolle **43** 45 5N 73 22W
Lacombe **61** 52 30N 113 44W
Lacon **76** 41 2N 89 24W
Lacona, U.S.A. **76** 41 11N 93 23W
Lacona, N.Y., U.S.A. **71** 43 37N 76 5W
Laconia **71** 43 32N 71 30W
Lacq **102** 43 25N 0 35W
Lacrosse **78** 46 51N 117 58W
Ladd **76** 41 23N 89 13W
Laddonia **76** 39 15N 91 39W
Lādiz **123** 28 55N 61 15 E
Ladner **66** 49 5N 123 4W
Ladon **101** 48 0N 2 30 E
Ladozhskoye Ozero **120** 61 15N 30 30 E
Ladrone Is. = Mariana Is. **14** 17 0N 145 0 E
Lady Ann Str. **65** 75 40N 79 50W
Lady Beatrix L. **34** 5 20N 76 50W
Ladysmith, Can. **62** 49 0N 123 49W
Ladysmith, S. Afr. **117** 28 32 S 29 46 E
Ladysmith, U.S.A. **74** 45 27N 91 4W
Lae **14** 6 40 S 147 2 E
Læsø **111** 57 15N 10 53 E
Lafayette, U.S.A. **77** 40 25N 86 54W
Lafayette, Colo., U.S.A. **74** 40 0N 105 2W
Lafayette, Ga., U.S.A. **73** 34 44N 85 15W
Lafayette, La., U.S.A. **75** 30 18N 92 0W
Lafayette, Tenn., U.S.A. **73** 36 35N 86 0W
Laferté **34** 48 37N 78 48W
Laferte, R. **54** 61 53N 117 44W
Lafia **114** 8 30N 8 34 E
Laflamme, R. **40** 49 17N 77 9W
Laflèche **43** 45 30N 73 28W
Lafleche **56** 49 45N 106 40W
Lafontaine **43** 45 48N 74 1W
Laforce **40** 47 32N 78 44W
Laforest **34** 47 4N 81 12W
Lagan, R. **97** 54 35N 5 55W
Lagarfljót **110** 65 40N 14 18W
Lagarto, Serra do **89** 23 0 S 57 15W
Lågen, R. **111** 61 30N 10 20 E
Laghman □ **123** 34 20N 70 0 E
Laghouat **114** 33 50N 2 59 E
Lagnieu **103** 45 55N 5 20 E
Lagny **101** 48 52N 2 40 E
Lagonoy Gulf **127** 13 50N 123 50 E
Lagoon **63** 48 25N 123 28W
Lagos, Nigeria **114** 6 25N 3 27 E
Lagos, Port. **104** 37 5N 8 41W
Lagos de Moreno **82** 21 21N 101 55W
Lagrange **77** 41 39N 85 25W
Laguépie **102** 44 8N 1 57 E
Laguna, Brazil **89** 28 30 S 48 50W
Laguna, U.S.A. **79** 35 3N 107 28W
Laguna Beach **81** 33 31N 117 52W
Laguna Dam **79** 32 55N 114 30W
Laguna Limpia **88** 26 32 S 59 45W
Laguna Madre **83** 27 0N 97 20W
Lagunas, Chile **88** 21 0 S 69 45W
Lagunas, Peru **86** 5 10 S 75 35W
Lagunillas **86** 10 8N 71 16W
Laha **130** 48 9N 124 30 E
Lahad Datu **127** 5 0N 118 30 E
Lahaina **67** 20 52N 156 41W
Lahat **126** 3 45 S 103 30 E
Lahewa **126** 1 22N 97 12 E
Lahijan **122** 37 10N 50 6 E
Lahn, R. **106** 50 52N 8 35 E
Laholm **111** 56 30N 13 2 E
Lahontan Res. **78** 39 28N 118 58W
Lahore **124** 31 32N 74 22 E
Lahore □ **124** 31 55N 74 5 E
Lahti **111** 60 58N 25 40 E
Lai (Béhagle) **114** 9 25N 16 30 E
Lai Chau **128** 22 5N 103 3 E
Laichow Wan **130** 37 30N 119 30 E
Laidlaw **63** 49 20N 121 36W
Laifeng **131** 29 30N 109 30 E
L'Aigle **100** 48 46N 0 38 E
Laignes **101** 47 50N 4 20 E
Laila **122** 22 10N 46 40 E
Laillahue, Mt. **86** 17 0 S 69 30W
Laipin **131** 23 45N 109 10 E
Laird **56** 52 43N 106 35W
Lairg **96** 58 1N 4 24W
Lais **126** 3 35 S 102 0 E
Laiyang **130** 37 0N 120 42 E
Laja, R. **82** 20 55N 100 46W
Lajes **89** 27 48 S 50 20W
Lakar **127** 8 15 S 128 17 E
Lake Alma **56** 49 9N 104 12W
Lake Alpine **80** 38 29N 120 0W
Lake Andes **74** 43 10N 98 32W
Lake Anse **72** 46 42N 88 25W
Lake Arthur **75** 30 8N 92 40W
Lake Bluff **77** 42 17N 87 50W
Lake Bronson **57** 48 44N 96 49W
Lake Cargelligo **136** 33 15 S 146 22 E
Lake Charles **75** 30 15N 93 10W
Lake City, Colo, U.S.A. **79** 38 3N 107 27W
Lake City, Fla., U.S.A. **73** 30 10N 82 40W
Lake City, Iowa, U.S.A. **77** 42 12N 94 42W
Lake City, Mich., U.S.A. **46** 44 20N 85 10W
Lake City, Minn., U.S.A. **74** 44 28N 92 21W
Lake City, Pa., U.S.A. **70** 42 2N 80 20W
Lake City, S.C., U.S.A. **73** 33 51N 79 44W
Lake Cowichan **62** 48 49N 124 3W
Lake District **98** 54 30N 3 10W
Lake Forest **77** 42 15N 87 50W
Lake Geneva **77** 42 36N 88 26W
Lake George **71** 43 25N 73 43W
Lake Harbour **65** 62 30N 69 50W
Lake Havasu City **81** 34 25N 114 29W
Lake Hill **63** 48 28N 123 22W
Lake Hughes **81** 34 41N 118 26W
Lake Isabella **81** 35 38N 118 28W
Lake Lenore **56** 52 24N 104 59W
Lake Linden **52** 47 11N 88 26W
Lake Louise **61** 51 30N 116 10W
Lake Mead Nat. Rec. Area **81** 36 0N 114 30W
Lake Michigan Beach **77** 42 13N 86 25W
Lake Mills, U.S.A. **77** 43 5N 88 55W
Lake Mills, Iowa, U.S.A. **74** 43 23N 93 33W
Lake Nebagamon **52** 46 30N 91 42W
Lake Odesse **77** 42 47N 85 8W
Lake of the Woods **69** 49 0N 95 0W
Lake Orion **77** 42 47N 83 14W
Lake Providence **75** 32 49N 91 12W
Lake River **34** 54 22N 82 31W
Lake St. Peter **47** 45 18N 78 2W
Lake Superior Prov. Park **53** 47 45N 84 45W
Lake Traverse **34** 45 56N 78 4W
Lake Tyers **136** 37 52 S 148 5 E
Lake Victoria Res. **136** 34 0 S 141 17 E
Lake View **50** 43 34N 79 33W
Lake Villa **77** 42 25N 88 5W
Lake Village **75** 33 20N 91 19W
Lake Wales **73** 27 55N 81 32W
Lake Worth **73** 26 36N 80 3W
Lakefield, Ont., Can. **47** 44 25N 78 16W
Lakefield, Qué., Can. **43** 45 45N 74 15W
Lakeland **73** 28 0N 82 0W
Lakemba, I. **133** 18 13 S 178 47W
Lakeport, Calif., U.S.A. **80** 39 1N 122 56W
Lakeport, Mich., U.S.A. **46** 43 7N 82 30W
Lakes Entrance **136** 37 50 S 148 0 E
Lakeside, Ariz., U.S.A. **79** 34 12N 109 59W
Lakeside, Calif., U.S.A. **81** 32 52N 116 55W
Lakeside, Nebr., U.S.A. **74** 42 5N 102 24W
Lakeview, Ont., Can. **48** 45 21N 75 50W
Lakeview, Qué., Can. **43** 45 53N 74 34W
Lakeview, Sask., Can. **58** 50 25N 104 38W
Lakeview, Mich., U.S.A. **46** 43 27N 85 17W
Lakeview, N.Y., U.S.A. **72** 42 43N 78 57W
Lakeview, Oreg., U.S.A. **78** 42 15N 120 22W
Lakewood, U.S.A. **80** 48 9N 122 12W
Lakewood, Calif., U.S.A. **81** 33 51N 118 8W
Lakewood, N.J., U.S.A. **71** 40 5N 74 13W
Lakewood, Ohio, U.S.A. **70** 41 28N 81 50W
Laki **110** 64 4N 18 14W
Lakin **75** 37 58N 101 18W
Lakitusaki, R. **34** 54 21N 82 25W
Lakonikós Kólpos **109** 36 40N 22 40 E
Lakor, I. **127** 8 15 S 128 17 E
Lakota **74** 48 0N 98 22W
Laksefjorden **110** 70 45N 26 50 E
Lakselv **110** 70 2N 24 56 E
Lakshadweep Is. **118** 10 0N 72 30 E
Lalín **104** 42 40N 8 5W
Lalinde **102** 44 50N 0 44 E
Lamaline **37** 46 52N 55 49W
Lamar, Colo., U.S.A. **74** 38 9N 102 35W
Lamar, Mo., U.S.A. **75** 37 30N 94 20W
Lamas **86** 6 28 S 76 31W
Lamastre **103** 44 59N 4 35 E
Lamatientze **130** 46 46N 124 46 E
Lamballe **100** 48 29N 2 31W
Lambaréné **116** 0 20 S 10 12 E
Lambay I. **97** 53 30N 6 0W
Lambayeque □ **86** 6 45 S 80 0W
Lambert **74** 47 44N 104 39W
Lambert Land **17** 79 12N 20 30W
Lambesc **103** 43 39N 5 16 E
Lambeth **46** 42 54N 81 18W
Lambi Kyun, (Sullivan I.) **128** 10 50N 98 20 E
Lambton **41** 45 50N 71 5W
Lambton, C. **64** 71 5N 123 9W
Lambton Mills **50** 43 39N 79 31W
Lame Deer **78** 45 45N 106 40W
Lamego **104** 41 5N 7 52W
Lamèque **39** 47 45N 64 38W
Lamesa **75** 32 45N 101 57W
Lamía **109** 38 55N 22 41 E
Lamitan **127** 6 40N 122 10 E
Lammermuir Hills **96** 55 50N 2 40W
Lamming Mills **63** 53 20N 120 15W
Lamoille **78** 40 47N 115 31W
Lamon Bay **127** 14 30N 122 20 E
Lamoni **76** 40 37N 93 56W
Lamont, Can. **60** 53 46N 112 50W
Lamont, U.S.A. **76** 42 35N 91 40W
Lamont, Calif., U.S.A. **81** 35 15N 118 55W
Lampa **86** 15 10 S 70 30W
Lampang **128** 18 18N 99 31 E
Lampasas **75** 31 5N 98 10W
Lampaul **100** 48 28N 5 7W
Lampazos de Naranjo **82** 27 2N 100 32W
Lampedusa, I. **108** 35 36N 12 40 E
Lampeter **95** 52 6N 4 6W
Lampman **56** 49 25N 102 50W
Lamprey **55** 58 33N 94 8W
Lampung **126** 1 48 S 115 0 E
Lamu **116** 2 10 S 40 55 E
Lamy **79** 35 30N 105 58W
Lan Tsan Kiang (Mekong) **119** 18 0N 104 15 E
Lan Yu, I. **131** 22 0N 121 30 E
Lanai City **67** 20 50N 156 56W
Lanai I. **67** 20 50N 156 55W
Lanao, L. **127** 7 52N 124 15 E
Lanark, Can. **47** 45 1N 76 22W
Lanark, U.K. **96** 55 40N 3 48W
Lancashire □ **94** 53 40N 2 30W
Lancaster, N.B., Can. **35** 45 17N 66 10W
Lancaster, Ont., Can. **47** 45 8N 74 30W
Lancaster, Ont., Can. **71** 45 10N 74 30W
Lancaster, Qué., Can. **43** 45 8N 74 30W
Lancaster, U.K. **94** 54 3N 2 48W
Lancaster, Calif., U.S.A. **81** 34 47N 118 8W
Lancaster, Ky., U.S.A. **77** 37 40N 84 40W
Lancaster, Minn., U.S.A. **57** 48 52N 96 48W
Lancaster, Mo., U.S.A. **76** 40 31N 92 32W
Lancaster, N.H., U.S.A. **71** 44 27N 71 33W
Lancaster, N.Y., U.S.A. **70** 42 53N 78 43W
Lancaster, Pa., U.S.A. **71** 40 4N 76 19W
Lancaster, S.C., U.S.A. **73** 34 45N 80 47W
Lancaster, Wis., U.S.A. **76** 42 48N 90 43W
Lancaster Sd. **65** 74 13N 84 0W
Lancer **56** 50 48N 108 53W
Lanchow **130** 36 4N 103 44 E
Lanciano **108** 42 15N 14 22 E
Lándana **116** 5 11 S 12 5 E
Landau **105** 49 12N 8 7 E
Landeck **106** 47 9N 10 34 E
Landen **105** 50 45N 5 3 E
Lander **78** 42 50N 108 49W
Landerneau **100** 48 28N 4 17W
Landes □ **102** 43 57N 0 48W
Landes, Les **102** 44 20N 1 0W
Landis **56** 52 12N 108 27W
Landivisiau **100** 48 31N 4 6W
Landrecies **101** 50 7N 3 40 E
Landrienne **40** 48 30N 77 50W
Land's End, Can. **17** 76 10N 123 0W
Land's End, U.K. **95** 50 4N 5 43W
Landshut **106** 48 31N 12 10 E
Landskrona **111** 56 53N 12 50 E
Lanesboro **71** 41 57N 75 34W
Lanett **73** 33 0N 85 15W
Lanfeng **131** 34 50N 114 58 E
Lang Bay **62** 49 45N 124 21W
Langara I. **62** 54 14N 133 1W
Langchung (Paoning) **131** 31 30N 106 0 E
Langdon **74** 48 47N 98 24W
Langeac **102** 45 7N 3 29 E
Langenburg **57** 50 51N 101 43W
Langfeng **130** 48 4N 121 10 E
Langford **63** 48 27N 123 29W
Langham **56** 52 22N 106 58W
Langholm **96** 55 9N 2 59W
Langjökull **110** 64 39N 20 12W
Langkawi, P. **128** 6 25N 99 45 E
Langkon **126** 6 30N 116 40 E
Langlade, Can. **34** 48 14N 76 10W
Langlade, St. P. & M. **37** 46 50N 56 20W
Langley **66** 49 7N 122 39W
Langlois **78** 42 54N 124 26W
Langogne **102** 44 43N 3 50 E
Langon **102** 44 33N 0 16W
Langøya **110** 68 45N 15 10 E
Langres **101** 47 52N 5 20 E
Langres, Plateau de **101** 47 45N 5 20 E
Langruth **57** 50 23N 98 40W
Langsa **126** 4 30N 97 57 E
Langson **128** 21 52N 106 42 E
Langstaff **50** 43 50N 79 25W
Langtry **75** 29 50N 101 33W
Languedoc **102** 43 58N 4 0 E
Lanigan **56** 51 51N 105 2W
Lannemezan **102** 43 8N 0 23 E
Lannilis **100** 48 35N 4 32W
Lannion **100** 48 46N 3 29W
Lanoraie **43** 45 58N 73 13W
Lanouaille **102** 45 24N 1 9 E
Lansdale **71** 40 14N 75 18W
Lansdowne **47** 44 24N 76 1W
Lansdowne House **34** 52 14N 87 53W
Lansford **71** 40 48N 75 55W
Lansing, Can. **50** 43 45N 79 25W
Lansing, U.S.A. **77** 42 47N 84 40W
Lanslebourg **103** 45 17N 6 52 E
Lantuna **127** 8 19 S 124 8 E
Lanus **88** 34 44 S 58 27W
Lanz I. **62** 50 49N 128 41W
Lanzville **62** 49 15N 124 5W
Lao Cai **128** 22 30N 103 57 E
Laoag **127** 18 7N 120 34 E
Laoang **127** 12 32N 125 8 E
Laois □ **97** 53 0N 7 20W

Laon
Lewisburg

Laon 101 49 33N 3 35E
Laona 72 45 32N 88 41W
Laos ■ 128 17 45N 105 0E
Lapa 89 25 46S 49 44W
Lapalisse 102 46 15N 3 44E
Laparan Cap, I. 127 6 0N 120 0E
Lapeer 46 43 3N 83 20W
Lapi □ 110 67 0N 27 0E
Lapland = Lappland 110 68 7N 24 0E
Laporte 71 41 27N 76 30W
Lappland 110 68 7N 24 0E
Laprairie 44 45 20N 73 30W
Laprairie □ 43 45 20N 73 30W
Laprida 88 37 34S 60 45W
Laptev Sea 121 76 0N 125 0E
Lapush 78 47 56N 124 33W
Lār 123 27 40N 54 14E
Lara □ 86 10 10N 69 50W
Laragne-Monteglin 103 44 18N 5 49E
Laramie 74 41 15N 105 29W
Laramie Mts. 74 42 0N 105 30W
Laranjeiras do Sul 89 25 23S 52 23W
Larantuka 127 8 5S 122 55E
Larap 127 14 18N 122 39E
Larat, I. 127 7 0S 132 0E
Larder Lake 34 48 5N 79 40W
Laredo 75 27 34N 99 29W
Laredo Sd. 62 52 30N 128 53W
Laren 105 52 16N 5 14E
Largentière 103 44 34N 4 18E
Largs 96 55 48N 4 51W
Lariang 127 1 35S 119 25E
Larimore 74 47 55N 97 35W
Lárisa 109 39 38N 22 28E
Lark Harbour 37 49 6N 58 23W
Lark, R. 95 52 26N 0 18E
Larnaca 122 35 0N 33 35E
Lárnax 122 35 0N 33 35E
Larne 97 54 52N 5 50W
Larne □ 97 54 55N 5 55W
Larned 74 38 15N 99 10W
Laroquebrou 102 44 58N 2 12E
Larrimah 134 15 35S 133 12E
Larrys River 39 45 13N 61 23W
Larsen Ice Shelf 91 67 0S 62 0W
Larus L. 52 51 17N 94 40W
Larvik 111 59 4N 10 0E
Laryak 120 61 15N 80 0E
Larzac, Causse du 102 44 0N 3 17E
Las Animas 75 38 8N 103 18W
Las Bonitas 86 7 50N 65 40W
Las Brenãs 88 27 5S 61 7W
Las Cascadas 84 9 5N 79 41W
Las Chimeneas 81 32 12N 116 5W
Las Cruces 79 32 25N 106 50W
Las Flores 88 36 0S 59 0W
Las Heras, Mendoza, Argent. 89 32 51S 68 49W
Las Heras, Santa Cruz, Argent. 90 46 30S 69 0W
Las Lajas 90 38 30S 70 25W
Las Lajitas 86 6 55N 65 39W
Las Lomitas 88 24 35S 60 50W
Las Mercedes 86 9 7N 66 24W
Las Palmas 88 27 8S 58 45W
Las Palmas □ 114 28 10N 15 28W
Las Palmas, R. 81 32 8N 116 33W
Las Piedras 89 34 35S 56 20W
Las Plumas 90 43 40S 67 15W
Las Rosas 88 32 30S 61 40W
Las Tablas 84 7 49N 80 14W
Las Termas 88 27 29S 64 52W
Las Tres Marías, Is. 82 20 12N 106 30W
Las Varillas 88 32 0S 62 50W
Las Vegas, Nev., U.S.A. 81 36 10N 115 5W
Las Vegas, N.M., U.S.A. 79 35 35N 105 10W
Lasalle 44 45 26N 73 38W
Lascano 89 33 35S 54 18W
Lascaux 102 45 5N 1 10E
Lashburn 56 53 10N 109 40W
Lashio 125 22 56N 97 45E
Lasqueti 62 49 30N 124 21W
Lasqueti I. 62 49 29N 124 16W
Lassay 100 48 27N 0 30W
Lassen, Pk. 78 40 35N 121 40W
Last Mountain L. 56 51 5N 105 14W
Lastchance Cr. 80 40 2N 121 15W
Lastoursville 116 0 55S 12 38E
Lastovo, I. 108 42 46N 16 55E
Latacunga 86 0 50S 78 35W
Latakia = Al Lādhiqiyah 122 35 30N 35 45E
Latchford 34 47 20N 79 50W
Lathrop 76 39 33N 94 20W
Lathrop Wells 81 36 39N 116 24W
Latina 108 41 26N 12 53E
Lating 130 39 23N 118 55E
Laton 80 36 26N 119 41W
Latouche 67 60 0N 148 0W
Latouche Treville, C. 134 18 27S 121 49E
Latrobe, Austral. 136 38 8S 146 44E
Latrobe, U.S.A. 70 40 19N 79 21W
Latulipe 40 47 26N 79 2W
Lau (Eastern) Group 133 17 0S 178 30W
Lauchhammer 106 51 35N 13 40E
Lauenburg 106 53 23N 10 33E
Laugarbakki 110 65 20N 20 55W
Launceston, Austral. 135 41 24S 147 8E
Launceston, U.K. 95 50 38N 4 21W
Laune, R. 97 52 5N 9 40W
Launglon Bok 128 13 50N 97 54E
Laura 135 15 32S 144 32E
Laurel, Ont., Can. 49 43 57N 80 13W
Laurel, Qué., Can. 43 45 51N 74 28W
Laurel, U.S.A. 77 39 31N 85 11W
Laurel, Miss., U.S.A. 75 31 50N 89 0W
Laurel, Mont., U.S.A. 78 45 46N 108 49W
Laurencekirk 96 56 50N 2 30W
Laurens 73 34 32N 82 2W
Laurentian Plat. 36 52 0N 70 0W
Laurentides 43 45 51N 73 46W
Laurentides, Parc Prov. des 41 47 45N 71 15W
Laurie I. 91 60 0S 46 0W
Laurie L. 55 56 35N 101 57W
Laurier 57 50 53N 99 33W
Laurier-Station 41 46 32N 71 38W
Laurierville 41 46 18N 71 39W
Laurinburg 73 34 50N 79 25W
Laurium 52 47 14N 88 26W
Lausanne 106 46 32N 6 38E
Laut Kecil, Kepulauan 126 4 45S 115 40E
Laut, Kepulauan 126 4 45N 108 0E
Lautoka 133 17 37S 177 27E
Lauzon 42 46 48N 71 10W
Lava Hot Springs 78 42 38N 112 1W
Laval, Can. 44 45 35N 73 45W
Laval, France 100 48 4N 0 48W
Laval-des-Rapides 44 45 33N 73 42W
Laval-Ouest 44 45 33N 73 52W
Laval-sur-le-Lac 44 45 32N 73 52W
Lavalle 88 28 15S 65 15W
Lavaltrie 43 45 53N 73 17W
Lavandou, Le 103 43 8N 6 22E
Lavant Sta. 47 45 3N 76 42W
Lavardac 102 44 12N 0 20E
Lavaur 102 43 42N 1 49E
Lavaveix 102 46 5N 2 8E
Lavelanet 102 42 57N 1 51E
Laverendrye Prov. Park 34 46 15N 17 15W
Laverlochère 40 47 26N 79 18W
Laverne 75 36 43N 99 58W
Laverton 134 28 44S 122 29E
Lavieille, L. 47 45 51N 78 14W
Lavillètte 39 47 16N 65 18W
Lavoy 60 53 27N 111 52W
Lavras 89 21 20S 45 0W
Lavrentiya 121 65 35N 171 0W
Lávrion 109 37 40N 24 4E
Lawas 126 4 55N 115 40E
Lawele 127 5 16S 123 3E
Lawn 37 46 57N 55 35W
Lawrence, Austral. 89 29 30S 153 8E
Lawrence, U.S.A. 77 39 50N 86 2W
Lawrence, Kans., U.S.A. 74 39 0N 95 10W
Lawrence, Mass., U.S.A. 71 42 40N 71 9W
Lawrence Station 39 45 26N 67 11W
Lawrenceburg, Ind., U.S.A. 77 39 5N 84 50W
Lawrenceburg, Ky., U.S.A. 77 38 2N 84 54W
Lawrenceburg, Tenn., U.S.A. 73 35 12N 87 19W
Lawrencetown 39 44 53N 65 10W
Lawrenceville, U.S.A. 77 38 44N 87 41W
Lawrenceville, Ga., U.S.A. 73 33 55N 83 59W
Laws 80 37 24N 118 20W
Lawson 76 39 26N 94 12W
Lawton, U.S.A. 75 34 33N 98 25W
Lawton, U.S.A. 77 42 10N 85 50W
Lawu Mt. 127 7 40S 111 13E
Laxford, L. 96 58 25N 5 10W
Laytonville 78 39 44N 123 29W
Lazio □ 108 42 10N 12 30E
Lea, R. 95 51 40N 0 3W
Leach I. 53 47 28N 84 57W
Lead 74 44 20N 103 40W
Leader 56 50 50N 109 30W
Leadhills 96 55 25N 3 47W
Leadville 79 39 17N 106 23W
Leaf L. 57 53 1N 102 8W
Leaf, R., Can. 36 58 47N 70 4W
Leaf, R., U.S.A. 75 31 45N 89 20W
Leakey 75 29 45N 99 45W
Leaksville 73 36 30N 79 49W
Lealui 117 15 10S 23 2E
Leamington, Can. 46 42 3N 82 36W
Leamington, N.Z. 14 37 55S 175 29E
Leamington, U.K. 95 52 18N 1 32W
Leamington, U.S.A. 78 39 37N 112 17W
Leandro Norte Alem 89 27 34S 55 15W
Learmonth 134 22 40S 114 10E
Leaside 50 43 42N 79 22W
Leask 56 53 5N 106 45W
Leavenworth, Mo., U.S.A. 74 39 25N 95 0W
Leavenworth, Wash., U.S.A. 78 47 44N 120 37W
Leavenworthth 77 38 12N 86 21W
Leawood 76 38 57N 94 37W
Lebak 127 6 32N 124 5E
Lebam 80 46 34N 123 33W
Lebanon, Ill., U.S.A. 76 38 38N 89 49W
Lebanon, Ind., U.S.A. 77 40 3N 86 20W
Lebanon, Kans., U.S.A. 74 39 50N 98 35W
Lebanon, Ky., U.S.A. 72 37 35N 85 15W
Lebanon, Mo., U.S.A. 76 37 40N 92 40W
Lebanon, N.H., U.S.A. 71 43 38N 72 15W
Lebanon, Ohio, U.S.A. 77 39 26N 84 13W
Lebanon, Oreg., U.S.A. 78 44 31N 122 57W
Lebanon, Pa., U.S.A. 71 40 20N 76 28W
Lebanon, Tenn., U.S.A. 73 36 15N 86 20W
Lebanon ■ 122 34 0N 36 0E
Lebanon Junction 77 37 50N 85 44W
Lebbeke 105 51 0N 4 8E
Lebec 81 34 46N 118 59W
Lebel sur Quévillon 40 49 3N 76 59W
Lebrija 104 36 53N 6 5W
Lebu 88 37 40S 73 47W
Lecce 109 40 20N 18 10E
Lecco 108 45 50N 9 27E
Lectoure 102 43 56N 0 38E
Łeczyca 107 52 5N 19 45E
Ledbury 95 52 3N 2 25W
Leduc 60 53 15N 113 30W
Lee, Mass., U.S.A. 71 42 17N 73 18W
Lee, Nev., U.S.A. 78 40 35N 115 36W
Lee, R. 97 51 51N 9 2W
Lee Vining 80 37 58N 119 7W
Leech L., Can. 56 51 5N 102 28W
Leech L., U.S.A. 52 47 9N 94 23W
Leedey 75 35 53N 99 24W
Leeds, U.K. 94 53 48N 1 34W
Leeds, U.S.A. 73 33 32N 86 30W
Leek 94 53 7N 2 2W
Lee's Summit 76 38 55N 94 23W
Leesburg, U.S.A. 77 39 21N 83 33W
Leesburg, Fla., U.S.A. 73 28 47N 81 52W
Leesville 75 31 12N 93 15W
Leetonia 70 40 53N 80 45W
Leeuwarden 105 53 15N 5 48E
Leeuwin, C. 134 34 20S 115 9E
Leeward Is. 85 16 30N 63 30W
Lefebvre 41 47 12N 69 49W
Lefors 75 35 30N 100 50W
Lefroy 46 44 16N 79 34W
Lefroy, L. 134 31 21S 121 40E
Legal 60 53 55N 113 45W
Légère 39 47 25N 64 56W
Leghorn = Livorno 108 43 32N 10 18E
Legnica 106 51 12N 16 10E
Leh 124 34 15N 77 35E
Lehi 78 40 20N 112 0W
Lehighton 71 40 50N 75 44W
Lehua, I. 67 22 1N 160 6W
Leicester 95 52 39N 1 9W
Leicester □ 95 52 40N 1 10W
Leichhardt, R. 135 17 50S 139 49E
Leichow = Haihang 131 20 55N 110 3E
Leichow Pantao 131 20 30N 110 0E
Leiden 105 52 9N 4 30E
Leie, R. 105 51 2N 3 45E
Leigh Creek 135 30 28S 138 24E
Leigh, R. 136 37 50S 144 0E
Leine, R. 106 52 35N 9 40E
Leinster □ 97 53 0N 7 10W
Leinster Downs 70 27 52S 120 34E
Leinster, Mt. 97 52 38N 6 47W
Leipzig 106 51 20N 12 23E
Leiria 104 39 46N 8 53W
Leishan 131 25 55N 108 15E
Leith 96 55 59N 3 10W
Leith Hill 95 51 10N 0 23W
Leitrim, Can. 48 45 20N 75 36W
Leitrim, Ireland 97 54 0N 8 5W
Leitrim □ 97 54 8N 8 0W
Leiyang 131 26 27N 112 50E
Lejeune 41 47 46N 68 34W
Lek, R. 105 51 54N 4 38E
Leksula 127 3 46S 126 31E
Leland 75 33 25N 90 52W
Leland Lakes 55 60 0N 110 59W
Leleque 90 42 15S 71 0W
Lelystad 105 52 30N 5 25E
Léman, Lac 106 46 26N 6 30E
Lemay 76 38 20N 90 16W
Lemberg 56 50 44N 103 12W
Lemery 127 13 58N 120 56E
Lemesós 122 34 42N 33 1E
Lemhi Ra. 78 44 30N 113 30W
Lemieux 41 46 18N 72 7W
Lemieux Is. 65 63 40N 64 20W
Lemieux, L. 40 50 19N 74 38W
Lemmer 105 52 51N 5 43E
Lemmon 74 45 59N 102 10W
Lemoine, L. 40 48 0N 78 0W
Lemon Grove 81 32 45N 117 2W
Lemont 77 41 40N 88 0W
Lemoore 80 36 23N 119 46W
Lemoyne 45 45 30N 73 30W
Lempdes 102 45 22N 3 17E
Lemvig 111 56 33N 8 20E
Lena, R. 121 64 30N 127 0E
Lencloître 100 46 50N 0 20E
Lengau de Vaca, Punta 88 30 14S 71 38W
Lenggong 128 5 6N 100 58E
Leninabad 120 40 17N 69 37E
Leninakan 120 41 0N 42 50E
Leningrad 120 59 55N 30 20E
Leninogorsk 120 50 20N 83 30E
Leninsk-Kuznetskiy 120 55 10N 86 10E
Leninskoye 121 47 56N 132 38E
Lenmalu 127 1 58S 130 0E
Lennoxville 41 45 22N 71 51W
Lenoir 73 35 55N 81 36W
Lenoir City 73 35 40N 84 20W
Lenora 74 39 39N 100 1W
Lenore L. 56 52 30N 104 59W
Lenox, U.S.A. 76 40 53N 94 34W
Lenox, Mass., U.S.A. 71 42 20N 73 18W
Lens 101 50 26N 2 50E
Lensk (Mukhtuya) 121 60 48N 114 55E
Lentini 108 37 18N 15 0E
Lenwood 81 34 53N 117 7W
Leoben 106 47 22N 15 5E
Leola 74 45 47N 98 58W
Leominster, U.K. 95 52 15N 2 43W
Leominster, U.S.A. 71 42 32N 71 45W
Léon 102 43 53N 1 18W
León, Mexico 82 21 7N 101 30W
León, Nic. 84 12 20N 86 51W
León, Spain 104 42 38N 5 34W
Leon 76 40 40N 93 40W
León □ 104 42 40N 5 55W
León, Montañas de 104 42 30N 6 18W
Leonardtown 72 38 19N 76 39W
Leongatha 136 38 30S 145 58E
Leonora 134 28 49S 121 19E
Léopold II, Lac = Mai-Ndombe 116 2 0S 18 0E
Leopoldina 89 21 28S 42 40W
Leopoldsburg 105 51 7N 5 13E
Léopoldville = Kinshasa 116 4 20S 15 15E
Leoti 74 38 31N 101 19W
Leoville 56 53 39N 107 33W
Lepellé, R. 36 59 58N 72 24W
Lepikha 121 64 45N 125 55E
Lepreau 39 45 10N 66 28W
Lerdo 82 25 32N 103 32W
Lérida 104 41 37N 0 39E
Lérins, Is. de 103 43 31N 7 3E
Lérouville 101 48 50N 5 30E
Leroy 56 52 0N 104 44W
Leroy, L. 36 55 10N 67 15W
Lerwick 96 60 10N 1 10W
Léry 44 45 21N 73 48W
Leskov, I. 91 56 0S 28 0W
Leskovac 109 43 0N 21 58E
Leslie, U.S.A. 77 42 27N 84 26W
Leslie, Ark., U.S.A. 75 35 50N 92 35W
Leslieville 61 52 23N 114 36W
Lesneven 100 48 35N 4 20W
Lesotho ■ 117 29 40S 28 0E
Lesozavodsk 121 45 30N 133 20E
Lesparre-Médoc 102 45 18N 0 57W
Lessay 100 49 14N 1 30W
Lesse, R. 105 50 15N 4 54E
Lesser Antilles 85 12 30N 61 0W
Lesser Slave L. 60 55 30N 115 25W
Lesser Slave Lake Prov. Park 60 55 26N 114 49W
Lessines 105 50 42N 3 50E
Lester 80 47 12N 121 29W
Lestock 56 51 19N 103 59W
Lésvos, I. 109 39 0N 26 20E
Leszno 106 51 50N 16 30E
Letchworth 95 51 58N 0 13W
Lethbridge, Alta., Can. 61 49 45N 112 45W
Lethbridge, Newf., Can. 37 48 22N 53 52W
Leti 127 8 10S 127 40E
Leti, Kepulauan 127 8 10S 128 0E
Leticia 86 4 0S 70 0W
Letsôk-aw-Kyun (Domel I.) 128 11 30N 98 25E
Letterkenny 97 54 57N 7 42W
Leucadia 81 33 4N 117 18W
Leucate 102 42 56N 3 3E
Leucate, Étang de 102 42 50N 3 0E
Leuser, G. 126 4 0N 96 51E
Leuven (Louvain) 105 50 52N 4 42E
Leuze 105 50 36N 3 37E
Levack 46 46 38N 81 23W
Levan 78 39 37N 111 32W
Levanger 110 63 45N 11 19E
Levelland 75 33 38N 102 17W
Leven 96 56 12N 3 0W
Leven, L. 96 56 12N 3 22W
Levens 103 43 50N 7 12E
Leveque C. 134 16 20S 123 0E
Levering 46 45 38N 84 47W
Leverkusen 105 51 2N 6 59E
Levet 101 46 56N 2 22E
Levick, Mt. 91 75 0S 164 0E
Levie 103 41 40N 9 7E
Levier 101 46 58N 6 8E
Levin 133 40 37S 175 18E
Lévis 42 46 48N 71 9W
Levis, L. 54 62 37N 117 58W
Levittown 71 40 10N 74 51W
Levkás, I. 109 38 40N 20 43E
Levkôsia = Nicosia 122 35 10N 33 25E
Levroux 101 47 0N 1 38E
Lewellen 74 41 22N 102 5W
Lewes, U.K. 95 50 53N 0 2E
Lewes, U.S.A. 72 38 45N 75 8W
Lewis, Butt of 96 58 30N 6 12W
Lewis Hills 37 48 48N 58 30W
Lewis, I. 96 58 10N 6 40W
Lewis, R. 80 45 51N 122 48W
Lewis Range 78 48 0N 113 15W
Lewisburg, U.S.A. 77 39 51N 84 33W

Lewisburg **Lobstick L**

Place	Page	Lat.	Long.
Lewisburg, Pa., U.S.A.	70	40 57N	76 57W
Lewisburg, Tenn., U.S.A.	73	35 29N	86 46W
Lewisport	77	37 56N	86 54W
Lewisporte	37	49 15N	55 3W
Lewiston, Idaho, U.S.A.	78	46 30N	117 0W
Lewiston, Mich., U.S.A.	46	44 53N	84 18W
Lewiston, N.Y., U.S.A.	49	43 12N	79 2W
Lewiston, Utah, U.S.A.	78	41 58N	111 56W
Lewistown, Ill., U.S.A.	76	40 24N	90 9W
Lewistown, Mont., U.S.A.	78	47 0N	109 25W
Lewistown, Pa., U.S.A.	70	40 37N	77 33W
Lewisville	39	46 6N	64 46W
Lexington, Ill., U.S.A.	77	40 37N	88 47W
Lexington, Ky., U.S.A.	77	38 6N	84 30W
Lexington, Mich., U.S.A.	46	43 15N	82 30W
Lexington, Miss., U.S.A.	75	33 8N	90 2W
Lexington, Mo., U.S.A.	76	39 7N	93 55W
Lexington, N.C., U.S.A.	73	35 50N	80 13W
Lexington, Nebr., U.S.A.	74	40 48N	99 45W
Lexington, Ohio, U.S.A.	70	40 39N	82 35W
Lexington, Oreg., U.S.A.	78	45 29N	119 46W
Lexington, Tenn., U.S.A.	73	35 38N	88 25W
Leyte, I.	127	11 0N	125 0E
Lezay	102	46 17N	0 0E
Lèze, R.	102	43 28N	1 25E
Lézignan-Corbières	102	43 13N	2 43E
Lezoux	102	45 49N	3 21E
Lhasa	129	29 50N	91 3E
Lhatse Dzong	129	29 10N	87 45E
Lhokseumawe	126	5 20N	97 10E
Liang Liang	127	5 58N	121 30E
Lianga	127	8 38N	126 6E
Liangpran, Gunong	126	1 0N	114 23E
Liangsiang	130	39 55N	116 15E
Liao Ho, R.	130	41 0N	121 55E
Liaocheng	130	36 30N	115 59E
Liaochung	130	41 35N	122 45E
Liaoning □	130	41 40N	122 30E
Liaotung	130	40 10N	123 0E
Liaotung Wan	130	40 0N	120 45E
Liaoyang	130	41 15N	123 10E
Liaoyüan	130	42 55N	125 10E
Liard, R.	54	61 51N	121 18W
Libby	78	48 20N	115 10W
Libenge	116	3 40N	18 55E
Liberal, Kans., U.S.A.	75	37 4N	101 0W
Liberal, Mo., U.S.A.	75	37 35N	94 30W
Liberec	106	50 47N	15 7E
Liberia	84	10 40N	85 30W
Liberia ■	114	6 30N	9 30W
Libertad	86	8 20N	69 37W
Libertad, La	84	16 47N	90 7W
Liberty, Can.	56	51 8N	105 26W
Liberty, U.S.A.	77	39 38N	84 56W
Liberty, Mo., U.S.A.	79	39 15N	94 24W
Liberty, N.Y., U.S.A.	71	41 48N	74 45W
Liberty, Tex., U.S.A.	75	30 5N	94 50W
Liberty Center	77	41 27N	84 1W
Libertyville	77	42 18N	87 57W
Lîbîya, Sahrâ'	112	27 35N	25 0E
Libourne	102	44 55N	0 14W
Libreville	116	0 25N	9 26E
Libya ■	114	28 30N	17 30E
Licantén	88	34 55S	72 0W
Licata	108	37 6N	13 55E
Lichfield	94	52 40N	1 50W
Lichtenburg	117	26 8S	26 8E
Lida	79	37 30N	117 30W
Liddon Gulf	64	75 3N	113 0W
Lidköping	111	58 31N	13 14E
Liechtenstein ■	106	47 8N	9 35E
Liège	105	50 38N	5 35E
Liège □	105	50 32N	5 35E
Lienhua	131	26 58N	113 59E
Lienkiang	131	26 11N	119 30E
Lienshankwan	130	41 0N	123 59E
Lienyunkang	131	34 45N	119 30E
Lienz	106	46 50N	12 46E
Liepāja	120	56 30N	21 0E
Lier	105	51 7N	4 34E
Lieshankwan	130	40 56N	124 51E
Liévin	101	50 24N	2 47E
Lièvre, R.	40	45 31N	75 26W
Liffey, R.	97	53 21N	6 20W
Lifford	97	54 50N	7 30W
Liffré	100	48 12N	1 30W
Ligny-en-Barrois	101	48 36N	5 20E
Ligny-le-Châtel	101	47 54N	3 45E
Ligua, La	88	32 30S	71 16W
Liguria □	108	44 30N	9 0E
Ligurian Sea	108	43 20N	9 0E
Lihou Reefs and Cays	135	17 25S	151 40E
Lihue	67	21 59N	159 24W
Likasi	116	10 55S	26 48E
Likati	116	3 20N	24 0E
Likely	63	52 37N	121 35W
Likiang	129	26 50N	100 15E
Likunpu	130	36 31N	106 12E
Liling	131	27 47N	113 30E
Lille	101	50 38N	3 3E
Lille Bælt	111	55 30N	9 45E
Lillebonne	100	49 30N	0 32E
Lillehammer	111	61 8N	10 30E
Lillers	101	50 35N	2 28E
Lillesand	111	58 15N	8 23E
Lillestrøm	111	59 58N	11 5E
Lillian L. (Daré, Le, L.)	38	51 17N	61 23W
Lillooet	63	50 44N	121 57W
Lillooet L.	63	50 18N	122 35W
Lillooet, R.	63	49 15N	121 57W
Lilongwe	117	14 0S	33 48E
Liloy	127	8 4N	122 39E
Lima, Austral.	136	36 44S	146 10E
Lima, Indon.	127	3 37S	128 4E
Lima, Peru	86	12 0S	77 0W
Lima, Mont., U.S.A.	78	44 41N	112 38W
Lima, Ohio, U.S.A.	77	40 42N	84 5W
Limages	71	45 20N	75 16W
Limassol	122	34 42N	33 1E
Limavady	97	55 3N	6 58W
Limavady □	97	55 0N	6 55W
Limay Mahuida	88	37 10S	66 45W
Limay, R.	90	39 40S	69 45W
Limbang	126	4 42N	115 6E
Limbour	48	45 29N	75 45W
Limbourg □	105	51 2N	5 25E
Limburg □	108	51 20N	5 55E
Limehouse	49	43 38N	79 58W
Limeira	89	22 35S	47 28W
Limerick, Can.	56	49 39N	106 16W
Limerick, Ireland	97	52 40N	8 38W
Limerick □	97	52 30N	8 50W
Limestone	70	42 2N	78 39W
Limestone B.	57	53 50N	98 53W
Limestone, R.	55	56 31N	94 7W
Limfjorden	111	56 55N	9 0E
Limia, R.	104	41 55N	8 8W
Limko	131	20 57N	109 43E
Limmen Bight	134	14 40S	135 35E
Límnos, I.	109	39 50N	25 5E
Limoeiro do Norte	87	5 5S	38 0W
Limoges, Can.	47	45 20N	75 15W
Limoges, France	102	45 50N	1 15E
Limón	85	10 0N	83 2W
Limon, Panama	84	9 20N	79 45W
Limon, U.S.A.	74	39 18N	103 38W
Limon B.	84	9 22N	79 56W
Limousin	102	46 0N	1 0E
Limousin, Plateau du	102	46 0N	1 0E
Limoux	102	43 4N	2 12E
Limpopo, R.	117	23 15S	32 5E
Limuru	116	1 2S	36 35E
Linares	88	35 50S	71 40W
Linàres	86	1 23N	77 31W
Linares, Mexico	83	24 50N	99 40W
Linares, Spain	104	38 10N	3 40W
Linares □	88	36 0S	71 0W
Linaria	84	54 19N	114 8W
Linch'eng	130	37 26N	114 34E
Lincheng	131	37 20N	114 30E
Lincoln, Argent.	88	34 55N	61 30W
Lincoln, Can.	49	43 10N	79 29W
Lincoln, N.Z.	133	43 38S	172 30E
Lincoln, U.K.	94	53 14N	0 32W
Lincoln, Calif., U.S.A.	80	38 54N	121 17W
Lincoln, Ill., U.S.A.	76	40 10N	89 20W
Lincoln, Kans., U.S.A.	74	39 6N	98 9W
Lincoln, Maine, U.S.A.	35	45 27N	68 29W
Lincoln, Mich., U.S.A.	46	44 41N	83 25W
Lincoln, N. Mex., U.S.A.	79	33 30N	105 26W
Lincoln, Nebr., U.S.A.	74	40 50N	96 42W
Lincoln □	94	53 14N	0 32W
Lincoln Park	77	42 15N	83 11W
Lincoln Sea	17	84 0N	55 0W
Lincoln Wolds	94	53 20N	0 5W
Lincolnton	73	35 30N	81 15W
Lincolnville	39	45 30N	61 33W
Lind	78	47 0N	118 33W
Linda	80	39 6N	121 34W
Lindell Beach	63	49 2N	122 1W
Linden, Can.	61	51 36N	113 28W
Linden, Guyana	86	6 0N	58 10W
Linden, U.S.A.	77	40 11N	86 54W
Linden, Calif., U.S.A.	80	38 1N	121 5W
Linden, Mich., U.S.A.	46	42 49N	83 47W
Linden, Tex., U.S.A.	75	33 0N	94 20W
Lindi	116	9 58S	39 38E
Lindsay, Can.	47	44 22N	78 43W
Lindsay, Calif., U.S.A.	80	36 14N	119 6W
Lindsay, Okla., U.S.A.	75	34 51N	97 37W
Lindsborg	74	38 35N	97 40W
Línea de la Concepcïõn, La	104	36 15N	5 23W
Lineville	76	40 35N	93 31W
Linfen	130	36 0N	111 30E
Lingayer	127	16 1N	120 14E
Lingayer G.	127	16 10N	120 15E
Lingen	105	52 32N	7 21E
Lingga, Kepulauan	126	0 10S	104 30E
Linghsien, Hunan, China	130	26 26N	113 45E
Linghsien, Shantung, China	130	37 21N	116 34E
Lingle	74	42 10N	104 18W
Lingling	131	26 15N	111 40E
Linglo	131	24 20N	105 25E
Lingshan	131	22 26N	109 17E
Lingshih	130	36 55N	111 45E
Lingshui	131	18 27N	110 0E
Lingt'ai	131	35 4N	107 37E
Linguéré	114	15 25N	15 5W
Linh Cam	128	18 31N	105 31E
Linhai	131	28 50N	121 8E
Linho	130	40 50N	107 30E
Linhsien	130	37 57N	110 57E
Lini	131	35 5N	118 20E
Linière	41	46 4N	70 32W
Link L.	62	52 25N	127 40W
Linkian	130	41 57N	126 59E
Linkiang	129	46 2N	133 56E
Linköping	111	58 28N	15 36E
Linkow	130	45 16N	130 18E
Linlithgow	96	55 58N	3 38W
Linn	76	38 29N	91 51W
Linn, Mt.	78	40 0N	123 0W
Linneus	76	39 53N	93 11W
Linney Head	95	51 37N	5 4W
Linnhe, L.	96	56 36N	5 25W
Linping	131	24 25N	114 32E
Lins	89	21 40S	49 44W
Linsi	130	43 30N	118 5E
Linsia	129	35 50N	103 0E
Lintan	129	34 37N	103 40E
Lintao	130	35 16N	103 38E
Lintien	129	46 8N	124 58E
Lintlaw	56	52 4N	103 14W
Linton, Ont., Can.	50	43 56N	79 40W
Linton, Qué., Can.	41	47 15N	72 16W
Linton, Ind., U.S.A.	77	39 0N	87 10W
Linton, N. Dak., U.S.A.	74	46 21N	100 12W
Lintsing	130	36 50N	115 45E
Lintung	130	43 59N	119 8E
Linwood	46	43 35N	80 43W
Linwu	131	25 25N	112 10E
Linxe	102	43 56N	1 13W
Linyi	130	37 10N	116 50E
Linz, Austria	106	48 18N	14 18E
Linz, Ger.	106	50 33N	7 18E
Lion-d'Angers, Le	100	47 37N	0 43W
Lion, G. du	102	43 0N	4 0E
Lion's Head	34	44 58N	81 15W
Lioyang	131	33 30N	106 0E
Lipari, Is.	108	38 40N	15 0E
Lipetsk	120	52 45N	39 35E
Liping	131	26 12N	109 0E
Lipo	131	25 33N	107 45E
Lippe, R.	105	51 40N	7 20E
Lipscomb	75	36 16N	100 28W
Lipton	56	50 54N	103 51W
Liptrap C.	136	38 50S	145 55E
Lira	116	2 17N	32 57E
Liria	104	39 37N	0 35W
Lisala	116	2 12N	21 38E
Lisboa	104	38 42N	9 10W
Lisbon, N. Dak., U.S.A.	74	46 30N	97 46W
Lisbon, N.H., U.S.A.	71	44 13N	71 52W
Lisbon, Ohio, U.S.A.	70	40 45N	80 42W
Lisbon = Lisboa	104	38 42N	9 10W
Lisburn	97	54 30N	6 9W
Lisburn □	97	54 30N	6 5W
Lisburne, C.	67	68 50N	166 0W
Liscannor	97	52 57N	9 24W
Liscannor, B.	97	52 57N	9 24W
Liscomb	35	45 2N	62 0W
Lishih	130	37 30N	111 7E
Lishui	131	28 27N	119 54E
Lisianski I.	14	25 30N	174 0W
Lisieux	100	49 10N	0 12E
Lisle-sur-Tarn	102	43 52N	1 49E
Lismore, Austral.	135	37 58S	143 21E
Lismore, Ireland	97	52 8N	7 58W
Lisse	105	52 16N	4 33E
Lista, Norway	111	58 7N	6 39E
Lista, Sweden	111	59 19N	16 16E
Lister, Mt.	91	78 0S	162 0E
Listowel, Can.	46	43 44N	80 58W
Listowel, Ireland	97	52 27N	9 30W
Lit-et-Mixe	102	44 2N	1 15W
Litang, China	131	23 6N	109 2E
Litang, Malay.	127	5 27N	118 31E
Litchfield, Calif., U.S.A.	80	40 24N	120 23W
Litchfield, Conn., U.S.A.	71	41 44N	73 12W
Litchfield, Ill., U.S.A.	76	39 10N	89 40W
Litchfield, Minn., U.S.A.	74	45 5N	94 40W
Lithgow	136	33 25S	150 8E
Lithinon, Ákra	109	34 55N	24 44E
Lithuania S.S.R. □	120	55 30N	24 0E
Litoměrice	106	50 33N	14 10E
Little Abaco I.	73	26 50N	77 30W
Little Abitibi, R.	53	50 29N	81 32W
Little America	91	79 0N	160 0W
Little Andaman I.	128	10 40N	92 15E
Little Barrier I.	133	36 12S	175 8E
Little Bay	37	49 36N	55 57W
Little Belt Mts.	78	46 50N	111 0W
Little Blue, R.	74	40 18N	97 45W
Little Bow, R.	61	49 53N	112 29W
Little Burnt Bay	37	49 25N	55 5W
Little Cadotte, R.	60	56 41N	117 6W
Little Cayman, I.	84	19 41N	80 3W
Little Churchill, R.	55	57 30N	95 22W
Little Coco I.	128	14 0N	93 15E
Little Colorado, R.	79	36 0N	111 31W
Little Corners	49	43 20N	80 17W
Little Current	46	45 55N	82 0W
Little Current, R.	53	50 57N	84 36W
Little Dover	39	45 15N	61 3W
Little Falls, Minn., U.S.A.	74	45 58N	94 19W
Little Falls, N.Y., U.S.A.	71	43 3N	74 50W
Little Fork, R.	52	48 31N	93 35W
Little Fort	63	51 26N	120 13W
Lit. Grand Rapids	57	52 0N	95 29W
Lit. Humboldt, R.	78	41 20N	117 27W
Lit. Inagua I.	85	21 40N	73 50W
Little Lake	81	35 58N	117 58W
Little Longlac	34	49 42N	86 58W
Little Marais	74	47 24N	91 8W
Little Mecatiná I.	35	50 30N	59 25W
Little Minch	96	57 35N	6 45W
Lit. Missouri R.	74	46 40N	103 50W
Little Narrows	39	45 59N	60 59W
Little Ouse, R.	95	52 25N	0 50E
Little Pic, R.	53	48 48N	86 37W
Little Quill L.	56	51 55N	104 5W
Little Red, R.	75	35 40N	92 15W
Little River	133	43 45S	172 49E
Little Rock	75	34 41N	92 10W
Little Rouge, R.	51	43 48N	79 8W
Little Sable Pt.	72	43 40N	86 32W
Little Sioux, R.	67	42 20N	95 55W
Little Smoky, R.	60	54 44N	117 11W
Little Snake, R.	78	40 45N	108 15W
Little Valley	70	42 15N	78 48W
Little Wabash, R.	77	38 40N	88 20W
Little Whale, R.	34	55 50N	75 0W
Little White, R.	46	46 23N	83 20W
Little York	76	41 1N	90 45W
Littlefield	75	33 57N	102 17W
Littlefork	74	48 24N	93 35W
Littlehampton	95	50 48N	0 32W
Littleton	71	44 19N	71 47W
Liuan	131	31 49N	116 29E
Liucheng	131	24 5N	109 3E
Liuchow	131	24 10N	109 10E
Liupa	131	33 40N	107 0E
Liupan Shan	130	35 40N	106 10E
Liuwa Plain	117	14 20S	22 30E
Livarot	100	49 0N	0 9E
Live Oak, Calif., U.S.A.	80	39 17N	121 40W
Live Oak, Fla., U.S.A.	73	30 17N	83 0W
Lively	46	46 26N	81 9W
Livermore	80	37 41N	121 47W
Livermore, Mt.	75	30 45N	104 8W
Liverpool, Austral.	136	33 54S	150 58E
Liverpool, Can.	39	44 5N	64 41W
Liverpool, U.K.	94	53 25N	3 0W
Liverpool Bay, Can.	67	70 0N	128 0W
Liverpool Bay, U.K.	98	53 30N	3 20W
Liverpool, C.	65	73 38N	78 6W
Liverpool Plains	136	31 15S	150 15E
Liverpool Ra.	136	31 50S	150 30E
Livingston, Guat.	84	15 50N	88 50W
Livingston, U.S.A.	76	42 54N	90 26W
Livingston, Calif., U.S.A.	80	37 23N	120 43W
Livingston, Mont., U.S.A.	78	45 40N	110 40W
Livingstone	75	30 44N	94 54W
Livingstone I.	91	63 0S	60 15W
Livingstone (Maramba)	117	17 46S	25 52E
Livingstonia	116	10 38S	34 5E
Livny	120	52 30N	37 30E
Livonia	46	42 25N	83 23W
Livorno	108	43 30N	10 18E
Livramento	89	30 55S	55 30W
Livron-sur-Drôme	103	44 46N	4 51E
Liwale	116	9 48S	37 58E
Lizard Pt.	95	49 57N	5 11W
Ljubljana	108	46 4N	14 33E
Ljungan, R.	110	62 30N	14 30E
Ljungby	111	56 49N	13 55E
Ljusdal	111	61 46N	16 3E
Ljusnan, R.	111	62 0N	15 20E
Ljusne	111	61 13N	17 7E
Llancanelo, Salina	88	35 40S	69 8W
Llandovery	95	51 59N	3 49W
Llandrindod Wells	95	52 15N	3 23W
Llandudno	94	53 19N	3 51W
Llanelli	95	51 41N	4 11W
Llanes	104	43 25N	4 50W
Llangollen	94	52 58N	3 10W
Llanidloes	95	52 28N	3 31W
Llano Estacado	68	34 0N	103 0W
Llano R.	75	30 50N	99 0W
Llanos	86	3 25N	71 35W
Llaoyang	130	41 14N	123 6E
Llera	83	23 19N	99 1W
Llico	88	34 46S	72 5W
Llobregat, R.	104	41 19N	2 9E
Lloret de Mar	104	41 41N	2 53E
Lloyd L.	55	57 22N	108 57W
Lloydminster	56	53 17N	110 0W
Lloyds, R.	37	48 35N	57 15W
Lloydtown	50	43 59N	79 42W
Llullaillaco, volcán	88	24 30S	68 30W
Lo Ho	131	34 15N	111 10E
Loa	79	38 18N	111 46W
Loa, R.	88	21 30S	70 0W
Lobatse	117	25 12S	25 40E
Lobería	88	38 10S	58 40W
Lobito	117	12 18S	13 35E
Lobos	88	35 2S	59 0W
Lobos, I.	82	21 27N	97 13W
Lobstick L.	36	54 0N	65 12W

Loc Binh **Lufkin**

Loc Binh 128 21 46N 106 54 E
Loc Ninh 128 11 50N 106 34 E
Locarno 106 46 10N 8 47 E
Lochaber 96 56 55N 5 0W
Lochdale 66 49 17N 122 58W
Loche, La 55 56 29N 109 26W
Loche, La, L. 55 56 40N 109 30W
Lochem 105 52 9N 6 26 E
Loches 100 47 7N 1 0 E
Lochgelly 96 56 7N 3 18W
Lochgilphead 96 56 2N 5 37W
Lochnagar, Mt. 96 56 57N 3 14W
Lochwan 130 35 59N 109 30 E
Lochy, R. 96 56 52N 5 3W
Lock Haven 70 41 7N 77 31W
Lockeford 80 38 10N 121 9W
Lockeport 39 43 47N 65 4W
Lockerbie 96 55 7N 3 21W
Lockhart 75 29 55N 97 40W
Lockport, U.S.A. 77 41 35N 88 3W
Lockport, N.Y., U.S.A. 70 43 12N 78 42W
Locminé 100 47 54N 2 51W
Locronan 100 48 7N 4 15W
Loctudy 100 47 50N 4 12W
Locust Cr. 76 39 40N 93 17W
Lod 115 31 57N 34 54 E
Loddon, R. 136 35 31 S 143 51 E
Lodève 102 43 44N 3 19 E
Lodge Grass 78 45 21N 107 27W
Lodgepole, Can. 61 53 6N 115 19W
Lodgepole, U.S.A. 74 41 12N 102 40W
Lodgepole Cr. 74 41 20N 104 30W
Lodhran 124 29 32N 71 30 E
Lodi 80 38 12N 121 16W
Lodja 116 3 30 S 23 23 E
Lodji 127 1 38 S 127 28 E
Lodwar 116 3 10N 35 40 E
Łodz 107 51 45N 19 27 E
Lofoten Is. 110 68 30N 15 0 E
Logan, Kans., U.S.A. 74 39 40N 99 35W
Logan, Ohio, U.S.A. 72 39 25N 82 22W
Logan, Utah, U.S.A. 78 41 45N 111 50W
Logan I. 52 50 7N 88 27W
Logan, Mount 38 48 53N 66 38W
Logan, Mt. 67 60 41N 140 22W
Logan Pass 61 48 41N 113 44W
Logandale 81 36 36N 114 29W
Logansport, U.S.A. 77 40 45N 86 22W
Logansport, La., U.S.A. 72 31 58N 93 58W
Loggieville 39 47 4N 65 23W
Logroño 104 42 28N 2 32W
Logy Bay 37 47 38N 52 40W
Lohardaga 125 23 27N 84 45 E
Loho 131 33 33N 114 5 E
Lohrville 76 42 17N 94 33W
Loikaw 125 19 40N 97 17 E
Loimaa 111 60 50N 23 5 E
Loir-et-Cher □ 101 47 40N 1 20 E
Loire □ 103 45 40N 4 5 E
Loire-Atlantique □ 100 47 25N 1 40W
Loire, R. 100 47 16N 2 10W
Loiret □ 101 47 58N 2 10 E
Loja, Ecuador 86 3 59 S 79 16W
Loja, Spain 104 37 10N 4 10W
Lokandu 116 2 30 S 25 45 E
Lokchong 131 25 15N 113 0 E
Lokeren 105 51 6N 3 59 E
Lokitaung 116 4 12N 35 48 E
Lokka 110 67 49N 27 45 E
Løkken 110 63 8N 9 45 E
Lokoja 114 7 47N 6 45 E
Lokolama 116 2 35 S 19 50 E
Loktung 131 18 41N 109 5 E
Lokwei 131 19 12N 110 30 E
Lola, Mt. 80 39 26N 120 22W
Loliondo 116 2 2 S 35 39 E
Lolland 111 54 45N 11 30 E
Lolo 78 46 50N 114 8W
Lom 109 43 48N 23 20 E
Loma 78 47 59N 110 29W
Loma Linda 81 34 3N 117 16W
Lomami, R. 116 1 0 S 24 40 E
Lomas de Zamóra 88 34 45 S 58 25W
Lombard, U.S.A. 77 41 53N 88 1W
Lombard, Mont., U.S.A. 78 46 7N 111 28W
Lombardia □ 108 45 35N 9 45 E
Lombardy = Lombardia 108 45 35N 9 45 E
Lombez 102 43 29N 0 55 E
Lomblen, I. 127 8 30 S 123 32 E
Lombok, I. 126 8 35 S 116 20 E
Lomé 114 6 9N 1 20 E
Lomela 116 2 5 S 23 52 E
Lomela, R. 116 1 30 S 22 50 E
Lometa 75 31 15N 98 25W
Lomie 116 3 13N 13 38 E
Lommel 105 51 14N 5 19 E
Lomond 61 50 24N 112 36W
Lomond, L. 96 56 8N 4 38W
Lompobatang, mt. 127 5 24 S 119 56 E
Lompoc 81 34 41N 120 32W
Łomza 107 53 10N 22 2 E
Loncoche 90 39 20 S 72 50W
Londa 124 15 30N 74 30 E
Londe, La 103 43 8N 6 14 E
Londinières 100 49 50N 1 25 E
London, Can. 46 42 59N 81 15W
London, U.K. 95 51 30N 0 5W
London, Ky., U.S.A. 72 37 11N 84 5W
London, Ohio, U.S.A. 77 39 54N 83 28W
London □ 95 51 30N 0 5W
London Mills 76 40 43N 90 11W
Londonderry, Can. 39 45 29N 63 36W
Londonderry, U.K. 97 55 0N 7 20W
Londonderry, C. 134 13 45 S 126 55 E
Londonderry, Co. 97 55 0N 7 20W
Londonderry, I. 90 55 0 S 71 0W
Londrina 89 23 0 S 51 10W
Lone Butte 63 51 33N 121 12W
Lone Pine, Can. 60 54 18N 115 7W
Lone Pine, U.S.A. 80 36 35N 118 2W
Lone Rock 56 53 3N 109 53W
Lonely I. 46 45 34N 81 28W
Long Beach, Can. 62 49 1N 125 40W
Long Beach, Calif., U.S.A. 81 33 46N 118 12W
Long Beach, N.Y., U.S.A. 71 40 35N 73 40W
Long Beach, Wash., U.S.A. 80 46 20N 124 1W
Long Branch, Can. 50 43 35N 79 32W
Long Branch, U.S.A. 71 40 19N 74 0W
Long Cr. 56 49 7N 102 59W
Long Eaton 94 52 54N 1 16W
Long I., Bahamas 85 23 20N 75 10W
Long I., Newf., Can. 37 47 34N 55 59W
Long I., N.W.T., Can. 36 54 50N 79 20W
Long I., U.S.A. 71 40 50N 73 20W
Long I. Sd. 71 41 10N 73 0W
Long L., Alta., Can. 60 54 22N 112 46W
Long L., Ont., Can. 53 49 30N 86 50W
Long L., U.S.A. 71 43 57N 74 25W
Long Lake, Can. 39 44 36N 63 38W
Long Lake, U.S.A. 46 44 25N 83 52W
Long Mynd 98 52 35N 2 50W
Long Pine 74 42 33N 99 50W
Long Pt., Man., Can. 57 53 2N 98 25W
Long Pt., Newf., Can. 37 48 47N 58 46W
Long Pt., Ont., Can. 46 42 38N 80 8W
Long Pt., Ont., Can. 46 42 35N 80 2W
Long Point B. 46 42 40N 80 10W
Long Pt. Bay 70 42 40N 80 20W
Long Range Mts 37 48 0N 58 30W
Long Range Mts. 37 49 30N 57 30W
Long Reach 39 45 28N 66 5W
Long Str. 17 70 0N 175 0 E
Long Xuyen 128 10 19N 105 28 E
Longeau 101 47 47N 5 20 E
Longford 97 53 43N 7 50W
Longford □ 97 53 42N 7 45W
Longhawan 126 2 15N 114 55 E
Longiram 126 0 5 S 115 45 E
Longlac 53 49 45N 86 25W
Longlegged L. 52 50 46N 94 8W
Longmont 74 40 10N 105 4W
Longnawan 126 21 50N 114 55 E
Longreach 135 23 28 S 144 14 E
Longs Peak 78 40 20N 105 50W
Longué 100 47 22N 0 8W
Longue-Pointe-de-Mingan 38 50 16N 64 9W
Longueuil, Can. 71 45 32N 73 28W
Longueuil, Qué., Can. 45 45 32N 73 30W
Longueuil-St-Hubert 43 45 29N 73 26W
Longuyon 101 49 27N 5 35 E
Longview, Can. 61 50 32N 114 10W
Longview, Tex., U.S.A. 75 32 30N 94 45W
Longview, Wash., U.S.A. 80 46 9N 122 58W
Longwy 101 49 30N 5 45 E
Loning 131 34 28N 111 42 E
Löningen 105 54 43N 7 44 E
Lonoke 75 34 48N 91 57W
Lonouaille 102 46 30N 1 35 E
Lons-le-Saunier 101 46 40N 5 31 E
Lønsdal 110 66 46N 15 26 E
Looc 127 12 20N 112 5 E
Loogootee 77 38 41N 86 55W
Lookout, C., Can. 34 55 18N 83 56W
Lookout, C., U.S.A. 73 34 30N 76 30W
Loomis 55 49 15N 108 45W
Loon L. 55 44 50N 77 15W
Loon Lake 56 54 2N 109 10W
Loon, R., Alta., Can. 60 57 8N 115 3W
Loon, R., Man., Can. 55 55 53N 101 59W
Loop Hd. 97 52 34N 9 55W
Lop Nor 129 40 20N 90 10 E
Lopatina, G. 121 50 0N 143 30 E
Lopei 130 47 40N 131 12 E
Lopez C. 116 0 47 S 8 40 E
Lopez I. 63 48 30N 122 54W
Lopphavet 110 70 27N 21 15 E
Lora, R. 124 32 0N 67 15 E
Lorain 70 41 20N 82 55W
Loraine 76 40 9N 91 13W
Loralai 124 30 29N 68 30 E
Lorca 104 37 41N 1 42W
Lord Howe I. 14 31 33 S 159 6 E
Lord Selkirk 58 49 56N 97 11W
Lord's Cove 37 46 53N 55 40W
Lordsburg 79 32 15N 108 45W
Loreburn 56 51 13N 106 36W
Loreto, Brazil 87 7 5 S 45 30W
Loreto, Italy 108 43 26N 13 36 E
Loreto, Mexico 82 26 1N 111 21W
Lorette 57 49 44N 96 52W
Loretteville 42 46 51N 71 21W
Lorgues 103 43 28N 6 22 E
Lorica 86 9 14N 75 49W
Lorient 100 47 45N 3 23W
Lorimor 76 41 7N 94 3W
Lorne, Austral. 136 38 33 S 143 59 E
Lorne, Can. 39 47 53N 66 8W
Lorne, U.K. 96 56 26N 5 10W
Lorne, Firth of 96 56 20N 5 40W
Lorne Park 50 43 32N 79 36W
Lorraine, Can. 44 45 41N 73 47W
Lorraine, France 101 49 0N 6 0 E
Lorrainville 40 47 21N 79 23W
Los Alamos, Calif., U.S.A. 81 34 44N 120 17W
Los Alamos, N. Mex., U.S.A. 79 35 57N 106 17W
Los Altos 80 37 23N 122 7W
Los Andes 88 32 50 S 70 40W
Los Angeles 88 37 28 S 72 23W
Los Angeles 81 34 0N 118 10W
Los Angeles Aqueduct 81 35 25N 118 0W
Los Banos 80 37 8N 120 56W
Los Blancos 88 23 45 S 62 30W
Los Gatos 80 37 15N 121 59W
Los Lamentos 82 30 36N 105 50W
Los Lunas 79 34 55N 106 47W
Los Mochis 82 25 45N 109 5W
Los Olivos 81 34 40N 120 7W
Los Palacios 84 22 35N 83 15W
Los Reyes 82 19 21N 99 7W
Los Roques, Is. 85 11 50N 66 45W
Los Testigos, Is. 86 11 23N 63 6W
Los Vilos 88 32 0 S 71 30W
Loshing 131 24 45N 108 58 E
Loshkalakh 121 62 45N 147 20 E
Lošinj, I. 108 44 30N 14 30 E
Lossiemouth 96 57 43N 3 17W
Lost River 43 45 50N 74 33W
Lot □ 102 44 39N 1 40 E
Lot-et-Garonne □ 102 44 22N 0 30 E
Lot, R. 102 44 18N 0 20 E
Lota 88 37 5 S 73 10W
Lothiers 101 46 42N 1 33 E
Loting 131 22 46N 111 34 E
Lott Cr. 59 51 0N 114 13W
Loudéac 100 48 11N 2 47W
Loudon 73 35 35N 84 22W
Loudonville 70 40 40N 82 15W
Loudun 100 47 0N 0 5 E
Loué 100 47 59N 0 9W
Loue, R. 100 47 4N 6 10 E
Loughborough 94 52 46N 1 11W
Lougheed 61 52 44N 111 33W
Lougheed I. 64 77 26N 105 6W
Loughrea 97 53 11N 8 33W
Loughros More, B. 97 54 48N 8 30W
Louhans 103 46 38N 5 12 E
Louis Creek 63 51 8N 120 7W
Louis Trichardt 117 23 0 S 29 55 E
Louis XIV, Pte. 36 54 37N 79 45W
Louisa 72 38 5N 82 40W
Louisa, L. 43 45 46N 74 25W
Louisbourg 39 45 55N 60 0W
Louisbourg Nat. Historic Park 39 45 58N 60 20W
Louisburg 76 38 37N 94 41W
Louisdale 39 45 36N 61 4W
Louise I. 62 52 55N 131 40W
Louiseville 41 46 20N 72 56W
Louisiade Arch. 14 11 10 S 153 0 E
Louisiana 76 39 25N 91 0W
Louisiana □ 75 30 50N 92 0W
Louisville, Ky., U.S.A. 77 38 15N 85 45W
Louisville, Miss., U.S.A. 75 33 7N 89 3W
Loulay 102 46 3N 0 30W
Loulé 104 37 9N 8 0W
Lount L. 55 50 10N 94 20W
Loup City 74 41 19N 98 57W
Loupe, La 100 48 29N 1 1 E
Loups Marins, Lacs des 36 56 30N 73 45W
Lourdes, Can. 37 48 39N 59 0W
Lourdes, France 102 43 6N 0 3W
Lourdus-du-Blanc-Sablon 37 51 24N 57 12W
Lourenço-Marques = Maputo 117 25 58 S 32 32 E
Louroux Béconnais, Le 100 47 30N 0 55W
Louth, Ireland 97 53 47N 6 33W
Louth, U.K. 94 53 23N 0 0W
Louth □ 97 53 55N 6 30W
Louvière, La 105 50 27N 4 10 E
Louviers 100 49 12N 1 10 E
Love 56 53 29N 104 10W
Loveland, U.S.A. 77 39 16N 84 16W
Loveland, Colo., U.S.A. 74 40 27N 105 4W
Lovell 78 44 51N 108 20W
Lovelock 78 40 17N 118 25W
Loverna 56 51 40N 110 0W
Loves Park 76 42 19N 89 3W
Loviisa = Lovisa 111 60 31N 26 20 E
Lovilia 76 41 8N 92 55W
Loving 75 32 17N 104 4W
Lovington, U.S.A. 77 39 43N 88 38W
Lovington, N.Mex., U.S.A. 75 33 0N 103 20W
Low 40 45 50N 76 0W
Low, C. 65 63 7N 85 18W
Low L. 36 55 54N 67 5W
Low Rocky Pt. 135 42 59 S 145 29 E
Lowa 116 1 25 S 25 47 E
Lowden 76 41 52N 90 56W
Lowe Farm 57 49 21N 97 35W
Lowell, Ind., U.S.A. 77 41 18N 87 25W
Lowell, Mass., U.S.A. 71 42 38N 71 19W
Lowell, Mich., U.S.A. 77 42 56N 85 20W
Lower Arrow L. 63 49 40N 118 5W
Lower Capilano 66 49 19N 123 7W
Lower Hutt 133 41 10 S 174 55 E
Lower L. 78 41 17N 120 3W
Lower Lake 80 38 56N 122 36W
Lower Manitou L. 52 49 15N 93 0W
Lower Neguac 35 47 20N 65 10W
Lower Nicola 63 50 12N 120 54W
Lower Post 54 59 58N 128 30W
Lower Red L. 52 48 0N 94 50W
Lower Sackville 35 44 45N 63 43W
Lower Seal, L. 34 56 30N 74 23W
Lower West Pubnico 39 43 38N 65 48W
Lower Wood Harbour 39 43 31N 65 44W
Lowestoft 95 52 29N 1 44 E
Łowicz 107 52 6N 19 55 E
Lowry City 76 38 8N 93 44W
Lowther 53 49 32N 83 2W
Lowville 71 43 48N 75 30W
Loxton 135 34 28 S 140 31 E
Loyalton 80 39 41N 120 14W
Loyalty Is. 14 21 0 S 167 30 E
Loyang 131 34 41N 112 28 E
Loyauté, Îles 14 21 0 S 167 30 E
Loyüan 131 26 25N 119 33 E
Loyung 131 24 25N 109 25 E
Lozère □ 102 44 35N 3 30 E
Lu-ta 130 39 0N 121 31 E
Lü-ta (Dairen-P. Arthur) 130 39 0N 121 31 E
Lü-Tao 131 22 47N 121 20 E
Luabo 85 18 30 S 36 10 E
Luacano 116 11 15 S 21 37 E
Lualaba, R. 116 5 45 S 26 50 E
Luan 127 6 10N 124 25 E
Luan Chau 128 21 38N 103 24 E
Luanda 116 8 58 S 13 9 E
Luang Prabang 128 19 45N 102 10 E
Luangwa, R. 117 14 25 S 30 25 E
Luanshya 117 13 3 S 28 28 E
Luapula, R. 116 12 0 S 28 50 E
Luarca 104 43 32N 6 32W
Luashi 116 10 50 S 23 36 E
Lubalo 116 9 10 S 19 15 E
Lubang Is. 127 13 50N 120 12 E
Lubbock 75 33 40N 101 55W
Lübeck 106 53 52N 10 41 E
Lubefu 116 4 47 S 24 27 E
Lubicon L. 60 56 23N 115 56W
Lubicon Lake 60 56 22N 115 52W
Lublin 107 51 12N 22 38 E
Lubny 120 50 3N 32 58 E
Lubok Antu 126 1 3N 111 50 E
Lubuagan 127 17 21N 121 10 E
Lubudi 116 6 50 S 21 20 E
Lubuhanbilik 126 2 33N 100 14 E
Lubuk Linggau 126 3 15 S 102 55 E
Lubuk Sikaping 126 0 10N 100 15 E
Lubumbashi 117 11 32 S 27 28 E
Lubutu 116 0 45 S 26 30 E
Luc-en-Diois 103 44 36N 5 28 E
Luc, Le 103 43 23N 6 21 E
Lucan 46 43 11N 81 24W
Lucania, Mt. 67 60 48N 141 25W
Lucca 108 43 50N 10 30 E
Luce Bay 96 54 45N 4 48W
Lucea 84 18 25N 78 10W
Lucedale 73 30 55N 88 34W
Lucena, Phil. 127 13 56N 121 37 E
Lucena, Spain 104 37 27N 4 31W
Lučenec 107 48 18N 19 42 E
Lucerne, Can. 63 52 52N 118 33W
Lucerne, Calif., U.S.A. 80 39 6N 122 48W
Lucerne, Wash., U.S.A. 63 48 12N 120 36W
Lucerne = Luzern 106 47 3N 8 18 E
Lucerne Valley 81 34 27N 116 57W
Lucero 82 30 49N 106 30W
Luceville 41 48 32N 68 22W
Luchow 131 28 57N 105 26 E
Lucira 117 14 0 S 12 35 E
Luck L. 56 51 5N 107 5W
Luckenwalde 106 52 5N 13 11 E
Luckey 77 41 27N 83 29W
Lucknow, Can. 46 43 57N 81 31W
Lucknow, India 125 26 50N 81 0 E
Lucky Lake 56 50 59N 107 8W
Luçon 102 46 28N 1 10W
Lüdenscheid 105 51 13N 7 37 E
Lüderitz 117 26 41 S 15 8 E
Ludhiana 124 30 57N 75 56 E
Ludington 72 43 58N 86 27W
Ludlow, Can. 39 46 29N 66 21W
Ludlow, U.K. 95 52 23N 2 42W
Ludlow, Calif., U.S.A. 81 34 43N 116 10W
Ludlow, Vt., U.S.A. 71 43 25N 72 40W
Ludvika 111 60 8N 15 14 E
Ludwigsburg 106 48 53N 9 11 E
Ludwigshafen 106 49 27N 8 27 E
Luebo 116 5 21 S 21 17 E
Luepa 86 5 43N 61 31W
Lufira R. 116 9 30 S 27 0 E
Lufkin 75 31 25N 94 40W

Manitou **Masi**

Manitou, Man., Can. 57 49 15N 98 32W
Manitou, Qué., Can. 38 50 18N 65 15W
Manitou Beach 77 41 58N 84 19W
Manitou I. 53 47 22N 87 30W
Manitou Is. 72 45 8N 86 0W
Manitou L., Ont., Can. 46 45 51N 82 0W
Manitou L., Ont., Can. 55 49 15N 93 0W
Manitou L., Qué., Can. 36 50 55N 65 17W
Manitou, R. 38 50 18N 65 15W
Manitoulin I. 46 45 40N 82 30W
Manitouwadge 53 49 8N 85 48W
Manitowaning 46 45 46N 81 49W
Manitowoc 72 44 8N 87 40W
Maniwaki 40 46 23N 75 58W
Manizales 86 5 5N 75 32W
Manja 117 21 26 S 44 20 E
Manjacaze 117 24 45 S 34 0 E
Manjhand 124 25 50N 68 10 E
Manjil 122 36 46N 49 30 E
Manjimup 134 34 15 S 116 6 E
Manjra, R. 124 18 20N 77 20 E
Mankato, Kans., U.S.A. 74 39 49N 98 11W
Mankato, Minn., U.S.A. 74 44 8N 93 59W
Mankota 56 49 25N 107 5W
Manlius 58 50 0N 97 2W
Manly 136 33 48 S 151 17 E
Manmad 124 20 18N 74 28 E
Manna 126 4 25 S 102 55 E
Mannar 124 9 1N 79 54 E
Mannar, G. of 124 8 30N 79 0 E
Mannar I. 124 9 5N 79 45 E
Mannheim, Can. 49 43 24N 80 33W
Mannheim, Ger. 106 49 28N 8 29 E
Manning, Can. 60 56 53N 117 39W
Manning, Oreg., U.S.A. 80 45 45N 123 13W
Manning, S.C., U.S.A. 73 33 40N 80 9W
Manning Park 63 49 4N 120 47W
Manning Prov. Park 63 49 5N 120 45W
Manning, R. 136 31 52 S 152 43 E
Mannington 72 39 35N 80 25W
Mannville 60 53 20N 111 10W
Manokwari 127 0 54 S 134 0 E
Manombo 117 22 57 S 43 28 E
Manono 116 7 15 S 27 25 E
Manor 57 49 36N 102 5W
Manosque 103 43 49N 5 47 E
Manotick 47 45 13N 75 41W
Manouane L. 36 50 45N 70 45W
Manouane, L. 41 47 33N 74 6W
Manresa 104 41 48N 1 50 E
Mans, Le 100 48 0N 0 10 E
Mansa 116 11 13 S 28 55 E
Manseau 41 46 22N 72 0W
Mansel I. 36 62 0N 79 50W
Mansfield, Austral. 136 37 4 S 146 6 E
Mansfield, U.K. 94 53 8N 1 12W
Mansfield, La., U.S.A. 75 32 2N 93 40W
Mansfield, Mass., U.S.A. 71 42 2N 71 12W
Mansfield, Ohio, U.S.A. 70 40 45N 82 30W
Mansfield, Pa., U.S.A. 70 41 48N 77 4W
Mansfield, Wash., U.S.A. 78 47 51N 119 44W
Mansle 102 45 52N 0 9 E
Manso, R. 87 14 0 S 52 0W
Manson 76 42 32N 94 32W
Manson Creek 54 55 37N 124 25W
Manta 86 1 0 S 80 40W
Mantalingajan, Mt. 126 8 55N 117 45 E
Manteca 80 37 50N 121 12W
Mantecal 86 7 34N 69 17W
Manteno 77 41 15N 87 50W
Manteo 73 35 55N 75 41W
Mantes-la-Jolie 101 49 0N 1 41 E
Manthani 124 18 40N 79 35 E
Manthelan 100 47 9N 0 47 E
Manti 78 39 23N 111 32W
Mantiqueira, Serra da 89 22 0 S 44 0W
Manton 46 44 23N 85 25W
Mántova 108 45 10N 10 47 E
Mänttä 110 62 0N 24 40 E
Mantua 70 41 15N 81 14W
Mantua = Mántova 108 45 10N 10 47 E
Manu 86 12 10 S 71 0W
Manua Is. 127 14 12 S 169 35W
Manucan 127 8 14N 123 3 E
Manuel Alves, R. 87 11 19 S 48 28W
Manuels 39 47 3N 64 59W
Manui I. 127 3 35 S 123 5 E
Manville 74 42 48N 104 36W
Many 75 31 36N 93 28W
Many Island L. 61 50 8N 110 3W
Manyara L. 116 3 40 S 35 50 E
Manyberries 61 49 24N 110 42W
Manyoni 116 5 45 S 34 55 E
Manzai 124 32 20N 70 15 E
Manzanares 104 39 0N 3 22W
Manzanillo, Cuba 84 20 20N 77 10W
Manzanillo, Mexico 82 19 0N 104 20W
Manzanillo, Pta. 84 9 30N 79 40W
Manzano Mts. 79 34 30N 106 45W
Maoke, Pengunungan 126 3 40 S 137 30 E
Mapastepec 83 15 26N 92 54W
Mapia, Kepulauan 127 0 50N 134 20 E
Mapimí 82 25 50N 103 31W
Mapimí, Bolsón de 82 27 30N 103 15W
Maple 50 43 51N 79 31W
Maple Bay 63 48 48N 123 37W
Maple Creek 56 49 55N 109 29W
Maple Falls 63 48 56N 122 5W
Maple Grove 44 45 19N 73 50W
Maple, R. 77 42 58N 84 56W
Maple Valley 80 47 25N 122 3W
Maples, The 49 43 52N 80 10W
Mapleton 78 44 4N 123 58W
Maplewood 74 38 33N 90 18W
Mapuera, R. 86 0 30 S 58 25W
Maputo 117 25 58 S 32 32 E
Maqnā 122 28 25N 34 50 E
Maquinchao 90 41 15 S 68 50W
Maquoketa 76 42 4N 90 40W
Mar Chiquita, L. 88 30 40 S 62 50W
Mar del Plata 88 38 0 S 57 30W
Mar, Serra do 89 25 30 S 49 0W
Maraã 86 1 43 S 65 25W
Marabá 87 5 20 S 49 5W
Maracá, I. de 87 2 10N 50 30W
Maracaibo 86 10 40N 71 37W
Maracaibo, Lago de 86 9 40N 71 30W
Maracaju 89 21 38 S 55 9W
Maracay 86 10 15N 67 36W
Marāgheh 122 37 30N 46 12 E
Marajó, Ilha de 87 1 0 S 49 30W
Maralal 116 1 0N 36 38 E
Marana 79 32 30N 111 9W
Marand 122 38 30N 45 45 E
Marandellas 117 18 5 S 31 42 E
Maranguape 87 3 55 S 38 50W
Maranhão = São Luis 87 2 31 S 44 16W
Maranhão □ 87 5 0 S 46 0W
Marañ n, R. 86 4 50 S 75 35W
Maranoa R. 135 27 50 S 148 37 E
Maraş 122 37 37N 36 53 E
Marathon 53 48 44N 86 23W
Marathón 109 38 11N 23 58 E
Marathon, U.S.A. 76 42 52N 94 59W
Marathon, N.Y., U.S.A. 71 42 25N 76 3W
Marathon, Tex., U.S.A. 75 30 15N 103 15W
Maratua, I. 127 2 10N 118 35 E
Marbella 104 36 30N 4 57W
Marble 52 47 19N 93 18W
Marble Bar 134 21 9 S 119 44 E
Marble Falls 75 30 30N 98 15W
Marblehead, Can. 63 50 15N 116 58W
Marblehead, U.S.A. 71 42 29N 70 51W
Marblemount 63 48 32N 121 26W
Marbleton 41 45 37N 71 35W
Marburg 106 50 49N 8 44 E
Marceau, L. 38 51 25N 66 41W
Marcelin 56 52 55N 106 47W
Marceline 76 39 43N 92 57W
March 95 52 33N 0 5 E
Marché 102 46 0N 1 20 E
Marche □ 108 43 22N 13 10 E
Marche-en-Famenne 105 50 14N 5 19 E
Marchin 105 50 28N 5 14 E
Marcigny 103 46 17N 4 2 E
Marcillac-Vallon 102 44 29N 2 27 E
Marcillat 102 46 12N 2 38 E
Marck 101 50 57N 1 57 E
Marckolsheim 101 48 10N 7 30 E
Marconi 58 49 55N 97 6W
Marcos Juárez 88 32 42 S 62 5W
Marcus I. 14 24 0N 153 45 E
Marcy Mt. 71 44 7N 73 55W
Mardan 124 34 20N 72 0 E
Marden 49 43 36N 80 18W
Mardin 122 37 20N 40 36 E
Maree L. 96 57 40N 5 30W
Mareeba 135 16 59 S 145 28 E
Marek 127 4 41 S 120 24 E
Marek = Stanke Dimitrov 109 42 17N 23 9 E
Marelan 43 45 38N 74 33W
Maremma 108 42 45N 11 15 E
Maremma, reg. 108 42 30N 11 0 E
Marengo, Can. 56 51 29N 109 47W
Marengo, U.S.A. 76 41 42N 92 5W
Marenisco 52 46 23N 89 40W
Mareuil-sur-Lay 102 46 32N 1 14W
Marfa 75 30 15N 104 0W
Margaree Forks 39 46 20N 61 5W
Margaree Harbour 35 46 26N 61 8W
Margaret Bay 67 51 20N 127 20W
Margaret L. 54 58 56N 115 25W
Margarita 84 9 20N 79 55W
Margarita, Isla de 86 11 0N 64 0W
Margate 95 51 23N 1 24 E
Margeride, Mts. de la 102 44 43N 3 38 E
Margo 56 51 49N 103 20W
Marguerite 63 52 30N 122 25W
Mari, A.S.S.R. □ 120 56 30N 48 0 E
Maria 38 48 10N 65 59W
María Elena 88 22 18 S 69 40W
María Grande 88 31 45 S 59 55W
Maria, I. 134 14 52 S 135 45 E
Maria I. 134 42 35 S 148 0 E
Maria van Diemen, C. 133 34 29 S 172 40 E
Marian L. 54 63 0N 116 15W
Mariana Is. 14 17 0N 145 0 E
Mariana Trench 14 13 0N 145 0W
Marianao 84 23 8N 82 24W
Marianna, Ark., U.S.A. 75 34 48N 90 48W
Marianna, Fla., U.S.A. 73 30 45N 85 15W
Marias, R. 78 48 26N 111 40W
Mariato, Punta 84 7 12N 80 52W
Maribor 108 46 36N 15 40 E
Maricopa, Ariz., U.S.A. 79 33 5N 112 2W
Maricopa, Calif., U.S.A. 81 35 7N 119 27W
Maricourt 36 56 34N 70 49W
Marie Galante, I. 85 15 56N 61 16W
Marie L. 60 54 38N 110 18W
Mariehamn (Maarianhamina) 111 60 5N 19 57 E
Marienberg 105 52 30N 6 35 E
Marienbourg 105 50 6N 4 31 E
Mariental 117 24 36 S 18 0 E
Marienville 70 41 27N 79 8W
Mariestad 111 58 43N 13 50 E
Marietta, Ga., U.S.A. 73 34 0N 84 30W
Marietta, Ohio, U.S.A. 72 39 27N 81 27W
Marieville 45 45 26N 73 10W
Marignane 103 43 25N 5 13 E
Mariinsk 120 56 10N 87 20 E
Marília 89 22 0 S 50 0W
Marin 104 42 23N 8 42W
Marina 80 36 41N 121 48W
Marinduque, I. 127 13 25N 122 0 E
Marine City 46 42 45N 82 29W
Marinel, Le 116 10 25 S 25 17 E
Marinette, Ariz., U.S.A. 79 33 41N 112 16W
Marinette, Wis., U.S.A. 72 45 4N 87 40W
Maringá 89 23 35 S 51 50W
Marion, Ala., U.S.A. 73 32 33N 87 20W
Marion, Ill., U.S.A. 76 37 45N 88 55W
Marion, Ind., U.S.A. 77 40 35N 85 40W
Marion, Iowa, U.S.A. 76 42 2N 91 36W
Marion, Kans., U.S.A. 74 38 25N 97 2W
Marion, Mich., U.S.A. 46 44 7N 85 8W
Marion, N.C., U.S.A. 73 35 42N 82 0W
Marion, Ohio, U.S.A. 77 40 38N 83 8W
Marion, S.C., U.S.A. 73 34 11N 79 22W
Marion, Va., U.S.A. 73 36 51N 81 29W
Marion I. 16 47 0 S 38 0 E
Marion, L. 73 33 30N 80 15W
Marion Reef 135 19 10 S 152 17 E
Maripa 86 7 26N 65 9W
Mariposa 80 37 31N 119 59W
Mariscal Estigarribia 88 22 3 S 60 40W
Maritsa, R. 109 42 15N 24 0 E
Marjan 123 32 5N 68 20 E
Markdale 46 44 19N 80 39W
Marked Tree 75 35 35N 90 24W
Markerville 61 52 7N 114 10W
Market Drayton 94 52 55N 2 30W
Market Harborough 95 52 29N 0 55W
Markham 50 43 52N 79 16W
Markham I. 17 84 0N 0 45W
Markham L. 55 62 30N 102 35W
Markham Mts. 91 83 0 S 164 0 E
Markleeville 80 38 42N 119 47W
Markovo 121 64 40N 169 40 E
Markstay 46 46 29N 80 32W
Marksville 75 31 10N 92 2W
Marl 105 51 39N 7 4 E
Marlbank 47 44 26N 77 6W
Marlboro, Can. 54 53 30N 116 50W
Marlboro, U.S.A. 71 42 19N 71 33W
Marlborough □ 133 41 45 S 173 33 E
Marlborough Downs 95 51 25N 1 55W
Marle 101 49 43N 3 47 E
Marlin 75 31 25N 96 50W
Marlow 75 34 40N 97 58W
Marmagao 124 15 25N 73 56 E
Marmande 102 44 30N 0 10 E
Marmara denizi 122 40 45N 28 15 E
Marmara, I. 109 40 35N 27 38 E
Marmara, Sea of = Marmara denizi 122 40 45N 28 15 E
Marmaris 122 36 50N 28 14 E
Marmarth 74 46 21N 103 52W
Marmion L. 52 48 55N 91 30W
Marmolada, Mte. 108 46 25N 11 55 E
Marmora 47 44 28N 77 41W
Marnay 101 47 20N 5 48 E
Marne □ 101 49 0N 4 10 E
Marne, R. 101 48 53N 2 25 E
Marnoo 136 36 40 S 142 54 E
Maroa 86 2 43N 67 33W
Maroantsetra 117 15 26 S 49 44 E
Maroni, R. 87 4 0N 52 0W
Marovoay 117 16 6 S 46 39 E
Marquesas Is. = Marquises 15 9 30 S 140 0W
Marquette, Can. 57 50 4N 97 44W
Marquette, U.S.A. 53 46 30N 87 21W
Marquette I. 46 45 58N 84 18W
Marquette, L. 41 48 54N 73 54W
Marquise 101 50 50N 1 40 E
Marquises, Is. 15 9 30 S 140 0W
Marrakech 114 31 40N 8 0W
Marrat 122 25 0N 45 35 E
Marree 135 29 39 S 138 1 E
Marromeu 117 18 40 S 36 25 E
Marrupa 117 13 8 S 37 30 E
Mars, Le 74 43 0N 96 0W
Marsabit 116 2 18N 38 0 E
Marsala 108 37 48N 12 25 E
Marsaxlokk (Medport) 108 35 47N 14 32 E
Marsden 56 52 51N 109 49W
Marseillan 102 43 23N 3 31 E
Marseille 103 43 18N 5 23 E
Marseilles 77 41 20N 88 43W
Marseilles = Marseille 103 43 18N 5 23 E
Marsh I. 75 29 35N 91 50W
Marshall, Can. 56 53 11N 109 47W
Marshall, Ark., U.S.A. 75 35 58N 92 40W
Marshall, Ill., U.S.A. 77 39 23N 87 42W
Marshall, Mich., U.S.A. 77 42 17N 84 59W
Marshall, Minn., U.S.A. 74 44 25N 95 45W
Marshall, Mo., U.S.A. 76 39 8N 93 15W
Marshall, Tex., U.S.A. 75 32 29N 94 20W
Marshall Is. 14 9 0N 171 0 E
Marshalltown 76 42 5N 92 56W
Marshfield, Mo., U.S.A. 75 37 20N 92 58W
Marshfield, Wis., U.S.A. 74 44 42N 90 10W
Marsoui 38 49 13N 66 4W
Marstrand 111 57 53N 11 35 E
Marsville 49 43 50N 80 13W
Mart 75 31 34N 96 51W
Martaban 125 16 30N 97 35 E
Martagne 100 46 59N 0 57W
Martapura 126 3 22 S 114 56 E
Martelange 105 49 49N 5 43 E
Marten River 46 46 44N 79 49W
Martensdale 76 41 23N 93 45W
Martensville 56 52 17N 106 40W
Martha's Vineyard 71 41 25N 70 35W
Martigné Ferchaud 100 47 50N 1 20W
Martigues 103 43 24N 5 4 E
Martin, S.D., U.S.A. 74 43 11N 101 45W
Martin, Tenn., U.S.A. 75 36 23N 88 51W
Martin, L. 73 32 45N 85 50W
Martinborough 133 41 14 S 175 29 E
Martinez 80 38 1N 122 8W
Martinique, I. 85 14 40N 61 0W
Martinique Passage 85 15 15N 61 0W
Martinópolis 89 22 11 S 51 12W
Martins Ferry 71 40 5N 80 46W
Martinsburg, Pa., U.S.A. 70 40 18N 78 21W
Martinsburg, W. Va., U.S.A. 72 39 30N 77 57W
Martinsville, Ill., U.S.A. 77 39 20N 87 53W
Martinsville, Ind., U.S.A. 77 39 29N 86 23W
Martinsville, N.Y., U.S.A. 49 43 2N 78 50W
Martinsville, Va., U.S.A. 73 36 41N 79 52W
Marton 133 40 4 S 175 23 E
Martos 104 37 44N 3 58W
Martre, L., La 64 63 0N 118 0W
Marudi 126 4 10N 114 25 E
Maruf 124 31 30N 67 0 E
Marugame 132 34 15N 133 55 E
Marvejols 102 44 33N 3 19 E
Marvine Mt. 79 38 44N 111 40W
Marwar 124 25 43N 73 45 E
Marwayne 60 53 32N 110 20W
Mary 120 37 40N 61 50 E
Mary Frances L. 55 63 19N 106 13W
Mary Kathleen 135 20 35 S 139 48 E
Maryborough, Queens., Austral. 135 25 31 S 152 37 E
Maryborough, Vic., Austral. 136 37 0 S 143 44 E
Maryborough = Port Laoise 97 53 2N 7 20W
Maryen, L. 38 51 20N 60 28W
Maryfield 57 49 50N 101 35W
Maryhill 49 43 32N 80 23W
Maryland □ 72 39 10N 76 40W
Maryport 94 54 43N 3 30W
Mary's Harbour 36 52 18N 55 51W
Marystown 37 47 10N 55 10W
Marysvale 79 38 25N 112 17W
Marysville, B.C., Can. 61 49 35N 116 0W
Marysville, N.B., Can. 39 45 59N 66 35W
Marysville, Calif., U.S.A. 80 39 14N 121 40W
Marysville, Kans., U.S.A. 74 39 50N 96 38W
Marysville, Mich., U.S.A. 46 42 55N 82 29W
Marysville, Ohio, U.S.A. 77 40 15N 83 20W
Marysville, Wash., U.S.A. 80 48 3N 122 11W
Maryville, U.S.A. 76 40 21N 94 52W
Maryville, Tenn., U.S.A. 73 35 50N 84 0W
Marzo, Punta 86 6 50N 77 42W
Marzuq 114 25 53N 14 10 E
Masaka 116 0 21 S 31 45 E
Masalima, Kepulauan 126 5 10 S 116 50 E
Masamba 127 2 30 S 120 15 E
Masan 130 35 11N 128 32 E
Masandam, Ras 123 26 30N 56 30 E
Masasi 116 10 45 S 38 52 E
Masaya 84 12 0N 86 7W
Mascarene Is. 16 22 0 S 55 0 E
Mascota 82 20 30N 104 50W
Mascouche 44 45 45N 73 36W
Mascouche, R. 44 45 41N 73 37W
Mascoutah 76 38 29N 89 48W
Masela 127 8 9 S 129 51 E
Maseme 85 18 46 S 25 3 E
Maseru 117 29 18 S 27 30 E
Mashābih 122 25 35N 36 30 E
Mashhad 123 36 20N 59 35 E
Mashike 132 43 31N 141 30 E
Mashki Chah 124 29 5N 62 30 E
Mashkode 34 47 2N 84 7W
Masi 110 69 26N 23 50 E

Masi-Manimba **Mendota**

Masi-Manimba **116** 4 40S 18 5E
Masindi **116** 1 40N 31 43E
Masisea **86** 8 35S 74 15W
Masjed Soleyman **122** 31 55N 49 25E
Mask, L. **97** 53 36N 9 24W
Maskinongé **41** 46 14N 73 1W
Masoala, C. **117** 15 59S 50 13E
Masohi **127** 3 2S 128 15E
Mason, Mich., U.S.A. **77** 42 35N 84 27W
Mason, Nev., U.S.A. **80** 38 56N 119 8W
Mason, Ohio, U.S.A. **77** 39 22N 84 19W
Mason, S.D., U.S.A. **74** 45 12N 103 27W
Mason, Tex., U.S.A. **75** 30 45N 99 15W
Mason City, Ill., U.S.A. **76** 40 12N 89 42W
Mason City, Iowa, U.S.A. **76** 43 9N 93 12W
Mason City, Wash., U.S.A. **78** 48 0N 119 0W
Masqat **123** 23 37N 58 36E
Massa **108** 44 2N 10 7E
Massachusetts □ **71** 42 25N 72 0W
Massachusetts B. **72** 42 30N 70 0W
Massangena **117** 21 34S 33 0E
Massat **102** 42 53N 1 21E
Massena **71** 44 52N 74 55W
Masset **62** 54 2N 132 10W
Masset Inlet **62** 53 43N 132 20W
Massey **46** 46 12N 82 5W
Massiac **102** 45 15N 3 11E
Massif Central **102** 45 30N 2 21E
Massillon **70** 40 47N 81 30W
Massinga **117** 23 15S 35 22E
Masson **40** 45 32N 75 25W
Masson I. **91** 66 10S 93 20E
Massueville **43** 45 55N 72 56W
Mastanli = Momchilgrad **92** 41 33N 25 23E
Masterton **133** 40 56S 175 39E
Mastigouche, Parc **41** 46 33N 73 41W
Mastuj **124** 36 20N 72 36E
Mastung **124** 29 50N 66 42E
Masuda **132** 34 40N 131 51E
Mataboor **127** 1 41S 138 3E
Matachewan **34** 47 56N 80 39W
Matad **129** 47 11N 115 27E
Matadi **116** 5 52S 13 31E
Matador **55** 50 49N 107 56W
Matagalpa **84** 13 10N 85 40W
Matagami **40** 49 45N 77 34W
Matagami, L. **40** 49 50N 77 40W
Matagorda **75** 28 43N 96 0W
Matagorda, B. **75** 28 30N 96 15W
Matagorda I. **75** 28 10N 96 40W
Matak, P. **126** 3 18N 106 16E
Matakana, I. **136** 37 32S 176 5E
Matamec, L. **38** 50 21N 65 58W
Matamoros, Campeche, Mexico **83** 25 53N 97 30W
Matamoros, Coahuila, Mexico **82** 25 45N 103 1W
Matamoros, Puebla, Mexico **83** 18 2N 98 17W
Matamoros, Tamaulipas, Mexico **83** 25 50N 97 30W
Matana, D. **127** 2 30S 121 25E
Matane **38** 48 50N 67 33W
Matane, Parc Prov. de **38** 48 40N 67 0W
Matane, R. **38** 48 50N 67 35W
Matanzá **86** 7 22N 73 2W
Matanzas **84** 23 0N 81 40W
Matapédia **39** 48 0N 66 59W
Matapédia, L. **38** 48 35N 67 35W
Matara **124** 5 58N 80 30E
Mataram **126** 8 41S 116 10E
Matarani **86** 16 50S 72 10W
Mataranka **134** 14 55S 133 4E
Mataura **133** 46 11S 168 51E
Matawin, R. **41** 46 54N 72 56W
Matawin, Rés. **41** 46 46N 73 50W
Matchi-Manitou, L. **40** 48 0N 77 4W
Matehuala **82** 23 40N 100 50W
Matera **108** 40 40N 16 37E
Matha **102** 45 52N 0 20W
Matheson Island **57** 51 45N 96 56W
Mathis **75** 28 4N 97 48W
Mathura **124** 27 30N 77 48E
Mati **127** 6 55N 126 15E
Matias Romero **83** 16 53N 95 2W
Matinenda L. **46** 46 22N 82 57W
Matlock **94** 53 8N 1 32W
Mato Grosso □ **87** 14 0S 55 0W
Mato Grosso, Planalto do **86** 15 0S 54 0W
Matochkin Shar **120** 73 10N 56 40E
Matour **103** 46 19N 4 29E
Matozinhos **104** 41 11N 8 42W
Matrah **123** 23 37N 58 30E
Matrûh **115** 31 19N 27 9E
Matsang Tsangpo (Brahmaputra), R. **125** 29 25N 88 0E
Matsue **132** 35 25N 133 10E
Matsumoto **132** 36 15N 138 0E
Matsuyama **132** 33 45N 132 45E
Mattagami L. **53** 47 54N 81 35W
Mattagami, R. **53** 50 43N 81 29W
Mattancheri **124** 9 50N 76 15E
Mattawa **34** 46 20N 78 45W
Mattawamkeag **35** 45 30N 68 30W
Mattawitchewan, R. **53** 49 52N 83 12W
Matterhorn, mt. **106** 45 58N 7 39E
Matteson **77** 41 30N 87 42W
Matthew Town **85** 20 57N 73 40W
Matthews **77** 40 23N 85 31W
Matthew's Ridge **86** 7 37N 60 10W
Mattice **53** 49 40N 83 20W
Mattituck **71** 40 58N 72 32W
Mattoon **77** 39 30N 88 20W
Matua **126** 2 58S 110 52E
Matucana **86** 11 55S 76 15W
Matun **124** 33 22N 69 58E
Maturín **86** 9 45N 63 11W
Mau-è-ele **117** 24 18S 34 2E
Mau Ranipur **124** 25 16N 79 8E
Mauagami, R. **34** 49 30N 82 0W
Maubeuge **101** 50 17N 3 57E
Maubourguet **102** 43 29N 0 1E
Maudheim **91** 71 5S 11 0W
Maudin Sun **125** 16 0N 94 30E
Maués **86** 3 20S 57 45W
Mauganj **125** 24 50N 81 55E
Maugerville **39** 45 52N 66 27W
Maui I. **67** 20 45N 156 20E
Mauke, I. **133** 20 09S 157 20W
Maulamyaing **125** 16 30N 97 40E
Maule □ **88** 36 5S 72 30W
Mauléon-Licharre **102** 43 14N 0 54W
Maumee **77** 41 35N 83 40W
Maumee, R. **77** 41 42N 83 28W
Maumere **127** 8 38S 122 13E
Maun **117** 20 0S 23 26E
Mauna Kea, Mt. **67** 19 50N 155 28W
Mauna Loa, Mt. **67** 19 50N 155 28W
Maungmagan Is. **125** 14 0S 97 48E
Maungmagan Kyunzu **128** 14 0N 97 48E
Maunoir, L. **64** 67 30N 124 55W
Maupin **78** 45 12N 121 9W
Maure-de-Bretagne **100** 47 53N 2 0W
Maurepas L. **75** 30 18N 90 35W
Maures, mts. **103** 43 15N 6 15E
Mauriac **102** 45 13N 2 19E
Maurice L. **134** 29 30S 131 0E
Mauricie, Parc Nat. de la **41** 46 45N 73 0W
Maurienne **103** 45 15N 6 20E
Mauritania ■ **114** 20 50N 10 0W
Mauritius ■ **16** 20 0S 57 0E
Mauron **100** 48 9N 2 18W
Maurs **102** 44 43N 2 12E
Mauston **74** 43 48N 90 5W
Mauvezin **102** 43 44N 0 53E
Mauzé-sur-le-Mignon **102** 46 12N 0 41W
Mavillette **39** 44 6N 66 11W
Mavinga **117** 15 50S 20 10E
Mawcook **43** 45 27N 72 47W
Mawer **55** 50 46N 106 22W
Mawkmai **125** 20 14N 97 50E
Mawlaik **125** 23 40N 94 26E
Mawson Base **91** 67 30N 65 0E
Max **74** 47 50N 101 20W
Maxcanú **83** 20 40N 90 10W
Maxhamish L. **54** 59 50N 123 17W
Maxixe **117** 23 54S 35 17E
Maxville **47** 45 17N 74 51W
Maxwell **80** 39 17N 122 11W
May Pen **84** 17 58N 77 15W
Maya Mts. **83** 16 30N 89 0W
Maya, R. **121** 58 20N 135 0E
Mayaguana Island **85** 21 30N 72 44W
Mayagüez **85** 18 12N 67 9W
Mayapán **83** 20 38N 89 27W
Mayarf **85** 20 40N 75 39W
Mayarí **85** 20 40N 75 41W
Maybell **78** 40 30N 108 4W
Mayenne **100** 48 20N 0 38W
Mayenne □ **100** 48 10N 0 40W
Mayer **79** 34 28N 112 17W
Mayerthorpe **60** 53 57N 115 8W
Mayfair **56** 52 58N 107 36W
Mayfield **73** 36 45N 88 40W
Mayhill **79** 32 58N 105 30W
Maykop **120** 44 35N 40 25E
Mayland **59** 51 3N 114 0W
Maymont **56** 52 34N 107 42W
Maymyo **128** 22 2N 96 28E
Maynard **80** 47 59N 122 55W
Mayne **63** 48 52N 123 17W
Mayne, Le, L. **35** 57 5N 68 30W
Maynooth, Can. **34** 45 14N 77 56W
Maynooth, Ireland **97** 53 22N 6 38W
Mayo **67** 63 38N 135 57W
Mayo □ **97** 53 47N 9 7W
Mayo L. **67** 63 45N 135 0W
Mayo, R. **82** 26 45N 109 47W
Mayon, Mt. **127** 13 15N 123 42E
Mayor I. **133** 37 16S 176 17E
Mayson L. **55** 57 55N 107 10W
Maysville, U.S.A. **76** 39 53N 94 21W
Maysville, U.S.A. **77** 38 39N 83 46W
Mayu, I. **127** 1 30N 126 30E
Mayville, N.D., U.S.A. **74** 47 30N 97 23W
Mayville, N.Y., U.S.A. **70** 42 14N 79 31W
Maywood **77** 41 53N 87 51W
Mayya **121** 61 44N 130 18E
Mazabuka **117** 15 52S 27 44E
Mazagão **87** 0 20S 51 50W
Mazama, Can. **54** 49 43N 120 8W
Mazama, U.S.A. **63** 48 37N 120 25W
Mazamet **102** 43 30N 2 20E
Mazán **86** 3 15S 73 0W
Mazapil **82** 24 38N 101 34W
Mazar-i-Sharif **123** 36 41N 67 0E
Mazarredo **90** 47 10S 66 50W
Mazarrón **104** 37 38N 1 19W
Mazaruni, R. **86** 6 15N 60 0W
Mazatán **82** 29 0N 110 8W
Mazatenango **84** 14 35N 91 30W
Mazatlán **82** 23 10N 106 30W
Mazenod **56** 49 52N 106 13W
Mazhabong L. **53** 46 58N 82 30W
Māzhān **123** 32 30N 59 0E
Mazinān **123** 36 25N 56 48E
Mazoe R. **117** 16 45S 32 30E
Mazomanie **76** 43 11N 89 48W
Mazon **77** 41 14N 88 25W
Mbabane **117** 26 18S 31 6E
M'Baiki **116** 3 53N 18 1E
Mbala **116** 8 46S 31 17E
Mbale **116** 1 8N 34 12E
Mbalmayo **116** 3 33N 11 33E
Mbamba Bay **116** 11 13S 34 49E
Mbandaka **116** 0 1S 18 18E
Mbanza Ngungu **116** 5 12S 14 53E
Mbarara **116** 0 35S 30 25E
Mbeya **116** 8 54S 33 29E
Mbini □ **114** 1 30N 10 0E
Mbuji-Mayi **116** 6 9S 23 40E
Mbulu **116** 3 45S 35 30E
Mburucuyá **88** 28 1S 58 14W
M'Clintock Chan. **64** 72 0N 102 0W
M'Clure Str., Can. **22** 75 0N 118 0W
M'Clure Str., N.W.T., Can. **64** 75 0N 119 0W
Mdina **108** 35 51N 14 25E
Meacham **56** 52 6N 105 45W
Meachen **61** 49 38N 116 17W
Mead L. **81** 36 1N 114 44W
Meade, Can. **34** 49 26N 83 51W
Meade, U.S.A. **75** 37 18N 100 25W
Meadow L. **56** 54 7N 108 20W
Meadow Lake **56** 54 10N 108 26W
Meadow Lake Prov. Park **55** 54 27N 109 0W
Meadow Valley Wash **81** 36 30N 114 24W
Meadowlands **52** 47 7N 92 49W
Meadville, U.S.A. **76** 39 47N 93 18W
Meadville, Pa., U.S.A. **70** 41 39N 80 9W
Meaford **46** 44 36N 80 35W
Meaghers Grant **39** 44 55N 63 15W
Mealy Mts. **35** 53 10N 59 30W
Meander, R. = Menderes, Büyük **122** 37 45N 27 40E
Meander River **54** 59 2N 117 42W
Meares, C. **78** 45 37N 124 0W
Meares I. **62** 49 12N 125 50W
Mearim, R. **87** 3 4S 44 35W
Meath □ **97** 53 32N 6 40W
Meath Park **56** 53 27N 105 22W
Meaulne **102** 46 36N 2 28E
Meaux **101** 48 58N 2 50E
Mecatina, Little, R. **38** 52 10N 60 40W
Mécatina, Petit-, R. **38** 50 40N 59 30W
Mecca **81** 33 37N 116 3W
Mechanicsburg **70** 40 12N 77 0W
Mechanicsville **76** 41 54N 91 16W
Mechanicville **71** 42 54N 73 41W
Mechelen **105** 51 2N 4 29E
Mechernich **105** 50 35N 6 39E
Méchins, Les **38** 48 59N 66 59W
Mecklenburger Bucht **106** 54 20N 11 40E
Meconta **117** 14 59S 39 50E
Meda, R. **134** 17 20S 124 30E
Medan **126** 3 40N 98 38E
Medanosa, Pta. **90** 48 0S 66 0W
Medaryville **77** 41 4N 86 55W
Medellín **86** 6 15N 75 35W
Medford, Oreg., U.S.A. **78** 42 20N 122 52W
Medford, Wis., U.S.A. **74** 45 9N 90 21W
Media Agua **88** 31 58S 68 25W
Media Luna **88** 34 45S 66 44W
Mediapolis **76** 41 0N 91 10W
Mediaş **107** 46 9N 24 22E
Medical Lake **78** 47 41N 117 42W
Medicine Bow **78** 41 56N 106 11W
Medicine Hat **61** 50 0N 110 45W
Medicine Lake **74** 48 30N 104 30W
Medicine Lodge **75** 37 20N 98 37W
Medina, Colomb. **86** 4 30N 73 21W
Medina, N.D., U.S.A. **74** 46 57N 99 20W
Medina, N.Y., U.S.A. **70** 43 15N 78 27W
Medina, Ohio, U.S.A. **70** 41 9N 81 50W
Medina = Al Madīnah **122** 24 35N 39 52E
Medina del Campo **104** 41 18N 4 55W
Medina L. **75** 29 35N 98 58W
Medina, R. **75** 29 10N 98 20W
Medina-Sidonia **104** 36 28N 5 57W
Mediterranean Sea **93** 35 0N 15 0E
Medley **60** 54 25N 110 16W
Médoc **102** 45 10N 0 56W
Medora **77** 38 49N 86 10W
Medstead **56** 53 19N 108 5W
Meductic **39** 46 0N 67 29W
Medvezhi, Ostrava **121** 71 0N 161 0E
Medvezhyegorsk **120** 63 0N 34 25E
Medway, R., Can. **39** 44 8N 64 36W
Medway, R., U.K. **95** 51 12N 0 23E
Meekatharra **134** 26 32S 118 29E
Meeker **78** 40 1N 107 58W
Meelpaeg L. **35** 48 18N 56 35W
Meerut **124** 29 1N 77 50E
Meeteetsa **78** 44 10N 108 56W
Mégantic **35** 45 36N 70 56W
Mégantic, L. **41** 45 32N 70 53W
Mégantic, Mt. **41** 45 28N 71 9W
Mégara **109** 37 58N 23 22E
Mégève **103** 45 51N 6 37E
Meghalaya □ **125** 25 50N 91 0E
Mégiscane, L. **40** 48 35N 75 55W
Mégiscane, R. **40** 48 29N 75 38W
Mehadia **107** 44 56N 22 23E
Meharry, Mt. **134** 22 59S 118 35E
Mehsana **124** 23 39N 72 26E
Mehun-sur-Yèvre **101** 47 10N 2 13E
Meighen I. **65** 80 0N 99 30W
Meihokow **130** 42 37N 125 46E
Meihsien **131** 24 18N 116 7E
Meiktila **125** 21 0N 96 0E
Meissen **106** 51 10N 13 29E
Meit'an **131** 27 45N 107 28E
Méjean, Causse **102** 44 15N 3 30E
Mejillones **88** 23 10S 70 30W
Mekambo **116** 1 2N 14 5E
Mekhtar **124** 30 30N 69 15E
Mékinac, L. **41** 47 3N 72 41W
Meklong = Samut Songkhram **128** 13 24N 100 1E
Meknès **114** 33 57N 5 33W
Mekong, R. **128** 18 0N 104 15E
Mekongga **127** 3 50S 121 30E
Mekoryok **67** 60 20N 166 20W
Melagiri Hills **124** 12 20N 77 30E
Melaka **128** 2 15N 102 15E
Melaka □ **128** 2 20N 102 15E
Melalap **126** 5 10N 116 5E
Melanesia **14** 4 0S 155 0E
Melbourne, Austral. **136** 37 50S 145 0E
Melbourne, U.S.A. **76** 41 57N 93 6W
Melbourne, Fla., U.S.A. **73** 28 13N 80 35W
Melcher **76** 41 13N 93 15W
Melchor Múzquiz **82** 27 50N 101 40W
Melchor Ocampo (San Pedro Ocampo) **82** 24 52N 101 40W
Meldrum Bay **46** 45 56N 83 6W
Meldrum Creek **63** 52 6N 122 21W
Mêle-sur-Sarthe, Le **100** 48 31N 0 22E
Mélèzes, R. **36** 57 40N 69 29W
Melfort **56** 52 50N 104 37W
Melilla **114** 35 21N 2 57W
Melilot **100** 31 22N 34 37E
Melipilla **88** 33 42S 71 15W
Melita **57** 49 15N 101 0W
Melitopol **120** 46 50N 35 22E
Melk **106** 48 13N 15 20E
Mellansel **110** 63 25N 18 17E
Melle **102** 46 14N 0 10W
Mellen **52** 46 19N 90 36W
Mellerud **111** 58 41N 12 28E
Mellette **74** 45 11N 98 29W
Mellish Reef **135** 17 25S 155 50E
Melo **89** 32 20S 54 10W
Melochville **44** 45 19N 73 56W
Melolo **127** 9 53S 120 40E
Melones Res. **80** 37 57N 120 31W
Melrose, U.K. **96** 55 35N 2 44W
Melrose, U.S.A. **76** 40 59N 93 3W
Melrose, N.Mex., U.S.A. **75** 34 27N 103 33W
Melstone **78** 46 40N 107 55W
Melton Mowbray **94** 52 46N 0 52W
Melun **101** 48 32N 2 39E
Melville **56** 50 55N 102 50W
Melville B. **135** 12 0S 136 45E
Melville Bugt **65** 75 30N 63 0W
Melville, C. **135** 14 11S 144 30E
Melville I., Austral. **134** 11 30S 131 0E
Melville I., Can. **64** 75 30N 111 0W
Melville, L. **35** 53 45N 59 40W
Melville Pen. **65** 68 0N 84 0W
Melvin, R. **54** 59 11N 117 31W
Memba **117** 14 11S 40 30E
Memboro **127** 9 30S 119 30E
Memmingen **106** 47 59N 10 12E
Memphis, U.S.A. **76** 40 28N 92 10W
Memphis, Mich., U.S.A. **46** 42 54N 82 46W
Memphis, Tenn., U.S.A. **75** 35 7N 90 0W
Memphis, Tex., U.S.A. **75** 34 45N 100 30W
Memphrémagog, L. **41** 45 8N 72 17W
Mena **75** 34 40N 94 15W
Menai Strait **94** 53 7N 4 20W
Ménaka **114** 15 59N 2 18E
Menard **75** 30 57N 99 58W
Ménardville **45** 45 17N 73 4W
Ménascouagama, L. **38** 51 13N 61 52W
Menasha **72** 44 13N 88 27W
Menate **126** 0 12S 112 47E
Mencheng **131** 33 27N 116 45E
Mendawai, R. **126** 1 30S 113 0E
Mende **102** 44 31N 3 30E
Mendenhall, C. **67** 59 44N 166 10W
Menderes, R. **122** 37 25N 28 45E
Mendez **83** 25 7N 98 34W
Mendham **56** 50 46N 109 40W
Mendip Hills **95** 51 17N 2 40W
Mendocino **78** 39 26N 123 50W
Mendon **77** 42 0N 85 27W
Mendota, Calif., U.S.A. **80** 36 46N 120 24W

Mendota, Ill., U.S.A.	**76**	41 35N	89 5W
Mendoza	**88**	32 50S	68 52W
Mendoza □	**88**	33 0S	69 0W
Mene Grande	**86**	9 49N	70 56W
Menemen	**122**	38 18N	27 10E
Menfi	**108**	37 36N	12 57E
Meng-so	**128**	22 33N	99 31E
Meng Wang	**128**	22 18N	100 31E
Menggala	**126**	4 20S	105 15E
Mengshan	**131**	24 2N	110 32E
Mengtsz	**129**	23 20N	103 20E
Mengyin	**130**	35 40N	117 55E
Menihek	**36**	54 28N	56 36W
Menihek L.	**36**	54 0N	67 0W
Menin	**105**	50 47N	3 7E
Menindee	**136**	32 20S	142 25E
Ménistouc, L.	**38**	52 52N	66 29W
Menlo Park	**80**	37 27N	122 12W
Menominee	**72**	45 9N	87 39W
Menominee, R.	**72**	45 30N	87 50W
Menomonee Falls	**77**	43 11N	88 7W
Menomonie	**74**	44 50N	91 54W
Menor, Mar	**104**	37 43N	0 48W
Menorca, I.	**104**	40 0N	4 0E
Mentawai, Kepulauan	**126**	2 0S	99 0E
Menton	**103**	43 50N	7 29E
Mentone	**77**	41 10N	86 2W
Mentor	**70**	41 40N	81 21W
Menzies	**134**	29 40S	120 58E
Meoqui	**82**	28 17N	105 29W
Meota	**56**	53 2N	108 27W
Meppel	**105**	52 42N	6 12E
Meppen	**105**	52 41N	7 20E
Mequon	**77**	43 14N	87 59W
Mer Rouge	**75**	32 47N	91 48W
Merabéllou, Kólpos	**109**	35 10N	25 50E
Merak	**127**	5 55S	106 1E
Meramec, R.	**76**	38 23N	91 21W
Merano (Meran)	**108**	46 40N	11 10E
Merasheen I.	**37**	47 25N	54 15W
Merauke	**127**	8 29S	140 24E
Merbabu, Mt.	**127**	7 30S	110 40E
Merbein	**136**	34 10S	142 2E
Merca	**115**	1 48N	44 50E
Mercara	**124**	12 30N	75 45E
Merced	**80**	37 18N	120 30W
Merced Pk.	**80**	37 36N	119 24W
Mercedes, Buenos Aires, Argent.	**88**	34 40S	59 30W
Mercedes, Corrientes, Argent.	**88**	29 10S	58 5W
Mercedes, San Luis, Argent.	**88**	33 5S	65 21W
Mercedes, Uruguay	**88**	33 12S	58 0W
Merceditas	**88**	28 20S	70 35W
Mercer, N.Z.	**133**	37 16S	175 5E
Mercer, U.S.A.	**76**	40 31N	93 32W
Mercer, Pa., U.S.A.	**70**	41 14N	80 13W
Mercier	**44**	45 19N	73 45W
Mercoal	**60**	53 10N	117 5W
Mercury	**81**	36 40N	116 0W
Mercy C.	**65**	65 0N	62 30W
Merdrignac	**100**	48 11N	2 27W
Meredith C.	**90**	52 15S	60 40W
Meredith, L.	**75**	35 30N	101 35W
Meredosia	**76**	39 50N	90 34W
Méréville	**101**	48 20N	2 5E
Mergui Arch.	**128**	12 30N	98 35E
Mergui Arch. = Myeik Kyunzu	**128**	11 30N	97 30E
Mérida, Mexico	**83**	20 50N	89 40W
Mérida, Spain	**104**	38 55N	6 25W
Mérida, Venez.	**86**	8 36N	71 8W
Mérida □	**86**	8 30N	71 10W
Mérida, Cord. de	**86**	9 0N	71 0W
Meriden	**71**	41 33N	72 47W
Meridian, Calif., U.S.A.	**80**	39 9N	121 55W
Meridian, Idaho, U.S.A.	**78**	43 41N	116 25W
Meridian, Miss., U.S.A.	**73**	32 20N	88 42W
Meridian, Tex., U.S.A.	**75**	31 55N	97 37W
Merigomish	**39**	45 38N	62 26W
Merimula	**136**	36 54S	149 54E
Meringur	**136**	34 20S	141 19E
Merirumã	**87**	1 15N	54 50W
Merivale	**48**	45 19N	75 43W
Merkel	**75**	32 30N	100 0W
Merksem	**105**	51 16N	4 25E
Merlebach	**101**	49 5N	6 52E
Merlerault, Le	**100**	48 41N	0 16E
Merowe	**115**	18 29N	31 46E
Merredin	**134**	31 28S	118 18E
Merrick, Mt.	**96**	55 8N	4 30W
Merrickville	**47**	44 55N	75 50W
Merrill, Mich., U.S.A.	**46**	43 25N	84 20W
Merrill, Oregon, U.S.A.	**78**	42 2N	121 37W
Merrill, Wis., U.S.A.	**74**	45 11N	89 41W
Merriton	**70**	43 12N	79 13W
Merritt	**63**	50 10N	120 45W
Merry I.	**36**	55 29N	77 31W
Merrygoen	**136**	31 51S	149 12E
Merryville	**75**	30 47N	93 31W
Mersch	**105**	49 44N	6 7E
Merseburg	**106**	51 20N	12 0E
Mersey, R., Can.	**39**	44 2N	64 43W
Mersey, R., U.K.	**94**	53 20N	2 56W
Merseyside □	**94**	53 25N	2 55W
Mersin	**122**	36 51N	34 36E
Mersing	**128**	2 25N	103 50E
Merthyr Tydfil	**95**	51 45N	3 23W
Mertoa	**136**	36 33S	142 29E
Mértola	**104**	37 40N	7 40E
Merton	**49**	43 25N	79 44W
Mertzon	**75**	31 17N	100 48W
Méru	**101**	49 13N	2 8E
Meru	**116**	0 3N	37 40E
Merville, Can.	**62**	49 48N	125 3W
Merville, France	**101**	50 38N	2 38E
Mervin	**56**	53 20N	108 53W
Méry-sur-Seine	**101**	48 31N	3 54E
Merzig	**105**	49 26N	6 37E
Mesa	**79**	33 20N	111 56W
Mesa, La, Colomb.	**86**	4 38N	74 28W
Mesa, La, Calif., U.S.A.	**81**	32 48N	117 5W
Mesa, La, N. Mex., U.S.A.	**79**	32 6N	106 48W
Mesgouez, L.	**36**	51 20N	75 0W
Meshed = Mashhad	**123**	36 20N	59 35E
Meshoppen	**71**	41 36N	76 3W
Mesick	**72**	44 24N	85 42W
Mesilinka, R.	**54**	56 6N	124 30W
Mesilla	**79**	32 20N	106 50W
Meslay-du-Maine	**100**	47 58N	0 33W
Mesolóngion	**109**	38 27N	21 28E
Mesopotamia, reg.	**122**	33 30N	44 0E
Mess Cr.	**54**	57 55N	131 14W
Messac	**100**	47 49N	1 50W
Messeix	**102**	45 37N	2 33E
Messina, Italy	**108**	38 10N	15 32E
Messina, S. Afr.	**117**	22 20S	30 12E
Messina, Str. di	**108**	38 5N	15 35E
Messine	**40**	46 14N	76 2W
Messíni	**109**	37 4N	22 1E
Messiniakós, Kólpos	**109**	36 45N	22 5E
Mesta, R.	**109**	41 30N	24 0E
Meta	**76**	38 19N	92 10W
Meta □	**86**	3 30N	73 0W
Meta, R.	**86**	6 20N	68 5W
Metagama	**34**	47 0N	81 55W
Metaline Falls	**63**	48 52N	117 22W
Metamora	**76**	40 47N	89 22W
Metán	**88**	25 30S	65 0W
Metchosin	**54**	48 15N	123 37W
Meteghan	**39**	44 11N	66 10W
Methuen	**71**	42 43N	71 10W
Methven	**133**	43 38S	171 40E
Methy L.	**55**	56 28N	109 30W
Metil	**117**	16 24S	39 0E
Métis-sur-Mer	**38**	48 40N	67 59W
Metlakatla	**67**	55 10N	131 33W
Metropolis	**75**	37 10N	88 47W
Mettur Dam	**124**	11 45N	77 45E
Metz	**101**	49 8N	6 10E
Meulaboh	**126**	4 11N	96 3E
Meulan	**101**	49 0N	1 52E
Meung-sur-Loire	**101**	47 50N	1 40E
Meureudu	**126**	5 19N	96 10E
Meurthe-et-Moselle □	**101**	48 52N	6 0E
Meurthe, R.	**101**	48 47N	6 9E
Meuse □	**101**	49 8N	5 25E
Meuse, R.	**105**	50 45N	5 41E
Mexborough	**94**	53 29N	1 18W
Mexia	**75**	31 38N	96 32W
Mexiana, I.	**87**	0 0	49 30W
Mexicali	**82**	32 40N	115 30W
México	**83**	19 20N	99 10W
Mexico, Me., U.S.A.	**71**	44 35N	70 30W
Mexico, Mo., U.S.A.	**76**	39 10N	91 55W
Mexico ■	**82**	20 0N	100 0W
México □	**82**	19 20N	99 10W
Mexico, G. of	**83**	25 0N	90 0W
Meymac	**102**	45 32N	2 10E
Meyrargues	**103**	43 38N	5 32E
Meyronne	**56**	49 39N	106 50W
Meyrueis	**102**	44 12N	3 27E
Meyssac	**102**	45 3N	1 40E
Mèze	**102**	43 27N	3 36E
Mezen	**120**	65 50N	44 20E
Mezen, R.	**120**	64 34N	46 30E
Mézidon	**100**	49 5N	0 1W
Mézilhac	**103**	44 49N	4 21E
Mézin	**102**	44 4N	0 16E
Mezökövesd	**107**	47 49N	20 35E
Mézos	**102**	44 5N	1 10W
Mezötúr	**107**	47 0N	20 41E
Mezquital	**82**	23 29N	104 23W
Mhow	**124**	22 33N	75 50E
Miahuatlán	**83**	16 21N	96 36W
Miami, Ariz., U.S.A.	**79**	33 25N	111 0W
Miami, Fla., U.S.A.	**73**	25 52N	80 15W
Miami, Tex., U.S.A.	**75**	35 44N	100 38W
Miami Beach	**73**	25 49N	80 6W
Miami, R.	**72**	39 20N	84 40W
Miamisburg	**77**	39 40N	84 11W
Miandowāb	**122**	37 0N	46 5E
Miandrivazo	**117**	19 50S	45 56E
Mīāneh	**122**	37 30N	47 40E
Mianwali	**124**	32 38N	71 28E
Miao Tao	**130**	38 10N	120 50E
Miaoli	**131**	24 33N	120 42E
Miarinarivo	**117**	18 57S	46 55E
Miass	**120**	54 59N	60 6E
Mica Creek	**63**	52 2N	118 35W
Mica Dam	**63**	52 5N	118 32W
Mica Res.	**54**	51 55N	118 00W
Michaudville	**43**	45 50N	73 4W
Michelson, Mt.	**67**	69 20N	144 20W
Michigan □	**69**	44 40N	85 40W
Michigan Center	**46**	42 14N	84 20W
Michigan City	**77**	41 42N	86 56W
Michigan, L.	**72**	44 0N	87 0W
Michih	**130**	37 58N	110 0E
Michipicoten	**53**	47 55N	84 55W
Michipicoten B.	**53**	47 53N	84 53W
Michipicoten I.	**53**	47 40N	85 50W
Michoacan □	**82**	19 0N	102 0W
Michurinsk	**120**	52 58N	40 27E
Micmac Lake	**39**	44 41N	63 33W
Micronesia	**14**	17 0N	160 0E
Mid Glamorgan □	**95**	51 40N	3 25W
Midai, P.	**126**	3 0N	107 47E
Midale	**56**	49 25N	103 20W
Midas	**78**	41 14N	116 56W
Middelburg, Neth.	**105**	51 30N	3 36E
Middelburg, S. Afr.	**117**	31 30S	25 0E
Middle Alkali L.	**78**	41 30N	120 3W
Middle Andaman I.	**128**	12 30N	92 30E
Middle Brook	**35**	48 40N	54 20W
Middle Church	**58**	49 59N	97 4W
Middle Fork Feather, R.	**80**	39 35N	121 25W
Middle Lake	**56**	52 29N	105 18W
Middle Musquodoboit	**39**	45 3N	63 9W
Middle, R.	**76**	41 26N	93 30W
Middle Raccoon, R.	**76**	41 35N	93 35W
Middleboro	**71**	41 56N	70 52W
Middleburg, N.Y., U.S.A.	**71**	42 36N	74 19W
Middleburg, Pa., U.S.A.	**70**	40 46N	77 5W
Middlebury, Ind., U.S.A.	**77**	41 41N	85 42W
Middlebury, Vt., U.S.A.	**71**	44 0N	73 9W
Middleport	**72**	39 0N	82 5W
Middlesbrough	**94**	54 35N	1 14W
Middlesex, Belize	**83**	17 2N	88 31W
Middlesex, U.S.A.	**71**	40 36N	74 30W
Middleton, Can.	**39**	44 57N	65 4W
Middleton, U.S.A.	**76**	43 6N	89 30W
Middleton I.	**67**	59 30N	146 28W
Middletown, Calif., U.S.A.	**80**	38 45N	122 37W
Middletown, Conn., U.S.A.	**71**	41 37N	72 40W
Middletown, N.Y., U.S.A.	**71**	41 28N	74 28W
Middletown, Ohio, U.S.A.	**77**	39 30N	84 21W
Middletown, Pa., U.S.A.	**71**	40 12N	76 44W
Middleville	**77**	42 43N	85 28W
Middlewood	**39**	44 14N	64 34W
Midi, Canal du	**102**	43 45N	1 21E
Midland, Man., Can.	**58**	49 54N	97 11W
Midland, Ont., Can.	**46**	44 45N	79 50W
Midland, Calif., U.S.A.	**81**	33 52N	114 48W
Midland, Mich., U.S.A.	**46**	43 37N	84 17W
Midland, Pa., U.S.A.	**70**	40 39N	80 27W
Midland, Tex., U.S.A.	**75**	32 0N	102 3W
Midland Junction	**134**	31 50S	115 58E
Midleton	**97**	51 52N	8 12W
Midlothian	**75**	32 30N	97 0W
Midnapore, Can.	**59**	50 55N	114 5W
Midnapore, India	**125**	22 25N	87 21E
Midvale	**78**	40 39N	111 58W
Midway	**63**	49 1N	118 48W
Midway Is.	**14**	28 13N	177 22W
Midway Wells	**81**	32 41N	115 7W
Midwest	**78**	43 27N	106 11W
Mie-ken □	**132**	34 30N	136 10E
Miedzychód	**106**	52 35N	15 53E
Miedzyrzec Podlaski	**107**	51 58N	22 45E
Miélan	**102**	43 27N	0 19E
Mienchih	**131**	34 47N	111 49E
Mienhsien	**131**	33 11N	106 35E
Mienyang, Hupei, China	**131**	30 10N	113 20E
Mienyang, Szechwan, China	**131**	31 18N	104 26E
Miercurea Ciuc	**107**	46 21N	25 48E
Mieres	**104**	43 18N	5 48W
Miette Hotsprings	**60**	53 8N	117 46W
Migennes	**101**	47 58N	3 31E
Miguel Alemán, Presa	**83**	18 15N	96 40W
Miguel Alves	**87**	4 11S	42 55W
Mihara	**132**	34 24N	133 5E
Milntown	**70**	40 34N	77 24W
Mikardo	**46**	44 34N	83 28W
Mikínai	**109**	37 43N	22 46E
Mikindani	**116**	10 15S	40 2E
Mikkeli	**111**	61 43N	27 25E
Mikkeli □	**110**	62 0N	28 0E
Mikkwa, R.	**60**	58 25N	114 46W
Míkonos, I.	**109**	37 30N	25 25E
Mikura-Jima	**132**	33 52N	139 36E
Milaca	**74**	45 45N	93 40W
Milagro	**86**	2 0S	79 30W
Milan, U.S.A.	**46**	42 5N	83 40W
Milan, Ill., U.S.A.	**76**	41 27N	90 34W
Milan, Mo., U.S.A.	**76**	40 10N	93 5W
Milan, Tenn., U.S.A.	**73**	35 55N	88 45W
Milan = Milano	**108**	45 28N	9 10E
Milano	**108**	45 28N	9 10E
Milâs	**122**	37 20N	27 50E
Milazzo	**108**	38 13N	15 13E
Milbank	**74**	45 17N	96 38W
Milden	**56**	51 29N	107 32W
Mildmay	**46**	44 3N	81 7W
Mildura	**136**	34 13S	142 9E
Miles, Austral.	**135**	26 40S	150 23E
Miles, U.S.A.	**75**	31 39N	100 11W
Miles City	**74**	46 30N	105 50W
Milestone	**56**	49 59N	104 31W
Milford, U.S.A.	**77**	42 35N	83 36W
Milford, U.S.A.	**77**	41 40N	87 43W
Milford, Conn., U.S.A.	**71**	41 13N	73 4W
Milford, Del., U.S.A.	**72**	38 52N	75 27W
Milford, Mass., U.S.A.	**71**	42 8N	71 30W
Milford, Pa., U.S.A.	**71**	41 20N	74 47W
Milford, Utah, U.S.A.	**79**	38 20N	113 0W
Milford Haven	**95**	51 43N	5 2W
Milford Haven, B.	**95**	51 40N	5 10W
Milford Sd.	**133**	44 34S	167 47E
Milford Station	**39**	45 3N	63 26W
Milk, R., Can.	**61**	49 0N	110 33W
Milk, R., U.S.A.	**78**	48 40N	107 15W
Milk River	**61**	49 10N	112 5W
Mill City	**78**	44 45N	122 28W
Mill Cr.	**59**	53 33N	113 29W
Mill Grove	**48**	43 20N	79 58W
Mill, I.	**91**	66 0S	101 30E
Mill Shoals	**77**	38 15N	88 21W
Mill Valley	**80**	37 54N	122 32W
Mill Village	**39**	44 9N	64 39W
Millau	**102**	44 8N	3 4E
Millbridge	**47**	44 41N	77 36W
Millbrook	**47**	44 10N	78 29W
Mille	**73**	33 7N	83 15W
Mille Îles, R. des	**44**	45 42N	73 32W
Mille Isles	**43**	45 49N	74 14W
Mille Lacs, L.	**52**	46 10N	93 30W
Mille Lacs, L. des	**52**	48 45N	90 35W
Milledgeville	**76**	41 58N	89 46W
Millen	**73**	32 50N	81 57W
Miller	**74**	44 35N	98 59W
Millerand	**39**	47 13N	61 59W
Millersburg, U.S.A.	**77**	41 32N	85 42W
Millersburg, Mich., U.S.A.	**46**	45 20N	84 4W
Millersburg, Ohio, U.S.A.	**70**	40 32N	81 52W
Millersburg, Pa., U.S.A.	**70**	40 32N	76 58W
Millerton	**71**	41 57N	73 32W
Millerton, L.	**80**	37 0N	119 42W
Millertown	**37**	48 49N	56 33W
Millet	**61**	53 6N	113 28W
Millevaches, Plat. de	**102**	45 45N	2 0E
Millicent	**135**	37 34S	140 21E
Milliken	**50**	43 49N	79 18W
Millington	**46**	43 17N	83 32W
Millinocket	**35**	45 45N	68 45W
Mills L.	**54**	61 30N	118 20W
Millsboro	**70**	40 0N	80 0W
Millstream	**39**	48 2N	67 2W
Milltown, N.B., Can.	**39**	45 10N	67 18W
Milltown, Newf., Can.	**37**	47 54N	55 46W
Milltown Malbay	**97**	52 51N	9 25W
Millview	**39**	44 43N	63 40W
Millville, Can.	**39**	46 8N	67 12W
Millville, U.S.A.	**72**	39 22N	75 0W
Millwood Res.	**75**	33 45N	94 0W
Milly	**101**	48 24N	2 20E
Milnesville	**50**	43 55N	79 16W
Milnor	**74**	46 19N	97 29W
Milo	**61**	50 34N	112 53W
Milolii	**67**	22 8N	159 42W
Mílos	**109**	36 44N	24 25E
Milot	**41**	48 54N	71 49W
Milroy	**77**	39 30N	85 28W
Milton, N.S., Can.	**39**	44 4N	64 45W
Milton, Ont., Can.	**49**	43 31N	79 53W
Milton, N.Z.	**133**	46 7S	169 59E
Milton, U.S.A.	**76**	40 41N	92 10W
Milton, U.S.A.	**77**	42 47N	88 56W
Milton, Calif., U.S.A.	**80**	38 3N	120 51W
Milton, Fla., U.S.A.	**73**	30 38N	87 0W
Milton, Pa., U.S.A.	**70**	41 0N	76 53W
Milton-Freewater	**78**	45 57N	118 24W
Milton Heights	**49**	43 31N	79 56W
Milton Keynes	**95**	52 3N	0 42W
Milton West	**70**	43 33N	79 53W
Milverton	**46**	43 34N	80 55W
Milwaukee	**77**	43 9N	87 58W
Milwaukie	**80**	45 27N	122 39W
Mimico Cr.	**50**	43 37N	79 30W
Miminegash	**39**	46 53N	64 14W
Miminiska L.	**52**	51 35N	88 37W
Mimizan	**102**	44 12N	1 14W
Mimosa	**49**	43 44N	80 13W
Min K.	**131**	26 0N	119 20E
Mina	**79**	38 21N	118 9W
Mina Pirquitas	**88**	22 40S	66 40W
Mina Saud	**122**	28 45N	48 20E
Minā'al Ahmadī	**122**	29 5N	48 10E
Mīnāb	**123**	27 10N	57 1E
Minago, R.	**57**	54 33N	98 59W
Minaki	**52**	49 59N	94 40W
Minamata	**132**	32 10N	130 30E
Minas Basin	**39**	45 20N	64 12W
Minas Channel	**39**	45 15N	64 45W
Minas de Rio Tinto	**104**	37 42N	6 22W
Minas Gerais □	**87**	18 50S	46 0W
Minas, Sierra de las	**84**	15 9N	89 31W
Minatitlán	**83**	17 58N	94 35W
Minbu	**125**	20 10N	95 0E
Mindanao, I.	**127**	8 0N	125 0E
Mindanao Sea	**127**	9 0N	124 0E
Mindanao Trench	**127**	8 0N	128 0E

Mindemoya **Monroe**

Mindemoya **46** 45 44N 82 10W
Minden, Can. **47** 44 55N 78 43W
Minden, Ger. **106** 52 18N 8 54 E
Minden, La., U.S.A. **75** 32 40N 93 20W
Minden, Nev., U.S.A. **80** 38 57N 119 48W
Mindiptana **127** 5 45 S 140 22 E
Mindona, L. **136** 33 6 S 142 6 E
Mindoro, I. **127** 13 0N 121 0 E
Mindoro Strait **127** 12 30N 120 30 E
Mindouli **116** 4 12 S 14 28 E
Mine Centre **52** 48 45N 92 37W
Ming, I. **38** 50 51N 64 43W
Minegan, Îles de **38** 50 12N 63 35W
Minehead **95** 51 12N 3 29W
Mineola **75** 32 40N 95 30W
Mineral King **80** 36 27N 118 36W
Mineral Point **76** 42 52N 90 11W
Mineral Wells **75** 32 50N 98 5W
Minersville, Pa., U.S.A. **71** 40 40N 76 17W
Minersville, Utah, U.S.A. **79** 38 14N 112 58W
Minerva **70** 40 43N 81 8W
Minette **73** 30 54N 87 43W
Minetto **71** 43 24N 76 28W
Mingan **38** 50 20N 64 0W
Mingan = Pangkiang **130** 43 4N 112 30 E
Mingan, R. **38** 50 18N 63 59W
Mingechaurskoye Vdkhr. **120** 40 56N 47 20 E
Mingin **125** 22 50N 94 30 E
Mingki (Kweihwa) **131** 26 10N 117 14 E
Minho □ **104** 41 25N 8 20W
Minho, R. **104** 41 58N 8 40W
Minhow = Foochow **131** 26 2N 119 12 E
Minhsien **131** 34 26N 104 2 E
Minidoka **78** 42 47N 113 34W
Minier **76** 40 26N 89 19W
Minilya **134** 23 55 S 114 0 E
Minipi, L. **38** 52 25N 60 45W
Miniss L. **52** 50 48N 90 50W
Minitonas **57** 52 5N 101 2W
Mink L. **54** 61 54N 117 40W
Minkiang **131** 32 30N 114 10 E
Minneapolis, Kans., U.S.A. **74** 39 11N 97 40W
Minneapolis, Minn., U.S.A. **74** 44 58N 93 20W
Minnedosa **57** 50 14N 99 50W
Minnesota □ **74** 46 40N 94 0W
Minnitaki L. **52** 49 57N 91 55W
Miño, R. **104** 41 58N 8 40W
Minonk **76** 40 54N 89 2W
Minooka **77** 41 27N 88 16W
Minorca = Menorca **104** 40 0N 4 0 E
Minot **74** 48 10N 101 15W
Minquiers, Les **100** 48 58N 2 8W
Minsk **120** 53 52N 27 30 E
Minsk Mazowiecki **107** 52 10N 21 33 E
Minster **77** 40 24N 84 23W
Minstrel Island **62** 50 37N 126 18W
Mintaka Pass **124** 37 0N 74 58 E
Minto, Can. **39** 46 5N 66 5W
Minto, U.S.A. **67** 64 55N 149 20W
Minto, L. **36** 57 13N 75 0W
Minton **56** 49 10N 104 35W
Mintsing **131** 26 8N 118 57 E
Minturn **78** 39 45N 106 25W
Minusinsk **121** 53 50N 91 20 E
Minutang **125** 28 15N 96 30 E
Minvoul **116** 2 9N 12 8 E
Minya Konka, mt. **129** 29 36N 101 50 E
Mio **46** 44 39N 84 8W
Mios Num, I. **127** 1 30 S 135 10 E
Miquelon, Can. **40** 49 25N 76 27W
Miquelon, St. P. & M. **37** 47 3N 56 20W
Miquelon, I. **37** 47 1N 56 20W
Miquelon, St. Pierre et, □ **37** 47 8N 56 24W
Mira **39** 46 2N 59 58W
Mira, R. **39** 46 2N 59 58W
Mirabel **44** 45 40N 74 10W
Mirabel Airport **44** 45 41N 74 2W
Miraflores **82** 23 21N 109 45W
Miraflores Locks **84** 8 59N 79 36W
Miraj **124** 16 50N 74 45 E
Miram Shah **124** 33 0N 70 0 E
Miramar **88** 38 15 S 57 50W
Miramas **103** 43 33N 4 59 E
Mirambeau **102** 45 23N 0 35W
Miramichi B. **39** 47 15N 65 0W
Miramichi, Little S.W., R. **39** 46 58N 65 38W
Miramichi, N.W., R. **39** 46 57N 65 55W
Miramichi, S.W., R. **39** 46 58N 65 38W
Miramont-de-Guyenne **102** 44 37N 0 21 E
Miranda **87** 20 10 S 56 15W
Miranda de Ebro **104** 42 41N 2 57W
Mirando City **75** 27 28N 98 59W
Mirandópolis **89** 21 9 S 51 6W
Miraporvos, I. **85** 22 9N 74 30W
Mirassol **89** 20 46 S 49 28W
Mirebeau, Côte d'Or, France **101** 47 25N 5 20 E
Mirebeau, Vienne, France **100** 46 49N 0 10 E
Mirecourt **101** 48 20N 6 10 E
Miri **126** 4 18N 114 0 E
Mirim, Lagoa **89** 32 45 S 52 50W
Mirimire **86** 11 10N 68 43W
Mirny **91** 66 0 S 95 0 E
Mirnyy **121** 62 33N 113 53 E
Mirond L. **55** 55 6N 102 47W
Mirool **136** 34 24 S 147 5 E
Mirpur Khas **124** 25 30N 69 0 E
Mirror **61** 52 30N 113 7W
Miryang **130** 35 34N 128 42 E
Mirzapur **125** 25 10N 82 45 E
Misantla **83** 19 56N 96 50W
Miscou Centre **39** 47 57N 64 34W
Miscou I. **39** 47 57N 64 31W
Miscouche **39** 46 26N 63 52W
Misehkow, R. **52** 51 26N 89 11W
Mish'āb, Ra'as al **122** 28 15N 48 43 E
Mishan **129** 45 31N 132 2 E
Mishawaka **77** 41 40N 86 8W
Mishima **132** 35 10N 138 52 E
Misión **81** 32 6N 116 53W
Misión, La **82** 32 5N 116 50W
Misiones □, Argent. **89** 27 0 S 55 0W
Misiones □, Parag. **88** 27 0 S 56 0W
Miskīn **123** 23 44N 56 52 E
Miskitos, Cayos **84** 14 26N 82 50W
Miskolc **107** 48 7N 20 50 E
Misoöl, I. **127** 2 0 S 130 0 E
Misrātah **114** 32 18N 15 3 E
Missanabie **53** 48 20N 84 6W
Missinaibi L. **53** 48 23N 83 40W
Missinaibi Lake Prov. Park **53** 48 25N 83 30W
Missinaibi, R. **53** 50 43N 81 29W
Mission, S.D., U.S.A. **74** 43 21N 100 36W
Mission, Tex., U.S.A. **75** 26 15N 98 30W
Mission City **63** 49 10N 122 15W
Missipuskiow, R. **56** 53 53N 103 18W
Missisa L. **34** 52 20N 85 7W
Missisicabi, R. **36** 51 14N 79 31W
Missisquoi □ **45** 45 5N 73 0W
Missisquoi, B. **43** 45 2N 73 9W
Mississagi Prov. Park **46** 46 30N 82 40W
Mississagi, R. **46** 46 15N 83 9W
Mississauga **50** 43 32N 79 35W
Mississinewa, R. **77** 40 46N 86 3W
Mississippi, Delta of the **75** 29 15N 90 30W
Mississippi L. **47** 45 5N 76 10W
Mississippi, R. **75** 35 29N 89 15W
Mississippi Sd. **75** 30 25N 89 0W
Missoula **78** 47 0N 114 0W
Missouri □ **74** 38 25N 92 30W
Missouri, Little, R. **78** 46 0N 111 35W
Missouri, R. **72** 40 20N 95 40W
Mist **80** 45 59N 123 15W
Mistake B. **55** 62 8N 93 0W
Mistanipisipou, R. **38** 51 32N 61 50W
Mistaouac, L. **40** 49 25N 78 41W
Mistassibi Nord-Est., R. **41** 49 31N 71 56W
Mistassibi, R. **41** 48 53N 72 13W
Mistassini **41** 48 53N 72 12W
Mistassini L. **36** 51 0N 73 40W
Mistassini, Parc. Prov. de **41** 50 20N 74 0W
Mistassini, R. **41** 48 42N 72 20W
Mistastin L. **35** 55 57N 63 20W
Mistatim **56** 52 52N 103 22W
Mistretta **108** 37 56N 14 20 E
Misty L. **55** 58 53N 101 40W
Mitchell, Austral. **135** 26 29 S 147 58 E
Mitchell, Can. **46** 43 28N 81 12W
Mitchell, Ind., U.S.A. **77** 38 42N 86 25W
Mitchell, Nebr., U.S.A. **74** 41 58N 103 45W
Mitchell, Oreg., U.S.A. **78** 44 31N 120 8W
Mitchell, S.D., U.S.A. **74** 43 40N 98 0W
Mitchell Corners, Ont., Can. **49** 43 55N 78 53W
Mitchell Corners, Qué., Can. **43** 45 2N 73 1W
Mitchell I. **66** 49 12N 123 5W
Mitchell L. **63** 52 52N 120 37W
Mitchell, Mt. **73** 35 40N 82 20W
Mitchell, R. **135** 15 12 S 141 35 E
Mitchelstown **97** 52 16N 8 18W
Mitchelton **97** 27 25 S 152 59 E
Mitchinamécus, Rés. **40** 47 19N 75 9W
Mitiaro, I. **133** 19 49 S 157 43W
Mitilíni = Lesvos **109** 39 0N 26 20 E
Mitla **83** 16 55N 96 24W
Mito **132** 36 20N 140 30 E
Mitsinjo **117** 16 1 S 45 52 E
Mitsiwa Channel **115** 15 30N 40 0 E
Mitta Mitta, R. **136** 36 14 S 147 10 E
Mittagong **136** 34 28 S 150 29 E
Mitú **86** 1 8N 70 3W
Mituas **86** 3 52N 68 49W
Mitumba, Chaîne des **116** 10 0 S 26 20 E
Mitwaba **116** 8 2N 27 17 E
Mitzick **116** 0 45N 11 40 E
Mixteco, R. **83** 18 11N 98 30W
Miyagi-Ken □ **132** 38 15N 140 45 E
Miyake-Jima **132** 34 0N 139 30 E
Miyako **132** 39 40N 141 75 E
Miyako-rettō **131** 24 47N 125 20 E
Miyakonojō **132** 31 32N 131 5 E
Miyazaki **132** 31 56N 131 30 E
Miyazaki-ken □ **132** 32 0N 131 30 E
Miyazu **132** 35 35N 135 10 E
Miyet, Bahr el **115** 31 30N 35 30 E
Miyun **130** 40 25N 116 50 E
Mizamis = Ozamiz **127** 8 15N 123 50 E
Mizen Hd., Cork, Ireland **97** 51 27N 9 50W
Mizen Hd., Wick., Ireland **97** 52 52N 6 4W
Mizoram □ **125** 23 0N 92 40 E
Mjölby **111** 58 20N 15 10 E
Mjøsa **111** 60 40N 11 0 E
Mkushi **117** 14 25 S 29 15 E
Mladá Boleslav **106** 50 27N 14 53 E
Mława **107** 53 9N 20 25 E
Mo i Rana **110** 66 15N 14 7 E
Moa, I. **127** 8 0 S 128 0 E
Moab **79** 38 40N 109 35W
Moabi **116** 2 24 S 10 59 E
Moala, I. **133** 18 36 S 179 53 E
Moama **136** 36 3 S 144 45 E
Moamba **136** 25 34 S 32 16 E
Moapo **81** 36 45N 114 37W
Moba **116** 7 0 S 29 48 E
Mobaye **116** 4 25N 21 5 E
Mobayi **116** 4 15N 21 8 E
Moberley **76** 39 25N 92 25W
Moberly, R. **54** 56 12N 120 55W
Mobert **34** 48 41N 85 40W
Mobile **73** 30 41N 88 3W
Mobile B. **73** 30 30N 88 0W
Mobile, Pt. **73** 30 15N 88 0W
Mobridge **74** 45 40N 100 28W
Mobutu Sese Seko, L. **116** 1 30N 31 0 E
Moçambique **117** 15 3 S 40 42 E
Mochudi **117** 24 27 S 26 7 E
Mocimboa da Praia **116** 11 25 S 40 20 E
Moclips **80** 47 14N 124 10W
Moç"medes □ **117** 16 35 S 12 30 E
Mocoa **86** 1 15N 76 45W
Mococa **89** 21 28 S 47 0W
Mocorito **82** 25 20N 108 0W
Moctezuma **82** 30 12N 106 26W
Moctezuma, R. **83** 21 59N 98 34W
Mocuba **117** 16 54 S 37 25 E
Modane **103** 45 12N 6 40 E
Módena **108** 44 39N 10 55 E
Modena **79** 37 55N 113 56W
Modesto **80** 37 43N 121 0W
Módica **108** 36 52N 14 45 E
Modjokerto **127** 7 29 S 112 25 E
Moe **135** 38 12 S 146 19 E
Moei, R. **128** 17 25N 98 10 E
Moëlan-sur-Mer **100** 47 49N 3 38W
Moengo **87** 5 45N 54 20W
Moffat, Can. **49** 43 31N 80 3W
Moffat, U.K. **96** 55 20N 3 27W
Mogadiscio = Mogadishu **115** 2 2N 45 25 E
Mogadishu **115** 2 2N 45 25 E
Mogami-gawa, R. **132** 38 45N 140 0 E
Mogaung **125** 25 20N 97 0 E
Mogi das Cruzes **89** 23 45 S 46 20W
Mogi-Guaçu, R. **89** 20 53 S 48 10W
Mogi-Mirim **89** 22 20 S 47 0W
Mogilev **120** 53 55N 30 18 E
Mogilla **136** 36 41 S 149 38 E
Mogincual **117** 15 35 S 40 25 E
Mogocha **121** 53 40N 119 50 E
Mogoi **127** 1 55 S 133 10 E
Mogok **125** 23 0N 96 40 E
Mogollon **79** 33 25N 108 55W
Mogollon Mesa **79** 35 0N 111 0W
Mohács **107** 45 58N 18 41 E
Mohall **74** 48 46N 101 30W
Mohammadābād **123** 37 30N 59 5 E
Mohave Desert **79** 35 0N 117 30W
Mohave L. **79** 35 25N 114 36W
Mohawk, Ariz., U.S.A. **79** 32 45N 113 50W
Mohawk, Mich., U.S.A. **52** 47 18N 88 26W
Mohembo **117** 18 15 S 21 43 E
Mohican, C. **67** 60 10N 167 30W
Möhne, R. **105** 51 29N 8 10 E
Moho **129** 53 15N 122 27 E
Mohon **101** 49 45N 4 44 E
Mohoro **116** 8 6 S 39 8 E
Moidart, L. **96** 56 47N 5 40W
Moille, La **76** 41 32N 89 17W
Moine, R, La **76** 39 58N 90 32W
Mointy **120** 47 40N 73 45 E
Moira, R. **47** 44 21N 77 24W
Moirans **103** 45 20N 5 33 E
Moirans-en-Montagne **103** 46 26N 5 43 E
Moisie **38** 50 12N 66 1W
Moisie, R. **38** 50 14N 66 5W
Moissac **102** 44 7N 1 5 E
Mojave **81** 35 8N 118 8W
Mojave Desert **81** 35 0N 116 30W
Mojikit L. **52** 50 40N 88 15W
Mojo **88** 21 48 S 65 33W
Mojo, I. **126** 8 10 S 117 40 E
Mokai **133** 38 32 S 175 56 E
Mokane **76** 38 41N 91 53W
Mokelumne Hill **80** 38 18N 120 43W
Mokelumne, R. **80** 38 23N 121 25W
Mokokchung **125** 26 15N 94 30 E
Mokpo **131** 34 50N 126 30 E
Mol **105** 51 11N 5 5 E
Molchanovo **120** 57 40N 83 50 E
Mold **94** 53 10N 3 10W
Moldavian S.S.R. □ **120** 47 0N 28 0 E
Molde **110** 62 45N 7 9 E
Molepolole **117** 24 28 S 25 28 E
Molfetta **108** 41 12N 16 35 E
Moline **76** 41 30N 90 30W
Molinos **88** 25 28 S 66 15W
Moliro **116** 8 12 S 30 30 E
Molise □ **108** 41 45N 14 30 E
Mollendo **86** 17 0 S 72 0W
Mölndal **111** 57 40N 12 3 E
Molokai, I. **67** 21 8N 157 0W
Molong **136** 33 5 S 148 54 E
Molopo, R. **117** 25 40 S 24 30 E
Molotov, Mys **121** 81 10N 95 0 E
Moloundou **116** 2 8N 15 15 E
Molsheim **101** 48 33N 7 29 E
Molson L. **57** 54 22N 95 32W
Molu, I. **127** 6 45 S 131 40 E
Molucca Sea **127** 4 0 S 124 0 E
Moluccas = Maluku, Is. **127** 1 0 S 127 0 E
Moma **117** 16 47 S 39 4 E
Mombasa **116** 4 2 S 39 43 E
Momchilgrad **109** 41 33N 25 23 E
Momence **77** 41 10N 87 40W
Mompós **86** 9 14N 74 26W
Møn **111** 54 57N 12 15 E
Mon, R. **125** 20 25N 94 30 E
Mona, Canal de la **85** 18 30N 67 45W
Mona, I. **85** 18 5N 67 54W
Mona Passage **85** 18 0N 67 40W
Mona, Punta **84** 9 37N 82 36W
Monach Is. **96** 57 32N 7 40W
Monaco ■ **103** 43 46N 7 23 E
Monadhliath Mts. **96** 57 10N 4 4W
Monagas □ **86** 9 20N 63 0W
Monaghan **97** 54 15N 6 58W
Monaghan □ **97** 54 10N 7 0W
Monahans **75** 31 35N 102 50W
Monarch **61** 49 48N 113 7W
Monarch Mt. **54** 51 55N 125 57W
Monaro Ra. **136** 36 20 S 149 0 E
Monashee Prov. Park **63** 50 30N 118 15W
Monastier-sur-Gazeille, Le **102** 44 57N 3 59 E
Monastir = Bitola **109** 41 5N 21 21 E
Moncayo, Sierra del **104** 41 48N 1 50W
Mönchengladbach **105** 51 12N 6 23 E
Monchique **104** 37 19N 8 38W
Monchique, Sa. de, **104** 37 18N 8 39W
Monck **49** 43 58N 80 29W
Monclova **82** 26 50N 101 30W
Moncontour **100** 48 22N 2 38W
Moncouche, L. **41** 48 45N 70 42W
Moncton **39** 46 7N 64 51W
Mondego, R. **104** 40 28N 8 0W
Mondeodo **127** 3 21 S 122 9 E
Mondonac, L. **41** 47 24N 73 58W
Mondoví **108** 44 23N 7 56 E
Mondovi **74** 44 37N 91 40W
Mondragon **103** 44 13N 4 44 E
Monessen **70** 40 9N 79 50W
Monestier-de-Clermont **103** 44 55N 5 38 E
Monet **34** 48 10N 75 40W
Monêtier-les-Bains, Le **103** 44 58N 6 30 E
Monett **75** 36 55N 93 56W
Monflanquin **102** 44 32N 0 47 E
Monforte **104** 39 6N 7 25W
Mong Cai **128** 21 27N 107 54 E
Möng Hsu **125** 21 54N 98 30 E
Möng Kung **125** 21 35N 97 35 E
Mong Lang **128** 20 29N 97 52 E
Möng Nai **125** 20 32N 97 55 E
Möng Pai **125** 19 40N 97 15 E
Mong Pawk **125** 22 4N 99 16 E
Mong Ton **125** 20 25N 98 45 E
Mong Wa **125** 21 26N 100 27 E
Mong Yai **125** 22 28N 98 3 E
Mongalla **115** 5 8N 31 55 E
Monger, L. **134** 29 25 S 117 5 E
Monghyr **125** 25 23N 86 30 E
Mongolia **49** 43 56N 79 13W
Mongolia ■ **129** 47 0N 103 0 E
Mongolia, Inner, □ **130** 44 15N 117 0 E
Mongoumba **116** 3 33N 18 40 E
Mongpang **128** 23 5N 100 25 E
Mongu **117** 15 16 S 23 12 E
Monistrol-St.-Loire **103** 45 17N 4 11 E
Monitor **61** 51 58N 110 34W
Monk **55** 47 7N 69 59W
Monkey River **83** 16 22N 88 29W
Monkoto **116** 1 38 S 20 35 E
Monkstown **37** 47 35N 54 26W
Monkton **46** 43 35N 81 5W
Monmouth, U.K. **95** 51 48N 2 43W
Monmouth, U.S.A. **76** 40 50N 90 40W
Monmouth Mt. **62** 51 0N 123 47W
Mono, L. **80** 38 0N 119 9W
Mono Mills **49** 43 57N 79 58W
Mono, Punta del **84** 12 0N 83 30W
Mono Road Station **49** 43 51N 79 51W
Monolith **81** 35 7N 118 22W
Monon **77** 40 52N 86 53W
Monona, Iowa, U.S.A. **76** 43 3N 91 24W
Monona, Wis., U.S.A. **76** 43 4N 89 20W
Monongahela **70** 40 12N 79 56W
Monópoli **108** 40 57N 17 18 E
Monroe, Iowa, U.S.A. **76** 41 31N 93 6W
Monroe, La., U.S.A. **75** 32 32N 92 4W
Monroe, Mich., U.S.A. **46** 41 55N 83 26W
Monroe, N.C., U.S.A. **73** 35 2N 80 37W
Monroe, N.Y., U.S.A. **71** 41 19N 74 11W
Monroe, Ohio, U.S.A. **77** 39 27N 84 22W
Monroe, Utah, U.S.A. **79** 38 45N 112 5W

Monroe **Mouchalagane, R**

Monroe, Wash., U.S.A. **80** 47 51N 121 58W
Monroe, Wis., U.S.A. **76** 42 38N 89 40W
Monroe City **76** 39 40N 91 40W
Monroe, Res. **77** 39 1N 86 31W
Monroeville, U.S.A. **77** 40 59N 84 52W
Monroeville, Ala., U.S.A. **73** 31 33N 87 15W
Monrovia, Liberia **114** 6 18N 10 47W
Monrovia, U.S.A. **79** 34 7N 118 1W
Mons **105** 50 27N 3 58E
Monse **127** 4 0S 123 10E
Monségur **102** 44 38N 0 4E
Mont-Carmel **41** 47 26N 69 52W
Mont-de-Marsan **102** 43 54N 0 31W
Mont d'Or, Tunnel **101** 46 45N 6 18E
Mont-Dore, Le **102** 45 35N 2 50E
Mont-Gabriel **43** 45 55N 74 10W
Mont-Joli **41** 48 37N 68 10W
Mont Laurier **40** 46 35N 75 30W
Mont-Louis **38** 49 15N 65 44W
Mont Luis **35** 42 31N 2 6E
Mont-Rolland **43** 45 57N 74 7W
Mont-Royal **44** 45 31N 73 39W
Mont-St-Grégoire **45** 45 20N 73 10W
Mont-St-Hilaire **43** 45 34N 73 12W
Mont St-Pierre **38** 49 13N 65 49W
Mont-St-Michel, Le **100** 48 40N 1 30W
Mont-Tremblant **40** 46 13N 74 36W
Mont Tremblant Prov. Park **41** 46 30N 74 30W
Montagnac **102** 43 29N 3 28E
Montagu, I. **82** 58 30S 26 15W
Montague, Can. **39** 46 10N 62 39W
Montague, Calif., U.S.A. **78** 41 47N 122 30W
Montague, Mass., U.S.A. **71** 42 31N 72 33W
Montague, I. **82** 31 40N 144 46W
Montague I. **67** 60 0N 147 0W
Montague Sd. **134** 14 28S 125 20E
Montaigu **100** 46 59N 1 18W
Montalbán **104** 40 50N 0 45W
Montalvo **81** 34 15N 119 12W
Montaña **86** 6 0S 73 0W
Montana □ **68** 47 0N 110 0W
Montañita **86** 1 30N 75 28W
Montargis **101** 48 0N 2 43E
Montauban **102** 44 0N 1 21E
Montauk **71** 41 3N 71 57W
Montbard **101** 47 38N 4 20E
Montbéliard **101** 47 31N 6 48E
Montbrison **103** 45 36N 4 3E
Montcalm □ **43** 45 59N 73 45W
Montcalm, Pic de **102** 42 40N 1 25E
Montceau-les-Mines **101** 46 40N 4 23E
Montcerf **40** 46 32N 76 3W
Montcevelles, L. **38** 51 7N 60 38W
Montclair **71** 40 53N 74 49W
Montcornet **101** 49 40N 4 0E
Montcuq **102** 44 21N 1 13E
Montdidier **101** 49 38N 2 35E
Monte Albán **83** 17 2N 96 45W
Monte Alegre **87** 2 0S 54 0W
Monte Bello Is. **134** 20 30S 115 45E
Monte-Carlo **103** 43 46N 7 23E
Monte Caseros **88** 30 10S 57 50W
Monte Comán **88** 34 40S 68 0W
Monte Cristi **85** 19 52N 71 39W
Monte, Le **76** 38 47N 93 27W
Monte Libano **93** 8 5N 75 29W
Monte Lindo, R. **88** 25 30S 58 40W
Monte Quemado **88** 25 53S 62 41W
Monte Rio **80** 38 28N 123 0W
Monte Sant' Ángelo **108** 41 42N 15 59E
Monte Santu, C. di **108** 40 5N 9 42E
Monte Visto **79** 37 40N 106 8W
Monteagudo **89** 27 14S 54 8W
Montebello **40** 45 40N 74 55W
Montebourg **100** 49 30N 1 20W
Montecito **81** 34 26N 119 40W
Montecristi **86** 1 0S 80 40W
Montego B. **84** 18 30N 78 0W
Montelíbano **86** 8 5N 75 29W
Montélimar **103** 44 33N 4 45E
Montello **74** 43 49N 89 21W
Montemorelos **83** 25 11N 99 42W
Montendre **102** 45 16N 0 26W
Montenegro **89** 29 39S 51 29W
Montepuez **117** 13 8S 38 59E
Montereau **101** 48 22N 2 57E
Monterey, U.S.A. **77** 41 11N 86 30W
Monterey, Calif., U.S.A. **80** 36 35N 121 57W
Monterey, B. **80** 36 50N 121 55W
Montería **86** 8 46N 75 53W
Monteros **88** 27 11S 65 30W
Monterrey **82** 25 40N 100 30W
Montes Claros **87** 16 30S 43 50W
Montesano **80** 47 0N 123 39W
Monteverde **116** 8 45S 16 45E
Montevideo **89** 34 50S 56 11W
Montezuma, U.S.A. **76** 41 32N 92 35W
Montezuma, U.S.A. **77** 39 47N 87 22W
Montfaucon, Haute-Loire, France **103** 45 11N 4 20E
Montfaucon, Meuse, France **101** 49 16N 5 8E
Montfort **43** 45 53N 74 20W
Montfort-l'Amaury **101** 48 47N 1 49E
Montfort-sur-Meu **100** 48 8N 1 58W
Montgenèvre **103** 44 56N 6 42E
Montgomery, Can. **59** 51 4N 114 10W
Montgomery, U.K. **95** 52 34N 3 9W
Montgomery, U.S.A. **77** 41 44N 88 21W
Montgomery, Ala., U.S.A. **73** 32 20N 86 20W
Montgomery, W. Va., U.S.A. **72** 38 9N 81 21W
Montgomery = Sahiwal **124** 30 45N 73 8E
Montgomery City **76** 38 59N 91 30W
Montguyon **102** 45 12N 0 12W
Monticello, Can. **49** 43 59N 80 24W
Monticello, U.S.A. **76** 40 7N 91 43W
Monticello, U.S.A. **76** 42 13N 91 11W
Monticello, Ark., U.S.A. **75** 33 40N 91 48W
Monticello, Fla., U.S.A. **73** 30 35N 83 50W
Monticello, Ill., U.S.A. **77** 40 1N 88 34W
Monticello, Ind., U.S.A. **77** 40 40N 86 45W
Monticello, Iowa, U.S.A. **74** 42 18N 91 18W
Monticello, Ky., U.S.A. **73** 36 52N 84 50W
Monticello, Minn., U.S.A. **74** 45 17N 93 52W
Monticello, Miss., U.S.A. **75** 31 35N 90 8W
Monticello, N.Y., U.S.A. **71** 41 37N 74 42W
Monticello, Utah, U.S.A. **79** 37 55N 109 27W
Montier **101** 48 30N 4 45E
Montignac **102** 45 4N 1 10E
Montigny-les-Metz **101** 49 7N 6 10E
Montigny-sur-Aube **101** 47 57N 4 45E
Montijo **104** 38 52N 6 39W
Montilla **104** 37 36N 4 40W
Montivideo **74** 44 55N 95 40W
Montlhéry **101** 48 39N 2 15E
Montluçon **102** 46 22N 2 36E
Montmagny **41** 46 58N 70 34W
Montmartre **56** 50 14N 103 27W
Montmédy **101** 49 30N 5 20E
Montmélian **103** 45 30N 6 4E
Montmirail **101** 48 51N 3 30E
Montmoreau-St.-Cybard **102** 45 23N 0 8E
Montmorency **42** 46 53N 71 11W
Montmorency, R. **42** 46 53N 71 7W
Montmorillon **102** 46 26N 0 50E
Montmort **101** 48 55N 3 49E
Monto **135** 24 52S 151 12E
Montoro **104** 38 1N 4 27W
Montour Falls **70** 42 20N 76 51W
Montpelier, Idaho, U.S.A. **78** 42 15N 111 20W
Montpelier, Ind., U.S.A. **77** 40 33N 85 17W
Montpelier, Ohio, U.S.A. **77** 41 34N 84 40W
Montpelier, Vt., U.S.A. **71** 44 15N 72 38W
Montpellier **102** 43 37N 3 52E
Montpezat-de-Quercy **102** 44 15N 1 30E
Montpon-Ménestrol **102** 45 2N 0 11E
Montréal, Can. **44** 45 31N 73 34W
Montréal, France **102** 43 13N 2 8E
Montreal I. **53** 47 19N 84 44W
Montréal, Île de **44** 45 30N 73 40W
Montreal L. **56** 54 20N 105 45W
Montreal Lake **56** 54 3N 105 46W
Montréal-Nord **44** 45 36N 73 38W
Montreal, R. **53** 47 14N 84 39W
Montredon-Labessonnié **102** 43 45N 2 18E
Montréjeau **102** 43 6N 0 35E
Montrésor **100** 47 10N 1 10E
Montreuil **101** 50 27N 1 45E
Montreuil-Bellay **100** 47 8N 0 9W
Montreuil, L. **40** 50 12N 77 40W
Montreux **106** 46 26N 6 55E
Montrevault **100** 47 17N 1 2W
Montrevel-en-Bresse **103** 46 21N 5 8E
Montrichard **100** 47 20N 1 10E
Montrose, B.C., Can. **63** 49 5N 117 35W
Montrose, Ont., Can. **49** 43 3N 79 8W
Montrose, U.K. **96** 56 43N 2 28W
Montrose, Col., U.S.A. **79** 38 30N 107 52W
Montrose, Mich., U.S.A. **46** 43 11N 83 54W
Montrose, Pa., U.S.A. **71** 41 50N 75 55W
Montrose, L. **76** 38 18N 93 50W
Monts, Pte des **38** 49 20N 67 12W
Montsalvy **102** 44 41N 2 30E
Montsauche **101** 47 13N 4 0E
Montserrat, I. **85** 16 40N 62 10W
Monveda **116** 2 52N 21 30E
Mônywa **125** 22 7N 95 11E
Monze **117** 16 17S 27 29E
Monze, C. **124** 24 47N 66 37E
Monzón **104** 41 52N 0 10E
Moonbeam **53** 49 20N 82 10W
Moonie, R. **136** 27 45S 150 0E
Moorcroft **74** 44 17N 104 58W
Moore, L. **134** 29 50S 117 35E
Moore Pt. **51** 43 48N 79 3W
Moorefield **72** 39 5N 78 59W
Moores Mill **39** 45 18N 67 17W
Moores Res. **71** 44 45N 71 50W
Mooresville, U.S.A. **77** 39 37N 86 22W
Mooresville, N.C., U.S.A. **73** 35 36N 80 45W
Moorfoot Hills **96** 55 44N 3 8W
Moorhead **74** 47 0N 97 0W
Mooroopna **136** 36 25S 145 22E
Moorpark **81** 34 17N 118 53W
Moose Creek **47** 45 15N 74 58W
Moose Factory **53** 51 16N 80 40W
Moose Heights **63** 53 4N 122 31W
Moose Hill **52** 48 15N 89 29W
Moose I. **57** 51 42N 97 10W
Moose Jaw **56** 50 24N 105 30W
Moose Jaw, R. **56** 50 34N 105 18W
Moose L. **57** 53 46N 100 8W
Moose Lake, Can. **57** 53 43N 100 20W
Moose Lake, U.S.A. **52** 46 27N 92 48W
Moose Mountain Cr. **56** 49 13N 102 12W
Moose Mtn. Prov. Park **57** 49 48N 102 25W
Moose, R. **53** 51 20N 80 25W
Moose River **53** 50 48N 81 17W
Moosehead L. **35** 45 40N 69 40W
Moosomin **57** 50 9N 101 40W
Moosonee **53** 51 17N 80 39W
Moosup **71** 41 44N 71 52W
Mopeia **117** 17 30S 35 40E
Mopti **114** 14 30N 4 0W
Moquegua **86** 17 15S 70 46W
Mora, Sweden **111** 61 2N 14 38E
Mora, Minn., U.S.A. **74** 45 52N 93 19W
Mora, N. Mex., U.S.A. **79** 35 58N 105 21W
Moradabad **124** 28 50N 78 50E
Morafenobe **117** 17 50S 44 53E
Morales **86** 2 45N 76 38W
Moramanga **117** 18 56S 48 12E
Moran, Kans., U.S.A. **75** 37 53N 94 35W
Moran, Mich., U.S.A. **46** 46 0N 84 50W
Moran, Wyo., U.S.A. **78** 43 53N 110 37W
Morant Cays **84** 17 22N 76 0W
Morant Pt. **84** 17 55N 76 12W
Morar L. **96** 56 57N 5 40W
Moratuwa **124** 6 45N 79 55E
Morava, R. **106** 49 50N 16 50E
Moravatío **82** 19 51N 100 25W
Moravia **76** 40 50N 92 50W
Morawhanna **86** 8 30N 59 40W
Moray Firth **96** 57 50N 3 30W
Morbihan □ **100** 47 55N 2 50W
Morcenx **102** 44 0N 0 55W
Mordelles **100** 48 5N 1 52W
Morden **57** 49 15N 98 10W
Mordialloc **136** 38 1S 145 6E
Mordovian S.S.R. □ **120** 54 20N 44 30E
Mordvinske A S S R **96** 54 20N 44 30E
More L. **96** 58 18N 4 52W
Møre og Romsdal □ **110** 63 0N 9 0E
Moreau, R. **74** 45 15N 102 45W
Morecambe **94** 54 5N 2 52W
Morecambe B. **94** 54 7N 3 0W
Moree **135** 29 28S 149 54E
Morehead **72** 38 12N 83 22W
Morehead City **73** 34 46N 76 44W
Moreira **86** 0 34S 63 26W
Morelia **82** 19 40N 101 11W
Morell **39** 46 25N 62 42W
Morella **104** 40 35N 0 5W
Morelos **82** 26 42N 107 40W
Morelos □ **83** 18 40N 99 10W
Morena, Sierra **104** 38 20N 4 0W
Morenci, U.S.A. **77** 41 43N 84 13W
Morenci, Ariz., U.S.A. **79** 33 7N 109 20W
Mores, I. **73** 26 15N 77 35W
Moresby I. **62** 52 30N 131 40W
Morestel **103** 45 40N 5 28E
Moret **101** 48 22N 2 58E
Moreton B. **135** 27 10S 153 10E
Moreton, I. **135** 27 10S 153 25E
Moreuil **101** 49 46N 2 30E
Morez **103** 46 31N 6 2E
Morgan **78** 41 3N 111 44W
Morgan City **75** 29 40N 91 15W
Morgan Hill **80** 37 8N 121 39W
Morganfield **72** 37 40N 87 55W
Morganton **73** 35 46N 81 48W
Morgantown, U.S.A. **77** 39 22N 86 16W
Morgantown, W. Va., U.S.A. **72** 39 39N 79 58W
Morgat **100** 48 15N 4 32W
Morhange **101** 48 55N 6 38E
Moriarty **79** 35 3N 106 2W
Morice L. **62** 53 50N 127 40W
Morice, R. **62** 54 12N 127 5W
Morichal **86** 2 10N 70 34W
Morichal Largo, R. **86** 8 55N 63 0W
Morin-Heights **43** 45 54N 74 15W
Morinville **60** 53 49N 113 41W
Morioka **132** 39 45N 141 8E
Moris **82** 28 8N 108 32W
Moriston, Glen **96** 57 10N 5 0W
Moriston, R. **96** 57 10N 5 0W
Morlaàs **102** 43 21N 0 18W
Morlaix **100** 48 36N 3 52W
Mormant **101** 48 37N 2 52E
Mornington **136** 38 15S 145 5E
Mornington I. **135** 16 30S 139 30E
Mornington, I. **90** 49 50S 75 30W
Moro G. **127** 6 30N 123 0E
Morocco **77** 40 57N 87 27W
Morocco ■ **114** 32 0N 5 50W
Morococha **86** 11 40S 76 5W
Morogoro **116** 6 50S 37 40E
Morokweng **117** 26 12S 23 45E
Moroleón **82** 20 8N 101 32W
Morombé **117** 21 45S 43 22E
Moron **88** 34 39S 58 37W
Morón **84** 22 0N 78 30W
Morón de la Frontera **104** 37 6N 5 28W
Morondava **117** 20 17S 44 17E
Morongo Valley **81** 34 3N 116 37W
Morotai, I. **127** 2 10N 128 30E
Moroto **116** 2 28N 34 42E
Morpeth **94** 55 11N 1 41W
Morrilton **75** 35 10N 92 45W
Morrin **61** 51 40N 112 47W
Morrinhos **87** 17 45S 49 10W
Morrinsville **133** 37 40S 175 32E
Morris, Can. **57** 49 25N 97 22W
Morris, Ill., U.S.A. **77** 41 20N 88 20W
Morris, Minn., U.S.A. **74** 45 33N 95 56W
Morris L. **39** 44 39N 63 30W
Morris, R. **57** 49 21N 97 21W
Morrisburg **47** 44 55N 75 7W
Morrison **76** 41 47N 90 0W
Morrisonville **76** 39 25N 89 27W
Morriston **49** 43 27N 80 7W
Morristown, U.S.A. **77** 39 40N 85 42W
Morristown, Ariz., U.S.A. **79** 33 54N 112 45W
Morristown, N.J., U.S.A. **71** 40 48N 74 30W
Morristown, S.D., U.S.A. **74** 45 57N 101 44W
Morristown, Tenn., U.S.A. **73** 36 18N 83 20W
Morro Bay **80** 35 27N 120 54W
Morro, Pta. **88** 27 6S 71 0W
Morrosquillo, Golfo de **85** 9 35N 75 40W
Morrow **77** 39 21N 84 8W
Morrumbene **117** 23 31S 35 16E
Morse **56** 50 25N 107 3W
Morson **52** 49 6N 94 19W
Mortagne **102** 45 28N 0 49W
Mortagne-au-Perche **100** 48 31N 0 33E
Mortagne, R. **101** 48 30N 6 30E
Mortain **100** 48 40N 0 57W
Morteau **101** 47 3N 6 35E
Morteros **88** 30 50S 62 0W
Mortes, R. das **87** 11 45S 50 44W
Mortlach **56** 50 27N 106 4W
Mortlake **136** 38 5S 142 50E
Morton, U.S.A. **76** 40 37N 89 28W
Morton, Tex., U.S.A. **75** 33 39N 102 49W
Morton, Wash., U.S.A. **80** 46 33N 122 17W
Morvan, Mts. du **101** 47 5N 4 0E
Morven, dist. **96** 56 38N 5 44W
Morvern **96** 56 38N 5 44W
Morwell **136** 38 10S 146 22E
Moscos Is. **128** 14 0N 97 30E
Moscow **78** 46 45N 116 59W
Moscow = Moskva **120** 55 45N 37 35E
Mosel, R. **105** 50 22N 7 36E
Moselle □ **101** 48 59N 6 33E
Moselle, R. **105** 50 22N 7 36E
Moses Inlet **62** 51 47N 127 23W
Moses Lake **78** 47 16N 119 17W
Mosgiel **133** 45 53S 170 21E
Mosher **53** 48 42N 84 12W
Moshi **116** 3 22S 37 18E
Mosjøen **110** 65 51N 13 12E
Moskenesøya **110** 67 58N 13 0E
Moskenstraumen **110** 67 47N 13 0E
Moskva **120** 55 45N 37 35E
Mosley Cr. **62** 51 18N 124 50W
Mosquera **86** 2 35N 78 30W
Mosquero **75** 35 48N 103 57W
Mosquitia **84** 15 20N 84 10W
Mosquito B. **36** 61 10N 78 0W
Mosquitos, Golfo de los **84** 9 15N 81 10W
Moss **111** 59 27N 10 40E
Moss Vale **136** 34 32S 150 25E
Mossaka **116** 1 15S 16 45E
Mossbank **56** 49 56N 105 56W
Mossburn **133** 45 41S 168 15E
Mosselbaai **117** 34 11S 22 8E
Mossendjo **116** 2 55S 12 42E
Mossman **135** 16 28S 145 23E
Mossoró **87** 5 10S 37 15W
Mossuril **117** 14 58S 40 42E
Mossy, R. **56** 54 5N 102 58W
Most **106** 50 31N 13 38E
Mosta **108** 35 54N 14 24E
Mostaganem **114** 35 54N 0 5E
Mostar **109** 43 22N 17 50E
Mostardas **89** 31 2S 50 51W
Mosul = Al Mawsil **122** 36 20N 43 5E
Mosun **131** 23 35N 109 30E
Motagua, R. **84** 15 44N 88 14W
Motala **111** 58 32N 15 1E
Mothe-Achard, La **100** 46 37N 1 40W
Mothe, La, Rés. **41** 48 46N 71 9W
Motherwell **96** 55 48N 4 0W
Motihari **125** 26 37N 85 1E
Motocurunya **86** 4 24N 64 5W
Motozintea de Mendoza **83** 15 21N 92 14W
Mott **74** 46 25N 102 14W
Motte-Chalançon, La **103** 44 30N 5 21E
Motte, L. la **40** 48 20N 78 2W
Motte, La **103** 44 20N 6 3E
Motueka **133** 41 7S 173 1E
Motul **83** 21 0N 89 20W
Mouchalagane, R. **36** 50 56N 68 41W

Moucontant 100 46 43N 0 36W
Moúdhros 109 39 50N 25 18 E
Mouila 116 1 50 s 11 0 E
Moulamein Cr. 136 35 6 s 144 3 E
Mould Bay 64 76 12N 119 25W
Moule, Le 85 16 20N 61 22W
Moulins 102 46 35N 3 19 E
Moulmein 125 16 30N 97 40 E
Moulton, U.S.A. 76 40 41N 92 41W
Moulton, Tex., U.S.A. 75 29 35N 97 8W
Moultrie 73 31 11N 83 47W
Moultrie, L. 73 33 25N 80 10W
Mound City, Mo., U.S.A. 74 40 2N 95 25W
Mound City, S.D., U.S.A. 74 45 46N 100 3W
Moundsville 70 39 53N 80 43W
Mount Airy 73 36 31N 80 37W
Mount Albert, Can. 70 44 10N 79 20W
Mount Albert, Ont., Can. 46 44 8N 79 19W
Mount Angel 78 45 4N 122 46W
Mount Assiniboine Prov. Park 61 50 53N 115 39W
Mount Ayr 76 40 43N 94 14W
Mount Baker 63 48 50N 121 40W
Mount Barker 134 34 38 s 117 40 E
Mount Brydges 46 42 54N 81 29W
Mount Carleton Prov. Park 39 47 25N 66 55W
Mount Carmel, Can. 37 47 9N 53 29W
Mount Carmel, Ill., U.S.A. 77 38 20N 87 48W
Mount Carmel, Pa., U.S.A. 71 40 46N 76 25W
Mount Carroll 76 42 6N 89 59W
Mount Clemens 46 42 35N 82 50W
Mount Darwin 117 16 47 s 31 38 E
Mount Dennis 50 43 41N 79 29W
Mount Desert I. 35 44 25N 68 25W
Mount Dora 73 28 49N 81 32W
Mount Eden 77 38 3N 85 9W
Mount Edgecumbe 67 57 8N 135 22W
Mount Enid 134 21 42 s 116 26 E
Mount Forest 46 43 59N 80 43W
Mount Gambier 136 37 50 s 140 46 E
Mount Goldsworthy 134 20 25 s 119 39 E
Mount Hamilton 48 43 14N 79 51W
Mount Henry 77 42 21N 88 16W
Mount Hope, Can. 48 43 9N 79 55W
Mount Hope, U.S.A. 72 37 52N 81 9W
Mount Horeb 76 43 0N 89 42W
Mount Hotham 136 37 2 s 146 52 E
Mount Isa 135 20 42 s 139 26 E
Mount Joy 71 40 6N 76 30W
Mount Laguna 81 32 52N 116 25W
Mount Lavinia 124 6 50N 79 50 E
Mount Lofty Ra. 135 34 35 s 139 5 E
Mount McKinley Nat. Pk. 67 64 0N 150 0W
Mount Magnet 134 28 2 s 117 47 E
Mount Maunganui 133 37 40 s 176 14 E
Mount Morgan 135 23 40 s 150 25 E
Mount Moriah 37 48 58N 58 2W
Mount Morris, Mich., U.S.A. 46 43 8N 83 42W
Mount Morris, N.Y., U.S.A. 70 42 43N 77 50W
Mount Nicholas 134 22 54 s 120 27 E
Mount Olive 76 39 4N 89 44W
Mount Olivet 77 38 32N 84 2W
Mount Orab 77 39 5N 83 56W
Mount Pearl 37 47 31N 52 47W
Mount Pleasant, Alta., Can. 59 51 4N 114 5W
Mount Pleasant, Ont., Can. 49 43 5N 80 19W
Mount Pleasant, Iowa, U.S.A. 76 41 0N 91 35W
Mount Pleasant, Mich., U.S.A. 46 43 35N 84 47W
Mount Pleasant, Pa., U.S.A. 70 40 9N 79 31W
Mount Pleasant, S.C., U.S.A. 73 32 45N 79 48W
Mount Pleasant, Tenn., U.S.A. 73 35 31N 87 11W
Mount Pleasant, Tex., U.S.A. 75 33 5N 95 0W
Mount Pleasant, Ut., U.S.A. 78 39 40N 111 29W
Mount Pocono 71 41 8N 75 21W
Mount Pulaski 76 40 1N 89 17W
Mount Rainier Nat. Park. 80 46 50N 121 43W
Mount Revelstoke Nat. Park 63 51 5N 118 30W
Mount Robson 54 52 56N 119 15W
Mount Robson Prov. Park 63 53 0N 119 0W
Mount Royal 58 50 27N 104 40W
Mount Seymour Prov. Park 66 49 24N 122 55W
Mount Shasta 78 41 20N 122 18W
Mount Signal 81 32 39N 115 37W
Mount Singleton 136 32 30 s 151 3 E
Mount Sterling, Ill., U.S.A. 76 40 0N 90 40W

Mount Sterling, Ky., U.S.A. 77 38 0N 84 0W
Mount Sterling, Ohio, U.S.A. 77 39 43N 83 16W
Mount Stewart 39 46 22N 62 52W
Mount Tolmie 63 48 28N 123 20W
Mount Tom Price 134 22 50 s 117 40 E
Mount Uniacke 39 44 54N 63 50W
Mount Union 70 40 22N 77 51W
Mount Vernon, Can. 49 43 6N 80 24W
Mount Vernon, Ill., U.S.A. 77 38 19N 88 55W
Mount Vernon, Ind., U.S.A. 77 38 17N 88 57W
Mount Vernon, Iowa, U.S.A. 76 41 55N 91 23W
Mount Vernon, N.Y., U.S.A. 71 40 57N 73 49W
Mount Vernon, Ohio, U.S.A. 72 40 20N 82 30W
Mount Vernon, Wash., U.S.A. 63 48 25N 122 20W
Mount Vernon, Wash., U.S.A. 80 48 27N 122 18W
Mount Washington 77 38 3N 85 33W
Mount Whaleback 134 23 18 s 119 44 E
Mount Zion 77 39 46N 88 53W
Mountain Center 81 33 42N 116 44W
Mountain City, Nev., U.S.A. 78 41 54N 116 0W
Mountain City, Tenn., U.S.A. 73 36 30N 81 50W
Mountain Grove 75 37 5N 92 20W
Mountain Home, Ark., U.S.A. 75 36 20N 92 25W
Mountain Home, Idaho, U.S.A. 78 43 11N 115 45W
Mountain Iron 74 47 30N 92 37W
Mountain Park. 61 52 50N 117 15W
Mountain Pass 81 35 29N 115 35W
Mountain View, Can. 61 49 8N 113 36W
Mountain View, Ark., U.S.A. 75 35 52N 92 10W
Mountain View, Calif., U.S.A. 79 37 26N 122 5W
Mountain Village 67 62 10N 163 50W
Mountainair 79 34 35N 106 15W
Mountmellick 97 53 7N 7 20W
Mountnorris 97 54 15N 6 29W
Moura 86 1 25 s 61 45W
Moure, La 74 46 27N 98 17W
Mourenx 102 43 23N 0 36W
Mourmelon-le-Grand 101 49 8N 4 22 E
Mourne Mts. 97 54 10N 6 0W
Mourne, R. 97 54 45N 7 39W
Mouscron 105 50 45N 3 12 E
Mouthe 101 46 44N 6 12 E
Moûtiers 103 45 29N 6 31 E
Moutong 127 0 28N 121 13 E
Mouy 101 49 18N 2 20 E
Movas 82 28 10N 109 25W
Moville 97 55 11N 7 3W
Moweaqua 76 39 37N 89 1W
Mowming 131 21 50N 110 32 E
Mowping 130 37 25N 121 34 E
Moy, R. 97 54 5N 8 50W
Moyahua 82 21 16N 103 10W
Moyale 116 3 30N 39 0 E
Moyie 54 49 17N 115 50W
Moyie Springs 61 48 43N 116 11W
Moyle □ 97 55 10N 6 15W
Moyobamba 86 6 0 s 77 0W
Mozambique = Moçambique 117 15 3 s 40 42 E
Mozambique ■ 117 19 0 s 35 0 E
Mozambique Chan. 117 20 0 s 39 0 E
Mozdok 120 43 45N 44 48 E
Mozyr 120 52 0N 29 15 E
Mpanda 116 6 23 s 31 40 E
Mpika 117 11 51 s 31 25 E
Mpwapwa 116 6 30 s 36 30 E
Msoro 117 13 35 s 31 50 E
Mtwara 116 10 20 s 40 20 E
Muaná 87 1 25 s 49 15W
Muang Chiang Rai 128 19 52N 99 50 E
Muang Kalasin 128 16 26N 103 30 E
Muang Lampang 128 18 16N 99 32 E
Muang Lamphun 128 18 40N 98 53 E
Muang Nan 128 18 52N 100 42 E
Muang Phetchabun 128 16 23N 101 12 E
Muang Phichit 128 16 29N 100 21 E
Muang Ubon 128 15 15N 104 50 E
Muang Yasothon 128 15 50N 104 10 E
Muar 128 2 3N 102 34 E
Muar, R. 128 2 15N 102 48 E
Muarabungo 126 1 45 s 101 10 E
Muaradjuloi 126 0 12 s 114 3 E
Muaraenim 126 3 40 s 103 50 E
Muarakaman 126 0 2 s 116 45 E
Muaratebo 126 1 30 s 102 26 E
Muaratembesi 126 1 42 s 103 2 E
Muaratewe 126 0 50 s 115 0 E
Mubairik 122 23 22N 39 8 E
Mubende 116 0 33N 31 22 E
Mucajaí, Serra do 86 2 23N 61 10W
Muchalat Inlet 62 49 38N 126 15W
Muchikan 129 53 2N 120 27 E
Muck, I. 96 56 50N 6 15W
Mucuri 87 18 0 s 40 0W

Mud B. 66 49 5N 122 53W
Mud L. 78 40 15N 120 15W
Muddy L. 56 52 19N 109 6W
Muddy, R. 79 38 30N 110 55W
Mudgee 136 32 32 s 149 31 E
Mudhnib 122 25 50N 44 18 E
Mudjatik, R. 55 56 1N 107 36W
Muenster 56 52 12N 105 0W
Muerto, Mar 83 16 10N 94 10W
Mufulira 117 12 32 s 28 15 E
Muğla 122 37 15N 28 28 E
Mugu 125 29 45N 82 30 E
Mühlig-Hofmann-fjella 91 72 30 s 5 0 E
Mui Bai Bung 128 8 35N 104 42 E
Mui Ron 128 18 7N 106 27 E
Muine Bheag 97 52 42N 6 59W
Mukah 126 2 55N 112 5 E
Mukalla 115 14 33N 49 2 E
Mukden = Shenyang 130 41 35N 123 30 E
Mukomuko 126 2 20 s 101 10 E
Muktsar 124 30 30N 74 30 E
Mukur 124 32 50N 67 50 E
Mukutawa, R. 57 53 10N 97 24W
Mukwonago 77 42 52N 88 20W
Mulanay 127 13 30N 122 30 E
Mulatas, Arch. de las 84 6 51N 78 31W
Mulberry Grove 76 38 55N 89 16W
Mulchén 88 37 45 s 72 20W
Mulde, R. 106 50 55N 12 42 E
Muldraugh 77 37 56N 85 59W
Mule Creek 74 43 19N 104 8W
Mulegé 82 26 53N 112 1W
Muleshoe 75 34 17N 102 42W
Mulgrave 39 45 38N 61 31W
Mulhacén 104 37 4N 3 20W
Mülheim 105 51 26N 6 53W
Mulhouse 101 47 40N 7 20 E
Mull I. 96 56 27N 6 0W
Mull, Sound of 96 56 30N 5 50W
Mullaittvu 124 9 15N 80 55 E
Mullen 74 42 5N 101 0W
Mullens 72 37 34N 81 22W
Muller, Pegunungan 126 0 30N 113 30 E
Mullet Pen. 97 54 10N 10 2W
Mullett L. 46 45 30N 84 30W
Mullewa 134 28 29 s 115 30 E
Mullin 75 31 33N 98 38W
Mullingar 97 53 31N 7 20W
Mullins 73 34 12N 79 15W
Mullion Creek 136 33 9 s 148 7 E
Multan 124 30 15N 71 30 E
Multan □ 124 30 29N 72 29 E
Mulvane 75 37 30N 97 15W
Mulwala 136 35 59 s 146 0 E
Mumbwa 117 15 0 s 27 0 E
Mun 128 15 17N 103 0 E
Muna, I. 127 5 0 s 122 30 E
Muna Sotuta 83 20 29N 89 43W
München 106 48 8N 11 33 E
Munchen-Gladbach = Mönchengladbach 105 51 12N 6 23 E
Muncho Lake 54 59 0N 125 50W
Muncie 77 40 10N 85 20W
Mundala, Puncak 127 4 30N 141 0 E
Mundare 60 53 35N 112 20W
Munday 75 33 26N 99 39W
Münden 106 51 25N 9 42 E
Mundo Novo 87 11 50 s 40 29W
Mungbere 116 2 36N 28 28 E
Mungindi 135 28 58 s 149 1 E
Munhango R. 117 11 30 s 19 30 E
Munich = München 106 48 8N 11 35 E
Munising 53 46 25N 86 39W
Muñoz Gamero, Pen. 90 52 30 s 73 5 E
Munroe L. 55 59 13N 98 35W
Munson 61 51 34N 112 45W
Munster 101 48 2N 7 8 E
Münster, Ger. 105 52 59N 10 5 E
Münster, Switz. 106 46 30N 8 17 E
Münster □ 97 52 20N 8 40W
Muntok 126 2 5N 105 10 E
Muon Pak Beng 128 19 51N 101 4 E
Muong La 128 22 52N 102 5 E
Muonio 110 67 57N 23 40 E
Muonio älv 110 67 48N 23 25 E
Mur-de-Bretagne 100 48 12N 3 0W
Múr, R. 106 47 7N 13 55 E
Murallón, Cuerro 90 49 55 s 73 30W
Murang'a 116 0 45 s 37 9 E
Murashi 120 59 30N 49 0 E
Murat 102 45 7N 2 53 E
Murchison I. 52 50 0N 88 21W
Murchison, R. 134 26 45 s 116 15 E
Murchison Ra. 134 20 0 s 134 10 E
Mure, La 103 44 55N 5 48 E
Mures R. 107 46 0N 22 0 E
Muret 102 43 30N 1 20 E
Murfreesboro 73 35 50N 86 21W
Murgab 120 38 10N 73 59 E
Murgon 135 26 15 s 151 54 E
Muriaé 89 21 8 s 42 23W
Muriel L. 60 54 9N 110 40W
Müritz-see 106 53 25N 12 40 E
Murjo Mt. 127 6 36 s 110 53 E

Murmansk 120 68 57N 33 10 E
Muro 103 42 34N 8 54 E
Muro, C. de 103 41 44N 8 37 E
Murom 120 55 35N 42 3 E
Muroran 132 42 25N 141 0 E
Muroto-Misaki 132 33 15N 134 10 E
Murphy 78 43 11N 116 33W
Murphy L. 63 52 3N 121 15W
Murphys 80 38 8N 120 28W
Murphysboro 76 37 50N 89 20W
Murray, U.S.A. 76 41 3N 93 57W
Murray, Ky., U.S.A. 73 36 40N 88 20W
Murray, Utah, U.S.A. 78 40 41N 111 58W
Murray Bridge 135 35 6 s 139 14 E
Murray Harbour 39 46 0N 62 28W
Murray, L. 73 34 8N 81 30W
Murray, R., S. Australia, Austral. 136 35 20 s 139 22 E
Murray, R., W. Australia, Austral. 135 32 33 s 115 45 E
Murray, R., Can. 54 56 11N 120 45W
Murray River 39 46 1N 62 37W
Murraysburg 117 31 58 s 23 47 E
Murrayville, Austral. 136 35 16 s 141 11 E
Murrayville, U.S.A. 76 39 35N 90 15W
Murree 124 33 56N 73 28 E
Murrieta 81 33 33N 117 13W
Murrumbidgee, R. 136 34 40 s 143 0 E
Murrumburrah 136 34 32 s 148 22 E
Murrurundi 136 31 42 s 150 51 E
Murtle L. 63 52 8N 119 38W
Murtoa 136 36 35 s 142 28 E
Murwara 125 23 46N 80 28 E
Murwillumbah 135 28 18 s 153 27 E
Mürzzuschlag 106 47 36N 15 41 E
Muş 122 38 45N 41 30 E
Musa Khel 124 30 29N 69 52 E
Musa Qala (Musa Kala) 124 32 20N 64 50 E
Musaffargarh 124 30 10N 71 10 E
Musala, I. 126 1 41N 98 28 E
Musalla, mt. 109 42 13N 23 37 E
Musan 130 42 12N 129 12 E
Muscat = Masqat 123 23 37N 58 36 E
Muscatine 76 41 25N 91 5W
Muscoda 76 43 11N 90 27W
Musgrave Harbour 37 49 27N 53 58W
Musgrave Ras. 134 26 0 s 132 0 E
Mushaboom 39 44 51N 62 32W
Mushie 116 2 56 s 17 4 E
Musi, R. 126 2 55 s 103 40 E
Muskeg B. 52 48 59N 95 5W
Muskeg L. 52 49 0N 90 2W
Muskeg, R. 54 60 20N 123 20W
Muskeg River 60 53 55N 118 39W
Muskego 77 42 54N 88 8W
Muskegon 46 43 15N 86 17W
Muskegon Hts. 77 43 12N 86 17W
Muskegon, R. 72 43 25N 86 0W
Muskogee 75 35 50N 95 25W
Muskoka, L. 46 45 0N 79 25W
Muskwa L. 60 56 9N 114 38W
Muskwa, R., Alta., Can. 60 56 15N 113 48W
Muskwa, R., B.C., Can. 54 58 47N 122 48W
Musoma 116 1 30 s 33 48 E
Musquanousse, L. 38 50 22N 61 5W
Musquaro, L. 38 50 10N 61 3W
Musquash 39 45 11N 66 19W
Musquodoboit Harbour 39 44 50N 63 9W
Mussel Inlet 62 52 53N 128 7W
Musselburgh 96 55 57N 3 3W
Musselshell, R. 78 46 30N 108 15W
Mussidan 102 45 2N 0 22 E
Mussooree 124 30 27N 78 6 E
Mustafa Kemalpaşa 122 40 3N 28 25 E
Mustang 129 29 10N 83 55 E
Musters, L. 90 45 20 s 69 25W
Muswellbrook 135 32 16 s 150 56 E
Mut 122 36 40N 33 28 E
Mutan Kiang 130 46 18N 129 31 E
Mutankiang 130 44 35N 129 30 E
Mutis 86 1 4N 77 25W
Mutshatsha 116 10 35 s 24 20 E
Muttaburra 135 22 38 s 144 29 E
Mutton Bay 35 50 50N 59 2W
Muxima 116 9 25 s 13 52 E
Muy, Le 103 43 28N 6 34 E
Muy Muy 84 12 39N 85 36W
Muya 121 56 27N 115 39 E
Muzaffarabad 124 34 25N 73 30 E
Muzaffarnagar 124 29 26N 77 40 E
Muzaffarpur 125 26 7N 85 32 E
Muzhi 120 65 25N 64 40 E
Muzillac 100 47 35N 2 30W
Muzo 86 5 32N 74 6W
Muztagh P. 129 36 30N 87 22 E
Mwanza, Congo 116 7 55 s 26 43 E
Mwanza, Tanz. 116 2 30 s 32 58 E
Mwaya 116 9 32 s 33 5 E
Mweelrea, Mt. 97 53 37N 9 48W
Mweka 116 4 50 s 21 40 E
Mwenga 116 3 1 s 28 21 E
Mweru, L. 116 9 0 s 29 0 E
Mwinilunga 117 11 43 s 24 51 E
My Tho 128 10 29N 106 23 E
Myall, R. 136 32 30 s 152 15 E
Myanaung 125 18 25N 95 10 E

Myaungmya Negra Pt

Myaungmya 125 16 30N 95 0 E
Mycenæ 109 37 44N 22 45 E
Myerstown 71 40 22N 76 18W
Myingyan 125 21 30N 95 30 E
Myitkyina 125 25 30N 97 26 E
Mymensingh 125 24 45N 90 24 E
Myndmere 74 46 23N 97 7W
Myogi 128 21 24N 96 28 E
Mýrdalsjökull 110 63 40N 19 6W
Myrnam 60 53 40N 111 14W
Myrtle Beach 73 33 43N 78 50W
Myrtle Creek 78 43 0N 123 9W
Myrtle Point 78 43 0N 124 4W
Myrtleford 136 36 34S 146 44 E
Mysore 124 12 17N 76 41 E
Mysore □ = Karnataka 124 13 15N 77 0 E
Mystery Lake 60 54 10N 114 55W
Mystic, U.S.A. 76 40 47N 92 57W
Mystic, Conn., U.S.A. 71 41 21N 71 58W
Myton 78 40 10N 110 2W
Mývatn 110 65 36N 17 0W

N

Naab, R. 106 49 10N 12 0 E
Naaldwijk 105 51 59N 4 13 E
Naalehu 67 19 4N 155 35W
Naantali 111 60 29N 22 2 E
Naas 97 53 12N 6 40W
Nabadwip 125 23 34N 88 20 E
Nabas 127 11 47N 122 6 E
Naberezhnyye Chelny 120 55 42N 52 19 E
Nabesna 67 62 33N 143 10W
Nabire 127 3 15S 136 27 E
Nabisipi, R. 36 50 14N 62 13W
Nablus = Nābulus 115 32 14N 35 15 E
Nābulus 115 32 14N 35 15 E
Nacala-Velha 117 14 32S 40 34 E
Nacaome 84 13 31N 87 30W
Nachako Res. 62 53 42N 127 30W
Naches 78 46 48N 120 49W
Naches, R. 80 46 38N 120 31W
Nachi 131 28 50N 105 25 E
Nachicapau, L. 36 56 40N 68 5W
Nachingwea 116 10 49S 38 49 E
Nachvak Fd. 36 59 3N 63 45W
Nacimento Res. 80 35 46N 120 53W
Nackawic 39 45 59N 67 17W
Nacmine 61 51 28N 112 47W
Naco, Mexico 82 31 20N 109 56W
Naco, U.S.A. 79 31 24N 109 58W
Nacogdoches 75 31 33N 95 30W
Nácori Chico 82 29 39N 109 1W
Nacozari 82 30 30N 109 50W
Nadern Harb. 62 54 0N 132 36W
Nadiad 124 22 41N 72 56 E
Nadina L. 62 53 53N 127 2W
Nadina, R. 62 53 58N 126 30W
Nadūshan 123 32 2N 53 35 E
Nadym 120 63 35N 72 42 E
Nadym, R. 120 65 30N 73 0 E
Naft Shāh 122 34 0N 45 30 E
Nafūd ad Dahy 122 22 0N 45 0 E
Naga, Japan 131 26 34N 127 43 E
Naga, Phil. 127 13 38N 123 15 E
Naga Hills 130 26 0N 94 30 E
Nagagami L. 53 49 25N 85 1W
Nagagami, R. 53 49 40N 84 40W
Nagagamisis L. 53 49 28N 84 40W
Nagaland □ 125 26 0N 94 30 E
Nagano 132 36 40N 138 10 E
Nagano-ken □ 132 36 15N 138 0 E
Nagaoka 132 37 27N 138 50 E
Nagappattinam 124 10 46N 79 51 E
Nagar Parkar 124 24 30N 70 35 E
Nagas Pt. 62 52 12N 131 22W
Nagasaki 132 32 47N 129 50 E
Nagasaki-ken □ 132 32 50N 129 40 E
Nagasin L. 53 47 48N 83 37W
Nagaur 124 27 15N 73 45 E
Nagercoil 124 8 12N 77 33 E
Nagineh 123 34 20N 57 15 E
Nago 131 26 36N 128 0 E
Nagoya 132 35 10N 136 50 E
Nagpur 124 21 8N 79 10 E
Nagua 85 19 23N 69 50W
Nagykanizsa 106 46 28N 17 0 E
Nagykörös 107 46 55N 19 48 E
Naha 131 26 12N 127 40 E
Nahanni Butte 54 61 2N 123 20W
Nahanni Nat. Pk. 54 61 15N 125 0W
Nahariya 115 33 1N 35 5 E
Nahāvand 122 34 10N 48 30 E
Nahlin 54 58 55N 131 38W
Naicá 82 27 53N 105 31W
Naicam 56 52 30N 104 30W
Naikoon Prov. Park 62 53 55N 131 55W
Nain 36 56 34N 61 40W
Nā'in 123 32 54N 53 0 E
Nainpur 124 22 30N 80 10 E
Naintré 100 46 46N 0 29 E
Naira, I. 127 4 28S 130 0 E
Nairn, Can. 46 46 20N 81 35W
Nairn, U.K. 96 57 35N 3 54W
Nairobi 116 1 17S 36 48 E
Naivasha 116 0 40S 36 30 E
Najac 102 44 14N 1 58 E
Najafābād 123 32 40N 51 15 E
Najd 122 26 30N 42 0 E
Najibabad 124 29 40N 78 20 E
Najin 130 42 12N 130 15 E
Nakamura 132 33 0N 133 0 E
Nakano Shima 132 29 50N 130 0 E
Nakelele Pt. 67 21 2N 156 35W
Nakhi Mubarak 122 24 10N 38 10 E
Nakhichevan A.S.S.R. □ 120 39 14N 45 30 E
Nakhodka 121 43 10N 132 45 E
Nakhon Phanom 128 17 23N 104 43 E
Nakhon Ratchasima (Khorat) 128 14 59N 102 12 E
Nakhon Sawan 128 15 35N 100 10 E
Nakhon Si Thammarat 128 8 29N 100 0 E
Nakina, B.C., Can. 54 59 12N 132 52W
Nakina, Ont., Can. 53 50 10N 86 40W
Naknek 67 58 45N 157 0W
Nakskov 111 54 50N 11 8 E
Naktong, R. 130 35 7N 128 57 E
Nakuru 116 0 15S 35 5 E
Nakusp 63 50 20N 117 45W
Nal, R. 124 27 0N 65 50 E
Nalayh 129 47 43N 107 22 E
Nalchik 120 43 30N 43 33 E
Nalgonda 124 17 6N 79 15 E
Nallamalai Hills 124 15 30N 78 50 E
Nalón, R. 104 43 35N 6 10W
Nam Dinh 128 20 25N 106 5 E
Nam-Phan 128 10 30N 106 0 E
Nam Phong 128 16 42N 102 52 E
Nam Tha 128 20 58N 101 30 E
Nam Tso 129 30 40N 90 30 E
Nama 131 23 45N 108 1 E
Namacurra 117 17 30S 36 50 E
Namakan L. 52 48 27N 92 35W
Namaland 117 26 0S 18 0 E
Naman 131 25 0N 118 30 E
Namangan 120 41 0N 71 40 E
Namapa 117 13 43S 39 50 E
Namber 127 1 2S 134 57 E
Nambour 135 26 32S 152 58 E
Namcha Barwa 129 29 40N 95 10 E
Nameh 126 2 34N 116 21 E
Namew L., Can. 57 54 10N 102 0W
Namew L., Sask., Can. 55 54 14N 101 56W
Namib Desert = Namib Woestyn 117 22 30S 15 0 E
Namib-Woestyn 117 22 30S 15 0 E
Namibia □ 117 22 0S 18 9 E
Namiquipa 82 29 15N 107 25W
Namja Pass 125 30 0N 82 25 E
Namlea 127 3 10S 127 5 E
Namoa tao 131 23 30N 117 0 E
Nampa 78 43 40N 116 40W
Nampula 117 15 6S 39 7 E
Namrole 127 3 46S 126 46 E
Namsen, R. 110 64 40N 12 45 E
Namsos 110 64 28N 11 0 E
Namtu 125 23 5N 97 28 E
Namu 62 51 52N 127 50W
Namur, Belg. 105 50 27N 4 52 E
Namur, Can. 40 45 54N 74 56W
Namur □ 105 50 17N 5 0 E
Namutoni 117 18 49S 16 55 E
Namwala 117 15 44S 26 30 E
Namyung 131 25 15N 114 5 E
Nan Shan 129 38 30N 99 0 E
Nanaimo 62 49 10N 124 0W
Nanam 130 41 44N 129 40 E
Nanango 135 26 40S 152 0 E
Nanao 132 37 0N 137 0 E
Nanchang, Hupei, China 131 31 50N 111 50 E
Nanchang, Kiangsi, China 131 28 34N 115 48 E
Nancheng 131 27 30N 116 28 E
Nancheng = Hanchung 131 33 10N 107 2 E
Nanchung 131 30 47N 105 59 E
Nanchwan 131 29 10N 107 15 E
Nancy 101 48 42N 6 12 E
Nanda Devi, Mt. 129 30 30N 80 30 E
Nander 124 19 10N 77 20 E
Nandi 133 17 25S 176 50 E
Nandurbar 124 21 20N 74 15 E
Nandyal 124 15 30N 78 30 E
Nanga Eboko 116 4 41N 12 22 E
Nanga Parbat, mt. 124 35 10N 74 35 E
Nangapinoh 126 0 20S 111 14 E
Nangarhar □ 124 34 20N 70 0 E
Nangatajap 126 1 32S 110 34 E
Nangfeng 131 27 10N 116 20 E
Nangis 101 48 33N 3 0 E
Nanika L. 62 53 47N 127 38W
Nanisivik 65 73 2N 84 33W
Nankang 131 25 42N 114 35 E
Nankiang 131 32 20N 106 50 E
Nanking 131 32 10N 118 50 E
Nannine 134 26 51S 118 18 E
Nanning 131 22 48N 108 20 E
Nanpi 130 38 0N 116 40 E
Nanping, Fukien, China 131 26 45N 118 5 E
Nanping, Szechwan, China 131 33 20N 103 56 E
Nanpu 131 31 17N 105 59 E
Nansei-Shotō, Japan 132 26 0N 128 0 E
Nansei-Shotō, Japan 132 29 0N 129 0 E
Nansen Sd. 65 81 0N 91 0W
Nant 102 44 1N 3 18 E
Nantan 131 25 0N 107 35 E
Nantes 100 47 12N 1 33W
Nanteuil-le-Haudouin 101 49 9N 2 48 E
Nantiat 102 46 1N 1 11 E
Nanticoke 71 41 12N 76 1W
Nanton 61 50 21N 113 46W
Nantou 131 23 57N 120 35 E
Nantua 103 46 10N 5 35 E
Nantucket I. 69 41 16N 70 3W
Nantung 131 32 0N 120 50 E
Nanuque 87 17 50S 40 21W
Nanyang 131 33 0N 112 32 E
Nanyuan 130 39 45N 116 30 E
Nanyuki 116 0 2N 37 4 E
Nao, C. de la 104 38 44N 0 14 E
Naococane L. 36 52 50N 70 45W
Naoetsu 132 37 12N 138 10 E
Napa 80 38 18N 122 17W
Napa, R. 80 38 10N 122 19W
Napamute 67 61 30N 158 45W
Napanee 47 44 15N 77 0W
Napanoch 71 41 44N 74 2W
Napartokh B. 36 58 1N 62 19W
Naperville 77 41 46N 88 9W
Napier 133 39 30S 176 56 E
Napierville 45 45 11N 73 25W
Napierville □ 44 45 10N 73 30W
Napinka 57 49 19N 100 50W
Naples, Fla., U.S.A. 73 26 10N 81 45W
Naples, N.Y., U.S.A. 70 42 35N 77 25W
Naples = Nápoli 108 40 50N 14 5 E
Napo □ 86 0 30S 77 0W
Napo, R. 86 3 5S 73 0W
Napoleon, N. Dak., U.S.A. 74 46 32N 99 49W
Napoleon, Ohio, U.S.A. 77 41 23N 84 7W
Nápoli 108 40 50N 14 5 E
Nappanee 77 41 27N 86 0W
Nara, Japan 132 34 40N 135 49 E
Nara, Mali 114 15 25N 7 20W
Nara-ken □ 132 34 30N 136 0 E
Nara Visa 75 35 39N 103 10W
Naracoorte 136 36 58S 140 45 E
Naradhan 136 33 34S 146 17 E
Narasapur 125 16 26N 81 50 E
Narathiwat 128 6 40N 101 55 E
Narayanganj 125 23 31N 90 33 E
Narayanpet 124 16 45N 77 30 E
Narbonne 102 43 11N 3 0 E
Nardò 109 40 10N 18 0 E
Narin 124 36 5N 69 0 E
Narinda, B. de 117 14 55S 47 30 E
Narino □ 86 1 30N 78 0W
Narmada, R. 124 22 40N 77 30 E
Narooma 136 36 14S 150 4 E
Narrabri 135 30 19S 149 46 E
Narrandera 136 34 42S 146 31 E
Narraway, R. 60 55 44N 119 55W
Narriah 136 33 56S 146 43 E
Narrogin 134 32 58S 117 14 E
Narromine 136 32 12S 148 12 E
Narsinghpur 124 22 54N 79 14 E
Narva 120 59 10N 28 5 E
Narvik 110 68 28N 17 26 E
Naryan-Mar 120 68 0N 53 0 E
Narym 120 59 0N 81 58 E
Narymskoye 120 49 10N 84 15 E
Naryn 120 41 26N 75 58 E
Nasa, mt. 110 66 32N 15 23 E
Naseby 133 45 1S 170 10 E
Naselle 80 46 22N 123 49W
Naser, Buheirat en 115 23 0N 32 30 E
Nash Creek 39 47 56N 66 6W
Nashua, Iowa, U.S.A. 76 42 55N 92 34W
Nashua, Mont., U.S.A. 78 48 10N 106 25W
Nashua, N.H., U.S.A. 71 42 50N 71 25W
Nashville, Ark., U.S.A. 75 33 56N 93 50W
Nashville, Ga., U.S.A. 73 31 13N 83 15W
Nashville, Ill., U.S.A. 76 38 21N 89 23W
Nashville, Ind., U.S.A. 77 39 12N 86 14W
Nashville, Mich., U.S.A. 77 42 36N 85 5W
Nashville, Tenn., U.S.A. 73 36 12N 86 46W
Nashwaak Bridge 39 46 14N 66 37W
Nashwaaksis 39 45 59N 66 38W
Nasik 124 20 2N 73 50 E
Nasirabad, Bangla. 125 24 42N 90 30 E
Nasirabad, India 124 26 15N 74 45 E
Naskaupi, R. 36 53 47N 60 51W
Nass, R. 54 55 0N 129 40W
Nassau, Bahamas 84 25 0N 77 30W
Nassau, U.S.A. 71 42 30N 73 34W
Nassau, Bahía 90 55 20S 68 0W
Nasser, L. = Naser, Buheiret en 115 23 0N 32 30 E
Nässjö 111 57 38N 14 45 E
Nastapoka, Is. 36 56 55N 76 50W
Nastapoka, R. 36 56 55N 76 33W
Nastopoka Is. 34 57 0N 77 0W
Nata 131 19 37N 109 17 E
Natā 122 27 15N 48 35 E
Nata 117 2 0S 34 25 E
Natagaima 86 3 37N 75 6W
Natal, Brazil 87 5 47S 35 13W
Natal, Can. 61 49 43N 114 51W
Natal, Indon. 126 0 35N 99 0 E
Natal □ 117 28 30S 30 30 E
Natalkuz L. 62 53 36N 125 20W
Natanz 123 33 30N 51 55 E
Natashquan 38 50 14N 61 46W
Natashquan-Est, R. 38 51 20N 61 40W
Natashquan Pt. 38 50 8N 61 40W
Natashquan, R. 38 50 7N 61 50W
Natchez 75 31 35N 91 25W
Natchitoches 75 31 47N 93 4W
Nathdwara 124 24 55N 73 50 E
Natick 71 42 16N 71 19W
Natih 123 22 25N 56 30 E
Nation, R. 54 55 30N 123 32W
National City 80 32 45N 117 7W
National Mills 55 52 52N 101 40W
Natividad, I. de 82 27 50N 115 10W
Natkyizin 128 14 57N 97 59 E
Natoma 74 39 14N 99 0W
Natron L. 116 2 20S 36 0 E
Natrona 70 40 39N 79 43W
Natuna Besar, Kepulauan 126 4 0N 108 15 E
Natuna Selatan, Kepulauan 126 2 45N 109 0 E
Natural Bridge 71 44 5N 75 30W
Naturaliste, C. 134 33 32S 115 0 E
Naturaliste Channel 134 25 20S 113 0 E
Naubinway 46 46 7N 85 27W
Naucelle 102 44 13N 2 20 E
Naugatuck 71 41 28N 73 4W
Naughton 46 46 24N 81 12W
Naumburg 106 51 10N 11 48 E
Nauru I. 14 0 25N 166 0 E
Naushahra 124 34 0N 72 0 E
Nauta 86 4 20S 73 35W
Nautanwa 125 27 20N 83 25 E
Nautla 83 20 20N 96 50W
Nauvoo 76 40 33N 91 23W
Nava 82 28 25N 100 46W
Navalcarnero 104 40 17N 4 5W
Navan = An Uaimh 97 53 39N 6 40W
Navarino, I. 90 55 0S 67 30W
Navarra □ 104 42 40N 1 40W
Navarre, France 102 43 15N 1 20 E
Navarre, U.S.A. 70 40 43N 81 31W
Navarrenx 102 43 20N 0 47W
Navarro 80 39 10N 123 32W
Navasota 75 30 20N 96 5W
Navassa I. 85 18 30N 75 0W
Naver, R. 96 58 34N 4 15W
Navidad 88 33 57S 71 50W
Navin 58 49 51N 97 0W
Navoi 120 40 9N 65 22 E
Navojoa 82 27 0N 109 30W
Navolato 82 24 47N 107 42W
Návpaktos 109 38 23N 21 42 E
Návplion 109 37 33N 22 50 E
Navsari 124 20 57N 72 59 E
Nawabshah 124 26 15N 68 25 E
Nawakot 125 28 0N 85 10 E
Nawalgarh 124 27 50N 75 15 E
Náxos 109 37 8N 25 25 E
Nay 102 43 10N 0 18W
Näy Band 123 27 20N 52 40 E
Naya 86 3 13N 77 22W
Naya, R. 86 3 13N 77 22W
Nayakhan 121 62 10N 159 0 E
Nayarit □ 82 22 0N 105 0W
Nazaré 87 13 0S 39 0W
Nazaré da Mata 87 7 44S 35 14W
Nazareth 115 32 42N 35 17 E
Nazas 82 25 10N 104 0W
Nazas, R. 82 25 20N 104 4W
Naze, The 95 51 43N 1 19 E
Nazir Hat 125 22 35N 91 55 E
Nazko 62 53 1N 123 37W
Nazko, R. 62 53 7N 123 34W
Ncheu 117 14 50S 34 37 E
Ndélé 116 8 25N 20 36 E
Ndendeé 116 2 29S 10 46 E
Ndjamena 114 12 4N 15 8 E
Ndjolé 116 0 10S 10 45 E
Ndola 117 13 0S 28 34 E
Neagh, Lough 97 54 35N 6 25W
Neah Bay 80 48 25N 124 40W
Near Is. 67 53 0N 172 0W
Neath 95 51 39N 3 49W
Neath, R. 98 51 46N 3 35W
Nebraska □ 74 41 30N 100 0W
Nebraska City 74 40 40N 95 52W
Nébrodi, Monti 108 37 55N 14 45 E
Necedah 74 44 2N 90 7W
Nechako, R. 63 53 30N 122 44W
Neche 57 48 59N 97 39W
Neches, R. 75 31 80N 94 20W
Neckar, R. 106 48 43N 9 15 E
Necochea 88 38 30S 58 50W
Needles 81 34 50N 114 35W
Needles, The 95 50 48N 1 19W
Ñeembucú □ 88 27 0S 58 0W
Neemuch (Nimach) 124 24 30N 74 50 E
Neenah 72 44 10N 88 30W
Neepawa 57 50 15N 99 30W
Negaunee 53 46 30N 87 36W
Negeri Sembilan □ 128 2 50N 102 10 E
Negoiu, Vf. 107 43 35N 24 31 E
Negombo 124 7 12N 79 50 E
Negotin 109 44 16N 22 37 E
Negra, La 88 23 46S 70 18W
Negra Pt. 127 18 40N 120 50 E

Negro, R — **Niemur**

Negro, R., Argent. **90** 40 0S 64 0W
Negro, R., Brazil **86** 0 25S 64 0W
Negro, R., Uruguay **89** 32 30S 55 30W
Negros, I. **127** 10 0N 123 0E
Neguac **39** 47 15N 65 5W
Nehalem **80** 45 40N 123 56W
Nehbandān **123** 31 35N 60 5E
Neidpath **56** 50 12N 107 20W
Neihart **78** 47 0N 110 52W
Neikiang **131** 29 35N 105 10E
Neila Gaari Post Office **136** 32 1S 142 48E
Neilburg **56** 52 50N 109 38W
Neil's Harbour **39** 46 48N 60 20W
Neilton **78** 47 24N 123 59W
Neisiang **131** 33 10N 112 0E
Neisse, R. **106** 51 0N 15 0E
Neiva **86** 2 56N 75 18W
Nejanilini L. **55** 59 33N 97 48W
Neksø **111** 55 4N 15 8E
Neligh **74** 42 11N 98 2W
Nelkan **121** 57 50N 136 15E
Nellore **124** 14 27N 79 59E
Nelma **121** 47 30N 139 0E
Nelson, Austral. **136** 38 3S 141 2E
Nelson, B.C., Can. **63** 49 30N 117 20W
Nelson, Ont., Can. **48** 43 23N 79 50W
Nelson, N.Z. **133** 41 18S 173 16E
Nelson, U.K. **94** 53 50N 2 14W
Nelson, Ariz., U.S.A. **79** 35 35N 113 24W
Nelson, Nev., U.S.A. **81** 35 46N 114 55W
Nelson □ **133** 42 11S 172 15E
Nelson, C. **136** 38 26S 141 32E
Nelson, Estrecho **90** 51 30S 75 0W
Nelson Forks **54** 59 30N 124 0W
Nelson House **55** 55 47N 98 51W
Nelson I. **67** 60 40N 164 40W
Nelson L. **55** 55 48N 100 7W
Nelson-Miramichi **39** 46 59N 65 34W
Nelson, R. **55** 54 33N 98 2W
Nelspruit **117** 25 29S 30 59E
Néma **114** 16 40N 7 15W
Neman (Nemunas), R. **120** 53 30N 25 10E
Nemegos **34** 47 40N 83 15W
Nemegosenda L. **53** 48 0N 83 7W
Nemeiben L. **55** 55 20N 105 20W
Némiscachingue, L. **40** 47 25N 74 30W
Nemiscau **36** 51 18N 76 54W
Nemiscau, L. **36** 51 25N 76 40W
Nemours **101** 48 16N 2 40E
Nemunas, R. **120** 55 25N 21 10E
Nemuro **132** 43 20N 145 35E
Nemuro-Kaikyō **132** 43 30N 145 30E
Nemuy **121** 55 40N 135 55E
Nenagh **97** 52 52N 8 11W
Nenana **67** 64 30N 149 0W
Nene, R. **94** 52 38N 0 7E
Nenusa, Kepulauan **127** 4 45N 127 1E
Neodesha **75** 37 30N 95 37W
Neoga **77** 39 19N 88 27W
Neosho **75** 36 56N 94 28W
Neosho, R. **75** 35 59N 95 10W
Neoskweskau **36** 51 52N 74 17W
Nepal ■ **125** 28 0N 84 30E
Nepalganj **125** 28 0N 81 40E
Nephi **78** 39 43N 111 52W
Nephin, Mt. **97** 54 1N 9 21W
Nepisiguit, R. **39** 47 37N 65 38W
Neptune **56** 49 22N 104 4W
Neptune City **71** 40 13N 74 4W
Nérac **102** 44 10N 0 20E
Nerchinsk **121** 52 0N 116 39E
Nerchinskiy Zavod **121** 51 10N 119 30E
Neret L. **36** 54 45N 70 44W
Neretva, R. **109** 43 30N 17 50E
Nerva **104** 37 42N 6 30W
Nes **110** 65 53N 17 24W
Neskaupstaður **110** 65 9N 13 42W
Nesle **101** 49 45N 2 53E
Nespelem **63** 48 10N 118 58W
Ness, Loch **96** 57 15N 4 30W
Nestaocano, R. **41** 49 38N 73 28W
Nestor Falls **52** 49 7N 93 56W
Nesttun **111** 60 19N 5 21E
Nèthe, R. **105** 51 5N 4 55E
Netherby **49** 42 57N 79 8W
Netherdale **135** 21 10S 148 33E
Netherlands ■ **105** 52 0N 5 30E
Netherlands Guiana = Surinam **87** 4 0N 56 0W
Nett L. **52** 48 6N 93 10W
Nettancourt **101** 48 51N 4 57E
Nettilling L. **65** 66 30N 71 0W
Netzahualcoyotl, Presa **83** 17 10N 93 30W
Neubrandenburg **106** 53 33N 13 17E
Neuchâtel **106** 47 0N 6 55E
Neuchâtel, Lac de **106** 46 53N 6 50E
Neudorf **56** 50 43N 103 1W
Neuf-Brisach **101** 48 0N 7 30E
Neufchâteau, Belg. **105** 49 50N 5 25E
Neufchâteau, France **101** 48 21N 5 40E
Neufchâtel, Can. **42** 46 51N 71 23W
Neufchâtel, France **101** 49 43N 1 30E
Neufchâtel-sur-Aisne **101** 49 26N 4 0E
Neuillé-Pont-Pierre **100** 47 33N 0 33E
Neuilly-St-Front **101** 49 10N 3 15E
Neumünster **106** 54 4N 9 58E
Neung-sur-Beuvron **101** 47 30N 1 50E
Neunkirchen **105** 49 23N 7 6E
Neuquén **90** 38 0S 68 0E
Neuquén □ **88** 38 0S 69 50W
Neuruppin **106** 52 56N 12 48E
Neuse, R. **73** 35 5N 77 40W
Neusiedler See **106** 47 50N 16 47E
Neuss **105** 51 12N 6 39E
Neussargues-Moissac **102** 45 9N 3 1E
Neustadt **46** 44 5N 81 0W
Neustrelitz **106** 53 22N 13 4E
Neuvic **102** 45 23N 2 16E
Neuville **101** 45 52N 4 51E
Neuville-aux-Bois **101** 48 4N 2 3E
Neuvy-St.-Sépulchure **102** 46 35N 1 48E
Neuvy-sur-Barangeon **101** 47 20N 2 15E
Neuwied **105** 50 26N 7 29E
Nevada, Iowa, U.S.A. **76** 42 1N 93 27W
Nevada, Mo., U.S.A. **76** 37 51N 94 22W
Nevada □ **78** 39 20N 117 0W
Nevada City **80** 39 20N 121 0W
Nevada de Sta. Marta, Sa. **86** 10 55N 73 50W
Nevada, Sierra, Spain **104** 37 3N 3 15W
Nevada, Sierra, U.S.A. **78** 39 0N 120 30W
Nevado, Cerro **88** 35 30S 68 20W
Nevado de Colima, Mt. **82** 19 35N 103 45W
Nevanka **121** 56 45N 98 55E
Nevers **101** 47 0N 3 9E
Nevertire **136** 31 50S 147 44E
Neville **56** 49 58N 107 39W
Nevis I. **85** 17 0N 62 30W
Nevşehir **122** 38 33N 34 40E
New Albany, Ind., U.S.A. **77** 38 20N 85 50W
New Albany, Miss., U.S.A. **75** 34 30N 89 0W
New Albany, Pa., U.S.A. **71** 41 35N 76 28W
New Amsterdam **86** 6 15N 57 30W
New Athens **76** 38 19N 89 53W
New Baltimore **46** 42 41N 82 44W
New Bedford **71** 41 40N 70 52W
New Berlin, U.S.A. **76** 39 44N 89 55W
New Berlin, U.S.A. **77** 42 59N 88 6W
New Bern **73** 35 8N 77 3W
New Bethlehem **70** 41 0N 79 22W
New Bloomfield **70** 40 24N 77 12W
New Boston **75** 33 27N 94 21W
New Braunfels **75** 29 43N 98 9W
New Brigden **61** 51 42N 110 29W
New Brighton **133** 43 29S 172 43E
New Britain **71** 41 41N 72 47W
New Brunswick **71** 40 30N 74 28W
New Brunswick □ **35** 46 50N 66 30W
New Buffalo **77** 41 47N 86 45W
New Byrd **91** 80 0S 120 0W
New Caledonia, I. **14** 21 0S 165 0E
New Canton **76** 39 37N 91 8W
New Carlisle, Can. **39** 48 1N 65 20W
New Carlisle, Ind., U.S.A. **77** 41 45N 86 32W
New Carlisle, Ohio, U.S.A. **77** 39 56N 84 2W
New Castile = Castilla La Neuva **104** 39 45N 3 20W
New Castle, Ind, U.S.A. **77** 39 55N 85 22W
New Castle, Ind., U.S.A. **77** 39 55N 85 23W
New Castle, Ky., U.S.A. **77** 38 26N 85 10W
New Castle, Pa., U.S.A. **70** 41 0N 80 20W
New City **71** 41 8N 74 0W
New Cristóbal **84** 9 25N 79 40W
New Cumberland **70** 40 30N 80 36W
New Cuyama **81** 34 57N 119 38W
New Delhi **124** 28 37N 77 13E
New Denmark **39** 47 2N 67 38W
New Denver **63** 50 0N 117 25W
New Dundee **49** 43 21N 80 31W
New Durham **49** 43 3N 80 34W
New England **74** 46 36N 102 47W
New England Ra. **135** 30 20S 151 45E
New Forest **95** 50 53N 1 40W
New Franklin **76** 39 1N 92 44W
New Germany **39** 44 33N 64 43W
New Glarus **76** 42 49N 89 38W
New Glasgow, N.S., Can. **39** 45 35N 62 36W
New Glasgow, Qué., Can. **43** 45 50N 73 53W
New Guinea, I. **14** 4 0S 136 0E
New Hamburg **46** 43 23N 80 42W
New Hampshire □ **71** 43 40N 71 40W
New Hampton **76** 43 2N 92 20W
New Harbour **39** 45 13N 61 29W
New Harmony **77** 38 7N 87 56W
New Haven, Conn., U.S.A. **71** 41 20N 72 54W
New Haven, Ill., U.S.A. **77** 37 55N 88 8W
New Haven, Ind., U.S.A. **77** 41 4N 85 1W
New Haven, Mich., U.S.A. **46** 42 44N 82 46W
New Haven, Mo., U.S.A. **76** 38 37N 91 13W
New Hazelton **54** 55 20N 127 30W
New Hebrides, Is. **14** 15 0S 168 0E
New Iberia **75** 30 2N 91 54W
New Ireland, I. **14** 3 20S 151 50E
New Jersey □ **71** 39 50N 74 10W
New Kensington **70** 40 36N 79 43W
New Lexington **72** 39 40N 82 15W
New Liskeard **34** 47 31N 79 41W
New London, Conn., U.S.A. **71** 41 23N 72 8W
New London, Iowa, U.S.A. **76** 40 55N 91 24W
New London, Minn., U.S.A. **74** 45 17N 94 55W
New London, Mo., U.S.A. **76** 39 35N 91 24W
New London, Ohio, U.S.A. **70** 41 4N 82 25W
New London, Wis., U.S.A. **74** 44 23N 88 43W
New Madison **77** 39 58N 84 43W
New Madrid **75** 36 40N 89 30W
New Market **71** 43 4N 70 57W
New Meadows **78** 45 0N 116 10W
New Mexico □ **68** 34 30N 106 0W
New Miami **77** 39 26N 84 32W
New Milford, Conn., U.S.A. **71** 41 35N 73 25W
New Milford, Pa., U.S.A. **71** 41 50N 75 45W
New Norfolk **135** 42 46S 147 2E
New Norway **61** 52 52N 112 57W
New Orleans **75** 30 0N 90 5W
New Palestine **77** 39 45N 85 52W
New Paris **77** 39 5N 84 48W
New Pekin **77** 38 31N 86 2W
New Philadelphia **70** 40 29N 81 25W
New Plymouth, Bahamas **84** 26 56N 77 20W
New Plymouth, N.Z. **133** 39 4S 174 5E
New Providence I. **84** 25 0N 77 30W
New Radnor **95** 52 15N 3 10W
New Richmond, Can. **38** 48 15N 65 45W
New Richmond, U.S.A. **77** 38 57N 84 17W
New Richmond, Wis., U.S.A. **74** 45 6N 92 34W
New Roads **75** 30 43N 91 30W
New Rochelle **71** 40 55N 73 46W
New Rockford **74** 47 44N 99 7W
New Ross, Can. **39** 44 44N 64 27W
New Ross, Ireland **97** 52 24N 6 58W
New Salem **74** 46 51N 101 25W
New Sarepta **60** 53 16N 113 8W
New Sharon **76** 41 28N 92 39W
New Siberian Is. = Novosibirskiye Os. **121** 75 0N 140 0E
New Smyrna Beach **73** 29 0N 80 50W
New South Wales □ **135** 33 0S 146 0E
New Toronto **50** 43 36N 79 30W
New Ulm **74** 44 15N 94 30W
New Vienna **77** 39 19N 83 42W
New Virginia **76** 41 11N 93 44W
New Waterford **39** 46 13N 60 4W
New Westminster **66** 49 13N 122 55W
New World I. **37** 49 35N 54 40W
New York □ **71** 42 40N 76 0W
New York City **71** 40 45N 74 0W
New Zealand ■ **14** 40 0S 176 0E
Newala **116** 10 58S 39 10E
Newark, U.K. **94** 53 6N 0 48W
Newark, Del., U.S.A. **72** 39 42N 75 45W
Newark, N.J., U.S.A. **71** 40 41N 74 12W
Newark, N.Y., U.S.A. **70** 43 2N 77 10W
Newark, Ohio, U.S.A. **70** 40 5N 82 30W
Newberg, U.S.A. **76** 37 55N 91 54W
Newberg, Oreg., U.S.A. **78** 45 22N 123 0W
Newberry **46** 46 20N 85 32W
Newberry Springs **81** 34 50N 116 41W
Newboro L. **47** 44 38N 76 20W
Newbrook **60** 54 24N 112 57W
Newburgh, Can. **47** 44 19N 76 52W
Newburgh, U.S.A. **77** 37 57N 87 24W
Newburgh, N.Y., U.S.A. **71** 41 30N 74 1W
Newbury, U.K. **95** 51 24N 1 19W
Newbury, U.S.A. **71** 44 7N 72 6W
Newburyport **71** 42 48N 70 50W
Newcastle, Austral. **136** 33 0S 151 40E
Newcastle, N.B., Can. **39** 47 1N 65 38W
Newcastle, Ont., Can. **70** 43 54N 78 34W
Newcastle, S. Afr. **117** 27 45S 29 58E
Newcastle, U.K. **97** 54 13N 5 54W
Newcastle, Calif., U.S.A. **80** 38 53N 121 8W
Newcastle, Me., U.S.A. **71** 43 4N 70 41W
Newcastle, Wyo., U.S.A. **74** 43 50N 104 12W
Newcastle Bridge **39** 46 5N 66 3W
Newcastle Emlyn **95** 52 2N 4 29W
Newcastle Ra. **135** 15 45S 130 15E
Newcastle-under-Lyme **94** 53 2N 2 15W
Newcastle-upon-Tyne **94** 54 59N 1 37W
Newcastle Waters **134** 17 30S 133 28E
Newcastle West **97** 52 27N 9 3W
Newdegate **134** 33 6S 119 0E
Newell **74** 44 48N 103 25W
Newell, L. **61** 50 26N 111 55W
Newenham, C. **67** 58 40N 162 15W
Newfoundland **35** 48 30N 56 0W
Newfoundland □ **35** 48 28N 56 0W
Newgate **61** 49 2N 115 12W
Newhalem **63** 48 41N 121 16W
Newhalen **67** 59 40N 155 0W
Newhall **81** 34 23N 118 32W
Newham **95** 51 31N 0 2E
Newhaven **95** 50 47N 0 4E
Newkirk **75** 36 52N 97 3W
Newman, U.S.A. **77** 39 48N 87 59W
Newman, U.S.A. **80** 37 19N 121 1W
Newman, Mt. **134** 23 20S 119 34E
Newmarket, Can. **46** 44 3N 79 28W
Newmarket, Ireland **97** 52 13N 9 0W
Newmarket, U.K. **95** 52 15N 0 23E
Newmarket, U.S.A. **71** 43 4N 70 57W
Newnan **73** 33 22N 84 48W
Newport, Austral. **136** 33 40S 151 20E
Newport, Can. **38** 48 16N 64 45W
Newport, Ont., Can. **49** 43 6N 80 14W
Newport, Gwent, U.K. **95** 51 35N 3 0W
Newport, I. of W., U.K. **95** 50 42N 1 18W
Newport, Salop, U.K. **95** 52 47N 2 22W
Newport, U.S.A. **77** 42 2N 83 22W
Newport, Ark., U.S.A. **75** 35 38N 91 15W
Newport, Ind., U.S.A. **77** 39 53N 87 26W
Newport, Ky., U.S.A. **77** 39 5N 84 23W
Newport, N.H., U.S.A. **71** 43 23N 72 8W
Newport, Oreg., U.S.A. **78** 44 41N 124 2W
Newport, Pa., U.S.A. **70** 40 28N 77 8W
Newport, R.I., U.S.A. **71** 41 30N 71 19W
Newport, Tenn., U.S.A. **73** 35 59N 83 12W
Newport, Vt., U.S.A. **71** 44 57N 72 17W
Newport, Wash., U.S.A. **63** 48 11N 117 2W
Newport Beach **81** 33 40N 117 58W
Newport News **72** 37 2N 76 30W
Newquay **95** 50 24N 5 6W
Newry **97** 54 10N 6 20W
Newry & Mourne □ **97** 54 10N 6 15W
Newton, Can. **66** 49 8N 122 51W
Newton, Ill., U.S.A. **77** 38 59N 88 10W
Newton, Iowa, U.S.A. **76** 41 40N 93 3W
Newton, Mass., U.S.A. **72** 42 21N 71 10W
Newton, N.C., U.S.A. **73** 35 42N 81 10W
Newton, N.J., U.S.A. **71** 41 3N 74 46W
Newton, Texas, U.S.A. **75** 30 54N 93 42W
Newton Abbot **95** 50 32N 3 37W
Newton Brook **50** 43 48N 79 24W
Newton Stewart **96** 54 57N 4 30W
Newtonabbey □ **97** 54 45N 6 0W
Newtown, Austral. **136** 37 38S 143 40E
Newtown, Can. **37** 49 12N 53 31W
Newtown, U.K. **95** 52 31N 3 19W
Newtown, U.S.A. **76** 40 22N 93 20W
Newtownabbey **97** 54 40N 5 55W
Newtownabbey □ **105** 54 45N 6 0W
Newtownards **97** 54 37N 5 40W
Newville **70** 40 10N 77 24W
Neyrīz **123** 29 15N 54 55E
Neyshābūr **123** 36 10N 58 20E
Nezhin **120** 51 5N 31 55E
Nezperce **78** 46 13N 116 15W
Ngabang **126** 0 30N 109 55E
Ngami Depression **117** 20 30S 22 46E
Ngandjuk **127** 7 32S 111 55E
Ngaoundéré **114** 7 15N 13 35E
Ngapara **133** 44 57S 170 46E
Ngau, I. **133** 18 2S 179 18E
Ngawi **127** 7 24S 111 26E
Ngha Lo **128** 21 33N 104 28E
Ngoring Nor **129** 34 50N 98 0E
Ngudu **116** 2 58S 33 25E
Nguru **114** 12 56N 10 29E
Nha Trang **128** 12 16N 109 10E
Nhill **136** 36 18S 141 40E
Nhulunbuy **135** 12 10S 136 45E
Niagara **72** 45 45N 88 0W
Niagara □, Can. **49** 43 15N 79 4W
Niagara □, U.S.A. **49** 43 16N 78 55W
Niagara Falls, Can. **49** 43 7N 79 5W
Niagara Falls, N. Amer. **34** 43 5N 79 5W
Niagara Falls, U.S.A. **49** 43 5N 79 0W
Niagara-on-the-Lake **49** 43 15N 79 4W
Niagara, R. **49** 43 16N 79 3W
Niah **126** 3 58N 113 46E
Nialia, L. **136** 33 20S 141 42E
Niamey **114** 13 27N 2 6E
Niangara **116** 3 50N 27 50E
Niangua, R. **76** 38 0N 92 48W
Nias, I. **126** 1 0N 97 40E
Nibong Tebal **128** 5 10N 100 29E
Nicaragua ■ **84** 11 40N 85 30W
Nicaragua, Lago de **84** 12 50N 85 30W
Nicastro **108** 39 0N 16 18E
Nice **103** 43 42N 7 14E
Niceville **73** 30 30N 86 30W
Nichinan **132** 31 38N 131 23E
Nicholas, Chan. **84** 23 30N 80 30W
Nicholasville **72** 37 54N 84 31W
Nichols **71** 42 1N 76 22W
Nicholson, Can. **34** 47 58N 83 47W
Nicholson, U.S.A. **71** 41 37N 75 47W
Nicobar Is. **118** 9 0N 93 0E
Nicoclí **86** 8 26N 76 48W
Nicola **63** 50 12N 120 40W
Nicola L. **63** 50 10N 120 32W
Nicolasville **77** 37 53N 84 34W
Nicolet **41** 46 17N 72 35W
Nicolls Town **84** 25 8N 78 0W
Nicomekl, R. **66** 49 3N 122 52W
Nicosia **122** 35 10N 33 25E
Nicoya **84** 10 9N 85 27W
Nicoya, G. de **84** 10 0N 85 0W
Nicoya, Pen. de **84** 9 45N 85 40W
Nidd, R. **94** 54 1N 1 32W
Niederbronn **101** 48 57N 7 39E
Niemur **136** 35 17S 144 9E

Nienburg Nosratābād

Nienburg	**106**	52 38N	9 15 E
Nientzeshan	**130**	47 38N	122 58 E
Nieuw Nickerie	**87**	6 0N	57 10W
Nieuwpoort	**105**	51 8N	2 45 E
Nièvre □	**101**	47 10N	3 40 E
Niğde	**122**	38 0N	34 40 E
Nigel I.	**62**	50 53N	127 43W
Niger ■	**114**	13 30N	10 0 E
Niger, R.	**114**	10 0N	4 40 E
Nigeria ■	**114**	8 30N	8 0 E
Nightcaps	**133**	45 57 S	168 14 E
Nii-Jima	**132**	34 20N	139 15 E
Niigata	**132**	37 58N	139 0 E
Niigata-ken □	**132**	37 15N	138 45 E
Niihama	**132**	33 55N	133 10 E
Niihau, I.	**67**	21 55N	160 10W
Nijkerk	**105**	52 13N	5 30 E
Nijmegen	**105**	51 50N	5 52 E
Nikel	**110**	69 30N	30 5 E
Nikiniki	**127**	9 40 S	124 30 E
Nikki	**114**	9 58N	3 21 E
Nikkō	**132**	36 45N	139 35 E
Nikolayev	**120**	46 58N	32 7 E
Nikolayevsk-na-Amur	**121**	53 40N	140 50 E
Nikolayevski	**120**	50 10N	45 35 E
Nikolski	**67**	53 0N	168 50W
Nikolskoye, Amur, U.S.S.R.	**121**	47 50N	131 5 E
Nikolskoye, Kamandorskiye, U.S.S.R.	**121**	55 12N	166 0 E
Nīkshahr	**123**	26 15N	60 10 E
Nikšić	**115**	42 50N	18 57 E
Nîl el Abyad, Bahr	**115**	9 30N	31 40 E
Nîl el Azraq □	**114**	12 30N	34 30 E
Nîl el Azraq, Bahr	**115**	10 30N	35 0 E
Nîl, Nahr el	**115**	27 30N	30 30 E
Nila	**127**	8 24 S	120 29 E
Niland	**81**	33 16N	115 30W
Nile, R. = Nîl, Nahr el	**115**	27 30N	30 30 E
Niles	**70**	41 8N	80 40W
Nimach = Neemuch	**124**	24 30N	74 50 E
Nimba, Mt.	**114**	7 39N	8 30W
Nîmes	**103**	43 50N	4 23 E
Nimingarra	**134**	20 31 S	119 55 E
Nimneryskiy	**121**	58 0N	125 10 E
Nimpkish L.	**62**	50 25N	126 59W
Nimpkish, R.	**62**	50 34N	126 58W
Nimpo L.	**62**	52 20N	125 10W
Nimule	**116**	3 32N	32 3 E
Ninemile	**54**	56 0N	130 7W
Ninette	**57**	49 24N	99 38W
Ninety Mile Beach	**14**	34 45 S	173 0 E
Ninety Mile Beach, The	**135**	38 15 S	147 24 E
Nineveh	**122**	36 25N	43 10 E
Ningan	**130**	44 23N	129 26 E
Ninghsien	**130**	35 30N	107 58 E
Ninghwa	**131**	32 58N	119 59 E
Ningkiang	**131**	32 52N	106 17 E
Ningming	**131**	22 10N	107 59 E
Ningpo	**131**	29 53N	121 33 E
Ningshan	**131**	33 12N	108 29 E
Ningsia Hui A.R. □	**130**	37 45N	106 0 E
Ningteh	**131**	26 45N	120 0 E
Ningtsin	**130**	37 40N	115 0 E
Ningtu	**131**	26 30N	115 58 E
Ningwu	**130**	39 2N	112 15 E
Ningyüan	**131**	25 36N	111 54 E
Ninh Binh	**128**	20 15N	105 55 E
Ninkiang	**131**	32 50N	106 20 E
Ninove	**105**	50 51N	4 2 E
Nioaque	**89**	21 5 S	55 50W
Niobrara	**74**	42 48N	97 59W
Niobrara R.	**74**	42 30N	103 0W
Nioki	**116**	2 47 S	17 40 E
Nioman	**36**	50 25N	66 5W
Nioro du Sahel	**114**	15 30N	9 30W
Niort	**102**	46 19N	0 29W
Nipawin	**56**	53 20N	104 0W
Nipawin Prov. Park	**56**	54 0N	104 37W
Nipekamew, R.	**56**	54 59N	104 52W
Nipigon	**52**	49 0N	88 17W
Nipigon B.	**53**	48 53N	87 50W
Nipigon, L.	**52**	49 50N	88 30W
Nipin, R.	**56**	55 46N	109 2W
Nipishish L.	**36**	54 12N	60 45W
Nipisi L.	**60**	55 47N	114 57W
Nipissing L.	**46**	46 20N	80 0W
Nipissis, L.	**38**	51 2N	66 10W
Nipissis, R.	**36**	50 30N	66 5W
Nipisso, L.	**38**	50 52N	65 50W
Nipomo	**81**	35 4N	120 29W
Nipper's Harbour	**37**	49 48N	55 52W
Nipton	**81**	35 28N	115 16W
Nirmal	**124**	19 3N	78 20 E
Nirmali	**125**	26 20N	86 35 E
Niš	**109**	43 19N	21 58 E
Nishinomiya	**132**	34 45N	135 20 E
Niskibi, R.	**34**	56 29N	88 9W
Nisqually, R.	**80**	47 6N	122 42W
Nisswa	**52**	46 31N	94 17W
Nisutlin, R.	**54**	60 14N	132 34W
Nitchequon	**36**	53 10N	70 58W
Niterói	**89**	22 52 S	43 0W
Nith, R., Can.	**46**	43 12N	80 23W
Nith, R., U.K.	**96**	55 20N	3 5W
Nitinat	**62**	48 56N	124 29W
Nitinat L.	**62**	48 45N	124 45W
Nitra	**107**	48 19N	18 4 E
Nitra, R.	**107**	48 30N	18 7 E
Niuafo'ou, I.	**133**	15 30 S	175 58W
Niue I. (Savage I.)	**14**	19 2 S	169 54W
Niut, Mt.	**126**	0 55N	109 30 E
Nivelles	**105**	50 35N	4 20 E
Nivernais	**101**	47 0N	3 40 E
Niverville	**57**	49 36N	97 3W
Nixon, Nev., U.S.A.	**78**	39 54N	119 22W
Nixon, Tex., U.S.A.	**75**	29 17N	97 45W
Nizamabad	**124**	18 45N	78 7 E
Nizamghat	**125**	28 20N	95 45 E
Nizhanaya Tunguska	**121**	64 20N	93 0 E
Nizhne Kolymsk	**121**	68 40N	160 55 E
Nizhne-Vartovskoye	**120**	60 56N	76 38 E
Nizhneangarsk	**121**	56 0N	109 30 E
Nizhneudinsk	**121**	55 0N	99 20 E
Nizhniy Tagil	**120**	57 55N	59 57 E
Nizip	**122**	37 5N	37 50 E
Nizké Tatry	**107**	48 55N	20 0 E
Njombe	**116**	9 20 S	34 50 E
Nkhata Bay	**116**	11 33 S	34 16 E
Nkhota Kota	**117**	12 56 S	34 15 E
Nkongsamba	**116**	4 55N	9 55 E
Nmai, R.	**125**	25 30N	98 0 E
Noakhali = Maijdi	**125**	22 50N	90 45 E
Noatak	**67**	67 32N	163 10W
Noatak, R.	**67**	68 0N	161 0W
Nobel	**46**	45 25N	80 6W
Nobeoka	**132**	32 36N	131 41 E
Noble	**77**	38 42N	88 14W
Nobleford	**61**	49 53N	113 3W
Noblesville	**77**	40 1N	85 59W
Nobleton	**50**	43 54N	79 40W
Nocera Inferiore	**108**	40 45N	14 37 E
Nochixtlán	**83**	17 28N	97 14W
Nocona	**75**	33 48N	97 45W
Noda	**121**	47 30N	142 5 E
Noel, Can.	**39**	45 18N	63 45W
Noel, U.S.A.	**75**	36 36N	94 29W
Noelville	**46**	46 8N	80 26W
Nogales, Mexico	**82**	31 36N	94 29W
Nogales, U.S.A.	**79**	31 33N	115 50W
Nōgata	**132**	33 48N	130 54 E
Nogent-en-Bassigny	**101**	48 0N	5 20 E
Nogent-le-Rotrou	**100**	48 20N	0 50 E
Nogent-sur-Seine	**101**	48 30N	3 30 E
Noginsk	**121**	64 30N	90 50 E
Nogoa, R.	**135**	23 33 S	148 32 E
Nogoyá	**88**	32 24 S	59 48W
Noi, R.	**128**	14 50N	100 15 E
Noirclair, L.	**38**	50 38N	60 23W
Noire, Mt.	**100**	48 11N	3 40W
Noire, R.	**40**	45 54N	76 57W
Noirétable	**102**	45 48N	3 46 E
Noirmoutier	**100**	47 0N	2 15W
Noirmoutier, Î. de	**100**	46 58N	2 10W
Nok Kundi	**124**	28 50N	62 45 E
Nokhtuysk	**121**	60 0N	117 45 E
Nokomis, Can.	**56**	51 35N	105 0W
Nokomis, U.S.A.	**76**	39 18N	89 18W
Nokomis L.	**55**	57 0N	103 0W
Nola	**116**	3 35N	16 10 E
Nolay	**101**	46 58N	4 35 E
Noman L.	**55**	62 15N	108 55W
Nombinnie	**136**	32 56 S	145 53 E
Nombre de Dios	**84**	9 34N	79 28W
Nome	**67**	64 30N	165 30W
Nominingue	**40**	46 24N	75 2W
Nominingue, L.	**40**	46 26N	74 59W
Nonacho L.	**55**	61 57N	109 28W
Nonancourt	**100**	48 47N	1 11 E
Nonant-le-Pin	**100**	48 42N	0 12 E
Nong Khae	**128**	14 29N	100 53 E
Nong Khai	**128**	17 50N	102 46 E
Nonoava	**82**	27 22N	106 38W
Nonopapa	**67**	21 50N	160 15W
Nontron	**102**	45 31N	0 40 E
Noonan	**56**	48 51N	102 59W
Noonkanbah	**126**	18 30 S	124 50 E
Noorvik	**67**	66 50N	161 14W
Nootka	**62**	49 38N	126 38W
Nootka I.	**62**	49 40N	126 50W
Noqui	**116**	5 55 S	13 30 E
Nora Springs	**76**	43 9N	92 1W
Norah Head	**136**	33 15 S	151 35 E
Noranda	**40**	48 20N	79 0W
Norborne	**76**	39 18N	93 40W
Norco	**81**	33 56N	117 33W
Nord □	**101**	50 15N	3 30 E
Nord, Grand L. du	**38**	50 54N	67 6W
Nord-Ostee Kanal	**106**	54 5N	9 15 E
Nord, Petit L. du	**38**	50 50N	67 10W
Nord, R.	**43**	45 31N	74 20W
Nord-Trondelag Fylke □	**110**	64 20N	12 0 E
Nordaustlandet	**17**	79 55N	23 0 E
Nordegg	**61**	52 29N	116 5W
Nordhausen	**106**	51 29N	10 47 E
Nordhorn	**105**	52 27N	7 4 E
Nordkapp, Norway	**110**	71 10N	25 44 E
Nordkapp, Svalb.	**17**	80 31N	20 0 E
Nordkinn	**93**	71 3N	28 0 E
Nordland Fylke □	**110**	65 40N	13 0 E
Nordrhein-Westfalen □	**106**	51 45N	7 30 E
Nordvik	**121**	73 40N	110 57 E
Nore R.	**97**	52 40N	7 20W
Norembega	**34**	48 59N	80 43W
Norfolk, Nebr., U.S.A.	**74**	42 3N	97 25W
Norfolk, N.Y., U.S.A.	**71**	44 47N	75 1W
Norfolk, Va., U.S.A.	**72**	36 52N	76 15W
Norfolk □	**94**	52 39N	1 0 E
Norfolk Broads	**94**	52 30N	1 15 E
Norfolk I.	**14**	28 58 S	168 3 E
Norfork Res.	**75**	36 25N	92 0W
Norg	**105**	53 4N	6 28 E
Norilsk	**121**	69 20N	88 0 E
Normal	**76**	40 30N	89 0W
Norman	**75**	35 12N	97 30W
Norman, R.	**135**	19 20 S	142 35 E
Norman Wells	**64**	65 17N	126 45W
Normanby, R.	**135**	14 23 S	144 10 E
Normandie	**100**	48 45N	0 10 E
Normandie, Collines de	**100**	48 55N	0 45W
Normandin	**41**	48 49N	72 31W
Normandy = Normandie	**100**	48 45N	0 10 E
Norman's Cove	**37**	47 33N	53 40W
Normanton	**135**	17 40 S	141 10 E
Normanview	**58**	50 28N	104 40W
Normétal	**40**	49 0N	79 22W
Norquay	**57**	51 53N	102 5W
Ñorquinco	**90**	41 51 S	70 55W
Norrby	**110**	64 55N	18 15 E
Nørresundby	**111**	57 5N	9 52 E
Norris	**78**	45 40N	111 48W
Norris Arm	**37**	49 5N	55 15W
Norris City	**77**	37 59N	88 20W
Norris Point	**37**	49 31N	57 53W
Norristown	**71**	40 9N	75 15W
Norrköping	**111**	58 37N	16 11 E
Norrland □	**110**	66 50N	18 0 E
Norrtälje	**111**	59 46N	18 42 E
Norsk	**121**	52 30N	130 0 E
Norte de Santander □	**86**	8 0N	73 0W
North Adams	**71**	42 42N	73 6W
North Andaman I.	**128**	13 15N	92 40 E
North Atlantic Ocean	**12**	30 0N	50 0W
North Aulatsivik I.	**36**	59 46N	64 5W
North Baltimore	**77**	41 11N	83 41W
North Battleford	**56**	52 50N	108 17W
North Bay	**46**	46 20N	79 30W
North Belcher Is.	**36**	56 50N	79 50W
North Bend, Can.	**63**	49 50N	121 35W
North Bend, Oreg., U.S.A.	**78**	43 28N	124 7W
North Bend, Pa., U.S.A.	**70**	41 20N	77 42W
North Bend, Wash., U.S.A.	**80**	47 30N	121 47W
North Berwick, U.K.	**96**	56 4N	2 44W
North Berwick, U.S.A.	**71**	43 18N	70 43W
North Buck L.	**60**	54 41N	112 32W
North Burnaby	**66**	49 17N	123 0W
North Canadian, R.	**75**	36 48N	103 0W
North C., Antarct.	**91**	71 0N	166 0 E
North C., Can.	**35**	47 2N	60 20W
North, Cape	**39**	47 2N	60 25W
North C., N.Z.	**133**	34 23 S	173 4 E
North C., Spitsbergen	**17**	80 40N	20 0 E
North Caribou L.	**34**	52 50N	90 40W
North Carolina □	**73**	35 30N	80 0W
North Cascades Nat. Park	**63**	48 45N	121 14W
North Channel, Br. Is.	**96**	55 0N	5 30W
North Channel, Can.	**46**	46 0N	83 0W
North Chicago	**77**	42 19N	87 50W
North College Hill	**77**	39 13N	84 33W
North Dakota □	**74**	47 30N	100 0W
North Down □	**97**	54 40N	5 45W
North Downs	**95**	51 17N	0 30W
North East	**70**	42 17N	79 50W
North English	**76**	41 31N	92 5W
North Esk, R.	**96**	56 44N	2 25W
North European Plain	**93**	55 0N	20 0 E
North Fabius, R.	**76**	39 54N	91 28W
N. Foreland, Pt.	**95**	51 22N	1 28 E
North Fork	**80**	37 14N	119 29W
North Fork, American, R.	**80**	38 45N	121 8W
North Fork, Feather, R.	**80**	39 17N	121 38W
North Fork, Salt R.	**76**	39 26N	91 5W
North French, R.	**53**	51 10N	80 50W
North Glanford	**48**	43 11N	79 54W
North Gower	**47**	45 8N	75 43W
North Grant	**39**	45 40N	62 2W
North Hatley	**41**	45 17N	71 58W
North Head, N.B., Can.	**39**	44 46N	66 45W
North Head, Newf., Can.	**37**	47 29N	52 38W
North Henik L.	**55**	61 45N	97 40W
North Highlands	**80**	38 40N	121 25W
North I.	**133**	38 0 S	175 0 E
North Judson	**77**	41 13N	86 46W
North Kamloops	**54**	50 40N	120 25W
North Kansas City	**76**	39 9N	94 35W
North Kingsville	**70**	41 53N	80 42W
North Knife, R.	**55**	58 53N	94 45W
North Korea ■	**130**	40 0N	127 0 E
N. Lakhimpur	**125**	27 15N	94 10 E
North Lancaster	**43**	45 13N	74 30W
N. Las Vegas	**81**	36 15N	115 6W
North Liberty	**77**	41 32N	86 26W
North Lonsdale	**66**	49 20N	123 4W
North Magnetic Pole	**65**	76 12N	100 36W
North Manchester	**77**	41 0N	85 46W
North Minch	**96**	58 5N	5 55W
North Nahanni, R.	**54**	62 15N	123 20W
North Ossetian A.S.S.R. □	**120**	43 30N	44 30 E
North Palisade	**80**	37 6N	118 32W
North Platte	**74**	41 10N	100 50W
North Platte, R.	**78**	42 50N	106 50W
North Pt.	**39**	47 5N	64 0W
North Pole	**17**	90 0N	0 0 E
North Portal	**57**	49 0N	102 33W
North Powder	**78**	45 2N	117 59W
North, R.	**36**	57 30N	61 50W
North Ram, R.	**61**	52 16N	114 38W
North Ronaldsay, I.	**96**	59 20N	2 30W
North Rustico	**39**	46 27N	63 19W
N. Saskatchewan R.	**56**	53 15N	105 5W
North Sea	**93**	56 0N	4 0 E
North Seneca	**49**	43 7N	79 56W
North Sentinel, I.	**128**	11 35N	92 15 E
North Star	**60**	56 51N	117 38W
North Stradbroke I.	**135**	27 35 S	153 28 E
North Sydney	**39**	46 12N	60 21W
North Thompson, R.	**63**	50 40N	120 20W
N. Tonawanda	**49**	43 5N	78 50W
North Troy	**71**	44 59N	72 24W
N. Truchas Pk.	**79**	36 0N	105 30W
North Twin I.	**36**	53 20N	80 0W
North Twin L.	**37**	49 45N	55 56W
North Tyne, R.	**94**	54 59N	2 7W
North Uist I.	**96**	57 40N	7 15W
North Vancouver	**66**	49 2N	123 3W
North Vermilion	**54**	58 25N	116 0W
North Vernon	**77**	39 0N	85 35W
North Wabasca L.	**60**	56 0N	113 55W
North Walsham	**94**	52 49N	1 22 E
North Webster	**77**	41 25N	85 48W
North West Highlands	**96**	57 35N	5 2W
North West River	**36**	53 30N	60 10W
North York	**50**	43 46N	79 30W
North York Moors	**94**	54 25N	0 50W
North Yorkshire □	**94**	54 15N	1 25W
Northallerton	**94**	54 20N	1 26W
Northam	**134**	31 35 S	116 42 E
Northampton, Austral.	**134**	28 21 S	114 33 E
Northampton, U.K.	**95**	52 14N	0 54W
Northampton, Mass., U.S.A.	**71**	42 22N	72 39W
Northampton, Pa., U.S.A.	**71**	40 38N	75 24W
Northampton □	**95**	52 16N	0 55W
Northbridge	**71**	42 12N	71 40W
N.E. Land	**17**	80 0N	24 0 E
N.E. Providence Chan.	**84**	26 0N	76 0W
Northeast Providence Channel	**84**	26 0N	76 0W
Northern Circars	**125**	17 30N	82 30 E
Northern Group	**133**	10 00 S	160 00W
Northern Indian L.	**55**	57 20N	97 20W
Northern Ireland □	**97**	54 45N	7 0W
Northern Light, L.	**52**	48 15N	90 39W
Northern Territory □	**134**	16 0 S	133 0 E
Northfield	**74**	44 30N	93 10W
Northland □	**133**	35 30 S	173 30 E
Northmount	**50**	43 46N	79 24W
Northome	**52**	47 53N	94 15W
Northport, Can.	**39**	45 56N	63 52W
Northport, Ala., U.S.A.	**73**	33 15N	87 35W
Northport, Mich., U.S.A.	**72**	45 8N	85 39W
Northport, Wash., U.S.A.	**63**	48 55N	117 48W
Northumberland □	**94**	55 12N	2 0W
Northumberland, C.	**135**	38 5 S	140 40 E
Northumberland Str.	**39**	46 20N	64 0W
Northville	**72**	43 13N	74 11W
Northway Junction	**67**	63 0N	141 55W
Northwest Gander, R.	**37**	48 55N	55 2W
N.W. Providence Chan.	**84**	26 0N	78 0W
Northwest Terr. □	**64**	65 0N	100 0W
N.W.Basin	**134**	25 45 S	115 0 E
Northwich	**94**	53 16N	2 30W
Northwood, Iowa, U.S.A.	**74**	43 27N	93 0W
Northwood, N.D., U.S.A.	**74**	47 44N	97 30W
Norton, Can.	**39**	45 38N	65 42W
Norton, U.S.A.	**74**	39 50N	100 0W
Norton B.	**67**	64 40N	162 0W
Norton Sd	**67**	64 0N	165 0W
Norton Shores	**77**	43 8N	86 15W
Norwalk, Calif., U.S.A.	**81**	33 54N	118 5W
Norwalk, Conn., U.S.A.	**71**	41 9N	73 25W
Norwalk, Ohio, U.S.A.	**70**	41 13N	82 38W
Norway	**72**	45 46N	87 57W
Norway ■	**111**	67 0N	11 0 E
Norway House	**57**	53 59N	97 50W
Norwegian B.	**65**	77 30N	90 0W
Norwegian Dependency	**91**	66 0N	15 0 E
Norwegian Sea	**12**	66 0N	1 0 E
Norwich, Can.	**46**	42 59N	80 36W
Norwich, U.K.	**94**	52 38N	1 17 E
Norwich, Conn., U.S.A.	**71**	41 33N	72 5W
Norwich, N.Y., U.S.A.	**71**	42 32N	75 30W
Norwood, Can.	**47**	44 23N	77 59W
Norwood, Mass., U.S.A.	**71**	42 10N	71 10W
Norwood, Ohio, U.S.A.	**77**	39 10N	89 27W
Nos Kaliakra, C.	**109**	43 21N	28 30 E
Nose Cr.	**59**	51 3N	114 1W
Noshiro	**132**	40 12N	140 0 E
Noshiro, R.	**132**	40 15N	140 15 E
Nosok	**120**	70 10N	82 20 E
Nosratābād	**123**	29 55N	60 0 E

Noss Hd Okehampton

Noss Hd. 96 58 29N 3 4W
Nossob, R. 117 25 15S 20 30E
Nosy Bé, I. 117 13 25S 48 15E
Nosy Mitsio, I. 117 12 54S 48 36E
Nosy Varika 117 20 35S 48 32E
Notigi Dam 55 56 40N 99 10W
Notikewin 54 56 55N 117 50W
Notikewin, R. 60 57 2N 117 38W
Notituchow 131 24 25N 107 20E
Noto 108 36 52N 15 4E
Noto-Hanto 132 37 0N 137 0E
Notre-Dame, N.B., Can. 39 46 18N 64 46W
Notre-Dame, Qué., Can. 45 45 28N 73 28W
Notre Dame B. 37 49 45N 55 30W
Notre Dame de Koartac 36 60 55N 69 40W
Notre-Dame-de-la-Doré 41 48 43N 72 39W
Notre-Dame-de-l'Île-Perrot 44 45 23N 73 56W
Notre Dame de Lourdes 57 49 32N 98 33W
Notre-Dame-de-Stanbridge 43 45 8N 73 2W
Notre-Dame-des-Bois 41 45 24N 71 4W
Notre-Dame-des-Laurentides 42 46 55N 71 18W
Notre-Dame-du-Bon-Conseil 41 46 0N 72 21W
Notre Dame du Lac 46 46 18N 80 11W
Notre-Dame-du-Lac 41 47 36N 68 48W
Notre-Dame-du-Laus 40 46 5N 75 37W
Notre-Dame-du-Nord 40 47 36N 79 30W
Notre-Dame-du-Portage 41 47 46N 69 37W
Notre-Dame, Les 38 48 10N 68 0W
Nottawasaga B. 46 44 35N 80 15W
Nottaway, R. 36 51 22N 78 55W
Nottingham 94 52 57N 1 10W
Nottingham □ 94 53 10N 1 0W
Nottingham I. 65 63 20N 77 55W
Nottingham Island 65 63 6N 77 50W
Nottoway, R. 72 37 0N 77 45W
Notukeu Cr. 56 49 56N 106 29W
Nouadhibou 114 21 0N 17 0W
Nouakchott 114 18 20N 15 50W
Nouméa 14 22 17S 166 30E
Noupoort 117 31 10S 24 57E
Nouveau Comptoir (Paint Hills) 36 53 0N 78 49W
Nouveau-Quebec, Reg. 36 56 0N 71 0W
Nouvelle 39 48 8N 66 19W
Nouvelle France, C. de 36 62 27N 73 42W
Nouvelle, R. 39 48 7N 66 19W
Nouzonville 101 49 48N 4 44E
Nova Chaves 116 10 50S 21 15E
Nova Cruz 87 6 28S 35 25W
Nova Esperança 89 23 8S 52 13W
Nova Friburgo 89 22 10S 42 30W
Nova Gaia 116 10 10S 17 35E
Nova Iguaçu 89 22 45S 43 28W
Nova Iorque 87 7 0S 44 5W
Nova Lima 89 19 59S 43 51W
Nova Lisboa = Huambo 117 12 42S 15 54E
Nova Mambone 117 21 0S 35 3E
Nova Preixo 117 14 45S 36 22E
Nova Scotia □ 35 45 10N 63 0W
Nova Sofala 117 20 7S 34 48E
Nova Venécia 87 18 45S 40 24W
Nova Zembla I. 65 72 11N 74 50W
Novalorque 87 6 48S 44 0W
Novar 46 45 27N 79 15W
Novara 108 45 27N 8 36E
Novato 80 38 6N 122 35W
Novaya Lyalya 120 58 50N 60 35E
Novaya Sibir, O. 121 75 10N 150 0E
Novaya Zemlya 120 75 0N 56 0E
Nové Zámky 107 48 2N 18 8E
Novelty 76 40 1N 92 12W
Novgorod 120 58 30N 31 25E
Novi-Pazar 109 43 25N 27 15E
Novi Sad 109 45 18N 19 52E
Novinger 76 40 1N 92 43W
Nôvo Hamburgo 89 29 37S 51 7W
Novo Luso 127 4 3S 126 6E
Novoataysk 120 53 30N 84 0E
Novocherkassk 120 47 27N 40 5E
Novokazalinsk 120 45 40N 61 40E
Novokuznetsk 120 54 0N 87 10E
Novomoskovsk 120 54 5N 38 15E
Novorossiysk 120 44 43N 37 52E
Novosibirsk 120 55 0N 83 5E
Novosibirskiye Ostrava 121 75 0N 140 0E
Novska 108 45 19N 17 0E
Novyy Port 120 67 40N 72 30E
Now Shahr 123 36 40N 51 40E
Nowgong 125 26 20N 92 50E
Nowingi 136 34 33S 142 15E
Nowra 136 34 53S 150 35E
Nowy Sącz 107 49 40N 20 41E
Nowy Tomyśl 106 52 19N 16 10E
Noxen 71 41 25N 76 4W
Noxon 78 48 0N 115 54W
Noyant 100 47 30N 0 6E
Noyers 101 47 40N 4 0E
Noyes, I. 54 55 30N 133 40W
Noyon 101 49 34N 3 0E
Nriquinha 117 16 0S 21 25E
Nsanje 117 16 55S 35 12E
Nuanetsi 117 21 15S 30 48E
Nubian Desert 115 21 30N 33 30E
Nûbîya, Es Sahrâ En 115 21 30N 33 30E
Ñuble □ 88 37 0S 72 0W
Nuboai 127 2 10S 136 30E
Nudo Ausangate, Mt. 86 13 45S 71 10W
Nudo de Vilcanota 86 14 30S 70 0W
Nueces, R. 75 28 18N 98 39W
Nueltin L. 55 60 30N 99 30W
Nueva Antioquia 86 6 5N 69 26W
Nueva Casas Grandes 82 30 25N 107 55W
Nueva Esparta □ 86 11 0N 64 0W
Nueva Gerona 84 21 53N 82 49W
Nueva Imperial 90 38 45S 72 58W
Nueva Palmira 88 33 52S 58 20W
Nueva Rosita 82 28 0N 101 20W
Nueva San Salvador 84 13 40N 89 25W
Nuéve de Julio 88 35 30S 61 0W
Nuevitas 84 21 30N 77 20W
Nuevo, Golfo 90 43 0S 64 30W
Nuevo Guerrero 83 26 34N 99 15W
Nuevo Laredo 83 27 30N 99 40W
Nuevo León □ 82 25 0N 100 0W
Nuevo Rocafuerte 86 0 55S 76 50W
Nugget Pt. 133 46 27S 169 50E
Nugssuaq Pen. 65 70 30N 53 0W
Nuhaka 133 39 3S 177 45E
Nuhurowa, I. 127 5 30S 132 45E
Nuits-St.-Georges 101 47 10N 4 56E
Nukey Bluff, Mt. 134 32 32S 135 40E
Nukus 120 42 20N 59 40E
Nulato 67 64 40N 158 10W
Nulki L. 62 53 55N 124 7W
Nulla Nulla 136 33 47S 141 28E
Nullagine 134 21 53S 120 6E
Nullarbor Plain 134 30 45S 129 0E
Numan 114 9 29N 12 3E
Numata 132 36 45N 139 4E
Numazu 132 35 7N 138 51E
Numfoor, I. 127 1 0S 134 50E
Numurkah 136 36 0S 145 26E
Nunaksaluk I. 36 55 49N 60 20W
Nuneaton 95 52 32N 1 29W
Nungan 130 44 29N 125 10E
Nungesser L. 52 51 28N 93 30W
Nunivak I. 67 60 0N 166 0W
Nunkiang 129 49 11N 125 12E
Nunkun, Mt. 124 33 57N 76 8E
Nunspeet 105 52 21N 5 45E
Nuorgam 108 70 5N 27 51E
Nuquí 86 5 42N 77 17W
Nurcoung 136 36 45S 141 42E
Nuremburg = Nürnberg 106 49 26N 11 5E
Nuri 82 28 2N 109 22W
Nürnberg 106 49 26N 11 5E
Nusa Barung 127 8 22S 113 20E
Nusa Kambangan 127 7 47S 109 0E
Nusa Tenggara □ 126 7 30S 117 0E
Nusa Tenggara Barat 126 8 50S 117 30E
Nusa Tenggara Timur 127 9 30S 122 0E
Nushki 124 29 35N 65 65E
Nut L. 56 52 22N 103 42W
Nutak 36 57 28N 61 52W
Nuvuk Is. 36 62 24N 78 3W
Nuwakot 125 28 10N 83 55E
Nuweveldberge 117 32 10S 21 45E
Nuyts Arch. 134 32 12S 133 20E
Nuyts, Pt. 134 35 4S 116 38E
Nyaake (Webo) 114 4 52N 7 37W
Nyabing 134 33 30S 118 7E
Nyack 71 41 5N 73 57W
Nyagyn 120 62 8N 63 36E
Nyah West 136 35 11S 143 21E
Nyahanga 116 2 20S 33 37E
Nyahururu 116 0 2N 36 27E
Nyâlâ 115 12 2N 24 58E
Nyarling, R. 54 60 41N 113 23W
Nyasa, L. = Malawi, L. 117 12 0S 34 30E
Nybro 111 56 44N 15 55E
Nyda 120 66 40N 73 10E
Nyenchen Tanglha Shan 129 30 30N 95 0E
Nyeri 116 0 23S 36 56E
Nyíregyháza 107 48 0N 21 47E
Nykarleby (Uusikaarlepyy) 110 63 32N 22 31E
Nykøbing 111 54 56N 11 52E
Nylstroom 117 24 42S 28 22E
Nynäshamn 111 58 54N 17 57E
Nyngan 136 31 30S 147 8E
Nyons 103 44 22N 5 10E
Nysa 107 50 40N 17 22E
Nysa, R. 106 52 4N 14 46E
Nyssa 78 43 56N 117 2W
Nyurba 121 63 17N 118 20E
Nzega 116 4 10S 33 12E

O

O-Shima 132 34 44N 139 24E
Oacoma 74 43 50N 99 26W
Oahe 74 44 33N 100 29W
Oahe Dam 74 44 28N 100 25W
Oahe Res 74 45 30N 100 15W
Oahu I. 67 21 30N 158 0W
Oak Bay, B.C., Can. 63 48 26N 123 18W
Oak Bay, N.B., Can. 39 45 14N 67 12W
Oak Bluff 58 49 46N 97 19W
Oak Creek, U.S.A. 77 42 52N 87 55W
Oak Creek, Colo., U.S.A. 78 40 15N 106 59W
Oak Harb. 80 48 20N 122 38W
Oak Hill, Can. 39 45 20N 67 20W
Oak Hill, U.S.A. 72 38 0N 81 7W
Oak I. 52 46 57N 90 51W
Oak Lake 57 49 46N 100 38W
Oak Lawn 77 41 43N 87 44W
Oak Park 72 41 55N 87 45W
Oak Point 57 50 30N 98 1W
Oak Ridge 73 36 1N 84 5W
Oak Ridges 50 43 57N 79 28W
Oak River 57 50 8N 100 26W
Oak View 81 34 24N 119 18W
Oakbank 58 49 57N 96 51W
Oakdale, Calif., U.S.A. 80 37 49N 120 56W
Oakdale, La., U.S.A. 75 30 50N 92 38W
Oakengates 94 52 42N 2 29W
Oakes 74 46 14N 98 4W
Oakesdale 78 47 11N 117 9W
Oakford 76 40 6N 89 58W
Oakham 94 52 40N 0 43W
Oakhurst 80 37 19N 119 40W
Oakland, Can. 49 43 2N 80 20W
Oakland, Calif., U.S.A. 80 37 50N 122 18W
Oakland, Ill., U.S.A. 77 39 39N 88 2W
Oakland City 77 38 20N 87 20W
Oakleigh 136 37 54S 145 6E
Oakley 78 42 14N 113 55W
Oakridge 78 43 47N 122 31W
Oaktown 77 38 52N 87 27W
Oakville, Can. 50 43 27N 79 41W
Oakville, U.S.A. 80 46 50N 123 14W
Oakville, R. 49 43 27N 79 41W
Oakwood, Ohio, U.S.A. 77 39 43N 84 11W
Oakwood, Ohio, U.S.A. 77 41 6N 84 23W
Oakwood, Tex., U.S.A. 75 31 35N 95 47W
Oamaru 133 45 5S 170 59E
Oasis, Calif., U.S.A. 81 33 28N 116 6W
Oasis, Nev., U.S.A. 80 37 29N 117 55W
Oates Coast 91 69 0S 160 0E
Oatman 81 35 1N 114 19W
Oaxaca 83 17 2N 96 40W
Oaxaca □ 83 17 0N 97 0W
Ob, R. 120 62 40N 66 0E
Oba 53 49 4N 84 7W
Oba L. 53 48 40N 84 16W
Obakamiga L. 53 49 9N 85 9W
Obalski, L. 40 48 43N 77 58W
Obamsca, L. 40 50 24N 78 16W
Oban, N.Z. 133 46 55S 168 10E
Oban, U.K. 96 56 25N 5 30W
Obatanga Prov. Park 53 48 20N 85 10W
Obatogamau L. 34 49 34N 74 26W
Obbia 115 5 25N 48 30E
Obed 60 53 30N 117 10W
Obedjwan 40 48 40N 74 56W
Obeh 124 34 28N 63 10E
Obera 89 27 21S 55 2W
Oberhausen 105 51 28N 6 50E
Oberlin, Kans., U.S.A. 74 39 52N 100 31W
Oberlin, La., U.S.A. 75 30 42N 92 42W
Oberlin, Ohio, U.S.A. 70 41 15N 82 10W
Obernai 101 48 28N 7 30E
Oberon 136 33 45S 149 52E
Obi, Kepulauan 127 1 30S 127 30E
Óbidos 87 1 50S 55 30W
Obihiro 132 42 25N 143 12E
Objat 102 45 16N 1 24E
Oblong 77 39 0N 87 55W
Obluchye 121 49 10N 130 50E
Obo 116 5 20N 26 32E
Obonga L. 52 49 57N 89 22W
Oboyan 120 51 20N 36 28E
Obozerskaya 120 63 20N 40 15E
Observatory Inlet 54 55 25N 129 45W
Obshchi Syrt 93 52 0N 53 0E
Obskaya Guba 120 70 0N 73 0E
Ocala 73 29 11N 82 5W
Ocampo 82 28 9N 108 8W
Ocaña 104 39 55N 3 30W
Ocanomowoc 74 43 7N 88 30W
Ocate 75 36 12N 104 59W
Occidental, Cordillera 86 5 0N 76 0W
Ocean City, N.J., U.S.A. 72 39 18N 74 34W
Ocean City, Wash., U.S.A. 80 47 4N 124 10W
Ocean Falls 62 52 18N 127 48W
Ocean I. 14 0 45S 169 50E
Ocean Park, Can. 66 49 2N 122 52W
Ocean Park, U.S.A. 80 46 30N 124 2W
Oceanlake 78 45 0N 124 0W
Oceano 81 35 6N 120 37W
Oceanport 71 40 20N 74 3W
Oceanside 81 33 13N 117 26W
Ochil Hills 96 56 14N 3 40W
Ochre River 57 51 4N 99 47W
Ocilla 73 31 35N 83 12W
Ocmulgee, R. 73 32 0N 83 19W
Oconee, R. 73 32 30N 82 55W
Oconomowoc 77 43 6N 88 30W
Oconto 72 44 52N 87 53W
Oconto Falls 72 44 52N 88 10W
Ocós 84 14 31N 92 11W
Ocosingo 83 18 4N 92 15W
Ocotal 84 13 41N 86 41W
Ocotlán 82 20 21N 102 42W
Octave 79 34 10N 112 43W
Octeville 100 49 38N 1 40W
Octyabrskoy Revolyutsii, Os. 121 79 30N 97 0E
Ocumare del Tuy 86 10 7N 66 46W
Ocussi 127 9 20S 124 30E
Odanah 52 46 38N 90 41W
Ódáoahraun 110 65 5N 17 0W
Odawara 132 35 20N 139 6E
Odda 111 60 3N 6 35E
Odei, R. 55 56 6N 96 54W
Odell 77 41 0N 88 31W
Ödemiş 122 38 15N 28 0E
Odense 111 55 22N 10 23E
Oder, R. 106 53 0N 14 12E
Odessa, Ont., Can. 47 44 17N 76 43W
Odessa, Sask., Can. 56 50 17N 103 47W
Odessa, U.S.A. 76 39 0N 93 57W
Odessa, Tex., U.S.A. 75 31 51N 102 23W
Odessa, Wash., U.S.A. 78 47 25N 118 35W
O'Donnell 75 33 0N 101 48W
Odorheiul Secuiesc 107 46 21N 25 21E
Odra, R. 106 52 40N 14 28E
Odžak 109 45 3N 18 18E
Odzi 117 19 0S 32 20E
Oeiras 87 7 0S 42 8W
Oelrichs 74 43 11N 103 14W
O'Fallon 76 38 50N 90 43W
Ofanto, R. 108 41 8N 15 50E
Offaly □ 97 53 15N 7 30W
Offenbach 106 50 6N 8 46E
Offranville 100 49 52N 1 0E
Ofotfjorden 110 68 27N 16 40E
Ogahalla 53 50 6N 85 51W
Ogaki 132 35 21N 136 37E
Ogallala 74 41 12N 101 40W
Ogascanane, L. 40 47 5N 78 25W
Ogbomosho 114 8 1N 3 29E
Ogden, Can. 59 51 0N 114 0W
Ogden, Iowa, U.S.A. 76 42 3N 94 0W
Ogden, Utah, U.S.A. 78 41 13N 112 1W
Ogdensburg 71 44 40N 75 27W
Ogeechee, R. 73 32 30N 81 32W
Ogema 56 49 35N 104 55W
Ogilby 81 32 49N 114 50W
Ogilvie Mts. 64 65 0N 140 0W
Oglesby 76 41 21N 89 3W
Oglio, R. 108 45 15N 10 15E
Ogmore Vale 95 51 35N 3 32W
Ognon, R. 101 47 16N 5 28E
Ogoki 53 51 38N 85 58W
Ogoki L. 53 50 50N 87 10W
Ogoki, R. 53 51 38N 85 57W
Ogoki Res. 52 50 45N 88 15W
Ogooué, R. 116 1 0S 10 0E
Ogowe, R. = Ogooué, R. 116 1 0S 10 0E
Ohai 133 44 55S 168 0E
Ohakune 133 39 24S 175 24E
Ohau, L. 133 44 15S 169 53E
Oheida 76 41 4N 90 13W
Ohey 105 50 26N 5 8E
O'Higgins □ 88 34 15S 71 1W
Ohio □ 72 40 20N 83 0W
Ohio City 77 40 46N 84 37W
Ohio, R. 72 38 0N 86 0W
Ohre, R. 106 50 10N 12 30E
Ohridsko, Jezero 109 41 8N 20 52E
Ohsweken 49 43 4N 80 7W
Oil City 70 41 26N 79 40W
Oil Springs 46 42 47N 82 7W
Oildale 81 35 25N 119 1W
Oise □ 101 49 28N 2 30E
Oise, R. 101 49 53N 3 50E
Oisterwijk 105 51 35N 5 12E
Oita 132 33 14N 131 36E
Oita-ken □ 132 33 15N 131 30E
Oiticica 87 5 3S 41 5W
Ojai 81 34 28N 119 16W
Ojinaga 82 29 34N 104 25W
Ojocaliente 82 30 25N 106 30W
Ojos del Salado 88 27 0S 68 40W
Oka 44 45 28N 74 5W
Oka, R. 120 56 20N 43 59E
Oka-sur-le-Lac 44 45 28N 74 6W
Okahandja 117 22 0S 16 59E
Okak 36 57 33N 61 58W
Okak Is. 36 57 30N 61 30W
Okanagan L. 63 50 0N 119 30W
Okanagan Mission 63 49 45N 119 30W
Okanagan Mountain Prov. Park 63 49 45N 119 30W
Okanogan 63 48 22N 119 35W
Okanogan, R. 78 48 40N 119 24W
Okarito 133 43 15S 170 9E
Okaukuejo 117 19 10S 16 0E
Okavango, R. = Cubango, R. 117 16 15S 18 0E
Okavango Swamp 117 19 30S 23 0E
Okawville 76 38 26N 89 33W
Okaya 132 36 0N 138 10E
Okayama 132 34 40N 133 54E
Okayama-ken □ 132 35 0N 133 50E
Okazaki 132 34 57N 137 10E
Okeechobee 73 27 16N 80 46W
Okeechobee L. 73 27 0N 80 50W
Okefenokee Swamp 73 30 50N 82 15W
Okehampton 95 50 44N 4 1W

Okha Otago □

Okha 121 53 40N 143 0 E
Okhotsk 121 59 20N 143 10 E
Okhotsk, Sea of 121 55 0N 145 0 E
Okhotskiy Perevoz 121 61 52N 135 35 E
Okhotsko Kolymskoy 121 63 0N 157 0 E
Oki no Erabu 131 27 15N 128 45 E
Oki-Shotō 132 36 15N 133 15 E
Okiep 117 29 39 S 17 53 E
Okinawa 131 26 40N 128 0 E
Okinawa-guntō 131 26 0N 127 30 E
Oklahoma □ 75 35 20N 97 30W
Oklahoma City 75 35 25N 97 30W
Okmulgee 75 35 38N 96 0W
Okolona, U.S.A. 75 34 0N 88 45W
Okolona, U.S.A. 77 38 8N 85 41W
Okondja 116 0 35 S 13 45 E
Oku 131 26 35N 127 50 E
Okuru 133 43 55 S 168 55 E
Okushiri-Tō 132 42 15N 139 30 E
Ola 75 35 2N 93 10W
Ólafsfjörður 110 66 4N 18 39W
Ólafsvík 110 64 53N 23 43W
Olancha 81 36 15N 118 1W
Olancha Pk. 81 36 15N 118 7W
Olanchito 85 15 30N 86 30W
Öland 111 56 45N 16 50 E
Olargues 102 43 34N 2 53 E
Olascoaga 88 35 15 S 60 39W
Olathe 74 38 50N 94 50W
Olavarría 88 36 55 S 60 20W
Ólbia 108 40 55N 9 30 E
Old Bahama Chan. 84 22 10N 77 30W
Old Baldy Pk = San Antonio, Mt. 81 34 17N 117 38W
Old Castile = Castilla la Vieja 104 41 55N 4 0W
Old Castle 97 53 46N 7 10W
Old Chelsea 48 45 30N 75 49W
Old Crow 64 67 30N 140 5 E
Old Dale 81 34 8N 115 47W
Old Factory 34 52 36N 78 43W
Old Forge, N.Y., U.S.A. 71 43 43N 74 58W
Old Forge, Pa., U.S.A. 71 41 20N 75 46W
Old Fort, R. 55 58 36N 110 24W
Old Harbor 67 57 12N 153 22W
Old Perlican 37 48 5N 53 1W
Old Speckle, Mt. 71 44 35N 70 57W
Old Town 35 45 0N 68 50W
Old Wives L. 56 50 5N 106 0W
Oldcastle 97 53 46N 7 10W
Oldenburg 105 53 10N 8 10 E
Oldham 94 53 33N 2 8W
Oldman, R. 61 49 57N 111 42W
Olds 61 51 50N 114 10W
Olean 70 42 8N 78 25W
O'Leary 39 46 42N 64 13W
Olekma, R. 121 58 0N 121 30 E
Olekminsk 121 60 40N 120 30 E
Olema 80 38 3N 122 47W
Olenek 121 68 20N 112 30 E
Olenek, R. 121 71 0N 123 50 E
Oléron, I. d' 102 45 55N 1 15W
Oleśnica 107 51 13N 17 22 E
Olga 121 43 50N 135 0 E
Olga, L. 40 49 47N 77 15W
Olga, Mt. 134 25 20 S 130 40 E
Olgastretet 17 78 35N 25 0 E
Olifants, R. 117 24 5 S 31 20 E
Ólimbos, Óros 109 40 6N 22 23 E
Olímpia 89 20 44 S 48 54W
Olimpo □ 88 20 30 S 58 45W
Olin 76 42 0N 91 9W
Oliva 88 32 0 S 63 38W
Olive Hill 77 38 18N 83 13W
Olivehurst 80 39 6N 121 34W
Oliveira 87 20 50 S 44 50W
Olivenza 104 38 41N 7 9W
Oliver 63 49 13N 119 30W
Oliver L. 55 56 56N 103 22W
Ollagüe 88 21 15 S 68 10W
Olmos, L. 88 33 25 S 63 19W
Olney, Ill., U.S.A. 77 38 40N 88 0W
Olney, Tex., U.S.A. 75 33 25N 98 45W
Olomane, R. 36 50 14N 60 37W
Olomouc 106 49 38N 17 12 E
Olongapo 121 14 30N 120 18 E
Oloron-Ste.-Marie 102 43 11N 0 38W
Olovyannaya 121 50 50N 115 10 E
Olsztyn 107 53 48N 20 29 E
Olt, R. 107 43 50N 24 40 E
Oltenița 107 44 7N 26 42 E
Olton 75 34 16N 102 7W
Oltu 122 40 35N 41 50 E
Olympia, Greece 109 37 39N 21 39 E
Olympia, U.S.A. 80 47 0N 122 58W
Olympic Mts. 80 47 50N 123 45W
Olympic Nat. Park 80 47 48N 123 30W
Olympus, Mt. 80 47 52N 123 40W
Olympus, Mt. = Olimbos, Oros 109 40 6N 22 23 E
Olyphant 71 41 27N 75 36W
Omachi 132 36 30N 137 50 E
Omagh 97 54 36N 7 20W
Omagh □ 97 54 35N 7 15W
Omaha 74 41 15N 96 0W
Omak 63 48 24N 119 31W
Omak L. 63 48 16N 119 23W
Oman ■ 122 23 0N 58 0 E
Oman, G. of 123 24 30N 58 30 E
Omaruru 117 21 26 S 16 0 E
Omate 86 16 45 S 71 0W
Ombai, Selat 127 8 30 S 124 50 E
Omboué 116 1 35 S 9 15 E
Ombrone, R. 108 42 48N 11 15 E
Omdurmân 115 15 40N 32 28 E
Omemee 47 44 18N 78 33W
Ometepe, Isla de 84 11 32N 85 35W
Ometepec 83 16 39N 98 23W
Omineca, R. 54 56 3N 124 16W
Ōmiya 132 35 54N 139 38 E
Ommanney B. 65 73 0N 101 0W
Ommen 105 52 31N 6 26 E
Omsk 120 55 0N 73 38 E
Omsukchan 121 62 32N 155 48 E
Omu 130 43 48N 128 10 E
Omul, Vf. 107 45 27N 25 29 E
Omura 132 33 8N 130 0 E
Omuramba, R. 117 19 10 S 19 20 E
Ōmuta 132 33 0N 130 26 E
Onaga 74 39 32N 96 12W
Onakawana 53 50 36N 81 27W
Onalaska 74 43 53N 91 14W
Onaman L. 53 50 0N 87 26W
Onaman, R. 53 49 59N 88 0W
Onamia 74 46 4N 93 38W
Onancock 72 37 42N 75 49W
Onang 127 3 2 S 118 55 E
Onanole 57 50 37N 99 58W
Onaping 46 46 37N 81 25W
Onaping L. 53 47 3N 81 30W
Onaping, R. 46 46 37N 81 18W
Onarga 77 40 43N 88 1W
Onatchiway, L. 41 49 3N 71 5W
Onavas 82 28 28N 109 30W
Onawa 74 42 2N 96 2W
Onaway 46 45 21N 84 11W
Oncocua 117 16 30 S 13 40 E
Onda 104 39 55N 0 17W
Öndörhaan 129 47 19N 110 39 E
Ondorhaan 130 47 22N 110 31 E
Ondverdarnes 110 64 52N 24 0W
One Tree 136 34 13 S 144 42 E
Onega 120 64 0N 38 10 E
Onega, G. of = Onezhskaya G. 120 64 30N 37 0 E
Onega, L. = Onezhskoye Oz. 120 62 0N 35 30 E
Onehunga 133 36 55N 174 30 E
Oneida 71 43 5N 75 40W
Oneida L. 71 43 12N 76 0W
O'Neill 74 42 30N 98 38W
Onekotan, Ostrov 121 49 59N 154 0 E
Oneonta, Ala., U.S.A. 73 33 58N 86 29W
Oneonta, N.Y., U.S.A. 71 42 26N 75 5W
Onezhskoye Ozero 120 62 0N 35 30 E
Ongarue 133 38 42 S 175 19 E
Ongiyn Gol 130 45 56N 103 0 E
Ongole 124 15 33N 80 2 E
Onida 74 44 42N 100 5W
Onilahy, R. 117 23 30 S 44 0 E
Onion Lake 56 53 43N 110 0W
Onitsha 114 6 6N 6 42 E
Onoda 132 33 59N 131 11 E
Onondaga 49 43 7N 80 7W
Onoway 60 53 42N 114 12W
Onslow 134 21 40 S 115 0 E
Onslow B. 73 34 30N 77 0W
Onstwedde 105 52 2N 7 4 E
Ontake-San 132 35 53N 137 29 E
Ontario, Calif., U.S.A. 81 34 2N 117 40W
Ontario, Oreg., U.S.A. 78 44 1N 117 1W
Ontario □ 34 52 0N 88 10W
Ontario, L. 48 43 40N 78 0W
Ontonagon 52 46 52N 89 19W
Onyx 81 35 41N 118 14W
Oodnadatta 134 27 33 S 135 30 E
Ooglaamie 17 72 1N 157 0W
Ookala 67 20 1N 155 17W
Ooldea 134 30 27 S 131 50 E
Oona River 62 53 57N 130 16W
Oostende 105 51 15N 2 50 E
Oosterhout 105 51 39N 4 52 E
Oosterschelde 105 51 33N 4 0 E
Ootacamund 124 11 30N 76 44 E
Ootmarsum 105 52 24N 6 54 E
Ootsa L. 62 53 50N 126 20W
Ootsa Lake 62 53 50N 126 5W
Opala, U.S.S.R. 121 52 15N 156 15 E
Opala, Zaïre 116 1 11 S 24 45 E
Opanake 124 6 35N 80 40 E
Opasatica, L. 40 48 5N 79 18W
Opasatika 53 49 30N 82 50W
Opasatika L. 53 49 4N 83 6W
Opasatika, R. 53 50 25N 82 25W
Opasquia 55 53 16N 93 34W
Opataca, L. 40 50 22N 74 55W
Opava 107 49 57N 17 58 E
Opawica, L. 40 49 35N 75 55W
Opelousas 75 30 35N 92 0W
Opémisca L. 36 50 0N 75 0W
Opémisca, L. 40 49 56N 74 52W
Opeongo L. 47 45 42N 78 23W
Opheim 56 48 52N 106 30W
Ophir 67 63 10N 156 40W
Ophthalmia Ra. 134 23 15 S 119 30 E
Opinaca L. 36 52 39N 76 20W
Opinaca, R. 36 52 15N 78 2W
Opiscoteo, L. 36 53 10N 68 10W
Opiskotish, L. 36 53 10N 67 50W
Opladen 105 51 4N 7 2 E
Opocopa, L. 38 52 38N 66 35W
Opole 107 50 42N 17 58 E
Oporto = Porto 104 41 8N 8 40W
Opotiki 133 38 1 S 177 19 E
Opp 73 31 19N 86 13W
Oppland fylke □ 111 61 15N 9 30 E
Opua 133 35 19 S 174 9 E
Opunake 133 39 26 S 173 52 E
Oquawka 76 40 56N 90 57W
Oracle 79 32 45N 110 46W
Oradea 107 47 2N 21 58 E
Öræfajökull 110 64 2N 16 39W
Orai 124 25 58N 79 30 E
Oraison 103 43 55N 5 55 E
Oran, Alg. 114 35 37N 0 39W
Oran, Argent. 88 23 10 S 64 20W
Orange, Austral. 136 33 15 S 149 7 E
Orange, France 103 44 8N 4 47 E
Orange, Calif., U.S.A. 81 33 47N 117 51W
Orange, Mass., U.S.A. 71 42 35N 72 15W
Orange, Tex., U.S.A. 75 30 10N 93 50W
Orange, Va., U.S.A. 72 38 17N 78 5W
Orange, C. 87 4 20N 51 30W
Orange Cove 80 36 38N 119 19W
Orange Free State □ 117 28 30 S 27 0 E
Orange Grove 75 27 57N 97 57W
Orange, R. = Oranje, R. 117 28 30 S 18 0 E
Orange Walk 83 18 6N 88 33W
Orangeburg 73 33 35N 80 53W
Orangeville, Can. 49 43 55N 80 5W
Orangeville, U.S.A. 76 42 28N 89 39W
Oranienburg 106 52 45N 13 15 E
Oranje, R. 117 28 30 S 18 0 E
Oranje Vrystaat □ 117 28 30 S 27 0 E
Oranjemund (Orange Mouth) 117 28 32 S 16 29 E
Orapa 117 21 13 S 25 25 E
Oras 127 12 9N 125 22 E
Orb, R. 102 43 17N 3 17 E
Orbec 100 49 1N 0 23 E
Orbetello 108 42 26N 11 11 E
Orbost 136 37 40 S 148 29 E
Orcas 63 48 36N 122 57W
Orchies 101 50 28N 3 14 E
Orchila, Isla 85 11 48N 66 10W
Orchy, Bridge of 96 56 30N 4 46W
Orchy, Glen 96 56 27N 4 52W
Orcutt 81 34 52N 120 27W
Ord, Mt. 134 17 20 S 125 34 E
Ord, R. 134 15 33 S 128 35 E
Orderville 79 37 18N 112 43W
Ordos 130 39 25N 108 45 E
Ordu 122 40 55N 37 53 E
Ordway 74 38 15N 103 42W
Ordzhonikidze 120 43 0N 44 35 E
Örebro 111 59 20N 15 18 E
Örebro län □ 111 59 27N 15 0 E
Oregon, U.S.A. 77 41 38N 83 25W
Oregon, Ill., U.S.A. 76 42 1N 89 20W
Oregon, Wis., U.S.A. 76 42 56N 89 23W
Oregon □ 78 44 0N 120 0W
Oregon City 80 45 21N 122 35W
Orel 120 52 57N 36 3 E
Orem 78 40 27N 111 45W
Orenburg 120 51 45N 55 6 E
Orense 104 42 19N 7 55W
Orepuki 133 46 19 S 167 46 E
Orford Ness 95 52 6N 1 31 E
Orgon 103 43 47N 5 3 E
Orhon Gol 129 49 30N 106 0 E
Orient 76 41 12N 94 25W
Orient Bay 34 49 20N 88 10W
Oriente 88 38 44 S 60 37W
Origny-Ste.-Benoîte 101 49 50N 3 30 E
Orihuela 104 38 7N 0 55W
Orillia 46 44 40N 79 24W
Orinoco, Delta del 85 8 30N 61 0W
Orinoco, R. 86 5 45N 67 40W
Orion, Can. 55 49 28N 110 49W
Orion, U.S.A. 76 41 21N 90 23W
Orissa □ 125 21 0N 85 0 E
Oristano 108 39 54N 8 35 E
Oristano, Golfo di 108 39 50N 8 22 E
Orizaba 83 18 50N 97 10W
Orkanger 110 63 18N 9 52 E
Orkla, R. 110 63 18N 9 51 E
Orkney □ 96 59 0N 3 0W
Orkney Is. 96 59 0N 3 0W
Orland, U.S.A. 77 41 47N 85 12W
Orland, Calif., U.S.A. 80 39 46N 122 12W
Orlando 73 28 30N 81 25W
Orléanais 101 48 0N 2 0 E
Orléans 101 47 54N 1 52 E
Orleans 71 44 49N 72 10W
Orléans, Î. d' 42 46 54N 70 58W
Ormara 124 25 16N 64 33 E
Ormiston 56 49 44N 105 24W
Ormoc 127 11 0N 124 37 E
Ormond, N.Z. 133 38 33 S 177 56 E
Ormond, U.S.A. 73 29 13N 81 5W
Ormstown 43 45 8N 74 0W
Ornans 101 47 7N 6 10 E
Orne □ 100 48 40N 0 0 E
Örnsköldsvik 110 63 17N 18 40 E
Oro Grande 81 34 36N 117 20W
Oro, R. 82 26 8N 105 58W
Orocué 86 4 48N 71 20W
Orogrande 79 32 20N 106 4W
Oromocto 39 45 54N 66 29W
Oromocto, L. 39 45 36N 67 0W
Oron, R. 121 69 21N 95 43 E
Orono 47 43 59N 78 37W
Oroquieta 127 8 32N 123 44 E
Orós 87 6 15 S 38 55W
Orosei 108 40 20N 9 40 E
Orotukan 121 62 16N 151 42 E
Oroville, Calif., U.S.A. 80 39 31N 121 30W
Oroville, Wash., U.S.A. 63 48 58N 119 30W
Oroville, Res. 80 39 33N 121 29W
Orr 52 48 3N 92 48W
Orrick 76 39 13N 94 7W
Orrville 70 40 50N 81 46W
Orsainville 42 46 51N 71 14W
Orsha 120 54 30N 30 25 E
Orsk 120 51 12N 58 34 E
Orșova 107 44 41N 22 25 E
Ortegal, C. 104 43 43N 7 52W
Orthez 102 43 29N 0 48W
Ortigueira 104 43 40N 7 50W
Orting 80 47 6N 122 12W
Ortles, mt. 108 46 31N 10 33 E
Ortón, R. 86 10 50 S 67 0W
Ortona 108 42 21N 14 24 E
Oruro 86 18 0 S 67 19W
Orvault 100 47 17N 1 38W
Orvieto 108 42 43N 12 8 E
Orwell 70 41 32N 80 52W
Orwell, R. 95 52 2N 1 12 E
Oryakhovo 109 43 40N 23 57 E
Osa, Pen. de 84 8 0N 84 0W
Osage, Iowa, U.S.A. 74 43 15N 92 50W
Osage, Wyo., U.S.A. 74 43 59N 104 25W
Osage City 74 38 43N 95 51W
Osage, R. 76 38 15N 92 30W
Ōsaka 132 34 30N 135 30 E
Osaka-fu □ 132 34 40N 135 30 E
Osawatomie 74 38 30N 94 55W
Osawin, R. 53 49 45N 85 19W
Osborne 74 39 30N 98 45W
Osborne Corners 49 43 13N 80 16W
Osceola, Ark., U.S.A. 75 35 40N 90 0W
Osceola, Iowa, U.S.A. 76 41 0N 93 20W
Osceola, Mo., U.S.A. 76 38 3N 93 42W
Oscoda-Au-Sable 46 44 26N 83 20W
Osgood 77 39 8N 85 18W
Osgoode 47 45 8N 75 36W
Osh 120 40 37N 72 49 E
Oshawa 51 43 50N 78 50W
Oshawa Cr. 51 43 52N 78 50W
Oshikango 117 17 9 S 16 10 E
Oshkosh, Nebr., U.S.A. 72 41 27N 102 20W
Oshkosh, Wis., U.S.A. 72 44 3N 88 35W
Oshogbo 114 7 48N 4 37 E
Oshwe 116 3 25 S 19 28 E
Osijek 109 45 34N 18 41 E
Oskaloosa 76 41 18N 92 40W
Oskarshamn 111 57 15N 16 27 E
Oskélanéo 40 48 5N 75 15W
Osler 56 52 22N 106 33W
Oslo 111 59 55N 10 45 E
Oslob 127 9 31N 123 26 E
Oslofjorden 111 59 20N 10 35 E
Osmanabad 124 18 5N 76 10 E
Osmaniye 122 37 5N 36 10 E
Osnabrück 105 52 16N 8 2 E
Osnaburgh L. 52 51 12N 90 9W
Osorio 89 29 53 S 50 17W
Osorno 90 40 25 S 73 0W
Osorno, Vol. 90 41 0N 72 30W
Osoyoos 63 49 0N 119 30W
Osoyoos L. 63 49 0N 119 27W
Ospika, R. 54 56 20N 124 0W
Osprey Reef 135 13 52 S 146 36 E
Ospringe 49 43 42N 80 7W
Oss 105 51 46N 5 32 E
Ossa, Mt. 135 41 52 S 146 3 E
Ossa, Oros 109 39 47N 22 42 E
Ossabaw I. 73 31 45N 81 8W
Ossineke 46 44 55N 83 26W
Ossining 71 41 9N 73 50W
Ossipee 71 43 41N 71 9W
Ossokmanuan L. 36 53 25N 65 0W
Ossora 121 59 20N 163 13 E
Ostaboningue, L. 40 47 9N 78 53W
Ostend = Oostende 105 51 15N 2 50 E
Österdalälven 111 61 30N 13 45 E
Östergötlands Län □ 111 58 35N 15 45 E
Östersund 110 63 10N 14 38 E
Østfold fylke □ 111 59 25N 11 25 E
Ostfriesische Inseln 106 53 45N 7 15 E
Ostfriesland 105 53 27N 7 30 E
Ostia 108 41 40N 12 20 E
Ostrava 107 49 51N 18 18 E
Ostróda 107 53 42N 19 58 E
Ostrołeka 107 53 4N 21 38 E
Ostrów Mazowiecka 107 52 50N 21 51 E
Ostrów Wielkopolski 107 51 36N 17 44 E
Ostrowiec-Swietokrzyski 107 50 55N 21 22 E
O'Sullivan L. 53 50 25N 87 2W
Osumi-Kaikyō 132 30 55N 131 0 E
Osumi-Shotō 132 30 30N 130 45 E
Osuna 104 37 14N 5 8W
Oswego 71 43 29N 76 30W
Oswestry 94 52 52N 3 3W
Otago □ 133 45 20 S 169 20 E

Otago Harb Panhandle

Otago Harb. 133 45 47 S 170 42 E
Otake 132 34 12N 132 13 E
Otaki 133 40 45 S 175 10 E
Otaru 132 43 10N 141 0 E
Otaru-Wan 132 43 25N 141 1 E
Otavalo 86 0 20N 78 20W
Otavi 117 19 40 S 17 24 E
Otelnuk L. 36 56 9N 68 12W
Othello 78 46 53N 119 8W
Otira Gorge 133 42 53 S 171 33 E
Otis 74 40 12N 102 58W
Otish, Mts. 36 52 22N 70 30W
Otjiwarongo 117 20 30 S 16 33 E
Otorohanga 133 38 12 S 175 14 E
Otoskwin, R. 34 52 13N 88 6W
Otosquen 57 53 17N 102 1W
Otranto 109 40 9N 18 28 E
Otranto, C.d' 109 40 7N 18 30 E
Otranto, Str. of 109 40 15N 18 40 E
Otsego 77 42 27N 85 42W
Ottawa, Can. 48 45 27N 75 42W
Ottawa, Ill., U.S.A. 77 41 20N 88 55W
Ottawa, Kans., U.S.A. 74 38 40N 95 10W
Ottawa, Ohio, U.S.A. 77 41 1N 84 3W
Ottawa-Carleton □ 48 45 23N 75 40W
Ottawa International Airport 48 45 19N 75 40W
Ottawa Is. 23 59 35N 80 16W
Ottawa, R. 44 45 20N 73 55W
Otter L. 55 55 35N 104 39W
Otter Lake 46 43 13N 83 28W
Otter Rapids, Ont., Can. 53 50 11N 81 39W
Otter Rapids, Sask., Can. 55 55 38N 104 44W
Otterbein 77 40 29N 87 6W
Otterburn Park 45 45 32N 73 13W
Otterville, Can. 46 42 55N 80 36W
Otterville, U.S.A. 76 38 42N 93 0W
Ottoville 77 40 57N 84 22W
Ottumwa 76 41 0N 92 25W
Otway, Bahía 90 53 30 S 74 0W
Otway, C. 136 38 52 S 143 30 E
Otwock 107 52 5N 21 20 E
Ötztaler Alpen 106 46 58N 11 0 E
Ou, R. 128 20 4N 102 13 E
Ou-Sammyaku 132 39 20N 140 35 E
Ouachita Mts. 75 34 50N 94 30W
Ouachita, R. 75 33 0N 92 15W
Ouadda 116 8 15N 22 20 E
Ouagadougou 114 12 25N 1 30W
Ouanda Djallé 116 8 55N 22 53 E
Ouango 116 4 19N 22 30 E
Ouareau, L., Rés. 41 46 17N 74 9W
Ouargla 114 31 59N 5 25 E
Ouasiemsca, R. 41 49 0N 72 30W
Oubangi, R. 116 1 0N 17 50 E
Ouche, R. 101 47 11N 5 10 E
Oude Rijn, R. 105 52 12N 4 24 E
Oudenaarde 105 50 50N 3 37 E
Oudenbosch 105 51 35N 4 32 E
Oudon 100 47 22N 1 19W
Oudon, R. 100 47 47N 1 2W
Oudtshoorn 117 33 35 S 22 14 E
Ouessant, Île d' 100 48 28N 5 6W
Ouesso 116 1 37N 16 5 E
Ouest, Pte. 38 49 52N 64 40W
Ougrée 105 50 36N 5 32 E
Ouimet 34 48 43N 88 35W
Ouistreham 100 49 17N 0 18W
Oulu 110 65 1N 25 29 E
Oulu □ 110 65 10N 27 20 E
Oulujärvi 110 64 25N 27 0 E
Oulujoki 110 64 45N 26 30 E
Ouray 79 38 3N 107 48W
Ouricuri 87 7 53 S 40 5W
Ourinhos 89 23 0 S 49 54W
Ouro Fino 89 22 16 S 46 25W
Ouro Prêto 89 20 20 S 43 30W
Ourthe, R. 105 50 29N 5 35 E
Ouse, Great, R. 94 52 12N 0 7 E
Ouse, Little, R. 95 52 25N 0 20 E
Ouse, R., Sussex, U.K. 95 50 58N 0 3 E
Ouse, R., Yorks., U.K. 94 54 3N 0 7 E
Oust 102 42 52N 1 13 E
Oust, R. 100 48 8N 2 49W
Oustic 49 43 42N 80 15W
Outaouais, R. 48 45 28N 75 38W
Outardes 41 50 20N 69 10W
Outardes, R. 41 49 24N 69 30W
Outer Hebrides, Is. 96 57 30N 7 40W
Outer I., Can. 36 51 10N 58 35W
Outer I., U.S.A. 52 47 5N 90 30W
Outjo 117 20 5 S 16 7 E
Outlook, Can. 56 51 30N 107 0W
Outlook, U.S.A. 56 48 53N 104 46W
Outreau 101 50 40N 1 36 E
Outremount 44 45 31N 73 37W
Ouyen 136 35 1 S 142 22 E
Ouzouer-le-Marché 100 47 54N 1 32 E
Ovalau, I. 133 17 40 S 178 48 E
Ovalle 88 30 33 S 71 18W
Ovamboland = Owambo 117 17 20 S 16 30 E
Ovar 104 40 51N 8 40W
Ovejas 86 9 32N 75 14W
Ovens, R. 136 36 2 S 146 12 E
Overflakkee 105 51 44N 4 10 E
Overflowing, R. 57 53 8N 101 5W
Overijssel □ 105 52 25N 6 35 E
Overland 76 38 41N 90 23W
Overland Park 76 38 58N 94 40W
Overton 81 36 32N 114 31W
Övertorneå 110 66 23N 23 40 E
Ovid, Colo., U.S.A. 74 41 0N 102 17W
Ovid, Mich., U.S.A. 46 43 1N 84 22W
Oviedo 104 43 25N 5 50W
Ovruch 120 51 25N 28 45 E
Owaka 133 46 27 S 169 40 E
Owambo 117 17 20 S 16 30 E
Owase 132 34 7N 136 5 E
Owatonna 74 44 3N 93 17W
Owego 71 42 6N 76 17W
Owen Sound 46 44 35N 80 55W
Owendo 116 0 17N 9 30 E
Owens L. 81 36 20N 118 0W
Owens, R. 80 36 32N 117 59W
Owensboro 77 37 40N 87 5W
Owensville, U.S.A. 77 38 16N 87 41W
Owensville, Mo., U.S.A. 76 38 20N 91 30W
Owenton 77 38 32N 84 50W
Owikeno L. 62 51 40N 126 50W
Owingsville 77 38 9N 83 46W
Owl, R. 55 57 51N 92 44W
Owosso 77 43 0N 84 10W
Owyhee 78 42 0N 116 3W
Owyhee, R. 78 43 10N 117 37W
Owyhee Res. 78 43 30N 117 30W
Ox Mts. 97 54 6N 9 0W
Oxbow 57 49 14N 102 10W
Oxelösund 111 58 43N 17 15 E
Oxford, Can. 39 45 44N 63 52W
Oxford, N.Z. 133 43 18 S 172 11 E
Oxford, U.K. 95 51 45N 1 15W
Oxford, U.S.A. 76 41 43N 91 47W
Oxford, Mich., U.S.A. 46 42 49N 83 16W
Oxford, Mich., U.S.A. 77 42 49N 83 16W
Oxford, Miss., U.S.A. 75 34 22N 89 30W
Oxford, N.C., U.S.A. 73 36 19N 78 36W
Oxford, Ohio, U.S.A. 77 39 30N 84 40W
Oxford □ 95 51 45N 1 15W
Oxford L. 55 54 51N 95 37W
Oxleys Pk. 136 31 51 S 150 22 E
Oxnard 81 34 10N 119 14W
Oya 126 2 55N 111 55 E
Oyama 63 50 7N 119 22W
Oyem 116 1 42N 11 43 E
Oyen 61 51 22N 110 28W
Oykell, R. 96 57 55N 4 26W
Oymyakon 121 63 25N 143 10 E
Oyo 114 7 46N 3 56 E
Oyonnax 103 46 16N 5 40 E
Oyster B. 71 40 52N 73 32W
Oyster River 62 49 53N 125 7W
Ozaka 132 34 40N 135 30 E
Ozamis (Mizamis) 127 8 15N 123 50 E
Ozark, Ala., U.S.A. 73 31 29N 85 39W
Ozark, Ark., U.S.A. 75 35 30N 93 50W
Ozark, Mo., U.S.A. 75 37 0N 93 15W
Ozark Plateau 75 37 20N 91 40W
Ozarks, L. of 76 38 10N 93 0W
Ozette, L. 80 48 6N 124 38W
Ozona 75 30 43N 101 11W
Ozuluama 83 21 40N 97 50W

P

Pa-an 125 16 45N 97 40 E
Pa Sak, R. 128 15 30N 101 0 E
Paan (Batang) 129 30 0N 99 3 E
Paarl 117 33 45 S 18 56 E
Paatsi, R. 110 68 55N 29 0 E
Paauilo 67 20 3N 155 22W
Pab Hills 124 26 30N 66 45 E
Pabna 124 24 1N 89 18 E
Pabos Mills 38 48 19N 64 42W
Pacajá, R. 87 1 56 S 50 50W
Pacasmayo 86 7 20 S 79 35W
Pacaudière, La 101 46 11N 3 52 E
Pacho 86 5 8N 74 10W
Pachpadra 124 25 58N 72 10 E
Pachuca 83 20 10N 98 40W
Pachung 131 31 58N 106 40 E
Pacific, Can. 54 54 48N 128 28W
Pacific, U.S.A. 76 38 29N 90 45W
Pacific Grove 80 36 38N 121 58W
Pacific Ocean 14 10 0N 140 0W
Pacific Rim Nat. Park 62 48 40N 124 45W
Pacifica 80 37 36N 122 30W
Packenham 47 45 22N 76 25W
Packwood 80 46 36N 121 40W
Pacofi 54 53 0N 132 30W
Pacquet 37 50 0N 55 53W
Pacy-sur-Eure 100 49 1N 1 23 E
Padaido, Kepulauan 127 1 5 S 138 0 E
Padalarang 127 7 50 S 107 30 E
Padang 126 1 0 S 100 20 E
Padang, I. 126 1 0 S 100 0 E
Padangsidimpuan 126 1 30N 99 15 E
Paddockwood 56 53 30N 105 30W
Paderborn 106 51 42N 8 44 E
Padlei 55 62 10N 97 5W
Padloping Island 65 67 0N 63 0W
Pádova 108 45 24N 11 52 E
Padre I. 75 27 0N 97 20W
Padstow 95 50 33N 4 57W
Padua = Pádova 108 45 24N 11 52 E
Paducah, Ky., U.S.A. 72 37 0N 88 40W
Paducah, Tex., U.S.A. 75 34 3N 100 16W
Paeroa 133 37 23 S 175 41 E
Pag, I. 108 44 30N 14 50 E
Pagadian 127 7 55N 123 30 E
Pagai Selatan, I. 126 3 0 S 100 15W
Pagai Utara, I. 126 2 35 S 100 0 E
Pagalu, I. 112 1 35 S 3 35 E
Pagaralam 126 4 0 S 103 17 E
Pagastikós Kólpos 109 39 15N 23 12 E
Pagatan 126 3 33 S 115 59 E
Page 74 47 11N 97 37W
Pagny-sur-Moselle 101 48 59N 6 2 E
Pago Pago 133 14 16 S 170 43W
Pagosa Springs 79 37 16N 107 4W
Pagwa River 53 50 2N 85 14W
Pagwachuan, R. 53 50 12N 84 43W
Pahala 67 20 25N 156 0W
Pahang □ 128 3 40N 102 20 E
Pahang, R. 128 3 30N 103 9 E
Pahiatua 133 40 27 S 175 50 E
Pahoa 67 19 30N 154 57W
Pahokee 73 26 50N 80 30W
Pahrump 81 36 15N 116 0W
Paia 67 20 54N 156 22W
Paicheng 130 45 50N 122 53 E
Paicines 80 36 44N 121 17W
Paignton 95 50 26N 3 33W
Päijänne 111 61 30N 25 30 E
Pailin 128 12 46N 102 36 E
Pailolo Chan. 67 21 5N 156 42W
Paimbœuf 100 47 17N 2 0W
Paimpol 100 48 48N 3 4W
Paimpont, L. 38 50 28N 61 34W
Painan 126 1 15 S 100 40 E
Painesdale 52 47 2N 88 41W
Painesville 70 41 42N 81 18W
Paint l. 55 55 28N 97 57W
Paint Rock 75 31 30N 99 56W
Painted Desert 79 36 40N 111 30W
Paintsville 72 37 50N 82 50W
Paipa 86 5 47N 73 7W
Paisley, Can. 46 44 18N 81 16W
Paisley, U.K. 96 55 51N 4 27W
Paisley, U.S.A. 78 42 43N 120 40W
Paita 86 5 5 S 81 0W
Paix, Îles de la 44 45 20N 73 51W
Paiyin 130 36 45N 104 4 E
Paiyü Shan, mts. 130 37 20N 107 30 E
Paiyunopo 130 41 46N 109 58 E
Pajares 104 39 57N 1 48W
Pak Lay 128 18 15N 101 27 E
Pakanbaru 126 0 30N 101 15 E
Pakaraima, Sierra 86 6 0N 60 0W
Pakashkan L. 52 49 21N 90 15W
Pakenham 71 45 18N 76 18W
Pakhoi 131 21 30N 109 10 E
Pakistan ■ 124 30 0N 70 0 E
Pakokku 125 21 30N 95 0 E
Pakonghow 131 23 50N 113 0 E
Pakowi L. 61 49 20N 111 0W
Pakse 128 15 5N 105 52 E
Paktya □ 124 33 0N 69 15 E
Pakwash L. 52 50 45N 93 30W
Pala 81 33 22N 117 5W
Palacios 75 28 44N 96 12W
Palagruza 108 42 24N 16 15 E
Palais, Le 100 47 20N 3 10W
Palam 124 19 0N 77 0 E
Palamós 104 41 50N 3 10 E
Palampur 124 32 10N 76 30 E
Palana 121 59 10N 160 10 E
Palanan 127 17 8N 122 29 E
Palanpur 124 24 10N 72 25 E
Palapye 117 22 30 S 27 7 E
Palatine 77 42 7N 88 3W
Palatka 73 29 40N 81 40W
Palau Is. 14 7 30N 134 30 E
Palauig 127 15 26N 119 54 E
Palauk 128 13 10N 98 40 E
Palavas 102 43 32N 3 56 E
Palawan, I. 126 10 0N 119 0 E
Palayancottai 124 8 45N 77 45 E
Palchewoflock 136 35 20 S 142 15 E
Paleleh 127 1 10N 121 50 E
Palembang 126 3 0 S 104 50 E
Palencia 104 42 1N 4 34W
Palermo, Can. 49 43 26N 79 47W
Palermo, Colomb. 86 2 54N 75 26W
Palermo, Italy 108 38 8N 13 20 E
Palermo, U.S.A. 78 39 30N 121 37W
Palestine, Asia 115 32 0N 35 0 E
Palestine, U.S.A. 75 31 42N 95 35W
Paletwa 125 21 30N 92 50 E
Palghat 124 10 46N 76 42 E
Palgrave 49 43 57N 79 50W
Pali 124 25 50N 73 20 E
Palinyuch'i (Tapanshang) 130 43 40N 118 20 E
Palisade 74 40 35N 101 10W
Palitana 124 21 32N 71 49 E
Palizada 83 18 18N 92 8W
Palk Bay 124 9 30N 79 30 E
Palk Strait 124 10 0N 80 0 E
Palm Beach 73 26 46N 80 0W
Palm Desert 81 33 43N 116 22W
Palm Is. 135 18 40 S 146 35 E
Palm Springs 81 33 51N 116 35W
Palma, Canary Is. 93 28 40N 17 50W
Palma, Mozam. 116 10 46 S 40 29 E
Palma, Bahía de 104 39 30N 2 39 E
Palma, La, Panama 84 8 15N 78 0W
Palma, La, Spain 104 37 21N 6 38W
Palma, R. 87 10 10N 71 50W
Palma Soriano 84 20 15N 76 0W
Palmares 87 8 41 S 35 36W
Palmarito 86 7 37N 70 10W
Palmarolle 40 48 40N 79 12W
Palmas 89 26 29 S 52 0W
Palmas, C. 114 4 27N 7 46W
Pálmas, G. di 108 39 0N 8 30 E
Palmdale 81 34 36N 118 7W
Palmeira dos Índios 87 9 25 S 36 37W
Palmer, Alaska, U.S.A. 67 61 35N 149 10W
Palmer, Mass., U.S.A. 71 42 9N 72 21W
Palmer Arch 91 64 15 S 65 0W
Palmer Lake 74 39 10N 104 52W
Palmer Pen. 91 73 0 S 60 0W
Palmer, R., N. Terr., Austral. 134 24 30 S 133 0 E
Palmer, R., Queens., Austral. 134 16 5 S 142 43 E
Palmerston, Can. 70 43 50N 80 40W
Palmerston, Ont., Can. 46 43 50N 80 51W
Palmerston, N.Z. 133 45 29 S 170 43 E
Palmerston, C. 135 21 32 S 149 29 E
Palmerston North 133 40 21 S 175 39 E
Palmerton 71 40 47N 75 36W
Palmetto 73 27 33N 82 33W
Palmi 108 38 21N 15 51 E
Palmira, Argent. 88 32 59 S 68 25W
Palmira, Colomb. 86 3 32N 76 16W
Palms 46 43 37N 82 47W
Palmyra, U.S.A. 77 42 52N 88 36W
Palmyra, Ill., U.S.A. 76 39 26N 90 0W
Palmyra, Mo., U.S.A. 76 39 45N 91 30W
Palmyra, N.Y., U.S.A. 70 34 5N 77 18W
Palmyra = Tadmor 122 34 30N 37 55 E
Palni Hills 124 10 14N 77 33 E
Palo Alto 80 37 25N 122 8W
Palo Verde 81 33 26N 114 45W
Paloe 127 8 20 S 121 43 E
Paloma, La 88 30 35 S 71 0W
Palomar 53 48 10N 82 16W
Palopo 127 3 0 S 120 16 E
Palos, Cabo de 104 37 38N 0 40W
Palos Verdes 81 33 48N 118 23W
Palos Verdes, Pt. 81 33 43N 118 26W
Palouse 78 46 59N 117 5W
Palu, Indon. 127 1 0 S 119 59 E
Palu, Turkey 122 38 45N 40 0 E
Paluan 127 13 35N 120 29 E
Pamamaroo, L. 136 32 17 S 142 28 E
Pamanukan 127 6 16 S 107 49 E
Pamekasan 127 7 10 S 113 29 E
Pameungpeuk 127 7 38 S 107 44 E
Pamiencheng 130 43 16N 124 4 E
Pamiers 102 43 7N 1 39 E
Pamirs, Ra. 120 37 40N 73 0 E
Pamlico, R. 73 35 25N 76 40W
Pamlico Sd. 73 35 20N 76 0W
Pampa 75 35 35N 100 58W
Pampa de las Salinas 88 32 1 S 66 58W
Pampa, La □ 88 36 50 S 66 0W
Pampanua 127 4 22 S 120 14 E
Pampas, Argent. 88 34 0 S 64 0W
Pampas, Peru 86 12 20 S 74 50W
Pamplona, Colomb. 86 7 23N 72 39W
Pamplona, Spain 104 42 48N 1 38W
Pana 76 39 25N 89 10W
Panaca 79 37 51N 114 50W
Panache, L. 46 46 15N 81 20W
Panaitan, I. 127 6 35 S 105 10 E
Panaji (Panjim) 124 15 25N 73 50 E
Panamá 84 9 0N 79 25W
Panama ■ 84 8 48N 79 55W
Panama Canal 84 9 10N 79 56W
Panama Canal Zone 84 9 10N 79 56W
Panama City 73 30 10N 85 41W
Panamá, Golfo de 84 8 4N 79 20W
Panamint Mts. 79 36 15N 117 20W
Panamint Springs 81 36 20N 117 28W
Panão 86 9 55 S 75 55W
Panarukan 127 7 40 S 113 52 E
Panay, G. 127 11 0N 122 30 E
Panay I. 127 11 10N 122 30 E
Pancake Ra. 79 38 30N 116 0W
Pančevo 109 44 52N 20 41 E
Pancorbo, Paso 104 42 32N 3 5W
Pandan 127 11 45N 122 10 E
Pandangpanjang 126 0 40 S 100 20 E
Pandeglang 127 6 25 S 106 0 E
Pandharpur 124 17 41N 75 20 E
Pando 89 34 30 S 56 0W
Panfilov 120 44 30N 80 0 E
Pang-Long 125 23 11N 98 45 E
Pangani 116 5 25 S 38 58 E
Pangi 116 3 10 S 26 35 E
Pangkalanberandan 126 4 1N 98 20 E
Pangkalansusu 126 4 2N 98 42 E
Pangkiang (Mingan) 130 43 4N 112 30 E
Pangkoh 126 3 5 S 114 8 E
Pangmar 56 49 39N 104 40W
Pangong Tso, L. 124 34 0N 78 20 E
Pangrango 127 6 46 S 107 1 E
Panguitch 79 37 52N 112 30W
Pangutaran Group 127 6 18N 120 34 E
Panhandle 75 35 23N 101 23W

Panjgur Pelican Rapids

Panjgur 124 27 0N 64 5 E
Panjim = Panaji 124 15 25N 73 50 E
Panjinad Barrage 124 29 22N 71 15 E
Pankadjene 127 4 46 S 119 34 E
Pankal Pinang 126 2 0 S 106 0 E
Panna 124 24 40N 80 15 E
Panny, R. 60 57 8N 114 51W
Panora 76 41 41N 94 22W
Panorama 89 21 21 S 51 51W
Panshan 130 41 15N 122 0 E
Panshih 130 42 59N 126 0 E
Pantano 79 32 0N 110 32W
Pantar, I. 127 8 28 S 124 10 E
Pantelleria, I. 108 36 52N 12 0 E
Pantjo 127 8 42 S 118 40 E
Pantukan 127 7 17N 125 58 E
Panuco 83 22 0N 98 25W
Paochang 130 41 46N 115 30 E
Paocheng 131 33 12N 107 0 E
Paokang 131 31 57N 111 21 E
Paoki 131 34 25N 107 15 E
Paoko 131 34 22N 107 12 E
Paola 74 38 36N 94 50W
Paoli 77 31 33N 86 28W
Paonia 79 38 56N 107 37W
Paoshan 125 25 7N 99 9 E
Paoteh 130 39 0N 110 45 E
Paoting 130 38 50N 115 30 E
Paotow 130 40 45N 110 0 E
Paotsing 131 28 35N 109 35 E
Paoua 116 7 25N 16 30 E
Papá 107 47 22N 17 30 E
Papagayo, Golfo de 84 10 4N 85 50W
Papagayo, R., Brazil 82 12 30 S 58 10W
Papagayo, R., Mexico 83 16 36N 99 43W
Papaikou 67 19 47N 155 6W
Papakura 133 37 4 S 174 59 E
Papaloapan, R. 82 18 2N 96 51W
Papantla 83 20 45N 97 21W
Papar 126 5 45N 116 0 E
Papenburg 105 53 7N 7 25 E
Papigochic, R. 82 29 9N 109 40W
Papineau-Labelle, Parc Prov. 40 46 10N 75 15W
Papineauville 40 45 37N 75 1W
Paposo 88 25 0 S 70 30W
Papua New Guinea ■ 14 8 0 S 145 0 E
Papudo 88 32 29 S 71 27W
Papun 125 18 0N 97 30 E
Pará = Belém 87 1 20 S 48 30W
Pará □ 87 3 20 S 52 0W
Paracatú 87 17 10 S 46 50W
Paracel Is. 126 16 49N 111 2 E
Paradip 125 20 15N 86 35 E
Paradis 40 48 15N 76 35W
Paradise, Calif., U.S.A. 80 39 46N 121 37W
Paradise, Mich., U.S.A. 46 46 38N 85 3W
Paradise, Mont., U.S.A. 78 47 27N 114 54W
Paradise, Nev., U.S.A. 81 36 4N 115 7W
Paradise Hill 56 53 32N 109 28W
Paradise, R. 36 53 27N 57 19W
Paradise Valley, Can. 61 53 2N 110 17W
Paradise Valley, U.S.A. 78 41 30N 117 28W
Parado 127 8 42 S 118 30 E
Paragould 75 36 5N 90 30W
Paragua, La 86 6 50N 63 20W
Paragua, R. 86 6 30N 63 30W
Paraguaçu Paulista 89 22 22 S 50 35W
Paraguaçu, R. 87 12 45 S 38 54W
Paraguai, R. 86 16 0 S 57 52W
Paraguaipoa 86 11 21N 71 57W
Paraguana, Pen. de 86 12 0N 70 0W
Paraguarí 88 25 36 S 57 0W
Paraguarí □ 88 26 0 S 57 10W
Paraguay ■ 88 23 0 S 57 0W
Paraguay, R. 88 27 18 S 58 38W
Paraíba = Joéo Pessoa 82 7 10 S 35 0W
Paraíba □ 87 7 0 S 36 0W
Paraíba do Sul, R. 89 21 37 S 41 3W
Parainen 111 60 18N 22 18 E
Paraíso 83 19 3 S 52 59W
Paraiso 83 18 24N 93 14W
Parakou 114 9 25N 2 40 E
Paramaribo 87 5 50N 55 10W
Paramillo, Nudo del 86 7 4N 75 55W
Paramushir, Ostrov 121 40 24N 156 0 E
Paraná 88 32 0 S 60 30W
Paranã 87 12 30 S 47 40W
Paraná □ 89 24 30 S 51 0W
Paraná, R. 88 33 43 S 59 15W
Paranã, R. 87 22 25 S 53 1W
Paranaguá 89 25 30 S 48 30W
Paranaíba, R. 87 18 0 S 49 12W
Paranapanema, R. 89 22 40 S 53 9W
Paranapiacaba, Serra do 89 24 31 S 48 35W
Paranavaí 89 23 4 S 52 28W
Parang, Jolo, Phil. 127 5 55N 120 54 E
Parang, Mindanao, Phil. 127 7 23N 124 16 E
Paratinga 87 12 40 S 43 10W
Paray-le-Monial 103 46 27N 4 7 E
Parbhani 124 19 8N 76 52 E
Parchim 106 53 25N 11 50 E
Pardee Res. 80 38 16N 120 51W
Pardo, R., Bahia, Brazil 87 15 40 S 39 0W
Pardo, R., Mato Grosso, Brazil 87 21 0 S 53 25W
Pardo, R., São Paulo, Brazil 87 20 45 S 48 0W
Pardubice 106 50 3N 15 45 E
Pare 127 7 43 S 112 12 E
Pare Pare 127 4 0 S 119 45 E
Parecis, Serra dos 86 13 0 S 60 0W
Paren 121 62 45N 163 0 E
Parent 40 47 55N 74 35W
Parent, Lac. 40 48 31N 77 1W
Parentis-en-Born 102 44 21N 1 4W
Parepare 127 4 0 S 119 40 E
Parfuri 117 22 28 S 31 17 E
Parham, Can. 71 44 40N 76 40W
Parham, Ont., Can. 47 44 39N 76 43W
Paria, Golfo de 86 10 20N 62 0W
Paria, Pen. de 86 10 50N 62 30W
Pariaguán 86 8 51N 64 43W
Pariaman 126 0 47 S 100 11 E
Paricutín, Cerro 82 19 28N 102 15W
Parigi 127 0 50 S 120 5 E
Parika 86 6 50N 58 20W
Parima, Serra 86 2 30N 64 0W
Parinari 86 4 35 S 74 25W
Parîngul-Mare, mt. 107 45 20N 23 37 E
Parintins 87 2 40 S 56 50W
Pariparit Kyun 125 14 55 S 93 45 E
Paris, Can. 49 43 12N 80 25W
Paris, France 101 48 50N 2 20 E
Paris, U.S.A. 76 39 29N 92 0W
Paris, Idaho, U.S.A. 78 42 13N 111 30W
Paris, Ill., U.S.A. 77 39 36N 87 42W
Paris, Ky., U.S.A. 77 38 12N 84 12W
Paris, Tenn., U.S.A. 73 36 20N 88 20W
Paris, Tex., U.S.A. 75 33 40N 95 30W
Parish 71 43 24N 76 9W
Pariti 127 9 55 S 123 30 E
Park 80 48 45N 122 18W
Park City 78 40 42N 111 35W
Park Falls 74 45 58N 90 27W
Park Head 70 44 36N 81 10W
Park Range 78 40 0N 106 30W
Park Rapids 74 46 56N 95 0W
Park Ridge 77 42 2N 87 51W
Park River 74 48 25N 97 50W
Park Royal 66 49 20N 123 8W
Park View 79 36 45N 106 37W
Parker, Can. 49 43 46N 80 35W
Parker, Ariz., U.S.A. 81 34 8N 114 16W
Parker, S.D., U.S.A. 74 43 25N 97 7W
Parker Dam 81 34 13N 114 5W
Parkersburg, U.S.A. 76 42 35N 92 47W
Parkersburg, W. Va., U.S.A. 72 39 18N 81 31W
Parkerview 56 51 21N 103 18W
Parkes, A.C.T., Austral. 135 35 18 S 149 8 E
Parkes, N.S.W., Austral. 136 33 9 S 148 11 E
Parkfield 80 35 54N 120 26W
Parkhill 46 43 15N 81 38W
Parkland 80 47 9N 122 26W
Parks L. 53 49 27N 87 38W
Parkside 56 53 10N 106 33W
Parkston 74 43 25N 98 0W
Parksville 62 49 20N 124 21W
Parma, Italy 108 44 50N 10 20 E
Parma, Idaho, U.S.A. 78 43 49N 116 59W
Parma, Ohio, U.S.A. 70 41 25N 81 42W
Parnaguá 87 10 10 S 44 10W
Parnaiba, Piauí, Brazil 87 3 0 S 41 40W
Parnaiba, São Paulo, Brazil 87 19 34 S 51 14W
Parnaíba, R. 87 3 35 S 43 0W
Parnassós, mt. 109 38 17N 21 30 E
Pärnu 120 58 12N 24 33 E
Paroo Chan. 135 30 50 S 143 35 E
Paroo, R. 135 30 0 S 144 5 E
Paropamisus Range = Fīroz Kohi 123 34 45N 63 0 E
Páros, I. 109 37 5N 25 12 E
Parowan 79 37 54N 112 56W
Parpaillon, mts. 103 44 30N 6 40 E
Parral 88 36 10 S 72 0W
Parramatta 136 33 48 S 151 1 E
Parras 82 25 30N 102 20W
Parrett, R. 95 51 7N 2 58W
Parris I. 73 32 20N 80 30W
Parrsboro 39 45 30N 64 25W
Parry 55 49 47N 104 41W
Parry, C. 67 70 20N 123 38W
Parry Is. 64 77 0N 110 0W
Parry Sound 46 45 20N 80 0W
Parshall 74 47 56N 102 11W
Parsnip, R. 54 55 10N 123 2W
Parson 63 51 5N 116 37W
Parsons 75 37 20N 95 10W
Parsons Pond 37 49 59N 57 37W
Parson's Pond 37 50 2N 57 43W
Parthenay 100 46 38N 0 16W
Partridge Pt. 37 50 10N 56 10W
Partridge, R. 53 51 19N 80 18W
Paru, R. 87 0 20 S 53 30W
Paruro 86 13 45 S 71 50W
Parvatipuram 125 18 50N 83 25 E
Parwan □ 124 35 0N 69 0 E
Pas-de-Calais □ 101 50 30N 2 30 E
Pasadena, Can. 37 49 1N 57 36W
Pasadena, Calif., U.S.A. 81 34 5N 118 9W
Pasadena, Tex., U.S.A. 75 29 45N 95 14W
Pasaje 86 3 10 S 79 40W
Pasaje, R. 88 25 35 S 64 57W
Pascagoula 75 30 30N 88 30W
Pascagoula, R. 75 30 40N 88 35W
Pasco 78 46 10N 119 0W
Pasco, Cerro de 86 10 45 S 76 10W
Pasfield L. 55 58 24N 105 20W
Pasir Mas 128 6 2N 102 8 E
Pasir Puteh 128 5 50N 102 24 E
Pasirian 127 8 13 S 113 8 E
Pasley, C. 134 33 52 S 123 35 E
Pasni 124 25 15N 63 27 E
Paso Cantinela 81 32 33N 115 47W
Paso de Indios 90 43 55 S 69 0W
Paso de los Libres 88 29 44 S 57 10W
Paso de los Toros 88 32 36 S 56 37W
Paso Robles 79 35 40N 120 45W
Paspébiac 39 48 3N 65 17W
Pass Island 37 47 30N 56 12W
Passage Pt. 64 73 29N 115 16W
Passage West 97 51 52N 8 20W
Passaic 71 40 50N 74 8W
Passau 106 48 34N 13 27 E
Passero, C. 108 36 42N 15 8 E
Passo Fundo 89 28 10 S 52 30W
Passos 87 20 45 S 46 37W
Passy 101 45 55N 6 41 E
Pastaza, R. 86 2 45 S 76 50W
Pasteur, L. 38 50 13N 66 58W
Pasto 86 1 13N 77 17W
Pasuruan 127 7 40 S 112 53 E
Patagonia, Argent. 90 45 0 S 69 0W
Patagonia, U.S.A. 79 31 35N 110 45W
Patan 124 23 54N 72 14 E
Patan (Lalitapur) 125 27 40N 85 20 E
Patani 127 0 20N 128 50 E
Pataokiang 130 41 58N 126 30 E
Patay 101 48 2N 1 40 E
Patchewollock 136 35 22 S 142 12 E
Patchogue 71 40 46N 73 1W
Patea 133 39 45 S 174 30 E
Paternò 108 37 34N 14 53 E
Paternoster, Kepulauan 126 7 5 S 118 15 E
Pateros 78 48 4N 119 58W
Paterson, Austral. 136 32 37 S 151 39 E
Paterson, U.S.A. 71 40 55N 74 10W
Pathankot 124 32 18N 75 45 E
Pathfinder Res. 78 42 30N 107 0W
Páti 127 6 45 S 111 3 E
Patiala 124 30 23N 76 26 E
Patjitan 127 8 12 S 111 8 E
Patkai Bum 125 27 0N 95 30 E
Pátmos, I. 109 37 21N 26 36 E
Patna 125 25 35N 85 18 E
Patos de Minas 87 18 35 S 46 32W
Patos, Lag. dos 89 31 20 S 51 0 E
Patquía 88 30 0 S 66 55W
Pátrai 109 38 14N 21 47 E
Pátraikos, Kólpos 109 38 17N 21 30 E
Patrick's Cove 37 47 3N 54 7W
Patrie, La 41 45 24N 71 15W
Patrocínio 87 18 57 S 47 0W
Pattani 128 6 48N 101 15 E
Patten 35 45 59N 68 28W
Patterson, Can. 50 43 54N 79 28W
Patterson, Calif., U.S.A. 80 37 30N 121 9W
Patterson, La., U.S.A. 75 29 44N 91 20W
Patterson, Mt. 80 38 29N 119 20W
Patti 108 38 8N 14 57 E
Patton 70 40 38N 78 40W
Pattonsburg 76 40 3N 94 8W
Patuakhali 125 22 20N 90 25 E
Patuca, Punta 84 15 49N 84 14W
Patuca, R. 84 15 20N 84 40W
Patung 131 31 0N 110 30 E
Pátzcuaro 82 19 30N 101 40W
Pau 102 43 19N 0 25W
Pauillac 102 45 11N 0 46W
Pauini, R. 86 1 42 S 62 50W
Pauk 125 21 55N 94 30 E
Paul I. 36 56 30N 61 20W
Paul-Sauvé, L. 40 50 15N 78 20W
Paulatuk 67 69 25N 124 0W
Paulding 77 41 8N 84 35W
Paulhan 102 43 33N 3 28 E
Paulistana 87 8 9 S 41 9W
Paullina 74 42 55N 95 40W
Paulo Afonso 87 9 21 S 38 15W
Paul's Valley 75 34 40N 97 17W
Pauma Valley 81 33 16N 116 58W
Pavia 108 45 10N 9 10 E
Pavlodar 120 52 33N 77 0 E
Pavlof Is. 67 55 30N 161 30W
Pavlovo 121 63 5N 115 25 E
Paw-Paw 76 41 41N 88 59W
Paw Paw 77 42 13N 85 53W
Pawhuska 75 36 40N 96 25W
Pawling 71 41 35N 73 37W
Pawnee, U.S.A. 76 39 35N 89 35W
Pawnee, Okla., U.S.A. 75 36 24N 96 50W
Pawnee City 74 40 8N 96 10W
Pawtucket 71 41 51N 71 22W
Paxton, Ill., U.S.A. 77 40 25N 88 0W
Paxton, Nebr., U.S.A. 74 41 12N 101 27W
Paya Bakri 128 2 3N 102 44 E
Payakumbah 126 0 20 S 100 35 E
Payen 129 45 57N 127 58 E
Payette 78 44 0N 117 0W
Payne 77 41 5N 84 44W
Payne = Bellin 36 60 1N 70 1W
Paynesville 74 45 21N 94 44W
Paysandú 88 32 19 S 58 8W
Payson, Ariz., U.S.A. 79 34 17N 111 15W
Payson, Utah, U.S.A. 78 40 8N 111 41W
Paz, Bahía de la 82 24 15N 110 25W
Paz Centro, La 84 12 20N 86 41W
Paz, La, Entre Ríos, Argent. 88 30 50 S 59 45W
Paz, La, San Luis, Argent. 88 33 30 S 67 20W
Paz, La, Boliv. 86 16 20 S 68 10W
Paz, La, Hond. 84 14 20N 87 47W
Paz, La, Mexico 82 24 10N 110 20W
Paz, La, Bahía de 82 24 20N 110 40W
Paz, R. 84 13 44N 90 10W
Pazar 122 41 10N 40 50 E
Pazardzhik 109 42 12N 24 20 E
Pe Ell 80 46 30N 123 18W
Peabody 71 42 31N 70 56W
Peace Point 54 59 7N 112 27W
Peace, R. 54 59 0N 111 25W
Peace River 60 56 15N 117 18W
Peace River Res. 54 55 40N 123 40W
Peach Springs 79 35 36N 113 30W
Peachland 63 49 47N 119 45W
Peak Hill 134 32 39 S 148 11 E
Peak Range 135 22 50 S 148 20 E
Peak, The 94 53 24N 1 53W
Peale Mt. 79 38 25N 109 12W
Pearblossom 81 34 30N 117 55W
Pearce 79 31 57N 109 56W
Pearl, Can. 52 48 40N 88 40W
Pearl, U.S.A. 76 39 28N 90 38W
Pearl City, U.S.A. 76 42 16N 89 50W
Pearl City, Hawaii, U.S.A. 67 21 24N 158 0W
Pearl Harbor 67 21 20N 158 0W
Pearl, R. 75 31 50N 90 0W
Pearsall 75 28 55N 99 8W
Pearse I. 54 54 52N 130 14W
Peary Land 17 82 40N 33 0W
Pease, R. 75 34 18N 100 15W
Pebane 117 17 10 S 38 8 E
Pebas 86 3 10 S 71 55W
Pebble Beach 80 36 34N 121 57W
Peć 109 42 40N 20 17 E
Pecatonica 76 42 19N 89 22W
Pecatonica, R. 76 42 26N 89 17W
Pechenga 120 69 30N 31 25 E
Pechora, R. 120 62 30N 56 30 E
Pechorskaya Guba 120 68 40N 54 0 E
Peck 46 43 16N 82 49W
Pecos 75 31 25N 103 35W
Pecos, R. 75 31 22N 102 30W
Pécs 107 46 5N 18 15 E
Pedasí 84 7 32N 80 3W
Pedernales 85 18 2N 71 44W
Pedjantan, I. 126 0 5 S 106 15 E
Pedra Azul 87 16 2 S 41 17W
Pedreiras 87 4 32 S 44 40W
Pedrera, La 86 1 18 S 69 43W
Pedro Afonso 87 9 0 S 48 10W
Pedro Antonio Santos 83 18 54N 88 15W
Pedro Cays 84 17 5N 77 48W
Pedro Chico 86 1 4N 70 25W
Pedro de Valdivia 88 22 33 S 69 38W
Pedro Juan Caballero 89 22 30 S 55 40W
Pedro Miguel Locks 84 9 1N 79 36W
Peebles, U.K. 96 55 40N 3 12W
Peebles, U.S.A. 77 38 57N 83 23W
Peekshill 71 41 18N 73 57W
Peel 94 54 14N 4 40W
Peel □ 50 43 45N 79 47W
Peel, R. 64 67 0N 135 0W
Peerless L. 60 56 37N 114 40W
Peerless Lake 60 56 40N 114 35W
Peers 60 53 40N 116 0W
Pegasus Bay 133 43 20 S 173 10 E
Peggy's Cove 39 44 30N 63 55W
Pegu 125 17 20N 96 29 E
Pegu Yoma, mts. 125 19 0N 96 0 E
Peh K. 131 24 20N 113 20 E
Pehan 129 48 17N 120 31 E
Pehpei 131 29 44N 106 29 E
Pehtaiho 130 39 50N 119 30 E
Pehuajó 88 36 0 S 62 0W
Peine 88 23 45 S 68 8W
Peiping 130 39 50N 116 20 E
Peixe 87 12 0 S 40 40W
Pekalongan 127 6 53 S 109 40 E
Pekan 128 3 30N 103 25 E
Pékans, R. 38 52 12N 66 49W
Pekin 76 40 35N 89 40W
Peking = Peiping 130 39 50N 116 20 E
Pelabuhan Ratu, Teluk 127 7 5 S 106 30 E
Pelabuhanratu 127 7 0 S 106 32 E
Pelaihari 126 3 55 S 114 45 E
Peleaga, mt. 107 45 22N 22 55 E
Pelee I. 46 41 47N 82 40W
Pelée, Mt. 85 14 40N 61 0W
Pelee, Pt. 46 41 54N 82 31W
Peleng, I. 127 1 20 S 123 30 E
Pelham, Can. 49 43 3N 79 21W
Pelham, U.S.A. 73 31 5N 84 6W
Pelham Union 49 43 5N 79 23W
Pelican 67 58 12N 136 28W
Pelican L. 57 52 28N 100 20W
Pélican, L. 36 59 47N 73 35W
Pelican L., U.S.A. 52 48 4N 92 58W
Pelican L., U.S.A. 52 46 36N 94 5W
Pelican Narrows 55 55 10N 102 56W
Pelican Portage 54 55 51N 113 0W
Pelican Rapids 57 52 45N 100 42W

Peligre, L. de Pine Flat Res

Peligre, L. de 85 19 1N 71 58W
Pelkosenniemi 110 67 6N 27 28E
Pella 76 41 30N 93 0W
Pelletier Sta. 41 47 33N 69 26W
Pellston 46 45 33N 84 47W
Pelly 57 51 52N 101 56W
Pelly Bay 65 68 0N 89 50W
Pelly Crossing 64 62 49N 136 34W
Pelly L. 64 66 0N 102 0W
Pelly Pt. 66 49 7N 123 12W
Pelly, R. 64 62 15N 133 30W
Peloponnese = Pelóponnisos 109 37 10N 22 0E
Pelopónnisos Kai Dhitikí Iprotikí Ellas □ 109 37 10N 22 0E
Peloro, C. 108 38 15N 15 40E
Pelorus Sound 133 40 59S 173 59E
Pelotas 89 31 42S 52 23W
Pelvoux, Massif de 103 44 52N 6 20E
Pemalang 127 6 53S 109 23E
Pematang Siantar 126 2 57N 99 5E
Pemba 117 16 30S 27 28E
Pemba, I. 117 5 0S 39 45E
Pemberton, Austral. 134 34 30S 116 0E
Pemberton, Can. 63 50 25N 122 50W
Pembina 57 48 58N 97 15W
Pembina, R., Alta., Can. 60 54 45N 114 17W
Pembina, R., Man., Can. 57 49 0N 98 12W
Pembine 72 45 38N 87 59W
Pembroke, Can. 47 45 50N 77 7W
Pembroke, N.Z. 133 44 33S 169 9E
Pembroke, U.K. 95 51 41N 4 57W
Pembroke, U.S.A. 73 32 5N 81 32W
Pen-y-Ghent 94 54 10N 2 15W
Peña de Francia, Sierra de 104 40 32N 6 10W
Peñalara, Pico 104 40 51N 3 57W
Penang = Pinang 128 5 25N 100 15E
Penápolis 89 21 30S 50 0W
Peñas, C. de 104 43 42N 5 52W
Peñas, G. de 90 47 0S 75 0W
Peñas, Pta. 86 11 17N 70 28W
Pend Oreille, L. 63 48 0N 116 30W
Pend Oreille, R. 78 49 4N 117 37W
Pendembu 114 9 7N 12 14W
Pendleton, U.S.A. 77 40 0N 85 45W
Pendleton, Calif., U.S.A. 81 33 16N 117 23W
Pendleton, Oreg., U.S.A. 78 45 35N 118 50W
Penedo 87 10 15S 36 36W
Penetanguishene, Newf., Can. 37 47 36N 52 45W
Penetanguishene, Ont., Can. 46 44 50N 79 55W
Pengalengan 127 7 9S 107 30E
Pengan 131 31 0N 106 18E
Pengchia Yu (Agincourt) Is. 131 25 4N 122 2E
Penghu (Pescadores) 131 23 34N 119 30E
Penglai (Tengchowfu) 130 37 50N 120 50E
Pengpu 131 33 0N 117 25E
Pengshui 131 29 20N 108 15E
Penhold 61 52 8N 113 52W
Peniche 104 39 19N 9 22W
Penida, I. 126 8 45S 115 30E
Penki 130 41 20N 132 50E
Penmarch 100 47 49N 4 21W
Penmarch, Pte. de 100 47 48N 4 22W
Pennant 56 50 32N 108 14W
Penner, R. 124 14 50N 78 20E
Penniac 39 46 2N 66 34W
Pennines 94 54 50N 2 20W
Pennington 80 39 15N 121 47W
Pennsylvania □ 72 40 50N 78 0W
Pennville 77 40 30N 85 9W
Penny 63 53 51N 121 20W
Penny Highland 65 67 19N 66 20W
Penny Str. 65 76 30N 97 0W
Pennyan 70 42 39N 77 7W
Penola 136 37 25S 140 47E
Penong 134 31 59S 133 5E
Penonomé 84 8 31N 80 21W
Penrhyn Is. 15 9 0S 150 30W
Penrith, Austral. 136 33 43S 150 38E
Penrith, U.K. 94 54 40N 2 45W
Pensacola 73 30 30N 87 10W
Pensacola Mts. 91 84 0S 40 0W
Pense 56 50 25N 104 59W
Pentecôte, L. 38 49 53N 67 20W
Pentecôte, R. 38 49 46N 67 10W
Penticton 63 49 30N 119 30W
Pentland 135 20 32S 145 25E
Pentland Corners 49 43 40N 80 30W
Pentland Firth 96 58 43N 3 10W
Pentland Hills 96 55 48N 3 25W
Penylan L. 55 61 50N 106 20W
Penza 120 53 15N 45 5E
Penzance 95 50 7N 5 32W
Penzhinskaya Guba 121 61 30N 163 0E
Peoria, Ariz., U.S.A. 79 33 40N 112 15W
Peoria, Ill., U.S.A. 76 40 40N 89 40W
Peoria Heights 76 40 45N 89 35W
Peotone 77 41 20N 87 48W
Pepperwood 78 40 23N 124 0W
Perabumilih 126 3 27S 104 15E
Peraki, R. 128 5 10N 101 4E
Percé 38 48 31N 64 13W
Perche 100 48 31N 1 1E
Perche, Collines de la 100 42 30N 2 5E
Percy, France 100 48 55N 1 11W
Percy, U.S.A. 76 38 5N 89 41W
Perdido, Mte. 104 42 40N 0 50E
Perdue 56 52 4N 107 33W
Pereira 86 4 49N 75 43W
Perez, I. 83 22 24N 89 42W
Pergamino 88 33 52S 60 30W
Perham 74 46 36N 95 36W
Perhentian, Kepulauan 128 5 54N 102 42E
Péribonca, L. 41 50 1N 71 10W
Péribonca, R. 36 48 45N 72 5W
Peribonka 41 48 46N 72 3W
Perico 88 24 20S 65 5W
Pericos 82 25 3N 107 42W
Périers 100 49 11N 1 25W
Périgord 102 45 0N 0 40E
Périgueux 102 45 10N 0 42E
Perija, Sierra de 86 9 30N 73 3W
Perkam, Tg. 127 1 35S 137 50E
Perlas, Arch. de las 84 8 41N 79 7W
Perlas, Punta de 84 11 30N 83 30W
Perlis □ 128 6 30N 100 15E
Perm (Molotov) 120 58 0N 57 10E
Pernambuco = Recife 87 8 0S 35 0W
Pernambuco □ 87 8 0S 37 0W
Péronne 101 49 55N 2 57E
Perouse Str., La 118 45 40N 142 0E
Perow 54 54 35N 126 10W
Perpignan 102 42 42N 2 53E
Perrington 77 43 12N 84 42W
Perris 81 33 47N 117 14W
Perros-Guirec 100 48 49N 3 28W
Perrot, Île 44 45 22N 73 57W
Perry, U.S.A. 77 42 50N 84 13W
Perry, Fla., U.S.A. 73 30 9N 83 40W
Perry, Ga., U.S.A. 73 32 25N 83 41W
Perry, Iowa, U.S.A. 76 41 48N 94 5W
Perry, Maine, U.S.A. 73 44 59N 67 20W
Perry, Mo., U.S.A. 76 39 26N 91 40W
Perry, N.Y., U.S.A. 70 42 44N 77 59W
Perry, Okla., U.S.A. 75 36 20N 97 20W
Perry River 65 67 43N 102 14W
Perrysburg 77 41 34N 83 38W
Perryton 75 36 28N 100 48W
Perryville, Alas., U.S.A. 67 55 54N 159 10W
Perryville, Mo., U.S.A. 76 37 42N 89 50W
Persepolis 123 29 55N 52 50E
Persia = Iran 123 35 0N 50 0E
Persian Gulf 123 27 0N 50 0E
Perth, Austral. 134 31 57S 115 52E
Perth, N.B., Can. 34 46 43N 67 42W
Perth, N.B., Can. 39 46 44N 67 42W
Perth, Ont., Can. 47 44 55N 76 15W
Perth, U.K. 96 56 24N 3 27W
Perth, U.S.A. 71 40 33N 74 36W
Perth Amboy 72 40 30N 74 25W
Perthus, Le 102 42 30N 2 53E
Pertuis 103 43 42N 5 30E
Peru, Ill., U.S.A. 76 41 18N 89 12W
Peru, Ind., U.S.A. 77 40 42N 86 0W
Peru ■ 86 8 0S 75 0W
Perúgia 108 43 6N 12 24E
Péruwelz 105 50 31N 3 36E
Pervouralsk 120 56 55N 60 0E
Pésaro 108 43 55N 12 53E
Pesca, La 83 23 46N 97 47W
Pescadores = Penghu 131 23 34N 119 30E
Pescara 108 42 28N 14 13E
Peshawar 124 34 2N 71 37E
Peshawar □ 124 35 0N 72 50E
Peshtigo 72 45 4N 87 46W
Pesqueira 87 8 20S 36 42W
Pesquiería 82 29 23N 110 54W
Pesquieria, R. 82 25 54N 99 11W
Pessac 102 44 48N 0 37W
Petaling Jaya 128 3 4N 101 42E
Petaluma 80 38 13N 122 39W
Petange 105 49 33N 5 55E
Petatlán 82 17 31N 101 16W
Petauke 117 14 14S 31 12E
Petawawa 47 45 54N 77 17W
Petén Itza, Lago 84 16 58N 89 50W
Peter 1st, I. 91 69 0S 91 0W
Peter Pond L. 55 55 55N 108 44W
Peterbell 53 48 36N 83 21W
Peterboro 71 42 55N 71 59W
Peterborough, S. Australia, Austral. 135 32 58S 138 51E
Peterborough, Victoria, Austral. 135 38 37S 142 50E
Peterborough, Can. 47 44 20N 78 20W
Peterborough, U.K. 95 52 35N 0 14W
Peterhead 96 57 30N 1 49W
Peters, L. 36 59 41N 70 53W
Petersburg, U.S.A. 76 40 1N 89 51W
Petersburg, Alas., U.S.A. 54 56 50N 133 0W
Petersburg, Ind., U.S.A. 77 38 30N 87 15W
Petersburg, Va., U.S.A. 72 37 17N 77 26W
Petersburg, W. Va., U.S.A. 72 38 59N 79 10W
Petersfield 57 50 18N 96 58W
Petit Bois I. 73 30 16N 88 25W
Petit-Brûlé 44 45 35N 74 2W
Petit-Cap 38 48 3N 64 30W
Petit-de-Grat 39 45 30N 60 58W
Petit Étang 39 46 39N 60 58W
Petit Goâve 85 18 27N 72 51W
Petit-Mécatina, I. du 36 50 30N 59 25W
Petit-Quevilly, Le 100 49 26N 1 0E
Petit-Rocher 39 47 46N 65 43W
Petitcodiac 39 45 57N 65 11W
Petite Baleine, R. 36 56 0N 76 45W
Petite-Cascapédia, Parc Prov. de la 38 48 30N 65 45W
Petite-Rivière 41 47 20N 70 33W
Petite Rivière Bridge 39 44 14N 64 27W
Petite Saguenay 41 48 15N 70 4W
Petitsikapau, L. 36 54 37N 66 25W
Petlad 124 22 30N 72 45E
Peto 83 20 10N 89 0W
Petone 133 41 13S 174 53E
Petoskey 46 45 22N 84 57W
Petra, Ostrova 17 76 15N 118 30E
Petrich 109 41 24N 23 13E
Petrolândia 87 9 5S 38 20W
Petrolia 46 42 54N 82 9W
Petrolina 87 9 24S 40 30W
Petropavlovsk 120 55 0N 69 0E
Petropavlovsk-Kamchatskiy 121 53 16N 159 0E
Petrópolis 89 22 33S 43 9W
Petroşeni 107 45 28N 23 20E
Petrovaradin 109 45 16N 19 55E
Petrovsk-Zabaykalskiy 121 51 26N 108 30E
Petrozavodsk 120 61 41N 34 20E
Petty Harbour Long Pond 37 47 31N 52 58W
Peumo 88 34 21S 71 19W
Peureulak 126 4 48N 97 45E
Pevek 121 69 15N 171 0E
Peyrehorade 102 43 34N 1 7W
Peyruis 103 44 1N 5 56E
Pézenas 102 43 28N 3 24E
Pforzheim 106 48 53N 8 43E
Phagwara 124 31 10N 75 40E
Phala 117 23 45S 26 50E
Phalodi 124 27 12N 72 24E
Phalsbourg 101 48 46N 7 15E
Phan Rang 128 11 40N 109 9E
Phan Thiet 128 11 1N 108 9E
Phangnga 128 8 28N 98 30E
Phanh Bho Ho Chi Minh 128 10 58N 106 40E
Phanom Dang Raek, mts. 128 14 45N 104 0E
Pharo Dzong 129 27 45N 89 14E
Phatthalung 128 7 39N 100 6E
Phelps, N.Y., U.S.A. 70 42 57N 77 5W
Phelps, Wis., U.S.A. 74 46 2N 89 2W
Phelps L. 55 59 15N 103 15W
Phenix City 73 32 30N 85 0W
Phetchabun 128 16 25N 101 8E
Phetchaburi 128 13 1N 99 55E
Phichai 128 17 22N 100 10E
Philadelphia, Miss., U.S.A. 75 32 47N 89 5W
Philadelphia, N.Y., U.S.A. 71 44 9N 75 40W
Philadelphia, Pa., U.S.A. 72 40 0N 75 10W
Philip 74 44 4N 101 42W
Philip Smith Mts. 67 68 0N 146 0W
Philippeville 105 50 12N 4 33E
Philippines ■ 127 12 0N 123 0E
Philipsburg, Can. 43 45 2N 73 5W
Philipsburg, Mont., U.S.A. 78 46 20N 113 21W
Philipsburg, Pa., U.S.A. 70 40 53N 78 10W
Phillip, I. 136 38 30S 145 12E
Phillips, Texas, U.S.A. 75 35 48N 101 17W
Phillips, Wis., U.S.A. 74 45 41N 90 22W
Phillipsburg, Kans., U.S.A. 74 39 48N 99 20W
Phillipsburg, Penn., U.S.A. 71 40 43N 75 12W
Philmont 71 42 14N 73 37W
Philomath 78 44 28N 123 21W
Phitsanulok 128 16 50N 100 12E
Phnom Penh 128 11 33N 104 55E
Phnom Thbeng 128 13 50N 104 56E
Phoenix, Ariz., U.S.A. 79 33 30N 112 10W
Phoenix, N.Y., U.S.A. 71 43 13N 76 18W
Phoenix Is. 14 3 30S 172 0W
Phoenixville 71 40 12N 75 29W
Phong Saly 128 21 42N 102 9E
Phra Chedi Sam Ong 128 15 16N 98 23E
Phra Nakhon Si Ayutthaya 128 14 25N 100 30E
Phrae 128 18 7N 100 9E
Phrao 128 19 23N 99 15E
Phu Doan 128 21 40N 105 10E
Phu Loi 128 20 14N 103 14E
Phu Ly (Ha Nam) 128 20 35N 105 50E
Phu Qui 128 19 20N 105 20E
Phuket 128 8 0N 98 28E
Phuoc Le (Baria) 128 10 39N 107 19E
Pi Ho 131 32 0N 116 20E
Piacenza 108 45 2N 9 42E
Pialba 135 25 20S 152 45E
Piana 103 42 15N 8 34E
Piapot 56 49 59N 109 8W
Piashti, L. 38 50 29N 62 52W
Piatra Neamţ 107 46 56N 26 21E
Piauí □ 87 7 0S 43 0W
Piave, R. 108 45 50N 13 9E
Piazza Armerina 108 37 21N 14 20E
Pic I. 53 48 43N 86 37W
Pic, R. 53 48 36N 86 18W
Pica 86 20 35S 69 25W
Picardie 101 50 0N 2 15E
Picardie, Plaine de 101 50 0N 2 0E
Picardy = Picardie 101 50 0N 2 15E
Picayune 75 30 40N 89 40W
Piccadilly 37 48 34N 58 55W
Pichieh 131 27 20N 105 20E
Pichilemu 88 34 22S 72 9W
Pickerel L. 52 48 40N 91 25W
Pickering 51 43 52N 79 2W
Pickering Beach 51 43 50N 78 59W
Pickford 46 46 10N 84 22W
Pickle Lake 52 51 30N 90 12W
Pico 93 38 28N 28 18W
Pico Truncado 90 46 40S 68 10W
Picquigny 101 49 56N 2 10E
Picton, Austral. 136 34 12S 150 34E
Picton, Can. 47 44 1N 77 9W
Picton, N.Z. 133 41 18S 174 3E
Pictou 39 45 41N 62 42W
Pictou I. 39 45 49N 62 33W
Picture Butte 61 49 55N 112 45W
Picún-Leufú 90 39 30S 69 5W
Pidurutalagala, mt. 124 7 10N 80 50E
Pie I. 52 48 15N 89 6W
Piedad, La 82 20 20N 102 1W
Piedecuesta 86 6 59N 73 3W
Piedmont, Can. 43 45 54N 74 8W
Piedmont, U.S.A. 73 33 55N 85 39W
Piedmont = Piemonte 108 45 0N 7 30E
Piedmont Plat. 73 34 0N 81 30W
Piedras Blancas Pt. 79 35 45N 121 18W
Piedras Negras 82 28 35N 100 35W
Piedras, R. de las 86 11 40S 70 50W
Piemonte □ 108 45 0N 7 30E
Pierce 78 46 40N 115 53W
Piercefield 71 44 13N 74 35W
Pierceland 56 54 20N 109 46W
Pierre, France 101 46 54N 5 13E
Pierre, U.S.A. 74 44 23N 100 20W
Pierrefeu 103 43 8N 6 9E
Pierrefonds, Can. 44 45 29N 73 52W
Pierrefonds, France 101 49 20N 3 0E
Pierrefontaine 101 47 14N 6 32E
Pierrefort 102 44 55N 2 50E
Pierrelatte 103 44 23N 4 43E
Pierreville 41 46 4N 72 49W
Pierson 57 49 11N 101 15W
Piestany 69 48 35N 17 50E
Piet Retief 117 27 1S 30 50E
Pietarsaari 110 63 41N 22 40E
Pietermaritzburg 117 29 35S 30 25E
Pietersburg 117 23 54S 29 25E
Pietrosul 107 47 35N 24 43E
Pigeon 46 43 50N 83 17W
Pigeon Hill 43 45 3N 72 56W
Pigeon L., Alta., Can. 61 53 1N 114 2W
Pigeon L., Ont., Can. 47 44 27N 78 30W
Pigeon, R. 34 48 1N 89 42W
Piggott 75 36 20N 90 10W
Pigü 88 37 36S 62 25W
Pike River 43 45 4N 73 6W
Pikes Peak 74 38 50N 105 10W
Piketberg 117 32 55S 18 40E
Pikeville 72 37 30N 82 30W
Pikwitonei 55 55 35N 97 9W
Pilar, Brazil 87 9 36S 35 56W
Pilar, Parag. 88 26 50S 58 10W
Pilas, I. 127 6 39N 121 37E
Pilbara Cr. 134 21 15S 118 22E
Pilcomayo, R. 88 25 21S 57 42W
Pilibhit 124 28 40N 79 50E
Pilica, R. 107 51 25N 20 45E
Pilos 109 36 55N 21 42E
Pilot Butte 56 50 28N 104 25W
Pilot Grove 76 38 53N 92 55W
Pilot Mound 57 49 15N 98 54W
Pilot Point 75 33 26N 97 0W
Pilot Rock 78 45 30N 118 58W
Pilsen = Plzen 106 49 45N 13 22E
Pimba 135 31 18S 136 46E
Pimenta Bueno 86 11 35S 61 10W
Pimentel 86 6 45S 79 55W
Pin-Blanc, L. 40 46 45N 78 8W
Pinacle, Le, mt. 43 45 2N 72 45W
Pinang, I. 128 5 25N 100 15E
Pinar del Río 84 22 26N 83 40W
Pinawa 57 50 9N 95 50W
Pincher Creek 61 49 30N 113 57W
Pinchi L. 54 54 38N 124 30W
Pinckneyville 76 38 5N 89 20W
Pinconning 46 43 52N 83 57W
Pincourt 44 45 23N 74 0W
Pinczów 107 50 30N 20 35E
Pindos Óros 109 40 0N 21 0E
Pindus Mts. = Pindos Óros 109 40 0N 21 0E
Pine 79 34 27N 111 30W
Pine Bluff 75 34 10N 92 0W
Pine, C. 37 46 37N 53 32W
Pine City 74 45 46N 93 0W
Pine Creek 134 13 50S 131 49E
Pine Dock 57 51 30N 96 48W
Pine Falls 57 50 34N 96 11W
Pine Flat Res. 80 36 50N 119 20W

Pine Grove — Pontian Kechil

Pine Grove **50** 43 48N 79 35W
Pine Hill **43** 45 44N 74 29W
Pine, La **78** 40 53N 80 45W
Pine Pass **54** 55 25N 122 42W
Pine Point **54** 60 50N 114 28W
Pine Portage **52** 49 20N 88 26W
Pine, R. **55** 58 50N 105 38W
Pine Ridge, Can. **58** 50 0N 96 50W
Pine Ridge, U.S.A. **74** 43 0N 102 35W
Pine River, Can. **57** 51 45N 100 30W
Pine River, U.S.A. **52** 46 43N 94 24W
Pine Valley **81** 32 50N 116 32W
Pinecrest **80** 38 12N 120 1W
Pinedale, Ariz., U.S.A. **79** 34 23N 110 16W
Pinedale, Calif., U.S.A. **80** 36 50N 119 48W
Pinega, R. **120** 64 20N 43 0 E
Pinerolo **108** 44 47N 7 21 E
Pinetop **79** 34 10N 109 57W
Pinetown **117** 29 48 S 30 54 E
Pinetree **74** 43 42N 105 52W
Pineview **63** 53 50N 122 38W
Pineville, Ky., U.S.A. **73** 36 42N 83 42W
Pineville, La., U.S.A. **75** 31 22N 92 30W
Pinewood **55** 48 45N 94 10W
Piney, Can. **55** 49 5N 96 10W
Piney, France **101** 48 22N 4 21 E
Ping, R. **128** 15 42N 100 9 E
Pinghua **131** 24 14N 117 2 E
Pingkiang **131** 28 45N 113 30 E
Pingliang **130** 35 20N 106 40 E
Pinglo, Kwangsi-Chuang, China **131** 24 30N 110 45 E
Pinglo, Ningsia Hui, China **130** 38 58N 106 30 E
Pingnam **131** 23 30N 110 15 E
Pingsiang, Kiangsi, China **131** 27 43N 113 50 E
Pingsiang, Kwangsi-Chuang, China **131** 22 2N 106 55 E
Pingtung **131** 22 36N 120 30 E
Pingyang **131** 27 45N 120 25 E
Pingyao **130** 37 12N 112 0 E
Pingyuan **130** 37 5N 106 40 E
Pinhal **89** 22 10 S 46 46W
Pinhel **104** 40 18N 7 0W
Pini, I. **126** 0 10N 98 40 E
Piniós, R. **109** 39 55N 22 10 E
Pinjarra **134** 32 37 S 115 52 E
Pink, R. **55** 56 50N 103 50W
Pinnacles **80** 36 33N 121 8W
Pinnaroo **136** 35 13 S 140 56 E
Pinon Hills **81** 34 26N 117 39W
Pinos **82** 22 20N 101 40W
Pinos, I. de **84** 21 40N 82 40W
Pinos, Mt **81** 34 49N 119 8W
Pinos Pt. **79** 36 50N 121 57W
Pinotepa Nacional **83** 16 25N 97 55W
Pinrang **127** 3 46 S 119 34 E
Pins, Pte. aux **46** 42 15N 81 51W
Pinsk **120** 52 10N 26 8 E
Pintados **86** 20 35 S 69 40W
Pintendre **42** 46 45N 71 8W
Pinting **130** 37 45N 113 34 E
Pinto Butte Mt. **55** 49 22N 107 27W
Pinware **37** 51 37N 56 42W
Pinware R. **37** 51 39N 56 42W
Pinyang **131** 23 17N 108 47 E
Pinyug **120** 60 5N 48 0 E
Pioche **79** 38 0N 114 35W
Piombino **108** 42 54N 10 30 E
Pioner, I. **121** 79 50N 92 0 E
Piorini, L. **86** 3 15 S 62 35W
Piotrków Trybunalski **107** 51 23N 19 43 E
Pip **123** 26 45N 60 10 E
Pipestone **74** 44 0N 96 20W
Pipestone Cr., Man., Can. **57** 49 38N 100 15W
Pipestone Cr., Sask., Can. **55** 53 37N 109 46W
Pipestone, R. **34** 52 53N 89 23W
Pipinas **88** 35 30 S 57 19W
Pipmuacan, Rés. **41** 49 45N 70 30W
Pipriac **100** 47 49N 1 58W
Piqua **77** 40 10N 84 10W
Piquiri, R. **89** 24 3 S 54 14W
Piracicaba **89** 22 45 S 47 30W
Piracuruca **87** 3 50 S 41 50W
Piræus = Piraiévs **109** 37 57N 23 42 E
Piraiévs **109** 37 57N 23 42 E
Pirajuí **89** 21 59 S 49 29W
Pirane **88** 25 25 S 59 30W
Pirapora **87** 17 20 S 44 56W
Pirgos **109** 37 40N 21 27 E
Piriac-sur-Mer **100** 47 22N 2 33W
Piribebuy **88** 25 26 S 57 2W
Pirin Planina **109** 41 40N 23 30 E
Pirineos, mts. **104** 42 40N 1 0 E
Piripiri **87** 4 15 S 41 46W
Piritu **86** 9 23N 69 12W
Pirmasens **105** 49 12N 7 30 E
Pirot **109** 43 9N 22 39 E
Pirtleville **79** 31 25N 109 35W
Piru **81** 34 25N 118 48W
Pisa **108** 43 43N 10 23 E
Pisagua **86** 19 40 S 70 15W
Pisco **86** 13 50 S 76 5W
Písek **106** 49 19N 14 10 E
Pising **127** 5 8 S 121 53 E
Pismo Beach **81** 35 9N 120 38W
Pissos **102** 44 19N 0 49W
Pistoia **108** 43 57N 10 53 E
Pistol B. **55** 62 25N 92 37W
Pistolet B. **37** 51 35N 55 45W
Pisuerga, R. **104** 42 10N 4 15W
Pitalito **86** 1 51N 76 2W
Pitcairn I. **15** 25 5 S 130 5W
Pite älv **110** 65 44N 20 50W
Piteå **110** 65 20N 21 25 E
Piteşti **107** 44 52N 24 54 E
Pithapuram **125** 17 10N 82 15 E
Pithiviers **101** 48 10N 2 13 E
Pitiquito **82** 30 42N 112 2W
Pitlochry **96** 56 43N 3 43W
Pitt I. **62** 53 30N 129 50W
Pitt L. **63** 49 25N 122 32W
Pitt Meadows **66** 49 13N 122 42W
Pitt, R. **66** 49 13N 122 46W
Pittsburg, Calif., U.S.A. **80** 38 1N 121 50W
Pittsburg, Kans., U.S.A. **75** 37 21N 94 43W
Pittsburg, Tex., U.S.A. **75** 32 59N 94 58W
Pittsburgh **70** 40 25N 79 55W
Pittsfield, Ill., U.S.A. **76** 39 35N 90 46W
Pittsfield, Mass., U.S.A. **71** 42 28N 73 17W
Pittsfield, N.H., U.S.A. **71** 43 17N 71 18W
Pittston **71** 41 19N 75 50W
Piura **86** 5 5 S 80 45W
Pivabiska, R. **53** 50 13N 82 52W
Pivijay **86** 10 28N 74 37W
Pixley **80** 35 58N 119 18W
Pizarro **86** 4 58N 77 22W
Pizzo **108** 38 44N 16 10 E
Placentia **37** 47 20N 54 0W
Placentia B. **37** 47 0N 54 40W
Placerville **80** 38 47N 120 51W
Placetas **84** 22 15N 79 44W
Plage-St-Blaise **43** 45 12N 73 16W
Plain **76** 43 17N 90 3W
Plain Dealing **75** 32 56N 93 41W
Plaine, La **44** 45 47N 73 46W
Plainfield, U.S.A. **77** 41 37N 88 12W
Plainfield, N.J., U.S.A. **71** 40 37N 74 28W
Plains, Kans., U.S.A. **75** 37 20N 100 35W
Plains, Mont., U.S.A. **78** 47 27N 114 57W
Plains, Tex., U.S.A. **75** 33 11N 102 50W
Plainview, Nebr., U.S.A. **74** 42 25N 97 48W
Plainview, Tex., U.S.A. **75** 34 10N 101 40W
Plainville **74** 39 18N 99 19W
Plainwell **72** 42 28N 85 40W
Plaisance **102** 43 36N 0 3 E
Pláka **109** 36 45N 24 26 E
Plakhino **120** 67 45N 86 5 E
Plamondon **60** 54 51N 112 32W
Plana Cays **85** 22 38N 73 30W
Planada **80** 37 18N 120 19W
Planaltina **87** 15 30 S 47 45W
Plancoët **100** 48 32N 2 13W
Planeta Rica **86** 8 25N 75 36W
Plankinton **74** 43 45N 98 27W
Plano **75** 33 0N 96 45W
Plant City **73** 28 0N 82 15W
Plant, La **74** 45 11N 100 40W
Plaquemine **75** 30 20N 91 15W
Plasencia **104** 40 3N 6 8W
Plaster City **81** 32 47N 115 51W
Plaster Rock **39** 46 53N 67 22W
Plata, La, Argent. **88** 35 0 S 57 55W
Plata, La, U.S.A. **76** 40 2N 92 29W
Plata, La, Río de **88** 35 0 S 56 40W
Platani, R. **108** 37 28N 13 23 E
Plateau **91** 70 55 S 40 0 E
Plateau du Coteau du Missouri **74** 47 9N 101 5W
Platí, Ákra **109** 40 27N 24 0 E
Platinum **67** 59 2N 161 50W
Plato **86** 9 47N 74 47W
Platte **74** 43 28N 98 50W
Platte City **76** 39 22N 94 47W
Platte, R., Minn., U.S.A. **52** 45 47N 94 17W
Platte, R., Nebr., U.S.A. **76** 41 04N 95 53W
Platteville, U.S.A. **76** 42 44N 90 29W
Platteville, Colo., U.S.A. **74** 40 18N 104 47W
Plattsburg **76** 39 34N 94 27W
Plattsburgh **71** 44 41N 73 30W
Plattsmouth **74** 41 0N 95 50W
Plauen **106** 50 29N 12 9 E
Playa Azul **82** 17 59N 102 24W
Playgreen L. **57** 54 0N 98 15W
Pleasant Bay **35** 46 51N 60 48W
Pleasant Hill, Ill., U.S.A. **76** 39 27N 90 52W
Pleasant Hill, Mo., U.S.A. **76** 38 48N 94 14W
Pleasant Ridge Park **77** 38 9N 85 50W
Pleasantdale **56** 52 35N 104 30W
Pleasanton **75** 29 0N 98 30W
Pleasantville, U.S.A. **76** 41 23N 93 18W
Pleasantville, N.J., U.S.A. **72** 39 25N 74 30W
Pléaux **102** 45 8N 2 13 E
Pledger L. **53** 50 53N 83 42W
Pleiku (Gia Lai) **128** 14 3N 108 0 E
Plélan-le-Grand **100** 48 0N 2 7W
Plémet **100** 48 11N 2 36W
Pléneuf-Val-André **100** 48 35N 2 32W
Plenty **56** 51 47N 108 38W
Plenty, Bay of **133** 37 45 S 177 0 E
Plentywood **74** 48 45N 104 35W
Plessisville **41** 46 14N 71 47W
Plestin-les-Grèves **100** 48 40N 3 39W
Pletipi L. **36** 51 44N 70 6W
Pleven **109** 43 26N 24 37 E
Plevlja **109** 43 21N 19 21 E
Plevna **47** 44 58N 76 59W
Ploëmeur **100** 47 44N 3 26W
Ploërmel **100** 47 55N 2 26W
Ploieşti **107** 44 57N 26 5 E
Plomb du Cantal **102** 45 2N 2 48 E
Plombières **101** 47 59N 6 27 E
Plonge, Lac La **55** 55 8N 107 20W
Plouay **100** 47 55N 3 21W
Ploudalmézeau **100** 48 34N 4 41W
Plougasnou **100** 48 42N 3 49W
Plouha **100** 48 41N 2 57W
Plouhinec **100** 48 0N 4 29W
Plovdiv **109** 42 8N 24 44 E
Plum Coulee **57** 49 11N 97 45W
Plum I. **71** 41 10N 72 12W
Plumas, Can. **57** 50 23N 99 5W
Plumas, U.S.A. **80** 39 45N 119 4W
Plummer **78** 47 21N 116 59W
Plumtree **117** 20 27 S 27 55 E
Plunkett **56** 51 55N 105 27W
Pluvigner **100** 47 46N 3 1W
Plymouth, U.K. **95** 50 23N 4 9W
Plymouth, U.S.A. **76** 40 29N 90 58W
Plymouth, Calif., U.S.A. **80** 38 29N 120 51W
Plymouth, Ind., U.S.A. **77** 41 20N 86 19W
Plymouth, Mass., U.S.A. **71** 41 58N 70 40W
Plymouth, Mich., U.S.A. **46** 42 22N 83 28W
Plymouth, N.C., U.S.A. **73** 35 54N 76 55W
Plymouth, N.H., U.S.A. **71** 43 44N 71 41W
Plymouth, Pa., U.S.A. **71** 41 17N 76 0W
Plymouth, Wis., U.S.A. **72** 43 42N 87 58W
Plymouth Sd. **95** 50 20N 4 10W
Plympton **39** 44 30N 65 55W
Plynlimon = Pumlumon Fawr **95** 52 29N 3 47W
Plzen **106** 49 45N 13 22 E
Po Hai **130** 38 30N 119 0 E
Po, R. **108** 45 0N 10 45 E
Pobedino **120** 49 51N 142 49 E
Pobedy Pik **120** 40 45N 79 58 E
Pocahontas, Arkansas, U.S.A. **75** 36 18N 91 0W
Pocahontas, Ill., U.S.A. **76** 38 50N 89 33W
Pocahontas, Iowa, U.S.A. **76** 42 41N 94 42W
Pocatello **78** 42 50N 112 25W
Pocatière, La **41** 47 22N 70 2W
Pochontas **54** 53 10N 117 51W
Pochutla **83** 15 50N 96 31W
Pocita Casas **82** 28 32N 111 6W
Pocomoke City **72** 38 4N 75 32W
Poços de Caldas **89** 21 50 S 46 45W
Podensac **102** 44 40N 0 22W
Podgorica = Titograd **109** 42 30N 19 19 E
Podkamennaya Tunguska **121** 61 50N 90 26 E
Pofadder **117** 29 10 S 19 22 E
Pogamasing **53** 46 55N 81 50W
Pogranichnyy **130** 44 21N 131 23 E
Poh **127** 0 46 S 122 51 E
Pohang **130** 36 1N 129 23 E
Pohsien **131** 33 53N 115 48 E
Poile, La **37** 47 41N 58 24W
Point Baker **67** 56 20N 133 35W
Point-du-Jour **45** 45 41N 72 59W
Point Edward **46** 43 0N 82 30W
Point Fortin **85** 10 9N 61 46W
Point Gatineau **40** 45 28N 75 42W
Point Hope **67** 68 20N 166 50W
Point L. **64** 65 15N 113 4W
Point Lay **67** 69 45N 163 10W
Point Leamington **37** 49 20N 55 24W
Point Pedro **124** 9 50N 80 15 E
Point Pelee Nat. Park **46** 41 57N 82 31W
Point Pleasant, Can **39** 44 37N 63 34W
Point Pleasant, U.S.A. **72** 38 50N 82 7W
Point Roberts **66** 48 59N 123 13W
Point Sapin **39** 46 58N 64 50W
Pointe-à-la-Frégate **38** 49 12N 64 55W
Pointe-à-la Hache **75** 29 35N 89 55W
Pointe-à-Maurier **38** 50 20N 59 48W
Pointe-à-Pitre **85** 16 10N 61 30W
Pointe au Baril Sta. **46** 45 35N 80 23W
Pointe-au-Pic **41** 47 38N 70 9W
Pointe-aux-Anglais **38** 49 41N 67 10W
Pointe-aux-Outardes **41** 49 3N 68 26W
Pointe-Aux-Trembles **43** 45 39N 73 30W
Pointe-aux-Trembles **45** 45 40N 73 30W
Pointe-Calumet **44** 45 30N 73 58W
Pointe-Cavagnal **44** 45 27N 74 4W
Pointe-Claire **44** 45 26N 73 50W
Pointe-des-Cascades **44** 45 20N 73 58W
Pointe du Bois **57** 50 18N 95 33W
Pointe-Fortune **43** 45 34N 74 23W
Pointe-Gatineau **48** 45 28N 75 42W
Pointe-Lebel **41** 49 10N 68 12W
Pointe-Noire **116** 4 48 S 12 0 E
Pointe-Parent **38** 50 8N 61 47W
Pointe Verte **39** 47 51N 65 46W
Poisson-Blanc, L. du **40** 46 0N 75 45W
Poissy **101** 48 55N 2 0 E
Poitiers **100** 46 35N 0 20 E
Poitou, Plaines du **102** 46 30N 0 1W
Poix **101** 49 47N 2 0 E
Poix-Terron **101** 49 38N 4 38 E
Pojoaque **79** 35 55N 106 0W
Pokaran **124** 27 0N 71 50 E
Pokegama Res. **52** 47 12N 93 39W
Poko **116** 5 41N 31 55 E
Pokotu **129** 48 47N 122 7 E
Pokpak **131** 22 20N 109 45 E
Pokrovsk **121** 61 29N 129 6 E
Pola **129** 57 30N 32 0 E
Polacca **79** 35 52N 110 25W
Polan **123** 25 30N 61 10 E
Poland ■ **107** 52 0N 20 0 E
Polar Bear Prov. Park **34** 54 30N 83 20W
Polcura **88** 37 10 S 71 50W
Polden Hills **95** 51 7N 2 50W
Polewali, Sulawesi, Indon. **127** 4 8 S 119 43 E
Polewali, Sulawesi, Indon. **127** 3 21 S 119 31 E
Poli **129** 45 43N 130 28 E
Poligny **101** 46 50N 5 42 E
Polillo I. **127** 14 56N 122 0 E
Polis **122** 35 3N 32 30 E
Políyiros **109** 40 23N 23 25 E
Polk **70** 41 22N 79 57W
Pollachi **124** 10 35N 77 0 E
Pollock **74** 45 58N 100 18W
Polnovat **120** 63 50N 66 5 E
Polo, Ill., U.S.A. **76** 42 0N 89 38W
Polo, Mo., U.S.A. **76** 39 33N 94 3W
Polotsk **120** 55 30N 28 50 E
Polson **78** 47 45N 114 12W
Poltava **120** 49 35N 34 35 E
Poltimore **40** 45 47N 75 43W
Polynesia **15** 10 0 S 162 0W
Pomaro **82** 18 20N 103 18W
Pombal, Brazil **87** 6 55 S 37 50W
Pombal, Port. **104** 39 55N 8 40W
Pomeroy, Ohio, U.S.A. **72** 39 0N 82 0W
Pomeroy, Wash., U.S.A. **78** 46 30N 117 33W
Pomme de Terre, Res. **76** 37 54N 93 19W
Pomona **81** 34 2N 117 49W
Pompano Beach **73** 26 12N 80 6W
Pompey **101** 48 50N 6 2 E
Pompeys Pillar **78** 46 0N 108 0W
Ponape I. **14** 6 55N 158 10 E
Ponask, L. **34** 54 0N 92 41W
Ponass L. **56** 52 16N 103 58W
Ponca **74** 42 38N 96 41W
Ponca City **75** 36 40N 97 5W
Ponce **85** 18 1N 66 37W
Ponchatoula **75** 30 27N 90 25W
Poncheville, L. **40** 50 10N 76 55W
Poncin **103** 46 6N 5 25 E
Pond **81** 35 43N 119 20W
Pond Inlet **65** 72 30N 77 0W
Pondicherry **124** 11 59N 79 50 E
Ponds, I. of **36** 53 27N 55 52W
Ponferrada **104** 42 32N 6 35W
Ponnani **124** 10 45N 75 59 E
Ponnyadaung **125** 22 0N 94 10 E
Ponoi, R. **120** 67 10N 39 0 E
Ponoka **61** 52 42N 113 40W
Ponorogo **127** 7 52 S 111 29 E
Pons **102** 45 35N 0 34W
Ponsonby **49** 43 38N 80 22W
Pont-à-Mousson **101** 45 54N 6 1 E
Pont Audemer **100** 49 21N 0 30 E
Pont Aven **100** 47 51N 3 47W
Pont-Château **44** 45 20N 74 12W
Pont-de-Roide **101** 47 23N 6 45 E
Pont-de-Salars **102** 44 18N 2 44 E
Pont-de-Vaux **101** 46 26N 4 56 E
Pont-de-Veyle **103** 46 17N 4 53 E
Pont-l'Abbé **100** 47 52N 4 15W
Pont Lafrance **35** 47 40N 64 58W
Pont-l'Evêque **100** 49 18N 0 11 E
Pont-Mousseau **43** 45 52N 73 39W
Pont-Rouge **41** 46 45N 71 42W
Pont-St.-Esprit **103** 44 16N 4 40 E
Pont-sur-Yonne **101** 48 18N 3 10 E
Pont-Viau **44** 45 34N 73 41W
Ponta Grossa **89** 25 0 S 50 10W
Ponta Pora **89** 22 20 S 55 35W
Pontacq **102** 43 11N 0 8W
Pontailler **101** 47 18N 5 24 E
Pontarlier **101** 46 54N 6 20 E
Pontaubault **100** 48 40N 1 20W
Pontaumur **102** 45 52N 2 40 E
Pontcharra **103** 45 26N 6 1 E
Pontchartrain, L. **75** 30 12N 90 0W
Pontchâteau **100** 47 25N 2 5W
Ponte Leccia **103** 42 28N 9 13 E
Ponte Nova **89** 20 25 S 42 54W
Pontedera **108** 43 40N 10 37 E
Pontefract **94** 53 42N 1 19W
Ponteix **56** 49 46N 107 29W
Pontemacassar Naikliu **127** 9 30 S 123 58 E
Pontevedra **104** 42 26N 8 40W
Pontiac, Ill., U.S.A. **77** 40 50N 88 40W
Pontiac, Mich., U.S.A. **77** 42 40N 83 20W
Pontiac, Parc **40** 46 30N 76 30W
Pontian Kechil **128** 1 29N 103 23 E

Pontianak Presidio

Pontianak 126 0 3S 109 15E
Pontine Mts. = Karadeniz D. 122 41 30N 35 0E
Pontivy 100 48 5N 3 0W
Pontoise 101 49 3N 2 5E
Ponton, R. 54 58 27N 116 11W
Pontorson 100 48 34N 1 30W
Ponts-de Cé, Les 100 47 25N 0 30W
Pontypool, Can. 47 44 6N 78 38W
Pontypool, U.K. 95 51 42N 3 1W
Pontypridd 95 51 36N 3 21W
Ponziane, Isole 108 40 55N 13 0E
Poole 33 50 42N 1 2W
Pooley I. 62 52 45N 128 15W
Poona = Pune 124 18 29N 73 57E
Pooncarie 136 33 22S 142 31E
Poopelloe, L. 136 31 40S 144 0E
Poopó, Lago de 86 18 30S 67 35W
Poorman 67 64 5N 155 48W
Popak 128 22 15N 109 56E
Popakai, Austral. 87 32 12S 141 46E
Popakai, Surinam 87 3 20N 55 30W
Popayán 86 2 27N 76 36W
Poperinge 105 50 51N 2 42E
Popigay 121 71 55N 110 47E
Poplar, Mont., U.S.A. 74 48 3N 105 9W
Poplar, Wis., U.S.A. 52 46 35N 91 48W
Poplar Bluff 75 36 45N 90 22W
Poplar Point 57 50 4N 97 59W
Poplar, R., Man., Can. 57 53 0N 97 19W
Poplar, R., N.W.T., Can. 54 61 22N 121 52W
Poplarfield 57 50 53N 97 36W
Poplarville 75 30 55N 89 30W
Popocatepetl, vol. 83 19 10N 98 40W
Popokabaka 116 5 49S 16 40E
Porbandar 124 21 44N 69 43E
Porcher I. 62 53 50N 130 30W
Porcupine 53 48 30N 81 11W
Porcupine Plain 56 52 36N 103 15W
Porcupine, R., Can. 55 59 11N 104 46W
Porcupine, R., U.S.A. 67 67 0N 143 0W
Pore 86 5 43N 72 0W
Pori 111 61 29N 21 48E
Porjus 110 66 57N 19 50E
Porkkala 111 59 59N 24 26E
Porlamar 86 10 57N 63 51W
Pornic 100 47 7N 2 5W
Poronaysk 121 49 20N 143 0E
Porreta Pass 108 44 0N 11 10E
Porsangen 110 70 40N 25 40E
Port 101 47 43N 6 4E
Port Alberni 62 49 40N 124 50W
Port Albert 136 38 42S 146 42E
Port Albert Victor 124 21 0N 71 30E
Port Alexander 67 56 13N 134 40W
Port Alfred, Can. 41 48 18N 70 53W
Port Alfred, S. Afr. 117 33 36S 26 55E
Port Alice 62 50 20N 127 25W
Port Allegany 70 41 49N 78 17W
Port Allen 75 30 30N 91 15W
Port Angeles 80 48 7N 123 30W
Port Antonio 84 18 10N 76 30W
Port Aransas 75 27 49N 97 4W
Port Arthur, Austral. 135 43 7S 147 50E
Port Arthur, U.S.A. 75 30 0N 94 0W
Port Arthur = Lüshun 130 38 51N 121 20E
Port Arthur = Thunder Bay 52 48 25N 89 10W
Port au Choix 37 50 43N 57 22W
Port au Port 37 48 33N 58 43W
Port au Port B. 37 48 40N 58 50W
Port-au-Prince 85 18 40N 72 20W
Port Augusta 135 32 30S 137 50E
Port Augusta West 135 32 29S 137 47E
Port Austin 46 44 3N 82 59W
Port Bergé Vaovao 117 15 33S 47 40E
Port Blair 128 11 40N 92 30E
Port Blandford 37 48 20N 54 10W
Port Bolivar 75 29 20N 94 40W
Port Burwell 46 42 40N 80 48W
Port Canning 125 22 17N 88 48E
Port Carling 46 45 7N 79 35W
Port-Cartier 38 50 2N 66 50W
Port-Cartier-Ouest 38 50 1N 66 52W
Port Chalmers 133 45 49S 170 30E
Port Chester 71 41 0N 73 41W
Port Clements 62 53 40N 132 10W
Port Clinton 77 41 30N 83 0W
Port Colborne 46 42 50N 79 10W
Port Coquitlam 66 49 15N 122 45W
Port Credit 50 43 33N 79 35W
Port Dalhousie 49 43 13N 79 16W
Port-Daniel, Parc Prov. de 38 48 11N 64 58W
Port Darwin 90 51 50S 59 0W
Port-de-Bouc 103 43 24N 4 59E
Port de Paix 85 19 50N 72 50W
Port Dickson 128 2 30N 101 49E
Port Dover 46 42 47N 80 12W
Port Dufferin 39 44 55N 62 23W
Port Edward 62 54 12N 130 10W
Port Elgin, N.B., Can. 39 46 3N 64 5W
Port Elgin, Ont., Can. 34 44 25N 81 25W
Port Elizabeth 117 33 58S 25 40E
Port Erin 94 54 5N 4 45W
Port Fairy 136 38 22S 142 12E
Port Gamble 80 47 51N 122 35W
Port-Gentil 116 0 47S 8 40E
Port Gibson 75 31 57N 91 0W
Port Glasgow 96 55 57N 4 40W
Port Greville 39 45 24N 64 33W
Port Guichon 66 49 5N 123 7W
Port Hammond 66 49 12N 122 39W
Port Harcourt 114 4 40N 7 10E
Port Hardy 62 50 41N 127 30W
Port Hastings 39 45 39N 61 24W
Port Hawkesbury 39 45 36N 61 22W
Port Hedland 134 20 25S 118 35E
Port Heiden 67 57 0N 158 40W
Port Henry 71 44 0N 73 30W
Port Hood 39 46 0N 61 32W
Port Hope, Can. 47 43 56N 78 20W
Port Hope, U.S.A. 46 43 57N 82 43W
Port Howe 39 45 51N 63 45W
Port Hueneme 81 34 7N 119 12W
Port Huron 46 43 0N 82 28W
Port Isabel 75 26 12N 97 9W
Port Jackson 135 33 50S 151 18E
Port Jefferson 71 40 58N 73 5W
Port Jervis 71 41 22N 74 42W
Port-Joinville 100 46 45N 2 23W
Port Kaituma 86 8 3N 59 58W
Port Kelang 128 3 0N 101 23E
Port Kells 66 49 10N 122 42W
Port Kembla 136 34 29S 150 56E
Port-la-Nouvelle 102 43 1N 3 3E
Port Laoise 97 53 2N 7 20W
Port Lavaca 75 28 38N 96 38W
Port Lewis 43 45 10N 74 17W
Port Lincoln 134 34 42S 135 52E
Port Loring 46 45 55N 80 0W
Port Lorne 39 44 57N 65 16W
Port Louis, France 100 47 42N 3 22W
Port Louis, Maur. 16 20 10S 57 30E
Port McNeill 62 50 35N 127 5W
Port Macquarie 135 31 25S 152 54E
Port Maitland 70 42 53N 79 35W
Port Mann 66 49 12N 122 49W
Port Maria 84 18 25N 76 55W
Port Medway 39 44 8N 64 35W
Port Mellon 63 49 32N 123 31W
Port-Menier 38 49 51N 64 15W
Port Moody 66 49 17N 122 51W
Port Morant 84 17 54N 76 19W
Port Moresby 14 9 24S 147 8E
Port Mouton 39 43 58N 64 50W
Port-Navalo 100 47 34N 2 54W
Port Nelson, Man., Can. 55 57 3N 92 36W
Port Nelson, Ont., Can. 48 43 20N 79 46W
Port Nolloth 117 29 17S 16 52E
Port Nouveau-Quebec (George R.) 36 58 30N 65 50W
Port O'Connor 75 28 26N 96 24W
Port of Spain 85 10 40N 61 20W
Port Orchard 80 47 31N 122 38W
Port Oxford 78 42 45N 124 28W
Port Pegasus 133 47 12S 167 41E
Port Perry 47 44 6N 78 56W
Port Phillip B. 136 38 10S 144 50E
Port Pirie 135 33 10S 137 58E
Port Pleasant 71 40 5N 74 4W
Port Renfrew 62 48 30N 124 20W
Port Robinson 49 43 2N 79 13W
Port Rowan 46 42 40N 80 30W
Port Royal 39 44 43N 65 36W
Port Ryerse 70 42 47N 80 15W
Port Said = Bûr Sa'îd 115 31 16N 32 18E
Port St. Joe 73 29 49N 85 20W
Port-St.-Louis-du-Rhône 103 43 23N 4 49E
Port St. Servain 35 51 21N 58 0W
Port Sanilac 46 43 26N 82 33W
Port Saunders 37 50 40N 57 18W
Port Severn 46 44 48N 79 43W
Port Shepstone 117 30 44S 30 28E
Port Simpson 54 54 30N 130 20W
Port Stanley 46 42 40N 81 10W
Port Stephens 136 32 38S 152 12E
Port Talbot 95 51 35N 3 48W
Port Townsend 80 48 7N 122 50W
Port-Vendres 102 42 32N 3 8E
Port Wallace 39 44 42N 63 33W
Port Washington 72 43 25N 87 52W
Port Weld 128 4 50N 100 38E
Port Weller East 49 43 14N 79 13W
Port Whitby 51 43 51N 78 56W
Port Wing 52 46 47N 91 23W
Portachuelo 86 17 10S 63 20W
Portadown (Craigavon) 97 54 27N 6 26W
Portage, Can. 35 46 40N 64 5W
Portage, U.S.A. 74 43 31N 89 25W
Portage B. 57 51 33N 98 50W
Portage L. 52 47 3N 88 30W
Portage La Prairie 57 49 58N 98 18W
Portage Mt. Dam 54 56 0N 122 0W
Portage, R. 77 41 32N 82 58W
Portageville 75 36 25N 89 40W
Portalegre 104 39 19N 7 25W
Portalegre □ 104 39 20N 7 40W
Portales 75 34 12N 103 25W
Portarlington 97 53 10N 7 10W
Porte City, La 76 42 19N 92 12W
Porte, La 77 41 36N 86 43W
Porter 77 41 36N 87 4W
Porter L., N.W.T., Can. 55 61 41N 108 5W
Porter L., Sask., Can. 55 56 20N 107 20W
Porterville 80 36 5N 119 0W
Portet 102 43 34N 0 11W
Porthill 61 49 0N 116 30W
Portile de Fier 107 44 42N 22 30E
Portimão 104 37 8N 8 32W
Portland, N.S.W., Austral. 136 33 20S 150 0E
Portland, Victoria, Austral. 136 38 20S 141 35E
Portland, Can. 47 44 42N 76 12W
Portland, Conn., U.S.A. 71 41 34N 72 39W
Portland, Ind., U.S.A. 77 40 26N 84 59W
Portland, Me., U.S.A. 35 43 40N 70 15W
Portland, Mich., U.S.A. 77 42 52N 84 58W
Portland, Oreg., U.S.A. 80 45 35N 122 40W
Portland B. 136 38 15S 141 45E
Portland Bill 95 50 31N 2 27W
Portland, C. 135 40 46S 148 0E
Portland Creek Pond 37 50 11N 57 32W
Portland, I. of 95 50 32N 2 25W
Portland Prom. 36 58 40N 78 33W
Portneuf 42 46 43N 71 55W
Portneuf, Parc Prov. de 41 47 10N 72 25W
Portneuf, R. 41 48 38N 69 5W
Pôrto 104 41 8N 8 40W
Pôrto Alegre, Mato Grosso, Brazil 87 21 40S 53 30W
Pôrto Alegre, Rio Grande do Sul, Brazil 89 30 5S 51 3W
Porto Alexandre 117 15 55S 11 55E
Pôrto de Moz 87 1 41S 52 22W
Porto Empédocle 108 37 18N 13 30E
Pôrto Esperança 86 19 37S 57 29W
Pôrto Franco 87 6 20S 47 24W
Porto, G. de 103 42 17N 8 34E
Porto Mendes 89 24 30S 54 15W
Porto Murtinho 86 21 45S 57 55W
Porto Nacional 87 10 40S 48 30W
Porto Novo 114 6 23N 2 42E
Pôrto São José 89 22 43S 53 10W
Pôrto Seguro 87 16 26S 39 5W
Porto Tórres 108 40 50N 8 23E
Pôrto União 89 26 10S 51 10W
Pôrto Válter 86 8 5S 72 40W
Porto-Vecchio 103 41 35N 9 16E
Pôrto Velho 86 8 46S 63 54W
Portobelo 84 9 35N 79 42W
Portoferráio 108 42 50N 10 20E
Portola 80 39 49N 120 28W
Portoscuso 108 39 12N 8 22E
Portoviejo 86 1 0S 80 20W
Portpatrick 96 54 50N 5 7W
Portree 96 57 25N 6 11W
Portrush 97 55 13N 6 40W
Portsall 100 48 37N 4 45W
Portsmouth, Can. 71 44 14N 76 34W
Portsmouth, Domin. 85 15 34N 61 27W
Portsmouth, U.K. 95 50 48N 1 6W
Portsmouth, N.H., U.S.A. 71 43 5N 70 45W
Portsmouth, Ohio, U.S.A. 72 38 45N 83 0W
Portsmouth, R.I., U.S.A. 71 41 35N 71 44W
Portsmouth, Va., U.S.A. 72 36 50N 76 20W
Porttipahta 110 68 5N 26 30E
Portugal ■ 104 40 0N 7 0W
Portuguesa □ 86 9 10N 69 15W
Portuguese Timor ■ = Timor 127 8 0S 126 30E
Portumna 97 53 5N 8 12W
Portville 70 42 3N 78 21W
Porvenir 90 53 10S 70 30W
Porvoo 111 60 24N 25 40E
Posadas 89 27 30S 56 0W
Poseh 131 23 50N 106 0E
Posen 46 45 16N 83 42W
Poseyville 77 38 10N 87 47W
Poso 127 1 20S 120 55E
Poso Colorado 88 23 30S 58 45W
Poso, D. 127 1 20S 120 55E
Posse 87 14 4S 46 18W
Possel 116 5 5N 19 10E
Possession I. 91 72 4S 172 0E
Post 75 33 13N 101 21W
Post Falls 78 47 50N 116 59W
Poste de la Baleine 36 55 17N 77 45W
Postiljon, Kepulauan 127 6 30S 118 50E
Postojna 107 45 46N 14 12E
Poston 81 34 0N 114 24W
Postville 76 43 5N 91 34W
Potchefstroom 117 26 41S 27 7E
Poteau 75 35 5N 94 37W
Poteet 75 29 4N 98 35W
Potenza 108 40 40N 15 50E
Poteriteri, L. 133 46 5S 167 10E
Potgietersrus 117 24 10S 29 3E
Potomac, R. 72 38 0N 76 23W
Potosí 86 19 38S 65 50W
Potosi 76 37 56N 90 47W
Potosí □ 86 20 31S 67 0W
Potosi Mt. 81 35 57N 115 29W
Potow 130 38 8N 116 31E
Potrerillos 88 26 20S 69 30W
Potros, Cerro del 88 28 32S 69 0W
Potsdam, Ger. 106 52 23N 13 4E
Potsdam, U.S.A. 71 44 40N 74 59W
Pottageville 50 43 59N 79 37W
Potter 74 41 15N 103 20W
Pottstown 71 40 17N 75 40W
Pottsville 71 40 39N 76 12W
Pottuvil 124 6 55N 81 50E
Pouancé 100 47 44N 1 10W
Pouce Coupé 54 55 40N 120 10W
Pouch Cove 37 47 46N 52 46W
Poughkeepsie 71 41 40N 73 57W
Pouilly 101 47 18N 2 57E
Poulaphouca Res. 97 53 8N 6 30W
Pouldu, Le 100 47 41N 3 36W
Poulin-de-Courval, L. 41 48 52N 70 27W
Poulsbo 80 47 45N 122 39W
Pouso Alegre, Mato Grosso, Brazil 87 11 55S 57 0W
Pouso Alegre, Minas Gerais, Brazil 89 22 14S 45 57W
Poutrincourt, L. 41 49 11N 74 7W
Pouzages 102 46 40N 0 50W
Povenets 120 62 50N 34 50E
Poverty Bay 133 38 43S 178 2E
Póvoa de Varzim 104 41 25N 8 46W
Povungnituk 36 60 2N 77 10W
Povungnituk, B. 36 60 0N 77 30W
Povungnituk, Mts. de 36 61 22N 75 5W
Povungnituk, R. 36 60 3N 77 15W
Powassan 46 46 5N 79 25W
Poway 81 32 58N 117 2W
Powder, R. 74 46 47N 105 12W
Powell 78 44 45N 108 45W
Powell Creek 134 18 6S 133 46E
Powell L. 62 50 2N 124 25W
Powell River 62 49 50N 124 35W
Powers, Mich., U.S.A. 72 45 40N 87 32W
Powers, Oreg., U.S.A. 78 42 53N 124 2W
Powers Lake 74 48 37N 102 38W
Powis, Vale of 98 52 40N 3 10W
Powys □ 95 52 20N 3 20W
Poyang 131 28 59N 116 40E
Poyang Hu 131 29 10N 116 10E
Poyarkovo 121 49 36N 128 41E
Poza Rica 83 20 33N 97 27W
Požarevac 109 44 35N 21 18E
Poznan 106 52 25N 17 0E
Pozo 81 35 20N 120 24W
Pozo Almonte 86 20 10S 69 50W
Pozoblanco 104 38 23N 4 51W
Prachin Buri 128 14 0N 101 25E
Prachuap Khiri Khan 128 11 49N 99 48E
Pradelles 102 44 46N 3 52E
Pradera 86 3 25N 76 15W
Prades 102 42 38N 2 23E
Prado 87 17 20S 39 13W
Prague = Praha 106 50 5N 14 22E
Praha 106 50 5N 14 22E
Prahecq 102 46 19N 0 26W
Praid 107 46 32N 25 10E
Prainha, Amazonas, Brazil 86 7 10S 60 30W
Prainha, Pará, Brazil 87 1 45S 53 30W
Prairie City 78 44 27N 118 44W
Prairie du Chien 76 43 1N 91 9W
Prairie du Rocher 76 38 5N 90 6W
Prairie, La 45 45 25N 73 30W
Prairie, R. 75 34 45N 101 15W
Prairies, R. des 44 45 42N 73 29W
Praja 126 8 39S 116 27E
Prapat 126 2 41N 98 58E
Prata, Minas Gerais, Brazil 87 19 25S 49 0W
Prata, Pará, Brazil 87 1 10S 47 35W
Prato 108 43 53N 11 5E
Prats-de-Mollo 102 42 25N 2 27E
Pratt 75 37 40N 98 45W
Prattville 73 32 30N 86 28W
Pravia 104 43 30N 6 12W
Pré-en-Pail 100 48 28N 0 12W
Precordillera 88 30 0S 69 1W
Preeceville 56 51 57N 102 40W
Préfailles 100 47 9N 2 11W
Pregonero 86 8 1N 71 46W
Preissac, L. 40 48 20N 78 20W
Prelate 56 50 51N 109 24W
Premier 54 56 4N 129 56W
Premier Downs 134 30 30S 126 30E
Premont 75 27 19N 98 8W
Prentice 74 45 31N 90 19W
Prenzlau 106 53 19N 13 51E
Prepansko Jezero 109 40 45N 21 0E
Preparis North Channel 128 15 12N 93 40E
Preparis South Channel 128 14 36N 93 40E
Prerov 107 49 28N 17 27E
Prescott, Can. 47 44 45N 75 30W
Prescott, Ariz., U.S.A. 79 34 35N 112 30W
Prescott, Ark., U.S.A. 75 33 49N 93 22W
Prescott □ 43 45 32N 74 30W
Prescott I. 62 54 6N 130 37W
Présentation, La 45 45 39N 73 3W
Preservation Inlet 133 46 8S 166 35E
Presho 74 43 56N 100 4W
Presidencia de la Plaza 88 27 0S 60 0W
Presidencia Roque Sáenz Peña 88 26 45S 60 30W
Presidente Dutra 82 5 15S 44 30W
Presidente Hayes □ 88 24 0S 59 0W
Presidente Hermes 86 11 0S 61 55W
Presidente Prudente 89 22 5S 51 25W
Presidente Rogue Saena Peña 88 34 33S 58 30W
Presidio, Mexico 82 29 29N 104 23W
Presidio, U.S.A. 75 29 30N 104 20W

Presque Isle Quilán, C

Presque Isle 35 46 40N 68 0W
Presteigne 95 52 17N 3 0W
Preston, Can. 49 43 23N 80 21W
Preston, U.K. 94 53 46N 2 42W
Preston, U.S.A. 76 42 6N 90 24W
Preston, Idaho, U.S.A. 78 42 10N 111 55W
Preston, Minn., U.S.A. 74 43 39N 92 3W
Preston, Nev., U.S.A. 78 38 59N 115 2W
Preston, C. 134 20 51S 116 12E
Prestonpans 96 55 58N 3 0W
Prestwick 96 55 30N 4 38W
Pretoria 117 25 44S 28 12E
Preuilly-sur-Claise 100 46 51N 0 56E
Préveza 109 38 57N 20 47E
Préville 45 45 29N 73 30W
Prevost 43 45 52N 74 5W
Prey-Veng 128 11 35N 105 29E
Pribilov Is. 17 56 0N 170 0W
Pribram 106 49 41N 14 2E
Price, Can. 38 48 36N 68 7W
Price, U.S.A. 78 39 40N 110 48W
Price I. 62 52 23N 128 41W
Prieska 117 29 40S 22 42E
Priest L. 63 48 30N 116 55W
Priest River 78 48 11N 116 55W
Priest Valley 80 36 10N 120 39W
Priestly 54 54 8N 125 20W
Prilep 109 41 21N 21 37E
Primrose L. 55 54 55N 109 45W
Prince 56 52 58N 108 23W
Prince Albert 56 53 15N 105 50W
Prince Albert Nat. Park 56 54 0N 106 25W
Prince Albert Pen. 64 72 30N 116 0W
Prince Albert Sd. 64 70 25N 115 0W
Prince Alfred C. 64 74 20N 124 40W
Prince Charles I. 64 67 47N 76 12W
Prince Edward I. □. 39 46 30N 63 30W
Prince Edward Is. 16 45 15S 39 0E
Prince Edward Island Nat. Pk. 39 46 26N 63 12W
Prince Edward Pt. 47 43 56N 76 52W
Prince George 63 53 55N 122 50W
Prince Gustav Adolf Sea 64 78 30N 107 0W
Prince of Wales, C. 67 65 50N 168 0W
Prince of Wales I. 67 73 0N 99 0W
Prince of Wales, I. 67 53 30N 131 30W
Prince of Wales Is. 135 10 40S 142 10E
Prince of Wales Str. 64 73 0N 117 0W
Prince Patrick I. 64 77 0N 120 0W
Prince Regent Inlet 65 73 0N 90 0W
Prince Rupert 62 54 20N 130 20W
Prince William Sd. 67 60 20N 146 30W
Princess Charlotte B. 135 14 25S 144 0E
Princess Margaret Range 65 80 30N 92 0W
Princess Royal Chan. 62 53 0N 128 31W
Princess Royal I. 62 53 0N 128 40W
Princeton, B.C., Can. 63 49 27N 120 30W
Princeton, Ont., Can. 49 43 10N 80 32W
Princeton, Calif., U.S.A. 80 39 24N 122 1W
Princeton, Ill., U.S.A. 76 41 23N 89 28W
Princeton, Ill., U.S.A. 76 41 25N 89 25W
Princeton, Ind., U.S.A. 77 38 20N 87 35W
Princeton, Ky., U.S.A. 72 37 6N 87 55W
Princeton, Mo., U.S.A. 76 40 23N 93 35W
Princeton, N.J., U.S.A. 71 40 18N 74 40W
Princeton, W. Va., U.S.A. 72 37 21N 81 8W
Princeville, Can. 41 46 10N 71 53W
Princeville, U.S.A. 76 40 56N 89 46W
Principe Chan. 62 53 28N 130 0W
Principe da Beira 86 12 20S 64 30W
Principe, I. de 112 1 37N 7 27E
Prineville 78 44 17N 120 57W
Prins Harald Kyst 91 70 0S 35 1E
Prinzapolca 84 13 20N 83 35W
Pripet, R. = Pripyat, R. 120 51 30N 30 0E
Pripyat, R. 120 51 30N 30 0E
Priština 109 42 40N 21 13E
Pritchard 73 30 47N 88 5W
Privas 103 44 45N 4 37E
Prizren 109 42 13N 20 45E
Probolinggo 127 7 46S 113 13E
Procter 63 49 37N 116 57W
Proddatur 124 14 45N 78 30E
Progreso 83 21 20N 89 40W
Prokopyevsk 120 54 0N 87 3E
Prome = Pyè 125 18 45N 95 30E
Prophet, R. 54 58 48N 122 40W
Prophetstown 76 41 40N 89 56W
Propriá 87 10 13S 36 51W
Propriano 103 41 41N 8 52E
Proserpine 135 20 21S 148 36E
Prosser 78 46 11N 119 52W
Prostějov 106 49 30N 17 9E
Protection 75 37 16N 99 30W
Prøven 65 72 10N 55 8W
Provence 103 43 40N 5 46E
Providence, Ky., U.S.A. 72 37 25N 87 46W
Providence, R.I., U.S.A. 71 41 41N 71 15W
Providence Bay 46 45 41N 82 15W
Providence, La 45 45 37N 72 57W
Providence Mts. 79 35 0N 115 30W
Providencia 86 0 28S 76 28W
Providencia, I. de 84 13 25N 81 26W
Provideniya 121 64 23N 173 18E
Province Wellesley 128 5 15N 100 20E
Provincetown 72 42 5N 70 11W
Provins 101 48 33N 3 15E
Provo 78 40 16N 111 37W
Provost 61 52 25N 110 20W
Prudhoe Bay 67 70 20N 148 20W
Prudhoe Land 17 78 1N 65 0W
Prud'homme 56 52 20N 105 54W
Pruszków 107 52 9N 20 49E
Prut, R. 107 46 3N 28 10E
Prydz B. 91 69 0S 74 0E
Pryor 75 36 17N 95 20W
Przemyśl 107 49 50N 22 45E
Przeworsk 107 50 6N 22 32E
Przhevalsk 120 42 30N 78 20E
Pskov 120 57 50N 28 25E
Puán 88 37 30S 63 0W
Pubnico 35 43 47N 65 50W
Pucallpa 86 8 25S 74 30W
Pucheng 131 28 0N 118 30E
Puchi 131 29 42N 113 54E
Pudukkottai 124 10 28N 78 47E
Puebla 83 19 0N 98 10W
Puebla □ 83 18 30N 98 0W
Pueblo 74 38 20N 104 40W
Pueblo Bonito 79 36 4N 107 57W
Pueblo Hundido 88 26 20S 69 30W
Pueblo Nuevo 86 8 26N 71 26W
Pueblonuevo 104 38 16N 5 16W
Puelches 88 38 5S 66 0W
Puelén 88 37 32S 67 38W
Puente Alto 88 33 32S 70 35W
Puente Genil 104 37 22N 4 47W
Puerco, R. 79 35 10N 109 45W
Puerh 129 23 11N 100 56E
Puerto Aisén 90 45 10S 73 0W
Puerto Angel 83 15 40N 96 29W
Puerto Arista 83 15 56N 93 48W
Puerto Armuelles 84 8 20N 83 10W
Puerto Ayacucho 86 5 40N 67 35W
Puerto Barrios 84 15 40N 88 40W
Puerto Belgrano 131 38 50S 62 0W
Puerto Bermejo 88 26 55S 58 34W
Puerto Bermúdez 86 10 20S 75 0W
Puerto Bolívar 86 3 10S 79 55W
Puerto Cabello 86 10 28N 68 1W
Puerto Cabezas 84 14 0N 83 30W
Puerto Cabo Gracias a Dios 84 15 0N 83 10W
Puerto Carreño 86 6 12N 67 22W
Puerto Casado 88 22 19S 57 56W
Puerto Castilla 84 16 0N 86 0W
Puerto Chicama 86 7 45S 79 20W
Puerto Coig 90 50 54S 69 15W
Puerto Columbia 86 10 59N 74 58W
Puerto Cortés, C. Rica 84 8 20N 82 20W
Puerto Cortés, Hond. 84 15 51N 88 0W
Puerto Cuemani 86 0 5N 73 21W
Puerto Cumarebo 86 11 29N 69 21W
Puerto de Morelos 83 20 49N 86 52W
Puerto de Santa María 104 36 36N 6 13W
Puerto Deseado 90 47 45S 66 0W
Puerto Heath 86 12 25S 68 45W
Puerto Huitoto 86 0 18N 74 3W
Puerto Juárez 83 21 11N 86 49W
Puerto La Cruz 86 10 13N 64 38W
Puerto Leguízamo 86 0 12S 74 46W
Puerto Libertad 82 29 55N 112 41W
Puerto Limón, Meta, Colomb. 86 3 23N 73 30W
Puerto Limón, Putumayo, Colomb. 86 1 3N 76 30W
Puerto Lobos 90 42 0S 65 3W
Puerto López 86 4 5N 72 58W
Puerto Madryn 90 42 48S 65 4W
Puerto Maldonado 86 12 30S 69 10W
Puerto Manotí 84 21 22N 76 50W
Puerto Mercedes 86 1 11N 72 53W
Puerto Montt 90 41 22S 72 40W
Puerto Natales 90 51 45S 72 25W
Puerto Nuevo 86 5 53N 69 56W
Puerto Ordaz 86 8 16N 62 44W
Puerto Padre 84 21 13N 76 35W
Puerto Páez 86 6 13N 67 28W
Puerto Peñasco 82 31 20N 113 33W
Puerto Pinasco 88 22 43S 57 50W
Puerto Pirámides 90 42 35S 64 20W
Puerto Plata 85 19 40N 70 45W
Puerto Quellón 90 43 7S 73 37W
Puerto Quepos 84 9 29N 84 6W
Puerto Rico 86 1 54N 75 10W
Puerto Rico ■ 85 18 15N 66 45W
Puerto Rico Trough 12 20 0N 63 0W
Puerto Sastre 88 22 25S 57 55W
Puerto Suárez 86 18 58S 57 52W
Puerto Tejada 86 3 14N 76 24W
Puerto Umbria 86 0 52N 76 33W
Puerto Vallarta 82 20 26N 105 15W
Puerto Villamizar 86 8 25N 72 30W
Puerto Wilches 86 7 21N 73 54W
Puertollano 104 38 43N 4 7W
Pueyrredón, L. 90 47 20S 72 0W
Pugachev 120 52 0N 48 55E
Puget Sd. 78 47 15N 122 30W
Puget-Théniers 103 43 58N 6 53E
Púglia □ 108 41 0N 16 30E
Pugwash 39 45 51N 63 40W
Puhute Mesa 80 37 25N 116 50W
Puigcerdá 104 42 24N 1 50E
Puisaye, Collines de 101 47 34N 3 28E
Puiseaux 101 48 11N 2 30E
Pukaki L. 133 44 4S 170 1E
Pukaskwa Nat. Park 53 48 20N 86 0W
Pukatawagan 55 55 45N 101 20W
Pukekohe 133 37 12S 174 55E
Pukoo 67 21 4N 156 48W
Pukow 131 32 15N 118 45E
Pula 108 39 0N 9 0E
Pulantien 130 39 25N 122 0E
Pulaski, N.Y., U.S.A. 71 43 32N 76 9W
Pulaski, Tenn., U.S.A. 73 35 10N 87 0W
Pulaski, Va., U.S.A. 72 37 4N 80 49W
Pulga 80 39 48N 121 29W
Pulicat, L. 124 13 40N 80 15E
Pullman 78 46 49N 117 10W
Pulog, Mt. 127 16 40N 120 50E
Puloraja 126 4 55N 95 24E
Pumlumon Fawr 95 52 29N 3 47W
Puna 86 19 45S 65 28W
Puna de Atacama 88 25 0S 67 0W
Puná, I. 86 2 55S 80 5W
Punakha 125 27 42N 89 52E
Punata 86 17 25S 65 50W
Punch 124 33 48N 74 4E
Pune 124 18 29N 73 57E
Punjab □ 124 31 0N 76 0E
Punnichy 56 51 23N 104 18W
Puno 86 15 55S 70 3W
Punta Alta 90 38 53S 62 4W
Punta Arenas 90 53 0S 71 0W
Punta de Díaz 88 28 0S 70 45W
Punta de Piedras 86 10 54N 64 6W
Punta del Lago Viedma 90 49 45S 72 0W
Punta Gorda, Belize 83 16 10N 88 45W
Punta Gorda, U.S.A. 73 26 55N 82 0W
Punta Prieta 82 28 58N 114 17W
Puntarenas 84 10 0N 84 50W
Punto Fijo 86 11 42N 70 13W
Puntzi L. 62 52 12N 124 2W
Punxsutawney 70 40 56N 79 0W
Punyu 131 22 58N 113 16E
Puquio 86 14 45S 74 10W
Pur, R. 120 65 30N 77 40E
Purace, vol. 86 2 21N 76 23W
Purbeck, Isle of 95 50 40N 2 5W
Purcell 75 35 0N 97 25W
Puri 125 19 50N 85 58E
Purificación 86 3 51N 74 55W
Purísima, La 82 26 10N 112 4W
Purmerend 105 52 30N 4 58E
Purnea 125 25 45N 87 31E
Pursat 128 12 34N 103 50E
Puruey 86 7 35N 64 48W
Purukcahu 126 0 35S 114 35E
Purulia 125 23 17N 86 33E
Purus, R. 86 5 25S 64 0W
Purwakarta 127 6 35S 107 29E
Purwodadi, Jawa, Indon. 127 7 51S 110 0E
Purwodadi, Jawa, Indon. 127 7 7S 110 55E
Purworejo 127 7 43S 110 2E
Pusan 130 35 5N 129 0E
Pushchino 121 54 20N 158 10E
Puskitamika L. 34 49 20N 76 30W
Puslinch 49 43 26N 80 5W
Puslinch, L. 49 43 25N 80 16W
Putahow L. 55 59 54N 100 40W
Putao 125 27 28N 97 30E
Putaruru 133 38 2S 175 50E
Putehachi (Chalantun) 129 48 4N 122 45E
Puthein Myit, R. 125 15 56N 94 18E
Putien 131 25 28N 119 0E
Putignano 108 40 50N 17 5E
Putnam 71 41 55N 71 55W
Putorana, Gory 121 69 0N 95 0E
Puttalam 124 8 1N 79 55E
Putten 105 52 16N 5 36E
Puttgarden 106 54 28N 11 15E
Putumayo □ 86 1 30S 70 0W
Putumayo, R. 86 1 30S 70 0W
Putussibau, G. 126 0 45N 113 50E
Puy-de-Dôme 102 45 46N 2 57E
Puy-de-Dôme □ 102 45 47N 3 0E
Puy-de-Sancy 102 45 32N 2 41E
Puy Guillaume 102 45 57N 3 28E
Puy, Le 102 45 3N 3 52E
Puy l'Évêque 102 44 31N 1 9E
Puyallup 80 47 10N 122 22W
Puyang 130 35 45N 115 22E
Puyjalon, L. 38 50 30N 63 25W
Puylaurens 102 43 35N 2 0E
Puyôo 102 43 33N 0 56W
Pweto 116 8 25S 28 51E
Pwllheli 94 52 54N 4 26W
Pyapon 125 16 5N 95 50E
Pyasina, R. 121 72 30N 90 30E
Pyatigorsk 120 44 2N 43 0E
Pyinmana 125 19 45N 96 20E
Pyŏngyang 130 39 0N 125 30E
Pyote 75 31 34N 103 5W
Pyramid L. 78 40 0N 119 30W
Pyramid Pk. 81 36 25N 116 37W
Pyrénées 102 42 45N 0 18E
Pyrenees = Pyrénées 102 42 45N 0 18E
Pyrénées-Atlantiques □ 102 43 15N 1 0W
Pyrénées-Orientales □ 102 42 35N 2 26E
Pyu 125 18 30N 96 35E

Q

Qadam 123 32 55N 66 45E
Qadhimah 122 22 20N 39 13E
Qala-i-Kirta 123 32 15N 63 0E
Qala Nau 123 35 0N 63 5E
Qala Punja 123 37 0N 72 40E
Qal'at al Akhdar 122 28 0N 37 10E
Qal'eh Shaharak 124 34 10N 64 20E
Qamruddin Karez 124 31 45N 68 20E
Qarachuk 122 37 0N 42 2E
Qarah 122 29 55N 40 3E
Qasr-e-Qand 123 26 15N 60 45E
Qatar ■ 123 25 30N 51 15E
Qattara Depression = Q. Munkhafed el 115 29 30N 27 30E
Qattâra, Munkhafed el 115 29 30N 27 30E
Qāyen 123 33 40N 59 10E
Qazvin 122 36 15N 50 0E
Qeisari, (Caesarea) 115 32 30N 34 53E
Qena 115 26 10N 32 43E
Qesari 115 32 30N 34 53E
Qeshm 123 26 55N 56 10E
Qeshm, I. 123 26 50N 56 0E
Qila Saifulla 124 30 45N 68 17E
Qom 123 34 40N 51 0E
Quadra I. 62 50 10N 125 15W
Quakerstown 71 40 27N 75 20W
Qualicum Beach 62 49 22N 124 26W
Quan Long 128 9 7N 105 8E
Quanan 75 34 20N 99 45W
Quang Nam 128 15 55N 108 15E
Quang Ngai 128 15 13N 108 58E
Quang Yen 128 21 3N 106 52E
Quantock Hills, The 95 51 8N 3 10W
Qu'Appelle 56 50 33N 103 53W
Qu'Appelle, R. 56 50 26N 101 19W
Quaraí 88 30 15S 56 20W
Quarré les Tombes 101 47 21N 4 0E
Quarryville 39 46 50N 65 47W
Quartzsite 81 33 44N 114 16W
Quathiaski Cove 62 50 3N 125 12W
Quatsino 62 50 30N 127 40W
Quatsino Sd. 62 50 25N 127 58W
Qūchān 123 37 10N 58 27E
Que Que 117 18 58S 29 48E
Queanbeyan 136 35 17S 149 14E
Québec 42 46 52N 71 13W
Québec □ 35 50 0N 70 0W
Queen Alexandra Ra. 91 85 0S 170 0E
Queen Bess Mt. 54 51 13N 124 35W
Queen Charlotte 62 53 15N 132 2W
Queen Charlotte Is. 62 53 20N 132 10W
Queen Charlotte Mts. 62 53 5N 132 15W
Queen Charlotte Sd. 62 51 30N 130 0W
Queen Charlotte Str. 62 51 0N 128 0W
Queen City 76 40 25N 92 34W
Queen Elizabeth Is. 10 76 0N 95 0W
Queen Mary Coast 91 70 0S 95 0E
Queen Maud G. 64 68 15N 102 30W
Queen's Chan. 134 15 0S 129 30E
Queens Sd. 62 51 57N 128 20W
Queensborough 66 49 12N 122 56W
Queenscliff 136 38 16S 144 39E
Queensland □ 135 15 0S 142 0E
Queenston 49 43 10N 79 3W
Queenstown, Austral. 135 42 4S 145 35E
Queenstown, Can. 39 45 41N 66 7W
Queenstown, N.Z. 133 45 1S 168 40E
Queenstown, S. Afr. 117 31 52S 26 52E
Queets 80 47 32N 124 20W
Queguay Grande, R. 88 32 9S 58 9W
Queimadas 87 11 0S 39 38W
Quela 116 9 10S 16 56E
Quelimane 117 17 53S 36 58E
Quelpart = Cheju Do 131 33 29N 126 34E
Quemado, N. Mex., U.S.A. 79 34 17N 108 28W
Quemado, Tex., U.S.A. 75 28 58N 100 35W
Quemoy = Kinmen 131 24 25N 118 24E
Quemú-Quemú 88 36 3S 63 36W
Quequén 88 38 30S 58 30W
Querétaro 82 20 40N 100 23W
Querétaro □ 82 20 30N 100 30W
Quesnel 63 53 0N 122 30W
Quesnel L. 63 52 30N 121 20W
Quesnel, R. 63 52 58N 122 29W
Questa 79 36 45N 105 35W
Questembert 100 47 40N 2 28W
Quetico 34 48 45N 90 55W
Quetico Prov. Park 52 48 30N 91 45W
Quetta 124 30 15N 66 55E
Quetta □ 124 30 15N 66 55E
Quévillon, L. 40 49 4N 76 57W
Quezaltenango 84 14 40N 91 30W
Quezon City 127 14 38N 121 0E
Qui Nhon 128 13 40N 109 13E
Quiaca, La 88 22 5S 65 35W
Quibaxi 116 8 24S 14 27E
Quibdó 86 5 42N 76 40W
Quiberon 100 47 29N 3 9W
Quibor 86 9 56N 69 37W
Quick 54 54 36N 126 54W
Quidi Vidi 37 47 35N 52 41W
Quiet L. 54 61 5N 133 5W
Quiindy 88 25 58S 57 14W
Quila 82 24 23N 107 13W
Quilán, C. 90 43 15S 74 30W

Quilcene Reefton

Quilcene 80 47 49N 122 53W
Quilchena 63 50 10N 120 30W
Quilengues 117 14 12S 14 12E
Quilimarí 88 32 5S 70 30W
Quilino 88 30 14S 64 29W
Quill Lake 56 52 4N 104 15W
Quillabamba 86 12 50S 72 50W
Quillagua 88 21 40S 69 40W
Quillaicillo 88 31 17S 71 40W
Quillan 102 42 53N 2 10E
Quillebeuf 100 49 28N 0 30E
Quillota 88 32 54S 71 16W
Quilmes 88 34 43S 58 13W
Quilon 124 8 50N 76 38E
Quilpie 135 26 35S 144 11E
Quilpué 88 33 5S 71 33W
Quimilí 88 27 40S 62 30W
Quimper 100 48 0N 4 9W
Quimperlé 100 47 53N 3 33W
Quinault, R. 80 47 23N 124 18W
Quincy, Calif., U.S.A. 80 39 56N 121 0W
Quincy, Fla., U.S.A. 73 30 34N 84 34W
Quincy, Ill., U.S.A. 74 39 55N 91 20W
Quincy, Mass., U.S.A. 72 42 14N 71 0W
Quincy, Wash., U.S.A. 78 47 22N 119 56W
Quines 88 32 13S 65 48W
Quinga 117 15 49S 40 15E
Quingey 101 47 7N 5 52E
Quinhagak 67 59 45N 162 0W
Quintana Roo □ 83 19 0N 88 0W
Quintanar de la Orden 104 39 36N 3 5W
Quintanar de la Sierra 104 41 57N 2 55W
Quintero 88 32 45S 71 30W
Quintin 100 48 26N 2 56W
Quinton 56 51 23N 104 24W
Quinze, L. des 40 47 35N 79 5W
Quirihue 88 36 15S 72 35W
Quiriquire 86 9 59N 63 13W
Quisiro 86 10 53N 71 17W
Quissac 103 43 55N 4 0E
Quissanga 117 12 24S 40 28E
Quitilipi 88 26 50S 60 13W
Quitman, Ga., U.S.A. 73 30 49N 83 35W
Quitman, Miss., U.S.A. 73 32 2N 88 42W
Quitman, Tex., U.S.A. 75 32 48N 95 25W
Quito 86 0 15S 78 35W
Quixadá 87 4 55S 39 0W
Quneitra 115 33 7N 35 48E
Quorn, Austral. 135 32 25S 138 0E
Quorn, Can. 34 49 25N 90 55W
Quruq Tagh, mts. 129 41 30N 90 0E
Quseir 115 26 7N 34 16E
Quyon 40 45 31N 76 14W

R

Raahe 110 64 40N 24 28E
Raanes Pen. 65 78 30N 85 45W
Raasay I. 96 57 25N 6 4W
Raasay, Sd. of 96 57 30N 6 8W
Raba 127 8 36S 118 55E
Rabastens, Hautes Pyrénées, France 102 43 25N 0 10E
Rabastens, Tarn, France 102 43 50N 1 43E
Rabat, Malta 108 35 53N 14 25E
Rabat, Moroc. 114 34 2N 6 48W
Rabaul 14 4 24S 152 18E
Rabbit L. 55 47 0N 79 38W
Rabbit Lake 56 53 8N 107 46W
Rabbit, R. 54 59 41N 127 12W
Rabbitskin, R. 54 61 47N 120 42W
Rabigh 122 22 50N 39 5E
Raccoon Cr. 77 39 47N 87 23W
Raccoon, R. 76 41 35N 93 37W
Race, C. 37 46 40N 53 5W
Rach Gia 128 10 5N 105 5E
Rachaya 115 33 30N 35 50E
Racine 77 42 41N 87 51W
Racine L. 53 48 2N 83 20W
Rackerby 80 39 26N 121 22W
Radauti 107 47 53N 25 48E
Radcliff 77 37 51N 85 57W
Radford 72 37 8N 80 32W
Radisson 56 52 30N 107 20W
Radium Hill 135 32 30S 140 42E
Radium Hot Springs 61 50 35N 116 2W
Radnor Forest 95 52 17N 3 10W
Radom 107 51 23N 21 12E
Radomir 109 42 37N 23 4E
Radomsko 107 51 5N 19 28E
Radstock 95 51 17N 2 25W
Radstock, C. 134 33 12S 134 20E
Radville 56 49 30N 104 15W
Radway 60 54 4N 112 57W
Rae 54 62 50N 116 3W
Rae Bareli 125 26 18N 81 20E
Rae Isthmus 65 66 40N 87 30W
Raeside, L. 134 29 20S 122 0E
Raetihi 133 39 25S 175 17E
Rafaela 88 31 10S 61 30W
Rafai 116 4 59N 23 58E
Rafhã 122 29 35N 43 35E
Rafsanjãn 123 30 30N 56 5E
Ragama 124 7 0N 79 50E
Raglan 133 37 55S 174 55E
Ragueneau 35 49 11N 68 18W
Ragusa 108 36 56N 14 42E
Raha 127 8 20S 118 40E
Raichur 124 16 10N 77 20E
Raigarh 125 21 56N 83 25E
Raiis 122 23 33N 38 43E
Raijua 127 10 37S 121 36E
Rainbow Lake 54 58 30N 119 23W
Rainier 80 46 4N 123 0W
Rainier, Mt. 80 46 50N 121 50W
Rainy L. 52 48 42N 93 10W
Rainy, R. 52 48 43N 94 29W
Rainy River 52 48 43N 94 29W
Raipur 125 21 17N 81 45E
Raith 34 48 50N 90 0W
Raj Nandgaon 125 21 0N 81 0E
Raja Empat, Kepulauan 127 0 30S 129 40E
Raja, Ujung 126 3 40N 96 25E
Rajahmundry 125 17 1N 81 48E
Rajang, R. 126 2 30N 113 30E
Rajapalaiyarm 124 9 25N 77 35E
Rajasthan □ 124 26 45N 73 30E
Rajasthan Canal 124 30 31N 71 0E
Rajgarh 124 24 2N 76 45E
Rajkot 124 22 15N 70 56E
Rajojooseppi 110 68 25N 28 30E
Rajpipla 124 21 50N 73 30E
Rajshahi 125 24 22N 88 39E
Rajshahi □ 125 25 0N 89 0E
Rakaia 133 43 45S 172 1E
Rakaia, R. 133 43 26S 171 47E
Rakan, Ras 123 26 10N 51 20E
Rakaposhi, mt. 124 36 20N 74 30E
Raleigh, Can. 37 51 34N 55 44W
Raleigh, U.S.A. 34 35 46N 78 38W
Raleigh B. 73 34 50N 76 15W
Ralls 75 33 40N 101 20W
Ralston 61 50 15N 111 10W
Rãm Allãh 115 31 55N 35 10E
Ram Hd. 136 37 47S 149 30E
Ram, R., Alta., Can. 61 52 23N 115 25W
Ram, R., N.W.T., Can. 54 62 1N 123 41W
Rama, Can. 56 51 46N 103 0W
Rama, Nic. 84 12 9N 84 15W
Ramadi 122 33 28N 43 15E
Ramah 36 58 52N 63 15W
Ramah B. 36 58 52N 63 13W
Ramanathapuram 124 9 25N 78 55E
Rambervillers 101 48 20N 6 38E
Rambipudji 127 8 12S 113 37E
Rambouillet 101 48 40N 1 48E
Rambre Kyun 125 19 0N 94 0E
Ramea, Can. 35 47 28N 57 4W
Ramea, Newf., Can. 37 47 31N 57 23W
Ramea Is. 37 47 31N 57 22W
Ramechhap 125 27 25N 86 10E
Ramelau, Mte. 127 8 55S 126 22E
Ramgarh, Bihar, India 125 23 40N 85 35E
Ramgarh, Rajasthan, India 124 27 30N 70 36E
Rãmhormoz 122 31 15N 49 35E
Ramla 115 31 55N 34 52E
Ramnad = Ramanathapuram 124 9 25N 78 55E
Ramona 81 33 1N 116 56W
Ramore 34 48 30N 80 25W
Ramos Arizpe 82 23 35N 100 59W
Ramos, R. 82 25 35N 105 3W
Rampart 67 65 0N 150 15W
Rampur 124 28 50N 79 5E
Rampurhat 125 24 10N 87 50E
Ramsay I. 62 52 33N 131 23W
Ramsayville 48 45 23N 75 34W
Ramsey, Can. 53 47 25N 82 20W
Ramsey, U.K. 94 54 20N 4 21W
Ramsey, U.S.A. 76 39 8N 89 7W
Ramsey L. 53 47 13N 82 15W
Ramsgate 95 51 20N 1 25E
Ramtek 124 21 20N 79 15E
Ranaghat 125 23 15N 88 35E
Ranau 126 6 2N 116 40E
Rancagua 88 34 10S 70 50W
Rance, R. 100 48 34N 1 59W
Rancheria, R. 54 60 13N 129 7W
Ranchester 78 44 57N 107 12W
Ranchi 125 23 19N 85 27E
Rand 136 35 33S 146 32E
Randall 52 46 9N 94 28W
Randan 102 46 2N 3 21E
Randers 111 56 29N 10 1E
Randle 80 46 32N 121 57W
Randolph, N.Y., U.S.A. 70 42 10N 78 59W
Randolph, Utah, U.S.A. 78 41 43N 111 10W
Randolph, Vt., U.S.A. 71 43 55N 72 39W
Random I. 37 48 8N 53 44W
Randsburg 81 35 20N 117 44W
Råne älv 110 66 26N 21 10E
Råneå 110 65 53N 22 18E
Ranfurly 60 53 25N 111 41W
Rang-des-Dusseau 43 45 11N 73 9W
Rangaunu B. 133 34 51S 173 15E
Rangeley 71 44 58N 70 33W
Rangely 78 40 3N 108 53W
Ranger 75 32 30N 98 42W
Ranger L. 53 46 52N 83 35W
Rangia 125 26 15N 91 20E
Rangiora 133 43 19S 172 36E
Rangitaiki 14 38 52S 176 23E
Rangitaiki, R. 133 37 54S 176 49E
Rangitata, R. 133 43 45S 171 15E
Rangkasbitung 127 6 22S 106 16E
Rangon, R. 125 16 28N 96 40E
Rangoon 125 16 45N 96 20E
Rangpur 125 25 42N 89 22E
Ranibennur 124 14 35N 75 30E
Raniganj 125 23 40N 87 15E
Raniwara 124 24 50N 72 10E
Rankin, U.S.A. 77 40 28N 87 54W
Rankin, Tex., U.S.A. 75 31 16N 101 56W
Rankin Inlet 65 62 30N 93 0W
Rankin's Springs 136 33 49S 146 14E
Rannoch 96 56 41N 4 20W
Rannoch L. 96 56 41N 4 20W
Ranohira 117 22 29S 45 24E
Ranoke 53 50 26N 81 35W
Ranong 128 9 56N 98 40E
Ransom 77 41 9N 88 39W
Ransomville 49 43 15N 78 55W
Rantau 126 4 15N 98 5E
Rantauprapat 126 2 15N 99 50E
Rantemario 127 3 15S 119 57E
Rantoul 77 40 18N 88 10W
Raon-l'Étape 101 48 24N 6 50E
Rapa Iti, I. 15 27 35S 144 20W
Rapang 127 3 45S 119 55E
Rãpch 123 25 40N 59 15E
Raper, C. 65 69 44N 67 6W
Rapid City, Can. 57 50 7N 100 2W
Rapid City, Mich., U.S.A. 46 44 50N 85 17W
Rapid City, S.D., U.S.A. 74 44 0N 103 0W
Rapid, R., Can. 54 59 15N 129 5W
Rapid, R., U.S.A. 52 48 42N 94 26W
Rapid River 72 45 55N 87 0W
Rapide-Blanc 41 47 48N 73 2W
Rapide-Mascouche 44 45 46N 73 40W
Rapide-Sept 40 47 46N 78 19W
Rapides des Joachims 40 46 13N 77 43W
Rarotonga, I. 15 21 30S 160 0W
Ras al Khaima 123 25 50N 56 5E
Ra's at Tannũrah 122 26 40N 50 10E
Ras Dashan, mt. 116 13 8N 37 45E
Rasa, Punta 90 40 50S 62 15W
Rasht 122 37 20N 49 40E
Raso, C. 87 1 50N 50 0W
Rason, L. 134 28 45S 124 25E
Rat Buri 128 13 30N 99 54E
Rat, Is. 67 51 50N 178 15E
Rat, R., Man., Can. 54 56 0N 99 30W
Rat, R., Man., Can. 57 49 35N 97 10W
Rat River 54 61 7N 112 36W
Ratangarh 124 28 5N 74 35E
Rath Luirc (Charleville) 97 52 21N 8 40W
Rathbun Res. 76 40 49N 93 53W
Rathdrum, Ireland 97 52 57N 6 13W
Rathdrum, U.S.A. 78 47 50N 116 58W
Rathenow 106 52 38N 12 23E
Rathkeale 97 52 32N 8 57W
Rathlin I. 97 55 18N 6 14W
Rathlin O'Birne I. 97 54 40N 8 50W
Ratlam 124 23 20N 75 0E
Ratnagiri 124 16 57N 73 18E
Raton 75 37 0N 104 30W
Rats, R. aux 41 48 53N 72 14W
Rattray Hd. 96 57 38N 1 50W
Ratz, Mt. 54 57 23N 132 12W
Raub 128 3 47N 101 52E
Rauch 88 36 45S 59 5W
Raufarhöfn 110 66 27N 15 57W
Raukumara Ra. 133 38 5S 177 55E
Rauma 111 61 10N 21 30E
Raung, Mt. 127 8 8S 114 4E
Rãvar 123 31 20N 56 51E
Ravena 71 42 28N 73 49W
Ravenna, Italy 108 44 28N 12 15E
Ravenna, U.S.A. 77 43 11N 85 56W
Ravenna, U.S.A. 77 37 42N 83 55W
Ravenna, Nebr., U.S.A. 74 41 3N 98 58W
Ravenna, Ohio, U.S.A. 70 41 11N 81 15W
Ravensburg 106 47 48N 9 38E
Ravenshoe 135 17 37S 145 29E
Ravensthorpe 134 33 35S 120 2E
Ravenswood 72 38 58N 81 47W
Raventasón 86 6 10S 81 0W
Ravenwood 76 40 23N 94 41W
Ravi, R. 124 31 0N 73 0E
Rawalpindi 124 33 38N 73 8E
Rawalpindi □ 124 33 10N 72 50E
Rawãndũz 122 36 40N 44 30E
Rawang 128 3 20N 101 35E
Rawdon 41 46 3N 73 40W
Rawene 133 35 25S 173 32E
Rawlinna 134 30 58S 125 28E
Rawlins 78 41 50N 107 20W
Rawlinson Range 134 24 40S 128 30E
Rawson 90 43 15S 65 0W
Ray 74 48 21N 103 6W
Ray, C. 37 47 33N 59 15W
Ray Mts. 67 66 0N 152 10W
Rayadrug 124 14 40N 76 50E
Rayagada 125 19 15N 83 20E
Raychikhinsk 121 49 46N 129 25E
Rayin 123 29 40N 57 22E
Rayleigh 63 50 49N 120 17W
Raymond, Can. 61 49 30N 112 35W
Raymond, U.S.A. 76 39 19N 89 34W
Raymond, Calif., U.S.A. 80 37 13N 119 54W
Raymond, Wash., U.S.A. 80 46 45N 123 48W
Raymondville 75 26 30N 97 50W
Raymore 56 51 25N 104 31W
Rayne 75 30 16N 92 16W
Rayón 82 29 43N 110 35W
Rayong 128 12 40N 101 20E
Raytown 76 39 1N 94 28W
Rayville 75 32 30N 91 45W
Raz, Pte. du 100 48 2N 4 47W
Razgrad 109 43 33N 26 34E
Razor Back Mt 54 51 32N 125 0W
Ré, Île de 102 46 12N 1 30W
Read Island 64 69 12N 114 31W
Reading, Can. 49 43 50N 80 13W
Reading, U.K. 95 51 27N 0 57W
Reading, Mich., U.S.A. 77 41 50N 84 45W
Reading, Ohio, U.S.A. 77 39 13N 84 26W
Reading, Pa., U.S.A. 71 40 20N 75 53W
Realicó 88 35 0S 64 15W
Réalmont 102 43 48N 2 10E
Ream 128 10 34N 103 39E
Reata 82 26 8N 101 5W
Reay 96 58 33N 3 48W
Rebais 101 48 50N 3 10E
Rebi 127 5 30S 134 7E
Rebun-jima 132 45 20N 142 45E
Recherche, Arch. of the 134 34 15S 122 50E
Recife 87 8 0S 35 0W
Recklinghausen 105 51 36N 7 10E
Reconquista 88 29 10S 59 45W
Recreo 88 29 25S 65 10W
Red Bank 71 40 21N 74 4W
Red Bay, Newf., Can. 36 51 44N 56 25W
Red Bay, Newf., Can. 37 51 44N 56 25W
Red Bluff 78 40 11N 122 11W
Red Bluff L. 75 31 59N 103 58W
Red Bud 76 38 13N 90 0W
Red Cloud 74 40 8N 98 33W
Red Deer 61 52 20N 113 50W
Red Deer L., Alta., Can. 61 52 43N 113 2W
Red Deer L., Man., Can. 57 52 55N 101 20W
Red Deer, R. 61 50 58N 110 0W
Red Deer R. 57 52 53N 101 1W
Red Hill South 136 38 25S 145 2E
Red I. 37 47 23N 54 10W
Red Indian L. 37 48 35N 57 0W
Red L. 52 51 3N 93 49W
Red Lake 52 51 3N 93 49W
Red Lake Falls 74 47 54N 96 15W
Red Lake Road 52 49 59N 93 25W
Red Lodge 78 45 10N 109 10W
Red Mountain 81 35 37N 117 38W
Red Oak 74 41 0N 95 10W
Red Pass 63 53 0N 119 0W
Red, R., Can. 58 50 24N 96 48W
Red, R., Minn., U.S.A. 74 48 10N 97 0W
Red, R., Tex., U.S.A. 75 33 57N 95 30W
Red River Floodway 58 49 50N 96 57W
Red Rock, B.C., Can. 63 53 42N 122 40W
Red Rock, Ont., Can. 52 48 55N 88 15W
Red Rock, L. 76 41 30N 93 15W
Red Sea 115 25 0N 36 0E
Red Slate Mtn. 80 37 31N 118 52W
Red Sucker L 55 54 9N 93 40W
Red Tower Pass = Turnu Rosu P. 107 45 33N 24 17E
Red Wing 74 44 32N 92 35W
Redberry L. 56 52 45N 107 14W
Redbridge 95 51 35N 0 7E
Redcar 94 54 37N 1 4W
Redcliff 61 50 10N 110 50W
Redding 78 40 30N 122 25W
Redditch 95 52 18N 1 57W
Redditt 52 49 59N 94 24W
Redfield 74 45 0N 98 30W
Redkey 77 40 21N 85 9W
Redknife, R. 54 61 14N 119 22W
Redlands 81 34 0N 117 11W
Redmond, Oreg., U.S.A. 78 44 19N 121 11W
Redmond, Wash., U.S.A. 80 47 40N 122 7W
Redon 100 47 40N 2 6W
Redonda, I. 85 16 58N 62 19W
Redonda Is. 62 50 15N 124 50W
Redondela 104 42 15N 8 38W
Redondo 104 38 39N 7 37W
Redondo Beach 81 33 52N 118 26W
Redondz Bay 62 50 17N 124 57W
Redrock Pt. 54 62 11N 115 2W
Redruth 95 50 14N 5 14W
Redvers 57 49 35N 101 40W
Redwater 60 53 55N 113 6W
Redwillow, R. 60 55 2N 119 18W
Redwood 71 44 18N 75 48W
Redwood City 80 37 30N 122 15W
Redwood Falls 74 44 30N 95 2W
Ree, L. 97 53 35N 8 0W
Reed City 72 43 52N 85 30W
Reed, L 55 54 38N 100 30W
Reed, Mt. 35 52 5N 68 5W
Reeder 74 46 7N 102 52W
Reedley 80 36 36N 119 27W
Reedsburg 74 43 34N 90 5W
Reedsport 78 43 45N 124 4W
Reef Pt. 133 35 10S 173 5E
Reefton 133 42 6S 171 51E

Reese	46	43 27N	83 42W
Refugio	75	28 18N	97 17W
Regensburg	106	49 1N	12 7E
Regent Park	58	50 28N	104 39W
Réggio di Calábria	108	38 7N	15 38E
Réggio nell' Emilia	108	44 42N	10 38E
Regina	58	50 27N	104 35W
Regina Beach	56	50 47N	105 0W
Registan □	124	30 15N	65 0E
Registro	89	24 29S	47 49W
Rehoboth	117	23 15S	17 4E
Reichenbach	106	50 36N	12 19E
Reid L.	56	50 0N	108 9W
Reid Lake	62	53 58N	123 6W
Reidsville	73	36 21N	79 40W
Reigate	95	51 14N	0 11W
Reims	101	49 15N	4 0E
Reina Adelaida, Arch.	90	52 20S	74 0W
Reinbeck	76	42 18N	92 0W
Reindeer I.	57	52 30N	98 0W
Reindeer L.	55	57 15N	102 15W
Reindeer, R.	55	55 36N	103 11W
Reine, La	40	48 50N	79 30W
Reinga, C.	133	34 25S	172 43E
Reinland	57	49 2N	97 52W
Reliance	55	63 0N	109 20W
Remanso	87	9 41S	42 4W
Rembang	127	6 42S	111 21E
Remedios, Colomb.	86	7 2N	74 41W
Remedios, Panama	84	8 15N	81 50W
Remer	52	47 3N	93 55W
Remeshk	123	26 55N	58 50E
Remi Lake Prov. Park	53	49 30N	82 15W
Rémigny	40	47 46N	79 12W
Remington	77	40 45N	87 8W
Remiremont	101	48 0N	6 36E
Remoulins	103	43 55N	4 35E
Remscheid	105	51 11N	7 12E
Remus	46	43 36N	85 9W
Renata	63	49 27N	118 7W
Rencontre East	37	47 38N	55 12W
Rend L.	76	38 2N	88 58W
Rendsburg	106	54 18N	9 41E
Rene	121	66 2N	179 25W
Renews	37	46 56N	52 56W
Renfrew, Can.	47	45 30N	76 40W
Renfrew, U.K.	96	55 52N	4 24W
Rengat	126	0 30S	102 45E
Rengo	88	34 24S	70 50W
Renison	53	50 58N	81 7W
Renkum	105	51 58N	5 43E
Renmark	135	34 11S	140 43E
Rennell Sd.	62	53 23N	132 35W
Renner Springs Teleg. Off.	134	18 20S	133 47E
Rennes	100	48 7N	1 41W
Rennie	57	49 51N	95 33W
Rennison I.	62	52 50N	129 20W
Reno	80	39 30N	119 50W
Reno, R.	108	44 45N	11 40E
Renovo	70	41 20N	77 47W
Rens	104	54 54N	9 5E
Rensselaer, Ind., U.S.A.	77	41 0N	87 10W
Rensselaer, N.Y., U.S.A.	71	42 38N	73 41W
Renton	80	47 30N	122 9W
Réole, La	102	44 35N	0 1W
Repentigny	45	45 44N	73 28W
Republic, Mich., U.S.A.	53	46 25N	87 59W
Republic, Wash., U.S.A.	63	48 38N	118 42W
Republican City	74	40 9N	99 20W
Republican, R.	74	40 0N	98 30W
Repulse B., Antarct.	91	64 30S	99 30E
Repulse B., Austral.	135	20 31S	148 45E
Repulse Bay	65	66 30N	86 30W
Requena, Peru	86	5 5S	73 52W
Requena, Spain	104	39 30N	1 4W
Reserve, Can.	56	52 28N	102 39W
Reserve, U.S.A.	79	33 50N	108 54W
Resht = Rasht	122	37 20N	49 40E
Resistencia	88	27 30S	59 0W
Reşiţa	107	45 18N	21 53E
Resolute	65	74 42N	94 54W
Resolution I., Can.	23	61 30N	65 0W
Resolution I., N.Z.	133	45 40S	166 40E
Restigouche, R.	39	47 50N	67 0W
Reston	57	49 33N	101 6W
Restrepo	86	4 15N	73 33W
Retalhuleu	84	14 33N	91 46W
Rethel	101	49 30N	4 20E
Réthímnon	109	35 15N	24 40E
Rétiers	100	47 55N	1 25W
Retiro	88	35 59S	71 47W
Réunion, Î.	16	22 0S	56 0E
Reutlingen	106	48 28N	9 13E
Revel	102	43 28N	2 0E
Revelstoke	63	51 0N	118 10W
Revigny	101	48 50N	5 0E
Revilla Gigedo, Is. de	15	18 40N	112 0W
Revillagigedo I.	54	55 50N	131 20W
Revin	101	49 55N	4 39E
Rewa	125	24 33N	81 25E
Rewari	124	28 15N	76 40E
Rex	67	64 10N	149 20W
Rexburg	78	43 55N	111 50W
Rexdale	50	43 43N	79 33W
Rexton, Can.	39	46 39N	64 52W
Rexton, U.S.A.	46	46 10N	85 14W

Rey Malabo	116	3 45N	8 50E
Reyes, Pt.	80	37 59N	123 2W
Reykjahlið	110	65 40N	16 55W
Reykjanes	110	63 48N	22 40W
Reykjavík	110	64 10N	21 57E
Reynolds, Can.	57	49 40N	95 55W
Reynolds, U.S.A.	76	41 20N	90 40W
Reynolds Ra.	134	22 30S	133 0E
Reynoldsville	70	41 5N	78 58W
Reynosa	83	26 5N	98 18W
Rezā'iyeh, Daryāchech-ye	122	37 30N	45 30E
Rhayader	95	52 19N	3 30W
Rhein	57	51 25N	102 15W
Rhein, R.	106	51 42N	6 20E
Rheine	105	52 17N	7 25E
Rheinland-Pfalz □	105	50 50N	7 0E
Rheydt	105	51 10N	6 24E
Rhinau	101	48 19N	7 43E
Rhine, R. = Rhein	106	51 42N	6 20E
Rhinelander	74	45 38N	89 29W
Rhode Island □	71	41 38N	71 37W
Rhodes = Ródhos	109	36 15N	28 10E
Rhodesia ■	117	20 0S	30 0E
Rhodope Mts. = Rhodopi Planina	109	41 40N	24 20E
Rhodopi Planina	109	41 40N	24 20E
Rhön, mts.	106	50 24N	9 58E
Rhondda	95	51 39N	3 30W
Rhône □	103	45 54N	4 35E
Rhône, R.	103	43 28N	4 42E
Rhum, I.	96	57 0N	6 20W
Rhyl	94	53 19N	3 29W
Riachão	87	7 20S	46 37W
Rialto	81	34 6N	117 22W
Rians	103	43 37N	5 44E
Riasi	124	33 10N	74 50E
Riau □	126	0 0	102 35E
Riau, Kepulauan	126	0 30N	104 20E
Ribadeo	104	43 35N	7 5W
Ribat	117	29 50N	60 55E
Ribatejo □	104	39 15N	8 30W
Ribble, R.	94	54 13N	2 20W
Ribe	111	55 19N	8 44E
Ribeauvillé	101	48 10N	7 20E
Ribécourt	101	49 30N	2 55E
Ribeirão Prêto	89	21 10S	47 50W
Ribémont	101	49 47N	3 27E
Ribérac	102	45 15N	0 20E
Riberalta	86	11 0S	66 0W
Ribstone Cr.	61	52 52N	110 5W
Riccarton	133	43 32S	172 37E
Rice	81	34 5N	114 51W
Rice L., Can.	47	44 12N	78 10W
Rice L., U.S.A.	52	46 30N	93 22W
Rice Lake	74	45 30N	91 42W
Riceburg	43	45 8N	72 56W
Riceton	56	50 [illegible]	104 19W
Rich, C.	46	44 [illegible]	80 38W
Rich Hill	75	38 5N	94 22W
Rich Valley	60	53 51N	114 21W
Richan	52	49 59N	92 49W
Richards Deep	13	25 0S	73 0W
Richards I.	64	68 0N	135 0W
Richards L.	55	59 10N	107 10W
Richardson	58	50 23N	104 27W
Richardson Mts.	64	68 20N	135 45W
Richardson Pt.	51	43 50N	78 59W
Richardson, R.	55	58 25N	111 14W
Richardson Springs	80	39 51N	121 46W
Richardton	74	46 56N	102 22W
Riche, Pte.	37	50 42N	57 25W
Richelieu, Can.	45	45 27N	73 15W
Richelieu, France	100	47 0N	0 20E
Richelieu □	43	45 55N	73 0W
Richelieu, R.	45	45 28N	73 18W
Richey	74	47 42N	105 5W
Richfield, Idaho, U.S.A.	78	43 2N	114 5W
Richfield, Utah, U.S.A.	79	38 50N	112 0W
Richford	71	45 0N	72 40W
Richibucto	39	46 42N	64 54W
Richland, Ga., U.S.A.	73	32 7N	84 40W
Richland, Iowa, U.S.A.	76	41 13N	91 58W
Richland, Mo., U.S.A.	76	37 51N	92 26W
Richland, Oreg., U.S.A.	78	44 49N	117 9W
Richland, Wash., U.S.A.	78	46 15N	119 15W
Richland Center	74	43 21N	90 22W
Richlands	72	37 7N	81 49W
Richmond, N.S.W., Austral.	136	33 35S	150 42E
Richmond, Queens., Austral.	135	20 43S	143 8E
Richmond, N.S., Can.	39	44 40N	63 36W
Richmond, Ont., Can.	47	45 11N	75 50W
Richmond, Qué., Can.	41	45 40N	72 9W
Richmond, N.Z.	133	41 4S	173 12E
Richmond, S. Afr.	117	29 51S	30 18E
Richmond, N. Yorks., U.K.	94	54 24N	1 43W
Richmond, Surrey, U.K.	95	51 28N	0 18W
Richmond, Calif., U.S.A.	80	38 0N	122 21W
Richmond, Ind., U.S.A.	77	39 50N	84 50W
Richmond, Ky., U.S.A.	77	37 40N	84 20W
Richmond, Mich., U.S.A.	46	42 47N	82 45W
Richmond, Mo., U.S.A.	74	39 15N	93 58W

Richmond, N.Y., U.S.A.	71	40 35N	74 6W
Richmond, Tex., U.S.A.	75	29 32N	95 42W
Richmond, Va., U.S.A.	72	37 33N	77 27W
Richmond □	66	49 9N	123 7W
Richmond Gulf	34	56 20N	75 50W
Richmond Hill	50	43 52N	79 27W
Richmound	56	50 27N	109 45W
Richton	73	31 23N	88 58W
Richvale	50	43 51N	79 26W
Richwood, U.S.A.	77	40 26N	83 18W
Richwood, W. Va., U.S.A.	72	38 17N	80 32W
Rideau Canal	48	44 53N	76 0W
Rideau, R.	48	45 27N	75 42W
Ridge Farm	77	39 54N	87 39W
Ridge, R.	53	50 25N	84 20W
Ridgecrest	81	35 38N	117 40W
Ridgedale	56	53 0N	104 10W
Ridgefield	80	45 49N	122 45W
Ridgeland	73	32 30N	80 58W
Ridgetown	46	42 26N	81 52W
Ridgeville	77	40 18N	85 2W
Ridgway, Ill., U.S.A.	77	37 48N	88 16W
Ridgway, Pa., U.S.A.	70	41 25N	78 43W
Riding Mt. Nat. Park	57	50 50N	100 0W
Ried	106	48 14N	13 30E
Rietfontein	117	26 44S	20 1E
Rieti	108	42 23N	12 50E
Rieupeyroux	102	44 19N	2 12E
Riez	103	43 49N	6 6E
Rifle	78	39 40N	107 50W
Rifstangi	110	66 32N	16 12W
Riga	120	56 53N	24 8E
Rigaud	43	45 29N	74 18W
Rigby	78	43 41N	111 58W
Riggins	78	45 29N	116 26W
Rignac	102	44 25N	2 16E
Rigolet	36	54 10N	58 23W
Riihimäki	111	60 45N	24 48E
Riiser-Larsen halvøya	91	68 0S	35 0E
Riishiri-Tō	132	45 11N	141 15E
Rijeka (Fiume)	108	45 20N	14 21E
Rijkevorsel	105	51 21N	4 46E
Rijssen	105	52 19N	6 30E
Rijswijk	105	52 4N	4 22E
Rilly	101	49 11N	4 3E
Rimbey	61	52 35N	114 15W
Rimini	108	44 3N	12 33E
Rîmnicu Sărat	107	45 26N	27 3E
Rîmnicu Vîlcea	107	45 9N	24 21E
Rimouski	41	48 27N	68 30W
Rimouski-Est	41	48 28N	68 31W
Rimouski, Parc Prov. de	41	48 0N	68 15W
Rimouski, R.	41	48 27N	68 32W
Rimrock	80	46 38N	121 10W
Rinca	127	8 45S	119 35E
Rincón de Romos	82	22 14N	102 18W
Rinconada	88	22 26S	66 10W
Rineanna	97	52 42N	85 7W
Ringkøbing	111	56 5N	8 15E
Ringling	78	46 16N	110 56W
Ringvassøy	110	69 36N	19 15E
Ringwood	50	43 58N	79 17W
Rinía, I.	109	37 23N	25 13E
Rio Arica	86	1 35S	75 30W
Rio Branco	86	9 58S	67 49W
Rio Branco	89	32 40S	53 40W
Rio Brilhante	89	21 48S	54 33W
Río Chico	86	10 19N	65 59W
Rio Claro, Brazil	89	22 19S	47 35W
Rio Claro, Trin	85	10 20N	61 25W
Rio Colorado	90	39 0S	64 0W
Río Cuarto	88	33 10S	64 25W
Rio de Janeiro	89	23 0S	43 12W
Rio de Janeiro □	89	22 50S	43 0W
Rio do Sul	89	27 95S	49 37W
Río Gallegos	90	51 35S	69 15W
Rio Grande	90	53 50S	67 45W
Rio Grande	89	32 0S	52 20W
Rio Grande, Mexico	82	23 50N	103 2W
Rio Grande, Nic.	84	12 54N	83 33W
Rio Grande City	75	26 30N	98 55W
Rio Grande del Norte, R.	68	26 0N	97 0W
Rio Grande do Norte □	87	5 40S	36 0W
Rio Grande do Sul □	89	30 0S	53 0W
Rio Grande, R.	79	37 47N	106 15W
Rio Hato	84	8 22N	80 10W
Rio Lagartos	83	21 36N	88 10W
Rio Largo	87	9 28S	35 50W
Rio Mulatos	86	19 40S	66 50W
Rio Muni □ = Mbini □	114	1 30N	10 0E
Rio Negro	89	26 0S	50 0W
Río Oriente	84	22 17N	81 13W
Rio Pardo, Minas Gerais, Brazil	87	15 55S	42 30W
Rio Pardo, Rio Grande do Sul, Brazil	89	30 0S	52 30W
Río Segundo	88	31 40S	63 59W
Río Tercero	88	32 15S	64 8W
Rio Verde	83	21 56N	99 59W
Rio Vista	80	38 11N	121 44W
Ríobamba	86	1 50S	78 45W
Riohacha	86	11 33N	72 55W
Rioja, La, Argent.	88	29 20S	67 0W
Rioja, La, Spain	104	42 20N	2 20W
Rioja, La □	88	29 30S	67 0W
Riom	102	45 54N	3 7E

Riom-ès-Montagnes	102	45 17N	2 39E
Rion-des-Landes	102	43 55N	0 56W
Riondel	63	49 46N	116 51W
Rionegro	86	6 9N	75 22W
Riosucio, Caldas, Colomb.	86	5 30N	75 40W
Riosucio, Choco, Colomb.	86	7 27N	77 7W
Riou L.	55	59 7N	106 25W
Ripley, Can.	46	44 4N	81 35W
Ripley, U.S.A.	77	38 45N	83 51W
Ripley, Calif., U.S.A.	81	33 32N	114 39W
Ripley, N.Y., U.S.A.	70	42 16N	79 44W
Ripley, Tenn., U.S.A.	75	35 43N	89 34W
Ripon, Can.	40	45 45N	75 10W
Ripon, U.K.	94	54 8N	1 31W
Ripon, Calif., U.S.A.	80	37 44N	121 7W
Ripon, Wis., U.S.A.	72	43 51N	88 50W
Riscle	102	43 39N	0 5W
Rising Sun	77	38 57N	84 51W
Risle, R.	100	48 55N	0 41E
Rison	75	33 57N	92 11W
Risør	111	58 43N	9 13E
Ritchie L.	38	52 58N	66 1W
Ritchie's Archipelago	128	12 5N	94 0E
Rittman	70	40 57N	81 48W
Ritzville	78	47 10N	118 21W
Riva Bella	100	49 17N	0 18W
Rivadavia, Buenos Aires, Argent.	88	35 29S	62 59W
Rivadavia, Mendoza, Argent.	88	33 13S	68 30W
Rivadavia, Salta, Argent.	88	24 5S	63 0W
Rivadavia, Chile	88	29 50S	70 35W
Rivas	84	11 30N	85 50W
Rive-de-Gier	103	45 32N	4 37E
River Hébert	39	45 42N	64 23W
River John	39	45 45N	63 3W
River Jordan	62	48 26N	124 3W
River of Ponds	37	50 32N	57 24W
River of Ponds L.	37	50 30N	57 20W
River Rouge	77	42 16N	83 9W
River Valley	46	46 35N	80 11W
Rivera	89	31 0S	55 50W
Rivercrest	58	50 0N	97 3W
Riverdale	80	36 26N	119 52W
Riverfield	43	45 9N	73 49W
Riverhead, Can.	37	46 58N	53 31W
Riverhead, U.S.A.	71	40 53N	72 40W
Riverhurst	56	50 55N	106 50W
Riverina	135	35 30S	145 20E
Riverport	39	44 18N	64 20W
Rivers	57	50 2N	100 14W
Rivers Inl.	62	51 40N	127 20W
Rivers Inlet	62	51 42N	127 15W
Rivers, L. of the	56	49 49N	105 44W
Riversdal	117	34 7S	21 15E
Riverside, Can.	70	42 17N	82 59W
Riverside, Calif., U.S.A.	81	34 0N	117 22W
Riverside, Wash., U.S.A.	63	48 29N	119 30W
Riverside, Wyo., U.S.A.	78	41 12N	106 57W
Riverside-Albert	39	45 42N	64 45W
Riverton, Can.	57	51 1N	97 0W
Riverton, N.Z.	133	46 21S	168 0E
Riverton, U.S.A.	76	39 51N	89 33W
Riverton, Wyo., U.S.A.	78	43 1N	108 27W
Riverview Heights	39	46 4N	64 48W
Rives	103	45 21N	5 31E
Rivesaltes	102	42 47N	2 50E
Rivière-Ste.-Marguerite	38	50 8N	66 37W
Rivière-à-la-Chaloupe	38	50 17N	65 6W
Rivière-à-Pierre	41	46 59N	72 11W
Rivière-au-Renard	38	48 59N	64 23W
Rivière-aux-Rats	41	47 13N	72 53W
Rivière-Beaudette	43	45 14N	74 20W
Rivière-Bersimis	41	48 56N	68 42W
Rivière-Bleue	35	47 26N	69 2W
Rivière-de-la-Chaloupe	38	49 8N	62 32W
Rivière-des-Hurons	45	45 30N	73 9W
Rivière-des-Prairies	44	45 39N	73 33W
Rivière-du-Loup	41	47 50N	69 30W
Rivière-Ouelle	41	47 26N	70 1W
Rivière-Pigou	38	50 16N	65 35W
Rivière-Pontecôte	38	49 57N	67 1W
Rivière-Portneuf	41	48 38N	69 6W
Rivière-St-Jean	38	50 17N	64 19W
Rivière Verte	39	47 19N	68 9W
Rivierre-au-Tonnère	38	50 16N	64 47W
Riyadh = Ar Riyād	122	24 41N	46 42E
Rize	122	41 0N	40 30E
Rizzuto, C.	108	38 54N	17 5E
Rjukan	111	59 54N	8 33E
Roachdale	77	39 51N	86 48W
Road Town	85	18 27N	64 37W
Roag, L.	96	58 10N	6 55W
Roanne	103	46 3N	4 4E
Roanoke, U.S.A.	77	40 58N	85 22W
Roanoke, Ala., U.S.A.	73	33 9N	85 23W
Roanoke, Va., U.S.A.	72	37 19N	79 55W
Roanoke I.	73	35 55N	75 40W
Roanoke, R.	73	36 15N	77 20W
Roanoke Rapids	73	36 36N	77 42W
Roatán	84	16 18N	86 35W
Robb	60	53 13N	116 58W
Robe, Mt.	136	31 40S	141 20E
Robe-Noire, L. de la	38	50 42N	62 42W

Robe, R **Ruel**

Robe, R.	**97**	53 38N	9 10W
Robert Lee	**75**	31 55N	100 26W
Roberts, U.S.A.	**77**	40 37N	88 11W
Roberts, Idaho, U.S.A.	**78**	43 44N	112 8W
Robert's Arm	**37**	49 29N	55 49W
Roberts Bank Superport	**66**	49 1N	123 9W
Roberts Creek	**63**	49 26N	123 38W
Roberts, Pt.	**63**	49 0N	123 6W
Robertson, Austral.	**134**	34 37S	150 36E
Robertson, S. Afr.	**117**	33 46S	19 50E
Robertson I.	**91**	68 0S	75 0W
Robertsonville	**41**	46 9N	71 13W
Robertville	**39**	47 42N	65 46W
Roberval	**41**	48 32N	72 15W
Robeson Kanal	**17**	82 0N	61 30W
Robinson	**77**	39 0N	87 44W
Robinson Ranges	**134**	25 40S	118 0E
Robinvale	**136**	34 40S	142 45E
Robla, La	**104**	42 50N	5 41W
Roblin	**57**	51 14N	101 21W
Roblin Park	**58**	49 52N	97 17W
Roboré	**86**	18 10S	59 45W
Robsart	**56**	49 23N	109 17W
Robson, Mt.	**63**	53 10N	119 10W
Robstown	**75**	27 47N	97 40W
Roca, C. da	**104**	38 40N	9 31W
Roca Partida, I.	**82**	19 1N	112 2W
Roçadas	**117**	16 45S	15 0E
Rocanville	**57**	50 23N	101 42W
Rocas, I.	**87**	4 0S	34 1W
Rocha	**89**	34 30S	54 25W
Rochdale	**94**	53 36N	2 10W
Roche-Bernard, La	**100**	47 31N	2 19W
Roche-Canillac, La	**102**	45 12N	1 57E
Roche, La	**103**	46 4N	6 19E
Roche Percée	**56**	49 4N	102 48W
Roche-sur-Yon, La	**100**	46 40N	1 25W
Rochebaucourt	**40**	48 41N	77 30W
Rochechouart	**102**	45 50N	0 49E
Rochefort, Belg.	**105**	50 9N	5 12E
Rochefort, France	**102**	45 56N	0 57W
Rochefort-en-Terre	**100**	47 42N	2 22W
Rochefoucauld, La	**102**	45 44N	0 24E
Rochelle	**76**	41 55N	89 5W
Rochelle, La	**102**	46 10N	1 9W
Rocher River	**54**	61 23N	112 44W
Roches, R.	**38**	50 2N	66 55W
Rocheservière	**100**	46 57N	1 30W
Rochester, Austral.	**136**	36 22S	144 41E
Rochester, Can.	**60**	54 22N	113 27W
Rochester, U.K.	**95**	51 22N	0 30E
Rochester, Ind., U.S.A.	**77**	41 5N	86 15W
Rochester, Mich., U.S.A.	**77**	42 41N	83 8W
Rochester, Minn., U.S.A.	**74**	44 1N	92 28W
Rochester, N.H., U.S.A.	**71**	43 19N	70 57W
Rochester, N.Y., U.S.A.	**70**	43 10N	77 40W
Rochester, Pa., U.S.A.	**70**	40 41N	80 17W
Rock Creek	**63**	49 4N	119 0W
Rock Falls	**76**	41 47N	89 41W
Rock Hill	**73**	34 55N	81 2W
Rock Island, Can.	**41**	45 26N	73 34W
Rock Island, U.S.A.	**76**	41 30N	90 35W
Rock Lake	**74**	48 50N	99 13W
Rock Port	**74**	40 26N	95 30W
Rock, R.	**54**	60 7N	127 7W
Rock Rapids	**74**	43 25N	96 10W
Rock River	**78**	41 49N	106 0W
Rock Sound	**84**	24 54N	76 12W
Rock Sprs., Ariz., U.S.A.	**79**	34 2N	112 11W
Rock Sprs., Mont., U.S.A.	**78**	46 55N	106 11W
Rock Sprs., Tex., U.S.A.	**75**	30 2N	100 11W
Rock Sprs., Wyo., U.S.A.	**78**	41 40N	109 10W
Rock Valley	**74**	43 10N	96 17W
Rockall I.	**93**	57 37N	13 42W
Rockburn	**43**	45 1N	74 1W
Rockcliffe Park	**48**	45 27N	75 41W
Rockdale, Tex., U.S.A.	**75**	30 40N	97 0W
Rockdale, Wash., U.S.A.	**80**	47 22N	121 28W
Rockefeller Plat.	**91**	84 0S	130 0W
Rockford, Ill., U.S.A.	**76**	42 20N	89 0W
Rockford, Iowa, U.S.A.	**76**	43 3N	92 57W
Rockford, Mich., U.S.A.	**77**	43 7N	85 34W
Rockford, Ohio, U.S.A.	**77**	40 41N	84 39W
Rockglen	**56**	49 11N	105 57W
Rockhampton	**135**	23 22S	150 32E
Rockingham	**39**	44 41N	63 39W
Rockingham For.	**95**	52 28N	0 42W
Rocklake	**57**	48 47N	99 15W
Rockland, Can.	**47**	45 33N	75 17W
Rockland, Idaho, U.S.A.	**78**	42 37N	112 57W
Rockland, Me., U.S.A.	**35**	44 0N	69 0W
Rockland, Mich., U.S.A.	**52**	46 40N	89 10W
Rocklands Reservoir	**136**	37 15S	142 5E
Rocklin	**80**	38 48N	121 14W
Rockmart	**73**	34 1N	85 2W
Rockport, U.S.A.	**77**	37 53N	87 3W
Rockport, Tex., U.S.A.	**75**	28 2N	97 3W
Rockport, Wash., U.S.A.	**63**	48 30N	121 38W
Rockton	**49**	43 17N	80 7W
Rockville, U.S.A.	**77**	39 46N	87 14W
Rockville, Conn., U.S.A.	**71**	41 51N	72 27W
Rockville, Md., U.S.A.	**72**	39 7N	77 10W
Rockwall	**75**	32 55N	96 30W
Rockway	**49**	43 6N	79 20W
Rockwell	**136**	32 3S	141 32E
Rockwell City	**76**	42 20N	94 35W
Rockwood, Can.	**49**	43 37N	80 8W
Rockwood, U.S.A.	**77**	42 4N	83 15W
Rockwood, Tenn., U.S.A.	**73**	35 52N	84 40W
Rocky Ford	**74**	38 7N	103 45W
Rocky Fork Lake	**77**	39 12N	83 23W
Rocky Harbour	**37**	49 36N	57 55W
Rocky Island L.	**53**	46 55N	83 0W
Rocky Lane	**54**	58 31N	116 22W
Rocky Mount	**73**	35 55N	77 48W
Rocky Mountain House	**61**	52 22N	114 55W
Rocky Mts.	**54**	55 0N	121 0W
Rocky Pt.	**134**	33 30S	123 57E
Rocky, R.	**61**	53 8N	117 59W
Rockyford	**61**	51 14N	113 10W
Rocroi	**101**	49 55N	4 30E
Rod	**124**	28 10N	63 5E
Roda, La	**104**	39 13N	2 15W
Rødby Havn	**111**	54 39N	11 22E
Roddickton	**37**	50 51N	56 8W
Roden	**105**	53 8N	6 26E
Roderick I.	**62**	52 38N	128 22W
Rodez	**102**	44 21N	2 33E
Ródhos	**109**	36 15N	28 10E
Ródhos, I.	**109**	36 15N	28 10E
Rodney	**46**	42 34N	81 41W
Rodney, C.	**133**	36 17S	174 50E
Rodoni, C.	**109**	41 32N	19 30E
Rodriguez, I.	**16**	20 0S	65 0E
Roe, R.	**97**	55 0N	6 56W
Roebling	**71**	40 7N	74 45W
Roebourne	**134**	20 44S	117 9E
Roebuck B.	**134**	18 5S	122 20E
Roermond	**105**	51 12N	6 0E
Roes Welcome Sd.	**65**	65 0N	87 0W
Roeselare	**105**	50 57N	3 7E
Rogagua, L.	**86**	14 0S	66 50W
Rogaland fylke □	**111**	59 12N	6 20E
Roger, L.	**40**	47 50N	78 59W
Rogers	**75**	36 20N	94 0W
Rogers City	**46**	45 25N	83 49W
Rogerson	**78**	42 10N	114 40W
Rogersville, Can.	**39**	46 44N	65 26W
Rogersville, U.S.A.	**73**	36 27N	83 1W
Roggan	**36**	54 25N	79 32W
Roggan L.	**36**	54 8N	77 50W
Rogliano	**103**	42 57N	9 30E
Rogoaguado, L.	**86**	13 0S	65 30W
Rogue, R.	**78**	42 30N	124 0W
Rohan	**100**	48 4N	2 45W
Rohault, L.	**41**	49 23N	74 20W
Rohnert Park	**80**	38 16N	122 40W
Rohrbach	**101**	49 3N	7 15E
Rohri	**124**	27 45N	68 51E
Rohtak	**124**	28 55N	76 43E
Roi Et	**128**	15 56N	103 40E
Roisel	**101**	49 58N	3 6E
Rojas	**88**	34 10S	60 45W
Rojo, C., Mexico	**83**	21 33N	97 20W
Rojo, C., W. Indies	**67**	17 56N	67 11W
Rokan, R.	**126**	1 30N	100 50E
Roland	**57**	49 22N	97 56W
Rolândia	**89**	23 5S	52 0W
Rolette	**74**	48 42N	99 50W
Rolfe	**76**	42 49N	94 31W
Rolla, Kansas, U.S.A.	**75**	37 10N	101 40W
Rolla, Missouri, U.S.A.	**76**	37 56N	91 42W
Rolla, N. Dak., U.S.A.	**57**	48 50N	99 36W
Rollet	**40**	47 55N	79 15W
Rolling Hills	**61**	50 13N	111 46W
Rolling, R.	**77**	38 0N	85 56W
Roma, Austral.	**135**	26 32S	148 49E
Roma, Italy	**108**	41 54N	12 30E
Roma, Sweden	**111**	57 32N	18 26E
Romaine, R.	**36**	50 18N	63 47W
Roman	**107**	43 8N	23 54E
Romana, La	**85**	18 27N	68 57W
Romang, I.	**127**	7 30S	127 20E
Romano, Cayo	**84**	22 0N	77 30W
Romanzof, C.	**67**	62 0N	165 50W
Rome, Ga., U.S.A.	**73**	34 20N	85 0W
Rome, N.Y., U.S.A.	**71**	43 14N	75 29W
Rome = Roma	**108**	41 54N	12 30E
Romenay	**103**	46 30N	5 1E
Romilly	**101**	48 31N	3 44E
Romney, Can.	**70**	42 9N	82 23W
Romney, U.S.A.	**72**	39 21N	78 45W
Romney Marsh	**95**	51 0N	1 0E
Romorantin-Lanthenay	**101**	47 21N	1 45E
Romsdalen	**110**	62 25N	7 50E
Ronan	**78**	47 30N	114 11W
Roncador Cay	**84**	13 40N	80 4W
Roncador, Serra do	**87**	12 30S	52 30W
Ronceverte	**72**	37 45N	80 28W
Ronda	**104**	36 46N	5 12W
Rondane	**111**	61 57N	9 50E
Rondeau Prov. Park	**46**	42 19N	81 51W
Rondón	**86**	6 17N	71 6W
Rondônia □	**86**	11 0S	63 0W
Rong, Koh	**128**	10 45N	103 15E
Ronge, La	**55**	55 5N	105 20W
Ronge, Lac La	**55**	55 6N	105 17W
Rønne	**111**	55 6N	14 44E
Ronne Land	**91**	83 0S	70 0W
Ronse	**105**	50 45N	3 35E
Roodepoort-Maraisburg	**117**	26 8S	27 52E
Roodhouse	**76**	39 29N	90 24W
Roof Butte	**79**	36 29N	109 5W
Roorkee	**124**	29 52N	77 59E
Roosendaal	**105**	51 32N	4 29E
Roosevelt, Minn., U.S.A.	**74**	48 51N	95 2W
Roosevelt, Utah, U.S.A.	**78**	40 19N	110 1W
Roosevelt I.	**91**	79 0S	161 0W
Roosevelt, Mt.	**54**	58 20N	125 20W
Roosevelt Res.	**79**	33 46N	111 0W
Roosville	**61**	49 0N	115 3W
Roper, R.	**134**	14 43S	135 27E
Ropesville	**75**	33 25N	102 10W
Roque Pérez	**88**	35 25S	59 24W
Roquefort	**102**	44 2N	0 20W
Roquefort-sur-Soulzon	**102**	43 58N	2 59E
Roquemaure	**103**	44 3N	4 48E
Roquevaire	**103**	43 20N	5 36E
Roraima □	**86**	2 0N	61 30W
Roraima, Mt.	**86**	5 10N	60 40W
Rorketon	**57**	51 24N	99 35W
Røros	**110**	62 35N	11 23E
Rosa, U.S.A.	**78**	38 15N	122 16W
Rosa, Zambia	**116**	9 33S	31 15E
Rosa, Monte	**106**	45 57N	7 53E
Rosalia	**78**	47 26N	117 25W
Rosalind	**61**	52 47N	112 27W
Rosamund	**81**	34 52N	118 10W
Rosans	**103**	44 24N	5 29E
Rosario	**88**	33 0S	60 50W
Rosário, Maran., Brazil	**87**	3 0S	44 15W
Rosário, Rio Grande do Sul, Brazil	**90**	30 15S	55 0W
Rosario, Baja California, Mexico	**82**	30 0N	116 0W
Rosario, Durango, Mexico	**82**	26 30N	105 35W
Rosario, Sinaloa, Mexico	**82**	23 0N	106 0W
Rosario, Venez.	**86**	10 19N	72 19W
Rosario de la Frontera	**88**	25 50S	65 0W
Rosario de Lerma	**88**	24 59S	65 35W
Rosario del Tala	**88**	32 20S	59 10W
Rosário do Sul	**89**	30 15S	54 55W
Rosarito, Mexico	**82**	28 38N	114 4W
Rosarito, U.S.A.	**81**	32 18N	117 4W
Rosas	**104**	42 19N	3 10E
Rosas, G. de,	**104**	42 10N	3 15E
Roscoe	**76**	37 58N	93 48W
Roscoff	**100**	48 44N	4 0W
Roscommon, Ireland	**97**	53 38N	8 11W
Roscommon, U.S.A.	**46**	44 27N	84 35W
Roscommon □	**97**	53 40N	8 15W
Roscrea	**97**	52 58N	7 50W
Rose Blanche	**37**	47 38N	58 45W
Rose City	**46**	44 25N	84 7W
Rose Harbour	**62**	52 15N	131 10W
Rose Pt.	**62**	54 11N	131 39W
Rose Valley	**56**	52 19N	103 49W
Roseau, Domin.	**85**	15 20N	61 30W
Roseau, U.S.A.	**57**	48 51N	95 46W
Rosebud, Austral.	**136**	38 21S	144 54E
Rosebud, U.S.A.	**75**	31 5N	97 0W
Rosebud, R.	**61**	51 25N	112 38W
Roseburg	**78**	43 10N	123 10W
Rosedale, Can.	**63**	49 10N	121 48W
Rosedale, U.S.A.	**77**	39 38N	87 17W
Rosedale, Miss., U.S.A.	**75**	33 51N	91 0W
Roseisle	**57**	49 30N	98 20W
Roseland	**80**	38 25N	122 43W
Rosemary	**61**	50 46N	112 5W
Rosemère	**44**	45 38N	73 48W
Rosemont	**58**	50 27N	104 39W
Rosenberg	**75**	29 30N	95 48W
Rosendaël	**101**	51 3N	2 24E
Rosendale	**76**	40 4N	94 51W
Rosenheim	**106**	47 51N	12 9E
Rosetown	**56**	51 35N	107 59W
Roseville, U.S.A.	**76**	40 44N	90 40W
Roseville, Calif., U.S.A.	**80**	38 46N	121 17W
Roseville, Mich., U.S.A.	**46**	42 30N	82 56W
Rosières	**101**	48 36N	6 20E
Rosignol	**86**	6 15N	57 30W
Roskilde	**111**	55 38N	12 3E
Roslavl	**120**	53 57N	32 55E
Rosporden	**100**	47 57N	3 50W
Ross, N.Z.	**133**	42 53S	170 49E
Ross, U.K.	**95**	51 55N	2 34W
Ross Dependency	**91**	70 0S	170 5W
Ross I.	**91**	77 30S	168 0E
Ross Ice Shelf	**91**	80 0S	180 0W
Ross L.	**63**	48 50N	121 5W
Ross on Wye	**95**	51 55N	2 34W
Ross Pt.	**51**	43 51N	78 54W
Ross River	**67**	62 30N	131 30W
Ross Sea	**91**	74 0S	178 0E
Rossan Pt.	**97**	54 42N	8 47W
Rossburn	**57**	50 40N	100 49W
Rosseau, Can.	**70**	45 26N	79 39W
Rosseau, Ont., Can.	**46**	45 16N	79 39W
Rosseau L.	**46**	45 10N	79 35W
Rosser	**58**	49 59N	97 27W
Rossford	**77**	41 36N	83 34W
Rossignol, L., N.S., Can.	**39**	44 12N	65 0W
Rossignol, L., Qué., Can.	**36**	52 43N	73 40W
Rossland	**63**	49 6N	117 50W
Rosslare	**97**	52 17N	6 23W
Rossmore	**47**	44 8N	77 23W
Rossosh	**120**	50 15N	39 20E
Rossport	**53**	48 50N	87 30W
Røssvatnet	**110**	65 45N	14 5E
Rossville	**77**	40 25N	86 35W
Rosthern	**56**	52 40N	106 20W
Rostock	**106**	54 4N	12 9E
Rostov	**120**	47 15N	39 45E
Rostrenen	**100**	48 14N	3 21W
Roswell	**75**	33 26N	104 32W
Rosyth	**96**	56 2N	3 26W
Rotan	**75**	32 52N	100 30W
Rothaargebirge	**106**	51 0N	8 20E
Rother, R.	**95**	50 59N	0 40W
Rotherham	**94**	53 26N	1 21W
Rothes	**96**	57 31N	3 12W
Rothesay, Can.	**39**	45 23N	66 0W
Rothesay, U.K.	**96**	55 50N	5 3W
Roti, I.	**127**	10 50S	123 0E
Roto	**136**	33 0S	145 30E
Rotoroa Lake	**133**	41 55S	172 39E
Rotorua	**133**	38 9S	176 16E
Rotorua, L.	**133**	38 5S	176 18E
Rotterdam	**105**	51 55N	4 30E
Rottweil	**106**	48 9N	8 38E
Rotuma, I.	**14**	12 25S	177 5E
Roubaix	**101**	50 40N	3 10E
Rouen	**100**	49 27N	1 4E
Rouergue	**103**	44 20N	2 20E
Rouge Hill	**51**	43 48N	79 8W
Rouge, R., Ont., Can.	**51**	43 48N	79 7W
Rouge, R., Qué., Can.	**40**	45 17N	74 10W
Rougemont	**45**	45 26N	73 3W
Rouillac	**102**	45 47N	0 4W
Rouleau	**56**	50 10N	104 56W
Round Hill, Alta., Can.	**61**	53 10N	112 38W
Round Hill, N.S., Can.	**39**	44 46N	65 24W
Round L., Newf., Can.	**37**	51 15N	56 32W
Round L., Ont., Can.	**47**	45 38N	77 30W
Round Mt.	**135**	30 26S	152 16E
Round Mountain	**78**	38 46N	117 3W
Round Pond	**37**	48 11N	56 0W
Round Valley	**60**	53 21N	114 57W
Roundup	**78**	46 25N	108 35W
Rousay, I.	**96**	59 10N	3 2W
Rouses Point	**43**	44 58N	73 22W
Rousse, L'Île	**103**	42 27N	8 57E
Roussillon, Can.	**43**	45 41N	74 26W
Roussillon, France	**103**	45 24N	4 49E
Routhierville	**38**	48 11N	67 9W
Rouville □	**45**	45 33N	73 10W
Rouvray, L.	**41**	49 18N	70 49W
Rouyn	**40**	48 20N	79 0W
Rovaniemi	**110**	66 29N	25 41E
Rovereto	**108**	45 53N	11 3E
Rovigo	**108**	45 4N	11 48E
Rovinj	**108**	45 5N	13 40E
Rovira	**86**	4 15N	75 20W
Rovno	**120**	50 40N	26 10E
Rowan L.	**52**	49 18N	93 32W
Rowatt	**58**	50 20N	104 37W
Rowley I.	**65**	69 6N	77 52W
Rowley Shoals	**134**	17 40S	119 20E
Rowood	**79**	32 18N	112 54W
Roxas	**127**	11 36N	122 49E
Roxboro, Can.	**44**	45 31N	73 48W
Roxboro, U.S.A.	**73**	36 24N	78 59W
Roxburgh, N.Z.	**133**	45 33S	169 19E
Roxburgh, U.K.	**96**	55 34N	2 30W
Roxton Falls	**41**	45 34N	72 31W
Roy, U.S.A.	**78**	47 17N	109 0W
Roy, N. Mex., U.S.A.	**75**	35 57N	104 8W
Roy, Le, U.S.A.	**77**	40 21N	88 46W
Roy, Le, Kans., U.S.A.	**75**	38 8N	95 35W
Royal Center	**77**	40 52N	86 30W
Royal Oak, Can.	**63**	48 29N	123 23W
Royal Oak, U.S.A.	**77**	42 30N	83 5W
Royan	**102**	45 37N	1 2W
Roye	**101**	47 40N	6 31E
Rozay	**101**	48 40N	2 56E
Rozier, Le	**102**	44 13N	3 12E
Rozoy-sur-Serre	**101**	49 40N	4 8E
Rtishchevo	**120**	52 35N	43 50E
Ruahine Ra.	**133**	39 55S	176 2E
Ruapehu	**133**	39 17S	175 35E
Ruapuke I.	**133**	46 46S	168 31E
Rub 'al Khali	**115**	21 0N	51 0E
Rubicon, R.	**80**	38 53N	121 4W
Rubicone, R.	**108**	44 0N	12 20E
Rubio	**86**	7 43N	72 22W
Rubtsovsk	**120**	51 30N	80 50E
Ruby	**67**	64 40N	155 35W
Ruby L.	**78**	40 10N	115 28W
Ruby Mts.	**78**	40 30N	115 30W
Rudbar	**123**	30 0N	62 30E
Rudh a'Mhail, C.	**96**	55 55N	6 25W
Rudnogorsk	**121**	57 15N	103 42E
Rudnyy	**120**	52 57N	63 7E
Rudok	**129**	33 30N	79 40E
Rudyard	**46**	46 14N	84 35W
Rue	**101**	50 15N	1 40E
Rue, La	**77**	40 35N	83 23W
Ruel	**53**	47 15N	81 28W

Ruelle St-Eustacht

Ruelle 102 45 41N 0 14E
Ruffec Charente 102 46 2N 0 12E
Rufiji, R. 116 7 50S 38 15E
Rufino 88 34 20S 62 50W
Rugby, U.K. 95 52 23N 1 16W
Rugby, U.S.A. 74 48 21N 100 0W
Rügen, I. 106 54 22N 13 25E
Rugles 100 48 50N 0 40E
Ruhr, R. 105 51 25N 7 15E
Ruidosa 75 29 59N 104 39W
Ruidoso 79 33 19N 105 39W
Ruisseau-des-Anges 43 45 48N 73 40W
Ruisseau-Vert 41 49 4N 68 28W
Rukwa L. 116 7 50S 32 10E
Rully 85 46 52N 4 44E
Rum Jungle 134 13 0S 130 59E
Rumāh 122 25 35N 47 10E
Rumania ■ 107 46 0N 25 0E
Rumford 71 44 30N 70 30W
Rumilly 103 45 53N 5 56E
Rummelhardt 49 43 27N 80 34W
Rumoi 132 43 56N 141 39W
Rumorosa, La 81 32 33N 116 4W
Rumsey 61 51 51N 112 48W
Runanga 133 42 25S 171 15E
Runaway, C. 133 37 32S 178 2E
Runcorn 94 53 20N 2 44W
Rungwa 116 6 55S 33 32E
Runton Ra. 136 23 35S 123 15E
Rupa 125 27 15N 92 30E
Rupat, I. 126 1 45N 101 40E
Rupert B. 36 51 35N 79 0W
Rupert House = Fort Rupert 36 51 30N 78 40W
Rupert, R. 36 51 29N 78 45W
Rupununi, R. 87 3 30N 59 30W
Rurrenabaque 86 14 30S 67 32W
Rusagonis 39 45 48N 66 37W
Rusape 117 18 35S 32 8E
Ruschuk = Ruse 109 43 48N 25 59E
Ruse 109 43 48N 25 59E
Rush L. 53 47 47N 82 11W
Rush Lake 56 50 24N 107 24W
Rushden 95 52 17N 0 37W
Rushford 74 43 48N 91 46W
Rushoon 37 47 21N 54 55W
Rushville, Ill., U.S.A. 76 40 6N 90 35W
Rushville, Ind., U.S.A. 77 39 38N 85 22W
Rushville, Nebr., U.S.A. 74 42 43N 102 20W
Rushworth 136 36 32S 145 1E
Russell, Man., Can. 55 50 50N 101 20W
Russell, Que., Can. 71 45 16N 75 21W
Russell, N.Z. 133 35 16S 174 10E
Russell, U.S.A. 74 38 56N 98 55W
Russell I. 65 74 0N 98 25W
Russell L., Man., Can. 55 56 15N 101 30W
Russell L., N.W.T., Can. 54 63 5N 115 44W
Russellkonda 125 19 57N 84 42E
Russelltown 43 45 4N 73 45W
Russellville, Ala., U.S.A. 73 34 30N 87 44W
Russellville, Ark., U.S.A. 75 35 15N 93 0W
Russellville, Ky., U.S.A. 73 36 50N 86 50W
Russian Mission 67 61 45N 161 25W
Russian, R. 80 38 27N 123 8W
Russian S.F.S.R. □ 121 62 0N 105 0E
Russiaville 77 40 25N 86 16W
Russkoye Ustie 17 71 0N 149 0E
Rustenburg 117 25 41S 27 14E
Ruston 75 32 30N 92 58W
Rutba 122 33 4N 40 15E
Ruteng 127 8 26S 120 30E
Ruth, Mich., U.S.A. 46 43 42N 82 45W
Ruth, Nev., U.S.A. 78 39 15N 115 1W
Rutherford 80 38 26N 122 24W
Rutherglen, Austral. 136 36 5S 146 29E
Rutherglen, U.K. 96 55 50N 4 11W
Rutland 71 43 38N 73 0W
Rutland I. 128 11 25N 92 40E
Rutledge L. 55 61 33N 110 47W
Rutledge, R. 55 61 4N 112 0W
Rutshuru 116 1 13S 29 25E
Rutter 46 46 6N 80 40W
Ruvuma, R. 116 11 30S 36 10E
Ruwaidha 122 23 40N 44 40E
Ruwandiz 122 36 40N 44 32E
Ruwenzori Mts. 116 0 30N 29 55E
Ruwenzori, mt. 116 0 30N 29 55E
Ruzomberok 107 49 3N 19 17E
Rwanda ■ 116 2 0S 30 0E
Ryan, L. 96 55 0N 5 2W
Ryans B. 36 59 35N 64 3W
Ryazan 120 54 50N 39 40E
Rybache 120 46 40N 81 20E
Rybinsk (Shcherbakov) 120 58 5N 38 50E
Ryckman 48 43 15N 79 54W
Rycroft 60 55 45N 118 40W
Ryde 95 50 44N 1 9W
Ryderwood 80 46 23N 123 3W
Rye 95 50 57N 0 46E
Rye Patch Res. 78 40 45N 118 20W
Rye, R. 94 54 12N 0 53W
Ryegate 78 46 21N 109 27W
Ryley 60 53 17N 112 26W
Rypin 107 53 3N 19 32E
Ryūkyū Is. = Nansei-Shotō 132 26 0N 128 0E
Ryūkyū-rettō 131 26 0N 127 0E
Rzeszów 107 50 5N 21 58E
Rzhev 120 56 20N 34 20E

S

Sa Dec 128 10 20N 105 46E
Sa'ādatābād 123 30 10N 53 5E
Saale, R. 106 51 25N 11 56E
Saanich 63 48 28N 123 22W
Saar, R. 106 49 25N 6 35E
Saar (Sarre), □ 101 49 20N 6 45E
Saarbrücken 105 49 15N 6 58E
Saaremaa 120 58 30N 22 30E
Saariselkä 110 68 16N 28 15E
Saarland □ 15 49 20N 6 45E
Saarlouis 105 49 19N 6 45E
Saba I. 85 17 30N 63 10W
Sabadell 104 41 28N 2 7E
Sabagalel 126 1 36S 98 40E
Sabah □ 126 6 0N 117 0E
Sabak 128 3 46N 100 58E
Sábana de la Mar 85 19 7N 69 40W
Sábanalarga 86 10 38N 74 55W
Sabang 126 5 50N 95 15E
Sabará 87 19 55S 43 55W
Sabarania 127 2 5S 138 18E
Sabattis 71 44 6N 74 40W
Sabaudia 108 41 17N 13 2E
Sabhah 114 27 9N 14 29E
Sabina 77 39 29N 83 38W
Sabinal, Mexico 82 30 50N 107 25W
Sabinal, U.S.A. 75 29 20N 99 27W
Sabinas 82 27 50N 101 10W
Sabinas Hidalgo 82 26 40N 100 10W
Sabinas, R. 82 27 37N 100 42W
Sabine 75 29 42N 93 54W
Sabine, R. 75 31 30N 93 35W
Sablayan 127 12 5N 120 50E
Sable 100 47 50N 0 21W
Sable, C., Can. 39 43 29N 65 38W
Sable, C., U.S.A. 84 25 5N 81 0W
Sable I. 35 44 0N 60 0W
Sable River 39 43 51N 65 3W
Sablé-sur-Sarthe 100 47 50N 0 20W
Sables-D'Olonne, Les 102 46 30N 1 45W
Sables, R. aux 46 46 13N 82 3W
Sabourin, L. 40 47 58N 77 41W
Sabrevois 43 45 12N 73 14W
Sabrina Coast 91 67 0S 120 0E
Sabtang I. 131 20 15N 121 30E
Sabula 76 42 5N 90 23W
Sabzevār 123 36 15N 57 40E
Sabzvāran 123 28 45N 57 50E
Sac City 76 42 26N 95 0W
Sachigo, L. 34 53 50N 92 12W
Sachigo, R. 34 55 6N 88 58W
Sachs Harbour 64 71 59N 125 15W
Sackett's Harbor 71 43 56N 72 38W
Sackville 39 45 54N 64 22W
Saco, Me., U.S.A. 73 43 30N 70 27W
Saco, Mont., U.S.A. 78 48 28N 107 19W
Sacramento 80 38 39N 121 30E
Sacramento Mts. 79 32 30N 105 30W
Sacramento, R. 80 38 3N 121 56W
Sacramento Valley 80 39 0N 122 0W
Sacré-Coeur-de-Jésus 41 48 14N 69 48W
Sadaba 104 42 19N 1 12W
Sa'dani 116 5 58S 38 35E
Sadao 128 6 38N 100 26E
Saddle Mt. 80 45 58N 123 41W
Sadieville 77 38 23N 84 32W
Sado 132 38 0N 138 25E
Sado, Shima 132 38 15N 138 30E
Saegerstown 70 80 10N 41 42W
Safaniya 122 28 5N 48 42E
Saffron Walden 95 52 2N 0 15E
Safi 114 32 18N 9 14W
Safiah 100 31 27N 34 46E
Sag Harbor 71 40 59N 72 17W
Saga 127 2 40S 132 55E
Saga-ken □ 132 33 15N 130 20E
Sagaing 125 23 30N 95 30E
Saganaga L. 52 48 14N 90 52W
Saganash L. 53 49 4N 82 35W
Sagar 124 23 50N 78 50E
Sagil 129 50 15N 91 15E
Saginaw 46 43 26N 83 55W
Saginaw B. 46 43 50N 83 40W
Sagleipie 103 45 25N 7 0E
Saglek B. 36 58 30N 63 0W
Saglek Fd. 36 58 29N 63 15W
Saglouc 36 62 14N 75 38W
Sagone 103 42 7N 8 42E
Sagone, G. de 103 42 4N 8 40E
Sagra, La, Mt. 104 38 0N 2 35W
Sagres 104 37 0N 8 58W
Sagua la Grande 84 22 50N 80 10W
Saguache 79 38 10N 106 4W
Saguenay, R. 41 48 22N 71 0W
Sagunto 104 39 42N 0 18W
Sahagún, Colomb. 86 8 57N 75 27W
Sahagún, Spain 104 42 18N 5 2W
Sahara 114 23 0N 5 0W
Saharanpur 124 29 58N 77 33E
Sahiwal 124 30 45N 73 8E
Sahtaneh, R. 54 59 2N 122 28W
Sahuaripa 82 29 30N 109 0W
Sahuarita 79 31 58N 110 59W
Sahuayo 82 20 4N 102 43W
Sa'idabad 123 29 30N 55 45E
Saidapet 124 13 0N 80 15E
Saidu 124 34 50N 72 15E
Säe 111 59 8N 12 55E
Saighan 123 35 10N 67 55E
Saignes 102 45 20N 2 31E
Saigon = Phanh Bho Ho Chi Minh 128 10 58N 106 40E
Saih-al-Malih 123 23 37N 58 31E
Saijō 132 34 0N 133 5E
Saikhoa Ghat 125 27 50N 95 40E
Saiki 132 32 58N 131 57E
Saillans 103 44 42N 5 12E
Sailolof 127 1 7S 130 46E
St-Hyacinthe 45 45 40N 72 58W
St-Jean-Port-Joli 41 47 15N 70 13W
St Jovite 40 46 8N 74 38W
St.-Julien-du-Sault 101 48 1N 3 17E
St. Abb's Head 96 55 55N 2 10W
St-Adalbert 41 46 51N 69 53W
St-Adolphe-d'Howard 43 45 58N 74 20W
St-Affrique 102 43 57N 2 53E
St-Agapitville 41 46 34N 71 26W
St-Agrève 103 45 0N 4 23E
St.-Aignan 100 47 16N 1 22E
St. Alban's 37 47 51N 55 50W
St. Albans, U.K. 95 51 44N 0 19W
St. Albans, Vt., U.S.A. 71 44 49N 73 7W
St. Albans, W. Va., U.S.A. 72 38 21N 81 50W
St. Alban's Head 95 50 34N 2 3W
St. Albert 60 53 37N 113 40W
St-Alexandre, Qué., Can. 41 47 41N 69 38W
St-Alexandre, Qué., Can. 45 45 14N 73 7W
St-Alexis 43 45 56N 73 37W
St-Alexis-des-Monts 41 46 28N 73 8W
St-Amable 45 45 39N 73 18W
St-Amand 101 50 25N 3 6E
St-Amand-en-Puisaye 101 47 32N 3 5E
St-Amand-Mont-Rond 102 46 43N 2 30E
St-Amarin 101 47 54N 7 0E
St-Ambroise 41 48 33N 71 20W
St-Amour 103 46 26N 5 21E
St-Anaclet 41 48 29N 68 26W
St-André 39 47 8N 67 45W
St-André-Avellin 40 45 43N 75 3W
St-André-de-Cubzac 102 44 59N 0 26W
St-André de l'Eure 100 48 54N 1 16E
St-André-Est 43 45 34N 74 20W
St-André-les-Alpes 103 43 58N 6 30E
St. Andrews 39 45 7N 67 5W
St. Andrew's 37 47 45N 59 15W
St. Andrews 96 56 20N 2 48W
St-Angèle-de-Monnoir 45 45 23N 73 6W
St-Anicet 43 45 8N 74 22W
St. Ann B. 39 46 22N 60 25W
St. Anne 100 49 43N 2 11W
St Anne 77 41 1N 87 43W
St. Annes 57 49 40N 96 39W
St. Anns 49 43 5N 79 30W
St. Ann's Bay 84 18 26N 77 15W
St-Anselme, N.B., Can. 39 46 4N 64 43W
St-Anselme, Qué., Can. 41 46 37N 70 58W
St. Anthony, N.B., Can. 39 46 22N 64 45W
St. Anthony, Newf., Can. 37 51 22N 55 35W
St. Anthony, U.S.A. 78 44 0N 111 49W
St-Antoine 44 45 46N 73 59W
St-Antoine-des-Laurentides 44 45 46N 73 59W
St-Antoine-sur-Richelieu 45 45 46N 73 11W
St-Antonin 41 47 46N 69 29W
St-Antonin-Noble-Val 102 44 10N 1 45E
St-Apolline 41 46 48N 70 12W
St. Arnaud 136 36 32S 143 16E
St. Arthur 39 47 33N 67 46W
St. Asaph 94 53 15N 3 27W
St-Astier 102 45 8N 0 31E
St-Aubert 41 47 11N 70 13W
St-Aubin-du-Cormier 100 48 15N 1 26W
St-Augustin 44 45 38N 73 59W
St-Augustin-de-Desmaures 42 46 45N 71 30W
St-Augustin, L. 42 46 45N 71 23W
St-Augustin, R. 36 51 16N 58 40W
St-Augustin-Saguenay 37 51 13N 58 38W
St. Augustine 73 29 52N 81 20W
St. Austell 95 50 20N 4 48W
St-Avold 101 49 6N 6 43E
St-Barnabé-Sud 45 45 44N 72 55W
St-Barthélémy 41 46 11N 73 8W
St. Barthélemy, I. 85 17 50N 62 50W
St-Basile 39 47 21N 68 14W
St-Basile-le-Grand 45 45 32N 73 17W
St-Basile-Sud 41 46 45N 71 49W
St. Bee's Hd. 94 54 30N 3 38E
St. Benedict 56 52 34N 105 23W
St-Benoît 44 45 34N 74 6W
St-Benoît-du-Sault 102 46 26N 1 24E
St-Bernard-de-Lacolle 45 45 5N 73 25W
St-Blaise 43 45 13N 73 17W
St. Boniface 58 49 53N 97 5W
St-Bonnet 103 44 40N 6 5E
St. Brendan's 37 48 52N 53 40W
St-Brévin-les-Pins 100 47 14N 2 10W
St-Brice-en-Coglès 100 48 25N 1 22W
St. Bride's 37 46 56N 54 10W
St. Bride's B. 95 51 48N 5 15W
St-Brieuc 100 48 30N 2 46W
St. Brieux 56 52 38N 104 54W
St-Bruno 41 48 28N 71 39W
St-Bruno-de-Montarville 45 45 32N 73 21W
St-Calais 100 47 55N 0 45E
St-Calixte-de-Kilkenny 43 45 57N 73 51W
St-Calixte-Nord 43 45 59N 73 55W
St-Canut 44 45 43N 74 5W
St-Casimir 41 46 40N 72 8W
St-Cast 100 48 37N 2 18W
St. Catharines 49 43 10N 79 15W
St. Catherines I. 73 31 35N 81 10W
St. Catherine's Pt. 95 50 34N 1 18W
St-Céré 102 44 51N 1 54E
St-Cernin 102 45 5N 2 25E
St-Césaire 45 45 25N 73 0W
St-Chamond 103 45 28N 4 31E
St. Charles 58 49 53N 97 19W
St-Charles 42 46 46N 70 57W
St. Charles, Ill., U.S.A. 77 41 55N 88 21W
St. Charles, Mich., U.S.A. 46 43 18N 84 9W
St. Charles, Mo., U.S.A. 76 38 46N 90 30W
St-Charles, L. 42 46 55N 71 23W
St-Charles, R. 42 46 49N 71 13W
St-Charles-sur-Richelieu 45 45 41N 73 11W
St-Chély-d'Apcher 102 44 48N 3 17E
St-Chinian 102 43 25N 2 56E
St. Christopher (St. Kitts) 85 17 20N 62 40W
St-Chrysostôme 43 45 6N 73 46W
St-Ciers-sur-Gironde 102 45 17N 0 37W
Saint Clair 76 38 21N 90 59W
St. Clair, Mich, U.S.A. 46 42 47N 82 27W
St. Clair, Pa., U.S.A. 71 40 42N 76 12W
St. Clair, L. 46 42 30N 82 45W
St. Clair, R. 46 42 40N 82 20W
St. Clairsville 70 40 5N 80 53W
St-Claud 102 45 54N 0 28E
St. Claude 57 49 40N 98 20W
St-Claude 103 46 22N 5 52E
St-Clet 43 45 21N 74 13W
St-Cloud 100 48 51N 2 12E
St. Cloud, Fla., U.S.A. 73 28 15N 81 15W
St. Cloud, Minn., U.S.A. 74 45 30N 94 11W
St-Coeur de Marie 41 48 39N 71 43W
St-Colomban 44 45 44N 74 8W
St-Côme 41 46 16N 73 47W
St-Constant 44 45 22N 73 37W
St-Croix 39 45 34N 67 26W
St. Croix Falls 74 45 18N 92 22W
St. Croix, I. 85 17 45N 64 45W
St. 39 45 5N 67 6W
St. Croix, R., U.S.A. 52 46 16N 91 35W
St. Croix, R., U.S.A. 74 45 20N 92 50W
St-Cyprien 102 42 37N 3 0E
St-Cyr 103 43 11N 5 43E
St-Cyrille-de-L'Islet 41 47 2N 70 17W
St. Cyrus 96 56 47N 2 25W
St-Damase 45 45 31N 73 1W
St. David 76 40 30N 90 3W
St-David-de-l'Auberivière 42 46 47N 71 12W
St-David-d'Yamaska 43 45 57N 72 51W
St. David's 37 48 12N 58 52W
St. Davids 49 43 10N 79 6W
St. David's 95 51 54N 5 16W
St. David's Head 95 51 54N 5 16W
St-Denis, Can. 45 45 47N 73 9W
St-Denis, France 101 48 56N 2 22E
St.-Denis 16 20 52S 55 27E
St-Denis-d'Orques 100 48 2N 0 17W
St-Dié 101 48 17N 6 56E
St-Dizier 101 48 40N 5 0E
St-Dominique 44 45 20N 74 8W
St-Donat-de-Montcalm 41 46 19N 74 13W
St-Edouard-de-Napierville 43 45 14N 73 31W
St-Egrève 103 45 14N 5 41E
St-Eleanors 39 46 25N 63 49W
St. Elias, Mt. 67 60 20N 141 59W
St Elias Mts. 54 60 33N 139 28W
Saint Elmo 77 39 2N 88 51W
St-Éloi 41 48 2N 69 14W
St-Élouthère 41 47 30N 69 15W
St.-Eloy-les-Mines 102 46 10N 2 51E
St-Emile 42 46 52N 71 20W
St-Émilion 102 44 53N 0 9W
St-Éphrem-de-Tring 41 46 2N 70 59W
St-Esprit 43 45 54N 73 40W
St-Étienne 103 45 27N 4 22E
St-Étienne-de-Tinée 103 44 16N 6 56E
St-Étienne-de-Beauharnois 44 45 15N 73 55W
St. Eugène 47 45 30N 74 28W
St-Eugène 43 45 30N 74 29W
St-Eusèbe 41 47 33N 68 55W
St. Eustache 57 49 59N 97 47W
St-Eustache 44 45 33N 73 54W

St. Eustatius I. 85 17 20N 63 0W
St-Fabien 41 48 18N 68 52W
St-Félicien 41 48 40N 72 25W
St-Félix-de-Valois 41 46 10N 73 26W
St-Félix-du-Cap-Rouge 42 46 45N 71 22W
St. Fintan's 35 48 10N 58 50W
St-Florent 103 42 41N 9 18 E
St-Florent-sur-Cher 101 46 59N 2 15 E
St-Florentin 101 48 0N 3 45 E
St-Flour 102 45 2N 3 6 E
St-Fons 103 45 42N 4 52 E
St. Francis 74 39 48N 101 47W
St. Francis C. 117 34 14 S 24 49 E
St-Francis, L. 43 45 10N 74 22W
St. Francis, R. 75 35 25N 90 36W
St. Francisville 77 38 36N 87 39W
St-François, Qué., Can. 41 46 48N 70 49W
St-François, Qué., Can. 44 45 40N 73 35W
St-François-du-Lac 41 46 5N 72 50W
St-François, L. 41 45 10N 74 22W
St-François, R. 41 46 7N 72 55W
St. François Xavier 57 49 55N 97 32W
St-Fulgence 41 48 27N 70 54W
St-Fulgent 100 46 50N 1 10W
St-Gabriel-de-Brandon 41 46 17N 73 24W
St-Gabriel-de-Gaspé 38 48 31N 64 32W
St-Gabriel-de-Rimouski 41 48 25N 68 10W
St-Gabriel-Ouest 42 47 2N 71 35W
St. Gallen 106 47 25N 9 20 E
St-Gaudens 102 43 6N 0 44 E
St-Gédéon 41 48 30N 71 46W
St-Gédéon-de-Beauce 41 45 45N 70 40W
St-Gengoux-le-National 103 46 37N 4 40 E
St-Geniez-d'Olt 102 44 27N 2 58 E
St. George, Austral. 135 28 1 S 148 41 E
St. George, N.B., Can. 39 45 11N 66 50W
St. George, Ont., Can. 49 43 15N 80 15W
St. George, S.C., U.S.A. 73 33 13N 80 37W
St. George, Utah, U.S.A. 79 37 10N 113 35W
St. George, C., Can. 37 48 30N 59 16W
St. George, C., U.S.A. 73 29 36N 85 2W
St. George West 55 50 33N 96 7W
St-Georges 105 50 37N 4 20 E
St. George's, Newf., Can. 35 48 26N 58 31W
St. George's, Newf., Can. 37 48 26N 58 31W
St-Georges 41 46 8N 70 40W
St. Georges, Can. 34 46 42N 72 35W
St. Georges, Fr. Gui. 87 4 0N 52 0W
St. George's 85 12 5N 61 43W
St. George's B. 37 48 24N 58 53W
St. George's Channel 67 52 0N 6 0W
St-Georges-de-Didonne 102 45 36N 1 0W
St-Georges-de-Bagot 43 45 40N 72 50W
St-Georges-de-Cacouna 41 47 55N 69 30W
St. Georges Head 136 35 12 S 150 42 E
St-Georges-Ouest 41 46 7N 70 40W
St-Gérard 41 45 46N 71 25W
St-Germain 101 48 53N 2 5 E
St-Germain-Lembron 102 45 27N 3 14 E
St-Germain-de-Calberte 102 44 13N 3 48 E
St-Germain-de-Grantham 41 45 50N 72 34W
St-Germain-des-Fossés 102 46 12N 3 26 E
St-Germain-du-Plain 101 46 42N 4 58 E
St.-Germain-Laval 103 45 50N 4 1 E
St-Gervais, Haute Savoie, France 103 45 53N 6 42 E
St-Gervais, Puy de Dôme, France 102 46 4N 2 50 E
St.-Gervais-les-Bains 101 45 53N 6 41 E
St-Gildas, Pte. de 100 47 8N 2 14W
St-Gilles Croix-de-Vie 100 46 41N 1 55W
St-Gilles-du-Gard 103 43 40N 4 26 E
St.-Girons 102 42 59N 1 8 E
St. Goar 105 50 31N 7 43 E
St-Godefroi 39 48 5N 65 6W
St. Gotthard P. = San Gottardo 106 46 33N 8 33 E
St.-Gualtier 100 46 39N 1 26 E
St-Guénolé 100 47 49N 4 23W
St-Guillaume-d'Upton 43 45 53N 72 46W
St-Hector-de-Bagot 43 45 35N 72 48W
St. Helena 78 38 29N 122 30W
St. Helena, I. 13 15 55 S 5 44W
St Helena, Mt. 80 38 40N 122 36W
St. Helenabaai 117 32 40 S 18 10 E
St. Helens, U.K. 94 53 28N 2 44W
St. Helens, U.S.A. 80 45 55N 122 50W
St. Helens, Mt. 80 46 12N 122 11W
St. Helier 100 49 11N 2 6W
St-Henri 41 46 42N 71 4W
St-Henri-de-Lévis 42 46 42N 71 4W
St-Hermas 44 45 36N 74 11W
St-Hilaire, Can. 45 45 33N 73 12W
St-Hilaire, France 100 48 35N 1 7W
St-Hilarion 41 47 34N 70 24W
St-Hippolyte 101 47 20N 6 50 E
St-Hippolyte-de-Kilkenny 43 45 56N 74 1W
St-Hippolyte-du-Fort 102 43 58N 3 52 E
St-Honoré, Can. 41 48 32N 71 5W
St-Honoré, France 101 46 54N 3 50 E
St-Hubert 45 45 30N 73 25W
St. Hubert 105 51 23N 6 26 E
St-Hubert-de-Témiscouata 41 47 49N 69 9W
St-Hugues 43 45 48N 72 52W
St-Hyacinthe □ 45 45 40N 73 0W
St-Ignace 39 46 42N 65 5W
St. Ignace 46 45 53N 84 43W
St. Ignace I. 53 48 45N 88 0W
St-Ignas-de-Stanbridge 43 45 10N 72 57W
St. Ignatius 78 47 25N 114 2W
St-Isidore, Qué., Can. 43 45 20N 73 42W
St-Isidore, Qué., Can. 44 45 18N 73 40W
St-Isidore-Jonction 44 45 21N 73 38W
St. Ives, Cambs., U.K. 95 52 20N 0 5W
St. Ives, Cornwall, U.K. 95 50 13N 5 29W
St. Jacobs 49 43 32N 80 33W
St-Jacques, N.B., Can. 39 47 26N 68 23W
St-Jacques, Qué., Can. 43 45 57N 73 34W
St-Jacques-le-Mineur 45 45 17N 73 25W
St-James 100 48 31N 1 20W
St. James, U.S.A. 76 38 0N 91 37W
St. James, Mich., U.S.A. 46 45 45N 85 31W
St. James, Minn., U.S.A. 74 43 57N 94 40W
St. James-Assiniboia 58 49 54N 97 15W
St. James C. 54 51 55N 131 0W
St-Janvier 44 45 42N 73 56W
St. Jean 45 45 20N 73 20W
St.-Jean 103 48 57N 3 1 E
St-Jean □ 45 45 15N 73 15W
St. Jean Baptiste 57 49 15N 97 20W
St-Jean-Baptiste-de-Restigouche 39 47 46N 67 13W
St-Jean-Baptiste-de-Rouville 45 45 31N 73 7W
St-Jean-Chrysostôme 42 46 43N 71 12W
St-Jean-de-Maurienne 103 45 16N 6 28 E
St-Jean-de-Boischatel 42 46 54N 71 9W
St-Jean-de-Dieu 41 48 0N 69 3W
St-Jean-de-Luz 102 43 23N 1 39W
St-Jean-de-Monts 100 46 47N 2 4W
St-Jean-du-Gard 102 44 7N 3 52 E
St-Jean-en-Royans 103 45 1N 5 18 E
St-Jean, L. 41 48 40N 72 0W
St-Jean, R., Qué., Can. 36 50 17N 64 20W
St-Jean, R., Qué., Can. 38 48 46N 64 26W
St-Jérôme, Qué., Can. 43 48 26N 71 53W
St-Jérôme, Qué., Can. 44 45 47N 74 0W
St-Joachim 41 47 4N 70 50W
St-Joachim-de-Tourelle 38 49 9N 66 25W
St. Joe 77 41 19N 84 54W
St. John, Can. 39 45 20N 66 8W
St. John, Kans., U.S.A. 75 37 59N 98 45W
St. John, N.D., U.S.A. 57 48 58N 99 40W
St. John B. 37 50 55N 57 9W
St. John, C. 37 50 0N 55 32W
Saint John Harbour 39 45 15N 66 2W
St. John I., Can. 37 50 49N 57 14W
St. John I., China 131 21 45N 112 45 E
St. John, I. 67 18 20N 64 45W
St. John, L. 37 48 23N 54 41W
St. John, R. 39 45 15N 66 4W
St. Johns, Antigua 85 17 6N 61 51W
St. Johns, Can. 58 49 55N 97 7W
St. John's 37 47 35N 52 40W
St. Johns, Ariz., U.S.A. 79 34 31N 109 26W
St. Johns, Mich., U.S.A. 77 43 0N 84 38W
St. John's Airport 37 47 6N 52 45W
St. John's B. 37 47 34N 52 38W
St. John's East 37 47 38N 52 42W
St. John's North 37 47 33N 52 49W
St. John's, R. 73 30 20N 81 30W
St. John's South 37 47 30N 52 43W
St. Johnsburg 49 43 5N 78 53W
St. Johnsbury 71 44 25N 72 1W
St. Johnsville 71 43 0N 74 43W
St-Joseph 45 45 38N 72 56W
St. Joseph, Ill, U.S.A. 77 40 7N 88 2W
St. Joseph, La., U.S.A. 75 31 55N 91 15W
St. Joseph, Mich., U.S.A. 72 42 5N 86 30W
St. Joseph, Mich., U.S.A. 77 42 5N 86 30W
St. Joseph, Mo., U.S.A. 76 39 40N 94 50W
St-Joseph-de-Beauce 41 46 18N 70 53W
St-Joseph-de-la-Rivière-Bleue 41 47 26N 69 3W
St-Joseph-de-Sorel 41 46 2N 73 7W
St-Joseph-du-Lac 44 45 32N 74 0W
St. Joseph, I. 46 46 12N 83 58W
St. Joseph, L. 52 51 10N 90 35W
St. Joseph, R. 77 42 7N 86 30W
St-Jude 45 45 46N 72 59W
St-Juéry 102 43 55N 2 42 E
St-Julien 103 46 8N 6 5 E
St-Julien-Chapteuil 103 45 2N 4 4 E
St-Junien 102 45 53N 0 55 E
St-Just-en-Chaussée 101 49 30N 2 25 E
St-Just-en-Chevalet 102 45 55N 3 50 E
St-Justin 102 43 59N 0 14W
St-Justine 41 46 24N 70 21W
St. Kilda 133 45 53 S 170 31 E
St. Kilda, I. 98 57 40N 8 50W
St. Kitts, I. 85 17 20N 62 40W
St-Lambert 45 45 30N 73 30W
St. Laurent 57 50 25N 97 58W
St-Laurent 44 45 30N 73 40W
St-Laurent d'Orléans 42 46 51N 71 1W
St-Laurent-du-Pont 103 45 23N 5 45 E
St-Laurent-en-Grandvaux 103 46 35N 5 45 E
Saint-Laurent, R. 45 45 25N 73 32W
St. Lawrence 37 46 54N 55 23W
St. Lawrence, Gulf of 35 48 25N 62 0W
St. Lawrence, I. 67 63 0N 170 0W
St. Lawrence, R. 35 49 30N 66 0W
St. Lazare 57 50 27N 101 18W
St-Lazare-Station 44 45 23N 74 6W
St-Léolin 39 47 46N 65 10W
St-Léon-le-Grand 38 48 23N 67 30W
St Leonard 39 47 12N 67 58W
St-Léonard 44 45 35N 73 35W
St-Léonard-de-Noblat 102 45 49N 1 29 E
St-Léonard-de-Portneuf 41 46 53N 71 55W
St-les-Dax 102 43 44N 1 3W
St. Lewis, R. 36 52 26N 56 11W
St-Liboire 43 45 39N 72 46W
St. Lin 34 45 44N 73 46W
St-Lô 100 49 7N 1 5W
St Louis 39 46 53N 64 8W
St. Louis, Can. 56 52 55N 105 49W
St. Louis, Senegal 114 16 8N 16 27W
St. Louis, Mich., U.S.A. 46 43 27N 84 38W
St. Louis, Mo., U.S.A. 76 38 40N 90 12W
St-Louis-de-Gonzague 43 45 13N 74 0W
St-Louis-de-Kent 39 46 44N 64 58W
St-Louis-de-Richelieu 43 45 51N 72 59W
St-Louis-de-Terrebonne 44 45 42N 73 47W
St-Louis, L. 44 45 24N 73 48W
St-Louis, Mts 36 46 13N 73 36W
St-Louis, R. 44 45 19N 73 53W
St. Louis R. 52 47 15N 92 45W
St-Loup-sur-Semouse 101 47 53N 6 16 E
St-Luc 45 45 22N 73 18W
St-Luc-de-Matane 38 48 48N 67 28W
St. Lucia Channel 85 14 15N 61 0W
St. Lucia I. 85 14 0N 60 50W
St. Lucia, Lake 117 28 5 S 32 30 E
St-Ludger 41 45 45N 70 42W
St. Lunaire-Griquet 37 51 31N 55 28W
St. Maarten, I. 85 18 0N 63 5W
St-Magloire 41 46 35N 70 17W
St-Maixent-l'École 102 46 24N 0 12W
St. Malo 57 49 19N 96 57W
St-Malo 100 48 39N 2 1W
St-Malo, G. de 100 48 50N 2 30W
St-Mandrier 103 43 4N 5 56 E
St-Marc 45 45 41N 73 12W
St. Marc 85 19 10N 72 50W
St-Marcel-de-Richelieu 43 45 52N 72 54W
St-Marcellin 103 45 9N 5 20 E
St-Marcouf, Îs. 100 49 30N 1 10W
St. Margarets 39 46 54N 65 11W
St. Maries 78 47 17N 116 34W
St-Martin, Can. 44 45 35N 73 44W
St-Martin, France 101 50 42N 1 38 E
St.-Martin, I. 85 18 0N 63 0W
St. Martin L. 57 51 40N 98 30W
St-Martin-Vésubie 103 44 4N 7 15 E
St. Martins 39 45 22N 65 25W
St. Martinsville 75 30 10N 91 50W
St-Martory 102 43 9N 0 56 E
St. Mary B. 35 46 50N 53 50W
St Mary L. 61 48 40N 113 30W
St. Mary, R. 61 49 37N 115 38W
St. Mary Res. 61 49 20N 113 11W
St. Marys 135 33 44 S 150 49 E
St. Mary's 35 46 56N 53 34W
St. Marys 46 43 16N 81 8W
St. Mary's 70 43 20N 81 10W
Saint Marys 76 37 53N 89 57W
St. Mary's 77 40 33N 84 20W
St. Marys 70 41 30N 78 33W
St. Mary's Alpine Prov. Park 61 49 50N 116 25W
St. Marys Bay 39 44 25N 66 10W
St. Mary's, C. 37 46 50N 54 12W
St. Mary's I. 95 49 55N 6 17W
St. Mary's Pk. 135 31 30 S 138 33 E
St. Marys, R. 39 45 2N 61 53W
St. Mathews I. = Zadetkyi Kyun 128 10 0N 48 25 E
St-Mathias 45 45 28N 73 16W
St-Mathieu 45 45 19N 73 31W
St-Mathieu, Pte. de 100 48 20N 4 45W
St. Matthews 77 38 15N 85 39W
St-Maur-des-Fosses 101 48 48N 2 30 E
St-Maurice, Parc Prov. du 41 47 5N 73 15W
St-Maurice, R. 41 46 21N 72 31W
St-Médard-de-Guizières 102 45 1N 0 4W
St-Méen-le-Grand 100 48 11N 2 12W
St. Meinrad 77 38 10N 86 49W
St. Michael 67 63 30N 162 30W
St. Michaels 79 35 45N 109 5W
St. Michael's Mt. 95 50 7N 5 30W
St-Michel, Can. 44 45 34N 73 37W
St-Michel, France 103 45 15N 6 29 E
St-Michel-de-Bellechasse 42 46 52N 70 55W
St-Michel-de-Napierville 43 45 14N 73 34W
St-Michel-de-Wentworth 43 45 46N 74 29W
St-Michel-des-Saints 41 46 41N 73 55W
St-Mihiel 101 48 54N 5 30 E
St-Nazaire, Can. 41 45 44N 72 37W
St-Nazaire, France 100 47 17N 2 12W
St. Neots 95 52 14N 0 16W
St-Nicolas 42 46 42N 71 24W
St-Nicolas-de-Port 101 48 38N 6 18 E
St-Niklaas 105 51 10N 4 8 E
St-Noël 38 48 35N 67 50W
St. Norbert 58 49 46N 97 9W
St-Octave-de-l'Aveniro 38 49 0N 66 33W
St. Ola Sta. 70 44 50N 77 38W
St-Omer, Can. 41 47 3N 69 43W
St-Omer, France 101 50 45N 2 15 E
St. Ouen 101 48 50N 2 20 E
St-Ours 43 45 53N 73 9W
St-Pacome 41 47 24N 69 58W
St-Palais 102 45 40N 1 8W
St-Pamphile 41 46 58N 69 48W
St-Pardoux-la-Rivière 102 45 29N 0 45 E
St. Paris 77 40 8N 83 58W
St. Pascal 41 47 32N 69 48W
St-Patrice, L. 40 46 22N 77 20W
St. Paul 60 54 0N 111 17W
St-Paul 43 45 26N 72 53W
St. Paul, U.S.A. 77 39 33N 85 38W
St. Paul, Minn., U.S.A. 74 44 54N 93 5W
St. Paul, Nebr., U.S.A. 74 41 15N 98 30W
St-Paul-de-Fenouillet 102 42 50N 2 28 E
St-Paul-de-Montmigny 41 46 44N 70 22W
St-Paul-d'Industrie 43 45 59N 73 27W
St-Paul-du-Nord 41 48 34N 69 14W
St. Paul, I., Atl. Oc. 12 0 50N 31 40W
St. Paul, I., Can. 39 47 12N 60 9W
St. Paul, I., Ind. Oc. 16 30 40 S 77 34 E
St-Paul-l'Ermite 45 45 45N 73 28W
St-Paul, R. 36 51 27N 57 42W
St-Paulin 41 46 25N 73 1W
St. Pauls 37 49 52N 57 49W
St. Paul's B. 35 49 48N 57 58W
St-Péray 103 44 57N 4 50 E
St-Père-en-Retz 100 47 11N 2 2W
St. Peter 74 44 15N 93 57W
St. Peter Port 100 49 27N 2 31W
St. Peters, N.S., Can. 39 45 40N 60 53W
St. Peters, P.E.I., Can. 39 46 25N 62 35W
St. Petersburg 73 27 45N 82 40W
St-Philbert-de-Grand-Lieu 100 47 2N 1 39W
St-Philemon 41 46 41N 70 27W
St-Philippe-d'Argenteuil 43 45 37N 74 25W
St-Philippe-de-Laprairie 45 45 21N 73 28W
St-Pie 43 45 30N 72 54W
St. Pierre 57 49 26N 96 59W
St Pierre 37 46 40N 56 0W
St-Pierre-d'Oleron 102 45 57N 1 19W
St-Pierre-Église 100 49 40N 1 24W
St-Pierre-en-Port 100 49 48N 0 30 E
Saint-Pierre et Miquelon □ 37 46 55N 56 10W
St. Pierre, I. 16 9 20 S 46 0 E
Saint-Pierre, I. 37 46 47N 56 11W
St-Pierre, L., Qué., Can. 41 50 8N 68 26W
St-Pierre, L., Qué., Can. 41 46 12N 72 52W
St-Pierre-le-Moûtier 101 46 47N 3 7 E
St. Pierre-sur-Dives 100 49 2N 0 1W
St-Placide 44 45 31N 74 13W
St. Pol 101 50 21N 2 20 E
St-Pol-de-Léon 100 48 41N 4 0W
St-Pol-sur-Mer 101 51 1N 2 20 E
St-Polycarpe 43 45 18N 74 18W
St-Pons 102 43 30N 2 45 E
St-Pourçain-sur-Sioule 101 46 18N 3 18 E
St-Prime 41 48 35N 72 20W
St-Quay-Portrieux 100 48 39N 2 51W
St. Quentin 39 47 30N 67 23W
St-Quentin 101 49 50N 3 16 E
St-Raphaël, Can. 41 46 48N 70 45W
St-Raphaël, France 103 43 25N 6 46 E
St-Raymond 41 46 54N 71 50W
St-Rédemptueur 42 46 42N 71 17W
St. Regis, Mont., U.S.A. 78 47 20N 115 3W
St. Regis, N.Y., U.S.A. 71 44 39N 74 34W
St-Rémi 44 45 16N 73 37W
St-Rémy-de-Provence 103 43 48N 4 50 E
St-Renan 100 48 26N 4 37W
St-Robert 43 45 58N 73 0W
St-Roch 41 47 18N 70 12W
St-Roch-de-l'Achigan 43 45 51N 73 36W
St-Roch-de-Richelieu 43 45 53N 73 10W
St-Romauld-d'Etchemin 42 46 45N 71 14W
St-Romuald 41 46 46N 71 20W
St-Rose 44 45 37N 73 47W
St-Saëns 100 49 41N 1 16 E
St-Sauveur 39 47 32N 65 20W
St-Sauveur-des-Montes 43 45 54N 74 10W
St-Sauveur-en-Puisaye 101 47 37N 3 12 E
St-Sauveur-le-Vicomte 100 49 23N 1 32W
St-Savin 102 46 34N 0 50 E
St-Savinien 102 45 53N 0 42W
St-Sébastien 43 45 47N 70 58W
St. Sebastien, C. 117 12 26 S 48 44 E
St-Seine-l'Abbaye 101 47 26N 4 47 E
St-Sernin 102 43 54N 2 35 E
St.-Servan-sur-Mer 100 48 38N 2 0W
St-Sever-Calvados 100 48 50N 1 3W
St-Simeon 41 47 51N 69 54W
St-Siméon-de-Bonaventure 39 48 5N 65 36W
St-Simon-de-Bagot 43 45 44N 72 52W
St-Simon-de-Rimouski 41 48 12N 69 3W
St-Stanislas-de-Kostka 43 45 11N 74 8W
St. Stephen 39 45 16N 67 17W

St-Sulpice San Gabriel

St-Sulpice **43** 45 50N 73 21W
St-Sulpice-Laurière **102** 46 3N 1 29E
St-Sulpice-la-Pointe **102** 43 46N 1 41E
St-Télesphore **43** 45 17N 74 23W
St-Thégonnec **100** 48 31N 3 57W
St. Thomas **46** 42 45N 81 10W
St-Thomas-d'Aquin **45** 45 39N 72 59W
St. Thomas, I. **85** 18 21N 64 55W
St-Timothée **44** 45 18N 74 2W
St-Tite **41** 46 45N 72 40W
St-Tite-des-Caps **41** 47 8N 70 47W
St-Tropez **103** 43 17N 6 38E
St-Ulric **38** 48 47N 67 42W
St-Urbain **41** 47 33N 70 32W
St-Urbain-de-Châteauguay **43** 45 13N 73 44W
St-Vaast-la-Hougue **100** 49 35N 1 17W
St-Valérien **43** 45 34N 72 43W
St-Valéry **101** 50 10N 1 38E
St-Valéry-en-Caux **100** 49 52N 0 43E
St.-Vallier **103** 45 11N 4 50E
St-Vallier-de-Thiey **103** 43 42N 6 51E
St.-Varent **100** 46 53N 0 13W
St-Vianney **38** 48 37N 67 25W
St. Victor **56** 49 26N 105 52W
St. Vincent **12** 18 0N 26 1W
St. Vincent C. **117** 21 58S 43 20E
St-Vincent-de-Tyrosse **102** 43 39N 1 18W
St-Vincent-de-Paul **44** 45 37N 73 39W
St. Vincent, G. **135** 35 0S 138 0E
St. Vincent, I. **85** 13 10N 61 10W
St. Vincent Passage **85** 13 30N 61 0W
St. Vincent's **37** 46 48N 53 38W
St. Vital **58** 49 51N 97 7W
St-Vith **105** 50 17N 6 9E
St. Walburg **56** 53 39N 109 12W
St-Yrieux-la-Perche **102** 45 31N 1 12E
St-Yvon **38** 49 10N 64 48W
St-Zotique **43** 45 15N 74 15W
Ste-Adèle **43** 45 57N 74 7W
Ste-Adresse **100** 49 31N 0 5E
Ste. Agathe **57** 49 34N 97 11W
Ste-Agathe **41** 46 23N 71 25W
Ste-Agathe-des-Monts **41** 46 3N 74 17W
Ste-Agnès-de-Dundee **43** 45 1N 74 25W
Ste-Angèle-de-Mérici **38** 48 32N 68 5W
Ste-Angèle-de-Monnoir **43** 45 23N 73 6W
Ste. Anne **85** 14 26N 60 53W
Ste Anne de Beaupré **41** 47 2N 70 58W
Ste-Anne-de-Bellevue **44** 45 24N 73 57W
Ste-Anne-de-Madawaska **39** 47 15N 68 2W
Ste. Anne de Portneuf **35** 48 38N 69 8W
Ste-Anne-de-Prescott **43** 45 26N 74 29W
Ste-Anne-des-Monts **38** 49 8N 66 30W
Ste-Anne-des-Plaines **44** 45 47N 73 49W
Ste-Anne-du-Lac **40** 46 48N 75 25W
Ste-Anne, L. **38** 50 0N 67 42W
Ste. Anne, Lac **60** 53 42N 114 25W
Ste-Blandine **41** 48 22N 68 28W
Ste-Brigide-d'Iberville **45** 45 19N 73 4W
Ste. Cecile **35** 47 56N 64 34W
Ste-Cécile-de-Milton **43** 45 29N 72 44W
Ste-Claire **41** 46 36N 70 51W
Ste-Clothilde-de-Châteauguay **43** 45 10N 73 41W
Ste-Croix, Can. **41** 46 38N 71 44W
Ste-Croix, Switz. **101** 46 49N 6 34W
Ste-Dorothée **44** 45 32N 73 49W
Ste-Enimie **102** 44 22N 3 26E
Ste-Famille **41** 46 58N 70 58W
Ste-Félicité **38** 48 54N 67 20W
Ste-Florence **38** 48 16N 67 14W
Ste-Foy **42** 46 47N 71 17W
Ste-Foy-la-Grande **102** 44 50N 0 13E
Ste-Françoise **41** 48 6N 69 4W
Ste-Geneviève **44** 45 29N 73 52W
Ste. Genevieve **76** 37 59N 90 2W
Ste. Germaine **35** 46 24N 70 24W
Ste-Hélène-de-Bagot **43** 45 44N 72 44W
Ste-Hermine **102** 46 32N 1 4W
Ste-Julie **45** 45 35N 73 19W
Ste-Julienne **43** 45 58N 73 43W
Ste-Justine-de-Newton **43** 45 22N 74 25W
Ste-Livrade-sur-Lot **102** 44 24N 0 36E
Ste-Madeleine **45** 45 36N 73 6W
Ste-Marguerite, R. **36** 50 9N 66 36W
Ste. Marie **85** 14 48N 61 1W
Ste-Marie-aux-Mines **101** 48 10N 7 12E
Ste-Marie de la Madeleine **41** 46 26N 71 0W
Ste. Marie, I. **117** 16 50S 49 55E
Ste-Marie-Salomé **43** 45 56N 73 30W
Ste-Marthe **43** 45 24N 74 18W
Ste-Marthe-de-Gaspé **38** 49 12N 66 10W
Ste-Marthe-sur-le-Lac **44** 45 32N 73 57W
Ste-Martine **43** 45 15N 73 48W
Ste-Maure-de-Touraine **100** 47 7N 0 37E
Ste-Maxime **103** 43 19N 6 39E
Ste-Menehould **101** 49 5N 4 54E
Ste-Mère-Église **100** 49 24N 1 19W
Ste-Monique **41** 48 44N 71 51W
Ste-Monique-des-Deux-Montagnes **44** 45 40N 74 0W
Ste-Pudentienne **41** 45 28N 72 40W
Ste-Rosalie **43** 45 38N 72 54W
Ste-Rose **43** 45 37N 73 48W
Ste. Rose **85** 16 20N 61 45W
Ste.-Rose du lac **57** 51 4N 99 30W
Ste-Sabine **43** 45 15N 73 2W
Ste-Scholastique **44** 45 39N 74 5W
Ste. Teresa **88** 33 33S 60 54W
Ste-Thècle **41** 46 49N 72 31W
Ste-Thérèse **44** 45 38N 73 51W
Ste-Thérèse-de-Lisieux **42** 46 56N 71 12W
Ste-Thérèse, Île, Qué., Can. **45** 45 40N 73 29W
Ste-Thérèse, Île, Qué., Can. **45** 45 41N 73 28W
Ste-Thérèse-Ouest **44** 45 37N 73 50W
Ste-Victoire **43** 45 57N 73 5W
Saintes **102** 45 45N 0 37W
Saintes, I. des **85** 15 50N 61 35W
Saintes-Maries-de-la-Mer **103** 43 26N 4 26E
Saintonge **102** 45 40N 0 50W
Sairang **125** 23 50N 92 45E
Sairecábur, Cerro **88** 22 43S 67 54W
Sairs, L. **40** 46 49N 78 26W
Saitama-ken □ **132** 36 25N 137 0E
Sajama, Nevada **86** 18 0S 68 55W
Sākahka **122** 30 0N 40 8E
Sakai **132** 34 30N 135 30E
Sakai Shimane **132** 35 30N 133 25E
Sakaimachi **132** 35 30N 133 15E
Sakami, L. **36** 53 15N 76 45W
Sakania **117** 12 43S 28 30E
Sakata **132** 36 38N 138 19E
Sakhalin, Ostrov **121** 51 0N 143 0E
Sakishima-guntō **131** 24 30N 124 0E
Sakon Nakhon **128** 17 10N 104 9E
Sala **111** 59 58N 16 35E
Sala-y-Gomez, I. **15** 26 28S 105 28W
Salaberry-de-Valleyfield **44** 45 15N 74 8W
Salaberry, Île de **44** 45 17N 74 7W
Salada, La **82** 24 30N 111 30W
Saladas **88** 28 15S 58 40W
Saladillo **88** 35 40S 59 55W
Salado, R., Buenos Aires, Argent. **88** 35 40S 58 10W
Salado, R., Santa Fe, Argent. **88** 27 0S 63 40W
Salado, R., Mexico **82** 26 52N 99 19W
Salamanca, Chile **88** 32 0S 71 25W
Salamanca, Spain **104** 40 58N 5 39W
Salamanca, U.S.A. **70** 42 10N 78 42W
Salamina **86** 5 25N 75 29W
Salamis **109** 37 56N 23 30E
Salamonie, R. **77** 40 47N 85 40W
Salamonie, Resvr. **77** 40 45N 85 35W
Salar de Atacama **90** 23 30S 68 25W
Salar de Uyuni **86** 20 30S 67 45W
Salatu **130** 44 25N 107 58E
Salaverry **86** 8 15S 79 0W
Salayar, I. **127** 6 15S 120 30E
Salbris **101** 47 25N 2 3E
Saldaña **104** 42 32N 4 48W
Saldanha **117** 33 0S 17 58E
Sale, Austral. **136** 38 6S 147 6E
Sale, U.K. **94** 53 26N 2 19W
Salebabu **127** 3 45N 125 55E
Sālehābād **123** 35 40N 61 2E
Salekhard **120** 66 30N 66 25E
Salem, Can. **49** 43 42N 80 27W
Salem, India **124** 11 40N 78 11E
Salem, U.S.A. **76** 38 38N 88 57W
Salem, Ind., U.S.A. **77** 38 38N 86 0W
Salem, Mass., U.S.A. **71** 42 29N 70 53W
Salem, Mo., U.S.A. **75** 37 40N 91 30W
Salem, N.J., U.S.A. **72** 39 34N 75 29W
Salem, Ohio, U.S.A. **70** 40 52N 80 50W
Salem, Oreg., U.S.A. **78** 45 0N 123 0W
Salem, Va., U.S.A. **72** 37 19N 80 8W
Salembu, Kepulauan **126** 5 35S 114 30E
Salen **111** 64 41N 11 27E
Salernes **103** 43 34N 6 15E
Salerno **108** 40 40N 14 44E
Salford **94** 53 30N 2 17W
Salies-de-Béarn **102** 43 28N 0 56W
Salima **117** 13 47S 34 28E
Salina **74** 38 50N 97 40W
Salina Cruz **83** 16 10N 95 10W
Salina, I. **108** 38 35N 14 50E
Salina, La **86** 10 22N 71 27W
Salinas, Brazil **87** 16 20S 42 10W
Salinas, Chile **88** 23 31S 69 29W
Salinas, Ecuador **86** 2 10S 80 50W
Salinas, Mexico **82** 23 37N 106 8W
Salinas, U.S.A. **80** 36 40N 121 31W
Salinas Ambargasta **88** 29 0S 65 30W
Salinas, B. de **84** 11 4N 85 45W
Salinas (de Hidalgo) **82** 22 30N 101 40W
Salinas Grandes **88** 30 0S 65 0W
Salinas, Pampa de las **88** 31 58S 66 42W
Salinas, R., Mexico **83** 16 28N 90 31W
Salinas, R., U.S.A. **80** 36 45N 121 48W
Saline **46** 42 12N 83 49W
Saline, R. **74** 39 10N 99 5W
Salinópolis **87** 0 40S 47 20W
Salins-les-Bains **101** 46 58N 5 52E
Salisbury, Can. **39** 46 2N 65 3W
Salisbury, Rhod. **117** 17 50S 31 2E
Salisbury, U.K. **95** 51 4N 1 48W
Salisbury, U.S.A. **76** 39 25N 92 48W
Salisbury, Md., U.S.A. **72** 38 20N 75 38W
Salisbury, N.C., U.S.A. **73** 35 42N 80 29W
Salisbury I. **65** 63 30N 77 0W
Salisbury Plain **95** 51 13N 1 50W
Salle, La **76** 41 20N 89 6W
Salles-Curan **102** 44 11N 2 48E
Sallisaw **75** 35 26N 94 45W
Sally's Cove **37** 49 44N 57 56W
Salmo **63** 49 10N 117 20W
Salmon **78** 45 12N 113 56W
Salmon Arm **63** 50 40N 119 15W
Salmon Falls **78** 42 55N 114 59W
Salmon, R., B.C., Can. **54** 54 3N 122 40W
Salmon, R., N.B., Can. **39** 46 6N 65 56W
Salmon, R., Qué., Can. **38** 49 25N 62 15W
Salmon, R., U.S.A. **78** 46 0N 116 30W
Salmon Res. **37** 48 05N 56 00W
Salmon River **39** 44 3N 66 10W
Salmon River Mts. **78** 45 0N 114 30W
Salo **111** 60 22N 23 3E
Salome **81** 33 51N 113 37W
Salon-de-Provence **103** 43 39N 5 6E
Salonta **107** 46 49N 21 42E
Salop □ **95** 52 36N 2 45W
Salsacate **88** 31 20S 65 5W
Salses **102** 42 50N 2 55E
Salso, R. **108** 37 6N 13 55E
Salt Fork R. **75** 37 25N 98 40W
Salt Lake City **78** 40 45N 111 58W
Salt, R., Can. **54** 60 0N 112 25W
Salt, R., U.S.A. **76** 39 29N 91 5W
Salt, R., U.S.A. **77** 37 54N 85 51W
Salt, R., Ariz., U.S.A. **79** 33 50N 110 25W
Salta **88** 24 47S 65 25W
Salta □ **88** 24 48S 65 30W
Saltair **62** 48 57N 123 46W
Saltcoats, Can. **57** 51 5N 102 15W
Saltcoats, U.K. **96** 55 38N 4 47W
Saltee Is. **97** 52 7N 6 37W
Saltery Bay **62** 49 47N 124 10W
Saltfjorden **110** 67 15N 14 20E
Salthólmavik **110** 65 24N 21 57W
Saltillo **82** 25 30N 100 57W
Salto, Argent. **88** 34 20S 60 15W
Salto, Uruguay **88** 31 20S 57 59W
Salto □ **88** 31 20S 57 59W
Salto Augusto, falls **88** 8 30S 58 0W
Salton City **81** 33 21N 115 59W
Salton Sea **81** 33 20N 115 50W
Saltspring **54** 48 54N 123 37W
Salula, R. **73** 34 12N 81 45W
Salûm **115** 31 31N 25 7E
Salur **125** 18 27N 83 18E
Saluzzo **108** 44 39N 7 29E
Salvador, Brazil **87** 13 0S 38 30W
Salvador, Can. **56** 52 10N 109 25W
Salvador ■ **82** 13 50N 89 0W
Salvador, L. **75** 29 46N 90 16W
Salvail **45** 45 40N 73 4W
Salvail, R. **45** 45 49N 73 58W
Salvisa **77** 37 54N 84 51W
Salwa **123** 24 45N 50 55E
Salween, R. **125** 16 31N 97 37E
Salzburg **106** 47 48N 13 2E
Salzburg □ **106** 47 15N 13 0E
Salzgitter **106** 52 2N 10 22E
Sam Neua **128** 20 29N 104 0E
Sam Ngao **128** 17 18N 99 0E
Sam Rayburn Res. **75** 31 15N 94 20W
Sama **120** 60 12N 60 22E
Sama de Langreo **104** 43 18N 5 40W
Samales Group **127** 6 0N 122 0E
Samana Cay **85** 23 3N 73 45W
Samanco **86** 9 10S 78 30W
Samangan □ **123** 36 15N 67 40E
Samar, I. **127** 12 0N 125 0E
Samarkand **120** 39 40N 67 0E
Samarra **122** 34 16N 43 55E
Samatan **102** 43 29N 0 55E
Sambalpur **125** 21 28N 83 58E
Sambas, S. **126** 1 20N 109 20E
Sambava **117** 14 16S 50 10E
Sambhal **124** 28 35N 78 37E
Sambhar **124** 26 52N 75 10E
Sambiase **108** 38 58N 16 16E
Sambor **128** 12 46N 106 0E
Sambre, R. **105** 50 27N 4 52E
Sambro **39** 44 28N 63 36W
Samchŏk **130** 37 30N 129 10E
Same **116** 4 2S 37 38E
Samer **101** 50 38N 1 44E
Samo Alto **88** 30 22S 71 0W
Samoan Is. **10** 14 0S 171 0W
Samoëns **103** 46 5N 6 45E
Samoorombón, Bahía **88** 36 5S 57 20W
Sámos, I. **109** 37 45N 26 50E
Samosir, P. **126** 2 35N 98 50E
Samothráki, I. **109** 40 25N 25 40E
Sampacho **88** 33 20S 64 50W
Sampang **127** 7 11S 113 13E
Sampit **126** 2 20S 113 0E
Samra **122** 25 35N 41 0E
Samshui **131** 23 7N 112 58E
Samsun **122** 41 15N 36 15E
Samut Prakan **128** 13 32N 100 40E
Samut Sakhon **128** 13 31N 100 20E
Samut Songkhram (Mekong) **128** 13 24N 100 1E
San Agustín **86** 1 53N 76 16W
San Agustin, C. **127** 6 20N 126 13E
San Agustín de Valle Fértil **88** 30 35S 67 30W
San Ambrosio, I. **15** 26 35S 79 30W
San Andreas **80** 38 17N 120 39W
San Andrés, I. de **84** 12 42N 81 46W
San Andres Mts. **79** 33 0N 106 45W
San Andrés Tuxtla **83** 18 30N 95 20W
San Angelo **75** 31 30N 100 30W
San Anselmo **80** 37 49N 122 34W
San Antonio, Belize **83** 16 15N 89 2W
San Antonio, Chile **88** 33 40S 71 40W
San Antonio, N. Mex., U.S.A. **79** 33 58N 106 57W
San Antonio, Tex., U.S.A. **75** 29 30N 98 30W
San Antonio, Venez. **86** 3 30N 66 44W
San Antonio, C., Argent. **88** 36 15S 56 40W
San Antonio, C., Cuba **84** 21 50N 84 57W
San Antonio de Caparo **86** 7 35N 71 27W
San Antonio de los Baños **84** 22 54N 82 31W
San Antonio de los Cobres **88** 24 16S 66 2W
San Antonio do Zaire **116** 6 8S 12 11E
San Antonio, Mt. (Old Baldy Pk.) **81** 34 17N 117 38W
San Antonio Oeste **90** 40 40S 65 0W
San Antonio, R. **75** 28 30N 97 14W
San Ardo **80** 36 1N 120 54W
San Augustine **75** 31 30N 94 7W
San Benedetto **108** 45 2N 10 57E
San Benedicto, I. **82** 19 18N 110 49W
San Benito **75** 26 5N 97 32W
San Benito Mt. **80** 36 22N 120 37W
San Benito, R. **80** 36 53N 121 50W
San Bernardino **81** 34 7N 117 18W
San Bernardo **88** 33 40S 70 50W
San Bernardo, I. de **86** 9 45N 75 50W
San Blas **82** 26 10N 108 40W
San Blas, C. **73** 29 40N 85 25W
San Blas, Cord. de **84** 9 15N 78 30W
San Borja **86** 15 0S 67 12W
San Buenaventura **82** 27 5N 101 32W
San Buenaventura = Ventura **81** 34 17N 119 18W
San Carlos, Argent. **88** 33 50S 69 0W
San Carlos, Chile **130** 36 25S 72 0W
San Carlos, Mexico **82** 29 0N 101 10W
San Carlos, Nic. **84** 11 12N 84 50W
San Carlos, Phil. **127** 10 29N 123 25E
San Carlos, Uruguay **89** 34 46S 54 58W
San Carlos, U.S.A. **79** 33 24N 110 27W
San Carlos, Amazonas, Venez. **86** 1 55N 67 4W
San Carlos, Cojedes, Venez. **86** 9 40N 68 36W
San Carlos de Bariloche **90** 41 10S 71 25W
San Carlos del Zulia **86** 9 1N 71 55W
San Carlos L. **79** 33 20N 110 10W
San Clara **57** 51 29N 101 26W
San Clemente, Chile **88** 35 30S 71 39W
San Clemente, U.S.A. **81** 33 29N 117 45W
San Clemente I. **81** 32 53N 118 30W
San Cristóbal, Argent. **88** 30 20S 61 10W
San Cristóbal, Dom. Rep. **85** 18 25N 70 6W
San Cristóbal, Venez. **86** 7 46N 72 14W
San Cristóbal de las Casas **83** 16 50N 92 33W
San Diego, Calif., U.S.A. **81** 32 43N 117 10W
San Diego, Tex., U.S.A. **75** 27 47N 98 15W
San Diego, C. **90** 54 40S 65 10W
San Diego de la Unión **82** 21 28N 100 52W
San Estanislao **88** 24 39S 56 26W
San Felipe, Chile **88** 32 43S 70 50W
San Felipe, Mexico **82** 31 0N 114 52W
San Felipe, Venez. **86** 10 20N 68 44W
San Felipe, R. **81** 33 12N 115 49W
San Feliu de Guixols **104** 41 45N 3 1E
San Félix **86** 8 20N 62 35W
San Felix, I. **15** 26 30S 80 0W
San Fernando, Chile **88** 34 30S 71 0W
San Fernando, Mexico **82** 30 0N 115 10W
San Fernando, Luzon, Phil. **127** 16 40N 120 23E
San Fernando, Luzon, Phil. **127** 15 5N 120 37E
San Fernando, Spain **104** 36 22N 6 17W
San Fernando, Trin **85** 10 20N 61 30W
San Fernando, U.S.A. **81** 34 15N 118 29W
San Fernando de Apure **86** 7 54N 67 28W
San Fernando de Atabapo **86** 4 3N 67 42W
San Fernando, R. **82** 25 0N 99 0W
San Francisco, Córdoba, Argent. **88** 31 30S 62 5W
San Francisco, San Luis, Argent. **88** 32 45S 66 10W
San Francisco, U.S.A. **80** 37 47N 122 30W
San Francisco de Macorís **85** 19 19N 70 15W
San Francisco del Monte de Oro **88** 32 36S 66 8W
San Francisco del Oro **82** 26 52N 105 50W
San Francisco, Paso de **88** 35 40S 70 24W
San Francisco, R. **79** 33 30N 109 0W
San Francisco Solano, Pta. **86** 6 18N 77 29W
San Francisville **75** 30 48N 91 22W
San Gabriel **86** 0 36N 77 49W

San German — Santa Rosa

San German 67 18 5N 67 3W
San Gil 86 6 33N 73 8W
San Gorgonio Mt. 81 34 7N 116 51W
San Gottardo, Paso del 106 46 33N 8 33 E
San Gregorio, Uruguay 89 32 37 S 55 40W
San Gregorio, U.S.A. 80 37 20N 122 23W
San Ignacio, Boliv. 86 16 20 S 60 55W
San Ignacio, Mexico 82 27 27N 112 51W
San Ignacio, Parag. 88 26 52 S 57 3W
San Ignacio, Laguna 82 26 50N 113 11W
San Ildefonso, C. 127 16 0N 122 10 E
San Isidro 88 34 29 S 58 31W
San Jacinto, Colomb. 86 9 30N 75 8W
San Jacinto, U.S.A. 81 33 47N 116 57W
San Javier, Misiones, Argent. 89 27 55 S 55 5W
San Javier, Santa Fe, Argent. 88 30 40 S 59 55W
San Javier, Boliv. 86 16 18 S 62 30W
San Javier, Chile 88 35 40 S 71 45W
San Jerónimo, Sa. de 86 8 0N 75 50W
San Joaquin 80 36 36N 120 11W
San Joaquín 86 10 16N 67 47W
San Joaquin R. 80 37 4N 121 51W
San Joaquin Valley 80 37 0N 120 30W
San Jorge 88 31 54 S 61 50W
San Jorge, Bahía de 82 31 20N 113 20W
San Jorge, Golfo de 90 46 0 S 66 0W
San Jorge, G. de 104 40 50N 0 55W
San José, Boliv. 86 17 45 S 60 50W
San José, C. Rica 84 10 0N 84 2W
San José, Guat. 82 14 0N 90 50W
San José, Luzon, Phil. 127 15 45N 120 55 E
San José, Mindoro, Phil. 127 10 50N 122 5 E
San Jose, U.S.A. 76 40 18N 89 36W
San Jose, Calif., U.S.A. 80 37 20N 121 53W
San Jose, N. Mex., U.S.A. 75 35 26N 105 30W
San José Carpizo 83 19 26N 90 32W
San José de Feliciano 88 30 26 S 58 46W
San José de Jáchal 88 30 5 S 69 0W
San José de Mayo 88 34 27 S 56 27W
San José de Ocuné 86 4 15N 70 20W
San José del Cabo 82 23 0N 109 50W
San José del Guaviare 86 2 35N 72 38W
San José, I. 82 25 0N 110 50W
San Juan, Argent. 88 31 30 S 68 30W
San Juan, Antioquía, Colomb. 86 8 46N 76 32W
San Juan, Meta, Colomb. 86 3 26N 73 50W
San Juan, Dom. Rep. 67 18 49N 71 12W
San Juan, Coahuila, Mexico 82 29 34N 101 53W
San Juan, Jalisco, Mexico 82 21 20N 102 50W
San Juan, Querétaro, Mexico 82 20 25N 100 0W
San Juan, Phil. 127 8 35N 126 20 E
San Juan, Pto Rico 85 18 28N 66 37W
San Juan □ 88 31 9 S 69 0W
San Juan Bautista, Parag. 88 26 37 S 57 6W
San Juan Bautista, U.S.A. 80 36 51N 121 32W
San Juan, C. 67 18 23N 65 37W
San Juan Capistrano 81 33 29N 117 40W
San Juan de Guadalupe 82 24 38N 102 44W
San Juan de los Cayos 86 11 10N 68 25W
San Juan de los Morros 86 9 55N 67 21W
San Juan de Norte, B. de 84 11 30N 83 40W
San Juan del Norte 84 10 58N 83 40W
San Juan del Río 83 24 47N 104 27W
San Juan del Sur 84 11 20N 86 0W
San Juan I. 80 48 32N 123 5W
San Juan Mts. 79 38 30N 108 30W
San Juan, Presa de 82 17 45N 95 15W
San Juan, R., Argent. 88 32 20 S 67 25W
San Juan, R., Colomb. 86 4 0N 77 20W
San Juan, R., Nic. 84 11 0N 84 30W
San Juan, R., Calif., U.S.A. 80 36 14N 121 9W
San Juan, R., Utah, U.S.A. 79 37 20N 110 20W
San Julián 90 49 15 S 68 0W
San Justo 88 30 55 S 60 30W
San Lázaro, C. 82 24 50N 112 18W
San Lázaro, Sa. de 82 23 25N 110 0W
San Leandro 80 37 40N 122 6W
San Lorenzo, Argent. 88 32 45 S 60 45W
San Lorenzo, Ecuador 86 1 15N 78 50W
San Lorenzo, Parag. 88 25 20 S 57 32W
San Lorenzo, Venez. 86 9 47N 71 4W
San Lorenzo, I., Mexico 82 28 35N 112 50W
San Lorenzo, I., Peru 86 12 20 S 77 35W
San Lorenzo, Mt. 90 47 40 S 72 20W
San Lorenzo, R. 82 24 15N 107 24W
San Lucas, Boliv. 86 20 5 S 65 0W
San Lucas, Baja California S., Mexico 82 22 53N 109 54W
San Lucas, Baja California S., Mexico 82 27 10N 112 14W
San Lucas, U.S.A. 80 36 8N 121 1W
San Lucas, C. de 82 22 50N 110 0W
San Luis, Argent. 88 33 20 S 66 20W
San Luis, Cuba 84 22 17N 83 46W
San Luis, Guat. 82 16 14N 89 27W
San Luis, U.S.A. 79 37 14N 105 26W
San Luis, Venez. 86 11 7N 69 42W
San Luis □ 88 34 0 S 66 0W
San Luís de la Loma 82 17 18N 100 55W
San Luís de la Paz 82 21 19N 100 32W
San Luís de Potosí 82 22 9N 100 59W
San Luís de Potosí □ 82 22 10N 101 0W
San Luis, I. 82 29 58N 114 26W
San Luis Obispo 79 35 21N 120 38W
San Luis Res. 80 37 4N 121 5W
San Luis Río Colorado 82 32 29N 114 48W
San Luis, Sierra de 88 32 25 S 66 10W
San Marcos, Guat. 84 14 59N 91 52W
San Marcos, U.S.A. 75 29 53N 98 0W
San Marcos, I. 82 27 13N 112 6W
San Marino 108 43 56N 12 25 E
San Marino ■ 108 43 56N 12 25 E
San Martín, Argent. 88 33 5 S 68 28W
San Martín, Colomb. 86 3 42N 73 42W
San Martín, L. 90 48 50 S 72 50W
San Mateo 80 37 32N 122 19W
San Matías 86 16 25 S 58 20W
San Matías, Golfo de 90 41 30 S 64 0W
San Miguel, El Sal. 84 13 30N 88 12W
San Miguel, Panama 84 8 27N 78 55W
San Miguel, U.S.A. 80 35 45N 120 42W
San Miguel, Venez. 86 9 40N 65 11W
San Miguel de Tucumán 88 26 50 S 65 20W
San Miguel del Monte 88 35 23 S 58 50W
San Miguel I. 81 34 2N 120 23W
San Miguel, R., Boliv. 86 16 0 S 62 45W
San Miguel, R., Ecuador/Ecuador 86 0 25N 76 30W
San Narcisco 127 15 2N 120 3 E
San Nicolás de los Arroyas 88 33 17 S 60 10W
San Nicolas I. 68 33 16N 119 30W
San Onafre 81 33 22N 117 34W
San Onofre 86 9 44N 75 32W
San Pablo, Boliv. 88 21 43 S 66 38W
San Pablo, Colomb. 86 5 27N 70 56W
San Pedro, Buenos Aires, Argent. 89 33 43 S 59 45W
San Pedro, Jujuy, Argent. 88 24 12 S 64 55W
San Pedro, Chile 88 21 58 S 68 30W
San Pedro, Colomb. 86 4 56N 71 53W
San Pedro, Dom. Rep. 85 18 30N 69 18W
San Pedro, Mexico 82 23 55N 110 17W
San Pedro □ 88 24 0 S 57 0W
San Pedro Channel 81 33 35N 118 25W
San Pedro de Arimena 86 4 37N 71 42W
San Pedro de Atacama 88 22 55 S 68 15W
San Pedro de Jujuy 88 24 12 S 64 55W
San Pedro de las Colonias 82 25 50N 102 59W
San Pedro de Lloc 86 7 15 S 79 28W
San Pedro del Norte 84 13 4N 84 33W
San Pedro del Paraná 88 26 43 S 56 13W
San Pedro Mártir, Sierra 82 31 0N 115 30W
San Pedro Mixtepec 83 16 2N 97 0W
San Pedro Ocampo = Melchor Ocampo 82 24 52N 101 40W
San Pedro, Pta. 88 25 30 S 70 38W
San Pedro, R., Chihuahua, Mexico 82 28 20N 106 10W
San Pedro, R., Michoacan, Mexico 82 19 23N 103 51W
San Pedro, R., Nayarit, Mexico 82 21 45N 105 30W
San Pedro, R., U.S.A. 79 32 45N 110 35W
San Pedro Sula 84 15 30N 88 0W
San Pedro Tututepec 83 16 9N 97 38W
San Pedro,Pta. 88 25 30 S 70 38W
San Quintín, Mexico 82 30 29N 115 57W
San Quintín, Phil. 127 16 1N 120 56 E
San, R. 107 50 25N 22 20 E
San Rafael, Argent. 88 34 40 S 68 30W
San Rafael, Colomb. 86 6 2N 69 45W
San Rafael, Calif., U.S.A. 80 38 0N 122 32W
San Rafael, N. Mex., U.S.A. 79 35 6N 107 58W
San Rafael, Venez. 86 10 42N 71 46W
San Rafael Mt. 81 34 41N 119 52W
San Ramón de la Nueva Orán 88 23 10 S 64 20W
San Remo 108 43 48N 7 47 E
San Román, C. 86 12 12N 70 0W
San Roque 88 28 15 S 58 45W
San Rosendo 88 37 10 S 72 50W
San Saba 75 31 12N 98 45W
San Salvador 84 13 40N 89 20W
San Salvador de Jujuy 88 23 30 S 65 40W
San Salvador (Watlings) I. 85 24 0N 74 40W
San Sebastián, Argent. 90 53 10 S 68 30W
San Sebastián, Spain 104 43 17N 1 58W
San Sebastián, Venez. 86 9 57N 67 11W
San Severo 108 41 41N 15 23 E
San Simeon 80 35 39N 121 11W
San Simon 79 32 14N 109 16W
San Telmo 82 30 58N 116 6W
San Tiburcio 82 24 8N 101 32W
San Valentin, Mte. 90 46 30 S 73 30W
San Vicente de la Barquera 104 43 30N 4 29W
San Vicente del Caguán 86 2 7N 74 46W
San Vicenzo 123 43 9N 10 32 E
San Yanaro 86 2 47N 69 42W
San Ygnacio 75 27 6N 99 24W
San Ysidro 79 32 33N 117 5W
San'a 115 15 27N 44 12 E
Sana, R. 108 44 40N 16 43 E
Sanaga, R. 116 3 35N 9 38 E
Sanak I 67 53 30N 162 30W
Sanaloa, Presa 82 24 50N 107 20W
Sanana 127 2 5 S 125 50 E
Sanandaj 122 35 25N 47 7 E
Sanandita 88 21 40 S 63 35W
Sanary 103 43 7N 5 48 E
Sancergues 101 47 10N 2 54 E
Sancerre 101 47 20N 2 50 E
Sancha Ho 131 26 20N 105 30 E
Sánchez 85 19 15N 69 36W
Sanco, Pt. 127 8 15N 126 24 E
Sancoins 101 46 47N 2 55 E
Sancti-Spíritus 84 21 52N 79 33W
Sand Creek, R. 77 39 5N 85 52W
Sand I. 52 46 59N 91 0W
Sand L. 52 50 10N 94 35W
Sand Lake 34 47 46N 84 31W
Sand Pt. 46 43 54N 83 27W
Sand Point 67 55 20N 160 32W
Sand, R. 60 54 23N 111 2W
Sand Springs 75 36 12N 96 5W
Sandakan 126 5 53N 118 10 E
Sandan 128 12 46N 106 0 E
Sanday, I. 96 59 15N 2 30W
Sandbank L. 53 51 8N 82 41W
Sanders, U.S.A. 77 38 40N 84 56W
Sanders, Ariz., U.S.A. 79 35 12N 109 25W
Sanderson 75 30 5N 102 30W
Sandfell 110 63 57N 16 48W
Sandfly L. 55 55 43N 106 6W
Sandhill 49 43 50N 79 52W
Sandía 86 14 10 S 69 30W
Sandikli 122 38 30N 30 20 E
Sandnes 111 58 50N 5 45 E
Sandoa 116 9 48 S 23 0 E
Sandomierz 107 50 40N 21 43 E
Sandona 86 1 17N 77 28W
Sandoval 76 38 37N 89 7W
Sandover, R. 135 21 43 S 136 32 E
Sandoway 125 18 20N 94 30 E
Sandpoint 78 48 20N 116 40W
Sandringham 94 52 50N 0 30 E
Sandspit 62 53 14N 131 49W
Sandstone 134 27 59 S 119 16 E
Sandusky, Mich., U.S.A. 46 43 26N 82 50W
Sandusky, Ohio, U.S.A. 70 41 25N 82 40W
Sandusky, R. 77 41 27N 83 0W
Sandviken 111 60 38N 16 46 E
Sandwich 77 41 39N 88 37W
Sandwich B. 36 53 40N 57 15W
Sandwich Group 91 57 0 S 27 0W
Sandwip Chan. 125 22 35N 91 35 E
Sandy, Nev., U.S.A. 81 35 49N 115 36W
Sandy, Oreg., U.S.A. 80 45 24N 122 16W
Sandy Beach 49 43 4N 78 59W
Sandy C., Queens., Austral. 135 24 42 S 153 15 E
Sandy C., Tas., Austral. 135 41 25 S 144 45 E
Sandy Cay 85 23 13N 75 18W
Sandy Cove 37 51 21N 56 40W
Sandy Cr. 78 42 20N 109 30W
Sandy Hook 76 38 5N 83 8W
Sandy L., Alta., Can. 60 53 47N 114 2W
Sandy L., Newf., Can. 37 49 15N 57 0W
Sandy L., Ont., Can. 34 53 2N 93 0W
Sandy Lake 34 53 0N 93 15W
Sandy Narrows 55 55 5N 103 4W
Sandy Point 39 43 42N 65 19W
Sandy, R. 36 55 30N 68 21W
Sandybeach L. 52 49 49N 92 21W
Sanford, Fla., U.S.A. 73 28 45N 81 20W
Sanford, Me., U.S.A. 71 43 28N 70 47W
Sanford, N.C., U.S.A. 73 35 30N 79 10W
Sanford, R. 134 27 22 S 115 53 E
Sanga Tolon 121 61 50N 149 40 E
Sangamner 124 19 30N 74 15 E
Sangamon R. 76 40 2N 90 21W
Sangar 121 63 55N 127 31 E
Sangasanga 126 0 29 S 117 13 E
Sangchih 131 29 25N 109 30 E
Sangeang, I. 127 8 12 S 119 6 E
Sanger 80 36 47N 119 35W
Sanggau 126 0 5N 110 30 E
Sangihe, Kep. 127 3 0N 126 0 E
Sangihe, P. 127 3 45N 125 30 E
Sangkan Ho 130 40 24N 115 19 E
Sangkapura 126 5 52 S 112 40 E
Sangli 124 16 55N 74 33 E
Sangmélina 116 2 57N 12 1 E
Sangonera, R. 104 37 39N 2 0W
Sangre de Cristo Mts. 75 37 0N 105 0W
Sangsang 129 29 30N 86 0 E
Sangudo 60 53 50N 114 54W
Sanguinaires, Is. 103 41 51N 8 36 E
Sanish 74 48 0N 102 30W
Sankiang 131 25 39N 109 30 E
Sankt Moritz 106 46 30N 9 50 E
Sankuru, R. 116 4 17 S 20 25 E
Sanlúcar de Barrameda 104 37 26N 6 18W
Sanmaur 41 47 54N 73 47W
Sanmen Hu 131 34 40N 111 0 E
Sanmen Wan 131 29 10N 121 45 E
Sanmenhsia 131 34 46N 111 30 E
Sannicandro Gargánico 108 41 50N 15 34 E
Sanok 107 49 35N 22 10 E
Sanquhar 96 55 21N 3 56W
Santa Ana, Ecuador 86 1 10 S 80 20W
Santa Ana, El Sal. 84 14 0N 89 40W
Santa Ana, Mexico 82 30 31N 111 8W
Santa Ana, U.S.A. 81 33 48N 117 55W
Santa Ana, El Beni 86 13 50 S 65 40W
Santa Bárbara, Brazil 87 16 0 S 59 0W
Santa Bárbara, Colomb. 86 5 53N 75 35W
Santa Barbara 84 14 53N 88 14W
Santa Bárbara 82 26 48N 105 50W
Santa Barbara 81 34 25N 119 40W
Santa Bárbara 86 7 47N 71 10W
Santa Barbara Channel 81 34 20N 120 0W
Santa Barbara I. 81 33 29N 119 2W
Santa Barbara Is. 79 33 31N 119 0W
Santa Catalina 86 10 36N 75 17W
Santa Catalina, G. of 81 33 0N 118 0W
Santa Catalina, I., Mexico 82 25 40N 110 50W
Santa Catalina, I., U.S.A. 81 33 20N 118 30W
Santa Catarina □ 89 27 25 S 48 30W
Santa Catarina, I. de 89 27 30 S 48 40W
Santa Cecília 89 26 56 S 50 27W
Santa Clara, Cuba 84 22 20N 80 0W
Santa Clara, Calif., U.S.A. 80 37 21N 122 0W
Santa Clara, Utah, U.S.A. 79 37 10N 113 38W
Santa Clara de Olimar 89 32 50 S 54 54W
Santa Clotilde 86 2 25 S 73 45W
Santa Cruz, Argent. 90 50 0 S 68 50W
Santa Cruz, Boliv. 86 17 43 S 63 10W
Santa Cruz, Canary Is. 114 28 29N 16 26W
Santa Cruz, Chile 88 34 38 S 71 27W
Santa Cruz, C. Rica 84 10 15N 85 41W
Santa Cruz, Phil. 127 14 20N 121 30 E
Santa Cruz, Calif., U.S.A. 80 36 55N 122 1W
Santa Cruz, N. Mexico, U.S.A. 79 35 59N 106 1W
Santa Cruz □ 86 17 43 S 63 10W
Santa Cruz de Barahona 85 18 12N 71 6W
Santa Cruz del Norte 84 23 9N 81 55W
Santa Cruz del Sur 84 20 50N 78 0W
Santa Cruz do Rio Pardo 89 22 54 S 49 37W
Santa Cruz do Sul 89 29 42 S 52 25W
Santa Cruz I. 68 34 0N 119 45W
Santa Cruz, Is. 14 10 30 S 166 0 E
Santa Cruz, R. 90 50 10 S 70 0W
Santa Elena, Argent. 88 30 58 S 59 47W
Santa Elena, Ecuador 86 2 16 S 80 52W
Santa Elena C. 85 10 54N 85 56W
Santa Fe, Argent. 88 31 35 S 60 41W
Santa Fe, U.S.A. 79 35 40N 106 0W
Santa Fé □ 88 31 50 S 60 55W
Santa Filomena 87 9 0 S 45 50W
Santa Genoveva, Mt. 82 23 18N 109 52W
Santa Inés, I. 90 54 0 S 73 0W
Santa Isabel, Argent. 88 36 10 S 67 0W
Santa Isabel, Brazil 87 13 45 S 56 30W
Santa Lucía, Corrientes, Argent. 88 28 58 S 59 5W
Santa Lucía, San Juan, Argent. 88 31 30 S 68 45W
Santa Lucia 88 34 27 S 56 24W
Santa Lucia Range 80 36 0N 121 20W
Santa Magdalena, I. 82 24 50N 112 15W
Santa Margarita, Argent. 88 38 18 S 61 35W
Santa Margarita, U.S.A. 80 35 23N 120 37W
Santa Margarita, I. 82 24 30N 112 0W
Santa Margarita, R. 81 33 13N 117 23W
Santa María, Argent. 88 26 40 S 66 0W
Santa Maria, Brazil 89 29 40 S 53 40W
Santa María, Mexico 82 27 40N 114 40W
Santa Maria 81 34 58N 120 29W
Santa María, Bahía de 82 25 10N 108 40W
Santa Maria da Vitória 87 13 24 S 44 12W
Santa María del Oro 82 25 30N 105 20W
Santa Maria di Leuca, C. 109 39 48N 18 20 E
Santa María, R. 82 31 0N 107 14W
Santa Marta 86 11 15N 74 13W
Santa Marta Grande, C. 89 28 43 S 48 50W
Santa Marta, Sierra Nevada de 67 10 55N 73 50W
Santa Monica 81 34 0N 118 30W
Santa Napa 78 38 28N 122 45W
Santa Paula 81 34 20N 119 2W
Santa Rita, U.S.A. 79 32 50N 108 0W
Santa Rita, Guarico, Venez. 86 8 8N 66 16W
Santa Rita, Zulia, Venez. 86 10 32N 71 32W
Santa Rosa, La Pampa, Argent. 88 36 40 S 64 30W
Santa Rosa, San Luis, Argent. 88 32 30 S 65 10W
Santa Rosa, Boliv. 86 10 25 S 67 20W
Santa Rosa, Brazil 89 27 52 S 54 29W
Santa Rosa, Colomb. 86 3 32N 69 48W
Santa Rosa, Hond. 82 14 40N 89 0W

Santa Rosa **Sebastopol**

Santa Rosa, Calif., U.S.A. **80** 38 26N 122 43W
Santa Rosa, N. Mexico, U.S.A. **75** 34 58N 104 40W
Santa Rosa, Amazonas, Venez. **86** 1 29N 66 55W
Santa Rosa, Apure, Venez. **86** 6 37N 67 57W
Santa Rosa de Cabal **86** 4 52N 75 38W
Santa Rosa de Copán **84** 14 47N 88 46W
Santa Rosa de Osos **86** 6 39N 75 28W
Santa Rosa de Río Primero **88** 31 8S 63 20W
Santa Rosa de Viterbo **86** 5 53N 72 59W
Santa Rosa I., Calif., U.S.A. **81** 34 0N 120 6W
Santa Rosa I., Fla., U.S.A. **73** 30 23N 87 0W
Santa Rosa Mts. **78** 41 45N 117 30W
Santa Rosalía **82** 27 20N 112 30W
Santa Sylvina **88** 27 50S 61 10W
Santa Tecla = Nueva San Salvador **82** 13 40N 89 25W
Santa Teresa, Argent. **88** 33 25S 60 47W
Santa Teresa, Mexico **83** 25 17N 97 51W
Santa Teresa, Venez. **86** 4 43N 61 4W
Santa Vitória do Palmar **89** 33 32S 53 25W
Santa Ynez **81** 34 37N 120 5W
Santa Ynez, R. **81** 34 37N 120 41W
Santa Ysabel **81** 33 7N 116 40W
Santana, Coxilha de **89** 30 50S 55 35W
Santana do Livramento **89** 30 55S 55 30W
Santander, Colomb. **86** 3 1N 76 28W
Santander, Spain **104** 43 27N 3 51W
Santander Jiménez **83** 24 11N 98 29W
Santaquin **78** 40 0N 111 51W
Santarém, Brazil **87** 2 25S 54 42W
Santarém, Port. **104** 39 12N 8 42W
Santaren Channel **84** 24 0N 79 30W
Santiago, Brazil **89** 29 11S 54 52W
Santiago, Chile **88** 33 24S 70 50W
Santiago, Dom. Rep. **85** 19 30N 70 40W
Santiago, Panama **84** 8 0N 81 0W
Santiago □ **88** 33 30S 70 50W
Santiago de Compostela **104** 42 52N 8 37W
Santiago de Cuba **84** 20 0N 75 49W
Santiago del Estero **88** 27 50S 64 15W
Santiago del Estero □ **88** 27 50S 64 20W
Santiago Ixcuintla **82** 21 50N 105 11W
Santiago Papasquiaro **82** 25 0N 105 20W
Santiaguillo, L. de **82** 24 50N 104 50W
Santo Amaro **87** 12 30S 38 50W
Santo Anastácio **89** 21 58S 51 39W
Santo André **89** 23 39S 46 29W
Santo Ângelo **89** 28 15S 54 15W
Santo Antonio **87** 15 50S 56 0W
Santo Corazón **86** 18 0S 58 45W
Santo Domingo, Dom. Rep. **85** 18 30N 70 0W
Santo Domingo, Baja Calif. N., Mexico **82** 30 43N 115 56W
Santo Domingo, Baja Calif. S., Mexico **82** 25 32N 112 2W
Santo Domingo, Nic. **84** 12 14N 84 59W
Santo Tomas **82** 31 33N 116 24W
Santo Tomás **86** 14 34S 72 30W
Santo Tomé **89** 28 40S 56 5W
Santoña **104** 43 29N 3 20W
Santos **89** 24 0S 46 20W
Santos Dumont **89** 22 55S 43 10W
Santu **131** 25 59N 107 52E
Santuaho **131** 26 36N 119 42E
Sanvignes-les-Mines **101** 46 40N 4 18E
Sanyüan **131** 34 39N 108 59E
Sanza Pombo **116** 7 18S 15 56E
São Anastacio **89** 22 0S 51 40W
São Borja **89** 28 45S 56 0W
São Carlos **89** 22 0S 47 50W
São Cristóvão **87** 11 15S 37 15W
São Domingos, Brazil **87** 13 25S 46 10W
São Domingos, Guin.-Biss. **87** 12 22N 16 8W
Sao Francisco **87** 16 0S 44 50W
São Francisco do Sul **89** 26 15S 48 36W
São Francisco, R. **87** 10 30S 36 24W
São Gabriel **89** 30 10S 54 30W
São Gonçalo **89** 22 48S 43 5W
São João da Boa Vista **89** 22 0S 46 52W
São João del Rei **89** 21 8S 44 15W
São João do Araguaia **87** 5 23S 48 46W
São João do Piauí **87** 8 10S 42 15W
São José do Rio Prêto **89** 20 50S 49 20W
São José dos Campos **89** 23 7S 45 52W
São Leopoldo **89** 29 50S 51 10W
São Lourenço **89** 16 30S 55 5W
São Lourenço, R. **87** 16 40S 56 0W
São Luís Gonzaga **89** 28 25S 55 0W
São Luís (Maranhão) **87** 2 39S 44 15W
São Marcelino **86** 1 0N 67 12W
Sao Marcelino **86** 1 0N 67 12W
São Marcos, B. de **87** 2 0S 44 0W
São Marcos, R. **87** 18 15S 47 37W
São Mateus **87** 18 44S 39 50W
São Miguel **93** 37 33N 25 27W
São Paulo **89** 23 40S 46 50W
São Paulo □ **89** 22 0S 49 0W
São Romão **86** 5 53S 67 50W
São Roque, C. de **87** 5 30S 35 10W
São Sebastião do Paraíso **89** 20 54S 46 59W
São Sebastião, I. **89** 23 50S 45 18W
São Tomé, C. de **89** 22 0S 41 10W
São Tomé, I. **112** 0 10N 7 0E
São Vicente **89** 23 57S 46 23W
São Vicente, Cabo de **104** 37 0N 9 0W
Saona, I. **85** 18 10N 68 40W
Saône-et-Loire □ **101** 46 25N 4 50E
Saône, R. **101** 46 25N 4 50E
Saonek **127** 0 28S 130 47E
Saparua, I. **127** 3 33S 128 40E
Sapelo I. **73** 31 28N 81 15W
Sapodnyy Sayan **121** 52 30N 94 0E
Saposoa **86** 6 55S 76 30W
Sappho **80** 48 4N 124 16W
Sapporo **132** 43 0N 141 15E
Sapudi, I. **127** 7 2S 114 17E
Sapulpa **75** 36 0N 96 10W
Saqqez **122** 36 15N 46 20E
Sar-i-Pul **123** 36 10N 66 0E
Sar Planina **109** 42 10N 21 0E
Sarāb **122** 38 0N 47 30E
Sarada, R. **125** 28 15N 80 30E
Saragossa = Zaragoza **104** 41 39N 0 53W
Saraguro **86** 3 35S 79 16W
Sarajevo **109** 43 52N 18 26E
Saran, G. **126** 0 30S 111 25E
Saranac **77** 42 56N 85 13W
Saranac Lake **71** 44 20N 74 10W
Sarandí del Yi **89** 33 18S 55 38W
Sarandí Grande **88** 33 20S 55 50W
Sarangani B. **127** 6 0N 125 13E
Sarangani Is. **127** 5 25N 125 25E
Sarangarh **125** 21 30N 82 57E
Saransk **120** 54 10N 45 10E
Sarapul **120** 56 28N 53 48E
Sarasota **73** 27 10N 82 30W
Saratoga, Calif., U.S.A. **80** 37 16N 122 2W
Saratoga, Wyo., U.S.A. **78** 41 30N 106 56W
Saratoga Springs **71** 43 5N 73 47W
Saratok **126** 3 5S 110 50E
Saratov **120** 51 30N 46 2E
Saravane **128** 15 43N 106 25E
Sarawak □ **126** 2 0N 113 0E
Sarbāz **123** 26 38N 61 19E
Sarbisheh **123** 32 30N 59 40E
Sardarshahr **124** 28 30N 74 29E
Sardegna, I. **108** 39 57N 9 0E
Sardinata **86** 8 5N 72 48W
Sardinia **77** 39 0N 83 49W
Sardinia = Sardegna **108** 39 57N 9 0E
Sardis **63** 49 8N 121 58W
Sarektjåkkå **110** 67 27N 17 43E
Sargasso Sea **12** 27 0N 72 0W
Sargent **74** 41 42N 99 24W
Sargodha **124** 32 10N 72 40E
Sargodha □ **124** 31 50N 72 0E
Sarh **114** 9 5N 18 23E
Sārī **123** 36 30N 53 11E
Sarichef C. **67** 54 38N 164 59W
Sarikamiş **122** 40 22N 42 35E
Sarikei **126** 2 8N 111 30E
Sarina **135** 21 22S 149 13E
Sarita **75** 27 14N 97 49W
Sariwōn **130** 38 31N 125 44E
Sark, I. **100** 49 25N 2 20W
Sarlat-la-Canéda **102** 44 54N 1 13E
Sarles **57** 48 58N 99 0W
Sarmi **127** 1 49S 138 38E
Sarnia **46** 42 58N 82 23W
Sarny **120** 51 17N 26 40E
Sarolangun **126** 2 30S 102 30E
Saronikós Kólpos **109** 37 45N 23 45E
Saros Körfezi **109** 40 30N 26 15E
Sarpsborg **111** 59 16N 11 12E
Sarralbe **101** 48 55N 7 1E
Sarre, La **40** 48 45N 79 15W
Sarre, R. **101** 48 49N 7 0E
Sarre-Union **101** 48 55N 7 4E
Sarrebourg **101** 48 43N 7 3E
Sarreguemines **101** 49 1N 7 4E
Sartène **103** 41 38N 9 0E
Sarthe □ **100** 47 58N 0 10E
Sarthe, R. **100** 47 33N 0 31W
Sartilly **100** 48 45N 1 28W
Sartynya **120** 63 30N 62 50E
Sarūr **123** 23 17N 58 4E
Sarvestōn **123** 29 20N 53 10E
Sary-Tash **120** 39 44N 73 15E
Saryshagan **120** 46 12N 73 48E
Sarzeau **100** 47 31N 2 48W
Sasaginnigak L. **57** 51 36N 95 39W
Sasaram **125** 24 57N 84 5E
Sasebo **132** 33 10N 129 43E
Saseginaga, L. **40** 47 6N 78 35W
Saser Mt. **124** 34 50N 77 50E
Saskatchewan □ **55** 54 40N 106 0W
Saskatchewan Landing Prov. Park **56** 50 38N 107 59W
Saskatchewan, R. **57** 53 12N 99 16W
Saskatoon **56** 52 10N 106 38W
Sassandra **114** 5 0N 6 8W
Sássari **108** 40 44N 8 33E
Sassnitz **106** 54 29N 13 39E
Sata-Misaki **132** 30 59N 130 40E
Satanta **75** 37 30N 101 0W
Satara **94** 17 44N 73 58E
Satilla, R. **73** 31 15N 81 50W
Satmala Hills **124** 20 15N 74 40E
Satna **125** 24 35N 80 50E
Sátoraljaújhely **107** 48 25N 21 41E
Satpura Ra. **124** 21 40N 75 0E
Satu Mare **107** 47 46N 22 55E
Satui **126** 3 50S 115 20E
Satun **128** 6 43N 100 2E
Saturna **63** 48 47N 123 11W
Saturnina, R. **86** 12 15S 58 10W
Saubosq, L. **38** 51 30N 64 53W
Sauce **88** 30 5S 58 46W
Sauceda **82** 25 46N 101 19W
Saucillo **82** 28 1N 105 17W
Sauda **111** 59 38N 6 21E
Sauðarkrókur **110** 65 45N 19 40W
Saudi Arabia ■ **122** 26 0N 44 0E
Sauerland **105** 51 0N 8 0E
Saugatuck **77** 42 40N 86 12W
Saugeen, R. **46** 44 30N 81 22W
Saugerties **71** 42 4N 73 58W
Saugues **102** 44 58N 3 32E
Saujon **102** 45 41N 0 55W
Sauk Center **74** 45 42N 94 56W
Sauk City **76** 43 17N 89 43W
Sauk Rapids **74** 45 35N 94 10W
Saulieu **101** 47 17N 4 14E
Saulnierville **39** 44 16N 66 8W
Sault **103** 44 6N 5 24E
Sault-au-Moulton **41** 48 33N 69 15W
Sault aux Cochons, R. **41** 48 44N 69 4W
Sault Ste. Marie, Can. **46** 46 30N 84 20W
Sault Ste. Marie, U.S.A. **46** 46 27N 84 22W
Saumlaki **127** 7 55S 131 20E
Saumur **100** 47 15N 0 5W
Saumur, L. **38** 51 16N 62 49W
Saunders **54** 52 58N 115 40W
Saunders C. **133** 45 53S 170 45E
Saunders I. **91** 57 30S 27 30W
Saunemin **77** 40 54N 88 24W
Saurbær, Borgarfjarðarsýsla, Iceland **110** 64 24N 21 35W
Saurbær, Eyjafjarðarsýsla, Iceland **110** 65 27N 18 13W
Sausalito **80** 37 51N 122 29W
Sautatá **86** 7 50N 77 4W
Sauvage, L. **40** 50 6N 74 30W
Sauveterre, B. **102** 43 25N 0 57W
Sauzé-Vaussais **102** 46 8N 0 8E
Savá **84** 15 32N 86 15W
Sava, R. **109** 44 40N 19 50E
Savage **74** 47 43N 104 20W
Savanna **76** 42 5N 90 10W
Savanna la Mar **84** 18 10N 78 10W
Savannah, Ga., U.S.A. **73** 32 4N 81 4W
Savannah, Mo., U.S.A. **76** 39 55N 94 46W
Savannah, Tenn., U.S.A. **73** 35 12N 88 18W
Savannah, R. **73** 33 0N 81 30W
Savannakhet **128** 16 30N 104 49E
Savant L. **52** 50 30N 90 25W
Savant Lake **52** 50 14N 90 40W
Savanur **124** 14 59N 75 28E
Save R. **117** 21 16S 34 0E
Saveh **122** 35 2N 50 20E
Savenay **100** 47 20N 1 55W
Saverdun **102** 43 14N 1 34E
Saverne **101** 48 39N 7 20E
Savigny-sur-Braye **100** 47 53N 0 49E
Savoie □ **103** 45 26N 6 35E
Savona, Can. **63** 50 45N 120 50W
Savona, Italy **108** 44 19N 8 29E
Sawahlunto **126** 0 52S 100 52E
Sawai **127** 3 0S 129 5E
Sawai Madhopur **124** 26 0N 76 25E
Sawara **132** 35 55N 140 30E
Sawatch Mts. **79** 38 30N 106 30W
Sawel, Mt. **97** 54 48N 7 5W
Sawmills **117** 19 30S 28 2E
Sawu, I. **127** 10 35S 121 50E
Sawu Sea **127** 9 30S 121 50E
Sawyerville **41** 45 20N 71 34W
Saxon **52** 46 29N 90 25W
Saxton **70** 40 12N 79 18W
Sayabec **38** 48 33N 67 41W
Sayán **86** 11 0S 77 25W
Sayan, Vostochnyy **121** 54 0N 96 0E
Sayan, Zapadnyy **121** 52 30N 94 0E
Sayda **115** 33 35N 35 25E
Saylorville Res. **76** 41 43N 93 41W
Saynshand **130** 44 55N 110 11E
Sayre, Okla., U.S.A. **75** 35 20N 99 40W
Sayre, Pa., U.S.A. **71** 42 0N 76 30W
Sayula **82** 19 50N 103 40W
Sayville **71** 40 45N 73 7W
Sazan **109** 40 30N 19 20E
Sázava, R. **106** 49 50N 15 0E
Sazin **124** 35 35N 73 30E
Sca Fell **94** 54 27N 3 14W
Scaër **100** 48 2N 3 42W
Scammon Bay **67** 62 0N 165 49W
Scandia **61** 50 20N 112 0W
Scandinavia **93** 64 0N 12 0E
Scapa Flow **96** 58 52N 3 6W
Scappoose **80** 45 45N 122 53W
Scarborough, Can. **50** 43 45N 79 12W
Scarborough, Trin **85** 11 11N 60 42W
Scarborough, U.K. **94** 54 17N 0 24W
Scarpe, R. **101** 50 31N 3 27E
Scatarie I. **39** 46 0N 59 44W
Scenic **74** 43 49N 102 32W
Sceptre **56** 50 51N 109 15W
Schaffhausen **106** 47 42N 8 39E
Schefferville **36** 54 48N 66 50W
Schelde, R. **105** 51 10N 4 20E
Schell City **76** 38 1N 94 7W
Schenectady **71** 42 50N 73 58W
Scheveningen **105** 52 6N 4 16E
Schiedam **105** 51 55N 4 25E
Schiermonnikoog, I. **105** 53 30N 6 15E
Schiltigheim **101** 48 35N 7 45E
Schio **108** 45 42N 11 21E
Schirmeck **101** 48 29N 7 12E
Schleswig **106** 54 32N 9 34E
Schleswig-Holstein □ **106** 54 10N 9 40E
Schneider **77** 41 13N 87 28W
Schofield **74** 44 54N 89 39W
Scholls **80** 45 24N 122 56W
Schoolcraft **77** 42 7N 85 38W
Schouten, Kepulauan **127** 1 0S 136 0E
Schouwen, I. **105** 51 43N 3 45E
Schraumberg **77** 42 0N 88 15W
Schreiber **53** 48 45N 87 20W
Schuler **61** 50 20N 110 6W
Schumacher **53** 48 30N 81 16W
Schurz **78** 38 57N 118 48W
Schuyler **74** 41 30N 97 3W
Schuylkill Haven **71** 40 37N 76 11W
Schwäbischer Alb **106** 48 30N 9 30E
Schwangcheng **130** 45 27N 126 27E
Schwangyashan **129** 46 35N 131 15E
Schwarzwald **106** 48 0N 8 0E
Schweinfurt **106** 50 3N 10 12E
Schwerin **106** 53 37N 11 22E
Schwyz **106** 47 2N 8 39E
Sciacca **108** 37 30N 13 3E
Scie, La **37** 49 57N 55 36W
Scilla **108** 38 18N 15 44E
Scilly, Isles of **95** 49 55N 6 15W
Scioto, R. **72** 39 0N 83 0W
Scobey **74** 48 47N 105 30W
Scone, Austral. **136** 32 0S 150 52E
Scone, U.K. **96** 56 25N 3 26W
Scoresby Sund **17** 70 20N 23 0W
Scotia, Calif., U.S.A. **78** 40 36N 124 4W
Scotia, N.Y., U.S.A. **71** 42 50N 73 58W
Scotia Sea **91** 56 5S 56 0W
Scotland, Can. **49** 43 1N 80 22W
Scotland, U.S.A. **74** 43 10N 97 45W
Scotland □ **96** 57 0N 4 0W
Scotland Neck **73** 36 6N 77 24W
Scotstown **41** 45 32N 71 17W
Scott, Antarct. **91** 77 0S 165 0E
Scott, Can. **56** 52 22N 108 50W
Scott, C. **91** 71 30S 168 0E
Scott Chan. **62** 50 45N 128 30W
Scott City **74** 38 30N 100 52W
Scott, I. **91** 67 0S 179 0E
Scott Inlet **65** 71 0N 71 0W
Scott Is. **62** 50 48N 128 40W
Scott-Jonction **41** 46 30N 71 4W
Scott L. **55** 59 55N 106 18W
Scott Reef **134** 14 0S 121 50E
Scottdale **70** 40 8N 79 35W
Scottsbluff **74** 41 55N 103 35W
Scottsboro **73** 34 40N 86 0W
Scottsburg **77** 38 40N 85 46W
Scottsdale **135** 41 9S 147 31E
Scottsville, Ky., U.S.A. **73** 36 48N 86 10W
Scottsville, N.Y., U.S.A. **70** 43 2N 77 47W
Scottville **72** 43 57N 86 18W
Scranton, Iowa, U.S.A. **76** 42 1N 94 33W
Scranton, Pa., U.S.A. **71** 41 22N 75 41W
Screggan **100** 53 15N 7 32W
Scugog, L. **47** 44 10N 78 55W
Scunthorpe **94** 53 35N 0 38W
Scutari (Üsküdar) **109** 41 0N 29 5E
Sea Breeze **70** 43 12N 77 32W
Sea I. **66** 49 12N 123 10W
Seaford, Austral. **136** 38 10S 145 11E
Seaford, U.S.A. **72** 38 37N 75 36W
Seaforth **46** 43 35N 81 25W
Seager Wheeler L. **56** 51 17N 103 31W
Seagraves **75** 32 56N 102 30W
Seahorse L. **38** 52 12N 65 48W
Seal Cove, N.B., Can. **39** 44 39N 66 51W
Seal Cove, Newf., Can. **37** 47 29N 56 4W
Seal Cove, Newf., Can. **37** 49 57N 56 22W
Seal L. **36** 54 20N 61 30W
Seal, R. **55** 58 50N 97 30W
Sealy **75** 29 46N 96 9W
Seaman **77** 38 57N 83 34W
Searchlight **81** 35 31N 114 55W
Searchmont **53** 46 47N 84 3W
Searcy **75** 35 15N 91 45W
Searle **58** 49 51N 97 15W
Searles, L. **81** 35 47N 117 17W
Seaside, Calif., U.S.A. **80** 36 37N 121 50W
Seaside, Oreg., U.S.A. **80** 46 0N 123 55W
Seattle **80** 47 41N 122 15W
Seaview Ra. **135** 18 40S 145 45E
Seba Beach **60** 53 35N 114 47W
Sebastián Vizcaíno, Bahía **82** 28 0N 114 30W
Sebastopol **80** 38 24N 122 49W
Sebastopol = Sevastopol **120** 44 35N 33 30E

Sebewaing Sheldon

Sebewaing	46	43 45N	83 27W
Sebinkarahisar	122	40 22N	38 28 E
Sebring, Fla., U.S.A.	73	27 36N	81 20W
Sebring, Ohio, U.S.A.	70	40 55N	81 2W
Sebringville	46	43 24N	81 4W
Sebuku, I.	126	3 30 S	116 25 E
Sebuku, Teluk	126	4 0N	118 10 E
Sechelt	62	49 25N	123 42W
Sechura, Desierto de	86	6 0 S	80 30W
Seclin	101	50 33N	3 2 E
Second Narrows	66	49 18N	123 2W
Secondigny	100	46 37N	0 26W
Secretary I.	133	45 15 S	166 56 E
Secunderabad	124	17 28N	78 30 E
Sedalia	76	38 40N	93 18W
Sedan, France	101	49 43N	4 57 E
Sedan, U.S.A.	75	37 10N	96 11W
Seddon	133	41 40 S	174 7 E
Seddonville	133	41 33 S	172 1 E
Sedgewick	61	52 48N	111 41W
Sedley	56	50 10N	104 0W
Sedova, Pik	120	73 20N	55 10 E
Sedro Woolley	80	48 30N	122 15W
Seeheim	117	26 32 S	17 52 E
Seeley's Bay	47	44 29N	76 14W
Sées	100	48 38N	0 10 E
Seg-ozero	120	63 0N	33 10 E
Segamat	128	2 30N	102 50 E
Seget	127	1 24 S	130 58 E
Segonzac	102	45 36N	0 14W
Ségou	114	13 30N	6 10W
Segovia	104	40 57N	4 10W
Segré	100	47 40N	0 52W
Segre, R.	104	41 40N	0 43 E
Seguam	67	52 0N	172 30W
Seguam Pass.	67	53 0N	175 30W
Séguéla	114	7 55N	6 40W
Segula I.	67	52 0N	178 5W
Segundo	75	37 12N	104 50W
Segundo, R.	88	30 53 S	62 44W
Segura, R.	104	38 9N	0 40W
Sehithwa	117	20 30 S	22 30 E
Sehore	124	23 10N	77 5 E
Seilandsjøkelen	110	70 25N	23 16 E
Seiling	75	36 10N	99 5W
Seille, R.	103	46 31N	4 57 E
Sein, I. de	100	48 2N	4 52W
Sein, R.	58	49 54N	97 7W
Seinäjoki	110	62 48N	22 43 E
Seine-Maritime □	100	49 40N	1 0 E
Seine □	101	49 0N	3 0 E
Seine-et-Marne □	101	48 45N	3 0 E
Seine, R.	100	49 28N	0 15 E
Seine-Saint-Denis □	101	48 58N	2 24 E
Seistan	123	30 50N	61 0 E
Sejal	86	2 45N	68 0W
Sekaju	126	2 58 S	103 58 E
Sekibi-shō	131	25 45N	124 35 E
Sekiu	78	48 30N	124 29W
Sekondi-Takoradi	114	5 0N	1 48W
Selah	78	46 44N	120 30W
Selama	128	5 12N	100 42 E
Selangor □	128	3 20N	101 30 E
Selaru, I.	127	8 18 S	131 0 E
Selawik	67	66 55N	160 10W
Selby, U.K.	94	53 47N	1 5W
Selby, U.S.A.	74	45 34N	99 55W
Selby Lake	43	45 6N	72 48W
Selden	74	39 24N	100 39W
Seldovia	67	59 30N	151 45W
Sele, R.	108	40 27N	15 0 E
Selenga, R. = Selenge Mörön	130	49 25N	103 45 E
Selenge	129	49 25N	103 59 E
Selenge Mörön	130	52 16N	106 16 E
Selenge Mörön, R.	129	52 16N	106 16 E
Sélestat	101	48 10N	7 26 E
Seletan, Tg.	126	4 10 S	114 40 E
Selfridge	74	46 3N	100 57W
Sélibaby	114	15 20N	12 15W
Seligman	79	35 17N	112 56W
Selkirk, Man., Can.	57	50 10N	96 55W
Selkirk, Ont., Can.	46	42 49N	79 56W
Selkirk, U.K.	96	55 33N	2 50W
Selkirk I.	57	53 20N	99 6W
Selkirk Mts.	54	51 15N	117 40W
Selles-sur-Cher	101	47 16N	1 33 E
Sellières	101	46 50N	5 32 E
Sells	79	31 57N	111 57W
Selma, Ala., U.S.A.	73	32 30N	87 0W
Selma, Calif., U.S.A.	80	36 39N	119 39W
Selma, N.C., U.S.A.	73	35 32N	78 15W
Selmer	73	35 9N	88 36W
Selongey	101	47 36N	5 10 E
Selpele	127	0 1 S	130 5 E
Selsey Bill	95	50 44N	0 47W
Seltz	101	48 48N	8 4 E
Selu, I.	127	7 26 S	130 55 E
Selukwe	117	19 40 S	30 0 E
Sélune, R.	100	48 38N	1 22W
Selva	88	29 50 S	62 0W
Selva Beach, La	80	36 56N	121 51W
Selvas	86	6 30 S	67 0W
Selwyn	135	21 30 S	140 29 E
Selwyn L.	55	60 0N	104 30W
Selwyn Mts.	67	63 0N	130 0W
Selwyn Ra.	135	21 10 S	140 0 E
Semani, R.	109	40 45N	19 50 E
Semans	56	51 25N	104 44W
Semarang	127	7 0 S	110 26 E
Semeru, Mt.	127	8 4 S	113 3 E
Semiahmoo B.	66	49 1N	122 50W
Seminoe Res.	78	42 0N	107 0W
Seminole, Okla., U.S.A.	75	35 15N	96 45W
Seminole, Tex., U.S.A.	75	32 41N	102 38W
Semiozernoye	120	52 22N	64 8 E
Semipalatinsk	120	50 30N	80 10 E
Semirara Is.	127	12 0N	121 20 E
Semisopochnoi I.	67	52 0N	179 40W
Semitau	126	0 29N	111 57 E
Semiyarskoye	120	50 55N	78 30 E
Semmering Pass.	106	47 41N	15 45 E
Semnān	123	35 55N	53 25 E
Semnan □	123	36 0N	54 0 E
Semois, R.	105	49 53N	4 44 E
Semporna	127	4 30N	118 33 E
Semuda	126	2 51 S	112 58 E
Semur-en-Auxois	101	47 30N	4 20 E
Sen, R.	128	13 45N	105 12 E
Sena Madureira	86	9 5 S	68 45W
Senai	128	1 38N	103 38 E
Senaja	126	6 49 S	117 2 E
Senanga	117	16 2 S	23 14 E
Senatobia	75	34 38N	89 57W
Sendai, Kagoshima, Japan	132	31 50N	130 20 E
Sendai, Miyagi, Japan	132	38 15N	141 0 E
Seneca, Oreg., U.S.A.	78	44 10N	119 2W
Seneca, S.C., U.S.A.	73	34 43N	82 59W
Seneca Falls	70	42 55N	76 50W
Seneca L.	70	42 40N	76 58W
Sénécal, L.	38	52 5N	63 20W
Senegal ■	114	14 30N	14 30W
Senegal, R.	114	16 30N	15 30W
Seney	53	46 25N	86 0W
Senge Khambab (Indus), R.	125	28 40N	70 10 E
Senhor-do-Bonfim	87	10 30 S	40 10W
Senigállia	108	43 42N	13 12 E
Senj	108	45 0N	14 58 E
Senja	110	69 25N	17 20 E
Senkaku-guntō	131	25 50N	123 30 E
Senlis	101	49 13N	2 35 E
Senmonorom	128	12 27N	107 12 E
Sennâr	115	13 30N	33 35 E
Senneterre	40	48 25N	77 15W
Senneville	44	45 27N	73 57W
Senonches	100	48 34N	1 2 E
Sens	101	48 11N	3 15 E
Senta	109	45 55N	20 3 E
Sentein	102	42 53N	0 58 E
Sentinel	79	32 56N	113 13W
Sentolo	127	7 55 S	110 13 E
Seo de Urgel	104	42 22N	1 23 E
Seoul = Sŏul	130	37 31N	127 6 E
Separation Point	36	53 37N	57 25W
Sepone	128	16 45N	106 13 E
Sept-Îles	36	50 13N	66 22W
Sequart L.	38	52 26N	63 47W
Sequim	80	48 3N	123 9W
Sequoia Nat. Park	80	36 30N	118 30W
Seraing	105	50 35N	5 32 E
Seram, I.	127	3 10 S	129 0 E
Seram Sea	127	2 30 S	128 30 E
Serampore	125	22 44N	88 30 E
Serang	127	6 8 S	106 10 E
Serasan, I.	126	2 29N	109 4 E
Serbia = Srbija	109	43 30N	21 0 E
Seremban	128	2 43N	101 53 E
Serena, La	88	29 55 S	71 10W
Serenje	117	13 14 S	30 15 E
Sergipe □	87	10 30 S	37 30W
Seria	126	4 37N	114 30 E
Serian	126	1 10N	110 40 E
Sérifontaine	101	49 20N	1 45 E
Sérignan	102	43 17N	3 17 E
Sérigny, R.	36	56 47N	66 0W
Serik	122	36 55N	31 10 E
Sermaize-les-Bains	101	48 47N	4 54 E
Sermata, I.	127	8 15 S	128 50 E
Sernovdsk	120	61 20N	73 28 E
Serov	120	59 36N	60 35 E
Serowe	117	22 25 S	26 43 E
Serpentine, R.	66	49 5N	122 51W
Serpent's Mouth	86	10 0N	61 30W
Serpukhov	120	54 55N	37 28 E
Serrai	109	41 0N	23 30 E
Serres	103	44 26N	5 43 E
Serrezuela	88	30 40 S	65 20W
Sertânia	87	8 5 S	37 20W
Sertanópolis	89	23 4 S	51 2W
Sertâo	87	10 0 S	40 20W
Serua, P.	127	6 18 S	130 1 E
Serui	127	1 45 S	136 10 E
Serule	117	21 57 S	27 11 E
Serviceton	136	36 25 S	141 55 E
Sesajap Lama	126	3 32N	117 11 E
Sesepe	127	1 30 S	127 59 E
Sesfontein	117	19 7 S	13 39 E
Sesheke	117	17 29 S	24 13 E
Sesser	76	38 7N	89 3W
Sessy	130	42 40N	110 30 E
Sestao	104	43 18N	3 0W
Sète	102	43 25N	3 42 E
Sete Lagoas	87	19 27 S	44 16W
Seto Naikai	132	34 20N	133 30 E
Seton L.	63	50 42N	122 8W
Seton Portage	63	50 42N	122 17W
Setté Cama	116	2 32 S	9 57 E
Setting L.	55	55 0N	98 38W
Settle	94	54 5N	2 18W
Settlement Pt.	73	26 40N	79 0W
Setúbal	104	38 30N	8 58W
Setúbal, B. de	104	38 40N	8 56W
Seul L.	34	50 25N	92 30W
Seul Réservoir, Lac	52	50 25N	92 30W
Seulimeum	126	5 27N	95 15 E
Sevastopol	120	44 35N	33 30 E
Seven Islands B.	36	59 25N	63 45W
Seven Sisters Falls	57	50 7N	96 2W
Seven Sisters, mt	54	54 56N	128 10W
Seventy Mile House	63	51 18N	121 23W
Sévérac-le-Château	102	44 20N	3 5 E
Severn L.	34	53 54N	90 48W
Severn, R., Can.	34	56 2N	87 36W
Severn, R., U.K.	95	51 35N	2 38W
Severnaya Zemlya	121	79 0N	100 0 E
Severo-Kurilsk	121	50 40N	156 8 E
Severodvinsk	120	64 27N	39 58 E
Sevier	79	38 39N	112 11W
Sevier L.	78	39 0N	113 20W
Sevier, R.	79	39 10N	112 50W
Sevilla, Colomb.	86	4 16N	75 57W
Sevilla, Spain	104	37 23N	6 0W
Seville = Sevilla	104	37 23N	6 0W
Seward	67	60 0N	149 40W
Seward Pen.	67	65 0N	164 0W
Sewell, Can.	62	53 47N	132 16W
Sewell, Chile	88	34 10 S	70 45W
Sewer	127	5 46 S	134 40 E
Sewickley	70	40 33N	80 12W
Sexsmith	60	55 21N	118 47W
Seychelles, Is.	16	5 0 S	56 0 E
Seyðisfjörður	110	65 16N	14 0W
Seymchan	121	62 40N	152 30 E
Seymour, Austral.	136	37 0 S	145 10 E
Seymour, U.S.A.	76	40 45N	93 7W
Seymour, Conn., U.S.A.	71	41 23N	73 5W
Seymour, Ind., U.S.A.	77	39 0N	85 50W
Seymour, Tex., U.S.A.	75	33 35N	99 18W
Seymour, Wis., U.S.A.	72	44 30N	88 20W
Seymour Arm	63	51 15N	118 57W
Seymour Heights	66	49 19N	123 0W
Seymour Inlet	62	51 3N	127 0W
Seymour L.	66	49 27N	122 57W
Seymour, Mt.	66	49 24N	122 57W
Seymour, R.	66	49 18N	123 1W
Seyne	103	44 21N	6 22 E
Seyne-sur-Mer, La	103	43 7N	5 52 E
Sézanne	101	48 40N	3 40 E
Sfax	114	34 49N	10 48 E
Sfintu Gheorghe	107	45 52N	25 48 E
Shaba	116	8 0 S	25 0 E
Shabani	117	20 17 S	30 2 E
Shabogamo L., Can.	35	48 40N	77 0W
Shabogamo L., Newf., Can.	36	53 15N	66 30W
Shabunda	116	2 40 S	27 16 E
Shabuskwia L.	52	51 15N	89 0W
Shackleton	91	78 30 S	36 1W
Shackleton Inlet	91	83 0 S	160 0 E
Shadrinsk	120	56 5N	63 58 E
Shafer, L.	77	40 46N	86 46W
Shafter	81	35 32N	119 14W
Shaftesbury	95	51 0N	2 12W
Shāhābād	123	37 40N	56 50 E
Shāhbād	122	34 10N	46 30 E
Shahcheng	130	40 18N	115 27 E
Shahdād	123	30 30N	57 40 E
Shahdadkot	124	27 50N	67 55 E
Shahgarh	124	27 15N	69 50 E
Shāhī	123	36 30N	52 55 E
Shaho	131	28 29N	113 2 E
Shahpūr	122	38 12N	44 45 E
Shahr Kord	123	32 15N	50 55 E
Shahraban	122	34 0N	45 0 E
Shahrezā	123	32 0N	51 55 E
Shahrig	124	30 15N	67 40 E
Shahriza	123	32 0N	51 50 E
Shāhrūd	123	36 30N	55 0 E
Shahrukh	123	33 50N	60 10 E
Shahsavār	123	36 45N	51 12 E
Shahsien	131	26 25N	117 50 E
Shajapur	124	23 20N	76 15 E
Shakespeare I.	52	49 38N	88 25W
Shakhty	120	47 40N	40 10 E
Shakhunya	120	57 40N	47 0 E
Shaki	114	8 41N	3 21 E
Shakopee	74	44 45N	93 30W
Shaktolik	67	64 30N	161 15W
Shalalth	63	50 43N	122 13W
Shallow Lake	46	44 36N	81 5W
Shalu	131	24 24N	120 26 E
Sham, J. ash	123	23 10N	57 5 E
Shamattawa	55	55 51N	92 5W
Shamattawa, R.	34	55 1N	85 23W
Shamil	123	27 30N	56 55 E
Shammar, Jabal	122	27 40N	41 0 E
Shamo (Gobi)	129	44 0N	111 0 E
Shamokin	71	40 47N	76 33W
Shamrock, Can.	56	50 10N	106 37W
Shamrock, U.S.A.	75	35 15N	100 15W
Shamva	117	17 20 S	31 32 E
Shan □	125	21 30N	98 30 E
Shanchengtze	130	42 29N	125 30 E
Shandon	80	35 39N	120 23W
Shangani, R.	117	18 35 S	27 45 E
Shangch'eng	131	31 44N	115 22 E
Shangchih, (Chuho)	130	45 10N	127 59 E
Shangchwan Shan	131	21 35N	112 45 E
Shanghai	131	31 10N	121 25 E
Shanghsien	131	33 30N	109 58 E
Shangjao	131	28 25N	117 57 E
Shangkao	131	28 16N	114 50 E
Shangkiu	131	34 28N	115 42 E
Shangpancheng	130	40 52N	118 4 E
Shangshui	131	33 42N	114 34 E
Shangsze	131	22 0N	107 45 E
Shangtu	130	41 31N	113 35 E
Shangyu	131	25 59N	114 29 E
Shanh	129	47 5N	103 5 E
Shaniko	78	45 0N	120 50W
Shannon, Greenl.	17	75 10N	18 30W
Shannon, N.Z.	133	40 33 S	175 25 E
Shannon I.	17	75 0N	18 0W
Shannon L., Can.	53	49 48N	83 24W
Shannon L., U.S.A.	63	48 37N	121 42W
Shannon, R.	97	53 10N	8 10W
Shansi □	130	37 30N	112 15 E
Shantar, Ostrov Bolshoi	121	55 9N	137 40 E
Shantou (Chan-t'eou)	131	23 23N	116 41 E
Shantow (Swatow)	131	23 25N	116 40 E
Shantung □	130	36 0N	117 30 E
Shanyang	131	33 39N	110 2 E
Shaohing	131	30 0N	120 32 E
Shaowu	131	27 25N	117 30 E
Shaoyang	131	27 10N	111 30 E
Shapinsay, I.	96	59 2N	2 50W
Shaqra	122	25 15N	45 16 E
Sharbot Lake	47	44 46N	76 41W
Sharhjui	123	32 30N	67 22 E
Shari	122	27 20N	43 45 E
Sharin Gol	129	49 12N	106 27 E
Sharjah	123	25 23N	55 26 E
Shark B.	134	11 20 S	130 35 E
Sharon, U.S.A.	77	42 30N	88 44W
Sharon, Mass., U.S.A.	71	42 5N	71 11W
Sharon, Pa., U.S.A.	70	41 18N	80 30W
Sharpe, L.	34	54 10N	93 21W
Sharpe L.	55	54 5N	93 40W
Sharpsburg	70	40 30N	79 56W
Sharpsville	70	41 16N	80 28W
Shashi	117	21 15 S	27 27 E
Shasi	131	30 16N	112 20 E
Shasta, Mt.	78	41 30N	122 0W
Shasta Res.	78	40 50N	122 15W
Shattuck	75	36 17N	99 55W
Shaunavon	56	49 35N	108 25W
Shaver Lake	80	37 9N	119 18W
Shaw, R.	134	20 21 S	119 17 E
Shawan	129	44 21N	85 37 E
Shawanaga	46	45 31N	80 17W
Shawano	72	44 45N	88 38W
Shawbridge	43	45 52N	74 5W
Shawinigan	41	46 35N	72 50W
Shawinigan Sud	41	46 31N	72 45W
Shawnee, U.S.A.	76	39 1N	94 43W
Shawnee, N.Y., U.S.A.	49	43 9N	78 53W
Shawnee, Okla., U.S.A.	75	35 15N	97 0W
Shawville	40	45 36N	76 30W
Shcherbakov = Rybinsk	120	58 5N	38 50 E
Shchuchinsk	120	52 56N	70 12 E
Shebandowan	52	48 38N	90 4W
Sheboygan	72	43 46N	87 45W
Shediac	39	46 14N	64 32W
Sheelin, Lough	97	53 48N	7 20W
Sheep Haven	97	55 12N	7 55W
Sheerness	95	51 26N	0 47 E
Sheet Harbour	39	44 56N	62 31W
Sheffield, Can.	49	43 19N	80 12W
Sheffield, N.Z.	94	43 23 S	172 2 E
Sheffield, U.K.	94	53 23N	1 28W
Sheffield, Ala., U.S.A.	73	34 45N	87 42W
Sheffield, Ill., U.S.A.	76	41 21N	89 44W
Sheffield, Iowa, U.S.A.	76	42 54N	93 13W
Sheffield, Mass., U.S.A.	71	42 6N	73 23W
Sheffield, Pa., U.S.A.	70	41 42N	79 3W
Sheffield, Tex., U.S.A.	75	30 42N	101 49W
Sheffield L.	37	49 20N	56 34W
Sheguiandah	46	45 54N	81 55W
Sheho	56	51 35N	103 13W
Sheila	39	47 29N	64 55W
Shekhupura	124	31 42N	73 58 E
Shekichen	131	33 10N	113 15 E
Shekki	131	22 30N	113 15 E
Sheklung	131	23 5N	113 55 E
Shelbina	76	39 47N	92 2W
Shelburn	77	39 10N	87 24W
Shelburne, N.S., Can.	39	43 47N	65 20W
Shelburne, Ont., Can.	46	44 4N	80 15W
Shelburne, U.S.A.	71	44 23N	73 15W
Shelburne B.	135	11 50 S	143 0 E
Shelburne Falls	71	42 36N	72 45W
Shelby, Mich., U.S.A.	72	43 34N	86 27W
Shelby, Mont., U.S.A.	78	48 30N	111 59W
Shelby, N.C., U.S.A.	73	35 18N	81 34W
Shelby, Ohio, U.S.A.	70	40 52N	82 40W
Shelbyville, U.S.A.	76	39 48N	92 2W
Shelbyville, Ill., U.S.A.	77	39 25N	88 45W
Shelbyville, Ind., U.S.A.	77	39 30N	85 42W
Shelbyville, Ky., U.S.A.	77	38 13N	85 14W
Shelbyville, Tenn., U.S.A.	73	35 30N	86 25W
Shelbyville, Res.	77	39 26N	88 46W
Sheldon, U.S.A.	76	37 40N	94 18W
Sheldon, Iowa, U.S.A.	74	43 6N	95 51W

Sheldon Point **Sinkiang-Uighur**

Sheldon Point **67** 62 30N 165 0W
Sheldrake **36** 50 20N 64 51W
Shelikef, Str. **67** 58 0N 154 0W
Shelikhova, Zaliv **121** 59 30N 157 0E
Shell Lake **56** 53 19N 107 2W
Shellbrook **56** 53 13N 106 24W
Shelley **63** 54 0N 122 37W
Shellharbour **136** 34 31S 150 51E
Shellmouth **57** 50 56N 101 29W
Shellsburg **76** 42 6N 91 52W
Shelter Bay **35** 50 30N 67 20W
Shelton, Conn., U.S.A. **71** 41 18N 73 7W
Shelton, Wash., U.S.A. **80** 47 15N 123 6W
Shenandoah, Iowa, U.S.A. **74** 40 50N 95 25W
Shenandoah, Pa., U.S.A. **71** 40 49N 76 13W
Shenandoah, Va., U.S.A. **72** 38 30N 78 38W
Shenandoah, R. **72** 38 30N 78 38W
Shenchih **130** 39 12N 112 2E
Shenmu **130** 38 56N 110 19E
Shensi □ **131** 34 50N 109 25E
Shentsa **129** 30 56N 88 25E
Shenyang (Mukden) **130** 41 35N 123 30E
Sheopur Kalan **124** 25 40N 76 40E
Shepard **59** 50 57N 113 55W
Shepherd **46** 43 32N 84 41W
Shepherdsville **77** 37 59N 85 43W
Shepparton **136** 36 23S 145 26E
Sheppton **71** 40 52N 76 10W
Sher Khan Qala **124** 29 55N 66 10E
Sherborne **95** 50 56N 2 31W
Sherbro I. **114** 7 30N 12 40W
Sherbrooke **39** 45 28N 71 57W
Sheridan, Can. **50** 43 31N 79 40W
Sheridan, U.S.A. **76** 40 31N 94 37W
Sheridan, Ark., U.S.A. **75** 34 20N 92 25W
Sheridan, Col., U.S.A. **74** 39 44N 105 3W
Sheridan, Ill., U.S.A. **77** 41 32N 88 41W
Sheridan, Ind., U.S.A. **77** 40 8N 86 13W
Sheridan, Wyo., U.S.A. **78** 44 50N 107 0W
Sheridan L. **63** 51 31N 120 54W
Sherman, Can. **66** 49 21N 123 14W
Sherman, U.S.A. **75** 33 40N 96 35W
Sherridon **55** 55 8N 101 5W
Sherrington **43** 45 10N 73 31W
Sherwood, U.S.A. **77** 41 17N 84 33W
Sherwood, N.D., U.S.A. **57** 48 59N 101 36W
Sherwood, Tex., U.S.A. **75** 31 18N 100 45W
Sherwood For. **94** 53 5N 1 5W
Sherwood Park **59** 53 31N 113 19W
Shesheke **117** 17 14S 24 22E
Sheslay **54** 58 17N 131 45W
Sheslay, R. **54** 58 48N 132 5W
Shethanei L. **55** 58 48N 97 50W
Shetland □ **96** 60 30N 1 30W
Shetland Is. **96** 60 30N 1 30W
Shevchenko **120** 44 25N 51 20E
Sheyenne **75** 47 52N 99 8W
Sheyenne, R. **74** 47 40N 98 15W
Shiawassea, R. **46** 43 38N 83 50W
Shibeli, R. **115** 2 0N 44 0E
Shiberghan □ **123** 35 45N 66 0E
Shibogama L. **34** 53 35N 88 15W
Shibushi **132** 31 25N 131 0E
Shiel, L. **96** 56 48N 5 32W
Shifnal **96** 52 40N 2 23W
Shiga-ken □ **132** 35 20N 136 0E
Shigatse **129** 29 10N 89 0E
Shih Ho **131** 31 45N 115 50E
Shihchwan **131** 33 5N 108 30E
Shihkiachwang **130** 38 0N 114 32E
Shihkwaikow **130** 40 59N 110 4E
Shihlu **131** 19 15N 109 0E
Shihpu **131** 29 12N 121 58E
Shihtao **130** 36 55N 122 25E
Shihtsien **131** 27 28N 108 3E
Shihwei **129** 51 28N 119 59E
Shikarpur **124** 27 57N 68 39E
Shikohabad **123** 27 6N 78 38E
Shikoku **132** 33 30N 133 30E
Shikoku □ **132** 33 30N 133 30E
Shikoku-Sanchi **132** 33 30N 133 30E
Shilka **121** 52 0N 115 55E
Shilka, R. **121** 37 30N 93 18E
Shillelagh **97** 52 46N 6 32W
Shillong **125** 25 35N 91 53E
Shilo **57** 49 49N 99 38W
Shimabara **132** 32 48N 130 20E
Shimada **132** 34 49N 138 19E
Shimane-ken □ **132** 35 0N 132 30E
Shimano-gawa **132** 36 50N 138 30E
Shimenovsk **121** 52 15N 127 30E
Shimizu **132** 35 0N 138 30E
Shimodate **132** 36 20N 139 55E
Shimoga **124** 13 57N 75 32E
Shimonoseki **132** 33 58N 131 0E
Shin Dand **124** 33 12N 62 8E
Shin, L. **96** 58 7N 4 30W
Shinankow **129** 48 40N 121 32E
Shingleton **53** 46 25N 86 33W
Shingu **132** 33 40N 135 55E
Shinkiachwang **130** 38 0N 114 31E
Shinyanga **116** 3 45S 33 27E
Shio-no-Misaki **132** 33 25N 135 45E
Ship I. **75** 30 16N 88 55W
Shipka **109** 42 46N 25 33E
Shipki La **124** 31 45N 78 40E
Shippegan **39** 47 45N 64 45W
Shippegan I. **39** 47 50N 64 38W
Shippensburg **70** 40 4N 77 32W
Shiprock **79** 36 51N 108 45W
Shir Kūh **123** 31 45N 53 30E
Shirāz **123** 29 42N 52 30E
Shire, R. **117** 16 30S 35 0E
Shiriya-Zaki **132** 41 25N 141 30E
Shirley **77** 39 53N 85 35W
Shirvan **123** 37 30N 57 50E
Shirwa L. = Chilwa L. **117** 15 15S 35 40E
Shishmaref **67** 66 15N 166 10W
Shiukwan **131** 24 58N 113 3E
Shively **77** 38 12N 85 49W
Shivpuri **124** 25 18N 77 42E
Shizuoka **132** 35 0N 138 30E
Shizuoka-ken □ **132** 35 15N 138 40E
Shkoder = Shkodra **109** 42 6N 19 20E
Shkodra **109** 42 6N 19 20E
Shkumbini, R. **109** 41 5N 19 50E
Shmidt, O. **121** 81 0N 91 0E
Shoal Cr. **76** 39 39N 93 35W
Shoal L. **52** 49 33N 95 1W
Shoal Lake **57** 50 30N 100 35W
Shoalhaven, R. **136** 34 54S 150 42E
Shoals **77** 38 40N 86 47W
Shoals Prov. Park **53** 47 50N 83 50W
Shoeburyness **95** 51 31N 0 49E
Shohsien **130** 39 30N 112 25E
Sholapur **124** 17 43N 75 56E
Shologontsy **121** 66 13N 114 14E
Shongopovi **79** 35 49N 110 37W
Shoshone, Calif., U.S.A. **81** 35 58N 116 16W
Shoshone, Idaho, U.S.A. **78** 43 0N 114 27W
Shoshone L. **78** 44 30N 110 40W
Shoshone Mts. **78** 39 30N 117 30W
Shoshong **117** 22 56S 26 31E
Shoshoni **78** 43 13N 108 5W
Show Low **79** 34 16N 110 0W
Showyang **130** 38 0S 113 4E
Shreveport **75** 32 30N 93 50W
Shrewsbury **94** 52 42N 2 45W
Shropshire (□) = Salop **95** 52 36N 2 45W
Shubenacadie **39** 45 5N 63 24W
Shucheng **131** 31 25N 117 2E
Shuikiahu **131** 32 14N 117 4E
Shulan **130** 44 27N 126 57E
Shullsburg **76** 42 35N 90 15W
Shumagin Is. **67** 55 0N 159 0W
Shumikha **120** 55 10N 63 15E
Shunan **131** 29 37N 119 0E
Shunchang **131** 26 52N 117 48E
Shungnak **67** 66 55N 157 10W
Shuntak **131** 22 54N 113 8E
Shur, R. **123** 28 30N 55 0E
Shūsf **123** 31 50N 60 5E
Shūshtar **122** 32 0N 48 50E
Shuswap L. **63** 50 55N 119 3W
Shuyak I. **67** 58 35N 152 30W
Shuyang **131** 34 9N 118 51E
Shwangcheng **130** 45 30N 126 20E
Shwangliao **130** 43 39N 123 40E
Shwebo **125** 22 30N 95 45E
Shwegu **125** 18 49N 95 26E
Shweli, R. **125** 23 45N 96 45E
Shyok **124** 34 15N 78 5E
Shyok, R. **124** 34 30N 78 15E
Si Racha **128** 13 10N 100 56E
Siah **122** 22 0N 47 0E
Siahan Range **124** 27 30N 64 40E
Siahoyen **130** 42 30N 120 30E
Siaksriinderapura **126** 0 51N 102 0E
Siakwan **129** 25 45N 100 10E
Sialkot **124** 32 32N 74 30E
Siam, G. of **128** 11 30N 101 0E
Sian **131** 34 2N 109 0E
Siang K., Hunan, China **131** 27 10N 112 45E
Siang K., Kwangsi-chuang, China **131** 23 20N 107 40E
Siangcheng **131** 33 16N 115 2E
Siangfan **131** 32 15N 112 2E
Siangning **130** 36 10N 110 50E
Siangsiang **131** 27 50N 112 30E
Siangtan **131** 28 0N 112 55E
Siangyang **131** 32 18N 111 0E
Siangyin **131** 28 45N 113 0E
Siantan, P. **126** 3 10N 106 15E
Siao Hingan Ling **129** 49 0N 127 0E
Siaohaotze **129** 46 52N 124 22E
Siapu **131** 26 53N 120 0E
Siāreh **123** 28 5N 60 20E
Siargao, I. **127** 9 52N 126 3E
Siasi **127** 5 34N 120 50E
Siau, I. **127** 2 50N 125 25E
Sibbald **55** 51 24N 110 10W
Sibenik **108** 43 48N 15 54E
Siberia **121** 60 0N 100 0E
Siberut, I. **126** 1 30S 99 0E
Sibi **124** 29 30N 67 48E
Sibil **127** 4 59S 140 35E
Sibiti **116** 3 38S 13 19E
Sibiu **107** 45 45N 24 9E
Sibley, U.S.A. **77** 40 35N 88 23W
Sibley, Iowa, U.S.A. **74** 43 21N 95 43W
Sibley, La., U.S.A. **75** 32 34N 93 16W
Sibley Prov. Park **52** 48 30N 88 45W
Sibolga **126** 1 50N 98 45E
Sibsagar **125** 27 0N 94 36E
Sibuco **127** 7 20N 122 10E
Sibuguey B. **127** 7 50N 122 45E
Sibuko **127** 7 20N 122 10E
Sibut **116** 5 52N 19 10E
Sibutu, I. **127** 4 45N 119 30E
Sibutu Passage **127** 4 50N 120 0E
Sibuyan, I. **127** 12 25N 122 40E
Sicamous **63** 50 49N 119 0W
Sicapoo **127** 18 9N 121 34E
Sicasica **68** 17 20S 67 45W
Sichang **129** 28 0N 102 10E
Sichwan **131** 33 6N 111 30E
Sicilia □ **108** 37 30N 14 30E
Sicilia, I. **108** 37 30N 14 30E
Sicily = Sicilia **108** 37 30N 14 30E
Sicuani **86** 14 10S 71 10W
Siddipet **124** 18 0N 79 0E
Sideburned L. **53** 47 45N 83 15W
Sidell **77** 39 55N 87 49W
Sidi-Bel-Abbès **114** 35 13N 0 10W
Sidlaw Hills **96** 56 32N 3 10W
Sidmouth **95** 50 40N 3 13W
Sidnaw **52** 46 30N 88 43W
Sidney, B.C., Can. **63** 48 39N 123 24W
Sidney, Man., Can. **57** 49 54N 99 4W
Sidney, Mont., U.S.A. **74** 47 51N 104 7W
Sidney, N.Y., U.S.A. **71** 42 18N 75 20W
Sidney, Ohio, U.S.A. **77** 40 18N 84 6W
Sidoardjo **127** 7 30S 112 46E
Sidon = Saydā **115** 33 35N 35 25E
Sidon, (Saida) **122** 33 38N 35 28E
Siedlce **107** 52 10N 22 20E
Siegburg **105** 50 48N 7 12E
Siegen **105** 50 52N 8 2E
Siem Reap **128** 13 20N 103 52E
Siena **108** 43 20N 11 20E
Sienfeng **131** 29 45N 109 10E
Sienyang **131** 34 20N 108 48E
Sierck-les-Bains **101** 49 26N 6 20E
Sierpe, Bocas de la **86** 10 0N 61 30W
Sierra Blanca **79** 31 11N 105 17W
Sierra Blanca, mt. **79** 33 20N 105 54W
Sierra City **80** 39 34N 120 42W
Sierra Colorado **90** 40 35S 67 50W
Sierra Gorda **88** 23 0S 69 15W
Sierra Leone ■ **114** 9 0N 12 0W
Sierra Majada **82** 27 19N 103 42W
Sierraville **80** 39 36N 120 22W
Sífnos **109** 37 0N 24 45E
Sifton **57** 51 21N 100 8W
Sifton Pass **54** 57 52N 126 15W
Sigaboy **127** 6 39N 126 10E
Sigean **102** 43 2N 2 58E
Sighetul Marmatiei **107** 47 57N 23 52E
Sighişoara **107** 46 12N 24 50E
Sigli **126** 5 25N 96 0E
Siglufjörður **110** 66 12N 18 55W
Sigma **127** 11 29N 122 40E
Signal **81** 34 30N 113 38W
Signal Hill **37** 47 35N 52 41W
Signal Pk. **81** 33 25N 114 4W
Signy I. **91** 60 45S 46 30W
Signy-l'Abbaye **101** 49 40N 4 25E
Sigourney **76** 41 20N 92 12W
Sigsig **86** 3 0S 78 50W
Sigtuna **111** 59 36N 17 44E
Sigüenza **104** 41 3N 2 40W
Siguiri **114** 11 31N 9 10W
Sigurd **79** 38 57N 112 0W
Sigutlat L. **62** 52 57N 126 12W
Sihanoukville = Kompong Som **128** 10 40N 103 30E
Siho **131** 34 0N 105 0E
Sihsien, Anwhei, China **130** 29 55N 118 23E
Sihsien, Shansi, China **131** 36 54N 111 0E
Siirt **122** 37 57N 41 55E
Sijsele **91** 51 12N 3 20E
Sikandra Rao **123** 27 43N 78 24E
Sikar **124** 27 39N 75 10E
Sikeston **75** 36 52N 89 35W
Sikhote Alin, Khrebet **121** 46 0N 136 0E
Sikinos, I. **109** 36 40N 25 8E
Sikkani Chief, R. **54** 57 47N 122 15W
Sikkim ■ **125** 27 50N 88 50E
Siku **131** 33 48N 104 18E
Sil, R. **104** 42 23N 7 30W
Silacayoapán **83** 17 30N 98 9W
Silamulun Ho **130** 43 30N 123 35E
Silchar **125** 24 49N 92 48E
Silcox **55** 57 12N 94 10W
Siler City **73** 35 44N 79 30W
Silesia **106** 51 0N 16 30E
Silesia = Slask **106** 51 0N 16 30E
Silgarhi Doti **125** 29 15N 82 0E
Silghat **125** 26 35N 93 0E
Silifke **122** 36 22N 33 58E
Siliguri **125** 26 45N 88 25E
Silin **131** 24 10N 105 36E
Silinhot **130** 43 16N 116 0E
Silistra **109** 44 6N 27 19E
Siljan, L. **111** 60 55N 14 45E
Silkeborg **111** 56 10N 9 32E
Sillajhuay, Cordillera **86** 19 40S 68 40W
Sillé-le Guillaume **100** 48 10N 0 8W
Sillery **42** 46 46N 71 15W
Siloam Springs **75** 36 15N 94 31W
Silogui **126** 1 10S 98 46E
Silsbee **75** 30 20N 94 8W
Silver Bay **52** 47 17N 91 16W
Silver City, Pan. C. Z. **84** 9 21N 79 53W
Silver City, Calif., U.S.A. **78** 36 19N 119 44W
Silver City, N. Mex., U.S.A. **79** 32 50N 108 18W
Silver Cr., R. **78** 43 30N 119 30W
Silver Creek **70** 42 33N 79 9W
Silver Grove **77** 39 2N 84 24W
Silver Islet **52** 48 20N 88 45W
Silver L. **80** 38 39N 120 6W
Silver Lake, Calif., U.S.A. **81** 35 21N 116 7W
Silver Lake, Ind., U.S.A. **77** 41 4N 85 53W
Silver Lake, Oreg., U.S.A. **78** 43 9N 121 4W
Silver Lake, Wis., U.S.A. **77** 42 33N 88 13W
Silver Ridge **57** 50 48N 98 52W
Silver Star Prov. Park **63** 50 23N 119 5W
Silver Water **46** 45 52N 82 52W
Silverlake **80** 38 38N 120 7W
Silvertip Mt. **63** 49 10N 121 13W
Silverton, Austral. **136** 31 52S 141 10E
Silverton, Can. **63** 49 57N 117 21W
Silverton, Colo., U.S.A. **79** 37 51N 107 45W
Silverton, Tex., U.S.A. **75** 34 30N 101 16W
Silverton, Wash., U.S.A. **63** 48 5N 121 34W
Silvia **86** 2 37N 76 21W
Silvies, R. **78** 43 57N 119 5W
Silvis **76** 41 33N 90 28W
Silwani **123** 23 18N 78 27E
Simanggang **126** 1 15N 111 25E
Simard, L. **40** 47 40N 78 40W
Simarun **123** 31 16N 51 40E
Simcoe **46** 42 50N 80 20W
Simcoe Co. **50** 43 59N 79 49W
Simcoe, L. **46** 44 25N 79 20W
Simenga **121** 62 50N 107 55E
Simeulue, I. **126** 2 45N 95 45E
Simferopol **120** 44 55N 34 3E
Simi Valley **81** 34 16N 118 47W
Simikot **125** 30 0N 81 50E
Simití **86** 7 58N 73 57W
Simla **124** 31 2N 77 15E
Simmie **56** 49 56N 108 6W
Simmler **81** 35 21N 119 59W
Simmons **48** 45 26N 75 49W
Simmons Pen. **65** 76 40N 89 7W
Simojärvi **110** 66 5N 27 10E
Simojoki **110** 65 46N 25 15E
Simojovel **83** 17 12N 92 38W
Simonette, R. **60** 55 9N 118 15W
Simonhouse **57** 54 26N 101 23W
Simpang **128** 4 50N 100 40E
Simplon Pass **106** 46 15N 8 0E
Simpson **56** 51 27N 105 27W
Simpson Des. **135** 25 0S 137 0E
Simpson I. **53** 48 46N 87 41W
Simpson Pen. **65** 68 34N 88 45W
Simpsons Corners **49** 43 46N 80 18W
Simunjan **126** 1 25N 110 45E
Simushir, Ostrov **121** 46 50N 152 30E
Sinabang **126** 2 30N 46 30E
Sinaloa **82** 25 50N 108 20W
Sinaloa □ **82** 25 0N 107 30W
Sinamaica **86** 11 5N 71 51W
Sincé **86** 9 15N 75 9W
Sincelejc **86** 9 18N 75 24W
Sincheng, Honan, China **131** 34 25N 113 56E
Sincheng, Kwangsi, China **131** 24 1N 108 35E
Sinchengtu **131** 23 55N 108 30E
Sinclair **78** 41 47N 107 35W
Sinclair Mills **54** 54 5N 121 40W
Sinclair Pass **61** 50 40N 115 58W
Sincorá, Serra do **87** 13 30S 41 0W
Sind Sagar Doab **124** 32 0N 71 30E
Sindangan **127** 8 10N 123 5E
Sindangbarang **127** 7 27S 107 9E
Sindjai **127** 5 0S 120 20E
Sines **104** 37 56N 8 51W
Sinfeng, Kiangsi, China **131** 25 28N 114 40E
Sinfeng, Kweichow, China **131** 26 59N 106 55E
Singa **115** 13 10N 33 57E
Singaparna **127** 7 23S 108 4E
Singapore ■ **128** 1 17N 103 51E
Singapore, Straits of **128** 1 15N 104 0E
Singaraja **126** 8 15S 115 10E
Singida **116** 4 49S 34 48E
Singitikós, Kólpos **109** 40 6N 24 0E
Singkang **127** 4 8S 120 1E
Singkawang **126** 1 0N 109 5E
Singkep, I. **126** 0 30S 104 20E
Singleton **136** 32 33S 151 10E
Singleton, Mt. **134** 29 27S 117 15E
Singtai **130** 37 2N 114 30E
Singtze **131** 29 30N 116 4E
Singyang **131** 32 10N 114 0E
Sinhailien **131** 34 31N 119 0E
Sinhsien **130** 38 25N 112 45E
Sinhwa **131** 27 36N 111 6E
Sining **129** 36 35N 101 50E
Sinkan **131** 27 45N 115 30E
Sinkiang **130** 35 35N 111 25E
Sinkiang-Uighur □ **129** 42 0N 86 0E

Sinkin South Bend

Sinkin 130 39 30N 122 29 E
Sinlo 130 38 25N 114 50 E
Sinmak 130 38 25N 126 15 E
Sinmin 130 42 0N 122 50 E
Sinni, R. 108 40 6N 16 15 E
Sinoia 117 17 20S 30 8 E
Sinop 122 42 1N 35 11 E
Sinpin 130 41 50N 125 0 E
Sinsiang 131 35 15N 113 55 E
Sinskoye 121 61 8N 126 48 E
Sint Eustatius, I. 85 17 30N 62 59W
Sint Maarten, I. 85 18 4N 63 4W
Sintai 131 30 59N 105 0 E
Sintaluta 56 50 29N 103 27W
Sintang 126 0 5N 111 35 E
Sinti, (Hunghu) 131 29 49N 113 30 E
Sinton 75 28 1N 97 30W
Sintra 104 38 47N 9 25W
Sinŭiju 130 40 5N 124 24 E
Sinuk 67 64 42N 166 22W
Sinyang 131 32 6N 114 2 E
Sióma 117 16 25S 23 28 E
Sion 106 46 14N 7 20 E
Sioux City 74 42 32N 96 25W
Sioux Falls 74 43 35N 96 40W
Sioux Lookout 52 50 10N 91 50W
Sioux Narrows 52 49 25N 94 10W
Sipa 131 33 34N 118 59 E
Sipera, I. 126 2 18S 99 40 E
Siping 131 33 25N 114 10 E
Sipiwesk L. 55 55 5N 97 35W
Siquia, R. 84 12 30N 84 30W
Siquijor, I. 127 9 12N 123 45 E
Siquirres 84 10 6N 83 30W
Siquisique 86 10 34N 69 42W
Sir Edward Pellew Group 135 15 40S 137 10 E
Sir Francis Drake, Mt. 62 50 49N 124 48W
Sir Sandford, Mt. 63 51 40N 117 52W
Siracusa 108 37 4N 15 17 E
Sirajganj 125 24 25N 89 47 E
Siret, R. 107 47 58N 26 5 E
Sirohi 124 24 52N 72 53 E
Sironj 124 24 5N 77 45 E
Síros, I. 109 37 28N 24 57 E
Sirretta Pk. 81 35 56N 118 19W
Sirsa 124 29 33N 75 4 E
Sisak 108 45 30N 16 21 E
Sisaket 128 15 8N 104 23 E
Sisiang 131 33 2N 107 48 E
Sisipuk I. 55 55 40N 102 0W
Sisipuk L. 55 55 45N 101 50W
Sisophon 128 13 31N 102 59 E
Sisseton 74 45 43N 97 3W
Sissonne 101 49 34N 3 51 E
Sistan-Baluchistan □ 123 27 0N 62 0 E
Sisteron 103 44 12N 5 57 E
Sisters 78 44 21N 121 32W
Sitapur 125 27 38N 80 45 E
Sitges 104 41 17N 1 47 E
Sitka 67 57 9N 134 58W
Sittang Myit, R. 125 18 20N 96 45 E
Sittard 105 51 0N 5 52 E
Situbondo 127 7 45S 114 0 E
Siuna 84 13 37N 84 45W
Siuwu 131 35 10N 113 30 E
Siuyen 130 40 20N 123 15 E
Sivand 123 30 5N 52 55 E
Sivas 122 39 43N 36 58 E
Siverek 122 37 50N 39 25 E
Sivrihisar 122 39 30N 31 35 E
Sivry 105 50 10N 4 12 E
Siwalik Range 125 28 0N 83 0 E
Siwan 125 26 13N 84 27 E
Sixteen Island Lake 43 45 56N 74 28W
Sizewell 95 52 13N 1 38 E
Sjaelland 111 55 30N 11 30 E
Sjiptjenski P. 109 42 46N 25 33 E
Sjumen = Kolarovgrad 109 43 27N 26 42 E
Skagafjörður 110 65 54N 19 35W
Skagastölstindane, mt. 111 61 25N 8 10 E
Skagen 111 68 37N 14 27 E
Skagerrak 111 57 30N 9 0 E
Skagit, R. 80 48 20N 122 25W
Skagway 67 59 30N 135 20W
Skaidi 110 70 26N 24 30 E
Skandia 53 46 25N 87 16W
Skanee 52 46 53N 88 20W
Skara 111 58 25N 13 30 E
Skaraborgs län □ 111 58 20N 13 30 E
Skardu 124 35 20N 75 35 E
Skeena Mts. 54 56 40N 128 30W
Skeena, R. 62 54 9N 130 5W
Skeggjastadir 110 66 3N 14 50W
Skegness 94 53 9N 0 20 E
Skeldon 86 6 0N 57 20W
Skellefte älv 110 65 30N 18 30 E
Skellefteå 110 64 45N 20 58 E
Skelleftehamn 110 64 41N 21 14 E
Skellig Rocks 97 51 47N 10 32W
Skerries, The 94 53 27N 4 40W
Skibbereen 97 51 33N 9 16W
Skiddaw, Mt. 94 54 39N 3 9W
Skidegate 62 53 15N 132 1W
Skien 111 59 12N 9 35 E
Skierniewice 107 51 58N 20 19 E
Skihist, Mt. 63 50 12N 121 54W
Skikda 114 36 50N 6 58 E
Skillett Fork, Little Wabash, R. 77 38 6N 88 9W
Skipton 94 53 57N 2 1W
Skíros, I. 109 38 55N 24 34 E
Skive 111 56 33N 9 2 E
Skjálfandafljót 110 65 15N 17 25W
Skjálfandi 110 66 5N 17 30W
Skoghall 111 59 20N 13 30 E
Skopje 109 42 1N 21 32 E
Skövde 111 58 15N 13 59 E
Skovorodino 121 54 0N 125 0 E
Skowhegan 35 44 49N 69 40W
Skownan 57 51 58N 99 35W
Skudeneshavn 111 59 10N 5 10 E
Skull 97 51 32N 9 40W
Skunk, R. 76 40 42N 91 7W
Skwaner, Pegunungan 126 1 0S 112 30 E
Skwierzyna 106 52 46N 15 30 E
Skye, I. 96 57 15N 6 10W
Skykomish 78 47 43N 121 16W
Slamet, G. 126 7 16S 109 8 E
Slaney, R. 97 52 52N 6 45W
Slaokan 131 30 57N 114 2 E
Slask 106 51 25N 16 0 E
Slate Is. 34 48 40N 87 0W
Slater 76 39 13N 93 4W
Slatina 107 44 28N 24 22 E
Slaton 75 33 27N 101 38W
Slave Lake 60 55 17N 114 50W
Slave Pt. 54 61 11N 115 56W
Slave, R. 54 61 18N 113 39W
Slavgorod 120 53 10N 78 50 E
Slavkov (Austerlitz) 106 49 10N 16 52 E
Sleaford 94 53 0N 0 22W
Sleat, Sd. of 96 57 5N 5 47W
Sleepy Eye 74 44 15N 94 45W
Sleman 127 7 40S 110 20 E
Slemon L. 54 63 13N 116 4W
Slidell 75 30 20N 89 48W
Sliedrecht 105 51 50N 4 45 E
Slieve Aughty 97 53 4N 8 30W
Slieve Bloom 97 53 4N 7 40W
Slieve Donard 97 54 10N 5 57W
Slieve Gullion 97 54 8N 6 26W
Slieve Mish 97 52 12N 9 50W
Slievenamon Mt. 97 52 25N 7 37W
Sligo 97 54 17N 8 28W
Sligo □ 97 54 10N 8 35W
Sligo B. 97 54 20N 8 40W
Slite 111 57 42N 18 48 E
Sliven 109 42 42N 26 19 E
Sloan 81 35 57N 115 13W
Sloansville 71 42 45N 74 22W
Slocan 63 49 48N 117 28W
Slocan L. 63 49 50N 117 23W
Slochteren 105 53 12N 6 48 E
Slough 95 51 30N 0 35W
Sloughhouse 80 38 26N 121 12W
Slovakia □ 107 48 30N 19 0 E
Slovenia = Slovenija 108 45 58N 14 30 E
Slovenija □ 108 45 58N 14 30 E
Slovenské Rhudhorie 107 48 45N 19 0 E
Slyne Hd. 97 53 25N 10 10W
Slyudyanka 121 51 40N 103 30 E
Smalltree L. 55 61 0N 105 0W
Smallwood Reservoir 35 54 20N 63 10W
Smartville 80 39 13N 121 18W
Smeaton 56 53 30N 104 49W
Smederevo 109 44 40N 20 57 E
Smethport 70 41 50N 78 28W
Smidovich 121 48 36N 133 49 E
Smilde 105 52 58N 6 28 E
Smiley 56 51 38N 109 29W
Smith 60 55 10N 114 0W
Smith Arm 54 66 15N 123 0W
Smith Center 74 39 50N 98 50W
Smith I. 36 54 13N 58 18W
Smith Pen. 65 77 12N 78 50W
Smith, R. 54 59 34N 126 30W
Smith Sund 65 78 30N 74 0W
Smithers 54 54 45N 127 10W
Smithfield 73 35 31N 78 16W
Smiths Cove 39 44 37N 65 42W
Smiths Falls 47 44 55N 76 0W
Smithville, Can. 49 43 6N 79 33W
Smithville, U.S.A. 76 39 23N 94 35W
Smithville, Tex., U.S.A. 75 30 2N 97 12W
Smjörfjöll 110 65 30N 15 42W
Smoky Falls 53 50 4N 82 10W
Smoky Hill, R. 74 38 45N 98 0W
Smoky Lake 60 54 10N 112 30W
Smoky, R. 60 56 10N 117 21W
Smola 110 63 23N 8 3 E
Smolensk 120 54 45N 32 0 E
Smolikas, Óros 109 40 9N 20 58 E
Smolyan 109 41 36N 24 38 E
Smooth Rock Falls 53 49 17N 81 37W
Smoothrock L. 52 50 30N 89 30W
Smoothstone L. 55 54 40N 106 50W
Smyrna = İzmir 122 38 25N 27 8 E
Snaefell 94 54 18N 4 26W
Snaefells Jökull 110 64 45N 23 25W
Snake I. 136 38 47S 146 33 E
Snake L. 55 55 32N 106 35W
Snake, R. 78 46 31N 118 50W
Snake Ra., Mts. 78 39 0N 114 30W
Snake River Plain 78 43 13N 113 0W
Snaring 61 53 5N 118 4W
Sneek 105 53 2N 5 40 E
Snelgrove 49 43 44N 79 49W
Snelling 80 37 31N 120 26W
Sněžka 106 50 14N 15 50 E
Snipe L. 60 55 7N 116 47W
Snizort, L. 96 57 33N 6 28W
Snohetta 110 62 19N 9 16 E
Snohomish 80 47 53N 122 6W
Snow Hill 72 38 10N 75 21W
Snow L. 55 54 52N 100 3W
Snow Mt. 80 39 22N 122 44W
Snowbird L. 55 60 45N 103 0W
Snowdon, Mt. 94 53 4N 4 8W
Snowdrift 55 62 24N 110 44W
Snowdrift, R. 55 62 24N 110 44W
Snowflake, Can. 57 49 3N 98 39W
Snowflake, U.S.A. 79 34 30N 110 4W
Snowshoe 54 53 43N 121 0W
Snowville 78 41 59N 112 47W
Snowy Mts. 136 36 30S 148 20 E
Snowy, R. 136 37 46S 148 30 E
Snug Corner 85 22 33N 73 52W
Snyder, Can. 49 42 57N 79 3W
Snyder, Okla., U.S.A. 75 34 40N 99 0W
Snyder, Tex., U.S.A. 75 32 45N 100 57W
Soacha 86 4 35N 74 13W
Soalala 117 16 6S 45 20 E
Soap Lake 78 47 29N 119 31W
Sobat, R. 115 8 32N 32 40 E
Sobral 87 3 50S 40 30W
Soc Trang = Khonh Hung 128 9 37N 105 50 E
Socha 86 6 0N 72 41W
Soche (Yarkand) 129 38 24N 77 20 E
Sochi 120 43 35N 39 40 E
Société, Is. de la 15 17 0S 151 0W
Society Is. = Société, Is. de la 15 17 0S 151 0W
Socompa, Portezuelo de 88 24 27S 68 18W
Socorro, Colomb. 86 6 29N 73 16W
Socorro, U.S.A. 71 34 3N 106 58W
Socorro, I. 82 18 45N 110 58W
Socotra, I. 115 12 30N 54 0 E
Soda Creek 54 52 25N 122 10W
Soda L. 79 35 7N 116 2W
Soda Springs 78 42 40N 111 40W
Söderhamn 111 61 18N 17 10 E
Söderköping 111 58 31N 16 35 E
Södermanlands län □ 111 59 10N 16 30 E
Södertälje 111 59 12N 17 50 E
Sodo 115 7 0N 37 57 E
Sodus 70 43 13N 77 5W
Sodus Pt. 70 43 15N 77 0W
Soest 105 51 34N 8 7 E
Soeurs, Île des 45 45 28N 73 33W
Sofia = Sofiya 109 42 45N 23 20 E
Sofia, R. 117 15 25S 48 40 E
Sofiya 109 42 45N 23 20 E
Sogad 127 10 30N 125 0 E
Sogamoso 86 5 43N 72 56W
Sogn og Fjordane fylke □ 111 61 40N 6 0 E
Sogndalsfjøra 111 61 14N 7 5 E
Sognefjorden 111 61 10N 5 50 E
Sohâg 115 26 27N 31 43 E
Soignies 105 50 35N 4 5 E
Sointula 62 50 38N 127 0W
Soissons 101 49 25N 3 19 E
Söke 122 37 48N 27 28 E
Sokhta Chinar 123 35 5N 67 35 E
Sokó'ka 107 53 25N 23 30 E
Sokoto 114 13 2N 5 16 E
Sol Iletsk 120 51 10N 55 0 E
Solano 127 16 25N 121 15 E
Soledad, Colomb. 86 10 55N 74 46W
Soledad, U.S.A. 80 36 27N 121 16W
Soledad, Venez. 86 8 10N 63 34W
Solemint 81 34 25N 118 27W
Solent, The 95 50 45N 1 25W
Solenzara 103 41 53N 9 23 E
Solesmes 101 50 10N 3 30 E
Solfonn, Mt. 111 60 2N 6 57 E
Solikamsk 120 59 38N 56 50 E
Solimões, R. 86 2 15S 66 30W
Solina 49 43 58N 78 47W
Solingen 105 51 10N 7 4 E
Sollefteå 110 63 12N 17 20 E
Soller 104 39 43N 2 45 E
Solok 126 0 55S 100 40 E
Sololá 84 14 49N 91 10 E
Solomon Is. 14 6 0S 155 0 E
Solomon, N. Fork, R. 74 39 45N 99 0W
Solomon, S. Fork, R. 74 39 25N 99 12W
Solon Springs 52 46 19N 91 47W
Solor, I. 127 8 27S 123 0 E
Solothurn 106 47 13N 7 32 E
Soltanābād 123 36 29N 58 5 E
Soltāniyeh 122 36 20N 48 55 E
Solun 129 46 40N 120 40 E
Solunska Glava 109 41 44N 21 31 E
Solvang 81 34 36N 120 8W
Solvay 71 43 5N 76 17W
Solvesborg 111 56 5N 14 35 E
Solway Firth 96 54 45N 3 38W
Solwezi 117 12 20S 26 21 E
Somali Rep. ■ 115 7 0N 47 0 E
Sombernon 101 47 20N 4 40 E
Sombor 109 45 46N 19 17 E
Sombra 46 42 43N 82 29W
Sombrerete 82 23 40N 103 40W
Sombrero I. 85 18 30N 63 30W
Somers 78 48 4N 114 18W
Somerset, Can. 57 49 25N 98 39W
Somerset, Colo., U.S.A. 79 38 55N 107 30W
Somerset, Ky., U.S.A. 72 37 5N 84 40W
Somerset, Mass., U.S.A. 71 41 45N 71 10W
Somerset, Pa., U.S.A. 70 40 1N 79 4 E
Somerset □ 95 51 9N 3 0W
Somerset East 117 32 42S 25 35 E
Somerset, I. 65 73 30N 93 0W
Somersworth 71 43 15N 70 51W
Somerton 79 32 41N 114 47W
Somerville 71 40 34N 74 38W
Someş, R. 107 47 15N 23 45 E
Somme □ 101 50 0N 2 20 E
Somme, B. de la 100 5 22N 1 30 E
Sommepy-Tahure 101 49 15N 4 31 E
Sommesous 101 48 44N 4 12 E
Sommières 103 43 47N 4 6 E
Somoto 84 13 28N 86 37W
Somovit 109 43 40N 24 45 E
Somport, Puerto de 104 42 48N 0 31W
Son La 128 21 20N 103 50 E
Soná 84 8 0N 81 10W
Sønderborg 111 54 55N 9 49 E
Söndre Stromfjord 17 66 30N 50 52W
Sonepat 124 29 0N 77 5 E
Sonepur 125 20 55N 83 50 E
Song Cau 128 13 20N 109 18 E
Songea 116 10 40S 35 40 E
Songeons 101 49 32N 1 50 E
Songkhla 128 7 13N 100 37 E
Sonmiani 124 25 25N 66 40 E
Sonningdale 56 52 23N 107 44W
Sono, R. 87 8 58S 48 11W
Sonora, Can. 39 45 4N 61 54W
Sonora, Calif., U.S.A. 80 37 59N 120 27W
Sonora, Texas, U.S.A. 75 30 33N 100 37W
Sonora □ 82 28 0N 111 0W
Sonora I. 62 50 22N 125 15W
Sonora P. 78 38 17N 119 35W
Sonora, R. 82 28 30N 111 33W
Sonoyta 82 31 51N 112 50W
Sonsonate 84 13 43N 89 44W
Soo Junction 72 46 20N 85 14W
Soochow 131 31 18N 120 41 E
Sooke 63 48 13N 123 43W
Sopi 127 2 40N 128 28 E
Sopot 107 54 27N 18 31 E
Sopron 106 47 41N 16 37 E
Sop's Arm 37 49 46N 56 56W
Sør-Rondane 91 72 0S 25 0 E
Sør Trøndelag fylke □ 110 63 0N 11 0 E
Sorata 86 15 50S 68 50W
Sorel 41 46 0N 73 10W
Sorento 76 39 0N 89 34W
Sorgono 108 40 0N 9 0 E
Sorgues 103 44 1N 4 53 E
Soria 104 41 43N 2 32W
Soriano 88 33 24S 58 19W
Soriano □ 90 33 30S 58 0W
Sorocaba 89 23 31S 47 35W
Sorong 127 0 55S 131 15 E
Sororoca 86 0 43N 61 31W
Soroti 116 1 43N 33 35 E
Soröy Sundet 110 70 25N 23 0 E
Soröya 110 70 35N 22 45 E
Sorrento 108 40 38N 14 23 E
Sorsele 110 65 31N 17 30 E
Sorsogon 127 13 0N 124 0 E
Soscumica, L. 40 50 15N 77 27W
Sosnowiec 107 50 20N 19 10 E
Sospel 103 43 52N 7 27 E
Soto la Marina, R. 83 23 40N 97 40W
Sotteville-lès-Rouen 100 49 24N 1 5 E
Souanké 116 2 10N 14 10 E
Soucy 40 48 10N 75 30W
Soúdhas, Kólpos 109 35 31N 24 10 E
Soufrière 85 13 51N 61 4W
Soufrière, vol. 85 13 10N 61 10W
Souillac 102 44 53N 1 29 E
Sŏul 130 37 31N 127 6 E
Soulac-sur-Mer 102 45 30N 1 7W
Soulanges □ 44 45 18N 74 3W
Soulanges, Canal de 44 45 20N 73 58W
Soultz 101 48 57N 7 52 E
Sound, The 111 56 7N 12 30 E
Sounding Cr. 61 52 6N 110 28W
Sounding L. 61 52 8N 110 29W
Sources, Mt. aux 117 28 45S 28 50 E
Sourdeval 100 48 43N 0 55W
Soure 87 0 35S 48 30W
Souris, Man., Can. 55 49 40N 100 20W
Souris, P.E.I., Can. 39 46 21N 62 15W
Souris, R. 57 49 40N 99 34W
Sousa 87 6 45S 38 10W
Sousel 87 2 38S 52 29W
Soustons 102 43 45N 1 19W
Souterraine, La 102 46 15N 1 30 E
South Africa, Rep. of, ■ 117 30 0S 25 0 E
South Aulatsivik I. 36 56 45N 61 30W
South Australia □ 134 32 0S 139 0 E
South Baldy, Mt. 79 34 6N 107 27W
South Baymouth 46 45 33N 82 1W
South Beloit 76 42 29N 89 2W
South Bend, Indiana, U.S.A. 77 41 38N 86 20W
South Bend, Wash., U.S.A. 80 46 44N 123 52W

South Bentinck Arm Stickney

South Bentinck Arm **62** 52 7N 126 47W
South Berwick **71** 43 15N 70 47W
South Boston **73** 36 42N 78 58W
South Branch **37** 47 55N 59 2W
South Brook **37** 49 26N 56 5W
South Burnaby **66** 49 13N 123 0W
South Cape **67** 18 58N 155 24 E
South Carolina □ **73** 33 45N 81 0W
South Charleston **72** 38 20N 81 40W
South China Sea **128** 7 0N 107 0 E
South Dakota □ **74** 45 0N 100 0W
South Downs **95** 50 53N 0 10W
South East C. **135** 43 40 S 146 50 E
South East Passage **39** 44 36N 63 28W
South Esk, R. **96** 56 44N 3 3W
South Foreland **95** 51 7N 1 23 E
S. Fork, American, R. **80** 38 45N 121 5W
South Fork, Feather, R. **80** 39 17N 121 36W
South Fork, Lucking R. **77** 38 40N 84 19W
South Fork, R. **78** 47 54N 113 15W
South Gamboa **82** 9 4N 79 40W
South Gate **81** 33 57N 118 12W
South Georgia **91** 54 30 S 37 0W
South Gillies **52** 48 14N 89 42W
South Glamorgan □ **95** 51 30N 3 20W
South Granby **43** 45 19N 72 43W
South Grand, R. **76** 38 17N 94 25W
South Haven **77** 42 22N 86 20W
South Hd. **37** 49 9N 58 22W
South Heart, R. **60** 55 34N 116 11W
South Henik, L. **55** 61 30N 97 30W
South Horr **116** 2 12N 36 56 E
South I. **133** 43 0 S 170 0 E
South International Falls **52** 48 35N 93 24W
South Invercargill **133** 46 26N 168 23 E
South Knife, R. **55** 58 55N 94 37W
South Korea ■ **130** 36 0N 128 0 E
South Lake Tahoe **80** 38 57N 119 59W
South Lancaster **43** 45 8N 74 30W
South Lyon **46** 42 28N 83 39W
South Magnetic Pole (1965) **91** 66 30 S 139 30 E
South Milwaukee **77** 42 50N 87 52W
South Monroe **46** 41 54N 83 25W
South Nahanni, R. **54** 61 3N 123 21W
South Nation, R. **47** 45 34N 75 6W
South Orkney Is. **91** 63 0 S 45 0W
South Pass **78** 42 20N 108 58W
South Pekin **76** 40 30N 89 39W
South Pines **73** 35 10N 79 25W
South Platte, R. **74** 40 50N 102 45W
South Pt. **46** 44 54N 83 19W
South Pole **91** 90 0 S 0 0 E
South Porcupine **53** 48 30N 81 12W
South River **46** 45 52N 79 29W
South Ronaldsay, I. **96** 58 46N 2 58W
S. Sandwich Is. **13** 57 0 S 27 0W
South Saskatchewan, R. **56** 53 15N 105 5W
South Seal, R. **55** 58 48N 98 8W
South Sentinel, I. **128** 11 1N 92 16 E
South Shetland Is. **91** 62 0 S 59 0W
South Shields **94** 54 59N 1 26W
South Sioux City **74** 42 30N 96 30W
South Taranaki Bight **133** 39 40 S 174 5 E
South Thompson, R. **63** 50 40N 120 20W
South Twin I. **36** 53 7N 79 52W
South Twin L. **37** 49 16N 55 47W
South Tyne, R. **94** 54 46N 2 25W
South Uist, I. **96** 57 4N 7 21W
South Wabasca L. **60** 55 55N 113 45W
South Wayne **76** 42 34N 89 53W
South West Africa ■ = Namibia **117** 22 0 S 18 9 E
South West Cape **133** 47 16 S 167 31 E
South West Port Moulton **39** 43 54N 64 49W
South Westminster **66** 49 12N 122 53W
South Whitley **77** 41 5N 85 38W
South Yemen ■ **115** 15 0N 48 0 E
South Yorkshire □ **94** 53 30N 1 20W
Southampton, N.S., Can. **39** 45 35N 64 15W
Southampton, Ont., Can. **46** 44 30N 81 25W
Southampton, U.K. **95** 50 54N 1 23W
Southampton, U.S.A. **71** 40 54N 72 22W
Southampton I. **65** 64 30N 84 0W
Southbank **62** 54 2N 125 46W
Southbridge, N.Z. **133** 43 48 S 172 16 E
Southbridge, U.S.A. **71** 42 4N 72 2W
Southdate **39** 44 40N 63 34W
Southeast C. **67** 62 55N 169 40W
Southend **55** 56 19N 103 14W
Southend-on-Sea **95** 51 32N 0 42 E
Southern Alps **133** 43 41 S 170 11 E
Southern Cross **134** 31 12 S 119 15 E
Southern Indian L. **55** 57 10N 98 30W
Southern Indian Lake **55** 57 0N 99 0W
Southern Ocean **91** 62 0 S 160 0W
Southern Uplands **96** 55 30N 3 3W
Southey **56** 50 56N 104 30W
Southington **71** 41 37N 72 53W
Southold **71** 41 4N 72 26W
Southport, Austral. **135** 27 58 S 153 25 E
Southport, U.K. **94** 53 38N 3 1W
Southport, U.S.A. **73** 33 55N 78 0W
Southwold **95** 52 19N 1 41 E
Soutpansberge **117** 23 0 S 29 30 E
Souvigny **102** 46 33N 3 10 E
Sovereign **56** 51 31N 107 43W
Sovetskaya Gavan **121** 48 50N 140 0 E
Sowden L. **52** 49 32N 91 12W
Sōya-Misaki **132** 45 30N 142 0 E
Soyopa **82** 28 41N 109 37W
Spa **105** 50 29N 5 53 E
Spain ■ **104** 40 0N 5 0W
Spalding, Can. **56** 52 20N 104 30W
Spalding, U.K. **94** 52 47N 0 9W
Spalding, U.S.A. **74** 41 45N 98 27W
Spandau **106** 52 35N 13 7 E
Spangler **70** 40 39N 78 48W
Spaniard's Bay **37** 47 38N 53 20W
Spanish **46** 46 12N 82 20W
Spanish Fork **78** 40 10N 111 37W
Spanish, R. **46** 46 11N 82 19W
Spanish Town **84** 18 0N 77 20W
Sparks **80** 39 30N 119 45W
Sparta, U.S.A. **76** 38 7N 89 42W
Sparta, U.S.A. **77** 43 10N 85 42W
Sparta, Ga., U.S.A. **73** 33 18N 82 59W
Sparta, Wis., U.S.A. **74** 43 55N 91 10W
Sparta = Spárti **109** 37 5N 22 25 E
Spartanburg, Pa., U.S.A. **70** 41 48N 79 43W
Spartanburg, S.C., U.S.A. **73** 35 0N 82 0W
Spárti **109** 37 5N 22 25 E
Spartivento, C., Calabria, Italy **108** 37 56N 16 4 E
Spartivento, C., Sard., Italy **108** 38 52N 8 50 E
Sparwood **61** 49 44N 114 53W
Spassk-Dalniy **121** 44 40N 132 40 E
Spatha Ákra. **109** 35 42N 23 43 E
Spatsizi, R. **54** 57 42N 128 7W
Spear, C. **37** 47 31N 52 37W
Spearfish **74** 44 32N 103 52W
Spearman **75** 36 15N 101 10W
Speed, R. **49** 43 23N 80 22W
Speedway **77** 39 47N 86 15W
Speers **56** 52 43N 107 34W
Speightstown **85** 13 15N 59 39W
Spenard **67** 61 5N 149 50W
Spencer, U.S.A. **77** 39 17N 86 46W
Spencer, Idaho, U.S.A. **78** 44 18N 112 8W
Spencer, Iowa, U.S.A. **74** 43 5N 95 3W
Spencer, Nebr., U.S.A. **74** 42 52N 98 43W
Spencer, N.Y., U.S.A. **71** 42 14N 76 30W
Spencer, W. Va., U.S.A. **72** 38 47N 81 24W
Spencer Bay **65** 69 32N 93 32W
Spencer, C. **135** 35 20 S 136 45 E
Spencer G. **135** 34 0 S 137 20 E
Spencerville, Can. **47** 44 51N 75 33W
Spencerville, U.S.A. **77** 40 43N 84 21W
Spences Bridge **63** 50 25N 121 20W
Spenser Mts. **133** 42 15 S 172 45 E
Sperling **57** 49 30N 97 42W
Sperrin Mts. **97** 54 50N 7 0W
Spessart **106** 50 0N 9 20 E
Spey, R. **96** 57 26N 3 25W
Speyer **106** 49 19N 8 26 E
Speyer, R. **99** 49 18N 7 52 E
Spezia = La Spézia **108** 44 7N 9 49 E
Spézia, La **108** 44 8N 9 50 E
Spickard **76** 40 14N 93 36W
Spillimacheen **54** 51 6N 117 0W
Spin Baldak **123** 31 3N 66 16 E
Spinazzola **108** 40 58N 16 5 E
Spincourt **101** 49 20N 5 39 E
Spirit Lake, Idaho, U.S.A. **78** 47 56N 116 56W
Spirit Lake, Wash., U.S.A. **80** 46 15N 122 9W
Spirit River **60** 55 45N 118 50W
Spiritwood **56** 53 24N 107 33W
Spithead **95** 50 43N 0 56W
Spitzbergen (Svalbard) **17** 78 0N 17 0 E
Split **108** 43 31N 16 26 E
Split L. **55** 56 8N 96 15W
Splügenpass **106** 46 30N 9 20 E
Spoffard **75** 29 10N 100 27W
Spokane **78** 47 45N 117 25W
Spoleto **108** 42 46N 12 47 E
Spoon, R. **76** 40 19N 90 4W
Spooner **74** 45 49N 91 51W
Sporyy Navolok, Mys **120** 75 50N 68 40 E
Spragge **46** 46 15N 82 40W
Sprague, Can. **57** 49 2N 95 38W
Sprague, U.S.A. **78** 47 25N 117 59W
Sprague River **78** 42 28N 121 31W
Spratly, I. **126** 8 20N 112 0 E
Spray **78** 44 56N 119 46W
Spree, R. **106** 52 23N 13 52 E
Spremberg **106** 51 33N 14 21 E
Sprigg's Pt. **37** 47 33N 52 40W
Spring City **78** 39 31N 111 28W
Spring Coulee **61** 49 20N 113 3W
Spring Garden **80** 39 52N 120 47W
Spring Green **76** 43 11N 90 4W
Spring Mts. **79** 36 20N 115 43W
Spring Valley, Can. **56** 49 56N 105 24W
Spring Valley, U.S.A. **76** 41 20N 89 14W
Spring Valley, Minn., U.S.A. **74** 43 40N 92 30W
Spring Valley, N.Y., U.S.A. **71** 41 7N 74 4W
Springbok **117** 29 42 S 17 54 E
Springbrook **49** 43 39N 79 47W
Springburn **133** 43 40 S 171 32 E
Springdale, Can. **37** 49 30N 56 6W
Springdale, Ark., U.S.A. **75** 36 10N 94 5W
Springdale, Wash., U.S.A. **63** 48 1N 117 50W
Springerville **79** 34 10N 109 16W
Springfield, Man., Can. **58** 49 56N 96 56W
Springfield, N.S., Can. **39** 44 38N 64 52W
Springfield, Ont., Can. **46** 42 50N 80 56W
Springfield, N.Z. **133** 43 19 S 171 56 E
Springfield, Colo., U.S.A. **75** 37 26N 102 40W
Springfield, Ill., U.S.A. **76** 39 48N 89 40W
Springfield, Ky., U.S.A. **77** 37 41N 85 13W
Springfield, Mass., U.S.A. **71** 42 8N 72 37W
Springfield, Mo., U.S.A. **75** 37 15N 93 20W
Springfield, Ohio, U.S.A. **72** 39 58N 83 48W
Springfield, Oreg., U.S.A. **78** 44 2N 123 0W
Springfield, Tenn., U.S.A. **73** 36 35N 86 55W
Springfield, Vt., U.S.A. **71** 43 20N 72 30W
Springfield, L. **76** 39 46N 89 36W
Springfontein **117** 30 15 S 25 40 E
Springhill **35** 45 40N 64 4W
Springhouse **63** 51 56N 122 7W
Springs **117** 26 13 S 28 25 E
Springside **56** 51 21N 102 44W
Springsure **135** 24 8 S 148 6 E
Springvale, Can. **48** 43 13N 79 59W
Springvale, U.S.A. **71** 43 28N 70 48W
Springville, Calif., U.S.A. **80** 36 8N 118 49W
Springville, N.Y., U.S.A. **70** 42 31N 78 41W
Springville, Utah, U.S.A. **78** 40 14N 111 35W
Springwater **56** 51 58N 108 23W
Sproat L. **62** 49 17N 125 2W
Spruce-Creek **70** 40 36N 78 9W
Spruce Grove **60** 53 32N 113 55W
Spruce I. **57** 53 5N 100 40W
Spruce Woods Prov. Park **57** 49 43N 99 5W
Sprucedale **46** 45 29N 79 28W
Spryfield **39** 44 37N 63 37W
Spur **75** 33 28N 100 50W
Spurgeon **77** 38 14N 87 15W
Spurn Hd. **94** 53 34N 0 8 E
Spuzzum **63** 49 37N 121 23W
Squamish **63** 49 45N 123 10W
Squamish, R. **63** 49 45N 123 8W
Square Islands **38** 52 47N 55 47W
Squatec **41** 47 53N 68 43W
Squaw Rapids **56** 53 41N 103 21W
Squillace **108** 38 50N 16 26 E
Sragen **127** 7 28 S 110 59 E
Srbija □ **109** 43 30N 21 0 E
Sre Umbell **128** 11 8N 103 46 E
Sredinyy Khrebet **121** 57 0N 160 0 E
Sredne Tambovskoye **121** 50 55N 137 45 E
Srednekolymsk **121** 67 20N 154 40 E
Srednevilyuysk **121** 63 50N 123 5 E
Sredniy Ural, mts. **84** 59 0N 59 0 E
Sremska Mitrovica **109** 44 59N 19 35 E
Sretensk **121** 52 10N 117 40 E
Sri Lanka ■ **124** 7 30N 80 50 E
Srikakulam **125** 18 14N 84 4 E
Srinagar **124** 34 12N 74 50 E
Srnetica **108** 44 25N 16 35 E
Staðarhólskirkja **110** 65 23N 21 58W
Stadlandet **110** 62 10N 5 10 E
Stadskanaal **105** 53 4N 6 48 E
Stafafell **110** 64 25N 14 52W
Staffa, I. **96** 56 26N 6 21W
Stafford, U.K. **96** 52 49N 2 9W
Stafford, U.S.A. **75** 38 0N 98 35W
Stafford □ **94** 52 53N 2 10W
Stafford Springs **71** 41 58N 72 20W
Staines **95** 51 26N 0 30W
Stalingrad = Volgograd **120** 48 40N 44 25 E
Stalybridge **94** 53 29N 1 30W
Stamford, Can. **49** 43 8N 79 6W
Stamford, U.K. **95** 52 39N 0 29W
Stamford, Conn., U.S.A. **71** 41 5N 73 30W
Stamford, Tex., U.S.A. **75** 32 58N 99 50W
Stamping Ground **77** 38 16N 84 41W
Stamps **75** 33 22N 93 30W
Stanberry **74** 40 12N 94 32W
Stanbridge East **43** 45 7N 72 55W
Standard **61** 51 7N 112 59W
Standerton **117** 26 55 S 29 13 E
Standish **72** 43 58N 83 57W
Stanford **78** 47 11N 110 10W
Stanhope **76** 42 17N 93 48W
Stanislaus, R. **80** 37 40N 121 15W
Stanke Dimitrov **109** 42 17N 23 9 E
Stanley, N.B., Can. **39** 46 20N 66 50W
Stanley, Sask., Can. **55** 55 24N 104 22W
Stanley, Falk. Is. **90** 51 40 S 58 0W
Stanley, Idaho, U.S.A. **78** 44 10N 114 59W
Stanley, N.D., U.S.A. **74** 48 20N 102 23W
Stanley, N.Y., U.S.A. **70** 42 48N 77 6W
Stanley, Wis., U.S.A. **74** 44 57N 91 0W
Stanleyville = Kisangani **116** 0 35N 25 15 E
Stann Creek **83** 17 0N 88 20W
Stanovoy Khrebet **121** 55 0N 130 0 E
Stanthorpe **135** 28 36 S 151 59 E
Stanton, Can. **67** 69 45N 128 52W
Stanton, Mich., U.S.A. **46** 43 18N 85 5W
Stanton, Tex., U.S.A. **75** 32 8N 101 45W
Stanwood **80** 48 15N 122 23W
Stapleton **74** 41 30N 100 31W
Star City **56** 52 50N 104 20W
Stara Planina **109** 43 15N 23 0 E
Stara Zagora **109** 42 26N 25 39 E
Staraya Russa **120** 57 58N 31 10 E
Starbuck **57** 49 46N 97 37W
Starbuck I. **15** 5 37 S 155 55W
Stargard **106** 53 29N 13 19 E
Starke **73** 30 0N 82 10W
Starkville, Colo., U.S.A. **75** 37 10N 104 31W
Starkville, Miss., U.S.A. **73** 33 26N 88 48W
Starogard **107** 53 55N 18 30 E
Start Pt., Devon, U.K. **95** 50 13N 3 38W
Start Pt., Orkney, U.K. **95** 59 17N 2 25W
Staryy Kheydzhan **121** 60 0N 144 50 E
State Center **76** 42 1N 93 10W
State College **70** 40 47N 77 49W
State Is. **53** 48 40N 87 0W
Stateline **80** 38 57N 119 56W
Staten I. **71** 40 35N 74 10W
Staten, I. = Los Estados, I. de **90** 54 40 S 64 0W
Statesboro **73** 32 26N 81 46W
Statesville **73** 35 48N 80 51W
Station-du-Côteau, La **43** 45 17N 74 14W
Stauffer **81** 34 45N 119 3W
Staunton, Ill., U.S.A. **76** 39 0N 89 49W
Staunton, Va., U.S.A. **72** 38 7N 79 4W
Stavanger **75** 58 57N 5 40 E
Stave Falls **63** 49 13N 122 22W
Stave L. **63** 49 22N 122 17W
Stavelot **105** 50 23N 5 55 E
Stavely **61** 50 10N 113 38W
Staveren **105** 52 53N 5 22 E
Stavern **111** 59 0N 10 1 E
Stavropol **120** 45 5N 42 0 E
Stawell **136** 37 5 S 142 47 E
Stayner, Can. **70** 44 25N 80 5W
Stayner, Ont., Can. **46** 44 25N 80 5W
Steamboat Springs **78** 40 30N 106 58W
Steele **74** 46 56N 99 52W
Steele, Mt. **64** 61 6N 140 23W
Steelton **70** 40 17N 76 50W
Steelville **76** 37 57N 91 21W
Steen, R. **54** 59 35N 117 10W
Steen River **54** 59 40N 117 12W
Steensby Inl. **65** 70 15N 78 35W
Steenvoorde **101** 50 48N 2 33 E
Steenwijk **105** 52 47N 6 7 E
Steep Pt. **134** 26 08 S 113 8 E
Steep Rock **57** 51 30N 98 48W
Steep Rock Lake **34** 48 50N 91 38W
Stefanie L. = Chew Bahir **116** 4 40N 30 50 E
Stefansson I. **64** 73 20N 105 45W
Steger **77** 41 28N 87 38W
Stehekin **63** 48 19N 120 39W
Steiermark □ **106** 47 26N 15 0 E
Steilacoom **80** 47 10N 122 36W
Steinbach **57** 49 32N 96 40W
Steinkjer **110** 63 59N 11 31 E
Steinkopf **117** 29 15 S 17 48 E
Stellarton **39** 45 32N 62 45W
Stellenbosch **117** 33 58 S 18 50 E
Stelvio, Paso dello **108** 46 32N 10 27 E
Stendal **106** 52 36N 11 50 E
Stephan **74** 48 30N 96 53W
Stephens I. **62** 54 10N 130 45W
Stephenville, Can. **37** 48 31N 58 35W
Stephenville, U.S.A. **75** 32 12N 98 12W
Stephenville Crossing **37** 48 30N 58 26W
Sterlego, Mys **17** 80 30N 90 0 E
Sterling, Colo., U.S.A. **74** 40 40N 103 15W
Sterling, Ill., U.S.A. **76** 41 45N 89 45W
Sterling, Kans., U.S.A. **74** 38 17N 98 13W
Sterling City **75** 31 50N 100 59W
Sterling Run **70** 41 25N 70 12W
Sterlitamak **120** 53 40N 56 0 E
Stettin = Szczecin **106** 53 27N 14 27 E
Stettler **61** 52 19N 112 40W
Steubenville **70** 40 21N 80 39W
Stevens **53** 49 33N 85 49W
Stevens Port **74** 44 32N 89 34W
Stevens Village **67** 66 0N 149 10W
Stevenson **80** 45 42N 121 53W
Stevenson L. **57** 53 55N 96 0W
Steveston **66** 49 8N 123 11W
Steward **76** 41 51N 89 1W
Stewardson **77** 39 16N 88 38W
Stewart, B.C., Can. **54** 55 56N 129 57W
Stewart, N.W.T., Can. **67** 63 19N 139 26W
Stewart, U.S.A. **80** 39 5N 119 46W
Stewart, I. **90** 54 50 S 71 30W
Stewart I. **133** 46 58 S 167 54 E
Stewart Valley **56** 50 36N 107 48W
Stewarts Point **80** 38 39N 123 20W
Stewartsville **76** 39 45N 94 30W
Stewiacke **39** 45 9N 63 22W
Steyr **106** 48 3N 14 25 E
Stickney **39** 46 23N 67 34W

Stigler **Sussex, W. □**

Stigler	75	35 19N	95 6W
Stikine, R.	67	58 0N	131 12W
Stillwater, Minn., U.S.A.	74	45 3N	92 47W
Stillwater, N.Y., U.S.A.	71	42 55N	73 41W
Stillwater, Okla., U.S.A.	75	36 5N	97 3W
Stillwater Mts.	78	39 45N	118 6W
Stilwell	75	35 52N	94 36W
Stimson	34	48 58N	80 30W
Štip	109	41 42N	22 10E
Stiring Wendel	101	49 12N	6 57E
Stirling, Alta., Can.	61	49 30N	112 30W
Stirling, Ont., Can.	47	44 18N	77 33W
Stirling, U.K.	96	56 17N	3 57W
Stirling Ra.	134	34 0S	118 0E
Stittsville	47	45 15N	75 55W
Stockbridge	46	42 27N	84 11W
Stockerau	106	48 24N	16 12E
Stockett	78	47 23N	111 7W
Stockholm, Can.	57	50 39N	102 18W
Stockholm, Sweden	111	59 20N	18 3E
Stockinbingal	136	34 30S	147 53E
Stockport	94	53 25N	2 11W
Stockton, Austral.	136	32 56S	151 47E
Stockton, Calif., U.S.A.	80	38 0N	121 20W
Stockton, Ill., U.S.A.	76	42 21N	90 1W
Stockton, Kans., U.S.A.	74	39 30N	99 20W
Stockton, Mo., U.S.A.	76	37 40N	93 48W
Stockton I.	52	46 57N	90 35W
Stockton-on-Tees	94	54 34N	1 20W
Stockton, Reservoir	76	37 42N	93 46W
Stoke-on-Trent	94	53 1N	2 11W
Stokes Bay, Can.	34	45 0N	81 22W
Stokes Bay, Can.	46	45 0N	81 28W
Stokkseyri	110	63 50N	20 58W
Stokksnes	110	64 14N	14 58W
Stolac	109	43 8N	17 59E
Stolberg	105	50 48N	6 13E
Stolbovaya	121	64 50N	153 50E
Stonecliffe	34	46 13N	77 56W
Stoneham	41	47 0N	71 22W
Stonehaven	96	56 58N	2 11W
Stonehenge	95	51 9N	1 45W
Stoner	63	53 38N	122 40W
Stonewall	57	50 10N	97 19W
Stoney Creek	48	43 14N	79 45W
Stonington	76	39 44N	89 12W
Stony L., Man., Can.	55	58 51N	98 40W
Stony L., Ont., Can.	47	44 30N	78 0W
Stony Mountain	57	50 5N	97 13W
Stony Plain	60	53 32N	114 0W
Stony Rapids	55	59 16N	105 50W
Stony River	67	61 48N	156 48W
Stony Tunguska = Tunguska, Nizhmaya	121	64 0N	95 0E
Stonyford	80	39 23N	122 33W
Stora Lulevatten	110	67 10N	19 30E
Stora Sjøfallet	110	67 29N	18 40E
Storavan	110	65 45N	18 10E
Store Bælt	111	55 20N	11 0E
Storen	110	63 3N	10 18E
Storkerson B.	64	72 56N	124 50W
Storm B.	135	43 10S	147 30E
Storm Lake	74	42 35N	95 5W
Stormberg	117	31 16S	26 17E
Stormy L.	52	49 23N	92 18W
Stornoway	96	58 12N	6 23W
Storsjön	110	62 50N	13 8E
Storuman, L.	110	65 5N	17 10E
Story City	76	42 11N	93 36W
Stouffville	50	43 58N	79 15W
Stoughton, Can.	56	49 40N	103 0W
Stoughton, U.S.A.	76	42 55N	89 13W
Stour, R., Dorset, U.K.	95	50 48N	2 7W
Stour, R., Heref. & Worcs., U.K.	94	52 25N	2 13W
Stour, R., Kent, U.K.	95	51 15N	0 57E
Stour, R., Suffolk, U.K.	95	51 55N	1 5E
Stourbridge	95	52 28N	2 8W
Stout, L.	55	52 0N	94 40W
Stove Pipe Wells Village	81	36 35N	117 11W
Stowmarket	95	52 11N	1 0E
Strabane	97	54 50N	7 28W
Strabane □	97	54 45N	7 25W
Strachan, Mt.	66	49 25N	123 12W
Strahan	135	42 9S	145 20E
Stralsund	106	54 17N	13 5E
Strand	117	34 9S	18 48E
Strangford	97	54 23N	5 34W
Strangford, L.	97	54 30N	5 37W
Stranraer, Can.	56	51 43N	108 29W
Stranraer, U.K.	96	54 54N	5 0W
Strasbourg, Can.	56	51 4N	104 55W
Strasbourg, France	101	48 35N	7 42E
Strasburg	74	46 12N	100 9W
Stratford, Austral.	136	37 59S	147 7E
Stratford, Can.	46	43 23N	81 0W
Stratford, N.Z.	133	39 20S	174 19E
Stratford, Calif., U.S.A.	80	36 10N	119 49W
Stratford, Conn., U.S.A.	71	41 13N	73 8W
Stratford, Tex., U.S.A.	75	36 20N	102 3W
Stratford-on-Avon	95	52 12N	1 42W
Strath Spey	96	57 15N	3 40W
Strathclyde □	96	56 0N	4 50W
Strathcona Prov. Park	62	49 38N	125 40W
Strathmore, Can.	61	51 5N	113 25W
Strathmore, U.K.	96	56 40N	3 4W
Strathmore, U.S.A.	80	36 9N	119 4W
Strathnaver	63	53 20N	122 33W
Strathroy	46	42 58N	81 38W
Strathy Pt.	96	58 35N	4 0W
Stratton, Can.	52	48 41N	94 10W
Stratton, U.S.A.	74	39 20N	102 36W
Straumnes	110	66 26N	23 8W
Strawberry Hill	66	49 8N	122 53W
Strawberry Point	76	42 41N	91 32W
Strawberry Res.	78	40 0N	111 0W
Strawn	75	32 36N	98 30W
Streaky Bay	134	32 48S	134 13E
Streator	77	41 9N	88 52W
Streetsville	50	43 35N	79 42W
Strelka	121	58 5N	93 10E
Strezhevoy	120	60 42N	77 34E
Strezhnoye	120	57 45N	84 2E
Strezlecki	136	38 16S	145 50E
Strómboli, I.	108	38 48N	15 12E
Strome	61	52 48N	112 4W
Stromeferry	96	57 20N	5 33W
Ströms Vattudal L.	110	64 0N	15 30E
Strömstad	111	58 55N	11 15E
Stromsund	110	63 51N	15 35E
Strongfield	56	51 20N	106 35W
Stronghurst	76	40 45N	91 55W
Strongs Corners	46	46 18N	84 55W
Stronsay, I.	96	59 8N	2 38W
Stroud, Can.	46	44 19N	79 37W
Stroud, U.K.	95	51 44N	2 12W
Stroud Road	136	32 18S	151 57E
Stroudsberg	71	40 59N	75 15W
Struer	111	56 30N	8 35E
Struma, R.	109	41 50N	23 18E
Strumica	109	41 28N	22 41E
Struthers, Can.	53	48 41N	85 51W
Struthers, U.S.A.	70	41 6N	80 38W
Stryker	61	48 40N	114 44W
Strzelecki Creek	135	29 37S	139 59E
Stuart, U.S.A.	76	41 30N	94 19W
Stuart, Fla., U.S.A.	73	27 11N	80 12W
Stuart, Nebr., U.S.A.	74	42 39N	99 8W
Stuart I.	67	63 55N	164 50W
Stuart L.	54	54 30N	124 30W
Stuart, R.	54	54 0N	123 35W
Stuart Range	134	29 10S	134 56E
Stuart Town	136	32 44S	149 4E
Stull, L.	55	54 24N	92 34W
Stung-Treng	128	13 31N	105 58E
Stupart, R.	55	56 0N	93 25W
Sturgeon B.	57	52 0N	97 50W
Sturgeon Bay	72	44 52N	87 20W
Sturgeon Cr.	58	49 52N	97 16W
Sturgeon Falls	46	46 25N	79 57W
Sturgeon L., Alta., Can.	60	55 6N	117 32W
Sturgeon L., Ont., Can.	47	44 28N	78 43W
Sturgeon L., Ont., Can.	52	50 0N	90 45W
Sturgeon L., Ont., Can.	52	48 29N	91 38W
Sturgeon, R., Alta., Can.	59	53 46N	113 10W
Sturgeon, R., Ont., Can.	46	46 35N	80 11W
Sturgeon, R., Sask., Can.	56	53 12N	105 52W
Sturgis, Can.	56	51 56N	102 36W
Sturgis, Mich., U.S.A.	77	41 50N	85 25W
Sturgis, S.D., U.S.A.	74	44 25N	103 30W
Sturt, R.	134	34 58S	138 31E
Stutterheim	117	32 33S	27 28E
Stuttgart, Ger.	106	48 46N	9 10E
Stuttgart, U.S.A.	75	34 30N	91 33W
Stuyvesant	71	42 23N	73 45W
Stykkishólmur	110	65 2N	22 40W
Suakin	115	19 0N	37 20E
Suancheng	131	30 58N	118 57E
Süanen	131	30 0N	109 30E
Suanhan	131	31 17N	107 46E
Suanhwa	130	40 35N	115 0E
Suao	131	24 32N	121 42E
Suaqui	82	29 12N	109 41W
Suay Rieng	128	11 9N	105 45E
Subang	127	7 30S	107 45E
Subansiri, R.	125	26 48N	93 50E
Subi, I.	126	2 58N	108 50E
Subotica	109	46 6N	19 29E
Success	56	50 28N	108 6W
Suceava	107	47 38N	26 16E
Suchil	82	23 38N	103 55W
Suchitoto	84	13 56N	89 0W
Süchow	131	34 10N	117 20E
Sucio, R.	86	6 40N	77 0W
Suck, R.	97	53 17N	8 10W
Sucre, Boliv.	86	19 0S	65 15W
Sucre, Venez.	86	10 25N	64 5W
Sucre □, Colomb.	86	8 50N	75 40W
Sucre □, Venez.	86	10 25N	63 30W
Sucunduri, R.	86	6 20N	58 35W
Sud-Ouest, Pte. du	38	49 23N	63 36W
Sud, Pte.	38	49 3N	62 14W
Sudan ■	115	15 0N	30 0E
Sudan, The	112	11 0N	9 0E
Sudbury	46	46 30N	81 0W
Sudetan Mts. = Sudety	106	50 20N	16 45E
Sudety	106	50 20N	16 45E
Sudirman, Pengunungan	127	4 30N	137 0E
Sueca	104	39 12N	0 21W
Sueur, Le	74	44 25N	93 52W
Suez = El Suweis	115	29 58N	32 31E
Suez Canal	115	31 0N	32 20E
Sufaina	122	23 6N	40 44E
Suffield	61	50 12N	111 10W
Suffolk	72	36 47N	76 33W
Suffolk □	95	52 16N	1 0E
Suffolk, East, □	95	52 16N	1 10E
Suffolk, West, □	95	52 16N	0 45E
Sufu	129	39 44N	75 53E
Sufuk	123	23 50N	51 50E
Sugar City	74	38 18N	103 38W
Sugar Cr.	76	40 12N	89 41W
Sugar L.	63	50 24N	118 30W
Sugar, R., Ill., U.S.A.	76	42 25N	89 15W
Sugar, R., Ind., U.S.A.	77	39 50N	87 23W
Sugarloaf Head	37	47 37N	52 39W
Sugarloaf Pt.	136	32 22S	152 30E
Suggi L.	56	54 22N	102 47W
Suhār	123	24 20N	56 40E
Suhbaatar	130	50 17N	106 10E
Suhsien	131	33 40N	117 0E
Suichung	130	40 20N	120 20E
Suichwan	131	26 26N	114 32E
Suifenho	130	44 30N	131 2E
Suihsien	131	31 58N	113 20E
Suihwa	130	46 40N	126 57E
Suiknai	131	21 17N	110 19E
Suining	131	26 11N	109 5E
Suiping	131	33 15N	114 6E
Suippes	101	49 8N	4 30E
Suir, R.	97	52 31N	7 59W
Suiteh	130	37 35N	110 5E
Sukabumi	127	6 56S	106 57E
Sukadana	126	1 10S	110 0E
Sukandja	126	2 28S	110 25E
Sukarnapura = Jajapura	127	2 28N	140 38E
Sukarno, G. = Jaja, Puncak	127	3 57S	137 17E
Sukhona, R.	120	60 30N	45 0E
Sukhumi	120	43 0N	41 0E
Sukkur	124	27 50N	68 46E
Sukkur Barrage	124	27 50N	68 45E
Sukunka, R.	54	55 45N	121 15W
Sula, Kepulauan	127	1 45S	125 0E
Sulaco, R.	84	15 2N	87 44W
Sulaiman Range	124	30 30N	69 50E
Sulawesi □	127	2 0S	120 0E
Sulawesi, I.	127	2 0S	120 0E
Sulina	107	45 10N	29 40E
Sulitälma	110	67 17N	17 28E
Sulitjelma	110	61 7N	16 8E
Sullana	86	5 0S	80 45W
Sullivan, B.C., Can.	66	49 7N	122 48W
Sullivan, Qué., Can.	40	48 7N	77 50W
Sullivan, Ill., U.S.A.	77	39 40N	88 40W
Sullivan, Ind., U.S.A.	77	39 5N	87 26W
Sullivan, Mo., U.S.A.	76	38 10N	91 10W
Sullivan Bay	62	50 55N	126 50W
Sullivan L.	61	52 0N	112 0W
Sully	76	41 34N	92 50W
Sully-sur-Loire	101	47 45N	2 20E
Sulphur, La., U.S.A.	75	30 20N	93 22W
Sulphur, Okla., U.S.A.	75	34 35N	97 0W
Sulphur Pt.	54	60 56N	114 48W
Sulphur Springs	75	33 5N	95 30W
Sulphur Springs, Cr.	75	32 50N	102 8W
Sultan, Can.	53	47 36N	82 47W
Sultan, U.S.A.	80	47 51N	121 49W
Sultanpur	125	26 18N	82 10E
Sulu Arch.	127	6 0N	121 0E
Sulu Sea	127	8 0N	120 0E
Suluq	115	31 44N	20 14E
Sulzbach-Rosenburg	105	49 30N	11 46E
Sumalata	127	1 0N	122 37E
Sumampa	88	29 25S	63 29W
Sumatera, I.	126	0 40N	100 20E
Sumatera Selatan □	126	3 30S	104 0E
Sumatera Tengah □	126	1 0S	100 0E
Sumatera Utara □	126	2 0N	99 0E
Sumatra	78	46 45N	107 37W
Sumatra = Sumatera	126	0 40N	100 20E
Sumba, I.	127	9 45S	119 35E
Sumba, Selat	127	9 0S	118 40E
Sumbawa	126	8 26S	117 30E
Sumbawa, I.	127	8 34S	117 17E
Sümber	129	46 21N	108 25E
Sumbing, mt.	127	7 19S	110 3E
Sumburgh Hd.	96	59 52N	1 17W
Sumedang	127	6 49S	107 56E
Sumenep	127	7 3S	113 51E
Summer L.	78	42 50N	120 50W
Summerford	37	49 29N	54 47W
Summerland	63	49 32N	119 41W
Summerside, Newf., Can.	37	48 59N	57 59W
Summerside, P.E.I., Can.	39	46 24N	63 47W
Summerstown	43	45 4N	74 32W
Summerville, Newf., Can.	37	48 27N	53 33W
Summerville, Ont., Can.	50	43 37N	79 34W
Summerville, Ga., U.S.A.	73	34 30N	85 20W
Summerville, S.C., U.S.A.	73	33 2N	80 11W
Summit, Can.	34	47 50N	72 20W
Summit, U.S.A.	67	63 20N	149 20W
Summit Lake	54	54 20N	122 40W
Summit Pk.	79	37 20N	106 48W
Summitt	77	41 48N	87 48W
Sumner, U.S.A.	77	38 42N	87 53W
Sumner, Iowa, U.S.A.	76	42 49N	92 7W
Sumner, Wash., U.S.A.	80	47 12N	122 14W
Sumperk	106	49 59N	17 0E
Sumter	73	33 55N	80 10W
Sumy	120	50 57N	34 50E
Sun City	81	33 41N	117 11W
Sun Prairie	76	43 11N	89 13W
Sunart, L.	96	56 42N	5 43W
Sunburst	61	48 56N	111 59W
Sunbury, Can.	66	49 9N	122 59W
Sunbury, U.S.A.	71	40 50N	76 46W
Sunchales	88	30 58S	61 35W
Suncho Corral	88	27 55S	63 14W
Sunchŏn	131	34 52N	127 31E
Suncook	71	43 8N	71 27W
Sunda Ketjil, Kepulauan	126	7 30S	117 0E
Sunda, Selat	126	6 20S	105 30E
Sundance	74	44 27N	104 27W
Sundarbans, The	125	22 0N	89 0E
Sundargarh	125	22 10N	84 5E
Sunderland, Can.	47	44 16N	79 4W
Sunderland, U.K.	94	54 54N	1 22W
Sunderland, U.S.A.	71	42 27N	72 36W
Sundown	57	49 6N	96 16W
Sundre	61	51 49N	114 38W
Sundridge	46	45 45N	79 25W
Sundsvall	110	62 23N	17 17E
Sung-hua Hu	130	43 0N	127 0E
Sung-hua Kiang (Sungari)	130	47 0N	130 50E
Sungaipakning	126	1 19N	102 0E
Sungaipenuh	126	2 1S	101 20E
Sungaitiram	126	0 45S	117 8E
Sungari = Sung-hua Kiang	130	47 0N	130 50E
Sungei Lembing	128	2 53N	103 4E
Sungei Patani	128	5 38N	100 29E
Sungei Siput	128	4 51N	101 6E
Sungguminasa	127	5 17S	119 30E
Sunghsien	131	34 10N	112 10E
Sungkiang	131	31 0N	121 20E
Sungpan	129	32 50N	103 20E
Sungtao	131	28 12N	109 12E
Sungtzu	131	30 25N	111 46E
Sungtzu Hu	131	30 10N	111 45E
Sungurlu	122	40 12N	34 21E
Sungyang	131	28 16N	119 29E
Sunny Corner	39	46 57N	65 49W
Sunnybrae	39	45 24N	62 30W
Sunnyside, Can.	37	47 51N	53 55W
Sunnyside, Utah, U.S.A.	78	39 40N	110 24W
Sunnyside, Wash., U.S.A.	78	46 24N	120 2W
Sunnyvale	80	37 23N	122 2W
Sunray	75	36 1N	101 47W
Sunshine	136	37 48S	144 52E
Suntar	121	62 15N	117 30E
Sunwapta Pass	61	52 13N	117 10W
Supai	79	36 14N	112 44W
Supaul	125	26 10N	86 40E
Superior, Ariz., U.S.A.	79	33 19N	111 9W
Superior, Mont., U.S.A.	78	47 15N	114 57W
Superior, Nebr., U.S.A.	74	40 3N	98 2W
Superior, Wis., U.S.A.	52	46 45N	92 5W
Superior, L.	69	47 40N	87 0W
Suphan Buri	128	14 30N	100 10E
Supu	131	27 57N	110 15E
Supung Hu	130	40 40N	125 0E
Sūr, Leb.	115	33 19N	35 16E
Sūr, Oman	123	22 34N	59 32E
Sur, Pt.	80	36 18N	121 54W
Sura, R.	120	55 30N	46 20E
Surabaja = Surabaya	127	7 17S	112 45E
Surabaya	127	7 17S	112 45E
Surakarta	127	7 35S	110 48E
Surat	124	21 12N	72 55E
Surat Thani	128	9 6N	99 14E
Suratgarh	124	29 18N	73 55E
Sûre, R.	105	49 51N	6 6E
Surf	81	34 41N	120 36W
Surf Inlet	54	53 8N	128 50W
Surgères	102	46 7N	0 47W
Suri	125	23 50N	87 34E
Suriapet	124	17 10N	79 40E
Surin	128	14 50N	103 34E
Surinam ■	87	4 0N	56 15W
Suriname, R.	87	4 30N	55 30W
Surprise L.	54	59 40N	133 15W
Surprise, L.	40	49 20N	74 55W
Surrey	66	49 12N	122 51W
Surrey □, Can.	66	49 9N	122 46W
Surrey □, U.K.	95	51 16N	0 30W
Surrey Centre	66	49 7N	122 45W
Surtsey	110	63 20N	20 30W
Suruga-Wan	132	34 45N	138 30E
Surup	127	6 27N	126 17E
Surur	123	23 20N	58 10E
Susa	108	45 8N	7 3E
Süsangerd	122	31 35N	48 20E
Susanino	121	52 50N	140 14E
Susanville	78	40 28N	120 40W
Susquehanna Depot	71	41 55N	75 36W
Susquehanna, R.	71	41 50N	76 20W
Susques	88	23 35S	66 25W
Sussex, Can.	39	45 45N	65 37W
Sussex, U.S.A.	71	41 12N	74 38W
Sussex, E. □	95	51 0N	0 0E
Sussex, W. □	95	51 0N	0 30W

Sustut, R Taohsien

Sustut, R.	54	56 20N	127 30W
Susuman	121	62 47N	148 10 E
Susuna	127	3 20 S	133 25 E
Sutherland, Can.	55	52 15N	106 40W
Sutherland, S. Afr.	117	32 33 S	20 40 E
Sutherland, U.S.A.	74	41 12N	101 11W
Sutherland Falls	133	44 48 S	167 46 E
Sutherland Pt.	135	28 15 S	153 35 E
Sutherlin	78	43 28N	123 16W
Sutlej, R.	124	30 0N	73 0 E
Sutter	80	39 10N	121 45W
Sutter Creek	80	38 24N	120 48W
Sutton, Can.	71	45 8N	72 36W
Sutton, Ont., Can.	46	44 18N	79 22W
Sutton, Qué., Can.	41	45 6N	72 37W
Sutton, U.S.A.	74	40 40N	97 50W
Sutton-in-Ashfield	94	52 8N	1 16W
Sutton, R.	34	55 15N	83 45W
Sutwik I.	67	56 35N	157 10W
Suva	133	17 40 S	178 8 E
Suva Planina	109	43 10N	22 5 E
Suvorov Is.	15	13 15 S	163 30W
Suwałki	107	54 8N	22 59 E
Suwannee, R.	73	30 0N	83 0W
Suwanose Jima	132	29 26N	129 30 E
Suwen	131	20 27N	110 2 E
Suwŏn	130	37 17N	127 1 E
Suyung	131	28 12N	105 10 E
Suze, La	100	47 54N	0 2 E
Suzuka	132	34 55N	136 36 E
Svalbard, Arctica	17	78 0N	17 0 E
Svalbard, Iceland	110	66 12N	15 43W
Svanvik	110	69 38N	30 3 E
Svappavaari	110	67 40N	21 03 E
Svartenhuk Pen.	65	71 50N	54 30W
Svartisen	110	66 40N	14 16 E
Svealand □	111	59 55N	15 0 E
Sveg	111	62 2N	14 21 E
Svendborg	111	55 4N	10 35 E
Sverdlovsk	120	56 50N	60 30 E
Sverdrup Chan.	65	79 56N	96 25W
Sverdrup Is.	65	79 0N	97 0W
Svishov	109	43 36N	25 23 E
Svobodnyy	121	51 20N	128 0 E
Svolvær	110	68 15N	14 34 E
Swain Reefs	135	21 45 S	152 20 E
Swainsboro	73	32 38N	82 22W
Swakopmund	117	22 37 S	14 30 E
Swale, R.	94	54 18N	1 20W
Swan Hill	136	35 20 S	143 33 E
Swan Hills	60	54 42N	115 24W
Swan Islands	84	17 22N	83 57W
Swan L.	57	52 30N	100 40W
Swan, R., Austral.	134	32 3 S	115 35 E
Swan, R., Alta., Can.	60	55 30N	115 18W
Swan, R., Man., Can.	57	52 30N	100 45W
Swan River	57	52 10N	101 16W
Swanage	95	50 36N	1 59W
Swansea, Austral.	136	33 3 S	151 35 E
Swansea, Can.	50	43 38N	79 28W
Swansea, U.K.	95	51 37N	3 57W
Swartz Creek	46	42 58N	83 50W
Swastika	34	48 7N	80 6W
Swatow = Shantow	131	23 25N	116 40 E
Swaziland ■	117	26 30 S	31 30 E
Sweden ■	111	67 0N	15 0 E
Sweet Home	78	44 26N	122 38W
Sweet Springs	76	38 58N	93 25W
Sweetwater, Nev., U.S.A.	80	38 27N	119 9W
Sweetwater, Tex., U.S.A.	75	32 30N	100 28W
Sweetwater, R.	78	42 31N	107 30W
Swellendam	117	34 1 S	20 26 E
Swidnica	106	50 50N	16 30 E
Swiebodzin	106	52 15N	15 37 E
Swift Current, Newf., Can.	37	47 53N	54 12W
Swift Current, Sask., Can.	56	50 20N	107 45W
Swiftcurrent Cr.	56	50 38N	107 44W
Swilly L.	97	55 12N	7 35W
Swindle, I.	62	52 30N	128 35W
Swindon	95	51 33N	1 47W
Swinemünde = Świnouśćje	106	53 54N	14 16 E
Świnouśćje	106	53 54N	14 16 E
Switzerland ■	106	46 30N	8 0 E
Swords	97	53 27N	6 15W
Sydenham, R.	46	42 33N	82 25W
Sydney, Austral.	136	33 53 S	151 10 E
Sydney, Can.	39	46 7N	60 7W
Sydney, U.S.A.	74	41 12N	103 0W
Sydney L.	52	50 41N	94 25W
Sydney Mines	39	46 18N	60 15W
Sydney River	39	46 7N	60 13W
Sydproven	17	60 30N	45 35W
Syktyvkar	120	61 45N	50 40 E
Sylacauga	73	33 10N	86 15W
Sylarna, Mt.	110	63 2N	12 11 E
Sylhet	125	24 54N	91 52 E
Sylvan L.	61	52 21N	114 10W
Sylvan Lake	61	52 20N	114 10W
Sylvania, Can.	56	52 42N	104 0W
Sylvania, U.S.A.	77	41 43N	83 42W
Sylvania, Ga., U.S.A.	73	32 45N	81 37W
Sylvester, Can.	60	55 0N	119 41W
Sylvester, U.S.A.	73	31 31N	83 50W
Sym	120	60 20N	87 50 E
Symón	82	24 42N	102 35W
Syr Darya	120	45 0N	65 0 E
Syracuse, U.S.A.	77	41 28N	85 47W
Syracuse, Kans., U.S.A.	75	38 0N	101 40W
Syracuse, N.Y., U.S.A.	71	43 4N	76 11W
Syria ■	122	35 0N	38 0 E
Syrian Des.	122	31 30N	40 0 E
Syuldzhyukyor	121	63 25N	113 40 E
Syzran	120	53 12N	48 30 E
Szczecin	106	53 27N	14 27 E
Szczecinek	106	53 43N	16 41 E
Szechwan □	129	30 15N	103 15 E
Szeged	107	46 16N	20 10 E
Székesfehérvár	107	47 15N	18 25 E
Szekszárd	107	46 22N	18 42 E
Szemao	129	22 50N	101 0 E
Szenan	131	27 50N	108 25 E
Szengen, Kwangsi-Chuang, China	131	23 20N	108 5 E
Szengen, Kwangsi-Chuang, China	131	24 50N	108 0 E
Szentes	107	46 39N	20 21 E
Szeping	130	43 10N	124 18 E
Szeshui	94	34 50N	113 20 E
Szewui	131	23 30N	112 35 E
Szolnok	107	47 10N	20 15 E
Szombathely	106	47 14N	16 38 E

T

Ta Fengman	130	43 45N	126 35 E
Ta Hinghan Ling	129	48 0N	121 0 E
Ta Liang Shan	129	28 0N	103 0 E
Tabacal	88	23 15 S	64 15W
Tabaco	127	13 22N	123 44 E
Tābah	122	26 55N	42 30 E
Tabas, Khorasan, Iran	123	32 48N	60 12 E
Tabas, Khorasan, Iran	123	33 35N	56 55 E
Tabasará, Serranía de	84	8 35N	81 40W
Tabasco □	83	17 45N	93 30W
Tabatière, La	37	50 50N	58 58W
Tabatinga	86	4 11 S	69 58W
Tabatinga, Serra da	87	10 30 S	44 0W
Taber	61	49 47N	112 8W
Tablas, I.	127	12 25N	122 2 E
Table B.	36	53 40N	56 25W
Table Grove	76	40 20N	90 27W
Table Mt.	117	34 0 S	18 22 E
Tábor	106	49 25N	14 39 E
Tabora	116	5 2 S	32 57 E
Tabrīz	122	38 7N	46 20 E
Tabūk	122	28 30N	36 25 E
Tacámbaro	82	19 14N	101 28W
Tacarigua, L. de	86	11 3N	68 25W
Tachick L.	62	53 57N	124 12W
Tachintala	130	45 13N	121 37 E
Tachira	86	8 7N	72 21W
Tachira □	86	8 7N	72 15W
Tachu	131	30 45N	107 13 E
Tacloban	127	11 15N	124 58 E
Tacna	86	18 0 S	70 20W
Tacoma	80	47 15N	122 30W
Tacuarembó	89	31 45 S	56 0W
Tademaït, Plateau du	114	28 30N	2 30 E
Tadmor, N.Z.	133	41 27 S	172 45 E
Tadmor, Syria	122	34 30N	37 55 E
Tado	86	5 16N	76 32W
Tadoule, L.	55	58 36N	98 20W
Tadoussac	41	48 11N	69 42W
Tadzhik S.S.R. □	120	35 30N	70 0 E
Taegu	130	35 50N	128 37 E
Taejŏn	130	36 20N	127 28 E
Taerh Hu	130	43 25N	116 40 E
Taf, R.	95	51 55N	4 36W
Tafalla	104	42 30N	1 41W
Tafermaar	127	6 47 S	134 10 E
Tafí Viejo	88	26 43 S	65 17W
Taft, Phil.	127	11 57N	125 30 E
Taft, Calif.., U.S.A.	81	35 10N	119 28W
Taft, Tex., U.S.A.	75	27 58N	97 23W
Taga Dzong	125	27 5N	90 0 E
Taganrog	120	47 12N	38 50 E
Tagbilaran	127	9 39N	123 51 E
Tagish	54	60 19N	134 16W
Tagish L.	67	60 10N	134 20W
Tagliamento, R.	108	45 38N	13 5 E
Tagua, La	86	0 3N	74 40W
Taguatinga	87	12 26 S	46 26W
Tagum (Hijo)	127	7 33N	125 53 E
Tagus = Tajo, R.	104	39 44N	5 50W
Tahahbala, I.	126	0 30 S	98 30 E
Tahakopa	133	46 30 S	169 23 E
Tahan, Gunong	128	4 45N	102 25 E
Tahcheng	129	46 50N	83 1 E
Taheiho	130	50 10N	127 20 E
Tāherī	123	27 43N	52 20 E
Tahiti, I.	15	17 37 S	149 27W
Tahoe	80	39 12N	120 9W
Tahoe, L.	80	39 0N	120 9W
Taholah	80	47 21N	124 17W
Tahoua	114	14 57N	5 16 E
Tahsien	131	31 17N	107 30 E
Tahsis	62	49 55N	126 40W
Tahulandang, I.	127	2 27N	125 23 E
Tahuna	127	3 45N	125 30 E
Tai Hu	131	31 10N	120 0 E
Taian	130	36 20N	117 0 E
Taichow	131	32 30N	119 50 E
Taichow Wan.	131	28 55N	121 10 E
Taichung	131	24 10N	120 35 E
Taieri, R.	133	46 3 S	170 12 E
Taihan Shan	130	36 0N	114 0 E
Taihape	133	39 41 S	175 48 E
Taiho	131	26 50N	114 54 E
Taihsien	130	39 9N	112 58 E
Taihu	131	30 30N	116 25 E
Taikang	131	34 3N	115 0 E
Taikiang	131	26 45N	108 44 E
Taiku	130	37 46N	112 28 E
Taikung	131	26 50N	108 40 E
Tailagein Shara	130	44 10N	106 0 E
Tailai	129	46 28N	123 18 E
Taīma	122	27 35N	38 45 E
Taimyr = Taymyr	121	75 0N	100 0 E
Taimyr, Oz.	121	74 20N	102 0 E
Tain	96	57 49N	4 4W
Tainan	131	23 0N	120 15 E
Taínaron, Ákra	109	36 22N	22 27 E
Taining	131	27 0N	117 15 E
Taipei	131	25 2N	121 30 E
Taiping	128	4 51N	100 44 E
Taishan	131	27 29N	119 34 E
Taitao, Pen. de	90	46 30 S	75 0W
Taitung	131	22 43N	121 4 E
Taivalkoski	110	65 33N	28 12 E
Taiwan (Formosa) ■	131	23 30N	121 0 E
Taiwara	123	33 30N	64 24 E
Taïyetos Óros	109	37 0N	22 23 E
Taiyüan	130	38 0N	112 30 E
Tajicaringa	82	23 15N	104 44W
Tajitos	82	30 58N	112 18W
Tajo, R.	104	40 35N	1 52W
Tajumulco, Volcán de	83	15 20N	91 50W
Tak	128	16 52N	99 8 E
Takada	132	37 7N	138 15 E
Takaka	133	40 51N	172 50 E
Takamatsu	132	34 20N	134 5 E
Takanabe	132	32 8N	131 30 E
Takaoka	132	36 40N	137 0 E
Takapuna	133	36 47 S	174 47 E
Takasaki	132	36 20N	139 0 E
Takatsuki	132	34 51N	135 37 E
Takaungu	116	3 38 S	39 52 E
Takayama	132	36 18N	137 11 E
Takefu	132	35 50N	136 10 E
Takeo	128	10 59N	104 47 E
Tākestān	122	36 0N	49 50 E
Takhing	131	23 10N	111 45 E
Takingeun	126	4 45N	96 50 E
Takiyuak L.	64	65 30N	113 5W
Takla L.	54	55 15N	125 45W
Takla Landing	54	55 30N	125 50W
Takla Makan	129	39 0N	83 0 E
Taku, R.	54	58 30N	133 50W
Takushan	130	39 55N	123 30 E
Takysie Lake	62	53 53N	125 53W
Tala, Uruguay	89	34 21 S	55 46W
Tala, U.S.S.R.	121	72 40N	113 30 E
Talachih	130	36 45N	105 0 E
Talagante	88	33 40 S	70 50W
Talai	130	45 30N	124 20W
Talamanca, Cordillera de	84	9 20N	83 20W
Talara	86	4 30 S	81 10 E
Talas	120	42 45N	72 0 E
Talaud, Kepulauan	127	4 30N	127 10 E
Talavera de la Reina	104	39 55N	4 46W
Talayan	127	6 52N	124 24 E
Talbot, C.	134	13 48 S	126 43 E
Talbot L.	57	54 0N	99 55W
Talbragar, R.	136	32 5 S	149 15 E
Talca	88	35 20 S	71 46W
Talca □	88	35 20 S	71 46W
Talcahuano	88	36 40 S	73 10W
Talcher	125	20 55N	85 3 E
Taldy Kurgan	120	45 10N	78 45 E
Talesh, Kūhā-Ye	122	39 0N	48 30 E
Talguppa	124	14 10N	74 45 E
Tali, Shensi, China	131	34 48N	109 48 E
Tali, Yunnan, China	129	25 45N	100 5 E
Taliabu, I.	127	1 45 S	125 0 E
Taliang Shan	130	28 0N	102 0 E
Talien, (Dairen)	130	38 53N	121 37 E
Talihina	75	34 45N	95 1W
Taling Sung	128	15 5N	99 11 E
Taliwang	126	8 50 S	116 55 E
Talkeetna	67	62 20N	150 0W
Talkeetna Mts.	67	62 20N	149 0W
Talladega	73	33 28N	86 2W
Tallahassee	73	30 25N	84 15W
Tallangatta	136	36 15 S	147 10 E
Tallering Pk	134	28 6 S	115 37 E
Tallinn (Reval)	120	59 29N	24 58 E
Tallulah	75	32 25N	91 12W
Talmage	55	49 46N	103 40W
Talmont	102	46 27N	1 37W
Talpa de Allende	82	20 23N	104 51W
Taltal	88	25 23 S	70 40W
Taltson L.	55	61 30N	110 15W
Taltson R.	54	61 24N	112 46W
Talunkwan I.	62	52 50N	131 45W
Talyawalka Cr.	136	32 28 S	142 22 E
Tama	76	41 56N	92 37W
Tama Abu, Pegunungan	126	3 10N	115 0 E
Tamalameque	86	8 52N	73 49W
Tamale	114	9 22N	0 50W
Tamano	132	34 35N	133 59 E
Tamanrasset	114	22 56N	5 30 E
Tamaqua	71	40 46N	75 58W
Tamar, R.	95	50 33N	4 15W
Támara	86	5 50N	72 10W
Tamaroa	76	38 8N	89 14W
Tamatave	117	18 10 S	49 25 E
Tamaulipas □	83	24 0N	99 0W
Tamaulipas, Sierra de	83	23 30N	98 20W
Tamazula	82	24 55N	106 58W
Tamazunchale	83	21 16N	98 47W
Tambelan, Kepulauan	126	1 0N	107 30 E
Tambo de Mora	86	13 30 S	76 20W
Tambora, G.	126	8 12 S	118 5 E
Tambov	120	52 45N	41 20 E
Tambuku, G.	127	7 8 S	113 40 E
Tame	86	6 28N	71 44W
Tamega, R.	104	41 12N	8 5W
Tamenglong	125	25 0N	93 35 E
Tamerfors	111	61 30N	23 50 E
Tamgak, Mts.	114	19 12N	8 35 E
Tamiahua, Laguna de	83	21 30N	97 30W
Tamil Nadu □	124	11 0N	77 0 E
Taming	130	36 20N	115 10 E
Tammisaari (Ekenäs)	111	60 0N	23 26 E
Tampa	73	27 57N	82 30W
Tampa B.	73	27 40N	82 40W
Tampere	111	61 30N	23 50 E
Tampico, Mexico	83	22 20N	97 50W
Tampico, U.S.A.	76	41 38N	89 47W
Tampin	128	2 28N	102 13 E
Tamsagbulag	130	47 15N	117 5 E
Tamu	125	24 13N	94 12 E
Tamworth, Austral.	135	31 0 S	150 58 E
Tamworth, Can.	47	44 29N	77 0W
Tamworth, U.K.	95	52 38N	1 41W
Tan Kiang	131	33 25N	111 0 E
Tana	110	70 7N	28 5 E
Tana, L.	115	13 5N	37 30 E
Tana, R.	116	0 50 S	39 45 E
Tanacross	67	63 40N	143 30W
Tanafjorden	110	70 45N	28 25 E
Tanahdjampea, I.	127	7 10 S	120 35 E
Tanahgrogot	126	1 55 S	116 15 E
Tanahmasa, I.	126	0 5 S	98 29 E
Tanahmerah	127	6 0 S	140 7 E
Tanami Des.	134	18 50 S	132 0 E
Tanana	67	65 10N	152 15W
Tanana, R.	67	64 25N	145 30W
Tananarive = Antananarivo	117	18 55 S	47 31 E
Tánaro, R.	108	44 9N	7 50 E
Tancarville	100	49 29N	0 28 E
Tanchai	131	25 58N	107 49 E
Tanchŏn	130	40 27N	128 54 E
Tanchow	131	19 33N	109 22 E
Tandag	127	9 4N	126 9 E
Tandil	88	37 15 S	59 6W
Tandjungpandan	126	2 43 S	107 38 E
Tando Adam	124	25 45N	68 40 E
Tandou L.	136	32 40 S	142 5 E
Tane-ga-Shima	132	30 30N	131 0 E
Taneatua	133	38 4 S	177 1 E
Tanen Range	128	19 40N	99 0 E
Tanen Tong Dan	125	16 30N	98 30 E
Tanezrouft	114	23 9N	0 11 E
Tanga	116	5 5 S	39 2 E
Tanganyika, L.	116	6 40 S	30 0 E
Tanger	114	35 50N	5 49W
Tangerang	127	6 12 S	106 39 E
Tanghing	131	21 30N	108 2 E
Tangho	131	32 47N	113 2 E
Tanghsien	130	38 48N	114 54 E
Tangier	39	44 48N	62 42W
Tangkak	128	2 18N	102 34 E
Tangku	130	39 0N	117 40 E
Tanglha Shan	129	33 0N	90 0 E
Tangshan, Anhwei, China	131	34 17N	116 25 E
Tangshan, Hopei, China	130	39 40N	118 10 E
Tangtu	131	31 37N	118 39 E
Tangyang	131	30 50N	111 45 E
Tanhsien (Nata)	131	19 30N	109 17 E
Tanimbar, Kepulauan	127	7 30 S	131 30 E
Taning = Wuki	131	31 27N	109 46 E
Tanjay	127	9 30N	123 5 E
Tanjore = Thanjavur	124	10 48N	79 12 E
Tanjung	126	2 10 S	115 25 E
Tanjungbalai	126	2 55N	99 44 E
Tanjungbatu	126	2 23N	118 3 E
Tanjungkarang	126	5 20 S	105 10 E
Tanjungpinang	126	1 5N	104 30 E
Tanjungpriok	127	6 8 S	106 55 E
Tanjungredeb	126	2 9N	117 29 E
Tanjungselor	126	2 55N	117 25 E
Tannin	34	49 40N	91 0W
Tannu Ola	129	51 0N	94 0 E
Tanout	114	14 50N	8 55 E
Tanshui	131	25 10N	121 28 E
Tansley	49	43 25N	79 48W
Tanta	115	30 45N	30 57 E
Tantallon	57	50 32N	101 50W
Tantoyuca	83	21 21N	98 10W
Tanu I.	62	52 46N	131 40W
Tanus	102	44 8N	2 19 E
Tanzania ■	116	6 40 S	34 0 E
Tanzilla, R.	54	58 8N	130 43W
Taohsien	131	25 37N	111 24 E

Taokow Teulon

Taokow	130	35 30N	114 30 E
Taolaihao	130	44 51N	125 57 E
Taonan	130	45 30N	122 20 E
Taos	79	36 28N	105 35W
Taoyuan, Hunan, China	131	29 8N	111 15 E
Taoyuan, Taiwan, China	131	25 0N	121 4 E
Tapa Shan	131	31 45N	109 30 E
Tapachula	83	14 54N	92 17W
Tapah	128	4 12N	101 15 E
Tapajós, R.	87	4 30 S	56 10W
Tapaktuan	126	3 30N	97 10 E
Tapanshang = Palinyuchi	130	43 40N	118 20 E
Tapanui	133	45 56 S	169 18 E
Tapauá	86	5 40 S	64 20W
Tapauá, R.	86	6 0 S	65 40W
Tapirapecó, Serra	86	1 10N	65 0W
Tapleytown	48	43 11N	79 44W
Tappahannock	72	37 56N	76 50W
Tapti, R.	124	21 25N	75 0 E
Tapuaenuku, Mt.	133	41 55 S	173 50 E
Tapul Group, Is.	127	5 35N	120 50 E
Taquara	89	29 36N	50 46W
Taquari, R.	89	18 10 S	56 0W
Tar Island	54	57 03N	111 40W
Tara, Can.	46	44 28N	81 9W
Tara, U.S.S.R.	120	56 55N	74 30 E
Tara, R.	109	43 5N	19 20 E
Tarabagatay, Khrebet	121	48 0N	83 0 E
Tarābulus, Leb.	122	34 31N	33 52 E
Tarābulus, Libya	114	32 49N	13 7 E
Tarakan	126	3 20N	117 35 E
Taranaki □	133	39 5 S	174 51 E
Taranga Hill	124	24 0N	72 40 E
Táranto	108	40 30N	17 11 E
Táranto, G. di	108	40 0N	17 15 E
Tarapacá	86	2 56 S	69 46W
Tarapacá □	88	20 45 S	69 30W
Tarare	103	45 54N	4 26 E
Tararua Range	133	40 45 S	175 25 E
Tarascon, Ariège, France	102	42 50N	1 37 E
Tarascon, Bouches-du-Rhône, France	103	43 48N	4 39 E
Tarauacá	86	8 6 S	70 48W
Tarauacá, R.	86	7 30 S	70 30W
Taravo, R.	103	41 48N	8 52 E
Tarawera	133	39 2 S	176 36 E
Tarawera L.	133	38 13 S	176 27 E
Tarbagatai	129	48 30N	99 0 E
Tarbat Ness	96	57 52N	3 48W
Tarbela Dam	124	34 0N	72 52 E
Tarbert, Can.	49	43 56N	80 20W
Tarbert, U.K.	96	57 54N	6 49W
Tarbes	102	43 15N	0 3 E
Tarboro	73	35 55N	77 30W
Tarcoola	134	30 44 S	134 36 E
Tardets-Sorholus	102	43 8N	0 52W
Tardin	129	37 16N	92 30 E
Taree	136	31 50 S	152 30 E
Tarentaise	103	45 30N	6 35 E
Tarfaya	114	27 55N	12 55W
Targon	102	44 44N	0 16W
Tari Nur	130	43 25N	116 40 E
Táriba	86	7 49N	72 13W
Tarifa	104	36 1N	5 36W
Tarija	88	21 30 S	64 40W
Tarija □	88	21 30 S	63 30W
Tarim, R.	129	41 5N	86 40 E
Taritoe, R.	127	3 0 S	138 5 E
Tarko Sale	120	64 55N	77 50 E
Tarlac	127	15 29N	120 35 E
Tarma	86	11 25 S	75 45W
Tarn □	102	43 49N	2 8 E
Tarn-et-Garonne □	102	44 8N	1 20 E
Tarn, R.	102	44 5N	1 2 E
Tarnów	107	50 3N	21 0 E
Tarnowskie Góry	107	50 27N	18 54 E
Taroom	135	25 36 S	149 48 E
Tarpon Springs	73	28 8N	82 42W
Tarragona	104	41 5N	1 17 E
Tarrasa	104	41 26N	2 1 E
Tarrytown	71	41 5N	73 52W
Tarsus	122	36 58N	34 55 E
Tartagal	88	22 30 S	63 50W
Tartas	102	43 50N	0 49W
Tartūs	122	34 55N	35 55 E
Tarutao, Ko	128	6 33N	99 40 E
Tarutung	126	2 0N	99 0 E
Taschereau	40	48 40N	78 40W
Taseko L.	62	51 15N	123 35W
Taseko, R.	62	52 4N	123 9W
Tashauz	120	42 0N	59 20 E
Tashi Chho Dzong	125	27 31N	89 45 E
Tashigong	129	33 0N	79 30 E
Tashihkao	130	40 47N	122 29 E
Tashkent	120	41 20N	69 10 E
Tashkumyr	120	41 40N	72 10 E
Tashkurgan	129	37 51N	74 57 E
Tashkurghan	123	36 45N	67 40 E
Tashtagol	120	52 47N	87 53 E
Tasi Ho	131	28 20N	119 40 E
Tasikmalaya	127	7 18 S	108 12 E
Tasin (Yangli)	131	22 57N	107 15 E
Tasjön	110	64 15N	15 45 E
Tasman Bay	133	40 59 S	173 25 E
Tasman Glacier	133	43 45 S	170 20 E
Tasman Mts.	133	41 3 S	172 25 E
Tasman Pen.	135	43 10 S	148 0 E
Tasman Sea	135	36 0 S	160 0 E
Tasmania, I., □	135	49 0 S	146 30 E
Tassialuk, L.	36	59 3N	74 0W
Tasu	62	52 45N	132 5W
Tasu Sd.	62	52 47N	132 2W
Tatamagouche	39	45 43N	63 18W
Tatar A.S.S.R. □	120	55 30N	51 30 E
Tatarsk	120	55 20N	75 50 E
Tatarskiy Proliv	121	54 0N	141 0 E
Tateyama	132	35 0N	139 50 E
Tathlina L.	54	60 33N	117 39W
Tatien	131	25 45N	118 0 E
Tating	131	27 0N	105 35 E
Tatinnai L.	55	60 55N	97 40W
Tatla L.	62	52 0N	124 20W
Tatlayoko L.	62	51 35N	124 24W
Tatnam, C.	55	57 16N	91 0W
Tatsaitan	129	37 55N	95 0 E
Tatsu	131	29 40N	105 45 E
Tatta	124	24 42N	67 55 E
Tatton	63	51 43N	121 22W
Tatuī	89	23 25 S	48 0W
Tatuk, L.	62	53 32N	124 14W
Tatum	75	33 16N	103 16W
Tatung	130	30 50N	117 45 E
Tatungkow	130	39 55N	124 10 E
Tatura	136	36 29 S	145 16 E
Tatvan	122	37 28N	42 27 E
Taubaté	89	23 5 S	45 30W
Tauern, mts.	106	47 15N	12 40 E
Taumarunui	133	38 53 S	175 15 E
Taumaturgo	86	9 0 S	73 50W
Taungdwingyi	125	20 1N	95 40 E
Taunggyi	125	20 50N	97 0 E
Taungup Taunggya	125	18 20N	93 40 E
Taunton, Can.	49	43 56N	78 49W
Taunton, U.K.	95	51 1N	3 7W
Taunus	106	50 15N	8 20 E
Taupo	133	38 41 S	176 7 E
Taupo, L.	133	38 46 S	175 55 E
Tauq	122	35 12N	44 29 E
Tauramena	86	5 1N	72 45W
Tauranga	133	37 35 S	176 11 E
Tauranga Harb.	133	37 30 S	176 5 E
Taureau, Lac	34	46 50N	73 40W
Taurianova	108	38 22N	16 1 E
Taurus Mts. = Toros Dağlari	122	37 0N	35 0 E
Tava Wan	131	22 35N	114 35 E
Tavani	55	62 10N	93 30W
Tavas	122	37 35N	29 8 E
Tavda	120	58 7N	65 8 E
Tavda, R.	120	59 30N	63 0 E
Taverny	101	49 2N	2 13 E
Taveta	116	3 31N	37 37 E
Taviche	83	16 38N	96 32W
Tavignano, R.	103	42 7N	9 33 E
Tavira	104	37 8N	7 40W
Tavistock, Can.	46	43 19N	80 50W
Tavistock, U.K.	95	50 33N	4 9W
Tavoy	128	14 7N	98 18 E
Tavoy, I. = Mali Kyun	125	13 0N	98 20 E
Taw, R.	95	50 58N	3 58W
Tawas City	46	44 16N	83 31W
Tawau	126	4 20N	117 55 E
Tawu	131	22 30N	120 50 E
Tay, Firth of	96	56 25N	3 8W
Tay, L.	96	56 30N	4 10W
Tay Ninh	128	11 20N	106 5 E
Tay, R.	96	56 37N	3 38W
Tayabamba	86	8 15 S	77 10W
Tayen	131	30 4N	115 0 E
Taylor, Can.	54	56 13N	120 40W
Taylor, Alaska, U.S.A.	67	65 40N	164 50W
Taylor, Pa., U.S.A.	71	41 23N	75 43W
Taylor, Tex., U.S.A.	75	30 30N	97 30W
Taylor Mt.	79	35 16N	107 50W
Taylorsville	77	38 2N	85 21W
Taylorville	76	39 32N	89 20W
Taymyr, Oz.	121	74 50N	102 0 E
Taymyr, P-ov.	121	75 0N	100 0 E
Tayport	96	56 27N	2 52W
Tayshet	121	55 58N	97 25 E
Tayside □	96	56 25N	3 30W
Taytay	127	10 45N	119 30 E
Tayu	131	25 38N	114 9 E
Tayulehsze	129	29 15N	98 1 E
Tayung	131	29 8N	110 30 E
Taz, R.	120	65 40N	82 0 E
Tazin L.	55	59 44N	108 42W
Tazin, R.	55	60 26N	110 45W
Tazovskiy	120	67 30N	78 30 E
Tbilisi (Tiflis)	120	41 50N	44 50 E
Tchad, Lac	114	13 30N	14 30 E
Tchentlo L.	54	55 15N	125 0W
Tchibanga	116	2 45 S	11 12 E
Tchpao (Tienpao)	131	23 25N	106 47 E
Te Anau L.	133	45 15 S	167 45 E
Te Aroha	133	37 32 S	175 44 E
Te Awamutu	133	38 1 S	175 20 E
Te Horo	133	40 48 S	175 6 E
Te Kuiti	133	38 20 S	175 11 E
Te Puke	133	37 46 S	176 22 E
Te Waewae B.	133	46 13 S	167 33 E
Teague	75	31 40N	96 20W
Teapa	83	17 35N	92 56W
Tebicuary, R.	88	26 36 S	58 16W
Tebing Tinggi	126	3 38 S	102 1 E
Tecapa	81	35 51N	116 14W
Tecate	82	32 34N	116 38W
Tecomán	82	18 55N	103 53W
Tecoripa	82	28 37N	109 57W
Tecuci	107	45 51N	27 27 E
Tecumseh, Can.	46	42 19N	82 54W
Tecumseh, U.S.A.	77	42 1N	83 59W
Tedzhen	120	37 23N	60 31 E
Tee Lake	40	46 40N	79 0W
Teepee Creek	60	55 22N	118 24W
Tees B.	94	54 37N	1 10W
Tees, R.	94	54 36N	1 25W
Teesside	94	54 37N	1 13W
Teeswater	46	43 59N	81 17W
Tefé	86	3 25 S	64 50W
Tegal	127	6 52 S	109 8 E
Tegid, L.	94	52 53N	3 38W
Tegucigalpa	84	14 10N	87 0W
Tehachapi	81	35 11N	118 29W
Tehachapi Mts.	81	35 0N	118 40W
Tehchow	130	37 29N	116 11 E
Tehping	130	37 26N	117 0 E
Tehrān	123	35 44N	51 30 E
Tehrān □	123	35 0N	49 30 E
Tehtsin (Atuntze)	129	28 45N	98 58 E
Tehuacán	83	18 20N	97 30W
Tehuantepec	83	16 10N	95 19W
Tehuantepec, Golfo de	83	15 50N	95 0W
Tehuantepec, Istmo de	83	17 0N	94 30W
Teich, Le	102	44 38N	0 59W
Teifi, R.	95	52 4N	4 14W
Teign, R.	95	50 41N	3 42W
Teignmouth	95	50 33N	3 30W
Teil, Le	103	44 33N	4 40 E
Teilleul, Le	100	48 32N	0 53W
Tejo, R.	104	39 15N	8 35W
Tejon Pass	81	34 49N	118 53W
Tekamah	74	41 48N	96 14W
Tekapo, L.	133	43 53 S	170 33 E
Tekax	83	20 20N	89 30W
Tekeli	120	44 50N	79 0 E
Tekirdağ	122	40 58N	27 30 E
Tekkali	125	18 43N	84 24 E
Tekoa	78	47 19N	117 4W
Tel Aviv-Jaffa	115	32 4N	34 48 E
Tel Aviv-Yafo	115	32 4N	34 48 E
Tela	84	15 40N	87 28W
Telanaipura = Jambi	126	1 38 S	103 30 E
Telegraph Cove	62	50 32N	126 50W
Telegraph Cr.	54	58 0N	131 10W
Telemark fylke □	111	59 25N	8 30 E
Telén	88	36 15 S	65 31W
Teles Pires (São Manuel), R.	86	8 40 S	57 0W
Telescope Peak, Mt.	81	36 6N	117 7W
Telford	94	52 42N	2 31W
Telisze	130	39 50N	112 0 E
Telkwa	54	54 41N	126 56W
Tell City	77	38 0N	86 44W
Teller	67	65 12N	166 24W
Tellicherry	124	11 45N	75 30 E
Telluride	79	37 58N	107 54W
Telok Anson	128	4 3N	101 0 E
Teloloapán	83	18 21N	99 51W
Telom, R.	128	4 20N	101 46 E
Telsen	90	42 30 S	66 50W
Telukbetung	126	5 29 S	105 17 E
Telukdalem	126	0 45N	97 50 E
Tema	114	5 41N	0 0 E
Temagami L.	34	47 0N	80 10W
Temanggung	127	7 18 S	110 10 E
Temapache	83	21 4N	97 38W
Temax	83	21 10N	88 50W
Tembeling, R.	128	4 20N	102 23 E
Temblor Ra, mts.	81	35 30N	120 0W
Teme, R.	95	52 23N	2 15W
Temecula	81	33 26N	117 6W
Temerloh	128	3 27N	102 25 E
Temir Tau	120	53 10N	87 20 E
Temirtau	120	50 5N	72 56 E
Temiscamie, R.	36	50 59N	73 5W
Témiscaming	40	46 44N	79 5W
Témiscamingue, L.	40	47 10N	79 25W
Temora	136	34 30 S	147 30 E
Temosachic	82	28 58N	107 50W
Tempe, S. Afr.	79	29 1 S	26 13 E
Tempe, U.S.A.	79	33 26N	111 59W
Temperance Vale	39	46 4N	67 15W
Temperanceville	50	43 56N	79 28W
Tempestad	86	1 20 S	74 56W
Tempino	126	1 55 S	103 23 E
Tempiute	80	37 39N	115 38W
Temple	75	31 5N	97 28W
Temple B.	135	12 15 S	143 3 E
Temple Sowerby	95	54 38N	2 33W
Templeman, Mt.	63	50 42N	117 12W
Templemore	97	52 48N	7 50W
Templeton, Can.	48	45 29N	75 35W
Templeton, U.S.A.	80	35 33N	120 42W
Tempoal	83	21 31N	98 23W
Temuco	90	38 50 S	72 50W
Temuka	133	44 14 S	171 17 E
Ten Mile L.	37	51 6N	56 42W
Tena	86	0 59 S	77 49W
Tenabo	83	20 2N	90 12W
Tenaha	75	31 57N	94 15W
Tenali	124	16 15N	80 35 E
Tenancingo	83	19 0N	99 33W
Tenango	83	19 0N	99 40W
Tenasserim	128	12 6N	99 3 E
Tenasserim □	128	14 0N	98 30 E
Tenay	103	45 55N	5 30 E
Tenby	95	51 40N	4 42W
Tende	103	44 5N	7 35 E
Tende, Col de	103	44 9N	7 32 E
Tenerife, I.	114	28 20N	16 40W
Teng, R.	128	20 30N	98 10 E
Tengah □	127	2 0 S	122 0 E
Tengah Kepulauan	126	7 5 S	118 15 E
Tengchowfu = Penglai	130	37 50N	120 50 E
Tenggara □	127	3 0 S	122 0 E
Tenghsien, Kwangsi-Chuang, China	131	23 20N	111 0 E
Tenghsien, Shantung, China	131	35 10N	117 10 E
Tengiz, Ozero	120	50 30N	69 0 E
Tengkow	130	39 45N	106 40 E
Tenille	73	32 58N	82 50W
Tenino	80	46 51N	122 51W
Tenkasi	124	8 55N	77 20 E
Tenke	116	10 32 S	26 7 E
Tennant Creek	134	19 30 S	134 0 E
Tennessee □	69	36 0N	86 30W
Tennyson	77	38 5N	87 7W
Tenom	126	5 4N	115 38 E
Tenosique	83	17 30N	91 24W
Tenryū-gawa, R.	132	35 39N	137 48 E
Tent L.	55	62 25N	107 54W
Tenterfield	135	29 0 S	152 0 E
Teófilo Otôni	87	17 50 S	41 30W
Tepalcatepec, R.	82	18 35N	101 59W
Tepehuanes	82	25 21N	105 44W
Tepetongo	82	22 28N	103 9W
Tepic	82	21 30N	104 54W
Teplice	106	50 39N	13 50 E
Tepoca, C.	82	29 20N	112 25W
Tequila	82	20 54N	103 47W
Ter Apel	105	52 53N	7 5 E
Ter, R.	104	42 0N	2 30 E
Téramo	108	42 40N	13 40 E
Terang	136	38 15 S	142 55 E
Tercan	122	39 50N	40 30 E
Terceira	93	38 43N	27 13W
Tercero, R.	88	32 58 S	61 47W
Terence Bay	39	44 28N	63 43W
Terengganu □	128	4 55N	103 0 E
Teresina	87	5 2 S	42 45W
Terezinha	86	0 44N	69 27W
Tergnier	101	49 40N	3 17 E
Termas de Chillan	88	36 50 S	71 31W
Termez	120	37 0N	67 15 E
Términi Imerese	101	37 59N	13 51 E
Términos, Laguna de	83	18 35N	91 30W
Térmoli	108	42 0N	15 0 E
Ternate	127	0 45N	127 25 E
Terneuzen	105	51 20N	3 50 E
Terney	121	45 3N	136 37 E
Terni	108	42 34N	12 38 E
Terra Bella	81	35 58N	119 3W
Terra Cotta	49	43 43N	79 56W
Terra Nova	37	48 30N	54 13W
Terra Nova B.	91	74 50 S	164 40 E
Terra Nova Nat. Park	37	48 33N	53 58W
Terra Nova, R.	37	48 40N	54 0W
Terrace	54	54 30N	128 35W
Terrace Bay	53	48 47N	87 5W
Terracina	108	41 17N	13 12 E
Terralba	108	39 42N	8 38 E
Terranova = Ólbia	108	40 55N	9 30 E
Terrasse-Vaudreuil	44	45 24N	73 59W
Terrasson	102	45 7N	1 19 E
Terre Haute	77	39 28N	87 25W
Terrebonne	44	45 42N	73 38W
Terrebonne □	44	45 50N	74 0W
Terrebonne B.	75	29 15N	90 28W
Terrebonne Heights	44	45 44N	73 38W
Terrell	75	32 44N	96 19W
Terrenceville	37	47 40N	54 44W
Terry	74	46 47N	105 20W
Terschelling, I.	105	53 25N	5 20 E
Teruel	104	40 22N	1 8W
Tervola	110	66 6N	24 49 E
Tešanj	109	44 38N	17 59 E
Teshio-Gawa, R.	132	44 53N	141 45 E
Tesiyn Gol	129	50 40N	93 20 E
Teslin	67	60 10N	132 43W
Teslin L.	54	60 15N	132 57W
Teslin, R.	54	61 34N	134 35W
Tessenderlo	105	51 4N	5 5 E
Tessier	55	51 48N	107 26W
Test, R.	95	51 7N	1 30W
Teste, La	102	44 37N	1 8W
Tetachuck L.	62	53 18N	125 55W
Tetas, Pta.	88	23 31 S	70 38W
Tete	117	16 13 S	33 33 E
Tête-à-la-Baleine	37	50 41N	59 20W
Teteven	109	42 58N	24 17 E
Tethull, R.	54	60 35N	112 12W
Tetlin	67	63 14N	142 50W
Tetlin Junction	67	63 29N	142 55W
Teton, R.	78	47 58N	111 0W
Tétouan	114	35 35N	5 21W
Tetovo	109	42 1N	21 2 E
Tetu L.	52	50 11N	95 2W
Tetuán = Tétouan	114	35 30N	5 25W
Tetyukhe	121	44 45N	135 40 E
Teuco, R.	88	25 30 S	60 25W
Teulon	57	50 23N	97 16W

Teutoburger Wald Togo

Teutoburger Wald 106 52 5N 8 20 E
Tevere, R. 108 42 30N 12 20 E
Teviot, R. 96 55 21N 2 51W
Tewkesbury 95 51 59N 2 8W
Texada I. 62 49 40N 124 25W
Texarkana, Ark., U.S.A. 75 33 25N 94 0W
Texarkana, Tex., U.S.A. 75 33 25N 94 3W
Texas □ 75 31 40N 98 30W
Texas City 75 29 20N 95 20W
Texel, I. 105 53 5N 4 50 E
Texhoma 75 36 32N 101 47W
Texline 75 36 26N 103 0W
Texoma L. 75 34 0N 96 38W
Teziutlán 83 19 50N 97 30W
Tezpur 125 26 40N 92 45 E
Tezzeron L. 54 54 43N 124 30W
Tha-anne, R. 55 60 31N 94 37W
Tha Nun 128 8 12N 98 17 E
Thabana Ntlenyana, Mt. 117 29 30 S 29 9 E
Thabazimbi 117 24 40 S 26 4 E
Thai Nguyen 128 21 35N 105 46 E
Thailand (Siam) ■ 128 16 0N 102 0 E
Thakhek 128 17 25N 104 45 E
Thal 124 33 28N 70 33 E
Thal Desert 124 31 0N 71 30 E
Thala La 125 28 25N 97 23 E
Thame 95 51 44N 0 58W
Thame, R. 95 51 52N 0 47W
Thames 70 42 35N 82 1W
Thames, R., Can. 46 42 20N 82 25W
Thames, R., N.Z. 133 37 32 S 175 45 E
Thames, R., U.K. 95 51 30N 0 35 E
Thames, R., U.S.A. 71 41 18N 72 9W
Thamesford 46 43 4N 81 0W
Thamesville 46 42 33N 81 59W
Thana 124 19 12N 72 59 E
Thanet, I. of 95 51 21N 1 20 E
Thang Binh 128 15 50N 108 20 E
Thanh Hoa 128 19 48N 105 46 E
Thanjavur (Tanjore) 124 10 48N 79 12 E
Thann 101 47 48N 7 5 E
Thaon 101 48 15N 6 25 E
Thar (Great Indian) Desert 124 28 25N 72 0 E
Tharad 124 24 30N 71 30 E
Thargomindah 135 27 58 S 143 46 E
Tharrawaddy 125 17 38N 95 48 E
Tharthār, Bahr ath 122 34 0N 43 0 E
Thásos, I. 109 40 40N 24 40 E
Thatcher, Ariz., U.S.A. 79 32 54N 109 46W
Thatcher, Colo., U.S.A. 79 37 38N 104 6W
Thaton 125 16 55N 97 22 E
Thau, Étang de 102 43 23N 3 36 E
Thaungdut 125 24 30N 94 40 E
Thayer 75 36 34N 91 34W
Thayetmyo 125 19 20N 95 18 E
Thazi 125 21 0N 96 5 E
The Bight 85 24 19N 75 24W
The Dalles 78 45 40N 121 11W
The Grampians, Mts. 136 37 0 S 142 30 E
The Great Divide 136 35 0 S 149 17 E
The Grenadines, Is. 85 12 30N 61 30W
The Hague = 's-Gravenhage 106 52 7N 7 14 E
The Lake 85 21 5N 73 34W
The Pas 57 53 45N 101 15W
The Rock 136 35 15 S 147 2 E
The Vale 136 33 34 S 143 49 E
Thedford, Can. 46 43 9N 81 51W
Thedford, U.S.A. 74 41 59N 100 31W
Thekulthili L. 55 61 3N 110 0W
Thelon, R. 55 62 35N 104 3W
Thénezay 100 46 44N 0 2W
Thenon 102 45 9N 1 4 E
Theodore, Austral. 135 24 55 S 150 3 E
Theodore, Can. 56 51 26N 102 55W
Thérain, R. 101 49 15N 2 27 E
Theresa 71 44 13N 75 50W
Thermaïkos Kólpos 109 40 15N 22 45 E
Thermopílai P. 109 38 48N 22 45 E
Thermopolis 78 43 35N 108 10W
Thesiger B. 64 71 30N 124 5W
Thessalía □ 109 39 30N 22 0 E
Thessalon 46 46 20N 83 30W
Thessaloníki 109 40 38N 23 0 E
Thessaly = Thessalía 109 39 30N 22 0 E
Thetford 95 52 25N 0 44 E
Thetford Mines 41 46 8N 71 18W
Theux 105 50 32N 5 49 E
Thévet, L. 38 51 50N 64 12W
Thiberville 100 49 8N 0 27 E
Thicket Portage 55 55 19N 97 42W
Thief River Falls 75 48 15N 96 10W
Thiérache 101 49 51N 3 45 E
Thiers 102 45 52N 3 33 E
Thies 114 14 50N 16 51W
Thika 116 1 1 S 37 5 E
Thikombia, I. 133 15 44 S 179 55W
Thillot, Le 101 47 53N 6 46 E
Thimphu (Tashi Chho Dzong) 125 27 31N 89 45 E
þingvallavatn 110 64 11N 21 9W
Thionville 101 49 20N 6 10 E
Thirá 109 36 23N 25 27 E
Thirsk 94 54 15N 1 20W
Thisted 111 56 58N 8 40 E
Thistle I. 134 35 0 S 136 8 E
Thistletown 50 43 44N 79 33W
Thiu Khao Phetchabun 128 16 20N 100 55 E
Thívai 109 38 19N 23 19 E
Thiviers 102 45 25N 0 54 E
Thizy 103 46 2N 4 18 E
þjorsa 110 63 47N 20 48W
Thlewiaza, R., Man., Can. 55 59 43N 100 5W
Thlewiaza, R., N.W.T., Can. 55 60 29N 94 40W
Thoa, R. 55 60 31N 109 47W
Thoissey 103 46 12N 4 48 E
Thom Bay 65 70 9N 92 25W
Thomas, Okla., U.S.A. 75 35 48N 98 48W
Thomas, W. Va., U.S.A. 72 39 10N 79 30W
Thomas Hubbard, C. 65 82 0N 94 25W
Thomas Resr. 76 39 34N 92 39W
Thomastown 97 52 32N 7 10W
Thomasville, Ala., U.S.A. 73 31 55N 87 42W
Thomasville, Ga.., U.S.A. 73 30 50N 84 0W
Thomasville, N.C., U.S.A. 73 35 55N 80 4W
Thompson, B.C., Can. 63 50 15N 121 24W
Thompson, Man., Can. 55 55 45N 97 52W
Thompson Falls 78 47 37N 115 26W
Thompson Landing 55 62 56N 110 40W
Thompson, R., Can. 63 50 15N 121 24W
Thompson, R., U.S.A. 74 39 46N 93 37W
Thompsons 79 39 0N 109 50W
Thompsonville, U.S.A. 77 37 55N 88 46W
Thompsonville, Vt., U.S.A. 71 42 0N 72 37W
Thomson 76 41 58N 90 6W
Thomson, R. 135 25 11 S 142 53 E
Thonburi 128 13 50N 100 36 E
Thônes 103 45 54N 6 18 E
Thonon-les-Bains 103 46 22N 6 29 E
Thorburn 39 45 34N 62 33W
Thorhild 60 54 10N 113 7W
þorlákshöfn 110 63 51N 21 22W
Thornaby on Tees 94 54 36N 1 19W
Thornburn Road 37 47 35N 52 51W
Thornbury 46 44 34N 80 26W
Thorne Glacier 91 87 30N 150 0 E
Thornhill, Man., Can. 57 49 12N 98 14W
Thornhill, Ont., Can. 50 43 48N 79 25W
Thornton 76 42 57N 93 23W
Thorntown 77 40 8N 86 36W
Thorold 49 43 7N 79 12W
Thorold South 49 43 6N 79 12W
Thorsby 60 53 14N 114 3W
Thouarcé 101 47 17N 0 30W
Thousand Oakes 81 34 10N 118 50W
Thrace = Thráki 109 41 10N 25 30 E
Thráki 109 41 9N 25 30 E
Three Forks 78 45 55N 111 40W
Three Hills 61 51 43N 113 15W
Three Kings Is. 133 34 10 S 172 10 E
Three Lakes 74 45 41N 89 10W
Three Mile Plains 39 44 58N 64 7W
Three Oaks 77 41 48N 86 36W
Three Rivers, U.S.A. 77 41 57N 85 38W
Three Rivers, Calif., U.S.A. 80 36 26N 118 54W
Three Rivers, Tex., U.S.A. 75 28 30N 98 10W
Three Sisters, Mt. 78 44 10N 121 52W
þ risvatn 110 64 50N 19 26W
Throop 71 41 24N 75 39W
Throssell Ra. 134 17 24 S 126 4 E
þ rshöfn 110 66 12N 15 20W
Thrumster 96 58 24N 3 8W
Thubun Lakes 55 61 30N 112 0W
Thuddungra 136 34 8 S 148 8 E
Thueyts 103 44 41N 4 9 E
Thuin 105 50 20N 4 17 E
Thuir 102 42 38N 2 45 E
Thule 65 77 30N 69 0W
Thun 106 46 45N 7 38 E
Thunder B., Can. 52 48 20N 89 0W
Thunder B., U.S.A. 70 45 0N 83 20W
Thunder Bay 52 48 25N 89 15W
Thunder Cr. 56 50 23N 105 32W
Thunder River 54 52 13N 119 20W
Thung Song 128 8 10N 99 40 E
Thunkar 125 27 55N 91 0 E
Thüringer Wald 106 50 35N 11 0 E
Thurles 97 52 40N 7 53W
Thursday I. 135 10 30 S 142 3 E
Thurso, Can. 40 45 36N 75 15W
Thurso, U.K. 96 58 34N 3 31W
Thurso, R. 96 58 36N 3 30W
Thurston 70 39 50N 82 33W
Thurston I. 91 72 0 S 100 0W
Thury-Harcourt 100 49 0N 0 30W
Thutade L. 54 57 0N 126 55W
Tiahualilo 82 26 20N 103 30W
Tiaret 114 30 52N 10 10 E
Tibagi 89 24 30 S 50 24W
Tibagi, R. 89 22 47 S 51 1W
Tibati 114 6 22N 12 30 E
Tiber = Tevere, R. 108 42 30N 12 20 E
Tiber Res. 78 48 20N 111 15W
Tiberias 115 32 47N 35 32 E
Tibesti 114 21 0N 17 30 E
Tibet □ 129 32 30N 86 0 E
Tibooburra 135 29 26 S 142 1 E
Tibugá, Golfo de 86 5 45N 77 20W
Tiburón, I. 82 29 0N 112 30W
Ticino □ 106 46 20N 8 45 E
Ticino, R. 108 45 23N 8 47 E
Ticonderoga 71 43 50N 73 28W
Ticul 83 20 20N 89 50W
Tiddim 125 23 20N 93 45 E
Tide Head 39 47 59N 66 47W
Tidore 127 0 40N 127 25 E
Tiehling 130 42 25N 123 51 E
Tiel 105 51 53N 5 26 E
Tielt 105 51 0N 3 20 E
Tien Shan 129 42 0N 80 0 E
Tienchen 130 40 32N 114 0 E
Tienen 105 50 48N 4 57 E
Tienho 131 24 58N 108 35 E
Tieno 131 25 3N 107 3 E
Tienpao 131 23 25N 106 47 E
Tienshui 131 34 30N 105 34 E
Tientsin 130 39 10N 117 0 E
Tientu 131 18 12N 109 33 E
Tientung 131 23 47N 107 2 E
Tierra Alta 86 8 11N 76 4W
Tierra Amarilla 88 27 28 S 70 18W
Tierra Colorada 83 17 10N 99 35W
Tierra de Campos 104 42 10N 4 50W
Tierra del Fuego, I. Gr. de 90 54 0 S 69 0W
Tiétar, R. 104 39 55N 5 50W
Tieté, R. 87 20 40 S 51 35W
Tiffin 77 41 8N 83 10W
Tiffin, R. 77 41 20N 84 24W
Tiflis = Tbilisi 120 41 50N 44 50 E
Tifton 73 31 28N 83 32W
Tifu 127 3 39 S 126 18 E
Tigalda I. 67 54 9N 165 0W
Tigil 121 58 0N 158 10 E
Tignish 39 46 58N 64 2W
Tigre, R. 86 3 30 S 74 58W
Tigyaing 125 23 45N 96 10 E
Tihua 129 43 40N 87 50 E
Tijiamis 127 7 16 S 108 29 E
Tijibadok 127 6 53 S 106 47 E
Tijuana 82 32 30N 117 3W
Tikal 84 17 2N 89 35W
Tikamgarh 124 24 44N 78 57 E
Tikang 131 31 7N 118 2 E
Tikhoretsk 120 45 56N 40 5 E
Tikrit 122 34 35N 43 37 E
Tiksi 121 71 50N 129 0 E
Tilamuta 127 0 40N 122 15 E
Tilburg 105 51 31N 5 6 E
Tilbury, Can. 46 42 17N 82 23W
Tilbury, U.K. 95 51 27N 0 24 E
Tilcara 88 23 30 S 65 23W
Tilden 74 42 3N 97 45W
Tilichiki 121 61 0N 166 5 E
Till, R. 94 55 35N 2 3W
Tillamook 78 45 29N 123 55W
Tilley 54 50 28N 111 38W
Tillsonburg 46 42 53N 80 44W
Tilos, I. 109 36 27N 27 27 E
Tilston 57 49 23N 101 19W
Tilt, R. 96 56 50N 3 50W
Tilton 71 43 25N 71 36W
Timaru 133 44 23 S 171 14 E
Timber Lake 74 45 29N 101 0W
Timber Mtn. 80 37 6N 116 28W
Timberlea 39 44 40N 63 45W
Timbilica 136 37 22 S 149 42 E
Timbío 86 2 20N 76 40W
Timbiqui 86 2 46N 77 42W
Timboon 136 38 30 S 142 58 E
Timbuktu = Tombouctou 114 16 50N 3 0W
Timişoara 107 45 43N 21 15 E
Timmins 53 48 28N 81 25W
Timok, R. 109 44 10N 22 40 E
Timon 87 5 8 S 42 52W
Timor, I. 127 9 0 S 125 0 E
Timor Sea 135 10 0 S 127 0 E
Timur □ 127 9 0 S 125 0 E
Tin Mtn. 80 36 54N 117 28W
Tinaca Pt. 127 5 30N 125 25 E
Tinaco 86 9 42N 68 20W
Tinambacan 127 12 5N 124 32 E
Tinaquillo 86 9 55N 68 18W
Tinchebray 100 48 47N 0 45W
Tindouf 114 27 50N 8 4W
Tingan 131 19 42N 110 18 E
Tinghai 131 30 0N 122 10 E
Tingnan 131 24 45N 114 50 E
Tingo Maria 86 9 10 S 76 0W
Tingpien 130 37 30N 107 50 E
Tingsi 130 35 50N 104 17 E
Tinnia 88 27 0 S 62 45W
Tinnoset 111 59 45N 9 3 E
Tinogasta 88 28 0 S 67 40W
Tinos 109 37 33N 25 8 E
Tinpak 131 21 40N 111 15 E
Tintagel 62 54 12N 125 35W
Tintina 88 27 2 S 62 45W
Tioga 70 41 54N 77 9W
Tioman, I. 128 2 50N 104 10 E
Tioman, Pulau, Is. 128 2 50N 104 10 E
Tionaga 34 48 0N 82 0W
Tionesta 70 41 29N 79 28W
Tipongpani 125 27 20N 95 55 E
Tipp City 77 39 58N 84 11W
Tippecanoe, R. 77 40 31N 86 47W
Tipperary 97 52 28N 8 10W
Tipperary □ 97 52 37N 7 55W
Tipton, U.K. 95 52 32N 2 4W
Tipton, Calif., U.S.A. 80 36 3N 119 19W
Tipton, Ind., U.S.A. 77 40 17N 86 0W
Tipton, Iowa, U.S.A. 76 41 45N 91 12W
Tipton, Mo., U.S.A. 76 38 41N 92 48W
Tipton, Mt. 81 35 32N 114 16W
Tiptonville 75 36 22N 89 30W
Tīrān 123 32 45N 51 0 E
Tirana 109 41 18N 19 49 E
Tiraspol 120 46 55N 29 35 E
Tire 122 38 5N 27 50 E
Tirebolu 122 40 58N 38 45 E
Tiree, I. 96 56 31N 6 55W
Tîrgovişte 107 44 55N 25 27 E
Tîrgu-Jiu 107 45 5N 23 19 E
Tîrgu Mureş 107 46 31N 24 38 E
Tirich Mir Mt. 124 36 15N 71 35 E
Tirodi 124 21 35N 79 35 E
Tirol □ 106 47 3N 10 43 E
Tirso, R. 108 40 33N 9 12 E
Tiruchchirappalli 124 10 45N 78 45 E
Tirunelveli (Tinnevelly) 124 8 45N 77 45 E
Tirupati 124 13 45N 79 30 E
Tiruvannamalai 124 12 10N 79 12 E
Tisa, R. 107 45 30N 20 20 E
Tisdale 56 52 50N 104 0W
Tishomingo 75 34 14N 96 38W
Tit-Ary 121 71 50N 126 30 E
Titicaca, L. 86 15 30 S 69 30W
Titograd 109 42 30N 19 19 E
Titov Veles 109 41 46N 21 47 E
Titovo Užice 109 43 55N 19 50 E
Tittabawassee, R. 46 43 23N 83 59W
Titule 116 3 15N 25 31 E
Titumate 86 8 19N 77 5W
Titusville 70 41 35N 79 39W
Tiverton, N.S., Can. 39 44 23N 66 13W
Tiverton, Ont., Can. 46 44 16N 81 32W
Tiverton, U.K. 95 50 54N 3 30W
Tivoli 108 41 58N 12 45 E
Tiwī 123 22 45N 59 12 E
Tizmín 83 21 0N 88 1W
Tiznados, R. 86 8 50N 67 50W
Tiznit 114 29 48N 9 45W
Tjalang 127 4 30N 95 43 E
Tjangkuang, Tg. 126 7 0 S 105 0 E
Tjareme, G. 127 6 55 S 108 27 E
Tjeggelvas 110 66 37N 17 45 E
Tjepu 127 7 12 S 111 31 E
Tjiandjur 127 6 51 S 107 7 E
Tjibatu 127 7 8 S 107 59 E
Tjikadjang 127 7 25 S 107 48 E
Tjimahi 127 6 53 S 107 33 E
Tjirebon = Cirebon 127 6 45 S 108 32 E
Tjörnes 110 66 12N 17 9W
Tjurup 126 4 26 S 102 13 E
Tlacolula 83 16 57N 96 29W
Tlacotalpan 83 18 37N 95 40W
Tlaquepaque 82 20 39N 103 19W
Tlaxcala 83 19 20N 98 14W
Tlaxcala □ 83 19 30N 98 20W
Tlaxiaco 83 17 10N 97 40W
Tlell 62 53 34N 131 56W
Tlemcen 114 34 52N 1 15W
Toad, R. 54 59 25N 124 57W
Toay 88 36 50 S 64 30W
Toba 132 34 30N 136 45 E
Toba Inlet 62 50 25N 124 35W
Toba Kakar 124 31 30N 69 0 E
Toba, L. 126 2 40N 98 50 E
Tobago, I. 85 11 10N 60 30W
Tobelo 127 1 25N 127 56 E
Tobermory, Can. 46 45 12N 81 40W
Tobermory, U.K. 96 56 37N 6 4W
Tobin 80 39 55N 121 19W
Tobin L. 56 53 35N 103 30W
Tobique, R. 39 46 46N 67 42W
Toboali 126 3 0 S 106 25 E
Tobol 120 52 40N 62 39 E
Toboli 127 0 38 S 120 12 E
Tobolsk 120 58 0N 68 10 E
Tobruk = Tubruq 115 32 7N 23 55 E
Toby Creek 63 50 20N 116 25W
Tobyhanna 71 41 10N 75 15W
Tocantinópolis 87 6 20 S 47 25W
Tocantins, R. 87 14 30 S 49 0W
Tocca 73 34 32N 83 17W
Tochigi 132 36 25N 139 45 E
Tochigi-ken □ 132 36 45N 139 45 E
Toconao 88 34 35N 83 19W
Tocópero 86 11 30N 69 16W
Tocopilla 88 22 5 S 70 10W
Tocumwal 136 35 45 S 145 31 E
Tocuyo, R. 86 10 50N 69 0W
Todeli 127 1 38 S 124 34 E
Todenyang 116 4 35N 35 56 E
Todjo 127 1 20 S 121 15 E
Todos os Santos, Baía de 87 12 48 S 38 38W
Todos Santos 82 23 27N 110 13W
Todos Santos, Bahia de 82 31 48N 116 42W
Tofield 60 53 25N 112 40W
Tofua I. 133 19 45 S 175 05W
Toghral Ombo 129 35 10N 81 40 E
Togian, Kepulauan 127 0 20 S 121 50 E
Togliatti 120 53 37N 49 18 E
Togo 57 51 24N 101 35W

Togo ■ 114 6 15N 1 35E
Tōhoku □ 132 39 50N 141 45E
Toirim 130 46 0N 106 50E
Tokaj 107 48 8N 21 27E
Tokala, G. 127 1 30S 121 40E
Tokamachi 132 37 8N 138 43E
Tokanui 133 46 34S 168 56E
Tokara-gunto 132 29 0N 129 0E
Tokara Kaikyō 132 30 0N 130 0E
Tokarahi 133 44 56S 170 39E
Tokat 122 40 22N 36 35E
Tokeland 80 46 42N 123 59W
Tokelau Is. 14 9 0S 172 0W
Tokong 128 5 27N 100 23E
Tokoto 130 40 18N 111 0E
Tokuno-shima 131 27 50N 129 2E
Tokushima 132 34 4N 134 34E
Tokushima-ken □ 132 35 50N 134 30E
Tokuyama 132 34 0N 131 50E
Tōkyō 132 35 45N 139 45E
Tōkyō-to □ 132 35 40N 139 30E
Tolaga Bay 133 38 21S 178 20E
Tolageak 67 70 2N 162 50W
Tolbukhin 109 43 37N 27 49E
Toledo, Spain 104 39 50N 4 2W
Toledo, U.S.A. 76 42 0N 92 35W
Toledo, U.S.A. 77 39 16N 88 15W
Toledo, Ohio, U.S.A. 72 41 37N 83 33W
Toledo, Oreg., U.S.A. 78 44 40N 123 59W
Toledo, Wash., U.S.A. 78 46 29N 122 58W
Toledo, Montes de 104 39 33N 4 20W
Tolfino 62 49 11N 125 55W
Tolga 114 34 46N 5 22E
Tolima □ 86 3 45N 75 15W
Tolima, Vol. 86 4 40N 75 19W
Tolitoli 127 1 5N 120 50E
Tolleson 79 33 29N 112 10W
Tollhouse 80 37 1N 119 24W
Tolo 116 2 50S 18 40E
Tolo, Teluk 127 2 20S 122 10E
Tolono 77 39 59N 88 16W
Tolosa 104 43 8N 2 5W
Tolstoi 57 49 5N 96 49W
Toluca 83 19 20N 99 50W
Tolun 130 42 22N 116 30E
Tomahawk 74 45 28N 89 40W
Tomales 80 38 15N 122 53W
Tomales B. 80 38 15N 123 58W
Tomar 104 39 36N 8 25W
Tomaszów Mazowiecki 107 51 30N 19 57E
Tomatlán 82 19 56N 105 15W
Tombigbee, R. 73 32 0N 88 6W
Tombodor, Serra do 87 12 0S 41 30W
Tombouctou 114 16 50N 3 0W
Tombstone 79 31 40N 110 4W
Tomé 88 36 36S 73 6W
Tomelloso 104 39 10N 3 2W
Tomiko L. 46 46 32N 79 49W
Tomini 127 0 30N 120 30E
Tomini, Teluk 127 0 10S 122 0E
Tommot 121 58 50N 126 20E
Tomo 86 2 38N 67 32W
Tomorong 136 35 0S 151 9E
Tomorrit, mt. 109 40 40N 20 30E
Tompkins 56 50 4N 108 47W
Toms Place 80 37 34N 118 41W
Toms River 71 39 59N 74 12W
Tomsk 120 56 30N 85 12E
Tonalá 83 16 8N 93 41W
Tonalea 79 36 17N 110 58W
Tonantins 86 2 45S 67 45W
Tonasket 63 48 45N 119 30W
Tonawanda 49 43 0N 78 54W
Tonbridge 95 51 12N 0 18E
Tondano 127 1 35N 124 54E
Tone-Gawa, R. 132 35 44N 140 51E
Tonga Is. ■ 133 20 0S 173 0W
Tonga Trench 133 18 0S 175 0W
Tongatapu, I. 133 21 10S 174 0W
Tongeren 105 50 47N 5 28E
Tongking = Bac-Phan 128 21 30N 105 0E
Tongking, G. of 128 20 0N 108 0E
Tongoy 88 30 25S 71 40W
Tongsa Dzong 125 27 31N 90 31E
Tongue, R. 78 48 30N 106 30W
Tonica 76 41 13N 89 4W
Tonk 124 26 6N 75 54E
Tonkawa 75 36 44N 67 22W
Tonlé Sap 128 13 0N 104 0E
Tonnay-Charente 102 45 56N 0 55W
Tonneins 102 44 24N 0 20E
Tonnerre 101 47 51N 3 59E
Tonopah 79 38 4N 117 12W
Tonosi 84 7 20N 80 20W
Tonsberg 111 59 19N 10 25E
Tooele 78 40 30N 112 20W
Toora-Khem 121 52 28N 96 9E
Toowoomba 135 27 32S 151 56E
Top 124 34 15N 68 35E
Top of the World Prov. Park 61 50 0N 115 35W
Topaz 80 38 41N 119 30W
Topeka 74 39 3N 95 40W
Topki 120 55 25N 85 20E
Topley 54 54 32N 126 5W
Topocalma, Pta. 88 34 10S 72 2W
Topock 81 34 46N 114 29W
Topolobampo 82 25 40N 109 10W
Toppenish 78 46 27N 120 16W
Tor Bay, Austral. 134 35 5S 117 50E
Tor Bay, U.K. 98 50 26N 3 31W
Torata 86 17 3S 70 1W
Torbat-e Heydārīyeh 123 35 15N 59 12E
Torbat-e Jām 123 35 8N 60 35E
Torbay, Can. 37 47 40N 52 42W
Torbay, U.K. 95 50 26N 3 31W
Torch, R. 56 53 50N 103 5W
Tordesillas 104 41 30N 5 0W
Torfajökull 110 63 54N 19 0W
Torgau 106 51 32N 13 0E
Torhout 105 51 5N 3 7E
Torigni-sur-Vire 100 49 3N 0 58W
Torin 82 27 33N 110 5W
Torino 108 45 4N 7 40E
Tormentine 35 46 6N 63 46W
Tormes, R. 104 41 7N 6 0W
Tormore 50 43 51N 79 42W
Tornado Mt. 54 49 55N 114 40W
Torne älv 110 65 50N 24 12E
Torneträsk 110 68 24N 19 15E
Torngat Mts. 36 59 0N 63 40W
Tornio 110 65 50N 24 12E
Tornionjoki 110 65 50N 24 12E
Tornquist 88 38 0S 62 15W
Toro, Cerro del 88 29 0S 69 50W
Toro Pk. 81 33 34N 116 24W
Toro, Pta. 84 9 22N 79 57W
Toronátos Kólpos 109 40 5N 23 30E
Toronto, Austral. 136 33 0S 151 30E
Toronto, Can. 50 43 39N 79 20W
Toronto, U.S.A. 70 40 27N 80 36W
Toronto □ 50 43 39N 79 23W
Toronto Harbour 50 43 38N 79 22W
Toronto I. 50 43 37N 79 23W
Toronto International Airport 50 43 42N 79 38W
Toronto, L. 82 27 40N 105 30W
Toropets 120 56 30N 31 40E
Tororo 116 0 45N 34 12E
Toros Dağlari 122 37 0N 35 0E
Torquay, Can. 56 49 9N 103 30W
Torquay, U.K. 95 50 27N 3 31W
Torrance 81 33 50N 118 19W
Torre Annunziata 108 40 45N 14 26E
Tôrre de Moncorvo 104 41 12N 7 8W
Torrelavega 104 43 20N 4 5W
Torremolinos 104 36 38N 4 30W
Torrens, L. 135 31 0S 137 50E
Torreón 82 25 33N 103 25W
Torres 82 28 46N 110 47W
Torres Strait 135 9 50S 142 20E
Torres Vedras 104 39 5N 9 15W
Torrevieja 104 37 59N 0 42W
Torrey 79 38 12N 111 30W
Torridge, R. 95 50 51N 4 10W
Torridon, L. 96 57 35N 5 50W
Torrington, Can. 61 51 48N 113 35W
Torrington, Conn., U.S.A. 71 41 50N 73 9W
Torrington, Wyo., U.S.A. 74 42 5N 104 8W
Torrowangee 136 31 22S 141 30E
Torsill Mts. 65 65 0N 84 30W
Tortola, I. 85 18 19N 65 0W
Tortosa 104 40 49N 0 31E
Tortosa C. 104 40 41N 0 52E
Tortue, I. de la 85 20 5N 72 57W
Tortue, R. de la 45 45 27N 73 56W
Tortuga, Isla la 85 11 8N 67 2W
Torūd 123 35 25N 55 5E
Torun 107 53 0N 18 39E
Tory Hill 70 44 56N 78 18W
Tory I. 97 55 17N 8 12W
Tosa-Wan 132 33 15N 133 30E
Toscana 108 43 30N 11 5E
Tostado 88 29 15S 61 50W
Toteng 117 20 22S 22 58E
Tôtes 100 49 41N 1 3E
Totma 120 60 0N 42 40E
Totonicapán 84 14 50N 91 20W
Tottenham, Austral. 136 32 14S 147 21E
Tottenham, Can. 46 44 1N 79 49W
Tottori 132 35 30N 134 15E
Tottori-ken □ 132 35 30N 134 12E
Touamotou, Archipel des 15 17 0S 144 0W
Toubkal, Djebel 114 31 0N 8 0W
Toubouai, Îles 15 25 0S 150 0W
Touchwood 56 51 21N 104 9W
Toucy 101 47 44N 3 15E
Touggourt 114 33 6N 6 4E
Toul 101 48 40N 5 53E
Toulnustouc Nord-Est., R. 38 50 56N 67 44W
Toulnustouc, R. 38 49 35N 68 24W
Toulon, France 103 43 10N 5 55E
Toulon, U.S.A. 76 41 6N 89 52W
Toulouse 102 43 37N 1 27E
Touques, R. 100 49 22N 0 8E
Touquet, Le 101 50 30N 1 36E
Tour-du-Pin, La 103 45 33N 5 27E
Touraine 100 47 20N 0 30E
Tourcoing 101 50 42N 3 10E
Tournai 105 50 35N 3 25E
Tournan-en-Brie 101 48 44N 2 46E
Tournay 102 43 13N 0 13E
Tournon 103 45 4N 4 50E
Tournon-St.-Martin 100 46 45N 0 58E
Tournus 103 46 35N 4 54E
Tours 100 47 22N 0 40E
Tovar 86 8 20N 71 46W
Towanda, U.S.A. 77 40 36N 88 53W
Towanda, N.Y., U.S.A. 71 41 46N 76 30W
Tower 52 47 49N 92 17W
Towner 74 48 25N 100 26W
Townsend 78 46 25N 111 32W
Townshend, C. 135 22 18S 150 30E
Townshend, I. 135 22 16S 150 31E
Townsville 135 19 15S 146 45E
Towshan 131 22 5N 112 50E
Towson 72 39 26N 76 34W
Toyah 75 31 20N 103 48W
Toyahvale 75 30 58N 103 45W
Toyama 132 36 40N 137 15E
Toyama-ken □ 132 36 45N 137 30E
Toyama-Wan 132 37 0N 137 30E
Toyohashi 132 34 45N 137 25E
Toyokawa 132 34 48N 137 27E
Toyonaka 132 34 50N 135 28E
Toyooka 132 35 35N 134 55E
Toyota 132 35 3N 137 7E
Trabzon 122 41 0N 39 45E
Tracadie 39 47 30N 64 55W
Tracy, N.B., Can. 39 45 41N 66 41W
Tracy, Qué., Can. 41 46 1N 73 9W
Tracy, Calif., U.S.A. 80 37 46N 121 27W
Tracy, Minn., U.S.A. 74 44 12N 95 30W
Tradom 129 30 0N 83 59E
Traer 76 42 12N 92 28W
Trafalgar, Austral. 136 38 14S 146 12E
Trafalgar, Can. 50 43 29N 79 43W
Trafalgar, C. 104 36 10N 6 2W
Trail 63 49 5N 117 40W
Trainor L. 54 60 24N 120 17W
Tralee 97 52 16N 9 42W
Tralee B. 97 52 17N 9 55W
Tramore 97 52 10N 7 10W
Tramping Lake 56 52 8N 108 57W
Tran Ninh, Cao Nguyen 128 19 30N 103 10E
Tranas 111 58 3N 14 59E
Trancas 88 26 20S 65 20W
Tranche-sur-Mer, La 100 46 20N 1 27W
Trang 128 7 33N 99 38E
Trangan, I. 127 6 40S 134 20E
Trangie 136 32 4S 148 0E
Trani 108 41 17N 16 24E
Tranqueras 89 31 8S 56 0W
Transcona 58 49 55N 97 0W
Transilvania 107 46 19N 25 0E
Transkei □ 117 32 15S 28 15E
Transvaal □ 117 25 0S 29 0E
Transylvania = Transilvania 107 46 19N 25 0E
Trápani 108 38 1N 12 30E
Trappe, La 44 45 29N 74 2W
Trappe Peak, Mt. 78 45 56N 114 29W
Traralgon 135 38 12S 146 34E
Tras os Montes e Alto-Douro □ 104 41 25N 7 20W
Trasimeno, L. 108 43 10N 12 5E
Trat 128 12 14N 102 33E
Travers, Mt. 133 42 1S 172 45E
Travers Res. 61 50 12N 112 51W
Traverse City 72 44 45N 85 39W
Traverse I. 91 48 0S 28 0E
Travnik 109 44 17N 17 39E
Traynor 55 52 20N 108 32W
Trebbia, R. 108 44 52N 9 30E
Trebinje 109 42 44N 18 22E
Třebon 106 48 59N 14 48E
Tredegar 95 51 47N 3 16W
Trégastel-Plage 100 48 49N 3 31W
Tréguier 100 48 47N 3 16W
Trégune 100 47 51N 3 51W
Treherne 57 49 38N 98 42W
Treignac 102 45 32N 1 48E
Treinta y Tres 89 33 10S 54 50W
Trelew 90 43 10S 65 20W
Trélissac 102 45 11N 0 47E
Trelleborg 111 55 20N 13 10E
Trélon 101 50 5N 4 6E
Tremblade, La 102 45 46N 1 8W
Tremblant, Mt. 40 46 16N 74 35W
Trementina 75 35 27N 105 30W
Tremonton 78 41 45N 112 10W
Tremp 104 42 10N 0 52E
Trenary 72 46 12N 86 59W
Trenche, R. 41 47 46N 72 53W
Trend Village 48 45 19N 75 48W
Trenggalek 127 8 5S 111 44E
Trenque Lauquen 88 36 0S 62 45W
Trent, R., Can. 47 44 6N 77 34W
Trent, R., U.K. 94 53 33N 0 44W
Trente et un Milles, L. des 40 46 12N 75 49W
Trentino-Alto Adige □ 108 46 5N 11 0E
Trento 108 46 5N 11 8E
Trenton, N.S., Can. 39 45 37N 62 38W
Trenton, Ont., Can. 47 44 10N 77 40W
Trenton, U.S.A. 77 42 8N 83 11W
Trenton, Mo., U.S.A. 76 40 5N 93 37W
Trenton, Nebr., U.S.A. 74 40 14N 101 4W
Trenton, N.J., U.S.A. 71 40 15N 74 41W
Trenton, Tenn., U.S.A. 75 35 58N 88 57W
Trepassey 37 46 43N 53 25W
Trepassey B. 37 46 37N 53 30W
Tréport, Le 100 50 3N 1 20E
Tres Arroyos 88 38 20S 60 20W
Três Corações 89 21 30S 45 30W
Três Lagoas 87 20 50S 51 50W
Tres Marías, Is. 82 21 25N 106 28W
Tres Montes, C. 90 47 0S 75 35W
Tres Pinos 80 36 48N 121 19W
Três Pontas 89 21 23S 45 29W
Tres Puentes 88 27 50S 70 15W
Três Puntas, C. 90 47 0S 66 0W
Tres Rios 89 22 20S 43 30W
Tres-St-Redempteur 43 45 26N 74 23W
Tres Valles 83 18 15N 96 8W
Trets 103 43 27N 5 41E
Treungen 111 59 1N 8 31E
Treuter Mts. 65 75 42N 82 30W
Trêve, L. la 40 49 56N 75 30W
Treviso 108 45 40N 12 15E
Trévoux 103 45 57N 4 47E
Triang 128 3 13N 102 27E
Triaucourt-en-Argonne 101 48 59N 5 2E
Tribulation, C. 135 16 5S 145 29E
Tribune, Can. 56 49 15N 103 49W
Tribune, U.S.A. 74 38 30N 101 45W
Trichur 124 10 30N 76 18E
Trier 105 49 45N 6 37E
Trieste 108 45 39N 13 45E
Triglav 108 46 25N 13 45E
Trikkala 109 39 34N 21 47E
Trikora, G. 127 4 11S 138 0E
Trilby 77 41 39N 83 37W
Trim 97 53 34N 6 48W
Trincomalee 124 8 38N 81 15E
Trindade, I. 13 20 20S 29 50W
Tring-Jonction 41 46 16N 70 59W
Trinidad, Boliv. 86 14 54S 64 50W
Trinidad, Colomb. 86 5 25N 71 40W
Trinidad, Cuba 84 21 40N 80 0W
Trinidad, Uruguay 88 33 30S 56 50W
Trinidad, U.S.A. 75 37 15N 104 30W
Trinidad & Tobago ■ 85 10 30N 61 20W
Trinidad, I., Argent. 90 39 10S 62 0W
Trinidad, I., S. Amer. 85 10 30N 61 15W
Trinidad, R. 83 17 49N 95 9W
Trinity, Can. 37 48 59N 53 55W
Trinity, U.S.A. 75 30 59N 95 20W
Trinity B., Austral. 135 16 30S 146 0E
Trinity B., Can. 37 48 20N 53 10W
Trinity Mts. 75 40 20N 118 50W
Trinity R. 75 30 30N 95 0W
Trion 73 34 35N 85 18W
Tripoli 76 42 49N 92 16W
Tripoli = Tarābulus 122 34 31N 33 52E
Tripolis 109 37 31N 22 25E
Tripp 74 43 16N 97 58W
Tripura □ 125 24 0N 92 0E
Triquet, L. 38 50 42N 59 47W
Tristan da Cunha, I. 13 37 6S 12 20W
Trivandrum 124 8 31N 77 0E
Trnava 107 48 23N 17 35E
Trochu 61 51 50N 113 13W
Trodely I. 36 52 15N 79 26W
Troglav, mt. 108 43 56N 16 36E
Troilus, L. 36 50 50N 74 35W
Trois-Pistoles 41 48 5N 69 10W
Trois-Rivières 41 46 25N 72 40W
Troitsk 120 54 10N 61 35E
Troitsko-Pechorsk 120 62 40N 56 10E
Trolladyngja 110 64 49N 17 29W
Tröllladyngja 110 64 54N 17 15W
Trollhättan 111 58 17N 12 20E
Tromelin I. 16 15 52S 54 25E
Troms fylke □ 110 68 56N 19 0E
Tromsø 110 69 40N 18 56E
Trona 81 35 46N 117 23W
Tronador, Mt. 90 41 53S 71 0W
Trondheim 110 63 25N 10 25E
Trondheimsfjorden 110 63 35N 10 30E
Troodos, mt. 122 34 58N 32 55E
Tropic 79 37 44N 112 4W
Trossachs, The 96 56 14N 4 24W
Trostan Mt. 97 55 4N 6 10W
Troup 75 32 10N 95 3W
Trout Creek, Can. 46 45 59N 79 22W
Trout Creek, U.S.A. 52 46 28N 89 1W
Trout L., N.W. Terr., Can. 54 60 40N 121 40W
Trout L., Ont., Can. 52 51 20N 93 15W
Trout Lake, Can. 63 50 35N 117 25W
Trout Lake, Mich., U.S.A. 46 46 10N 85 2W
Trout Lake, Wash., U.S.A. 80 45 60N 121 32W
Trout, R. 54 61 19N 119 51W
Trout River, Newf., Can. 37 49 29N 58 8W
Trout River, Qué., Can. 43 45 3N 74 17W
Trouville 100 49 21N 0 5E
Trowbridge 95 51 18N 2 12W
Troy, N.S., Can. 39 45 42N 61 26W
Troy, Ont., Can. 49 43 16N 80 11W
Troy, Turkey 122 39 55N 26 20E
Troy, Alabama, U.S.A. 73 31 50N 85 58W
Troy, Ill., U.S.A. 76 38 44N 89 54W
Troy, Ind., U.S.A. 77 38 0N 86 48W
Troy, Kans., U.S.A. 74 39 47N 95 2W
Troy, Mo., U.S.A. 76 38 56N 90 59W
Troy, Montana, U.S.A. 78 48 30N 115 58W
Troy, N.Y., U.S.A. 71 42 45N 73 39W
Troy, Ohio, U.S.A. 77 40 0N 84 10W

Troyes **Udmurt, A.S.S.R. □**

Troyes	**101**	48 19N	4 3 E
Trucial States = Utd. Arab Emirates	**123**	24 0N	54 30 E
Truckee	**80**	39 20N	120 11W
Truite, L. à la	**40**	47 20N	78 20W
Trujillo, Colomb.	**86**	4 10N	76 19W
Trujillo, Hond.	**84**	16 0N	86 0W
Trujillo, Peru	**86**	8 0 S	79 0W
Trujillo, Spain	**104**	39 28N	5 55W
Trujillo, U.S.A.	**75**	35 34N	104 44W
Trujillo, Venez.	**86**	9 22N	70 26W
Truk Is.	**15**	7 25N	151 46 E
Trumann	**75**	35 42N	90 32W
Trumbull, Mt.	**79**	36 25N	113 32W
Trun	**100**	48 50N	0 2 E
Trundle	**136**	32 53 S	147 42 E
Truro, Can.	**39**	45 21N	63 14W
Truro, U.K.	**95**	50 17N	5 2W
Truth or Consequences	**79**	33 9N	107 16W
Trutnov	**106**	50 37N	15 54 E
Truyère, R.	**102**	44 38N	2 34 E
Tryon	**73**	35 15N	82 16W
Tryonville	**70**	41 42N	79 48W
Tsacha L.	**62**	53 3N	124 50W
Tsagaan-Ükr	**129**	50 20N	105 3 E
Tsaidam	**129**	37 0N	95 0 E
Tsamkong = Chan Kiang	**131**	21 15N	110 20 E
Tsanghsien	**130**	38 24N	116 57 E
Tsangpo	**129**	29 40N	89 0 E
Tsaochwang	**86**	35 11N	115 28 E
Tsaohsien	**131**	34 50N	115 45 E
Tsaratanana	**117**	16 47 S	47 39 E
Tsaring Nor	**129**	34 40N	97 20 E
Tsau	**117**	20 8 S	22 29 E
Tsawassen	**66**	49 1N	123 6W
Tselinograd	**120**	51 10N	71 30 E
Tsenkung	**131**	27 3N	108 40 E
Tsetserleg	**129**	47 36N	101 32 E
Tsetserling	**130**	47 29N	101 10 E
Tshabong	**117**	26 2 S	22 29 E
Tshane	**117**	24 5 S	21 54 E
Tshela	**116**	5 4 S	13 0 E
Tshikapa	**116**	6 17 S	21 0 E
Tshofa	**116**	5 8 S	25 8 E
Tshwane	**117**	22 24 S	22 1 E
Tsian	**130**	41 12N	126 5 E
Tsiaotso	**131**	35 11N	113 37 E
Tsihombe	**117**	25 10 S	45 41 E
Tsimlyanskoye Vdkhr.	**120**	48 0N	43 0 E
Tsimo	**130**	36 25N	120 29 E
Tsin Ling Shan	**131**	34 0N	107 30 E
Tsinan	**130**	34 50N	105 40 E
Tsincheng	**130**	35 30N	113 0 E
Tsinghai	**129**	35 10N	96 0 E
Tsinghsien	**131**	26 30N	109 30 E
Tsingkiang	**131**	27 50N	114 38 E
Tsingliu	**131**	26 0N	116 50 E
Tsinglo	**130**	38 40N	112 0 E
Tsingning	**130**	35 25N	105 50 E
Tsingshih	**131**	29 43N	112 13 E
Tsingshuiho	**130**	39 56N	111 55 E
Tsingsi	**130**	38 1N	114 4 E
Tsingsi (Kweishun)	**131**	23 6N	106 25 E
Tsingtao	**130**	36 0N	120 25 E
Tsingtung Hu	**130**	37 34N	105 40 E
Tsingyuan	**130**	37 43N	104 35 E
Tsingyun	**131**	23 45N	112 55 E
Tsining	**131**	35 30N	116 35 E
Tsitsihar	**129**	47 20N	124 0 E
Tsitsutl Pk.	**62**	52 43N	125 47W
Tsivory	**117**	24 4 S	46 5 E
Tsowhsien	**131**	35 29N	117 0 E
Tsu	**132**	34 45N	136 25 E
Tsu L.	**54**	60 40N	111 52W
Tsuchiura	**132**	36 12N	140 15 E
Tsugaru-Kaikyō	**132**	41 35N	141 0 E
Tsuiluan	**130**	47 58N	28 27 E
Tsumeb	**117**	19 9 S	17 44 E
Tsumis	**117**	23 39 S	17 29 E
Tsungfa	**131**	23 35N	113 35 E
Tsungming Tao	**131**	31 40N	121 40 E
Tsungsin	**130**	35 2N	107 0 E
Tsungtso	**131**	22 26N	107 34 E
Tsunhwa	**130**	40 10N	117 57 E
Tsuniah L.	**62**	51 33N	124 4W
Tsuruga	**132**	35 45N	136 2 E
Tsushima, I.	**132**	34 20N	129 20 E
Tsushima-kaikyō	**132**	34 20N	130 0 E
Tsuyama	**132**	35 0N	134 0 E
Tual	**127**	5 30 S	132 50 E
Tuam	**97**	53 30N	8 50W
Tuamotu Arch = Touamotou	**15**	17 0 S	144 0W
Tuan	**131**	23 59N	108 3 E
Tuao	**127**	17 47 S	121 30 E
Tuatapere	**133**	46 8 S	167 41 E
Tuba City	**79**	36 8N	111 12W
Tubac	**79**	31 45N	111 2W
Tubai Is. = Toubouai, Îles	**15**	25 0 S	150 0W
Tuban	**126**	6 57 S	112 4 E
Tubarão	**89**	28 30 S	49 0W
Tubau	**126**	3 10N	113 40 E
Tubbergen	**105**	52 24N	6 48 E
Tübingen	**106**	48 31N	9 4 E
Tubruq, (Tobruk)	**115**	32 7N	23 55 E
Tucacas	**86**	10 48N	68 19W
Tuchang	**131**	29 15N	116 15 E
Tuchodi, R.	**54**	58 17N	123 42W
Tucson	**79**	32 14N	110 59W
Tucumán	**88**	26 50 S	65 20W
Tucumán □	**88**	26 48 S	66 2W
Tucumcari	**75**	35 12N	103 45W
Tucupido	**86**	9 17N	65 47W
Tucupita	**86**	9 14N	62 3W
Tucuracas	**86**	11 45N	72 22W
Tucuruí	**87**	3 42 S	49 27W
Tudela	**104**	42 4N	1 39W
Tudor, Lac	**36**	55 50N	65 25W
Tugaske	**56**	50 52N	106 17W
Tugidak I.	**67**	56 30N	154 40W
Tuguegarao	**127**	17 35N	121 42 E
Tugur	**121**	53 50N	136 45 E
Tuhshan	**131**	25 40N	107 30 E
Tukangbesi, Kepulauan	**127**	6 0 S	124 0 E
Tukarak I.	**36**	56 15N	78 45W
Tuktoyaktuk	**64**	69 27N	133 2W
Tukuyu	**116**	9 17 S	33 35 E
Tukzar	**124**	35 55N	66 25 E
Tula, Hidalgo, Mexico	**83**	20 0N	99 20W
Tula, Tamaulipas, Mexico	**83**	23 0N	99 40W
Tula, U.S.S.R.	**120**	54 13N	37 32 E
Tulak	**123**	33 55N	63 40 E
Tulan	**129**	37 24N	98 1 E
Tulancingo	**83**	20 5N	98 22W
Tulare	**80**	36 15N	119 26W
Tulare Basin	**80**	36 0N	119 48W
Tulare Lake	**79**	36 0N	119 53W
Tularosa	**79**	33 4N	106 1W
Tulbagh	**117**	33 16 S	19 6 E
Tulcán	**86**	0 48N	77 43W
Tulcea	**107**	45 13N	28 46 E
Tuléar	**117**	23 21 S	43 40 E
Tulemalu L.	**55**	62 58N	99 25W
Tuli, Indon.	**127**	1 24 S	122 26 E
Tuli, Rhod.	**117**	21 58 S	29 13 E
Tulkarm	**115**	32 19N	35 10 E
Tulla	**75**	34 35N	101 44W
Tullahoma	**73**	35 23N	86 12W
Tullamore, Can.	**50**	43 47N	79 46W
Tullamore, Ireland	**97**	53 17N	7 30W
Tulle	**102**	45 16N	1 47 E
Tullins	**103**	45 18N	5 29 E
Tullow	**97**	52 48N	6 45W
Tulsa	**75**	36 10N	96 0W
Tulsequah	**54**	58 39N	133 35W
Tulua	**86**	4 6N	76 11W
Tulun	**121**	54 40N	100 10 E
Tulungagung	**127**	8 5 S	111 54 E
Tum	**127**	3 28 S	130 21 E
Tuma, R.	**84**	13 18N	84 50W
Tumaco	**86**	1 50N	78 45W
Tumatumari	**86**	5 20N	58 55W
Tumba, L.	**116**	0 50 S	18 0 E
Tumbarumba	**136**	35 44 S	148 0 E
Tumbaya	**88**	23 50 S	65 20W
Tumbes	**86**	3 30 S	80 20W
Tumen	**130**	42 58N	129 49 E
Tumen K.	**130**	42 30N	130 0 E
Tumeremo	**86**	7 18N	61 30W
Tumkur	**124**	13 18N	77 12 E
Tummel, L.	**96**	56 43N	3 55W
Tummo	**114**	22 45N	14 8 E
Tump	**124**	26 7N	62 16 E
Tumpat	**128**	6 11N	102 10 E
Tumucumaque, Serra de	**87**	2 0N	55 0W
Tumut	**136**	35 16 S	148 13 E
Tumwater	**78**	47 0N	122 58W
Tuna, Pta.	**67**	17 59N	65 53W
Tunas de Zaza	**84**	21 39N	79 34W
Tunbridge Wells	**95**	51 7N	0 16 E
Tunduru	**116**	11 0 S	37 25 E
Tundzha, R.	**109**	42 0N	26 35 E
Tung-Pei	**121**	44 0N	126 0 E
Tung-Shan	**131**	23 40N	117 25 E
Tungabhadra, R.	**124**	15 30N	77 0 E
Tungcheng	**131**	31 0N	117 3 E
Tungchow	**130**	39 58N	116 50 E
Tungchuan	**131**	35 4N	109 2 E
Tungfanghsien, (Paso)	**131**	18 50N	108 33 E
Tunghwa	**130**	41 46N	126 0 E
Tungien	**131**	27 45N	109 3 E
Tungjen	**131**	27 40N	109 10 E
Tungkang	**131**	22 18N	120 29 E
Tungkiang, Heilungkiang, China	**130**	47 40N	132 30 E
Tungkiang, Szechwan, China	**131**	31 55N	107 30 E
Tungkingcheng	**130**	44 5N	129 15 E
Tungkun	**131**	23 0N	113 45 E
Tungkwan	**131**	34 40N	110 10 E
Tungla	**84**	13 24N	84 15W
Tunglan	**131**	24 30N	107 23 E
Tungliao	**130**	43 42N	122 11 E
Tungliu	**131**	31 0N	117 54 E
Tunglu	**131**	29 50N	119 35 E
Tungnafellsjökull	**110**	64 45N	17 55W
Tungping	**130**	35 50N	116 20 E
Tungshan, Fukien, China	**131**	23 40N	117 31 E
Tungshan, Hupeh, China	**131**	29 36N	114 28 E
Tungsheng	**130**	39 57N	110 0 E
Tungsten, Can.	**54**	61 57N	128 16W
Tungsten, U.S.A.	**78**	40 50N	118 10W
Tungtai	**131**	32 55N	120 15 E
Tungtao	**131**	26 15N	109 25 E
Tungting Hu	**131**	29 15N	112 30 E
Tungtze	**131**	27 59N	106 56 E
Tunguska, Nizhmaya, R.	**121**	64 0N	95 0 E
Tunguska, Podkammenaya, R.	**121**	61 0N	98 0 E
Tungyang	**131**	29 12N	120 12 E
Tunhwa	**130**	43 27N	128 16 E
Tunhwang	**129**	40 5N	94 46 E
Tunia	**86**	2 41N	76 31W
Tunica	**75**	34 43N	90 23W
Tunis	**114**	36 50N	10 11 E
Tunisia ■	**114**	33 30N	9 10 E
Tunja	**86**	5 40N	73 25W
Tunkhannock	**71**	41 32N	75 56W
Tunki	**131**	29 44N	118 4 E
Tunliu	**130**	36 15N	112 54 E
Tunnsjøen	**110**	64 45N	13 25 E
Tuntatuliag	**67**	60 20N	162 45W
Tunulic, R.	**36**	58 57N	66 50W
Tunungayualok I.	**36**	56 0N	61 0W
Tunuyán	**88**	33 55 S	69 0W
Tunuyán, R.	**88**	33 33 S	67 30W
Tuolumne	**80**	37 59N	120 16W
Tuolumne, R.	**80**	37 36N	121 13W
Tuoy-Khaya	**121**	62 32N	111 18 E
Tupã	**89**	21 57 S	50 28W
Tuparro, R.	**86**	5 0N	68 40W
Tupelo	**73**	34 15N	88 42W
Tupik	**121**	54 26N	119 57 E
Tupinambaranas, I.	**86**	3 0 S	58 0W
Tupiza	**88**	21 30 S	65 40W
Tupman	**81**	35 18N	119 21W
Tupper	**54**	55 32N	120 1W
Tupper L.	**71**	44 18N	74 30W
Tupungato, Cerro	**88**	33 15 S	69 50W
Tuque, La	**41**	47 30N	72 50W
Túquerres	**86**	1 5N	77 37W
Tura	**121**	64 20N	99 30 E
Turagua, Serrania	**86**	7 20N	64 35W
Türän	**123**	35 45N	56 50 E
Turan	**121**	51 38N	101 40 E
Turek	**107**	52 3N	18 30 E
Turen	**86**	9 17N	69 6W
Turfan	**129**	43 6N	89 24 E
Turfan Depression	**129**	42 45N	89 0 E
Turgeon, L.	**40**	49 2N	79 4W
Turgeon, R.	**40**	50 0N	78 56W
Turgutlu	**122**	38 30N	27 48 E
Turhal	**122**	40 24N	36 19 E
Turia, R.	**104**	39 43N	1 0W
TuriaçI	**87**	1 40 S	45 28W
TuriaçI, R.	**87**	3 0 S	46 0W
Turin, Can.	**54**	49 47N	112 24W
Turin, Alta., Can.	**61**	49 58N	112 31W
Turin = Torino	**108**	45 3N	7 40 E
Turiy Rog	**130**	45 5N	131 45 E
Turkana, L.	**116**	4 10N	32 10 E
Turkestan	**120**	43 10N	68 10 E
Turkey ■	**122**	39 0N	36 0 E
Turkey, R.	**76**	42 43N	91 2W
Turkmen S.S.R. □	**120**	39 0N	59 0 E
Turks Is.	**85**	21 20N	71 20W
Turks Island Passage	**85**	21 30N	71 20W
Turku (Åbo)	**111**	60 30N	22 19 E
Turlock	**80**	37 30N	120 55W
Turnagain, C.	**133**	40 28 S	176 38 E
Turnagain, R.	**54**	59 12N	127 35W
Turnberry	**55**	53 25N	101 45W
Turneffe Is.	**83**	17 20N	87 50W
Turner	**78**	48 52N	108 25W
Turner Valley	**61**	50 40N	114 17W
Turners Falls	**71**	42 36N	72 34W
Turnhout	**105**	51 19N	4 57 E
Turnor L.	**55**	56 35N	108 35W
Turnour I.	**62**	50 36N	126 27W
Turnovo	**109**	43 5N	25 41 E
Turnu Măgurele	**107**	43 46N	24 56 E
Turnu Rosu Pasul	**107**	45 33N	24 17 E
Turnu-Severin	**107**	44 39N	22 41 E
Turon	**75**	37 48N	98 27W
Turriff	**96**	57 32N	2 28W
Turtle L., Can.	**56**	53 36N	108 38W
Turtle L., U.S.A.	**74**	45 22N	92 10W
Turtle Lake	**74**	47 30N	100 55W
Turtle Mt. Prov. Park	**57**	49 3N	100 15W
Turtle, R.	**52**	48 51N	92 45W
Turtleford	**56**	53 23N	108 57W
Turūbah	**122**	28 20N	43 15 E
Turukhansk	**121**	65 50N	87 50 E
Turun ja Porin lä?ni □	**111**	60 27N	22 15 E
Tuscaloosa	**73**	33 13N	87 31W
Tuscar Rock	**97**	52 10N	6 15W
Tuscola, Ill., U.S.A.	**77**	39 48N	88 15W
Tuscola, Tex., U.S.A.	**75**	32 15N	99 48W
Tuscumbia, U.S.A.	**76**	38 14N	92 28W
Tuscumbia, Ala., U.S.A.	**73**	34 42N	87 42W
Tushikow	**130**	41 25N	115 55 E
Tuskar Rock	**97**	52 12N	6 10W
Tuskegee	**73**	32 24N	85 39W
Tusket	**39**	43 52N	65 58W
Tusket, R.	**39**	43 41N	65 57W
Tutóia	**87**	2 45 S	42 20W
Tutong	**126**	4 47N	114 34 E
Tutrakan	**109**	44 2N	26 40 E
Tutshi L.	**54**	59 56N	134 30W
Tuttlingen	**106**	47 59N	8 50 E
Tutuaia	**127**	8 25 S	127 15 E
Tutuila, I.	**133**	14 19 S	170 50W
Tuul Gol, R.	**130**	48 30N	104 25 E
Tuva, A.S.S.R. □	**121**	51 30N	95 0 E
Tuxedo	**58**	49 52N	97 13W
Tuxford	**56**	50 34N	105 35W
Tuxpan	**83**	20 50N	97 30W
Tuxtla Gutiérrez	**83**	16 50N	93 10W
Tuy	**104**	42 3N	8 39W
Tuy Hoa	**128**	13 5N	109 17 E
Tuya L.	**54**	59 7N	130 35W
Tuyen Hoa	**128**	17 50N	106 10 E
Tuyun	**131**	26 15N	107 32 E
Tuz Gölü	**122**	38 45N	33 30 E
Tuz Khurmatli	**122**	34 52N	44 41 E
Tūz Khurmātu	**122**	34 50N	44 45 E
Tuzla	**109**	44 34N	18 41 E
Twain	**80**	40 1N	121 3W
Twain Harte	**80**	38 2N	120 14W
Tweed	**47**	44 29N	77 19W
Tweed, R.	**94**	55 42N	2 10W
Tweedmuir	**56**	53 34N	105 57W
Tweedside, N.B., Can.	**39**	45 38N	67 1W
Tweedside, Ont., Can.	**49**	43 10N	79 41W
Tweedsmuir Prov. Park	**62**	53 0N	126 20W
Twelve Mile L.	**56**	49 29N	106 14W
Twelve Pins	**97**	53 32N	9 50W
Twenty Mile Creek, R.	**49**	43 10N	79 22W
Twentynine Palms	**81**	34 10N	116 4W
Twillingate	**37**	49 42N	54 45W
Twin Bridges	**78**	45 33N	112 23W
Twin City	**52**	48 22N	89 25W
Twin Falls	**78**	42 30N	114 30W
Twin Valley	**74**	47 18N	96 15W
Twisp	**63**	48 21N	120 5W
Two Creeks	**60**	54 18N	116 21W
Two Harbors	**52**	47 1N	91 40W
Two Hills	**60**	53 43N	111 45W
Two Rivers	**72**	44 10N	87 31W
Twofold B.	**136**	37 8 S	149 59 E
Tyler, Minn., U.S.A.	**74**	44 18N	96 15W
Tyler, Tex., U.S.A.	**75**	32 18N	94 58W
Tyndall	**57**	50 5N	96 40W
Tyndinskiy	**121**	55 10N	124 43 E
Tyne & Wear □	**94**	54 55N	1 35W
Tyne, R.	**94**	54 58N	1 28W
Tyne Valley	**39**	46 35N	63 56W
Tynemouth	**94**	55 1N	1 27W
Tyre = Sūr	**115**	33 19N	35 16 E
Tyrell Creek	**136**	35 22 S	143 0 E
Tyrell L.	**136**	35 22 S	143 0 E
Tyrifjorden	**111**	60 2N	10 8 E
Tyrma	**130**	50 0N	132 2 E
Tyrol = Tirol	**106**	46 50N	11 20 E
Tyrone	**70**	40 39N	78 10W
Tyrone □	**97**	54 40N	7 15W
Tyrone, Co.	**97**	54 40N	7 15W
Tyrrell Arm	**55**	62 27N	97 30W
Tyrrell, L.	**136**	35 20 S	142 50 E
Tyrrell L.	**55**	63 7N	105 27W
Tyrrell, R.	**136**	35 26 S	142 51 E
Tyrrhenian Sea	**108**	40 0N	12 30 E
Tysfjörden	**110**	68 10N	16 10 E
Tyumen	**120**	57 0N	65 18 E
Tywi, R.	**95**	51 48N	4 20W
Tzaneen	**117**	23 47 S	30 9 E
Tzechung	**131**	29 47N	104 50 E
Tzehsien	**130**	36 25N	114 24 E
Tzeki	**131**	27 40N	117 5 E
Tzekwei	**131**	31 0N	110 46 E
Tzepo	**130**	36 28N	117 58 E
Tzetung	**131**	31 31N	105 1 E
Tzuyang	**131**	35 44N	116 51 E

U

Uainambi	**86**	1 43N	69 51W
Uasadi-jidi, Sierra	**86**	4 54N	65 18W
Uato-Udo	**127**	4 3 S	126 6 E
Uatumã, R.	**86**	1 30 S	59 25W
Uaupés	**86**	0 8 S	67 5W
Uaxactún	**84**	17 25N	89 29W
Ubá	**89**	21 0 S	43 0W
Ubaitaba	**87**	14 18 S	39 20W
Ubangi, R. = Oubangi	**116**	1 0N	17 50 E
Ubaté	**86**	5 19N	73 49W
Ubauro	**124**	28 15N	69 45 E
Ube	**132**	33 56N	131 15 E
Ubeda	**104**	38 3N	3 23W
Uberaba	**87**	19 50 S	47 55W
Uberlândia	**87**	19 0 S	48 20W
Ubon Ratchathani	**128**	15 15N	104 50 E
Ubundi	**116**	0 22 S	25 30 E
Ucayali, R.	**86**	6 0 S	75 0W
Uchi Lake	**52**	51 5N	92 35W
Uchiura-Wan	**132**	42 25N	140 40 E
Ucluelet	**62**	48 57N	125 32W
Uda, R.	**121**	54 42N	135 14 E
Udaipur	**124**	24 36N	73 44 E
Udaipur Garhi	**125**	27 0N	86 35 E
Uddevalla	**111**	58 21N	11 55 E
Uden	**105**	51 40N	5 37 E
Udgir	**124**	18 25N	77 5 E
Udhampur	**124**	33 0N	75 5 E
Údine	**108**	46 5N	13 10 E
Udipi	**124**	13 25N	74 42 E
Udmurt, A.S.S.R. □	**120**	57 30N	52 30 E

Udon Thani	128	17 29N	102 46 E
Ueda	132	36 24N	138 16 E
Uedineniya, Os.	17	78 0N	85 0 E
Uelen	121	66 10N	170 0W
Uelzen	106	53 0N	10 33 E
Uere, R.	116	3 45N	24 45 E
Ufa	120	54 45N	55 55 E
Ugad R.	117	20 55 S	14 30 E
Ugalla, R.	116	6 0 S	32 0 E
Uganda ■	116	2 0N	32 0 E
Ugine	103	45 45N	6 25 E
Uhrichsville	70	40 23N	81 22W
Uiju	130	40 15N	124 35 E
Uinta Mts.	78	40 45N	110 30W
Uitenhage	117	33 40 S	25 28 E
Uithuizen	105	53 24N	6 41 E
Uivuk, C.	36	58 29N	62 34W
Uji-guntō	131	31 15N	129 25 E
Ujjain	124	23 9N	75 43 E
Újpest	107	47 22N	19 6 E
Ujung Pandang	127	5 10 S	119 20 E
Uka	121	57 50N	162 0 E
Ukerewe Is.	116	2 0 S	33 0 E
Ukhrul	125	25 10N	94 25 E
Ukhta	120	63 55N	54 0 E
Ukiah	80	39 10N	123 9W
Ukraine S.S.R. □	120	48 0N	35 0 E
Ulaan Nuur	130	44 30N	103 40 E
Ulaanbaatar	130	47 54N	106 52 E
Ulaangom	129	50 0N	92 10 E
Ulak I.	67	51 24N	178 58W
Ulan-Bator = Ulaanbaatar	130	47 54N	106 52 E
Ulan Ude	121	52 0N	107 30 E
Ulanhot	130	46 5N	122 1 E
Ulcinj	109	41 58N	19 10 E
Uldz Gol	130	49 30N	114 0 E
Ulhasnagar	124	19 15N	73 10 E
Ulladulla	136	35 21 S	150 29 E
Ullapool	96	57 54N	5 10W
Ullswater, L.	94	54 35N	2 52W
Ullŭng Do	130	37 30N	130 30 E
Ulm	106	48 23N	10 0 E
Ulricehamn	111	57 46N	13 26 E
Ulster □	97	54 45N	6 30W
Ulverston	94	54 13N	3 7W
Ulverstone	135	41 11 S	146 11 E
Ulya	121	59 10N	142 0 E
Ulyanovsk	120	54 25N	48 25 E
Ulyasutay, (Javhlant)	129	47 56N	97 28 E
Ulysses	75	37 39N	101 25W
Umala	86	17 25 S	68 5W
Umánaé	17	70 40N	52 10W
Umánaé Fjord	10	70 40N	52 0W
Umanak	65	70 58N	52 0W
Umaria	125	23 35N	80 50 E
Umarkot	70	25 15N	69 40 E
Umatilla	78	45 58N	119 17W
Umba	120	66 50N	34 20 E
Umbrella Mts.	133	45 35 S	169 5 E
Umbria □	108	42 53N	12 30 E
Ume, R.	110	64 45N	18 30 E
Umeå	110	63 45N	20 20 E
Umera	127	0 12 S	129 30 E
Umfreville L.	52	50 18N	94 45W
Umiat	67	69 25N	152 20W
Umm al Qaiwain	123	25 30N	55 35 E
Umm az Zamul	123	22 35N	55 18 E
Umm Lajj	122	25 0N	37 23 E
Umm Said	123	25 0N	51 40 E
Umnak.	67	53 20N	168 20W
Umnak I.	67	53 0N	168 0W
Umniati, R.	117	18 0 S	29 0 E
Umpang	128	16 3N	98 54 E
Umpqua, R.	78	43 30N	123 30W
Umtali	117	18 58 S	32 38 E
Umtata	117	31 36 S	28 49 E
Umvuma	117	19 16 S	30 30 E
Umzimvubu, R.	117	31 38 S	29 33 E
Unac, R.	108	44 42N	16 15 E
Unadilla	71	42 20N	75 17W
Unalanaska I.	67	54 0N	164 30W
Uncia	86	18 25 S	66 40W
Uncompahgce Pk., Mt.	79	38 5N	107 32W
Underbool	136	35 10 S	141 51 E
Ungarie	136	33 38 S	146 56 E
Ungava B.	36	59 30N	67 30W
Ungava Pen.	36	60 0N	75 0W
Unggi	130	42 16N	130 28 E
União	87	4 50 S	37 50W
União da Vitória	89	26 5 S	51 0W
Unimak I.	67	54 30N	164 30W
Unimak Pass.	67	53 30N	165 15W
Union, Mo., U.S.A.	76	38 25N	91 0W
Union, N.J., U.S.A.	71	40 47N	74 3W
Union, S.C., U.S.A.	73	34 49N	81 39W
Union Bay	62	49 35N	124 53W
Union City, N.J., U.S.A.	71	40 47N	74 5W
Union City, Ohio, U.S.A.	77	40 11N	84 49W
Union City, Pa., U.S.A.	70	41 53N	79 50W
Union City, Tenn., U.S.A.	71	36 25N	89 0W
Union Gap	73	46 38N	120 29W
Union Grove	77	42 41N	88 3W
Union I.	62	50 0N	127 16W
Unión, La, Chile	90	40 10 S	73 0W
Unión, La, Colomb.	86	1 35N	77 5W
Unión, La, El Sal.	83	13 20N	87 50W
Uníon, La	82	17 58N	101 49W
Unión, La	86	7 28N	67 53W
Union, Mt.	79	34 34N	112 21W
Union of Soviet Soc. Rep. ■	121	47 0N	100 0 E
Union Springs	73	32 9N	85 44W
Union Star	76	39 59N	94 36W
Uniontown, U.S.A.	77	37 47N	87 56W
Uniontown, Pa., U.S.A.	72	39 54N	79 45W
Unionville, Can.	50	43 52N	79 18W
Unionville, U.S.A.	76	40 29N	93 1W
Unionville, Mich., U.S.A.	46	43 39N	83 28W
United Arab Emirates ■	123	23 50N	54 0 E
United Arab Republic ■	113	27 5N	30 0 E
United States of America ■	69	37 0N	96 0W
United States Range	65	82 25N	68 0W
Unity	56	52 30N	109 5W
University City	76	38 40N	90 20W
University, R.	53	47 55N	85 12W
Unnao	125	26 35N	80 30 E
Unst, I.	96	60 50N	0 55W
Unturán, Sierra de	86	1 35N	64 40W
Unuk, R.	54	56 5N	131 3W
Ünye	122	41 5N	37 15 E
Upata	86	8 1N	62 24W
Upemba, L.	116	8 30 S	26 20 E
Upernavik	65	72 49N	56 20W
Upington	117	28 25 S	21 15 E
Uplands, B.C., Can.	63	48 27N	123 17W
Uplands, Sask., Can.	58	50 29N	104 36W
Upolu, I.	133	13 58 S	172 0W
Upolu Pt.	67	20 16N	155 52W
Upper Alkali Lake	78	41 47N	120 0W
Upper Arlington	77	40 0N	83 4W
Upper Arrow L.	63	50 30N	117 50W
Upper Blackville	39	46 39N	65 52W
Upper Campbell L.	62	49 55N	125 39W
Upper Foster L.	55	56 47N	105 20W
Upper Goose L.	52	51 43N	92 43W
Upper Humber R.	37	49 11N	57 28W
Upper Hutt	133	41 8 S	175 5 E
Upper Klamath L.	78	42 16N	121 55W
Upper L. Erne	97	54 14N	7 22W
Upper Lachute	43	45 40N	74 14W
Upper Lake	80	39 10N	122 55W
Upper Manitou L.	52	49 24N	92 48W
Upper Musquodoboit	39	45 10N	62 58W
Upper Red L., U.S.A.	52	48 10N	94 40W
Upper Red L., U.S.A.	74	48 0N	95 0W
Upper Sandusky	77	40 50N	83 17W
Upper Stewiacke	39	45 13N	63 0W
Upper Volta ■	114	12 0N	0 30W
Uppsala	111	59 53N	17 38 E
Uppsala län □	111	60 0N	17 30 E
Upsala	52	49 3N	90 28W
Upton, Can.	41	45 39N	72 41W
Upton, U.S.A.	74	44 8N	104 35W
Ur	122	30 55N	46 25 E
Urabá, Golfo de	86	8 25N	76 53W
Uracará	86	2 20 S	57 50W
Ural Mts. = Uralskie Gory	120	60 0N	59 0 E
Ural, R.	120	49 0N	52 0W
Uralsk	120	51 20N	51 20 E
Uralskie Gory	120	60 0N	59 0 E
Urana	136	35 15 S	146 21 E
Urandangi	135	21 32 S	138 14 E
Uranium City	55	59 34N	108 37W
Uraricaá, R.	86	3 20N	61 56W
Urawa	132	35 50N	139 40 E
Uray	120	60 5N	65 15 E
Urbana, U.S.A.	76	37 51N	93 10W
Urbana, Ill., U.S.A.	77	40 7N	88 12W
Urbana, Ohio, U.S.A.	77	40 9N	83 44W
Urbana, La	86	7 8N	66 56W
Urbandale	76	41 38N	93 43W
Urbino	108	43 43N	12 38 E
Urbión, Picos de	104	42 1N	2 52W
Urcos	86	13 30 S	71 30W
Urdinarrain	88	32 37 S	58 52W
Urdos	102	42 51N	0 35W
Urdzhar	120	47 5N	81 38 E
Ure, R.	94	54 20N	1 25W
Ures	82	29 30N	110 30W
Urfa	122	37 12N	38 50 E
Urfahr	106	48 19N	14 17 E
Urgench	120	41 40N	60 30 E
Urgun	123	32 55N	69 12 E
Uribante, R.	86	7 25N	71 50W
Uribe	86	3 13N	74 24W
Uribia	86	11 43N	72 16W
Uriondo	88	21 41 S	64 41W
Urique	82	27 13N	107 55W
Urique, R.	82	26 29N	107 58W
Urk	105	52 39N	5 36 E
Urla	122	38 20N	26 55 E
Urmia, L.	122	37 30N	45 30 E
Urmia (Rezā'iyeh)	122	37 40N	45 0 E
Urrao	86	6 20N	76 11W
Ursula Chan.	62	53 25N	128 55W
Uruaca	87	15 30 S	49 41W
Uruapán	82	19 30N	102 0W
Urubamba	86	13 5 S	72 10W
Urubamba, R.	86	11 0 S	73 0W
Uruçuí	87	7 20 S	44 28W
Uruguai, R.	89	24 0 S	53 30W
Uruguaiana	88	29 50 S	57 0W
Uruguay ■	88	32 30 S	55 30W
Uruguay, R.	88	28 0 S	56 0W
Urumchi = Wulumuchi	129	43 40N	87 50 E
Urungu	129	46 30N	88 50 E
Urup, I.	121	43 0N	151 0 E
Uruyén	86	5 41N	62 25W
Uruzgan □	124	33 30N	66 0 E
Usa	120	2 23 S	36 52 E
Uşak	122	38 43N	29 28 E
Usakos	117	22 0 S	15 31 E
Usedom	106	53 50N	13 55 E
Useko	116	5 8 S	32 24 E
Ush-Tobe	120	45 16N	78 0 E
Ushakova, O.	17	82 0N	80 0 E
Ushant = Ouessant, Île d'	100	48 25N	5 5W
Ushuaia	90	54 50 S	68 23W
Ushumun	121	52 47N	126 32 E
Usk, R.	95	51 37N	2 56W
Üsküdar	122	41 0N	29 5 E
Usolye Sibirskoye	121	52 40N	103 40 E
Uspallata, P. de	88	32 30 S	69 28W
Uspenskiy	120	48 50N	72 55 E
Ussel	102	45 32N	2 18 E
Ussuriysk	130	43 40N	131 50 E
Ust Aldan = Batamay	121	63 30N	129 15 E
Ust Amginskoye = Khandyga	121	62 30N	134 50 E
Ust-Bolsheretsk	121	52 40N	156 30 E
Ust Ilga	121	55 5N	104 55 E
Ust Ilimpeya = Yukti	121	63 20N	105 0 E
Ust-Ilimsk	121	58 3N	102 39 E
Ust Ishim	120	57 45N	71 10 E
Ust Kamchatsk	121	56 10N	162 0 E
Ust Kamenogorsk	120	50 0N	82 20 E
Ust Karenga	121	54 40N	116 45 E
Ust Khayryuzova	121	57 15N	156 55 E
Ust Kut	121	56 50N	105 10 E
Ust Kuyga	121	70 1N	135 36 E
Ust Maya	121	60 30N	134 20 E
Ust Mil	121	59 50N	133 0 E
Ust Nera	121	64 35N	143 15 E
Ust Olenek	121	73 0N	120 10 E
Ust-Omchug	121	61 9N	149 38 E
Ust Port	120	70 0N	84 10 E
Ust Tsilma	120	65 25N	52 0 E
Ust-Tungir	121	55 25N	120 15 E
Ust Urt = Ustyurt	120	44 0N	55 0 E
Ust Vorkuta	120	67 7N	63 35 E
Ustaritz	102	43 24N	1 27W
Ustí nad Labem	106	50 41N	14 3 E
Ustica, I.	108	38 42N	13 10 E
Ustye	121	55 30N	97 30 E
Ustyurt, Plato	120	44 0N	55 0 E
Usuki	132	33 8N	131 49 E
Usulután	84	13 25N	88 28W
Usumacinta, R.	83	17 0N	91 0W
Utah □	78	39 30N	111 30W
Utah, L.	78	40 10N	111 58W
Ute Cr.	75	36 5N	103 45W
Utete	116	8 0 S	38 45 E
Uthai Thani	128	15 22N	100 3 E
Uthmaniyah	122	25 5N	49 6 E
Utiariti	86	13 0 S	58 10W
Utica, Mich., U.S.A.	46	42 38N	83 2W
Utica, N.Y., U.S.A.	71	43 5N	75 18W
Utica, Ohio, U.S.A.	70	40 13N	82 26W
Utik L.	55	55 15N	96 0W
Utikuma L.	60	55 50N	115 30W
Utrecht, Neth.	105	52 3N	5 8 E
Utrecht, S. Afr.	117	27 38 S	30 20 E
Utrecht □	105	52 6N	5 7 E
Utrera	104	37 12N	5 48W
Utsjoki	110	69 51N	26 59 E
Utsunomiya	132	36 30N	139 50 E
Uttar Pradesh □	124	27 0N	80 0 E
Uttaradit	128	17 36N	100 5 E
Utterson	70	45 13N	79 20W
Uttoxeter	94	52 53N	1 50W
Uudenmaan lä ni □	111	60 25N	25 0 E
Uuldza	130	49 8N	112 10 E
Uusikaarlepyy	110	63 32N	22 31 E
Uusikaupunki	111	60 47N	21 25 E
Uvalde	75	29 15N	99 48W
Uvat	120	59 5N	68 50 E
Uvinza	116	5 5 S	30 24 E
Uvira	116	3 22 S	29 3 E
Uvs Nuur	129	50 20N	92 30 E
Uwainid	122	24 50N	46 0 E
Uwajima	132	33 10N	132 35 E
Uxbridge	46	44 6N	79 7W
Uxmal	83	20 22N	89 46W
Uyuni	88	20 35 S	66 55W
Uyuni, Salar de	88	20 10 S	68 0W
Uzbekistan S.S.R. □	120	40 5N	65 0 E
Uzerche	102	45 25N	1 35 E
Uzès	103	44 1N	4 26 E

V

Vaal, R.	117	27 40 S	25 30 E
Vaasan lääni □	110	63 2N	22 50 E
Vabre	102	43 42N	2 24 E
Vác	107	47 49N	19 10 E
Vacaria	89	28 31 S	50 52W
Vacaville	80	38 21N	122 0W
Vach, R.	120	60 56N	76 38 E
Vache, I.-à	85	18 2N	73 35W
Vadodara	124	22 20N	73 10 E
Vadsø	110	70 3N	29 50 E
Vaerøy	110	67 40N	12 40 E
Vagney	101	48 1N	6 43 E
Váh, R.	107	49 10N	18 20 E
Vaigach	120	70 10N	59 0 E
Vaiges	100	48 2N	0 30W
Vaihsel B.	91	75 0 S	35 0W
Vailly Aisne	101	49 25N	3 30 E
Vaison	103	44 14N	5 4 E
Val-Alain	41	46 24N	71 45W
Val-Barrette	40	46 30N	75 21W
Val Brillant	38	48 32N	67 33W
Val Caron	46	46 37N	81 1W
Val d' Ajol, Le	101	47 55N	6 30 E
Val-de-Marne □	101	48 45N	2 28 E
Val-des-Bois	40	45 54N	75 35W
Val-d'Espoir	38	48 31N	64 24W
Val-d'Oise □	101	49 5N	2 0 E
Val d'Or	40	48 7N	77 47W
Val Marie	56	49 15N	107 45W
Val-St-Michael	42	46 52N	71 27W
Valahia	107	44 35N	25 0 E
Valcheta	90	40 40 S	66 20W
Valcourt	41	45 29N	72 18W
Valdahon, Le	101	47 8N	6 20 E
Valdepeñas	104	38 43N	3 25W
Valdes I.	63	49 4N	123 39W
Valdes Pen.	90	42 30 S	63 45W
Valdez	67	61 14N	146 10W
Valdezia	97	23 5 S	30 14 E
Valdivia	90	39 50 S	73 14W
Valdivia □	90	40 0 S	73 0W
Valdivia, La	88	34 43 S	72 5W
Valdosta	73	30 50N	83 20W
Vale	78	44 0N	117 15W
Valemount	63	52 50N	119 15W
Valença	87	13 20 S	39 5W
Valença do Piauí	87	6 20 S	41 45W
Valence	103	44 57N	4 54 E
Valence-d'Agen	102	44 8N	0 54 E
Valencia, Spain	104	39 27N	0 23W
Valencia, Venez.	86	10 11N	68 0W
Valencia □	104	39 20N	0 40W
Valencia, Albufera de	104	39 20N	0 27W
Valencia de Alcántara	104	39 25N	7 14W
Valencia, G. de	104	39 30N	0 20 E
Valencia, L. de	85	10 13N	67 40W
Valenciennes	101	50 20N	3 34 E
Valensole	103	43 50N	5 59 E
Valentia Hr.	97	51 56N	10 17W
Valentia I.	97	51 54N	10 22W
Valentine, Nebr., U.S.A.	74	42 50N	100 35W
Valentine, Tex., U.S.A.	75	30 36N	104 28W
Valenton	78	48 45N	2 28 E
Valera	86	9 19N	70 37W
Valier	78	48 25N	112 9W
Valinco, G. de	103	41 40N	8 52 E
Valjevo	109	44 18N	19 53 E
Valkeakoski	111	61 16N	24 2 E
Valkenswaard	105	51 21N	5 29 E
Valladolid, Mexico	83	20 30N	88 20W
Valladolid, Spain	104	41 38N	4 43W
Valle d'Aosta □	108	45 45N	7 22 E
Valle de la Pascua	86	9 13N	66 0W
Valle de las Palmas	81	32 20N	116 43W
Valle de Santiago	82	20 25N	101 15W
Valle de Zaragoza	82	27 28N	105 49W
Valle del Cauca □	86	3 45N	76 30W
Valle Fértil, Sierra del	88	30 20 S	68 0W
Valle Hermosa	83	25 35N	102 25 E
Valle Nacional	83	17 47N	96 19W
Vallecas	104	40 23N	3 41W
Valledupar	86	10 29N	73 15W
Vallée-Jonction	41	46 22N	70 55W
Vallejo	80	38 12N	122 15W
Vallenar	88	28 30 S	70 50W
Valleraugue	102	44 6N	3 39 E
Vallet	100	47 10N	1 15W
Valletta	108	35 54N	14 30 E
Valley Center	81	33 13N	117 2W
Valley City	74	46 57N	98 0W
Valley Falls	78	42 33N	120 8W
Valley Park	76	38 33N	90 29W
Valley Springs	80	38 11N	120 50W
Valley Station	77	38 10N	85 50W
Valley Wells	81	35 27N	115 46W
Valleyfield	34	45 15N	74 8W
Valleyview, Alta., Can.	60	55 5N	117 17W
Valleyview, B.C., Can.	63	50 10N	120 13W
Vallimanca, Arroyo	88	35 40 S	59 10W
Vallon	103	44 25N	4 23 E
Valls	104	41 18N	1 15 E
Valmeyer	76	38 18N	90 19W
Valmont	100	49 45N	0 30 E
Valmy	101	49 5N	4 45 E
Valognes	100	49 30N	1 28W
Valora	52	49 46N	91 13W
Valparaíso, Chile	88	33 2 S	71 40W
Valparaíso, Mexico	82	22 50N	103 32W
Valparaiso	77	41 27N	87 2W
Valparaiso □	88	33 2 S	71 40W
Valréas	103	44 24N	5 0 E
Valrita	53	49 27N	82 33W

Vals-les-Bains Villa Guillermina

Place	Page	Lat.	Long.
Vals-les-Bains	103	44 42N	4 24 E
Vals, Tanjung	127	8 32 S	137 32 E
Valsbaai	117	34 15 S	18 40 E
Valverde del Camino	104	37 35N	6 47W
Van	122	38 30N	43 20 E
Van Alstyne	75	33 25N	96 36W
Van Bruyssel	41	47 56N	72 9W
Van Buren, Can.	39	47 10N	67 55W
Van Buren, Ark., U.S.A.	75	35 28N	94 18W
Van Buren, Me., U.S.A.	73	47 10N	68 1W
Van Buren, Mo., U.S.A.	75	37 0N	91 0W
Van Diemen, C.	135	11 9 S	130 24 E
Van Diemen G.	134	11 45 S	131 50 E
Van Gölü	122	38 30N	43 0 E
Van Horn	79	31 3N	104 55W
Van Horne	76	42 1N	92 4W
Van Tassell	74	42 40N	104 3W
Van Wert	77	40 52N	84 31W
Vananda	62	49 46N	124 33W
Vanavara	121	60 22N	102 16 E
Vanceburg	77	38 36N	83 19W
Vancouver, Can.	66	49 15N	123 10W
Vancouver, U.S.A.	80	45 44N	122 41W
Vancouver Harb.	66	49 18N	123 5W
Vancouver I.	62	49 50N	126 0W
Vancouver I. Ranges	62	49 30N	125 40W
Vancouver International Airport	66	48 12N	123 11W
Vandalia, Ill., U.S.A.	76	38 57N	89 4W
Vandalia, Mo., U.S.A.	76	39 19N	91 29W
Vandalia, Mo., U.S.A.	76	39 18N	91 30W
Vandalia, Ohio, U.S.A.	77	39 54N	84 12W
Vandenburg	81	34 35N	120 44W
Vanderbijlpark	118	26 42 S	27 54 E
Vanderbilt	46	45 9N	84 40W
Vandergrift	70	40 36N	79 33W
Vanderhoof	62	54 0N	124 0W
Vanderlin I.	135	15 44 S	137 2 E
Vandry	41	47 52N	73 34W
Vänern	111	58 47N	13 30 E
Vänersborg	111	58 26N	12 27 E
Vanessa	49	42 58N	80 24W
Vang Vieng	128	18 58N	102 32 E
Vanga	116	4 35 S	39 12 E
Vangaindrano	117	23 21 S	47 36 E
Vanguard	56	49 55N	107 20W
Vanier, Ont., Can.	48	45 27N	75 40W
Vanier, Qué., Can.	42	46 49N	71 15W
Vankleek Hill	47	45 32N	74 40W
Vanna	110	70 6N	19 50 E
Vannas	110	63 58N	19 48 E
Vannes	100	47 40N	2 47W
Vanoise, Massif de la	103	45 25N	6 40 E
Vanrhynsdorp	117	31 36 S	18 44 E
Vans, Les	103	44 25N	4 7 E
Vansbro	111	60 32N	14 15 E
Vanscoy	56	52 0N	106 59W
Vansittart B.	134	14 3 S	126 17 E
Vansittart I.	65	65 50N	84 0W
Vanua Levu, I.	133	16 33 S	178 8 E
Vanua Mbalavu, I.	133	17 40 S	178 57W
Var □	103	43 27N	6 18 E
Varades	100	47 25N	1 1W
Varanasi (Benares)	125	25 22N	83 8 E
Varangerfjorden	110	70 3N	29 25 E
Varazdin	108	46 20N	16 20 E
Varberg	111	57 17N	12 20 E
Vardar, R.	109	41 25N	22 20 E
Varennes	43	45 39N	73 28W
Varennes-sur-Allier	102	46 19N	3 24 E
Varese	108	45 49N	8 50 E
Varginha	89	21 33 S	45 25W
Varillas	88	24 0 S	70 10W
Värmlands län □	111	59 45N	13 20 E
Varna, Bulg.	109	43 13N	27 56 E
Varna, U.S.A.	76	41 2N	89 14W
Varnamo	111	57 10N	14 3 E
Vars	47	45 21N	75 21W
Varto	122	39 10N	41 28 E
Varzaneh	123	32 25N	52 40 E
Varzy	101	47 22N	3 20 E
Vasa	110	63 6N	21 38 E
Vasa Barris, R.	87	11 10 S	37 10W
Vascongadas	104	42 50N	2 45W
Vasht = Khash	123	28 [illegible]	61 [illegible] E
Vaslui	107	46 38N	27 42 E
Vassa	110	63 6N	21 38 E
Vassar, Can.	57	49 10N	95 55W
Vassar, U.S.A.	46	43 23N	83 33W
Västerås	111	59 37N	16 38 E
Västerbottens län □	110	64 58N	18 0 E
Västerdalälven	111	60 50N	13 25 E
Västernorrlands län □	110	63 30N	17 40 E
Västervik	111	57 43N	16 43 E
Västmanland □	111	59 55N	16 30 E
Vasto	108	42 8N	14 40 E
Vatan	101	47 4N	1 50 E
Vatnajökull	110	64 30N	16 48W
Vatneyri	110	65 35N	24 0W
Vatoa, I.	133	19 50 S	178 13W
Vatomandry	117	19 20 S	48 59 E
Vatra-Dornei	107	47 22N	25 22 E
Vättern, L.	111	58 25N	14 30 E
Vaucluse	43	45 54N	73 26W
Vaucluse □	103	44 3N	5 10 E
Vaucouleurs	101	48 37N	5 40 E
Vaudreuil	44	45 24N	74 1W
Vaudreuil □	44	45 25N	74 15W
Vaudreuil-sur-le-Lac	44	45 25N	74 3W
Vaughan	79	34 37N	105 12W
Vaughn	78	47 37N	111 36W
Vaupés □	86	1 0N	71 0W
Vaupés, R.	86	1 0N	71 0W
Vauvert	103	43 42N	4 17 E
Vauxhall	61	50 5N	112 9W
Vavâu, I.	133	18 36 S	174 0W
Vavenby	63	51 36N	119 43W
Vavincourt	101	48 49N	5 12 E
Växjö	111	56 52N	14 50 E
Vaygach, Ostrov	120	70 0N	60 0 E
Vaza Barris, R.	87	10 0 S	37 30W
Vedea, R.	107	44 0N	25 20 E
Vedia	88	34 30 S	61 31W
Vedrin	105	50 30N	4 52 E
Veendam	105	53 5N	6 52 E
Vefsna	110	65 48N	13 10 E
Vega	75	35 18N	102 26W
Vega Baja	67	18 27N	66 23W
Vega Fd.	110	65 37N	12 0 E
Vega, I.	110	65 42N	11 50 E
Vega, La	85	19 20N	70 30W
Veghel	105	51 37N	5 32 E
Vegreville	60	53 30N	112 5W
Veinticino de Mayo	88	38 0 S	67 40W
Vejer de la Frontera	104	36 15N	5 59W
Vejle	111	55 43N	9 30 E
Velarde	79	36 11N	106 1W
Velas, C.	84	10 21N	85 52W
Velasco	75	29 0N	95 20W
Velasco, Sierra de.	88	29 20 S	67 10W
Velay, Mts. du	102	45 0N	3 40 E
Velebit Planina	108	44 50N	15 20 E
Vélez	86	6 1N	73 41W
Vélez Málaga	104	36 48N	4 5W
Vélez Rubio	104	37 41N	2 5W
Velhas, R.	87	17 13 S	44 49W
Velikiye Luki	120	56 25N	30 32 E
Velikonda Range	124	14 45N	79 10 E
Velletri	108	41 43N	12 43 E
Vellir	110	65 55N	18 28W
Vellore	124	12 57N	79 10 E
Velsen-Noord	105	52 27N	4 40 E
Velva	74	48 6N	100 56W
Venado	82	22 50N	101 10W
Venado Tuerto	88	33 50 S	62 0W
Venarey-les-Laumes	101	47 32N	4 26 E
Vence	103	43 43N	7 6 E
Vendée □, France	100	46 50N	1 35W
Vendée □, France	102	46 40N	1 20W
Vendée, Collines de	100	46 35N	0 45W
Vendée, R.	100	46 30N	0 45W
Vendeuvre-sur-Barse	101	48 14N	4 28 E
Vendôme	100	47 47N	1 3 E
Venetie	67	67 0N	146 30W
Véneto □	108	45 40N	12 0 E
Venézia	108	45 27N	12 20 E
Venézia, Golfo di	108	45 20N	13 0 E
Venezuela ■	86	8 0N	65 0W
Venezuela, Golfo de	86	11 30N	71 0W
Vengurla	124	15 53N	73 45 E
Venice = Venézia	108	45 27N	12 20 E
Venise	43	45 5N	73 8W
Vénissieux	103	45 43N	4 53 E
Venkatapuram	125	18 20N	80 30 E
Venlo	105	51 22N	6 11 E
Venosta	40	45 52N	76 1W
Venraij	105	51 31N	6 0 E
Venta, La	83	18 8N	94 3W
Ventana, Punta de la	82	24 4N	109 48W
Ventnor	95	50 35N	1 12W
Ventspils	111	57 25N	21 32 E
Ventuari, R.	86	5 20N	66 0W
Ventucopa	81	34 50N	119 29W
Ventura	81	34 16N	119 18W
Ventura, La	82	24 38N	100 54W
Venturosa, La	86	6 8N	68 48W
Vera, Argent.	88	29 30 S	60 20W
Vera, Spain	104	37 15N	1 15W
Veracruz	83	19 10N	96 10W
Veracruz □	83	19 0N	96 15W
Veraval	124	20 53N	70 27 E
Vercelli	108	45 19N	8 25 E
Verchères	45	45 47N	73 21W
Verchères □	45	45 45N	73 15W
Verdalsøra	110	63 48N	11 30 E
Verde, R., Argent.	90	41 55 S	66 0W
Verde, R., Chihuahua, Mexico	82	26 59N	107 58W
Verde, R., Oaxaca, Mexico	82	15 59N	97 50W
Verde, R., Veracruz, Mexico	83	21 10N	102 50W
Verde, R., Parag.	88	23 9 S	57 37W
Verden	107	52 58N	9 18 E
Verdi	80	39 31N	119 59W
Verdigre	74	42 38N	98 0W
Verdon-sur-Mer, Le	102	45 33N	1 4W
Verdun, Can.	44	45 27N	73 34W
Verdun, France	101	49 12N	5 24 E
Verdun-sur-le Doubs	101	46 54N	5 0 E
Vereeniging	117	26 38 S	27 57 E
Veregin	57	51 35N	102 5W
Vérendrye, Parc Prov. de la	40	47 20N	76 40W
Vergennes	71	44 9N	73 15W
Vergt	102	45 2N	0 43 E
Verkhoyansk	121	67 50N	133 50 E
Verkhoyanskiy Khrebet	121	66 0N	129 0 E
Verlo	56	50 19N	108 35W
Vermenton	101	47 40N	3 42 E
Vermeulle, L.	36	54 43N	69 24W
Vermilion	60	53 20N	110 50W
Vermilion, B.	75	29 45N	91 55W
Vermilion Bay	52	49 51N	93 34W
Vermilion Chutes	54	58 22N	114 51W
Vermilion L.	52	50 3N	92 13W
Vermilion Pass	63	51 15N	116 2W
Vermilion, R., Alta., Can.	60	53 22N	110 51W
Vermilion, R., Qué., Can.	41	47 38N	72 56W
Vermilion, R., Ill., U.S.A.	77	41 19N	89 5W
Vermilion, R., Ind., U.S.A.	77	39 57N	87 27W
Vermillion	74	42 50N	96 56W
Vermillion L.	52	47 53N	92 25W
Vermont	76	40 18N	90 26W
Vermont □	71	43 40N	72 50W
Vernal	78	40 28N	109 35W
Vernalis	80	37 36N	121 17W
Verner	46	46 25N	80 8W
Verneuil-sur-Avre	100	48 45N	0 55 E
Vernon, Can.	63	50 20N	119 15W
Vernon, France	100	49 5N	1 30 E
Vernon, U.S.A.	75	34 10N	99 20W
Vernon, U.S.A.	76	38 48N	89 5W
Vernon, U.S.A.	73	38 59N	85 36W
Vernonia	80	45 52N	123 11W
Vero Beach	73	27 39N	80 23W
Véroia	109	40 34N	22 18 E
Véron, L.	38	51 48N	65 7W
Verona, Can.	47	44 29N	76 42W
Verona, Italy	108	45 27N	11 0 E
Verona, U.S.A.	76	42 59N	89 32W
Veropol	121	66 0N	168 0 E
Versailles, France	101	48 48N	2 8 E
Versailles, Ill., U.S.A.	76	39 53N	90 39W
Versailles, Ind., U.S.A.	77	39 4N	85 15W
Versailles, Ky., U.S.A.	77	38 3N	84 44W
Versailles, Mo., U.S.A.	76	38 26N	92 51W
Versailles, Ohio, U.S.A.	77	40 13N	84 29W
Vert I.	52	48 55N	88 3W
Verte, I.	41	48 2N	69 26W
Vertou	100	47 10N	1 28W
Vertus	101	48 54N	4 0 E
Verviers	105	50 37N	5 52 E
Vervins	101	49 50N	3 53 E
Verwood	55	49 30N	105 40W
Vesle, R.	101	49 17N	3 50 E
Vesoul	101	60 40N	6 11 E
Vest-Agder fylke □	111	58 30N	7 15 E
Vesta	84	9 43N	83 3W
Vesterålen	110	68 45N	14 30 E
Vestfjorden	110	67 55N	14 0 E
Vestfold fylke □	111	59 15N	10 0 E
Vestmannaeyjar	110	63 27N	20 15W
Vestspitsbergen	17	78 40N	17 0 E
Vestvågøy	110	68 18N	13 50 E
Vesuvio	108	40 50N	14 22 E
Vesuvius, Mt. = Vesuvio	108	40 50N	14 22 E
Veszprém	107	47 8N	17 57 E
Veteran	61	52 0N	111 7W
Vetlanda	111	57 24N	15 3 E
Vetlugu, R.	120	57 0N	45 25 E
Vettore, Mte.	108	44 38N	7 5 E
Vevay	77	38 45N	85 4W
Veys	122	31 30N	49 0 E
Vézelise	101	48 30N	6 5 E
Vezhen, mt.	109	42 50N	24 20 E
Viacha	86	16 30 S	68 5W
Viana, Brazil	87	3 0 S	44 40W
Viana, Port.	104	38 20N	8 0W
Viana do Castelo	104	41 42N	8 50W
Vianópolis	87	16 40 S	48 35W
Vibank	56	50 20N	103 56W
Viborg	111	56 27N	9 23 E
Vic-en-Bigorre	102	43 24N	0 3 E
Vic-Fézensac	102	43 47N	0 19 E
Vic-sur-Cère	102	44 59N	2 38 E
Vic-sur-Seille	101	48 45N	6 33 E
[illegible]	100	[illegible]	11 21 E
Viceroy	56	49 28N	105 22W
Vich	104	41 58N	2 19 E
Vichada □	86	5 0N	69 30W
Vichy	102	46 9N	3 26 E
Vicksburg, Ariz., U.S.A.	81	33 45N	113 45W
Vicksburg, Mich., U.S.A.	77	42 10N	85 30W
Vicksburg, Miss., U.S.A.	75	32 22N	90 56W
Viçosa, Min. Ger., Brazil	87	20 45 S	42 53W
Viçosa, Pernambuco, Brazil	87	9 28 S	36 14W
Victor, Colo., U.S.A.	74	38 43N	105 7W
Victor, N.Y., U.S.A.	70	42 58N	77 24W
Victor Harbour	135	35 30 S	138 37 E
Victor, L.	38	50 35N	61 50W
Victoria, Argent.	88	32 40 S	60 10W
Victoria, Camer.	116	4 1N	9 10 E
Victoria, B.C., Can.	63	48 30N	123 25W
Victoria, Newf., Can.	37	47 46N	53 14W
Victoria, Ont., Can.	49	43 46N	79 53W
Victoria, Chile	90	38 13 S	72 20W
Victoria, H. K.	131	22 25N	114 15 E
Victoria, Malay.	126	5 20N	115 20 E
Victoria, Seychelles	16	5 0 S	55 40 E
Victoria, U.S.A.	76	41 2N	90 6W
Victoria, Kans., U.S.A.	74	38 52N	99 8W
Victoria, Tex., U.S.A.	75	28 50N	97 0W
Victoria & Albert Mts.	65	80 45N	72 0W
Victoria □	136	37 0 S	144 0 E
Victoria Beach	57	50 40N	96 35W
Victoria de las Tunas	84	20 58N	76 59W
Victoria Falls	117	17 58 S	25 45 E
Victoria, Grand L.	40	47 31N	77 30W
Victoria Harbour	46	44 45N	79 45W
Victoria I.	64	71 0N	111 0W
Victoria, L., Austral.	136	38 2 S	147 34 E
Victoria, L., E. Afr.	116	1 0 S	33 0 E
Victoria, La	86	10 14N	67 20W
Victoria Ld.	91	75 0 S	160 0 E
Victoria Pk.	61	49 18N	114 8W
Victoria Pk	62	50 3N	126 5W
Victoria, R.	134	15 10 S	129 40 E
Victoria Res.	37	48 20N	57 27W
Victoria Square	50	43 54N	79 22W
Victoria Taungdeik	125	21 15N	93 55 E
Victoria West	117	31 25 S	23 4 E
Victoriaville	41	46 4N	71 56W
Victorica	88	36 20 S	65 30W
Victorino	86	2 48N	67 50W
Victorville	81	34 32N	117 18W
Vicuña	88	30 0 S	70 50W
Vicuña Mackenna	88	33 53 S	64 25W
Vidal	81	34 7N	114 31W
Vidalia	73	32 13N	82 25W
Vidauban	103	43 25N	6 27 E
Vidin	109	43 59N	22 28 E
Vidisha (Bhilsa)	124	23 28N	77 53 E
Viedma	90	40 50 S	63 0W
Viedma, L.	90	49 30 S	72 30W
Viejo Canal de Bahama	84	22 10N	77 30W
Vien Pou Kha	128	20 45N	101 5 E
Vienna, Can.	46	42 41N	80 48W
Vienna, U.S.A.	76	38 11N	91 57W
Vienna, Illinois, U.S.A.	75	37 29N	88 54W
Vienna = Wien	106	48 12N	16 22 E
Vienne	103	45 31N	4 53 E
Vienne □	102	46 30N	0 42 E
Vienne, R.	100	47 5N	0 30 E
Vientiane	128	17 58N	102 36 E
Vieques, I.	67	18 8N	65 25W
Viersen	105	51 15N	6 23 E
Vierzon	101	47 13N	2 5 E
Vietnam ■	128	19 0N	106 0 E
Vieux-Boucau-les-Bains	102	43 48N	1 23W
Vif	103	45 5N	5 41 E
Vigan	127	17 35N	120 28 E
Vigan, Le	102	44 0N	3 36 E
Vigia	87	0 50 S	48 5W
Vigia Chico	83	19 46N	87 35W
Vignacourt	101	50 1N	2 15 E
Vignemale, Pic du	102	42 47N	0 10W
Vigneulles	101	48 59N	5 40 E
Vigo	104	42 12N	8 41W
Vihiers	100	47 10N	0 30W
Vijayawada (Bezwada)	125	16 31N	80 39 E
Viking	61	53 7N	111 50W
Vikna	111	64 52N	10 57 E
Vikulovo	120	56 50N	70 40 E
Vila Arriaga	117	14 35 S	13 30 E
Vila Bittencourt	86	1 20 S	69 20W
Vila Coutinho	117	14 37 S	34 19 E
Vila da Maganja	117	17 18 S	37 30 E
Vila de Aljustrel	117	13 30 S	19 45 E
Vila de Liquica	127	8 40 S	125 20 E
Vila de Manica	117	18 58 S	32 59 E
Vila Fontes	117	17 51 S	35 24 E
Vila Franca de Xira	104	38 57N	8 59W
Vila Machado	117	19 15 S	34 14 E
Vila Marechal Carmona = Uige	116	7 30 S	14 40 E
Vila Murtinho	86	10 20 S	65 20W
Vila Nova do Seles	117	11 35 S	14 22 E
Vila Real	104	41 17N	7 48W
Vila Real de Santo Antonio	104	37 10N	7 28W
Vila Salazar	127	5 25 S	123 50 E
Vila Velha	90	20 20 S	40 17W
Vila Verissimo Sarmento	116	8 15 S	20 50 E
Vilaine, R.	100	47 35N	2 10W
Vilanculos	117	22 1 S	35 17 E
Vilhelmina	110	64 35N	16 39 E
Vilhena	86	12 30 S	60 0W
Viliga	121	60 2N	156 56 E
Villa Abecia	88	21 0 S	68 18W
Villa Ahumada	82	30 30N	106 40W
Villa Ana	88	28 28 S	59 40W
Villa Ángela	88	27 34 S	60 45W
Villa Bella	86	10 25 S	65 30W
Villa Cañás	88	34 0 S	61 35W
Villa Cisneros = Dakhla	114	23 50N	15 53W
Villa Colón	88	31 38 S	68 20W
Villa Constitución	88	33 15 S	60 20W
Villa de Cura	86	10 2N	67 29W
Villa de Maria	88	30 0 S	63 43W
Villa de Rosario	88	24 30 S	57 35W
Villa Dolores	88	31 58 S	65 15W
Villa Franca	88	26 14 S	58 20W
Villa Frontera	82	26 56N	101 27W
Villa Grove	77	39 52N	88 10W
Villa Guillermina	88	28 15 S	59 29W

W

Walton Wendesi

Walton, N.Y., U.S.A. 71 42 12N 75 9W
Waltonville 76 38 13N 89 2W
Walvis Ridge 13 30 0S 3 0 E
Walvisbaai 117 23 0S 14 28 E
Wamba 116 2 10N 27 57 E
Wamego 74 39 14N 96 22W
Wamena 127 3 58S 138 50 E
Wampsville 71 43 4N 75 42W
Wamsasi 127 3 27S 126 7 E
Wan Ta Shan 130 46 20N 132 20 E
Wana 124 32 20N 69 32 E
Wanaka L. 133 44 33S 169 7 E
Wanan 131 26 25N 114 50 E
Wanapiri 127 4 30S 135 50 E
Wanapitei 34 46 30N 80 45W
Wanapitei L. 46 46 45N 80 40W
Wanapitei, R. 46 46 2N 80 51W
Wanchuan 130 40 53N 114 32 E
Wang Saphung 128 17 18N 101 46 E
Wangal 127 6 8S 134 9 E
Wanganui 133 39 35S 175 3 E
Wangaratta 136 36 21S 146 19 E
Wangching 130 43 15N 129 37 E
Wangerooge I. 106 53 47N 7 52 E
Wangiwangi, I. 127 5 22S 123 37 E
Wangkiang 131 30 6N 116 45 E
Wanham 60 55 44N 118 24W
Wanhsien, Kansu, China 130 36 45N 107 24 E
Wanhsien, Szechwan, China 131 30 50N 108 30 E
Wankie 117 18 18S 26 30 E
Wanless 57 54 11N 101 21W
Wanning 131 18 45N 110 28 E
Wannon, R. 136 37 38S 141 25 E
Wantsai 131 28 5N 114 22 E
Wanyang Shan, mts. 131 26 30N 113 45 E
Wanyüan 131 32 4N 108 5 E
Wapakoneta 77 40 35N 84 10W
Wapato 78 46 30N 120 25W
Wapawekka L. 55 54 55N 104 40W
Wapella 57 50 16N 101 58W
Wapello 76 41 11N 91 11W
Wapikopa L. 34 42 50N 88 10W
Wapiti, R. 34 55 5N 118 18W
Wappingers Fs. 71 41 35N 73 56W
Wapsipinicon, R. 76 41 44N 90 19W
Waranga Res. 136 36 32S 145 5 E
Warangal 124 17 58N 79 45 E
Waratah B. 136 38 54S 146 5 E
Warba 52 47 9N 93 16W
Warburg 61 53 11N 114 19W
Warburton 136 37 47S 145 42 E
Warburton, R. 133 27 30S 138 30 E
Ward 133 41 49S 174 11 E
Ward Cove 54 55 25N 132 10W
Ward Mt. 80 37 12N 118 54W
Wardha 124 20 45N 78 39 E
Wardha, R. 124 19 57N 79 11 E
Wardlow 61 50 56N 111 31W
Wardner 61 49 25N 115 26W
Wardoan 135 25 59S 149 59 E
Ware, Can. 54 57 26N 125 41W
Ware, U.S.A. 71 42 16N 72 15W
Wareham 71 41 45N 70 44W
Warendorf 105 51 57N 8 0 E
Warfield 63 49 6N 117 46W
Warialda 135 29 29S 150 33 E
Wariap 127 1 30S 134 5 E
Warkopi 127 1 12S 134 9 E
Warley 95 52 30N 2 0W
Warm Springs, Mont., U.S.A. 78 46 11N 112 56W
Warm Springs, Nev., U.S.A. 79 38 16N 116 32W
Warman 56 52 19N 106 30W
Warmbad, Namibia 117 19 14S 13 51 E
Warmbad, S. Afr. 117 24 51S 28 19 E
Warmeriville 101 49 20N 4 13 E
Warncoort 136 38 30S 143 45 E
Warnemünde 106 54 9N 12 5 E
Warner 61 49 17N 112 12W
Warner Range, Mts. 78 41 30S 120 20W
Warner Robins 73 32 41N 83 36W
Warracknabeal 136 36 9S 142 26 E
Warragul 136 38 10S 145 58 E
Warrego, R. 135 30 24S 145 21 E
Warrego Ra. 135 25 15S 146 0 E
Warren, Austral. 136 31 42S 147 51 E
Warren, Can. 46 46 27N 80 18W
Warren, U.S.A. 77 42 31N 83 2W
Warren, Ark., U.S.A. 75 33 35N 92 3W
Warren, Ill., U.S.A. 76 42 30N 89 59W
Warren, Ohio, U.S.A. 70 41 18N 80 52W
Warren, Pa., U.S.A. 70 41 52N 79 10W
Warren, R.I., U.S.A. 71 41 43N 71 19W
Warrender, C. 65 74 28N 81 46W
Warrenpoint 97 54 7N 6 15W
Warrens Corners 49 43 13N 78 45W
Warren's Landing 55 53 40N 98 0W
Warrensburg, Ill., U.S.A. 76 39 56N 89 4W
Warrensburg, Mo., U.S.A. 74 38 45N 93 45W
Warrenton, S. Afr. 117 28 9S 24 47 E
Warrenton, U.S.A. 76 38 49N 91 9W
Warrenton, Oreg., U.S.A. 80 46 11N 123 59W
Warrina 134 28 12S 135 50 E
Warrington, U.K. 94 53 25N 2 38W
Warrington, U.S.A. 73 30 22N 87 16W
Warrnambool 136 38 25S 142 30 E
Warroad 52 48 54N 95 19W
Warsaw, Ill., U.S.A. 76 40 22N 91 26W
Warsaw, Ind., U.S.A. 77 41 14N 85 50W
Warsaw, Ky., U.S.A. 77 38 47N 84 54W
Warsaw, Mo., U.S.A. 76 38 15N 93 23W
Warsaw, N.Y., U.S.A. 70 42 46N 78 10W
Warsaw, Ohio, U.S.A. 70 40 20N 82 0W
Warsaw = Warszawa 107 52 13N 21 0 E
Warszawa 107 52 13N 21 0 E
Warta, R. 106 52 40N 16 10 E
Warthe, R. = Warta, R. 106 52 40N 16 10 E
Waru 127 3 30S 130 36 E
Warwick, Austral. 135 28 10S 152 1 E
Warwick, U.K. 95 52 17N 1 36W
Warwick, U.S.A. 71 41 43N 71 25W
Warwick □ 95 52 20N 1 30W
Wasa 54 49 45N 115 50W
Wasaga Beach 46 44 31N 80 1W
Wasatch, Mt., Ra. 78 40 30N 111 15W
Wascana Cr. 58 50 39N 104 55W
Wascana L. 58 50 26N 104 36W
Wasco, Calif., U.S.A. 81 35 37N 119 16W
Wasco, Oreg., U.S.A. 78 45 45N 120 46W
Waseca, Can. 56 53 6N 109 28W
Waseca, U.S.A. 74 44 3N 93 31W
Wasekamio L. 55 56 45N 108 45W
Wash, The 94 52 58N 0 20W
Washago 46 44 45N 79 20W
Washburn, U.S.A. 76 40 55N 89 17W
Washburn, N.D., U.S.A. 74 47 23N 101 0W
Washburn, Wis., U.S.A. 52 46 38N 90 55W
Washi L. 53 51 24N 87 2W
Washington, Can. 49 43 18N 80 35W
Washington, Calif., U.S.A. 80 39 22N 120 48W
Washington, D.C., U.S.A. 72 38 52N 77 0W
Washington, Ga., U.S.A. 73 33 45N 82 45W
Washington, Ind., U.S.A. 77 38 40N 87 8W
Washington, Iowa, U.S.A. 76 41 20N 91 45W
Washington, Mo, U.S.A. 76 38 35N 91 20W
Washington, N.C., U.S.A. 73 35 35N 77 1W
Washington, N.J., U.S.A. 71 40 45N 74 59W
Washington, Pa., U.S.A. 70 40 10N 80 20W
Washington, Utah, U.S.A. 79 37 10N 113 30W
Washington □ 78 47 45N 120 30W
Washington Court House 77 39 34N 83 26W
Washington I., Pac. Oc. 15 4 43N 160 25W
Washington I., U.S.A. 72 45 24N 86 54W
Washington Mt. 71 44 15N 71 18W
Washir 124 32 15N 63 50 E
Washougal 80 45 35N 122 21W
Wasian 127 1 47S 133 19 E
Wasior 127 2 43S 134 30 E
Waskada 57 49 6N 100 48W
Waskaiowaka, L. 55 56 33N 96 23W
Waskateena Beach 56 53 45N 105 15W
Waskatenau 60 54 7N 112 47W
Waskesiu L. 56 53 56N 106 12W
Waskesiu Lake 56 53 55N 106 5W
Waskish 52 48 11N 94 28W
Wassenaar 105 52 8N 4 24 E
Wassy 101 48 30N 4 58 E
Waswanipi 40 49 40N 75 59W
Waswanipi, L. 40 49 35N 76 40W
Waswanipi, R. 40 49 40N 76 25W
Watangpone 127 4 29S 120 25 E
Watawaha, P. 127 6 30S 122 20 E
Water Valley 75 34 9N 89 38W
Waterberg 117 20 30S 17 18 E
Waterbury, Conn., U.S.A. 71 41 32N 73 0W
Waterbury, Vt., U.S.A. 71 44 22N 72 44W
Waterbury L. 55 58 10N 104 22W
Waterdown 48 43 20N 79 53W
Waterford, Can. 46 42 56N 80 17W
Waterford, Ireland 97 52 16N 7 8W
Waterford, U.S.A. 77 42 46N 88 13W
Waterford, Calif., U.S.A. 80 37 38N 120 46W
Waterford □ 97 51 10N 7 40W
Waterford Harb. 97 52 10N 6 58W
Waterford, R. 37 47 33N 52 43W
Waterhen L., Man., Can. 57 52 10N 99 40W
Waterhen L., Sask., Can. 55 54 28N 108 25W
Waterloo, Belg. 105 50 43N 4 25 E
Waterloo, Ont., Can. 49 43 30N 80 32W
Waterloo, Ont., Can. 52 43 45N 80 30W
Waterloo, Qué., Can. 41 45 21N 72 31W
Waterloo, Que., Can. 71 45 22N 72 32W
Waterloo, U.S.A. 77 41 24N 85 2W
Waterloo, Ill., U.S.A. 76 38 22N 90 6W
Waterloo, Iowa, U.S.A. 76 42 27N 92 20W
Waterloo, N.Y., U.S.A. 70 42 54N 76 53W
Waterloo, Wis., U.S.A. 76 43 11N 88 59W
Waterman 77 41 46N 88 47W
Watermeet 74 46 15N 89 12W
Waterpoint 70 43 19N 78 15W
Waterton Lakes Nat. Park 61 49 5N 114 15W
Waterton Park 61 49 3N 113 55W
Watertown, Conn., U.S.A. 71 41 36N 73 7W
Watertown, N.Y., U.S.A. 71 43 58N 75 57W
Watertown, S.D., U.S.A. 74 44 57N 97 5W
Watertown, Wis., U.S.A. 77 43 15N 88 45W
Waterville, N.S., Can. 39 45 3N 64 41W
Waterville, Qué., Can. 41 45 16N 71 54W
Waterville, Me., U.S.A. 35 44 35N 69 40W
Waterville, N.Y., U.S.A. 71 42 56N 75 23W
Waterville, Pa., U.S.A. 70 41 19N 77 21W
Waterville, Wash., U.S.A. 78 47 45N 120 1W
Watervliet, U.S.A. 77 42 11N 86 18W
Watervliet, N.Y., U.S.A. 71 42 46N 73 43W
Wates 127 7 53S 110 6 E
Watford, Can. 46 42 57N 81 53W
Watford, U.K. 95 51 38N 0 23W
Watford City 74 47 50N 103 23W
Wathaman, R. 55 57 16N 102 59W
Watkins Glen 70 42 25N 76 55W
Watlings I. 85 24 0N 74 35W
Watonga 75 35 51N 98 24W
Watrous, Can. 56 51 40N 105 25W
Watrous, U.S.A. 75 35 50N 104 55W
Watsa 116 3 4N 29 30 E
Watseka 77 40 45N 87 45W
Watshishou, L. 38 50 20N 60 50W
Watson 56 52 10N 104 30W
Watson Lake 67 60 6N 128 49W
Watsonville 80 36 55N 121 49W
Wattle Hill 136 38 42S 143 17 E
Watubela, Kepulauan 127 4 28S 131 54 E
Waubamik 46 45 27N 80 1W
Waubaushene 46 44 45N 79 42W
Waubay 74 45 42N 97 17W
Waubra 136 37 21S 143 39 E
Wauchope 136 31 28S 152 45 E
Wauchula 73 27 35N 81 50W
Waugh 57 49 40N 95 2W
Waukegan 77 42 22N 87 54W
Waukesha 77 43 0N 88 15W
Waukon 74 43 14N 91 33W
Wauneta 74 40 27N 101 25W
Waupaca 74 44 22N 89 8W
Waupun 74 43 38N 88 44W
Waurika 75 34 12N 98 0W
Wausau 74 44 57N 89 40W
Wauseon 77 41 33N 84 8W
Wautoma 74 44 3N 89 20W
Wauwatosa 77 43 6N 87 59W
Wave Hill 134 17 32S 131 0 E
Waveland 77 39 53N 87 3W
Waveney, R. 95 52 24N 1 20 E
Waverley, Can. 39 44 47N 63 36W
Waverley, N.Z. 133 39 46S 174 37 E
Waverly, Ill., U.S.A. 76 39 36N 89 57W
Waverly, Iowa, U.S.A. 76 42 40N 92 30W
Waverly, Mo., U.S.A. 76 39 13N 93 31W
Waverly, N.Y., U.S.A. 71 42 0N 76 33W
Wavre 105 50 43N 4 38 E
Wâw 115 7 45N 28 1 E
Wawa 53 47 59N 84 47W
Wawagosic, R. 40 49 58N 79 6W
Wawanesa 57 49 36N 99 40W
Wawang L. 52 49 25N 90 34W
Wawasee, L. 77 41 24N 85 42W
Wawona 80 37 32N 119 39W
Waxahachie 75 32 22N 96 53W
Way Way 136 33 30S 151 18 E
Wayabula Rau 127 2 29N 128 17 E
Wayagamac, L. 41 47 21N 72 39W
Waycross 73 31 12N 82 25W
Wayland 77 42 40N 85 39W
Wayne, Mich., U.S.A. 46 42 17N 83 23W
Wayne, Nebr., U.S.A. 76 42 16N 97 0W
Wayne, W. Va., U.S.A. 72 38 15N 82 27W
Wayne City 77 38 21N 88 35W
Waynesboro, Miss., U.S.A. 73 31 40N 88 39W
Waynesboro, Pa., U.S.A. 72 39 46N 77 32W
Waynesboro, Va., U.S.A. 72 38 4N 78 57W
Waynesburg 72 39 54N 80 12W
Waynesville, U.S.A. 76 37 50N 92 12W
Waynesville, U.S.A. 77 39 32N 84 5W
Waynesville, N.C., U.S.A. 73 35 31N 83 0W
Waynoka 75 36 38N 98 53W
Waza 124 33 22N 69 22 E
Wazirabad, Afghan. 123 36 44N 66 47 E
Wazirabad, Pak. 124 32 30N 74 8 E
We 126 6 3N 95 56 E
Weald, The 95 51 7N 0 9 E
Wear, R. 94 54 55N 1 22W
Weatherford, Okla., U.S.A. 75 35 30N 98 45W
Weatherford, Tex., U.S.A. 75 32 45N 97 48W
Weaubleau 76 37 54N 93 32W
Webb 56 50 11N 108 12W
Webb City 75 37 9N 94 30W
Webbwood 46 46 16N 81 52W
Webster, Mass., U.S.A. 71 42 4N 71 54W
Webster, N.Y., U.S.A. 70 43 11N 77 27W
Webster, S.D., U.S.A. 74 45 24N 97 33W
Webster, Wis., U.S.A. 74 45 53N 92 25W
Webster City 76 42 30N 93 50W
Webster Green 74 38 38N 90 20W
Webster Springs 72 38 30N 80 25W
Weda 127 0 30N 127 50 E
Weda, Teluk 127 0 30N 127 50 E
Weddell I. 90 51 50S 61 0W
Weddell Sea 91 72 30S 40 0W
Wedge I. 134 30 50S 115 11 E
Wedgeport 39 43 44N 65 59W
Weed 78 41 29N 122 22W
Weed Heights 80 38 59N 119 13W
Weedon-Centre 41 45 42N 71 27W
Weedsport 71 43 3N 76 35W
Weedville 70 41 17N 78 28W
Weekes 56 52 34N 102 52W
Weert 105 51 15N 5 43 E
Weesp 105 52 18N 5 2 E
Wei Ho, R. 131 34 38N 110 20 E
Weichow Tao 131 21 0N 109 1 E
Weifang 130 36 47N 119 10 E
Weihai 130 37 30N 122 10 E
Weimar 106 51 0N 11 20 E
Weinan 131 34 30N 109 35 E
Weipa 135 12 24S 141 50 E
Weir, R. 55 56 54N 93 21W
Weir River 55 56 49N 94 6W
Weirdale 56 53 27N 105 15W
Weirton 70 40 22N 80 35W
Weiser 78 44 10N 117 0W
Weiyüan 130 35 10N 104 10 E
Wejherowo 107 54 35N 18 12 E
Wekusko 55 54 30N 99 45W
Wekusko L. 55 54 40N 99 50W
Welby 55 50 33N 101 29W
Welch 72 37 29N 81 36W
Weldon 56 53 1N 105 8W
Welkom 117 28 0S 26 50 E
Welland 49 43 0N 79 15W
Welland Canal 49 43 3N 79 13W
Welland, R., Can. 49 43 4N 79 3W
Welland, R., U.K. 94 52 43N 0 10W
Wellandport 49 43 0N 79 29W
Weller Park 49 43 14N 79 13W
Wellesley Is. 135 17 20S 139 30 E
Wellin 105 50 5N 5 6 E
Wellingborough 95 52 18N 0 41W
Wellington, Austral. 136 32 35S 148 59 E
Wellington, B.C., Can. 62 49 13N 123 58W
Wellington, Newf., Can. 37 48 53N 53 58W
Wellington, Ont., Can. 47 43 57N 77 20W
Wellington, P.E.I., Can. 39 46 27N 64 0W
Wellington, N.Z. 133 41 19S 174 46 E
Wellington, U.K. 94 50 58N 3 13W
Wellington, U.S.A. 76 39 8N 93 59W
Wellington, Col., U.S.A. 74 40 43N 105 0W
Wellington, Kans., U.S.A. 75 37 15N 97 25W
Wellington, Nev., U.S.A. 80 38 47N 119 28W
Wellington, Ohio, U.S.A. 70 41 9N 82 12W
Wellington, Tex., U.S.A. 75 34 55N 100 13W
Wellington □, Can. 49 43 50N 80 30W
Wellington □, N.Z. 133 40 8S 175 36 E
Wellington Chan. 65 75 0N 93 0W
Wellington, I. 90 49 30S 75 0W
Wellington, L. 136 38 6S 147 20 E
Wellington (Telford) 94 52 42N 2 31W
Wells, Can. 63 53 6N 121 36W
Wells, Norfolk, U.K. 94 52 57N 0 51 E
Wells, Somerset, U.K. 95 51 12N 2 39W
Wells, Me., U.S.A. 71 43 18N 70 35W
Wells, Minn., U.S.A. 74 43 44N 93 45W
Wells, Nev., U.S.A. 78 41 8N 115 0W
Wells Gray Prov. Park 63 52 30N 120 15W
Wells L. 134 26 44S 123 15 E
Wells River 71 44 9N 72 4W
Wellsboro 70 41 46N 77 20W
Wellsburg 70 40 15N 80 36W
Wellsville, Mo., U.S.A. 76 39 4N 91 30W
Wellsville, N.Y., U.S.A. 70 42 9N 77 53W
Wellsville, Ohio, U.S.A. 70 40 36N 80 40W
Wellsville, Utah, U.S.A. 78 41 35N 111 59W
Wellton 79 32 46N 114 6W
Wels 106 48 9N 14 1 E
Welsford 39 45 27N 66 20W
Welshpool 95 52 40N 3 9W
Welwyn 55 50 20N 101 30W
Wem 94 52 52N 2 45W
Wembley 60 55 9N 119 8W
Wenasaga, R. 52 50 38N 93 10W
Wenatchee 78 47 30N 120 17W
Wenchang 131 19 45N 110 50 E
Wenchow 131 28 0N 120 35 E
Wendell 78 42 50N 114 51W
Wenden 81 33 49N 113 33W
Wendesi 127 2 30S 134 10 E

Wendover **Williamston**

Wendover	**78**	40 49N	114 1W
Wenebegon L.	**53**	47 23N	83 6W
Wenebegon, R.	**53**	46 53N	83 12W
Wengniu	**130**	43 2N	118 54 E
Wengteng	**130**	37 15N	122 10 E
Wenlock Edge	**98**	52 30N	2 43W
Wenlock, R.	**135**	12 2 S	141 55 E
Wenona	**76**	41 3N	89 3W
Wensi	**131**	35 25N	111 7 E
Wensiang	**131**	34 35N	110 40 E
Wensu	**129**	41 15N	80 14 E
Wenteng	**130**	37 10N	122 0 E
Wentworth, Austral.	**136**	34 2 S	141 54 E
Wentworth, Can.	**39**	45 38N	63 33W
Wentzville	**76**	38 49N	90 51W
Wenut	**127**	3 11 S	133 19 E
Weott	**78**	40 19N	123 56W
Wepener	**117**	29 42 S	27 3 E
Werda	**117**	25 24 S	23 15 E
Weri	**127**	3 10 S	132 30 E
Werne	**105**	51 38N	7 38 E
Werra, R.	**105**	51 0N	10 0 E
Werribee	**136**	37 54 S	144 40 E
Werris Creek	**136**	31 18 S	150 38 E
Wersar	**127**	1 30 S	131 55 E
Wesel	**105**	51 39N	6 34 E
Weser, R.	**106**	53 33N	8 30 E
Wesiri	**127**	7 30 S	126 30 E
Weslemkoon L.	**47**	45 2N	77 25W
Wesleyville, Can.	**37**	49 8N	53 36W
Wesleyville, U.S.A.	**70**	42 9N	80 1W
Wessel Is.	**135**	11 10 S	136 45 E
Wessington	**74**	44 30N	98 40W
Wessington Springs	**74**	44 10N	98 35W
West	**75**	31 50N	97 5W
West Allis	**77**	43 1N	87 0W
West, B.	**75**	29 5N	89 27W
West Bend	**72**	43 25N	88 10W
West Bengal □	**125**	25 0N	90 0 E
West Branch	**46**	44 16N	84 13W
West Bromwich	**95**	52 32N	2 1W
West Carrollton	**77**	39 33N	84 17W
West Chazy	**71**	44 49N	73 28W
West Chester	**72**	39 58N	75 36W
West Chicago	**77**	41 53N	88 12W
West Columbia	**75**	29 10N	95 38W
West Covina	**81**	34 4N	117 54W
West Des Moines	**76**	41 30N	93 45W
West Don, R.	**50**	43 42N	79 20W
West Duffin, R.	**51**	43 51N	79 4W
West End	**84**	26 41N	78 58W
West Falkland Island	**90**	51 30 S	60 0W
West Fork, Cuivre, R.	**76**	39 2N	90 58W
West Frankfort	**76**	37 56N	89 0W
West Glamorgan □	**95**	51 40N	3 55W
West Harbour	**15**	45 51 S	170 33 E
West Hartford	**71**	41 45N	72 45W
West Haven	**71**	41 18N	72 57W
West Helena	**75**	34 30N	90 40W
West Hill	**50**	43 47N	79 12W
West Humber, R.	**50**	43 44N	79 33W
West Indies	**74**	15 0N	70 0W
West Kildonan	**58**	49 56N	97 8W
West Lafayette	**77**	40 27N	86 55W
West Liberty, Iowa, U.S.A.	**76**	41 34N	91 16W
West Liberty, Ky., U.S.A.	**77**	37 55N	83 16W
West Liberty, Ohio, U.S.A.	**77**	40 15N	83 45W
West Lorne	**46**	42 36N	81 36W
West Louisville	**77**	37 42N	87 17W
West Magpie, R., Can.	**38**	51 2N	64 42W
West Magpie, R., Qué., Can.	**36**	52 0N	65 0W
West Manchester	**77**	39 55N	84 38W
West Memphis	**75**	35 5N	90 3W
West Midlands □	**95**	52 30N	1 55W
West Milton	**77**	39 58N	84 20W
West Monroe	**75**	32 32N	92 7W
West Montrose	**49**	43 35N	80 29W
West Newton	**70**	40 14N	79 46W
West Nicholson	**117**	21 2 S	29 20 E
West Palm Beach	**73**	26 44N	80 3W
West Paris	**128**	44 18N	70 30W
West Pittston	**71**	41 19N	75 49W
West Plains	**75**	36 45N	91 50W
West Point, Jamaica	**84**	18 14N	78 30W
West Point, Ga., U.S.A.	**73**	32 54N	85 10W
West Point, Ill., U.S.A.	**76**	40 15N	91 11W
West Point, Iowa, U.S.A.	**76**	40 43N	91 27W
West Point, Ky., U.S.A.	**77**	37 59N	85 57W
West Point, Miss., U.S.A.	**73**	33 36N	88 38W
West Point, Nebr., U.S.A.	**74**	41 50N	96 43W
West Point, Va., U.S.A.	**72**	37 35N	76 47W
West Poplar	**56**	49 0N	106 22W
West Road R.	**63**	53 18N	122 53W
West Salem	**77**	38 31N	88 1W
West Spitsbergen	**17**	78 40N	17 0 E
West Sussex □	**95**	50 55N	0 30W
West Terre Haute	**77**	39 27N	87 27W
West Thurlow I.	**62**	50 25N	125 35W
West Union, Iowa, U.S.A.	**76**	42 57N	91 49W
West Union, Ohio, U.S.A.	**77**	38 48N	83 33W
West Unity	**77**	41 35N	84 26W
West Vancouver	**66**	49 21N	123 8W
West Virginia □	**72**	39 0N	81 0W
West Walker, R.	**80**	38 54N	119 9W
West Wyalong	**136**	33 56 S	147 10 E
West Yellowstone	**78**	44 47N	111 4W
West Yorkshire □	**94**	53 45N	1 40W
Westbank	**54**	49 50N	119 40W
Westbourne	**57**	50 8N	98 35W
Westbrook, Maine, U.S.A.	**72**	43 40N	70 22W
Westbrook, Tex., U.S.A.	**75**	32 25N	101 0W
Westby, Austral.	**136**	35 30 S	147 24 E
Westby, U.S.A.	**74**	48 52N	104 3W
Westdale	**48**	43 17N	79 53W
Westend	**81**	35 42N	117 24W
Western Australia □	**134**	25 0 S	118 0 E
Western Duck I.	**46**	45 45N	83 0W
Western Ghats	**124**	15 30N	74 30 E
Western Isles □	**96**	57 30N	7 10W
Western Pen.	**52**	49 30N	94 50W
Western Samoa ■	**133**	14 0 S	172 0W
Western Shore	**39**	44 32N	64 19W
Westernport	**72**	39 30N	79 5W
Westerschelde, R.	**105**	51 25N	4 0 E
Westerwald, mts.	**105**	50 39N	8 0 E
Westfield, Can.	**39**	45 22N	66 14W
Westfield, Ill., U.S.A.	**77**	39 27N	88 0W
Westfield, Ind., U.S.A.	**77**	40 2N	86 8W
Westfield, Mass., U.S.A.	**71**	42 9N	72 49W
Westfield, N.Y., U.S.A.	**70**	42 20N	79 38W
Westfield, Pa., U.S.A.	**70**	41 54N	77 32W
Westfriesche Eilanden	**105**	53 20N	5 10 E
Westham I.	**66**	49 5N	123 10W
Westhope	**57**	48 55N	101 0W
Westland □	**133**	43 33 S	169 59 E
Westland Bight	**133**	42 55 S	170 5 E
Westlock	**60**	54 9N	113 55W
Westmeath □	**97**	53 30N	7 30W
Westminster	**72**	39 34N	77 1W
Westmorland	**79**	33 2N	115 42W
Westmount	**44**	45 29N	73 36W
Weston, Can.	**50**	43 43N	79 31W
Weston, Malay.	**126**	5 10N	115 35 E
Weston, Ohio, U.S.A.	**77**	41 21N	83 47W
Weston, Oreg., U.S.A.	**78**	45 50N	118 30W
Weston, W. Va., U.S.A.	**72**	39 3N	80 29W
Weston I.	**36**	52 33N	79 36W
Weston-super-Mare	**95**	51 20N	2 59W
Westover	**49**	43 19N	80 5W
Westphalia	**76**	38 26N	92 0W
Westport, Newf., Can.	**37**	49 47N	56 38W
Westport, N.S., Can.	**39**	44 15N	66 22W
Westport, Ont., Can.	**47**	44 40N	76 25W
Westport, Ireland	**97**	53 44N	9 31W
Westport, N.Z.	**133**	41 46 S	171 37 E
Westport, U.S.A.	**77**	39 11N	85 34W
Westport, Ore., U.S.A.	**80**	46 10N	123 23W
Westport, Wash., U.S.A.	**78**	46 48N	124 4W
Westray	**57**	53 36N	101 24W
Westray, I.	**96**	59 18N	3 0W
Westree	**53**	47 26N	81 34W
Westsyde	**63**	50 47N	120 21W
Westview	**54**	49 50N	124 31W
Westville, Can.	**39**	45 34N	62 43W
Westville, Calif., U.S.A.	**80**	39 8N	120 42W
Westville, Ill., U.S.A.	**77**	40 3N	87 36W
Westville, Ind., U.S.A.	**77**	41 35N	86 55W
Westville, N.Y., U.S.A.	**43**	44 58N	74 20W
Westville, Okla., U.S.A.	**75**	36 0N	94 33W
Westwood	**78**	40 26N	121 0W
Wetar, I.	**127**	7 30 S	126 30 E
Wetaskiwin	**61**	52 55N	113 24W
Wetteren	**105**	51 0N	3 53 E
Wetupoa	**136**	35 16 S	143 46 E
Wetzlar	**106**	50 33N	8 30 E
Wewaka	**75**	35 10N	96 35W
Wexford, Can.	**50**	43 45N	79 18W
Wexford, Ireland	**97**	52 20N	6 28W
Wexford □	**97**	52 20N	6 25W
Wexford Harb.	**97**	52 20N	6 25W
Weyburn	**56**	49 40N	103 50W
Weyburn L.	**54**	63 0N	117 59W
Weymouth, Can.	**39**	44 30N	66 1W
Weymouth, U.K.	**95**	50 36N	2 28W
Weymouth, U.S.A.	**71**	42 13N	70 53W
Weymouth, C.	**135**	12 37 S	143 27 E
Wezep	**105**	52 28N	6 0 E
Whakatane	**133**	37 57 S	177 1 E
Whale Cove	**55**	62 11N	92 36W
Whale, R.	**36**	58 15N	67 40W
Whales	**91**	78 0 S	165 0W
Whaletown	**62**	50 7N	125 2W
Whalsay, I.	**96**	60 22N	1 0W
Whampoa	**131**	23 5N	113 20 E
Whangamomona	**133**	39 8 S	174 44 E
Whangarei	**133**	35 43 S	174 21 E
Whangarei Harbour	**133**	35 45 S	174 28 E
Wharfe, R.	**94**	53 55N	1 30W
Wharton, N.J., U.S.A.	**71**	40 53N	74 36W
Wharton, Pa., U.S.A.	**70**	41 31N	78 1W
Wharton, Tex., U.S.A.	**75**	29 20N	96 6W
Whatcom, L.	**63**	48 43N	122 20W
Wheatfield	**77**	41 13N	87 4W
Wheatland, Calif., U.S.A.	**80**	39 1N	121 25W
Wheatland, Ind., U.S.A.	**77**	38 40N	87 19W
Wheatland, Wyo., U.S.A.	**74**	42 4N	105 58W
Wheatley	**46**	42 6N	82 27W
Wheaton, U.S.A.	**77**	41 52N	88 6W
Wheaton, Minn., U.S.A.	**74**	45 50N	96 29W
Wheelbarrow Pk.	**80**	37 26N	116 5W
Wheeler, Oreg., U.S.A.	**78**	45 45N	123 57W
Wheeler, Tex., U.S.A.	**75**	35 29N	100 15W
Wheeler Peak, Mt.	**78**	38 57N	114 15W
Wheeler, R., Qué., Can.	**36**	57 2N	67 13W
Wheeler, R., Sask., Can.	**55**	57 34N	104 15W
Wheeler Ridge	**81**	35 0N	118 57W
Wheeling	**70**	40 2N	80 41W
Whernside, Mt.	**94**	54 14N	2 24W
Whidbey I.	**63**	48 15N	122 40W
Whidbey Is.	**134**	34 30 S	135 3 E
Whiskey Gap	**61**	49 0N	113 3W
Whiskey Jack L.	**55**	58 23N	101 55W
Whistler	**73**	30 50N	88 10W
Whitbourne	**37**	47 25N	53 32W
Whitby, Can.	**51**	43 52N	78 56W
Whitby, U.K.	**94**	54 29N	0 37W
Whitcombe, Mt.	**15**	43 12 S	171 0 E
Whitcombe, P.	**15**	43 12 S	171 0 E
White B.	**37**	50 0N	56 35W
White Bear	**56**	50 53N	108 13W
White Bear Res.	**37**	48 10N	57 5W
White Bird	**78**	45 46N	116 21W
White Butte	**72**	46 23N	103 25W
White City	**74**	38 50N	96 45W
White Cliffs	**133**	43 26 S	171 55 E
White Deer	**75**	35 30N	101 8W
White Fox	**56**	53 27N	104 5W
White Hall	**76**	39 25N	90 27W
White Haven	**71**	41 3N	75 47W
White I.	**133**	37 30 S	177 13 E
White L., Ont., Can.	**47**	45 18N	76 31W
White L., Ont., Can.	**53**	48 47N	85 37W
White L., U.S.A.	**75**	29 45N	92 30W
White Mts.	**80**	37 30N	118 15W
White, Mts.	**71**	44 15N	71 15W
White Nile = Nîl el Abyad, Bahr	**115**	9 30N	31 40 E
White Otter L.	**52**	49 5N	91 55W
White Owl L.	**53**	47 10N	82 35W
White Pass, Can.	**67**	59 40N	135 3W
White Pass, U.S.A.	**80**	46 38N	121 24W
White Pigeon	**77**	41 48N	85 39W
White Pine	**52**	46 44N	89 35W
White Plains	**71**	41 2N	73 44W
White, R., Can.	**53**	48 33N	86 16W
White, R., U.S.A.	**77**	38 25N	87 45W
White, R., Ark., U.S.A.	**75**	36 28N	93 55W
White, R., Colo., U.S.A.	**78**	40 8N	108 52W
White, R., Ind., U.S.A.	**72**	39 25N	86 30W
White, R., S.D., U.S.A.	**74**	43 10N	102 52W
White, R., Wash., U.S.A.	**80**	47 12N	122 15W
White River, Can.	**53**	48 35N	85 20W
White River, U.S.A.	**74**	43 48N	100 45W
White River Junc.	**71**	43 38N	72 20W
White Rock	**66**	49 2N	122 48W
White Sulphur Springs, Mont., U.S.A.	**78**	46 35N	111 0W
White Sulphur Springs, W. Va., U.S.A.	**78**	37 50N	80 16W
White Swan	**80**	46 23N	120 44W
Whiteclay L.	**52**	50 53N	88 45W
Whitecourt	**60**	54 10N	115 45W
Whiteface	**75**	33 35N	102 40W
Whiteface R.	**52**	46 58N	92 48W
Whitefield	**71**	44 23N	71 37W
Whitefish, Can.	**46**	46 23N	81 19W
Whitefish, U.S.A.	**78**	48 25N	114 22W
Whitefish Bay	**77**	43 23N	87 54W
Whitefish Falls	**46**	46 7N	81 44W
Whitefish L., Can.	**55**	62 41N	106 48W
Whitefish L., U.S.A.	**52**	46 40N	94 10W
Whitefish Pt.	**53**	46 45N	85 0W
Whitegull, L.	**36**	55 27N	64 17W
Whitehall, Mich., U.S.A.	**72**	43 21N	86 20W
Whitehall, Mont., U.S.A.	**78**	45 52N	112 4W
Whitehall, N.Y., U.S.A.	**71**	43 32N	73 28W
Whitehall, Wis., U.S.A.	**74**	44 20N	91 19W
Whitehaven	**94**	54 33N	3 35W
Whitehorse	**67**	60 43N	135 3W
Whitehorse, Vale of	**95**	51 37N	1 30W
Whiteman	**76**	38 45N	93 40W
Whitemouth	**57**	49 57N	95 58W
Whitemouth L.	**57**	49 15N	95 40W
Whitemouth, R.	**57**	50 7N	96 2W
Whitemud Cr.	**59**	53 31N	113 34W
Whitesail, L.	**54**	53 35N	127 45W
Whitesand, R.	**56**	51 34N	102 56W
Whitesboro, N.Y., U.S.A.	**71**	43 8N	75 20W
Whitesboro, Tex., U.S.A.	**75**	33 40N	96 58W
Whiteshell Prov. Park	**57**	50 0N	95 40W
Whiteside	**76**	39 12N	91 2W
Whiteswan Ls.	**56**	54 5N	105 10W
Whitetail	**56**	48 54N	105 15W
Whitevale	**50**	43 53N	79 9W
Whiteville	**73**	34 20N	78 40W
Whitewater	**77**	42 50N	88 45W
Whitewater Baldy, Mt.	**79**	33 20N	108 44W
Whitewater, Cr.	**56**	49 0N	108 0W
Whitewater L.	**52**	50 50N	89 10W
Whitewood	**57**	50 20N	102 20W
Whithorn	**96**	54 55N	4 25W
Whitianga	**133**	36 47 S	175 41 E
Whiting	**77**	41 41N	87 29W
Whitman	**71**	42 4N	70 55W
Whitmire	**73**	34 33N	81 40W
Whitney	**47**	45 31N	78 14W
Whitney, Mt.	**80**	36 35N	118 14W
Whitney Pt.	**71**	42 19N	75 59W
Whitstable	**95**	51 21N	1 2 E
Whitsunday I.	**135**	20 15 S	149 4 E
Whittemore	**76**	43 4N	94 26W
Whittier	**67**	60 46N	148 48W
Whittington	**49**	43 59N	80 10W
Whitwell	**73**	35 15N	85 30W
Wholdaia L.	**55**	60 43N	104 20W
Whyalla	**135**	33 2 S	137 30 E
Whycocomagh	**39**	45 59N	61 7W
Wiarton	**46**	44 40N	81 10W
Wibaux	**74**	47 0N	104 13W
Wichita	**75**	37 40N	97 29W
Wichita Falls	**75**	33 57N	98 30W
Wick	**96**	58 26N	3 5W
Wicked Pt.	**47**	43 52N	77 15W
Wickenburg	**79**	33 58N	112 45W
Wickett	**75**	31 37N	102 58W
Wickham	**41**	45 45N	72 30W
Wickliffe	**70**	41 46N	81 29W
Wicklow	**97**	53 0N	6 2W
Wicklow □	**97**	52 59N	6 25W
Wicklow Hd.	**97**	52 59N	6 3W
Wicklow Mts.	**97**	53 0N	6 30W
Widnes	**94**	53 22N	2 44W
Wieliczka	**107**	50 0N	20 5 E
Wielun	**107**	51 15N	18 40 E
Wien	**106**	48 12N	16 22 E
Wiener Neustadt	**106**	47 49N	16 16 E
Wiesbaden	**105**	50 7N	8 17 E
Wigan	**94**	53 33N	2 38W
Wiggins, Colo., U.S.A.	**74**	40 16N	104 3W
Wiggins, Miss., U.S.A.	**75**	30 53N	89 9W
Wight, I. of	**95**	50 40N	1 20W
Wigtown	**96**	54 52N	4 27W
Wigtown B.	**96**	54 46N	4 15W
Wikwemikong	**46**	45 48N	81 43W
Wilber	**74**	40 34N	96 59W
Wilberforce, Can.	**47**	45 2N	78 13W
Wilberforce, U.S.A.	**77**	39 43N	83 52W
Wilburton	**75**	34 55N	95 15W
Wilcannia	**136**	31 30 S	143 26 E
Wilcock Lake	**50**	43 56N	79 25W
Wilcocks L.	**50**	43 57N	79 26W
Wilcox, Can.	**56**	50 6N	104 44W
Wilcox, U.S.A.	**70**	41 34N	78 43W
Wildcat Creek, R.	**77**	40 28N	86 48W
Wildfield	**50**	43 49N	79 44W
Wildgoose L.	**53**	49 44N	87 11W
Wildhay, R.	**60**	53 59N	117 20W
Wildrose, Calif., U.S.A.	**81**	36 14N	117 11W
Wildrose, N. Dak., U.S.A.	**74**	48 36N	103 17W
Wildwood, Can.	**60**	53 37N	115 14W
Wildwood, U.S.A.	**72**	38 59N	74 46W
Wilhelm II Coast	**91**	67 0 S	90 0 E
Wilhelmina, Mt.	**87**	3 50N	56 30W
Wilhelmshaven	**106**	53 30N	8 9 E
Wilkes-Barre	**71**	41 15N	75 52W
Wilkes Land	**91**	69 0 S	120 0 E
Wilkesboro	**73**	36 10N	81 9W
Wilkie	**56**	52 27N	108 42W
Wilkinsburg	**70**	40 26N	79 50W
Willamina	**78**	45 9N	123 32W
Willandra Billabong Creek	**136**	33 22 S	145 52 E
Willapa, B.	**78**	46 44N	124 0W
Willapa Hills	**80**	46 35N	123 25W
Willard, N. Mex., U.S.A.	**79**	34 35N	106 1W
Willard, Utah, U.S.A.	**78**	41 28N	112 1W
Willcox	**79**	32 13N	109 53W
Willebroek	**105**	51 4N	4 22 E
Willemstad	**85**	12 5N	69 0W
William A. Switzer Prov. Park	**60**	53 30N	117 48W
William L.	**57**	53 54N	99 21W
William, R.	**55**	59 8N	109 19W
Williams, Ariz., U.S.A.	**79**	35 16N	112 11W
Williams, Calif., U.S.A.	**80**	39 9N	122 9W
Williams, Minn., U.S.A.	**52**	48 45N	94 54W
Williams L.	**52**	51 48N	90 45W
Williams Lake	**63**	52 10N	122 10W
Williamsburg, Can.	**49**	43 24N	80 30W
Williamsburg, Ky., U.S.A.	**73**	36 45N	84 10W
Williamsburg, Pa., U.S.A.	**70**	40 27N	78 14W
Williamsburg, Va., U.S.A.	**72**	37 17N	76 44W
Williamsfield	**76**	40 55N	90 1W
Williamson, N.Y., U.S.A.	**70**	43 14N	77 15W
Williamson, W. Va., U.S.A.	**72**	37 46N	82 17W
Williamsport, Ind., U.S.A.	**77**	40 17N	87 17W
Williamsport, Pa., U.S.A.	**70**	41 18N	77 1W
Williamston, U.S.A.	**77**	42 41N	84 17W

X

Yaan Zeeland □

Y

Yaan 129 30 0N 102 59 E
Yaapeet 136 35 45 S 142 3 E
Yablonovyy Khrebet 121 53 0N 114 0 E
Yabrīn 122 23 7N 48 52 E
Yacuiba 88 22 0 S 63 25W
Yadgir 124 16 45N 77 5 E
Yadkin, R. 73 36 15N 81 0W
Yahatahama 132 33 25N 132 40 E
Yahk 61 49 6N 116 10W
Yahuma 116 1 0N 22 5 E
Yaicheng 131 18 14N 109 7 E
Yakataga 67 60 5N 142 32W
Yakima 78 46 42N 120 30W
Yakima, R. 78 47 0N 120 30W
Yakoshih 129 49 13N 120 35 E
Yakut A.S.S.R. □ 121 62 0N 130 0 E
Yakutat 67 59 50N 139 44W
Yakutsk 121 62 5N 129 40 E
Yala 128 6 33N 101 18 E
Yalabusha, R. 75 33 53N 89 50W
Yale, Can. 80 49 34N 121 25W
Yale, U.S.A. 46 43 9N 82 47W
Yalgoo 134 28 16 S 116 39 E
Yalinga 116 6 20N 23 10 E
Yalkubul, Punta 83 21 32N 88 37W
Yallourn 136 38 10 S 146 18 E
Yalu K. 130 41 30N 126 30 E
Yalung K. 129 32 0N 100 0 E
Yalutorovsk 120 56 30N 65 40 E
Yam Kinneret (L. Tiberias) 115 32 49N 35 36 E
Yamagata 132 38 15N 140 15 E
Yamagata-ken □ 132 38 30N 140 0 E
Yamaguchi 132 34 10N 131 32 E
Yamaguchi-ken □ 132 34 20N 131 40 E
Yamal, Poluostrov 120 71 0N 70 0 E
Yamana 122 24 5N 47 30 E
Yamanashi-ken □ 132 35 40N 138 40 E
Yamantau 120 54 20N 57 40 E
Yamantau, Gora 120 54 15N 58 6 E
Yamaska 41 46 0N 72 55W
Yamaska □ 43 46 50N 72 50W
Yamaska, Mt. 43 45 27N 72 52W
Yamaska, R. 45 45 17N 72 55W
Yambol 109 42 30N 26 36 E
Yamdena 127 7 45 S 131 20 E
Yamdrok Tso 129 29 0N 90 40 E
Yamethin 125 20 29N 96 18 E
Yamhsien 131 21 45N 108 31 E
Yamma-Yamma L. 135 26 16 S 141 20 E
Yampa, R. 78 40 37N 108 0W
Yampi Sd. 134 16 8 S 123 38 E
Yamuna (Jumna), R. 125 27 0N 78 30 E
Yana, R. 121 69 0N 134 0 E
Yanac 136 36 8 S 141 25 E
Yanaul 120 56 25N 55 0 E
Yanbu 'al Bahr 122 24 0N 38 5 E
Yanco 136 34 38 S 146 27 E
Yandoon 125 17 0N 95 40 E
Yangambi 116 0 47N 24 20 E
Yangchow 131 32 25N 119 25 E
Yangchuan 130 38 0N 113 29 E
Yangi-Yer 120 40 17N 68 48 E
Yangkao 130 40 20N 113 40 E
Yangshui (Hinghwa) 131 29 53N 115 3 E
Yangso 131 24 36N 110 32 E
Yangtsun 130 39 29N 117 4 E
Yangtze Kiang 131 31 40N 122 0 E
Yanhee Res. 128 17 30N 98 45 E
Yankton 74 42 55N 97 25W
Yanping 131 22 25N 112 0 E
Yao Shan 131 24 0N 110 0 E
Yaomen 130 44 31N 125 8 E
Yaoundé 116 3 50N 11 35 E
Yap Is. 127 9 30N 138 10 E
Yapen 127 1 50 S 136 0 E
Yapen, Selat 127 1 20 S 136 10 E
Yapero 127 4 59 S 137 11 E
Yapo, R. 86 0 30 S 77 0W
Yaqui, R. 82 28 28N 109 30W
Yar-Sale 120 66 50N 70 50 E
Yaracuy □ 86 10 20N 68 45W
Yaraka 135 24 53 S 144 3 E
Yare, R. 95 52 36N 1 28 E
Yarensk 120 61 10N 49 8 E
Yarí, R. 86 1 0N 73 40W
Yarkand (Soche) 129 38 24N 77 20 E
Yarker 47 44 23N 76 46W
Yarkhun, R. 124 36 30N 72 45 E
Yarmouth 39 43 50N 66 7W
Yaroslavl 120 57 35N 39 55 E
Yarra, R. 136 37 50 S 144 53 E
Yarrawonga 136 36 0 S 146 0 E
Yarrow 63 49 5N 122 2W
Yartsevo 121 60 20N 90 0 E
Yarumal 86 6 58N 75 24W
Yasawa Group 133 17 00 S 177 23 E
Yasinski, L. 36 53 16N 77 35W
Yasothon 128 15 50N 104 10 E
Yass 136 34 49 S 148 54 E
Yass, Res. 136 34 50 S 149 0 E
Yates Center 75 37 53N 95 45W
Yathkyed L. 55 62 40N 98 0W
Yatsushiro 132 32 30N 130 40 E
Yauyos 86 12 10 S 75 50W
Yavari R. 86 4 50 S 72 0W
Yayama-rettō 131 24 30N 123 40 E
Yazd (Yezd) 123 31 55N 54 27 E
Yazdan 123 33 30N 60 50 E
Yazoo City 75 32 48N 90 28W
Yazoo, R. 75 32 35N 90 50W
Yding Skovhøj 111 55 59N 9 46 E
Yebyu 125 14 15N 98 13 E
Yecla 104 38 35N 1 5W
Yécora 82 28 20N 108 58W
Yegros 88 26 20 S 56 25W
Yehsien 130 37 12N 119 58 E
Yehuda, Midbar 115 31 35N 34 57 E
Yelanskoye 121 61 25N 128 0 E
Yelets 120 52 40N 38 30 E
Yell, I. 96 60 35N 1 5W
Yell Sd. 96 60 33N 1 15W
Yellow Creek 56 52 45N 105 15W
Yellow Grass 56 49 48N 104 10W
Yellow Mt. 136 32 31 S 146 52 E
Yellow River = Hwang Ho 131 38 0N 117 20 E
Yellow Sea 130 35 0N 123 0 E
Yellowhead P. 63 52 53N 118 25W
Yellowknife 54 62 27N 114 21W
Yellowknife, R. 54 62 31N 114 19W
Yellowstone L. 78 44 30N 110 20W
Yellowstone National Park 78 44 35N 110 0W
Yellowstone, R. 74 46 35N 105 45W
Yemen ■ 115 15 0N 44 0 E
Yemen, South ■ 115 15 0N 48 0 E
Yenangyaung 125 20 30N 95 0 E
Yenchang 130 36 44N 110 2 E
Yencheng, Honan, China 131 33 43N 114 10 E
Yencheng, Kiangsu, China 131 33 22N 120 12 E
Yenchwan 130 37 0N 110 5 E
Yenda 136 34 13 S 146 14 E
Yengchun 131 22 10N 111 27 E
Yenisey, R. 120 68 0N 86 30 E
Yeniseysk 121 58 39N 92 4 E
Yeniseyskiy Zaliv 120 72 20N 81 0 E
Yenki, Kirin, China 130 43 12N 129 30 E
Yenki, Sinkiang, China 129 42 12N 86 30 E
Yenking 130 40 30N 116 0 E
Yenne 103 45 43N 5 44 E
Yenshih 131 34 42N 112 50 E
Yentai 130 37 30N 121 22 E
Yenyuka 121 58 20N 121 30 E
Yeo, L. 134 28 0 S 124 30 E
Yeo, R. 95 51 1N 2 46W
Yeola 124 20 0N 74 30 E
Yeotmal 124 20 20N 78 15 E
Yeovil 95 50 57N 2 38W
Yeppoon 135 23 5 S 150 47 E
Yerbent 120 39 30N 58 50 E
Yerbogachen 121 61 16N 108 0 E
Yerevan 120 40 10N 44 20 E
Yerington 80 38 59N 119 10W
Yermakovo 121 52 35N 126 20 E
Yermo 81 34 58N 116 50W
Yerofey Pavlovich 121 54 0N 122 0 E
Yershov 120 51 15N 48 27 E
Yerville 100 49 40N 0 53 E
Yes Tor, Mt. 95 50 41N 3 59W
Yeso 75 34 29N 104 37W
Yeu, I. d' 100 46 42N 2 20W
Yeungchun 131 22 15N 111 40 E
Yeungkong 131 21 55N 112 0 E
Yeungshan 131 24 27N 112 15 E
Yeysk Staro 120 46 40N 38 12 E
Yhati 88 25 45 S 56 35W
Yhú 89 25 0 S 56 0W
Yi, R. 88 33 7 S 57 8W
Yiannitsa 109 40 46N 22 24 E
Yihsien 131 34 50N 117 50 E
Yilan 131 24 47N 121 44 E
Yin Shan, mts. 130 41 0N 112 0 E
Yincheng 131 31 0N 113 40 E
Yinchwan 130 38 30N 106 20 E
Yingcheng 131 31 0N 113 44 E
Yingchow 130 39 45N 113 30 E
Yingkiang 131 28 10N 108 40 E
Yingkow 130 40 43N 122 9 E
Yingshan 131 30 50N 115 45 E
Yingtak 131 24 10N 113 5 E
Yingtan 131 28 12N 117 0 E
Yinmabin 125 22 10N 94 55 E
Yipang 128 22 15N 101 26 E
Yithion 109 36 46N 22 34 E
Yitu 130 36 40N 118 25 E
Yixian 131 41 32N 121 15 E
Yiyang 131 28 45N 112 16 E
Ylitornio 110 66 19N 23 39 E
Ylivieska 110 64 4N 24 28 E
Ynykchanskiy 121 60 15N 137 43 E
Yoakum 75 29 20N 97 10W
Yog Pt. 127 13 55N 124 20 E
Yogyakarta 127 7 49 S 110 22 E
Yoho Nat. Park 63 51 25N 116 30W
Yojoa, L. de 84 14 53N 88 0W
Yokadouma 116 3 35N 14 50 E
Yōkaichi 132 35 6N 136 12 E
Yokkaichi 132 35 0N 136 30 E
Yokohama 132 35 27N 139 39 E
Yokosuka 132 35 20N 139 40 E
Yola 114 9 10N 12 29 E
Yolaina, Cordillera de 84 11 30N 84 0W
Yolgali 136 34 20 S 146 7 E
Yom Mae Nam 128 15 15N 100 20 E
Yonago 132 35 25N 133 19 E
Yonaguni 131 24 28N 122 59 E
Yong Peng 128 2 0N 103 3 E
Yŏngchŏn 130 35 55N 128 55 E
Yŏngwŏl 130 37 18N 128 20 E
Yonker 55 52 40N 109 40W
Yonkers 71 40 57N 73 51W
Yonne □ 101 47 50N 3 40 E
Yonne, R. 101 48 23N 2 58 E
York, Austral. 134 31 52 S 116 47 E
York, Ont., Can. 50 43 1N 79 53W
York, Ont., Can. 50 43 42N 79 27W
York, U.K. 94 53 58N 1 7W
York, Ala., U.S.A. 73 32 30N 88 18W
York, Nebr., U.S.A. 74 40 55N 97 35W
York, Pa., U.S.A. 72 39 57N 76 43W
York □ 49 43 55N 79 30W
York, C., Austral. 135 10 42 S 142 31 E
York, C., Can. 65 76 30N 68 0W
York Factory 55 57 0N 92 18W
York, Kap 17 75 55N 66 25W
York Mills 50 43 45N 79 25W
York, R. 38 48 49N 64 34W
York Sd. 134 14 50 S 125 5 E
York, Vale of 98 54 15N 1 25W
Yorke Pen. 135 34 50 S 137 40 E
Yorkshire, reg. 94 54 54N 1 0W
Yorkshire Wolds 94 54 0N 0 30W
Yorkton 57 51 11N 102 28W
Yorktown 75 29 0N 97 29W
Yorkville, U.S.A. 77 41 38N 88 27W
Yorkville, Calif., U.S.A. 80 38 52N 123 13W
Yoro 84 15 9N 87 7W
Yosemite National Park 80 38 0N 119 30W
Yosemite Village 80 37 45N 119 35W
Yŏsu 131 34 47N 127 45 E
Yotsing 131 28 10N 120 55 E
Youbou 62 48 53N 124 13W
Youghal 97 51 58N 7 51W
Youghal B. 97 51 55N 7 50W
Youghal Har. 97 51 55N 7 50W
Young, Austral. 136 34 19 S 148 18 E
Young, Can. 56 51 47N 105 45W
Young, Uruguay 88 32 44 S 57 36W
Young, U.S.A. 79 34 9N 110 56W
Youngstown, Can. 61 51 35N 111 10W
Youngstown, N.Y., U.S.A. 49 43 16N 79 2W
Youngstown, Ohio, U.S.A. 70 41 7N 80 41W
Youngsville 70 41 51N 79 21W
Yoyang 131 29 27N 113 10 E
Yozgat 122 39 51N 34 47 E
Ypané, R. 88 23 29 S 57 19W
Yport 100 49 45N 0 15 E
Ypsilanti 77 42 18N 83 40W
Yreka 78 41 44N 122 40W
Ysleta 79 31 45N 106 24W
Yssingeaux 103 45 9N 4 8 E
Ystad 111 55 26N 13 50 E
Ythan, R. 96 57 26N 2 12W
Ytyk-Kel 121 62 20N 133 28 E
Yu Shan, Mt. 131 23 30N 121 0 E
Yuan Kiang 131 28 40N 110 30 E
Yuanling 131 28 30N 110 5 E
Yuanyang 129 23 10N 102 58 E
Yuba City 80 39 12N 121 37W
Yuba, R. 80 39 8N 121 36W
Yūbetsu 132 43 13N 144 5 E
Yucatán □ 83 21 30N 86 30W
Yucatán Basin 12 20 0N 84 0W
Yucatán Channel 84 22 0N 86 30W
Yucca 81 34 56N 114 6W
Yucca Valley 81 34 8N 116 30W
Yucheng 130 36 55N 116 40 E
Yudino 120 55 10N 67 55 E
Yugoslavia ■ 109 44 0N 20 0 E
Yühsien 130 34 10N 113 30 E
Yuhsien 131 39 45N 114 33 E
Yuhwan 131 28 1N 121 12 E
Yukan 131 28 43N 116 35 E
Yukikow 131 31 29N 118 17 E
Yukon, R. 67 65 30N 150 0W
Yukon Territory □ 64 63 0N 135 0W
Yukti 121 63 20N 105 0 E
Yule, R. 134 20 24 S 118 12 E
Yülin 130 18 10N 109 31 E
Yülin (Watlam) 131 22 30N 110 50 E
Yuma, Ariz., U.S.A. 81 32 45N 114 37W
Yuma, Colo., U.S.A. 74 40 10N 102 43W
Yuma, B. de 85 18 20N 68 35W
Yumbo 86 3 35N 76 28W
Yumen 129 41 13N 96 55 E
Yun Ho 129 35 0N 117 0 E
Yün Ho, R. 131 33 15N 119 45 E
Yunaska I. 67 52 40N 170 40W
Yundamindra 136 29 4 S 122 3 E
Yungan 131 25 50N 117 25 E
Yungas 86 17 0 S 66 0W
Yungay 88 37 10 S 72 5W
Yungchun 131 25 20N 118 15 E
Yungfu 131 24 59N 109 59 E
Yunghing 131 26 12N 113 3 E
Yunghwo 130 36 58N 110 56 E
Yungshun 131 29 3N 109 50 E
Yungsin 131 26 55N 114 10 E
Yungtsi 131 34 50N 110 25 E
Yungyun 131 24 31N 113 28 E
Yunhsien 131 32 30N 111 0 E
Yunhwo 131 28 0N 119 32 E
Yunlin 131 23 45N 120 30 E
Yunnan □ 129 25 0N 102 30 E
Yunsiao 131 24 0N 117 20 E
Yur 121 59 52N 137 49 E
Yurga 120 55 42N 84 51 E
Yuribei 120 71 20N 76 30 E
Yurimaguas 86 5 55 S 76 0W
Yuscarán 84 13 58N 86 51W
Yushu = Fyekundo 129 33 6N 96 48 E
Yütu 131 26 0N 115 24 E
Yutze 130 37 45N 112 45 E
Yuyang 131 28 44N 108 46 E
Yuyao 131 30 0N 121 20 E
Yuyu 130 40 20N 112 30 E
Yuzhno-Sakhalinsk 121 47 5N 142 5 E
Yvelines □ 101 48 40N 1 45 E
Yvetot 100 49 37N 0 44 E

Z

Zaandam 105 52 26N 4 49 E
Zabaykalskiy 121 49 40N 117 10 E
Zābol 123 31 0N 61 25 E
Zābolī 123 27 10N 61 35 E
Zabrze 107 50 18N 18 46 E
Zacapa 84 14 59N 89 31W
Zacapu 82 19 50N 101 43W
Zacatecas 82 22 49N 102 34W
Zacatecas □ 82 23 30N 103 0W
Zacatecolua 84 13 29N 88 51W
Zacaultipán 83 20 39N 98 36W
Zacoalco 82 20 10N 103 40W
Zadar 108 44 8N 15 8 E
Zadetkyi Kyun 128 10 0N 98 25 E
Zafra 104 38 26N 6 30W
Zagan 106 51 39N 15 22 E
Zagreb 108 45 50N 16 0 E
Zāgros, Kudhā-ye 123 33 45N 47 0 E
Zāhedān 123 29 30N 60 50 E
Zahlah 115 33 52N 35 50 E
Zaïre, R. 116 1 30N 28 0 E
Zaïre, Rep. of ■ 116 3 0 S 23 0 E
Zaječar 109 43 53N 22 18 E
Zakamensk 121 50 23N 103 17 E
ZāKhū 122 37 10N 42 50 E
Zákinthos 109 37 47N 20 54 E
Zákinthos, I. 109 37 45N 27 45 E
Zambèze, R. 117 18 46 S 36 16 E
Zambezi, R. 117 18 46 S 36 16 E
Zambia ■ 117 15 0 S 28 0 E
Zamboanga 127 6 59N 122 3 E
Zambrano 86 9 45N 74 49W
Zamora, Mexico 82 20 0N 102 21W
Zamora, Spain 104 41 30N 5 45W
Zamość 107 50 50N 23 22 E
Zamuro, Sierra del 86 4 0N 62 30W
Zanaga 116 2 48 S 13 48 E
Zandvoort 105 52 22N 4 32 E
Zanesville 70 39 56N 82 2W
Zanjan 122 36 40N 48 35 E
Zanthus 134 31 2 S 123 34 E
Zanzibar 116 6 12 S 39 12 E
Zanzibar I. 116 6 12 S 39 12 E
Zaouiet El Kahla 114 27 10N 6 40 E
Zaouiet Reggane 114 26 32N 0 3 E
Zapadnaya Dvina 120 56 15N 32 3 E
Západné Beskydy 107 49 30N 19 0 E
Zapala 90 39 0 S 70 5W
Zapaleri, Cerro 88 22 49 S 67 11W
Zapata 75 26 56N 99 17W
Zaporozhye 120 47 50N 35 10 E
Zara 122 39 58N 37 43 E
Zaragoza, Colomb. 86 7 30N 74 52W
Zaragoza, Coahuila, Mexico 82 28 30N 101 0W
Zaragoza, Nuevo León, Mexico 83 24 0N 99 36W
Zaragoza □ 104 41 35N 1 0W
Zarand 123 30 46N 56 34 E
Zarate 88 34 7 S 59 0W
Zaraza 86 9 21N 65 19W
Zarembo I. 54 56 20N 132 50W
Zaria 114 11 0N 7 40 E
Zaruma 86 3 40 S 79 30W
Zary 106 51 37N 15 10 E
Zarzal 86 4 24N 76 4W
Zashiversk 121 67 25N 142 40 E
Zaskar Mountains 124 33 15N 77 30 E
Zavareh 123 33 35N 52 28 E
Zavitinsk 121 50 10N 129 20 E
Zavodoski, I. 91 56 0 S 27 45W
Zawiercie 107 50 30N 19 13 E
Zāyandeh, R. 123 32 35N 32 0 E
Zayarsk 121 56 20N 102 55 E
Zaysan 120 47 28N 84 52 E
Zaysan, Oz. 120 48 0N 83 0 E
Zdunska Wola 107 51 37N 18 59 E
Zealand Station 39 46 3N 66 56W
Zealandia 56 51 37N 107 45W
Zearing 76 42 10N 93 20W
Zeballos 62 49 59N 126 50W
Zeebrugge 105 51 19N 3 12 E
Zeeland 77 42 49N 86 1W
Zeeland □ 105 51 30N 3 50 E

Acknowledgment is made to the following for providing the photographs used in the atlas

Agent-Général for Québec; Air India; Brazilian Embassy, London; British Aircraft Corporation; British Airways; British Leyland; British Petroleum; British Rail; British Steel Corporation; British Tourist Authority; Calgary City Hall; Canadian National Railways; Central Electricity Generating Board; D. Chanter; Danish Embassy, London; Edmonton City Hall; Egypt Air; R. Estall; Fiat (England) Ltd.; Finnish Tourist Bureau; Freightliners Ltd.; H. Fullard; M. H. Fullard; Gas Council Exploration Ltd.; Commander H. R. Hatfield/Astro Books; H. Hawes; Israeli Govt. Tourist Office; Japan Air Lines; Lufthansa; M.A.T. Transport Ltd.; Meteorological Office, London; Moroccan Tourist Office; N.A.S.A. (Space Frontiers); National Coal Board, London; National Maritime Museum, London; Offshore Co.; Pan American World Airways; M. Rentsch; Royal Astronomical Society, London; Shell International Petroleum Co. Ltd.; Swan Hunter Group, Ltd.; Swiss National Tourist Office; Toronto City Hall; Vancouver City Engineers Dept.; B. M. Willett; Woodmansterne Ltd.

Geographical Terms

This is a list of some of the geographical words from foreign languages which are found in the place names on the maps and in the index. Each is followed by the language and the English meaning.

Afr. afrikaans
Alb. albanian
Amh. amharic
Ar. arabic
Ber. berber
Bulg. bulgarian
Bur. burmese

Chin. chinese
Cz. czechoslovakian
Dan. danish
Dut. dutch
Fin. finnish
Flem. flemish
Fr. french

Gae. gaelic
Ger. german
Gr. greek
Heb. hebrew
Hin. hindi
I.-C. indo-chinese
Ice. icelandic

It. italian
Jap. japanese
Kor. korean
Lapp. lappish
Lith. lithuanian
Mal. malay
Mong. mongolian

Nor. norwegian
Pash. pashto
Pers. persian
Pol. polish
Port. portuguese
Rum. rumanian
Russ. russian

Ser.-Cr. serbo-croat
Siam. siamese
Sin. sinhalese
Som. somali
Span. spanish
Swed. swedish
Tib. tibetan
Turk. turkish

A. (Ain) *Ar.* spring
–á *Ice.* river
a *Dan., Nor., Swed.* stream
–abad *Pers., Russ.* town
Abyad *Ar.* white
Ad. (Adrar) *Ar., Ber.* mountain
Ada, Adasi *Tur.* island
Addis *Amh.* new
Adrar *Ar., Ber.* mountain
Aïn *Ar.* spring
Ăkra *Gr.* cape
Akrotíri *Gr.* cape
Alb *Ger.* mountains
Albufera *Span.* lagoon
–ålen *Nor.* islands
Alpen *Ger.* mountain pastures
Alpes *Fr.* mountains
Alpi *It.* mountains
Alto *Port.* high
–älv, –älven *Swed.* stream, river
Amt *Dan.* first-order administrative division
Appennino *It.* mountain range
Arch. (Archipiélago) *Span.* archipelago
Arcipélago *It.* archipelago
Arq. (Arquipélago) *Port.* archipelago
Arr. (Arroyo) *Span.* stream
–Ås, –åsen *Nor., Swed.* hill
Autonomna Oblast *Ser.-Cr.* autonomous region
Ayios *Gr.* island
Ayn *Ar.* well, waterhole

B(a). (Baía) *Port.* bay
B. (Baie) *Fr.* bay
B. (Bahía) *Span.* bay
B. (Ben) *Gae.* mountain
B. (Bir) *Ar.* well
B. (Bucht) *Ger.* bay
B. (Bugt.) *Dan.* bay
Baai, –baai *Afr.* bay
Bäb *Ar.* gate
Bäck, –bäcken *Swed.* stream
Back, backen, *Swed.* hill
Bad, –baden *Ger.* spa
Bådiya,-t *Ar.* desert
Baek *Dan.* stream
Baelt *Dan.* strait
Bahía *Span.* bay
Bahr *Ar.* sea, river
Bahra *Ar.* lake
Baía *Port.* bay
Baie *Fr.* bay
Bajo, –a, *Span.* lower
Bakke *Nor.* hill
Bala *Pers.* upper
Baltă *Rum.* marsh, lake
Banc *Fr.* bank
Bander *Ar., Mal.* port
Bandar *Pers.* bay
Banja *Ser.-Cr.* spa. resort
Barat *Mal.* western
Barr. (Barrage) *Fr.* dam
Barracão *Port.* dam, waterfall
Bassin *Fr.* bay
Bayt *Heb.* house, village
Bazar *Hin.* market, bazaar
Be'er *Heb.* well
Beit *Heb.* village
Belo-, Belyy, Belaya,

Beloye, *Russ.* white
Ben *Gae.* mountain
Bender *Somal.* harbour
Berg,(e) –berg(e) *Afr.* mountain(s)
Berg, –berg *Ger.* mountain
–berg, –et *Nor., Swed.* hill, mountain, rock
Bet *Heb.* house, village
Bir, Bîr *Ar.* well
Birket *Ar.* lake, bay, marsh
Bj. (Bordj) *Ar.* port
–bjerg *Dan.* hill, point
Boca *Span.* river mouth
Bodden *Ger.* bay, inlet
Bogaz, Boğaz, –ı *Tur.* strait
Boka *Ser.-Cr.* gulf, inlet
Bol. (Bolshoi) *Russ.* great, large
Bordj *Ar.* fort
–borg *Dan., Nor., Swed.* castle, fort
–botn *Nor.* valley floor
bouche(s) *Fr.* mouth
Br. (Burnu) *Tur.* cape
Bratul *Rum.* distributary stream
–breen *Nor.* glacier
–bruck *Ger.* bridge
–brunn *Swed.* well, spring
Bucht *Ger.* bay
Bugt, –bugt *Dan.* bay
Buheirat *Ar.* lake
Bukit *Mal.* hill
Bukten *Swed.* bay
–bulag *Mong.* spring
Bûr *Ar.* port
Burg. *Ar.* fort
Burg, –burg *Ger.* castle
Burnu *Tur.* cape
Burun *Tur.* cape
Butt *Gae.* promontory
–by *Dan., Nor., Swed.* town
–byen *Nor., Swed.* town

C. (Cabo) *Port., Span.* headland, cape
C. (Cap) *Fr.* cape
C. (Capo) *It.* cape
Cabeza *Span.* peak, hill
Camp *Port., Span.* land, field
Campo *Span.* plain
Campos *Span.* upland
Can. (Canal) *Fr., Span.* canal
Canale *It.* canal
Canalul *Ser.-Cr.* canal
Cao Nguyên *Thai.* plateau, tableland
Cap *Fr.* cape
Capo *It.* cape
Cataracta *Sp.* cataract
Cauce *Span.* intermittent stream
Causse *Fr.* upland (limestone)
Cayi *Tur.* river
Cayo(s) *Span.* rock(s), islet(s)
Cerro *Span.* hill, peak
Ch. (Chaîne(s)) *Fr.* mountain range(s)
Ch. (Chott) *Ar.* salt lake
Chaco *Span.* jungle
Chaîne(s) *Fr.* mountain range(s)
Chap. (Chapada) *Port.* hills, upland

Chapa *Span.* hills, upland
Chapada *Port.* hills, upland
Chaung *Bur.* stream, river
Chen *Chin.* market town
Ch'eng *Chin.* town
Chiang *Chin.* river
Ch'ih *Chin.* pool
Ch'ŏn *Kor.* river
–chŏsuji *Kor.* reservoir
Chott *Ar.* salt lake, swamp
Chou *Chin.* district
Chu *Tib.* river
Chung *Chin.* middle
Chute *Fr.* waterfall
Co. (Cerro) *Span.* hill, peak
Coch. (Cochilla) *Port.* hills
Col *Fr., It.* Pass
Colline(s) *Fr.* hill(s)
Conca *It.* plain, basin
Cord. (Cordillera) *Span.* mountain chain
Costa *It., Span.* coast
Côte *Fr.* coast, slope, hill
Cuchillas *Spain* hills
Cu-Lao *I.-C.* island

D. (Dolok) *Mal.* mountain
Dágh *Pers.* mountain
Dağ *Tur.* mountain(s)
Dağları *Tur.* mountain range
Dake *Jap.* mountain
–dal *Nor.* valley
–dal, -e *Dan., Nor.* valley
–dal, –en *Swed.* valley, stream
Dalay *Mong.* sea, large lake
–dalir *Ice.* valley
–dalur *Ice.* valley
–damm, –en *Swed.* lake
Danau *Mal.* lake
Dao *I.-O.* island
Dar *Ar.* region
Darya *Russ.* river
Daryächeh *Pers.* marshy lake, lake
Dasht *Pers.* desert, steppe
Daung *Bur.* mountain, hill
Dayr *Ar.* depression, hill
Debre *Amh.* hill
Deli *Ser.-Cr.* mountain(s)
Denizi *Tur.* sea
Dépt. (Département) *Fr.* first-order administrative division
Desierto *Span.* desert
Dhar *Ar.* region, mountain chain
Dj. (Djebel) *Ar.* mountain
Dō *Jap., Kor.* island
Dong *Kor.* village, town
Dong *Thai.* jungle region
–dorf *Ger.* village
–dorp *Afr.* village
–drif *Afr.* ford
–dybet *Dan.* marine channel
Dzong *Tib.* town, settlement

Eil.-eiland(en) *Afr., Dut.* island(s)
–elv *Nor.* river
–'emeq *Heb.* plain, valley
'erg *Ar.* desert with dunes
Estrecho *Span.* strait
Estuario *Span.* estuary

Étang *Fr.* lagoon
–ey(jar) *Ice.* island(s)

F. (Fiume) *It.* river
F. Folyó *Hung.* river
Fd. (Fjord) *Nor.* Inlet of sea
–feld *Ger.* field
–fell *Ice.* mountain, hill
–feng *Chin.* mountain
Fiume *It.* river
Fj. (–fjell) *Nor.* mountain
–fjall *Ice.* mountain(s), hill(s)
–fjäll(et) *Swed.* hill(s), mountain(s), ridge
–fjällen *Swed.* mountains
–fjard(en) *Swed.* fjord, bay, lake
Fjeld *Dan.* mountain
–fjell *Nor.* mountain, rock
–fjord(en) *Nor.* inlet of sea
–fjorden *Dan.* bay, marine channel
–fjörður *Ice.* fjord
Fl. (Fleuve) *Fr.* river
Fl. (Fluss) *Ger.* river
–flói *Ice.* bay, marshy country
Fluss *Ger.* river
foce,–i *It.* mouth(s)
Folyó *Hung.* river
–fontein *Afr.* fountain, spring
–fors, –en, *Swed.* rapids, waterfall
Foss *Ice., Nor.* waterfall
–furt *Ger.* ford
Fylke *Nor.* first-order administrative division

G. (Gebel) *Ar.* mountain
G. (Gebirge) *Ger.* hills, mountains
G. (Golfe) *Fr.* gulf
G. (Golfo) *It.* gulf
G. (Gora) *Bulg., Russ., Ser.-Cr.* mountain
G. (Gunong) *Mal.* mountain
–gang *Kor.* river
Ganga *Hin., Sin.* river
–gat *Dan.* sound
–gau *Ger.* district
Gave *Fr.* stream
–gawa *Jap.* river
Geb. (Gebirge) *Ger.* hills, mountains
Gebel *Ar.* mountain
Geziret *Ar.* island
Ghat *Hin.* range of hills
Ghiol *Rum.* lake
Ghubbat *Ar.* bay, inlet
Gji *Alb.* bay
Gjol *Alb.* lagoon, lake
Gl. (Glava) *Ser.-Cr.* mountain, peak
Glen. *Gae.* valley
Gletscher *Ger.* glacier
Gobi *Mong.* desert
Gol *Mong.* river
Golfe *Fr.* gulf
Golfo *It., Span.* gulf
Gomba *Tib.* settlement
Gora *Bulg., Russ., Ser.-Cr.* mountain(s)
Góry *Pol., Russ.* mountain
Gölü *Tur.* lake
–gorod *Russ.* small town
Grad *Bulg., Russ., Ser-Cr.* town, city

Grada *Russ.* mountain range
Guba *Russ.* bay
–Guntō *Jap.* island group
Gunong *Mal.* mountain
Gură *Rum.* passage

H. Hadabat *Ar.* plateau
–hafen *Ger.* harbour, port
Haff *Ger.* bay
Hai *Chin.* sea
Haihsia *Chin.* strait
–hale *Dan.* spit, peninsula
Hals *Dan., Nor.* peninsula, isthmus
Halvø *Dan.* peninsula
Halvøya *Nor.* peninsula
Hāmad, Hamada, *Ar.* stony desert, plain
Hammādah *Ar.* stony desert, plain
–hamn *Swed., Nor.* harbour, anchorage
Hāmūn *Ar.* plain
Hāmūn *Pers.* low-lying marshy area
–Hantō *Jap.* peninsula
Harju *Fin.* hill
Hassi *Ar.* well
–haug *Nor.* hill
Hav *Swed.* gulf
Havet *Nor.* sea
–havn *Dan., Nor.* harbour
Hegyseg *Hung.* forest
Heide *Ger.* heath
Hi. (hassi) *Ar.* well
Ho *Chin.* river
–hø *Nor.* peak
Hochland *Afr.* highland
Hoek, –hoek *Afr., Dut.* cape
Höfn *Ice.* harbour, port
–hög, –en, –högar, –högarna *Swed.* hill(s), peak, mountain
Höhe *Ger.* hills
Holm *Dan.* island
–holm, –holme, –holzen, *Swed.* island
Hon *I.-C.* island
Hora *Cz.* mountain
–horn *Nor.* peak
Hory *Cz.* mountain range, forest
–hoved *Dan.* point, headland, peninsula
Hráun *Ice.* lava
–hsi *Chin.* mountain, stream
–hsiang *Chin.* village
–hsien *Chin.* district
Hu *Chin.* lake
Huk *Dan., Ger.* point
Huken *Nor.* head

I. (Île) *Fr.* island
I. (Ilha) *Port.* island
I. (Insel) *Ger.* island
I. (Isla) *Span.* island
I. (Isola) *It.* island
Idehan *Ar., Ber.* sandy plain
Île(s) *Fr.* island(s)
Ilha *Port.* island
Insel(n) *Ger.* island(s)
Irmak *Tur.* river
Is. (Inseln) *Ger.* islands
Is. (Islas) *Span.* islands
Is. (Isola) *It.* island
Isola, –e *It.* island(s)
Istmo *Span.* isthmus

J. (Jabal) *Ar.* mountain
J. (Jazira) *Ar.* island
J. (Jebel) *Ar.* mountain
J. (Jezioro) *Pol.* lake
Jabal *Ar.* mountain, range
–jaur *Swed.* lake
–järvi *Fin.* lake, bay, pond
Jasovir *Bulg.* reservoir
Jazä'ir *Ar.* islands
Jazira *Ar.* island
Jazireh *Pers.* island
Jebel *Ar.* mountain
Jezero *Ser.-Cr.* lake
Jezioro *Pol.* lake
–Jima *Jap.* island
Jøkelen *Nor.* glacier
–joki *Fin.* stream
–jökull *Ice.* glacier
Jūras Licis *Lat.* bay, gulf

K. (Kap) *Dan.* cape
K (Khalig) *Ar.* gulf
K. (Kiang) *Chin.* river
K. (Kuala) *Mal.* confluence, estuary
Kaap *Afr.* cape
Kai *Jap.* sea
Kaikyō *Jap.* strait
Kamennyy *Russ.* stony
Kampong *Mal.* village
Kan. (Kanal) *Ser.-Cr.* channel, canal
Kanaal *Dut., Flem.* canal
Kanal *Dan.* channel, gulf
Kanal *Ger., Swed.* canal, stream
kanal *Ser.-Cr.* channel, canal
Kang *Kor.* river, bay
Kangri *Tib.* mountain glacier
Kap *Dan., Ger.* cape
Kapp *Nor.* cape
Kas *I.-C.* island
–kaupstaður *Ice.* market town
–kaupunki *Fin.* town
Kavïr *Pers.* salt desert
Kébir *Ar.* great
Kéfar *Heb.* village, hamlet
–ken *Jap.* first-order administrative division
Kep *Alb.* cape
Kepulauan *Mal.* archipelago
Ketjil *Mal.* lesser, little
Khalig, Khalij *Ar.* gulf
khamba, –ldg *Tib.* source, spring
Khawr *Ar.* wadi
Khirbat *Ar.* ruins
Kho Khot *Thai.* isthmus
Khôr *Pers.* creek, estuary
Khrebet *Russ.* mountain range
Kiang *Chin.* river
–klint *Dan.* cliff
–Klintar *Swed.* hills
Kloof *Afr.* gorge
Knude *Dan.* point
Ko *Jap.* lake
Ko *Thai.* island
Kohi *Pash.* mountains
Kol *Russ.* lake
Kolymskoye *Russ.* mountain range
Kólpos *Gr., Tur.* gulf, bay
Kompong *Mal.* landing place
–kop *Afr.* hill

-köping *Swed.* market town
Körfezi *Tur.* gulf
Kosa *Russ.* spit
-koski *Fin.* cataract, rapids
-kraal *Afr.* native village
Krasnyy *Russ.* red
Kryash *Russ.* ridge, hills
Kuala *Mal.* confluence, estuary
kuan *Chin.* pass
Kuh –hha *Pers.* mountains
Kul *Russ.* lake
Kulle *Swed.* hill, shoal
Kum *Russ.* sandy desert
Kumpu *Fin.* hill
Kurgan *Russ.* mound
Kwe *Bur.* bay, gulf
Kyst *Dan.* coast
Kyun, –zu, –umya *Bur.* island(s)

L. (Lac) *Fr.* lake
L. (Lacul) *Rum.* lake
L. (Lago) *It., Span.* lake, lagoon
L. (Lagoa) *Port.* lagoon
L. (Límni) *Gr.* lake
L. (Loch) *Gae.* (lake, inlet)
L. (Lough) *Gae.* (lake, inlet)
La *Tib.* pass
La (Lagoa) *Port.* lagoon
-laagte *Afr.* watercourse
Läani *Fin.* first-order administrative division
Län *Swed.* first-order administrative division
Lac *Fr.* lake
Lacul *Rum.* lake, lagoon
Lago *It., Span.* lake, lagoon
Lagoa *Port.* lagoon
Laguna *It., Span.* lagoon, intermittent lake
Lagune *Fr.* lake
Lahti *Fin.* bay, gulf, cove
Lakhti *Russ.* bay, gulf
Lampi *Fin.* lake
Land *Ger.* first-order administrative division
-land *Dan.* region
-land *Afr., Nor.* land, province
Lido *It.* beach, shore
Liehtao *Chin.* islands
Lilla *Swed.* small
Límni *Gr.* lake
Ling *Chin.* mountain range, ice
Linna *Fin.* historical fort
Llano *Span.* prairie, plain
Loch *Gae.* (lake)
Lough *Gae.* (lake)
Lum *Alb.* river
Lund *Dan.* forest
-lund, -en *Swed.* wood(s)

M. (Maj, Mai) *Alb.* mountain, peak
M. (Mont) *Fr.* mountain peak
M. (Mys) *Russ.* cape
Madīna(h) *Ar.* town, city
Madiq *Ar.* strait
Maj *Alb.* peak
Mäki *Fin.* hill, hillside
Mal *Alb.* mountain
Mal *Russ.* little, small
Mal/a, –i, –o *Ser.-Cr.* small, little
Man *Kor.* bay
Mar *Span.* lagoon, sea
Mare *Rum.* great
Marisma *Span.* marsh
-mark *Dan., Nor.* land
Marsâ *Ar.* anchorage, bay, inlet
Masabb *Ar.* river mouth
Massif *Fr.* upland, plateau
Mato *Port.* forest
Mazar *Pers.* shrine, tomb
Meer *Afr., Dut., Ger.* lake sea

Mi., Mti. (Monti) *It.* mountains
Miao *Chin.* temple, shrine
Midbar *Heb.* wilderness
Mif. (Massif) *Fr.* upland, plateau
Misaki *Jap.* cape, point
-mo *Nor., Swed.* heath, island
-mon *Swed.* heath
Mong *Bur.* town
Mont *Fr.* hill, mountain
Montagna *It.* mountain
Montagne *Fr.* hill, mountain
Montaña *Span.* mountain
Monte *It., Port., Span.* mountain
Monti *It.* mountains
More *Russ.* sea
Mörön *Hung.* river
Mt. (Mont) *Fr.* mountain
Mt. (Monti) *It.* mountain
Mt. (Montaña) *Span.* mountain range
Mte. (Monte) *It., Port., Span.* mountain
Mţi. (Munţi) *Rum.* mountain
Mts. (Monts) *Fr.* mountains
Muang *Mal.* town
Mui *Ar., I.-C.* cape
Mull *Gae.* (promontory)
Mund, –mund *Afr.* mouth
Munkhafed *Ar.* depression
Munte *Rum.* mount
Munţi(i) *Rum.* mountain(s)
Muong *Mal.* village
Myit *Bur.* river
Myitwanya *Bur.* mouths of river
-mýri *Ice.* bog
Mys *Russ.* cape

N. (Nahal) *Heb.* river
Naes *Dan.* point, cape
Nafūd *Ar.* sandy desert
Nahal *Heb.* river
Nahr *Ar.* river, stream
Najd *Ar.* plateau, pass
Nakhon *Thai.* town
Nam *I.-C.* river
-nam *Kor.* south
-näs *Swed.* cape
-nes *Ice.* cape
Ness, -ness *Gae.* promontory, cape
Nez *Fr.* cape
-niemi *Fin.* cape, point, peninsula, island
Nizhne, -iy *Russ.* lower
Nizmennost *Russ.* plain, lowland
Nísos, Nísoi *Gr.* island(s)
Nor *Chin.* lake
Nor *Tib.* peak
Nos *Bulg., Russ.* cape, point
Nudo *Span.* mountain
Nuruu *Mong.* mountain range
Nuur *Mong.* lake

O. (Ostrov) *Russ.* island
Ō (Ouâdi, Uued) *Ar.* wadi
-ö *Swed.* island, peninsula, point
-öar, (-na) *Swed.* islands
Oblast *Russ.* administrative division
Öbor *Mong.* inner
Occidental *Fr., Span.* western
Odde *Dan., Nor.* point, peninsula, cape
Oji *Alb.* bay
Ojo *Span.* spring
Oki *Jap.* bay
-ön *Swed.* island peninsula
Ondör *Mong.* high, tall

-ör *Swed.* island, peninsula, point
Orasul *Rum.* city
Ord *Gae.* point
Óri *Gr.* mountains
Oriental *Span.* eastern
Órmos *Gr.* bay
Óros *Gr.* mountain
Ort *Ger.* point, cape
Ostrov(a) *Russ.* island(s)
Otok(-i) *Ser.-Cr.* island(s)
Ouadi, –edi *Ar.* dry watercourse, wadi
Ouzan *Pers.* river
Ova (–si) *Tur.* plains, lowlands
–øy, (-a) *Nor.* island(s)
Oya *Hin.* point
Oya *Sin.* river
Oz. (Ozero, a) *Russ.* lake(s)

P. (Passo) *It.* pass
P. (Pasul) *Rum.* pass
P. (Pico) *Span.* peak
P. (Prokhod) *Bulg.* pass
–pää *Fin.* hill(s), mountain
Pahta *Lapp.* hill
Pampa, –s *Span.* plain(s) salt flat(s)
Pan. (Pantano) *Span.* Reservoir
Pantao *Chin.* peninsula
Parbat *Urdu* mountain
Pas *Fr.* gap
Paso *Span.* pass, marine channel
Pass *Ger.* pass
Passo *It.* pass
Pasul *Rum.* pass
Patam *Hin.* small village
Patna, –patnam *Hin.* small village
Pegunungan *Mal.* mountain, range
Pei, –pei *Chin.* north
Pélagos *Gr.* sea
Pen. (Península) *Span.* peninsula
Peña *Span.* rock, peak
Península *Span.* peninsula
Per. (Pereval) *Russ.* pass
Pertuis *Fr.* channel
Peski *Russ.* desert, sands
Phanom *I.-C., Thai.* mountain
Phnom *I.-C.* mountain
Phu *I.-C.* mountain
Pic *Fr.* peak
Pico(s) *Span.* peak(s)
Pik *Russ.* peak
Piz., pizzo *It.* peak
Pl. (Planina) *Ser.-Cr.* mountain, range
Plage *Fr.* beach
Plaine *Fr.* plain
Planalto *Span.* plateau
Planina *Bulg., Ser.-Cr.* mountain, range
Plat. (Plateau) *Fr.* level upland
Plato *Russ.* plateau
Playa *Span.* beach
P-ov. (Poluostrov) *Russ.* peninsula
Pointe *Fr.* point, cape
Pojezierze *Pol.* lakes plateau
Polder *Dut.* reclaimed farmland
-pólis *Gr.* city, town
Poluostrov *Russ.* peninsula
Połwysep *Pol.* peninsula
Pont *Fr.* bridge
Ponta *Port.* point, cape
Ponte *It.* bridge
Poort *Afr.* passage, gate
-poort *Dut.* port
Porta *Port.* pass
Portil, –e *Rum.* gate
Portillo *Span.* pass
Porto *It.* port
Porto *Port., Span.* port

Pot. (Potámi, Potamós) *Gr.* river
Poulo *I.-C.* island
Pr. (Průsmyk) *Cz.* pass
Pradesh *Hin.* state
Presa *Span.* reservoir
Presqu'île *Fr.* peninsula
Prokhod *Bulg.* pass
Proliv *Russ.* strait
Prusmyk *Cz.* pass
Pso. (Passo) *It.* pass
Pta. (Ponta) *Port.* point, cape
Pta. (Punta) *It., Span.* point, cape, peak
Pte. (Pointe) *Fr.* point cape
Puerto *Span.* port, pass
Puig *Cat.* peak
Pulau *Mal.* island
Puna *Span.* desert plateau
Punta *It., Span.* point, peak
Puy *Fr.* hill

Qal'at *Ar.* fort
Qanal *Ar.* canal
Qasr *Ar.* fort
Qiryat *Heb.* town
Qolleh *Pers.* mountain

Ramla *Ar.* sand
Rann *Hin.* swampy region
Rao *I.-C.* river
Ras *Amh.* cape, headland
Rās *Ar.* cape, headland
Recife(s) *Port.* reef(s)
Reka *Bulg., Cz., Russ.* river
Repede *Rum.* rapids
Represa *Port.* dam
Reshteh *Pers.* mountain range
-Rettō *Jap.* group of islands
Ría *Span.* estuary, bay
Ribeirão *Port.* river
Rijeka *Ser.-Cr.* river
Rio *Port.* river
Río *Span.* river
Riv. (Riviera) *It.* coastal plain, coast, river
Rivier *Afr.* river
Riviera *It.* coast
Rivière *Fr.* river
Roche *Fr.* rock
Rog *Russ.* horn
–rück *Ger.* ridge
Rūd *Pers.* stream, river
Rudohorie *Cz.* ore mountains
Rzeka *Pol.* river

S. (Sungei) *Mal.* river
Sa. (Serra) *It., Port.* range of hills
Sa. (Sierra) *Span.* range of hills
-saari *Fin.* island
Sadd *Ar.* dam
Sagar, –ara *Hin., Urdu* lake
Saharā *Ar.* desert
Sahrâ *Ar.* desert
Sa'id *Ar.* highland
Sakar *Fin.* mountain
-Saki *Jap.* point
Sal. (Salar) *Span.* salt pan
Salina(s) *Span.* salt flat(s)
-salmi *Fin.* strait, sound, lake, channel
Saltsjöbad *Swed.* resort
Sammyaku *Jap.* mountain, range
Samut *Thai.* gulf
-San *Jap.* hill, mountain
Sap. (Sapadno) *Russ.* west
Sasso *It.* mountain
Se, Sé *I.-C.* river
Sebkha, –kra *Ar.* salt flats
See *Ger.* lake
-see *Ger.* sea
-şehir *Turk.* town
Selat *Mal.* strait
-selkä *Fin.* bay, lake, sound, ridge, hills

Selva *Span.* forest, wood
Seno *Span.* bay, sound
Serír *Ar.* desert of small stones
Serra *It., Port.* range of hills
Serranía *Span.* mountains
Sev. (Severo) *Russ.* north
-shahr *Pers.* city, town
Shan *Chin.* hills, mountains, pass
Shan-mo *Chin.* mountain range
Shatt *Ar.* river
-Shima *Jap.* island
Shimāli *Ar.* northern
-Shotō *Jap.* group of islands
Shuik'u *Chin.* reservoir
Sierra *Span.* hill, range
Sjö, sjön *Swed.* lake, bay, sea
Sjøen *Dan.* sea
Skär *Swed.* island, rock, cape
Skog *Nor.* forest
-skog, -skogen *Swed.* wood(s)
-skov *Dan.* forest
Slieve *Gae.* range of hills
-sø *Dan., Nor.* lake
Sør *Nor.* south, southern
Solonchak *Russ.* salt lake, marsh
Souk *Ar.* market
Spitze *Ger.* peak, mountain
-spruit *Afr.* stream
-stad *Afr., Nor., Swed.* town
-stadt *Ger.* town
Staður *Ice.* town
Stausee *Ger.* reservoir
Stenón *Gr.* strait, pass
Step *Russ.* plain
Str. (Stretto) *It.* strait
-strand *Dan., Nor.* beach
-strede *Nor.* straits
Strelka *Russ.* spit
-strete *Nor.* straits
Stretto *It.* strait
Stroedet *Dan.* strait
-ström, -strömmen *Swed.* stream(s)
-stroom *Afr.* large river
Suidō *Jap.* strait, channel
Sûn *Bur.* cape
Sund *Dan.* sound
-sund, -sundet *Swed.* sound, estuary, inlet
-sund(et) *Nor.* sound
Sungai, -ei *Mal.* river
Sungei *Mal.* river
Sur *Span.* south, southern
Sveti *Bulg.* pass
Syd *Dan., Swed.* south

Tai -tai *Chin.* tower
Tal *Mong.* plain, steppe
-tal *Ger.* valley
Tall *Ar.* hills, hummocks
Tandjung *Mal.* cape, headland
Tao *Chin.* island
Tassili *Ar.* rocky plateau
Tau *Russ.* mountain, range
Taung *Bur.* mountain, south
Taunggya *Bur.* pass
Tělok *I.-C., Mal.* bay bight
Teluk *Mal.* bay, gulf
Tg. (Tandjung) *Mal.* cape, headland
-thal *Ger.* valley
Thok *Tib.* town
Tierra *Span.* land, country
-tind *Nor.* peak
Tjärn, -en, -et *Swed.* lake
Tong *Nor.* village, town
Tong *Bur., Thai.* mountain range
Tonle *I.-C.* large river, lake
-träsk *Swed.* bog, swamp
Tsangpo *Tib.* large river
Tso *Tib.* lake

Tsu *Jap.* entrance, bay
Tulur *Ar.* hill
T'un *Chin.* village
Tung *Chin.* east
Tunnel *Fr.* tunnel
Tunturi *Fin.* hill(s), mountain(s), ridge

Uad *Ar.* dry watercourse, wadi
Udjung *Mal.* cape
Udd, udde, udden *Swed.* point, peninsula
Uebi *Somal.* river
Us *Mong.* water
Ust *Russ.* river mouth
Uul *Mong., Russ.* mountain, range

V. (Volcán) *Span.* volcano
-vaara *Fin.* hill, mountain, ridge, peak
-våg *Nor.* bay
Val *Fr., It.* valley
Valea *Rum.* valley
-vall, -vallen *Swed.* mountain
Valle *Span.* valley
Vallée *Fr.* valley
Valli *It.* lake, lagoon
Väst *Swed.* west
-vatn *Ice., Nor.* lake
Vatten *Swed.* lake
Vdkhr. (Vodokhranilishche) *Russ.* reservoir
-ved, -veden *Swed.* range, hills
Veld, -veld *Afr.* field
Velik/a, -e, -i, -o *Ser.Cr.* large
-vesi *Fin.* water, lake, bay sound, strait
Vest *Dan., Nor.* west
Vf. (vîrful) *Rum.* peak, mountain
-vidda *Nor.* plateau
Vig *Dan.* bay, inlet, cove, lagoon, lake, bight
-vik, -vika, -viken *Nor., Swed.* bay, cove, gulf, inlet, lake
Vila *Port.* small town
Villa *Span.* town
Ville *Fr.* town
Vinh *I.-C.* bay
Vîrful *Rum.* peak, mountain
-vlei *Afr.* pond, pool
Vodokhranilishche *Russ.* reservoir
Vol. (Volcán) *Span.* volcano, mountain
Vorota *Russ.* gate
Vostochnyy *Russ.* eastern
Vozyshennost *Russ.* heights, uplands
Vrata *Bulg.* gate, pass
Vrchovina *Cz.* mountainous country
Vrchy *Cz.* mountain range
Vung *I.-C.* gulf
-vuori *Fin.* mountain, hill

W. (Wādī) *Ar.* dry watercourse
Wâhât *Ar.* oasis
Wald *Ger.* wood, forest
Wan *Chin., Jap.* bay
Webi *Amh.* river
Woestyn *Afr.* desert

Yam *Heb.* sea
Yang *Chin.* ocean
Yazovir *Bulg.* reservoir
Yoma *Bur.* mountain range
-yüan *Chin.* spring

Zaki *Jap.* peninsula
Zalew *Pol.* lagoon, swamp
Zaliv *Russ.* bay
Zan *Jap.* mountain
Zatoka *Pol.* bay
Zee *Dut.* sea
Zemlya *Russ.* land, island(s)

Principal Cities of the World

The population figures used are from censuses or more recent estimates and are given in thousands for towns and cities over 200 000 (over 500 000 in China and over 250 000 in Japan and U.S.S.R.). Where possible the population of the metropolitan areas is given e.g. Greater London, Greater New York, etc.

AFRICA

ALGERIA (1974)
Algiers ... 1 504
Oran ... 485
Constantine ... 350
Annaba ... 313
Tizi-Ouzou ... 224
ANGOLA (1970)
Luanda ... 475
CAMEROON (1975)
Douala ... 486
Yaoundé ... 274
CANARY ISLANDS (1970)
Las Palmas ... 287
CONGO (1974)
Brazzaville ... 290
EGYPT (1974)
Cairo ... 5 715
Alexandria ... 2 259
El Giza ... 854
Suez ... 368
Subra el Khelma ... 346
Port Said ... 342
El Mahalla el Kubra ... 288
Tanta ... 278
Aswan ... 246
El Mansura ... 232
ETHIOPIA (1975)
Addis Abeba ... 1 161
Asmera ... 318
GABON (1974)
Libreville ... 251
GHANA (1970)
Accra ... 738
Kumasi ... 345
GUINEA (1972)
Conakry ... 526
IVORY COAST (1976)
Abidjan ... 850
Bouaké ... 318
KENYA (1973)
Nairobi ... 630
Mombasa ... 301
LIBYA (1973)
Tripoli ... 551
Benghazi ... 282
MADAGASCAR (1971)
Tananarive ... 378
MOROCCO (1973)
Casablanca ... 1 753
Rabat-Salé ... 596
Marrakesh ... 436
Fès ... 426
Meknès ... 403
Oujda ... 349
Kénitra ... 341
Tétouan ... 308
Safi ... 215
Tanger ... 208
MOZAMBIQUE (1970)
Maputo ... 384
NIGERIA (1975)
Lagos ... 1 477
Ibadan ... 847
Ogbomosho ... 432
Kano ... 399
Oshogbo ... 282
Ilorin ... 282
Abeokuta ... 253
Port Harcourt ... 242
Zaria ... 224
Ilesha ... 224
Onitsha ... 220
Iwo ... 214
Ado-Ekiti ... 213
Kaduna ... 202
RHODESIA (1973)
Salisbury ... 502
Bulawayo ... 307
SENEGAL (1973)
Dakar ... 726
SIERRA LEONE (1974)
Freetown ... 214
SOMALI REP. (1972)
Mogadishu ... 230
SOUTH AFRICA (1970)
Johannesburg ... 1 434
Cape Town ... 1 096
Durban ... 843
Pretoria ... 562
Port Elizabeth ... 489
Germiston ... 281
SUDAN (1973)
Khartoum ... 784
TANZANIA (1975)
Dar-es-Salaam ... 517
TOGO (1971)
Lomé ... 214
TUNISIA (1966)
Tunis ... 648
UGANDA (1969)
Kampala ... 331
ZAÏRE (1972-4)
Kinshasa ... 2 008
Kananga ... 601
Lubumbashi ... 404
Mbuji Mayi ... 337
Kisangani ... 311
ZAMBIA (1972)
Lusaka ... 448
Kitwe ... 331
Ndola ... 235

ASIA

AFGHANISTAN (1976)
Kabul ... 588
BANGLADESH (1974)
Dacca ... 1 730
Chittagong ... 889
Narayanganj ... 443
Khulna ... 437
BURMA (1973)
Rangoon ... 3 189
Mandalay ... 401
CAMBODIA (1973)
Phnom Penh ... 2 000
CHINA (1970)
Shanghai ... 10 820
Peking ... 7 570
Tientsin ... 4 280
Shenyang ... 2 800
Wuhan ... 2 560
Canton ... 2 500
Chungking ... 2 400
Nanking ... 1 750
Harbin ... 1 670
Luta ... 1 650
Sian ... 1 600
Lanchow ... 1 450
Taiyuan ... 1 350
Tsingtao ... 1 300
Chengtu ... 1 250
Changchun ... 1 200
Kunming ... 1 100
Tsinan ... 1 100
Fushun ... 1 080
Anshan ... 1 050
Chengchow ... 1 050
Hangchow ... 960
Tangshan ... 950
Paotow ... 920
Tzepo ... 850
Changsha ... 825
Shihkiachwang ... 800
Tsitsihar ... 760
Soochow ... 730
Kirin ... 720
Suchow ... 700
Foochow ... 680
Nanchang ... 675
Kweiyang ... 660
Wusih ... 650
Hofei ... 630
Hwainan ... 600
Penki ... 600
Loyang ... 580
Nanning ... 550
Huhehot ... 530
Sining ... 500
Wulumchi ... 500
HONG KONG (1967)
Kowloon ... 2 195
Victoria ... 849
INDIA (1971)
Calcutta ... 7 005
Bombay ... 5 969
Delhi ... 3 630
Madras ... 2 470
Hyderabad ... 1 799
Bangalore ... 1 648
Ahmedabad ... 1 588
Kanpur ... 1 273
Nagpur ... 866
Pune ... 853
Lucknow ... 826
Agra ... 638
Jaipur ... 613
Varanasi ... 583
Indore ... 573
Madurai ... 548
Jabalpur ... 534
Allahabad ... 514
Patna ... 490
Surat ... 472
Vadodara ... 467
Jamshedpur ... 465
Cochin ... 438
Dhanbad ... 433
Amritsar ... 433
Trivandrum ... 410
Gwalior ... 407
Srinagar ... 404
Ludhiana ... 401
Sholapur ... 398
Bhopal ... 392
Hubli-Dharwar ... 380
Meerut ... 268
Visakhapatnam ... 362
Mysore ... 356
Coimbatore ... 353
Vijaywada ... 344
Calicut ... 334
Bareilly ... 326
Jodhpur ... 319
Salem ... 308
Tiruchurapalli ... 306
Rajkot ... 300
Jullundur ... 296
Moradabad ... 272
Guntur ... 270
Ajmer ... 262
Kolhapur ... 259
Ranchi ... 256
Aligarh ... 254
Durg-Bhilainagar ... 245
Chandigarh ... 233
Gorakhpur ... 231
Bhavnagar ... 226
Saharanpur ... 226
Jamnagar ... 215
Mangalore ... 214
Belgaum ... 214
Kota ... 213
Ujjain ... 209
Durgapur ... 207
Warangul ... 207
Raipur ... 206
INDONESIA (1971)
Jakarta ... 4 576
Surabaya ... 1 556
Bandung ... 1 202
Semarang ... 647
Medan ... 636
Palembang ... 583
Ujung Pandang ... 435
Malang ... 422
Surakarta ... 414
Yogyakarta ... 342
Banjarmasin ... 282
Pontianak ... 218
IRAN (1973)
Tehran ... 4 002
Esfahan ... 605
Mashhad ... 592
Tabriz ... 510
Shiraz ... 373
Abadan ... 312
Ahvaz ... 302
Kermanshah ... 249
IRAQ (1970)
Baghdad ... 2 969
Basra ... 371
Mosul ... 293
Kirkuk ... 208
ISRAEL (1974)
Tel Aviv-Jaffa ... 1 157
Haifa ... 354
Jerusalem ... 344
JAPAN (1973)
Tokyo ... 11 623
Osaka ... 2 780
Yokohama ... 2 620
Nagoya ... 2 080
Kyoto ... 1 460
Kobe ... 1 360
Sapporo ... 1 240
Kitakyushu ... 1 060
Kawasaki ... 1 020
Fukuoka ... 1 000
Hiroshima ... 761
Chiba ... 613
Sendai ... 576
Amagasaki ... 538
Higashiosaka ... 501
Okayama ... 501
Hamamatsu ... 467
Kumamoto ... 467
Nagasaki ... 446
Kagoshima ... 444
Shizuoka ... 444
Himeji ... 432
Niigata ... 413
Gifu ... 407
Kurishiki ... 405
Funabashi ... 391
Wakayama ... 387
Nishinomiya ... 384
Kanazawa ... 383
Yokosuka ... 382
Toyonaka ... 381
Matsuyama ... 366
Sagamihara ... 359
Iwaki ... 335
Utsunomiya ... 335
Kawaguchi ... 334
Matsudo ... 324
Urawa ... 322
Omiya ... 321
Takatsuki ... 318
Asahikawa ... 316
Naha ... 306
Oita ... 305
Hakodate ... 303
Nagano ... 303
Hachioji ... 299
Takamatsu ... 296
Ichikawa ... 294
Fukuyama ... 293
Suita ... 289
Toyama ... 287
Hirakata ... 285
Toyohashi ... 279
Kochi ... 275
Shimonoseki ... 266
Aomori ... 263
Sasebo ... 261
Fujisawa ... 261
Koriyama ... 258
Akita ... 254
JORDAN (1974)
Amman ... 598
Az Zarqa ... 226
KOREA, NORTH (1967-70)
Pyongyang ... 1 500
Chongjin ... 265
KOREA, SOUTH (1975)
Seoul ... 6 889
Pusan ... 2 454
Taegu ... 1 311
Inchon ... 800
Kwangju ... 607
Taejon ... 506
Masan ... 372
Chonju ... 311
Seongnam ... 272
Ulsan ... 253
Suweon ... 224
KUWAIT (1975)
Kuwait ... 295
LEBANON (1971)
Beirut ... 939
MACAU (1971)
Macau ... 248
MALAYSIA (1970)
Kuala Lumpur ... 452
Georgetown ... 270
Ipoh ... 248
MONGOLIA (1971)
Ulan Bator ... 282
PAKISTAN (1972)
Karachi ... 3 469
Lahore ... 2 148
Lyallpur ... 820
Hyderabad ... 624
Rawalpindi ... 615
Multan ... 544
Gujranwala ... 366
Peshawar ... 273
Sialkot ... 212
Sargodha ... 203
PHILIPPINES (1975)
Manila ... 1 438
Quezon City ... 995
Davao ... 591
Cebu ... 419
Caloocan ... 364
Zamboanga ... 250
Iloilo ... 248
Pasay ... 241
SAUDI ARABIA (1974)
Riyadh ... 667
Jedda ... 561
Mecca ... 367
Taif ... 205
SINGAPORE (1975)
Singapore ... 2 250
SRI LANKA (1973)
Colombo ... 618
SYRIA (1970)
Damascus ... 923
Aleppo ... 639
Homs ... 215
TAIWAN (1970-73)
Taipei ... 1 922
Kaohsiung ... 915
Tainan ... 495
Taichung ... 490
Chilung ... 334
Chiai ... 237
Shanchung ... 229
Hsinchu ... 205
THAILAND (1973)
Bangkok ... 3 967
TURKEY (1973)
Istanbul ... 3 135
Ankara ... 1 554
Izmir ... 819
Abana ... 454
Bursa ... 427
Gaziantep ... 353
Konya ... 324
Eskisehir ... 303
Kayseri ... 297
Diyarbakir ... 251
Samsun ... 242
Maras ... 237
Malatya ... 234
Izmit ... 233
Erzurum ... 226
Sivas ... 213
Siirt ... 211
UNITED ARAB EMIRATES (1976)
Abu Dhabi ... 236
Dubai ... 207
VIETNAM (1973)
Ho Chi Minh City ... 1 825
Hanoi ... 920
Da-Nang ... 492
Haiphong ... 390
Nha-trang ... 216
Qui-Nhon ... 214
Hue ... 209

AUSTRALASIA

AUSTRALIA (1973)
Sydney ... 2 874
Melbourne ... 2 584
Brisbane ... 911
Adelaide ... 868
Perth ... 739
Newcastle ... 358
Canberra ... 211
Wollongong ... 206
NEW ZEALAND (1976)
Auckland ... 743
Wellington ... 327
Christchurch ... 295

EUROPE

AUSTRIA (1971)
Vienna ... 1 859
Linz ... 357
Graz ... 314
BELGIUM (1971)
Brussels ... 1 075
Antwerp ... 673
Liège ... 440
Gent ... 225
Charleroi ... 214
BULGARIA (1974)
Sofia ... 962
Plovdiv ... 305
Varna ... 270
CZECHOSLOVAKIA (1974)
Prague ... 1 096
Brno ... 354
Bratislava ... 325
Ostrava ... 291
DENMARK (1974)
Copenhagen ... 1 378
Århus ... 245
FINLAND (1976)
Helsinki ... 868
Tampere ... 237
Turku ... 235
FRANCE (1975)
Paris ... 9 863
Lyon ... 1 167
Marseille ... 1 004
Lille ... 922
Bordeaux ... 589
Toulouse ... 495
Nantes ... 433
Nice ... 433
Rouen ... 389
Grenoble ... 389
Toulon ... 378
Strasbourg ... 356
St-Etienne ... 335
Lens ... 313
Nancy ... 278
Le Havre ... 265
Grasse-Cannes ... 254
Tours ... 246
Clermont-Ferrand ... 225
Valenciennes ... 224
Montpellier ... 223
Mulhouse ... 219
Rennes ... 213
Orléans ... 209
Dijon ... 208
Douai ... 203
GERMANY, EAST (1975)
East Berlin ... 1 094
Leipzig ... 569
Dresden ... 508
Karl-Marx-Stadt ... 304
Magdeburg ... 277
Halle ... 239
Rostock ... 212
Erfurt ... 203
GERMANY, WEST (1974)
West Berlin ... 2 048
Hamburg ... 1 752
München ... 1 337
Cologne ... 832
Essen ... 674
Frankfurt am Main ... 663
Dortmund ... 632
Düsseldorf ... 628
Stuttgart ... 625
Bremen ... 584
Nürnberg ... 515
Hannover ... 505
Duisburg ... 435
Wuppertal ... 410
Bochum ... 338

Gelsenkirchen 333
Mannheim 325
Bielefeld 321
Bonn 283
Kiel 266
Karlsruhe 261
Augsburg 257
Wiesbaden 252
Aachen 241
Oberhausen 241
Lübeck 236
Krefeld 221
Braunschweig 219
Kassel 213
Münster 200

GREECE (1971)

Athens 2 540
Thessaloniki 557
Piraeus 439

HUNGARY (1974)

Budapest 2 055

IRISH REPUBLIC (1971)

Dublin 815

ITALY (1975)

Rome 2 868
Milano 1 731
Napoli 1 223
Torino 1 202
Genova 805
Palermo 663
Bologna 491
Firenze 466
Catánia 399
Bari 376
Venézia 365
Trieste 271
Verona 271
Messina 261
Padova 240
Táranto 240
Cágliari 237
Bréscia 216

NETHERLANDS (1974)

Rotterdam 1 040
Amsterdam 1 002
s'Gravenhage 685
Utrecht 463
Eindhoven 350
Arnhem 277
Heerlen-Kerkrade 265
Enschede-Hengelo 238
Haarlem 235
Tilburg 211
Nijmegen 210
Groningen 203

NORWAY (1974)

Oslo 469
Bergen 215

POLAND (1974)

Warsaw 1 400
Lódz 784
Kraków 663
Wroclaw 565
Poznań 503
Gdańsk 402
Szczecin 360
Katowice 320
Bydgoszcz 311
Lublin 259
Gdynia 212
Zabrze 202

PORTUGAL (1974)

Lisbon 1 612
Oporto 1 315

RUMANIA (1977)

Bucharest 1 934
Constanța 290
Iasi 284
Timişoara 283
Cluj 262
Braşov 262
Ploeşti 255
Craiova 249
Galati 246

SPAIN (1974)

Madrid 3 520
Barcelona 1 810
Valencia 713
Sevilla 589
Zaragoza 547
Bilbao 458
Málaga 403
Las Palmas de Gran Canaria 328
Valladolid 275
Córdoba 249
Palma de Mallorca 267
Hospitalet 242
Murcia 241

SWEDEN (1974)

Stockholm 1 353
Göteborg 688
Malmö 454

SWITZERLAND (1974)

Zürich 721
Basel 379
Genève 323
Berne 288
Lausanne 231

U.S.S.R. (1975)

Moscow 7 632
Leningrad 4 311
Kiyev 1 947
Tashkent 1 595
Baku 1 383
Kharkov 1 357
Gorkiy 1 283
Novosibirsk 1 265
Kuybyshev 1 164
Sverdlovsk 1 147
Minsk 1 147
Tbilisi 1 006
Odessa 1 002
Chelyabinsk 969
Omsk 968
Dnepropetrovsk 958
Donetsk 950
Kazan 946
Perm 939
Volgograd 900
Erevan 899
Ufa 895
Rostov 888
Alma-Ata 836
Saratov 834
Riga 796
Krasnoyarsk 748
Voronezh 746
Zaporozhye 744
Krivoy Rog 628
Lvov 617
Yaroslavl 568
Karaganda 564
Krasnodar 532
Novokuznetsk 524
Vladivostok 511
Irkutsk 508
Izhevsk 506
Barnaul 502
Khabarovsk 500
Tula 500
Frunze 486
Zhdanov 459
Ivanovo 453
Astrakhan 452
Kishinev 452
Tolyatti 438
Dushanbe 436
Komarovo 435
Vilnius 433
Voroshilovgrad 432
Penza 426
Nikolayev 424
Ulyanovsk 424
Ryazan 419
Orenburg 419
Tomsk 399
Makeyevka 398
Nizhniy Tagil 394
Kalinin 389
Magnitogorsk 388
Arkhangelsk 369
Groznyy 375
Kirov 371
Bryansk 366
Murmansk 358
Lipetsk 351
Kursk 351
Kaunas 344
Gorlovka 342
Kaliningrad 338
Gomel 337
Tyumen 323
Kherson 307
Samarkand 299
Tallin 299
Ulan Ude 295
Ashkhabad 289
Chimkent 288
Kurgan 287
Chita 283
Simferopol 280
Taganrog 277
Vinnitsa 277
Orel 273
Vitebsk 272
Vladimir 271
Semipalatansk 271
Ordzhonikidze 270
Prokopyevsk 268
Sevastopol 267
Cheboksary 264
Poltava 263
Ust-Kamenogorsk 257
Tambov 257
Mogilev 255
Smolensk 250

UNITED KINGDOM (1974)

London 7 168
Birmingham 1 003
Glasgow 816
Liverpool 561
Manchester 516
Sheffield 507
Leeds 499
Edinburgh 450
Bristol 419
Teesside 387
Belfast 374
Coventry 334
Bradford 290
Nottingham 288
Leicester 287
Hull 279
Cardiff 276
Wolverhampton 268
Stoke-on-Trent 258
Plymouth 251
Derby 218
Sunderland 213
Southampton 213
Newcastle-upon-Tyne 209
Portsmouth 200

YUGOSLAVIA (1971)

Belgrade 1 204
Zagreb 602
Skopje 388
Sarajevo 292
Ljubljana 258
Novi Sad 214

NORTH AMERICA

CANADA (1976)

Toronto 2 803
Montréal 2 802
Vancouver 1 166
Ottawa 693
Winnipeg 578
Edmonton 554
Québec 542
Hamilton 529
Calgary 470
St. Catharines 302
Kitchener 272
London 270
Halifax 268
Windsor 248
Victoria 218

COSTA RICA (1973)

San Jose 395

CUBA (1970)

Havana 1 755
Holguin 422
Santa Clara 332
Santiago de Cuba 276
Cienfuegos 226

DOMINICAN REPUBLIC (1970)

Santo Domingo 818
Santiago de los Caballeros 245

EL SALVADOR (1971)

San Salvador 337

GUATEMALA (1973)

Guatemala City 707

HAITI (1971)

Port-au-Prince 494

HONDURAS (1973)

Tegucigalpa 302

JAMAICA (1971)

Kingston 573

MEXICO (1975)

Mexico City 11 340
Guadalajara 1 963
Monterrey 1 637
Ciudad Juárez 520
León de los Aldamas 496
Tijuana 495
Puebla de Zaragoza 482
Torreón 364
Chihuahua 346
Mexicali 331
Acapulco de Juárez 353
Tampico 343
San Luis Potosí 282
Cuernavaca 273
Veracruz Llave 266
Hermosillo 248
Culiacán 245
Mérida 239
Aguascalientes 222
Saltillo 211
Morelia 209

NICARAGUA (1974)

Managua 500

PANAMA (1975)

Panama 404

PUERTO RICO (1970)

San Juan 695

UNITED STATES (1970)

New York 11 571
Los Angeles 7 032
Chicago 6 979
Philadelphia 4 818
Detroit 4 200
San Francisco 3 109
Washington 2 861
Boston 2 754
Pittsburgh 2 401
St. Louis 2 363
Baltimore 2 071
Cleveland 2 064
Houston 1 985
Newark 1 957
Minneapolis-St. Paul 1 814
Dallas 1 556
Seattle 1 422
Anaheim-Santa Ana 1 420
Milwaukee 1 404
Atlanta 1 390
Cincinnati 1 385
Paterson 1 359
San Diego 1 358
Buffalo 1 349
Miami 1 268
Kansas City 1 254
Denver 1 228
San Bernardino 1 143
Indianapolis 1 110
San Jose 1 065
New Orleans 1 046
Tampa-St. Petersburg 1 013
Portland 1 009
Phoenix 968
Columbus 916
Providence 911
Rochester 883
San Antonio 864
Dayton 850
Louisville 827
Sacramento 801
Memphis 770
Fort Worth 762
Birmingham 739
Albany 722
Toledo 693
Norfolk 681
Akron 679
Hartford 664
Oklahoma City 641
Syracuse 636
Gary 633
Honolulu 629
Fort Lauderdale 620
Jersey City 609
Greensboro 604
Salt Lake City 558
Allentown 544
Nashville 541
Omaha 540
Grand Rapids 539
Youngstown 536
Springfield 530
Jacksonville 529
Richmond 518
Wilmington 499
Flint 497
Tulsa 477
Orlando 428
Fresno 413
Tacoma 411
Harrisburg 411
Charlotte 409
Knoxville 400
Wichita 389
Bridgeport 389
Lansing 378
Mobile 377
Oxnard 376
Canton 372
Davenport 363
El Paso 359
New Haven 356
Tucson 352
West Palm Beach 349
Worcester 344
Wilkes-Barre 342
Peoria 342
Utica 341
York 330
Bakersfield 329
Little Rock 323
Columbia 323
Lancaster 320
Beaumont 316
Albuquerque 316
Chattanooga 305
Trenton 304
Charleston 304
Binghamton 303
Greenville 300
Reading 296
Austin 296
Shreveport 295
Newport News 292
Madison 290
Stockton 290
Spokane 287
Des Moines 286
Baton Rouge 285
Corpus Christi 285
Fort Wayne 280
South Bend 280
Appleton 277
Las Vegas 273
Rockford 272
Duluth 265
Santa Barbara 264
Erie 264
Johnstown 263
Jackson 259
Lorain 257
Huntington 254
Augusta 253
Salinas 250
Vallejo 249
Pensacola 243
Columbus 239
Colorado Springs 236
Scranton 234
Ann Arbor 234
Evansville 233
Lawrence 232
Charleston 230
Raleigh 228
Huntsville 228
Hamilton 226
Saginaw 220
Eugene 213
Lowell 213
Fayetteville 212
Waterbury 209
New London 208
Stamford 206
Macon 206
Santa Rosa 205
Kalamazoo 202
Montgomery 201

SOUTH AMERICA

ARGENTINA (1970)

Buenos Aires 8 925
Rosario 811
Córdoba 799
La Plata 506
Mendoza 471
San Miguel de Tucumán 366
Mar del Plata 300
Santa Fé 245
San Juan 224

BOLIVIA (1975)

La Paz 697
Sucre 263

BRAZIL (1970)

São Paulo 5 870
Rio de Janeiro 4 252
Belo Horizonte 1 228
Recife 1 046
Salvador 1 005
Pôrto Alegre 863
Fortaleza 829
Nova Iguaçu 725
Belém 603
Curitiba 584
Brasília 517
Santo André 417
Duque de Caxias 404
Goiania 363
Santos 344
Campinas 336
Niterói 292
Manaus 284
Osasco 283
Natal 258
Maceió 252
Guarulhos 222
Juiz de Fora 220
João Pessoa 214

CHILE (1975)

Santiago 3 263
Valparaíso 592
Concepción 500
Viña del Mat 229

COLOMBIA (1973)

Bogotá 2 855
Medellin 1 100
Cali 923
Barranquilla 662
Cartagena 313
Bucaramanga 298
Cucuta 270
Manizales 231
Pereira 210
Ibague 205

ECUADOR (1974)

Guayaquil 814
Quito 597

PARAGUAY (1972)

Asunción 473

PERU (1972)

Lima 3 302
Arequipa 303
Callao 297
Trujillo 240

URUGUAY (1975)

Montevideo 1 230

VENEZUELA (1971)

Caracas 2 175
Maracaibo 652
Valencia 367
Barquisimeto 331
Maracay 255

Principal Countries of the World

Country	Area in thousands of square km	Population in thousands	Density of population per sq. km	Capital Population in thousands
Afghanistan	647	19 803	31	Kabul (588)
Albania	29	2 548	88	Tirana (175)
Algeria	2 382	17 304	7	Algiers (1 504)
Angola	1 247	6 761	5	Luanda (475)
Argentina	2 777	25 719	9	Buenos Aires (8 925)
Australia	7 687	14 078	2	Canberra (211)
Austria	84	7 514	89	Vienna (1 859)
Bangladesh	144	76 815	533	Dacca (1 730)
Belgium	31	9 889	319	Brussels (1 075)
Belize	23	144	6	Belmopan (5)
Benin	113	3 197	28	Porto-Novo (104)
Bhutan	47	1 202	26	Thimphu (10)
Bolivia	1 099	5 789	5	Sucre (263) La Paz (697)
Botswana	600	693	1	Gaborone (18)
Brazil	8 512	109 181	13	Brasilia (517)
Brunei	6	177	31	Bandar Seri Begawan (41)
Bulgaria	111	8 761	79	Sofia (962)
Burma	677	30 834	46	Rangoon (3 189)
Burundi	78	3 864	138	Bujumbura (107)
Cambodia	181	8 354	46	Phnom Penh (2 000)
Cameroon	475	6 591	14	Yaoundé (274)
Canada	9 976	23 143	2	Ottawa (693)
Central African Emp.	623	1 716	3	Bangui (187)
Chad	1 284	4 116	3	Ndjamena (193)
Chile	757	10 454	14	Santiago (3 263)
China	9 597	852 133	89	Peking (7 570)
Colombia	1 139	24 372	21	Bogota (2 855)
Congo	342	1 390	4	Brazzaville (290)
Costa Rica	51	2 012	39	San José (395)
Cuba	115	9 405	82	Havana (1 755)
Cyprus	9	639	69	Nicosia (116)
Czechoslovakia	128	14 918	117	Prague (1 096)
Denmark	43	5 073	118	Copenhagen (1 378)
Djibouti	22	108	5	Djibouti (62)
Dominican Republic	49	4 895	99	Santo Domingo (818)
Ecuador	284	7 305	26	Quito (597)
Egypt	1 001	38 067	38	Cairo (5 715)
El Salvador	21	4 123	196	San Salvador (337)
Equatorial Guinea	28	316	11	Rey Malabo (37)
Ethiopia	1 222	28 688	23	Addis Ababa (1 161)
Fiji	18	580	32	Suva (96)
Finland	337	4 727	14	Helsinki (868)
France	547	52 915	97	Paris (9 863)
French Guiana	91	62	1	Cayenne (25)
Gabon	268	530	2	Libréville (251)
Gambia	11	538	49	Banjul (48)
Germany, East	108	16 786	155	East Berlin (1 094)
Germany, West	249	61 498	247	Bonn (283)
Ghana	239	10 309	43	Accra (738)
Greece	132	9 165	69	Athens (2 540)
Greenland	2 176	50	0.02	Godthaab (4)
Guatemala	109	6 256	57	Guatemala (707)
Guinea	246	4 529	18	Conakry (526)
Guinea-Bissau	36	534	15	Bissau (65)
Guyana	215	783	4	Georgetown (164)
Haiti	28	4 668	167	Port-au-Prince (494)
Honduras	112	2 831	25	Tegucigalpa (302)
Hong Kong	1	4 383	4 174	Victoria (849)
Hungary	93	10 596	114	Budapest (2 055)
Iceland	103	220	2	Reykjavik (98)
India	3 288	610 077	186	Delhi (3 630)
Indonesia	1 904	139 616	73	Jakarta (4 576)
Iran	1 648	33 400	20	Tehran (4 002)
Iraq	435	11 505	26	Baghdad (2 969)
Irish Republic	70	3 162	45	Dublin (815)
Israel	21	3 584	171	Jerusalem (344)
Italy	301	56 323	187	Rome (2 868)
Ivory Coast	322	6 677	21	Abidjan (850)
Jamaica	11	2 060	187	Kingston (573)
Japan	372	112 768	303	Tokyo (11 623)
Jordan	98	2 779	28	Amman (598)
Kenya	583	13 847	24	Nairobi (630)
Korea, North	121	16 246	134	Pyongyang (1 500)
Korea, South	98	35 860	345	Seoul (6 889)
Kuwait	16	1 031	67	Kuwait (295)
Laos	237	3 383	14	Vientiane (174)
Lebanon	10	2 961	296	Beirut (939)
Lesotho	30	1 214	40	Maseru (29)
Liberia	111	1 751	16	Monrovia (172)
Libya	1 760	2 444	1	Tripoli (551)
Luxembourg	3	358	138	Luxembourg (78)
Madagascar	587	8 266	14	Tananarive (378)
Malawi	118	5 175	44	Lilongwe (102)
Malaysia	330	12 300	37	Kuala Lumpur (452)
Mali	1 240	6 035	5	Bamako (197)
Malta	0.3	304	950	Valletta (14)
Mauritania	1 031	1 481	1	Nouakchott (135)
Mauritius	2	895	448	Port Louis (141)
Mexico	1 973	62 329	32	Mexico (11 340)
Mongolia	1 565	1 488	1	Ulan Bator (282)
Morocco	447	17 828	40	Rabat (596)
Mozambique	783	9 444	12	Maputo (384)
Namibia	824	852	1	Windhoek (36)
Nepal	141	12 904	92	Katmandu (333)
Netherlands	41	13 825	339	Amsterdam (1 002)
New Zealand	269	3 140	12	Wellington (327)
Nicaragua	130	2 233	17	Managua (500)
Niger	1 267	4 727	4	Niamey (130)
Nigeria	924	64 750	70	Lagos (1 477)
Norway	324	4 035	12	Oslo (469)
Oman	212	791	4	Muscat (25)
Pakistan	804	72 368	90	Islamabad (77)
Panama	76	1 719	23	Panama (404)
Papua New Guinea	462	2 829	6	Port Moresby (76)
Paraguay	407	2 724	7	Asunción (473)
Peru	1 285	16 090	13	Lima (3 302)
Philippines	300	43 751	146	Manila (1 438)
Poland	313	34 636	111	Warsaw (1 400)
Portugal	92	9 449	103	Lisbon (1 612)
Puerto Rico	9	3 213	361	San Juan (695)
Rhodesia	391	6 530	17	Salisbury (502)
Rumania	238	21 446	90	Bucharest (1 934)
Rwanda	26	4 289	165	Kigali (54)
Saudi Arabia	2 150	9 240	4	Riyadh (667)
Senegal	196	5 115	26	Dakar (726)
Sierra Leone	72	3 111	43	Freetown (214)
Singapore	0.6	2 295	3 825	Singapore (2 250)
Somali Republic	638	3 261	5	Mogadishu (230)
South Africa	1 221	26 129	21	Pretoria (562) Cape Town (1 096)
Spain	505	35 971	71	Madrid (3 520)
Sri Lanka	66	14 270	216	Colombo (618)
Sudan	2 506	16 126	6	Khartoum (784)
Surinam	163	435	3	Paramaribo (182)
Swaziland	17	497	29	Mbabane (21)
Sweden	450	8 222	18	Stockholm (1 353)
Switzerland	41	6 346	155	Berne (288)
Syria	185	7 596	41	Damascus (923)
Taiwan	36	15 500	431	Taipei (1 922)
Tanzania	945	15 607	17	Dar-es-Salaam (517)
Thailand	514	42 960	84	Bangkok (3 967)
Togo	56	2 283	41	Lomé (214)
Trinidad and Tobago	5	1 067	209	Port of Spain (68)
Tunisia	164	5 737	35	Tunis (648)
Turkey	781	40 163	51	Ankara (1 554)
Uganda	236	11 943	51	Kampala (331)
United Arab Emirates	84	229	3	Abu Dubai (236)
U.S.S.R.	22 402	256 900	11	Moscow (7 632)
United Kingdom	244	55 928	228	London (7 168)
United States	9 363	215 800	23	Washington (2 861)
Upper Volta	274	6 174	23	Ouagadougou (125)
Uruguay	178	3 101	17	Montevideo (1 230)
Venezuela	912	12 361	14	Caracas (2 175)
Vietnam	330	46 523	140	Hanoi (920)
Western Samoa	2.8	159	56	Apia (33)
Yemen (Sana)	195	6 870	35	Sana (150)
Yemen (South)	333	1 749	6	Aden (285)
Yugoslavia	256	21 560	84	Belgrade (1 204)
Zaïre	2 345	25 629	11	Kinshasa (2 008)
Zambia	753	5 138	7	Lusaka (448)